THE BRONTËS

THE
BRONTËS

Juliet Barker

WEIDENFELD AND NICOLSON

London

First published in Great Britain in 1994
by Weidenfeld and Nicolson

The Orion Publishing Group,
Orion House, 5 Upper Saint Martin's Lane, London WC2H 9EA

ISBN 0 297 81290 4

A catalogue record for this book is available
from the British Library

Typeset by Selwood Systems, Midsomer Norton
Printed in Great Britain by Butler & Tanner Ltd, Frome and London

CONTENTS

Contents

ILLUSTRATIONS

Plates

Mrs Lydia Robinson (Walsall Area Health Authority)

Broughton-in-Furness (photograph by Simon Warner)

Branwell's poem, 'Real Rest', in the *Halifax Guardian* (British Newspaper Library)

Branwell Brontë, 'Lydia Gisborne' (Brontë Society)

between pp. 684–685

The Heger family (by courtesy of Monsieur René Rechere, Brussels)

A view of Brussels showing the Pensionnat Heger (Brontë Society)

The gateway to the Pensionnat Heger

Charlotte's caricature of herself in a letter to Ellen Nussey (Brontë Society)

Prospectus for the proposed school at Haworth Parsonage (Brontë Society)

Charlotte Brontë, drawn by Richmond (National Portrait Gallery)

George Smith (Brontë Society)

William Smith Williams (Brontë Society)

Mrs Gaskell (by courtesy of the Director and University Librarian, the John Rylands Library, University of Manchester)

Arthur Bell Nicholls (Brontë Society)

Campaigning letter by Patrick Brontë in the *Leeds Intelligencer* (British Newspaper Library)

Letter from Branwell to J. B. Leyland, October 1846 (Brotherton Collection, University of Leeds)

Letter from Anne to Ellen Nussey (Brontë Society)

Anne's gravestone

All uncredited reproductions are from the author's collection, out of copyright, or untraceable.

For James
Edward and Sophie

ACKNOWLEDGEMENTS

Throughout the many years it has taken to complete this book I have naturally incurred many debts. First and foremost amongst these is to my immediate family, my parents, husband and children, who have suffered endlessly (but not always in silence) because of my obsession. Without their practical assistance, encouragement and forbearance, this biography could never have been written. Secondly, I owe a debt I can never repay to Ian Beck, consultant gynaecologist and obstetrician, who saw me through the worst year of my existence. His quite exceptional kindness, good humour and medical skill saved my sanity and my health; his goddaughter, Sophie Jane, owes her life to him. Thirdly, though it is invidious to single out only some of those who have helped me with my research, I would like to make a special mention of Margaret Smith, who read through my entire manuscript and, with her meticulous eye for detail, saved me from an embarrassing number of errors. She also pinpointed the locations of many Brontë manuscript holdings which I would not have otherwise found. Sue Lonoff of Harvard University, Professor Victor Neufeldt of the University of Victoria, British Columbia, and Rebecca Fraser all gave extensive assistance and much moral support. Special mention is also due to Diana Chardin of Trinity College, Cambridge, for letting me know about her discovery of transcripts of Branwell's letters and to Eileen Maughan of the Cumbria Record Office, Barrow in Furness, for undertaking research on my behalf in an effort to identify Branwell's illegitimate child.

Acknowledgements

I am grateful to the staff and governing bodies of the following institutions for assisting me in my research and giving me permission to quote from manuscripts in their care: Beinecke Library, Yale University; Berg Collection, New York Public Library; Birmingham University Library; Bodleian Library, Oxford; Borthwick Institute of Historical Research, York; Boston Public Library, Massachusetts; British Library and British Newspaper Library; British and Foreign Bible Society; British Museum's Central Archives; Brontë Parsonage Museum, Haworth; Brotherton Collection, University of Leeds; Brown University Library, Rhode Island; Buffalo and Erie County Public Library, New York; Cambridge University Library; Casterton School, Kirkby Lonsdale; Church of England Record Centre; Church Missionary Society; Church Pastoral Aid Society; Columbia University, New York; Cumbria Record Office, Barrow in Furness; Cumbria Record Office, Kendal; Ella Strong Denison Library, Scripps College, California; Essex Record Office; Fales Library, New York University; Fitzwilliam Museum, Cambridge; Friends Historical Library of Swarthmore College, Pennsylvania; Guildhall Library, London; Harry Ransom Humanities Research Center, University of Texas at Austin; Historical Society of Pennsylvania; Houghton Library, Harvard University; Huntington Library, San Merino; John Murray (Publishers) Ltd; John Rylands University Library of Manchester; King's School, Canterbury; Knox College, Illinois; Law Society, London; Leeds City Museum; Leicestershire Record Office; The Library, Morrab Gardens, Penzance; Library and Museum of the United Grand Lodge of England; Maine Historical Society; Manchester Publ´ Library; Margaret Clapp Library, Wellesley College, Massachusett National Library of Scotland; Pforzheimer Collection, New York Publ: Library; Pierpont Morgan Library, New York; Princeton University; Public Record Office; Quaker Collection, Haverford College, Haverford; Robinson Library, University of Newcastle upon Tyne; Rosenbach Museum and Library, Philadelphia; Royal Academy of Arts, London; St John's College, Cambridge; Shropshire Record Office; Society for Promoting Christian Knowledge; Staffordshire Record Office; State University of New York at Buffalo; Trinity College Library, Cambridge; Trinity College Library, Dublin; United Society for the Propagation of the Gospel; University College, Durham; University Library, Durham; University Library, Sheffield; University of Illinois at Urbana-Champaign; University of Kentucky, Lexington; University of Rochester, Rochester, New York; West Yorkshire Archive Service at Bradford, Halifax, Huddersfield, Leeds and Wakefield; Whitby Literary and Philosophical Society, Whitby; Woodhouse Grove School, Bradford; Wordsworth Trust, Dove Cottage, Grasmere.

I would also like to give particular thanks to those individuals fortunate enough to possess Brontë material and generous enough to allow me to use it: Roger Barrett; Alan Gill; Lynda Glading; the late Lady Graham, Norton

Conyers; Sarah Greenwood; Arthur Hartley; Angelina F. Light; Barbara Malone; A. I. F. Parmeter; William Self; June Ward-Harrison. Thanks, too, to Joan Coleridge for permission to quote from Hartley Coleridge's draft letter to Branwell Brontë. Gratitude is also due to the following people who went out of their way to assist me: Dr Alan Betteridge, WYAS, Halifax; Peter Dyson, Braintree; Donald Hathaway, Newton Abbot; Canon S. M. Hind, Kirk Smeaton; G. I. Holloway, Headmaster of the Grammar School, Appleby; Professor Ian Jack, Cambridge University; Professor R. D. S. Jack, University of Edinburgh; Marjorie McCrea, All Saints' Parish Church, Wellington, Shropshire; Mrs Rita Norman, Secretary of the Wethersfield Historical Group; Dr Ray Refaussé, Representative Church Body Library, Dublin; Revd William Seale of Drumgooland Parish, County Down; Revd John Shead, Priest in Charge, Wethersfield; Dr Katherine Webb, York Health Authority. Not forgetting Mrs Chris Swift for her kindness to a total stranger: without her I might still be wandering round the streets of Wellington.

It will be apparent that I have received whole-hearted assistance and support in my research from many quarters. I regret that the one exception was the Brontë Society, whose Director and Council felt it necessary, for their own commercial reasons, to refuse permission for the reproduction of a carefully chosen selection of Brontë drawings from their collections as chapter headings. As a former employee and a Life Member of the Society I particularly deplore this action which has forced me to make alternative arrangements and delayed publication of this book.

I do, however, have many friends in the Brontë Society for whose support I am grateful. I would particularly like to thank the Rev Colin Spivey who kindly lent me photocopies of the Haworth church registers and the late Eunice Skirrow whose enthusiasm for and knowledge of Haworth were an inspiration. Among the staff of the Brontë Parsonage Museum, I am particularly grateful to Margery Raistrick, Kathryn White and Ann Dinsdale. Allegra Huston, my editor at Weidenfeld & Nicolson, has been endlessly patient and supportive and made many helpful suggestions. Finally, I acknowledge my debt to all the many enthusiasts who read in the library while I was Curator and Librarian of the Brontë Parsonage Museum: they interested, informed and infuriated me and they are ultimately responsible for prompting me to write this book.

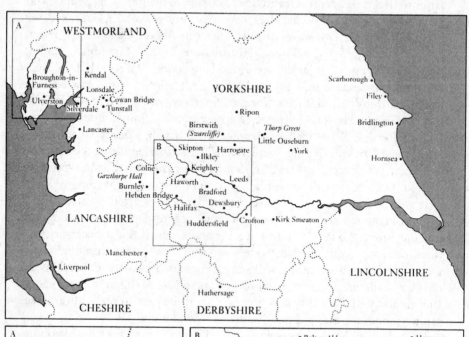

A

WESTMORLAND

Broughton-in-Furness
Kendal
Ulverston
Lonsdale
Silverdale • Cowan Bridge
Tunstall
Lancaster

YORKSHIRE

Scarborough
Filey

Bridlington

Ripon

Birstwith
(Swarcliffe)
Thorp Green
Little Ouseburn
Hornsea

B
Skipton
Colne
Gawthorpe Hall
Burnley
Hebden Bridge
Halifax
Huddersfield
Ilkley
Harrogate
Keighley
Haworth
Bradford
Dewsbury
Crofton
York
Leeds
Kirk Smeaton

LANCASHIRE

Manchester
Liverpool

LINCOLNSHIRE

Hathersage

CHESHIRE   DERBYSHIRE

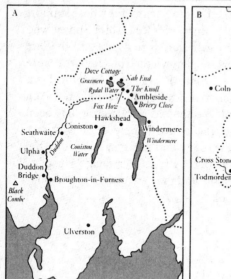

A

Dove Cottage
Grasmere   Nab End
Rydal Water   The Knoll
Fox How   Ambleside
Briery Close
Hawkshead
Seathwaite   Coniston   Windermere
Ulpha   Duddon   Windermere
Coniston
Water
Duddon
Bridge   Broughton-in-Furness
Black
Combe

Ulverston

B

Bolton Abbey   Harrogate
Skipton
Ilkley
Lothersdale
(Stone Gappe)
Guiseley
Keighley   Bingley   Rawdon (Woodhouse Grove)
Colne   Worth   Kirkstall Abbey
Stanbury   Haworth   Aire
Oxenhope   Leeds
Denholme   Allerton
Thornton   Bradford
Hebden   Clayton
Bridge   Luddenden
Foot   Law Hill
Cross Stone   Calder   Halifax   Gomersal
Todmorden   Birstall (Brookroyd,
The Ridings)
Sowerby   Clifton   Dewsbury
Bridge   Hartshead   Crofton
Mirfield
Huddersfield   (Roe Head,
Blake Hall)

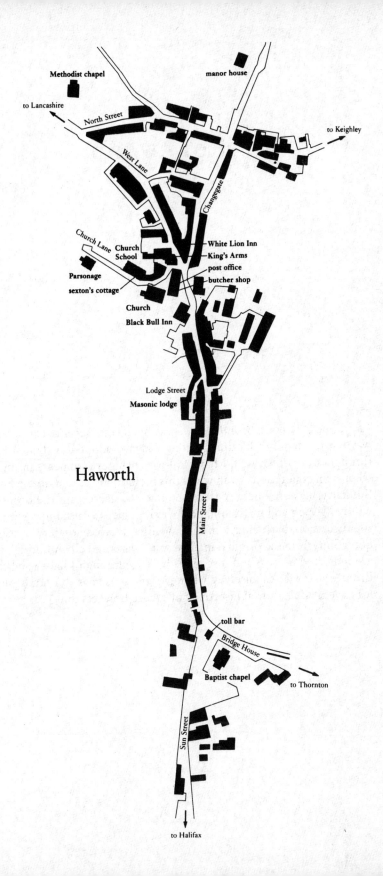

Haworth

FOREWORD

The now famous Brontë name was spelt and accented in a variety of ways in the family's lifetime. Though I have adopted a standard 'Brontë' throughout my own text, I have followed whatever appears in my sources when using quotations, even when this includes no accent on the final letter. Similarly, because I believe that the policy of 'correcting' the Brontës' often wildly ill-spelt and ungrammatical writings gives a false impression of their sophistication, particularly in the juvenilia, I have chosen to transcribe my quotations from the original manuscripts 'warts and all'. Authorial deletions are indicated by < > and insertions by \ /; although I have tried to let the Brontës speak for themselves, whenever the sense has absolutely demanded it I have made editorial insertions in square brackets thus [ ].

INTRODUCTION

Yet another biography of the Brontës requires an apology, or at least an explanation. Their lives have been written so many times that there ought to be nothing left to say. Mrs Gaskell's *Life of Charlotte Brontë*, published within two years of her subject's death, set a new standard in literary biography and is still widely read. In more recent times, Winifred Gérin and Rebecca Fraser have added considerably to our knowledge by publishing material which was not available to, or was suppressed by, Mrs Gaskell. The Brontës' lives and works have been taken apart and reassembled according to theories of varying degrees of sanity by literally hundreds of other biographers and literary critics.

What is surprising is that, despite so much activity, the basic ideas about the Brontës' lives have remained unchanged. Charlotte is portrayed as the long-suffering victim of duty, subordinating her career as a writer to the demands of her selfish and autocratic father; Emily is the wild child of genius, deeply misanthropic yet full of compassion for her errant brother; Anne is the quiet, conventional one who, lacking her sisters' rebellious spirit, conforms to the demands of society and religion. The men in their lives have suffered an even worse fate, blamed first of all by Mrs Gaskell, and since then by feminists, for holding the Brontë sisters back from achieving literary success and even, at times, for simply existing. Patrick is universally depicted as cold, austere and remote, yet given to uncontrollable rages, alternately neglecting and tyrannizing his children. Branwell is a selfish braggart, subordinating his sisters' lives to his own by right of his masculinity, and negating the value of this sacrifice by squandering his talent and the family's money on drink and drugs. Arthur Bell Nicholls, who cannot be portrayed as either mad or bad, is simply dull.

These stereotypes have been reinforced by the practice of writing separate biographies for each member of the family. Yet the most remarkable thing about the Brontës is that one family produced three, if not four, talented writers, and it is the fact that they were such an extraordinarily close family that is the key to their achievements. Taking one of them out of context creates the sort of imbalance and distortion of facts that has added considerably to the Brontë legend. A love poem by Anne, for instance, can be interpreted as autobiographical – unless one is aware that Emily was writing on the same subject at the same time in a Gondal setting. Though many have tried, it is impossible to write an authoritative biography of either of the two youngest Brontë sisters. The known facts of their lives could be written on a single sheet of paper; their letters, diary papers and drawings would not fill two dozen. Understandably but, I believe, misguidedly, biographers have fallen back on literary criticism to fill the void. Trawling through the Brontës' fiction in search of some deeply hidden autobiographical truth is a subjective and almost invariably pointless exercise.

In this biography I have deliberately chosen to write about the whole Brontë family, hoping that this will redress the balance and enable the reader to see the Brontës as they lived, not in isolation but as a tightly knit group. I am well aware that some members of the household are more prominent than others. Aunt Branwell and Tabby Aykroyd, despite my best endeavours, remain mere ciphers. Regrettably, Emily and Anne are also shadowy figures. This is the inevitable result of lack of biographical information but it is, I think, preferable to fanciful interpretation of their fiction. Virginia Moore's misreading of 'Love's Farewell' as 'Louis Parensell', resulting in an elaborate theory about Emily's secret lover, is a dire warning as to where such a method can lead.

The Brontë story has always been riddled with myths. Charlotte herself started the process in an attempt to explain why her sisters had written novels which had both shocked and titillated the literary critics. Mrs Gaskell ably extended this argument to Charlotte herself, producing in her *Life of Charlotte Brontë* a persuasive and powerful polemic which has never been seriously challenged. Instead of being writers of 'naughty books', who revelled in vulgarity and brutality, the Brontës thus became graduates of the school of adversity, writing in all innocence about the barbarous society in which they lived because that was all they knew. Their work took on a new, moral quality: that of Truth. However distasteful *Jane Eyre, Wuthering Heights* or *The Tenant of Wildfell Hall* might be, they were simply an accurate representation of provincial life. A bizarre offshoot of this argument is the belief that every one of the Brontës' fictional creations must have had its counterpart in reality. The search for originals of the places, characters and incidents in the Brontës' novels is as fanatical as it is irrelevant. Similarly, by a peculiar inversion of the normal process, literalists argue the facts of the Brontës' lives from their fiction, which they persist in regarding as autobiographical. It is not surprising that the myths survive.

The astonishing fact is that there is a wealth of material available to the biographer which has never before been used. No one has ever looked through the local newspapers, for instance, even though this is a basic source for the historian. Two years spent reading contemporary papers in local archives may have addled my brain but it has also provided an unexpectedly large haul of information which should, once and for all, scotch the myth that Haworth was a remote and obscure village where nothing ever happened. It was a township, a small, industrial town in the heart of a much larger chapelry, where politics and religion were hotly disputed and culture thrived. As a leading figure in Haworth, whose activities were constantly recorded and whose letters were regularly published, Patrick emerges as a tireless campaigner and reformer, a man of liberal beliefs rather than the rampant Tory he is so often labelled. The rest of his family, brought into the public domain by Mrs Gaskell's *Life of Charlotte Brontë*, were the subject of letters and reports by their friends and acquaintances, many of which contradict Mrs Gaskell's wilder flights of fancy from first-hand experience.

The Brontës have been ill-served by their biographers. Vast numbers of their letters, poems, stories, drawings, books and personal memorabilia have been preserved, though they are scattered throughout libraries and private collections in the United Kingdom and the United States. This is inconvenient. Many of the manuscripts are themselves divided and housed in different collections; they are often written in the Brontës' minute and cramped hand, which requires patience and good eyesight to decipher. This is even more inconvenient. But it is inexcusable that, almost without exception, the Brontës' biographers have preferred to do their research in the bowdlerized and inadequate texts which are all that are currently available in print. Where no published edition exists, that body of information has been virtually ignored. This is true of the bulk of Branwell's juvenilia and of Charlotte and Emily's French essays, leading to sweeping and highly inaccurate statements about their content. Even Charlotte's letters, though more readily accessible in manuscript, are quoted from the Shakespeare Head Brontë, which was compiled by the notorious forger, Thomas J. Wise, and his sidekick, J. A. Symington. Any derogatory remarks which did not live up to their idealized and sanitized image of Charlotte were simply omitted, as were passages difficult to read or carelessly transcribed. Margaret Smith's forthcoming monumental edition of Charlotte's letters will rectify all this but, for the moment, the conscientious biographer must rely on the manuscripts.

I have made it a point of honour to go back to the original manuscripts of all my material wherever possible, quoting them in preference to printed versions. Much of my material is therefore published here for the first time, including not only letters but also juvenilia, poetry and French essays. I have not followed the usual editorial practice of correcting the Brontës' appalling spelling and punctuation. Though this can make for difficult reading on occasion, I hope that the reader will appreciate that this is done to ensure that he can get as close as possible to the original. Correction is not just an interference with the Brontës' own words: it creates a very misleading impression of the sophistication of their writing, particularly when they were children.

I sincerely hope that this biography will sweep away the many myths which have clung to the Brontës for so long. They are no longer necessary. Unlike their contemporaries, we can value their work without being outraged or even surprised by the directness of the language and the brutality of the characters. It is surely time to take a fresh look at the Brontës' lives and recognize them for who and what they really were. When this is done, I believe, their achievements will shine brighter than ever before. For Patrick and Branwell, in particular, the time is long overdue. With due humility, I echo the words of Charlotte Brontë: 'This notice has been written, because I felt it a sacred duty to wipe the dust off their gravestones, and leave their dear names free from soil.'

Juliet R. V. Barker
May 1994

Chapter One

༷

AN AMBITIOUS MAN

On the first day of October 1802 a twenty-five-year-old Irishman walked through the imposing gateway of St John's College, Cambridge. Tall and thin, with sandy red hair, his aristocratic features and bearing marked him out as one of the gentlemen of the university. His appearance was deceptive, however, for this young man had only recently arrived in England and had not yet embarked on a university career. Indeed, his purpose in coming to St John's that day was to register as an undergraduate of the college.

He had an inauspicious start to his new life. Defeated by his Irish accent, the registrar attempted a phonetic spelling of the name he gave, entering 'Patrick Branty' as 'no 1235' in the admissions book of the college. After putting down 'Ireland' as the new undergraduate's 'county of residence', the registrar gave up his task as hopeless and left the other columns blank; the names of Patrick's parents, his date and place of birth and his educational background were all omitted.[1] Two days later, when Patrick returned to take up residence in the college, he found that the bursar had copied the mistaken spelling of his name into the college Residence Register. This time, however, he did not allow it to go unchallenged and the entry was altered from

[1]

'Branty' to the now famous 'Brontë'.[2] In this way, Patrick Brontë stepped from the obscurity of his Irish background into the pages of history.

It is difficult now to appreciate the full extent of Patrick's achievement in getting to Cambridge. To be Irish in an almost exclusively English university was in itself unusual, but what made him virtually unique was that he was also poor and of humble birth. Many years later, when Mrs Gaskell came to write her *Life of Charlotte Brontë*, Patrick gave her a brief account of his early years in Ireland.

My father's name, was Hugh Brontë – He was a native of the South of Ireland, and was left an orphan at an early age – It was said that he was of an Ancient Family. Whether this was, or was not so, I never gave myself the trouble to inquire, since his lot in life, as well as mine, depended, under providence, not on Family descent, but our own exertions – He came to the North of Ireland, and made an early, but suitable marriage. His pecuniary means were small – but renting a few acres of land, He, and my mother, by dint of application, and industry, managed to bring up a Family of ten Children, in a respectable manner. I shew'd an early fondness for books, and continued at school for several years – At the age of sixteen, knowing that my Father, could afford me no pecuniary aid I began to think of doing something for myself – I therefore opened a public school – and in this line, I continued five or six years; I was then a Tutor in a Gentleman's Family – from which situation I removed to Cambridge, and enter'd St John's College –[3]

The matter-of-fact way in which Patrick related these astonishing details is significant. For him, life effectively began only when he shook the dust of Ireland from his feet and was admitted to Cambridge. His first twenty-five years were an irrelevance, even though they must have been amongst the most formative of his life.

The bare bones of Patrick's account of his youth in Ireland can be fleshed out only a little. Nothing more is known about his father,[4] and his mother, Eleanor, sometimes called Alice, McClory, is an equally shadowy figure. According to a tradition originating at the end of the nineteenth century, she was a Roman Catholic, but this seems unlikely as all the family records of the Irish Brontës are associated with the Protestant Church and Patrick would hardly have described a mixed marriage as 'suitable'.[5] At a time when literacy was extremely rare, especially in rural districts of Ireland, the unusual Brontë name was spelt in a variety of ways, ranging from Prunty to Brunty and Bruntee, with no consistent version until Patrick himself decided on 'Bronte'.[6]

Patrick was born on 17 March 1777, apparently in a two-roomed, white-washed, thatched peasant cabin at Emdale, in the parish of Drumballyroney, County Down.[7] Over the next nineteen years, Hugh and Eleanor produced four more sons, followed by five daughters.[8] Despite the demands which this ever-growing family must have made on his slender resources, Hugh seems to have succeeded in substantially advancing the family fortunes. By 1781, when their third son, Hugh, was born, the Brontës were living in a larger house at Lisnacreevy, in the same parish, and before the arrival of their last daughter, Alice, in 1796, they had moved again. Their new home, a short distance away at Ballynaskeagh, was a large, two-storey, stone-built house, which was the epitome of respectability.⁹ Hugh Brontë may have been only a 'poor farmer' but he was not the impoverished peasant of Brontë legend.¹⁰

It is a further indication of the fact that the Brontës were not in desperate financial straits that Patrick escaped the customary fate of the eldest child in a large family. Instead of being put to work on his father's farm or apprenticed out so that he could make a contribution to the family income, he was allowed to remain at school much longer than was usual at the time.¹¹ The school itself has never been satisfactorily identified, but if it was simply the local village one at Glascar, it seems likely that Patrick may have stayed on as an usher or pupil-teacher in order to extend his education and prepare him for a future career as a teacher.¹²

Given the scarcity of written records in Ireland at this time, it is all the more remarkable that there is confirmation of Patrick's startling claim to have established his own school at the age of only sixteen. In November 1793, when Patrick was indeed sixteen, John Lindsay of Bangrove, Rathfriland, recorded the payment of one pound to 'Pat Prunty for David's school bill' in his account book.¹³ Nothing else is known about Patrick's school, not even its precise location, though the fact that it must have catered for the sons of the gentry, rather than village children, is indicated by the size of the fee charged and by David Lindsay's subsequent appointment as an officer in the local militia.¹⁴ If this was the case, then Patrick must have been able to offer more than the basics of reading, writing and arithmetic to his young pupils. Whether he was self-taught or whether his evident talents had already attracted the attention of local clergymen, who alone were in the position to give him higher education, is not known.¹⁵ Patrick's abilities and ambition must have made him an outstanding figure in the parish; his brothers simply followed in their father's footsteps, taking on the family farm and, apparently, extending into keeping an ale-house, shoemaking and building roads.¹⁶

On the surface, Patrick's decision to exchange the independence of keeping his own school for the comparatively humble role of tutor in a gentleman's family is surprising. But this was 1798, one of the most momentous years in Irish history.¹⁷ The rebellion of that year had its roots in the French Revolution, which had inspired the formation of a Society of United Irishmen who, like their French contemporaries, had gradually grown more extreme in their views. By 1797, they no longer simply advocated Protestantism and nationalism but had openly dedicated themselves to the violent overthrow of the Anglican ruling minority and the establishment in Ireland of social and political reform along French lines. When the new lord lieutenant determined to crush the United Irishmen by disarming Ulster, he drove them into open revolt. County Down, where the Brontë family lived, was at the epicentre of the rebellion. At the very least this must have disrupted Patrick's school; at worst, it may have caused its closure. More importantly, at least one member of the Brontë family, the second son, William, was himself a United Irishman. He joined the rebels and fought at the battle of Ballanahinch in June 1798, when the United Irishmen were crushed by government forces, and was lucky to escape capture and punishment.[18]

Where Patrick's loyalties lay at this time is unclear, but in later life he was an impassioned defender of the 1801 Act of Union, which suppressed Ireland's independent Parliament and administration, effectively transferring all executive power to London. He was equally fervent in denouncing rebellion, which suggests that this first-hand experience of popular revolt left him deeply scarred. For the rest of his life, his political opinions would be swayed by his fear of revolution, even to the point of aligning him with the Tory party which, in many other respects, was not his natural allegiance.[19]

The likelihood is that Patrick's political views were already diametrically opposed to his brother's and that the rebellion simply confirmed him in them. By the time it was over, the rebels disbanded, their leaders hanged and a supporting French invasion, which came too late to be of any assistance, repelled, Patrick's life had changed irrevocably. In taking up the appointment as tutor to the children of Thomas Tighe, he had publicly distanced himself from his brother and his brother's cause and declared his own allegiance to the establishment.

The Reverend Thomas Tighe was more than just the local clergyman, vicar of Drumballyroney and rector of Drumgooland. He was the third son of William Tighe, MP, of Rosanna in County Wicklow, and half-brother to two members of the Irish Parliament. Thomas Tighe himself was a justice of the peace and chaplain to the Earl of Glandore. As such he was one of the wealthy landed gentry of Ireland and a man of considerable influence. He had been educated in England, at Harrow, had graduated from St John's College, Cambridge, and been a fellow of Peterhouse before returning to take up his ministry in the Established Church of Ireland.[20] He had been vicar of Drumballyroney since 1778, so he must have known Patrick almost from birth and had had plenty of opportunity to observe his character and his single-minded pursuit of an education. His decisive intervention at such a late stage in Patrick's career, when the young man was already twenty-one, suggests that, for whatever reason, he saw the need to redirect his energies: undoubtedly, too, he had recognized in Patrick a potential recruit for the ministry of his church.

Although Thomas Tighe was a member of the Church of Ireland, he belonged firmly within the Evangelical camp. This was a reforming movement which sought to revive and reinspire a church whose ministry was corrupt and careless and whose congregations were disaffected. Through charismatic preachers, most notably the Wesleys, the Evangelicals' message was taken out of the somnolent parish churches and into the highways and byways of Britain. They preached a faith of personal commitment which began with a positive act of conversion.[21] Habitual self-examination, a sense of one's own sinfulness and an awareness of the imminence of the Day of Judgement, all combined to ensure that a life once dedicated to God remained positively and actively employed in His service. Because the Evangelicals placed great emphasis on the Bible, their ministers were particularly enthusiastic about the need for education and literacy among their congregations, promoting Sunday schools, holding 'cottage meetings' and producing simple, didactic pamphlets. This was a faith that demanded a missionary zeal in its ministers; there was simply no place for the idle or the half-hearted. Though the day was not far off when the Evangelicals would have to decide whether to remain within the Established Church or become a separate movement, as those who chose to become Methodists did in 1812, at this time there was no such conflict. Itinerant Evangelical preachers had been welcomed by Thomas Tighe and his relatives at both Rosanna, the family home, and Drumballyroney Rectory; John Wesley was a personal friend of the family and had stayed with the Tighes at Rosanna in June 1789 on his last visit to Ireland, eighteen months before his death.[22]

In the long term, Tighe's Evangelical sympathies were to be far more important to Patrick than his political and social connections. They were to be the inspiration for the whole of his future career. It has often been suggested that Patrick's choice of the Church was dictated by worldly ambition: the Church or the army, it is argued, were the only means by which talented but poor young men could seek to better themselves. This is singularly unfair to Patrick. Though his ambition cannot be doubted, neither can his personal faith. His writings and his activities are eloquent testimony to the sincerity of his belief, and the fact that he entered the ministry under the aegis of the Evangelicals is further proof of his commitment. By doing so he was effectively curtailing his chances of future promotion, for Evangelical clergymen were, as yet, only a small group within the Church and their progress met with considerable resistance from the all-powerful High Church party. It was difficult to find bishops willing to ordain them or grant them livings, and even the most venerated of all Evangelical clergymen, Charles Simeon, was never anything more than a simple vicar.[23] Had Patrick been ambitious for temporal, rather than spiritual, glory, he had enlisted under the wrong banner.

There were considerable difficulties to overcome if Patrick was to reach his goal of ordination, not the least being that he could not become a clergyman unless he graduated from one of the universities. To do that, he had first to be proficient in Latin and Greek. As these were not on the syllabus of the ordinary village school in Ireland, it seems likely that Patrick was instructed in the Classics by Thomas Tighe, perhaps in part-payment for his services as a tutor to the family. Interestingly, the story was current as early as 1855 that Patrick adopted the 'Bronte' spelling of his surname in response to pressure from Thomas Tighe, who disliked the plebian 'Brunty' and thought the Greek word for thunder a more appropriate and resonant version of the name.[24]

Having overcome his first hurdle, acquiring the gentleman's prerequisite, a classical education, Patrick faced the problem of obtaining entrance to university. Ostensibly there were three choices open to him: Trinity College in Dublin, the natural choice for an Irishman, Oxford or Cambridge.[25] In reality, however, Cambridge – and indeed St John's College – was Patrick's only option. It was not simply that Thomas Tighe pushed him to go to his own college, which both his half-brothers and, more recently, his nephew, had attended.[26] St John's was renowned for its Evangelical connections and, perhaps most important of all as far as Patrick was concerned, it had the largest funds available of any college in any of the universities for assisting poor but able young men to get a university education. Unlike most other college foundations, these scholarships were not all tied to specific schools or particular areas of the country, so if Patrick was to get into any university, St John's at Cambridge offered him the greatest chance of doing so.[27] To be admitted, all that he required were letters from Thomas Tighe attesting to his ability, confirming that he had reached the necessary standard of education and recommending him for an assisted place as a sizar.

Four long years after taking up the post as tutor to Thomas Tighe's children, Patrick finally achieved his ambition. Leaving behind his family, his friends and his home, he embarked for England with his meagre savings in his pocket and, it would appear, with scarcely a backward glance.

From the moment that he arrived in Cambridge in July 1802[28] to the day he graduated in 1806, Patrick Brontë was a distinctive and somewhat eccentric figure. His humble Irish background marked him out immediately, as did the fact that he was one of only four sizars in his year, though fortunately the menial tasks which went with the sizarship, such as waiting on the wealthier undergraduates at table, had recently been abolished.[29] Although some of the other men were already graduates of other universities when they came to St John's, Patrick, at twenty-five, was up to ten years older than many of his contemporaries. Most were wealthy young men who had been taught by private tutors or at public school; at worst they had been to long-established grammar schools which had links with the university going back centuries. For some, going to Cambridge was simply an opportunity for indulgence and a pleasant way of passing a few years before returning to the family estates or business.[30] A degree was desirable but not essential. For Patrick, it was the passport to a promising future and he had no intention of being distracted from his purpose. He was, in every sense, an outsider and he had only to open his mouth to betray his origins. No doubt he suffered from the snobbery and élitism of some of his contemporaries but, on the other hand, he did not pass unnoticed. At the very least, the unorthodox and rather romantic circumstances of his arrival at Cambridge made an impression and within a couple of years he was already a legend at the college.

Henry Martyn, for example, a leading Evangelical who was then a fellow of St John's, wrote to William Wilberforce, the great anti-slavery campaigner, in February 1804, describing Patrick's progress to college as having

[a] singularity [which] has hardly been equalled, I suppose, since the days of Bp Latimer – He left his native Ireland at the age of 22 with seven pounds having been able to lay by no more after superintending a school ten years. He reached Cambridge before that was expended, & there received an unexpected supply of £5 from a distant friend. On this he subsisted some weeks before entering at St John's, & has since had no other assistance than what the college afforded.[31]

Another contemporary was the poet Henry Kirke White, who is now perhaps best remembered for his hymn 'Oft in danger, oft in woe'. The son of a Nottingham butcher, he was admitted as a sizar to St John's in April 1804. Beset by financial problems himself, he was filled with admiration for Patrick, who managed to get by on an even lower income than he did. In a letter home, written on 26 October 1805, he told his mother:

I have got the bills of Mr [Brontë], a Sizar of this college, now before me, and from them, and his own account, I will give you a statement of what my college bills will amount to … 12£ or 15£ a-year at the most … The Mr [Brontë], whose bills I have borrowed, has been at college three years. He came over from [Ireland], with 10£ in his pocket, and has no friends, or any income or emolument whatever, except what he receives for his Sizarship; yet he does support himself, and that, too, very genteelly.[32]

Life in the college would certainly be gracious compared to the farmhouse at Ballynaskeagh. Patrick probably shared rooms with John Nunn, a fellow sizar, who was to become his closest friend, in the third storey of the front quadrangle, provided free of charge by the college. Most rooms were already furnished, though Patrick may have been unlucky, like Henry Kirke White, and found himself assigned unfurnished rooms which would have cost him about fifteen pounds to equip. Economies were possible, however, and White got away with spending 'only' four pounds by sleeping on a horsehair mattress on the floor instead of a proper bed.[33] He would also have had to pay for wood or coals to heat his rooms and candles to enable him to work outside daylight hours, though savings could be made even in this area. His own tutor, James Wood, the son of Lancashire weavers, had also once been a poor sizar at the college. He had lived in a small garret at the top of the turret in the southeast corner of the Second Court called 'the Tub' where, to save money, he used to study by the light of the rush candles on the staircase, with his feet wrapped in straw.[34] All the sizars dined in hall and the provision of food was generous, as Henry Kirke White explained:

Our dinners and suppers cost us nothing; and if a man choose to eat milk-breakfasts, and go without tea, he may live absolutely for nothing; for his college emoluments will cover the rest of his expenses. Tea is indeed almost superfluous, since we do not rise from dinner till half-past three, and the supper-bell rings a quarter before nine. Our mode of living is not to be complained of, for the table is covered with all possible variety; and on feast-days, which our fellows take care are pretty frequent, we have wine[35]

St John's was far and away the largest of all the colleges, its closest rival in terms of size being Trinity, next door. Most of the other dozen or so colleges were little more than small halls, lacking the grandeur of their two big brothers, though the magnificent Gothic chapel of King's College dominated the townscape then as now. The libraries offered the opportunity for recreation as well as study to someone like Patrick, for whom the purchase of a book meant considerable financial self-sacrifice. The churches and college chapels, too, with their enviable choirs and organs, provided music of a quality that Patrick could never have heard before. More importantly, they were the platform for the Evangelical preachers who, led by Charles Simeon himself from his pulpit at Holy Trinity Church, were inspiring a new generation of clergymen with the missionary faith of Evangelism.[36] If Patrick had not already been an Evangelical by the time he left Thomas Tighe in Ireland, he had every opportunity and incentive for conversion at Cambridge. He certainly seems to have been one of those ardent young men who met in Simeon's rooms and were taught the necessity of preaching 'to humble the sinner, to exalt the Saviour, and to promote holiness'.[37]

Beyond the insular life of the colleges there was the town of Cambridge, with its bustling markets which served the surrounding countryside and the Cam, which was not the sleepy river of today, but an important and busy waterway.[38] By comparison with the rural Ireland of Patrick's earlier years, the town must have seemed like a metropolis, though the drab Fenlands must have been a poor substitute for the beautiful mountains of Mourne, especially to a great walker like Patrick.

Though his sizarship relieved him of much of the burden of his living expenses at Cambridge, Patrick would still have had a struggle to make ends meet. The biggest expense was the fees payable to his college and the university. These were worked out on a sliding scale, so that where a fellow commoner (a nobleman) would pay £25 on admission and 17/6d. quarterly for tuition fees to his college, a pensioner (younger sons of the aristocracy, the gentry and professional classes) would pay £15 and 11/6d., but Patrick, as a sizar, would pay only £10 and 6/4d. respectively.[39] The university, too, demanded fees on matriculation and on graduation so that it was vital to Patrick to maintain an income of some kind. He did this in two ways – both dependent on his academic success. Firstly, he taught pupils in his leisure hours, a practice which might earn him up to fifteen guineas for four months' work in the long vacation. If he was lucky, there might be the additional bonus of gifts from grateful pupils, like the invaluable Lemprière's *Bibliotheca Classica*, presented to him by Mr Toulmen.[40] Secondly, he won exhibitions and books through excelling in his college examinations.

Patrick was fortunate in having three outstanding tutors at St John's: James Wood, Joshua Smith and Thomas Catton. All three had held sizarships themselves, so they fully understood the difficulties of and actively encouraged the sizars in their care. James Wood, an Evangelical who later became Master of the college and a Vice Chancellor of the university, was especially active on Patrick's behalf.[41] Under their guidance, Patrick's academic career flourished.

Fortunately, the records of the college examinations still exist, so we can see exactly how well he did in comparison with the rest of his year. It is significant that the lowest he ever came in the order of merit was in his very first attempt, in December 1802, when he came twenty-fifth out of thirty-seven in an examination on the geometry of Euclid and the theology of Beausobre and Doddridge.[42] It is a mark of his achievement that, despite lacking the advantages of a public school or private tutor which were available to most of his contemporaries,[43] Patrick still managed to scrape into the first class in this examination. James Wood noted against his name and those of the three men immediately above him that they were 'Inferior to the above but entitled to prizes if in the first class at the next examination'.[44]

From this moment on, Patrick's academic career never faltered. In each of the half-yearly exams that followed, Patrick maintained his place in a first class which grew steadily smaller over the years. The set books were alternately in Greek for the June examinations and Latin for the December ones, but all were chosen from the standard classics of the ancient world. In 1803 the set texts were histories: in June the *Anabasis* of Xenophon and in December, Tacitus' *Agricola*, at which point his friend, John Nunn, slipped from the first to the second class. In 1804 the subject was poetry with Euripides' verse tragedy *Iphigenia in Aulis* set for June, and books 1 and 4 of Virgil's *Georgics* set for December, when poor Nunn, whose Latin was obviously not as good as his Greek, dropped even further down into the third class. In June 1805, Patrick's last college examinations, the set book was Mounteney's edition of the speeches of Demosthenes, the Athenian orator and statesman. To crown his college career, Patrick was one of only seven men to get into the first class and, even more impressively, one of only five who had managed to maintain an unbroken record of first-class successes.[45]

Those who were in the first class in both the annual examinations were entitled to prize books. It is surprising, therefore, that only two of Patrick's are still extant, especially as he clearly regarded them with great pride. They were both standard works: Richard Bentley's 1728 edition of the works of Horace and Samuel Clarke's 1729 edition of Homer's *Iliad* in a dual Greek and Latin text.[46] Though both were nearly eighty years old, they had been rebound in stout leather and, as he pointed out in his inscriptions at the beginning, each bore the college arms on the front cover. On the title page of the *Iliad*, Patrick carefully noted: 'My Prize Book, for having always kept in the first Class, at St John's College – Cambridge – P. Brontê, A.B. To be retained – semper – '. A similar statement was inscribed in the Horace. The odd phrase 'To be retained – semper' (always) was one that Patrick was to use again and again over the years in books and manuscripts and it was a habit he was to pass on to his children.[47]

Patrick's pride was natural and justified. He had worked hard and the prize books were concrete evidence of his achievement. Another tangible result was the awarding of college exhibitions which, though not in themselves very substantial sums, together made an invaluable contribution towards his income. They were paid half-yearly, at the end of June and the end of December, following the college examinations. The most valuable was the Hare exhibition, worth £5 a year, which he was awarded in February 1803 and which was paid to him from June 1803 until December 1807 – a full eighteen months after he had left the college. The Suffolk exhibition, which should have been worth £3 6s. 8d. annually, was only worth half that amount because Patrick had to share it with a graduate, Dr A. Brown; although awarded at Christmas 1803, he had to wait till the following June for his first payment, but again it was paid to him up to and including December 1807. Finally, he held the Goodman exhibition for the six months from June to December 1805, receiving the half-yearly payment of 14s. at the end of that time.[48] Altogether, the exhibitions would give him an annual income of £6 13s. 4d., rising to £7 7s. 4d. for the short period when he held the Goodman exhibition.

By scrimping and saving, Patrick contrived to make ends meet, but by his own account to Henry Kirke White he needed between twelve and fifteen pounds a year for college bills alone. The shortfall had to be made up somehow – and in a way that would not detract from his studies. The obvious solution was to seek sponsorship of some kind and so, at the beginning of 1804, Patrick sought out Henry Martyn, who, though four years younger than Patrick, was already a fellow of St John's. Martyn, who had been Senior Wrangler (the student with the highest marks) of the university in 1801, was Charles Simeon's curate at Holy Trinity Church and therefore sympathetic towards a young man with Evangelical aspirations.[49] He took up Patrick's case immediately, writing first of all to John Sargent:

An Irishman, of the name of Bronte entered at St John's a year & half ago as a sizar. During this time he has received <u>no</u> assistance from his friends who are incapable of affording him any – Yet he has been able to get on in general pretty well by help of Exhibitions &c which are given to our sizars. Now however, he finds himself reduced to great straits & applied to me just before I left Cambridge to know if assistance could be procured for him from any of those societies, whose object is to maintain pious young men designed for the ministry.[50]

Patrick had now taken the plunge and committed himself to a career in the Church of England. Sargent contacted Henry Thornton, patron of one of the Evangelical societies, who, with his more famous cousin, William Wilberforce, himself a graduate of St John's College, agreed personally to sponsor Patrick through university. Martyn wrote to Wilberforce to thank him:

I availed myself as soon as possible of your generous offer to Mr Bronte & left it without hesitation to himself to fix the limits of his request. He says that £20 per annm. will enable him to go on with comfort, but that he could do with less.[51]

Wilberforce himself endorsed the letter 'Martyn abt Mr Bronte Heny. & I to allow him 10L. each anny.' The fact that Patrick was able to attract the attention of men of the calibre of Martyn, Thornton and Wilberforce is further proof of his commitment to his faith and his outstanding qualities. Henry Martyn himself had no doubts about him, telling Sargent unequivocally, 'For the character of the man I can safely vouch as I know him to be studious, clever, & pious – '. Recounting Patrick's long struggle to get to Cambridge from Ireland to Wilberforce, Martyn added another unsolicited testimonial: 'There is reason to hope that he will be an instrument of good to the church, as a desire of usefulness in the ministry seems to have influenced him hitherto in no small degree.'[52]

The fact that Patrick was now joining the majority of St John's undergraduates in working towards a career in the Church did not prevent him, or them, from taking part in the more secular activities of the university. Most prominent among these were the preparations for an invasion of England by the French which, after the renewal of hostilities by Napoleon and the declaration of war by Great Britain on 18 May 1803, seemed a daily possibility. Throughout the summer of 1803 Napoleon was putting together an invasion flotilla and restructuring the defences of his Channel ports. Volunteers were called for and by December 1803, 463,000 men had enrolled in the local militia of the three kingdoms. Among them was Patrick Brontë, who had a lifelong passion for all things military.[53] By September of that year the gentlemen of the university had obtained leave to drill as a separate volunteer corps from the men of the town. The following month, the heads of colleges and tutors gave reluctant permission for all lay members of the university to be allowed one hour a day for military drill, on condition that none of the officers were to be gazetted so as to be called up into the regular army; those who were already ordained were, of course, excluded from taking any active part in the drilling.[54]

On 25 February 1804 the *Cambridge Chronicle* published a list of 154 gentlemen of the university who, 'in the present crisis', had been instructed in the use of arms by Captain Bircham of the 30th Regiment.[55] The St John's men were headed by Lord Palmerston, who had been admitted to the college on 4 April 1804.[56] Though he was only eighteen, his social standing made him the obvious candidate to be elected as officer in charge of the fourth division, which was made up of the men of St John's and Peterhouse. Patrick Brontë, with his friend John Nunn, had joined the corps before Christmas and for nine months they trained in the Market Square under the command of Palmerston and under the watchful eye of Captain Bircham. Just before the university volunteer corps was effectively temporarily disbanded with the advent of the long vacation, they gathered to drill at Parker's Piece; after performing a series of manoeuvres, the volunteers formed into a hollow square to witness the presentation to the Captain by Palmerston of a letter containing two hundred guineas as 'a token of their acknowledgment for his unremitted attention to them ... and to express the high sense they entertained of his services'.[57] For the rest of his life Patrick was to be inordinately proud of the fact that he had drilled under Lord Palmerston, not least because by 1809, when he was still only a humble curate, Palmerston had been appointed Minister for War, and was already embarking on a long political career which was to make him an outstanding foreign secretary and prime minister.

The country continued in a state of constant alarms and invasion scares throughout Patrick's remaining years at Cambridge and, indeed, for many more years to come. Nelson's great victory at Trafalgar on 21 October 1805 ended the immediate and serious threat, however, and was celebrated in Cambridge with a general illumination[58] when candles and lamps were lit in the streets and all the windows of the colleges, shops and houses.

At the beginning of Michaelmas term 1805 Patrick was entering his fourth year at the university, at the end of which he would have completed his minimum residence requirement for taking his degree. His finances would not allow him to continue there any longer and, unless he won a fellowship to one of the colleges, he would have to look for employment as a curate. He therefore gave his name to his tutor so that the proctors could be informed of his decision to proceed to the degree of Bachelor of Arts. It was important to Patrick to do well, not only to maintain the academic reputation of sizars at his college, but also to justify the sums expended on him by his patrons.

Some time in the Lent term of 1806 Patrick would have been called to appear in the examination schools as a Disputant. He would have been given a fortnight in which to prepare a dissertation, in Latin, upon a Proposition taken from one of the three heads of the course. This gave him a choice of Natural Philosophy (Mathematics), Moral Philosophy (including the works of modern philosophers such as Locke and Hume) or *Belles Lettres* (Classical literature). He would have read his dissertation aloud and three other men of his year would then have attacked his Proposition, again in Latin, offering their own arguments in syllogistical form. The best men of the year, which, given his college performances, would probably have included Patrick, appeared eight times in Schools in this manner: twice as a Disputant, proposing a thesis, and six times as an Opponent. As if public oral examination in Latin were not enough, the degree candidates then had to undergo a formal written examination with the best candidates being put forward for Honours.[59] Patrick did not, apparently, proceed to an Honours degree, which suggests that, at this final hurdle, he failed to reach the required standard.

There was evidently also some sort of minor hitch in the granting of Patrick's degree, perhaps because he was absent on matters connected with his ordination. In December 1805 he had made arrangements for Thomas Tighe to write certifying his age since he could not produce a certificate of baptism, there being no baptismal registers in Drumballyroney before September 1778.[60] On 22 March 1806 he had also obtained a certification from Professor Fawcett to confirm that he had attended forty-seven lectures in Divinity, missing only three: 'one omission was occasioned by indisposition, two by necessary business in the Country'.[61]

Perhaps because he was too busy gathering his ordination documentation, Patrick missed the official degree day so that his name appears 'Post Comm.', that is, after the usual date for receiving degrees.[62] Another anomaly was that he signed the University Subscriptions Register, recording his having taken the oath to abide by the Thirty-Nine Articles of the Church of England, (a necessity which excluded Dissenters and Catholics from taking degrees), in person, on 22 April 1806 – the day before, instead of after, the conferral of his degree.[63] However the confusion arose, Patrick formally graduated as a Bachelor of Arts on St George's Day, 23 April 1806, and thereafter was entitled to write 'B.A.' or, more usually, 'A.B.' after his name. St John's gave him the customary four pounds for obtaining his degree and Patrick, in a moment of uncharacteristic profligacy, celebrated by buying a copy of Walter Scott's newly published *The Lay of the Last Minstrel*. He proudly inscribed it 'P. Brontë. B.A. St John's College, Cambridge –' and carefully put it into his tiny collection of books.[64]

For a little while longer, Patrick remained in his college, sorting out his affairs. He had no need to worry about future employment for he was now within the charmed circle of Cambridge graduates. Perhaps he received reassurance as to his prospects from his tutor, like Henry Kirke White, who was told, 'We make it a rule ... of providing for a clever man, whose fortune is small; & you may therefore rest assured, Mr White, that after you have taken your degree, you will be provided for with a genteel competency <u>by the college</u>.'[65] If no fellowship was available at St John's, White was advised, then he might be recommended to another college or, if all else failed, they could always get him a situation as a private tutor in a gentleman's family.[66]

Interestingly, Patrick seems to have had ambitions to become a college fellow. Despite the fact that it meant he had to continue paying tutorage fees and certain college bills, even after he was no longer in residence, Patrick left his name on the boards for a full two years after he had taken his degree.[67] This was an accepted method of indicating that a graduate was offering himself as a candidate for a fellowship and it was not incompatible with ordination. In the event, however, no offer was forthcoming, probably because he did not have an Honours degree.

By 28 June Patrick had a sworn document from Joseph Jowett, Regius Professor of Civil Law at Cambridge, appointing him his curate in the parish of Wethersfield in Essex at a salary of £60 a year.[68] Having secured his first curacy, Patrick allowed his name to be put forward for ordination immediately. The very next day, Samuel Chilcote, the curate at All Saints' Church in Cambridge, gave public notice that 'Mr Patrick Bronte intended to offer himself a Candidate for Holy Orders.'[69] Three days later, on 2 July, the Master and Senior Fellows of St John's signed letters testimonial on his behalf, attesting to the fact that he had behaved 'studiously and regularly' during his residence and that he had never believed or maintained anything contrary to the doctrine and discipline of the Church of England.[70] Patrick sent the letters, together with the certificates from Samuel Chilcote, Thomas Tighe and Professor Fawcett, to the secretary of the Bishop of London. In his accompanying letter he offered himself as a candidate for holy orders at the next ordination and asked which books he would be examined in by the bishop.[71]

The next ordination was on 10 August so Patrick had a full month to prepare himself for his bishop's examination. He made his last farewells in Cambridge and travelled up by coach to London. Perhaps he made his first acquaintance with the Chapter Coffee House in Paternoster Row at this time, but certainly he emerged from Fulham chapel on 10 August 1806 a deacon in holy orders.[72] His friend and fellow sizar, John Nunn, had been ordained deacon by the Bishop of Lichfield at the parish church of Eccleshall in Staffordshire on 1 June and was already officiating as a curate at St Chad's in Shrewsbury,[73] so Patrick must have felt some impatience to emulate him and make his own way in the world. In four years he had come a very long way from his humble origins in Ireland. His degree had made him a gentleman, his ordination would make him a clergyman; his future lay in his own hands, make of it what he would.

After his ordination, Patrick had a couple of months in hand before he was required in Wethersfield and it is possible that, despite an expense he could ill afford, he took the opportunity to make what would be his last trip to Ireland. No doubt there were ties of affection and duty that induced him to return; the Tighes, as well as his own family, would wish to hear how he had got on at Cambridge and to find out whether he had fulfilled his early promise. He may also have been influenced by the fact that Drumballyroney Church, where he had been baptized and where his first benefactor was still the vicar, was undoubtedly the most appropriate place for him to preach his first sermon to a congregation composed of his family, old friends and neighbours.[74]

Before taking a final leave of his family, Patrick obtained two letters from his father swearing (mistakenly) that he was twenty-eight years of age; these were required for his ordination as priest since he had no record of his baptism. Though the two letters are almost identical, one of them used the 'Bronte' name unaccented, but the other used 'Brontë',[75] a form which had appeared for the first time on all the letters for Patrick's ordination as deacon, except that supplied by his college.

If the visit to Ireland took place, it was brief. He seems to have left Ireland with few regrets. Though he retained a sentimental attachment to the land of his birth, his contacts with his relatives were to be few and far between and confined principally to the sending of occasional sums of money.[76] He never expressed any wish to return to Ireland and did not inspire any curiosity in his children to seek out their father's relatives or his first home.[77] Patrick had plainly seen that his future lay in England and he was eager to take up his first curacy there.

Wethersfield was – and still is – a small village in one of the prettiest parts of Essex. Less than thirty-five miles from Cambridge, the countryside between Wethersfield and its nearest neighbour, Finchingfield, rises above the surrounding flat fenlands; the two villages are set in gently rolling hills, large enough to give variety to the landscape but not so steep as to tire the walker. The patchwork of arable fields, divided up by hedgerows, narrow winding roads and small areas of woodland, looks as though it has changed little over the years though hops are no longer the main crop of the rich brown soil. The ancient windmills that dot the landscape are an attractive reminder of the huge amount of grain also grown in this area. The farmhouses, some of such antiquity that they still retain the vestiges of their moats, speak eloquently of the wealth of past and present generations. Patrick could hardly have chosen a more attractive place to launch his clerical career and yet, despite its seeming remoteness, the village was only seven miles from the bustling town of Braintree and about forty-five miles from the heart of London.

Wethersfield itself is still the same cluster of houses, less than half a mile long, built around the village green which also formed the junction of the three roads, leading to Braintree, Finchingfield and Sible Hedingham. Just over 1,300 people lived there, most of them employed on the land.[78] The village had a windmill and a brewery, with a school somewhat inappropriately placed between them, and several public houses.[79] Most of the buildings date from the seventeenth and eighteenth centuries and are an attractive mix of half-timbering and red brick, pargeting and weatherboarding. The most important house in the village, Wethersfield Manor, a huge eighteenth-century mansion, still stands in its own parkland on the approach from the Braintree road.

Close by, at the top of an incline rising from the village green, stands the magnificent church of St Mary Magdalene. There has been a church on this site since before the Norman Conquest and the hotchpotch of buildings reflects the styles of the different periods when additions were made. Built mainly of brick and knapped flint, it is dominated by a massive, square, twelfth-century tower and two huge porches, one to the south door, facing Wethersfield Manor, dating from around 1500, and a more modern one to the north door, giving access to the village, which was rebuilt in brick in 1750. Inside, the church is equally impressive, with a twelfth-century nave, and aisles and arcades added in the thirteenth and fourteenth centuries.[80] The walls and floor are covered with memorials, mainly to the Mott family, and near the altar is the splendid alabaster tomb of the Wentworths, with its recumbent male and female figures in late fifteenth-century dress. Even when Patrick first saw it in 1806 this tomb had already been defaced with graffiti from the two previous centuries.

It was in St George's House, a pleasant eighteenth-century building opposite the church gate, that Patrick took lodgings on his arrival at Wethersfield. Its frontage is deceptively narrow, for the house extends a long way back from the road and was apparently large enough to provide rooms for not only a clerical lodger but also the local doctor; it belonged to a Miss Mildred Davy.[81]

A few doors down, facing the green, is one of the biggest houses in the village, a large, three-storey, brick-built manse, standing next to the Congregational chapel. Nonconformity had a long and honourable history in Wethersfield extending back to the Reformation and there had been an independent chapel in the village for almost as long. Richard Rogers, son of the editor of the Matthews Bible, which had been approved by Henry VIII, had been a lecturer at the church for about forty-six years and had been burned at the stake during the Marian persecutions. Stephen Marshall, his successor and a Presbyterian, had been a highly influential chaplain to the Long Parliament which opposed Charles I and waged war on him. John Cole, the minister appointed during the Commonwealth, had been expelled from the living because he refused to use the Book of Common Prayer for his services; imprisoned for eight years, he set up an independent congregation by holding services in his own house after his release.[82] During the 1620s, emigrants from Wethersfield had travelled to the New World, founding a town in Connecticut which they named after their own village and, in 1635, establishing the third oldest of the Congregational chapels in America there.[83] Unlike the Wesleyans and other Methodists who were, as yet, still within the communion of the Church of England, the Congregationalists were fiercely independent and there was little love lost between the two. This was to be a decisive factor in one of the most important decisions of Patrick's life.

Joseph Jowett, vicar of Wethersfield, combined his clerical duties with a full-time post as Regius Professor of Civil Law at Cambridge. Or rather, he lived and worked in Cambridge and was part-time vicar of Wethersfield, spending only the three months of the long vacation in residence.[84] The living, which was in the gift of his college, Trinity Hall, was, of course, a valuable increment to his salary. For nine months of the year the curate was, in practical terms, in sole charge of the parish – a rather uncomfortable position for a newly ordained clergyman in his first curacy.

Patrick took his first duties on 12 October 1806 with a marriage and a baptism on the same day. Over the next week he performed three more marriages, catching up on a backlog that had built up over the summer, but thereafter there was only an average of just over one marriage a month.[85] Similarly, the number of baptisms averaged out at only two a month, though as Patrick seems to have specialized in multiple baptisms and held them, almost without exception, during his Sunday services, they hardly added a great deal to his workload.[86] The number of burials fluctuated considerably and Patrick was unfortunate that, soon after his arrival, there was an outbreak of typhus fever, the perennial disease of the poor. A neighbouring hamlet of wretched, damp cottages housing agricultural labourers was particularly badly affected. There was little that the parish doctor could do to ease their condition or prevent the outbreak spreading within the community and out of the forty people who fell ill, a quarter died.[87]

Despite the typhus outbreak, Patrick's formal duties at Wethersfield were relatively light, leaving him most of his time free to occupy as he wished. As a conscientious parish priest, he undoubtedly visited the sick, comforted the dying and helped to administer charitable aid to those in need. He may also have taught the Scriptures in the local charity school, where, according to the terms of Dorothy Mott's foundation, twenty girls were to be taught their catechism and had to attend the parish church regularly, in addition to learning how to sew and knit. Patrick, as the clergyman present in the parish, would have had to distribute the excess funds from Dorothy Mott's foundation to the poor 'whether Churchmen or Dissenters' on 21 December each year but he seems to have been excluded from all the decision-taking, which was dealt with by the vicar, on his brief visits, with the churchwardens.[88] Indeed, in the somewhat jaundiced view of the village doctor (a Nonconformist), Patrick was almost totally without influence: 'I had no acquaintance with him or notice from him, and nobody took any notice of him.'[89]

The curacy of Wethersfield was hardly a place for a man to make his mark; it was a pleasant and gentle way of breaking Patrick into his new career but he was ambitious, a man with a mission to convert and to minister, so he must have found his position, cut off from the mainstream of Evangelical activity in the depths of Essex, increasingly frustrating. Perhaps this is what took him to Colchester in the summer of 1807. While Jowett was in residence at Wethersfield, Patrick's presence was no longer needed in the parish and sometime after 9 July, when he performed a marriage, he removed to Colchester, some fifteen miles east of Braintree.

Two considerations must have influenced him. The first was the possibility of visiting John Nunn, whose family home was in Colchester.[90] The second, and more important, reason was that St Peter's Church, the largest in the town, was an outstanding centre of Evangelism. The right of presentation to the living had been bought with the specific purpose of ensuring that only Evangelicals were appointed and one of the trustees was Charles Simeon of Cambridge. The Reverend Robert Storry, who had been vicar of St Peter's since 1781, was a staunch Evangelical; he described himself as a 'gospel clergyman' and during his ministry had tried to attract Methodists to his church.[91] Patrick was drawn to the church like a moth to a flame and for the few weeks he resided in Colchester, though he took no actual duties there, he certainly used the opportunity to cultivate a friendship with Storry. Perhaps he hoped to secure his next curacy at St Peter's, but even though this was not to be, Storry was prepared to aid his promotion by attaching his all-important name to Patrick's letters testimonial.[92]

While he was at Colchester Patrick put the finishing touches to the arrangements for the second stage of his ordination. In his absence, Joseph Jowett gave the required declaration of Patrick's intention to proceed to the order of priests in the church at Wethersfield on 12, 19 and 26 July and supplied him with a certificate promising to keep him as his curate 'until he shall be provided with some other place'.[93] The rector of Panfield and the vicars of Gosfield and Thaxted, two villages and a small town within a six-mile radius of Wethersfield, who clearly knew Patrick better than Jowett, supplied letters testimonial to his character.[94] Although Patrick evidently rushed to put together all the necessary papers, he still appears to have missed the next ordination and had to wait till just before Christmas to become a fully fledged clergyman. He was finally ordained as a priest on 21 December 1807 in the splendid surroundings of the Chapel Royal of St James, Westminster.[95]

Patrick was now in a position to be looking actively for promotion to his own parish but, at this moment, he had little incentive to do so. He had fallen in love with the young daughter of a local farmer and was intent on marrying her. Mary Mildred Davy Burder[96] was the niece of the lady with whom Patrick lodged. The eldest of four children, she was eighteen years old, twelve years younger than Patrick; she lived with her mother, brothers and sister at a large farm, known as The Broad, just a mile across the fields from St George's House, halfway between Wethersfield and Finchingfield. Her father had died shortly before Patrick's arrival and her uncle, Mr Burder's brother, who lived at nearby Great Yeldham, had assumed responsibility for the family.

According to Mary's daughter,[97] Mary met Patrick when she was sent with a present of game to her aunt's house. She was in the kitchen, preparing it for dinner, when Patrick walked in. She was pretty and lively, and there was an instant and mutual attraction. The 'errands and messages to "Aunt Davy"' became more frequent and Patrick returned her visits, walking with her round the woods to The Broad. Some fifteen years later, Patrick was still to remember her as 'affectionate, kind, and forgiving, agreeable in person, and still more agreeable in mind'.[98] They shared an interest in books and Patrick apparently lent her some of his own – of the likes of *The Lay of the Last Minstrel*, one presumes, rather than his classical texts. There is no doubt that Patrick fell head over heels in love with her, nor that she returned his feelings:

You were the first whose hand I solicited, and no doubt I was the first to whom you promised to give that hand ... I am sure you once loved me with an unaffected innocent love, and I feel confident that after all which you have seen and heard, you cannot doubt my love for you.[99]

What is in considerable doubt is the reason why the courtship which, by Patrick's own admission, had become an engagement, was broken off. The accepted version of the story, which was told for the first time by Augustine Birrell in 1887, is that Mary's uncle intervened. He questioned the curate about his Irish origins, upon which he had apparently kept a sinister silence, and his future prospects, which the uncle evidently did not rate highly. The marriage was forbidden and Mary was then swept off to her uncle's house, where she was kept a virtual prisoner until Patrick had left Wethersfield. Patrick's letters to her were intercepted and destroyed and her uncle made him return all her letters. When Mary opened the parcel containing her own letters she found in it a small card with Patrick's likeness in profile on it and beneath it the words: 'Mary, you have torn the heart; spare the face.' Hearing no more from her lover, Mary eventually gave up all hope and resigned herself to the end of her engagement.[100]

Though there is clearly an element of truth in this account, it still begs a lot of questions. Mary was financially Patrick's superior and, once she was of age or married, would possess 'a handsome competency'.[101] The Broad was a substantial house, constructed of lath and plaster, with four rooms and a dairy downstairs, five bedrooms upstairs and attics used as servants' quarters. The house was surrounded by farm buildings and there was a large duck pond which also supplied all the water for the house and farm. In 1842 it was valued at £230 10d. and its appurtenances included a cottage and garden, arable fields, three grass lots and a wood.[102] Some time before April 1823, the Burders moved a few miles away to another farm, The Park, near Finchingfield, which was owned by Mary's brother. The house was larger, more modern and more manorial in style than Broad Farm, though it was valued in December 1842 at only £196 1s.[103] Undoubtedly land-owning wealth on this scale would compare badly with Patrick's curacy, worth only £60 a year, but his prospects were surely good: he was not slow to tell the Burders of his aristocratic friends and patrons and they must have recognized his ambition would take him beyond the narrow confines of a country parish in Essex. The relative financial status of the pair was not an insuperable problem.

Nor was it true that Patrick's letters to Mary were intercepted and destroyed: in August 1823 she told him she had recently perused 'many letters of yours bearing date eighteen hundred and eight, nine and ten addressed to myself and my dear departed Aunt'.[104] She had, therefore, not only received and kept his letters but also she or Miss Davy had continued to receive them for a full two years after Patrick had left Wethersfield. These letters, which, Patrick declared,

were written in your absence and which I entreat you never more to read, but to burn, were written when my mind was greatly distressed, and the only object of which was to hasten your return. These letters, I say, greatly distressed me soon after, and have greatly distressed me many a time since.[105]

They evidently made Mary deeply bitter, which suggests that Patrick, rather than her family, had been the cause of the breach of the engagement. Her review of his letters, she told Patrick,

excites in my bosom increased gratitude and thankfulness to that wise, that indulgent, Providence which then watched over me for good and withheld me from forming in very early life an indissoluble engagement with one whom I cannot think was altogether clear of duplicity. A union with you under then existing circumstances must have embittered my future days...[106]

These are the sentiments of a jilted woman and Mary's vitriolic bitterness against Patrick, even at the distance of fifteen years, suggests that she considered herself to have been wrongfully repudiated.

We can only guess at what happened. Marriage was definitely in the air in the early summer of 1808, for Patrick at long last arranged for his name to be removed from the boards at Cambridge on 26 May.[107] This meant that he had given up the possibility of being elected a college fellow, and the only reason for doing so, after two years, was that he intended to get married: only unmarried men could hold fellowships. Over the next few months he seems to have encountered opposition from the Burder family, which obliged him to give up his engagement because Mary was under the legal age to marry without consent. To ensure that there were no clandestine meetings, Mary was removed to Great Yeldham, perhaps under the impression that Patrick would wait for her until she was old enough to marry without her guardian's permission. The lovers were allowed a last meeting at which to say their farewells and Mary seems to have promised that, if Patrick came to Wethersfield again, she would receive him as a friend.[108] While Mary was kept away from her suitor and had to face the wrath and curiosity of her family and neighbours, Patrick's position was equally difficult. His authority in Wethersfield had been considerably compromised by the affair, not least because the Burders refused to accept his assurance that he would not pursue Mary. There was nothing else for him to do but to look for another post.

Some time at the end of September or the beginning of October, Patrick travelled to Glenfield, a small parish just outside Leicester, where he had been offered a curacy. The then curate, John Campbell, and his vicar, Robert Cox, were both Patrick's contemporaries from Cambridge: Campbell was a graduate of Queens' College and Cox had been a sizar in the year below Patrick at St John's.[109]

On 12 November 1808 Patrick wrote to John Campbell, telling him that he had decided not to accept the curacy at Glenfield. His letter is important, as it holds the key to the mystery of why Patrick never married Mary Burder.

Since I returned here, I have enjoyed more peace, & contentment than I expected I should have done. The Lady I mentioned, is always in exile; her Guardians can scarcely believe me, that I have given the affair entirely up forever. All along, I violated both the dictates of my conscience, and my judgment. 'Be not unequally yoked', says the Apostle. But Virgil was not far wrong, when he said, 'Omnia vincit Amor'; & no one can deny Solomons Authority, who tells us that 'Love is stronger than Death'. But for Christs sake we are, to cut off a right hand, or to pluck out a right eye, if requisite. May he by his grace enable me always to conform to his will.[110]

Patrick's quotation from St Paul has usually been taken to mean his acknowledgement of the unbridgeable social gulf which yawned between himself and Mary Burder. The quotation was used advisedly, however, for St Paul was actually referring to the marriage of Christians with non-Christians, which gives a completely different gloss on the matter. For Mary Burder, though not of course an 'unbeliever', was a Nonconformist, a worshipper at the Congregational chapel in Wethersfield, and not a member of the Church of England.¹¹¹ As such, had Patrick married her, he would almost certainly have placed immense difficulties in his own path of future promotion; who would have appointed as their curate or minister a man who had a wife belonging to a completely different religious group? This would seem to be the explanation behind one of Mary's most sarcastic and wounding comments:

Happily for me I have not been the ascribed cause of hindering your promotion, of preventing any brilliant alliance, nor have those great and affluent friends that you used to write and speak of withheld their patronage on my account, young, inexperienced, unsuspecting, and ignorant as I then was of what I had a right to look forward to.¹¹²

No wonder Patrick recoiled in dismay from the 'spirit of hatred, scorn, and revenge' which bristled off the pages of her letters when he tried to renew the friendship in 1823. Clearly he did not see the injury she felt he had done to her:

However, you may hate me <u>now</u> – I am sure you <u>once</u> loved me – and perhaps, as you may yet find, better than you will ever love another. But did I ever in any one instance take advantage of this or of your youth or inexperience? <u>You know</u> I did <u>not</u>. I, in all things, as far as it was then in my power, behaved most honourably and uprightly.¹¹³

It is a measure of his love for Mary Burder that he had allowed his heart to rule his head to the extent of asking for her hand in marriage. When her family opposed the match, Patrick saw this as the hand of God directing his affairs: however much he loved her, his service to God came first and he was prepared to suffer personally (and make Mary suffer) in the process. This was no easy decision to make, however, and Patrick's letter to John Campbell shows that he agonized over the choice between his love and his duty:

who is he that can say he has not a wish unfullfilld? Oh! that I could make my God and Saviour, my home, my Father, my all! But this happy state is reserved for better men than I <me>. I hope my dear Friend it is your portion. I often wish myself in your place: but Gods will be done; in due time he may bring me nearer to himself, & consequently nearer to heaven and happiness.¹¹⁴

He wrote to John Nunn too, pouring out his grief and anguish over the decision he had to make and describing the turmoil of his own spiritual state in terms so dark that Nunn felt obliged to destroy the letters.¹¹⁵ It should not be forgotten that, ambitious as he was, the Church was not the only career open to Patrick: he could easily have returned to teaching or private tutoring as a profession and, with his qualifications, he would not have been short of offers. Nor would teaching have been incompatible with marriage. It is perhaps the strongest evidence we have of Patrick's faith and his commitment to the Church that he chose to give up the woman he loved in order to serve his God.

Patrick may have made up his own mind as to where his duty lay by November 1808 but all the evidence suggests that Mary continued to believe he might marry her. Her references in 1823 to Patrick's letters of 1809 and 1810 and her insistence that it was the events of 'the last eleven or twelve years', rather than the last fifteen, which had placed an 'insuperable bar' to any revival of their friendship, point to the fact that it was not until some time after Patrick's departure from Wethersfield that she realized there was no hope. We know that Patrick had continued to write to her, either personally or through Miss Davy, after he had left Wethersfield. This, and the fact that, when they parted, Patrick assured her that he would return 'if his circumstances changed for the better',[116] seem to have led Mary to think that their engagement might be renewed, though it does not account for the complete absence of her replies. Perhaps Mary had even expected Patrick to return to claim her as his bride when he had settled in a living and she had reached her majority. It is significant, therefore, that Mary was twenty-one in 1811 or 1812, exactly the period when the breach really occurred. Coincidentally – or perhaps not – this was also the period of Patrick's wooing of Maria Branwell, so it could be that Mary believed Patrick had actually jilted her to marry someone else.

In his own defence, Patrick claimed that he had written twice to Miss Davy from Dewsbury in 1810 and received no reply; that even after that, when he was vicar of Hartshead, he received no answer to the letters he wrote to the south: 'from whence I concluded that all my Friends there were either dead or had forgotten me'. The only letter which had elicited any response was one to Mary's sister, Sarah, which led him to believe that Mary herself had married in the meantime.[117] Patrick's genuine surprise and mortification at Mary's reaction to his renewal of correspondence in 1823 suggest that he had no idea of either the misery he had caused her or the unfulfilled hopes she had cherished concerning him. Perhaps, in the end, one can only accuse him of insensitivity to Mary Burder's feelings.

On 22 December 1808 Patrick took a burial service at Wethersfield followed, on the last day of the old year, by a marriage service. His final official duty in the parish was to register the burial, which he did on 1 January 1809.[118] He then turned his back on Wethersfield, which had had such a momentous influence on his personal life, and set out for the grimmer pastures of the industrial north: there, he knew, he could fight the good fight for the Evangelicals and, if not wholeheartedly, at least completely, dedicate his life and work to the service of Christ.

It seems likely that Patrick secured his new post in Shropshire through the good offices of John Nunn, who was curate at Shrewsbury. Wellington could not have been more different from Wethersfield. Sheltering under the slopes of the Wrekin, which towers 1,100 feet above the flat marshes stretching northwards as far as the eye can see, Wellington was a busy town in the fast-developing industrial heartland of England. The River Severn and the Shropshire Union Canal, both nearby, had opened up the area for import and export and Wellington, like Ironbridge and Coalbrookdale less than five miles away, had a fast-growing trade in coal and iron. Industrial success had brought both wealth and poverty; the town was prosperous, with a regular Thursday market and four fairs a year, but rapid growth had brought an influx of impoverished immigrants seeking employment in the mines and foundries.[119]

Crammed into the narrow, bustling streets of the town were half-timbered houses from the sixteenth and seventeenth centuries, hemmed in by the more elegant proportions of the red brick houses of the eighteenth. There were a great many shops, mainly around the Market Square, where weekly markets had been held since 1244. There was a bank, set up in 1805 by the local squire and two industrial entrepreneurs, and a bookseller, recently turned printer and publisher, Edward Houlston. The large number of coaching inns around the town reflected the fact that Wellington straddled the routes to the midlands and the north: coaches ran several times daily to both Shrewsbury and London. The church, close to the Market Square, stood opposite the small green and was flanked on one side by the town prison and on the other by a large, plain, brick-built school, two storeys high, which during the week housed sixty day pupils and on Sundays a hundred Sunday Scholars.[120]

When Patrick arrived in Wellington, early in January 1809, the parish was just celebrating the wedding of the son of Thomas Eyton, the local squire, who lived at Eyton Hall, with the distribution of food and money to the poor at his expense.[121] Despite its burgeoning industry, Wellington was still very much dominated by its squirearchical family and, as was traditional, Thomas Eyton had presented his third son, John, to the living of the parish, which was in his gift.[122] John Eyton, however, was no ordinary gentleman parson. Like his new curate, Eyton had been to St John's College, Cambridge; though three years younger than Patrick, he had graduated in 1799 and gained his Master of Arts degree in 1802, so their university careers had not coincided. At Cambridge Eyton had fallen under the all-pervasive influence of Charles Simeon, converted to Evangelical precepts and abandoned his previously gay and fashionable way of life. In 1802 he became vicar of the joint parishes of Wellington and Eyton on the Weald Moors and promptly alienated many of his closest relatives and friends by the zeal with which he prosecuted the Evangelical cause. He rapidly made a name for himself as a powerful preacher and conscientious pastor, regularly visiting the sick and the poor. He was also personally responsible for turning the Wellington Free School into a model of its kind, bringing education to poor children long before the establishment of the National School Society. By the time Patrick arrived in Wellington, John Eyton was already renowned as a man of piety who had had at least one sermon published and was to have two volumes of them collected and published after his death.[123] Though Patrick had much to learn from his new vicar, there was an immediate bond of shared Evangelical conviction and university experience between them. Eyton made him welcome and, according to local tradition, provided him with lodgings in his own rather splendid Georgian vicarage, which was set in the fields off the turnpike road leading to Shrewsbury.[124]

All Saints' Church, like Wellington itself, was totally different from anything Patrick had known before. A modern building, less than twenty years old, it looked externally more like assembly rooms or a chapel than a Church of England. It had an elegant grey stone façade, with regular rows of huge, plain rectangular windows, surmounted by smaller arched windows; its only conventional church features were the clock and bell tower, set just behind the classical frontage, and the graveyard in front. Inside, it was light and airy, with a gallery to three sides held up by iron pillars cast at Coalbrookdale – an innovatory use of iron which was highly appropriate to the area.[125]

With a population of 8,000 people scattered over a wide area of countryside around the town, church business was brisk and Patrick would have found his time considerably more taken up with formal duties than at Wethersfield. This was particularly the case as John Eyton's health was already beginning to fail. Frequently he was unable to take any duty at all and even on the occasions when he attempted to conduct some part of the service, he would often be obliged to desist and hand over to his curate.[126] For this reason he employed not one, but two curates in his populous parishes. In the single year that Patrick spent at All Saints', there were 164 burials and 271 baptisms. As the registers were kept by the parish clerk and did not give the acting minister's name, it is impossible to tell at what proportion of these services Patrick personally officiated. From the marriage register, however, where the minister himself filled in the details, we can see that out of the fifty marriages performed throughout 1809, nearly half were performed by Patrick who, in the press of business, had begun to adopt a more hurried accent in the spelling of his name.[127]

Though All Saints' dominated parish life, there were also duties to take at the tiny red brick church of St Catherine at Eyton on the Weald Moors. Built in 1743 as a chapel of ease, and practically engulfed by the barns and farmyards of the prosperous farm next door, the little church served a population of nearly 400 souls. The duties here were obviously much lighter and seem mainly to have been taken by the other, more senior, curate, though on 25 May Patrick, together with the churchwarden and overseer of the poor, made and signed an assessment for the relief of the poor in the parish of Eyton.[128]

There were other clerical duties throughout the year. Wednesday, 8 February, had been set aside as a day of national fast and humiliation; these expressions of public mortification were held irregularly, throughout Patrick's career, as a response to moments of national crisis. Shops and mills were shut, special services were held in churches and personal penitence was expected to be observed; it was hoped that public contrition for the sinful state of the nation would appease God's wrath and avert the danger. On 1 June there was an important meeting at Wellington of all the contributors to the fund for the relief of clergymen's widows and orphans in the archdeaconry of Salop to host and organize; and on 11 June the annual sermons for the benefit of the Sunday schools at Wellington were preached by the Reverend Mr Waltham of Darlaston in Staffordshire, raising the enormous sum of £72 14s. 7½d. in collections.[129]

Undoubtedly the most memorable event, though, was the celebration on 25 October of the fiftieth anniversary of George III's accession. In Shrewsbury, John Nunn preached a sermon on the text 'Let the king live for ever' to the mayor and aldermen of the town and bonfires on all the hills in the area, including the Wrekin, were clearly visible.[130] In Wellington, the inhabitants were 'second to none in manifestions of loyalty and temperate joy'. Every house was brilliantly illuminated, the poorer inhabitants being generously supplied with candles for the purpose by Thomas Eyton; the squire's own house was resplendent with the motto 'Fear God Honor [sic] the King' formed out of variegated lamps. In addition to the Wrekin bonfire, there was a display of fireworks and a commemorative subscription raised enough money to buy four oxen, the meat being distributed among the poor. Not to be outdone by his father, the Reverend John Eyton committed himself to the establishment of a Lancasterian school at Ketley, as a permanent memorial of the jubilee.[131]

The increased scale and scope of Patrick's duties at Wellington would have provided a much-needed distraction from his personal unhappiness. So, too, would his burgeoning friendships in the unusually close-knit clerical community of Shropshire. His old college friend, John Nunn, was only ten miles away, a distance short enough to walk along the banks of the slow, wide Severn though there were several coaches a day, if he could afford the fare. Patrick must have visited him many times, for he made other friends in Shrewsbury too. There was Nunn's vicar, Thomas Stedman, an Oxford man, who had been at St Chad's since 1783.[132] It was during his incumbency that the church had been completely destroyed when its tower fell on to the nave. Stedman was responsible for the quite remarkable new church which replaced it, designed by the same George Steuart who had built All Saints' at Wellington and very similar to it in style, apart from its one aberration, the largest circular nave, at one hundred feet in diameter, in England. Stedman, like John Eyton, was also a writer, the author of several tracts and sermons and editor of the letters of Orton and Stonehouse.[33]

Another literary friend from Shrewsbury was Charles Hulbert, the antiquarian and historian of Shropshire, whose house Patrick visited regularly. Hulbert was a man of many parts; originally from Manchester he had set up Shrewsbury's one and only cotton factory in 1803 but he was also a Methodist Circuit Steward, a preacher on the Shrewsbury circuit which included Wellington.[34] Hulbert must have been one of the first of Patrick's many Methodist friends. Another, whose friendship was to help shape Patrick's future, was John Fennell, master of the day school at Wellington. Though he was later to choose ordination into the Established Church, Fennell, like so many of the clergymen in this area, was also a follower of the Wesleys.[35]

The closest, if perhaps not the most important, of Patrick's new friends was his fellow curate at All Saints', William Morgan. A Welshman, and five years younger than Patrick, he had been at All Saints' since 1806. The two men shared more than their duties, both being ambitious and enthusiastic by temperament and intensely committed to their faith. Morgan was also a friend of Charles Hulbert and John Fennell, whose daughter he was later to marry. He introduced Patrick to many new friends, including Samuel Walter, the curate whose place Patrick had taken on his promotion to Madeley, some six miles away.[36]

Madeley, though undistinguished as a town, was a place of immense spiritual significance, the inspirational source and guiding light which bound together all these men and profoundly affected their lives. It was the home of the aged widow of John Fletcher,[37] the great charismatic preacher who had been vicar of Madeley from 1760 till his death in 1785. Born John William de la Flechère at Nyon in Switzerland in 1729, he had spent most of his adult life in England. Among the hard-drinking and often violent workers in the collieries and ironworks around Madeley he had become a byword for saintly personal piety. He was fearless in his denunciation of sin, assiduous in his itinerant preaching and so generous in his charity that his household frequently found itself without either money or food. An intimate friend of both John and Charles Wesley, he was the author of a number of books and tracts which had had an enormous impact on the Evangelicals and the Methodists alike. With his insistence on the need for conversion to faith, his rebuttal of the Calvinistic doctrine of the Elect and his affection for St Paul, Fletcher became the model and inspiration for the many young clergymen, including Patrick, who converged on his home.

In 1781, only four years before his death, he married the woman he had loved for many years, Mary Bosanquet. As his widow, she faithfully continued his work long after his death and still held open house for all the many disciples to whom he had been such an inspiration. Like him, she worked hard to secure committed Evangelists for the northern counties of

England, where the growth in population consequent upon the Industrial Revolution, much of it in new towns outside the old centres of population, had far outstripped the number of churches established there and where, therefore, there was a crying need for ministers.

At John Fletcher's house, and in his widow's company, Patrick found comfort and encouragement for his professed purpose in life. He met other like-minded men, such as Joshua Gilpin, vicar of Wrockwardine, the pretty red sandstone village less than two miles from Wellington. Gilpin was a devoted follower of Fletcher, had lived in his house before his own ordination and been present at the great man's deathbed. He had translated from its original French and published in two volumes John Fletcher's treatise *The Portrait of St Paul*, appending his own account of the life of its author and, when Patrick met him, was working on a new edition of John Bunyan's *The Pilgrim's Progress*.[138] His own vicar, John Eyton, who had introduced William Morgan to Mary Fletcher, was a frequent visitor, as were Samuel Walter, Eyton's former curate, and John Fennell, the schoolmaster who was also John Fletcher's godson.[139]

It is possible, too, that Patrick met at Madeley Mary Fletcher's lifelong friend, John Crosse, who had been vicar of Bradford, in the West Riding of Yorkshire, since 1784. Patrick later told William Morgan, when the latter was writing his biography of John Crosse, that he considered 'Mr C[rosse] and Mrs F[letcher] as very similar to each other in their Christian simplicity, zeal, and manner of speaking to their friends, on the leading subjects of religion'.[140]

John Crosse, like so many of this circle, was firmly attached to the Arminian school of theology and a strong supporter of John Wesley, whom he had allowed to preach from his own pulpit. After the Methodists had withdrawn from the Church of England and become a separate sect in 1812, he actually considered resigning his living and joining them as a minister, only being dissuaded on the grounds that his usefulness would be greater as vicar of Bradford.[141] 'Usefulness' was the watch-word of the Evangelicals, implying activity and commitment, and it is significant that as early as 1804 Patrick had similarly been marked out as someone who had a 'desire for usefulness in the ministry'.[142]

Patrick was entirely at home in this atmosphere and as long as he lived, even after the Methodists had separated from the Church of England and it was no longer fashionable or even really acceptable to support them, he continued to maintain cordial relations with Methodists in general and Wesleyans in particular. After the emotional traumas of having to give up Mary Burder, it was no doubt a relief to find spiritual comfort and support in the Madeley circle.

Through his contacts here, if not from John Crosse himself, Patrick learnt that Bradford was one of the fastest growing parishes in terms of population and one of the least well served in terms of clergymen in the country. He had always wanted to live and work in Yorkshire,[143] which was regarded by the Evangelicals as a sort of 'Promised Land' of opportunity: the Bradford area now became an obvious and attractive choice. The first vacancy there that was brought to his attention was the post of curate in Dewsbury, an industrial town near Bradford. The vicar of Dewsbury, John Buckworth, was not yet the semi-permanent invalid he later became but, like John Eyton, his health was already suffering from the zeal with which he carried out his duties and he was in desperate need of support. He was anxious to secure someone committed to Evangelical beliefs and Patrick was therefore offered, and accepted, a post as his assistant.[144]

The decision was not entirely simple, however, for Patrick was once more at a crossroads in his life and had to make a decision that would determine his future. Just before he accepted Dewsbury, he had a letter from James Wood, his old tutor at St John's, offering him the post of chaplain to the governor of Martinique in the West Indies.[145] The island, a French colony, had recently been captured by the British, placing virtually all the West Indies under British rule. The appointment of a governor (and his chaplain) was therefore a new one, resulting from military success in the war against Napoleon. The position would offer prestige, excitement (as Martinique was still in the war zone) and an opportunity to be 'useful' converting the Negroes and attempting to work towards the abolition of slavery, a cause dear to Evangelical hearts.

It is not clear whether Patrick had solicited Wood's aid in trying to find another post, or whether Wood, remembering his former pupil's Evangelical commitment, simply thought he would be a suitable man for the job. The letter took some three weeks to find him, which suggests that the latter explanation was the more likely. When Patrick eventually replied at the end of November 1809, it was with two questions: was the post likely to be permanent and would he receive any salary in advance that would enable him to pay for the expense of his voyage? The questions were extremely pertinent and Wood's answers, which are not known, may have been the deciding factor in Patrick's decision.[146] In any event, Martinique lost its potential chaplain and Yorkshire gained the father of its most famous family.

Patrick performed his last marriage at Wellington on 18 November 1809, though he no doubt continued his other duties until his departure on 4 December.[147] His residence in Wellington had been very brief, less than a year, but the spiritual influences and the friendships of the Madeley circle were to remain with him for life. William Morgan, who, like John Fennell, was soon to follow Patrick to Yorkshire, presented him with a practical farewell present: a leather-bound volume of *Sermons or Homilies appointed to be read in churches* on the flyleaf of which he wrote:

The Reverend P. Bronte's Book – Presented to him by his Friend W: Morgan as a Memorial of the pleasant & agreeable friendship, which subsisted between them at Wellington, – & as a Token of the same Friendship, which, as is hoped, will continue for ever.[148]

Armed with his letters testimonial from Wethersfield, signed by Joseph Jowett, Robert Storry and John Thurlow, vicar of Gosfield, and from Wellington, signed by John Eyton, Joshua Gilpin and Thomas Stedman,[149] Patrick set off for Yorkshire.

Chapter Two

❧

THE PROMISED LAND

The fell hand of the twentieth century has destroyed most of the Dewsbury that Patrick Brontë knew. Its once proud and separate identity has been lost, swallowed up in the vast and characterless urban sprawl which oozes southwards from Bradford and Leeds. Today, its most dominant feature is the road system – a Gordian knot of flyovers, dual carriageways and underpasses apparently designed to prevent anyone either entering or leaving the town. The shabby remnants of late Victorian municipal splendour are dwarfed by the concrete stanchions of modern bridges. Semi-derelict mills, empty warehouses and demolition sites are a depressing foretaste of the town centre. Dewsbury is a town which has lost its way; having obliterated its past it gives the impression it has no confidence in its future. Yet in December 1809, when Patrick arrived, Dewsbury was a distinct entity, a town with a venerable history and a prosperous future in the boom years of the late nineteenth-century wool trade.

Dewsbury lies in a natural basin, on a loop in the River Calder which flows wide and deep down towards the Yorkshire coast. Surrounded then by fields and woods, the town had an open and pleasant aspect. Dotted about the hill tops overlooking it were many small villages which have now become indistinguishable parts of the Kirklees district. The town was built of grey stone, long since blackened with soot, and had many fine buildings, all of which have been demolished. There were some beautiful medieval buildings, including the large, timber-framed fourteenth-century vicarage, with its rows of tiny stone mullions and its huge chimneys, and, just behind it, a stone moot hall dating from the thirteenth century or even earlier. There was a late seventeenth-century manor house and, at Crow Nest, a mid-eighteenth-century mansion set amid parkland. Most of the architectural splendour of the town dated from the prosperous years of the eighteenth century. Three free schools had been founded by local philanthropists, including the Wheelwright Charity school for boys and girls. Great improvements in communications also took place over these years. Two new bridges were built over the Calder to replace the ferries, two new canals had been constructed to make the river navigable down its entire length and three turnpike roads connected the town to Halifax, Elland and Wakefield.[1]

The mid-eighteenth century had also seen the rebuilding of the medieval parish church. Tradition had it that All Saints' had been founded by Paulinus on a preaching mission to the Northumbrians in 627. In fact, Dewsbury lay within the old British kingdom of Elmet and it seems most likely that the story evolved from the preservation of Paulinus' altar in a monastery at Dewsbury after a devastating Welsh raid on a nearby Northumbrian royal palace in 633. The monastery had disappeared by 1066, but fragments of ninth- and tenth-century stone crosses and gravestones were still preserved in All Saints' when Patrick came. In consequence of the church having once been a minster, sending out priests to serve the outlying communities, many churches in the West Riding, including those of Bradford and Huddersfield, still paid tithes to Dewsbury.[2]

The town itself had a rapidly growing population which, in 1811, stood at 5,059; the parish also included the 7,539 inhabitants of Soothill, Ossett and Hartshead-cum-Clifton, which were separately administered by their own clergymen, subject to the vicar of Dewsbury.[3] The textile trade dominated the town. At least five mills had been established as early as the 1780s, their numbers increasing rapidly after the invention of the steam loom in 1807, but a large proportion of the population still produced cloth on hand looms in their own homes.[4]

As in both Patrick's previous parishes, there was a very strong element of religious nonconformity. John Wesley had preached there in 1742 on the first day of his tour of Yorkshire and thereafter both he and his brother were regular visitors. The Methodists had established their own meeting house in 1764 but remained on good terms with the vicar and his congregation. There were also several small Moravian settlements in the area. They seem to have been tolerated, if not actively encouraged, by the Anglicans, though their relations with the Methodists, whom they saw as rivals, were less happy.[5]

In Dewsbury, Patrick had his hands full. John Buckworth performed a marriage on the day his new curate arrived, 5 December 1809, but thereafter the full burden of the church offices was carried almost singlehandedly by Patrick. In the sixteen months of his curacy he personally performed nearly 130 marriages. Four hundred and twenty-six baptisms were carried out in the parish church, most of them during the Sunday services or on church festivals. Most onerous of all was the number of burials. At first these averaged around twenty a month, but then they rose sharply: from October 1810 to February 1811 there were over fifty a month, peaking at seventy-three in November when, on two occasions, there were eight burials in one day.[6] Almost two-thirds of the burials occurred within the last six months of Patrick's curacy, suggesting that Dewsbury had suffered one of the outbreaks of typhus or influenza which periodically struck the population. There was immense hardship at this time, the failure of the harvest adding to the problems of industrial depression and unemployment.

Conditions in the town, brought forcibly home to him by the number of burials he was called upon to perform, must have been a severe test of Patrick's faith and commitment to his pastoral work. But he did not shirk the task. In his vicar he had a shining exemplar of a parish priest. Cheerful, kind and courteous, John Buckworth was outstanding, even among Evangelicals, for his personal faith and humility and for his public exertions on behalf of his parishioners. He had been converted at the age of sixteen and, although apprenticed to a chemist, had been head-hunted by the Evangelicals, who paid for him to go to St Edmund Hall, Oxford. He had spent all his clerical career in Dewsbury, arriving there in 1804 as a curate and taking over as vicar, at the age of twenty-six, on the death of the previous incumbent in December 1806. Two years younger than Patrick, he was a talented preacher; determined to save sinners, he went about it with characteristic energy, as his biographer describes:

The sacred truths of the Gospel, he felt were of eternal importance to his hearers; and under the influence of this feeling, he would sometimes declare the terrors of the law in language sufficient to make the ears of every one that heard him to tingle. On these occasions, his manner might be regarded by some as too vehement, but he had before the eyes of his mind the awful realities of sin, and he felt excited to stretch every nerve to place them before his people in the strongest language possible.[7]

He had filled the half-empty parish church by his preaching skills, but he also seized every opportunity to preach and teach while out fulfilling his parish duties. A typical occasion was recorded in his journal for 1808; visiting a sick woman at Daw Green he called in her neighbours, some fifteen or twenty of whom came straight from their looms, so that he could spend three-quarters of an hour with them expounding the scriptures and praying.[8] With so many of his parishioners scattered over a large area, he had to make the most of such opportunities to 'preach in the kitchen' like the Methodists. Before his death in 1835, three more churches would have been built within the bounds of his own parish, but in 1810 there was only himself and his curate to minister to the needs of the whole population. There is no doubt that Patrick would have been drawn into Buckworth's habits and, indeed, the vicar actually drew up a set of notes for the guidance of his curate. Whether or not they were intended for Patrick personally, they clearly had an influence on his conduct, as the same traits were discerned in him by later observers:

Preach to the feelings, as well as to the understanding; and to the understanding as well as to the feelings. Let a due proportion of close and weighty application be made to different classes of hearers, either by way of inference or pointed address, in every sermon...

The mornings seem to be best for private reading, and preparing for the pulpit; and the afternoons are usually found most convenient to the people to be visited...

Guard, as you would against the plague, against a newsy, chit-chat, familiar trifling with them. Elevate the standard of Christian experience and conduct as high as possible, in your conversations with them...[9]

Buckworth also expected his curate to take a leading role in the Sunday school, the first in Yorkshire, which had been established in 1783. In addition to supervising the erection of a new building, which was funded by sub-scription and opened in 1810, Patrick had to attend the classes each week, opening the meetings with prayers and a hymn, then addressing the whole school and inspecting the pupils.[10] As well as religious instruction, Patrick also taught the basic skills of reading and writing; one of his former pupils declared that he was 'resolute about being obeyed, but was very kind, and we always liked him'.[11] Buckworth was also an enthusiastic supporter of the Church Missionary Society, so no doubt Patrick would also have had to assist at his twice-weekly evening meetings, held in the vicarage, for the instruction and preparation of pious young men for potential ordination. The young men, many of whom went on to be missionaries in India or ministers of the Church, were taught the rudiments of Latin and Greek, as well as theological subjects, so Patrick, whose own background was similar to theirs, was ideally placed to help them.[12]

Between his formal duties and pastoral visiting, there can have been little time available for pleasure. He is said to have enjoyed walking along the banks of the River Calder, which flowed just behind the church.[13] On one such occasion in the winter of 1809–10, as he walked past a group of boys playing rough and tumble near the flooded river, a simple boy was pushed, lost his balance and fell in. Hearing the commotion, Patrick turned back and plunged into the river to rescue the boy, who was being swept away by the current. He then carried him back to his mother, a poor widow living at Daw Green, before returning to the vicarage to change his clothes. On the way back he met the boys again and stopped to lecture them; when the culprit (whose son recounted the story) confessed, saying 'I only picked [pushed] him, to make him wet his shoon' Patrick relented, and let them off after making them promise to go and apologize to the victim and his mother.[14]

Another example of Patrick's muscular Christianity occurred during the Whit walk of 1810, when all the scholars and teachers of the Sunday school walked in procession through Dewsbury to nearby Earlsheaton. The vicar, who should have led the procession, was away in Oxford, taking his Master of Arts degree,[15] so Patrick had to take his place. Suddenly, a drunk obstructed their path, threatening them and refusing to let them pass. Seeing no other option, Patrick apparently seized the man by the collar and threw him into the ditch, much to the delight of the Sunday school children, who remembered the incident (and probably embroidered it) for years to come.[16]

A curious tale is also told on the authority of Joseph Tolson, a young man who sometimes officiated informally as parish clerk. It had been agreed that Patrick would take the morning and afternoon services at Hartshead for the Reverend William Lucas, who was ill. John Buckworth wanted to spend the evening at the Aldams, home of his wife's family, the Hallileys, so Patrick had agreed to take that service for him in Dewsbury. While returning from Hartshead, he and Tolson were caught in a thunderstorm and soaked to the skin, so they rode on to the Aldams to ask Buckworth to take the evening service while Patrick got changed. They were met by John Halliley, owner of the town's largest mill, who on hearing that Patrick wanted his son-in-law to take the service declared, 'What! keep a dog and bark himself!' Deeply insulted, Patrick turned on his heel and walked off; he performed the evening service, as arranged, but before giving his sermon declared publicly that he had been grievously insulted (without indicating by whom) and would not preach again from the pulpit at Dewsbury. According to Tolson, Patrick kept his word.[17]

Though there may be some truth in the story, Patrick was in no position to withdraw from the pulpit: had he done so, Buckworth could have terminated his curacy and would certainly not have promoted him to the living of Hartshead, when it came vacant, or maintained his friendship with Patrick afterwards. Nor is it likely that Patrick would have continued on good terms with John Halliley, junior,[18] if he had quarrelled with his father and brother-in-law. It is possible, however, that Patrick took offence at what was meant to be a jocular remark and, in the heat of the moment, threatened never to preach again. His promotion to Hartshead soon afterwards might have been construed by Tolson as a fulfilment of his threat.

Patrick was later described by one of his parishioners as 'a very earnest man, but a little peculiar in his manner'.[19] He was, like his vicar, a strict Sabbatarian and once angered the parish bell-ringing team by stopping them practising on a Sunday in preparation for a competition. Other personal habits were attributed to his Irishness and his poverty: his carrying a stick (magnified, in the light of later knowledge, into a shillelagh) led to him being called jokingly 'Old Staff' by some of his clerical friends; his frugal meals, too, were evidently a matter for comment in the parish.[20] Fortunately, at least for the first few months of his curacy, Patrick was able to live at the vicarage, thus saving the cost of renting a house; later he is said to have moved into lodgings nearby, possibly because Buckworth had opened 'a sort of college in his house' to prepare young men for ordination and train them for missionary work in India.[21]

There certainly seems to have been an unexplained hiatus in Patrick's curacy, which may have coincided with his departure from the vicarage. Within six months of his arrival, Patrick started making plans for promotion to his first full ministerial post. On 6 June 1810 he wrote to the Archbishop of York's secretary to confirm that he had certificates for the last three years of his ministry but explaining that he was not 'at present' licensed to the curacy of Dewsbury.[22] This may simply have been yet another administrative muddle of the kind which seems to have affected Patrick at every step in his career. On the other hand it is possible that Patrick had not been licensed to the curacy at Dewsbury because he was expecting an imminent promotion to Hartshead-cum-Clifton. The incumbent there, William Lucas, had been seriously ill for some time and the constant need to provide deputies to take his duties had been a severe strain on the already overworked clergy of Dewsbury. The living was in Buckworth's gift and it is likely that he had promised it to Patrick when trying to persuade him to leave Wellington; certainly he needed a fairly major incentive to leave the Madeley circle. Having brought Patrick to Dewsbury, Buckworth may then have discovered that his action was premature: as a 'perpetual curate', nothing short of death or resignation could make Lucas vacate his living. This would explain Patrick's lack of a formal position for the first seven months of his curacy.

In his letter, Patrick explained that he wanted to secure the licence to the curacy of Dewsbury, be inducted to the living of Hartshead and also obtain a licence for non-residence so that he did not have to remove to his new parish. With a rather touching naivety, he crossed out the references to Dewsbury in his letters testimonial from Wethersfield and Wellington and entered 'Hartshead' in its place. These, together with letters testimonial from Dewsbury, signed by John Buckworth, the curate of Batley and the ministers of Ossett and Woodkirk, Patrick sent off to the Archbishop of York on 28 June.[23] In the event, William Lucas did resign the living and Buckworth was able to write the nomination papers on 19 July.[24] The following day, the archbishop formally licensed Patrick to Hartshead-cum-Clifton. It is therefore somewhat surprising that Patrick continued to sign the registers at Dewsbury as 'curate' (he would have been entitled to write 'Officiating Minister') and that he did not appear in the registers at Hartshead as 'minister' till the end of March 1811.[25] The appointment seems to have made no difference to his life at all; he apparently continued to live and work in Dewsbury just as before. What is even stranger is that, until he actively took over the ministry eight months later, his duties at Hartshead appear to have been taken by David Jenkins, the new curate who had been appointed to replace him at Dewsbury.[26]

Whatever the cause of the delay in Patrick's removal to Hartshead, the result was that he was still in Dewsbury on 25 September when a young man, William Nowell, of Daw Green, was arrested as an army deserter and taken from his parents for committal to Wakefield prison. The only prosecution witness was James Thackray, the soldier who said he had enlisted Nowell eight days before at one of the annual fairs in the Dewsbury area. Though Nowell's parents had been to Lee Fair, Nowell himself had stayed behind in Dewsbury and, though he had a number of witnesses to prove this alibi, the magistrate at the committal refused to accept their evidence or allow time for more witnesses to be gathered. Nowell was sent to prison as a deserter and stayed there for ten weeks.[27] There was an immediate outcry in Dewsbury and Patrick took a leading role in the events that followed.

On the Friday after Nowell's committal, four gentlemen from Dewsbury, including Patrick, called upon the magistrate in Wakefield with two witnesses who were prepared to swear that they had been with Thackray all afternoon and that he had not enlisted any new recruits at Lee Fair; Mr Dawson, the magistrate, again refused to examine the new witnesses. A memorial signed by Patrick, the churchwardens and the principal inhabitants of Dewsbury, was then sent to the commander-in-chief of the army asking him to set Nowell free or, at least, to investigate the facts of the case. The letter was referred to the Office of the Secretary at War, which responded asking 'The Clergyman' to state whether the facts in the memorial were true to his own knowledge or whether he only believed them to be true. Patrick called a vestry meeting and took signed depositions from all the witnesses; he sent them to his old commander of the volunteers, Lord Palmerston, who was now the Secretary at War. Palmerston, however, felt that he could not interfere in the decision of a civil magistrate so impasse had been reached again.

Patrick did not despair: he called into action on Nowell's behalf another of his Cambridge connections, William Wilberforce, who was also one of the members of Parliament for Yorkshire. John Halliley, the vicar's father-in-law, who was in London at the time, was despatched with a letter to Wilberforce and accompanied him to the War Office. Palmerston was out of town so all that could be done was to request Dawson, through Wilberforce, to re-examine the evidence. Again he refused. Frustrated once more, Patrick and his allies sent the news to Wilberforce and asked him to seek an urgent personal interview with Palmerston. At last, Wilberforce succeeded and an 'imperative order' was sent to Dawson to review the case.[28]

On 27 November, Patrick, Mr Hague (a banker from Dewsbury), John Halliley, junior, and Mr Rylah (their solicitor) went to Wakefield for the third time, bringing fifteen witnesses to be examined. The depositions, together with an unexpected one from a Wakefield hairdresser who swore on oath that Thackray had told him the whole story was a pack of lies, were sent off to London and five days later, William Nowell was set free. Patrick had the satisfaction of not only co-ordinating the campaign to free an innocent man, but also of calling in on his behalf those 'great and affluent friends' of whom Mary Burder complained.[29] There was further gratification on seeing a detailed account of the whole story printed in the *Leeds Mercury* of 15 December 1810 but nothing, surely, could have given him as much pleasure as the appending, at the end of the report, of a letter from Palmerston addressed to Patrick himself:

War-Office, 5th Dec. 1810.

No 22,429.
SIR,
Referring to the correspondence relative to William Nowell, I am to acquaint you, that I feel so strongly the injury that is likely to arise to the service from an unfair mode of recruiting, that if by the indictment which the lad's friends are about to prefer against James Thackray they shall establish the fact of his having been guilty of perjury, I shall be ready to indemnify them for the reasonable and proper expences which they shall incur on the occasion.

I am, Sir, Yours, &c.
PALMERSTON.

The Rev. P. Bronte,
Dewsbury, near Leeds.[30]

William Nowell's case ended triumphantly nearly a year later, on 7 August 1811, when James Thackray was found guilty of wilful and corrupt perjury at the York Assizes and sentenced to transportation for the term of seven years.[31] It is worth pointing out that Patrick had pursued this case throughout one of the most difficult periods of his ministry so far: Nowell's imprisonment and the campaign coincided with the heaviest casualties in the epidemic which struck Dewsbury in the winter months of 1810–11.[32]

Patrick must have felt a genuine sense of relief when he finally exchanged his curacy at Dewsbury for the living at Hartshead. Leaving behind the muck, smoke, poverty and disease of Dewsbury, he travelled the four miles up hill to Hartshead, a journey familiar to him from the many times he had gone over to take services there during the previous incumbent's illness. Unlike most of the nearby churches, built in a more confident age, which defy the elements on the skylines and hill tops of Yorkshire, the church of St Peter at Hartshead lies huddled into the hill top as though sheltering from the wind. Low and squat, with a stubby, square Norman tower and a roof that comes unusually low down, giving only room for a single storey at the north and south elevations, the church was ancient and unpretentious. When Patrick came there, it had sash windows, wooden pillars, a Norman chancel arch and a flat ceiling to the nave. There was a double-decker pulpit for the preacher and, at the lower level, the parish clerk, high box pews which would almost conceal the congregation, and a gallery at the west end for the musicians and singers. It was already in a state of disrepair and had been for many years; the churchyard was cluttered with the box tombs which Mrs Gaskell found so unusual at Haworth but which are typical of the area and was dominated by a gigantic and very ancient yew tree.[33]

Patrick found convenient lodgings just opposite the church at a farm, then known as Lousy Thorn, a peculiarly appropriate name for its windswept and bleak aspect. The church stands in glorious isolation some distance from the village of Hartshead which even then was only a cluster of seventeenth- and eighteenth-century farmhouses. Just over a mile or so away, but seeming much further as it is down one steep hill and up another, was the village of Clifton. Today, the gulf is accentuated by the M62 motorway, which has sliced the old parish in half and made the two parts almost completely inaccessible to each other. Clifton, like Hartshead, is perched on the top of an immense escarpment and enjoys panoramic views over the hills in all directions; Dewsbury to the southeast and Brighouse, with Halifax beyond, to the southwest are clearly visible in the valleys below; Bradford lies to the northwest and Leeds to the northeast. The parish was ideally placed for Patrick to become involved in the affairs of the major industrial towns of the West Riding.

Though there was no church at Clifton, the village would have occupied more of Patrick's time as it had a population of 1,181, compared to Hartshead's 547. It was wealthier, too, with several magnificent sixteenth- and seventeenth-century stone-built farms and a large number of public houses. Men, women and children from Hartshead and Clifton, and from nearby Hightown and Roberttown, which also fell within Patrick's parish, worked in both the cottage woollen industry and the mills in neighbouring towns. There appears to have been only one large mill within the parish, the Little John Mill on the outskirts of Clifton which, by 1802, had already installed six carding machines. Open-cast coal mining, stone-hewing and wire-drawing, the last based at Clifton, were the other main occupations.[34]

What made the parish different from Patrick's previous industrial ones, at Dewsbury and Wellington, was the fact that between Hartshead and Clifton, on the slopes of the hill, stood Kirklees Hall, the seventeenth-century pile belonging to Sir George Armitage, Baronet.[35] A huge, rambling and unattractive mansion, built in a variety of styles with little to connect them, the house and its estate nevertheless dominated the area. In the grounds which spread out along the river known as the Nunbrook, just below Hartshead, stood the ruins of Kirklees Priory, a Benedictine nunnery founded in the reign of Henry II. Though little remained of the original medieval buildings except a delightful stone and half-timbered gatehouse and an enormous tithe barn, the place was renowned as the site of Robin Hood's grave. Legend had it that while recovering from wounds at the gatehouse, Robin was treacherously bled to death by the prioress and buried 660 yards away, where the arrow he shot from his deathbed had landed.[36] Mr and Mrs Bedford, Patrick's landlords at Lousy Thorn, had been upper servants at Kirklees Hall before their marriage.[37]

Patrick arrived in Hartshead with a determination to do well. John Buckworth gave him a useful present to assist and inspire him in the preparation of his own sermons; it was a copy of his latest book, snappily titled *A Series of Discourses Containing a System of Doctrinal Experimental and Practical Religion, Particularly Calculated for the Use of Families, Preached in the Parish Church of Dewsbury Yorkshire*, upon the flyleaf of which he had written: 'Revd. P. Brontè 1811. A Testimony of sincere esteem from the Author'.[38]

At the end of March 1811 the annual ritual of signing off the registers was carried out, and Patrick entered his name for the first time as minister, witnessed by the churchwardens.[39] Even then, on the admittedly flawed evidence of the marriage register alone, he does not appear to have taken full responsibility for the duties until the following August. Thereafter, he was thoroughly conscientious, taking virtually all the formal services that occurred. Compared with Dewsbury, though, his duties were extremely light; there were only, on average, eleven or twelve weddings a year. Baptisms, which, following Buckworth's advice, he almost invariably performed during the hours of public worship on Sundays, averaged around ninety-three a year, or less than two a week. Burials, too, fell within the more acceptable levels of fifty-six or fifty-seven a year – a total for the whole year smaller than the numbers he had been burying monthly at Dewsbury.[40] For a less committed man this might have been an opportunity for taking things more easily, but Patrick seems to have devoted his leisure hours to assisting his hard-pressed colleagues in Dewsbury.[41]

Within the area he soon acquired a number of friends, many of whom were to prove important in later life. The Evangelical Hammond Roberson, for instance, himself a former curate of Dewsbury and incumbent of Hartshead, whose martial Christianity Charlotte was to caricature in *Shirley*;

David Jenkins, the new curate at Dewsbury, who would assist Patrick's daughters in Brussels; most important of all, William Morgan, who had at last secured his own promotion to Yorkshire, becoming curate to John Crosse at Bradford Parish Church.[42]

What little time Patrick had left to himself he devoted to the cultivation of his mind and talents. Until 1814, when he could afford his own subscription, he would pay a weekly visit to the house of Abraham Lawford to read one of the local papers, the *Leeds Mercury*.[43] Significantly, this was a Whig publication, which would not have met with the approval of at least two of Patrick's High Tory friends, Roberson and Morgan; already Patrick was displaying that independence of mind which would lead him into frequent challenges to the political establishment.

It was at this time, too, that Patrick embarked on a literary career. It was clearly expected of him, since his vicars at Wellington and Dewsbury, as well as friends like Joshua Gilpin, the vicar of Wrockwardine in Shropshire, had all taken up the pen in the service of Christ. Like the Methodists, the Evangelicals believed in the importance of getting their message across to a wider audience than their own congregations. Even if most of their poorer parishioners were illiterate, hymns and simple verses, designed to be sung or read aloud, in Sunday school or in informal 'kitchen meetings', were an ideal way of communicating the faith.

Patrick had already dabbled in the art. His first identifiable piece, *Winter Evening Thoughts*, seems to have been a response to a Day of National Humiliation for the war against France, which was held on 28 February 1810. Subtitled 'A Miscellaneous Poem', it had been published anonymously in 1810, while he was curate at Dewsbury, but Patrick sent a copy to Shrewsbury with the inscription 'To my dear Friend Nunn, with my unfeigned love, and christian regards. P. Brontè.', adding 'By P. Brontè. B. A.' to ensure that his authorship was recognized.[44] On the title page, Patrick paraphrased a line from Horace to declare, in Latin, 'Although an insignificant man, I create elaborate verses in the hope that some will be worthy of publication.' A similar idea was expressed more fully in his introduction to the poem:

In this Miscellaneous Poem, now offered to the Public, which in due time will probably be followed by others of a similar nature, and upon the same plan, the Author's intention is, to 'Become all things to all men, that he might by all means save some':

He wishes by a judicious mixture of the *Profitable* and *Agreeable*, to gain access to the libraries of certain characters, who would shut their doors against anything savouring of *Austerity*.

Should the Author succeed, in being made the happy instrument of adding to the comforts of any individual, or of reclaiming but *one*, from the error of his ways, he will esteem himself amply recompensed for his labours.[45]

The quotation from St Paul, about wishing to 'become all things to all men, that he might by all means save some', was to be almost a trademark with Patrick: he used it again in two of his other publications as his justification for undertaking the work.[46]

Though reflecting the purpose of the Day of National Humiliation, the poem was indeed miscellaneous; 265 lines describing the sufferings of poor cottagers, an innocent girl, seduced in her youth, and now reduced to prostitution and a ship lost at sea with all hands in winter storms. Interwoven with these disparate subjects were patriotic references to the war against France:

> O! Britain fair, thou Queen of isles!
> Nor hostile arms, nor hostile wiles,
> Could ever shake thy solid throne,
> But for thy sins – thy sins alone,
> Can make thee stoop thy royal head,
> And lay thee prostrate, with the dead.[47]

The message was simple, though not very clearly expressed: sin was the root of all the problems facing the country and people alike.

> Where Sin abounds Religion dies,
> And Virtue seeks her native skies;
> Chaste Conscience, hides for very shame,
> And Honour's but an empty name.[48]

The same sort of didactic purpose lay behind Patrick's next publication, a collection of twelve poems entitled, in the Evangelical tradition, *Cottage Poems*. The poems were

chiefly designed for the lower classes of society ... For the convenience of the unlearned and poor, the Author has not written much, and has endeavoured not to burthen his subjects with matter, and as much as he well could, has aimed at simplicity, plainness, and perspicuity, both in manner and style.[49]

The Advertisement, which Patrick prefixed to the text, is a neat summary of the message of the poems. The Bible is the 'Book of Books ... in which the wisest may learn that they know nothing, and fools be made wise'; all those who wish to be truly happy must first be truly religious; the simple and natural manners of the poor, when refined by religion, 'shine ... with a peculiar degree of gospel simplicity ... wonderfully calculated to disarm prejudice, and to silence, and put infidelity to the blush'. There is also a rather touching confession of the almost guilty pleasure Patrick took in the composition of his verses:

When released from his clerical avocations, he was occupied in writing the Cottage Poems; from morning till noon, and from noon till night, his employment was full of real, indescribable pleasure, such as he could wish to taste as long as life lasts.[50]

Included in the collection was an adaptation of 'Winter Evening Thoughts', retitled 'Winter-night Meditations', and five poems extolling the virtues of a poor and simple life when coloured by religion. The highly sanitized descriptions of cottage life with its cheerful but welcoming cottagers who, though poor, are contented with their lot because they look to a better future in heaven, obviously bore little relation to the misery, poverty and disease of the labouring poor in Patrick's parish which was about to explode in the violence of the Luddite riots. Patrick's aim was not to paint a portrait from life, however, but to point out that faith alone offered salvation and the prospect of happiness.

Though all the poems have a religious theme, at least two had personal relevance to Patrick. The very first poem in the book was dedicated to 'The Rev. J— B—, whilst journeying for the recovery of his health'; a generous tribute to Buckworth's character and style of religion, the poem makes Patrick's admiration for and love of the man abundantly clear. Joshua Gilpin, a friend from the Wellington days, came in for his share of praise too, with a poem extolling the benefits of his newly published 'improved' edition of John Bunyan's *Pilgrim's Progress*.[51]

Cottage Poems bears all the hallmarks of having been written, as Patrick himself described, under pressure of time and with a specific, didactic purpose in mind. It has little literary merit, though it displays that 'faculty for verse' which Robert Southey later described Charlotte Brontë as possessing.[52] Bearing in mind the limitations imposed by the readership for whom it was intended, it was no worse than most clerical productions of the time.

If *Cottage Poems* had a didactic purpose, this was doubly true of Patrick's sermons, which are an unequivocal statement of his beliefs. Only two survive in manuscript, both dating from the Hartshead period, before he had the assurance to deliver his sermons without notes. Significantly, both are on the subject of conversion, which was central to Evangelical belief. The first sermon, a defence of baptism, urged his congregation not to put too much reliance on the outward act of baptism as an act of regeneration in itself; it was the inward, spiritual cleansing of the heart by the Holy Ghost that was the essence of baptism. Without inner conversion, adherence to the mere formalities of religion was useless:

When a man is converted, he is made a new creature in Christ Jesus old things have passed away – Worldly desires – evil propensities, and passions, mistaken notions of religion, spiritual indifference, and enmity to Godliness, are taken away: all the feelings, and inclinations, are sanctified, the mind is enlightened, and the heart is filled with godly zeal and love. From this inward radical change of principle, necessarily proceeds a total change of the outward conduct. The man who before uttered oaths and imprecations, will now sing praises unto God. Indifference, in spiritual things, and consequent inactivity, in good works, will be followed, by Godly zeal, and every corresponding holy action – In the place of gross sins, will be found, all the deeds of < charity > faith, hope, and charity. Faith will enable the converted soul to get the victory over the world; to evade its snares, overcome its temptations, to live above its fears and desires, and to get comfortable views of another and a better < world > country.[53]

There is a ring of conviction about these words that leads one to believe that Patrick was describing his own conversion.

His other sermon is on a similar theme, urging the necessity of inward conversion as well as outward observation of the forms of religion.

Wherever the heart is reformed, there of necessity, the conduct will be reformed also. No one can be righteous, and in a state of salvation, who will indulge in any allowed sin, or habitually omit opportunities of doing good. Faith and works, go hand in hand, & [ar]e inseperable, – But there may [be] an outwardly moral conduct whilst the heart is unchanged, & the soul under sentence of eternal condemnation ... Constant, & regular attendance at church, and a strict conformity to every christian right and ceremony, is no positive proof that a man is a child of God. Under these circumstances, he may still continue ignorant of divine truths ... to be a genuine Christian, and in a state of salvation, it is necessary, not only that we should be outwardly moral, but that our morality should spring from faith in Christ –[54]

A belief in conversion, the mainspring of Evangelical teaching, was also the cornerstone of Patrick's own life; it explains his frequent and repeated efforts to secure the baptism of his parishioners and also his own particular love for St Paul, the most dramatically converted of all the apostles, whose words he quoted frequently.

Patrick was so preoccupied with his pastoral duties and his poetical exertions that it was not until the end of July 1811 that he made an awful discovery. He had forgotten to make the required formal announcements on successive Sundays in the church at Hartshead and was not therefore legally the minister there. He wrote, in panic, to the Archbishop of York's secretary:

For want of proper information on the subject, I neglected, reading myself in, in due time, in consequence of which I find that I am not lawfully possessed of this Living I therefore take the liberty of requesting that you will be so kind as to inform me how I am to proceed, in order to regain right and lawful possession. though this Living is but small it merits particular attention; as Hartshead Church is the only one for several miles round, and there is an increasing number of people here, who are far from being friendly towards the Establishment. It is my intention to get a parsonage-House builded, and to make as far as I can, other necessary improvements, but I cannot proceed, till I get every impediment removed in the way of my retaining the Living. I beg, therefore, that as soon as convenient, you will give the instructions how I am to act.[55]

Almost a month later, having obtained a new set of letters testimonial from Dewsbury and a new nomination to the perpetual curacy of Hartshead-cum-Clifton from John Buckworth, Patrick was relicensed, read himself in properly and took lawful possession.[56]

There was no time to sit back and relax, however, for problems were already building up in the parish. Caught in a terrible trap of inescapable poverty, the working classes of the industrial West Riding had little hope of relief. The interminable war with France disrupted supplies of wool and cotton and cut off important markets for finished cloth and textiles: unemployment, already high, spiralled further and those still working had to accept reduced wages. The cottage-based industries were being forced out of business by the introduction of new, more efficient machinery in the mills which produced more cloth, of a more consistent quality, at a much reduced cost in terms of labour. In many of the West Riding towns Poor Rates, the parochial taxes calculated on property values to provide food, fuel and clothing for the poor, which were intended only as a last resort, were levied four times during the year 1812. At a time when a loaf of bread cost 1/8d., some 50,000 people in the manufacturing districts had only 2½d. a day, less than a tenth of that, for food.[57] In desperation and urged on by Jacobin sympathizers who hoped to imitate the French Revolution in England, malcontents began to meet in secret. Calling themselves Luddites, after Ned Lud, the semi-mythical Leicestershire man who had led the first rioters in the destruction of machinery, they took revenge on the only identifiable cause of the problems which was close at hand: the new machines.

The first attacks in the West Riding began in February 1812 in the Huddersfield area, about six miles south of Hartshead. Inspired by the Nottingham Luddites, whose activities had been recorded in the *Leeds Mercury* (no wonder Patrick made such a point of reading it!), the local Luddites made their first move right under Patrick's nose. They attacked a consignment of cropping machines as it crossed Hartshead Moor on its way to Rawfolds Mill, near Cleckheaton. Throughout February and March there were a number of attacks on mills in the Huddersfield area and many shearing frames were smashed to pieces. It must have been a considerable blow to Patrick when, despite his admonitions from the pulpit and in print, his parishioners not only actively joined in but also took a leading role in two of the worst incidents of Luddite violence.[58]

Under cover of darkness, on the night of 11 April, a large force of Luddites drawn mainly from Hartshead, Clifton, Roberttown and Hightown, all within Patrick's parish, gathered in the fields belonging to Sir George Armitage behind the Three Nuns public house. Their leaders were mainly from Huddersfield, but included William Hall, a cropper from Hartshead who lived in Hightown.[59] With military precision, the men were drawn into ranks and formed into companies according to their weapons: musketmen, hammermen, axemen, pistoliers and the unarmed who were to use whatever came to hand. Then, in silence – but surely not unobserved – the massed bands marched across Hartshead Moor, passing close to both the church and Patrick's lodgings at Lousy Thorn farm. Their objective was Rawfolds Mill, a couple of miles from Hartshead. William Cartwright, the mill owner, had been a leading light in introducing new machinery and in publicly defying the Luddites to attack him. He was supported, enthusiastically, by Patrick's friend, the Reverend Hammond Roberson, though Patrick himself seems to have taken a much less prominent role in the politics of the affair.

Cartwright was prepared for the attack, with lookouts posted and a number of soldiers and other armed men positioned inside the mill. At 12.30 in the morning, there was a violent assault on the building which broke the windows and showered a volley of shots into the mill. While the Luddites tried repeatedly to force an entrance, to the accompaniment of shouts of 'Bang up!', 'Murder them!' and 'Pull down the door!', the guards fired continuously at them. After about twenty minutes, the attempt was given up and the Luddites withdrew, taking their wounded with them but leaving two behind. Samuel Hartley of Halifax and John Booth of Huddersfield, both mortally wounded, were carried on litters to the Star Inn at Roberttown by Cartwright's men but died a few hours later: the inquest found judgements of 'justifiable homicide'. The defeated Luddites fled towards Huddersfield, passing through Hightown and Clifton, where they received food and help for their injuries: it was said that the road was stained with their blood for four miles from Rawfolds. There were no casualties at all among Cartwright's men, though one soldier, who had refused to fire on the Luddites, was court-martialled and sentenced to 300 lashes, which would probably have proved fatal; when the sentence was about to be carried out at Rawfolds the following Tuesday, the crowd was in such an ugly mood that Cartwright secured its commutation to twenty-five lashes.[60]

The Luddites, then as now, attracted both sympathy and hostility. Their appalling living conditions, their unemployment and poverty and the sheer desperation which drove them to violence provoked concern among the more liberal minded; and there is still something inherently romantic about this last-ditch attempt of a doomed band of men fighting the inexorable tide of industrial progress. But violence was no solution and, by causing widespread fear and alarm, did nothing to help the Luddites' case. Patrick undoubtedly sided with the establishment in condemning the attack, though he did not go as far as Hammond Roberson, who turned up when the alarm sounded at Rawfolds Mill with sword in hand. He probably also approved of the signing of a testimonial to Cartwright and the presentation to him of a subscription which raised £3,000 in recognition of his spirited defence of the mill.[61]

Given the fact that there was a strong feeling in favour of the Luddites in his parish, Patrick may have feared reprisals. It seems likely that it was in this period that he acquired his lifelong habit of keeping a loaded pistol in the house overnight. The discharging of the bullet out of the window each morning would become a ritual which aroused much future comment.[62]

The threat of assassination was real. A week to the day after the attack on Rawfolds Mill, an attempt was made on the life of William Cartwright. As he was returning from Huddersfield, presumably in the vicinity of Hartshead and Clifton, shots were fired at him from behind the hedges on each side of the road; the attack took place in broad daylight but Cartwright escaped unhurt.[63] William Horsfall, a woollen manufacturer from Marsden, a village about ten miles away on the other side of Huddersfield, was not so lucky. On 28 April he was ambushed and murdered by four armed working men, presumed to be Luddites. He, too, had been unremitting in his efforts to catch the men who had attacked Rawfolds and had, for some years, employed highly efficient cropping machinery in his mill at Marsden.[64]

The murder of Horsfall, and the vigorous prosecution of the search for those responsible, marked the virtual end of active Luddite resistance, though groups of armed men continued to meet and drill in secret on the moors above and around Huddersfield. The following January, a full nine months after the events had taken place, sixty-six Luddites were tried at York Castle under a special commission: seventeen were executed, including three for the murder of Horsfall and five for the attack on Rawfolds.[65] The Reverend Thomas Atkinson, Patrick's successor at Hartshead, later told his servant that some of the bodies of the executed men were brought back to Hartshead and buried secretly at dead of night in the churchyard there. Patrick had seen the disturbed state of the churchyard and discovered that the burial had taken place, but let it pass without comment, seeing that no harm had been done and believing it was wisest not to inflame popular feeling.[66] This story is clearly apocryphal as there was no need for secrecy in the burial of any of the Luddites, most of whom received public funerals. Nevertheless, it indicates a belief in Hartshead that Patrick was not totally without sympathy for the Luddite cause.

Though the excitements and turmoil of the uprisings must have given Patrick worry and work, by the middle of the year he had something else to occupy his mind. He was now thirty-five years old, 'a man of very retired habits, but attentive to his clerical duties'.[67] He had a wide acquaintance among the clergymen of the district and still enjoyed the company of the young men he had taught in the Sunday school at Dewsbury, many of whom, like the Newsome brothers, made the effort to come over regularly to Hartshead to hear him preach.[68] There was the pleasant and inspirational company of the Buckworths at the vicarage in Dewsbury and the renewal of friendship with William Morgan in Bradford. But now that he had his own parish and a post as perpetual curate from which he could not be evicted, short of some major catastrophe, Patrick could afford to consider marriage. No doubt Mary Burder sprang instantly to mind, but her faith and the fact that his letters to Wethersfield remained unanswered effectively ruled her out. It was no easy task to find an eligible bride who was capable of inspiring at least affection, if not love, in him. Fortunately, Patrick was to find a woman who possessed all the qualities he held most dear.

In January 1812, the Wesleyan Methodists had opened a new boarding school for the sons of ministers and preachers at Woodhouse Grove, an elegant, stone-built Georgian mansion at Rawdon, on the northern outskirts of Bradford and Leeds. It was set in seven acres of garden and had a further eight acres of rich parkland running down to the River Aire.[69] As their first headmaster and acting 'Commercial and Mathematical Master' they had appointed John Fennell, Patrick's friend from Wellington; he was expected to be resident and his wife, assisted by their daughter, Jane, was to act as matron and housekeeper to the establishment.[70] It was only a matter of time till Patrick, a dozen or so miles away at Hartshead, came over to renew his friendship with the family.

Doubtless there were earlier informal visits, but the first important one was made in July when Fennell, anxious to satisfy his board of governors as to the quality of the teaching at the new school, invited Patrick to come to Woodhouse Grove for a few days to examine the boys in the Classics. Patrick did so and presented his report to the committee; it was an unsatisfactory one and, on his recommendation, Mr Burgess, the 'Classical Master', was dismissed shortly afterwards.[71] While he was there, Patrick was introduced to Maria Branwell, Fennell's niece by marriage, who was helping her aunt with the domestic side of running the school.

Maria was twenty-nine years old, petite and elegant though not pretty; pious and something of a blue-stocking but also of a bright, cheerful and witty disposition. She was the daughter of a successful, property-owning grocer and tea merchant of Penzance, Thomas Branwell, who had died in 1808; her mother, Anne Carne, the daughter of a silversmith in the town, had died a year after her husband. Maria had grown up in a totally different world from Patrick. The eighth of eleven children, at least three of whom had not survived infancy, Maria had enjoyed all the benefits of belonging to a prosperous family in a small town.[72]

Penzance at the turn of the nineteenth century was a busy sea port, visited by traders from all over the world. Its position, at almost the southernmost tip of the Cornish peninsula, made it somewhat isolated from the rest of the country but also placed it in the forefront of the war against France. Indeed, the people of Penzance had been the first in England to learn of the victory of Trafalgar and the death of Nelson when two fishermen had intercepted the ship bringing home the news.[73] Though the land routes to London were only just being developed, Penzance was a regular port of call for ships passing between the capital, Bristol and Plymouth, so trade was brisk. The townsmen exported local pilchards, tin and copper and imported luxury goods such as tea, brandy, wines and snuff, which had to lie in their bonded warehouses until they had passed through the customs house beside the quay. The Branwell family were heavily involved in the import trade. Maria's father owned cellars at the quay, retailing and wholesaling the goods through his grocery shop in Market Square. He also owned a substantial amount of property in and around Penzance, including a brewery, the Golden Lion Inn on Market Square and Tremenheere House, the only mansion in the town. Maria's brother, Benjamin, continued the businesses after his father's death and, like him, was a prominent member of the town corporation, serving as mayor in 1809.[74]

Penzance in Maria's day was therefore a thriving market town of some three to four thousand inhabitants and, because of its trade, with a far wider outlook than its isolated and provincial position would otherwise have merited. It was the most important banking centre in Cornwall, banks like that of the Bolitho family being founded and funded out of the profits of the local tin smelting industry.[75] The Branwells not only had substantial sums invested in this bank but Maria's cousin, Joseph, who married her sister, joined its staff after abandoning his career as a schoolteacher.[76] There was also plenty of intellectual and artistic activity. The town had had its own Ladies' Book Club, Agricultural, Provident, Humane, Scientific and Literary Societies and a Penzance Institute since before Maria was born. There were concert rooms behind the Old Turk's Head Inn and Assembly Rooms, funded by public subscription and built in 1791 by Maria's uncle, Richard Branwell, where balls were held throughout the winter months.[77]

Equally important in the life of the town was the Wesleyan Methodist community, of which the Branwells and the Carnes were prominent members. The ubiquitous John Wesley himself had preached regularly in Penzance, including on at least three occasions in the 1780s when, as small children, Maria and her elder sister, Elizabeth, might have joined the crowds to hear him.[78] In 1790 Maria's aunt, Jane Branwell, had married John Fennell, then the headmaster and class leader of the Wesleyan Methodist school in Penzance. Ten years later, Maria's eldest sister, Jane, had married the Wesleyan minister, John Kingston, and emigrated with him to America. This marriage was not a happy one and, in a bold move extremely rare in those days, Jane left her husband and four older children there in 1809 and returned, with only her baby, to Penzance. When the Wesleyan Conference split away from the Church of England in 1812, the Branwells preferred to join the Wesleyans and were largely instrumental in the construction, in 1814, of Penzance's first purpose-built chapel, only a few yards up the street from Maria's old home.[79]

Visiting Penzance today it is not difficult to see why the place had such a

hold on the affections of Maria and Elizabeth. The oldest part of the town
is Chapel Street, where the Branwell home lay within a few hundred yards
of the sea to front and rear. The street is built along the ridge of a rocky
promontory protruding into the vast sweep of Mount's Bay. Then, as now,
the eye is immediately drawn to the spectacular outline of the island castle
of St Michael's Mount a couple of miles away. The long sandy beaches and
fertile agricultural land around the bay remain unchanged, but virtually all
traces of the tin industry have disappeared. In Maria's day Penzance was
surrounded by smelting works and mines, the most renowned of which was
the Wherry Mine, whose main shaft lay thirty fathoms under the sea and
half a mile out from the shore. At high tide all that was visible from the
shore was the steam engine's chimney, rising twelve feet above the waves,
and the miners had to walk across the sea along a plank bridge to reach the
entrance.[80]

The old heart of Penzance, centred around Chapel Street and Market
Jew Street, is also relatively unchanged though engulfed by the larger
modern town. Chapel Street itself is like something out of a picture book,
steep, narrow and cobbled, winding up from the quay to the Market Place
and lined with higgledy-piggledy eighteenth-century cottages. Most are
built of granite though some, like number 25 where the Branwells lived, are
faced with brick. Apart from this pretension to gentility, the house is simple
and of a kind with its neighbours, having five rooms on each floor, two attic
rooms and a south-facing walled garden to the rear. At the front, like its
neighbours, it is straight on to the street. Originally, the house backed on to
the graveyard of the ancient Chapel of St Mary but now it is dwarfed by the
new parish church built on the chapel site in 1835.[81] Above it, Chapel Street
climbs past the picturesque smugglers' inn, the Admiral Benbow, and the
faded grandeur of the Union Hotel before opening out into the commercial
bustle of Market Jew Street.

With all that the town had to offer and a climate so famously mild that
camellias bloom in February, Penzance must have been a very pleasant
home for the Branwell family. The impression one gets of life there when
Maria and her sisters were young is of a whirl of social entertainment and
visiting of the sort so vividly described by Jane Austen. Maria, too, with her
ready wit, charming manners and simple piety could have been a Jane
Austen heroine, living a comfortably middle-class life in a provincial town.
All this was to end, however, when a series of misfortunes struck. After the
death of her father in 1808, the ownership of 25 Chapel Street passed to his
brother, Richard, the tenant of the Golden Lion Inn. He allowed his brother's
family to continue living in the house, even after the death of his sister-in-
law the following year meant that it was only occupied by his three unmarried nieces, Elizabeth, now aged thirty-three, Maria, aged twenty-six, and
Charlotte, aged eighteen. They were quite comfortably situated as they each

had a life annuity of fifty pounds, secured against the property in their father's will.[82] Then, on Christmas Eve 1811, Richard's son, Thomas, a thirty-three-year-old lieutenant in the navy, was drowned in the wreck of the *St George* off the coast of Denmark.[83] Within a few months Richard himself was dead and this seems to have precipitated the break-up of the family. Maria's youngest sister, Charlotte, accepted an offer of marriage from her cousin, Richard's son, Joseph,[84] and Maria herself decided to leave Penzance and travel to Yorkshire to live with her aunt and uncle. John Fennell, like Patrick before him, had been promoted from his schoolmastership in Wellington in Shropshire to be head of the newly opened boarding school for Methodist ministers' sons at Woodhouse Grove. The school had expanded so rapidly that Mrs Fennell was unable to manage the domestic arrangements single-handedly. Maria therefore had the opportunity of earning her keep in a genteel manner while still remaining within her own family.

Elizabeth's fate is unknown: her annuity was not sufficient to enable her to remain in the family home alone and it seems likely that she moved in with her married sister.[85]

From the softness of the Cornish climate and the comfortable, close-knit social world of Penzance, Maria travelled over 400 miles to the comparative austerity and friendlessness of a boys' boarding school in the heart of a depressed and restless industrial West Riding. Though she soon became close friends with her cousin, Jane Branwell Fennell, who was eight years her junior, she must have felt the change in her circumstances and the loss of her family life. No doubt, therefore, she was more disposed to be receptive towards the courtship of the young minister of Hartshead than she might otherwise have been. The fact that Patrick enjoyed the confidence and esteem of her aunt and uncle, too, allowed him to be admitted into an intimate friendship with a speed which would otherwise have flouted social convention. Another important factor in Patrick's favour was that he was also the best friend of William Morgan, who was now actively courting her cousin Jane. It was natural for the two clergymen to visit the two cousins and the inevitable pairing off led to an engagement within only a few months.

Patrick lovingly preserved the series of letters written to him by Maria at this period; his side of the correspondence is unfortunately lost, but hers provides a unique and touching insight into the growing intimacy and affection between them. It is worth quoting extensively from them for this reason alone, but there is an added poignancy in that these letters, written during her engagement, contain virtually all we know about the mother of the Brontës.

On 26 August 1812, Maria wrote her first letter to Patrick, having agreed, at their last meeting, to become his wife.

My dear Friend,
This address is sufficient to convince you that I not only permit, but approve of yours to me – I do indeed consider you as my <u>friend</u>; yet, when I consider how short a time I have had the pleasure of knowing you, I start at my own rashness, my heart fails, and did I not think that you would be disappointed and grieved at it, I believe I should be ready to spare myself the task of writing. Do not think that I am so wavering as to repent of what I have already said. No, believe me, this will never be the case, unless you give me cause for it. You need not fear that you have been mistaken in my character. If I know anything of myself, I am incapable of making an ungenerous return to the smallest degree of kindness, much less to you whose attentions and conduct have been so particularly obliging. I will frankly confess that your behaviour and what I have seen and heard of your character has excited my warmest esteem and regard, and be assured that you shall never have cause to repent of any confidence you may think proper to place in me, and that it will always be my endeavour to deserve the good opinion which you have formed, although human weakness may in some instances cause me to fall short. In giving you these assurances I do not depend upon my own strength, but I look to Him who has been my unerring guide through life, and in whose continued protection and assistance I confidently trust.[86]

The receipt of a letter from Patrick had caused her some embarrassment as the Fennells had teased her about its contents though they did not, as yet, know of her engagement. Maria felt herself in some difficulty as to the etiquette of her own letter: she wanted to speak her heart but was afraid of appearing too forward:

If you knew what were my feelings whilst writing this you would pity me. I wish to write the truth and give you satisfaction, yet fear to go too far, and exceed the bounds of propriety. But whatever I may say or write I will <u>never deceive</u> you, or <u>exceed the truth</u>.[87]

By 5 September she felt emboldened enough to tease Patrick a little: 'I do, indeed, <u>sometimes</u> think of you, but I will not say how often, lest I raise your vanity.' She was worried by Patrick's haste in announcing his engagement to his friends, particularly as she had not yet told the Fennells:

But I think there is no need, as by some means or other they seem to have a pretty correct notion how matters stand betwixt us; and as their hints, etc., meet with no contradiction from me, my silence passes for confirmation. Mr Fennell has not neglected to give me some serious and encouraging advice, and my aunt takes frequent opportunities of dropping little sentences which I may turn to some advantage. I have long had reason to know that the present state of things would give pleasure to all parties.[88]

Toiling up the hill from Woodhouse Grove to take tea at Mr Tatham's she thought about

the evening when I first took the same walk with you, and on the change which had taken place in my circumstances and views since then – not wholly without a wish that I had your arm to assist me, and your conversation to shorten the walk.[89]

Six days later, she gave him a half-jocular berating for forgetting to pass on a note from Jane to William Morgan.[90] Patrick was apparently visiting fairly regularly at this time, walking the dozen or so miles in each direction in the day. The journey was not without hazard, as there were still ominous rumblings from the Luddites. John Abbott, who lived at Woodhouse Grove at this time and was, as he said, intimately acquainted with both Patrick and Maria, recalled the scares and alarms of those days:

I well remember how frightened she was when one night on my return from Leeds on foot – a walk of eleven miles I told her and her cousin Jane Fennel, afterwards Mrs Morgan, how that I had been met on my way and stopped by a regularly organised body of men (Luddites) marching along with military precision. As I approached it, a man in command gave the word 'halt' when the the [sic] moving body, it was too dark to distinguish individuals, became stationary and the man stepped out from it to confront me asking, in a harsh rough voice, as he did so, 'who goes there?'

'A friend', was the ready, and, under the circumstances of the case, the most prudent answer to the challenge.

'Pass friend', was the instant rejoinder, followed without even so much as a 'comma's' pause, with the word of command, 'quick march'! and the black mass of men with still blacker hearts moved on[91]

Sometimes Patrick would stay overnight or longer, as, for instance, in September, so that he could join the party in a walk along the banks of the River Aire to Kirkstall Abbey on the 16th.[92] Two days afterwards, Maria wrote again, feeling the need to explain her position to him. Like Emma Woodhouse, she had been accustomed to independence and reliance on her own judgement.

For some years I have been perfectly my own mistress, subject to no <u>control</u> whatever – so far from it, that my sisters who are many years older than myself, and even my dear mother, used to consult me in every case of importance, and scarcely ever doubted the propriety of my opinions and actions.[93]

Unlike Jane Austen's heroine, however, Maria had no confidence in her own judgement: she had

deeply felt the want of a guide and instructor. At such times I have seen and felt the necessity of supernatural aid, and by fervent applications to a throne of grace I have experienced that my heavenly Father is able and willing to supply the place of every earthly friend. I shall now no longer feel this want, this sense of helpless weakness, for I believe a kind Providence has intended that I shall find in you every earthly friend united; nor do I fear to trust myself under your protection, or shrink from your control. It is pleasant to be subject to those we love, especially when they never exert their authority but for the good of the subject.[94]

For the second time, Patrick was taken to task for failing to deliver a message, this time to the Fennells. In an attempt to get work for his parish and to help his friends, he had acted as an intermediary to place an order for blankets for the school. The Bedfords, with whom he still lodged, had been over to Woodhouse Grove to discuss the order and, because Patrick had forgotten to forewarn the Fennells, had found no one there. The Fennells, with affectionate indulgence, accused Patrick of being 'mazed' with love and talked of sending him to York Lunatic Asylum.[95]

Maria at last plucked up the courage to tell her sisters of her engagement:

Mr Fennell has crossed my letter to my sisters. With his usual goodness he has supplied my <u>deficiencies</u>, and spoken of me in terms of commendation of which I wish I were more worthy. Your character he has likewise displayed in the most favourable light; and I am sure they will not fail to love and esteem you though unknown.[96]

By the end of September the lovers were planning where they were to live. Patrick had intended to take a house but then decided that, with some alteration, his present lodgings would be adequate. Maria willingly acquiesced in his arrangements. 'My heart earnestly joins in your comprehensive prayers', she added, 'I trust they will unitedly ascend to a throne of grace, and through the Redeemer's merits procure for us peace and happiness here and a life of eternal felicity hereafter. Oh, what sacred pleasure there is in the idea of spending an eternity together in perfect and uninterrupted bliss!'[97]

Ten days later she took herself to task for writing anxiously and at length because she had not had a hoped-for letter from Patrick.

But what nonsense am I writing! Surely after this you can have no doubt that you possess all my heart. Two months ago I could not possibly have believed that you would ever engross so much of my thoughts and affections, and far less could I have thought that I should be so forward as to tell you so. I believe I must forbid you to come here again unless you can assure me that you will not steal any more of my regard. Enough of this; I must bring my pen to order, for if I were to suffer myself to revise what I have written I should be tempted to throw it in the fire ... I trust in your hours of retirement you will not forget to pray for me. I assure you I need every assistance to help me forward; I feel that my heart is more ready to attach itself to earth than heaven. I sometimes think there never was a mind so dull and inactive as mine is with regard to spiritual things.[98]

At the beginning of October there was another walk to Kirkstall Abbey, this time to celebrate Jane Fennell's twenty-first birthday. Patrick was invited to stay for a few days at Woodhouse Grove and Jane demanded a long poem in honour of her birthday, no doubt having read Patrick's verses sent to a lady on her eighteenth birthday in his *Cottage Poems*.[99] This visit gave Maria renewed confidence in the man she called 'him whom I love beyond all others'. 'Unless my love for you were very great', she reassured him,

how could I so contentedly give up my home and all my friends – a home I loved so much that I have often thought nothing could bribe me to renounce it for any great length of time together, and friends with whom I have been so long accustomed to share all the vicissitudes of joy and sorrow? Yet these have lost their weight, and though I cannot always think of them without a sigh, yet the anticipation of sharing with you all the pleasures and pains, the cares and anxieties of life, of contributing to your comfort and becoming the companion of your pilgrimage, is more delightful to me than any other prospect which this world can possibly present.[100]

Patrick and Maria's next meeting was in Bradford, where Maria was on a short visit and Patrick had to address the first anniversary meeting of the Bradford Auxiliary Bible Society. Over £150 had been raised in subscriptions throughout the year, half of which had been used to purchase bibles for free distribution among the poor of the neighbourhood.[101] The society was interdenominational but four Evangelicals, John Crosse, Patrick Brontë, William Morgan and Samuel Redhead, the last of whom was to reappear many times in Patrick's life, were among the chosen speakers. They declared, with pardonable exaggeration, that the society 'was one of the most pious, liberal, and useful Institutions, that have attracted the notice of mankind since the creation of the world till the present moment'.[102]

In her next letter, Maria Branwell addressed this eminent divine as 'My dear saucy Pat', commenting naughtily, 'Both the Dr [William Morgan] and his lady very much wish to know what kind of address we make use of in our letters to each other – I think they would scarcely hit on this!!' She and Patrick had enjoyed a lovers' dispute as to which one loved the other most: 'I firmly believe the Almighty has set us apart for each other –', she told him, 'may we by earnest, frequent prayer, & every possible exertion, endeavour to fulfill his will in all things! I do not, cannot, doubt your love, & here, I freely declare, I love you above all the world besides!'[103] She went on to tell him that disaster had struck for the first time since she had left her home in Penzance.

I suppose you never expected to be much the richer for me but I am sorry to inform you that I am still poorer than I thought myself. – I mentioned having sent for my books clothes &c On Saturday evg about the time when you were writing the description of your imaginary shipwreck, I was reading <the> & feeling the effects of a real one, having then received a letter from my sister giving me an account of the vessel in which she had sent my box, being stranded on the coast of Devonshire, in consequence of which the box was dashed to pieces with the violence of the sea &

all my little property, with the exception of a very few articles, swallowed up in the mighty deep –[104]

By the time Maria wrote her last letter, on 5 December, the wedding date had been set for the 29th of the month and the ladies were about to make the cakes: Mrs Bedford was asked to make another one for distribution among the 'fifteen or twenty' people in the Hartshead area on Patrick's list.[105] For this was to be no ordinary wedding, but a double one, shared with Jane Fennell and William Morgan, for which a special licence had to be procured: John Fennell would give away his daughter and his niece, the two clergymen would act alternately as bridegroom and officiating minister and the two cousins would be both bridesmaid and bride.

With the wedding imminent, Maria gave way to a classic state of pre-marital nerves. 'So you <u>thought</u> that <u>perhaps</u> I <u>might</u> expect to hear from you', she lashed her fiancé with unexpected ferocity.

As the case was so doubtful, and you were in such great haste, you might as well have deferred writing a few days longer, for you seem to suppose it is a matter of perfect indifference to me whether I hear from you or not. I believe I once requested you to judge of my feelings by your own – am I to think that <u>you</u> are thus indifferent?

Perceiving that she had over-reacted, she was immediately contrite. 'I am too serious on the subject', she confessed;

I only meant to rally you a little on the beginning of your last, and to tell you that I fancied there was a coolness in it which none of your former letters had contained. If this fancy was groundless, forgive me for having indulged it, and let it serve to convince you of the sincerity and warmth of my affection. Real love is ever apt to suspect that it meets not with an equal return; you must not wonder then that my fears are sometimes excited. My pride cannot bear the idea of a diminution of your attachment, or to think that it is stronger on my side than yours ... I am certain no one ever loved you with an affection more pure, constant, tender, and ardent than that which I feel. Surely this is not saying too much; it is the truth, and I trust you are worthy to know it. I long to improve in every religious and moral quality, that I may be a help, and if possible an ornament to you. Oh let us pray much for wisdom and grace to fill our appointed stations with propriety, that we may enjoy satisfaction in our own souls, edify others, and bring glory to the name of Him who has so wonderfully preserved, blessed, and brought us together.[106]

Who could doubt, on reading this letter, that Patrick had won a woman of superlative qualities?

The momentous year of 1812 drew to a close, a year which had seen riots at home and, abroad, war on two fronts, against France and the United States. During the months of Patrick's courtship of Maria, Napoleon had invaded Russia, marched in triumph on Moscow and, his fortunes changing at last, retreated in disastrous disarray. It was hardly an auspicious time to get married but, on 29 December 1812, in the ancient parish church at Guiseley, Patrick Brontë married Maria Branwell; immediately afterwards he officiated at the wedding of William Morgan and Jane Branwell Fennell. Maria had to borrow her white lace bridal veil as her own had been among the items lost at sea.[107] Their wedding breakfast, though undocumented, must have taken place at Woodhouse Grove before the newly weds departed, the Morgans to Bierley, where Morgan had just been appointed incumbent, and the Brontës to Hartshead. It cannot have simply been a coincidence in such a closely knit family that on exactly the same day there was another Branwell marriage. Far away in Penzance, Charlotte and Joseph Branwell were married at Madron Church, on the hill overlooking the bay.[108]

Married life at Hartshead must have been very different from Patrick's bachelor days, though his new bride seems to have made no impression on folk memory there.[109] They were not as comfortably off as perhaps they could have wished: Patrick's living was worth only sixty-two pounds a year[110] but Maria had her annuity of fifty pounds, enough to make them modestly respectable. At some stage, either on their marriage or possibly before the birth of their first child, they moved from Lousy Thorn to a home of their own. Clough House was at Hightown, nearly a mile away from Hartshead Church; built of stone, with a central door and two windows on each of its three storeys, the house was a small but comfortable gentleman's residence. It stood opposite the top of Clough Lane, which wound steeply down one hill and then up the next before eventually reaching the church, so it was not a particularly convenient location for conducting the services and offices. On the other hand, unlike Lousy Thorn, it was in the village of Hightown so Maria was not isolated and would have the opportunity of easily visiting her neighbours and the parish sick.

Patrick's personal happiness during his courtship and the first months of his marriage was reflected in his next literary venture, *The Rural Minstrel: A Miscellany of Descriptive Poems* which was printed and published for the author in September 1813 by P. K. Holden of Halifax. As with *Cottage Poems*, Patrick had again endeavoured to write a book

which, from its size, the nature and manner of its composition, and the matter it contained, would have some tendency to convey useful instruction, in a mode not unacceptable, and which, in the perusal and purchase, would require no great portion of money or time.[111]

The little book contained eleven poems of a much higher standard than those in *Cottage Poems*. This was partly because they had been written over a two-year period, whenever inspiration had struck, rather than specifically for the publication. The poems are again didactic homilies but the moral is not thrust down the reader's throat, as in his former work, but more attractively clad in descriptive verse which sugars the pill without detracting from its purpose. Even the message itself is more subtly expressed. Instead of pictures of impoverished but happy cottagers, we now, more realistically, have deathbed scenes. In one the good man has succumbed to disease and penury but comfort is offered to his widow and children in the assurance of his eternal salvation and the knowledge that God, not man, will now be their protector. The same message is pushed in another poem, 'Winter', which also includes an impassioned appeal to God for the physical relief of the distressed and suffering poor.[112]

The whole tone is much more sympathetic and sensitive to the plight of the poor; it seems that the terrible winters of 1811 and 1812 had left their mark on Patrick and influenced his poetry as well as his heart. The ephemeral nature of life is frequently touched upon and in several poems the sinner is warned, through hearing the Sabbath bell or the song of the Harper of Erin, for instance, that life is short and he must make time to repent his sins if he is to win eternal life.[113]

Two poems are much more personal: 'Kirkstall Abbey', which appears to have been part of a longer, possibly prose, tale which Patrick had contemplated writing, and 'Lines addressed to a lady on her birthday'. Kirkstall Abbey had been the objective of several of the family walks which Patrick had enjoyed during his courtship of Maria. The ruin of a medieval Cistercian abbey on the banks of the River Aire, it was a romantic and beautiful place in its own right but it is also said to be the place where Patrick actually proposed to Maria, so it had particularly happy associations for him.[114] The birthday verses, written only a few months after their marriage, were addressed to Maria, who was thirty on 15 April 1813. The poem is a rapturous description of the beauties of an April morning:

> Maria, let us walk, and breathe, the morning air,
>   And hear the cuckoo sing, –
> And every tuneful bird, that woos the gentle spring.
>   Throughout the budding grove,
>   Softly coos the turtle-dove,
>   The primrose pale,
>   Perfumes the gale.
> The modest daisy, and the violet blue,
> Inviting, spread their charms for you.
>
> How much enhanced is all this bliss to me,
> Since it is shared, in mutual joy with thee![115]

Echoing the sentiments expressed by Maria in her letters to him before they were married, Patrick ended the poem with a prayer that the rest of their lives should be spent with 'undivided heart' under the influence of pure religion, followed by 'endless bliss, without alloy' together in heaven.

In all these poems, whatever their subject, Patrick's love of the natural world shines through:

> With heart enraptured, oft have I surveyed,
> The vast, and bounteous works, that God has made.
> The tinkling rill, the floods astounding roar,
> The river's brink, and ocean's frothy shore,
> The feathered songster's notes, and winter's howl,
> The sky serene, and frowning ether's scowl,
> The softest sound, the hoarsest thunder's roll,
> Have each, their sweetest pleasures for my soul.
>
> As roves my mind, o'er nature's works abroad,
> It sees, reflected, their creative God,
> The insects, dancing in the sunny beam, –
> Whose filmy wings, like golden atoms gleam,
> The finny tribe, that glance across the lake,
> The timid hare, that rustles through the brake,
> The squirrel blithe, that frisks on yonder spray,
> The wily fox, that prowls about for prey,
> Have each a useful lesson for my heart,
> And sooth[e] my soul, and rural sweets impart.[116]

The beauties of the natural world were, to Patrick, the manifestation of God; it was a belief that he was to pass on to his children, who would all share the passion for nature which he first expressed in these verses. Interestingly, too, the influence of the poems in *The Rural Minstrel* can be traced through to their work, particularly the poetry of Branwell and Emily.[117]

The Brontës' happiness at Hartshead was crowned with the arrival of their first child, a daughter, the exact date of whose birth is not known. On St George's Day, 23 April 1814, seventeen days after the abdication of Napoleon and eight years to the day since Patrick had received his degree from Cambridge, the young Maria Brontë was baptized at Hartshead Church by William Morgan.[118] Though there is no evidence one way or the other, it seems more than likely that the Morgans and Fennells stood as her godparents. Their ties of relationship and friendship made them the ideal candidates, more especially as John Fennell was preparing for ordination into the Church of England. The decision had not been taken lightly and seems to have been prompted by the resolution of the Methodist Conference to separate from the Established Church in 1812. Fennell had always been more Methodist than Evangelical in his leanings, but this was the final straw. In April 1813 he had given notice to the governors of Woodhouse Grove of his intention to seek ordination in the Established Church and, in consequence, was dismissed from his post. He was allowed to remain at the school till the end of August, so that a replacement could be found, then he and his wife moved to Bradford, where he began the long process of preparing for ordination under the auspices of John Crosse.[119]

For Patrick, the clerical round continued. The abdication of Napoleon and the Peace of Paris, which followed shortly afterwards, heralded the end of decades of warfare. Combined with the improvements in trade, these events had brought new optimism to his parish, no less than to the rest of the country. In Dewsbury, the ceremony of proclaiming the peace on 7 July 1814 was turned into a huge celebration: at nine in the morning a procession of clergymen, gentry, members of friendly societies and Sunday school children made its way to the parish church. As over a thousand Sunday school children are said to have taken part, it seems certain that Patrick and his pupils too were involved. The celebration was marred by a dramatic incident: such was the press of people in the church that one of the galleries began to collapse under the sheer weight of the crowd. The congregation scattered, some making for the doors, others jumping out of the windows and out into the churchyard. Fortunately, no one was seriously injured but the service was postponed until the afternoon when John Buckworth preached to the assembled multitudes. While the inhabitants of the outlying districts, including Hartshead, returned home, Mr Brooke and John Halliley, junior, owners of the largest carpet mill in Dewsbury, entertained the 300 Sunday school children from the town and the workmen of their mills with roast beef and (inappropriately, one would have thought) strong ale.[120]

As 1813 progressed and, more often than not, John Buckworth was absent in a fruitless search to regain his health, Patrick found himself more and more drawn into the circle of John Crosse and the parish of Bradford. He was present, for instance, at the inaugural meeting of a new Church Missionary Association at Bradford, whose object was to fund the sending of bibles and missionaries to Africa and the East. Significantly, Patrick's co-founders in the new association included, once again, that select band of Evangelicals, John Crosse, William Morgan and Samuel Redhead, though its activities were to be nondenominational. As their circular grandly declaimed:

There is no need here for unholy rivalry. The wide world is before us. There is more than room for all the efforts, which the various denominations of Christians may be able to make for ages to come. The field of labour is most ample: the prospects of usefulness are great: and the call on Christians in general, and particularly on the members of the Church of England is now made with a confident expectation that it will be felt and answered.[121]

Out of the nineteen areas of Bradford where collectors had been appointed, only Patrick, at Hartshead, was outside the actual town; they were to meet with the officers once every three months and hold an annual general meeting on Easter Tuesday. Patrick himself took out a subscription of 10/6d.

a year which entitled him to receive *The Register*, the association's monthly journal. The following year he invited John Buckworth to give a sermon on behalf of the Church Missionary Society at Hartshead on 25 September, which resulted in a liberal collection for the society's funds.[122]

The Bradford Bible Society was also thriving and Patrick again addressed its anniversary meeting on 15 October 1814. The society had redoubled its efforts to purchase bibles for free distribution after discovering that nearly half the families in the parish did not possess one. Sunday school children, too, were being encouraged to subscribe a penny a week towards the cost of purchasing their own bibles which the society made available to them at reduced rates.[123] Though Hartshead is not mentioned in the reports of the society, there is no doubt that Patrick would have implemented these poli-cies, so dear to his heart, in his own parish and, before he left, he had the satisfaction of helping to set up a Dewsbury Auxiliary of the Bible Society, based at the parish church.[124]

Through his friendship with William Morgan and John Fennell, and his involvement in church missionary activities, Patrick had become a familiar figure in the parish of Bradford. For this reason, when he was approached by the Reverend Thomas Atkinson, perpetual curate of Thornton, with the proposition that they should exchange livings, Patrick was not displeased. Though he loved the countryside around Hartshead and Clifton, and had done much to improve the spiritual lot of his parishioners, he was never unwilling to accept a challenge and Bradford, with John Crosse, the ven-erable and now nearly blind vicar, at its head, had been his ultimate aim since Wellington. Thornton offered him the prospect of deeper involvement in a much larger parish and a considerably increased income as the living was worth £140 a year.[125] This was to be more important to him as on 8 February 1815, Maria had given birth to a second daughter, who was named after Maria's elder sister, Elizabeth.[126]

Thomas Atkinson was a nephew of Hammond Roberson, who may have suggested the exchange, and, like Patrick, a graduate of Cambridge. His sudden desire to move to Hartshead was apparently not inspired by spiritual but temporal motives. Through the Firth family of Thornton, he had been introduced to one of their relatives, Frances Walker of Lascelles Hall, near Huddersfield, and was now anxious to court her seriously. The incumbency of Hartshead-cum-Clifton would bring him nearer to her and facilitate their courtship, or, as one of his parishioners later put it, 'he had a bird to catch, near Hartshead'.[127]

By the middle of March 1815, the arrangements had been made and Patrick had been nominated and appointed by John Crosse as the new perpetual curate of Thornton.[128] Perhaps because Maria was in too delicate a state to move so rapidly after the birth of her daughter, the actual exchange was delayed for a couple of months. Patrick took his final services at Hartshead, a burial and three baptisms (there was evidently a last-minute rush to get babies baptized by the old minister instead of the new one) on 18 May. The next day, a Saturday, Patrick and Maria and their two little daughters travelled the thirteen or so miles across Bradford to a new parish and a new home at Thornton.[129]

Chapter Three

❧

GOOD FRIENDS AND KIND NEIGHBOURS

After what had seemed like the ending of decades of warfare with the abdication of Napoleon and the Peace of Paris, the whole of Europe was once again thrown into turmoil with news of Napoleon's escape from Elba. Since March, he had been back in power and the whole machinery of war had had to be cranked up into action again. The Brontës had been at Thornton for just a month when, on 16 June 1815, Wellington fought an indecisive battle at Quatre-Bras against the French commanded by Marshal Ney; the engagement prevented him sending aid to the Prussians, who were therefore heavily defeated by Napoleon at Ligny, losing 20,000 men. Fortunately, before news of these disasters had reached Yorkshire, the reversals had been completely overthrown with the triumph of the allies at Waterloo. The allied victory, under the command of Wellington and Blücher, was such a uniquely important event that, for the rest of the Brontës' lives, 18 June would be celebrated as 'Waterloo Day' throughout the kingdom. Napoleon had been crushed and, though his spectre was to continue to haunt Europe for another six years while he lived on in exile on St Helena, the long years of unremitting warfare had finally ended. One of Patrick's first services at Thornton, on 23 July, was dedicated to a thanksgiving for the victory at Waterloo, and the collections were taken in aid of the widows and orphans of those who fell.[1] He had to wait another six months, however, before he could finally give thanks for the restoration of peace in Europe – the first peace in Patrick's adult life.[2]

Against the background of these cataclysmic events in Europe, the Brontës arrived and settled in Thornton. In 1815 Thornton was a small township, less than four miles from the centre of Bradford. Like so many of the West Riding villages of the time, it was perched on a hillside, a vantage point from which Bradford could be seen in the valley bottom to the east. Within a radius of about two and a half miles, and also clinging independently to their own hill tops, the villages of Clayton to the south, Denholme to the west and Allerton to the north were all clearly visible from Thornton Heights; also to the north, but some three or four miles away and hidden in the lee of a hill, was Wilsden. All four villages, and the scattered hamlets between them, fell within Patrick's ministry.[3] Though Thornton itself was centrally placed, Patrick had considerable distances to cover – distances not made any easier by being all up hill and down dale and his not being able to afford a horse. Mrs Gaskell described the neighbourhood as 'desolate and wild; great tracts of bleak land, enclosed by stone dykes'[4] but then Mrs Gaskell, coming from the softer side of the Pennines, was never particularly attracted to the wilder countryside of Yorkshire.

The moorland was broken up not just by grey dry-stone walls but by grand, sturdy, square farmhouses, with gables and stone mullioned windows, built by wealthy yeomen farmers in the late Middle Ages. There were also quite a few stone quarries, particularly up on Thornton Heights above the town itself, where the concentration of names like 'World's End', 'Egypt', 'The Walls of Jericho' and 'Jerusalem Farm' are indicative of the strong traditions of Nonconformity in the area. Thornton, after all, had been the stronghold of men like Accepted Lister and Oliver Heywood and even in Patrick's time, the population divided into church and chapel, without the leavening of moderates like the Wesleyan Methodists.[5]

Like Hartshead-cum-Clifton, Thornton was a perpetual curacy and therefore subject to financial and administrative ties with, in this case, Bradford. In 1811 there were nearly 5,500 souls in the chapelry; by 1821, just after the Brontës had left, there were just over 9,000.[6] As in Hartshead, most were employed as agricultural labourers, in the stone quarries or as hand-loom weavers, working in their own cottages with the specially adapted long line of windows to the upper storey to give them maximum light. What has always seemed to make Thornton a much more pleasant and social place in the Brontës' time than either Hartshead or Haworth is the fact that, uniquely, there is an extant diary, kept by Miss Elizabeth Firth of Kipping House at Thornton, which records the day to day social life of the place. As it is little more than a list of engagements, it is immensely frustrating to those hoping for insights into the Brontës as people, but it does provide a fascinating glimpse of the sort of life they led in Thornton.[7]

For the first time, the Brontës were to live in a proper parsonage, provided by the parish. Though Patrick complained of it being 'very ill-constructed', 'inconvenient' and requiring 'annually, no small sum to keep it in repair', at least it obviated the need for paying rent.[8] Smaller than Clough House, with only three rooms on each of its two floors, the parsonage stood on Market Street, the main thoroughfare from Bradford; only a narrow strip of garden, surrounded by railings, separated it from the street. Built four square, with a large double window each side of the door and three above, the house was low and unpretentious but marginally more substantial than the other twenty-two houses in the street. If the front of the house was noisy and dirty with the daily passing of waggons and coaches, the back was quieter with a large yard and barns carved out of the hillside which rose up steeply behind the house. The rest of the hillside was a maze of narrow cobbled streets and ginnels bounded by higgledy-piggledy cottages and opening out at unexpected corners into flagged yards. The whole village was surrounded by fields with the open moorland, which Mrs Gaskell so disdained, crowning the hills.

The parsonage at Thornton was much more conveniently placed for the church than Clough House had been. The Old Bell Chapel, as it was known, lay at the Bradford end of Market Street, just above Thornton Hall and looking down over it to the pretty Pinchbeck Valley where the fields gave way to woods and Clayton Beck. Now a picturesque ruin, its squat bell tower humbled in the dust and its broken walls overgrown with weeds and shrubs, the chapel was in a dilapidated state even in 1815 when Patrick arrived. Built in 1620, it was a functional and unlovely building, with no pretensions to architectural beauty or merit. Small and narrow, on the north side it had two rows of square cottage windows and on the south, five Late Perpendicular pointed windows; inside it was gloomy and cramped. Francis Leyland, writing many years later – and after Patrick had 'repaired and beautified' the chapel – gives an evocative description:

The interior is blocked, on the ground floor, with high-backed, unpainted deal pews. Two galleries hide the windows almost from view, and cast a gloom over the interior of the edifice. The area under the pews, and in the aisles, is paved with gravestones, and a fetid, musty smell floats through the damp and mouldering interior.[9]

Despite the physical extent of his parish, Patrick was not hard pressed by official duties. The burials ran at about the same level as at Hartshead but there were only about half the number of baptisms: widespread Nonconformity in the Thornton area meant many children were not baptized into the Church of England.[10]

Patrick had a great deal of freedom to utilize his time as he wished. Though most biographers would have us believe he spent his hours either in social chitchat with the Firths and their friends or wandering through the Pinchbeck Valley, pen in hand, indulging his literary muse,[11] this was far from the case. In fact, most of the social visiting appears to have been between the ladies; Patrick only called in person at Kipping House approximately twice a month, sometimes more when business had to be conducted with Mr Firth or if the latter was ill. This was hardly excessive, given that the Firths were amongst his most important parishioners, though, inevitably, in a place so small, Patrick or his family sometimes met the Firths while visiting other neighbours.

When the Brontës moved to Thornton, Elizabeth Firth was actually away, staying at Lascelles Hall with her cousin, Frances Walker, for whose sake Thomas Atkinson had exchanged livings with Patrick. She returned to Thornton on 6 June, and the next day made it her first job to call on the new incumbent and his family. Two days later, she met them again while on a visit to the Kayes at Allerton Hall, and the following Sunday heard Patrick preach for the first time, his sermon being on the parable of the Sower.[12] Thereafter, there appears to have been a growing intimacy between Elizabeth Firth and Maria Brontë. Elizabeth was very young, only eighteen, and it was just less than a year since she had lost her mother, killed when the gig she had been travelling in had overturned and she had been thrown into the road. Her father, John Scholefield Firth, was a doctor, like his father before him, but at fifty-seven years of age, he was a comparatively old man. Elizabeth was an only child, but she had compensated for this by having a wide circle of her own friends who, with various members of the family, were always exchanging visits with her.[13]

It was natural for Maria to be drawn into this circle which was so like the old days of Penzance. No doubt she was eased into the friendship by having her own sister, Elizabeth Branwell, staying with her; she is first mentioned in the diaries on 12 June, but it seems more than likely that she had come to the Brontës in time to help the family move to Thornton. Her presence would have made it more comfortable for the new parson's wife to visit her neighbours, particularly when her husband was employed on other business. At least once a week, but occasionally more often, the ladies took tea together.[14]

The intimacy was evidently strong enough after two months for the Brontës to feel that they could ask Mr Firth and his daughter to be godparents to their second daughter, Elizabeth, who, nearly seven months after her birth, had not yet been christened. On Saturday, 26 August 1815, Elizabeth was baptized in her father's church by John Fennell, who had just been admitted to the Anglican priesthood. No doubt his wife and the Morgans were there, as well as the Firths and Elizabeth Branwell who was the second godmother.[15] Though she may not yet have known it, Maria was already expecting another child when her second daughter was christened.

While Maria and her sister enjoyed taking tea and going for pleasant summer walks with Elizabeth Firth, Patrick was once more engaged in writing. Since February, William Morgan had been running a series of short pieces on the subject of conversion in the little magazine he edited called *The Pastoral Visitor*. This was a subject dear to Patrick's heart. In a somewhat turgid style, peppered with biblical references, Morgan had listed the sins of the unconverted and taught how, through self-catechism, they could learn to know themselves and seek to be converted. Apart from an exemplary death-scene, quoted from Joshua Gilpin's *Monument of Parental Affection to a Dear and Only Son*, the little articles made dry and impersonal reading. Patrick recognized this and in a short story, which Morgan published in three sections over the months of July, September and October, fleshed out the moral precepts with an emotive and personal account, written in the first person, of the conversion of a sinner. He prefixed it with a short letter, addressed to the editor, which echoed those words from St Paul which were so frequently on his lips:

Rev. Sir,
Should you judge the following to be a just representation of the views and feelings of an awakened sinner, before he had got proper notions of the all sufficiency of Christ; by giving it a place in your useful little work, you may benefit some, and will much oblige your obedient servant,

P. B.[16]

The first part of Patrick's story described the sufferings of the sinner who knows his own guilt:

'Tis true, I have not robbed, I have not murdered, I have not actually committed any enormous crime, but in thought, and inclination (and these speak aloud in the ears of God,) I have been guilty of robbery, and murder, a hundred times over. How often have I coveted that which was not my own! How often have I been angry at my brother, without a cause! What was it but fear kept me from the most guilty deeds![17]

In the second part, the sinner has now spent two months pondering his sins and, through the Scriptures and the Liturgy, has begun to find consolation; 'The conflict may be long and severe; but I hope through Christ Jesus to obtain the victory and the prize.' Finally, the sinner has achieved conversion, not in a sudden and dramatic flash like St Paul, but gradually, with many stumblings along the way; he knows that he must still 'watch and pray' but, through Christ, he has now the certainty of salvation and death no longer has any terror for him.[18]

Though the story is in the typical Evangelical mould, with the terrors of damnation and the flames of hell threatening the sinner, it is full of humanity too; the author, one feels, sympathizes with and understands the feelings of the sinner and tries to convert him through love rather than fear. Interestingly, too, the division of the story into three self-contained but interdependent chapters reflects a certain literary sophistication in Patrick, particularly at the end of the first episode where the reader is left with the sinner, trembling on the brink of damnation, with only a 'glimmering ray of hope' breaking in on his 'benighted soul'.[19]

At about the same time as he was writing his article 'On Conversion', Patrick was also preparing for the press another story which, because it was longer and had four poems annexed to it, was to be published as a little book or pamphlet in its own right. *The Cottage in the Wood*, subtitled 'Or the art of becoming rich and happy', was very much in the same vein as *Cottage Poems* and was intended for the same class of readers. Possibly as a result of criticism of *Cottage Poems*, Patrick included a short disclaimer at the beginning of the book, pointing out that the blessings enjoyed by his cottagers were not the result of either their poverty or the rural beauties of their situation:

The truth is, that happiness and misery have their origin within, depending comparatively little on outward circumstances. The mind is its own place. Put a good man any where and he will not be miserable – put a bad man any where and he cannot be happy. The reason is obvious; the good man carries his mind with him, and thence he draws his remedies, his antidote, his comforts: the bad man also carries his mind with him, but it is a source of unruly desires, vain expectation, heavy disappointment, and keen remorse.[20]

The Cottage in the Wood told the story of Mary, the pious young daughter of an impoverished cottager, who attracted the attentions of a wealthy, drunken rake. Mary refused either to be his mistress, in return for financial assistance for her parents, or to marry him, because she could not bind herself to a man who was both immoral and, more importantly, an atheist. It was not Mary's piety, however, that persuaded her suitor to reform but his providential escape from almost certain death on two occasions. From that moment on he was a converted man and took up good works with alacrity. One day, while teaching poor children free of charge in the Sunday school, he again encountered Mary and renewed his suit; his conversion and reformation of character made him acceptable and the two were married, lived a long and happy life together, were blessed with good children and died, in an exemplary manner, within six months of each other.

The Cottage in the Wood contains most of Patrick's favourite themes: the story was a peg on which to hang expositions on the Bible, Sunday schools and the evils of drink. The importance of the education offered by Sunday schools is stressed throughout; the cottagers had themselves been unconverted until their daughter went to Sunday school and, in consequence, began to read the Scriptures to them each day; Mary herself was so apt a pupil that she was appointed a teacher and therefore earned a small but valuable salary which enabled her to pay for lessons in writing and grammar at a day school; and the genuine nature of Bower's conversion is publicly displayed in his offering a free education to those too poor to be able to afford one. Education is the key to moral and social improvement in the story and, as we shall see, in life as well as in fiction, Patrick, his wife and his children were passionately committed to this belief.

The Cottage in the Wood was the first of all the Brontë books to bear the name 'Brontë', spelt with the diaeresis, on the title page – though this appears to have been the result of a printing error rather than a deliberate change on Patrick's part.[21] It enjoyed quite a little local success. Priced fairly cheaply, at 1/6d., and having an illustrated frontispiece, it was regarded highly enough to be reprinted, without the poetry section, in *The Cottage Magazine* in June 1817, and as a whole in a second edition in 1818.[22] Its success was no doubt attributable to its being used in Sunday schools, though it must have been helped by William Morgan's review of it in *The Pastoral Visitor* in August 1816:

This is a very amusing and instructive tale, written in a pure and plain style. Parents will learn in this little Book the Advantages of Sunday Schools, while their Children will have an example well worthy of their closest imitation. Young women may here especially obtain a knowledge that the path of virtue leads to happiness. We would therefore most cordially recommend this Book to all sorts of Readers.[23]

While Patrick was enjoying local literary celebrity, his wife had not been idle. Perhaps inspired by the example of her cousin, Jane Morgan, who had already had her work published in her husband's *The Pastoral Visitor*,[24] Maria had taken up her own pen in support of Patrick's twin passions for conversion and education. Apart from her letters to Patrick before they were married, 'The Advantages of Poverty, in Religious Concerns' is the only extant manuscript by Maria. As such, it was carefully preserved by Patrick who wrote upon it, 'The above was written by my dear Wife, and sent for insertion in one of the periodical publications – Keep it, as a memorial of her –'.[25]

In the manuscript, which does not appear to have been published, Maria considered the question of poverty. She argued that it was not an absolute evil but, when combined with religion, was an actual benefit: salvation is easier for the poor man to attain as he does not have the opportunity or temptation to sin like the rich man. Though callous in its simplicity, the message was expressed with sympathy for the temporal sufferings of the poor.

Perhaps, some, who are daily, & hourly sinking under the distresses & privations, which attend extreme poverty ... may indignantly exclaim, 'Is it not an evil to be deprived of the necessaries of life? Can there be any anguish equal to that occasioned by the sight of objects, dear as your own soul, famishing with cold & hunger? Is it no evil, to hear the heart-rending cries of your children, craving for that, which you have it not in your power to give them? And, as an aggravation of this distress to know, that some are surfeited by abundance, at the same time, that you, & yours are perishing for want?' Yes, these are evils indeed of peculiar bitterness; & he must be less than man, that can behold them without sympathy, & an active desire to relieve them.[26]

In such straits, Maria argued, Christian charity is always there to relieve the worldly needs of the poor and religion will bring solace and contentment. She ended with a pious exhortation:

It surely is the duty of all christians, to exert themselves, in every possible way, to promote the instruction, & conversion of the Poor; &, above all, to pray with all the ardor of christian faith, & love, that every poor man, may be a religious man.[27]

It is easy to mock the naivety of Maria's sentiments and to dismiss her arguments as 'the usual Methodist palliative', but there is no question of her sincerity or her genuine piety. What is more, Maria was setting an example of female literary activity to her daughters which, together with Patrick's publications, was to be an inspiration to the future novelists. The article was probably intended for *The Pastoral Visitor*, or possibly for John Buckworth's *The Cottage Magazine*; it would have been equally appropriate for either publication.[28]

Literary activity aside, there was plenty to occupy the Brontës. On 6 September 1815, there was excitement in the township when Elizabeth Firth's father married Ann Greame of Exley, near Halifax, and brought her back to Kipping House to be introduced to the neighbours.[29] A few weeks later, there were three evenings of concerts in Bradford, featuring Handel's oratorio *The Messiah*, to celebrate the consecration on 12 October of a brand new church, Christ Church, at the top of Darley Street. It is more than likely that Patrick would have attended the consecration, not only as a mark of respect to the Archbishop of York, who performed the ceremony, but also to support William Morgan who, immediately afterwards, was nominated minister of the new church by John Crosse. It was to be an important post, making Morgan a dominant influence (not always to the good) in church affairs in Bradford. Unusually, instead of renting out its pews to the congregation, who had to pay for the privilege of taking their place in them, Christ Church had 500 free places. This made it an ideal base from which to carry the Evangelical message to the poor though such altruism had its price: a year after its consecration, the church was still over £1,000 in debt on its building costs.[30]

The day after the consecration, there was the satisfaction of attending the annual meeting of the Bradford Auxiliary of the Bible Society and hearing that it had gone from strength to strength in the town.[31] In Bradford, too,

Patrick joined the Library and Literary Society, though the annual subscription of a pound a year soon proved to be an expense he could ill afford and he only kept up his membership for a year.[32]

The year 1816 opened more hopefully than its predecessor. On Thursday, 18 January, there were national celebrations for the restoration of peace in Europe and Patrick, like ministers in churches and chapels throughout the land, held special services of public thanksgiving in the Old Bell Chapel.[33] On the domestic front, too, there were significant changes in the Brontë household during the year. On 21 April, Maria gave birth to her third daughter who, as had now become established practice, was named after another Branwell, Maria's youngest sister, Charlotte. Elizabeth Firth presented the new baby with a little cap which she had hand-worked herself, but this time it was her cousin, Frances Walker, who was asked to be a godmother. Charlotte Brontë was baptized by William Morgan in Thornton on Saturday, 29 June; her godfather was the former incumbent, Frances Walker's fiancé, Thomas Atkinson, and it seems likely that Charlotte Branwell, though absent in Penzance, was her other godmother.[34] A little celebration dinner was held at Kipping House some two weeks later, to which all the Brontë family were invited and the new baby was shown off to the Misses Haigh and Glover and Mrs Outhwaite.[35]

Elizabeth Branwell, Maria's sister, had been living with the family for well over a year and now, having seen Maria safely through her latest confinement, she was anxious to return home to Penzance. On 25 July, the two sisters drank tea together at Kipping House for the last time and the following Sunday, after Patrick had preached on the text, 'Jesus Christ is the same yesterday and today and for ever', the two Elizabeths bade each other farewell. For once, Elizabeth Firth's diary was, for her, positively effusive: 'I took leave of Miss Branwell. She kissed me and was much affected. She left Thornton that evening.'[36]

Maria must have felt the loss of her sister particularly badly though Elizabeth Firth kindly called the next day, and two days later, and then invited the family to tea with the Misses Marshall and Ibbotson and John Outhwaite, the Bradford surgeon.[37] Her assistance in running the household was especially missed now that Maria had three children, all under the age of three. The solution was to get either a housekeeper or a nursemaid – and preferably someone who could fill both roles. Perhaps on the advice of his church friends in Bradford, Patrick applied to the Bradford School of Industry for a girl to take the position of nursemaid at the parsonage. The School of Industry was a charity school, set up in rooms in Kirkgate in 1806, to 'train … girls of poor parents in habits of industry'. Some sixty girls, attending either in the morning or the afternoon only, were taught to sew, knit and read (in that order); their clothes were provided for them out of the proceeds of their own work and if they attended the parish church regularly, learnt their collects and psalms, and always had their scissors and sheath, thimble and handkerchief to hand, they were rewarded with 1½d. a quarter. The obsessions of the school with cropping hair short, forbidding any sort of personal adornment and meting out (by today's standards) barbaric punishments for relatively minor offences, are strongly reminiscent of Lowood School in *Jane Eyre*.[38]

The girl who was selected for the Brontës was Nancy Garrs, one of the twelve children of Richard Garrs of Westgate in Bradford, who was thirteen years old.[39] The first of remarkably few servants employed by the Brontës, she, like her successors, was devoted to them and remained a loyal friend long after she had left their service. In her capable hands, the young Brontës could be safely entrusted while their parents were occupied in parish affairs.

Domestic upheaval was more than matched by events in the parish. On 17 June 1816, the Reverend John Crosse, vicar of Bradford, died. An immense loss to the parish which he had served for thirty-two years, his death was also a blow to Patrick and his family. Despite his blindness, he had been an exemplary parish priest and he represented all the beliefs that Patrick held most dear. An Evangelical, friend of the Fletchers of Madeley, he had actively promoted missionary activity at home and abroad: he had supported the Sunday school movement and initiated the building of Christ Church in Bradford; he had been involved in the formation of Bradford Auxiliaries of the Bible Society and the Society for Promoting Christianity among the Jews.[40] In each and every one of his causes he was backed to the hilt by the men he had taken care to appoint to the ministry in the Bradford area – men who, like himself, had come from the charmed circles of Cambridge and Madeley – men who included his curate, John Fennell, and his ministers, William Morgan and Patrick Brontë. Indeed, only two weeks before his death, Patrick had preached an excellent sermon on the appropriate text 'for the earth shall be full of the knowledge of the Lord as the waters cover the sea' at the parish church to the Bradford Female Auxiliary Society for Promoting Christianity among the Jews.[41] Perhaps Patrick, like Morgan and Fennell, visited John Crosse on his deathbed and was encouraged and inspired by the serenity with which he went to meet his Maker.

after having lived *an useful life*, he died, as might be expected, *a comfortable death*: his sun set with splendour, without the least appearance of a cloud to darken his mind, or to obscure his prospect of heaven. All was tranquil and serene as the summer's evening: and so complete was the conquest that he gained over the fears of death, that he said more than once, to his friends and attendants, 'Dying is no more to me than the passing from one chamber to another. I have no fears of death. I had rather die than live. I long to depart and to be with Christ.'[42]

One of the few churchmen to be genuinely regretted by all classes of society, including the Dissenters with whom he had been on good terms, John Crosse was held up as an example to all by both John Fennell, in the funeral sermon which he preached on 23 June, and by William Morgan who, after a stormy relationship with a later vicar of Bradford, looked back with nostalgia to the days of the blind vicar and wrote a eulogistic biography of him, significantly titled *The Parish Priest.*[43]

It was a matter of some moment who would be appointed to replace John Crosse and it must necessarily have been some disappointment when the Reverend Henry Heap, from Todmorden in the Calder Valley, was appointed. A mild and affable man, his main claims to fame were that he had been noticed as a youth by John Crosse, when the latter was vicar of Todmorden and Cross-stone, and that he had trained for the ministry at his suggestion.[44] Henry Heap could not fill his predecessor's illustrious shoes. His equally long tenure of the vicarage of Bradford was to be marked by a sharp decline in the good relations previously enjoyed between churchmen and Dissenters and, indeed, between the parish and its daughter churches. It was perhaps appropriate that the year should come to a close with the greatest eclipse of the sun for over fifty years: in Yorkshire, five-sixths of the sun was obscured for just over two hours between 8 a.m. and 10.15 a.m. on 19 November. Elizabeth Firth noted in her diary, 'We observed a beautiful eclipse of the sun; the sky was very clear till it arrived at its greatest obscurity; it was thereafter enveloped in clouds[:] a great gloom.'[45]

There was indeed a great gloom over Thornton and the rest of the country throughout the winter of 1816 to 1817. The ending of the war had not brought economic revival, and the combination of a downturn in trade and a hard winter brought great distress amongst the poor. The pages of the *Leeds Mercury* for these months make grim reading: had it not been for the provision of soup kitchens and public subscriptions, all raised through the work of volunteers, there is no doubt that the mortality rates would have risen even higher than they did. Patrick, too, must have been active in trying to alleviate local distress; in his first year at Thornton he had initiated an annual collection for the poor in Ireland, so it is hardly likely that he would ignore the suffering on his own doorstep.[46]

As it was, the distress brought a repeat of the problems of 1812. The number of mechanized mills had increased rapidly since then and skilled workers like the croppers, to take only one example out of many, found that out of a total of 3,378 men employed in the trade in 1817, a third were unemployed and a further third were only partly employed.[47] It was no surprise when the Luddites began to meet again and there were fears of a general insurrection. These proved to be mainly alarmist, though one particular incident must have been a shock to Patrick: in June, ten Dewsbury men were arrested for plotting rebellion, including the former keeper of the Yew Tree Inn at Roberttown and a card maker from Hightown, both of whom must have been known personally to Patrick. It turned out that the 'plot' was simply the wild talk of desperate men and that the main 'plotter' was actually a government *agent provocateur*.⁴⁸ Nevertheless, it was a time of deep concern for Patrick and he must have had to redouble his efforts to ensure that those who needed charity received it.

At the parsonage, the even tenor of life was undisturbed by the turmoil in the country. Maria was pregnant again, though this did not restrict her social activities as it might have done in the more prudish Victorian age. She continued to take tea with Elizabeth Firth each week and doubtless met the other ladies of the township on a regular basis too. In March, a new visitor came to stay with the Brontës. Miss Thomas, as Elizabeth Firth noted, came to stay on 18 March and remained for at least two months.⁴⁹ Her relationship to the household is not known. She cannot have been a servant or nurse to assist in Maria's latest confinement, as this did not occur till the end of June, by which time she appears to have left; nor would Miss Firth of Kipping House have admitted Miss Thomas to her tea drinkings, visits and rambles around Thornton unless, like Elizabeth Branwell, she was a lady of some social standing. It is unlikely that she was a governess, as the Brontës' eldest child, Maria, was only just three years old and not yet ready for schooling. The only alternatives left are that she was either a relative, most likely from Penzance, or a friend from either Penzance or the Harts-head area.

On 11 May, Patrick persuaded Miss Thomas, Elizabeth Firth and her guest, Miss Fanny Greame, who was a relative of her stepmother, to begin attending the Sunday school as teachers.⁵⁰ Patrick was particularly anxious to nurture his Sunday school, which was still in its infancy. Despite his best efforts, it attracted only a hundred pupils, whereas the four Dissenting Sunday schools in his chapelry taught 770 children between them. The strength of the Dissenting interest meant that Patrick was hamstrung in his efforts to finance the school and had to rely on the voluntary contributions of his congregation. Nevertheless, he battled on, introducing the new method of instruction recommended by the National Society and per-suading his better-educated parishioners to act as teachers.⁵¹

On 12 May, he and Mr Firth travelled together to Wakefield, some twenty miles away, to vote in the election for a registrar for the West Riding. The election took place in the courthouse at Wakefield and was, at this period of limited suffrage, only open to gentlemen possessing freehold property worth at least one hundred pounds a year and clergymen with salaries worth a similar amount. Both Patrick and Mr Firth voted for the Tory, Mr Scott, who had to withdraw from the election the following Friday when it became clear from the poll that he could not win.⁵²

In the early hours of the morning of 26 June 1817, the latest Brontë arrived on the scene. For Maria, and more especially for Patrick, this was a particularly welcome moment, for this child was the long-awaited and much-wished-for son. In honour of the occasion the boy was given two names, Patrick, after his father, and Branwell, after his mother's maiden name, though at first there appears to have been some confusion over which name came first. The day after his birth, his three sisters, Maria, Elizabeth and Charlotte, were invited down to Kipping House to join a large party of ladies who, no doubt, made much of the little girls.[53] It did not take long to sort out their brother's name and, for the first time in the Brontë family, there was no delay in baptizing the child: on Wednesday, 23 July, John Fennell performed the ceremony at the Old Bell Chapel and Patrick Branwell Brontë acquired his God-given name. His godparents were Elizabeth Firth's father and stepmother.[54]

Branwell's safe arrival into the world must have been an even greater cause for thankfulness when, on 6 November, the much-loved Princess Charlotte of Wales, only daughter of the Prince Regent, died giving birth to a stillborn son. Her death was seen as a national tragedy and there seems to have been a genuine sense of personal loss throughout the country, reflected in the newspaper coverage of her death and funeral. It was announced that everyone was expected to go into general mourning, which would include the formal adoption of mourning dress, and Patrick, in common with other ministers of the Established Church, had to deck his pulpit in black cloth. On 19 November, when she was buried, all the shops and places of business had to close for the day and the churches opened in their stead, holding special services and tolling muffled bells to mark her passing.[55]

The day Princess Charlotte died, Patrick had escorted Elizabeth Firth to Bradford to attend a missionary meeting tea at the house of Mr Lambert, a prominent Bradford churchman; the following day, they were privileged to hear Legh Richmond, the popular Evangelical, preach at the Church Missionary meeting.[56] On 12 November, five days after the meeting, there was a more informal gathering of Evangelicals at Kipping House: Patrick and his fellow founder of the Bradford Bible Society, Samuel Redhead, were invited to dinner with the Firths; there they met the Firths' visitors, the Reverend James Franks and his wife, of Sowerby Bridge, whose son, James Clarke Franks, then enjoying a prestigious career at Patrick's old college at Cambridge, was later to marry Elizabeth Firth.[57] The year ended with the news from Hartshead that Thomas Atkinson had married Frances Walker on 23 December and that the pair had set up home in Mirfield at Green House, an elegant small mansion more suited to their affluence than Patrick's old homes at Lousy Thorn and Clough House.[58]

The new year, 1818, was marked throughout the Bradford district with the spectacular Bishop Blaize festivities. These were held once every seven years to celebrate the patron saint of woolcombers and included special services in the places of religious worship, colourful processions through the streets of the towns with the participants marching under the banners of their particular part of the woollen trade and dinners in the inns and public houses.[59]

For Patrick, this mood of celebration was to continue throughout the year. The April issue of *Blackwood's Magazine*, a national journal, carried the following advertisement in its monthly list of new publications: '*The Maid of Killarney, or Albion and Flora; a modern tale; in which are interwoven some cursory remarks on religion and politics*, 12mo. 3s.6d.'[60] Though no author was mentioned in the advertisement – nor, indeed, in the book itself – this was Patrick's most ambitious literary project to date. A novella, substantially longer than anything he had previously published, it boasted the imprint of Baldwin, Cradock & Joy, one of the small publishing houses based in Paternoster Row, London.[61] Curiously, given Patrick's preoccupations of the previous sixteen years, it is the most Irish of all his works. It is set in contemporary Ireland which is seen through the eyes of the appropriately named English hero, Albion. The beauties of the Irish lakes and mountains are evocatively painted in a detail which must reflect personal knowledge though Killarney, on the most southwestern tip of Ireland, could hardly be further away from Patrick's home in County Down. Similarly, the pitiable poverty of the Irish peasant is described at length and with the accuracy of personal observation.

On the title page, Patrick quoted several lines from his favourite classical poet, Horace, suggesting that he wished to instruct while amusing his readers. In his Preface he quoted, once again, his favourite apostle, St Paul, to explain how as an author, 'though following at an immense distance, he has endeavoured to walk in the footsteps of him of Tarsus, who became all things to all men, that he might by all means save some'.[62] He continued with a candid explanation of his choice of anonymity:

Perhaps he is not altogether insensible to praise or blame; and this might have been one reason why he preferred being anonymous, that at a safer distance, and through a wary loop-hole, he might so behold the fate of his little work, that whatever it might be, he who intended no harm, might receive none.[63]

Another reason for the anonymity might have been that *The Maid of Killarney* is actually a love story and, though the Evangelical teachings familiar from his earlier works feature prominently, the general impression is that Patrick's characters and the development of his plot interested him just as much as, if not more than, his didactic purpose. The conscientious clergyman was clearly being seduced by the 'real, indescribable pleasure, such as he could wish to taste as long as life lasts'[64] of literary composition for its own sake.

Nevertheless, the book is, as its full title suggests, an excuse for the exposition of Patrick's religious and political views. The hero, in order to make him a fit husband for the pious and lovely Flora but at the prompting of his dying father, undergoes conversion, 'that change, without which no man shall see the kingdom of heaven'.[65] The Society for Promoting Christian

Knowledge is compared, unfavourably, with the British and Foreign Bible Society in a powerful simile; the former is like the River Thames, flowing through and enriching its own London, but the latter is like the Nile, with countless tributaries, winding its irresistible course through different climates and nations until, 'disdaining its prescribed limits', it floods over the delta and brings riches to all. Playing at cards, dancing and the 'meretricious ornament' of the stage are all attacked as murderers of time, though not an evil in themselves.[66]

The most important arguments, however, are reserved for the discussion of Roman Catholic Emancipation. Though Patrick allows the virulent anti-Catholic sentiments of Dr O'Leary to be overthrown by the more moderate arguments of Albion and Captain Loughlean, it is clear that he did not think Catholics should be allowed to vote or sit in Parliament because their loyalty to the king would be continually compromised by their loyalty to the pope. His dislike of the practice of Catholicism is illustrated throughout *The Maid of Killarney*, but particularly at the beginning, where there are savage caricatures of an Irish wake and of the village priest who refuses to allow his parishioners to read the Bible: 'He says such like books are not fit for any but *larned* men like himself; and that all ignorant people who read them turn crack-brained, and full of vagaries, and die *harryticks*.'[67] For an Evangelical, the Catholic reliance on the priesthood rather than on individual effort to read the Bible was totally repugnant. Though Patrick later changed his mind on Roman Catholic Emancipation, he never lost his dislike of Catholicism itself.[68]

In his political arguments, Patrick proved more liberal – surprisingly so for a man who is always branded a rampant Tory. Perhaps the most important of his arguments concerned the system of criminal justice which, in his opinion, required a thorough overhaul. The law should be universally obeyed, but to be obeyed it had to be universally understood. This was simply impractical, given the impenetrable phraseology of the law and the obscurity of legal documentation. Its delays and its great expense put it beyond the reach of the ordinary man.

Consider, moreover, the inadequacy of punishment. A man will be hanged for stealing a fat sheep, though he be hungry; – he will incur no greater punishment for murdering twenty men! In the name of common sense, what is the necessary tendency of this? Most undoubtedly, the man who robs, will find it [in] his interest to murder also, for by so doing, he will be more likely to prevent discovery, and will, at all events, incur no greater punishment. It has always been a sorrowful reflection to me, when I have heard of robbers being hanged on the evidence of the person robbed, that in all probability they came to their melancholy end, through that little remains of conscience, and tenderness of heart, which they still possessed, and which prevented them, even at their own peril, from imbruing their hands in their fellow creatures' blood.[69]

Patrick was to return several times to this theme and despite feeling, on occasion, that he was a lone voice crying in the wilderness, he campaigned vigorously to get the criminal law reformed and its savagery moderated.[70]

The Maid of Killarney is Patrick's most important literary work, not only because it contains his views on so many subjects dear to his heart, but also because it was to have a tremendous influence on his children. They imitated his style, particularly his inclusion of poems as songs in the text, and borrowed his characters, especially the lovely Flora who, together with her harp, provides the model for many of the heroines of the juvenilia.[71] Many passages from *The Maid of Killarney*, on subjects as diverse as describing the beauties of the landscape or singing the praises of the Duke of Wellington, could just as easily have been written by one of the Brontë children.

In 1818 when the book was first published, however, Patrick's children were too young to appreciate its value to them. One of the first sales was to Elizabeth Firth, who purchased the book in May though apparently she did not read it till the following October. She was more preoccupied with reading the *Remains of Henry Kirke White*, which she seems to have taken up on the recommendation of Patrick, after he had walked with her and Fanny Outhwaite to Ogden Kirk, midway between Denholme and Halifax.[72]

On 30 July, Maria Brontë gave birth to yet another daughter, the fifth of her six children. Perhaps because the baby was sickly (though there is no indication of this in any of the sources), she was christened within three weeks of her birth, the shortest lapse of time for any of the Brontë children. William Morgan performed the baptism at the Old Bell Chapel on Thursday, 20 August; his wife, Jane, and her parents, the Fennells, are said to have been the baby's godparents and one of them presented the baby with a delicate white china christening mug with her name spelt out in gilt lettering around it, 'Emily Jane Bronte'.[73] It is appropriate that the most singular of the Brontë children should have been given a name unique in the family; there were neither Branwells nor Brontës named Emily, though her second name – and again she was unique in being the only one of Patrick and Maria's daughters to merit two forenames – was inspired by her godmother, Maria's cousin.

Patrick was invited to dinner at Kipping House on the eve of the christening and Jane Branwell Morgan, who had clearly come to stay for the ceremony, called in to renew her old friendship with Elizabeth Firth.[74] Perhaps the two ladies urged Patrick to get extra help for Maria who, with five infants all under five years of age, could no longer manage with only the help of one nursery maid. Nancy Garrs was therefore promoted to the position of cook and assistant housekeeper, and her younger sister, Sarah, who had also been trained at the Bradford School of Industry, came to take her place as nursemaid.[75]

The remainder of the year was a busy time for Patrick. There were the usual annual meetings in Bradford of the British and Foreign Bible Society and the Society for promoting Christianity Among the Jews in October and

Legh Richmond returned to preach at the beginning of November.[76] More time-consuming and of more importance locally was the complete reno-vation of the Old Bell Chapel, which Patrick began in the late autumn of 1818. The gallery at the east end of the chapel had become unsafe and had to be closed. For many years it had housed the singers and instrumentalists who provided the church music because there was no organ; the churchwardens' account books show that there were two treble violins, one tenor violin and a violoncello belonging to the chapel, plus some half-dozen manuscript music books, ranging from Holroyd's *Psalmody* to Purcell's *Te Deum*. The musicians were, naturally enough, somewhat disgruntled at being brought down from the sanctuary of their gallery to sit in a pew under the parson's eye. Perhaps it was in an attempt to placate them that new music books were purchased for the singers and the old ones, under the supervision of Elizabeth Firth, were repaired.[77]

Most of the expenditure went on work on the fabric of the building, repairing and making good the neglect of many years. On 10 November Elizabeth Firth made a special visit to the chapel to see 'the angel', pre-sumably a new or at least newly restored statue or painting.[78] On completion of the work a new board was installed at the entrance to the chapel which declared to all: 'This Chapel was repaired and beautified, A.D. 1818. The Rev. P. Bronte, B. A., Minister. Joseph Robertshaw, Joseph Foster, John Hill, John Lockwood and Tim Riley, churchwardens.' Under the names was painted a royal coat of arms, surmounted by the letters 'G.R.', and at the very bottom, in small lettering, 'Painted by Thomas Rembrandt Driver'.[79] Perhaps the death of Queen Charlotte, wife of George III, on 17 November, after a long illness, inspired this gesture of loyalty, particularly as the chapel was closed on the day of her funeral when Patrick should have preached a funeral sermon on her behalf.[80]

The new year, 1819, began quietly enough with an invitation to tea on 8 January at Kipping House for the three oldest Brontë children, Maria, Elizabeth and Charlotte.[81] In March there was an important occasion for the chapelry: a large party of about sixty young people was taken to Bradford to be confirmed in the parish church. As they reached Bradford – a distance of some four miles – the weather turned against them. Patrick was concerned, particularly as the young people still had to walk back to Thornton after the ceremony. He therefore went into the Talbot Hotel, just off the top of Darley Street, and ordered hot dinners to be prepared and waiting for the whole party as they came out of church. Thus fortified, and having sheltered from the worst of the storm, the young people returned safely to Thornton. This unexpected act of kindness was long remembered in the parish.[82]

Not long afterwards there was a parting of the ways for the Brontës and their family. John Fennell who, since leaving Woodhouse Grove School, had lived and worked in Bradford as a curate to John Crosse and then to his son-in-law at Christ Church, was appointed by the vicar of Halifax to the parish of Cross-stone, which lay between Hebden Bridge and Todmorden.[83] Though only some ten or eleven miles away from Thornton as the crow flies, it was actually much further because many miles of untracked moorland lay between; its inaccessibility was increased during the winter months as it stood high up in the Pennines and was almost invariably cut off by snow.

By an extraordinary coincidence, Patrick was almost immediately offered a new post which would take him into the same area. On 25 May, the Reverend James Charnock, perpetual curate of Haworth since 1791, died after a long illness.[84] Henry Heap, the vicar of Bradford, no doubt foreseeing the contest that was to come, acted with almost unseemly haste. Knowing that Patrick was an Evangelical, which would appeal to the inhabitants of Haworth, that he had had experience of similar chapelries at Thornton and Hartshead and that he was struggling to make ends meet in his present, less valuable post, Henry Heap offered him the incumbency. Patrick was taken by surprise but accepted the nomination as 'a gift and a call of Providence'.[85]

Unaware of the poisoned chalice he had been handed, Patrick set about securing the necessary papers. On 1 June, Michael Stocks, a friend who was a well-known and respected magistrate in the Halifax area, wrote to Mr Greenwood, one of the church trustees at Haworth, recommending Patrick as a successor to James Charnock. Though only a short letter, it contained an ominous phrase which foreshadowed the troubles to come: 'I trust that you will feel no objection to him on account of his possessing the confidence of the vicar of Bradford.'[86]

Unfortunately for Patrick, the trustees did object and on precisely this ground. What Patrick does not appear to have known, or perhaps failed to appreciate, was that the church trustees at Haworth did not simply exercise the usual powers of recommendation or approval but claimed an absolute right to appoint their own minister. The church at Haworth was a medieval foundation and, like Thornton, was originally a chapel-of-ease built to provide services for the remoter districts and manned by a perpetual curate who remained subject to Bradford. The vicars of Bradford had always had the right to nominate and appoint to the living of Haworth but, since at least 1559, this had effectively been in the hands of the church trustees. When Elizabeth I re-established the Protestant Church in England, after Queen Mary's attempt to restore Catholicism, the inhabitants of Haworth had raised the sum of thirty-six pounds which they then handed over to a trust. In an indenture, made on 18 December 1559, the trustees were empowered to purchase land at Stanbury and use the income from it to pay the salary of the 'lawfully licensed and admitted minister' of Haworth. The trustees were under an obligation to hand over the rents, dues and profits unless – and this was the crucial phrase – the trustees, their heirs or successors or a major part of them 'shall at any time hereafter be debarred in their choice or in the nomination of a minister'. An incumbent minister who was negligent in his duties, of infamous character or litigious could similarly be deprived of the income from the church lands, in which case the money had to be distributed among the poor of the parish.[87] While the vicar of Bradford claimed the right to nominate and appoint a minister at Haworth, the church trustees could make or break that appointment by declining to pay his salary.

The trust deed had been invoked before. In 1741, the then vicar of Bradford had declined to nominate the most famous of all Haworth's previous clergymen, William Grimshaw, but the trustees were determined to have him and succeeded in securing his appointment by refusing to pay the salary to anyone else. Even John Crosse, that mildest of men, had crossed swords with the trustees over his nomination of James Charnock in 1791 though, typically, he avoided a public conflict by obtaining their full consent before the appointment went forward.[88] It was therefore inevitable that there would be a dispute over Charnock's successor, which is why Henry Heap acted so quickly in nominating his replacement.

Perhaps hoping to complete his coup and ensure victory for Bradford before the trustees had had time to meet and rally opposition, Henry Heap made the mistake of going over to Haworth himself. On Whit Sunday, one of the most important festivals in the church calendar, which happened to fall between the death of James Charnock and Patrick's nomination, the vicar arrived at Haworth Church to take the day's services. The trustees actually shut the church doors in his face '& told him they would have nothing to do with any Person he might nominate, without their Consent previously obtained – They claim the ancient Privilege of chusing their own Minister –'.[89]

Henry Heap's response was equally belligerent: on 2 June, still only nine days after James Charnock's death, he wrote to the Archbishop of York requesting a licence for Patrick to the perpetual curacy of Haworth which 'doth of Right belong to my Nomination'.[90] The very wording of the nomination was calculated to antagonize the Haworth trustees whose rights, real or assumed, he had completely ignored in the hope of forestalling a reaction. He should have known better. On 14 June the *Leeds Intelligencer* carried this report:

We hear that the Rev. P. Bronte, curate of Thornton, has been nominated by the vicar of Bradford, to the valuable perpetual curacy of Haworth, vacant by the death of the Rev. James Charnock; but that the inhabitants of the chapelry intend to resist the *presentation*, and have entered a caveat at York accordingly.[91]

At this stage, Patrick decided to invoke the aid of the one Haworth church trustee with whom he had personal contact: Stephen Taylor, a gentleman farmer living at the Manor House in Stanbury, who was the father of Mercy Kaye of Allerton Hall.[92] Patrick had probably met him on the numerous occasions when he called at Allerton Hall, the Kayes being his friends as well as among the more prominent of his parishioners at Thornton.

Patrick paid a visit to Haworth and learnt from Stephen Taylor and some of the other trustees what the facts of the case were and what was the basis of their opposition to him. They had nothing against him personally, but would resist his appointment to the bitter end if it was forced upon them by the vicar of Bradford. Caught in the middle, Patrick evidently felt that it was beneath his dignity to get involved in such a sordid squabble for power, and decided to resign. Perhaps this was seen as an act of betrayal by the vicar who had looked for a sterner stance from his colleague; Patrick was told in no uncertain terms that he could not withdraw 'with honour, and with propriety' and was threatened with incurring the archbishop's displeasure. The latter offered to allow him to hold both Thornton and Haworth until the matter was satisfactorily settled, so Patrick had no choice but 'with the help of God, to go on till I see the conclusion'.[93] He wrote on 8 July to explain his decision to Stephen Taylor and seek his support:

I have resided for many years in the neighbourhood, where I am well known – I am a good deal conversant with the affairs of mankind – and I do humbly trust that it is my unvarying practice to preach Christ faithfully, as the only Way, the Truth, and the Life. From considerations such as these, I do think that Providence has called me to labour in His vineyard at Haworth, where so many great and good men have gone before me. I therefore request your kindness, and your prayers, and that when I come to preach amongst you, you will use your endeavours to prevent people from leaving the Church, and will exhort them to hear with candour and attention, in order that God's name may be glorified, and sinners saved...[94]

It is possible that Patrick went to Haworth on 12 July, the Sunday following this letter, in order to take the services and that, despite his request to Stephen Taylor, the congregation walked out or drowned his sermon with shouting and cat-calls; exactly the same thing was to happen to Samuel Redhead soon afterwards. This seems the likeliest explanation for Patrick's sudden change of heart, for on 14 July, two days later, he wrote again to Stephen Taylor and told him that he had written to both the vicar of Bradford and the Archbishop of York to resign Haworth.[95]

The trustees had won the first round and got their own way once more. They were now prepared to be gracious and sent to Patrick saying that they might be prepared to consider nominating him themselves if he would come over to Haworth and give them a sample of his preaching. The cool impudence of the suggestion, particularly if Patrick had indeed been driven from the pulpit at Haworth the week before, deserved the repudiation it got. Patrick's response, however angry he must have felt, was a masterpiece of tact and contained only the most veiled of reprimands: 'through divine grace my aim has been, and I trust, always will be, to preach Christ and not myself, and I have been more desirous of being made the instrument of benefit rather than pleasure to my own congregation'. If they wanted to hear him preach, let them come to him and hear him preach at a time when he did not expect them: 'It is an easy matter to compose a fine sermon or two for a particular occasion but no easy thing always to give satisfaction.' They might then take the opportunity to learn about him from his parishioners in Thornton, for, 'believe me, the character and conduct of man out of the pulpit is as much to be considered as his character and conduct in, and we are most likely to know those best who live nearest us –'.[96]

Whether or not the trustees made the effort to come and hear him preach, matters remained at an impasse for several months. Other clergymen took the duties at Haworth so that Patrick was not drawn into the fray again. He did take care to let the trustees know that, if they so wished, they could hear him preaching on behalf of the Church Missionary Society at both the morning and afternoon services at Keighley on 1 August.[97]

The ugly mood at Haworth was more than matched by what was going on in the country as a whole. The summer of 1819 had added bad harvests to industrial depression, leading to political discontent which had manifested itself in increasingly violent agitation for reform. The culmination of weeks of popular unrest was the great Manchester meeting on 16 August, when over 50,000 people gathered to hear the Radical, Henry Hunt; the magistrates, terrified of violence, ordered Hunt's arrest and then turned the attendant soldiers on the crowd. The result was the 'Manchester Massacre' or the 'Battle of Peterloo' in which one man was killed and forty were wounded. Instead of condemning the outrage, the government sent messages of support to the magistrates and reacted with extraordinary severity, clamping down on all forms of meetings and empowering magistrates to seize arms and prevent the publication of seditious pamphlets. Radicalism was temporarily and brutally suppressed; criticism was silenced by repression.

The events of the previous months were serious enough to merit comment at the eighth annual meeting of the Bible Society, held in the Friends' Meeting House in Bradford on 15 October; there were 'very animated' speeches from a number of clergymen, including Patrick, William Morgan, Samuel Redhead and Robinson Pool, the Dissenting minister of Thornton.

All these speakers alluded, more or less, to the crisis of the times, as loudly calling upon every Christian to join in disseminating the Word of God, as the only sure guide in life, the sole support of the soul in death, and as alone capable of raising us, through a Saviour's merits to everlasting happiness.[98]

Though Patrick had wished to keep out of the quarrel at Haworth, too much was at stake for him to be allowed to do so. The stalemate had to be broken somehow and on 8 October the Archbishop of York wrote to him, ordering him to take the duty at Haworth the following Sunday. Patrick reluctantly preached there on 10 October, having forewarned the trustees that he was acting 'very contrary to my inclination' but pointing out that he could not disobey his archbishop.⁹⁹ Things cannot have gone too well, for eleven days later his formal resignation was finally accepted, and Patrick was at last free to resume his ministry at Thornton.¹⁰⁰

The burden of Haworth was passed to his old friend, Samuel Redhead, who was to fare no better. The vicar of Bradford, backed by the archbishop, seemed determined not to give in and Redhead's appointment, like Patrick's, was made without reference to the trustees. On 30 October, the *Leeds Mercury* carried the bald statement that he had been licensed to the perpetual curacy of Haworth 'upon the nomination of the Rev. Henry Heap, vicar of Bradford'.¹⁰¹

Mrs Gaskell gives the now famous account of the torments endured by Samuel Redhead at the hands of the congregation of Haworth: how the entire congregation walked out of his first service, how a man was driven, face to tail, on the back of an ass down the aisles in his second and how, at the third and last service, a drunken chimney sweep was prompted to climb into the pulpit, embrace the unfortunate preacher, chase him into the churchyard and then empty a bag of soot over him.¹⁰² This picturesque story has entered Brontë mythology but her information, supplied by Dr Scoresby, a later vicar of Bradford, and the landlord of the Black Bull, who claimed a leading role in helping Redhead to escape the wrath of the crowd, is almost completely untrue. After *The Life of Charlotte Brontë* appeared in print, Samuel Redhead's son-in-law wrote to the *Leeds Intelligencer* and, in defence of his father-in-law and the people of Haworth, quoted the relevant extracts from Redhead's diary.¹⁰³ He also confirmed the details himself, saying that he had heard Redhead's own account of the events when he had visited Haworth with him in 1844.

According to his diary, Samuel Redhead arrived in Haworth on 31 October to take his first duty, accompanied by Mr Rand, a prominent Bradford lay churchman. He was admitted to the church on producing his licence but the churchwardens refused to allow the bells to be rung for the service so that it began with a very small congregation which gradually increased to some 500. All went well till Mr Redhead entered the pulpit, at which point 'on a signal given by the churchwardens, trustees &c.' the whole congregation got to its feet and stomped out of church, shouting 'Come out, come out'. No attempt was made to restrain the disorder and on leaving the church 'Mr Rand and I were pursued and hooted and insulted by considerable numbers out of the village.'

The following Sunday, 7 November, Redhead tried again, this time taking Mr Crossley, a Bradford churchwarden, with him as witness and moral support. The large congregation was evidently restless, waiting for a signal from their own churchwardens who, on the minister entering the pulpit, immediately left their pew. Utmost confusion followed with people coming in and out of the church without any regard for the service.

The afternoon service commenced in the midst of uproar and confusion, all decency seemed thrown aside, and laughing, talking, and noise frequently interrupted the prayers ... great numbers leaping over the tops of the pews, throwing to the pew doors with great violence, stamping with their feet, shouting and rushing out in the most outrageous and tumultuous manner. The whole scene was perfectly indescribable, and to the end of the prayers nothing but tumult prevailed.

Redhead retired to the comparative safety of the vestry, where he put himself under the protection of the churchwardens and demanded that if they could not control the tumult then they should call the respectable inhabitants of the town to assist them. The churchwardens refused, insisting that the respectable inhabitants would refuse to act, so strong was the feeling against the vicar of Bradford. Redhead insisted that the churchwardens should remain with him until he had interred a corpse, the funeral passing off in relative quiet; as he left, however, he was pursued out of the town with 'hootings and pushing and shouting and insult'.

Matters were now so serious that the next day Redhead, accompanied by Mr Fawcett from Bradford, set out for a personal interview with the Archbishop at York and obtained from him a threat that, if the tumults did not cease, the church would be shut up and the whole affair laid before the Lord Chancellor.

Samuel Redhead was a persistent man. On Sunday, 14 November, he returned to Haworth with Mr Crossley, hoping that the archbishop's remonstrance would have ensured him a quieter reception. He was sadly mistaken.

When we entered the village we were saluted with shoutings and insults, and pursued with the most indecent insolence. The same irreverent conduct was displayed all the way to the church, and we had no prospect but of the greatest disorder. Indecency and impiety marked their conduct during the prayers, and when I entered the pulpit all was uproar and confusion. I felt obliged to close the service without preaching. I gave directions to the churchwardens to shut up the church till they received instructions from the Archbishop, as I should lay the whole matter before him on the following day. I further told them that I should expect their protection through the town, with which they complied, and we went as we came, pursued more like wild beasts than human beings. Their shoutings continued, and we heard them for more than a mile and a half. The day after, Monday, 15, I wrote to the Archbishop and obtained his consent to my resignation.

This was a scandal that would not go away. The *Leeds Intelligencer* took Haworth to task:

We regret to learn from a correspondent, that scenes, scarcely possible in an heathen village, have been witnessed on three successive Sundays, in the church of Haworth, merely in consequence of the minister officiating under the appointment of the Vicar of Bradford, and the licence of the Archbishop of York. The churchwardens are certainly liable to a prosecution for the wilful neglect of their duty and deserve to feel, that the house of God, and the hallowed ground of a church-yard, are not proper places in which to allow, by disturbance and howlings, the loudest and lowest marks of irreverence and insult.[104]

Patrick must have felt some relief that he had not pursued his own appointment with as much vigour as his unfortunate friend. As one of the ministers living nearest to Haworth, however, he could not escape all contact. On 17 November, the Wednesday following Samuel Redhead's last attempt to take duty there, Patrick had to go to Haworth to perform two funerals and a baptism; eleven days later he had to go again, this time to perform a marriage.[105] No doubt he went with some reluctance and one can only guess what sort of reception he received. Perhaps the trustees took the opportunity to talk to him again, but to no effect, for he did not perform any more duties until he finally agreed to become minister of Haworth. He returned to Thornton to take up the threads of his old life, though the increased frequency of his visits to Kipping House[106] suggests that he was unsettled and still considering his position with regard to the continuing vacancy at Haworth. Through the Firths, he could maintain a suitably distant line of communication between himself and the Haworth trustees.

On 17 January 1820, the last of the Brontë children was born while her brother and sisters spent the day safely out of the way at Kipping House. The fifth of five daughters, the new baby was named Anne, after her maternal grandmother, and Elizabeth Firth called round the next day to see mother and baby.[107]

Anne's birth seems to have precipitated a small crisis. The little house in Market Street must have been bursting at the seams with six children, their parents and two young servants all living under one roof. The promise of a larger house and greater income at Haworth had appeared as the answer to prayer, only to be taken away, and Patrick was left feeling decidedly hard done by. If he could not improve his family's standard of living by relocating, then something would have to be done to supplement his income at Thornton. Ten days after Anne's birth, he wrote miserably to the governors of Queen Anne's Bounty, a charity which augmented the salaries of underpaid clergymen.

Thornton has generally been returned for one hundred and forty pounds a year; but in this have been included, the dues, which average about five pounds, and a voluntary contribution, frequently made under exceedingly unpleasant circumstances – amounting for the most part to seven or eight pounds. Nothing arises from Pews, or from any other service. The Inhabitants, too, are so poor, in general, that presents, which in some situations are very considerable, are here, not worth mentioning. So that all things truly weighed, and the proper deductions being made, the regular and certain salary of the Living, is not more than one hundred and twenty seven pounds yearly.

Patrick pointed out the size of his chapelry and that it 'swarms with disaffected people, who omit no opportunity that offers, to bring our excellent Establishment into contempt'. Though he had often felt inclined to give up the yearly voluntary contribution towards his salary, the respect due to his position had induced him to continue with it.

If I were a single man, I might find what I have sufficient, but as I have a wife, and six small children, with two maidservants, as well as myself to support, without I can obtain something more, in a just and honourable way, I greatly fear, that with the most rigorous economy, I shall be unable, any longer to uphold in appearance the due degree of Clerical respectability.[108]

A week later, he sent a copy of the letter to the Archbishop of York with a request that he would use his influence on Patrick's behalf to secure a grant.[109] Perhaps it was the receipt of this letter which stung the conscience of the archbishop and prompted him to a final resolution of the problem of Haworth. He had, too, just received a letter from Henry Heap suggesting that he, as vicar of Bradford, should hold Haworth himself, together with Bradford, in an attempt to bypass the problem of the appointment. The archbishop replied, pointing out the insuperable difficulties of this solution and suggesting that there should be a meeting between the vicar and trustees to settle the business.[110] A meeting was arranged.

After <u>many Altercations</u> they have at last agreed to take Mr Brontè on my permitting them <u>to join with me</u> in a Nomination similar to what was done by Mr Kennett late Vicar of Bradford, when Mr Grimshaw was appointed to Haworth – I had offered to do this some time ago, but the Trustees <u>positively refused</u> then to have Mr Brontè –[111]

Just four days after Patrick had written to the archbishop, not suspecting the sudden change in his fortunes, he was offered the perpetual curacy of Haworth once more, this time with the assurance that his appointment would have the blessing of all the parties concerned. On 8 February, a new nomination was drawn up and witnessed by Richard Lambert, a Bradford attorney, and William Tetley, the parish clerk: Henry Heap, the vicar of Bradford, jointly with William Greenwood, John Beaver, James Greenwood, Stephen Taylor and Robert Heaton, the trustees of the church lands at Haworth, nominated Patrick to the cure of Haworth and requested the archbishop's licence on his behalf. A codicil provided the necessary element of face-saving, establishing that the manner of this appointment did not set a precedent for future ones and did not prejudice the claims of either party.[112]

A rather more Christian spirit of reconciliation prevailed in Patrick's letters testimonial, which were also drawn up on 8 February: Samuel Redhead, despite his own claim to Haworth, added his signature to those of Henry Heap and William Morgan.[113]

Though the vicar had been forced to back down in his claim, he ensured that Patrick, if not the trustees, was in no doubt of his subjection to Bradford: as at Thornton, he was required to pay half the dues he received for marriages, funerals, baptisms and churchings (the ritual purification of women after childbirth) to the vicar and, if required to do so by the vicar, had to preach a sermon in the parish church every Trinity Sunday 'as a mark of Reverence to the Mother Church'.[114]

The day after the formalities had been completed, both Patrick and Henry Heap wrote to the archbishop. Patrick's letter was simply a prudent request that the archbishop would include the names of both vicar and trustees in his licence: 'for if the Vicar's name only, were to be inserted; on my reading myself in, it would in all probability give rise to very serious tumults in the Church, and might ultimately lead to the necessity of my resignation'.[115]

Henry Heap's letter was a report on the satisfactory resolution of a quarrel which had left the ministry of Haworth vacant for over eight months. Perhaps feeling his own share of guilt in the trouble caused to Patrick, he asked that the archbishop would allow Patrick to take his oath for his licence before him, in Bradford, instead of having to trail all the way to York: 'some expense would be saved by this means, which to Mr Brontè with six small Children, is certainly an object'.[116] The licence was finally granted on 25 February and Patrick was, in name at least, perpetual curate of Haworth once more.[117] Whether or not the inhabitants would be prepared to accept him this time remained to be seen.

No doubt it was the uncertainty about Patrick's welcome in Haworth that delayed the Brontës' removal for nearly two months. It would be fruitless to uproot the whole family to a new home if Patrick was to face opposition and ultimately a second resignation. For the moment, therefore, Patrick alone made the journey of some five or six miles over the moorland hills to Haworth to take duty as and when required – a testament to the strength of his constitution as well as his commitment. Patrick took his last baptism in Thornton on Sunday, 13 February 1820, and performed his last burial there on 10 April; thereafter, the duties at Thornton were taken by officiating ministers, including William Bishop, Henry Heap's curate, who was finally to be appointed in Patrick's stead in July.[118]

On 29 January, an era had ended with the death of George III; the only king most of his subjects, including the Brontës, had ever known, he had been on the throne of Great Britain and Ireland since 1760. His successor, proclaimed on 5 February, was George IV who, as Prince Regent, had been a much despised byword for profligacy and immorality. His past did not augur well for his reign, nor did he show any signs, like Prince Hal, of turning over a new leaf on attaining the crown. Ash Wednesday, 16 February, was a day of national mourning, therefore, not just officially for the old king, who was buried on that day, but also unofficially for the new; all the shops and places of business were closed and special services were held in the churches and chapels throughout the land.[119]

The country was also in a period of deep depression, particularly in the late winter of 1820, when huge public subscriptions for the relief of the poor did little more than provide temporary alleviation to tide over the worst of the distress.[120] Violent uprisings were daily expected: indeed, Elizabeth Firth's diary records how on Good Friday, 'We sat up expecting the Radicals.' The fears were real enough, though no doubt exaggerated by Patrick's frightening tales of the Luddites. Elizabeth Firth's son later told how Patrick 'used to come in to Kipping & frighten my mother and her step mother with tales of the outrages past or probable. But when they came there they only asked for bread, & that given, went off peaceably'.[121]

It was hardly an auspicious time to move to Haworth but this had now become a necessity; Patrick was clearly going to be accepted in his new post and some permanent provision had to be made for his old one. On 25 March, the extended family and their friends gathered for the last time in the Old Bell Chapel at Thornton to witness the baptism of Anne Brontë. William Morgan officiated and Elizabeth Firth and her great friend, Fanny Outhwaite, daughter and sister of two leading surgeons in Bradford, who had been present at the first dinner at Kipping House attended by the Brontës, stood as godmothers.[122] On 5 April, Elizabeth Firth said her farewells as she was about to depart on a visit and would miss the Brontës' departure. Finally, some time between 10 and 20 April, the contents of the parsonage on Market Street were packed on to two flat wagons, sent over from Stanbury for the purpose by Stephen Taylor, and the Brontës set out for what was to be their final home.[123]

Chapter Four

~❧~

A STRANGER IN A STRANGE LAND

In her *Life of Charlotte Brontë*, Mrs Gaskell declared, quite correctly,

For a right understanding of the life of my dear friend, Charlotte Brontë, it appears to me more necessary in her case than in most others, that the reader should be made acquainted with the peculiar forms of population and society amidst which her earliest years were passed...[1]

The Brontë novels have held such an honoured place in the corpus of English literature for so long that it is difficult today to conceive the shock and moral outrage that greeted their first publication. *Jane Eyre, Wuthering Heights* and *The Tenant of Wildfell Hall*, in particular, flouted almost every convention. It was not simply the unprecedented passion with which they were written that dismayed the critics: the stories and characters, too, displayed all those qualities which polite Victorians most feared – a disregard for social niceties, an obsession (as it was seen then) with violence, cruelty and vice, and a complete lack of that satisfying morality which doled out rewards to the innocent and good and punished those who had done wrong. To quote a random selection of snippets from contemporary reviews: *Jane*

Eyre combines 'masculine hardness, coarseness, and freedom of expression', Mr Rochester possesses 'the profanity, brutality, and slang of the misanthropic profligate' and the whole book expresses 'a total ignorance of the habits of society, a great coarseness of taste, and a heathenish doctrine of religion'; *Wuthering Heights* is 'coarse and loathsome', showing the 'brutalizing influence of unchecked passion' and 'there is such a general roughness and savageness ... as never should be found in a work of art'; *The Tenant of Wildfell Hall* brings the reader 'into the closest proximity with naked vice, and there are conversations such as we had hoped never to see printed in English'.[2] G. H. Lewes neatly summed up the reaction: 'Books, coarse even for men, coarse in language and coarse in conception, the coarseness apparently of violence and uncultivated men –'.[3]

Charlotte was stung by the venom of the reviews into a defence of her sisters: in her preface to the reissue of their novels, published after both were dead, she portrayed them as quiet, naive and simple spinsters, living a dull, inoffensive life of feminine piety and duty in the isolation of 'a remote district where education had made little progress, and where, consequently, there was no inducement to seek social intercourse beyond our own domestic circle...'[4]

Mrs Gaskell followed Charlotte's cue and sought to explain the 'coarseness' of the Brontës' writings as being the result of their own innocence and the peculiarities of their isolation in the primitive surroundings of the provinces. For Mrs Gaskell the Brontës' Haworth is still the Haworth of the 1700s where life is 'nasty, brutish and short'.[5] Village life is dominated by drunkenness and profligacy, with football matches and horse races on the Sabbath and drunken orgies at wedding and funeral feasts. There is much colourful quotation from the *Life of William Grimshaw*, a minister of Haworth in the middle of the eighteenth century, who was perhaps most famous for giving out a long psalm during his services so that he had time to go round the village public houses and horsewhip the sinners into church. Even the wealthier and more educated classes are no better: a local squire orders an arrangement of mirrors on his deathbed so that, though unable to move, he can still view his favourite cocks fighting in his bedchamber. The weirdness of the wild, rough men of Haworth, with their 'repellent' air of independence, dogged power of will and strange grim sense of humour, is accentuated by the incomprehensible dialect they speak. These eccentric characters, Mrs Gaskell does not fail to point out, are the raw material of *Wuthering Heights* and *The Tenant of Wildfell Hall*.[6]

This view of Haworth was accepted unquestioningly at the time. 'For practical purposes,' the *Christian Remembrancer* declared, '[Charlotte Brontë] lived in a less refined age than our own. Her early experience is drawn from a society a hundred years behindhand in these matters.' This was hardly surprising, given that Mrs Gaskell's main source was, as she herself admitted, the biography of a 'clergyman 100 years ago at Haworth'.[7] Yet the accuracy of her portrayal of Haworth has never been questioned. Her wonderfully evocative picture of a family of genius, growing up in physical and social isolation, excluded from all the normal preoccupations of ordinary life, let alone genteel society, has become the essence of Brontë mythology.

It comes as something of a shock to discover that historic Haworth was a dramatically different place from the one of popular legend. Mrs Gaskell's description may be a fairly accurate picture of Haworth in the seventeenth and eighteenth centuries, but it completely ignores the Industrial Revolution and the major impact it had had on life in the nineteenth-century township. 'Isolated', 'solitary', 'lonely' are the epithets on every page. But in reality, Haworth was a busy, industrial township not some remote rural village of *Brigadoon*-style fantasy. What is more, the period of Patrick Brontë's ministry there, from 1820 to 1861, saw some of the fastest growth and biggest changes that were to take place in Haworth and the surrounding area. The population of the chapelry had already risen by over seventeen per cent in the years 1811 to 1821. By 1821, there were 4,668 inhabitants, a figure that was to increase by over thirty-three per cent in the next twenty years. The population increased by a quarter during Patrick's first decade of residence alone.[8]

Haworth was equidistant from three major towns, lying about a dozen miles away from Bradford to the east, Halifax to the south and Burnley to the west, over the border in Lancashire. The nearest large town, Keighley, was only some three or four miles away down the Worth Valley, but, historically, Haworth's affiliations were much stronger with Bradford, because it fell within that parish, and Halifax, because of the trading links. Though small by comparison with these places, Haworth was important for several reasons. First of all, it lay on one of the main routes between Yorkshire and Lancashire, so there was a substantial volume of traffic passing continually through the township. Most of the business was connected with the wool trade, raw wool going on to Bradford to be treated and then to Halifax or Huddersfield to be made into cloth; there was also a substantial border manufacture, based at Hebden Bridge, of needlecord and moleskin, which were made from a combination of wool and cotton.

Secondly, its position in the hills above Keighley and Bradford gave it an ample supply of water so it was an ideal place to site factories. The mills built along the River Worth were among the first in Yorkshire and, despite its rural reputation, there were already thirteen small textile mills in the chapelry of Haworth when the Brontës arrived.[9] Those inhabitants who were not directly employed in the mills were involved in various trades, most of them connected with wool. As at Thornton and Hartshead, there were a large number of hand-loom weavers working in their own homes but there was also a very substantial cottage industry of wool-combing. This involved the creation of great amounts of heat and steam in confined quarters and was a major contributor to ill health in the town. Haworth was therefore in the unusual position of being able to run its own worsted trade from start to finish. The staplers sorted and graded wool brought in from the outlying farms, wool combers carded and combed it in their cottages, top manufacturers gathered the long fibres into coils of even length ready for the yarn spinners to turn it into thread, which, in turn, was passed on to the worsted manufacturers who turned it into cloth. The noils, or shorter fibres, which were of a lower grade than the tops used in worsted manufacturing, were sold on to woollen mills.[10]

Quarrying the sandstone of the surrounding hills provided further employment. There were also a large number of small farms cultivating oats, the only crop that would grow eight hundred feet up in the acidic peat soil of the Pennines, and keeping livestock, principally sheep and the pigs for which the district was famous. In the village itself there were a respectable number of professional people and tradesmen: Haworth boasted its own resident surgeon, Thomas Andrew, a wine and spirit merchant, William Thomas, and a watchmaker, James Barraclough. In addition there were five butchers, two confectioners, eleven grocers and three cabinetmakers; six public houses served the needs of the travellers passing through as well as providing rooms and dinners for the various meetings of inhabitants of the town.[11]

As at Thornton, Patrick had to minister to the needs of a large and rapidly increasing population spread out over many miles of open countryside. Stanbury, to the west, and Oxenhope to the south, were both less than three miles from Haworth but the church registers show that places as far away as Trawden, eight miles away to the west on the Lancashire side of the border, not to mention Cullingworth to the east and Oakworth to the north, fell within his ambit. The chapelry of Haworth, bordering the parishes of Bradford and Halifax, effectively covered the whole sweep of moorland between Heptonstall, Keighley and his old chapelry of Thornton.

As the Brontës travelled the five miles from Thornton to Haworth in April 1820 they would have observed that the moorland grew wilder, with less land under cultivation, and that the hills grew steeper. Whether they travelled by Denholme and Oxenhope and then along the river valley into Haworth or by Wilsden and Cullingworth over Brow Moor,[12] they would have had the opportunity to pause on the crest of a hill to see the whole of the chapelry spread out before them. To those who love bleak and dramatic scenery there is something almost heart-wrenching in the beauty of the sweep of moorlands round Haworth. The great hills rise, one after another, horizon beyond horizon: as Mrs Gaskell described it to a friend after her first visit to Haworth, 'the sinuous hills seemed to girdle the world like the great Norse serpent, and for my part I don't know if they don't stretch up to the North Pole'.[13] Apart from a few short weeks in September, when the moors are covered with the purple bloom of the heather and the air is heavy with its scent, the predominant colours of the landscape are an infinite variety of subtle shades of brown, green and grey. There are no hedgerows and the few trees which brave the elements on the skyline are stunted and grow aslant, bent under the power of the prevailing wind. The whole landscape is in thrall to the sky, which is rarely cloudless and constantly changing; each season it absorbs a peculiar and different quality of light and the wind sends cloud-shadows dancing or creeping over the hills, according to mood. Whether the sun shines or there is snow or rain, there is always a wind at Haworth; the days in the year when it is still are so exceptional as to cause comment. Even the field walls, which stake man's claim to earn a living from a hostile and acquisitive landscape, are of dry-stone construction so as to offer less resistance to the wind which passes safely through the gaps. The buildings, too, are made of stone to withstand the wind: stone walls, stone-flagged roofs and stone-mullioned windows. Built low and solid, the scattered farmsteads and the cottages, which huddle together as if seeking protection from the onslaught of the elements, seem to be a part of the natural landscape.

Much of the scenery remains as it was in the Brontës' day, but the insatiable greed of the twentieth century is swallowing it up at a frightening pace. The narrow valleys were heavily wooded then but are now rapidly filling with housing estates; the River Worth and its tributaries, once powerful enough to drive the machinery that provided employment for most of the population, are considerably depleted by the building of reservoirs on the tops; what the water authorities have not drowned, the electricity generators have smothered, stalking pylons and wind turbines across the horizons.

Haworth itself has become a monument to the grosser excesses of the tourism industry: the village, surrounded by a sea of carparks, is choked with coaches and cars; the shops, with a few honourable exceptions serving the people who live there, are full of tat, prostituting the Brontë name. It is the power of the legend, not the reality, that continues to lure the visitor to Haworth.

It requires some perseverance to find the remnants of the Brontës' Haworth[14], though the distinctive shape of Main Street is still clearly visible, the houses following the contour of the road which snakes up the hill to the church. Tucked away in the valley bottom are the mills on which the local economy depended: Ebor Mill, owned for many generations by the Merrall family, and the vast complex of Bridgehouse Mills. Just above the latter and set well back from the road in several acres of grounds, now considerably reduced by new building, stands Woodlands, perhaps the most gracious mill owner's house in early nineteenth-century Haworth. It had a chequered history, changing hands according to the fortunes of trade.[15]

From Bridgehouse the road begins to climb steeply and is lined with small cottages which overlooked open fields where Haworth Fair was held in the Brontë era. Just below the junction with the bottom of Main Street was the old toll gate, its site marked by a white milestone in the wall; travellers, carriers and even pedestrians and animal droves were stopped at the toll gates and charged for the right to continue their journey. At the junction itself the large, stone-built Hall Green Baptist Chapel, built in 1825, stands facing Haworth Old Hall, a sixteenth-century manor house, once owned by the lords of the manor of Haworth, which was divided into tenements in the Brontës' day. In front of the Old Hall, just along Sun Street, then known as Stubbing Lane, was the old village green, complete with a ducking well for nagging wives, which has long since disappeared. Sun Street is little changed, its cottages petering out as the road climbs along and up the hill, past the old Haworth Grammar School, to Marsh and Oxenhope.[16]

A section of the houses at the bottom of Main Street was demolished in the 1960s, but once past this point little has changed since the Brontës' day. On each side of the road there is an unbroken stretch of two-storey cottages jostling for position with three-storey houses; most of them date from the eighteenth and early nineteenth centuries. The small frontages are deceptive, particularly on the lower side of Main Street, where the hill falls away so steeply that a house with only two or three storeys fronting the street often has five or six storeys behind. Invariably built of stone, begrimed with the factory smoke and peat fires of many generations, the houses seem to crowd in over the narrow street separating them. The road itself, from Bridgehouse to the top of Main Street, was once paved with setts, rectangular blocks of stone larger and flatter than cobbles but much smaller than flags, though only the Main Street section has escaped tarmac today.[17] The hill rises so steeply that many of the shops and houses are only accessible by a series of steps and raised pavements sometimes two or three feet above the road.

Three-quarters of the way up Main Street is Lodge Street, which is as all the alleys and sidestreets in Haworth used to be: a narrow dirt track, six to eight feet wide, with a pavement of stone flags to keep the pedestrian out of the muck. As late as 1850, there were still no sewers and few covered drains; the surface water, combined with household waste and what a report into the sanitation of Haworth politely called the 'effluvium' of privies and midden-steads, ran along open channels and gutters down the streets.[18] Lodge Street is typical of the many that once honeycombed the hill below Main Street, but which have long since been demolished.

Gone too, as recently as the 1960s, are the higgledly-piggledy cottages, built round cobbled yards and reached by narrow alleyways and ginnels, which once covered the triangle of land at the top of Main Street between Changegate, West Lane and Back Lane (now North Street).[19] This was the most populous part of Haworth in the nineteenth century where the working classes lived, the shopkeepers and professionals preferring the larger houses in Main Street and the outskirts of the town. Most of the cottages were back-to-back and many had stone stairs and railed landings outside, with doors, separately numbered, at this level and in the cellar, indicating that, small though they were, they were shared by several families. The cellar dwellings, of which there were twenty-five in Haworth in 1850, consisted of just two rooms: damp, because they were below street level and poorly ventilated, one room would serve as a wool-combing shop, the other as kitchen, living room and bedroom for six or seven people.[20]

Ill health was exacerbated by the poor quality of the water supply. By 1850 there were eleven pumps, only nine of which were in use, and seven wells (one belonging to the parsonage) of which only two were public. One hundred and fifty inhabitants were dependent on the supply from Head Well which, in summer, ran so slowly that the poor had to start queuing there at two or three o'clock in the morning in order to get their water for the Monday wash; sometimes it ran so green and putrid that even the cattle refused to drink it. The water was tainted by the overflow from the midden-steads, which every house with access to a back yard seems to have possessed. These were walled enclosures into which all the solid household waste was thrown, including offal, ashes and the refuse of the privies. Every now and again, the local farmers would come round and take away the contents to spread on the fields, but sometimes the tips were overflowing, as in the case of the druggist's house where the midden-stead was actually against the back wall of the house and was piled up to the height of the larder window.[21] There was not a single water closet in the whole of Haworth and only sixty-nine privies: some two dozen houses, including the parsonage, had their own, but most households had to share and there were at least two instances where twenty-four households were sharing a single privy. The 1850 Report notes that

Two of the privies used, by a dozen families each, are in the public street, not only within view of the houses, but exposed to the gaze of passers by, whilst a third, as though even such a situation were too private, is perched upon an eminence, commanding the whole length of the main street.[22]

It was no surprise to the inspector to find that the mortality rates in Haworth rivalled those in the worst districts of London: in Haworth, as Patrick was soon to discover, over forty-one per cent of children died before reaching their sixth birthday and the average age at death was twenty-five. His own bereavements were no worse than those suffered by his parishioners.[23]

At the top of Main Street the road widens and divides into West Lane and Changegate. Among the houses and cottages are old warehouses three or four storeys high, with winches and pulleys set in the gables: here the wool, at varying stages of treatment, was stored. This part of Haworth is also notable for a remarkable number of public houses, perhaps to serve pedestrians who have slogged the three-quarters of a mile up the hill from the valley bottom. At the foot of the church steps is the Black Bull, notorious as the supposed haunt of Branwell Brontë, which then boasted its own barn, stables and brew-house; facing it is the White Lion, where the manorial courts of Haworth were held.[24]

There has been a church, or more properly, a chapel-of-ease, in Haworth since medieval times, but the building during Patrick's ministry was substantially one of the eighteenth century. Only fifty-seven feet long and thirty-two feet wide, it was demolished in 1879 and swallowed up in a new church thirty-six feet longer and twenty feet wider; only the tower, with the addition of an extra few feet above the second window to take the clock, remains from the original church.[25] The old church had a double-gabled roof with three arched windows in the gables facing out over the top of Haworth; on each side of the church there were six similar arched windows, all set with eighteenth-century glazing bars rather than leaded lights. With so many large windows, the interior should have been light and airy but, over the years, as the population increased, wooden galleries were built which effectively blocked out much of the light. On the north side, a butcher's shop and house, back kitchen, stable and privy belonging to Joseph Hartley stood so close to the church that they blocked up the windows and created what the parish clerk euphemistically called 'an intolerable nuisance'.[26]

A row of pillars, supporting the roof, ran down the centre of the church and every available space was filled with shoulder-high box pews, each one painted with the name and address of its owner, who paid for the privilege of sitting in that particular pew for each of the three Sunday services. The square Brontë pew, with its green baize seats and worn hassocks, was on the east wall, next to the altar, and the two were uncomfortably crammed in beneath the organ loft. Charlotte apparently preferred the corner seat, even though it meant she sat with her back to the pulpit, perhaps because it avoided the problem of facing the rest of the congregation.[27]

To maintain some sort of order and so that the congregation could be seen by the officiating minister, there was a high, three-decker wooden pulpit on the south wall. Above the third level there was a sounding board, on the underside of which was painted 'I determined not to know anything among you, save Jesus Christ, and him crucified. – I Cor. 2.2. For to me, to live is Christ, and to die is gain. – Ph. 1.21. William Grimshaw A. B. Minister 1742'.[28] The parish clerk, who had to make the responses and lead the congregation through the services, sat at the lowest level; above him sat the minister who conducted the service from that level and then went up to the third level to read the Gospel and preach his sermon. The dominance of the pulpit, rather than the altar, in the arrangement of the church reflected the fact that, at that time, the sermon was the central part of the service and communion was taken much less frequently than it is today. Despite being directly under the eagle eye of the clerk and minister, the congregation sometimes grew restive listening to a service which most of them, being virtually illiterate, could not follow in the prayer books. Ellen Nussey, Charlotte's schoolfriend, visiting in 1833, gives a wonderful description of a service:

The people assembled, but it was apparently to <u>listen</u>, any part beyond that was quite out of their reckoning. All through the Prayers a stolid look of apathy was fixed in the generality of their faces, then they sat or leaned in their pews; (some few perhaps were resting after a long walk over the moors). The children from the school pattered in after service had commenced, and pattered out again before the sermon. < began > The sexton with a long staff continually walked round in the aisles 'knobbing' sleepers when he dare, shaking his head at and threatening unruly children, but when the sermon began there was a change, attitudes took the listening form, eyes were turned on the speaker. It was curious now to note < to note > the expression, a rustic untaught intelligence gleamed in their faces, in some a daring doubting questioning look as if the lips would like to say something defiant.[29]

Aware of the limitations of his congregation, Patrick usually preached extempore, setting his watch out before him and preaching for exactly one hour; he tended to choose texts from the Gospels and addressed his audience with that 'simple, yet dignified air, not inaccessible to the poorest, and most illiterate hearer' which he himself had praised in *The Maid of Killarney*.[30]

The church, dedicated to St Michael and All Angels, was only a stone's throw from the National Church Sunday School which Patrick had built, and which still stands on the other side of Church Lane, facing the church-yard. The schoolroom was a low, small, single-storey building, with a bell (now replaced by a cross) at the top end. Just above the schoolroom was a low stone barn belonging to the King's Arms but rented by the sexton and his sons to pursue their trade as stonemasons.[31] At the top end of Church Lane, the highest point in the village itself, stands the parsonage. Within this comparatively small area, around the churchyard, all the most important elements of Patrick Brontë's life were brought together: his faith represented by the church, his belief in education represented by the school, and his family represented by their home of forty-one years.

In 1820 the parsonage was virtually the last house in the village; it faced down into Haworth but at the back it looked over the miles of open moorland where Yorkshire meets Lancashire. Today it has been surrounded by car-parks and modern housing and there is only one window (and that not in the original Brontë home) from which the moors can still be glimpsed. The churchyard, where 44,000 burials are said to have taken place, was closed in 1856; the trees, planted eight years later to help disperse the corpses, now obscure the views over Haworth towards Brow Moor, Oakworth Moor and Steeton Moor.[32] Visitors today understandably receive the impression that the outlook of the house was dominated by the churchyard but, from their vantage point at the parsonage, the Brontës would have looked, not down at the churchyard but across and up to the sweep of moorland hills stretching as far as the Yorkshire Dales: even Mrs Gaskell, who preferred the softer scenery of her native Cheshire, was moved to comment, on her visit to the parsonage in September 1853, that the view from the sitting room and her bedroom above it 'was really beautiful in certain lights, moon-light especially'. She also found the exposed position of the house rather unsettling: 'The wind goes piping and wailing and sobbing round the square unsheltered house in a very strange unearthly way.'[33]

The main part of the parsonage is little changed from when the Brontës lived there. A low, grey-stone, rather elegant house, built in 1779, it has simplicity and symmetry: its frontage, facing the church, has a central doorway with pilasters and pediment, two long Georgian sashed windows with glazing bars on each side and five on the floor above. At the rear of the house there were stone-mullioned windows, now gone, and a large arched window on the stairs which still remains.[34] At some stage, though when is not known, Patrick had a large wash kitchen built on the back of the house on the side nearest Church Lane; in the back yard was the privy, a two-seater with large and small seats for adults and children, and a well, fed by spring water running off the moor.[35]

The entrance from Church Lane was a gate, set in the wall which ran round the perimeter of the yard and the square garden plot at the front which occupied an area slightly larger than the house.[36] The Brontës were not enthusiastic gardeners and the constant war against the elements did not encourage growth in anything except the green moss which thrives on the damp stone and soil. There were a few fruit bushes, some straggling lilacs, thorns and elders and a semicircular gravel walk; in the narrow flowerbed under the windows of the house Emily, prompted by Ellen Nussey, attempted to grow cornflowers and Sicilian peas, but there was no sign of life there when Mrs Gaskell visited in 1853.[37]

Though the garden was neglected, the house was not. Mrs Gaskell commented that

Everything about the place tells of the most dainty order, the most exquisite cleanliness. The door-steps are spotless; the small old-fashioned window-panes glitter like looking-glass. Inside and outside of that house cleanliness goes up into its essence, purity.[38]

By the time Mrs Gaskell visited, Charlotte, her father and their servants, Tabitha Aykroyd and Martha Brown, were the only inhabitants of the parsonage and substantial changes had been made to its fabric and decoration.

Ellen Nussey, visiting Haworth for the first time some twenty years earlier, also found the parsonage scrupulously clean but considerably more austere. There were no curtains at the windows because, she said, of Patrick's fear of fire[39] though internal wooden shutters more than adequately supplied their place.

There was not much carpet any where except in the Sitting room, & and [sic] on the centre of the Study floor. The hall floor and stairs were done with sand stone, always beautifully clean as everything about the house was, the walls were not papered but coloured in a pretty dove-coloured tint, hair-seated chairs and mahogany tables, book-shelves in the Study but not many of these elsewhere. Scant and bare indeed many will say, yet it was not a scantness that made itself felt –[40]

No doubt the austerity was more evident because of the stone-flagged floors, which extended beyond the kitchen to all the downstairs rooms. The two larger rooms at the front of the house were the main living rooms; the one on the left of the hall became the family dining room, or parlour, as Mrs Gaskell called it, and the one on the right became Patrick's study. Behind the dining room was a small storeroom, also used as a pantry, and behind the study was the kitchen with a large cooking range built into the chimney. A passageway, giving access through the back door to the yard, eventually separated this kitchen from the wash kitchen added by Patrick. Upstairs, the basic room layout was the same, with two larger bedrooms at the front and two smaller ones at the back: over the hall was the little room which the Brontë servants called 'the children's study'. There were no attic rooms but there was a double-vaulted cellar beneath the house, reached from the hall by a flight of stone stairs.

To this house, provided free of rent by the trustees of the church lands, Patrick brought his wife, six small children and two servants in April 1820. Though Mrs Gaskell and probably every visitor after her wondered where on earth they all slept,[41] the house was larger and better proportioned than the parsonage at Thornton: it also had the all-important addition of a comparatively large garden where the children could play safely, well away from a busy main thoroughfare. While the children settled happily into their new home, Patrick and, to a lesser extent, Maria had to face an uncertain reception. As Patrick later told his friend and former vicar, John Buckworth: 'When I first came to this place, though the angry winds which had been previously excited, were hushed, the troubled sea was still agitated, and the vessel required a cautious and steady hand at the helm.'[42]

Patrick launched into his new duties with his customary conscientious fervour, performing burials on 20, 21 and 22 April, followed by four baptisms and two marriages on the 23rd and two more marriages on the 24th, which, as the official birthday of the new king, was celebrated by ringing the church bells. Thereafter, he settled into a steady routine of duty. Over the first ten years of his ministry he had to take an average of 290 baptisms a year, the equivalent of more than five a week. There were so many baptisms that he was unable to perform them all during the Sunday services and a large proportion of his time, week in and week out, was taken up with christenings. The high numbers owed something to his own missionary zeal, as well as the birth rate in the chapelry: the registers show that multiple baptisms were commonplace and that baptisms of between fifteen and thirty children a day were not uncommon. As many of these were older brothers and sisters being baptized at the same time as the infant, it would seem that Patrick made a point of visiting parents at the time of birth and persuading them to have all their children christened. The high number of bastard children he baptized also suggests that, while condemning the immorality that had begotten them, he did not extend his condemnation to the children themselves.[43]

The high birth rate in the chapelry was matched by a high mortality rate: in the same period, 1820 to 1830, Patrick conducted, on average, 111 burials a year, rising in 1824 and 1830 to 140. Even the marriages ran at the comparatively high rate of about twenty-eight a year, with a surprising number of minors being married with their parents' consent. No doubt many of these took place because a baby was on the way but, with life expectancy so low, marriages did take place at an earlier age than today.[44]

Patrick faced an immense task in Haworth, especially compared to his previous ministry. Though the population was only one eighth as big again as that of Thornton, Patrick had to perform – singlehandedly – more than double the number of burials and marriages and nearly seven times as many baptisms as he had had to carry out in Thornton. Faced with such a relentless round of official duty, it was remarkable that Patrick found any time for visiting the sick, dying and bereaved in the far-flung corners of his chapelry.

Nevertheless, Patrick made it clear, right from the start of his ministry at Haworth, that he cared deeply about the plight of his parishioners and that he would be active on their behalf. It was not simply their spiritual welfare that concerned him but also their physical needs and he was to prove an indefatigable campaigner on their behalf. On 6 June 1820, for instance, he assisted the overseer of the poor in drawing up a petition addressed to the committee of the charity at Harrogate responsible for enabling 'the Afflicted and Distressed Poor' to receive the spa waters there. The petition, which Patrick was the first to sign, stated that James Parker, a wool-comber of Haworth, had been unable to provide for his family because of unemployment and a severe scorbutic complaint and requested financial assistance to enable him to take the waters at Harrogate in the hope of either relieving or curing his condition.[45]

On the same day that he signed the petition, Patrick travelled over to Thornton, where he stayed the night at Kipping House so that early the next morning he could go into Bradford for the annual visitation of the diocese. He was to break his journey into Bradford by staying overnight at Kipping House several times over the next few months, but it was not until 8 September that Elizabeth Firth and her father braved the journey to Haworth to dine with the Brontës in their new home.[46] This was to be the first and last time that the two families would meet at Haworth for, at the beginning of December, Mr Firth fell ill. Patrick visited him on the 13th and again on the 21st, when it became clear that his friend was dying. He was in deep depression of spirits, but Patrick comforted him and 'By God's blessing and Mr Bronte's conversation [he] became more happy', spending all the following day in 'holy ecstacies'. On 27 December, he died.[47]

The new year of 1821 began sorrowfully enough as Patrick returned to Thornton on 2 January 1821 to officiate at the burial, but this was as nothing compared to the grief that was to come.[48] Shortly after his return home, on 29 January, Maria, his wife, was suddenly taken dangerously ill. It was obvious from the start that her illness was mortal and Patrick was at his wits' end, expecting her imminent demise 'During every week and almost every day' of the seven and a half months it took her to die. Patrick called in Thomas Andrew, the local surgeon, and consulted several other medical men 'but all their skill was in vain'. She had cancer, probably of the uterus, and there was little anyone could do to help her.[49] Nevertheless, Patrick bought the medicines and tried every remedy available, noting in his copy of Graham's *Modern Domestic Medicine*, purchased a few years later, in the margin of the pages on cancer that 'Drinking a table spoonful of brandy, & water \and salt,/ four times a day, and bathing with this mixture; the parts affected, is said to be good for a cancer'. Beneath this he added the grim postscript: 'This remains to be proved – B.' He may even have called in a surgeon in a vain effort to save his wife for, having noted that excision was the surest method of removing cancer in its earliest stages, he went on to write, 'As I have read, and seen, sometimes but not always – when a cancer, is radically cut out in one part, it breaks out in another – B.'[50]

As Maria gradually grew weaker and needed more care than Patrick's duties would permit him to give her, he was forced to employ a nurse. She bathed and tended the invalid during the day but it was Patrick, and Patrick alone, who nursed his 'beloved sufferer' during the long, lonely hours of the night.[51] Though his heart cannot have been in his work and he must have been exhausted, mentally and physically, by the strain of Maria's illness, Patrick was meticulous in performing his ministerial duties. Throughout the long, terrible months, until Maria died, he missed only one burial out of sixty-three and two baptisms out of 192, performing all twenty-one marriages.[52]

Torn between the relentless round of his duties and the long hours spent nursing his wife, Patrick felt the loneliness of his situation for the first time. 'Had I been at D[ewsbury] I should not have wanted kind friends;' he told

John Buckworth, 'had I been at H[artshead], I should have seen them, and others, occasionally; or had I been at T[hornton], a family there, who were ever truly kind, would have soothed my sorrows; but I was at [Haworth], a stranger in a strange land.'[53]

This was a pardonable exaggeration. Though it was not the same as having her just down the road in Thornton, Elizabeth Firth came over several times to visit the stricken household. On 9 February she found Maria 'very poorly' so she came again on 21 February and in March. When she could not visit in person, she wrote. Even more kindly, and demonstrating the practical consideration that Patrick needed so much, she arrived in Haworth on 26 May in a post chaise with her friend and fellow godmother to the Brontë children, Fanny Outhwaite. The two ladies carried off the young Maria and Elizabeth, taking them back to Kipping House for a month.[54]

If Elizabeth Firth did so much to help, it is inconceivable that Maria's relatives, the Morgans and the Fennells, did not offer some assistance.[55] Though both William Morgan and John Fennell were heavily committed in their own parishes and could offer Patrick no assistance in his ministerial duties, they must have visited the family in their plight. The sheer distances involved, however, meant that those to whom the Brontës were closest were unable to be in constant attendance. After only eight months in Haworth, and those spent in difficult circumstances trying to heal the differences that had arisen over Patrick's appointment, the Brontës were not yet on intimate terms with anyone in the town. The situation was not improved by the fact that Patrick was too proud to admit that he was in trouble and that he needed help.[56] Despite this, the family was still shown kindness by, for example, the Greenwoods of Bridge House, who were 'remarkably attentive and kind to Mrs Brontë in her illness, and ... paid the children the attention of asking them occasionally to tea'.[57] If the Greenwoods, who were Particular Baptists and had no obligation to the family, responded in the crisis, it seems unlikely that members of Patrick's own congregation and his supporters among the trustees would not have assisted their minister.

For Patrick the lowest point came on 'a gloomy day, a day of clouds and darkness', when Maria seemed at death's door, lying cold and silent, hardly seeming to notice what was happening around her. That day, three of the children were taken ill with scarlet fever. As if Patrick had not already enough to bear, the next day, the other three were also taken ill with the same infection. Scarlet fever was then a mortal sickness, so death threatened not only his wife but all six of his children. His faith severely tested by the trials he was forced to endure, Patrick nearly broke under the weight of 'the greatest load of sorrows that ever pressed on me' and prayed for relief. It came. All the children recovered, Maria's condition improved slightly and a few weeks later, her sister, Elizabeth Branwell, arrived from Penzance to help.[58]

Aunt Branwell's arrival was a godsend: she was not only an affectionate relative who could truly sympathize but also a competent and efficient manager. The nurse could be dismissed and Maria given over to her sister's loving care; for Patrick particularly, there was relief in having someone who loved his wife to tend her and an adult to whom he could talk. Elizabeth's presence 'afforded great comfort to my mind, which has been the case ever since, by sharing my labours and sorrows, and behaving as an affectionate mother to my children'.[59]

The sense of impending doom cannot have been helped by the death of Queen Caroline, wife of George IV, on 7 August; the paraphernalia of public mourning were everywhere to be seen and even Patrick's pulpit had to be draped in funereal black as if in preparation for the death that had to come. At the end of the month there came further sad news: his old friend and first patron, Thomas Tighe, had died in Ireland on 21 August.[60] Maria's own condition was fast deteriorating:

Death pursued her unrelentingly. Her constitution was enfeebled, and her frame wasted daily; and after above seven months of more agonizing pain than I ever saw anyone endure, she fell asleep in Jesus, and her soul took its flight to the mansions of glory. During many years, she had walked with God; but the great enemy, envying her life of holiness, often disturbed her mind in the last conflict. Still, in general, she had peace and joy in believing; and died, if not triumphantly, at least calmly, and with a holy, yet humble confidence, that Christ was her Saviour, and heaven her eternal home.[61]

It must have added considerably to Patrick's mental anguish that the gentle and pious woman he loved so much was unable to die 'triumphantly' as a good Evangelical should. In one of her love letters she had once told him that her heart was more ready to attach itself to earth than to heaven. As she lay dying it was the thought of her soon-to-be motherless children which tormented her, rather than her own spiritual plight. The nurse had heard her crying out continually, 'Oh God my poor children – oh God my poor children!'[62] On 15 September 1821, Maria died, as she had lived, in the midst of her family. Patrick and her sister sat on either side of her bed and the children, the eldest of whom was only seven years old, the youngest not yet two, stood at the foot of the bed with Sarah Garrs, their nursemaid.[63]

For two weeks Patrick was prostrate with grief and unable to perform his duties. William Anderton, who had officiated during the vacancy at Haworth, stepped into the breach again but Patrick called on his old friend, William Morgan, who, in happier times, had married Patrick and Maria and christened four of their six children, to officiate at Maria's funeral. On Saturday, 22 September, Maria was buried in the vault near the altar under Haworth Church. She was thirty-eight years old.[64]

And when my dear wife was dead, and buried, and gone, and when I missed her at every corner, and when her memory was hourly revived by the innocent, yet distressing prattle, of my children, I do assure you, my dear Sir, from what I felt, I was happy in the recollection, that to sorrow, not as those without hope, was no sin; that our Lord himself had wept over his departed friend; and that he had promised us grace and strength sufficient for such a day.[65]

Whatever may have been his personal inclination, Patrick could not afford the indulgence of shutting himself away to mourn his loss. Within a week of his wife's funeral he was again performing all the official duties required of him, even though there were moments when the tide of grief threatened to overwhelm him. He had serious financial problems, too, for Maria's illness, the medication, the doctors and the nurse, had all required a large expenditure which Patrick had given unstintingly and, in the process, left himself deeply in debt. Maria's annuity, which had provided the comfortable sum of fifty pounds per annum, ceased on her death and was not transferable to her children.[66] Patrick, totally dependent on his salary of £170 a year, had no savings and nothing of value which he could capitalize to pay his debts.

Too proud to seek help, he felt it was an answer to prayer when his old friends in Bradford rallied round and held a subscription on his behalf. Elizabeth Firth contributed two guineas and doubtless wealthy clerical friends like John Buckworth and Samuel Redhead gave more: the total sum raised was £150.[67] In addition, 'my old and very kind friend at B[radford]', presumably William Morgan, sent a few pounds and one of the church charities sent him a donation of fifty pounds. A few days later he received a bank post bill for a further fifty pounds from 'a benevolent individual, a wealthy lady, in the West Riding of Yorkshire'. Though the benefactress' name is not known, it seems more than likely that this was Patrick's first encounter with Miss Currer, of Eshton Hall, who was the patron of William Morgan's former living at Bierley. She was renowned for her generosity to all kinds of charities and a gift to a widowed clergyman with six small children was entirely in character for her.[68] Characteristically, Patrick was scrupulous in paying back that portion of the money which had been loaned to him; as soon as possible – but probably several years later – he paid a personal visit to William Tetley, the Bradford parish clerk, and repaid him the fifty pounds he had received through his hands.[69]

The generosity of his friends relieved Patrick of his most pressing debts and ensured that the family did not go in need, but he was still left with the major problem of how he was to provide for the care of his children. For the moment Aunt Branwell was prepared to stay, but her home was in Penzance, where all her friends were and where she had other responsibilities to the families of her brothers and sisters. Her residence at the parsonage could only be a temporary arrangement and then what was Patrick to do? Nancy and Sarah Garrs were good and loyal servants, but they could not take the place of a parent or guardian. Driven half out of his mind with worry about the future and his judgement still clouded by grief, Patrick made the mistake of taking decisive action.

On 8 December he went to stay at Kipping House for a couple of nights, presumably because he had business to transact in Bradford. Elizabeth Firth was no doubt sympathetic and understanding: she had known and loved Maria, taken an interest in the children and was godmother to at least two of them. In the midst of his despair, Patrick suddenly saw a glimmer of hope. Although she was only twenty-four, Elizabeth Firth could supply virtually everything the Brontës needed. She was quite capable of running the household as she had already proved by successfully managing her father's house until his remarriage; she was every inch a lady and would therefore be an ideal model and instructress to his daughters; since her father's death she had been a wealthy woman in her own right and her money would provide for his children in a way that Patrick could not; and, perhaps most important of all, she was already known and liked by the children themselves. On his return home he wrote to Elizabeth Firth and asked her to marry him.[70] Always an honest man, Patrick no doubt set out the practical advantages to his family which she could bring as his wife as well as expressing his personal esteem for her. She received his letter on 12 December and was appalled. Maria had been dead for scarcely three months and here was her widower, a penniless clergyman with six small children, asking her to throw herself away on him. Her anger was probably compounded by the fact that she was at the same time being courted by an eminently more eligible clergyman, James Clarke Franks. Two days later, she wrote a decided entry in her diary: 'I wrote my last letter to Mr Bronte.' She kept her word for nearly two years, refusing to have anything more to do with the Brontës.[71] By this disastrous proposal Patrick had succeeded only in alienating one of his few female friends and thereby lost his daughters the chance of being taken under their godmother's wing. He could not even take the obvious step of proposing to Elizabeth Branwell, despite the fact that she decided to stay on at Haworth until the children were old enough to go to school, because marriage to a deceased wife's sister was then against the law. Any idea of a second marriage would have to be abandoned, at least for the foreseeable future.

But what of the children themselves? Most of the biographers would have us believe that their childhood was no childhood: no toys, no children's books, no playmates; only newspapers to read and their own precocious, vivid imaginations to amuse them. Mrs Gaskell set the trend when she described them as 'grave and silent beyond their years' and quoted their mother's nurse: 'You would not have known there was a child in the house, they were such still, noiseless, good little creatures ... I used to think them spiritless, they were so different to any children I had ever seen.'[72]

The nurse, however, as Nancy and Sarah Garrs were quick to point out, seems to have borne a grudge about her dismissal. Though she may have left simply because Aunt Branwell arrived, the Garrs sisters said that she was 'sent away by Mr Bronte for reasons which he thought sufficient'. Perhaps, like Mrs Gamp, she had helped herself too frequently to the beer which Aunt Branwell kept under lock and key in the cellar.[73] It was certainly Patrick who bore the brunt of her vitriolic accounts of life in the parsonage during Maria's illness. She blamed him for the supposed listlessness of his children:

I set it down to a fancy Mr Brontë had of not letting them have flesh-meat to eat. It was from no wish for saving, for there was plenty and even waste in the house, with young servants and no mistress to see after them; but he thought that children should be brought up simply and hardily: so they had nothing but potatoes for their dinner.[74]

Patrick, in a letter to Mrs Gaskell, called this 'the principal mistake in the memoir' and flatly denied that he restricted his children to a vegetable diet. He was backed up by his cook, Nancy Garrs, who pointed out to visitors the meat jack from the parsonage which Patrick had requested should be sent to her on his death and stated categorically that the children had had meat to eat every day of their lives.[75] References in the Brontës' letters and diary notes to cooking meals confirm that their diet consisted of oatmeal porridge for breakfast, meat, vegetables and a milk pudding or fruit pie for dinner and bread and butter, with fruit preserve, for tea.[76] If the children were at all pale and subdued while the nurse was at the Parsonage it was probably because they were just recovering from scarlet fever; they must have been anxious about their mother, too. Even so, Patrick's reference to 'the innocent, yet distressing prattle of my children' in the couple of months following Maria's death suggests that the young Brontës were perfectly normal, noisy young children.

Mrs Gaskell explained her inclusion of the sensational stories about Patrick's 'eccentricities' by saying, 'I hold the knowledge of them to be necessary for a right understanding of the life of his daughter.'[77] Yet those who knew Patrick well, including his friends and his servants, did not recognize him in Mrs Gaskell's portrait: the words they used to describe him were uniformly 'kind', 'affable', 'considerate' and 'genial'. Like her picture of 'barbaric' Haworth, Mrs Gaskell's portrayal of Patrick as a half-mad recluse who wanted nothing to do with his children was intended to explain away those characteristics of his daughter's writings which the Victorians found unacceptable.

Most of the stories were completely untrue, including those illustrative of Patrick's supposedly explosive temperament. Again, they came from the nurse who had been dismissed, embellished, no doubt, by Lady Kay Shuttleworth, who knew her and reported back to Mrs Gaskell with all the malicious glee of a sitting-room gossip. Both Patrick and Nancy Garrs denied that there was any foundation in fact to the 'Eccentrick Movements' of sawing the backs off chairs and burning hearth rugs in the heat of his Irish temper and Mrs Gaskell was compelled, albeit reluctantly, to remove the accounts from her third edition of *The Life of Charlotte Brontë*.[78]

Nancy also declared that the story of Patrick's burning the coloured boots put out by the nurse for his children to wear because they were 'too gay and luxurious for his children, and would foster a love of dress' was simply untrue: the incident could not have happened without Nancy's knowledge as she was seldom absent from the kitchen for more than five minutes. She also denied that Patrick 'worked off his volcanic wrath by firing pistols out of the back-door in rapid succession'. Patrick only carried loaded pistols when he took the long and lonely walk across the moors from Thornton to Haworth during periods of popular unrest and would discharge them before entering the house simply to make them safe.[79]

The only story to which Nancy gave any credence at all – and its tone she hotly denied – was that Patrick had cut one of his wife's dresses into ribbons because it was 'not according to his consistent notions of propriety'. Nancy's version of the story was that Patrick had bantered his wife good-humouredly on a new dress, 'commenting with special awe and wonder on the marvellous expanse of sleeves'. Maria took the dress off, but when she later returned to her room she found that Patrick had been there before her and cut off the sleeves. Maria gave the dress to Nancy and, soon afterwards, Patrick came into the kitchen bearing a new silk dress which he had gone to Keighley to buy for his wife.[80]

If Patrick was not the half-mad and violent eccentric described by Mrs Gaskell, neither was he a weird recluse who 'did not require companionship, therefore he did not seek it'.[81] Though this has again become part of Brontë mythology, it was not true that, during his wife's illness, Patrick shut himself away in his study and began a lifelong habit of taking his meals in there alone. A schoolmaster friend of Patrick and Branwell, William Dearden, interviewed Nancy on the point and was roundly informed 'Whether Mr Brontë was troubled with indigestion or not, Nancy says she cannot tell, as she never heard him complain on that score; but, up to the time of her leaving his service, she declares that he dined with his family every day.'[82]

Dearden also drew on his own intimacy with the family to take up the cudgels on behalf of Patrick's role as a father. 'His children were the frequent companions of his walks', Dearden insisted. 'I have seen him, more than once, conversing kindly and affably with them in the studio of a clever artist who resided in Keighley; and many others, both in that town and in Haworth, can bear testimony to the fact of his having been often seen accompanied by his young family in his visits to friends, and in his rambles among the hills.'[83]

It is difficult to recognize in this picture the same 'domestic hyena'[84] described by Mrs Gaskell which sadly remains the popular image of the father of the Brontës. Yet it is entirely consistent with everything we can learn of the man through his life and his work. Patrick was clearly not only concerned for, but interested in, his children. William Dearden is the witness on his behalf again:

We are led to infer from Mrs Gaskell's narrative, that their father – if he felt – at least, did not manifest much anxiety about their physical and mental welfare; and we are told that the eldest of the motherless group, then at home, by a sort of premature inspiration, under the feeble wing of a maiden aunt, undertook their almost entire supervision. Branwell … told me, when accidentally alluding to this mournful period in the history of his family, that his father watched over his little bereaved flock with truly paternal solicitude and affection – that he was their constant guardian and instructor – and that he took a lively interest in all their innocent amusements.[85]

The truth of this remark is borne out by Patrick himself in the letters he wrote to Mrs Gaskell as she was preparing her biography of Charlotte, which she actually quoted in the book.

When mere children, as soon as they could read and write, Charlotte and her brother and sisters, used to invent and act little plays of their own, in which the Duke of Wellington my Daughter Charlotte's Hero, was sure to come off, the conquering hero – when a dispute [would] not infrequently [arise] amongst them regarding [the] comparative merits of him, Buonaparte, Hannibal, and Caesar – When the argument got warm, and rose to its height, as their mother was then dead, I had sometimes to come in as arbitrator, and settle the dispute, according to the best of my judgement.[86]

The children clearly had no fear of dragging their supposedly ferocious and reclusive father into their games. Equally, Patrick was interested enough to break off from his own demanding work to enter into the spirit of the thing, listening to the arguments and weighing their merits. On another occasion, Patrick 'just happened' to have a mask in the house:

When my children were very young, when as far as I can rem[em]ber, the oldest was about ten years of age and the youngest about four – thinking that they knew more, than I had yet discover'd, in order to make them speak with less timidity, I deem'd that if they were put under a sort of cover, I might gain my end – and happen[in]g to have a mask in the house, I told them all to stand, and speak boldly from under \cover of/ the mask – I began with the youngest – I asked what a child like her most wanted – She answer'd, age and experience – I asked the next what I had best do with her brother Branwell, who was sometimes, a naughty boy, She answered, reason with him, and when he won't listen to reason whip him – I asked Branwell, what was the best way of knowing the difference between the intellects, of men and women – he answer'd by considering the difference between them as to their bodies – I then asked Charlotte, what was the best Book in the world, she answered, the Bible – and what was the next best, she answer'd the Book of Nature – I then asked the next, what was the best mode of education for a woman, she answered, that which would make her rule her house well – Lastly I asked the oldest, what < wait > was the best mode of spending time she answer'd, by laying it out in preparation for a happy eternity – I may not have given precisely their words, but I have nearly done so as they made a deep and lasting impression on my memory –[87]

Though the anecdote is usually cited as an example of the young Brontës' undoubted precocity, it also demonstrates once more than their father took a keen interest in their personal and intellectual development. One more story, narrated this time by Sarah Garrs, shows that the children enjoyed the usual escapades of childhood: Sarah had been roped into playing a part in one of their plays:

As an escaping Prince, with a counterpane for a robe, I stepped from a window on the limb of a cherry tree, which broke and let me down. There was great consternation among the children, as it was Mr Brontë's favourite tree, under which he often sat. I carried off the branch and blackened the place with soot, but the next day, Mr Brontë detained them a moment and began with the youngest, asking each pleasantly, 'Who spoiled my tree?' The answer was, 'Not I,' until it came to my turn. They were always loyal and true.[88]

This again is a far cry from Mrs Gaskell's picture of the subdued children closeted in their 'study', listening to the seven-year-old Maria reading the newspapers. If Mrs Gaskell, and those who have followed in her path, are so wide of the mark in their description of the Brontës' childhood, what then was life at Haworth parsonage really like at this time? Fortunately, Sarah Garrs, the person who was probably most involved in their day-to-day care, has left her own account of a typical day.[89]

After the children had been washed and dressed, the day began with the whole family, including the servants, assembling in Patrick's study for prayers. The children then accompanied him across the hall for a 'plain but abundant' breakfast of porridge and milk, bread and butter. Apart from the baby, Anne, they then returned to the study for a morning session of lessons with their father. Once that was over, they were then committed to Sarah's care till dinner-time: she taught the girls how to sew and, by the age of five, Charlotte had made a linen chemise for her own wear, aided only in the cutting out and basting by Sarah. The children dined at two o'clock with their father. They were given plain roast or boiled meat and for dessert there were bread and rice puddings, custards and other slightly sweetened preparations of eggs and milk. While Patrick went out to do his parish visiting in the afternoons, the children walked out on the moors every day unless the weather was too bad. These walks were the highlight of their day:

Their afternoon walks, as they sallied forth, each neatly and comfortably clad, were a joy. Their fun knew no bounds. It never was expressed wildly. Bright and often dry, but deep, it occasioned many a merry burst of laughter. They enjoyed a game of romps, and played with zest.

On their return home they found tea waiting for them in the kitchen. Patrick came in later and took his tea in his study. When the tea-tray was removed, he gathered the children about him 'for recitation and talk, giving them oral lessons in history, biography or travel' while the girls sewed.[90] While their mother was still alive and able to listen to them, the children said their nightly prayers at her bedside, kissed her goodnight and went to their own 'warm clean beds'. On Sunday evenings, the whole family gathered in Patrick's study once more for Bible study and catechism: the servants were again included but, as Sarah noted, they were always treated as superiors in the presence of the children.[91]

Sarah's account would suggest that the Brontës had a perfectly normal childhood. Though the loss of their mother at such an early age could not be anything other than a personal tragedy for the children she left behind, its importance should not be exaggerated. It was, after all, a commonplace occurrence – much more commonplace than it is today – and therefore accepted more readily. In a more pious age, too, there was the comfort of knowing that she had gone to a better place and that her soul, if not her body, was immortal. In later life, Charlotte, who always said that she began to observe and analyze character at five years old, had no more than two or three memories of her mother, including one of her playing with Branwell in the parlour one evening.[92] Though she and her brother and sisters felt the lack of a mother figure, their real mother, as a person, was someone the younger four simply did not remember. Her loss, terrible though it may have been at the time, did not permanently blight their young lives.

Their home life was secure and stable, with their father always ready to spend time with them, despite the pressures of his own work. Their aunt, too, was an 'affectionate mother', supervising their lessons and their household work and nursing the infant Anne.[93] Nancy and Sarah Garrs were playmates and confidantes, closely involved, as we have seen, in the children's games.

Like all large families, particularly those with children close together in age, the Brontës were self-sufficient. They had no need to seek friends of their own age in the town when they had companions with the same tastes and enthusiasms in their own home. Maria, as the eldest, seems to have taken the lead. Sarah Garrs tells us that 'Their "games" were founded upon what Maria read to them from the newspapers, and the tales brought forth from the father's mines of tradition, history, and romance. Nothing escaped them.'[94]

Mrs Gaskell found the idea of small children reading the newspapers unnerving in its precocity and later biographers have assumed that they read newspapers because they had no other, more suitable books.[95] In fact, the local newspapers of this period, such as the *Leeds Mercury* and the *Leeds Intelligencer*, were a fascinating source of information and had plenty to interest bright young children. The political reports and coverage of parliamentary debates were written in a lively – sometimes even libellous – strain that brought the characters vividly to life. There was no nonsense about editorial fairhandedness and political neutrality: the papers screamed their political affiliation from every page with a savagery that sometimes amounted to hysteria. Though Patrick and his family were Tory, they took or had access to Whig papers too, so that the children were able to recognize political bias and see the arguments from both ends of the spectrum. Patrick used to say that he could converse with Maria on any of the leading topics of the day as freely and with as much pleasure as with any adult.[96]

Though the newspapers undoubtedly provided the political raw material which was to feed the Brontës' hero-worship of men like the Duke of Wellington, they had many other elements too. They carried reviews of books and magazines, including extensive quotation of interesting incidents from new works and old. There were descriptions of the latest fashions and accounts of life in high society, complete with all its scandal and gossip. There was also the local news where, sandwiched between the lurid detail of the criminal courts and the trivia of outsize mushrooms and other 'amazing phenomena', the Brontës would frequently see their father's name. Here was endless material for the children's plays and stories.

Patrick, in the meantime, was as busy as ever. Despite his extensive duties he found time for his special interests. In the summer of 1822 there was a national effort on behalf of the Irish poor who were suffering extreme deprivation and hardship. Henry Heap, the vicar of Bradford, preached a sermon and raised a subscription on their behalf and it seems likely that Patrick would have followed suit. Perhaps coincidentally, Patrick's own mother is said to have died in Ireland in the course of this year, so that the strongest remaining tie between him and the land of his birth had now been broken.[97] On 17 December there was a meeting of the Keighley Auxiliary Bible Society, chaired by Patrick's friend, the Reverend Theodore Dury; although Patrick's name is not mentioned, it is likely that he was there, particularly as William Morgan was one of the main speakers. If he did attend, he would have met, possibly for the first time, the Reverend William Carus Wilson, vicar of Tunstall in Westmorland, who was soon to play such an important role in his family's life.[98]

The winter of 1822 was one of the most severe in living memory; it snowed solidly for five days and nights, cutting off Clayton Heights and Blackstone Edge, and preventing the mail and stage coaches getting through.[99] Nevertheless, Patrick seems to have been a fairly frequent visitor to Keighley over the winter, giving rise to local gossip. Though he had been friendly with Theodore Dury since at least as far back as his days at Thornton, when he had preached for the Missionary Society in Keighley, it was now said that Patrick had proposed to Isabella Dury, the vicar's sister. Whether the rumour was true or not, Isabella wrote to her friend, Miss Mariner, daughter of a Keighley manufacturer:

I heard before I left Keighley that my brother & I had quarrelled about poor Mr Bronte, I beg if you ever hear such a report that you will contradict it as I can assure you it is perfectly unfounded, I think I never should be so very silly as to have the most distant idea of marrying anybody who had not some fortune, and six children into the bargain. It is too ridiculous to imagine any truth in it.[100]

It seems likely enough that Patrick had proposed to Isabella Dury. Like Elizabeth Firth, she was a gentlewoman of independent means and therefore a suitable stepmother for his children; presumably, too, like her brother, she was of the Evangelical persuasion so she would have been a fitting wife for Patrick.

It is a measure of his desperation at this time that when Isabella Dury also turned him down, Patrick's thoughts turned back fifteen years to the days of his first curacy at Wethersfield and to a woman who had then welcomed his attentions. When Patrick was at the beginning of his career, Mary Burder's religion had stood in the way of their marriage but now, as perpetual curate of Haworth, he felt secure enough to risk a wife who might not be prepared to give up her faith for his. Undoubtedly, there would have been grave difficulties but Patrick was determined on remarriage as the only solution to his problems. Two months after his presumed rejection by Isabella Dury, Patrick wrote a tentative letter to Mary Burder's mother, sounding out the ground and trying to discover whether Mary had married in the intervening years. The excuse for his letter, having lost contact with Wethersfield for so many years, was that he intended to travel south in the summer and might pass through the neighbourhood. 'I long to revisit the scene of my first ministerial labours', he told her, 'and to see some of my old friends.' He took care, however, to give Mrs Burder a brief résumé of his career to date, mentioning his wife, ' a very amiable and respectable Lady, who has been dead for nearly two years, so that I am now left a widower', but not his six children. On the offchance that Mary was still unmarried, he made sure that her mother was aware of his eligibility as a potential suitor: he had been at Haworth for three years, he explained,

where, in all human probability, I shall continue during the remainder of my life. This Living is what is here called a Benefice, or Perpetual Curacy. It is mine for life, no one can take it from me. The only difference between it and a Vicarage is that in a Vicarage the salary arises from tithes, and in the Living I have it arises from the rent of Freehold Estates, which I like much better. My salary is not large, it is only about two hundred a year. But in addition to this two hundred a year I have a good House, which is mine for life also, and is rent free.

Just in case Mrs Burder had not taken the hint, but not wishing to be too blatant, he continued: 'I should like to know whether Miss Davy be still alive, how you are yourself, how all your children are, whether they be married or single, and whether they be doing well, both as it respects this life, and that which is to come.'[101]

Not knowing that the family had moved to The Park, a farm nearer Finchingfield owned by Mary's brother, Patrick addressed his letter to their old home, The Broad, and then waited for a reply.

While he waited he was approached by the chairman of the committee at Woodhouse Grove School and asked to examine the boys in classical learning. The last time he had done this was in 1812 and the occasion had been the start of his serious courtship of Maria Branwell. It must have been acutely distressing, therefore, to have to return to the school where he had met and wooed his wife and where so many happy memories must have been revived. Patrick was never one to shirk his duty, however, and this time he was able to give a satisfactory report to the committee. As a clergyman in the Church of England he then had the curious distinction of being thanked by the Methodist Conference for his 'valuable and gratuitous services' in examining the boys and presenting his report.[102]

At the end of July Patrick received the long-awaited reply to his letter. Mary Burder herself wrote to him, but in terms which made it clear she had no wish to renew the acquaintance. Patrick chose to ignore her expressions of dislike, for she was still single and might be won round:

It is now almost fifteen years since I last saw you. This is a long interval of time and may have effected many changes. It has made me look something older. But, I trust I have gained more than I have lost, I hope I may venture to say I am <u>wiser</u> and better... Though I have had much bitter sorrow in consequence of the sickness and death of my dear Wife, yet I have ample cause to praise God for his numberless mercies. I have a <u>small</u> but <u>sweet</u> little family that often soothe my heart and afford me pleasure by their endearing little ways, and I have what I consider a competency of the good things of this life. I am <u>now settled</u> in a part of the country <u>for life</u> where I have many friends, and it has pleased God in many respects to give me favour in the eyes of the people, and to prosper me in my ministerial labours. I want but <u>one</u> addition to my comforts, and then I think I should wish for no more on this side [of] eternity. I want to see a dearly Beloved Friend, kind as I <u>once</u> saw her, and as <u>much</u> disposed to promote my happiness. If I have ever given her any pain I only wish for an opportunity to make her ample amends, by every attention and kindness.[103]

Patrick even referred her to John Buckworth for references, in case she doubted his own words! She clearly did, and in a letter full of 'disdain, hatred, and revenge"[104] she gave a '<u>decided</u> negative' to Patrick's proposed visit, telling him, 'I know of no ties of friendship *ever* existing between us which the last eleven or twelve years have not severed or at least placed an insuperable bar to any revival.' She also firmly quashed any idea that Patrick might have had about her continued unmarried state: 'My present condition upon which you are pleased to remark has hitherto been the state of my choice and to me a state of much happiness and comfort.' Somewhat maliciously, in view of his proposal, she told him that the Lord could supply all his and his children's needs, and expressed the hope that he would be as faithful, zealous and successful at Haworth as his illustrious predecessor, William Grimshaw.[105]

After such an assault, it took Patrick some months before he could summon his courage to pursue his object once more. On 1 January 1824, he wrote in terms of mild reproach for her unkindness and sought her forgiveness:

For this, and every other word or action towards you and yours in which I have been wrong, I ask your pardon. I do not remember the things you allude to, but as far as I can collect from your letter I must have said something or other highly unbecoming and improper. Whatever it was, as a Christian Minister and a gentle-man, I feel myself called upon to acknowledge my great sorrow for it. Such an apology becomes me, and is, I deem, required of me. And such an apology I now make.[106]

Had he left it at that, Mary Burder might have thought better of him but, with characteristic obstinacy, Patrick refused to give up this last chance of securing a mother for his children. Returning to the touchy subject of her unmarried state, he affirmed, 'I <u>have not</u> the <u>least doubt</u> that if you had <u>been mine</u> you would have been happier than you <u>now</u> are or <u>can</u> be as one in <u>single</u> life. You would have had other and kindlier views and feelings."[107] Despite all that she had said, he renewed his request to be allowed to visit her more urgently than before. Mary Burder seems to have left this, Patrick's last letter, unanswered. He had abased himself to no avail.

Patrick was now nearly forty-seven years of age. His lack of fortune and position made him an unattractive marriage prospect among the ranks of his wealthier friends. He had tried and failed to win back someone who, having once loved him for himself alone, now hated him for the same reason. There could have been no clearer sign that God did not intend Patrick to take a second wife. He would have to abandon any idea of remarrying, resign himself to celibacy and, most important of all, make alternative plans for the future of his children.

Chapter Five

❧

CHARITY-CHILDREN

On 4 October 1823, Patrick called at Kipping House for the first time in nearly two years to renew his acquaintance with Elizabeth Firth and her stepmother. Perhaps he apologized for his ill-advised proposal two years before; perhaps he simply explained the desperation which had led him to make it. Certainly he was forgiven and invited to stay for a couple of nights.[1] He may well have taken the opportunity to discuss with Elizabeth Firth the problem of what he was to do with his young family. Aunt Branwell had been with him for just over two years and was anxious to return to Cornwall. If she went, there would only be the two Garrs girls to look after the children and, with the best will in the world, they were not themselves sufficiently well educated to take on the responsibility of bringing up his daughters. They needed a role model to learn the social niceties that would be expected of them as the daughters of a clergyman. More importantly, as it was obvious that their father would be unable to provide financially for them all, they needed to have the sort of education that would equip them to earn their own living.

There were not many options open to the daughters of impoverished clergymen. The most likely course was a suitable marriage but, as Patrick had found to his own cost, without money behind them they were unlikely to attract husbands of substance. If they moved in the right circles, however, their chances of a good marriage were improved; the correct sort of education, with girls of similar social standing but greater fortune, would be an important step in the right direction. Equally, it was unlikely that all five would marry, or marry well. If the option of marriage was not open to them, then a career had to be considered. There was, of course, no question of them entering a profession as this was simply unheard of in the early nineteenth century. Dressmaking, shopkeeping, nursing[2] and going into service were all working-class occupations and could not be considered. All that remained was teaching, either in a private school or in a private household, or becoming the companion of a wealthy lady. In either case, the right education was essential. It was not simply that the girls would have to be able to read and write; they would have to walk, talk and behave correctly in a society which condemned any deviation from the accepted standards of conduct. They would have to have the right sort of feminine attainments too, including an ability to draw, play the piano and do needlework; a smattering of French, Italian and (if the girl was bookish) German was an advantage, but the classical languages or mathematics were the prerogative of the male sex. The contemporary view of a woman's role is perfectly put by one of Patrick's characters in *The Maid of Killarney*.

The education of a female ought, most assuredly, to be competent, in order that she might enjoy herself, and be a fit companion for man. But, believe me, lovely, delicate, and sprightly woman, is not formed by nature, to pore over the musty pages of Grecian and Roman literature, or to plod through the windings of Mathematical Problems; nor has Providence assigned for her sphere of action, either the cabinet or the field. Her forte is softness, tenderness, and grace.[3]

With the acquisition of these qualities in mind, Patrick sought the advice of Elizabeth Firth, who seems to have recommended her own old school as the ideal place for his daughters.

Crofton Hall, near Wakefield, was a country house run as a boarding school for young ladies. It had been founded and run for nearly thirty years by Miss Richmal Mangnall, a lady whose name was pre-eminent in education circles. Pious and charitable – she gave one fifth of her annual income to the poor – she was also something of a blue-stocking. Not content with running her own school, ' a highly respected ladies' academy', she was the author of one of the standard text books, Mangnall's *Historical Questions*.[4] She had died some four years before, on 1 May 1820, but her school continued to be run on the lines she had set down.[5]

Elizabeth Firth and Fanny Outhwaite, another Brontë godmother, had both been to Crofton Hall and had been very happy there. There seems to have been a mixture of carrot and stick in the learning process. Elizabeth was proud of, and preserved, the tiny prize cards she had won for learning and repeating her lessons correctly.[6] Misdemeanours, such as failing in lessons, were punished by having to learn Bible verses or dictionary excerpts, wearing the dunce's cap or being sent early to bed; graver offences, such as lying, thieving or obstinacy, merited whipping. Elizabeth's diary for the period reveals a cheerful round of lessons, half-holidays, concerts, dancing and the usual boarding-school obsession of eating.[7]

Elizabeth Firth had been fifteen when she went to Crofton Hall; Maria and Elizabeth Brontë were now only nine and eight years old respectively, but they were still old enough to go away to boarding school and were certainly of an age when a formal education was beginning to be a necessity. It is possible that their two godmothers contributed at least some of their expenses.[8] The exact dates of the Brontës' time at Crofton Hall are not known. Patrick himself simply said that they went to a good school in Wakefield and briefly described his two eldest daughters: 'Maria had a powerfully intellectual mind – Elizabeth had good solid sense.'[9] One imagines that with those qualities they would have done well. It seems likely that their stay was of fairly brief duration, given it was an expense Patrick could ill afford. Moreover, there was the problem of his three other daughters to contend with; it was only fair that they, too, should receive as good an education as was possible.

On 4 December 1823, an advertisement for a new school appeared in the *Leeds Intelligencer*. For Patrick it must have seemed like the answer to prayer. 'School for Clergymen's Daughters' ran the headline. The advertisement announced that a property had been purchased at Cowan Bridge in the parish of Tunstall, one governess had already been engaged and a school would open on the premises in March or April.

The House will be enlarged and altered for the Accommodation of Sixty Pupils: each Girl is to pay £14 a Year (Half in Advance) for Clothing, Lodging, Boarding, and Education: and £1 Entrance towards the Expense of Books, &c. The Education will be directed according to the Capacities of the Pupils, and the Wishes of their Friends. In all Cases, the great Object in View will be their intellectual and religious Improvement; and to give that plain and useful Education, which may best fit them to return with Respectability and Advantage to their own Homes, or to maintain themselves in the different Stations of Life to which Providence may call them. If a more liberal Education is required for any who may be sent to be educated as Teachers and Governesses, an extra Charge will probably be made.[10]

The school was to be open to daughters of clergymen throughout the country, but it was primarily intended for those in most need and of the Evangelical persuasion.

Donors and Subscribers will of course gain the first Attention in the Recommendation of Pupils: and every Effort will be made to confine the Benefits of the School to the *really* necessitous Clergy; and especially to those who are the most exemplary in their Life and Doctrine.[11]

The school appeared to be tailor-made for the Brontës: they were certainly in straitened circumstances and Patrick was a committed Evangelical clergyman. At only fourteen pounds a year, the fees were half those of comparable schools, including Crofton Hall, so Patrick could afford to educate two daughters for the price of one.[12]

A cheap education could have its drawbacks. At almost exactly the same time as the advertisement for the Clergy Daughters' School appeared in the *Leeds Intelligencer*, the same paper ran at least two horrific accounts of 'Cheap Schools'. On 6 November 1823, it reported a case in the Court of Common Pleas concerning a young men's seminary at Bowes in Yorkshire. Between 260 and 300 boys were boarded and educated there 'for the very moderate sum of twenty guineas per annum'. Apart from enduring appalling physical conditions, the boys had only two towels to share between them and, in consequence, most of them suffered from the itch, a contagious skin disease caused by a mite burrowing under the skin. Eighteen boys were particularly badly afflicted, some of them partially losing their sight and others becoming totally blind.[13]

Another court case was reported on 22 January 1824: a schoolmaster near Richmond in Yorkshire, also charging twenty guineas a year for some eighty pupils, kept his boys in a similar state of deprivation. Up to eight pupils at a time shared a single bed, sleeping on a straw mattress, with only one sheet, two blankets (one of which covered the mattress) and a quilt in winter. Three of the bedrooms had no ceiling or under-drawing so the boys slept under the slates of the roof with buckets set out to catch the rain and snow. Virtually all of them were infested with head lice and fleas.[14]

Any fears Patrick might have had about the Clergy Daughters' School must have vanished when he saw the list of patrons annexed to the advertisement. This was no cheap Yorkshire school of the Dotheboys Hall[15] variety: the list included some of the most eminent people in the land as well as a number of names well known to Patrick himself. There was Mrs Powley of Ossett, daughter of the poet William Cowper's great friend, Mary Unwin, and widow of the Reverend Matthew Powley, John Buckworth's predecessor at Dewsbury; Mrs Hannah More, the famous moralist whose exemplary works were the staple diet of female education; Joshua Fawcett of Leeds, whom Patrick had known since at least his visits to Woodhouse Grove, if not before; the Reverend Charles Simeon, the Evangelical who had been an inspiration to Patrick at Cambridge. There were even two of Patrick's own patrons on the list: William Wilberforce, who had enabled him to finish his education at St John's, and Miss Currer of Eshton Hall, who had sent him money to pay his debts when his wife had died.[16] With the backing of such a host of the great and good, Patrick could not doubt the quality of the school. He even had personal knowledge of the founder, the Reverend William Carus Wilson, a renowned missionary preacher who had espoused the same Evangelical causes as Patrick himself and who regularly preached in the Bradford area.[17] If Patrick had not met him in December 1822, then he would at least have had a personal recommendation of him from their mutual friend, Theodore Dury, who was also one of the early trustees of the school.[18] There was, therefore, no question of Patrick hastily packing off his daughters to some terrible institution simply because it was cheap and he wanted them out from under his feet at home.

The story of the young Brontës at the Clergy Daughters' School has become inextricably entwined with that of the young Jane Eyre at Lowood School. Charlotte's account of the sufferings of Helen Burns and Jane at the hands of Mr Brocklehurst and Miss Scatcherd is written with such raw passion and such a burning sense of injustice that it is impossible not to identify with the girls against their persecutors. There is also no doubt that the novel was based upon Charlotte's real experiences at the Clergy Daughters' School, so it is easy to fall into the trap of believing that the fictional characters and place are accurate representations of the people at Cowan Bridge and the school itself.[19] This is to do less than justice to both the much-maligned Carus Wilson, who is seen as the villain of the piece, and Charlotte herself, who, while protesting the truth of her account, also clearly recognized that it was not impartial. As she told Mrs Gaskell several times,

she had not considered it necessary, in a work of fiction, to state every particular with the impartiality that might be required in a court of justice, nor to seek out motives, and make allowances for human feelings, as she might have done, if dispassionately analysing the conduct of those who had the superintendence of the institution.[20]

Lowood is seen through the eyes of the child suffering there, not the dispassionate adult. On the other hand, the novel clearly struck a chord in those who knew the Clergy Daughters' School. Charlotte herself wrote to William Smith Williams, her editor, less than three months after the novel had been published:

'Jane Eyre' has got down into Yorkshire; a copy has even penetrated into this neighbourhood: I saw an elderly clergyman reading it the other day, and had the satisfaction of hearing him exclaim 'Why – they have got — School, and Mr — here, I declare! and Miss — (naming the originals of Lowood, Mr. Brocklehurst and Miss Temple) He had known them all: I wondered whether he would recognize the portraits, and was gratified to find that he did and that moreover he pronounced them faithful and just – he said too that Mr — (Brocklehurst) 'deserved the chastisement he had got'.[21]

The unidentified clergyman was not alone in recognizing the school and Charlotte later confessed

she should not have written what she did of Lowood in *Jane Eyre*, if she had thought the place would have been so immediately identified with Cowan Bridge, although there was not a word in her account of the institution but what was true at the time when she knew it…[22]

Those who did not recognize the school from the novel were left in no doubt of its identity by Mrs Gaskell, who named names and laid the blame for Charlotte's future ill health and the deaths of her sisters squarely on the institution and its founder.[23] *The Life of Charlotte Brontë* therefore caused a furore, provoking not only legal action from Carus Wilson but also a flood of letters to the newspapers from former pupils. Their accounts, some supporting Mrs Gaskell, some emphatically contradicting her, help to build up a picture of what life was really like at the Clergy Daughters' School.

The school itself was a row of low stone cottages, built at right angles to and adjoining the main turnpike road which ran high over the fells of the Yorkshire Dales from Kendal, in the Lake District, to Leeds in the West Riding of Yorkshire. These cottages, which are still standing, were the teachers' quarters, the kitchen and dining room and some small bedrooms. At right angles to the cottages, facing the road, was an old bobbin mill which Carus Wilson had had converted into the schoolroom, with the main dormitory above. Opposite this wing of the school and backing on to the road, was a long, covered walkway where the girls could exercise in bad weather. The schoolroom, cottages and walkway formed three sides of a square; in the middle, stretching down to the river, were the small plots of garden which were tended by the pupils themselves.[24]

Although only the cottages now remain and the hamlet of Cowan Bridge has been engulfed by a modern industrial estate, it is still possible to feel the isolation of the school's position. It stands on the lower slopes of Leck Fell, from which vantage point it looks out over an immense vista of low-lying wooded hills and lush green river valleys. In the distance lies the rough moorland terrain of the fells, rising to the mountains of the southern Lake District to the west and Ingleborough, Whernside and Penyghent to the east. There are a few scattered sheep farms, the houses built like the Cowan Bridge cottages, with stone walls several feet thick and tiny windows to withstand the excesses of the weather. When it is not hidden in low-lying cloud and mist, pulverized by torrential rain or lost in the white-out of snow blizzards, the situation is magnificent. Its dramatic beauty could not have been lost on the young Brontës.

The regime at Cowan Bridge was undoubtedly strict and austere, but this was by no means unusual at the time. Woodhouse Grove, the academy founded in 1812 to provide a free education for the sons of Methodist ministers, is especially relevant as a comparison. It was founded for similar reasons to the Clergy Daughters' School and had the same aims in mind. Patrick had a thorough working knowledge of its arrangements, having served twice as an examiner and stayed there several times during his courtship of Maria.[25] Unlike the Clergy Daughters' School, however, Woodhouse Grove never produced a pupil who wrote a blazing indictment of the regime in one of the most popular novels of the day. Woodhouse Grove therefore maintained its reputation as an excellent academic institution providing a charitable service to the Methodist Church. It is a typical example of the better boarding schools of the day, including places as famous as Dr Arnold's Rugby or as ancient as Oundle.

The girls at Cowan Bridge had to wear a distinctive uniform, which Charlotte undoubtedly resented because it labelled them 'charity-children'.[26] On the other hand, they were required to be equipped with a plentiful supply of clothing: four day shifts (shirts) and three night shifts, three night caps, two pairs of stays, two flannel, one grey stuff (wool) and three white upper petticoats, two pairs of pockets, four pairs of white cotton stockings and three of black worsted, one nankeen spencer (a short jacket), four brown and two white holland pinafores, one short coloured dressing-gown and two pairs of shoes. In addition they had to bring gloves and a pair of pattens, which were wood and metal overshoes for outdoor wear. Their frocks, bonnets and cloaks were provided by the school at the cost of three pounds per child. In summer they wore plain straw cottage bonnets with white frocks on Sundays and nankeen (buff-coloured cotton) frocks on other days; in winter they had purple stuff frocks and purple cloaks.[27] The simple fact that they had to bring so many duplicate items suggests that the school was concerned about cleanliness, enabling them to have regular laundry days without depriving the girls of their clothing. This is not so ridiculous as it sounds. The boys at the 'cheap' Bowes school sometimes went four or five days without jackets or trousers when these were taken away to be mended, and even at Woodhouse Grove School, which was a model of its kind, the boys were only provided with one suit of clothes a year.[28]

Cowan Bridge was capable of taking up to seventy-two pupils, but when the Brontës arrived the school had only been open a few months and there was never anything like this number in their time. Maria and Elizabeth were only the seventeenth and eighteenth pupils to enter the school, and by the time Charlotte and Emily left on 1 June 1825, there were still only fifty-three pupils on the register. The ages of the pupils varied widely, the youngest on entry being six, the oldest twenty-two. Thirty of the forty-four pupils at the school when Emily came on 25 November 1824 were in the eight to fourteen bracket, including her own sisters. Emily, at nearly six and a half, was one of only three six-year-olds, who were clearly the babies of the school as there were no seven-year-olds; they appear to have been treated quite differently from the older pupils.[29] At eight, Charlotte would have been one of the youngest and smallest girls in the mainstream of the school – an obvious disadvantage in terms of the daily scramble for food and places next to the fire. Like Jane Eyre, however, Charlotte was fortunate in finding an older girl who took her under her wing. Perhaps surprisingly, given their closeness at home, this was not either of her elder sisters, but a seventeen-year-old named Mellany Hane. She came from Bedfordshire and, with her twenty-two-year-old sister, had entered the school exactly seven weeks after Charlotte; her fees were paid by the Clergy Orphan Society. Charlotte later told her father that Mellany had frequently defended her against the encroachments of the older girls.[30]

As was the normal practice at boarding schools, most of the girls slept two to a bed in the single large dormitory which ran the length of the upper floor over the schoolroom. If *Jane Eyre* is an accurate description of life at Cowan Bridge, the girls rose before dawn, dressed by rush-light, washed each morning in basins shared between six girls (when the water in the pitchers had not frozen overnight) and went downstairs to an hour and a half of prayers before being allowed to eat breakfast.[31] To young children straight from a loving home, where they had had a nursemaid to wait on them, this must have been a great hardship. However, it was not unusual – indeed, it was actually an improvement on common practice in many schools at this time. At one of the 'cheap' schools near Richmond in Yorkshire, there were at least three boys to one bed, and often as many as eight. Their sheets remained unchanged for two months, their under-blankets were never washed and the straw mattresses were ridden with fleas. Even at Woodhouse Grove in 1822 there were forty-eight beds in one dormitory, twenty in another and twelve in the third. The boys had to go down into the basement to wash in three long wooden troughs filled with clean water; there was always a scramble to get there as the first boys got the cleanest water and the first use of the towels.[32] The insistence on personal cleanliness at Cowan Bridge, which may have seemed onerous to the girls at the time, was actually prompted by a desire to safeguard their health.

The strictness of the daily regime at *Jane Eyre*'s Lowood has been called cruel in the extreme. After their dawn rising and prayers the girls had a quarter of an hour for a breakfast of porridge before lessons from nine till twelve. They then had a period of recreation and exercise in the garden before dinner. Lessons then recommenced and went on till five, when there was a short break for half a slice of bread and a small mug of coffee, followed by half an hour's recreation then study. The evening ended with a glass of water and a piece of oatcake before prayers and bed. On Sundays there was a variation in the routine. The girls had to walk two miles across the fields to their patron's church for the morning service. It was too far to return to school for a meal, so the girls had to eat a cold packed lunch in the church before enduring the afternoon service and the walk back again. Their reward was a whole – instead of the usual half – slice of bread with a scraping of butter on their return. The remainder of the evening was spent in repeating by heart the catechism and biblical texts and listening to a sermon read aloud by one of the teachers.[33]

This fictional account seems to be rooted in fact. For the first year or so of the school's existence, the girls attended Sunday services at Tunstall Church, where Carus Wilson was vicar. The church is two miles across the fields from Cowan Bridge and still has a room over the porch which is pointed out as the place where the girls ate their food between the services. The church is even now dark and gloomy inside and bone-chillingly cold as only damp, fifteenth-century churches can be.[34]

Remarking on the Cowan Bridge method of instilling religion into its girls, one of the Brontës' fellow pupils later wrote:

I trust I have ever been a firm advocate for making religion the groundwork of all education but the hours devoted to sermons, lectures scripture lessons &c &c were so unreasonably <u>long</u> at Cowan Bridge, that I feel they were calculated to hinder not promote the salvation of immortal souls.[35]

Certainly the young Jane Eyre seems to have spent more time thinking about her frozen limbs and her empty stomach than in learning the lessons of the Scriptures. Another Cowan Bridge pupil, who later died of consumption, was a more apt pupil and turned the religious tables on her teachers:

It was usual for each pupil to repeat on Sunday morning a text of her own choice; and one who had, I believe, been punished for stealing bread, repeated in her turn, the verse which declares that men do not despise a thief who steals bread to satisfy his hunger.[36]

Again, however, the regime at Cowan Bridge was no worse, and in some respects more lenient, than at other comparable schools. At Woodhouse Grove – and this in the days of John Fennell's headmastership – the boys rose daily at six, had a public prayer meeting from six-thirty to seven, then spent an hour in school at reading and exercises. This was followed by family prayer and breakfast, after which lessons began at nine and continued till twelve, or half past if music lessons were on the child's syllabus. An hour was then given over to dinner and exercise, followed by lessons from one-thirty to four-thirty. The next hour and a half was spent in preaching and reading, followed by two hours, from six till eight, of public prayer, ending with supper and family prayer before bed. At Woodhouse Grove there was a chapel on site, converted from the stables of the old house, so there was no long walk to worship on a Sunday. Instead, the boys spent virtually all day at their bibles. Private prayer, reading the Scriptures and preaching replaced their usual lessons and were simply added to the normal daily diet of prayer meetings.[37]

Nor was the discipline at the Clergy Daughters' School out of the ordinary. In Jane Eyre's Lowood, the punishments range from wearing badges for being untidy to beatings in front of the whole school. Seen through the eyes of the passionate Jane, these are terrible injustices and unwarranted cruelty, especially when inflicted on the gentle and patient Helen Burns. Once more, we find that these were standard practices in even the best schools. At Woodhouse Grove, one early governor would beat offenders on the bare flesh with a birch rod in front of the assembled pupils, having first ensured that he could not run away by 'horsing' him, putting him on the back of one of the biggest boys who held him firmly by the hands. Another slightly later, governor would indiscriminately cane twenty or thirty boys every Monday, without enquiring if they were guilty of any misdemeanour. Delinquents were forced to wear boards on their backs for several days at a time, which were printed in large letters with legends such as 'Guilty of lying' or 'Guilty of going out of bounds'. Even at Crofton Hall, the select academy for young ladies, offences as minor as impertinence or accidental breakages were punished with the public labelling of offenders and whipping.[38]

More than anything else, however, it was the account of the food in *Jane Eyre* and subsequently in *The Life of Charlotte Brontë* which roused most passion, largely because Mrs Gaskell blamed it for Charlotte's 'stunted' growth and the ill health which eventually killed her sisters. In *Jane Eyre*, the housekeeper was 'a woman after Mr Brocklehurst's own heart, made up of equal parts of whalebone and iron'. The breakfast porridge was regularly served up so burnt that it was inedible and dinner, 'redolent of rancid fat', was a mess of 'indifferent potatoes and strange shreds of rusty meat, mixed and cooked together'.[39] Unable to eat these disgusting main meals, the girls became so weak that half the school fell victim to a fever.

This account seems to reflect the genuine state of affairs. Charlotte herself told Mrs Gaskell that the food at Cowan Bridge was 'spoilt by the dirty carelessness of the cook, so that she and her sisters disliked their meals exceedingly'. She was so hungry, she said, that she would have been thankful for even a piece of bread, though unlike some of her contemporaries, Charlotte did not resort to stealing.[40] Another pupil and her sister, Elizabeth and Maria Gauntlett, who came from the south of England, were unable to stomach the north-country diet of oatmeal porridge and therefore went without breakfast for six months. When forced to eat it on one occasion,

Elizabeth vomited – and was promptly dosed with an emetic. The dinner Maria Gauntlett described as 'sufficient, but not good'.

Three days in the week it consisted of what the girls called Hot-pot or potato pie – pieces of meat, fat &c cut up & baked or boild with potatoes – the only vegetable ever seen – on two days there was salt beef, often ill-cured, on the other two days, fresh beef or veal – rarely if ever, mutton.[41]

The Carus Wilson lobby, led by Miss Andrews, a teacher who had also temporarily been superintendent of the school during the Brontë period, denied there had ever been a scarcity of food. 'The daily dinner consisted of meat, vegetables, and pudding, in abundance; the children were permitted and expected to ask for whatever they desired, and they were never limited.'[42] As Charlotte's husband and staunch defender pointed out, however,

what about the <u>cooking</u> that spoiled these provisions; boiled the puddings in unclean water; compounded the Saturday's nauseous mess from the fragments accumulated in a dirty larder during the week; and too often sent up the porridge, not merely burnt, but with offensive fragments of other substances discoverable in it![43]

Yet another Cowan Bridge girl of the Brontë period sent a horrific account to substantiate the accusations, pointing out that 'on first reading "Jane Eyre" several years ago I recognized immediately the picture there drawn and was far from considering it in any way exaggerated, in fact I thought at the time, and still think, the matter rather understated than otherwise'. She then went on to say:

The housekeeper was very dirty with the cooking and very unkind to the girls generally. I have frequently seen grease swim[m]ing on the milk and water we had for breakfast, in consequence of its having been boiled in a greasy copper and I perfectly remember having once been sent for a cup of tea for a teacher who was ill in bed, and no teaspoon being at hand the housekeeper stirred the tea with her finger she being engaged in cutting raw meat at the time. If space would allow I could give you scores of such instances as these which fell under my own observation and which after nearly twenty five years have elapsed dwell unpleasantly in my memory. Our food was almost always badly cooked, and besides that we certainly had not enough of it whatever may be said to the contrary.[44]

Charlotte herself had seen the doctor, who was soon to become Carus Wilson's brother-in-law, actually spit out a portion of food he had tasted. Even Miss Andrews had to confess that when the doctor was called in during the spring of 1825 to attend the girls smitten with 'low fever', he had spoken 'rather scornfully' of a baked rice pudding. Her protest that 'as the ingredients of this dish were chiefly rice, sugar, and milk, its effects could hardly have been so serious as have been affirmed' suggests that the teachers may not have been sympathetic to the girls' complaints about the food.[45]

If the skimmed milk used at the school was sour, it would have been difficult to detect until tasted, because it does not curdle or smell bad. There was no excuse for the dirty cooking utensils, however, or the slovenliness of the housekeeper. Unfortunately, Cowan Bridge does not appear to have been an isolated case; complaints about the food at Woodhouse Grove have a familiar ring about them. As late as the 1850s, one schoolboy complained:

Breakfast consisted of a thick slice of dry bread and about half a pint of skimmed milk, occasionally sour, and sometimes slightly warmed in winter. At dinner we generally had two courses; and supper, at six o'clock, was an exact repetition of breakfast … my stomach rebels at this moment at the thought of the rice, it was either boiled very dry (into 'snowballs') and then anointed with a thin unguent composed of treacle and warm water, or else baked in huge black tins, in which it looked as if it had been 'trodden under foot of men'. You had to eat it all up, or Mrs Farrar would probably give you a box on the ear, and stand over you till you did. I have many a time gone away from the table with food in my handkerchief to throw away, because, had I been forced to eat it, I should have been ill.[46]

As everyone, including Charlotte and Mrs Gaskell, was careful to point out, the filthy cook at Cowan Bridge was eventually dismissed and replaced by a clean and efficient woman, who produced a marked improvement in the food.

The school register supports Mrs Gaskell's claim that ill health was commonplace among the girls during the early years of the school, resulting in many being sent home. Of the fifty-three pupils there at the same time as the Brontës, one died at Cowan Bridge and eleven left school in ill health; six of them died soon after reaching home. There clearly was a particular problem in the first nine months of 1825, when twenty girls (including the four Brontës) were withdrawn from the school, nine of them in ill health.[47] Carus Wilson therefore lost more than a third of his pupils in only the second year of the Clergy Daughters' School's existence. Nor did the general state of health even start to improve until 1832 – the year the school relocated to Casterton – by which time another two, if not three, girls had actually died at Cowan Bridge and a further fifteen had left school in ill health, six of them to die.[48] Though it may seem horrendous today that any child should die of fever at school, in defence of Cowan Bridge it should be noted that epidemics and consequent fatalities were an unfortunate but ordinary fact of nineteenth-century boarding school life. Woodhouse Grove lost eleven boys in a period of about ten years and there were similarly fatal epidemics at Rugby, Rossall and other public schools of the day.[49]

All in all, therefore, the Brontës were unfortunate to be at the Clergy Daughters' School during its difficult early years. On the other hand, even then the school was no worse than many of its renowned and much-praised contemporaries and in certain instances it was actually better. Apart from the significant problem of the dirty housekeeper, there was an insistence on personal cleanliness, neatness and discipline which was not only necessary for the smooth and healthy running of the school but also inculcated the sort of personal habits that would commend themselves to the Brontës in later years.[50] There is no doubt that Charlotte endured great hardship there: her fastidious nature was revolted by the unavoidable evils of communal school life, she rebelled against the loss of freedom and she resented the feeling that she was a 'charity child'. What she could not forgive, however, was the fact that her two older sisters died as a direct result, as she saw it, of their own experience at the school.

Maria and Elizabeth Brontë arrived at the Clergy Daughters' School on 21 July 1824. They should have gone earlier, but because they were still delicate from having had whooping cough and measles in the spring, their entry was delayed. Patrick himself escorted his daughters the forty-five miles from Haworth to Cowan Bridge; they travelled by the daily coach from Leeds, which conveniently stopped at Keighley. He stayed overnight and dined at the same table as his children so that he was able to see for himself how the school was run; he was evidently satisfied as he returned home without comment.[51] Had there been the slightest hint of anything unusual or wrong he would undoubtedly have complained, as he was not the sort of person to allow such things to pass.

The girls were assessed by the superintendent, Miss Andrews, and their details entered into the school register. It was noted, for instance, that both were being paid for by Patrick himself, not by one of the charitable societies or by their godmothers. They had both been vaccinated and Maria had also had chicken pox. Their 'Acquirements on Entering' seem unimpressive. (It should be explained that 'ciphering' meant arithmetic, 'working' meant plain sewing and 'accomplishments' meant French, music and drawing.) Against Maria, aged ten, it was recorded:

Reads tolerably – Writes pretty well – Ciphers a little – Works very badly – Knows a little of Grammar, very little of Geography & History. Has made some progress in reading French but knows nothing of the language grammatically

Elizabeth, aged nine, fared even worse: 'Reads little – Writes pretty well – Ciphers none – Works very badly. Knows nothing of Grammar, Geography, History or Accomplishments'.[52] The apparently damning reports, which are often cited as evidence of Patrick's failure to educate his daughters, are actually almost identical to every other entry in the register, regardless of age or background.[53] There was obviously a motive to understate achievements on entry so that the school could take the credit for greater improvements. Many girls, even some of the oldest entrants who were in their late teens, did no better than the Brontës: Maria was exceptional in being able to read French at the age of ten, even if she could not parse it.

It is interesting to note that Patrick had a clear notion of his daughters' capabilities and future prospects. Maria, 'a girl of fine imagination and extra-ordinary talents', as even the teacher who is supposed to have persecuted her readily admitted, was to be educated for a governess. She therefore received lessons in French and drawing, for which Patrick had to pay an extra three pounds a year. Elizabeth, who possessed 'sound common sense' but was not as intellectual as her sisters, was clearly earmarked by Patrick to be the family housekeeper; she was the only one of his daughters not to be instructed in the 'accomplishments'.[54]

Life at the school at this time was probably not unpleasant. Both Maria and Elizabeth were used to being away from home, having already experi-enced the rigours of boarding school at Crofton Hall. There were only sixteen other girls there to begin with and, of these, at least two were already acquaintances, if not actual friends. Margaret Plummer, who had been at the school since 21 February, was the fourteen-year-old daughter of the Reverend Thomas Plummer, headmaster of the Free Grammar School at Keighley, who sometimes officiated for Patrick. She must have become a friend, as Maria gave her a needlecase she had made herself, suitably inscribed. Ten-year-old Harriet Jenkins, who had been there since 4 March, was the daughter of the Reverend David Jenkins, Patrick's fellow curate at Dewsbury, who had undertaken duty for him so often at Hartshead.[55]

On 10 August, just under three weeks after their own arrival, Maria and Elizabeth had a welcome visit from their father when he brought Charlotte, who was now well enough to join her sisters at the school. Patrick again stayed the night and dined with his daughters. At the end of September there was another visitor, Elizabeth Firth, now Mrs James Clarke Franks, who was on her wedding tour; she gave each of the girls 2/6d. before leaving.[56]

For Charlotte, the change in her circumstances was traumatic. It was the first time she had ever been away from home and she had no prospect of returning there for nearly a year: the only holidays were the customary five weeks in the summer. She could not even keep in regular contact with her father and the younger members of the family because letter writing was confined to once a quarter.[57] Even though her elder sisters were there it must have seemed like a perpetual banishment from the home and the family which meant so much to her. Her own entry in the school register noted that she had been vaccinated and that she had had whooping cough. Her acquirements on entering were listed as: 'Reads tolerably – Writes indiffer-ently – Ciphers a little and works neatly. Knows nothing of Grammar, Geography, History or Accomplishments'. To this was added an unusual and perceptive note: 'Altogether clever of her age but knows nothing sys-tematically'. Like her eldest sister, she was entered for the higher level of education which would train her to be a governess.[58]

Despite her own later recollection of herself as having a very quiet career, being 'plodding and industrious', and 'very grave', the entrance register assessment is backed up by Miss Andrews, who described her as

a very bright, clever, and happy little girl, a general favorite; to the best of my recollection she was never under disgrace, however slight; punishment she certainly did <u>not</u> experience while she was at Cowan Bridge.[59]

While their older sisters were settling into their new environment and, according to Miss Andrews, doing well,[60] the three younger Brontë children were still at home in the care of Aunt Branwell and Nancy and Sarah Garrs. Branwell was now seven, Emily just six and Anne four. They must have missed Maria, Elizabeth and Charlotte taking the lead in their study and play, but this was not the first time they had had to manage without the two eldest girls. Their ordinary routine was enlivened by two exciting incidents.

On Tuesday, 31 August 1824, Haworth was honoured by a rare visit from Edward Harcourt, the Archbishop of York. The reason for his visit was somewhat grim: he had come to consecrate a new piece of ground which was to be added to the then overflowing churchyard. An immense concourse of people gathered to watch the ceremony and, despite the fact that Harcourt had backed the vicar of Bradford against the trustees over Patrick's and Samuel Redhead's appointment to Haworth, 'the strictest order and decorum prevailed'. The three Brontë children must have had prime positions for viewing the ceremony and afterwards, to add to their excitement, the archbishop and some of his fellow clergy came back to the parsonage to 'partake of good English fare' prepared by a no doubt flustered Nancy Garrs.[61] To see in the flesh, in their own home, one of the two premier spiritual lords of the land, about whom they read constantly in the newspapers, must have been a great thrill for the impressionable children.

The second event was even more memorable and certainly more spectacular. Two days after the archbishop's visit, on Thursday, 2 September, at about six o'clock in the evening, the bog four miles up on the moor behind the parsonage at Crow Hill burst, causing a landslip and flooding. Patrick described what happened in a sermon he preached ten days later in Haworth Church:

As the day was exceedingly fine, I had sent my little children, who were indisposed, accompanied by the servants, to take an airing on the common, and as they stayed rather longer than I expected, I went to an upper chamber to look out for their return. The heavens over the moors were blackening fast. I heard muttering of distant thunder, and saw the frequent flashing of the lightning. Though, ten minutes before, there was scarcely a breath of air stirring; the gale freshened rapidly, and carried along with it clouds of dust and stubble; and, by this time, some large drops of rain, clearly announced an approaching heavy shower. My little family had escaped to a place of shelter, but I did not know it. I consequently watched every movement of the coming tempest with a painful degree of interest. The house was perfectly still. Under these circumstances, I heard a deep, distant explosion, something resembling, yet something differing from thunder, and I perceived a gentle tremour in the chamber in which I was standing, and in the glass of the window just before me, which, at the time, made an extra-ordinary impression on my mind; and which, I have no manner of doubt now, was the effect of an Earthquake at the place of eruption.[62]

The picture of the anxious father looking out for his children because they were late and then fearing dreadfully for their safety as he watched the storm develop should forever dispel any suggestion that Patrick was a cold and uncaring parent. What he did not say, but was later reported by Sarah Garrs' family, was that when he realized that his children were in actual danger, he set out in search of them. They had been caught in the full horror of the storm, 'and they were frightened, and hid themselves under Sarah's cloak, and Mr Bronte went in search of them and found them in a Porch ... terrified, and so was he till he found them'.[63] He then discovered just how close he had come to losing them. A seven-foot-high torrent of mud, peat and water had swept down the valley from Crow Hill towards Ponden. Fortunately, it was seen in time and someone gave the alarm, 'and thereby saved the lives of some children, who would otherwise have been swept away'.[64]

Once he had his beloved children safely back at home, Patrick had time to think over his experience. As an Evangelical, he was certain that the world would one day end in the apocalyptic style of the Revelation of St John. There was a general belief at the time, particularly in Evangelical circles, that the end of the world was imminent and Patrick's immediate response was probably that it was happening at that moment. When it became clear that it was not, he then realized that this was a solemn warning,

to turn sinners from the error of their ways, and as solemn forerunners of that last and greatest day, when the earth shall be burnt up – and the heavens shall pass away with a great noise – and the universal frame of nature shall tremble, and break, and dissolve.[65]

In his intense excitement, Patrick wrote to both the *Leeds Intelligencer* and the *Leeds Mercury* giving an account of the bog-burst, which he attributed to an earthquake, and 'improving' the event by pointing out its moral.[66] The day after the bog-burst, he had been up to Crow Hill to view the damage. One solid stone bridge had been swept away, two others had been breached, four or five mills had had their workings entirely clogged up, fields of corn, hedges and walls had been flattened in the deluge and some houses had been swamped. Two huge areas of moorland bog had sunk without trace, swept down along the valleys by the volume of water absorbed in the undrained peat in the heavy rainfall of the previous days. The effects were felt as far away as Leeds: 200 stone of perch and trout were taken out of the River Aire at Horsforth, poisoned, or rather suffocated, by the volume of peat, mud and detritus flowing from the bog-burst. Virtually the entire woollen industry in the area ground to a halt for several days as it was impossible to use the water because it was so filthy.[67]

Patrick's letters caused further consternation – not for the spiritual thoughts he had hoped to inspire, but for the more prosaic reason that, if an earthquake had caused an underground reservoir to open up, then the woollen trade might be permanently affected. A team of investigators from the *Leeds Mercury* joined the supposed 10,000 sightseers who came from all over Yorkshire to view the dramatic sight. They concluded that the bog-burst was the result of a water spout, not an earthquake.[68]

Patrick obstinately refused to change his opinion. The day the *Leeds Mercury* published its report, Patrick wrote another letter in great haste to the paper, defending his claim that it was an earthquake. The electrical discharge of the lightning, combined with the intense heat of the day, had caused the eruption, he believed.[69] The next day he delivered a powerful sermon to his parishioners on an appropriate text from the ninety-seventh psalm: 'His lightnings enlightened the world; the earth saw, and trembled. The hills melted like wax at the presence of the Lord, at the presence of the Lord of the whole earth.' He explained the physical causes of earthquakes and some of the reasons why God sent them. Finally, he declared:

We have just seen something of the mighty power of God: he has unsheathed his sword, and brandished it over our heads, but still the blow is suspended in mercy – it has not yet fallen upon us. As well might he have shaken and sunk all Haworth, as those parts of the uninhabited moors on which the bolts of his vengeance have fallen. Be thankful that you are spared. – Despise not this merciful, but monitory voice of Divine Wisdom.[70]

Patrick's warnings were not treated with uniform respect. A correspondent from Haworth, signing himself 'JPJ', wrote to the newspapers:

That it may have alarmed our worthy minister, terrified the clerk, electrified our grave-digger, and have been a subject for all women in the parish both now, and probably as long as they live after, to talk about, are truths, according to hearsay, that I am not now about to dispute: but that any reasonable person should construe a simple thing like [this] into an earthquake, or an irruption, or what not, is really preposterous.[71]

This cynic had not dared to publish in a local newspaper, however, but in the *Liverpool Mercury*, reflecting the widespread interest and controversy that Patrick's letters had sparked off. This justified Patrick in having the sermon printed for wider circulation by Thomas Inkersley, the Bradford printer and publisher, who printed some of Patrick's earlier works.[72] At the same time he rewrote the sermon in simpler terminology, added a verse description of the bog-burst and published it as a reward book for the higher classes in Sunday schools. A major shift of emphasis, dictated by the fact that the poem was intended for children, was that the poem ended, not with the threat of the end of the world, but with the promise of the Second Coming.

> But, O! what heavenly joy will then impart
> Its strongest impulse to the pious heart,
> When the great Judge will loud approving say –
> 'Come with me, to the heaven of heavens, away!'
> Whilst the seraphic choirs strike all their strings,
> And sing *Hosannah* to the King of kings!
> And the new earth and heavens wide echo round,
> The sweet, triumphal, loud, immortal sound![73]

If the bog-burst caused such excitement and trauma to Patrick, one wonders what effect it had on his children, particularly as the apocalyptic interpretations could not have been lost on them. None of their writings for this period are extant, however, and only one poem by Emily, written twelve years later, even approaches the experience,[74] so we cannot tell what they felt about their own brush with death.

As interest in the bog-burst gradually faded, Emily's approaching departure for the Clergy Daughters' School became the most urgent problem. On 10 November, Patrick wrote to his banker, Mr Mariner, a worsted manufacturer of Keighley:

I take this opportunity to give you notice that in the course of a fortnight it is my intention to draw about twenty pounds out of your savings bank: I am going to send another of my little girls to school, which at the first will cost me some little – but in the end I shall not loose [sic] – as I now keep two servants but am only to keep one elderly woman now, who, when my other little girl is at school – will be able to wait I think on my remaining children and myself.[75]

This letter suggests that Patrick believed he had at last found a satisfactory solution to his family's future. With four daughters established at school and knowing that a place would be available for Anne when she was old enough, he had only himself and his son to consider. There was no one better qualified than himself to teach Branwell, either academically or morally; with a servant to look after the running of the house, they would be provided with everything they needed. Aunt Branwell would be free to return home to Penzance and the Garrs girls could be dismissed. Nancy had been engaged for some time and would be glad to be able to leave and marry her young man who, by coincidence, was also called Pat. When one of his daughters told Patrick this, he came especially into the kitchen to speak to her,

and said, in his pleasant way 'Why, Nancy, is it true that you are going to marry a Pat?' 'Yes, sir,' I replied, 'it is, and if he only proves one-tenth as kind a husband as you have been, I shall think myself very happy in having made a Pat my choice.'[76]

Sarah, the nursemaid, was less fortunately placed. Patrick took it upon himself to provide her with new employment and, at his recommendation, she found a post travelling for two years with a wealthy widow and her daughter. Unfortunately, her mother objected so strongly to the plan that Sarah was obliged to give it up and had to return to her old home in Bradford. She became apprenticed to a dressmaker and, in 1829, married William Newsome with whom she later emigrated to the United States. Both the Garrs girls left with the affection of the whole Brontë family and they, in their turn, remained devoted to them. Sarah even took with her to America a lock of hair from each member of the family, ranging in colour from the pale gold of Anne to the dark brown of her sister Maria.[77]

In place of Nancy and Sarah Garrs, Patrick engaged a fifty-three-year-old widow from Haworth, Tabitha Aykroyd, who was to remain with the family for the rest of her life and, in the process, outlived all but Patrick and Charlotte. For the moment, however, she was an unknown quantity and Emily, leaving home for the first time, had to say a final farewell to the two servant girls who had been a part of her life for as long as she could remember.

On 25 November 1824 Patrick took Emily to Cowan Bridge to join her sisters.[78] For the third time in five months, he had the opportunity to observe the running of the school and to see how his daughters were faring. Maria may, by this stage, have had a slight cough but then his children were always susceptible to colds and coughs. None of them can have been so unhappy that they complained to their father as he would not have left without making some reference to this to the superintendent. He returned home unaware of the tragedy that was brewing.

The six-year-old Emily, 'a darling child' and 'little petted Em', as Miss Evans, the new superintendent of the school, called her, was an immediate favourite. Even her entry in the admissions register reflected her position as 'quite the pet nursling of the school'. It simply said 'Reads very prettily & Works a little'. Though it was obvious she did not have the other acquirements, she nevertheless escaped the usual damning litany 'Knows nothing of Grammar, Geography or History and nothing of Accomplishments'. Like all three of her sisters she had had whooping cough, but there is no record of her having been vaccinated; this may simply have been an omission on the part of the school, as Patrick is unlikely to have had some and not all of his children vaccinated. Like Maria and Charlotte, she was to be educated as a governess and Patrick paid the extra fees necessary.[79]

As the weather grew colder with the approach of winter, the hardships of the pupils intensified. Wearing only pattens over their thin shoes, instead of changing into boots, they regularly suffered wet feet, particularly in the trail across the fields to and from church each Sunday. Charlotte, in the voice of Jane Eyre, described the 'torture of thrusting the swelled, raw and stiff toes into my shoes' and another pupil at the school ascribed her own, near fatal, illness at Cowan Bridge to having had to sit in church all Sunday with wet feet.[80] In December, Maria began to show signs of being consumptive, but her father was not informed. This was not an isolated case. The former pupil who complained of her wet feet later wrote:

I suffered so severely from the treatment that I was never in the schoolroom the last three months I was there until about a week before I left and was considered to be far gone in a consumption. My Mother (whose only child I was) was never informed of my illness and I might certainly have died there without her being informed of it had not a severe illness of her own caused her hastily to summon me home. She was so much shocked at my appearance that she refused to allow me to return although pressed to do so. I was some time before my constitution recovered the blow it then received.[81]

Charlotte herself suggested that her own sister, Maria, was the original of Helen Burns in *Jane Eyre*. She later told her editor, William Smith Williams:

You are right in having faith in the reality of Helen Burns's character: she was real enough: I have exaggerated nothing there: I abstained from recording much that I remember respecting her, lest the narrative should sound incredible. Knowing this, I could not but smile at the quiet, self-complacent dogmatism with which one of the journals lays it down that 'such creatures as Helen Burns are very beautiful but very untrue'.[82]

If Helen Burns was a literal portrait of Maria Brontë, Charlotte's eldest sister was truly a model of fortitude. Patient and long-suffering in her illness, Helen bore the casual cruelties inflicted on her by Miss Scatcherd in a spirit of martyrdom. When Miss Scatcherd made her wear the 'slattern' or 'untidy' badge or whipped her for not having clean fingernails, she refused to see this as persecution, admitting that she was indeed careless, untidy and forgetful. Her punishment was therefore just and it was her duty to suffer the consequences of her misdemeanours; 'it is weak and silly to say you *cannot bear* what it is your fate to be required to bear', Helen told the rebellious Jane Eyre.[83]

One genuine incident which occurred between Maria Brontë and Miss Andrews seems typical of the sort of treatment the fictional teacher meted out to her pupil, though it did not appear in *Jane Eyre*. There was a day when Maria was so ill that the doctor had applied a blister to her side. In great pain and feeling very ill, she wished to remain in bed but, fearing Miss Andrews' wrath, had got up and slowly begun to dress. Before she could do so, Miss Andrews had pounced on her, pulled her into the centre of the room, regardless of her blistered side, and loudly abused her for her dirty and untidy habits. Begging some of the more indignant girls to keep calm, Maria had slowly continued to dress, gone downstairs and was then punished for being late. Mrs Gaskell's unnamed informant, who had witnessed the whole scene, 'spoke as if she saw it yet, and her whole face flashed out undying indignation'.[84]

It seems unfortunate, to say the least, that Miss Evans did not put a stop to Miss Andrews' persecutions. The superintendent was highly thought of by all the girls at the school, including Charlotte, but 'she had her energies severely tasked and I believe did not at all times know the manner in which we were treated'. Nor did the Reverend William Carus Wilson intervene, though later pupils expressed gratitude for the personal interest and concern he showed over their state of health.[85]

Perhaps this was just as well, for his form of religion might have distressed the dying child. Like her father, Carus Wilson was an Evangelical. Unlike Patrick, he was also a Calvinist[86] and believed in predestination: that only a small band of 'the elect' had been chosen by God for salvation and that, even before they were born, most men were condemned to eternal damnation. Such a doctrine left no place for the individual to earn a place in heaven through genuine piety, repentance or the performance of good works. The emphasis of his religion was on sin and the certainty of punishment, not on conversion or the hope of salvation. Nor did he feel any necessity to soften or lighten this message for the children in his care.

Like Patrick, he wrote many pieces for schoolchildren. His *Child's First Tales*, published in 1836, was a typical example. The stories were all deliberately written in monosyllables and were short, usually less than two pages long, so that they were easy for children to read. Each one had an accompanying woodcut but the illustrations were of unpleasant subjects like dead children, dead mothers and executions. A typical story was 'Child in a pet'.

Do look at that bad child. She is in the pet. She would have her own way. Oh! how cross she looks. And oh! what a sad tale have I to tell you of her. She was in such a rage, that all at once God struck her dead. She fell down on the floor, and died. No time to pray. No time to call on God to save her poor soul. She left this world in the midst of her sin. And oh! where do you think she is now? I do not like to think of it. But we know that bad girls go to hell when they die, as well as bad men. I do not think that this poor girl's rage is now at an end, though she is in hell. She is in a rage with her-self. She is in a rage to think of her bad deeds here on earth.

My child, take care of such sins. Pray that you may be meek and low-ly in heart, like your dear Lord and Sa-vi-our.[87]

Carus Wilson's most famous and most widely read book was *The Children's Friend*, which was published locally each month and was in use at the Clergy Daughters' School. A familiar Evangelical mix of missionary tales and exemplary stories, much like John Buckworth's *Cottage Magazine*, the issue of December 1826 contains the story of the death of Sarah Bicker, who had died at Cowan Bridge on 28 September, aged eleven. She had been at the school since 21 February 1824 and was therefore well known to all the Brontës. She died of an extremely painful inflammation of the bowels but her faith in Christ never faltered. When asked if she should like to die, she answered 'Not yet' because 'I should wish to have time to repent, and be a better child.' Carus Wilson ended his account of her elevating death-scene with the comment:

I bless God that he has taken from us the child of whose salvation we have the best hope and may her death be the means of rousing many of her school-fellows to seek the Lord while he may be found.[88]

Other books at the school reveal the same attitude towards and pre-occupation with infant mortality. In the little library at Cowan Bridge, for instance, was a newly purchased copy of Richard Baxter's *Dying Thoughts, with Meditations from Owen*; a seventeenth-century Puritan divine, Baxter's works cannot have made easy reading for young schoolgirls.[89] Even the prize books awarded at the school were morbid in the extreme. *Hymns for Infant Minds*, awarded to Isabella Turner 'for attention to Spelling' in the second class on 19 December 1826, sounds innocent enough. The frontispiece, however, was a woodcut illustration of a little girl weeping over her mother's grave in the churchyard with the caption, 'Oh! if she would but come again, I think I'd vex her so no more.'[90] Though death, and death in childhood, was an ever-present threat at the time, Carus Wilson and his school seem to have shared an extreme and even unhealthy obsession with it.

Fortunately for her, Maria was spared Carus Wilson's deathbed ministrations. By the middle of February 1825 it was obvious that she was seriously ill. Patrick was at last informed of his daughter's condition. He came immediately to Cowan Bridge and, when he saw the state of his eldest daughter, he took her straight back home.[91] The distress and confusion which Maria's sudden removal from the school must have caused her sisters was compounded by the fact that they were never to see her again. For just over eleven weeks she lingered on in the final stages of consumption, nursed, as her mother had been nursed such a short time before, by Patrick and Aunt Branwell. Comforted by her father's more benevolent faith, 'She exhibited during her illness many symptoms of a heart under divine influence.'[92] On Friday, 6 May 1825, Maria died. She was eleven years old. Six days later, appropriately enough on Ascension Day, she was buried in the vault under Haworth Church, next to her mother. William Morgan again came to officiate, burying the child he had baptized eleven years before. Patrick, Aunt Branwell, Branwell and Anne were able to make their last farewells and attend the funeral but Elizabeth, Charlotte and Emily, still at school, were denied the comfort of observing these last ceremonies.[93]

While Patrick was nursing one dying child, he was presumably unaware that Elizabeth, too, was sickening. Her own fatal symptoms may have been masked by the general outbreak of 'low fever', a sort of typhus probably caused by the insanitary conditions and practices in the kitchen. So many girls went down with it that the doctor was called in. He recommended the removal of the girls from the seat of infection and all those who were fit enough for the journey were sent to Silverdale, a pleasant sandy cove on the Lancashire coast near Morecambe, where Carus Wilson had a holiday house.[94] Among those too ill to benefit from the sea air was Elizabeth Brontë. On 31 May, the day her sisters, Charlotte and Emily, travelled with the other girls to Silverdale, Elizabeth was quietly put in the charge of a confidential servant, Mrs Hardacre, and sent home. They travelled by public coach to Keighley and then by private gig to Haworth.[95] For the second time in just over three months, Charlotte and Emily could only watch helplessly as a beloved elder sister was taken away from them.

Patrick probably had no forewarning that Elizabeth was returning home, for he would undoubtedly have insisted on his younger daughters being sent home with her. One can only guess at his feelings when a second daughter was brought home to die. Seeing the signs of consumption on Elizabeth's face, his thoughts immediately flew to his remaining daughters still at the school. Perhaps they, too, were in danger. The very next day he went straight to Silverdale and removed both Charlotte and Emily from the school.[96] They were never to go back. Their joy at escaping from the hardships of the Clergy Daughters' School and returning to their beloved home would be tempered by the knowledge that it was a home without Maria and soon to be without Elizabeth. All Carus Wilson's dire predictions and stories of the deaths of small children must have sprung to mind as they watched Elizabeth die. Perhaps fortunately for them all, the process was not prolonged. She was already far gone in consumption and on Tuesday, 15 June 1825, at the age of ten, she followed her sister to an early grave. William Morgan returned yet again to Haworth on 18 June to perform the melancholy task of burying the third member of his friend's family.[97]

The deaths of Maria and Elizabeth had a traumatic effect on the remaining children. It was not simply that they lost two of their sisters, but that they lost their two *eldest* sisters. The younger children had naturally looked to them for the leadership and support which elder children provide. In their case this role had taken on even greater importance because Maria, and to a lesser extent Elizabeth, had helped to fill the void caused by their mother's death so early in their lives. Once again they had been deprived of the maternal figure in the family.

The profound nature of their loss was to be reflected in all their later work. Motherless children and orphans were a feature not only of their juvenile writings but also of their novels. All Charlotte's heroines, from Frances Henri in her first novel, *The Professor,* to the schoolgirl in *Emma,* her last, unfinished work, were orphans. The absence of maternal love is a major factor in determining not only their future prospects but also their sense of loneliness and deprivation. In *Shirley*, this was of particular significance as the discovery of her long-lost mother is the crucial factor in Caroline's recovery from an apparently hopeless illness. 'My own mamma,' Caroline says, 'who belongs to me, and to whom I belong! I am a rich girl now: I have something I can love well, and not be afraid of loving.'[98]

In *Wuthering Heights*, Emily too seems to have created an orphan world. Virtually every child, including Heathcliff, Catherine and Hindley in the first generation and Linton, the young Catherine and Hareton in the second, loses at least one parent, usually the mother. Though the effect is less crucial on the development of the personalities of her characters than in Charlotte's novels, the motherless state of so many of them must be significant. The relationship between the two cousins, Linton and Catherine, particularly, is essentially that of a mother surrogate and her child.[99]

By contrast, Anne, the youngest child, who was also closest to her aunt, creates the most normal families. Agnes Grey has a happy home with father, mother and sister and, unlike Jane Eyre, only goes to be a governess at her own insistence. Helen Graham, the heroine of *The Tenant of Wildfell Hall*, has an ordinary home life with her uncle and aunt even though her parents are apparently dead.[100] Her suitor, Gilbert Markham, is fatherless, but not from childhood, and enjoys a robust and normal family life with his mother, brother and sister. Anne, who was only five when Maria and Elizabeth died, seems to have been the least affected, if only because she still had older sisters to look up to in Charlotte and Emily.

Though Branwell never published a novel, the loss of his sisters made a deep and abiding impression on him. For him there was no confusion between the loss of his mother and his two eldest sisters. It was the deaths of Maria and Elizabeth that made most impact. Ten years later, writing to the editor of *Blackwood's Magazine*, Branwell described the delight he had taken in the magazine as a child and quoted from memory the following lines:

'Long Long long ago seems the time when we danced hand in hand with our golden haired Sister whom all that looked on loved long long long ago the day on which she died. That hour so far more dreadful than any hour that now can darken us on this earth – When She her coffin and that velvet pall descended – and descended – Slowly – slowly – into the horrid clay and we were born[e] deathlike and wishing to die out of the churchyard that < for > from that moment we thought we could never enter more.' Passages like these Sir, (and when that last was written my Sister died) Passages like these, read then and remembered now afford feelings which I repeat I cannot describe.[101]

In a long poem he wrote about the same time, he described the death of a beloved sister and her funeral solemnities. While it is dangerous to consider the poem autobiographical, as it owed more to *Blackwood's* than to the deaths of Maria and Elizabeth, there are certain graphic and haunting lines which suggest that Branwell was drawing on actual experience. When lifted to see the dead child in her coffin, for instance,

> And, to this moment, I can feel
> The voiceless gasp – the sickening chill –
> With which I hid my whitened face

The funeral, too, is described in terms redolent of personal experience:

> All else seems blank – the mourning march,
> The proud parade of woe,
> The passage 'neath the churchyard arch,
> The crowd that met the show.
> My place or thoughts amid the train
> I strive to recollect, in vain –
> I could not think or see:
> I cared not whither I was borne:
> And only felt that death had torn
> My Caroline from me...
> Long years have never worn away
> The unnatural strangeness of that day[102]

But it was Charlotte who was the most vulnerable and probably the most affected. She had witnessed her sisters' sufferings at the Clergy Daughters' School and she was closest to them in age. She must have felt a bewildering sense of divine injustice in the deaths of sisters she considered so eminently superior to herself. More importantly, having always been one of the 'little ones', her sisters' deaths promoted her to the role of eldest child. It was a responsibility she was always to feel and her own sense of inadequacy as to the way she filled that role may help to explain her subsequent veneration for Maria. A later schoolfriend described how

She used to speak of her two elder sisters, Maria and Elizabeth, who died at Cowan Bridge. I used to believe them to have been wonders of talent and kindness. She told me, early one morning, that she had just been dreaming: she had been told that she was wanted in the drawing-room, and it was Maria and Elizabeth ... she wished she had not dreamed, for it did not go on nicely; they were changed; they had forgotten what they used to care for. They were very fashionably dressed, and began criticizing the room, etc.[103]

As late as 1849, Charlotte still refused to believe that a fellow pupil at Cowan Bridge might remember her, rather than her sisters:

none of them can possibly remember me. They might remember my eldest sister, Maria; her prematurely developed and remarkable intellect, as well as the mildness, wisdom, and fortitude of her character, <u>might</u> have left an indelible impression on some observant mind amongst her companions. My second sister, Elizabeth, too, may perhaps be remembered, but I cannot conceive that I left a trace behind me.[104]

It was not Charlotte, but Elizabeth, who left least impression on her contemporaries at the school. Obviously less brilliant than Maria, Charlotte or Emily, as Patrick had recognized when entering her for the lower level of education, she shared their outstanding moral fortitude. The only incident concerning her which anyone brought to mind was the way she suffered 'with exemplary patience' a cut on the head so severe that she had to spend several days and nights in the superintendent's room.[105]

On 23 September 1825, Patrick received the final settlement of his account with the Clergy Daughters' School in a long letter of condolence from the superintendent, Miss Evans. She had been ill herself, she told him, and the school had still not recovered fully from the outbreak of typhus in the spring:

though cast down we have not been in despair but enabled to look beyond the dark valley of the shadow of death to that glorious life and immortality which are brought to light by the Gospel. May we but be enabled to hold on and to hold out to the end and the tears which now so often dim our eyes by reason of the sorrow which saddens our hearts, shall all be wiped away then when there shall be no more death neither sorrow nor crying neither shall there be any more pain seeing the former things are passed away.[106]

Miss Evans had no inkling of the resentment Charlotte harboured against the school, for there was no connection in her mind between Cowan Bridge and the deaths of Maria and Elizabeth. She ended her letter, 'Our circle unite in kind respects to yourself with love to dear Charlotte and little petted Em.' Patrick was to be credited with £2 14s. 2d. One year of education at the Clergy Daughters' School had cost him £80 2s. 2d., nearly half his annual income.[107] It had also cost him two beloved daughters.

Chapter Six

⌁

SCRIBBLEMANIA

For Charlotte and Emily the summer of 1825 was a welcome return to Haworth and the family. While all the household mourned Maria and Elizabeth, there was at least the consolation of grief shared and of certainty in believing that they had gone to a better world. These would be months of physical and mental recovery from the sufferings of Cowan Bridge, watched over by Patrick, Aunt Branwell, who now had to give up all hope of returning to Penzance, and Tabby Aykroyd. With good food, daily walks in the fresh air of the moors and the re-establishment of a routine of lessons with their father and aunt, the children would gradually return to something like normality.

No doubt Patrick kept his anxiety about their finances to himself but, despite the brave words to his friends, his position and future were not as secure as they might have seemed. On 25 August, some two months after bringing his daughters home from Cowan Bridge, he wrote once more to the governors of Queen Anne's Bounty. He had looked at the deeds for the parsonage and found that the trustees were not bound in law to let the incumbent live there but could rent it out or otherwise do as they liked with it. Even his salary was uncertain as the trustees had ample excuses for withholding it, in part or as a whole, 'however circumspectly he may walk'. Worst of all, Patrick was personally responsible for paying for any repairs or maintenance work carried out on the Church lands: this he had recently found out to his cost, when the trustees presented him with several bills 'to a very large amount, rendering the salary inadequate to support my family, even with the most rigorous economy'.[1] Despite being urged to pursue his case by Henry Heap, the vicar of Bradford, Patrick once again came up against an immovable block. Whatever the real merits of the case, the fact that his annual salary was valued by his archbishop at over £150 made it impossible for the governors of Queen Anne's Bounty to intervene. Patrick had to struggle on and economize wherever possible.[2]

He had founded an Auxiliary Bible Society in Haworth in 1823 and on 19 September 1825 it held its second anniversary meeting in a packed church. Patrick, as President, took the chair and delivered a 'very animated speech', followed by twelve others, including ones by the Reverends Henry Heap and William Morgan from Bradford and Moses Saunders, minister of the newly built Baptist chapel at Hall Green at the bottom of Main Street. The Haworth Auxiliary had raised the amazing sum of £350 and distributed eighty copies of the Bible during the previous year. One newspaper report stated:

We never saw speakers more in earnest, nor any Meeting of the kind more attentive. And we venture to predict, that Haworth which has been so long blessed with the light of the gospel, will increase its labours in diffusing that light among the benighted inhabitants of the universe.[3]

A few weeks later, Patrick, supported by his two secretaries, James Greenwood, a manufacturer, and Thomas Andrew, the surgeon, wrote to the Parent Society to express deep concern about the inclusion of the Apocrypha in the Bibles issued by the society. This practice was

pregnant with the seeds of Discord, and if not speedily, and forever abandoned, will counteract, whatever partial good it may do, by a <u>vast</u> preponderance of evil; and will <u>entirely</u> dissolve that spell, which can exist, only as long as the Inspired Books <u>alone</u>, shall be distributed.[4]

At the end of November 1825, under orders from the vicar of Bradford, every minister in the parish had to present to his congregation for signature a requisition to Mr Fontayne Wilson, requesting him to stand as a candidate for Parliament in the next election because he was opposed to Roman Catholic Emancipation. Most ministers made the requisition available for signature in the vestry after the service but some of the more zealous, including William Morgan, introduced and read it during divine service.[5] As Patrick was in favour of partial reform by 1829, he is unlikely to have adopted such a provocative stance.

Politics were also intruding into the working life of his parishioners. At the end of September, fifty-six mill owners and manufacturers in Keighley followed Bradford's example and declared that they would dismiss any combers or weavers who joined or supported trade unions. The effect of this, combined with poor trade and the collapse of a number of banks throughout the country, was to increase unemployment dramatically. At the end of December the failure of a major manufacturer in Keighley, Butterworths, had such a terrible knock-on effect that many small businesses in the area also collapsed. A committee for the relief of the suffering poor was set up, but a public subscription in the district failed because the distress was too general, among masters as well as the men.[6] By May, out of 6,691 factory operatives surveyed in Keighley, 4,524 were completely unemployed and the remainder were only working a three-day week. Two months later, six mills were shut altogether, and the poor rates had risen to sixteen shillings in the pound. The situation in Haworth, though unrecorded, must have been similar.[7]

The poverty and unemployment were to continue throughout the year, adding considerably to Patrick's workload because, as the incumbent, he was partly responsible for organizing the raising of poor rates and their distribution. In addition, he did what he could to help individuals. In a judgement of Solomon, for instance, and 'owing to the hardness of the times, and very nearly an equality of merit', he appointed not one but two parish clerks who were to officiate in alternate months and share the dues and Easter collection between them. Both men could therefore look forward to a certain, if reduced, income for the forthcoming year. This was a highly unorthodox settlement of what had obviously been a long-running and acrimonious dispute. With quiet humour, Patrick observed, 'I think I see Mr Taylor <u>smile</u> whilst he reads it.'[8] Patrick's charities were, of necessity, small-scale and unobtrusive. He did not have the financial status to enable him to perform grand gestures, like Theodore Dury who annually treated 500 Sunday-school children and their teachers to a fête and tea at the vicarage at Keighley.[9] The two men were friends, however, and committed to the same ends. Later in the year Theodore Dury preached a sermon at Haworth on behalf of the Sunday school and Patrick reciprocated by addressing the Keighley Auxiliary Bible Society. On the latter occasion Patrick had the dubious honour of sharing the platform with William Carus Wilson, the first time he had met the man since the deaths of Maria and Elizabeth. One can only guess at his thoughts, particularly as by this time he must have been made aware of Charlotte's views on the Clergy Daughters' School. It may perhaps be significant that he does not appear to have attended the following year, when Carus Wilson was once again one of the principal speakers.[10]

Distress in the manufacturing districts continued unabated. Violent electrical storms throughout the summer, which had set fire to many of the surrounding moorlands, gave way to a harsh winter. On 9 December, Patrick buried Timothy Feather, the schoolmaster at Heptonstall, who had got lost on the moors returning from a visit to his father; his body had been discovered in trackless snow seven miles out of his way.[11] Typhus fever was virulent in the neighbourhood: one of Patrick's parishioners, Benjamin Burwin of Far Oxenhope, lost his wife, four daughters, three sons and a grandson in under three months. Conditions were so bad that Haworth merited its own separate grant of £100 for the relief of the poor in February 1827.[12] It was to be three full months after that before the woollen trade began to revive.

On 12 July 1827, William Wilberforce arrived in Keighley for a four-day visit to Theodore Dury. The presence of 'The African's Friend' was marked by a pink flag flying from the church tower and peals of bells.[13] Given his friendship with Theodore Dury and his own connections with Wilberforce, it seems more than likely that Patrick was one of those fortunate enough to be invited to Keighley vicarage to meet the great man. The Sunday after Wilberforce's departure, the vicar of Bradford came to Haworth and preached on behalf of the Sunday school to an overflowing church. In scenes reminiscent of Grimshaw's days, several hundred people were said to have crowded the churchyard in an attempt to hear his sermon.[14] The Brontë children were doubtless prominent in the congregation. A great deal more exciting for them was the balloon flight from Keighley to Colne of Mr Green, 'the celebrated aeronaut'. Huge crowds gathered in Keighley to watch his ascent, but the Brontës would have enjoyed a perfect view of the intrepid balloonist from their own home or the moors behind it. The event clearly made an impression on them, as balloon flights feature frequently in the juvenilia.[15]

Throughout the terrible years of distress and the reprieve that followed, life at Haworth Parsonage continued in its daily routine of lessons, walks and play. From the books that we know the Brontës possessed, it is possible to deduce something of the education Patrick offered his children. Standard educational texts of the day which they owned included Thomas Salmon's *New Geographical and Historical Grammar*, Oliver Goldsmith's four-volume *History of England* condensed into one volume, Rollin's *History* and J. Goldsmith's *A Grammar of General Geography*.[16] The last is heavily annotated throughout by all the Brontë children and obviously provided inspiration for the maps and place names of the fictional kingdoms they were soon to invent. There was also a copy of Hannah More's *Moral Sketches*, purchased by Patrick while he was at Thornton, which was required reading in all literate households at the time.[17] Three other favourite books of the period were in their little library: a 1743 edition of John Bunyan's *Pilgrim's Progress*, a 1791 edition of the hymn writer Isaac Watts' *Doctrine of the Passions* and a 1797 edition of John Milton's *Paradise Lost*. All three were to be seminal influences on the young Brontës and a constant source of quotation, just as they had been for their father.[18]

The fact that so many of the Brontës' books were second-hand reflects not only the high price of books at the time but also their own lack of funds to spend on such extravagances. Patrick still had his classical texts from Cambridge – his Homer, Horace, Lemprière's *Bibliotheca Classica* – and his copy of Walter Scott's *Lay of the Last Minstrel*. Maria had a small collection of books from Penzance, which had survived the shipwreck of her box just before her marriage. Among these were her copy of Thomas à Kempis' *Extract of the Christian's Pattern*, a well-thumbed edition of *The Seasons* by the poet James Thomson, and *The Union Dictionary*, a compilation of the dictionaries of Johnson, Sheridan and Walker.[19]

Undoubtedly, too, there must have been books belonging to Aunt Branwell. She was, like her sister, something of a blue-stocking, 'lively and intelligent' and more than capable of holding her own against Patrick in an argument. It is tempting to see her collection depicted in that of Caroline Helstone's Aunt Mary in Charlotte's novel, *Shirley*:

some venerable *Lady's Magazines*, that had once performed a sea-voyage with their owner, and undergone a storm, and whose pages were stained with salt water; some mad, *Methodist Magazines*, full of miracles and apparitions, of preternatural warnings, ominous dreams, and frenzied fanaticism.[20]

It is likely that Aunt Branwell possessed copies of both magazines. The 1799 edition of the *Methodist Magazine*, for example, contained a memoir of the life of John Kingston who had married her own sister, Jane, in 1800. The *Lady's Magazines* could well have survived Maria's shipwreck and Charlotte certainly read them as a child:

I recollect when I was a child getting hold of some; antiquated odd volumes and reading them by stealth with the most exquisite pleasure. You give a correct description of the patient Grizzles of those days – my Aunt was one of them and to this day she thinks the tales of the Lady's Magazine infinitely superior to any trash of Modern Literature. So do I for I read them in childhood and childhood has a very strong faculty of admiration but a very weak one of Criticism.[21]

In addition to the wilder side of religion, there were any number of the basic religious texts. In all his teaching and writing Patrick had emphasized the importance of reading the Bible and his children knew their Bibles inside out. In addition to their father's copies, the children each had their own Bible and Prayer Book. 13 February 1827 must have been a day worth com-

memorating, for Emily was given a Bible 'by her affectionate Father' and
Anne was given a Book of Common Prayer by her godmother, Fanny
Outhwaite. Anne had already been given a Bible by her other godmother,
Elizabeth Firth, in October 1823, when her father and Elizabeth Firth
'renewed their acquaintance' after Patrick's disastrous proposal. Charlotte's
New Testament was a gift from the Morgans. Jane Morgan, Maria's cousin,
died in the last week of September 1827 and was buried in her father's
churchyard at Cross-stone. Patrick was too busy in Haworth to stay with
the bereaved family at Cross-stone, but he must have attended the funeral
and visited again two days later, when William Morgan presented him with
his wife's copy of the Prayer Book in Greek as a memorial of her.[22]

Patrick was to use the various copies of the Bible and Prayer Books as a
tool for instructing his children in the classics. Their familiarity would make
it easier to learn the new language in which they were written. In his
vernacular copy of the New Testament, for instance, Branwell marked his
progress in translating to and from the Latin text.[23] Though it is generally
supposed that only Branwell received instruction in the classics from his
father, there is evidence to suggest that his sisters shared at least some of his
lessons. When William Makepeace Thackeray read *Jane Eyre* in 1847, he
commented, 'Who the author can be I can't guess; if a woman she knows
her language better than most ladies do, or has had a classical education.'[24]

While it was commonplace for ladies to speak and write the modern
languages, it was rare to find one who was familiar with Latin, Greek and
Ancient History. Unlike Branwell, Charlotte never quotes from the Greek
and only rarely uses Latin tags, but her work is littered with classical
references, which suggest more than a passing acquaintance with the writings of the ancient world. At the very least she was thoroughly familiar
with the translations from the classics, like John Dryden's English verse
version of the works of Virgil, which was already at the parsonage at this
time.[25] Emily and Anne, too, were familiar with classical language as well as
literature. Emily was adept enough at Latin to be able to translate and make
notes on Virgil's *Aeneid* and Anne bought a copy of a Latin text book
in November 1843, presumably as an aid to teaching her pupil, Edmund
Robinson.[26]

The books available to the young Brontës at home were to be the core
of their reading and were to shape their ideas for the future. In addition,
they had access to books outside the parsonage, as their astonishingly
wide range of reading makes clear. Much weight has been given to
two particular sources, the library of the Keighley Mechanics' Institute
and the private library at Ponden Hall, near Stanbury, which belonged to
the Heaton family who were among the trustees of Haworth Church
lands.[27] It is often suggested that the young Brontës spent hours browsing
through these libraries and that this was where they saw the periodicals,

biographies, travel books and works of fiction which had such an impact on their intellectual development.

The role of both libraries had been greatly over-emphasized; indeed, it has not been proven in either case that the Brontës ever used them at all, let alone on a regular basis. The Keighley Mechanics' Institute was founded in 1825, setting up a programme of fortnightly lectures, which included practical demonstrations of chemistry and talks on subjects as diverse as physical astronomy and the wheel and axle. Though primarily intended for the working classes, the lectures were open to ladies and gentlemen, so Patrick and his children had the opportunity to improve their scientific knowledge cheaply and conveniently. This was not the case with the library, however, which would not have been available to them until Patrick became a member in 1833. Though he kept up his membership for ten years, his children clearly had access to books beyond those in their own home for many years long before this. The rules of the Institute, too, were not calculated to encourage family usage; only two books could be borrowed at one time if the member lived more than a mile from Keighley and only sons (not daughters) could accompany their father to the library.[28] The collection was in any case heavily biased towards the sciences and though it contained many books which the Brontës read and enjoyed, their interests were not particularly served by it.

The same is true of the library at Ponden Hall. Again it contained books which the Brontës undoubtedly read, but the collection as a whole was dominated by eighteenth-century literature. This was the period with which the Brontës were least familiar and with which they had least affinity. Among the books mentioned in the Brontës' juvenile writings are many which were at Ponden Hall: Samuel Johnson's *Lives of the Poets*, Gilbert White's *Natural History of Selborne*, Alexander Pope's translation of the *Iliad*, the poetry of Burns, Moore and Butler. These were, however, standard works which any good library would have possessed and there is virtually no overlap between the rest of the collection at Ponden Hall and the Brontës' known sources.[29] In all probability they did borrow books occasionally, but the simple fact that a library existed at Ponden Hall does not mean that it was regularly used by the Heatons' literary-minded neighbours.

The most likely source of books was, in fact, the circulating libraries in Keighley. Mrs Gaskell herself said that the Brontës had used one, though the idea has been dismissed by later biographers on the grounds that Charlotte told her friend Ellen Nussey 'we do not subscribe to a circulating library in Haworth'.[30] This does not, however, preclude the idea that they used one in Keighley, for which there is strong circumstantial evidence. Mrs Milligan, wife of the Keighley surgeon, was from Haworth herself and claimed that the sisters called in at her house on their way 'to change books at a Keighley Circulating Library'.[31] The son of the Haworth tailor also said that 'he frequently saw the sisters trudging down to Keighley'; he added that Charlotte procured her books, periodicals and reviews from a lending library kept by Mr Hudson, a bookseller in the High Street, who also published the short-lived *Keighley and Haworth Argus*.[32] Another newspaper connection, Robert Aked, the printer of *The Keighley Visitor*, Haworth Church hymnsheets and, among other things, two of Patrick's pamphlets, also kept a circulating library, established as early as 1822.[33] Although there are no extant catalogues for their collections, they were undoubtedly similar to other circulating libraries of the time and offered the usual diet of history, biography and travel books with a leavening of fiction, poetry and periodicals. A library of this kind, with its emphasis on the arts and on nineteenth-century publications, would seem to be a more likely source for the Brontës' reading.

Of all the books and periodicals that the Brontë children read, one truly did change their lives. This was *Blackwood's Magazine*, a monthly journal published from 1817 by William Blackwood of Edinburgh. They borrowed it from a Mr Driver, who may have been the Reverend Jonas Driver who lived in Haworth and died at the end of December 1831.[34] A potent miscellany of satire and comment on contemporary politics and literature, *Blackwood's Magazine* formed the tastes and fed the interests of the Brontës for many years. They absorbed its Tory politics, made its heroes, from the Duke of Wellington to Lord Byron, into their own heroes and copied its serio-comic style. Its tremendously long and detailed reviews of new works of biography, history, travel, politics and, to a lesser extent, fiction, gave them access to books and knowledge which were otherwise beyond their reach, especially as extensive quotations were given from the books under review. The soon-to-be thirteen-year-old Charlotte described it as

the most able periodical there is the editor is Mr Christopher North an old man 74 years of age the 1st of April is his Birthday his company are Timothy Ticklar Morgan Odoherty Macrabin Mordecai Mullion [?Warrell] and James Hogg a < 12 Mar > man of most extraordinary genius a Scottish Sheppherd.[35]

The fictitious names she quotes were, with the real James Hogg, a poet also known as the Ettrick Shepherd, members of an informal drinking club whose rumbustious imaginary conversations at Ambrose's Tavern, Elysium' were recorded under the title *Noctes Ambrosianae*. These were tremendously influential on the young Brontës and were responsible for the conversational style and tavern setting of many of their own writings. No doubt the *Noctes* lent themselves to being performed as plays by the children too, or at least read aloud in character. One can imagine their delight when a version of their own unusual surname appeared in the character of O'Bronte, even if it was only as the Ettrick Shepherd's dog.[36]

In addition to these rather precocious tastes, the young Brontës enjoyed the usual children's books of the time. They had copies of Aesop's *Fables*, for example, and the *Arabian Nights' Entertainment*, both of which provided inspiration for their early writings. They would also seem to have had Dyche's *Spelling Book*, which recounted familiar fables for children, and another immensely influential model for future writing, an edition of Sir Walter Scott's *Tales of a Grandfather*, which was a particularly thoughtful present to her nephew and nieces from Aunt Branwell.[37]

They had several books illustrated with the charming woodcuts of Thomas Bewick, including his most famous *History of British Birds*, but also, in all probability, his editions of *Fables* for children. Bewick's vignettes are delightful scenes of human and animal life but they have an additional appeal for observant children in that they often contain irrelevant but crudely funny details, such as a man relieving himself behind a hedge. The simple lines but great detail of the vignettes were endlessly copied by the young Brontës with varying degrees of success.[38] As most of the Brontë drawings seem to date from 1829, it seems likely that this was the year that they began to have art lessons from John Bradley of Keighley. Bradley was one of the founder members and first secretary of the Keighley Mechanics' Institute, later becoming the architect of its new building. He was also a well-known local artist and William Dearden, a schoolmaster of Keighley, remembered meeting Patrick, Charlotte and Branwell 'many times' in Bradley's studio, 'where they hung in close-gazing inspection and silent admiration over some fresh production of the artist's genius'. Perhaps it was Bradley who encouraged the young Brontës to copy Bewick's vignettes and, recognizing Branwell's particular talent, urged him to more difficult work, such as copying Hogarth's portrait of the *Idle Apprentices*.[39]

Keighley not only provided the children with an art master but also a music master, Abraham Sunderland, the parish organist. It is even possible that Branwell had an academic tutor in the Reverend Thomas Plummer, headmaster of the Free Grammar School at Keighley.[40] Despite his straitened circumstances, Patrick did everything he could to promote the education and talents of his children.

It would be wrong to create the impression that life for the young Brontës was all work and no play. They had plenty of toys. They had painted wooden alphabet blocks, a wooden lion, a toy barrel and a set of ninepins. For the girls there were wax-headed dolls with hats and frocks, a wickerwork doll's cradle, a children's tea service and even a tiny working model of an iron in brass.[41] Branwell, too, acquired at least three sets of wooden soldiers from Bradford, Keighley and Leeds, two sets of Turkish musicians from Keighley and Halifax and one set of Indians from Haworth in only four years.[42]

Like any normal children, the Brontës played with their toys, gave them characters and invented stories around them. Their wide range of reading, especially in *Blackwood's Magazine*, gave them endless scope for adventure and a constant stimulus to their imaginations. Just as they had done with Maria and Elizabeth in the days before Cowan Bridge, they made up plays and acted them out with unrestrained enthusiasm. Despite the best efforts of Aunt Branwell to instil some decorum into her female charges, the Brontës, like any children of their age, were full of energy and their games were noisy and exciting. Such was their glee in these performances that on one occasion their servant, Tabby Aykroyd, was driven to take refuge in her nephew's house, declaring

'William! yah mun gooa up to Mr Brontë's, for aw'm sure yon childer's all gooin mad, and aw darn't stop 'ith hause ony longer wi' 'em; an' aw'll stay here woll yah come back!' When the nephew reached the parsonage, 'the childer set up a great crack o' laughin',' at the wonderful joke they had perpetrated on faithful Tabby.[43]

Their childhood plays were about to take on a new dimension, for they were now old enough and literate enough to be able to record their adventures in writing. In 1829, Charlotte looked back over the most important plays they had invented.

Our plays < whe > were established Young Men June < 1827 > 1826 Our fellows July 1827 islanders December 1827. those are our thre[e] great plays that are not kept secret. Emily's and my Bed play's where Established the 1st December 1827 and the other March 182< 7 >8 – Bed plays < are > mean< s > secret plays they are very nice ones < the young men > all our plays are very strange ones there nature I need not write on paper for I think I shall always remember them. the young man play took its rise from some wooden soldier's Branwell had Our fellows from Esops fable < and are > and the Islanders … from several events whi[c]h happened.[44]

The Young Men plays would develop into the complex, imaginary world of Glasstown and, ultimately, Angria. The bed plays, which have given rise to much prurient speculation, were simply secret because they excluded Branwell and Anne, not because they had any sexual element. Charlotte and Emily shared a bed, as was commonplace at the time and a necessity in the cramped conditions at the parsonage. Perhaps inevitably, they invented plays together to while away the hours of darkness and probably, if Emily and Anne's later partnership is anything to go by, their characters were feminine rather than the soldiers and politicians who dominated the daytime plays.

We know more about the play of the islanders, as Charlotte later wrote a graphic account of their origin.

The play of the Islanders was formed in December 1827 in the following maner. One night about the time when the cold sleet and < ? > \dreary/ fogs of November are succeeded by the snow storms & high peircing nightwinds of confirmed < ? > winter we where all sitting round < by a > the warm blazing kitchen fire having just concluded a quarel with Taby concerning the propriety \of/ lighting a candle from which she came of victorious no candles having been produced a long pause suceeded which was at last broken by B saying in a lazy maner I dont know what to do this was reechoed by E & A

T   wha ya may go t'bed

B   Id rather do anything [than] that

& C   Your so glum tonight T < well > supose we had each an Island.

B   if we had I would choose the Island of Man

C   & I would choose Isle of Wight

E   the Isle of Arran for me

A   & mine should be Guernsey

C   the D[uke] of Wellington should be my cheif man

B   Her[r]ies should be mine.

E   Walter \Scott/ should be mine

A   I should have Benti[n]ck

here our conversation was interupted by < the > to us dismal sound of the clock striking 7 & we where sumoned of to bed. the next day we added several others to our list of names till we had got allmost all the cheif men in the Kingdom.[45]

The 'Tales of the Islanders' went on for several years and were chronicled by Charlotte in four volumes, but eventually they were absorbed into the plays of the Young Men.[46]

Only one story is extant from Our Fellows, Branwell's 'History of the Rebellion in My Fellows', which he wrote in 1828, when he was eleven. Written on music paper, it begins, 'Good man was A Rascal and did want to Raise a Rebellion' and tells the story of events in the autumn of 1827. The play was set in Lorraine, which was ruled by Branwell's character, Boaster, and follows the rebellion, besieging at Loos and defeat in battle of Good Man, Charlotte's character. After sending embassies to 'Charlotte's Country' and negotiating a peace, Boaster 'began to fortify my country I built c[h]ur-ches castles and other publick Buildings in abundance'. The fact that the children enacted the parts of their characters is quite clear; the story even includes a letter addressed to 'little Branwell' by Charlotte as Good Man, declaring war on him.[47]

All the elements of the Brontës' juvenile writings are already present in this story: battles, rebellions and politics were to be their staple diet, reflect-ing not only their origins in the toy soldiers but also Branwell's dominant role in the plays. The story also presaged future efforts in form as well as subject, for it was written in a hand-made little book, less than thirteen centimetres square. At first it was probably the fact that paper was expensive and in short supply that persuaded the young Brontës to write their stories in such tiny books, which they made themselves from scraps of paper, sewn into covers made from odd bits of sugar bags, parcel wrappings and wallpaper. The handwriting was proportionately tiny and, as the children grew older and more skilful, they developed a minuscule hand, designed to look like bookprint, which allowed them to write many more words to the page. The writing cannot be read easily without a magnifying glass, but as all the young Brontës were shortsighted, this would not have been so much of a problem to them. The tiny hand also had the advantage of being illegible to their father and aunt, so the children enjoyed the delicious thrill of knowing that the contents of the little books were a secret shared only among themselves.

Looking at the apparently painstakingly written pages and the hundreds of thousands of words they contain, it is easy to fall into the same trap as Mrs Gaskell and assume that the Brontë children's interests were 'of a sedentary and intellectual nature'. The popular image is of young children with a compulsion to write, pouring out precocious and mature literary works at an age when most children can barely form their letters.[48] This is only a very small part of the story and, indeed, in some ways a major distortion of the truth.

The invention of fantasy kingdoms and the chronicling of imaginary adventures in little books was not unique to the Brontës. At the age of seven, their exact contemporary, John Ruskin, wrote over fifty pages of a little book, measuring only fifteen by ten centimetres, in a minuscule print similarly modelled on book print. Like the Brontës, his own reading, in his case the *Scientific Dialogues* of Joyce and the dramatic poem *Manfred* by Byron, provided the inspiration for his stories and poems.[49] Equally literate, though less eminent than Ruskin, were the four Winkworth children, who were growing up in Manchester at about the same time as the Brontës. They, too, were highly imaginative and, because they were allowed very few works of fiction to read, they drew their inspiration from reading travelogues and histories. Every game they played had an associated story behind it. They took to dividing up the realms of Nature among themselves and developing stories round their own special possessions. 'Thus each of the children had a Continent and a kingdom of Natural History, each choosing their representative beast as "king" of the animals.'[50] The young Catherine Winkworth, who was later to become a friend of Charlotte Brontë, also kept a personal journal which was written in minute printed characters.[51] For whatever reason, bright children at this period were drawn to writing little books and inventing fictitious kingdoms.

It is easy also to over-emphasize the maturity of the young Brontës by drawing attention to the complexity of their childhood writings, the elaborate and exotic descriptive passages, the wide range of references and the rich vocabulary used. Less often mentioned is the highly imitative nature of much of the writing, in both style and subject matter. Their slap-dash writing, appalling spelling and non-existent punctuation well into their late teenage years is usually glossed over,[52] as is the frequent immaturity of thought and characterization. These elements in the juvenilia do not detract from the Brontës' achievement in producing such a volume of literature at so early an age, but they do extensively undermine the view that they were born novelists.

The Brontës were unique in their total absorption in the fantasy worlds they had created – an involvement that was at times to bring them into conflict with the real world. Equally unique is the fact that the play element continued to be an important part of the creative process even into adulthood. As late as 1845, when they were in their middle twenties, Emily and Anne whiled away a train journey by pretending to be Royalist prisoners escaping from Gondal.[53]

The play origin of the books and the mixing of fact and fiction is perhaps best illustrated by the story of the Young Men, also known as the Twelves, which gradually came to dominate the children's imaginations. Both Charlotte and Branwell recorded their origin. On 5 June 1826,

papa bought Branwell some soldiers at Leeds when papa came home it was night and we where in Bed so next morning Branwell came to our Door with a Box of soldiers Emily and I jumped out of Bed and I snat[c]hed up one and exclaimed this is the Duke of Wellington it shall be mine‼ \Auther/ when I said this \Athur/ Emily likewise took one and said it should be hers when Anne came down she took one also. Mine was the prettiest of the whole and perfect in every part Emilys was a Grave Looking ferllow we called him Gravey Anne's was a queer litle thing very much like herself. he was called waiting Boy Branwell chose Bonaparte[54]

The children invented a previous history for their soldiers, which was recorded by Branwell in his 'History of the Young Men'. The Twelves were a brave band of Englishmen who had sailed from England, fought against and slaughtered the Dutch on Ascension Island and then landed in the kingdom of Ashantee on the coast of Africa. While exploring the interior they were seized by

an Immense and terreble monster his head touched the clouds was encircled with a red and fiery Halo his nostrils flashed forth flames and < smo > smoke and he was enveloped in dim misty and indefinable robe[55]

The monster, as Branwell explained in a footnote, turned out to be the redheaded and nightgown-clad Branwell himself, bringing the soldiers to show his sisters on that morning of 5 June.

the tallest of the 3 new monsters seized Arthur Wellesly the next seized E W Parry and the least seized J Ross For a long time they continued looking at them in silence which however was broken by The monster who brought them < their > there he saying 'Know you then that I give into your protection but not for your own these mortals whom you hold in your hands' ... 'I am the cheif Genius Brannii < the > with me there are 3 others she wellesly who protects you is named Tallii she who protects Parry is named Emmii she who protects Ross is called Annii'[56]

Branwell's own soldier, Bonaparte, was also called Sneaky; later he developed into Rogue and ultimately into Branwell's alter ego, Northangerland. Emily's Gravey swiftly became Sir William Edward Parry, the Arctic explorer who had just returned from his third expedition to find the North-West Passage. Anne's oddly named Waiting Boy similarly turned into the more charismatic Sir James Clarke Ross, who had accompanied Parry on his expeditions. Both explorers had featured prominently in *Blackwood's Magazine*.[57] Charlotte, already obsessive about her hero, the Duke of Wellington, named her soldier after him. He was to feature as 'her man' in most of the plays, regardless of their origin, and her fixation with him as a fictional character did not really end until he was superseded by his more malleable sons, the fictional Arthur and Charles Wellesley.

Blackwood's Magazine provided not only the characters of many of the Young Men but also the setting for the plays. In 1819 it had printed an eighteen-page review of T. Edward Bowditch's *Mission from Cape Coast Castle to Ashantee; with a statistical account of that kingdom, and geographical notices of the other parts of the interior of Africa*. The Brontës placed their Young Men on the west coast of Africa in the kingdom of Ashantee and they adopted not only its capital, Coomassie, but also at least two of its Ashantee kings, Sai TooToo and Sai Quamina, as their enemies.[58] The rivers Gambia and Niger flowed through their imaginary land, which was divided up into a confederacy of states, each belonging to one of the soldiers of each child: Wellingtonsland, Sneakysland, Parrysland and Rossesland. A number of islands just off the coast belonged to other soldiers, Monkeysland and Stumpsland playing the most prominent role. The lands, their populations and their characteristics were faithfully recorded not only in stories but also in maps and censuses.[59]

Each state had its own capital, called a Glasstown, and at the mouth of the Gambia was the Great Glasstown itself. Under Branwell's classical influence it was translated into Verdopolis and under Charlotte's French influence it became a hybrid, Verreopolis. Whatever its name, the city was a heady mixture of London, Paris and Babylon. Dominated by the Tower of All Nations, which was inspired by the biblical Tower of Babel, the Great Glasstown had all the excitement and bustle of a great metropolis. Public buildings on the scale of John Martin's biblical paintings vied with mills drawn from the Brontës' own experience. The city had its fashionable aristocratic society, like the London of which they read in the newspapers, and its low life haunting the inns in the manner of pre-revolutionary France. All life was here depicted, arts, learning, politics, fashionable and unfashionable scandal, thrown together in a potent brew that could never be matched in reality.

Branwell's fictional interpretation of real events in 'The History of the Young Men' is indicative of the Brontës' whole approach to the plays. The battles were played out for real in the garden or on the moors, where the toy soldiers could shoot down their enemies with cannon and wash them away by damming the streams. The parsonage cellars, with their peeling walls and atmospheric darkness, could be turned into dungeons for political prisoners or cells for punishing naughty schoolchildren.[60] The enthusiasm, amounting to violence, with which the children played with the Twelves is reflected in the fate of the toy soldiers themselves. During the year his sisters were away at Cowan Bridge, Branwell 'Maimed Lost burnt or destroyed' two dozen soldiers. Of the Twelves themselves, bought in June 1826, only two or three lasted until 1830, when Branwell wrote their history, and the 'Ashantees', a set of ninepins, fared even worse.[61] The children even invented an ancient language for their heroes, 'the old young men tongue', which they reproduced phonetically in their stories. It appears to have been Yorkshire dialect spoken out loud while holding the nose.[62]

Real events impinged on the fictional world. The king of the Young Men, Frederick Guelph, Duke of York, was allowed to be killed in battle because 'at the time we let this battle take place (ie in the beggining of AD 1827) The real Duke of York died of a mortification'. The arrival of a party of Peninsular War veterans in Ashantee, under the leadership of the Duke of Wellington, was caused by Branwell's purchase of a new set of Turkish Musicians in Halifax in 1827 who had to be given a role in the plays. Even more dramatically, the children themselves sometimes appeared in the stories, either as Genii intervening to save their Young Men from a nasty fate or even to restore them to life,[63] or in their own persons. We have already seen how 'little Branwell' and Charlotte appeared alongside Boaster and Good Man in 'The History of the Rebellion in My Fellows'. In Charlotte's first volume of 'Tales of the Islanders', the fictional aristocratic pupils of the Islanders' school are kept in order by Branwell who has 'a large black club with which he thumps the children upon ocasion and that most unmercifully'; the children would be tortured without detection in the school's dungeons 'if it was not that I keep the key of the dungeon & Emily keeps the key of the cell's'.[64]

So real were their imaginary characters and worlds to the young Brontës that the two frequently became confused. Emily, writing one of her occasional diary papers in November 1834, places equal emphasis on both; she moves from describing the practicalities of daily life to her imaginary world of Gondal as if there is no discernible difference between the two: 'papa opened the parlour Door and < said B > gave Branwell a Letter saying here Branwell read this and show it to your Aunt and Charlotte – The Gondals are < disc > discovering the interior of Gaaldine Sally mosley is washing in the back Kitchin'.[65]

An even more graphic demonstration of this is given in Charlotte's second volume of 'Tales of the Islanders'. Having described how a school had been established by the Islanders, Charlotte suddenly breaks off – just as the young Brontës clearly broke off from their play – distracted by the burning issue of Roman Catholic Emancipation.

O those < times from > 3 months from the time of the Kings speech to the end! nobody could think speak or write on anything but the catholic question and the Duke of Wellington or Mr Peel I remember the < ? >day when the Intelligence extraordinary came with Mr Peels speech in it containing the terms on which the catholics were to be let in with what eagerness papa tore off the cover & how we all gathered round him & with what breathless anxiety we listend as one by one they were disclosed & explained & argued upon so ably & so well & then when it was all out how aunt said she thought it was excellent & that the catholics [could] do no harm with such good security. I remember also the doubts as to wether it would pass into the house of Lord & the prophecys that it would not & when the paper came which was to decide the question the anxiety was almost dreadful with which we listened to the whole affair the opening of the < L > doors the hush the Royal Dukes in theire robes & the Great Duke in green sash & waistcoat the rising of all the peeresses when he rose the reading of his speech papa saying that his words were like precious gold & lastly the majority one to 4 in favour of the bill. but this is a digression...[66]

The passions aroused in the children by the possibility of Roman Catholic Emancipation, which would give Catholics the right to sit in Parliament, hold civil office and vote, providing they met the necessary property qualifications, was inspired in them by their father. Patrick had already written three letters to the *Leeds Intelligencer* on the subject, which were published in as many weeks, between 15 January and 5 February 1829. The letters, calmly reasoned and remarkably liberal in attitude, belie his popular image as a rabid Tory. His stance was completely out of line with that of his contemporaries and friends on the Evangelical wing of the Church: Hammond Roberson and William Morgan, for instance, were violently opposed to any concessions to the Catholics.[67] So unusual was Patrick's advocacy of emancipation, especially in a Tory newspaper, that the editor felt obliged to point out that he was not a subversive or a Radical. 'This much is due, from us to Mr Bronte to declare – that, whatever his speculative opinions, he has, *to our knowledge*, been always at his post, as a practical supporter of Church and State.'[68] It must have taken some courage to come forward publicly and, under his own name, declare his support for emancipation, particularly as, being an Irishman, he was an easy target for charges of suspect loyalty.

Like the opponents of emancipation, Patrick believed that no Catholic oath of loyalty to the state could be trusted because the Pope had the power to release his subjects from their obligations. He also took it for granted that a Catholic state was an evil to be avoided at all costs. Where he differed from his friends was in believing that Catholics, like Dissenters, should have civil rights, providing that the Protestant establishment was secured by allowing the Protestant monarch or legislature to remove Catholics from 'all places of trust or influence' if danger threatened. Speaking with the authority of one who had witnessed the last bloody Irish rebellion of 1798, Patrick declared:

we cannot continue as we now are, even for a few years longer, without the manifest danger of a general convulsion, that might shock the whole empire to its centre, and dissever for ever Ireland from Great Britain.[69]

In his second letter, he reiterated his views and defended his own attachment to the establishment.

I am in no way changed in reference to this mighty subject. A warm and true, but liberal friend to Church and State, I still am, and, I trust, ever will be. – But I would not suffer prejudice to mislead me, nor error to warp my judgement, or turn it aside from the path of justice and truth.[70]

In his last letter, he emphasized the pragmatism of offering Catholics some measure of emancipation as an antidote to the sort of extremism, embodied in the Roman Catholic Association, which could only lead to popular violence. Again, however, he pointed out that, 'without the safest securities, it would be rash, it would be hazardous in the extreme, to permit Roman Catholics to have any share in our Legislation'.[71] Given Patrick's unpopular but publicly stated views, it is easy to see why his children took such a fervent interest in the subject and to understand their relief in seeing emancipation pass through Parliament with the safeguards their father deemed necessary.

At almost the same time, Patrick was also writing to the newspapers on another favourite subject of his: the severity of the criminal code. In a letter to the *Leeds Mercury*, written on 22 December 1828 but not published till 10 January 1829, he offered support to the paper's attempt to start a campaign for liberalization. Patrick now took one stage further the views he had expressed in *The Maid of Killarney*. It was not only morally wrong to make no differentiation between stealing a sheep and murdering a fellow human, by hanging a man for either crime:

Shame and guilt rest on the heads of those who enacted such laws, and of those who connive at them, or willingly endure their continuance. Nor can they be innocent who execute them. The counsel who argues against the criminal is not innocent – the jury that convict, and the judge who delivers the fatal sentence, are not innocent – the reckless wretch that ties the fatal noose is not innocent. On the bench, on the jury-box, on the snowy ermine, on the fatal platform, there is a bloody stain, which no fancied duty of submission to the higher powers, can ever wash away.[72]

Patrick's sudden outburst into print at the beginning of 1829 was reflected in an explosion of literary activity in his children. There are only three extant little books for the preceding years,[73] but there are at least eighteen for 1829 alone. While, to some extent, this may be because the Brontës kept only the pieces they considered worth preserving, it also demonstrates the more conscious creation of literary works rather than simple records of what had happened in their plays. Though the extant works are all by Branwell and Charlotte, the dominant pair in the plays, it is inconceivable that Emily and Anne, already nearly eleven and nine, did not have their own plays and books. These, like all their later prose books in the Gondal sagas, appear to have been lost or destroyed.

In January 1829, Branwell launched the first issue of 'Branwell's Blackwood's Magazine'. It was, as its name declared, an outright imitation of *Blackwood's Magazine* and, although Branwell staked his claim to having founded it in its very title, Charlotte was almost certainly a contributor right from the start. The first issue, its cover made from an advertisement for *The Life of John Wesley* and Thomas à Kempis' *Imitation of Christ*, began with a short account of gigantic mythical fish. It is headed 'Natural History O Dear', which suggests that it originated in the play of the 'O Dears', giant men based on characters from Aesop's *Fables* inhabiting islands.[74] It is followed by a poetry section which contains a seven-line adaptation for the Americans of the National Anthem, urging them to abolish slavery and end their disputes with Britain. Beneath it, Branwell has copied out a comment from Charlotte in her Young Men character of Captain Tree: 'this was sung at the < Young Men > our oratiorio and was much approved CT'.[75] Charlotte, too, seems to be responsible for the next short piece, a letter addressed to Branwell in the old tongue of the Young Men, signed by 'Good', Good Man being her character in Our Fellows. 'Bany do ought not to – Punit de Doung moan< s > for having rebelled agains[t] do—for dhey did deir Duty – Good – '.[76] Finally, the little magazine ends with 'Travels No 1', an unfinished account of a voyage across the South Atlantic.

This tiny magazine, only five and a half by three and a half centimetres, written in the special book print with – it has to be remembered – a quill pen, set the pattern for the forthcoming monthly issues which were to appear regularly for the next two years. Most of them took only a couple of days to write, so they were often written several months before the supposed date of issue, and they followed closely the genuine *Blackwood's Magazine* format of prose tales, reviews of books and pictures and poetry. Branwell wrote the magazines for the first six months, contributing most of the material himself under a variety of pseudonyms, including Captain John Bud, the historian of Glasstown and later Angria, and Young Soult, the poet based on the real Marshal Soult, one of Napoleon's commanders. Sometimes, like a real editor, he reproduced works by 'other authors', that is, Charlotte. The June issue of 1829, for example, contains Branwell's transcript of her short story 'The Enfant'.[77] Another innovation was Branwell's own version of *Noctes Ambrosianae*, the series first published in *Blackwood's Magazine* in March 1822 and still appearing in 1829. Branwell's 'Nights' were set in Bravey's Inn in

Glasstown and the participants included some of the characters associated with each child, suggesting that the conversations may have been 'played out' first by the children and then recorded. After six months of 'editing' his 'Blackwood's Magazine', Branwell decided enough was enough and it was time to go on to pastures new. In a concluding address to his July 1829 issue, Branwell announced:

We have hitherto conducted this Magazine we hope to the satisfaction of most. (No one can please all) but as we are conducting a Newspaper which requires all the time and attention we can spare from ot[h]er employiments we hav[e] fouund it expedient to relenquish the editorship of this Magazine but we recommend our readers t[o] be to the new Editor as they were to me the new one is < Cha > the Chief Genius Charlotte she wil[l] conduct it in future tho I shall write now and then for it – $\Delta\Theta H^i$ July 1829 P B Brontë[78]

This was a typical pattern of events. Branwell initiated a new idea, dominated its early development and then, getting bored, would go off to do something else. Charlotte was to keep the general outline of Branwell's magazine, which she renamed the 'Young Men's Magazine', adding more of her own short stories and giving greater weight to her characters, Arthur Wellesley and his younger brother, Charles.

Charlotte's editions of the 'Young Men's Magazine' reflected her own preoccupations. The Duke of Wellington becomes a distinct character in his own right, one more firmly based on the real duke. Arthur becomes the duke's eldest son, the Marquis of Douro, a romantic and ideal hero, while his younger brother, Charles, more interestingly, becomes an increasingly waspish and sarcastic observer of events. Hero-worship of the duke emerges time and again, even in seemingly irrelevant passages. His tomb is described, set in the middle of a desolate plain:

Over his < grave > tomb you see no monument of human erection but there the light of his glory stands fixed in the heavens & \it/ shall eternally illuminate the small spot of earth where lie the bones of that mighty one[79]

A little later, she compiled a series of laudatory anecdotes about the life of the duke, culled from a variety of sources, including Walter Scott's *Life of Napoleon.*[80]

Charlotte's editions of the 'Young Men's Magazine', written in the second half of 1829 and throughout 1830, are full of tales of magic, mystery and the supernatural. They included large-scale adaptations from the *Arabian Nights*, such as her story of Houssain, an old man from Isphahan in Persia, who sought an heir to his fortune by considering the candidates' reactions to a revelation of Paradise through a magic silver tube.[81] Other, less exotic stories, which feature spectral apparitions, premonitory dreams and fairy transformations, owe more to *Blackwood's Magazine* which, since 1818, had been running irregular serials on superstitions, legends and traditions from Wales, Ireland and Scotland.[82] In one particularly macabre story, inspired by an article on 'The Buried Alive', Charles Wellesley dreams he loses all powers of speech and motion and is taken for dead and buried alive by his family.

Now I dreaded that they would suppose I was dead & tried in vain to give some sign of life, the emotions of horror which filled my mind are unutterable indescribable as I heard my father say he is gone & both he & Arthur burst into tears … mortal lips must not attempt the relation of my sufferings as the idea of being buried with dead bodies amid stench & putrefaction, while my soul yet held & animated its tenement, took possession of my mind.[83]

In this case, as in all the children's stories, the 'corpse' is revived and all is well again.[84] The power of restoring to life may reflect the Brontë children's deep-seated need to be able to give life back to their creations after the irreversible deaths of their sisters, but it also owes much to their reluctance to part permanently with their favourite characters.

Much of Charlotte's writing at this time is given up simply to descriptive passages – something which had inevitably been missing from the plays but which in the magazines she could indulge in to her heart's content. Again, the *Arabian Nights* was a fertile source for exotic settings and, in imitation, Charlotte set her stories in the deserts and lush vegetation of the East. The Duke of Wellington, for example, lives in a white marble palace, surrounded by olive trees, myrtles, palms, almonds, vines, jasmine, lilies and roses, in an oasis three days' journey into the Sahara desert.[85] Interiors are just as fabulous: the Genii sit

upon thrones of pure and massive gold in the midst of an immense hall surrounded by pillars of fine & brilliant diamond the pavement sparkles with ameythst jasper & saphire a large & cloudlike canopy hangs over the heads of the geni all studded with bright rubies from which a red clear light streams irradiating all around with its burning glow & forming a fine contrast to the mild flood of glory which pours from the magnificent emerald dome & invests every thing with a solemn shadowy grandeur < wich >\which/ reminds you that you are gazing on the production of a mighty imagination[86]

The tongue-in-cheek remark at the end of the passage is a reminder that Charlotte was usually aware when her hyperbole threatened to get the better of her. The joy of the imaginary kingdoms was that different elements, no matter how incompatible or incongruous in real life, could be brought together to form the backdrop for the stories. Descriptions of rural Britain provided a salutary check on the more fantastic elements of African and Eastern scenery though, in their own way, they are just as exuberant and florid. Charlotte describes a summer morning walk in Ireland:

snails & worms luxuriate in < for > dampness – under the heat[h] & hawthorn hedges glittring \with dew/ or white with blossoms & star-eyed robin-flowers and < t > stately < caps > fairy-caps are seen gleaming from trailing underwood by the roadside; or crowning with crimson bells the sloping green banks. music at that happy hour is above below & around: larks warble in the sky – thrushe[s] sing in the hedge & grasshoppers chirp in the feilds.[87]

The descriptive passages were not always a simple indulgence. In 'Conversations' in Bravey's Inn the characters of the two Wellesley brothers are deftly illuminated by their different perceptions of winter:

> Marquis of Duro
> O I like such weather when the snow is drifted up into great curling wreaths like a garland of lilies woven for the coffin of a giant or to crown his head with when he is wrapped in his shroud when the crystal icicles are hanging from the eaves of the houses & the bushy evergreens are all spangled with snow flakes as if twas spring & they were flourishing in full blossom –
> Lord Charles Wellesley
> when all the old women traverse the streets in great woollen cloaks & clacking iron pattons. When apothecarys are seen rushing about with gargles & tinctures & washes for sprained ancles chilblains & frost bitten noses. When you can hardly feel your hands & feet for the cold & < are > forced to stand shuddering over the fire on pain of being petrified by the frost how pleasant that is Arthur?[88]

The sheer sense of fun which leaps off every page makes it clear that the imaginary worlds were not simply a retreat from reality but a hugely enjoyable frolic. Charlotte frequently used her characters to poke fun at her brother and sisters – and they responded in kind. In a review of the *Causes of the Late War*, a book which purported to be written by the Duke of Wellington himself, Charlotte detected the hand of Branwell in his character of Sergeant Bud:

> Firstly, because the margins are uncommonly narrow; secondly because the style is like that of a rule to show cause why a prosecution for libel should not be tried against some unhappy individual; thirdly, because Bud, at the time when it was writing, was often out of the way when we wanted him ... fourthly and lastly, because we are sure His Grace never would have the patience to write such a long, dry thing.[89]

Emily and Anne were targeted in 'A Day at Parry's Palace', Parry being Emily's chief character. Clearly, Emily and Anne had already broken away from Glasstown even at this early period, to the extent of forming their own distinct and separate country. The sardonic Charles Wellesley

> was imediately struck with the changed aspect of every thing. instead of tall strong muscular men going about seeking whom they may devour, with \guns/ on their shoulders or in their hands – I saw none but little shiftless milk-and-water-beings, in clean blue linen jackets & white < ? > aprons < ? > all the houses were ranged in

formal rows. they contained four rooms each with a little garden in front. No proud castle or splendid palace Toweres insultingly over the cottages around.⁹⁰

Their neat, ordered and ordinary world was apparently inhabited by dolls rather than soldiers and even the meals (roast beef, Yorkshire pudding, mashed potatoes, apple pies and preserved cucumbers) are unexciting compared to the feasts at Glasstown. Charlotte, in her Wellesley character, is very patronizing of her younger sisters. They speak a 'scarcely intelligible jargon' which is a mix of baby talk and Yorkshire dialect, the conversation is all of the new clothes they have made for their dolls and Parry offers Wellesley a napkin at dinner to pin to his clothes saying 'that he supposed they were my best as I had come on a visit & that perhaps my mama would be angry if they got stained'.⁹¹

On 18 June 1830, Charlotte wrote a piece by Charles Wellesley about the resurrectionists disturbed in their digging up corpses for anatomical dissection by a group of Glasstown worthies bent on recovering the public library books they have stolen and hidden in coffins in the churchyard. Branwell was so incensed at this scurrilous attack on so many of the chief characters that the next day he wrote an answer to it, 'The Liar Detected'.

Homer had his Zoilus Virgil his Mearius – and CAPTAIN TREE his Wellesly all these were & are alike contemptible in character and Influence and like vipers can do no more than bite the heels of their Enimies⁹²

After effectively demolishing the lies of 'the little shop boy', he also attacks Wellesley's conceit:

O how I fancy I can see the yong Author brimfull of himself after having finished this passage rise up take the Manuscript in his greasy hand rubb his head stick out his shirt frill give a few hems pop into Popes homer to see if their was a passage their equal to it then sit down \his self esteem/ no way abated and fag < o > away like one on a wager⁹³

Only a few weeks later, Charlotte responded with a similar but much more prolonged attack on one of Branwell's favourite characters, Young Soult, a poet with grandiose aspirations. Insultingly caricaturing him as 'Henry Rhymer', she dedicated two whole volumes to the 'Poetaster', as she called him, mocking his pomposity and his exalted sense of his own calling. Rhymer, sitting alone in his garret, starts at a sudden noise:

What's that? Oh! 'twas but the wind, mournfully serenading me on its passage through the sky. Methinks I will apostrophize it. Yea, the thoughts are crowding into my mind. Dost thou, oh wind, look from thy ever resounding halls with pity on me, the Forsaken? Dost thou send forth thy blasts to moan thy compassion in my disconsolate ear? I will believe that thou dost, though no articulate response comes on the winged breeze. Let me see. That's good poetry. I'll versify it.

<u>Thinks</u>. No, it'll not do. The thoughts should come spontaneously as I write or they're not the inspirations of genius. But I'll try again.
<u>Seizes a bit of paper, pen and ink.</u>
How my hand trembled. I'm certainly in a consumption brought on by excessive drink¡ – study, I mean. Or was it only the effect of those fervid flashes from one of the Muses' lamps that just then passed through my mind?[94]

Though this long play owed much, including its title, to Ben Jonson, Charlotte was also taking the opportunity to get her own back. With sarcasm bordering on savagery, she depicts the hapless Rhymer on the gallows offering his writings as his legacy. A voice from the crowd cries 'Thank you lad. They'll do to light our pipes.' The final insult is that Rhymer is only saved from execution on condition that he becomes Charles Wellesley's secretary, reducing Glasstown's greatest poet to the mere amanuensis of his rival.[95]

There were two serious points behind the heavy irony of 'The Poetaster'. One is that the Brontës were widening their scope in their writings, drawing on new forms and styles for imitation and inspiration; the other is that they had become interested in investigating and analysing the whole nature of the arts and literature.

It was Branwell again who led the way. After handing over 'Branwell's Blackwood's Magazine' to Charlotte, he had turned to newspaper writing. Although there is only one extant, later, example of this, his 'Monthly Intelligencer' of March to April 1833,[96] it is clear that the newspaper format gave Branwell greater opportunity to explore the political scene in Glasstown, reporting debates and the progress of events as they unfolded with an immediacy to which the monthly magazines could not aspire. As early as June 1829, Bravey's Inn took 'the Young Mans Intelligencer', 'the Opposition', 'the Greybottle' 'the Glasstown Intelligencer', the 'Courier du francais' and the 'Quatre Deinne'; any one of these could have been taken up and developed by Branwell as a vehicle for his political interests.[97]

His literary ambitions were developing too. On 30 September 1829 he 'published' two volumes of poems by Young Soult which were extensively annotated by Monsieur de la Chateaubriand, a fictitious version of the real French writer and statesman whose work had been featured in *Blackwood's Magazine*. The flippant style of some of the notes – 'this Poem is an exceedingly rambling and irregular < ? > meter and contains a great many things for which he ought to be punished Yong Soult – wrote it while drunk'[98] – masks an extensive knowledge of France under Napoleon. A similar venture was his edition, supposedly in twenty-eight volumes, of the poems of Ossian, edited by Sergeant Bud. In a splendidly satirical send-up of learned commentaries, which he was no doubt obliged to use in his classical studies with his father, Branwell added dull and obvious notes to virtually every line. A note to the word 'thistle', for example, reads 'The Thistle: Latin carduus

Greek σκολυμος, a prickley weed abounding in Scotland & usually growing in cornfields'. He ends his review 'this is one of the most long winded Books that have ever been printed we must now conclude for we are dreadfuly tired'.[99]

Between 18 and 23 December 1829, Branwell produced his first verse play, 'Laussane: a Dramatic Poem' by Young Soult, set in France in 1423 and charting the restoration to power of the exiled Count Laussane. Once again the subject, style and language seem to have been inspired by *Blackwood's Magazine*, in this case by the 'Horae Germanicae' series of translated extracts from German tragedies.[100] More poems were to follow in the same mould. Six months later, as Young Soult, he wrote another dramatic poem, 'Caractacus', telling the story of the ancient Briton's betrayal to the Romans. Six months after 'Caractacus' he produced 'The Revenge', another medieval 'tradgedy in 3 Acts', similar to but much more sophisticated than 'Laussane'.[101] On the title page of 'Caractacus' and 'The Revenge', he quoted himself, as Captain John Bud:

In dramatic poetry the cheif thing to be attained Is an excellence in describing the passions and in proportion as this excelence is attained so are we To judge of the merits of the peice. J BUDS synop[s]is of The Drama Vol I p130[102]

In all three dramas but especially in the last two, the thirteen-year-old Branwell achieved some moments of genuine poetry, despite using archaic language and borrowing heavily from Byron, Milton and Shakespeare. While Charlotte may have mocked his pretension to heroic verse and his choice of grandiose subjects in 'The Poetaster' (significantly her only large scale verse drama), there is no escaping the fact that Branwell's work was both more mature and more adventurous than her own at this time.

Glasstown was not forgotten, but Branwell did find a new way of approaching it. On 6 September 1830 he began the first in a series of six 'Letters from an Englishman', which described the travels and adventures of James Bellingham in Africa.[103] The letter format allowed Branwell to write in character but, because his author was an outsider, they were also a convenient vehicle for describing what amounted to first impressions of the scenery and characters he encountered.

Throughout their little books in the fertile period of 1829 to 1830, Charlotte and Branwell were continually exploring the idea of creative art and the role of the artist. It is, for instance, no accident that the juvenilia is full of references to drunkenness. Biographers have taken this to mean that Branwell was a habitual drunkard from his teenage years,[104] but in fact the references date back as early as 1829 when the boy was only twelve years old and it defies the imagination to believe that he was already a hardened drinker. In addition, there are just as many allusions to drinking in Charlotte's poetry and prose of this period, though no one has yet suggested she, too, was an alcoholic. The apparent obsession with drunkenness can be traced to two sources, *Blackwood's Magazine* and the classics. In both cases, alcohol is the source or at least the backdrop to creativity. The *Noctes Ambrosianae* were set in Ambrose's public house and the convivial poets, writers and artists meeting there take plenty of Madeira, whisky, punch and brandy during their gatherings. The mood is set by the motto which appears at the beginning of each session, quoting from the Greek of Phocylides:

> ... 'Tis right for good winebibbing people,
> Not to let the jug pace round the board like a cripple;
> But gaily to chat while discussing their tipple.[105]

The main protagonists kept up their heavy drinking image in other contributions to the magazine, including, most famously, Morgan O'Doherty's 142 'Maxims', which are almost exclusively on drinking.[106] In classical poetry, too, the ancient Greeks and Romans found inspiration in the wine cup; drinking was supposed to induce the poetic muse and drunkenness betokened possession by poetic frenzy. Perhaps surprisingly, it was Charlotte who was most drawn to this type of poetry, producing several poems extolling the virtues of wine and brandy, including one, 'Haste bring us the wine cup', which is an imitation of the classical format.[107]

The children's education at this time permeated their juvenile writings. Branwell flaunted his knowledge of Latin and Greek in his pseudo-scholarly notes to the works of Young Soult and Sergeant Bud,[108] but Charlotte was equally at home with the classics. Her stories and poems, too, are peppered with casual references to Scipio Africanus, Socrates, Ovid, Virgil's *Eclogues* and Herodotus and it is clear from their context that she knew more about them than simply their brief entries in her father's Lemprière's *Bibliotheca Classica*.[109] 'The Violet', for instance, a long poem written on 14 November 1830, is full of allusions to not only the greatest literary men but also the landscape of ancient Greece and Rome. In the poem Charlotte seeks the gift of poetic inspiration and is given a violet, rather than the customary laurel, as a symbol that she will have that gift but only to a lesser degree than the ancients.[110]

The children were also beginning to study French. France and all things connected with Napoleon had long held a fascination for them. Their elder sister, Maria, could read French by the time she went to the Clergy Daughters' School, but Charlotte was fourteen before she began to make a serious study of the language. It is interesting to speculate who taught the children French. Patrick's knowledge of the language would seem to have been fairly basic: in 1842, when he had to escort his daughters to Belgium, he drew up a book of simple phrases of the most elementary kind to assist him.[111] Aunt Branwell, however, was well read and had had the conventional education of her day. It seems very likely that she shared the predilection for French novels of her sex, generation and class and so it is not beyond the bounds of possibility that she was responsible for instructing her nieces in the language. Charlotte was sufficiently interested to spend three shillings of her precious money on a copy of Voltaire's epic poem *La Henriade*, which she bought in May 1830. On 11 August she translated the first book, transcribing it into one of her own miniature books.[112] The exercise inspired her to include more French in her writings, as two days later she began a new series in her 'Young Men's Magazine' entitled 'Journal of a Frenchman', in which her characters converse in French – except when the vocabulary was beyond her.[113]

The activities of the real world were not always reflected in the children's writing, even when they were unusual. A major concert of sacred music in Haworth Church on 20 July 1829 left no impression, even though there was an orchestra of eighty, conducted by Mr White, and performances from some of the most famous professional singers in Yorkshire, including Thomas Parker, the tenor from Haworth itself, and Master Wilde, from York.[114] Similarly, a visit away from home, with all the excitement of its new experiences, passed unnoticed. Accompanied by Aunt Branwell, the four children spent a few days in September at the parsonage at Cross-stone with the recently widowed John Fennell.[115] The weather was poor so they were not able to explore the dramatic hills and valleys between Hebden Bridge and Todmorden but, from the tiny parsonage perched on the hillside, the young Brontës looked straight across the valley to Stoodley Pike. A huge stone obelisk, built on top of the moors and thrusting belligerently into the sky, Stoodley Pike was a memorial to the Allies' seizure of Paris and the victory of Waterloo, a visible symbol of the Duke of Wellington's success. Charlotte wrote a letter to her father, which he lovingly endorsed 'Charlotte's First Letter' and carefully preserved, describing how they had spent their time:

very pleasantly, between reading, working, and learning our lessons, which Uncle Fennell has been so kind as to teach us every day. Branwell has taken two sketches from nature, and Emily, Anne, and myself have likewise each of us drawn a piece from some views of the lakes which Mr Fennell brought with him from West-moreland.[116]

The day she returned home, in some sort of bizarre ritual, Charlotte recorded on a tiny scrap of folded paper, 'on September the 25 I put in the Life of the Duke of W a piece of paper burnt at one end and on it was inscribed – Charles & Arthur Charlotte Brontë Sept 25 1829'. The act perhaps symbolized her return to the imaginary world.[117]

Patrick, too, was busy, campaigning for reform at home and abroad. In November he returned to his attack on the criminal code, writing yet again to the *Leeds Mercury* and calling on all men to work for the abolition of the death penalty except for murder, so that 'the scales of justice and mercy are poised with even hand, and cruelty and oppression can nowhere be found'.[118] Disappointingly, there was no response, but with characteristic persistence, Patrick did not give up. The following April, in common with Evangelicals all over the country, he organized petitions for the abolition of slavery to both Houses of Parliament. Unlike any of his fellow ministers, he also took the opportunity to raise petitions for the revision and mitigation of the criminal code.[119] Having got nowhere with the supposedly reforming *Leeds Mercury* he wrote to the *Leeds Intelligencer*, pointing out that

all the Dissenting and Methodist ministers in the parish gave their consent and assistance with a cheerful alacrity that did credit alike to their piety, good sense, and humanity; and out of a population of more than four thousand, not one objected to – but all approved of, those measures of mercy and justice which we had in contemplation.[120]

Once again, Patrick's clarion call for liberalization of the criminal law fell on deaf ears. Worn out by his campaigning efforts, by an unpleasant contested election for the post of parish overseer and the relentless round of parish duties,[121] he fell seriously ill for the first time in his career. An inflammation of the lungs, neglected at first, reduced him to such a state that for three weeks in June and July he was too ill to get out of bed and his life was held to be in imminent danger. The duties that he was so reluctant to neglect were taken by Thomas Plummer, headmaster of the grammar school at Keighley.[122] The children were alarmed by their father's sudden weakness. One incident impressed itself so deeply on Charlotte that she broke off from her Glasstown imaginings to record it.

The following strange occurence happened on the 22 of June 1830. At that time papa was very ill, confined to his bed and so weak that he could not rise without assistance. Tabby and I were alone in the kitchen, about half past 9 ante-meridian. Suddenly we heard a knock at the door. Tabby rose and opened it. An old man appeared standing without, who accosted her thus:
Old Man: Does the parson live here?
Tabby: Yes.
Old Man: I wish to see him.
Tabby: He is poorly in bed.
Old Man: Indeed. I have [a] message for him.
Tabby: Who from?
Old Man: From the LORD.
Tabby: Who?
Old Man: The LORD. He desires me to say that the bridegroom is coming and that he must prepare to meet him; that the cords are about to be loosed and the golden bowl broken; the pitcher broken at the fountain and the wheel stopped at the cistern. Here he concluded his discourse and abruptly went away. As Tabby closed the door I asked her if she knew him. Her reply was that she had never seen

him before nor anyone like him. Though I am fully persuaded that he was some fanatical enthusiast, well-meaning, perhaps, but utterly ignorant of true piety, yet I could not forbear weeping at his words, spoken so unexpectedly at that particular period.

Charlotte Brontë
June the 22, 1830
6 o'clock pm
Haworth near Bradford[123]

Charlotte, obsessed with tales of supernatural apparitions and omens, was particularly vulnerable to the implicit threat in the visitor's prophecy, but Patrick's illness must have shaken the whole household out of its ordinary routine. Though the immediate danger passed, Patrick remained physically weak and consequently very depressed in spirits for six months, finding his return to his duties a constant struggle.[124] He was fifty-three years old and he could not live for ever. On his death his children would lose everything, even the roof over their heads. Aunt Branwell, though now permanently established with the Brontës at Haworth, was in no position to support them financially. The problem of providing for the future of his children loomed large again, no doubt adding to Patrick's depression. The eldest, Charlotte, was already fourteen and in a few years' time would be capable of earning her own living. As yet she had had only one year's schooling, which could hardly equip her to find a good post as a teacher or governess. Whatever the advantages of the wide-ranging education she had had at home, any future employer would expect at least some formal qualifications. It was time for her to go to school again.

Chapter Seven

❧

Emulation Rewarded

Roe Head School was everything that the Clergy Daughters' School was not. It was based in a large house on the outskirts of Mirfield, about half a mile down the hill from Patrick's old church at Hartshead. A rather grand three-storey grey stone building, with an unusual double-bowed frontage, it had been built for the Marriott family in 1740. It has changed little in appearance over the years, despite being surrounded by the more mundane buildings of the much larger school it has become. It still enjoys large and pleasant gardens, with lawns to the front and woods and shrubbery at the rear and side to screen it from the road into Mirfield and Dewsbury beyond. Most of all, however, it retains its open aspect. Though lower than Hartshead, its elevated site gives spectacular views over the wooded grounds of Kirklees Hall. The stark outlines of the surrounding hills are broken only by the hill villages lying between Huddersfield and Halifax. Down in the valley bottom to the left can be seen the mills of Mirfield, the nearest town, which like Brighouse and Raistrick to the right, has spilt out beyond its nineteenth-century limits. Only the scar of the M62 motorway and the hum of its traffic are alien intrusions into the landscape as Charlotte knew it.

Roe Head had been taken over from the Marriotts in 1830 by Miss Margaret Wooler and her sisters, Catherine, Susan, Marianne and Eliza.¹ Unfortunately, there are almost no relevant records, so it is impossible to tell whether this represented the actual setting up of their school or whether they had moved from another house in the area. By 1831 it had established a reputation and attracted as pupils the daughters of some of the leading manufacturers in the area. Among them were families well known to Patrick: the Brookes, granddaughters of John Halliley of Dewsbury, for instance, and the Haighs, who were friends or relations of the Firths of Thornton.² The school had only a very small number of pupils, apparently between seven and ten at a time, and there was no great disparity in their ages. Most of the girls, like Charlotte, seem to have been in their early teens and there were no infants as there had been at Cowan Bridge. All appear to have been boarders, though most of them came from within a radius of a few miles of the school, Charlotte being the exception in that her home was some twenty miles from Roe Head.³

The school was run as well as owned by Miss Margaret Wooler and her sisters. It says much for the character of Margaret Wooler that Patrick described her as a 'clever, decent and motherly woman' and that she became Charlotte's lifelong friend. In appearance she was short and stout, but graceful in her movements; her voice was sweet and she was fluent in conversation. One of her pupils described her as being like a lady abbess, dressed in white robes, with her hair bound into a plaited coronet and falling in ringlets to her shoulders. Catherine Wooler, whose disposition Charlotte thought had been soured by her continuing spinsterhood, was equally cultivated and intellectual in her tastes.⁴ The regime they had instituted at Roe Head was disciplined but kindly. With so few pupils it was possible to take into account each girl's foibles and capabilities and there is no doubt that Charlotte not only benefited from the education offered, but also actually enjoyed her time at the school.

The choice of Roe Head seems odd at first. There were many schools closer to Haworth: Keighley, for instance, had two ladies' boarding schools and there were plenty of others in Bradford and Halifax.⁵ Although the scale of its fees is not known, there is no reason to suppose it was any cheaper than those, more convenient schools. The choice must have been dictated by Patrick's personal knowledge of the place. He had walked past the building many times on his parish rounds at Dewsbury and Hartshead, so he was aware that it was in a healthy and open position. He knew the parents of some of the pupils and that they were men wealthy and powerful enough to pick and choose the education offered to their daughters, unlike the poor clergymen of Cowan Bridge. He knew that Charlotte's godparents, the Reverend Thomas Atkinson and his wife, the former Frances Walker, lived at Green House in Mirfield, less than a mile from the school and that the

Reverend James Clarke Franks and his wife, the former Elizabeth Firth, lived at the vicarage in Huddersfield a few miles further away. Both Mrs Atkinson and Mrs Franks were acquainted with not only the pupils and their families, but also the Misses Wooler who ran the school.[6] It is possible that Frances Atkinson actually suggested Roe Head to Patrick, as her own niece Amelia Walker was already at the school. The story that she paid the school fees for her goddaughter seems to be apocryphal,[7] but she did keep a watchful eye over Charlotte's progress there. This time Patrick would not be left in ignorance of his daughter's welfare.

On 17 January 1831 Charlotte Brontë began the new term at Roe Head School. Mary Taylor, who was to become a lifelong friend, described her arrival:

I first saw her coming out of a covered cart, in very old-fashioned clothes, and looking very cold and miserable. She was coming to school at Miss Wooler's. When she appeared in the schoolroom her dress was changed, but just as old. She looked a little old woman, so short-sighted that she always appeared to be seeking something, and moving her head from side to side to catch a sight of it. She was very shy and nervous, and spoke with a strong Irish accent.[8]

A week later, the strangeness of her surroundings had still not worn off. Charlotte was homesick and lonely, missing the closeness of her family life and finding it difficult to mix with her school-fellows, who found her eccentric and something of an object of fun. It was therefore opportune that eight days after her own arrival, another new girl arrived. Ellen Nussey was almost exactly a year younger than Charlotte, her birthday being the day after Charlotte's. A quiet and gentle girl herself, she was immediately drawn to the girl she found shrinking into the bay window of the schoolroom and weeping silently while the others played outside. A mutual sense of being new and out of place played its part in bringing them together, as did their shared homesickness.[9]

Charlotte was immediately marked out as different from her fellow pupils, not just by her old-fashioned clothes and odd Irish accent, but also by her appearance and mannerisms. Mary Taylor, never one to mince her words, told her directly that she was very ugly. Ellen Nussey's judgement was kinder.

She never seemed to me the unattractive little person others designated her, but certainly she was at this time anything but *pretty*, even her good points were lost. Her naturally beautiful hair of soft silky brown being then dry and frizzy-looking, screwed up in tight little curls, showing features that were all the plainer from her exceeding thinness and want of complexion, she looked 'dried in.' A dark, rusty green stuff dress of old-fashioned make detracted still more from her appearance[10]

The girls found her short-sightedness a particular source of amusement:

'When a book was given her she dropped her head over it till her nose nearly touched it, and when she was told to hold her head up, up went the book after it, still close to her nose, so that it was not possible to help laughing.' Though the girls urged her to join in the more active outdoor games, it was soon discovered that she could not see the ball and she was unceremoniously 'put out' again and left to her own devices. In any case, Charlotte was happier sitting or standing under the trees in the playground.

She endeavoured to explain this, pointing out the shadows, the peeps of sky, etc. We understood but little of it. She said that at Cowan Bridge she used to stand in the burn, on a stone, to watch the water flow by. I told her she should have gone fishing; she said she never wanted."

The energetic and boisterous Mary Taylor found Charlotte physically feeble in everything. Not only did she not play games but she refused to eat any animal food, remembering the horrors of the meat at Cowan Bridge. Her foibles were accepted at Roe Head, however, and something was always specially provided for her to eat. Gradually, as she grew more confident and happy, she was persuaded to try gravy with her vegetables and was eventually won round to the normal school diet.[12]

If her fellow pupils were swift to notice Charlotte's oddities, they were soon forced to recognize her unusually brilliant mind. At first the general impression, typified by Mary Taylor's comments, was remarkably similar to her entry in the register of the Clergy Daughters' School seven years before: 'We thought her very ignorant, for she had never learnt grammar at all, and very little geography.' It was soon realized that her knowledge and abilities were of quite a different sort.

She would confound us by knowing things that were out of our range altogether. She was acquainted with most of the short pieces of poetry that we had to learn by heart: would tell us the authors, the poems they were taken from, and sometimes repeat a page or two, and tell us the plot ... She used to draw much better, and more quickly, than anything we had seen before, and knew much about celebrated pictures and painters. Whenever an opportunity offered of examining a picture or cut of any kind, she went over it piecemeal, with her eyes close to the paper, looking so long that we used to ask her 'what she saw in it'. She could always see plenty, and explained it very well. She made poetry and drawing at least exceedingly interesting to me; and then I got the habit, which I have yet, of referring mentally to her opinion on all matters of that kind...[13]

Charlotte's evident mental superiority and her diffident way of sharing her knowledge, rather than flaunting it, won her the respect and affection of her fellow pupils; her peculiarities were soon forgotten and she was accepted as one of the girls. Within a few weeks of arriving at the school, she had settled in happily.

The system of education at the school was almost entirely class-based, which meant that new pupils were at first taught individually until they were of the required standard. Even when they were in their classes, the girls could proceed at their own pace, reciting their lessons to Miss Wooler as and when they had learnt them, rather than waiting for the whole class to complete the allotted task. The lessons were the standard ones of the day: geography, history, English grammar and French, with a leavening of music and drawing. Richmal Mangnall's *Historical and Miscellaneous Questions* was the staple diet, passages being learnt off by heart and recited back to the teacher. Charlotte arrived at Roe Head with her own copy of this and of Tocquot's *New and Easy Guide to the Pronunciation and Spelling of French*, both of which she inscribed with her name and the first date of term. Both books are heavily annotated and scribbled in: the Mangnall has most of its annotations in the section on the history of ancient Greece where names, dates and further information have been added. On the endpapers and inside the back cover of the Tocquot, Charlotte scribbled lists of Shakespearian characters and Latin versions of place names. During her eighteen months at the school she acquired further books, reflecting her grammatical weakness: Pinnock's *Comprehensive Grammar of the English Language* and Lindley Murray's *English Grammar*.[14]

Charlotte made such rapid progress in her studies that by the end of her first half year she had risen to the top of her class, carrying off three prizes and being awarded the silver medal for achievement, suitably inscribed 'Emulation' on one side and 'Rewarded' on the other. She was never to lose her place at the top of the class and so was awarded the medal at the end of each of the three terms she spent at Roe Head. At the end of her second term she also won the school French prize, a copy of the New Testament in French inscribed on the fly leaf 'French Prize adjudged to Miss Bronte & presented with the Miss Woolers' kind love. Roe Head Decr 14th 1831'.[15]

In the 'accomplishments' Charlotte also made advances. Like all the young Brontës she had always loved drawing and from 1828 onwards she had spent much time and effort in producing increasingly detailed and skilful pencil drawings and watercolours. By 1830 she was capable of exquisite and delicate paintings, a simple spray of wild roses taken from nature, a prettified copy of a portrait of her mother or a highly coloured copy of J. H. Fuessli's illustrations to John Milton.[16] Her lessons with John Bradley had given her a head start over her fellow pupils, but at Roe Head she was forced to go back to basics. Among her extant pieces are a whole series of pencil studies of mouths, noses, eyes, ears and profiles produced in the first two months of school. She then progressed to pencil head-and-shoulder portraits, copied from the cartoons of Raphael which appeared in the *Penny Magazine* at the time: at least two of these reminded her of her school-fellows, for one was labelled 'Amelia Walker' and another 'Susan Ledgard'. Thereafter, it was pencil copies of botanical illustrations and landscapes, drawings from life not being encouraged except for the single instance of a drawing of Roe Head.[7] Though the course did not foster originality, it gave a sound basis for future artistic effort.

Charlotte's instinctive love of and ear for music were quietly discouraged, not because she was without talent but because she could not see her notes without stooping so dreadfully that it was feared she might permanently affect her posture.[8]

What Charlotte had initially lacked in formal education, she more than made up for by her application to study. She had a set purpose in mind and she deeply felt the responsibility that rested on her: she was an object of expense to those at home and she must use every opportunity to attain the knowledge which would fit her for her chosen path of being a governess. Ellen Nussey, who was not inclined to intellectual interests, felt that Charlotte had almost too much opportunity for her conscientious diligence. Once the set lessons for the day had been accomplished, the girls were free to do as they liked. Charlotte was so quick to learn that she would have had ample time for recreation, but she chose instead to spend her free hours in extra lessons.

She liked the stated task to be over, that she might be free to pursue her self-appointed ones ... When her companions were merry round the fire, or otherwise enjoying themselves during the twilight, which was always a precious time of relaxation, she would be kneeling close to the window busy with her studies, and this would last so long that she was accused of seeing in the dark[19]

Self-improvement was Charlotte's goal, not only in the formal attainments but in cultivating her tastes.

She always said there was enough of hard practicality and *useful* knowledge forced on us by necessity, and that the thing most needed was to soften and refine our minds. She picked up every scrap of information concerning painting, sculpture, poetry, music, etc., as if it were gold.[20]

At Roe Head Charlotte was free to indulge her passion for poetry and the visual arts, though there was no time to spare for her other obsession, the fictional world of Glasstown. The fourteen-year-old Charlotte saw no reason to hide or be ashamed of her family's absorption in the imaginary worlds of their own creation. She told her school friends all about the monthly issues of the 'Young Men's Magazine' and how they were written in characters to make them look as if they had been printed. She even told the girls a story out of one of them and promised to show the magazines to Mary Taylor – a promise she afterwards retracted and could never be induced to fulfil.[21]

Charlotte did find some outlet for her highly active imagination, however, and in the process won herself a reputation as a storyteller. On one occasion, she thrilled her audience with the terrifying story of the wanderings of a sleepwalker:

She brought together all the horrors her imagination could create, from surging seas, raging breakers, towering castle walls, high precipices, invisible chasms and dangers. Having wrought these materials to the highest pitch of effect, she brought out, in almost cloud-height, her somnambulist, walking on shaking turrets, – all told in a voice that conveyed more than words alone can express.

So powerful was the effect she created that one girl, who had recently been ill, was reduced to shivering terror; help had to be called for and Charlotte felt so guilty that she refused to tell her frightening stories ever again. After some time and by popular demand, however, she was induced to revert to telling stories after hours in the dormitory – until she and all her listeners were fined by Miss Catherine Wooler for 'late talking'.[22]

Charlotte had found a role at the school which enabled the otherwise shy and retiring girl to blossom. When it was decided to enact a 'coronation performance' one half-day holiday, Charlotte naturally assumed the organizational role she had always held at home. She drew up the programme, arranged the titles of the performers and wrote both the invitations and the central speech for the coronation:

Powerful Queen! accept this crown, the symbol of dominion, from the hands of your faithful and affectionate subjects! And if their earnest and united wishes have any efficacy, you will long be permitted to reign over this peaceful, though circumscribed empire.[23]

In such a role Charlotte was in her element: she had, after all, been writing similar speeches for many years and the only difference now was that she had a wider audience than simply her devoted family.

Living too far away to travel home, except for the summer and Christmas holidays, Charlotte was fortunate in that her school-fellows often invited her to their houses for the weekend or short holidays. As most of them were daughters of wealthy manufacturers, their houses were much grander than Haworth Parsonage. The Nusseys lived at The Rydings, an elegant, castellated old house set in landscaped grounds in Birstall. Ellen's father, John Nussey, had been a wealthy cloth manufacturer, with mills at Birstall Smithies; he had died in 1826 but the business had been continued by his sons. Ellen was the youngest of twelve children: there was a wide disparity in their ages, the oldest being more than twenty years older than Ellen. Life at The Rydings was genteel but busy with all the comings and goings of the vast circle of Nussey friends and relations, who spent their time in paying social visits to one another. Charlotte was welcomed with friendly courtesy and unobtrusive kindness.[24]

By contrast, Mary Taylor's family were boisterous and did not stand on ceremony. Mary and her sister, Martha, who was also at Roe Head, were the fourth and fifth of six children, but they were all very close in age and consequently the household was dominated by the young people. Their father, Joshua Taylor, was also a manufacturer and a banker but in the same year that Ellen's father died he had gone bankrupt as a result of the failure of his own bank in London.[25] He spent many years paying back his debts and trying to restore the fortunes of his business. Like his children, he was an ardent Radical and his vociferously expressed beliefs were the absolute antithesis of Charlotte's High Tory politics. At the Red House, their gracious but unusually brick-built home in Gomersal, Charlotte was drawn into political argument and a defence of her hero the Duke of Wellington:

We used to be furious politicians, as one could hardly help being in 1832. She knew the names of the two Ministries; the one that resigned, and the one that succeeded and passed the Reform Bill. She worshipped the Duke of Wellington, but said that Sir Robert Peel was not to be trusted; he did not act from principle, like the rest, but from expediency. I, being of the furious Radical party, told her, 'How could any of them trust one another? they were all of them rascals!' Then she would launch out into praises of the Duke of Wellington, referring to his actions; which I could not contradict, as I knew nothing about him. She said she had taken interest in politics ever since she was five years old. She did not get her opinions from her father – that is, not directly – but from the papers, etc., he preferred … At our house she had just as little chance of a patient hearing, [as at school] for though not school-girlish we were more intolerant. We had a rage for practicality, and laughed all poetry to scorn. Neither she nor we had any idea but that our opinions were the opinions of all the *sensible* people in the world, and we used to astonish each other at every sentence.[26]

Charlotte's visits to the Red House and her friendship with Mary Taylor, in particular, were to be stimulating, exciting and constantly surprising.

Much less enjoyable were the duty visits Charlotte had to pay to her father's friends. With the best of intentions, she was occasionally invited over to spend the day with the Franks at the vicarage in Huddersfield or with the Atkinsons at Green House. For Charlotte, these visits were an ordeal. Even the servant sent to fetch her to the Atkinsons' found her exceedingly shy, timid and shrinking, 'spare of speech and nice in manners, though somewhat awkward, and evidently observant'.[27] On her best behaviour in company and terrified of committing a *faux pas* among people whom she did not know well, Charlotte found most pleasure in retreating into the garden. One visit to an unnamed family who had known Patrick when he was curate in their parish was particularly mortifying. Charlotte's shyness and smallness were taken as indications of extreme youth: 'They took me for a child, and treated me just like one … one tall lady would nurse me.'[28] Always hypersensitive to anything that smacked of patronage, Charlotte resented the intended, if misplaced, kindness. Similarly, she clearly felt her own poverty, especially when contrasted with the wealth of her own and her father's friends. A note to Mrs Franks, written during Charlotte's first half year to thank her for the present of a frock and muslin and Miss Outhwaite for a shawl, is polite in the extreme but hardly breathes a spirit of genuine appreciation.[29] No doubt Mary Taylor and the other girls had mocked her old-fashioned and second-hand clothing as they had her lack of personal good looks. The gifts, meant in kindness, were perceived as charity and served only as a reminder to Charlotte of her inferior status.

Patrick, on the other hand, was grateful for his old friends' attentions to his daughter and wrote to thank them on her behalf. He also took the opportunity to set the record straight on his own position, which had become increasingly isolated over the last few months. His liberal stance on Roman Catholic Emancipation and, more particularly his campaign to revise the criminal code, had angered many of his former friends, including William Morgan, the Franks and the Outhwaites. His campaign over the winter of 1830 and spring of 1831 for the restoration to the magistracy of Michael Stocks was only marginally less controversial. Stocks, who was a Whig, had been humiliatingly removed from office when charged with perjury and perverting the course of justice; eventually he was to be triumphantly vindicated when his accuser turned out to be a proven liar who was simply seeking revenge on a magistrate who had sentenced him in the past. Patrick, with all the other clergymen of the parish of Bradford, had signed a memorial to the Lord High Chancellor seeking Stocks' reinstatement as early as December 1830, though the affair dragged on as a party political issue throughout the following year.[30]

It was Patrick's support for the Whigs' Reform Bill of 1831 which most annoyed his High Tory friends. The bill would disenfranchise the rotten boroughs, enfranchise some of the new towns which had grown up since the Industrial Revolution and halve the property qualification for registering as a voter. Once more Patrick had to defend himself against charges of having become an enemy to the establishment.

A warmer, or truer friend to Church, and state, does not breathe the vital air. But, after many years, mature deliberation, I am fully convinced, that, unless, the real friends of our Excellent Institutions, come forward, and advocate the cause of Temperate reform – the inveterate enemies – will avail themselves of the opportunity, which this circumstance would give them, and will work on the popular feeling – already but too much excited – so as to cause, in all probability, general insurrectionary movements, and bring about a revolution – ... Both, then, because, I think moderate, or temperate reform, is wanted – and that this would satisfy all wise & reasonable people, and weaken the hands of our real enemies, & preserve the Church and State from ruin – I am an advocate for the Bill, which has been just thrown out of Parli[a]ment – It is with me, merely an affair of conscience and judgement, and sooner than violate the dictates of either of these, I would run the hazard of poverty, imprisonment, and death.[31]

It is a measure of the independence of thought Patrick inspired in his children that both Branwell and Charlotte took completely the opposite view on the question of the Reform Bill. A year later, on 17 May 1832, Charlotte addressed her weekly letter home to Branwell, 'As usual...because to you I find the most to say'.

Lately I had begun to think that I had lost all the interest which I used formerly to take in politics but the extreme pleasure I felt at the news of the Reform-bill's being thrown out \by/ < of > by the House of Lords and of the expulsion or resignation of Earl Grey, &c. &c. convinced me that I have not as yet lost all my penchant for politics.[32]

This particular letter had been preceded by a totally unexpected visit from Branwell, who had arrived at Roe Head, having walked the twenty-odd miles from Haworth, to visit his sister. He brought news that Aunt Branwell had decided to subscribe to *Fraser's Magazine*, which, though less interesting to the children than *Blackwood's*, was nevertheless better than nothing. They discussed politics and, almost certainly, Branwell's progress with the Glasstown saga. His stay, of necessity short, threw Charlotte into such a confusion of excitement that it was only after he had left that she remembered all the questions she had wanted to ask him.[33]

In Charlotte's absence, Branwell had been preoccupied with a major retrospective of the establishment and growth of Glasstown, which he entitled 'The History of the Young Men'. The biggest enterprise yet undertaken in terms of both physical size and imaginative scale, it was finally completed on 7 May 1831, about six weeks before Charlotte came home for the summer holidays.[34] The real threat of revolution in England, as the Reform Bill looked likely to be rejected by Parliament, prompted Branwell to tackle two more volumes of his occasional series, 'Letters from an Englishman', in June 1831. The first carried James Bellingham away from the Great Glasstown to Wellington's Glasstown in the African interior, in the company of the Marquis of Douro (Arthur Wellesley), his brother Charles and the poet Young Soult. During their journey they encounter cattle rustlers led by Pigtail, 'the greatest vender of white bread and Prussian Butter', stay overnight with a gang of poachers and 'rare lads' and are then summoned dramatically back to the Great Glasstown by news that it is on the point of revolution.[35] This little book was sabotaged by one of his sisters, probably Emily, who wrote on the back of the title page in her best schoolgirl French: 'ma cher frère vous l'avez ecris tres bien je croyais non vraiment vous n'avez pas. Ma foi que vous étes un mauvais garçon et vous serez un choquant homme.'[36]

The second volume, drawing heavily on newspaper accounts of the 1830 revolutions in Paris, Belgium, Poland, Germany and Italy, gives an account of the transformation of Alexander Rogue into a demagogue, including a verbatim report of his speech to Parliament, which results in his expulsion. It also vividly describes, from Bellingham's point of view, the resulting revolution and destruction of the Great Glasstown. Peace is only brought about by the intervention of the venerable patriarch, Crashey, one of the original Twelves.[37] Though his future importance was not yet apparent, in Alexander Rogue, whom he consistently calls 'Rougue', Branwell had created one of the greatest figures in all the juvenilia and one who was to haunt him for the rest of his life.

By contrast, Charlotte seems to have used the summer holiday as a period of relaxation from her self-imposed burden of education. The fact that she did not seize the opportunity to rush straight back into the affairs of Glasstown suggests that she had found her first term both intellectually demanding and fulfilling. There is only one extant piece of writing from her holiday in 1831 and that is a fragment. Far from referring to Branwell's destruction of Glasstown or advancing the fates of her own preferred characters, the fragment is a desultory and half-hearted descriptive piece, an excuse for a long poem by Marian Hume lamenting her abandonment by her lover, the Marquis of Douro, who has fallen in love with another woman. The love affair and the marquis's subsequent attraction to Lady Zenobia Ellrington had already been the subject of Charlotte's short story 'Albion and Marina', written in the October before she went to school, so this was little more than a reworking of an old story.[38]

Similarly, in the Christmas vacation, Charlotte produced only two poems. 'The trumpet hath sounded' is generally portrayed as the death knell for Glasstown, representing the fulfilment of the children's decision to destroy their whole imaginary world. This is to give the poem an arbitrary and isolated importance, however, which is not justified by subsequent events in the juvenilia. It would seem that Charlotte was simply toying with an idea suggested by Branwell's devastation of the city of Great Glasstown by Rogue and his revolutionaries. Charlotte, who had always preferred the magic and supernatural element in their stories, simply reinterpreted his story, attributing the destruction to a biblical-style visitation from the Angel of Death. The Genii, too, who had disappeared from Branwell's most recent work, reappear in Charlotte's poem, even if it is only so that they can be swept away with all the living souls of the Glasstown. The poem reflects Charlotte's passion for Isaiah, which Ellen Nussey had noted at school, and her growing love for Byron, upon whose poem, 'The Destruction of Sennacherib', it is based. It did not, however, mark the end of the kingdoms or characters of Glasstown, which were to continue to flourish long after the creation of Angria.[39] Within two weeks Charlotte was writing a second poem extolling the beauties of her imaginary Africa as if nothing had happened.[40] Again, however, she had neither the time nor the inclination to pursue her fictional writings in the month between her second and third terms at Roe Head.

In June 1832, at the end of her third term at Roe Head, Charlotte had to announce that she would not be returning after the summer holidays. She had had eighteen months' schooling but, through her own determination and self-discipline, had achieved far more than the syllabus would normally have allowed. She left the school covered with glory. She had won the silver medal for achievement three terms in succession and it was now presented to her to keep as a permanent memorial of her success. She had never had to wear the black sash for breach of rules, unladylike manners or incorrect grammar, and she had only once been awarded a black mark for failing to learn what Miss Wooler finally admitted, on protest from her other pupils, was an excessively long portion of Blair's *Belles-Lettres*.[41] After preparation by the Reverend Edward Carter, who was curate of Mirfield and engaged to Susan Wooler, Charlotte had been confirmed, probably during September 1831 when the Archbishop of York had visited the locality.[42] In every aspect of her life she had made dramatic improvements during those eighteen months.

Not the least important of these was in her social life. Alone among the Brontë girls, Charlotte made friends with girls of her own age and class which were to last a lifetime. There is no recorded instance of Emily ever having befriended anyone outside the family and Anne's only friend, Ann Cook, died only a year or so after she left Roe Head.[43] Charlotte's two closest friends were Ellen Nussey and Mary Taylor. The quiet, ladylike and kind Ellen, who had comforted her when she had been in the throes of home-sickness in her first weeks at school, became her bed-fellow in the dormitory and a spur to further achievement in the classroom. Even while they were both still at school, Charlotte and Ellen were already exchanging letters, probably, it must be admitted, as part of a school exercise. Ellen's older sister, Mercy, had invited them both to hear Mr Murray's lectures on Galvanism but, as it would have meant asking for an extra half-holiday, Charlotte observed that they would have to refuse, 'compelled "to bend our inclinations to our duty" (as Miss Wooler observed the other day)'. 'Besides', she added, 'we should perhaps have got behind-hand with our lessons.'[44]

In the Christmas holidays, 'knowing that when Schoolgirls once get home they willingly abandon every recollection which tends to remind them of school', Charlotte was surprised and gratified to receive letters from both Ellen and Mary. It is a measure of the comparative importance of each friendship that Charlotte's reply to Ellen was taken up with messages to Mary: she was glad Mr Taylor had liked Mary's drawings but was somewhat alarmed to hear that she was reading the 'lucubrations' of the Radical, William Cobbett.

I beg she will on no account burden her memory with passages to be repeated for my edification lest I should not justly appreciate either her kindness or their merit since that worthy personage & his principles whether private or political are no great favourites of mine.[45]

Ellen was intelligent but neither intellectual nor mentally adventurous. Mary, on the other hand, could follow Charlotte intellectually where Ellen could not and, though differing wildly in their views and thoughts, the two had much in common. Her two friends represented the two halves of Charlotte's life. Ellen, with her quiet domesticity, unquestioning conformity to social and moral codes of behaviour and complete conventionality, was a model which Charlotte strove to emulate in order to achieve a peaceful acceptance of her fate as a clergyman's daughter and middle-class spinster. In her friendship Charlotte found a certain restfulness and the ease of companionship. Throughout the many years of correspondence between them, Ellen was Charlotte's confidante for family problems and an emotional prop.

Mary, on the other hand, with her intellectual curiosity, utter disregard for appearances or the opinions of others and fearless pursuit of self-improvement, was a stimulus to Charlotte's longing to do and be something in the world. Mary was a born fighter and her example was both a frequent reproach to Charlotte and a constant reminder that she should use her abilities and talents to the full. Nothing gives a better indication of the characters of the three friends than their reactions to the fate which overcame each of them in turn: the necessity of facing a future without the security of family wealth or marriage. Ellen Nussey retreated into genteel poverty, keeping up appearances but entirely (and often querulously) dependent on the charity of her brothers. Mary Taylor, or Polly as she was affectionately known to her friends, packed her bags and emigrated to set up shop in New Zealand where she made enough money to return home and live in comfortable independence. Charlotte, torn between duty and inclination, lacking the courage to stand on her own two feet but afraid of the consequences of not doing so, submitted to second best, taking a series of hated governessing posts before giving in to literary ambition. It is more than unfortunate that virtually all Charlotte's letters to Mary Taylor have been destroyed. Their different emphasis would have given us more insight into Charlotte's development, particularly as a writer, than the commonplaces of her correspondence with Ellen.[46]

In early June 1832, Charlotte returned home to Haworth, parting with some reluctance from her friends. On her last day at Roe Head, she flung off her studious character, telling Ellen:

I should for once like to feel <u>out and out</u> a school-girl; I wish something would happen! Let us run round the fruit garden (running was what she never did); perhaps we shall meet some one, or we may have a fine for trespass.[47]

Nothing did happen, however, and Charlotte left school in the same quiet manner she had spent her time there. Her homecoming was no doubt boisterous enough. She was now sixteen and old enough not only to take charge of her own studies but also to direct those of her fourteen- and twelve-year-old sisters.

It must have been a relief to Patrick to relinquish the supervision of his daughters' education to Charlotte. The demands on his time were so great that he can have had little or no time to indulge in private reading and his health had never fully recovered from the attack on his lungs in 1830. Despite this, he was relentless in his campaigns. Like his old friend and vicar, John Buckworth, he tried to encourage pious men in his parish to go for ordination. He wrote several times on behalf of one, Anthony Metcalfe, who was the brother of a Keighley schoolmaster, but the archbishop refused to bend his rules to ordain a non-graduate who was already over thirty years of age.[48] Another campaign, of much wider significance to his district, was more successful.

In the summer of 1831 he had obtained a grant of eighty pounds from the National School Society towards the building of a Sunday school in Haworth. The church trustees had given some land adjacent to the parsonage for the site of the school and the remainder of the money was to be raised by a public subscription. Foreseeing future problems with his belligerent trustees, Patrick requested that the National School Society should 'peremptorily demand' that the incumbent should always have a considerable share in the management of the school. To add to the funds, Patrick invited local preachers of distinction to address his congregation and donate the collections to the subscription: among those who came were Edwin Smith of Keighley, who was soon to go as a missionary to India, and Thomas Crowther of Halifax, the champion of factory children, who was to become a regular preacher at Haworth. The new building was erected and opened in the summer of 1832 with a plaque, surely devised by Patrick, which noted that 'this National Church Sunday School is under the management of trustees of whom the Incumbent for the time being is one'.[49] All the Brontës were to take their turn as teachers in the Sunday school, a duty they could hardly escape as children of the minister. Anne 'looked the nicest and most serious like' and Branwell was notorious for his impatience:

He was very rapid and impulsive in his manner: he could not bear slowness of reading from the scholars; he could hardly wait till they got through their verses; he wanted to be getting on. Well, there was one scholar in the class who was extremely slow, and who spelled his way through almost every word. On one occasion Branwell got quite out of patience with him, and sharply remarked, 'Get on, or I'll turn you out of the class.' The boy's answer was characteristic of the rough and outspoken character of the Haworth people of the period. In angry tones he replied, 'Tha' willn't, tha' old Irish —.' And having had his say, he took his cap and walked out of the school … After school hours we were taken to the church, and placed in a large square pew under the north gallery. Branwell accompanied us. He used to retire to one corner close to the window, where he read with avidity during the service some book which was not the Prayer-book. If any of us disturbed him he was very cross. He would come to the interrupter, and twining a lock of the lad's hair round his finger, he would lift the offender from the floor and finish by giving him a sharp rap with his knuckles.[50]

Given the amount of time the Brontës would have to spend in the Sunday school, it is not surprising that one of Charlotte's first duties on returning from Roe Head was to entertain the female teachers to tea.[51]

It was over a month after leaving school before Charlotte got a letter from Ellen Nussey. How much she had missed her friend and longed to hear from her is an indication of how happy she had been at Roe Head.

My dearest Ellen
Your kind and interesting letter gave me the sincerest pleasure – I have been expecting to hear from you almost every day since my arrival at home and I \at/ length began to despair of receiving the wished-for letter … I do hope my dearest – that you will return to School again for your own sake though for mine I had rather you would remain at home as we shall then have more frequent opportunities of correspondence with each other … accept all the fondest expressions of genuine attachment, from Your real friend
Charlotte Brontë
P.S. Remember the mutual promise we made of a regular correspondence with each other … Farewell my dear dear dear Ellen.[52]

Ellen's letter had been full of chat about their school-friends and their circle, almost all of whom Ellen saw on a regular basis, in the holidays as well as at school to which she did return for the next term. Charlotte felt the contrast with her own life very deeply.

You ask me to give you a description of the manner in which I have passed every day since I left School: this is soon done as an account of one day is an account of all. In the Morning from nine o'clock till half-past twelve – I instruct my Sisters & draw, then we walk till dinner after dinner I sew till tea time, and after tea I either read, write, do a little fancy-work or draw, as I please. Thus in one delightful, though somewhat monotonous course my life is passed.[53]

It may have pleased Charlotte to give her friend a dull account of her life which would inspire sympathy, but this was scarcely the whole truth. In the same letter she admits to having been out to tea twice in the last month, expecting company at the parsonage that afternoon and the following Tuesday and to having had a letter from Leah Brooke, a former pupil at Roe Head.[54] Charlotte was fortunate in receiving letters from her school-friends, however intermittent, as this was an extravagance the family could ill afford; in these days before the introduction of the Penny Post system, it was the recipient, not the sender, who had to pay the postage, which was often quite arbitrarily and extravagantly high.

Part of Charlotte's sense of dullness may be attributable to her inability to work up any enthusiasm for the fictional world of Glasstown at this time. Far from allowing her to plunge back into the imaginary worlds with all the renewed vigour of someone who had been deprived of them for the last eighteen months, her release from school routine seems to have left her feeling only regret and lack of purpose. It was a month after her return before she tried her hand at any writing and even then her verse play, 'The Bridal', was only a half-hearted reworking of her 'Albion and Marina' of nearly two years before. Telling of Lady Zenobia Ellrington's efforts to win the Marquis of Douro from his fiancée, Marian Hume, by invoking magical and demonical arts, the story shows little advance in subject or style on Charlotte's previous efforts. It lacks even the interest of being seen through the eyes of the malicious and amusing Charles Wellesley.[55]

Though it is always dangerous to argue from absence of evidence, since manuscripts may well have been lost or destroyed, the six months following Charlotte's return from Roe Head appear to have been remarkably barren. Apart from 'The Bridal', which she had completed by 20 August, Charlotte seems to have written only two poems during the rest of 1832 – neither of them on Glasstown subjects. 'St John in the Island of Patmos', written on 30 August, is a competent but conventional poem of fifty-six lines based on the Revelation of St John. 'Lines on the Celebrated Bewick', completed three months later, is a longer and more evocative poem conjuring up the much loved woodcuts by Thomas Bewick which the young Brontës had copied so often.[56] Both poems are a departure from Charlotte's earlier efforts, not only in subject matter, but also in showing signs of being carefully thought out and worked upon. It seems likely that they were written for 'public' consumption rather than for inclusion in the juvenilia like her earlier poetry. These were poems she could show openly to her father and aunt as tangible proof of the benefit her education at Roe Head had bestowed on her.

Charlotte's lack of interest in the fictional worlds is in sharp contrast to Branwell's undimmed enthusiasm. Typically, he had found a new way of describing events in Glasstown, inspired by his reading of the classics and of John Milton. In 'The Fate of Regina', a poem of over 400 lines divided into two books, Branwell imitated the heroic verse of Homer's *Iliad* and Milton's *Paradise Lost* to describe the bloody battle for the city of Regina between the four kings and Rogue's revolutionary followers. He followed this with two odes, in the classical tradition, both written on his fifteenth birthday. 'Ode on the Celebration of the Great African Games' is interesting as one of the most direct comparisons between the world of the ancients and that of the Glasstown confederacy.[57] Not only are there parallels in landscape but, more importantly, the role of the Genii is seen as directly comparable to that of the gods of ancient Greece and Rome.

> Awful Branii < cloudy > gloomy giant
> Shaking oer earth his blazing air
> Brooding on blood with drear and vengeful soul
> He sits enthroned in clouds to hear his thunder roll
> < Em > \Dread/ Tallii next like a dire Eagle flies
> And on our mortal miseries feasts her bloody eyes
> Emmii and Annii last with boding cry
> Famine and war fortell and mortal misery

The role of the Twelves, too, is seen as similar to that of the heroes of the ancient world, fighting against the vengeful whims of the gods, voyaging far and wide and leading their people to found a new civilization.

'Ode to the Polar Star' is probably the finest Branwell had yet produced. It sings the praises of the travellers' 'guardian in the sky' which guides sailors through the stormy seas.

> Blesser of Mortals! Glorious guide
> Nor turning ever from thy course aside
> Eternal Pilot while time passes by
> > While Earthly Guides decay and die
> > Thou holdst thy throne
> > Fixed and alone
> In the vast concave of the nightly sky[58]

In August Branwell also completed the final three volumes of his 'Letters from an Englishman'. After the rebellion, James Bellingham continued his sightseeing trip to Sneaky's Glasstown in the company of the Marquis of Douro, his brother Charles Wellesley and Young Soult. For a second time, the party was caught up in Rogue's machinations: they heard one of his rabble-rousing speeches fomenting revolt against the aristocrats, were captured by his newly raised army and forced to witness his taking and burning of the city of Fidena. Branwell's juvenilia is usually (and unfairly) characterized as an endless description of campaign and battle but even at this early date, when he was more interested in warfare for its own sake, all the elements of his later work are present. Rogue is not simply a general but a demagogue whose political ambition is far more important than any military manoeuvring. The crux of the fifth volume is not the burning of Fidena but the desertion of his commander, O'Connor, which imperils the success of the siege. The theme of the sixth volume is the rivalry between Highlanders and Lowlanders in Rogue's army which leads to in-fighting and ultimately causes the defeat of the rebels and Rogue's own execution by the kings of the Glasstown states. Defiant to the end, dressed in black and with a countenance pale as death, Rogue faces the firing squad and orders them to fire in 'a firm clear but sepulchral tone'.[59]

The death of what was fast becoming his favourite character seems to have put rather a damper on Branwell's writing for the time being and, like his sister, he seems to have temporarily lost his enthusiasm for Glasstown. Charlotte had other excitements to distract her. At the end of September, only three months after leaving school, she was invited to stay for a fortnight at The Rydings with Ellen Nussey, her older sister, Mercy, and their mother. Escorted by Branwell, Charlotte travelled the twenty-odd miles to Birstall in a two-wheeled gig – a rather more refined mode of transport than the covered cart which had taken her to Roe Head. The battlemented old house and its beautiful grounds sent Branwell into ecstasies and he returned reluctantly to Haworth, telling his sister that he 'was leaving her in Paradise and if she were not intensely happy she never would be!' Charlotte's extreme shyness, which manifested itself most of all on formal occasions, made her a difficult guest. On one occasion, she trembled and nearly burst into tears when led into dinner by a stranger but, on the whole, the visit was a great success. The two girls were allowed to retreat to the garden away from the daily round of visitors and the time passed pleasantly enough.[60]

In the middle of October, Branwell returned to fetch Charlotte home again. Laden with apples, sent by Ellen for her sisters, she received a rapturous welcome, as if, she told Ellen, she had been away for more than a year rather than just a fortnight. The two friends had agreed to write alternately once a month and, at Charlotte's insistence, to continue their correspondence in French. Ellen, lacking Charlotte's single-minded pursuit of self-improvement, lost her nerve and so the good intentions did not outlast Charlotte's first letter after her return home.[61] In the school-marmish tone she often adopted towards Ellen in the early days of their correspondence, Charlotte wrote in the new year of 1833:

The first day of January always presents to my mind a train of very solemn and important reflections and a question< s > more easily asked than answered frequently occurs viz: How have I improved the past year and with [what] good intentions do I view the dawn of its successor? these my dearest Ellen are weighty considerations which (young as we are) neither you nor I can too deeply or too seriously ponder. I am sorry your too great diffidence arising I think from the want of sufficient confidence in your own capabilities prevented you from writing to me in French as I think the attempt would have materially contributed to your improvement in that language.

Ellen's refusal to write in French was perhaps wise, given Charlotte's reaction to her effort at literary criticism of Walter Scott's novel, *Kenilworth*. 'I was exceedingly amused at the characteristic and naive manner in which you expressed your detestation of Varney's character so much so indeed that I could not forbear laughing aloud.'[62] Though she might mock Ellen's prosaic inability to appreciate the arts, she felt humbled by her friend's willingness to conform to social pressures and to submit patiently to duty. Six months later, Charlotte wrote to Ellen lamenting the difference in their characters and her own inability to maintain that single-minded pursuit of self-improvement which had so marked her progress at Roe Head:

unhappily all the good thoughts that enter m[y mind] evaporate almost before I have had time [to] ascertain their existence, every right resolution < that > \which/ I form is so transient, so fragile, and so easily broken that I sometimes fear I shall never be what I ought.[63]

The reason for this sudden remorse was that Charlotte had been lured back into the Glasstown fold and was now deeply immersed in writing about the fictional world. Her determination to devote her free time to study had been gradually worn away over the first few months of 1833.

Branwell had no such sense of conflict. After a five-month silence – which may again be due simply to lost manuscripts – he had launched back into Glasstown with one of his most ambitious projects to date. Between 30 January and 8 February 1833, he resurrected (without explanation) his hero, Alexander Rogue, and wrote his first full-scale story about him. Finally abandoning the miniature books in which he had written earlier, he adopted a much larger format which he had used only once before but which he was to use consistently from now on. The story, 'The Pirate', was written in a booklet, 114mm by 185mm, which was at least four times larger than previous books.[64] As he still adopted the minuscule script of the earlier stories, the whole scale of the project was much more ambitious than all his earlier works except 'The History of the Young Men'.

'The Pirate' marks the first serious attempt in the Brontë juvenilia to develop the role of one particular figure. Rogue was not one of the original Twelves, but his character had been delineated by Charlotte as early as December 1829.

Rogue is about 47 years of age. He is very tall, rather spare. His countenance is handsome, except that there is something very startling in his fierce, grey eyes and formidable forehead. His manner is rather polished and gentlemanly, but his mind is deceitful, bloody and cruel. His walk (in which he much prides himself) is stately and soldier-like, and he fancies that it greatly resembles that of the Duke of Wellington. He dances well and plays cards admirably, being skilled in all the sleight-of-hand blackleg tricks of the gaming table. And, to crown all, he is excessively vain of this (what he terms) accomplishment.[65]

Despite being a 'celebrated character' in 1829, Rogue merited only the briefest of passing mentions until, during Charlotte's absence at school, Branwell had turned him into the political demagogue and revolutionary whose exploits had been observed in 'Letters from an Englishman'. In 'The Pirate' Branwell adopted his same English narrator, the merchant James Bellingham,[66] and described how Rogue had turned pirate, preying on the shipping of both Napoleon and Wellington and, in the process, attacking some of Bellingham's own vessels. The spoils he had disposed of through his company, Rogue, Sdeath and Co., and by this means financed his extravagant lifestyle in Verdopolis. For the first time the portrait of Rogue is fleshed out. He still has the same tall, thin and erect bearing and the handsome face still bears the cynical sneering expression which had marked him out in 'Letters from an Englishman'. Now, however, he is portrayed as a heavy drinker, sinking prodigious amounts of raw brandy and wine, and also, more shockingly, the suggestion of atheism hangs about him.

I say sir Im as near foundering as Life can be be [sic] I say Im a Perfect wreck why (< dir drinkig > drinking again largly) why I couldn't keep body and soul together if it wasnt for this Body and soul did I say. fool who in the name of nonsense ever heard of two thing[s] seperating that were never together?[67]

In 'The Pirate' Branwell was able to give full vent to his fascination for this increasingly satanic character, who was modelled on Lord Byron's Conrad, Walter Scott's Richard Varney and Milton's Lucifer. The story also introduces the symbiotic relationship between Rogue and his evil genius, Robert Patrick Sdeath, which draws heavily on the story of Robert Wringhim and his association with the devil in James Hogg's *Confessions of a Justified Sinner.*[68] In creating a real and complex character out of Rogue, Branwell had found a counterbalance to Charlotte's fixation with her hero, Arthur Wellesley, the Marquis of Douro. Middle-aged, debauched, cruel, evil and an inciter of popular revolt, he is the antithesis of the young, handsome, high-minded, romantic and aristocratic marquis. The conflict between them, which was to shape much of the future writing of both Charlotte and Branwell, is already foreshadowed in 'The Pirate'. At the end of the story, Rogue suddenly and unexpectedly marries Lady Zenobia Ellrington, the magnificent Italian blue-stocking whom Charlotte had invented as a rival to Marian Hume for the Marquis of Douro's affections.[69]

The few fragments Charlotte wrote in the spring of 1833 suggest she was at least thinking about the development of the Glasstown stories at this time. Branwell's creation of Rogue had clearly intrigued her. One of her fragments was a poem, 'Lord Ronan', which depicted Rogue on his deathbed reluctantly having to fulfil his pact with the devil and surrender his soul to him.[70] Fascinated as she was by the emergence of this new character, Charlotte could not allow Rogue to be placed centre stage at the expense of her own Marquis of Douro. The old childhood rivalry between brother and sister reasserted itself and her response was to restore the marquis to his dominant role in Glasstown in a story of comparable length to 'The Pirate'.

'Something About Arthur', which she finished on 1 May, is a curious, disjointed piece written under her favourite pseudonym of Lord Charles Wellesley, the malicious brother of her hero. Surprisingly, in view of their respective reputations, it is Charlotte, not Branwell, who in this tale introduces the first fully developed picture of low life in Verdopolis. For six months Charles Wellesley's only companions had been 'Tavern Keepers, poachers, park-breakers, Highwaymen, murderers, the Flashmen about Town, &c &c my only places of Resort pothouses, the Rend[e]zvous of Robbers & the open fields'. The story is full of heavy-drinking 'rare lads', racy slang and incidents of casual cruelty, which form a long and incongruous introduction to the main theme, the fifteen-year-old Arthur Wellesley's love affair with a peasant girl, Mina Laury, who is discovered to be the daughter of his own childhood nurse.[71]

In writing about the Marquis of Douro's first love affair, before his meeting with and marriage to Marian Hume, the seventeen-year-old Charlotte had found the one great subject which was to dominate her subsequent juvenilia and even her published novels. Like any teenage girl, Charlotte had a romantic concept of love which had been fostered by her addiction to the novels of Walter Scott. The development of a love affair between the marquis and Mina Laury, which almost seems to have been an afterthought in 'Something About Arthur', touched a chord in Charlotte's nature. The story itself suddenly takes life: it also sparked off a whole series of increasingly long and complex stories about the triumph of love over apparently insuperable difficulties. For the next two years Charlotte would be constantly employed on the romantic affairs of the Glasstowners. As soon as one story ended, she began another.

Her heroes and heroines are invariably extraordinarily beautiful. The men are tall, usually fair and have effeminate features. The women are either dark, bold, dashing beauties with voluptuous figures or small, delicate, golden-haired and virginal young girls. Charlotte seized every opportunity in her writing to linger lovingly over descriptions of the physical beauty and splendid dress of her characters, particularly her heroines. The future creator of small, plain Jane Eyre, who was herself described as 'very ugly' to her face by Mary Taylor, was still spellbound by matchless figures and features. Apart from one or two female characters, such as Lily Hart, whose beauty, in true fairytale fashion, makes her worthy of elevation to the higher echelons of society, Charlotte's heroes and heroines are also invariably aristocratic. Cold, proud and haughty to those beneath them, they also exhibit the 'aristocratic' qualities of nobility, courage and enthusiasm.[72] It is a curious contradiction that these passionate creatures, capable of enduring and overcoming every sort of obstacle to union with their loved ones, are completely sexless. We know they are in love because we are told they are, but there is no real attempt to describe the attraction or to develop it. There is no lingering over love scenes, which are limited to declarations of undying love, an occasional chaste kiss on the hand and an even more infrequent 'fervent embrace'. Clearly it is the romance of the situation rather than the nature of the love itself which attracts Charlotte's attention. It is equally clear from the naivety of the relationships that Charlotte's knowledge of the grand passion was entirely formed from books.

Charlotte's love stories reflect her immaturity in other ways. She had never lost her childhood addiction to mystery and the magical and super-natural. This now found a new outlet in the creation of dashing young men of seemingly obscure origins who, like Arthurian knights, have to prove their aristocratic origins before they can marry the beautiful and spirited heroines. Edward Sydney, son of the Duke of York, is introduced as a foundling child, the Earl of St Clair woos the Lady Emily as plain Mr Leslie and Lily Hart is secretly married to her Mr Seymour for three years before she discovers that he is really John, Duke of Fidena and heir to Sneakysland.[73] The revelations of true identity are often made through magical means. The foundling Edward Sydney, for example, is guided by mysterious apparitions and supernatural voices to the Philosopher's Isle where Byron's magician, Manfred, reveals that he is none other than the long-lost son of Frederick, Duke of York. Similarly, a vision of the drowned figure of her fiancé, Henry Percy, allows Marian Hume to put aside her scruples about his dis-appearance and marry the Marquis of Douro.[74]

Though Branwell was impressed enough with the introduction of affairs of the heart to create his own pairs of lovers,[75] he firmly rejected the magical element which Charlotte introduced so often to resolve her stories. Since adopting Rogue as his chief character, his interest was firmly in the sphere of human motivation and actions and their consequences. The Genii had only been mentioned once in his writings since the summer of 1832 whereas they were still playing a significant interventionary role in Charlotte's stories a year later.[76] Similarly, though he willingly accepted all her new characters, he took some delight in knocking all the romance out of them and putting them firmly into the real world. Her dashing and lovesick heroes, Edward Sydney and Earl St Clair, for instance, become in Branwell's stories cynical and self-seeking leaders of the powerful Aristocratic Party opposed to the Democrats.[77]

In the old tit-for-tat which had been a feature of their childhood writings before Charlotte went away to school, she responded by bringing the roman-tic touch to Branwell's arch-demagogue, Alexander Rogue himself. In 'The Pirate' and 'Real Life in Verdopolis', a story written in the summer of 1833, Branwell had made the revolutionary a former buccaneer and a robber baron with a hideout in the hills.[78] Charlotte explained that Rogue had been driven to this life of crime by sixteen years spent in exile from Glasstown, a punishment which was imposed on him for attempting to secure the execution of the Earl of St Clair for treason. He had also been forced to adopt Alexander Rogue as his pseudonym: 'Few now can recognize in that seditious demagogue that worn-out & faded debauchee Alexander Rogue Viscount Ellrington, the once brilliant & handsome young soldier Colonel Augustus Percy.' His rivalry with the Marquis of Douro she also extended to cover their respective wives: Zenobia, the wife from whom Rogue has derived his new title, is increasingly depicted as being still in love with the marquis, while Ellrington himself has designs on the marchioness.[79]

How close the partnership between brother and sister was at this time is illustrated by two stories which they wrote contemporaneously: Charlotte's 'The Foundling', written between 31 May and 27 June 1833, and Branwell's more ambitious two-volume story 'Real Life in Verdopolis', begun in May and finished in September of the same year.[80] Each story introduces a new young and bold outsider to the Verdopolitan scene, Edward Sydney and Viscount Castlereagh, who align themselves with the Marquis of Douro and Viscount Ellrington respectively. Both Sydney and Castlereagh fall in love with and eventually marry, after many trials of their devotion, a Julia who has almost been forced into a marriage with a rival lover against her will. In 'The Foundling', the Glasstowners riot and attack the Tower of All Nations, thinking that their leader, Ellrington, is imprisoned there and similarly, Ellrington himself in 'Real Life in Verdopolis' leads a popular attack on the prison in Glasstown to release some of his fellow conspirators who might betray his secrets.

Both stories also introduce a new and sinister element in Glasstown life, a secret society. Charlotte's was based on the Philosopher's Isle, where the nobles of Glasstown were sent for their education; under the instruction of Manfred the magician, the students learnt the secrets of life and death but were sworn not to misuse the knowledge. Branwell's, typically, is not concerned with magic but with politics. Castlereagh is ritually initiated into the society, which is called the Paradise of Souls or the Elysium, and swears never to divulge its secrets: he is then free to join in its activities which, for the moment, consist chiefly of gambling, drinking and fighting. Ellrington is the President, the Marquis of Douro its Vice-President. Interestingly, these accounts of secret societies coincide with the revival of a masonic society, the Lodge of the Three Graces, in Haworth. At the very time Branwell was writing about the Elysium Society, his father was preaching a sermon to the masons of the surrounding area who had gathered in Haworth to celebrate the opening of the lodge's first private meeting rooms.[81]

If the stories had a great deal in common, they were also used to score points against their respective authors. In 'The Foundling' Edward Sydney makes a great maiden speech in Parliament against Ellrington and succeeds in defeating his motion against the government: Branwell responds by having 'that hat[e]ful spider Sydny' soundly drubbed in a speech by Montmorenci,

Ellrington's ally, which accuses him of being unfit for office.[82] Charlotte makes Zenobia bewail the fact that she ever married Ellrington and declare that she married him solely in a fit of pique at the marquis whom she truly loves. Branwell gets his own back by having the marquis become well and truly embroiled in all the disreputable activities of the Elysium Society: 'till I read this admirable work', responded Charlotte as Charles Wellesley, 'I was ignorant to what a hopeless depth he had sunk in the black gulphs of sin & dissipation'.[83]

The interchange of characters and ideas and the interweaving of often complex story-lines demanded a close partnership between brother and sister. Although they did not necessarily discuss their plots beforehand, they were quick to respond to developments in each other's writing. The very act of writing thus became a sort of game in which each attempted to outdo or outmanoeuvre the other. As soon as one story ended, another began so that they constantly had some writing on hand. No writings by Emily and Anne exist from this period. It is possible that they were as deeply absorbed in the imaginary worlds as their older siblings, but this seems unlikely. A thundering editorial in Branwell's 'Monthly Intelligencer', written between March and April of this year, suggests that the fourteen- and thirteen-year-old girls had 'absconded' from Glasstown, leaving the fate of their characters in Charlotte and Branwell's hands.

A Few words to The Cheif Genii
When a Parent leaves his Childern young and inexperienced, and without a cause absconds, never more troubling himself about them those Childern according to received notions among men if they by good fortune should happen to survive this neglect and become of repute in society are by no means bound to believe that he has done < their > his duty to them as a parent, merely because they have risen, nor are they indeed required to own or treat him as a parent. this is all very plain. and we believe that 4 of our readers will understand our aim in thus speaking.
A child of the G—ii[84]

This suggests that the foundation of the kingdom of Angria gave Emily and Anne an excuse to break away and establish their own independent world of Gondal, though there are no specific references to it until November of the following year. It seems unlikely that they had simply abandoned Glasstown and giving up writing altogether.

Charlotte and Branwell's absorption in the affairs of Glasstown was of necessity put aside for a few weeks in the summer. At long last Charlotte was able to return the kindness she had been shown at The Rydings the previous autumn and invite Ellen to stay at the parsonage. In July 1833, Ellen paid her first visit to Haworth and, though recorded many years later, we have her own detailed account of her impressions of the Brontës and their home. This is the first comprehensive description of the family on record.

From the very start, Ellen stood in awe of Patrick. At fifty-six and with his hair already snow white, he must have seemed very old to his sixteen-year-old visitor: she politely described him as looking 'very venerable' and his old-fashioned manner and mode of speech as having 'a tone of high-bred courtesy'. She clearly did not believe in his poor state of health, regarding him as a hypochondriac and the enormous white silk cravat which he wound round his throat to protect him from bronchial complaints as an eccentric affectation. His habit of sleeping with a loaded pistol to hand, which he discharged from his bedroom window each morning, filled her with alarm; the 'strange stories' told to him by some of his oldest parishioners, which he recounted to his family, were 'full of grim humour & interest' to them but made Ellen 'shiver and shrink from hearing'.[85]

Aunt Branwell, who was a year older than Patrick, Ellen also found something of a curiosity, describing her as 'a very small antiquated little lady', wearing silk dresses, huge old-fashioned caps and a false hair-piece – a row of 'light auburn curls' – on her forehead. She had 'a horror' of the Yorkshire climate and amused Ellen by clicking about inside the parsonage wearing pattens, normally only worn outside, to protect her feet from the cold stone floors.

She talked a great deal of her younger days, the gaities of her native town, Penzance in Cornwall, the soft warm climate &c She very probably had been a belle \among her acquaintances/ the social life of her younger days she appeared to recall with regret

The thoroughly modern Ellen was shocked when Aunt Branwell teasingly offered her a pinch of snuff from her pretty gold snuffbox, this being a habit that had died out among gentlewomen in the early years of the century. She was still responsible for Anne's lessons and sewing, though Emily had begun to have the disposal of her own time.[86]

Even Tabby, 'the faithful trustworthy old servant', was, according to Ellen, 'very quaint in appearance'. She was also extremely active, and still regarded it as her duty to accompany her 'childer' when they walked any distance from home if Branwell was unavailable as an escort. Intensely loyal to the Brontës, she always rebuffed the curious enquiries from the Haworth people who wished to know if they were not 'fearfully larn'd', refused to indulge in gossip and went off in a huff to recount the story to her charges.[87]

With the younger generation, Ellen had more empathy. Emily, now fifteen, had a 'lithesome graceful figure' and was the tallest in the house after her father.

her hair which was naturally as beautiful as Charlotte's was in the same unbecoming tight curl and frizz, and there was the same want of complexion. She had very beautiful eyes, kind< ly >, kindling, liquid eyes, sometimes they looked grey, some-times dark blue but she did not often look at you, she was too reserved. She talked very little. She and Anne were \like twins/ inseparable companions, \and/ in the very closest sympathy which never had any interruption.

Anne, dear gentle Anne, was quite different in appearance to the others. She was her Aunt's favorite. Her hair was a very pretty light brown and < in falling curls > fell on her neck in graceful curls. She had lovely violet blue eyes, fine pencilled eye-brows, a clear, almost transparent complexion.[88]

Anne's hair was actually darker than Ellen remembered: a little plait, cut off and carefully preserved by Patrick on 22 May 1833, suggests that it had deepened to a rich brown with a hint of auburn, though it remained fairer than her sisters'.[89]

Of Branwell, whose later career rendered him unmentionable in Ellen's eyes, she had nothing to say, except that he studied regularly with his father and was already learning to paint in oils because, even at this early date, all the family expected him to have a distinguished career as an artist.[90] From other sources at the time, however, we learn that he was small for his age but good-looking, with his father's aquiline nose and a high forehead. Afflicted with his sisters' poor eyesight, he was obliged to wear glasses and he wore his hair, which was the reddest in the family, rather long in what he considered an artistic fashion. With somewhat untypical self-deprecating humour, Branwell caricatured himself as a colour grinder to the great Verdopolitan portrait painter, Sir Edward de Lisle, in one of his stories of the following year.

This grinder < fe > was a fellow of singular aspect he was a Lad of perhaps 17. years of age but from his appearance he seemed at le[a]st half a score years older and < ? > his meagre freckled visage < and rom > and large Roman nose thatched by a thick matt of red hair constantly changed and twisted themselves into an endless variety of incomprehensible movements As he spoke instead of looking his auditor streight in the face he turned his eyes which were further beautified by a pair of spectacles, either toward his toes nose or fingers and while one word issued stammering from his mouth it< s > was straightway contradicted or confused by a < mor? > chaos of strange suceeding jargon.[91]

Like his hero, Viscount Ellrington, Branwell was an intellectual with an extensive knowledge of the classics and a passion for music. Unlike his hero, he was excitable and emotional and unable to conceal his feelings.

It must have been about this time that Branwell went to Keighley Feast with his friend Michael Merrall, son of a local mill owner. The town was crowded with stalls, booths and sideshows which were lit up as evening fell. Branwell was in such a state of excitement that he was barely able to control himself and insisted on seeing and trying everything. When he and Michael Merrall went on one of the fairground rocking boats, however, he was so overwrought that each time the boat plunged downwards, he screamed 'Oh! my nerves! my nerves! Oh! my nerves!' Later, as the friends made their way on foot back to Haworth, they wrestled with each other and Branwell lost his glasses, resulting in a sleepless night as he worried about having to confess to his father how he had lost them. Fortunately for him, the confession was avoided as Michael Merrall found the glasses, undamaged, the next morning and returned them to Branwell without his father being any the wiser.[92]

Branwell was also apparently involved in a village boxing club which met in an upper room of one of the public houses. No doubt part of the attraction of 'the noble art' was that it asserted Branwell's masculinity in a house full of girls. On the other hand, he was also following in the footsteps of his much admired Lord Byron and even *Blackwood's Magazine*, which had formed so many of his other tastes, dedicated articles to the subject on a regular basis. Branwell's new interest was carried over into his writing; about this time both Ellrington and the Marquis of Douro take up pugilism in the halls of the Elysium Society.[93]

Odd references indicate the daily routine of life at the parsonage at this time. Breakfast – at least for Emily and Anne – was oatmeal porridge – a somewhat surprising choice to the fastidious Ellen. A portion of this meal was always reserved by them for the dog, Grasper, which appears to have been a terrier of some kind. In the afternoons the young people would walk out on the moors if the weather was favourable. Emily – her reserve temporarily forgotten – Anne and Branwell would go ahead, fording the streams and placing stepping-stones for Charlotte and Ellen who followed in their wake. Emily and Anne's favourite walk was along Sladen Beck to a place where several springs converged on the stream: with typical hyperbole, which suggests it may have played a role in their fictional writing, they called it 'The Meeting of the Waters'. It was here that Emily, 'half reclining on a slab of stone played like a young child with the tad-poles in the water, making them swim about, and \then/ fell to moralising on the big and the little, the brave and cowardly as she chased them \about/ with her hand'. The adults spent the afternoon more sedately, Aunt Branwell reading aloud to Patrick and arguing the issues with him. Sometimes the discussions would continue throughout tea, which the family all took together, and Ellen observed, with some admiration, that Aunt Branwell would tilt her arguments against Patrick 'without fear'. The household assembled once again at eight o'clock for family worship and then at nine Patrick retired to bed, pausing only to tell his 'children' not to stay up too late and to wind the grandfather clock halfway up the stairs.[94]

The sole exception to this daily routine was the now customary annual ritual of inviting the Sunday school teachers to tea, which Ellen witnessed for the first time. Her genteel manners were shocked by the way these robust factory girls called their employers by their Christian names and, much to the amusement of the Brontës, she suggested that they should be taught a more respectful form of address. 'Vain attempt!' was Emily's typically laconic response. Ellen had her revenge, however, when the girls undertook to initiate the Brontë sisters into playing some games. 'The Brontë faces were worth anything as a study', she gleefully reported, 'they had such a puzzled, amused, submissive expression, intently anxious though, to give pleasure and gratify others.'[95]

Ellen Nussey's description of the parsonage suggests that it was an austere and comfortless home: the Brontës' lack of money meant that the furnishings were 'scant and bare' and she implied that because Patrick was 'remarkably independent of the luxuries and comforts of life' he chose to impose this on his children. Though by comparison with Ellen's own, much wealthier, home the parsonage appeared sparsely furnished and unfashionable, it was nothing like as austere as she suggests. The son of the Haworth tailor, who had been sent to do some work at the parsonage, was fascinated by the pictures in the study; noticing his interest, Patrick took him round and explained the various subjects depicted. These included black-and-white engravings of a number of dramatic pictures by John Martin, the celebrated allegorical painter of biblical scenes. The tailor's son mentioned 'The Last Judgement' and 'The Plains of Heaven', and the 1861 bill of sale for the parsonage lists 'The Deluge', 'Belshazzar's Feast' and 'Joshua commanding the Sun to Stand'. There may also have been an engraving of Martin's 'Queen Esther', as the thirteen-year-old Branwell copied the picture in December 1830. In addition, there were at least three other framed engravings, 'St Paul preaching at Athens', 'The Resurrection announced to the Apostles' and 'The Passage of the Red Sea', and two oil paintings, 'Bolton Abbey' and 'Kirkstall Abbey', the last two of which were also copied by Charlotte.[96] The presence of so many pictures in a financially hard-pressed household is an indication of the importance the Brontës attached to art.

Towards the end of Ellen's visit, there was a clubbing together of pocket money to secure an excursion to Bolton Abbey. Branwell procured a phaeton to convey the little party of young people and they set off from the parsonage at between five and six in the morning. Though this was his first trip to Bolton Abbey, 'Branwell seemed to know every inch of the way, could tell the names of the hills that would be driven over, or walked over, their exact height above the sea, the views to be seen, and the places to be passed through.' The only pall on the occasion was the mortification which the Brontës felt when their 'shabby-looking conveyance' was regarded with disdain by the hotel attendants at the Devonshire Arms where they break-fasted. No doubt this was not helped by Ellen's family arriving in 'a handsome carriage-and-pair' to take her home. The two parties had a pleasant walk in the abbey grounds, Emily and Anne barely speaking, except to each other, but Branwell, who was 'in a phrenzy of pleasure', talking 'fast and brilliantly' and amusing everyone. 'He had any amount of poetry ready for quotation, and this day he was well off in an appreciative audience whenever he chose to recite', Ellen explained, adding, somewhat grudgingly, 'it was one of the things he did well'.[97]

Ellen's visit to Haworth had lasted only a fortnight, but she won the hearts of all at the parsonage, as Charlotte was delighted to tell her:

Were I to tell you of the impression you have made on every one here, you would accuse me of flattery. Papa and Aunt are continually adducing you as an example for me to shape my actions and behaviour by, Emily & Anne say 'they never saw any one they liked so well as Miss Nussey' and Tabby whom you have absolutely fascinated talks a great deal more nonsense about your Ladyship than I choose to report[98]

The only incident of note, Charlotte reported, in the two months since her visit was that Emily had been very ill with what was described as 'erysipelas', or red and painful inflammation of the arm, resulting in severe bilious attacks and a general weakness. Her arm eventually had to be cut to remove the infection.[99] Though it is pure speculation, it is tempting to identify this 'illness' with the incident Charlotte described to Mrs Gaskell and put into her novel *Shirley*. Emily, whose love of animals was always stronger than any concern for her own wellbeing, had seen a dog running past the parsonage with its head lolling and its tongue hanging out. Thinking only to relieve it, she went out to give it a drink of water, only to have it snap at her and draw blood. Well aware of the dangers if the dog was rabid and had infected her, Emily went straight into the kitchen and, taking one of Tabby's red-hot irons from the fire, cauterized the wound herself. The bite and the cauterization could well have caused the inflammation and consequent biliousness which the doctor and her family diagnosed as erysipelas; her own powerful imagination, alive to the horrors of rabies, may have contributed to her general weakness. With characteristic fortitude, Emily told no one of the incident until all danger of infection was past, fearing that her family might over-react and make an intolerable fuss over her.[100]

As usual, Charlotte's letter to Ellen made no reference to the important developments which were taking place in the Glasstown stories. One of the most significant was Branwell's rapid erosion of the Marquis of Douro's clean-cut, romantic image in the second half of 1833. This had remained relatively unchanged since Charlotte had described him in December 1829:

In appearance he strongly resembles his noble mother. He has the same tall, slender shape, the same fine and slightly Roman nose. His eyes, however, are large and brown like his father's, and his hair is dark auburn, curly and glossy, much like what his father's was when he was young. His character also resembles the Duchess's, mild and humane but very courageous, grateful for any favour that is done and ready to forgive injuries, kind to others and disinterested in himself. His mind is of the highest order, elegant and cultivated. His genius is lofty and soaring, but he delights to dwell among pensive thoughts and ideas rather than to roam in the bright regions of fancy.[101]

Branwell made the marquis plunge into the dissipation of the Elysium Society where, presiding in the absence of Ellrington, he is an enthusiastic participant in the gambling, card playing, drinking and fighting. This was only the beginning of his fall from grace. In November, Branwell wrote a story describing Napoleon's invasion of Glasstown from Frenchysland. The marquis, like Ellrington, is appointed one of the leaders of the Verdopolitan army. Instead of setting his former example of moral rectitude and inspiring his troops in their fight against overwhelming odds, the marquis imperils the whole enterprise by leading a mutiny when some of his men are disciplined. Even more seriously, when the ministry refuse to allow the army to consolidate its success in battle against the French by raising more money, men and arms, the marquis and Ellrington lead a military coup, execute the Prime Minister, Earl St Clair, and set up a ruling Council of Six.[102] The Machiavellian Ellrington is, of course, manoeuvring behind the scenes and is the prime instigator of the coup, but he prefers to remain an *éminence grise* while the marquis enjoys the limelight. In the space of three books and six months, therefore, Branwell turned his sister's effete and lovelorn hero into a hardened soldier, a proud, overbearing and ruthless tyrant.

Perhaps surprisingly, Charlotte does not seem to have reacted to Branwell's perversion of her favourite character. Similarly, she seems to have been quite happy to sit back and let him dictate the course of events in the Glasstown kingdoms. In October, while she made a number of false starts on new stories which she eventually grouped together and called 'Arthuriana: or Odds and Ends', he began a new story, 'The Politics of Verdopolis'.[103] Despite its title, the book was largely taken up with introducing a new heroine, Mary Percy, the proud and haughty, beautiful and intellectual seventeen-year-old daughter of Viscount Ellrington by his first wife, Mary Henrietta, who had died at the age of twenty-one. The rest of the story, inspired by the agitation throughout the United Kingdom in the build-up to and in the wake of the Reform Bill of 1832, is taken up with the dissolution of the Glasstown Parliament and the subsequent general election. There are lively scenes depicting the preparation for the campaign and the hustings, which must reflect Branwell's personal experience of electioneering the previous year. Despite its beautiful heroine, who was to become a leading figure in future juvenilia, the story is far removed from the exotic locations and magical interventionism of Charlotte's Glasstown. For the first time, the location is typically English: Percy Hall is an ancient country house, set in oak woodlands and deer-filled parklands, rather than the almost oriental splendour of Verdopolis. Branwell's evocative description of the place, which Charlotte found inspirational,[104] was to set a new tone of realism in the juvenilia which removed it one stage further from its original African concept.

This approach was consolidated in the next two books Branwell wrote. Five days after finishing 'Politics in Verdopolis', he began 'An Historical

Narrative of the "War of Enroachment"', which was followed immediately by 'An Historical Narrative of the War of Aggression'.[105] Between them, these two stories turned the world of the Glasstown Confederacy upside down, threatening its very existence by the invasion of highly trained French armies rather than native Ashantees. In its defence, the Verdopolitans march out to the eastern city of Angria, with its villages of Zamorna and Northangerland. Continuing the theme he had begun in 'Politics in Verdopolis', Branwell gave Angria an English, even specifically Yorkshire setting. The Angrians are depicted as stubborn and unhelpful provincials, epitomized by their leader Warner Howard Warner who lives in a thinly disguised Haworth (Howard), 'a wild villiage seated amid barren uncultivated Hills'.[106] Despite the mutiny led by Ellrington and Douro and overwhelming numbers of French opposing them, the Glasstown army wins a famous victory at the Heights of Velino. Even at such a glorious moment, Branwell cannot resist a dig at his sister. Lord Lofty is killed in the battle leading a gallant charge against the enemy in an effort to wipe out the stains 'so needlessly stuck to his character from the ridiculous transactions mentioned in a manner so lively in "Arthuriana" by Lord Charles Wellesley'.[107] The military coup which puts Ellrington and the Marquis of Douro in total control of the government of Verdopolis, as well as its armies, is followed up by a second great victory 'on the feilds of Zamorna and Northangerland' which 'decided the fate of all Africa'.[108] On this auspicious note Branwell ended his last story of the year 1833. The victory had indeed decided not only the fate of all Africa but also the future course of the juvenilia. The focus of interest would now move on from the exotic and Babylonic city of Glasstown to the more prosaic and provincial world.

Chapter Eight

ANGRIANS ARISE!

The increasing amount of time spent in writing at the parsonage did not go unnoticed. Patrick could not be unaware that his children were spending many hours poring over their manuscripts but when he saw the minute cramped hand in which they were writing he was deeply concerned. His children's eyesight would be strained, their posture ruined and, perhaps more importantly, there was something obsessively and unhealthily secret about the sheer volume of diminutive writing. He clearly knew at least something of its nature, for he observed to Mrs Gaskell that as the children grew older 'their compositions and plots were more matur'd, and had less of romance and more of taste, and judgement'.[1] Wisely, Patrick made no attempt to put a stop to the writing but he did encourage them to channel their energies into less secretive projects. At Christmas 1833, he presented Charlotte with a manuscript notebook in which he had written on the top of the first page, '1833. All that is written in this book, must be in a good, plain <u>and legible hand</u>. PB.' Charlotte made an effort to please her father by copying into it a series of long poems on heroic subjects which were unconnected with the imaginary worlds and therefore fit for public consumption.

The first, 'Richard Coeur de Lion & Blondel', was written on 27 December 1833, the second, 'Death of Darius Codomanus', on 2 May 1834 and the third, 'Saul', on 7 October 1834.[2] She added only two more poems during the course of the next year, so Patrick's attempt to give a less introverted direction to his daughter's writing failed miserably.

Charlotte was far too absorbed in the delicious prospects held out by the creation of a new kingdom of Angria to allow herself to be deflected from writing about the imaginary worlds for long. The marquis and Ellrington had both been rewarded for their services in defeating the French: taking their titles from the site of their great victory in Angria, the marquis had become Duke of Zamorna, Ellrington the Earl of Northangerland. This was not enough to satisfy the ambition of either man, however, and Zamorna now demanded that the huge, fertile but thinly populated eastern province of Angria should be ceded to him unconditionally and that he should be allowed to rule it as its monarch. In a great speech to the Assembly, Branwell had Northangerland support Zamorna's claim:

My Lords Can the workman mean his master harm when after having done that Masters Bidding he comes to receive his rightful wages ... how can Arthur Wellesly mean the country Harm when after having caste himself as a sheild before his country in her hour of peril he but – the hour of defeat averted – turns round to beg from her one kiss of love and gratitude ... My lords you believe that the Duke of Zamorna has done you service you believe that he deserves reward for that service you believe that he is the son of a King and that thus he is qualified to receive a Kingdom and as in this case these are the only < tu > true grounds to proceed upon you would you <?> would readily give to him a Kingdom.[3]

Despite the Earl of St Clair's claim that the proposal was putting 'a premium upon insubordination rebellion and immorality' and despite a foolishly arrogant and tactless speech from Zamorna himself,[4] Northangerland's oratory won the day. Zamorna was created King of Angria, though the new kingdom was to remain part of the Glasstown union.

While Branwell advanced the political career of the newly avaricious Zamorna, Charlotte decided to develop his personal life. It was quite clear from the profound changes that had taken place in his own character that Zamorna had outgrown his child-bride, Marian Hume, whose sweet innocence was entirely out of place in the brave new world of Angria. Charlotte therefore disposed of her, writing her last will and testament on 5 January 1834 and having her die of a broken heart caused by her husband's neglect. Free now to marry a woman of more spirit and better suited to his new character, Charlotte married him to Branwell's new creation, Mary Percy, daughter of Northangerland. Branwell had originally intended her for one of his politicians, the slippery Sir Robert Pelham, but for once Charlotte took the initiative, hijacked his heroine and married her off before her brother could object.[5] The marriage was to be fundamental to the future development of the juvenilia as Mary, beloved by both Zamorna and Northangerland, became a pawn in, and victim of, their ever-deepening rivalry.

Not content with simply providing Zamorna with a new wife, Charlotte gave him an increasingly complex and immoral love-life, reflecting the twist Branwell had given to his character and political career. He acquires a bastard child, an evil and misshapen dwarf called Finic, by a Negress with whom he had an adulterous affair when he was eighteen. A first wife, Helen Victorine, is revealed, by whom he has a son of doubtful legitimacy: like her successor, Marian Hume, Helen Victorine was neglected by her husband and died of a broken heart.[6] It is also announced that Zamorna transferred his attentions to Mary Percy while Marian was still alive and that he actually courted her in his wife's presence. Within three months of his marriage to Mary he was already blatantly flirting with other women. There is even a suggestion that Mina Laury, his first love who has become the nurse of his children by previous marriages and affairs, is being kept as his mistress in the seclusion of Grassmere Manor.[7] No doubt Zamorna's exotic and Byronic style of life was a powerful antidote to the enforced piety and chaste normality of life at Haworth Parsonage.

Similarly, the idea of depicting real life in Haworth as she knew it had no attraction for Charlotte. In 'High Life in Verdopolis', written between 20 February and 20 March 1834, she opened her story with a defence of her love of the aristocratic way of life:

I like high life, I like its manners, its splendors, its luxuries, the beings which move in its enchanted sphere. I like to consider the habits of those beings, their way of thinking, speaking acting. Let fools talk about the artificial, voluptuous, idle existences spun out by Dukes, Lords Ladies, knights & squires of high degree. Such cant is not for me, I despise it, what is there \of/ artificial in the lifeves of our Verdopolitan Aristocracy? what is there of idle? Voluptuous they are to a proverb, splendidly, magnificently voluptuous, but not inactive, not unnatural.[8]

If Charlotte was unwilling to leave the glittering social world she had created in Verdopolis for the bleaker provincialism of Angria, Branwell had no such reluctance. He countered her obsession with the higher echelons of society by introducing the more familiar and mundane world of the woollen industry to the juvenilia. Mills had always been present on the Verdopolitan scene, but 'The Wool is Rising', which Branwell completed on his seventeenth birthday, was the first story to chart the rise of a mill owner and be set, in part at least, in the counting house of a mill. Edward Percy is the eldest son of Northangerland by his second wife Mary Henrietta. He and his younger brother, William, were supposed to have been killed at birth on Northangerland's orders but, for reasons best known to himself, had been preserved by Sdeath. Left to their own devices, they had lived in abject poverty until the driving ambition of Edward had set them up as working wool-combers. Such was his success in the trade that he soon became a mill owner, employing workmen in his mills and his brother and a clerk in the counting house and earning himself a fortune. His business methods were as under-hand as his father's political machinations, but the profits enabled him to buy land in Adrianopolis, the new city Zamorna was building as his capital in Angria, and to set up mills in the kingdom. Having made his fortune he becomes a member of the Verdopolitan Parliament as a member of the Angrian party and sets up in grand style at Edwardston Hall in Angria. In sharp contrast to Charlotte's effete and wordy lovers, Edward Percy is both passionate and decisive: his successful wooing of the princess, Maria Sneachie, is almost brutal in its directness and he has no qualms about clasping his lover in his arms and 'imprinting on her lips one ardent kiss'.[9]

The scenes in the counting house, in which Edward Percy bullies his 'spirited but weak' brother and his 'grovelling' clerk, who are respectively reading poetry and Wesley's hymns instead of working at their ledgers, were later to be lifted by Charlotte to form the opening chapters of her first novel, *The Professor*.[10] Her conversion to the less glamorous world of her own experience was some way off, however, and her next venture, 'The Spell', was a violent reaction against Branwell's attempts to tone down her extravagances. The story is a reversion to the old world of magic, omens and mysterious strangers. Zamorna nearly dies as the result of a curse put on him at birth and it is revealed that he has an identical twin brother, Valdacella, who is really responsible for all the arbitrary and cruel deeds and the sudden change in character of Charlotte's great hero. Here again, the influence of James Hogg's *Confessions of a Justified Sinner* is very evident, the devil-like figure of Valdacella assuming Zamorna's persona.

their past lives are inextricably interwoven, the achievements of one cannot now be distinguished from the achievements of the other, their writings, their military actions their political manoeuvres, are all blended, all twisted into the same cord, a cord which none but themselves can unravel & which they will not.

If the story set out to restore Zamorna back to his former good character and extricate him from all the consequences of his pride and ambition by attributing them to his twin, it failed. Branwell had pushed the story on too far and Charlotte was too completely seduced by Zamorna's Byronic incarnation to allow him to revert to his former self. As Charlotte ruefully acknowledged in a tail-piece to the story:

If the young King of Angria has no alter Ego he ought to have such a convenient representative, For no single man having one corporeal & one spiritual nature ... should in right reason & in the ordinance [of] common sense & decency, speak & act in that capricious, double-dealing, unfathomable, incomprehensible, torturing,

Sphinx-like manner which he constantly assumes for reasons known only to himself."

If Charlotte rather regretted the way Zamorna was turning out, Branwell had no such doubts about Northangerland. During the spring of 1834 he wrote the first volume of 'The Life of feild Marshal the Right Honourable Alexander Percy. Earl of Northangerland' under the alias of John Bud. The story developed Northangerland's descent from the Northumbrian Percy family which Charlotte had first outlined some six months previously in 'The Green Dwarf'. His father, a crude, violent and dissipated man, sold his family estates to gratify his profligate habits, fled to Ireland after fighting a duel and carrying off a lady and ended up in Africa attempting to escape justice.

the birth of Northangerland was marked by a rough and stormy day. certai[nly th]eir appeared no prodigy either on heaven or earth. But clouds and wind and rain beat rou[nd th]e ancient Hall when its Young lord < appeared > first opened his eyes upon that life whic[h for] him [h]as seldom been one of happiness[12]

The young Alexander Percy has a powerful mind and quickly masters Greek, Latin, modern languages and mathematics; when he is sent to St Patrick's College on the Philosopher's Isle, he applies himself so single-mindedly to his studies that he becomes Senior Wrangler. Already he has proved himself to be driven by that ambition which will not permit him to be anything but the first in everything he does. In addition to his intellectual gifts, Percy is extraordinarily sensitive to music, bursting into tears as a child when he hears an Italian flute player and seeing visions of angels when he plays on the organ. Pious in the extreme, he spends hours reading his Bible and questions his tutor, John Bud, endlessly: 'Mr Bud where shall we go when we die', 'What are our spirits like Sir', 'Why doesnt the judgement day come now when men are so wicked'. As a result of this 'overmuch unassisted thinking of an < Impass >Impassioned melancholy and unbridled mind', young Percy came to a crisis of faith and then lapsed into that 'fixed and hopeless and rayless Atheism' which was to blight the rest of his days with melancholia and fear of death.[13]

Percy's atheism, which had gradually become more explicit in the juvenilia, is one of the few indications of rebellion among the Brontë children against the religious atmosphere in which they were brought up. It is often cited as proof that Branwell himself was an atheist, but this is no more true than to suggest that Charlotte's obsession with the adulterous affairs of her hero is an indication that she indulged in liaisons with married men.[14] In both cases, the attraction of such piquantly shocking characteristics in their creations was that they were so alien to the conventionality of life at the parsonage.

On the other hand, the juvenilia also provided a useful outlet for Branwell's deepening sense of disgust at religious hypocrisy. Interestingly, he seems to depict this as being almost exclusively the preserve of those outside the Established Church, in particular the inspirational sects. In 'An Historical Narrative of the War of Aggression', he had made Percy himself deliver an ironical impromptu prayer, aided by his wicked confederates, Sdeath and Montmorenci. Kneeling beside a chair, his eyes raised to heaven, his hands clasped, 'a heavenly pensiveness' diffused over his countenance, he prays:

Oh – may we be saved. – may we be all saved. (Sdeath – may we be saved). Saved to life everlasting saved to ever lasting life. (Mont. just so) Oh Grace. – Oh Grace. come down upon us (S. come) (Mont. come) … oh. save us. save thy lambs save thy sheep. save thy lambs (Thornton. 'It would be better If he told you how to save your Hams')[15]

Timothy Steaton, too, the clerk in 'The Wool is Rising', conceals his villainy under a cloak of pretended piety.

while thanking the Lord for his abundant loving kindness a light as that which fell upon Saul of Tarshish broke in upon my mind. I bethought me at a venture upon the Lost Sheep of the house of Israel and I said to my soul Truely it hath pleased the Lord to send rain upon the earth whereby perchance many of his creatures have been delectated and many damaged < per adventure that > But as his mercy endureth for ever he hath so ordered it that none of this damage shall if we < per > use the sense he has given us fall upon the head of sinful and erring man. now peradventure there shall have been in this wet season a plenitude of sheep and lambs of his fold < new born > found upon the pasturage seized with the < rot and > rot. and that to them frail mortals death shall have come thereby[.] now greedy and lucre loving mortals may at first sight on this case feel cause to mourn but thou < ar > a ministering angel flys and chases misery from their soul. I said to my soul oh frail tenant of a frail clay, why art thou not awake to sing thy Creators praise. Lo may not my master < perch > perchance sojourn into the far country and gather together as sheaves into a garner all the fleeces of sheep fallen through the rot these fleeces can he take at a small trifle and resell at an< d > enlarged sum.[16]

The association between evil and a façade of religion is developed most fully in the character of Sdeath in 'The Life of feild Marshal the Right Honourable Alexander Percy'. Despite being the faithful servant of Edward Percy for thirty years, his attitude towards father and son is ambivalent, encouraging each to plot against the other. After one quarrel between them, Sdeath urges Alexander to kill his father, justifying the murder on scriptural grounds.

thaw mun look to the lord man and abide by his will. Theres a Providence ower were heads which alluss provides for the best and what says the Scripture – come unto me all ye that are heavy laden and I will give you rest – and agean though your Sins be as scarlet yet they shall be as white as wool. Naw them texts were never intended for ought but the help of the needy and Aw hev often and often thought on Em as aw read that blessed book...'[7]

The powerful combination of religious cant and Yorkshire dialect, which Emily was later to use as her model for Joseph in *Wuthering Heights*, was probably derived as much from the servants John Barnet in James Hogg's *Confessions of a Justified Sinner*, and Andrew Fairservice in Walter Scott's *Rob Roy*, as from personal observation of Haworth Methodists.[8]

Alexander Percy's own atheism is curiously combined with an increasing identification of him with the devil. Like Robert Wringhim's satanic incarnation in Hogg's novel, Percy is always dressed in black rather than the brilliant dress of the other Verdopolitan and Angrian nobles. Like Milton's Satan, he possesses great physical beauty but his lack of moral principle is evident in the scornful sneer which is always on his lips and his broad expanse of forehead; like him, too, Percy is driven by overweening ambition. 'Augusta', Percy tells his wife, 'if there be a Satan I am he!'[9]

Percy's wife, whom he marries in defiance of his father's wishes, is Lady Augusta Romana di Segovia. A passionate, beautiful, ambitious and unprincipled woman, she is also a 'determined and unthinking Atheist', committed to the vanities and dissipations of the world, though she despises its customs and conventions. Augusta, as Sdeath recognized, is Percy's female counterpart and ideal mate. Their love for each other, which inspired some of Branwell's best poetry, commits both to a life of crime. Percy's creed, which determines all his future conduct, is neatly summarized in the initiation oaths of the secret society he founds on the Philosopher's Isle: its members are sworn to achieve the extermination of all religious creeds and modes of belief, the overthrow of the whole religion and theocracy of the Verdopolitan Union, the utter extermination of all kingly government and the overthrow of the present constitution and twelveship of Africa.[20]

Having begun this process of destruction of the established order of things by securing the creation of the kingdom of Angria for Zamorna, Northangerland then set about undermining Zamorna's power. In his books written in the second half of 1834, Branwell symbolically has Northangerland perform the coronation of Zamorna and then, in a dramatic volte-face, raise the standard of democratic revolt against the tyranny of the new king.[21] In one of the few instances where brother and sister appear to have worked side by side on a single story, Charlotte contributed Zamorna's addresses to the Angrians and at the opening of Parliament.

Charlotte's main work of the autumn was 'My Angria and the Angrians', which she finished on 14 October. For the first time, she seems to have realized that the provincial setting of Angria, which she had originally resisted as being too mundane, provided her with the possibility of caricaturing her family and home. The lengthiest of these is her portrait of her brother as Benjamin Patrick Wiggins,

a low, slightly built man attired in a black coat and raven grey trowsers, his hat placed nearly at the back of his head, revealing a bush of carroty hair so arranged that at the sides it projected almost like two spread hands, a pair of spectacles placed across a prominent Roman nose, black neckerchief adjusted with no great attention to precision, and, to complete the picture, a little black ratan flourished in the hand.[22]

Wiggins is a garrulous braggart, boasting that he has consumed two bottles of Glasstown ale and a double quart of porter when he has really had only two or three cups of tea. In this character, Charlotte thoroughly mocks Branwell's ambition and pretensions to greatness. Wiggins' mind 'was always looking above my station. I wasn't satisfied with being a sign-painter at Howard, as Charlotte and them things were with being sempstresses.' His own epitaph, Wiggins declared, would be

As a musician he was greater than Bach; as a poet he surpassed Byron; as a painter, Claude Lorrain yielded to him; as a rebel he snatched the palm from Alexander Rogue; as a merchant Edward Percy was his inferior; as a mill-owner, Grenville came not near him; as a traveller De Humbolt, Ledyard, Mungo Park, etc., etc., never braved half his dangers or overcame half his difficulties...

In sharp contrast to Wiggins' inflated opinion of himself and his talents was his dismissive attitude towards his sisters.

'I've some people who call themselves akin to me in the shape of three girls. They are honoured by possessing me as a brother, but I deny that they're my sisters...'
'What are your sisters' names?'
'Charlotte Wiggins, Jane Wiggins and Anne Wiggins.'
'Are they as queer as you?'
'Oh, they are miserable silly creatures not worth talking about. Charlotte's eighteen years old, a broad dumpy thing, whose head does not come higher than my elbow. Emily's sixteen, lean and scant, with a face about the size of a penny, and Anne is nothing, absolutely nothing.'
'What! Is she an idiot?'
'Next door to it.'

Equally scathing is Charlotte's depiction of Haworth. When asked where he was born Wiggins replies, in typically exaggerated fashion:

I was born partly at Thorncliffe, that is, after a fashion, but then I always account myself a native of Howard, a great city among the Warner Hills, under the dominion of that wonderful and superhuman gentleman Warner Howard Warner, Esqr' (here he took off his hat and bowed low). 'It has four churches and above twenty grand hotels, and a street called the Taan Gate, far wider than Bridgenorth in Free Town.' 'None of your humbug, Wiggins!' said I. 'I know well enough Howard is only a miserable little village, buried in dreary moors and moss-hags and marshes. I question whether it has one church or anything nearer an hotel than that way side ale-house you are now eyeing so longingly'.²³

Charlotte's jaundiced view of Haworth at this time was also reflected in the letters she wrote to her friends. On 11 February 1834, for example, she wrote to Ellen Nussey:

My letters are scarcely worth the postage and therefore I have till now, delayed answering your last communication; but upwards of two months having elapsed since I received it, I have at length determined to take up the pen in reply lest your anger should be roused by my apparent negligence ... According to custom I have no news to communicate indeed I do not write either to retail gossip or to impart solid information; my motives for maintaining our mutual correspondence are in the first place to get intelligence from you, and in the second that we may remind each other of our separate existences; without some such medium of reciprocal converse; according to the nature of things you, who are surrounded by society and friends, would soon forget that such an \insignificant/ being as myself, ever lived; I however in the solitude of our wild little hill village, think of my only un-related friend, my dear ci-devant school companion daily, nay almost hourly. Now Ellen, don't you think I have very cleverly contrived to make a letter out of nothing?²⁴

Within a week, she had a letter from Ellen herself, reporting that she was in London where she was to stay for six months with her older brother, John, a physician.²⁵ Judging Ellen by what would have been her own response to 'that great city, which has been called the mercantile metropolis of Europe', Charlotte was astonished that in the midst of the excitements of London, Ellen had remembered to write to her old school-friend. Ellen, however, was not as impressed as Charlotte herself would have been.

I was greatly amused at the tone of nonchalance which you assumed while treating of London, and its wonders, which seem to have excited anything rather than surprise in your mind: did you not feel awed while gazing at St Paul's and Westminster Abbey? had you no feeling of intense, and ardent interest, when in St James' you saw the Palace, where so many of England's Kings, had held their courts ... Have you yet seen any of the Great Personages whom the sitting of Parliament now detains in London? The Duke of Wellington, Sir Robert Peel, Earl Grey, Mr Stanley, Mr O'Connel &c.?

Charlotte, eaten up with longing to visit the city which had provided the model for the Great Glasstown, was unable to comprehend that the stolid Ellen's indifference could be anything other than assumed. 'You should not be too much afraid of appearing country-bred', she advised Ellen, 'the magnificence of London has drawn exclamations of astonishment from travelled-men, experienced in the World, its wonders, and beauties.'²⁶

Compared to all the imagined glories of London, it is not surprising that Haworth and its neighbourhood seemed dull and unexciting to Charlotte.

Her constant complaints to Ellen of lack of news and 'the solitude of our wild little hill village' have done much to create the impression that the Brontës were cut off from all society and culture at Haworth. It has to be remembered, however, that Ellen was able to gossip to Charlotte about her friends, neighbours and relations because they were nearly all known to Charlotte from her schooldays. Gossip about Haworth, on the other hand, would have meant little or nothing to Ellen, since she had only had a single brief visit there. Discussion about politics, art or literature, which was more to Charlotte's taste, was wasted on Ellen and shared with Mary Taylor – of whom Ellen was clearly jealous.[27] As Charlotte's letters to Mary are not extant, this side of her life at Haworth has been almost completely overlooked. There were many opportunities to indulge in the very things the Brontës loved best, not only in the nearby towns such as Keighley, Halifax and Bradford, but also in Haworth itself. The local newspapers at this time are full of accounts of music, art and politics.

As Benjamin Binns, the son of the Haworth tailor, later noted, 'Haworth in those days was remarkable for its cultivation of music, and the goddess was wooed for herself rather than for any pecuniary gain.'[28] The Haworth Philharmonic Society, which had been founded in or about 1780, held regular concerts, including an annual combined vocal and instrumental concert in the large room of the Black Bull Inn on 5 November. The concerts catered for a wide variety of tastes: the annual performance of 1834, for example, included a selection from Haydn's *Seasons* as well as songs, glees and catches. The presence in the village of Thomas Parker, one of the leading Yorkshire tenors of the day, gave added stimulus to local concerts. Both he and his numerous family, all of whom were picturesquely named after famous musicians, took time out from their professional careers to foster musical performances in their home town.[29] Haworth had the usual church orchestra to accompany the hymns and psalms but it also had its own band, apparently associated with Merralls' mill, which travelled throughout the local area fulfilling engagements. An added dimension was given to musical performance by the installation of an organ in Haworth Church. The money to build the organ was raised by public subscription and supported by sermons on behalf of the fund. The organ was finally unveiled to the public at a performance of Handel's *Messiah* on 23 March 1834. The church thus became an alternative and much larger venue for concerts, though the Haworth Philharmonic held a successful concert in the Black Bull a few days later and continued to play the leading role in music in the village.[30]

There is no doubt that the Brontës attended concerts in the village. Patrick was 'passionately fond of oratorio' and, according to the son of the Haworth tailor, often took his family to concerts 'and other meetings of an elevating tendency'. It was his invariable practice to leave for home at nine o'clock, though presumably Aunt Branwell and the children were allowed to remain to the end.[31] The concert to celebrate the installation of the organ was such a high point in the Brontës' lives that it actually found its way into the juvenilia. Abraham Sunderland, who arranged the concert, was caricatured as 'one Mr Sudbury Figgs, who resided within four miles of Howard, and who, being a pianist by profession, was accustomed to give music lessons to various families in the neighbourhood'. John Greenwood, the former Keighley organist who had gone to live in London and returned to the district to christen the organ, appeared as himself, returning from Stumpsland, and as the object of Branwell's hero-worship. In a vicious satire on her brother, Charlotte depicted his response as Benjamin Patrick Wiggins to Greenwood's arrival in Haworth.

yes, I remember the moment when he entered the church, walked up to the organ gallery where I was, kicked Sudbury Figgs, who happened to be performing Handel's 'And the Glory of the Lord', from the stool, and assuming it himself, placed his fingers on the keys, his feet on the pedals, and proceeded to electrify us with 'I Know that My Redeemer Liveth'.

'Then', said I, 'this is a god and not a man!' As long as the music sounded in my ears, I dared neither speak, breathe, nor even look up. When it ceased, I glanced furtively at the performer. My heart had previously been ravished by the mere knowledge of his fame and skill, but how resistlessly was it captivated, when I saw in Mr Greenwood a tall man dressed in black, with a pair of shoulders, light complexion and hair inclining to red – my very beau ideal of personal beauty, carrying even some slight and dim resemblance to the notion I had formed of Rogue. Instantly I assumed that inverted position which with me is always a mark of highest astonishment, delight and admiration. In other words I clapt my pate to the ground and let my heels fly up with a spring. They happened to hit Mr Sudbury Figgs's chin, as he stood in his usual way, picking his teeth and projecting his under jaw a yard beyond the rest of his countenance. He exclaimed so loud as to attract Mr Greenwood's attention. He turned round and saw me. 'What's that fellow playing his mountebank tricks here for?' I heard him say, Before anybody could answer I was at his feet licking the dust under them and crying aloud, 'O Greenwood! The greatest, the mightiest, the most famous of men! Doubtless you are ignorant of a nit, the foal of a louse, like me, but I have learnt to know you through the medium of your wonderful works. Suffer the basest of creatures to devote himself utterly to your service, as a shoe-black, a rosiner of fiddlesticks, a greatcoat-carrier, a port-music, in short as a thorough-going toadie...'[32]

It is possible that the younger Brontës were also personally involved in the performances. Branwell had played the flute since at least November 1831, when he began to compile a book of his favourite arrangements. These ranged from church music, such as the Old Hundredth psalm and a funeral march, through to Scottish ballads such as 'Scots, wha hae wi Wallace bled' and 'Ye Banks and Braes o' Bonny Doon', via such ephemera as 'Oh no, we never mention her'. The choice of music suggests that Branwell may well have been involved in both the church orchestra and the Haworth Philharmonic Society. He could also play the piano and when the organ was installed in the church, Branwell seems to have learnt to play this too, under the tuition of Abraham Sunderland. Like his father, he was enthusiastically fond of sacred music, particularly Handel's oratorio *Samson* and the masses of Haydn and Mozart, and though he did not play well he was an appreciative listener.[33]

His sisters, too, were keenly interested in music. Emily and Anne both played the piano, though Charlotte had been discouraged from doing so at Roe Head because of her poor eyesight. Patrick, ever anxious to foster any signs of rising talent in his children, bought a cottage piano some time in late 1833 or in 1834. Acquired from John Green, a music agent of Soho Square in London, but probably purchased in one of the many music shops in Leeds, Halifax or Bradford, the piano was a comparatively cheap one but probably the best Patrick could afford. Though cased in mahogany, it had only five octaves and its strings were hidden behind an upright pleated silk screen. Abraham Sunderland was still coming regularly to the parsonage to give Emily and Anne their lessons as late as November 1834.[34]

If the Brontës' passion for music was not fulfilled in Haworth, they had plenty of opportunity to go elsewhere. Halifax was less than a dozen miles away, within walking distance for Branwell at least, and had a remarkable reputation for music. Its concerts attracted musicians, composers and performers of international standing. Paganini, the virtuoso violinist, played there on 9 February 1832 and he was followed by Johann Strauss, 'The Waltz King', and his orchestra, a youthful Franz Liszt and Felix Mendelssohn.[35]

On a much less grand scale, but more accessible, were the frequent concerts held in Keighley, sponsored by the Mechanics' Institute and the Keighley Philharmonic Society, especially during the winter season. On 27 November 1833, for example, the musical amateurs of the Keighley, Haworth and Bingley districts all gathered for their annual meeting at the National School in Keighley; the highlight of the evening was a performance of the Dettingen *Te Deum*. In January 1834 the town held a music festival which drew some of the biggest audiences ever seen in the area. The Brontës are likely to have attended as their music teacher, Abraham Sunderland, conducted the orchestra and choirs in the selection of sacred music and Thomas Parker was the principal soloist. Mr Greenwood again returned from London to play the organ of the Wesleyan Methodist chapel and performed 'an astonishing extempore fugue'. The *Leeds Mercury* declared that 'The performances have given a great impetus to the musicians in the town and neighbourhood.' Another special concert was given on 29 December 1834 in the large hall of the new Keighley Mechanics' Institute building which had just been opened the day before: the singers included professionals from Leeds and the hall was packed with 'the most respectable families of the town and the surrounding district for several miles'.[36]

Keighley was an increasingly prosperous town and in the 1830s it was expanding rapidly. A new market place, with handsome buildings round it, was begun in 1833 and a new National Church Sunday School and Mechanics' Institute in 1834.[37] The place had much to offer the Brontës by way of entertainment. In addition to its concerts and circulating libraries, the town held regular lectures, mostly sponsored by the Mechanics' Institute, of which Patrick became a member after Charlotte's return from Roe Head. The lectures were increasingly varied in subject matter by this time and were a more attractive prospect than the purely scientific ones of the early days. One of the most popular was a course of lectures in 1832 on ancient British poetry. Again, the Brontës are likely to have attended as the subject was one in which they were keenly interested and the lectures were given by a former schoolmaster of Keighley, William Dearden, who was an old family friend. By the winter season of 1835, free lectures were being given fortnightly in the new Mechanics' Institute on subjects as diverse as Napoleon, geography and Poland, and Patrick himself had been enlisted as one of the lecturers.[38]

Keighley was also the source of drawing lessons for the Brontë children. John Bradley, the architect of the new Mechanics' Institute, had taught them since at least 1828–9 and had encouraged them in their pursuit of art. It is curious that both Charlotte and Branwell hoped to pursue an artistic career at this time. On her return from Roe Head, Charlotte had immersed herself in her drawing, copying with minute detail the plates and engravings which appeared in annuals and albums, such as *Friendship's Offering* and *The Keepsake*. Her work seems fairly evenly divided between what Mrs Gaskell called the 'nimini-pimini' pencil reproductions of mountains scenes such as 'Santa Maria' and 'Geneva',[39] and the lighter touch of pencil and watercolour portraits. The latter are particularly interesting for the fact that they are all, without exception, of young and beautiful people in romantic poses. Charlotte was always obsessed with the notion of her own physical unattractiveness and was obviously uninterested in portraying anything less than physical perfection. Many of her portraits were associated with one of her favourite poets, Lord Byron. She copied ones of Byron himself and his patroness, the beautiful Countess Blessington, Lady Jersey, whose portrait had appeared in Moore's *Life of Byron* and even illustrations to his poems such as 'The Maid of Saragossa'. The women are invariably large-eyed, long-necked, ringletted and bejewelled; the men are effete in feature and form, with elaborately curled hair and military dress.[40] Undoubtedly these idealized portraits represented the heroes and heroines of Charlotte's imaginary world as well as being a serious exercise in draughtsmanship.[41]

The Brontës were also familiar with the art world in Leeds. It seems likely, for instance, that Patrick's engravings of 'Belshazzar's Feast' and 'Joshua Commanding the Sun' were purchased there when the originals were exhibited at the Music Hall in Albion Street from 1 November 1823 to the end of

January 1824.[42] The Northern Society for the Encouragement of the Arts had held an annual summer exhibition in Leeds since 1808, drawing together paintings of old masters in private collections and new works for sale to put on public display. The Brontës may have attended the exhibition of 1833 when, among the forty sculptures and 417 paintings and drawings, they would have seen fourteen by William Robinson, the society portrait painter from Leeds. Francis Leyland, a friend of Branwell's, tells us that they were among the 2,000 visitors to the exhibition the following year who saw his brother's colossal sculpted head of Satan and group of English greyhounds, before the former was taken to London where it achieved great critical acclaim. On display then were also three portraits of gentlemen, two of ladies and two of groups of children painted by William Robinson, 'all largely partaking of the skill and care which distinguish the works of this excellent portrait painter'.[43]

Some time after the exhibition, possibly in 1834 but probably not until the following year, Patrick secured the services of Robinson as a tutor to his son, apparently paying out the huge sum of two guineas per lesson for the privilege.[44] In terms of prestige and contacts, the money was well spent. Robinson was only a young man, in his mid-thirties, but he had been a free pupil of the great Sir Thomas Lawrence who had died in 1830. Lawrence himself was an innkeeper's son who had studied at the Royal Academy and eventually succeeded Sir Joshua Reynolds as Painter-in-Ordinary to the King. Robinson had studied with Lawrence and learnt to imitate his style, even his most famous portrait of the Duke of Wellington being but an adaptation of one by Lawrence. Whether Robinson was the right person to instruct Branwell is a more difficult point. He seems to have needed money as he died only a few years later, in 1838, leaving his widow and children in absolute penury.[45] This may have led him to encourage Branwell's artistic ambitions which, he must have realized, were far greater than his talent could support. As Leyland, who frequented artistic circles, pointed out, Robinson failed to teach Branwell the correct way to mix his pigments and how to apply them properly. He was therefore unable to depict the delicacy of fleshy tints and the variations of light and shade; the colours he used faded rapidly leaving behind only the tint of the boiled oil with which he mixed his pigments. It is striking, too, that the hard features and sometimes wooden, formal poses of Branwell's subjects are the very points on which Robinson himself was criticized.[46]

Branwell had decided as early as 1833 that he wanted to become a professional portrait painter. When Ellen Nussey visited that summer, he was already painting in oils.[47] By the following year, whether he was still studying under John Bradley or had progressed to William Robinson, he was copying the work of other artists and, most famously, twice persuaded or bullied his sisters into sitting for him. Both oil paintings included himself as well as his sisters, though in one, which Mrs Gaskell described as a 'rough, common-looking oil-painting', he immediately painted himself out again, probably because the composition was too cramped in the upright format he had chosen. The ghostly image of Branwell, together with the delicate pencil sketching which formed the basis of his portraits, is gradually re-emerging as the badly mixed paint becomes transparent with age. This is the famous 'Three Sisters' or 'Pillar Portrait' which, by an irony of fate, is now one of the most popular paintings in the National Portrait Gallery.[48]

The second portrait was done in a landscape format, giving greater room for Branwell and his sisters. They are gathered round a table on which Branwell, gun in hand, has just placed his trophies of the day's shoot. This portrait was described by one visitor to the parsonage in 1858, who saw it hanging in pride of place on the stairs, as 'a shocking daub, not up to the rudest sign board style'. Though Charlotte's husband, the Reverend Arthur Bell Nicholls, can hardly be said to have been a man of artistic judgement, it is worth noting that he destroyed this portrait on the grounds that the likenesses were so bad, keeping only the fragment which had the delicate and sensitive profile of Emily. The composition of the original picture is now only known from a photograph of it belonging to Martha Brown, the Brontës' servant, and a set of tracings of the three girls made by John Greenwood, the Haworth stationer.[49]

Whatever the merits of the paintings as art, they are invaluable, if unflattering, portrayals of the four Brontës as they were in 1834, a year after Ellen's visit to Haworth. Charlotte, at eighteen, is the only one to wear her hair long and put up into a bun at the back, with long sausage shaped ringlets framing her face. As befits her age, she is also the only one to wear a high-collared dress. Her face is square-jawed, with a high forehead, large nose and prim mouth. Emily and Anne, at sixteen and fourteen, are physically more alike, with longer and thinner faces, and wearing their hair loosely curled at shoulder length. In the gun group they both wear the same unflattering scoop-neck dresses as Charlotte, but without her modest high-necked collar. In the other portrait they all wear simple V-necked dresses with large fichu-type collars. Branwell, who has significantly made himself appear the tallest in both portraits, though he was actually shorter than Emily, wears his bright red hair parted and artistically arranged in wisps and tendrils over his remarkably wide and high forehead. It says much for the closeness of the Brontë family that, even after Branwell's downfall, they preferred to display the gun group, which included him, in the parsonage, even though it was a poorer painting.[50]

Charlotte was also producing portraits from life at this time. Within fourteen months, between 17 April 1833 and 17 June 1834, she drew one delicate pencil portrait and two watercolour portraits of Anne. All are in profile, though in one watercolour the face is slightly turned towards the artist.

They are recognizably the same person as Branwell's portraits of Anne, with her long neck, thin features and pronounced mouth. It is possible, though unlikely, that the portraits were painted under William Robinson's supervision and that Charlotte may have had some share in her brother's lessons. Whatever the reason behind her sudden excursion into portrait painting, it seems that she was only able to persuade the more pliant Anne to sit for her as there are no known portraits of Emily by either of her sisters.[51]

If 1833 and 1834 were busy years for the arts in Haworth, possibly culminating in Branwell's pupillage to William Robinson, they were also increasingly fraught on the political front. The Church of England was no longer the indissoluble and monopolist partner of the state: the repeal of the Test and Corporation Acts in 1828 and the emancipation of Roman Catholics in 1829 had admitted Dissenters and, to a lesser degree, Catholics, to civil liberty and public office. Over the next decade, however, the cry would increasingly be for more rights and more equal status, particularly for Dissenters, who had the backing of the powerful and wealthy mercantile classes. Behind these demands and the outcry over the compulsory payment of church rates by all sects loomed the ultimate horror of the spectre of the disestablishment of the Anglican Church. The relations between the Established Church and Dissenters, which Patrick had always striven to keep open and mutually beneficial, gradually deteriorated over the decade in Haworth as elsewhere.

A symptom of this was the declining fortunes of Patrick's beloved Haworth Auxiliary of the Bible Society, which had relied heavily on the support and co-operation of the different sects in the township. On 3 September 1833 Patrick had to write to the society in London cancelling the visit of one of their speakers because he was unable to rouse sufficient interest for a meeting. This, he explained somewhat incoherently, was 'owing to changes effected by death – in some cases, and by political, and Trades Unions, in others'.[52] Patrick's own health, as he explained, was still poor and he was not yet equal to the struggle of persuading his fellow ministers to put aside their differences and promote the interests of the society.

Ill health, which had dogged Patrick since his dramatic collapse three years before, was also doubtless the reason why in July 1833 he tried to obtain his first curate for the parish. He prepared, but never completed, the nomination papers for a young man, James Bardsley, who had not yet been fully admitted to holy orders. The day before his ordination, the Archbishop of York, 'for some private reason of his own', refused to sanction the arrangement and assigned Bardsley instead to the curacy of Keighley. Nevertheless, Bardsley remained on friendly terms with the Brontës and frequently took his young wife to the parsonage on Saturday afternoons to drink tea.[53] Thwarted in his plans to obtain more permanent help in the chapelry, Patrick must have been doubly grateful to visiting clergymen friends, such as Thomas Crowther and William Morgan, who preached the annual Sunday school sermons on his behalf.[54]

At the beginning of 1834, Patrick landed himself in the middle of a furious and bitter row, which became increasingly characterized by personal invective. Towards the end of December 1833 there had been a number of meetings in Bradford of Dissenters from the independent and Baptist denominations, who were fiercely arguing for the removal of their grievances.[55] In response to these meetings, which were reported in detail in the local press, Patrick wrote a series of three letters to the *Leeds Intelligencer* defending the Anglican Church establishment and attacking Dissenters' proposals to remove the bishops from the House of Lords, abolish tithes and other Church dues and open the universities to non-Anglicans. The letters were written anonymously, perhaps in a fruitless attempt to avoid offending the strong dissenting element in Haworth, but signed with his initials.[56] His authorship was soon discovered and brought to the attention of the Reverend John Winterbotham, minister of the Baptist chapel in West Lane at Haworth, who responded:

I knew that very many people, both men and women, were seen to flock to the head inn, in this village, to hear, whilst some one read aloud, the wonderful discoveries which a learned gentleman had made concerning Dissenters, and that his College store of learned lore had found out that they were hypocrites, selfish persons, and, moreover, traitors to the King.[57]

The correspondence, most of which was unfortunately published in the columns of the local newspapers, soon descended from the wider issues which had prompted it to local and personal accusation. Patrick poured scorn on the presumption of his uneducated colleague's attempt to instruct Parliament and the clergy. If Winterbotham wanted the universities opening,

I would seriously ask him, what good this opening would do to him? He seems not to be aware that, however the universities might be opened, it would be requisite, that before any one entered them, he should have at least a competent knowledge of Greek and Latin. When he went therefore to procure admission, the inexorable examiner would put Homer and Horace into his hands, and just then and there, alas! would for ever terminate the university peregrination of the Rev. John Winterbotham.[58]

His opponent was not slow to respond, accusing him of 'storms and rages' which 'in my estimation, resemble more the vapourings of an empty mind, than the sober language of a man of letters'. He pointed out that Patrick had obtained his present position and salary through 'the kind influence of Dissenters' and that his recent repairs to the church, which included a new roof, a new and ornamented under-drawing and complete painting and redecoration, had been paid for out of church rates imposed on Dissenters and Anglicans alike.[59] Though the newspaper correspondence ended when Patrick, wisely, refused to be provoked into further replies, the matter did not stop there. Winterbotham was to be a vociferous opponent of church rates for many years to come and Patrick himself would return to the fray the following year in his pamphlet, *The Signs of the Times*.[60]

Patrick's attack on the Dissenters does not seem to have soured his relations with the Church trustees, many of whom, by a curious irony, were non-Anglicans. Both clergyman and trustees seem to have been working to put things on a more formal and efficient footing. On 1 February 1834, they all signed a document agreeing to the appointment of four out of the twelve to be acting trustees in rotation, with Joseph Greenwood of Springhead, their chairman, present at all meetings to sign any necessary documents. In addition to creating a more manageable-sized committee, Patrick also initiated a reform in the payment of his salary: ten pounds a year was, in future, to be deducted before it was paid to him. This was to be used for the repair and upkeep of buildings on the Church lands, for which he was responsible. The fixed sum, and its prior deduction, would avoid arguments about the excessive amounts sometimes charged to him in the past and about reclaiming sums which had already been handed over.[61]

Patrick's good relations with Joseph Greenwood of Springhead extended beyond Church affairs. On 11 August 1834, he wrote to the Lord Lieutenant of the Shire, the Earl of Harewood, requesting him, as a matter of urgency, to appoint a magistrate for the Haworth district because 'Our neighbourhood, is populous, and in some parts, has been – and soon may be again, somewhat turbulent.'[62] The suggestion was rejected as two new magistrates had recently been appointed for Keighley, but Patrick tried again in November after the dismissal of Lord Melbourne's Whig ministry had put the Tory party back in office. Joseph Greenwood, being a major landowner, 'warmly attached to the best Institutions of our Country, ... of sound principles – and a regular Churchman', was the obvious candidate for the magistracy, as Patrick pointed out in a letter soliciting his support, to Henry Heap, the vicar of Bradford. The application was again refused, though Greenwood was eventually appointed a magistrate for the area in 1836.[63]

One of the reasons Patrick cited for needing a magistrate in Haworth itself was to enforce the new factory regulations of 1833 which restricted the hours children under eleven could work in the mills to a maximum of forty-eight, those under eighteen to a maximum of sixty-nine and insisted on a minimum of two hours' schooling per day.[64] Patrick is likely to have been a supporter not only of the Factory Act of 1833 but also of the Ten Hours lobby, which wanted further restrictions to be imposed. On 11 September 1834 he entertained the Reverend George Bull at the parsonage and, at very short notice, gave him a platform in the schoolroom to defend himself against accusations of being a 'Tory Demagogue, under the MASK of pleading for the poor factory children'. Bull's accuser was the vitriolic Baptist minister, John Winterbotham, which may have increased Patrick's sympathy for his clerical colleague, but the two men were already friends and Patrick greatly admired George Bull's commitment to the cause of the Ten Hours bill.[65]

Patrick's last major campaign of the year 1834 was for a Temperance Society in Haworth. An inaugural meeting on 17 November, held in the National School-Room, was so well attended that it had to move to the larger premises of the Methodist chapel on West Lane. Reviving the spirit of co-operation with other sects which had existed before he had incurred Winterbotham's wrath, Patrick called on the support of the other ministers in Haworth, inviting them, Theodore Dury and James Bardsley from Keighley and a number of other ministers from the district to address the meeting. Patrick was appointed President of the Society and given three secretaries, the two Baptist ministers, Moses Saunders and John Winterbotham, and his own son, Branwell. At the close of the meeting 'a considerable number' of people came forward to sign the temperance pledge. Their membership cards declared, 'We agree to abstain from Distilled Spirits, except for Medicinal Purposes, and to discountenance the Causes and Practice of Intemperance.' Perhaps it was the good effect of the Temperance Society, but when Babbage came to Haworth to investigate the sanitary conditions in 1850 he noted that the total consumption of beer and spirits was considerably below the average of other places.[66] This certainly belies the drunken image given the town by Mrs Gaskell.

Ellen Nussey had returned from London in the summer and, to Charlotte's evident surprise, not only remained unchanged by the experience of living in the metropolis but also as firmly attached to her old friend as ever. Mrs Gaskell was struck by Charlotte's lack of optimism in later life, but this was evidently a characteristic she had developed by the age of eighteen.

> I am slow, _very_ slow to believe the protestations of another ... I have long seen 'friend' in your mind, in your words, in your actions, but _now_ distinctly visible, and clearly written in characters that cannot be distrusted, I discern _true_ friend! I am really grateful for your mindfulness of so obscure a person as myself...[67]

Ellen tried to fall back into the old ways of gaining Charlotte's attention in their correspondence, seeking her opinion on various subjects. Would Charlotte give her a list of her faults so that she could seek to improve herself? – she would not, 'Why child – I've neither time nor inclination to reflect on your _faults_ when you are so far from me and when besides kind letters and presents and so forth are continually bringing forward your goodness in the most prominent light.' Did Charlotte think dancing between young men and women an objectionable amusement? – she did not, unless it encouraged frivolity and wasted time.[68] Would Charlotte recommend some books for her to read? – she would, 'in as few words as I can'. The list she gave Ellen is unexceptionable and is simply a summary of the standard works of the day, reflecting not Charlotte's own, more adventurous reading but what she thought would suit her conventional friend.

If you like poetry let it be first rate, Milton, Shakespeare, Thomson, Goldsmith, Pope (if you will though I don't admire him) Scott, Byron, Campbell, Wordsworth and Southey. Now Ellen don't be startled at the names of Shakespeare and Byron. Both these were great men and their works are like themselves, you will know how to choose the good and avoid the evil, the finest passages are always the purest, the bad are invariably revolting you will never wish to read them over twice; Omit the Comedies of Shakspeare and the Don Juan, perhaps the Cain of Byron though the latter is a magnificent poem and read the rest fearlessly.[69]

As Shakespeare had been one of Miss Wooler's favourite authors, there was little chance of shocking Ellen there. Byron, more feared for his moral reputation than for his often execrable verse, was the only unusual inclusion and, as Charlotte pointed out, poems like his 'Hebrew Melodies' were free from any taint of moral perversion. What she did not tell Ellen was that she had not only read both *Don Juan* and *Cain* herself, but had lingered over the more salacious passages.[70]

For History read Hume, Rollin, and the Universal History if you <u>can</u> – <u>I</u> never did. For Fiction – read Scott alone all novels after his are worthless. For Biography, read Johnson's Lives of the Poets, Boswell's Life of Johnson, Southey's Life of Nelson, Lockhart's Life of Burns, Moore's Life of Sheridan, Moore's Life of Byron, Wolfe's Remains. For Natural History, read Bewick, and Audubon, and Goldsmith and White of Selborne. For Divinity, but your brother Henry will advise you there.

The whole tenor of the list was summed up in Charlotte's final comment: 'I only say adhere to standard authors and don't run after novelty.'[71] One wonders, by contrast, what she might have suggested Mary Taylor should read.

On 24 November 1834, Emily and Anne together drew up a diary paper which gives a brief but eloquent vignette of life at Haworth Parsonage. It is signed by them both but written by Emily, on a scrap of paper less than 10cm by 6cm, in a mixture of her ordinary hand and the same tiny script as Charlotte and Branwell used in their miniature books.

November the 24 1834 Monday
Emily Jane Brontë
Anne Brontë
I fed Rainbow, Diamond, Snowflake Jasper phesant (alias this morning Branwell went down to Mr Drivers and brought news that Sir Robert peel was going to be invited to stand for Leeds Anne and I have been peeling Apples \for/ Charlotte to

make an apple pudding \and for Aunts [?] and apple/ Charlotte said she made puddings perfectly and she was of a quick but lim[i]ted intellect[.] Taby said just now come Anne pillopatate (ie pill a potato Aunt has come into the Kitchen just now and said where are you feet Anne Anne answered < onthe > on the floor Aunt papa opened the parlour Door and < said B > gave Branwell a Letter saying here Branwell read this and show it to your Aunt and Charlotte – The Gondals are < disc > discovering the interior of Gaaldine
Sally mosley is washing in the back Kitchin
It is past Twelve o'clock Anne and I have not tid[i]ed ourselvs, done our bed work \or/ done our lessons and we want to go out to play We are going to have for < dinner > Dinner Boiled Beef Turnips potato's and applepudding the Kitchin is in avery untidy state Anne and I have not Done our music excercise which consists of b majer Taby said on my putting a pen in her face Ya pitter pottering there instead of pilling a potate I answered O Dear, O Dear, O Dear I will derictly with that I get up, take a Knife and begin pilling (finished pilling the potatos papa going to walk Mr Sunderland expected
Anne and I say I wonder what we shall be like < if all be well > and what we shall be and where we shall be < this year > if all goes on well in the year 1874 – in which year I shall be in my 57th year Anne will be going in her 55th year Branwell will be going in his 58th year And Charlotte in her 59th year hoping we shall all be well at that time We close our paper

Emily and Anne November the 24 1834[72]

Down the side of the first page Anne contributed a sketch of a flowing ringlet, which Emily captioned 'A bit of Lady Julet's hair done by Anne'. While the diary paper is a lively evocation of the hustle and bustle of a wash-day Monday at the parsonage, the dreadful handwriting and spelling are scarcely credible as the work of a highly intelligent sixteen-year-old. The reference to Sir Robert Peel being invited to stand as Member of Parliament for Leeds was an indication of a revived interest in politics which swept the family – and indeed the whole country – in the first half of 1835. The King seized the opportunity of Viscount Althorp's removal to the House of Lords to dismiss the Whig ministry and impose a minority Tory government, led by Sir Robert Peel. Without the support of the House of Commons, Peel's ministry lasted only a brief hundred days before he was forced to resign. The King's high-handed action, which caused outrage in the country, ensured the return of a Whig government for the next six years. As the fate of future reforms hung in the balance in the struggle for power, the whole tenor of life was disrupted. Even Ellen Nussey, who normally showed no interest in politics, was caught up in the enthusiasm. Shortly after returning from a two-week visit to The Rydings in February, and just before Peel's resignation, Charlotte wrote to her:

What do you think of the course Politics are taking? I make this inquiry because I now think you have a wholesome interest in the matter; formerly you did not care greatly about it. Brougham you see is triumphant. Wretch! I am a hearty hater, and if there is any one I thoroughly abhor, it is that man. But the Opposition is divided, red hots, and luke warms; and the Duke (par excellence <u>the</u> Duke) and Sir Robert Peel show no sign of insecurity, though they have already been twice beat; so 'courage, mon amie.' Heaven defend the right! as the old chevaliers used to say, before they joined battle. Now Ellen, laugh heartily at all this rodomontade, but you have brought it on yourself; don't you remember telling me to write such letters to you as I write to Mary Taylor? Here's a specimen; hereafter should follow a long disquisition on books, but I'll spare you that.[73]

At the beginning of April, Haworth, in common with many other towns in West Yorkshire, sent an address to Sir Robert Peel in support of his minority government. The address was clearly instigated by Patrick, who was the first to sign it, and it bears all the hallmarks of his style, from its grandiose opening to its tentative conclusion.

SIR – With glowing and unfeigned delight we hail all your measures of Reform, and witness the glorious struggle which you and your colleagues, in conjunction with our gracious Sovereign, are making at the present eventful crisis, in order to stem the factious torrent which assails you, and which threatens to overwhelm the best institutions of our country: and in the name and on behalf of the numerous Friends to Church and State in our chapelry, we entreat you *not* to resign your high office, but to *persevere* even to the *dissolution* of Parliament, if necessary, being fully convinced, as we are, that by such an event you would find a great accession of true and loyal hearts to support you from every quarter of the United Kingdom. We are not sure that in this address we have proceeded according to the regular and prescribed form, but we have obeyed the best feelings of our hearts, and the genuine dictates of our consciences and judgements.[74]

The publication of the address in the *Leeds Intelligencer* caused a furore in Haworth. John Foster wrote in indignation to denounce it as un-representative of the views of the Haworth voters. There were 124 registered voters in the township of whom ninety-six had declared their support for the Whigs, Lord Morpeth and George Strickland, in the forthcoming election. Far from expressing the views of all the voters, therefore, the address only represented those of at most twenty-eight men – led by the incumbent and churchwardens who, Foster suggested, acted out of fear of the parliamentary proposals to disestablish the Church of England. Foster also poured scorn on the 'Conservative Committee' whose chairman had signed the address: its existence in Haworth was such a closely guarded secret that no one had heard of it until the address was published.[75]

At the end of April Lord Morpeth himself appeared on the hustings in Haworth to a 'cordial' reception from the reformers of Haworth. Charlotte was unimpressed, but gave her detailed opinion to Mary Taylor rather than Ellen Nussey, so her assessment of the future Earl of Carlisle, whom she was to meet again many years later in London, is unrecorded. Well might Charlotte exclaim, 'The Election! The Election! that cry has rung even amongst our lonely hills like the blast of a trumpet', as the Dissenters gathered forces in Haworth. While Charlotte urged Ellen to entreat her brothers 'if necessary on your knees to stand by their Country and Religion in this day of danger', in Yorkshire it was the Whigs, once again, who were returned for the West Riding.[76] This reflected the general state across the country and a Whig ministry, under Lord Melbourne, was returned to office, meaning that the pace of reform would continue unchecked. 'A genuine Friend', signing himself 'O. P. Q.', addressed himself to the reformers of Haworth in the first glow of victory, congratulating them on withstanding 'FALSEHOOD, BRIBERY and INTIMIDATION' and urging them to establish a Reform Association in the township. One of the moral victories he claimed for the reformers was that they had effected a volte-face by Patrick: 'the clergyman, once a flaming reformer, has joined the ranks of those who support corruption in church and state'.[77] The threat of the disestablishment of the Church was one reform Patrick could not accept and would fight to the end of his days, but the accusation was hardly fair.

Shortly after the election, Patrick wrote and published, through Robert Aked of Keighley, a pamphlet which he entitled *The Signs of the Times.*[78] In a measured and restrained style which was the antithesis of the violent and accusatory tone adopted by John Winterbotham, John Foster and 'O. P. Q.', he set out the 'signs of the times' as he saw them. By far the greatest part of the pamphlet was given over to a defence of the Established Church of England and Ireland. He argued that, like a good father, the state had a moral duty to lay down a system of religious instruction for its people and that the Church of England was the best suited to be the church supported by the state. At the same time, however, all religions should be tolerated and there should be full liberty of conscience. Patrick was far from saying that the Established Church was perfect, but he argued, as he always had done, that reform not destruction was needed. It was obvious that tithes should be fairly commuted and church rates, in their present form, abolished. It was equally obvious that the Church of England should be financed by some fairer system which did not impose on Dissenters but it should not lose state support.[79] If it had to rely on voluntary contributions alone it could not survive, as men would always find other ways of spending their money. The same argument did not apply to Dissenters. If they wanted to attend university and have their own burial grounds, then they should build their own and endow them with their own funds; in this way they could follow the dictates of their own consciences without destroying the basic principles of the universities and the Church.

Another 'sign of the times' Patrick noted was the 'growing conviction that, in our generation, we are wiser than our forefathers'. Looking back to the great law-givers, philosophers and poets of biblical and classical times, he pointed out that though more people now had a little knowledge, fewer knew much. Finally, he objected to the party violence of the last elections: 'If there be one privilege greater than another, in all our charter of liberty, it is that which consists in full permission to write and speak our sentiments with propriety and decorum.'[80] Without the right to free speech, the whole fabric of freedom was undermined.

The Signs of the Times is an important summary of Patrick's political beliefs and does much to redress his image as a rampant high Tory, opposed to all change. His children, with the tendency of youth to see things in black and white, were much more extreme in their views. The excitement of the election inspired Branwell to introduce one in the juvenilia. Allowing Northangerland to return from his exile in Stumps Isle and moving on from the Angrians' successes in their military campaigns against the Ashantee,[81] he introduced a Reform Ministry to Verdopolis. In a vivid depiction of the hustings, drawn from his own observations, Branwell had Northangerland give a powerful speech denouncing the peculation, corruption and rottenness of the ministry:

I passed that evening through Elrington Square and beheld workmen erecting a spacious Hustings in front of the splendid Elrington Hall while directly opposite another was in progress for the yellows and their speaker Montmorency ... Orange Crimson Scarlet and Blood red favours mingled in tumultous confusion. at 7 o clock the yellow Hustings began to fill with the Ministeral grandees ... amid the hoarse applause of their Partisans ... Ere I was aware Another Person stood in the full front of the Bloody hustings But the Roars of Hate and Triumph rose in such deafning volleys that I could hardly steady my eyes to see him.[82]

Just as had happened in real life, the meeting of the Verdopolitan Parliament was brought to a close by the four kings, Parry, Ross, Stumps and Moncay, who prorogued it to prevent discussion of Northangerland's bill for the reform of the navy.[83]

The rapid changes on the national political scene were followed by no less momentous changes in the Brontë family. On 2 July 1835, Charlotte wrote to Ellen:

We are all about to divide, break up, separate, Emily is going to school, Branwell is going to London, and I am going to be a Governess. This last determination I formed myself, knowing that I should have to take the step sometime, and 'better sune as syne' to use the Scotch proverb and knowing also that Papa would have enough to do with his limited income should Branwell be placed at the Royal Academy, and Emily at Roe-Head. Where am I going to reside? you will ask – within four miles of yourself dearest at a place neither of us are wholly unacquainted with, being no other than the identical Roe-Head mentioned above. Yes I am going to teach in the very school where I was myself taught –. Miss Wooler made me the offer and I preferred it to one or two proposals of Private Governessship which I had before received – I am sad, very sad at the thoughts of leaving home but Duty – Necessity – these are stern mistresses who will not be disobeyed.[84]

Though leaving home would be a terrible wrench, for Charlotte and Emily there was at least the consolation of being together. At the end of the month only Anne would be left at home with her father and aunt. The seventeen-year-old Emily was going to school for the first time since her few brief months at Cowan Bridge and Charlotte and Branwell were launching out into the world in their chosen careers.

Chapter Nine

✦

THE INFERNAL WORLD

While Charlotte and Emily packed their bags ready for their departure to Roe Head on 29 July 1835,[1] Branwell sat down in some excitement to draft a letter to the Royal Academy in London.

Sir,
Having an earnest desire to enter as Probationary Student in the Royal Academy but not being possessed of information as to the means of obtaining my desire I presume to request from you as Secretary to the Insti< t >ution an answer to the questions –
    Where am I to present my drawing?
    At what time – ?
      and especialy
   Can I do it in August or September[2]

It has been argued and, in recent years, it has been taken for granted that in consequence of this letter Branwell did indeed travel up to London to present himself at the Royal Academy. There, according to the accepted version of events, it is assumed he was overwhelmed by the discovery of his

[226]

own lack of talent in the face of the brilliant portraits on display in the metropolis and that he returned home in disgrace to Haworth, having spent all his father's money on drink and dissipation in an attempt to drown his sorrows.[3]

There is some evidence to support this view. In letters written on 2 July and 6 July 1835, both Charlotte and Patrick refer to the plan to send Branwell to the Royal Academy, though there are no references to Branwell's actually travelling to London or taking up his place there.[4] This could suggest that the family maintained a conspiracy of silence about the failure of the venture. Equally, as there are no extant letters from Charlotte to Ellen for the second half of 1835, it may be that Ellen, ever mindful of her friend's reputation, destroyed them in an effort to obliterate all reference to Branwell's first step on the slippery downward slope.

The positive evidence for the London fiasco is provided by two of Branwell's friends from the 1840s who were his earliest biographers. Francis Leyland, who was also the brother of Branwell's greatest friend, Joseph Bentley Leyland, refers to a 'short stay' in London, during which Branwell toured most of the public institutions and paid a visit to the Castle tavern at Holborn. Another railway friend, Francis Grundy, remembered Branwell drawing a finished elevation of one portion of Westminster Abbey from memory 'having been but once in London some years before'.[5]

In addition to the evidence of his friends, a story written by Branwell the following year is usually cited as being an autobiographical account of his own disastrous trip to London and the key to his failure there. The story, which is part of an incomplete and dismembered manuscript, describes the first visit of a young Angrian, Charles Wentworth, to Verdopolis. Dazed by the sights and glories of Verdopolis, particularly the splendour of St Michael's Cathedral, Wentworth allowed his letters of introduction to remain unused in his pocket, fortified himself with regular 'little squibs of rum' and spent all day walking about 'objectless'.[6]

There are serious problems with all these arguments, beginning with the very letter written by Branwell to the Royal Academy. The letter exists only in draft form and so little importance was attached to it that it was torn into several pieces and used as scrap paper for writing poetry. The Royal Academy has no record of this letter, a reply or any other correspondence with or about him; his name does not appear as either a probationer or student in their files. Branwell, it would appear, never made a formal approach for entrance.[7]

The obvious reason for this is that Branwell had discovered his plans were premature and did not send his letter. His claim that he was not 'possessed of information as to the means of obtaining my desire' is further evidence to suggest that he had not yet begun to study with William Robinson. As

Robinson himself had trained at the Royal Academy, he would have known that Branwell was not sufficiently prepared for entrance and that he would need to have an extensive portfolio of anatomical studies and drawings of classical sculptures and works of art to show before he could be admitted. This is exactly the sort of work which is totally absent from Branwell's extant drawings and paintings, which would explain, at least in part, why the Academy scheme was deferred. Branwell had a lot of work to do before he qualified for admission and Robinson was the ideal man to help him. It seems likely that he began a course of lessons with Robinson in the summer of 1835, travelling over to the artist's studio in Leeds, so that he could prepare himself for future entrance.[8]

The supposed 'conspiracy of silence' surrounding Branwell's failure at the Royal Academy may therefore simply reflect the fact that he never actually went there. Mrs Gaskell believed this was the case and actually wrote to Ellen Nussey to ask why the scheme had come to nothing. Ellen's reply, though hardly flattering to Branwell, clearly indicates her own belief that this was so: 'I do not know whether it was conduct or want of finances that prevented Branwell from going to the Royal Academy. Probably there were impediments of both kinds.'[9]

Neither Leyland nor Grundy, who provide the only positive evidence that Branwell did go to London, knew him at the time of the Royal Academy scheme. Both were writing some fifty years after this period and after only a comparatively brief acquaintance with Branwell. Even so, neither of them suggests that Branwell made any attempt to enter the Royal Academy, only that he visited London for a short time. Grundy's claim that Branwell could draw the façade of Westminster Abbey from memory is not proof that he had ever seen it in real life. From childhood he had been surrounded by books such as *A Description of London*, which not only described such buildings in detail but also reproduced illustrations of them.[10] It would have been the easiest thing in the world for Branwell to have carelessly sketched a copy of one of these illustrations from memory for the amusement of his friends, perhaps deliberately leaving them with the impression that he was recalling it from personal observation. This is precisely what he did with the maps of London he obtained in preparation for his proposed entry at the Royal Academy, as another acquaintance, George Searle Phillips, later described.

So enthusiastic was he about London at this time, that he got hold of all the maps he could find, illustrating its highways and byways, its alleys, and back slums, and short cuts, and studied them so closely that he knew them all by heart, and often cheated the 'commercial gents' who came to the Black Bull into the belief that he, though a young man, was an old Londoner, and knew more about the ins and outs of the mighty Babylon than many a man who had passed his life within its walls.

Then Branwell would astonish them by saying that he was never in London in his life."

Leyland's account is less easy to dismiss because it is more detailed. But it is clear from the way he writes of Branwell's adventures in London that he is merely guessing at what happened rather than writing from first-hand knowledge. His account draws on that of Francis Grundy and cites one 'Mr Woolven', who, while later working on the construction of the Manchester and Leeds Railway, met and remembered Branwell from the Castle tavern at Holborn." Apart from the unlikelihood of Woolven's recognizing someone in Yorkshire whom he had once seen briefly in a London tavern five or six years before, his account of Branwell's confident assumption of the role of public arbiter in a quarrel there is entirely at odds with the timidity and lack of self-esteem which Leyland himself, and later biographers, would have us believe drove Branwell home in confusion and led him to abandon his Academy ambitions.

Again, it seems more than likely that this was simply bluff on Branwell's part. He was completely familiar with the setting and the *habitués* of the Castle tavern at Holborn from his reading of the works of Pierce Egan, the author who had possibly inspired his own love of boxing. Branwell had certainly read extracts from his five-volume work *Boxiana; or Sketches of Antient and Modern Pugilism,* in *Blackwood's Magazine,* if not the work itself. He also regularly read Egan's sporting journal, *Bell's Life in London,* for which he had to send to the Shake Hands public house between Keighley and Oakworth. In all probability Branwell would also have read Egan's *Book of Sports,* published only three years earlier in 1832, which gave a detailed description of the Castle tavern, its landlord, its clientele and a typical evening of jollities there." With his facility for conversation and his remarkably retentive memory, Branwell would easily have been able to give an apparently personal impression of the Castle tavern and talk with its famous landlord, the retired pugilist, Tom Spring. Among his much more worldly and better travelled friends at the railway, Branwell was always anxious to foster a sophisticated image of himself, so it would not have been unnatural for him to pretend a genuine knowledge of the metropolis which was, in fact, simply derived from books.

Even if we take at face value the accounts of both Grundy and Leyland, the most that can be claimed is that Branwell spent a short time in London, possibly in connection with his artistic endeavours. Such a trip could have occurred after his course of lessons with Robinson had finished in September 1835 or possibly in March the following year. The September date is more likely as being the period that Branwell himself suggested in his draft letter. The Royal Academy was, however, closed in September, so any intention of even calling in there to enquire about future admission would have been foiled.[14] On 8 April 1836, he told the editor of *Blackwood's Magazine* that 'Absence from home has for a long time prevented my again addressing you', which might suggest he had been away in London. At the very least, this seems to have been an exaggeration as Branwell was certainly in Haworth on 29 February and on 28 March, when he attended meetings of the Three Graces Lodge.[15] Any trip to London can only have been of a very short duration, therefore, and, on the whole, the available evidence would tend to suggest that such a visit was unlikely.

Many years later, when disillusion with his prospects really had set in, Branwell wrote to his friend, the sculptor, J. B. Leyland:

I used to think that if I could have for a week the free range of the British Museum – the Library included – I could feel as though I were placed for seven days in paradise, but now really, dear Sir, my eyes would roam over the Elgin marbles, the Egyptian saloon and the most treasured volumes like the eyes of a dead cod fish.[16]

The implication of this statement is surely that Branwell had never had the opportunity to visit the British Museum and Library. Though there is no visitors' book for that period, the records of the Reading Room show that he was never issued with a ticket. Yet if Branwell had gone to London in the autumn of 1835, either to prepare for entry to the Academy or to enter as a probationer, the British Museum and Library is precisely where he would have gone. The Elgin Marbles and the Egyptian saloon, in particular, would have furnished him with exactly the material he was lacking – ancient statuary and artefacts to draw 'from the antique'. It is inconceivable, too, that the bookish Branwell would not have seized the opportunity to browse, if not to study, in the Reading Room.

Branwell's own writings at the time of the supposed London venture do not support the idea of a catastrophic failure, despite the Angrian story of Charles Wentworth. It is always dangerous to argue autobiographical facts from fiction and there is nothing to suggest that Branwell identified himself with Wentworth, who does not appear in the juvenilia until May 1836 and even then plays only a relatively minor role.[17] Wentworth's background and reasons for his visit to the metropolis could hardly be more different from those of Branwell. Wentworth is a wealthy young man, soon to inherit a large fortune on his twenty-first birthday, who is troubled by the Calvinist doctrine of predestination. He asks 'shall I perish for ever for doing what I could not avoid' and then, following the 'most mistaken advice' of the poet who advises 'Pursue what fate or Chance proclaimeth best', he decides to visit Verdopolis 'to seek in its pleasures and dissipation and wild approaching turmoil the good which fate and Chance should hold out to him'.[18] This could hardly be further from the fixed purpose of the eighteen-year-old Branwell's journey.

As for Wentworth's 'little squibs of rum', rum was the only drink Branwell disdained. Whisky was his own favourite tipple and when he could not afford that he drank gin.[19] In a story written the following year as part of his chronicles of Angria, Branwell has Wentworth, Hastings and his sister's creation, Townsend, drinking in an inn at Aynsham. There, brandy is declared 'the highest Liquor the prince and sovereign of the lot'; the man who chooses to drink it 'exhibits Ambition a love of the grand in art and Nature – a poetical feeling'. Gin is 'a witty but dissipated sort of Liquor' whose choice 'exhibits a quick mind but a fondness < of > for the foundations of society – the lowest'. Rum, on the other hand, which Wentworth is again drinking, is castigated sharply: 'Catch me a harsher meaner clumsier fluid and I'm yours … A love of Rum declares a mind naturally grovelling. and fourpennorth betokens it stingy parsimonious and abominable'.[20] Quite clearly Branwell did not intend Wentworth as a self-portrait.

Wentworth's dazed reaction to the glorious buildings and bustling streets of Verdopolis is typical of all newcomers to that great city but is not the beginning, crux or even end of his story. The news that finally moves him to action is the outbreak of war, at which point he decides to join the forces of Northangerland and seek glory in the ensuing military campaign to protect Angria from the Reformist Ministry in Verdopolis.[21] In fact, Wentworth owes his creation to Branwell's need to have an informant among Northangerland's troops, just as he already had Henry Hastings on the side of Zamorna and John Flower, now Baron Richton, with Fidena and the Constitutionalists.[22] He fills a fictional void and assumes a minor and rather disreputable role in the continuation of the Angrian chronicles. In short, therefore, there is no reason to believe Wentworth and his experiences in Verdopolis are literal and autobiographical accounts of Branwell himself and his supposed adventures in London. The story cannot and should not be taken out of its context as a very minor incident in a long train of much more important events.

Had Branwell undergone the traumatic experience of rejection or personal failure at the Royal Academy, one would have expected this to be reflected in his writing. But Branwell was in a buoyant mood throughout the autumn of 1835 and the following spring. He was not only constantly employed on his writing but also had several works on hand at once, including a massive undertaking writing the chronicles of Angria. On 3 October 1835 he began an important new chapter in the first volume of a chronicle which, over the summer, had followed the fortunes of Angria after Zamorna's victory over the Ashantee at Loanga and the excitement of the subsequent elections. The new chapter was almost exclusively concerned with the political consequences of the Marquis of Ardrah's Reform Ministry being elected to power and his introduction of a 'Bill for the Reform of the Angrian Kingdom'. The Angrians were to be faced with the stark choice of complete independence from the Verdopolitan Union, with the subsequent loss of their estates and rights elsewhere in Africa, or the abolition of their own monarchy and legislature which would be submerged in that of Verdopolis. These events, inspired by the return of Viscount Melbourne's reforming Whig ministry in the April elections of 1835, set the scene for the forthcoming civil war which was to be the most climactic event in the whole history of the imaginary kingdoms of Africa.[23]

Throughout October and November Branwell was also heavily involved in completing the second volume of 'The Life of Alexander Percy'. In one of the best and most interesting stories he had yet written, he followed the fortunes of Northangerland's wife and evil genius, Augusta di Segovia. Their passionate, destructive and death-defying love, which is based on an almost instinctive and complete knowledge and understanding of each other, fore-shadows and possibly inspired the more famous love between Heathcliff and Catherine in Emily's novel, *Wuthering Heights*. Northangerland tells Augusta, for example:

I know thee and thou knowest how I love thee We will not confess what needs no confession but rather let me live an hour of heaven here in the arms of one with whom I sacrifice all hope of it hereafter – O Augusta with you here I do < almost > feel < I am joy. you here > happy. as I or you can feel I know I am Alexander Percy who thinks that years with thee are bought cheaply by Eternity –[24]

At Augusta's instigation, Percy arranges for Sdeath to murder his father so that he can inherit his fortune and estates immediately and pay off his own huge gambling debts. Although parricide is suspected it cannot be proved, but greed proves their downfall. Augusta persuades Percy to renege on his debts and he returns to their house to find her lying dead in her room, murdered by Sdeath at the instigation of the moneylenders. Augusta's death finally drives Percy into the atheism with which he had flirted for so many years, tainting his mourning with the blackest despair. Like Heathcliff, he too is haunted by the image of his dead beloved:

> Thou art gone but I am here
> Left behind and mourning on
> Doomed in dreams to Deem thee near
> But to awake and find thee gone[25]

Though the loss of Augusta explains Percy's future atheism and melancholy, the continuation of his story is envisaged at the end with the introduction of Mary Henrietta Wharton, Percy's future wife and mother of his daughter, Mary Percy. As soon as this retrospective was finished, Branwell went on to a new venture, writing poetry with the specific purpose in mind of securing its publication in *Blackwood's Magazine*. In the new year he launched into yet another new project, plunging the fortunes of Angria into a horrendous spiral of war against the Government forces of Verdopolis which rapidly gave way to civil war within the kingdom itself.[26]

Branwell's confidence in himself and his own abilities cannot be better summarized than in the letter he wrote to *Blackwood's Magazine* on 8 December 1835. This was at least the third attempt he had made to be accepted as a contributor to the magazine. In previous letters, he now admitted:

I have perhaps spoken too openly respecting the extent of my powers, But I did so because I determined to say what I beleived; I <u>know</u> that I am not one of the wretched writers of the day, I < beleive > know that I possess strength to assist you beyond some of your own contributors; but I wish to make you the Judge in this case and give you the benefit of its desiscion [decision].[27]

Branwell had been prompted to write again by the news that James Hogg, the Ettrick Shepherd, who had had such a profound influence on the young Brontës as a poet, author and figure in the *Noctes Ambrosianae*, had died on 21 November. Having had no reply to his previous letters, Branwell was determined to receive a reply this time and began in a way calculated to attract attention. 'Sir,' he demanded of the editor, 'Read what I write.' He continued in less aggressive mood, citing his favourite passages from *Blackwood's Magazine* and offering himself as a contributor in place of James Hogg.

He and others like him gave your Magazine the peculiar character which made it famous:- As these men die it will decay, unless thier places be supplied by others like them. – Now Sir, to you I appear writing with conceited assurance, – < by > but <u>I am not</u> – for I know myself so far as to beleive in my own originality; and on that ground I desire of you admittance into your ranks; And do not wonder that I apply so determinedly, for the remembrances I spoke of, have < fik > fixed you and your Magazine in such a manner upon my mind that the Idea of striving to aid another periodical is <u>horribly repulsive</u>. My resolution is to devote my ability to you, and for Gods sake, till you see wether or not I can serve you do not so < coldy > coldly refuse my aid...

Now Sir, do not act like a common place person, but like a man willing to examine for himself. Do not t[urn] from the naked truth of my letters but <u>prove me</u> – and if I do not stand the proof I will not farther press myself on you – If I do stand it – Why – you have lost an able writer in James Hogg and God grant you may gain one in

Patrick Branwell Brontë[28]

Though Branwell's obviously sincere desire to become a contributor to *Blackwood's Magazine* shone through his letter, the careless spellings, numerous crossings out and frequent, startling changes of handwriting did little to substantiate his claims to the editor's attention. His apparent arrogance and hectoring style, though hardly diplomatic, were not sufficient in themselves to merit rejection. Similar letters regularly appeared in the pages of *Blackwood's* – though Branwell may have misjudged his recipient in assuming that the jocose house style of the magazine was also appropriate for a genuine letter to the editor.[29]

Branwell faced the new year of 1836 in confident mood: if his future as yet appeared unclear it was only because he had a plethora of talents. If the Royal Academy scheme never materialized then a career in letters beckoned. For the moment he would hedge his bets by pursuing both.

For the rest of his family the second half of 1835 had not been a particularly happy time. Charlotte had taken up her post as a teacher at Roe Head with deep reluctance. 'Did I not once say Ellen you ought to be thankful for your independence?' she asked her friend. 'I felt what I said at the time, and I repeat it now with double earnestness'.[30] At least, however, as she also admitted, 'my lines have fallen in pleasant places'. She was going to a place she knew, to work for Miss Wooler whom she loved and respected; her sister Emily would be with her and both Ellen and Mary Taylor would be near at hand. It is probable, too, that the prospect of teaching young girls was not as yet unpleasant to her. It is often forgotten in the despair and bitterness of her later experiences, particularly as a governess, that Charlotte could devise no happier fate for the heroines of her novels, if they had no hope of marriage, than to run their own school.[31]

Though she was now entering the teaching profession, Charlotte herself was, at nineteen, very much of a marriageable age. As yet no suitor had approached her, but as an independent young woman earning her own living at Roe Head she might well attract the attention of a prospective husband. She was, after all, replacing a teacher who had left Roe Head to get married.[32] It was undoubtedly the possibility of her forming an unsuitable attachment, away from the careful supervision of her father and aunt, that prompted Patrick to write once more to his old friend, Elizabeth Firth Franks:

As two of my dear children, are soon to be placed near you, I take the liberty of writing to you a few lines, in order to request both you and Mr Franks, to be so kind, as to interpose with your advice and counsel, to them, in any case of necessity – and if expedient to write to Miss Branwell, or me, if our interference should be requisite. I will charge them, strictly, to attend to what you may advise ... They, both, have good abilities, & as far as I can judge their principles are good also, but they are very young, and unacquainted with the ways of this delusive, and insnaring world, and though, they will be placed under the superintendence, of Miss Wooler, who will I doubt not, do what she can for their good, Yet, I am well aware, that neither they, nor any other, can ever, in this land of probation, lie beyond the reach of temptation.[33]

Aware of how indignant such a letter would make Charlotte, Patrick did not tell either of his daughters that he had written, contenting himself with the thought that Mrs Franks would be his eyes and ears.

In the end, however, it was not Charlotte but Emily who was to cause the family concern. Apart from the brief six months she had spent at the Clergy Daughters' School nearly ten years earlier, she had never spent any length of time away from home before. As if to reinforce the separation from her family, her first full day at school actually fell on her seventeenth birthday, the first she had ever passed away from home. Life as a schoolgirl at Roe Head had been difficult for Charlotte and it is unlikely to have been any easier for Emily, despite the advantages she had over her sister. She was neither as absolutely alone nor as unprepared as Charlotte had been, having had the benefit of lessons from her older sister based on what Charlotte herself had learnt at Roe Head. On the other hand, she had several disadvantages. Her relationship to a teacher may have made her vulnerable to unpleasantness from, or even ostracism by, her fellow pupils. The round of school routine would leave the sisters little time for private conversation and Charlotte may have slept in her own room away from the dormitory.[34] Perhaps most important of all was her age, for at seventeen she would have been one of the oldest pupils in the school. Miss Wooler's practice of teaching new girls separately until they had reached the required standard to join the rest of the class must have been particularly galling when pupils much younger than herself had already earned their places. Even when she joined them, she is likely to have been self-conscious both physically and mentally. Being tall for her age, she must have attracted even more malicious attention than Charlotte had done by her inexpensive and unfashionable clothing. Her intelligence, which a later teacher was to rate more highly than Charlotte's,[35] must have added to her frustration with the learning by rote which formed such a large part of the school syllabus.

Added to all these problems was the fact that the pervasive nature of school routine effectively ensured that Emily had no time to spend in Gondal fantasies. Though nothing remains of the Gondal stories written before 1838, there is no doubt that these had already reached the same levels of complexity and sophistication as Charlotte and Branwell's Angria.[36] Until now, Emily had always been free to let her imagination wander at will: though she had had lessons and household duties to perform, so long as these were completed satisfactorily, she had effectively had the rest of her time at her own disposal. Now, for the first time in her life, virtually every hour of her day was organized for her and there was scarcely a spare moment even to think about Gondal, let alone write about it. She could not even indulge in Gondal talk, for Anne, her playing partner, was far away at home in Haworth. For Emily the need to follow through her Gondal fantasies was so intense that it transcended the bounds of the imagination and affected her physical wellbeing. Deprived of the stimulus of Gondal, she had nothing to make the rigid routine of daily school life bearable.

When a schoolgirl herself, Charlotte had been able to turn her imaginative powers to good account by telling stories which won her friends, but Emily's extreme reticence, which Ellen had remarked on two years before during her visit to Haworth, made this impossible for her. After the quiet and privacy of life at Haworth Parsonage, it must have been anathema to the seventeen-year-old Emily to be compelled to spend all her waking and sleeping hours in the company of boisterous, unimaginative and unsympathetic girls whom Charlotte herself, in one of her more vitriolic moods, described as 'fat-headed oafs'. Though having at least some time at her own disposal, Charlotte, too, suffered from the loss of privacy attendant on boarding school life.

The Ladies went into the school-room to do their exercises & I crept up < in >to the bed-room to be <u>alone</u> for the first time that day < day >. Delicious was the sensation I experienced as I laid down on the spare-bed & resigned myself to the Luxury of twilight & Solitude.[37]

If Charlotte felt the need for privacy, how much more must Emily have done so when she had to share even her bed with one of her fellow pupils? At seventeen, too, it must have been difficult to change the habits of the past ten years and adapt to the oppressive rigidity of the daily routine. Her misery was compounded by the fact that from the schoolroom and dormitory windows she could see the surrounding moorland hills slowly turning from the green and russet hues of summer to the glorious purple of flowering heather as July gave way to August and September.[38] A tantalizing reminder of her own beloved moors at Haworth, which she was free to wander at will, this served only to reinforce the confining atmosphere of school. Her homesickness became so overpowering that she became literally ill, as Charlotte later explained:

Liberty was the breath of Emily's nostrils; without it, she perished. The change from her own home to a school, and from her own very noiseless, very secluded, but unrestricted and inartificial mode of life, to one of disciplined routine (though under the kindliest auspices), was what she failed in enduring. Her nature proved here too strong for her fortitude. Every morning when she woke, the vision of home and the moors rushed on her, and darkened and saddened the day that lay before her. Nobody knew what ailed her but me – I knew only too well. In this struggle her health was quickly broken: her white face, attenuated form, and failing strength threatened rapid decline. I felt in my heart she would die if she did not go home, and with this conviction obtained her recall.[39]

Emily's symptoms, so forcibly recalling the spectre of the consumption which had carried off Maria and Elizabeth, did not allow of any delay. By the end of October, just three months after setting out for Roe Head, Emily was back again in the regenerative atmosphere of her home at Haworth. She was fortunate that Charlotte, too, was suffering from the enforced deprivation of her own imaginative world: it was quite true that 'nobody knew what ailed her but me', for who else but one her own siblings could have recognized the importance of allowing the imagination free rein? That such indulgence was inextricably linked with home, Charlotte also recognized quite clearly. Eighteen months later, when her own sense of deprivation was beginning to overpower her, she wrote:

How few would believe that from sources purely imaginery such happiness could be derived – Pen cannot pourtray the deep Interest of the scenes, of the continued trains of events, I have witnessed in that little room with the low narrow bed & bare \white-washed/ walls – twenty miles away – What a treasure is thought! What a privilege is reverie – I am thankful that I have the power of solacing myself with the dream of creations whose reality I shall never behold – May I never lose that power may I never feel it growing weaker – If I should how little pleasure will life afford me – its lapses of shade are so wide so gloomy Its gleams of sunshine so limited & dim –![40]

That liberty, so vital to Emily, which Charlotte took pains to imply to the outside world was physical and dependent on the moorlands of home, was actually the liberty of mind and imagination. Home was the only place which could offer her the unbridled indulgence of Gondal fantasy.

Emily's place at school was immediately taken by Anne, whose dependence on Gondal was much less extreme than her sister's.[41] Anne's career at Roe Head was undistinguished. Quiet and diligent, she left no abiding impression on either her teachers or her school-fellows, though she apparently won the prize for good conduct in December 1836 and made at least one, much younger friend. Even Charlotte made only passing references to her presence: Anne tells her that George Nussey had just gone past or appears as a 'quiet < face > image, sitting at her lessons on the opposite side of the table –'.[42] Yet this apparent ordinariness concealed a struggle that was just as intense, if not as dramatic, as Emily's. It was the first time that Anne, now nearly sixteen, had ever left home to go to school. All her life she had been the cherished and protected 'little one', the baby of the family, who was always spoken of in terms of more than ordinary affection. Patrick had initially dismissed the idea of sending her away to school, preferring to keep 'my dear little Anne' at home for another year 'under her Aunt's tuition, and my own'.[43]

Later, as a governess, Anne was to pour out her longing for home in poetry and there is no reason to believe that she was not just as homesick at Roe Head as Emily. Like her older sister Charlotte, however, Anne had a core of steel, a sense of duty and obligation which seems to have been flawed, if not altogether missing, in Emily. She could not fail to be aware that financial sacrifices were being made at home and by Charlotte, whose teaching salary was almost totally absorbed in the cost of providing her with an education. 'After clothing herself and Anne,' Charlotte was to confess to Mary Taylor, 'there was nothing left, though she had hoped to be able to save something.'[44] Like Charlotte, Anne clearly believed it was her duty to get an education that would enable her to earn her own living. She therefore bravely embarked upon her schooldays, pragmatically determined to make the best of things.

Charlotte herself was faced with an uphill task, but she made a determined effort to succeed in her chosen profession, throwing all her energies into teaching. There would appear to have been no more than about half a dozen boarding pupils, though Charlotte's weariness suggests that there may have been more day pupils. Of those whose names are mentioned, Anne Brontë was by far the oldest at nearly sixteen; Ann Cook, Anne's friend, and her sister, Ellen, were ten- and eight-year-old sisters from Dewsbury; there was a Miss Upton and a Miss Caris, and Charlotte's *bêtes noires*, the Misses Lister and Marriott, who were possibly related.[45] Most of Charlotte's day was taken up with the endless routine of taking and hearing lessons, supervising the girls during their hours of study or escorting them on their daily walks. Here and there she was able to snatch the odd half hour for herself. These opportunities, doubly precious because they were so rare, she seized upon to dream or write about her beloved Angria. Branwell, deeply immersed in the chronicling of Angria at home, fed her imagination with bulletins on the latest developments.

About a week since I got a letter from Branwell containing a most exquisitely characteristic epistle from Northangerland to his daughter – It is astonishing what a soothing and delightful tone that letter seemed to speak – I lived on its contents for days, < & > in every pause of employment – it came chiming in like some sweet bar of music – bringing with it agreeable thoughts such as I had for many weeks been a stranger to –[46]

So compulsive was Charlotte's need to escape from the mundanities of life at Roe Head that the exotic Angrian figures and scenes of her imagination acquired a reality of their own. One particular moment in the winter term of 1835 made such a deep impression on her that she wrote about it on her return home at Christmas.

Never shall I Charlotte Brontë forget what a voice of wild & wailing music Now came thrillingly to my mind's almost to my body's ear nor how distinctly I < I saw > sitting in the schoolroom at Roe-head < & saw > saw the Duke of Zamorna leaning against that obelisk with the mute marble Victory above him, the fern waving at his feet his black horse turned loose grazing among the heather, the moonlight so mild & so exquisitely tranquil sleeping upon that vast & vacant road & the African sky quivering & shaking with stars expanded above all, I was quite gone I had really utterly forgot where I was and all the gloom & cheerlessness of my situation I felt myself breathing quick & short as I beheld < Zamorna > the Duke lifting up his sable crest which undulated as the plume of a hearse waves to the wind & knew that that music which < seems > as mournfully triumphant as the Scriptural verse

> 'Oh Grave where is thy sting Oh Death where
> is thy victory'

was exciting him & quickening his ever rapid pulse 'Miss Brontë what are you thinking about?' said a voice that dissipated all the charm & Miss Lister thrust her little rough black head into my face, 'Sic transit' &c.[47]

The Christmas holidays at the end of 1835 must have come as a welcome relief. At home, where there was the stimulation and encouragement of a sympathetic brother and sisters, the Angrian dream could be followed through without interruption and recorded at blissful length. It is no surprise, therefore, to find that as soon as she arrived home Charlotte launched into a long poem looking back over the foundation of the imaginary worlds and celebrating their continued power to excite her.

> When I sat 'neath a strange roof-tree
> With nought I knew or < loved round > loved around me
> Oh how my heart < shrank > shrank back to thee
> Then I felt how fast thy ties had bound \me/ ...
>
> Then < wildly > sadly I longed for my own dear home
> For a sight of the old familliar faces
> I drew near the casement & sat in its gloom
> And looked forth on the tempests desolate traces
>
> < Still Suddenly > Ever anon that < wild & > wolfish breeze
> The dead leaves & sere from their boughs < were > was shaking
> And I gazed on the hills through the leafless trees
> And felt as if my heart was breaking
>
> Where was I e're an hour had past
> Still list'ning to that dreary blast
> Still in that mirthless lifeless room
> Cramped, chilled & deadened by its gloom
>
> No! thanks to that bright darling dream
> Its power had shot one kindling gleam
> Its voice had sent one wakening cry
> And bade me lay my sorrows by
> And called me earnestly to come
> And borne me to my moorland home
> < Alas! I had lost > I heard no more the senseless sound
> Of task & chat that hummed around
> I saw no more that grisly night
> closing the day's sepulchral light[48]

For a few brief weeks, Charlotte was free to indulge her fantasies though the need to do so was less compelling in the liberating atmosphere of home.

Charlotte and Anne discovered that all had not gone smoothly at home in their absence. Their father, too, had had a difficult six months. The campaign by Dissenters to disestablish the Church of England, which Patrick had so vigorously opposed in his quarrel with John Winterbotham, the Baptist minister, had suddenly taken on a new and alarming form. On 22 September 1835, the annual meeting had been held in Haworth Church to elect the surveyors and constable and lay a rate on the parish to cover church expenses for the forthcoming year. The former constable had been a political partisan in the summer Parliamentary elections, so his candidature was vehemently contested. Even more stormy was the attempt to impose a church rate which met with 'the most marked opposition by the people generally. They seemed to be fully determined not to submit any longer to the gross injustice of taxing all to support the religion of one sect.'[49]

Haworth, with its large Dissenting population, was in the forefront of what was to become a national and annual campaign to oppose the granting of church rates. Even more seriously, the chief role in the anti-church rate lobby was assumed by James Greenwood, the Baptist mill owner of Bridge End Mills in Haworth. He was not only a more influential and heavyweight opponent than Winterbotham, but also, following a bitter family dispute, bore a serious grudge against his brother, Joseph Greenwood of Spring Head, who was the main church trustee.[50] As the churchwardens already had a surplus of ten pounds from the rate of the previous year, the Anglicans were not in a good position to argue their need. James Greenwood took the lead in denouncing as 'impolitic and improper' a proposal from one of the churchwardens, George Taylor, that they should draw on the poor rate once the ten pounds had been expended. He followed this up by taking advantage of the turbulent state of the meeting to propose that the question of laying a church rate should be deferred to the following year. Though this might appear a compromise position, it was effectively a victory for the Dissenters, who had successfully fought off the imposition of a church rate. This left the churchwardens (and Patrick) with the impossible task of maintaining and repairing the church for a year out of a sum of only ten pounds – which would not even pay the salaries of the two parish clerks.[51]

The sudden refusal to approve a church rate, which in the past had always gone through on the nod, seems to have thrown Patrick into a panic. The spectre of a disestablished Church of England loomed closer, achieved, not by Parliamentary measure, but by the wilful and concerted opposition of determined Dissenters at the local level. James Greenwood's influence could only be counteracted by promoting his brother. The day after the meeting, Patrick wrote to the Earl of Harewood, urgently renewing his plea to have Joseph Greenwood appointed to the magistracy. Two weeks later he signed a petition got up by the gentlemen of Keighley, requesting the earl, as Lord Lieutenant, to act swiftly in replacing the late Mr Ferrand in the magistracy.

Fearing to be thought too importunate, Patrick wrote once more to the earl, explaining that the petition did not originate or have any connection with him and that he had not divulged the contents of the earl's letters to himself.[52] No positive response was forthcoming and on 26 December Patrick wrote in a state of high excitement and distress to Henry Heap, vicar of Bradford, asking him to intervene and lead a personal deputation to the Lord Lieutenant.

Our case is now becoming very Urgent, as the Enemies, of the Church, in this place, are in active cooperation, and are determined to apply to Government, through the medium of Lord Morpeth, and Mr Baines, in order, to have a Whig Magistrate appointed for Haworth, <u>over the head of the Lord Lieutenant</u>!!! – as they <u>have</u> already, insolently, and shamefully done in many other parts of the Kingdom – I wish, that the Lord Lieutenant, could be informed of this, as soon as <u>possible</u> – I have written to his Lordship, on the subject, so frequently, that I am ashamed to trouble Him in this way, any more –[53]

Henry Heap reluctantly forwarded Patrick's letter, apologizing for its vehemence by pointing out that Patrick 'is a very warm Conservative', but adding his own, rather weary, plea: 'If Mr Greenwood could be <u>soon</u> admitted to the Privilege of becoming a Magistrate for that truly <u>important</u> part of my Parish, I should be grateful to your Lordship –'.[54] At last galvanized into action, the Lord Lieutenant made enquiries about Joseph Greenwood's suitability and put arrangements in train for his appointment. Patrick's campaign, which had lasted well over a year, was finally vindicated when Joseph Greenwood was sworn in as a Justice of the Peace on 28 June 1836.[55]

The problems Patrick was facing with the Dissenters in Haworth came at a time when he was increasingly unable to cope with the sheer weight of his parish duties. The population had expanded by over a third since he had first become minister of Haworth. With nearly 6,000 people in the chapelry, the number of funerals and baptisms had increased dramatically. In 1834 and again in 1835 he performed 135 burials, compared to around only a hundred in his first few years. Even more startling was the number of baptisms, which reflects not only the population increase but also an active campaign on Patrick's part. By 1834 these had risen to 286, rising again to 301 – an average of twenty-five baptisms a month – the following year. On occasions, he personally baptized twenty children a day.[56] Once in a while one of the neighbouring clerics, such as Thomas Brooksbank Charnock, son of the former minister of Haworth,[57] would help out, but most of the ceaseless round of duty was performed by the fifty-eight-year-old Patrick himself. Permanent assistance had now become an absolute necessity and at about the same time as his daughters returned from Roe Head, Patrick employed a curate.

The Reverend William Hodgson's origins are obscure, but he was certainly of humble birth and may have been an Irishman. He was newly ordained and Haworth was his first and only curacy; in 1837 he was promoted to the incumbency of Christ Church at Colne, on the Lancashire side of the moors behind Haworth, where he remained for the rest of his life.[58] By temperament he was a fiery and somewhat tactless young man who proved to be a voluble advocate of the Established Church and a vigorous opponent of Dissenters both in the pulpit and in print. His position in Haworth seems to have been awkward from the start. Though he took his first duty, a burial, on Christmas Day 1835, following this with two baptisms on 27 December, he did not begin signing the church registers with his title as 'curate' until the middle of April the following year. This coincided with Patrick's first grant of fifty pounds from the Church Pastoral Aid Society towards the cost of his curate's salary, which would make a formal appointment financially possible. Until this point, however, it would seem that the arrangement was informal and that the curate was paid either out of Patrick's own pocket (which seems extremely unlikely) or by means of a subscription among the wealthier Anglicans in the chapelry.[59]

Never one to shirk his responsibilities, Patrick continued to take the larger proportion of the baptisms, marriages and burials, but Hodgson was able to stand in for him on a regular basis, take the Sunday schools and also relieve him of some of the Sunday duties. Indeed, on the first or second Sunday after his arrival he found himself flung in at the deep end.

It had been arranged that Mr Hodgson should preach in the morning and Mr Brontë in the afternoon, but while Mr Hodgson was in the afternoon Sunday School Mr Brontë sent for him and told him that he felt unequal to the task of preaching and that Mr Hodgson must take his place. To this Mr Hodgson demurred, urging that he had no sermon ready. 'Oh,' said Mr Brontë, 'you must preach extempore; the people like it better.' Poor Mr Hodgson with much sinking of heart had to do as he was bid, and the Haworth folk used to remind him of that first extempore sermon and say that he never preached a better one.[60]

Though the sudden appearance of a young, unmarried curate in the village might have been expected to cause at least a flutter of interest at the parsonage, William Hodgson's entire curacy seems to have passed unremarked by the younger Brontës.[61] Apparently they saw little of him. He had taken lodgings at Cook Gate with a lady of independent means called Grace Ogden who lived there with her daughter, Susanna, and her three-year-old granddaughter, Grace. He paid the occasional duty visit to Patrick but was not, it appears, admitted into the family on any terms of intimacy. Perhaps not unnaturally, Hodgson formed the impression that pride was largely responsible for the girls' shyness and reserve, though he had a great deal of respect for Patrick and 'scouted with indignation' Mrs Gaskell's tales of his outbursts of intemperate rage.[62]

Charlotte and Anne's time at home was too short and precious to be wasted on civilities towards a young clergyman. Indeed, Charlotte seems to have spent most of her holiday steeling herself for the return to Roe Head. It is possible that she talked to her father about her unhappiness at the prospect of teaching for the rest of her life and told him something about her passionate need to write. Perhaps Branwell's recent letters to *Blackwood's Magazine* prompted her to imagine that she, too, might earn her living by her pen. If she was already nurturing ambitions in that quarter, Patrick firmly quashed them, pointing out the unlikelihood of her succeeding as a writer. It seems likely also that he warned her against allowing herself to be seduced away from her duties by Angrian fantasies which poisoned her mind against her daily life. Patrick knew what he was talking about. Many years before he had himself felt the pull of literary ambition but, having conquered it, he gave short shrift to those who did not. In the preface to his *The Cottage in the Wood* he had written:

The sensual novelist and his admirer, are beings of depraved appetites and sickly imaginations, who having learnt the art of *self-tormenting*, are diligently and zealously employed in creating an imaginary world, which they can never inhabit, only to make the real world, with which they must necessarily be conversant, gloomy and insupportable.[63]

He urged Charlotte to attend more closely to her duties, to contrive to become more interested in them and to confine her literary activities to the purely recreational. There was no harm in pursuing flights of the imagination as an amusement in leisure hours but when this became so obsessive that it interfered with the mechanics of real life, then it was time to crush it. Acknowledging in her heart the justice of these remarks, Charlotte later wrote, rather sadly, that

Following my father's advice – who from my childhood has counselled me ... I have endeavoured not only attentively to observe all the duties a woman ought to fulfil, but to feel deeply interested in them. I don't always succeed, for sometimes when I'm teaching or sewing I would rather be reading or writing; but I try to deny myself; and my father's approbation amply rewarded me for the privation.[64]

It was perhaps Patrick, too, who suggested that piety, not Angria, should be Charlotte's mental crutch for the future. In one of the poems she wrote during the Christmas holidays, Charlotte reflected on what she was increasingly to see as a conflict between her religion and her imagination. She looked back with nostalgia to the simple and unquestioning faith of her youth:

> My heart was better then than now
> Its hopes < were higher far > soared far more free
> I felt a blind, but ardent glow
> Of love for piety

Even as a child, however, her imagination had betrayed her. Her fascination with stories of ghosts and spectral hauntings had undermined her certainty and wrought on her nerves to such an extent that she 'almost feared to pray'. Now 'other visions' of Angria haunt her, which, though not as painful, 'yet fever the blood in its flow'. Such is their potency that a poem which clearly began with the intention of seeking solace in religion ends up as yet another digression into the hot-house world of Angria. This Charlotte felt called upon to justify: her imagination is already her solace:

> Is it not well, that < oft > thou can'st call
>   Her hallowing scenes < around > to thee
> When haply in thy spirit all
>   Sinks chill & hopelessly
>
> Is it not well when severed far
> From those thou lovedst to see
> That she has hung her golden star
> O'er alien hill & tree[65]

Charlotte did make an effort to turn from Angria, however futile it turned out to be. During the whole month of her holiday, she made no attempt to write a prose story despite the fact that Branwell had completed one Angrian adventure on 7 January 1836 and promptly begun another the same day.[66] For him there was no hint of conflict but, on the other hand, his Angrian obsession had less of idolatry in it. In another poem written the day before her return to Roe Head, Charlotte recognized the unpalatable fact of her blasphemy; Zamorna was

> … not the temple but the god
>   the idol in his marble shrine
> Our grand dream is his wide abode
> And there for me he dwells divine

Knowing that she must go back to Roe Head the next day, she bade farewell to each of her beloved Angrian characters in turn and resolved to shut them out of her mind until she returned home again.

> But no more now of the wondrous dream
> My time of pleasant holiday
> Is faded like a sunny beam
> And I must here no longer stay
> may we all meet in joy again
> And then I'll sing a lighter strain
> This evening hear the solemn Knell
> Farewell! & yet again farewell!![67]

On 20 January 1836, Charlotte and Anne returned to school, leaving Emily and Branwell at home with Patrick and Aunt Branwell. At nineteen, Charlotte's future stretched out before her in a seemingly endless and uninviting prospect; she had no alternative but to teach. For Branwell, however, there was an embarrassment of riches. The Royal Academy plan may have been shelved but even more exciting schemes were being put forward. It was now suggested that he should make a study tour of the Continent.

In preparation for this plan, Branwell joined the Freemasons, hoping to benefit from their network of contacts while he was abroad. His name was put forward and approved at a meeting of the Three Graces Lodge in Haworth on 1 February 1836. There was one important obstacle to his initiation: Branwell was only eighteen years old and the minimum age for admittance was twenty-one. On 8 February John Brown and Joseph Redman, the Worshipful Master and Secretary of the Lodge, who also happened to be the church sexton and parish clerk respectively, wrote to the Provincial Lodge at Wakefield seeking a dispensation to allow Branwell to be admitted. They made light of his age, passing him off as 'about 20 Years of Age' and pointed out that his father 'is Minister of the Chapelry of Haworth, and always appears to be very favourable to Masonry'.[68] The application was unexpectedly refused, provoking a second letter from Brown and Redman explaining

we doubted not but our request would be complyed with, being, as we thought agreable to the laws of the Craft – vide Book of Constitutions, Page 90, – where going abroad is not mentioned, but in fact, this young Gentleman is a Pourtrait Painter and for the purpose of acquiring information or instruction intends going on to the Continent this Summer –[69]

This explanation 'quite alters the case' and a dispensation was immediately issued for Branwell to become a member of the Lodge of the Three Graces. He was initiated as one of the brethren in a ceremony on 29 February 1836.[70]

The fact that Branwell was planning an ambitious artistic tour of the Continent within a few months of the supposedly devastating failure of his Royal Academy ambitions, is further evidence that he never made that fateful trip to London the previous autumn. It suggests not only that he was still preparing himself for eventual entry to the Royal Academy but also that he had the full backing of his father, without whom he could not have afforded to go abroad. It is hardly likely that Patrick would have sanctioned a tour of Europe if Branwell had already proved himself totally untrustworthy, financially and morally, only a couple of hundred miles away from home in London.

Branwell was also still pursuing *Blackwood's Magazine* with a single-mindedness which suggests that he was less than committed to the idea of an artistic career. The brothers Blackwood were not noted for their punctiliousness in replying to correspondence and all Branwell's letters had so far remained unanswered. Undeterred, he wrote again on 8 April prefacing his letter with 'Sir, Read now at least,' written in large characters across the top of the page.[71] With the letter he enclosed two scenes from a long poem somewhat infelicitously entitled 'Misery'. If the editor would not ask Branwell for a sample of his writing, then he would have it thrust upon him.

The poem drew on a typical Angrian scenario and told of the defeated Count Albert's flight through a stormy night, his unexpected discovery of his dying wife, Maria, and his own subsequent death on the battlefield, where he is tortured by fear of there being no life beyond the tomb. Branwell planned, but did not attempt, a third concluding scene in which the soul of Count Albert was followed to its final misery after death.[72] Though the poem did not substantiate Branwell's claims to originality or especial powers, being highly imitative of Byron, it was nevertheless as good as, if not better than, much of the poetry that was then appearing in *Blackwood's*. Unusually, Branwell took a great deal of trouble over the lines, drafting and redrafting them until he was satisfied with the result. The first scene, a resonant description of a lone horseman struggling through the storm to reach his home, was substantially written within ten days of sending his letter of 8 December 1835; the second scene, which brought the total number of lines up to 728, was finished on 2 March 1836.[73] The final version was neatly written up and far more polished and considered than the accompanying letter. Branwell had at least the grace to offer an apology for his frequent changing over from right-handed to left-handed writing: he had hurt his right hand while boxing and had, till now, been unable to use it. With assumed carelessness, he sought the editor's opinion of his verse.

The affair which accompan< yes >ies my letter is certainly sent for insertion in Blackwood < but > as a Specimen, whi[c]h, wether bad or good, I earnestly desire you to look over, it may be dis-agreeable – but you will then Know wether in putting \it/ into the fire you – would gain or lose

It would now be impudent in me to speak of my powers since in five minutes you can tell wether or not they are < the worst? > Fudge and nonsense but this I know that if they are such I have no intention of stooping under them. New powers I will get if I can and provided I keep them you Sir shall see them.[74]

Branwell's laudable determination to persevere with and improve his poetry suggests that the eighteen-year-old was torn between his desire to be an artist and a poet. His hope of becoming a contributor to *Blackwood's* did not necessarily exclude the possibility of his becoming a successful portrait painter, but it inevitably raised doubts about whether he would have the determination to overcome the hurdles in his path should he ever attempt to enter the Royal Academy. At this moment he clearly wanted nothing more than to be accepted as one of the élite band of *Blackwood's* contributors.

In case the editor found his subject matter morbidly off-putting, Branwell urged him:

But dont think Sir that I write nothing but miseries my day is far too much < un > in the morning for such continual shadow – Nor think either (and this I intreat) that I wish to deluge you with Poetry. I send it because it is soonest read and comes from the heart – If it goes <u>to</u> yours print it and write to me on the subject of <u>contribution</u> then I will send Prose – But if < I > what I <u>now</u> send is worthless what I have said has only been conceit and folly – Yet CONDEMN NOT UNHEARD – P B Brontë[75]

While he waited for a reply, his masonic career was proceeding with extra-ordinary rapidity. At an emergency meeting on 20 April he was promoted to the degree of Fellowcraft and five days later, at the ordinary meeting, he was raised to the sublime degree of Master Mason. Though this would suggest that his departure for the Continent was imminent, in fact this never materialized, probably abandoned on the grounds of expense, and Branwell's presence is recorded at virtually every monthly meeting in Haworth throughout 1836 and 1837.[76]

It is next to impossible to discover what Branwell was doing during these two years. He was certainly of an age to be earning his own living and it is doubtful whether Patrick would have allowed him sit around at home without at least ensuring that he was preparing himself for gainful employ-ment. Given Patrick's own background, it is surprising that a university career never seems to have been considered. Financial considerations can only have played a part in this for, while Branwell could not look to ecclesi-astical charities for patronage, since he refused even to contemplate taking orders, there were still a number of scholarships available for talented laymen. With sufficient commitment, Branwell could have made his way through either Oxford or Cambridge University but there was little point in doing so unless he intended to go into the church. A university education would not have gained him an automatic *entrée* elsewhere though it might have assisted him had he chosen to enter the legal or teaching professions.

It seems likely that Branwell spent the years 1836 and 1837 trying to establish himself as a professional painter. Excluding those of his sisters, there are only eleven extant oil portraits known to be by Branwell. Of these, all but three are of people whose associations were with Haworth, rather than Bradford, where he later set up a studio. All, except one, are undated, but it seems likely that they belong to these two years which Branwell spent at home, having completed his lessons with William Robinson. With Charlotte and Anne away at Roe Head it was more practical for him to appropriate a bedroom as his studio.

The people he painted were, as one might expect, the well-to-do men of the area: Michael Merrall, his friend from boyhood who was now a substantial mill owner in Haworth and Keighley, William Thomas, the brandy merchant of Haworth, Henry Foster, the mill owner of Denholme, and James Fletcher, a mill owner from Skipton. Three other portraits of less substantial men, John Brown, the Haworth sexton, his brother, William Brown, and Thomas Parker, the well-known Haworth tenor, may have been simply presents to friends or commissions from the Three Graces Lodge, with which the Browns were associated, and one of the Haworth Music societies.[77] All the portraits are almost identical in style and pose, half-length and either full face or turned slightly to the right, with an indeterminate background. The only strikingly different details are in the portraits of Thomas Parker, who holds a violin as a symbol of his musical profession, and of Michael Merrall, which is said to have had the names of great musicians scrolled around the border in homage to Merrall's patronage of music in Haworth. The only woman Branwell is known to have painted at this period was Maria Taylor, sister of George Taylor of Stanbury, one of the Haworth church trustees. Though Branwell's male sitters show the expected diversity of appearance, it is interesting that this portrait bears a remarkable likeness to those Branwell had painted of his sisters. Indeed, it could almost be mistaken for the 'Pillar Portrait' of Anne, which suggests that it is too easy to read into the 'sad, earnest, shadowed faces' of the Brontës those mysterious portents of early death which Mrs Gaskell was so convinced she saw.[78]

Whatever Branwell was actually doing during the years 1836 and 1837, he had plenty of free time to devote to his writing. Angrian stories simply poured out of him without interruption. In the spring of 1836, continuing the theme he had launched the previous winter, he plunged Africa into civil war. Secretly aided by Northangerland, who was playing his usual double game, the Verdopolitan Reform Ministry invaded Angria, placed its people under martial law, quartered its murderous French, Ashantee and Bedouin allies on them and began a reign of terror. When its leader, the Marquis of Ardrah, refused to withdraw or restore its legislature and king, the Marquis of Fidena and the Duke of Wellington rallied to Zamorna and declared war on the Reform Ministry.[79] Despite the warlike setting, Branwell was clearly more interested in the political developments of this period. He reports at length, for instance, the angry debates in the Verdopolitan Parliament over the expulsion of Angria from the Verdopolitan Union, reproducing characteristic speeches and revealing a detailed knowledge of Parliamentary procedure which owed much to his reading of the political sections of the newspapers. Similarly, the dramatic arrest in the Verdopolitan Parliament of the Angrian Members who refused to resign their seats was inspired by Charles I's arrest of five members of his Parliament in 1642.[80]

Charlotte, back at school again, was simply a passive spectator in these events. Branwell had always been the one to force the pace and dominate the storyline but, with their partnership weakened by separation, she could not influence the developments taking place. Indeed, she had little time or opportunity to do so. One evening, shortly after her return, she snatched a few moments to muse on her position:

Well here I am at Roe-Head., it is seven o'clock at night the young ladies are all at their lessons the school-room is quiet the fire is low, a stormy day is at this moment passing off in a murmuring and bleak night. I now resume my own thoughts my mind relaxes from the stretch on which it has been for the last twelve hours & falls back onto the rest which no-body in this house knows of but myself. I now after a day's weary wandering return to the ark which for me floats alone on the face of this world's desolate & boundless deluge it is strange. I cannot get used < to the ongoings that surround > to the ongoings that surround me. I fulfil my duties strictly & well, I < not > so to speak if the illustration be not profane as God was not in the wind nor the fire nor the earth-quake so neither is my heart in the task, < that > the theme or the exercicese. it is the still small voices alone that comes to me at eventide, that which like a breeze with a voice in it over the deeply blue hills & out of the now leafless forests & from the cities on distant river banks < it is that now calling > of a far & bright < continent it is that which > continent, it is that which wakes my spirit & engrosses all my living feelings all my energies which are not merely mechanical & like Haworth & home wakes sensations which lie dormant elsewhere. last night I did indeed < hav > lean upon the thunder-wakening wings of such a stormy blast as I have seldom heard blow & it < whirl > whirled me away like heath in the wilderness for five seconds of ecstasy, and as I sat by < myself in > myself in the dining-room while all the rest were at tea the trance seemed to descend on a sudden & verily this foot trod the war-shaken shores of the Calabar & these < light > eyes saw the defiled & violated Adrianopolis shedding its lights on the river from lattices whence the invader looked out & was not darkened; ... while this apparition was before me the dining-room door opened and Miss W[ooler] came in with a plate of butter in her hand. 'A very stormy night my dear!' said she 'it is ma'am'. said I[81]

The constant interruptions gave Charlotte no opportunity to 'play out' her fantasies and she had to be content with sketching the odd vignette of Angrian scenes or scenery. A few days later, on 4 February 1836, for example, she wrote:

Now as I have a little bit of time there being no French lessons this afternoon I should like to write something. I can't enter into any continued narrative my mind is not settled enough for that but if I could call up some slight & pleasant sketch, I would amuse myself by jotting it down –[82]

Having been deprived of the indulgence of anything more than the odd Angrian scene during the term, Charlotte flung herself wholeheartedly into Branwell's scenario on her return for the Easter holidays. Now that there was nothing to impede her she could write a good long story and, for the first time since October 1834,[83] she sat down to compose a whole volume. Whether it was the sheer excitement of having the unaccustomed freedom to write or a feeling of being overwhelmed by the pace of events dictated by Branwell in her absence, Charlotte found it difficult to choose a subject. The beginning of her story, 'Passing Events', is a kaleidoscope of changing scenes and moods as she sought to establish a theme out of the many that presented themselves. Several pages into the book, she apologized:

Reader, as yet I have written \nothing/, I would fain fall into some regular strain of composition, but I cannot, my mind is like a prism full of coulours but not of forms. A thousand tints are there brilliant & varied & if they would resolve into the shade of some flower or bird or gem, I could < fling > fling a picture before you. I feel I < could > could.[84]

Eventually, the book resolved itself into three separate vignettes based on Mina Laury, Mary Percy and Charles Townshend, encompassing an irrelevant and viciously sardonic portrayal of a Wesleyan Methodist meeting in the 'Slugg Street' Chapel. The unlearned and extravagantly self-abasing style of the Methodist preachers obviously caused amusement in the parson's household. Charlotte's Mr Bromley addresses his congregation:

'Filthy rags are we, potsherds were with the leper has scraped himself, bowls of the putrid blood of the sacrifices, sweepings of the courts of thy temple Straws of the dunghill, refuse of the Kennel, Thieves murderers, slanderers, false-swearers.' Amen, Amen! groaned every hearer from his inmost soul[85]

As usual, the immediate inspiration for this sketch was Branwell who, at exactly the same time, was engaged in writing an equally virulent skit in which Alexander Percy adopts the role of 'Mr Ashworth', a hypocritical Methodist preacher. This role had been foreshadowed two years earlier, when Percy had broken out in a ranting religious speech which was observed with deepest cynicism by his friends.[86] Now, for the first time, he explicitly impersonates a Methodist preacher but his sermon is a terrible inversion of the real message of the Gospel. He urges his congregation to pray for their own damnation as this will be proof to God that they are humbled and therefore, paradoxically, deserve salvation.

I hate you all I Hate you as filthy and Abominable Sinners – as such I abhor you. but there is a Hope of your Salvation and while that hope lasts I will strive to make it a certainty – So start not when now I tell you to fly from salvation such doctrine < th > has not been preached before but I said The whole world had been D[am]ned till now – the whole world has been preached to therefore < su > if such insults could follow that preaching such preaching must be very vain – now I am commanded and commissioned from Heaven to save therefore my Doctrine must not be like that which has ended only in condemnation – I speak as my Creator directs me and I say – Fly from Salvation![87]

The argument was certainly logical, but it should not be seen as an exposition of Branwell's own views. The sermon was entirely in keeping with the misanthropic and whimsical character of Northangerland, who was to adopt the role of Mr Ashworth at other points in his career, as, for instance, when he urgently needed to raise cash or simply when the whim took him.

It is a measure of the difference in their styles and purposes in writing that Charlotte's sketch is simply a sharply observed and sardonic description of a Methodist meeting while Branwell's equally jaundiced account has an important purpose: as 'Mr Ashworth', Northangerland is able to give a new twist to his demagogic skills to whip up anti-government sentiment and obtain the ruin of the people he professes to support.

It is not surprising to find the children of the parsonage mocking the Dissenters who flourished in their father's parish. What is surprising is that their sarcasm was aimed specifically at the Methodists, rather than the Baptists and stricter sects who were a thorn in Patrick's flesh. The Methodists had always been Patrick's most reliable allies and reasonable opponents and Maria and Elizabeth Branwell, their own mother and aunt, had even been brought up as Wesleyan Methodists, though both had become members of the Church of England. For the young Brontës, however, Methodism was equated with hypocrisy and from this period on the Methodists frequently appear in their writings as figures of either contempt or fun.[88]

Charlotte's first foray into religious criticism – or rather, criticism of the practitioners of religion – coincided with a spiritual crisis of her own. The conflict between her sense of what she ought to be and her knowledge of what she actually was had become acutely painful to her. 'Duty' and 'Necessity' demanded that she should commit all her energies to teaching the young girls in her care and earning her own living. This, with her usual sense of commitment, she had determined to do and she flung herself into her duties with an excess of zeal that troubled Miss Wooler. Invitations to spend Saturday and Sunday with the Nusseys or the Taylors, which would have provided a welcome relief from the monotony of school routine, were turned down by Charlotte on the grounds that allowing herself a holiday was a dereliction of her duty. Occasionally, Miss Wooler would positively compel her to go. At the end of May, for instance, Charlotte wrote to Ellen:

You are far too kind and frequent in your invitations. You puzzle me; I hardly know how to refuse, and it is still more embarrassing to accept. At any rate I cannot come this week, for we are in the very thickest melee of the Repetitions. I was hearing the terrible fifth section when your note arrived. But Miss Wooler says I must go to Gomersal next Friday as she promised for me on Whit-Sunday; and on Sunday morning I will join you at church if it be convenient, and stay at Rydings till Monday morning. There's a free and easy proposal! Miss Wooler has driven me to it; she says her character is implicated![89]

Mary Taylor also observed that Charlotte 'seemed to have no interest or pleasure beyond the feeling of duty' and it was clear to all her friends that she was making herself ill with her insistence on performing her duties to the letter.[90]

Even the summer holidays offered no respite from the deepening mood of gloom which gradually enveloped Charlotte at Roe Head. School broke up on 17 June but the pleasure of going straight to Haworth was deferred by an invitation to spend a week at Huddersfield Vicarage. As unwelcome as it was unexpected, Charlotte attempted to cut short the visit to a weekend, using the excuse that 'papa I fear will scarcely be willing to dispense with us longer at home even though we should be staying with so valued a friend as yourself'.[91] Unfortunately, Patrick did not take the same view and wrote to Mrs Franks countermanding his daughter's arrangements:

I esteem it, as a high privilege, that they should be under your roof, for a time – where, I am sure, they will see, and hear nothing, but what, under Providence, must necessarily tend, to their best interest, in both the worlds –[92]

The visit, which took up the whole of the first week of the vacation, was not a great success. The eldest child, John Firth Franks, recollected that Charlotte never spoke to him during the whole time she was there though Anne brought toys to him in the nursery.[93] The sisters arrived at the vicarage to find Charlotte's old school-fellow, Amelia Walker, and her family, waiting there to receive them. 'They were wondrously gracious,' Charlotte sourly remarked to Ellen,

Amelia almost enthusiastic in her professions of friendship!! She is taller, thinner, paler and more delicate looking than she used to be. very pretty still, very lady-like and polished, but spoilt utterly spoilt by the most hideous affectation[94]

The Walkers also pressed an invitation on the reluctant Brontës, who duly travelled over to Lascelles Hall the following Tuesday. There, Charlotte was grudgingly forced to admit, they had 'on the whole a very pleasant day'. Amelia, dispensed from having to earn a living by her family fortune, again attracted Charlotte's jaundiced comment.

Miss Amelia changed her character every half hour. now she assumed the sweet sentimentalist, now the reckless rattler. Sometimes the question was 'Shall I look prettiest lofty?' and again 'Would not tender familiarity suit me better?' At one moment she affected to inquire after her old school-acquaintance the next she was detailing anecdotes of High Life.[95]

One can only guess at the relief Charlotte and Anne felt when they were finally released from social duty and allowed to come home. Not only was the family complete again, but the old playing partnerships could be re-established.

For once, Haworth and the restoration to her family failed to cure Charlotte's growing disillusionment with the general tenor of her life. The contrast between her own existence, toiling in the schoolroom at the beck and call of Miss Wooler and her girls, with that of Branwell and Emily, living at home and having their time at their own disposal, must have struck her forcibly. From the sheer volume of his output it is clear that Branwell had a great deal of spare time and energy. Not for him the snatched moments of solitude and the feverish scribbling of Angrian fragments; nor, most painfully, the sense of frustration and guilt which built up when imagination could not be indulged.

Emily too, released from the bondage of school life, was deep in the throes of Gondal composition. Though no Gondal prose tales are extant, some of her poems of this period are preserved, written in her minuscule print on tiny scraps of paper. They are the earliest of her fictional writings in existence and reveal a mind that, in stark contrast to her elder sister's, was calm and content. She had already established the pattern of her future work, taking her inspiration from the beauties of nature or even simple contemplation of the weather before progressing to Gondal scenes and characters. The earliest recorded poem, probably written earlier that year, is typical.

> Cold clear and blue the morning heaven
> Expands its arch on high
> Cold clear and blue Lake Wernas water
> Reflects that winters sky
> The moon has set but Venus shines
> A silent silvery star[96]

Such tranquil moments were out of Charlotte's reach. Lacking both the incentive and the energy to write, she made only the feeblest of efforts to retain her hold on Angria. On her return from Huddersfield Vicarage, she began a prose tale, drawing on Branwell's newspaper reports about the cataclysmic events of the last few months. Either the subject failed to interest her or, more likely, the recent pace of events in Africa left her slightly bemused. The story remained unfinished and this fragment and a single Angrian poem were all she produced throughout the whole five weeks of her vacation.[97] This was despite the fact that Branwell had placed her own hero, Zamorna, in the worst crisis of his career. The Verdopolitan Reform Ministry which had invaded Angria had been overthrown by a popular revolution led by the old arch-demagogue himself, Northangerland, who had established himself at the head of a Provisional Government. Zamorna had been defeated at the battle of Edwardston, captured and exiled in the company of Sdeath by Northangerland; in a scene reminiscent of Shakespeare, his eldest son Edward had also been captured, blinded and put to death. All Angria was at last completely under Northangerland's sway and he ruled with a reign of terror, supported by the Ashantee, French and Bedouin invaders. Zamorna's sole prospect of revenge lay in breaking

Northangerland's heart by divorcing his wife, Percy's beloved daughter, and banishing her to Alnwick where, he knew, she would die of a broken heart.[98]

Such a scenario would once have provoked a sharp retort from Charlotte and a swift turning of the tables on her brother's abasement of her great hero. It is an indication of the profound lethargy which had her in its grasp that Charlotte did not respond or react, but accepted Branwell's dictation of events. One spark of interest remained. In a long and dreary poem of 576 lines, completed on 19 July just before she returned to Roe Head, she depicted Zamorna on board the ship taking him into exile mourning the fate of his wife and son and being comforted by his mistress, Mina Laury, who had chosen to accompany him.[99] Then, like her hero, she returned to her own, self-imposed, exile at Roe Head.

The hopeless and bitter state of her defeated and exiled hero seems to have suited Charlotte's mood in the autumn of 1836. The reluctance with which she resumed her second year as a teacher at Roe Head soon deepened into revolt. She continued to add to the diary fragments which she had jotted down in her notebook at odd moments over the past year[100] but their tone became increasingly harsh and resentful. Instead of finding relief in spending her precious leisure moments in writing reflective vignettes of Angria, her impatience and frustration were vented in splenetic outbursts against her pupils. On 11 August, a few weeks into the new term, she wrote:

All this day I have been in a dream half-miserable & half ecstatic miserable because I could not follow it out uninterruptedly, ecstatic because it shewed almost in the vivid light of reality the ongoings of the infernal world. I had been toiling for nearly an hour with Miss Lister, Miss Marriott & Ellen Cook striving to teach them the distinction between an article and a substantive. The parsing lesson was completed, a dead silence had succeeded it in the school-room & I sat sinking from irritation & weariness into a kind of lethargy. The thought came over me am I to spend all the best part of my life in this wretched bondage, forcibly suppressing my rage at the idleness the apathy and the hyperbolical & most asinine stupidity of these fat-headed oafs and on compulsion assuming an air of kindness, patience & assiduity?

must I from day to day sit chained to this chair prisoned with in these four bare-walls, while these glorious summer suns are burning in heaven & the year is revolving in its richest glow & declaring at the close of every summer day \the time I am losing/ < it > will never come again? Stung to the heart with this reflection I started up & mechanically walked to the window – a sweet August morning was smiling without The dew was not yet dried off the field. the early shadows were stretching cool & dim from the hay-stack \&/ the roots of the grand old oaks & thorns scattered along the sunk fence. All was still except the murmur of the scrubs about me over their tasks, I flung up the sash. an uncertain sound of inexpressible sweetness came on a dying gale from the south, I looked in that direction Huddersfield & the hills beyond it were all veiled in blue mist, the woods of Hopton & Heaton Lodge were clouding the waters-edge & the Calder silent but bright was shooting among them < like > like a – silver arrow. I listened the sound sailed full &

liquid down the descent. It was the bells of Huddersfield Parish church. I shut the window & went back to my seat. Then came on me rushing impetuously. all the mighty phantasm that this had conjured from nothing from nothing [sic] to a system strong as some religious creed. I felt as if I could < have > have written gloriously – I longed to write. The Spirit of all Verdopolis of all the mountainous North of all the < woodland the > woodland West of all the river-watered East came crowding into my mind. if I had < it > had time to indulge it I felt that the vague sensations of that moment would have settled down into some narrative better at least than any thing I ever produced before. But just then a Dolt came up with a lesson. I thought I should have vomited[101]

Charlotte's own quick intellect made her unsympathetic to her slower-minded pupils, so that sometimes she would almost boil with rage and frustration at their 'asinine stupidity'. The need to keep such feelings hidden beneath the patient demeanour of the schoolmistress simply added further tension to her already taut nerves.

In the afternoon Miss E L[ister] was < triger > trigonometrically oecumenical about her French Lessons she nearly killed me between the violence of the irritation her horrid wilfulness excited and the labour it took to subdue it to a moderate < appearan? > appearance of calmness. My fingers trembled as if I had had twenty four hours tooth-ache, & my spirits felt worn down to a degree of desperate despondency. Miss Wooler tried to make me talk at tea time and was exceedingly kind to me but I could not have roused if she had offered me worlds. After tea we took a long weary walk. I came back abymè to the last degree < fro > for Miss L[ister] & Miss M[arriot]t had been boring me with their vulgar familliar trash all the time we were out if those Girls knew how I loathe their company they would not seek mine as much as they do[102]

Angria could still provide some solace and there were moments of quiet daydreaming, even in the classroom.

I'm just going to write because I cannot help it Wiggins might indeed talk of scriblemania if he were to see me just now encompassed by the bulls (query calves of Bashen) all wondering why I write with my eyes shut – staring, gaping hang their astonishment – A C[oo]k on one side of me E L[iste]r on the other and Miss W[oole]r in the back-ground, Stupidity the atmostphere, school-books the employment, asses the society, what in all this is there to remind me of the divine, silent, unseen land of thought.[103]

The sound of the wind gusting round Roe Head conjured up thoughts of home:

that wind I know is heard at this moment far away on the moors at Haworth. Branwell & Emily hear it and as it sweeps over our house down the church-yard & round the old church, they think perhaps of me & Anne – < Nort > Glorious! that blast was mighty it reminded me of Northangerland ... O it has wakened a feeling that I cannot satisfy – a thousand wishes rose at its call which must die with me for they will never be fulfilled. now I should be agonized if I had not the dream to repose on., its existences, its forms its scenes do fill a little of the craving vacancy[104]

Sometimes, however, as Charlotte herself realized, the golden dream of Angria could be oppressive. One evening, lying on her bed in the school dormitory, she became so wrapt up in the scene her imagination had conjured up that she could not physically rouse herself.

I knew I was wide awake & that it was dark, & that moreover the ladies were now come into the room to get their curl-papers – they perceived me lying on the bed & I heard them talking about me. I wanted to speak – to rise – it was impossible – I felt that this was a frightful predicament – that it would not do – the weight pressed me as if some huge animal had flung itself across me. a horrid apprehension quickened every pulse I had. I must get up I thought & I did so with a start. I have had enough of morbidly vivid realisations. every advantage has its corresponding disadvantage –[105]

If even Angria could not bring relief, then where could Charlotte turn?

Chapter Ten

❧

LOSING BATTLES

While Charlotte fought a losing battle to keep up a semblance of normality at Roe Head, her father was also coming under increasing pressure at Haworth. Patrick's beloved Auxiliary Bible Society had become the latest victim in the antipathy between Baptists and Anglicans. General meetings had become impossible, due to 'unpleasant differences between the officers and friends', though it was still hoped to salvage something by holding a meeting sanctioned by Patrick and the Wesleyan Methodists.[1] The hard-line sects were flourishing in Haworth. The Baptists had raised over £1,500 to establish a school for the religious instruction of their children and the Primitive Methodists were engaged in building a brand new chapel, which was formally opened on 20 November 1836.[2] Worse still, the vexed question of church rates had come to the fore again as the date of the meeting adjourned from the previous year approached. Patrick seems to have been determined to keep a low profile. He allowed a meeting to take place in the church, which was advertised by placard as an 'opportunity of stating in vestry assembled whether they did really consider it right for one sect to tax all others to support its own religion'. He appears to have taken no part in the meeting, which was chaired by John Hartley, and voted almost unanimously to adjourn the laying of the 1835 rate to September 1837, despite vociferous interventions by George Taylor, one of the churchwardens. Nor did Patrick allow his churchwardens to attempt to raise a new rate for the current year.[3]

The softening of his attitude, which had gradually taken place over the year, was made apparent in a letter he wrote to the *Leeds Mercury* at the end of October. He declared once more that he had never favoured church rates in their present form but that he still considered that they were necessary as long as the church was 'a kind of public property'. He argued that vestry meetings, which organized parish affairs, were held for the benefit of all denominations, Dissenters owned pews in the church for which they received rents and all the parish benefited from the giving out of public notices in church, the church clock and the church bells. Most telling of all, so long as Dissenters had burial places in the church and churchyard, which had to be kept in good repair, then they should make a contribution to their upkeep.[4] Instead of relying on arguments from the Scriptures, Patrick had turned to the pragmatic considerations which could justify laying a rate.

Despite his defence of the system, Patrick clearly no longer desired any confrontation. A few weeks later, at the beginning of December, he quietly opened a voluntary subscription to defray the expenses of the church. If he had hoped to avoid publicity, this was denied him, for one of the Dissenters, probably John Winterbotham, who was then agitating to start an Anti-Church Rates Society in Bradford, wrote to the *Leeds Mercury* trumpeting 'the Death of a Church Rate'. While taking the opportunity to praise Patrick and the Dissenting ministers for pledging themselves to a peaceful pursuit of their vocations, the anonymous author made a vicious attack on Patrick's curate, William Hodgson.

The only drawback ... arises from the wild zeal and boisterous denunciations of a certain young man, who has lately assumed the gown, and who discredits his holy vocation by repeated *tirades* and invective against those who do not attend the place where he is permitted to officiate. Having been suddenly raised from a very humble situation in life, his head seems too weak to bear the elevation ... There is nothing more seemly in young men, and especially young ministers, than modesty. There is nothing more unbecoming the pulpit than a bold, condemnatory spirit.[5]

With his usual skill at personal invective, Winterbotham succeeded in provoking Hodgson into an indignant and defensive reply. While acknowledging his own humble birth, he emphatically denied that he had anathematized the Dissenters:

The reason, I believe, of these accusations, is my preaching on certain doctrines, which have not a place in Zigzag's creed; which are on Ecclesiastical Establishment, Episcopacy, Infant Baptism, the use of a Liturgy, and the purity of our Formularies.[6]

Hodgson somewhat undermined his defence against the accusations by then submitting the same letter to the Tory *Leeds Intelligencer*, requesting its inclusion as 'an exhibition of a few "pious frauds" of a Dissenter'.[7]

The Christmas vacation, which reunited the Brontë family at the end of December 1836, was marred when a terrible accident befell Tabby Aykroyd, their servant for the last ten years. A few days after Charlotte and Anne's return home, Tabby had gone down the village on an errand, slipped on a patch of ice and fallen heavily. As it was dark, it was some time before she was able to attract attention and was carried into the druggist's shop nearby. There it was discovered that she had completely shattered and dislocated her leg. No surgeon could be got to set the fracture till six o'clock the following morning, so she was brought back to the parsonage in 'a very doubtful and dangerous state'. 'Of course we are all exceedingly distressed at the circumstance', Charlotte told Ellen, 'for she was like one of our own family'. The girls rallied round, performing all her household tasks between them, with the occasional assistance of 'a person [who] has dropped in now and then to do the drudgery', and taking Tabby's nursing upon themselves.[8] This Aunt Branwell strongly deprecated, urging that Tabby should be sent to her sister's house until she was fully recovered. The girls insisted that it was their duty to nurse Tabby in her old age and infirmity when she had looked after them so well for so many years. There then followed a dramatic clash of wills, Aunt Branwell urging practical difficulties and economy, the sisters urging compassion and sentiment. The war of words turned into a war of action: the girls went on strike, refusing to eat until their aunt at last gave way and allowed them the privilege of nursing Tabby back to health in their own house. Tabby remained in a very delicate state throughout the holiday, so that Charlotte was reluctantly obliged to cancel a visit by Ellen: 'I would urge your visit yet, I would entreat and press it – but the thought comes across me "Should Tabby die while you are in the house?" I should never forgive myself.'[9] Fortunately, and probably due to the careful nursing of her former charges, Tabby did eventually recover and was able to resume most of her household duties.

Despite the extra burden of work caused by Tabby's illness, the Christmas holidays saw a flurry of literary activity. Anne's earliest extant poem, which, from its polished nature, was clearly not the first she had ever written, dates from this time. 'Verses by Lady Geralda' is also the first of many poems by both Anne and Emily depicting a typical Gondal scenario: an orphan girl lamenting the fact that the beauties of nature no longer have power to soothe her troubled spirit.

> Why, when I hear the stormy breath
>   Of the wild winter wind
> Rushing o'er the mountain heath,
>   Does sadness fill my mind?

> For long ago I loved to lie
>   Upon the pathless moor,
> And hear the wild wind rushing by
>   With never ceasing roar;
>
> Its sound was music then to me;
>   Its wild and lofty voice
> Made my heart beat exultingly
>   And my whole soul rejoice.
>
> But now, how different is the sound?
>   It takes another tone,
> And howls along the barren ground
>   With melancholy moan.[10]

Resonant with echoes of Wordsworth's 'Intimations of Immortality' ode, the poem is the only glimpse we have of Gondal at this time. It shows that Emily and Anne had not allowed their stories to lapse in Anne's absence and that Gondal, like Angria, had a setting which owed at least something to the moorlands around their own beloved home.

Meanwhile, Branwell was bringing the affairs of Angria to a new climax: Northangerland's reign of terror was coming to an end. Inspired by a powerful speech by Warner Howard Warner, those Angrians still loyal to Zamorna won a great victory over Northangerland and were now bent on redeeming Angria from his clutches.[11] Branwell did not envisage Zamorna's return from exile till the summer, but for the first time in many years, Charlotte intervened and forced the pace of events. Perhaps surprisingly, it was not the fact that Branwell had sent her beloved Zamorna off into exile which goaded her into a response, but that he had killed Zamorna's wife, Mary Percy. She had died of grief and loneliness in exile, divorced and disgraced by her husband and ruined by her father. Branwell had described her death-bed quite movingly, in terms foreshadowing Cathy's death in *Wuthering Heights*.

This was not like the death bed of her mother there was no mingling of Heaven with earth nothing of that Angelic hope of glory, that real triumph over death This was the end of a Child of earth all whose soul and spirit were < centered > rooted in < the > earth and perishing on being torn away from it < Her burden > Her thoughts were expressed plainly by her a day or two before this time

It does not matter where I am going I know I am going and I know from whom I am going —

Death in such a state is more terrible than < at t? > any anticipations of the future can be[12]

Charlotte, away at Roe Head, had not believed it possible that Branwell would kill his favourite heroine and had waited in some suspense to know whether he would actually do so.[13] It had evidently taken some steeling of his nerve, though the deathbed scenes were among the best he had ever written. 'Reader I cannot do otherwise than drop a tear to her memory', he wrote, 'for recollect that I it was whose pen first brought her to your notice who from her rising to her setting have so long recorded the different phases of her glory.'[4] Branwell was ruthless enough to sacrifice Mary for the effect it would have on his two protagonists, Northangerland and Zamorna: for him, it was a necessary part of their story. Charlotte, however, was appalled and dismayed by Mary's fate. Just as she had done in their earliest childhood writings, she determined to make Mary come to life again. It was no longer acceptable to ascribe this to magical means, so Charlotte justified Mary's resurrection by declaring that Branwell's author, Lord Richton, had spread the rumour of Mary's death to rouse the Angrians to greater fury against their oppressor, Northangerland. 'In our land we take methods such as were never known in the political world before for exciting a party to our wish.'[5]

In the first long narrative she had written for over two years, she described how Mary had been saved from death by the brief reappearance, in disguise, of Zamorna whom she had thought drowned at sea on his voyage into exile. Having given Mary a reason to live, Zamorna then moved on to reveal himself to his faithful allies and inspire the Angrians to victory once more.[16] The story is confidently told and, despite changes of scene and character, is much more closely interwoven than many of her previous efforts. This time Charlotte had no trouble choosing her subject, nor in following it through to its conclusion.

There is no doubt that Branwell regarded Charlotte as playing a very subsidiary role in the partnership. His reaction to Charlotte's intervention was to ignore it almost completely. Mary remained dead, as Charlotte was soon forced to acknowledge, though Zamorna's return from exile to lead his troops to victory over Northangerland does seem to have been brought forward.[17]

Charlotte was unmoved by Branwell's contempt. The pent-up flow of creativity which had been released continued unabated throughout January, sparking off a number of long poems reflecting on the trials of war-torn Angria and its king.[18] However it was no longer simply the attraction of the current storyline which inspired her. During the vacation, Charlotte and Branwell decided that they should attempt to turn their writing skills to good account and, if possible, earn a living from them. To do this they needed the advice and judgement of those who were already professional writers, so both embarked upon a course of letter-writing to their literary idols. On 29 December 1836 Charlotte wrote to Robert Southey, the Poet Laureate, sending him some of her poems and requesting his opinion of them. Charlotte's letter is not extant, but Southey referred to it as 'flighty', an epithet which is also entirely appropriate for the letter she wrote some years later to Hartley Coleridge,[19] Southey's nephew and son of Samuel

Taylor Coleridge. It was also fulsome in its praise of Southey himself, if his quotes from her letter are an indication of its content. As Southey was away from Keswick at the time, Charlotte was forced to wait over two months for his reply. When it finally came, it was not very encouraging.

you live in a visionary world & seem to imagine that this is my case also, when you speak of 'stooping from a throne of light & glory' ... You who so ardently desire 'to be for ever known' as a poetess, might have had your ardour in some degree abated, by seeing a poet in the decline of life ... You evidently possess, and in no inconsiderable degree, what Wordsworth calls the 'faculty of verse'. I am not depreciating it when I say that in these times it is not rare. Many volumes of poems are now published every year without attracting public attention, any one of which, if it had appeared half a century ago, would have obtained a high reputation for its author. Whoever, therefore, is ambitious of distinction in this way ought to be prepared for disappointment.

The sting was in the tail, however, as the elderly poet administered his 'dose of cooling admonition' to those ardent hopes and burning ambitions of the young girl who had written to him.

there is a danger of which I would, with all kindness and all earnestness, warn you. The day dreams in which you habitually indulge are likely to induce a distempered state of mind; and, in proportion as all the ordinary uses of the world seem to you flat and unprofitable, you will be unfitted for them without becoming fitted for anything else. Literature cannot be the business of a woman's life, and it ought not to be. The more she is engaged in her proper duties, the less leisure will she have for it, even as an accomplishment and a recreation. To those duties you have not yet been called, and when you are you will be less eager for celebrity ... Write poetry for its own sake; not in a spirit of emulation, and not with a view to celebrity; the less you aim at that the more likely you will be to deserve and finally to obtain it.[20]

Though ironic in that the Poet Laureate could see no worthwhile future, except in the traditional roles of wife and mother, for a woman whose novels were later to achieve far more lasting fame than his own works, Southey's attitude was a general one in the nineteenth century. It was just what Patrick Brontë had always advised his daughter, urging her to content herself with fulfilling her duty and not to allow her seemingly unattainable ambitions to sour her daily life. Perhaps it was hardly surprising that a constant theme throughout Charlotte's future novels was the fact that there were practicable alternatives to the conventional role of woman as goddess of the hearth: 'I believe single women should have more to do – better chances of interesting and profitable occupation than they possess now.'[21]

Charlotte's initial reaction to Southey's letter was one of gloom. The shining prospect of literary fame had been snatched from her. On 16 March she wrote more soberly to thank him for his advice.

At the first perusal of your letter I felt only shame and regret that I had ever ventured to trouble you with my crude rhapsody; I felt a painful heat rise to my face when I thought of the quires of paper I had covered with what once gave me so much delight, but which now was only a source of confusion … I trust I shall never more feel ambitious to see my name in print; if the wish should rise, I'll look at Southey's letter, and suppress it.[22]

As further proof of her intention to take the Poet Laureate's advice to heart, she ritualized her putting away of literary ambition by writing upon the letter wrapper: 'Southey's Advice To be kept for ever Roe-Head April 21 1837 My twenty-first birthday'.[23]

While Southey's letter had apparently closed an avenue of escape from teaching for Charlotte, Branwell was not even rewarded with replies to his letters. On 4 January 1837, he had made 'one last attempt' on *Blackwood's Magazine*. 'I will at last and most <u>earnestly</u> ask of you a Personal Interview'. Branwell's somewhat startling proposition was to show the editor either his chronicles of Angria or his 'Life of Alexander Percy':

In a former letter, I hinted, that I was in possession of something the design of which, whatever might be its execution, would be superior to that of any <u>series</u> of articles which has yet appeared in Blackwood's Magazine – But, being prose, of course, and of great length, as well as peculiar in character, a description of it by letter would be impracticable.

With a singular lack of tact Branwell then lectured the editor on why he must at last respond.

Now, is the trouble of writing a single line, to outweigh the certainty of doing good to a fellow Creature and the possibility of doing good to Yourself? – Will you still so wearisomly < f > refuse me a word, when You can neither know what you refuse or whom you are refusing? – Do you think your Magazine so < powerful > perfect that no addition to its power would be either possible or desirable? – Is it pride which actuates you – or Custom – or Prejudice? – Be a Man – Sir! and think no more of these things! <u>Write</u> to me – Tell me that you <u>will</u> receive a visit –[24]

Even this letter, despite being written much more neatly and with evidently more care than his earlier ones, met with no response. Undeterred, Branwell next chose, like his sister, to write to one of the literary luminaries of the day, William Wordsworth. His overwhelming desire to please the poet who, with Byron, had most influenced his own style, led him to some injudicious flattery. He tried to depict himself as a Wordsworthian child of nature, growing up among the mountains of the north:

Sir,

I most earnestly entreat you to read and pass your Judgement upon what I have sent you, because from the day of my birth to this the nineteenth year of my life I have lived among wild and secluded hills where I could neither know what I was or what I could do. – I read for the same reason that I eat or drank, – because < if > it was a real craving of Nature. I wrote on the same principle as I spoke, – out of the impulse and feelings of the mind; – nor could I help it, for what came, came out and there was the end of it

He had now reached an age when 'I must do something for myself'; if his literary talents were indeed worthless then he must pursue an alternative career. He hoped that Wordsworth would be able to assess their value.

Do Pardon me, Sir, that I have ventured to come before one whose works I have most loved in our Literature and who most has been with me a divinity of the mind – < for > laying before him one of my writings, and asking of him a Judgement of its contents, – I must come before some < m > one from whose sentence there is no appeal, and such an one he is who has developed the theory of Poetry as well as its Practice, and both in such a way as to claim a place in the memory of a thousand years to come.

My aim Sir is to push out into the open world and for this I trust not poetry alone that might launch the vessel but could not bear her on – Sensible and scientific prose bold and vigorous efforts in my walk in Life would give a farther title to the notice of world and <u>then</u> again poetry ought to brighten and crown that name with glory – but nothing of all this can be even begun without <u>means</u> and < m > as I dont posess these < s > I must in every shape strive to gain them; Surely in this day when there is not a <u>writing</u> poet worth a sixpence the feild must be open if a better man can step forward…

Forgive undue warmth because my feelings in this matter cannot be cool and beleive me to be Sir

With deep respect
Your really humble Servant
P B Brontë[25]

Branwell's obviously youthful sincerity and enthusiasm did not outweigh his maladroit comments in the eyes of the great poet. Nor did the fact that the poem Branwell enclosed, 'The Struggles of flesh with Spirit Scene I – Infancy',[26] had obvious echoes of Wordsworth's own 'Intimations of Immortality'. Wordsworth was 'disgusted with the letter', though he certainly exaggerated in saying that it contained 'gross flattery and plenty of abuse of other poets'.[27] Like the editor of *Blackwood's Magazine*, he did not deign to reply.

Despite the singular lack of success which writing to the leading literary men of the day had produced, Branwell did not abandon the idea of future fame in that field. While still continuing with his Angrian chronicles, on 9 March he began a serious retrospective of his work, collecting the best poems from stories he had written as long ago as December 1833 and then correcting and transcribing them into a notebook he designated for the purpose.[28] He kept the notebook for just over a year, adding to it regularly and including some of his most recent compositions, so that it was to become an important reference work for future attempts at publication. As the earliest of both Emily and Anne's surviving dated poems also belong to roughly the same period,[29] it suggests that they too had seen the importance of preserving their poetry independent of the bulky Gondal manuscripts.

Even Patrick seems to have put pen to paper in the new year, writing a skittish 'Ode to that Unruly Member the Tongue' which was published in the *Leeds Intelligencer* on 21 January 1837. The poem drew on the old tale of a man who arranged an expensive cure for his wife's dumbness, only to be driven mad by her continual nagging. In what one can only call doggerel, the poem made the point that Daniel O'Connell, the Irish nationalist leader, who was a vociferous opponent of church tithes, had similarly driven his audiences mad with the use of his tongue. It was not surprising, given the subject and tone of the poem, that Patrick chose to submit it under his initials alone.[30]

Politics were very much in the minds of both Patrick and his son throughout 1837. On 27 January Branwell took the lead in establishing a Haworth Operative Conservative Society at a meeting in the church Sunday school room. He acted as secretary for that meeting and was appointed chairman for the second quarter of the year. The objectives of the society were 'to maintain loyalty to the King attachment to the connection between church and State respect for the independance and prerogatives of the House of Lords and a proper regard for the Commons House of Parliament'. The society must have had the backing of Patrick, who gave its members the use of the Sunday school room for two hours every day of the week except Wednesday and Sunday. It also enjoyed the support of Joseph Greenwood of Spring Head, who presented the society with a donation of five shillings and his copies of the London *Times* newspaper, the day after he had received them.[31]

The support of such a society would have been important to Patrick at a time when he was once more in open opposition to the Government. On 22 February he called and chaired a meeting of the inhabitants of the township in the Sunday school room. Its object was to petition Parliament to repeal the Poor Law Amendment Act of 1834 whose measures were just beginning to be put into practice in Yorkshire. Its severity has become legendary, lambasted by the enduring images of Charles Dickens' *Oliver Twist*. The Act ended outdoor relief, which had been administered locally by the parish vestry and had supplemented the incomes of the poor during periods of unemployment or need. Poor Law unions, administered centrally by commissioners in London, had been formed out of groups of parishes, and those who through old age, infirmity or unemployment were no longer able to support themselves could only obtain assistance by residing in the workhouse. There the able-bodied had to work to earn their keep, and the work was invariably hard labour, such as breaking or grinding stones. The greatest hardship of all, and the one which inflamed most passions, was the separation of the sexes: husbands and wives, parents and children, however old or young, were strictly segregated with little or no prospect of ever being reunited. The provisions of the Poor Law Act were now being enforced in Yorkshire and Lancashire, where the vagaries of the textile trade meant that many honest and hardworking factory operatives would find themselves at one time or another in the workhouse – or die of starvation if they wanted to keep their families together.

Despite threats from local Whig mill owners, so many people turned up for the meeting that it had to be adjourned into the open air. There Patrick addressed the assembled crowds, declaring that 'upon that occasion neither speakers nor hearers had met to promote the interests of party, but to plead the cause of the poor'. He entreated the people of Yorkshire and Lancashire to rouse themselves and oppose the Act, for 'if dear times and general distress should come on, starvation, deprived of relief, would break into open rebellion'.[32]

Patrick was supported by several others who spoke with equal passion. Abraham Wildman, the Keighley Chartist, displayed to the meeting the food given to a pauper for a whole day's consumption: a single potato pared down to bring it within the regulation, a solitary mouthful of beef and a penny's weight of cheese. He declared the Act contrary to the Scriptures and the constitution of England. Abraham Leighton, a wool-comber who lived in Main Street, Haworth, and the Reverend William Hodgson, Patrick's curate, were also among the speakers; Branwell read and moved the petition, which was carried unanimously and sent to one of the local members of Parliament and the Archbishop of Canterbury for presentation to the Houses of Commons and Lords respectively. The meeting achieved unlooked-for publicity, not only in the local press but also in *The Times*, which carried a full report of the speeches and resolutions made.[33] Once again, Patrick's sense of justice had placed him in an otherwise unlikely political alliance. It was an irony that Patrick himself could not fail to appreciate that he thus classed himself with the Radicals, Chartists and revolutionaries who, only a few months later, were addressing an anti-Poor Law rally of thousands on Hartshead Moor.[34]

Haworth had not one but two public meetings in a week. On 27 February Hall Green Baptist Chapel hosted a meeting to petition Parliament for the total abolition of church rates. Patrick, Branwell and William Hodgson made a point of attending 'with the intention of disturbing the harmony of the meeting', as one hostile newspaper reported, 'but finding themselves unsupported they prudently contented themselves with holding up their hands against the resolution'. This caused much laughter, as they were the only opponents in an otherwise unanimous meeting.[35] John Winterbotham, as might be expected, was one of the main speakers and used the opportunity to accuse Branwell publicly of sending false statements to the *Intelligencer*. 'The accused party proclaimed by his blushes and his silence the truth of the charge alleged against him.'[36]

Straight after this meeting, as the correspondent to the *Leeds Intelligencer* mischievously remarked, the company adjourned to the Black Bull Inn 'to make a night of it'. In fact, the object was not to make merry but to found a reform association which would set up newsrooms throughout the township, giving the poor access to Radical newspapers which were otherwise beyond their pocket. It is interesting that it was felt necessary to establish a reform association, as this was clearly a reaction to the foundation of the Conservative Operative Society:

the political clergymen and their satellites take a good deal of pains to wheedle the Radicals and 'unwashed' artisans; but the people of Haworth are too shrewd to be gulled by them … They know how to distinguish between those who are but moderate or partial Reformers, and those who are no Reformers at all, but conservators of all abuses and abominations.[37]

Patrick's reaction to the decision to send an anti-church rate petition to Parliament in the name of the inhabitants of Haworth was apparently one of great anger, if the hostile *Bradford Observer* is to be believed.

The church parson and his curate have been in a dreadful state of excitement ever since. On last Sabbath morning one of them commenced a fierce attack upon all Dissenters; and in the afternoon both of those meek-spirited clergymen let loose a whole volley of vulgar abuse, in a double lecture in the church, to the great consternation of the congregation. It is feared they are both in a rabid state; some say they believe if any one had challenged the old gentleman that he would have *fought*, for he declared that he cared for no man or woman, and made great professions of valour. And the young *potato eater* is really boiling with rage, and offering the most frightful menaces to the whole race of dissenters.[38]

William Hodgson was the more fiery of the two and undoubtedly gave the morning sermon attacking Dissenters. He had already written a provocative letter to the *Leeds Intelligencer*, trumpeting the fact that on Sunday, 26 February, he and Patrick between them baptized seventy-two children, followed by a further sixty over the next two days. For so many baptisms to take place on the eve of the introduction of civil registration, which would allow Dissenters to perform their own baptisms, marriages and burials, was proof, in Hodgson's eyes, that they actually preferred the services of the Established Church.[39]

Political tensions in Haworth heightened over the next few months. The Tory Guardians of the Poor, William Thomas, Robert Ogden and Nathan Ogden, all withdrew their names from the list of guardians because of their opposition to the Poor Law Amendment Act. Branwell drew up their public declaration and noted on it that the Conservative Committee not only supported them but also would refuse to put up any other Tory candidates in the forthcoming elections for parish officers as a means of expressing their 'most decided *Abhorrence* of this Unjust Tyrannical Unconstitutional and unintelligible Act'. The Dissenting and Whig/Radical constables of Haworth had no hesitation in putting forward their own names as candidates and, being all large manufacturers, were said to have threatened their work-people with instant dismissal if they did not vote for them. The constables then called the election meeting for midday on Easter Monday in the church vestry. This was a move calculated to cause trouble, for the church service on that day always began at twelve o'clock and the sermon was usually preached by the vicar of Bradford, to whom Haworth traditionally had to pay substantial church rates.[40]

In the event, wiser counsels prevailed. The Reverend Henry Heap sensibly absented himself for the first time since he had taken up his post as vicar of Bradford, pleading ill health. Patrick successfully persuaded the constables to adjourn the meeting to the Sunday school after the service and took the chair himself. The meeting, which had to appoint all the new parish officials, lasted four hours but did not degenerate into an unseemly row. Patrick's 'able, patient, and impartial conduct' as chairman was unanimously appreciated in a vote of thanks, prompting the *Leeds Intelligencer* to add its own eulogy.

though he is far advanced in years, and has suffered much from ill health, [he] displayed his pristine energies and faithfulness. That his life and services in his place may be long continued, is the fervent prayer of every churchman, to which every dissenter, who has the cause of religion at heart, will not fail to add his hearty Amen.[41]

The Baptists in Haworth did not share this view. Both John Winterbotham and Moses Saunders were prominent in organizing a petition from the whole of the parish of Bradford to Government ministers, demanding the abolition of church rates. So strong was the depth of feeling it raised that it eventually secured 19,700 signatures.[42] On the morning of a great meeting in Bradford in connection with this petition, there was an incident which the *Bradford Observer* gleefully reported as 'a specimen of Church conservatism'. The Haworth band and a number of ' "bonny Haworth" lads' were walking to the meeting when they were overtaken by 'a Haworth *blue* on horseback' who deliberately rode into their midst. Several men were knocked down and injured, one so seriously he had to be left behind on the roadside. 'This outrage', the *Bradford Observer* darkly opined, 'was planned by a little party of fierce & malignant Tories, with a sion [sic] of the Church at their head, who chuckled vastly at the success of their plot'.[43] Whether or not Branwell was the actual perpetrator of the incident, the Baptists had no difficulty in seeing his hand in the matter.

Patrick relied on more peaceable means, continuing his campaign against the Poor Law Amendment Act through the newspapers. On 17 April, he wrote a powerful and emotive letter to the *Leeds Intelligencer*, calling on all men to do their duty and seek its repeal. 'Petition, remonstrate, and resist *powerfully* but *legally*', he urged. 'We have religion, reason, justice and humanity, on our side, and by these we are determined to stand or fall.'[44] Not for the first time in his career, his appeal fell on deaf ears and the provisions of the Act were to remain in force throughout his lifetime and beyond.

Perhaps because he had incurred such virulent opposition and personal invective during this period, William Hodgson decided that the time had come for him to leave Haworth. Patrick was appalled at the prospect of losing his curate and rallied to his defence, drawing up a requisition which was a testament to the standing Hodgson had already achieved among the Anglican congregation.

We the undersigned inhabitants of Haworth ... being fully satisfied with your faithful and diligent services, both in the desk, pulpit, Sunday School, and parish, earnestly desire (if you can see it to be the path of duty pointed out by Providence) that you would continue in your present situation for another year, at least, or as long as you conveniently can. And at the same time we wish to state it is our hope and belief that, notwithstanding trade is depressed, your subscription will be conducted in a spirit, similar to that which gave rise to it, last year.

To this Patrick added a note stating that the 236 signatures to the requisition, which included his own and Branwell's, had been collected in a few hours only and that he was convinced that all the church people of the chapelry would sign it, if given the opportunity. Unfortunately for Patrick, Hodgson had been offered the post of vicar of Christ Church at Colne so there was no real prospect of him remaining in Haworth. He signed the registers as curate for the last time on 11 May 1837[45] and then crossed over the moors into Lancashire to take up his first and last incumbency. In the short time he had been at Haworth, this colourful and lively young man had been Patrick's right-hand man; he would be sorely missed, particularly as it was to take nearly two years before a replacement could be found. Patrick had once more to shoulder the whole burden of parish duties at a time when he was busier than ever campaigning on a wider stage.

The turmoil in Haworth culminated in the election campaign which took place in the summer. King William IV died on 20 June 1837 and, in consequence, Parliament was dissolved and a general election called. Haworth, despite its comparatively small size, was dignified by visits from at least two of the main candidates. On 17 July, the Tory James Stuart Wortley spoke at the hustings there and, surprisingly, 'had a patient and quiet hearing', though when questioned by a Radical on his opinion of the

Poor Law Amendment Act his views did not come up to those professed by his committee and friends, who included the Brontës, father and son.[46] Three days later, the Whig candidate, Lord Morpeth, arrived, obliging Patrick to put off an invitation to tea with the Taylors at Stanbury.

As Lord Morpeth is coming to Haworth, tomorrow evening at four O'Clock and Miss Branwell and my Children, wish to see and hear him – and it is likely that there will be a good deal of drunkness, and confusion on the roads, I must request that you will excuse us, for not accepting your kind invitation –[47]

Patrick was being modest when he said that his family only wished to hear Lord Morpeth, for he took a prominent role in the proceedings himself. The son of the Haworth tailor has left us a vivid account of that day.

Elections at Haworth in those days were very violent affairs ... The Tories, or 'Blues', were very few in number, and dared hardly show their faces. On this occasion the platforms for the two parties were erected nearly opposite each other, the Liberals being located against a laithe which stood on the now open space in front of the Black Bull Inn. The vicar and his son Branwell were on the 'Blue' platform ... The Liberals were there in great numbers. Robert Pickles, a noted politician, having brought a considerable body from the outskirts. When Mr Brontë began to question Lord Morpeth a regular 'hullabulloo' was set up. Branwell, in his impetuous way, rushed to the front crying, 'If you won't let my father speak, you shan't speak'.[48]

Another contemporary said that Branwell first became publicly known at this election, not only for this intervention but also because, as Secretary for the Conservative Committee of the District, he displayed his great abilities, 'notably his powers of conversation & the facility with which he wrote with either hand or with both at one time'. Certainly Branwell made himself conspicuous, so much so that he became the object of revenge.

After that election Branwell's effigy, bearing a herring in one hand and a potato in the other, in allusion to his nationality, was carried through the main street of Haworth and afterwards burned. Branwell witnessed the procession from a shop in the village.[49]

The Brontës' efforts were unavailing; Lord Morpeth was returned for the West Riding and Lord Melbourne and his Whig ministry took up office once more.

Apart from the single instance of attending the election hustings, the tumultuous events in Haworth seem to have passed the Brontë sisters by. There is no reference to them in any of Charlotte's letters and, unlike the election of 1835, they were not reflected in Angria or Gondal. Indeed, Charlotte seems to have deliberately clung to quite a different view of Haworth. One dull Saturday afternoon at Roe Head, she amused herself by conjuring up a vision of home.

Remembrance yields up many a fragment of past twilight hours – spent in that little unfurnished room – There have I sat on the low bed-stead my eyes fixed on the window, through which appeared no other landscape than a monotonous stretch of moorland, a grey church tower, rising from the centre of a church-yard so filled with graves, that the rank-weed & coarse grass scarce had room to shoot up between the monuments. Over these hangs in the eye of memory a sky of such grey clouds as often veil the chill close of an October day & low on the horizon < appear > glances at intervals through the rack the orb of a lurid & haloed moon.⁵⁰

Emily's view of Haworth was equally remote from what was actually going on. Despite the fact that she was at home and therefore in the thick of things, she seems to have been oblivious to all but the narrow confines of life in the parsonage and the wider expanse of her own imagination. The diary paper she wrote with Anne on 26 June, Branwell's twentieth birth-day, is startling evidence of the lack of impact the outside world had upon her.

Monday evening June 26 1837
A bit past 4 o'Clock Charolotte working in Aunts room Branwell reading Eugene Aram to her Anne and I writing in the drawing room – Anne a poem beginning 'fair was the evening and brightly the sun – I Agustus Almedas life Ist vol – 4th page from the last a fine rather coolish thin grey cloudy but Sunny day Aunt working in the little Room papa gone out. Tabby in the Kitchin – the Emperors and Empresses of Gondal and Gaaldine preparing to depart from Gaaldine to Gondal to prepare for the coranation which will be on the 12th of July Queen Victoria ascended the throne this month. Northangerland in Monceys Isle – Zamorna at Eversham. all tight and right in which condition it is to be hoped we shall all be on this day 4 years at which time Charollote will be 25 and 2 months – Branwell just 24 it being his birthday – myself 22 and 10 months and a peice Anne 21 and nearly a half I wonder where we shall be and how we shall be and what kind of a day it will be then let us hope for the best

Emily Jane Brontë – Anne Brontë⁵¹

Under the diary note, Emily drew a rough, labelled sketch of herself and Anne sitting at the table with 'The Papers' and 'The Tin Box' in which they were stored strewn across its surface. In this, as in her other diary papers, Emily deliberately drew only a back view of herself as if the sketch was done by someone standing a few paces behind her. Her own face is concealed; that of Anne is a blank. Below the sketch, Emily reported the conversation that evidently followed its completion.

Aunt. come Emily its past 4 o'clock Emily Yes Aunt
Anne \Well/ do you intend to write in the evening
Emily well what think you
(we agreed to go out ıst to make sure if we get into a humor we may Stay [out? in?])

Evidently further discussion about their condition four years hence then took place for up the right-hand margin of the drawing Emily added:

I guess that this day 4 years we shall all be in this drawing room comfortable I hope it may be so
  Anne guesses we shall all be gone somewhere together comfortable we hope it may be either[52]

The sole external event which percolated through into the diary paper was the accession of the eighteen-year-old Queen Victoria. Even then, one suspects that the interest was solely because the romantic accession of a young girl, the same age as Emily herself, was the very stuff of Gondal – and may indeed have inspired the forthcoming coronation in the imaginary kingdom.

The diary paper reveals that Emily and Anne were perfectly *au fait* with what was happening in Angria; they must have read Branwell's work as soon as he produced it, as the events they mention were entirely topical. Without the prose stories of Gondal, which have been lost or destroyed, it is next to impossible to re-create that world.[53] However, it is clear from the poems which survive that Gondal owed much to Angria both in the general sweep of events and scenes and in the detail of character and plot.

We have some clues to its layout. In her copy of *A Grammar of General Geography* by the Reverend J. Goldsmith, Emily carefully inserted in minuscule script the names and brief details of some of the imaginary places in a gazetteer of real ones. We learn that Gondal was a large island in the north Pacific and that Regina was its capital. Just as Branwell and Charlotte had moved on from the Verdopolitan Union to conquer and found the new kingdom of Angria, Emily and Anne had expanded into new territory. Gaaldine was 'a large Island newly discovered in the south pacific' which was divided up into a large province, Zedora, governed by a Viceroy, and a number of kingdoms, Alexandra, Almedore, Elseraden, Zelona and Ula.[54] The last of these, in a manner reminiscent of the early days of the four Genii, was ruled by four sovereigns.

Echoes of Angria occur constantly. There is the same sharp contrast between the harsh climate and scenery in the north, with its moorlands and snow-capped mountains, and the soft, wooded landscape of the south. Names, and possibly characters too, are borrowed: a young pair of lovers, for instance, are called Alexander and Zenobia after Alexander Percy and his third wife.[55] The lives and destinies of these characters, who are all of aristocratic or royal birth, are closely bound up in the fate of their kingdoms. Like the Angrians, they endure wars, civil wars and revolutions: Gondal in 1837 saw the siege and capture of Tyndarum and victory for the kingdom of Almedore, which, like Angria, displayed the crimson ensign.[56] Even in death, whether pining for a long-lost lover or fatally wounded in battle, they are, like Mary Percy, children of the earth, torn reluctantly from the beauties of nature.

> And there he lay among the bloom
> His red blood dyed a deeper hue
> Shuddering to feel the ghostly gloom
> That coming Death around him threw –
> Sickening to think one hour would sever
> The sweet, sweet world and him for ever
> To think that twilight gathering dim
> Would never pass away to him –[57]

The format of the stories, we can assume, was much the same as for Angria. Emily tells us in her diary paper that she was working on the first volume of a life of Augusta Almeda, a fact that was reflected in the number of poems she produced about Augusta at this time.[58] This is consistent with Branwell's recent preoccupation with writing a life of Alexander Percy in several volumes, which also spawned many poems. Like Branwell, Emily had the freedom to pursue her imaginings and capture them on paper and, if the number of poems written in 1837 is anything to go by, she, like him, was the dominant member of the partnership. Anne, like Charlotte, was away from home too much to contribute anything more than the occasional poem.

Though Gondal clearly owed much to Angria, there were subtle differences in style and character which seem to have arisen, in part at least, because this was a world created and directed by women. Warfare and politics were the backdrop for all the stories, but this was not a man's world in which women were simply the beautiful playthings of leisure time. Gondal women play a far greater and more active role than their counterparts in Angria and from Queen Augusta Almeda downwards they are strong-minded, ambitious and resourceful. The passive beauties, literally dying for a kind look from Zamorna, are unknown in Gondal.

Nor was the Gondal landscape simply a re-creation of the moorlands of Haworth. Though frequently bleak and undoubtedly hill country, Haworth does not have the snow-capped mountains, ruined castles and wandering deer which are features of Gondal.[59] These are borrowed from the novels and ballads of Sir Walter Scott. The wilderness of the northern mountains reflects the Scottish Highlands and the lusher wooded hills of the south conjure up the richer beauty of the Borders. Scott's influence on the Brontës was extremely marked, so much so that Branwell paused at the beginning of a new chapter he was writing in December 1837, to comment on it:

Among all the descriptions I have read I do not recollect one to me more beautiful than that in the commencement of the Tales of My Landlord which describes the Burial-place of the Covenanters at the Valley Head among the lonely Lowland Hills, and I like it so much because there is not about it that selection of the sublime or beautiful in Nature wherewith to seize the mind independently of power in the writer or of sentiment in his subject for exepting in the Grave stones themselves half buried it is only the picture of one among many 'lone vales of green Bracken' with a rude ill cultivated Country below and a brown fern Hidden brook within and dull stony swells around and a Marshy monotonous Moor beyond But I born and bred upon the Hill sides want no more of the great or striking to make me adore that discription for I feel enough of the Associations called up at sight of those < Hill > linnet peopled Hills and well indeed the quiet nook of Grave stones tells me of times when the perils of Life and the sternness of man fitly accorded with the Moors and Mosses of their Mountain Land.[60]

These sentiments were certainly shared by Emily and Anne, though probably not by Charlotte, who had always had a hankering for the exotic. Branwell was obviously getting at his older sister when he continued:

I would doubt the genius of that writer who loved more to dwell upon Indian Palm Groves or Genii palaces than on the Wooded Manors and cloudy skies of England So when I see upon that page the reflection of objects which I have always been surrounded with I must the more delight in the description itself and in the Noble Head that framed it for it shews me both its own Sacred Grave yard and what I have only to lift my eyes from the paper to look on[61]

Walter Scott had always been one of Emily's passions: as long ago as December 1827, when she was a child of nine, she had chosen him for her chief man and Arran for her island for the play of 'Tales of the Islanders'. Now she and Anne borrowed the Scottish scenery of his novels for Gondal, and adapted his romantic stories and his characters. There is a strong preponderance of Scottish names among the heroes and heroines of Gondal and Gaaldine. In addition to references in the poems and diary papers, there are at least three extant lists of Gondal characters, scrawled haphazardly on fragments of paper and on the backs of poems. Among the names are Ronald Stew[a]rt and his wife Flora, Una Campbell, Lucia MacElgin, Halbert Clifford, Archibald Muray and Helen Douglas.[62]

Another significant Scottish influence, particularly on Emily, was David Moir, whose poetry was published extensively in *Blackwood's Magazine* under the pseudonym 'Delta'. In terms of subject, style and treatment, his work struck a responsive chord in Emily. Like her, he was frequently moved to rapture by the beauties of nature and included descriptive passages in almost all his poems. Like her, he had a predilection for graveside laments and elegiac stanzas: in his spare and deceptively simple style, with his fondness for words such as 'drear' and 'stirless', one can see a model for much of Emily's own poetry. Indeed, complete lines, even whole poems, are occasionally echoed in her verse and his ballad tales of Scottish history and the deeds of Douglas set the scene for many Gondal lyrics and stories.[63]

As in the novels and ballads of Scott and Delta, and indeed, in Angria, Emily and Anne's Gondal creations live in stirring times. However, on the admittedly fragile evidence of the poems alone, it appears that the personal relationships between the characters, rather than the grand scheme of things, is the dominant theme. Emily and Anne clearly shared with their sister a romantic interest in the affairs of the heart, but its manifestation is very different. Charlotte's love affairs are nearly all one-sided, the women, whether the Marchioness of Douro, Mina Laury or Mary Percy, being so abjectly in love with Zamorna that they are his slaves, dependent on his whims and caprices for their happiness. Zamorna himself, despite the fact that Charlotte was more than a little in love with him, is a distinctly unpleasant character in his personal life, treating his wives and mistresses with an amused and cynical contempt and accepting their homage as his natural right. It is difficult to see why he exerted such an irresistible spell over his women, including Charlotte.

By contrast, Emily and Anne's lovers are more equal and, like Scott's lovers, are brave, passionate and faithful unto death. The scenario of *Old Mortality*, for instance, where Henry Morton and Edith are separated by political loyalties, which result in Morton being banished for so many years that Edith believes him to be dead, is repeated many times in Gondal.[64] In that world, love is often the result of the close sympathy arising out of growing up together, developing gradually and usually because of separation, into the passion of adulthood. Heathcliff and Catherine are prefigured in Gondal stories some ten years before their creator put pen to paper to write *Wuthering Heights*. The inevitable separation as one or the other leaves to seek his or her fortune or, more usually, becomes the victim of politics and is exiled or imprisoned, inspired poem after poem. Longing for the loved one and the native land, grief sinking to despair at separation and mourning when death intervenes are the principal themes. In spare and simple language, as different as it is possible to be from the frequently turgid and hyperbolical versification of their sister, Emily and Anne created a hauntingly elegiac mood for Gondal. Typical of these is a poem written by Anne at Haworth at the end of January 1838, a few days after her eighteenth birthday. Alexandrina Zenobia, imprisoned in a southern dungeon, is comforted by the sound of the wind.

> That wind is from the North, I know it well.
> No other breeze could have so wild a swell.
> Now deep \and/ loud it thunders round my cell,
> > Then faintly dies,
> > And softly sighs,
> And moans and murmers mournfully
> I know its language thus it speaks to me –

'I have passed over thy own mountains dear,
Thy northern mountains – and they still are free,
Still lonely, wild, majestic, bleak, and drear,
And stern, and lovely, as they used to be

When thou a young enthusiast,
As wild and free as they,
O'er rocks and glens and snowy heights,
Didst often love to stray.

I've blown the wild untrodden snows
In whirling eddies from their brows,
And I have howled in caverns wild
Where thou, a joyous mountain child,
Didst dearly love to be.
The sweet world is not changed, but Thou
Art pining in a dungeon now,
Where thou must ever be;
No voice but mine can reach thine ear,
And Heaven has kindly sent me here,
To mourn and sigh with thee,
And tell the[e] of the cherished land
Of thy nativity.'[65]

It is tempting to see the recurring pictures of dungeons and captivity as reflecting Anne's own feelings at being confined to Roe Head, particularly as the sound of the wind also conjured up visions of home and Angria to Charlotte.[66] This cannot be taken too far, however, as the same image occurs just as frequently in Emily's poems even though she was in full enjoyment of her liberty at home. For Emily's prisoners, it is not just the natural world which has the power to console: the great comforter – and one which all the young Brontës recognized – was the imagination.

I'll come when thou art sadest
laid alone in the darkend room
When the mad days mirth has vanished
And the smile of joy is banished
From evenings chilly gloom

Ill come when the hearts real feeling
Has entire unbiassed sway
And my influence oer thee stealing
greif deepening, joy congealing
Shall bear thy soul away

Listen 'tis just the hour
The awful time for thee
dost thou not feel upon thy Soul

A Flood of strange sensations roll
Forunners of a sterner power
Heralds of me[67]

Again, it is tempting to regard this poem as a personal statement by Emily, describing the visitation of imagination as if it had some sort of quasi-mystical external embodiment. It is comparable to Charlotte's diary fragments written at Roe Head and it is clear from many of Emily's other poems that evening was the time she habitually devoted to the imagination and her writings. While the poem may have been based on personal experience, it almost certainly belongs to the Gondal cycle: it has the initial O at the top of the manuscript, which usually indicates a Gondal pseudonym, and the reference to 'mad days mirth' seems an unlikely description of Emily's own life.

While Emily, assisted by the occasional contribution from Anne, pursued her heroes and heroines through the tangled web of Gondal intrigues, Branwell was still working on his own chronicles of Angria. He had already been working on this project for over three years but his ingenuity in developing new storylines showed no sign of flagging. After their victory over Northangerland and his Revolutionists at the battle of Evesham, Zamorna and Fidena set about retaking and restoring order to the rest of Angria and Verdopolis. Already, though, there were suggestions that all was not well: Zamorna's self-conceit made him a difficult partner and he was jealous of all Fidena's successes, believing that his own role as victor was being undermined. Charles Wentworth, who had once been one of Zamorna's greatest admirers, now mocked his pretensions thoroughly: 'it has pleased his Majesty to be out parading through the whole night through Drudgery which any Subaltern General would have done more fitly – under the idea that he was acting the Monarch Warrior'.[68]

Northangerland, defeated once more and in a state of mental and physical exhaustion, had retired to his country estate, Ennerdale House, where he sought the forgiveness and support of his long-suffering wife, Zenobia. Like the Duchess of Zamorna, Zenobia had had to put up with her husband's many mistresses and his neglect of herself, so she was reluctant to take him back. However, in a scene which foreshadowed Helen Huntingdon's decision to return and nurse her own debauched and dying husband in Anne's second novel, *The Tenant of Wildfell Hall,* Zenobia devoted herself to caring for Northangerland and was rewarded by the return of some of his affection.[69] It seems probable that Branwell intended Northangerland to die at this point as Zenobia, watching him sink into an unaccustomed calmness of spirit, wondered whether this change was simply the 'prelude to another and awful change'. The manuscript, incomplete either because Branwell could not bring himself to kill his great hero or because the ending has been lost, ends with a poem definitively titled 'PERCYS LAST SONNET'.

Cease, Mourner, cease thy sorrowing for the Dead
    for, if their Life be lost its Toils are oer
    And Woe and Want shall visit them no more
Nor ever slept they in an earthly bed
Such sleep as that which lulls them dreamless laid
    In the lone chambers of the eternal Shore
    Where Sacred Silence seals each guarded door.
Oh! Turn from tears for these thy bended head
    And mourn the <u>Dead Alive</u> whose pleasure flies
And < Hopes > Life departs before their death has come;
    Who lose the Earth from their benighted eyes;
Yet see no Heaven gleam through the rayless gloom.
    These only feel the worm that never dies
The Quenchless fire – the <u>Horrors</u> of a Tomb!'[70]

While Northangerland lay dying at Ennerdale, his former associates were being hunted down in Angria. Wentworth had fallen in with Henry Hastings and Charles Townshend and the three of them went on a drinking spree which eventually took them to an inn at Aynsham. There Hastings, abandoned by his companions, had become entangled with a new set of associates, led by the notorious debauchees George Ellen, esquire, and Parson Joynes. Their carousing sessions, which may have owed something to Branwell's attendance at masonic meetings throughout the year, were chiefly taken up with inventing childish and frequently blasphemous toasts. Hastings, for instance, raised his glass and proposed

'< The > Its speedy entombement in our stomachs and its ressurection with us in another world!'
    The President himself contradicted such a toast swearing that He had enough to do with < it > resurrection \of its ghost/ next morning and Crofton < ?had been > vowed that after a full dinner and flowing glass he had too often been troubled with the resurrection the next minute[71]

In a later incident, Hector Montmorency revived Quashia who had been knocked out in a wrestling match by Parson Joynes:

he held and poured whiskey down the throat of the Ethiop swore the parson must pardon him for administering Infant Baptism But he thought they had better all be confirmed and hoped he should stand excused if he \likewise/ practised upon himself Baptism for such as are of riper years!'[72]

These scenes of debauchery, which are totally unconvincing as portrayals of real life, were evidently regarded by Branwell as an opportunity to display his wit as a man of the world.
    If Branwell really did kill off Northangerland at the end of October 1837, he soon found he could not write without him. Before the year was out, he began an unfinished story relating to Northangerland's early career when,

like Walter Scott's Rob Roy, he was a simple cattle drover. More interesting, and written with a great deal more flair than his efforts at depicting low life, the story centres round Darkwall, a lonely farmhouse on the edge of the moors:

with large black walls and mossy mistal and a plantation of gloomy firs one clump of which the oldest and the highest stretched their horizontal arms above one Gable like the Genii of that desolate scene. Beyond this House its long feild walls made a line with the November sky and the path across them led on to an interminable Moor whose tracks might furnish a long days sport after Snipe or Heathcock, but no birds flew near the House except the Linnets twittering by hundreds on some wet old wall. and yet despite its loneliness this House was one of no common note in the Extensive Parish and half the fireside tales of times gone by were sure to take 'Darkwall' for their scene and its owners for their < Actors > subject.[73]

Like Wuthering Heights or Wildfell Hall, Darkwall has its secrets: its owner, Mr Thurston, is a drunkard and a violent man who alternately neglects and harasses his beautiful wife, Maria, who is going to fall in love with Alexander Percy. Though the story was abandoned, it had potential which Branwell later recognized, attempting to develop it into a full-scale novel.[74]

Charlotte's contribution to Angria throughout the year 1837 was negligible. In the summer holidays she wrote another volume by Charles Townshend, but again it was simply a collection of unconnected scenes rather than a developed narrative: Julia Thornton flirting with Captain Hastings, Louisa Vernon, Northangerland's opera singer mistress, now trying to ingratiate herself with Zamorna, and yet another attack on the hypocrisy of Methodist preachers.[75] Most of her effort was directed towards poetry. Robert Southey had not forbidden her to write or described her work as utterly without merit; he had advised her to write poetry for its own sake and, once she had got over the disappointment his letter had caused her, she found renewed energy. Between January 1837 and July 1838, she produced sixty poems, by far the highest number she had written in such a short time since the early days of the 'Young Men's Magazines'.[76] Though most of them were still Angrian in context, increasingly she produced shorter, lyrical pieces, more like her sisters' poems than the long narratives she had favoured before. Undoubtedly this change reflected the fact that her time was not at her own disposal: short poems were easier to write in the odd half hour or so of snatched leisure between lessons and supervision duties. Unlike prose narratives, which were so often interrupted and broken off, poems could be thought over and redrafted to achieve at least a measure of completeness – though the number of poems which Charlotte left unfinished suggests that even this was difficult.

Charlotte's last extant diary fragment was written about the time she received her reply from Southey[77] and thereafter she used the poems as an

alternative vehicle for the expression of her frustrations and sense of iso-
lation at Roe Head. A typical poem, later reworked as 'The Teacher's
Monologue' for her first publication, was written between 12 May and 15
May 1837.

> The room is quiet thoughts alone
> People its mute tranquillity
> The yoke put off, the hard toil done
> I am, as it is bliss to be,
> Still and untroubled, now I see
> For the first time, how soft the day
> O'er waveless water and stirless tree
> Silent & sunny wings its way
> Now as I watch that distant hill
> So faint so blue so far removed
> Sweet dreams of home my heart may fill
> That home where I am known & loved
> It lies beyond, that azure brow
> Parts me from all earth holds for me
> And morn & eve my yearnings flow
> Thither ward tending, changelessly...
>
> For youth departs, & pleasure flies
>   And life consumes away
> And youth's rejoicing ardour dies
>   Beneath this drear delay
> And patience weary with her yoke
>   Is yielding to despair
> And health's elastic spring broke
>   Submits to tyrant care[78]

In the end, however, it was not Charlotte but Anne whose spirit and health
broke under the regime at Roe Head. We have no account and no hint from
Anne herself of what happened, but Charlotte wrote to Ellen Nussey during
the Christmas holidays of 1837 to explain:

You were right in your conjectures respecting the cause of my sudden departure –
Anne continued – wretchedly ill – neither the pain nor the difficulty of breathing
left her – and how could I feel otherwise than very miserable? I looked upon her
case in a different light to what I could < hope > wish or expect any uninterested
person to view it in – Miss Wooler thought me a fool – and by way of proving her
opinion treated me with marked coldness – we came to a little eclairsissement one
evening – I told her one two rather plain truths – which set her a crying – and the
next day unknown to me she wrote to Papa – telling him that I had reproached
her – bitterly – taken her severely to task &c.&c. – Papa sent for us the day after he
had received her letter – Meantime I had formed a firm resolution – to quit Miss
Wooler and her concerns for ever – but just before I went away she took me into

her room – and giving way to her feelings which in general she restrains far too rigidly – gave me to understand that in spite of her cold repulsive manners She had a considerable regard for me and would be very sorry to part with me – If any body likes me I can't help liking them – and remembering that she had in general been very kind to me – I gave in and said I – would come back if she wished me – so – we're settled again for the present – but I am not satisfied I should have respected her far more if she had turned me out of doors instead of crying for two days and two nights together – I was in a regular passion my 'warm temper' quite got the better of me – Of which I don't boast for it was a weakness – nor am I ashamed of it for I had reason to be angry – Anne is now much better – though she still requires a great deal of care – however I am relieved from my worst fears respecting her –[79]

Knowing how taut Charlotte's nerves were at the time, it is easy to accept Mrs Gaskell's verdict that Miss Wooler's diagnosis of a common cold was correct and that Charlotte simply over-reacted to the whole situation. However, Mrs Gaskell not only placed the incident in December 1838, a year later than it actually happened, but also wrongly believed that it occurred at Dewsbury Moor, where the school relocated at the beginning of that year.[80] More importantly, there is independent evidence to corroborate Charlotte's account of the seriousness of Anne's illness. The Reverend James de la Trobe, the minister and teacher of the Moravian chapel and school at Well House in Mirfield, visited Anne several times during her illness. 'She was suffering from a severe attack of gastric fever which brought her very low, and her voice was only a whisper; her life hung on a slender thread.'[81]

If Charlotte was right to be concerned about Anne's state of health, it is even more interesting to discover that Anne's illness seems to have been exacerbated by a religious crisis. Once she had overcome her natural shyness at meeting a total stranger, Anne was deeply grateful to James de la Trobe for his visits:

I found her well acquainted with the main truths of the Bible respecting our salvation, but seeing them more through the law than the gospel, more as a require-ment from God than His gift in His Son, but her heart opened to the sweet views of salvation, pardon, and peace in the blood of Christ, and she accepted His welcome to the weary and heavy laden sinner, conscious more of her not loving the Lord her God than of acts of enmity to Him, and, had she died then, I should have counted her His redeemed and ransomed child.[82]

This account raises at least two important questions: why was quiet, gentle, pious Anne in any sort of religious doubt and why was a Moravian minister called in to administer to her?

In her biography of Anne Brontë, Winifred Gérin laid the blame for Anne's religious sufferings squarely on the shoulders of Aunt Branwell, whom she labelled a staunch Methodist. She depicts her as constitutionally gloomy and of an arid temperament, dogmatically expounding her

Methodism as a religion of fear rather than love. This is totally at odds with Ellen Nussey's picture of the sprightly little woman who had been a belle of the ball in her younger days, teased her prim and proper guest by offering her snuff and tilted arguments against Patrick 'without fear'.[83] Aunt Branwell is the most shadowy of all the members of the Brontë household but to portray her as ruling the young Brontës 'by a tyranny of the spirit', subjecting them to a harsh regime of discipline and continually reminding them of their own mortality with threats of hell-fire and damnation, is a travesty. Aunt Branwell, like her sister, Maria Brontë, was brought up as a Wesleyan Methodist. Unlike the more extreme forms of Methodism, which the young Brontës caricatured so mercilessly, the Wesleyans had much in common with Anglicans – so much so, indeed, that when the two congregations finally parted in 1812 many Wesleyans, including Maria Branwell and her uncle, John Fennell, chose to become members of the Established Church. Both Maria and Elizabeth Branwell attended Patrick's services in the Anglican church and both chose to be buried within its precincts.[84] At the very least this implies that Aunt Branwell found the doctrines Patrick preached acceptable. In all probability, then, she shared Patrick's belief in the essential goodness and infinite mercy of God and hoped, through faith, good works and the intercession of Christ, to win her place in heaven. Even if she did not, it is inconceivable that Patrick would have allowed his sister-in-law to indoctrinate his children with the harsh tenets of Calvinism, with its belief that only the elect few were predestined for salvation.

Although Aunt Branwell undoubtedly had more influence with Anne than her brother and sisters, having brought her up from being a baby, this is no reason to ascribe Anne's religious problems to her. It is surely significant that the religious crisis occurred, not at home under Aunt Branwell's eye, but at school. James de la Trobe described Roe Head as a school 'where a Christian influence pervaded the establishment and its decided discipline'.[85] Two of the five Wooler sisters who had assisted in the running of the school had married local clergymen: Susan had married the Reverend Edward Carter, then curate but now incumbent of Mirfield, on 30 December 1830 and Marianne had married the Reverend Thomas Allbutt, vicar of Dewsbury, on 9 July 1835. Though the Roe Head girls attended Mirfield Church each Sunday,[86] because it was nearer, both clergymen seem to have exercised considerable influence over the school. Allbutt, in particular, seems to have been a stickler for discipline who followed the Scriptures to the letter. In 1834, for instance, it was his harsh strictures against dancing, especially between the two sexes, which led Ellen Nussey to seek Charlotte's opinion on the subject.[87] The whole circle of Dewsbury clergymen seems to have been hard-line and unduly censorious in its attitudes: Patrick himself had incurred their disapproval with his liberal views on politics and religion and, much later, Charlotte was to shock them with *Jane Eyre*.[88] With two clergymen virtually on the staff at Roe Head, Patrick's old friends Thomas Atkinson at Hartshead and James Clarke Franks at Huddersfield and Ellen Nussey's brother Henry, the newly ordained curate of Dewsbury,[89] Anne had an almost embarrassing choice of ministers to call on in her hour of need. The fact that she, an Anglican clergyman's daughter herself, chose instead to turn to a stranger and a minister of the Moravian church, suggests a rejection of the values of the Dewsbury circle.

What these values were can be inferred from Charlotte's letters written throughout the time she was a teacher at Roe Head. Charlotte herself also underwent a prolonged religious crisis during these same years and, like Anne, ended up doubting the prospect of her own salvation. Her introspective and highly critical self-examination was shared and encouraged by Ellen, herself a devoted churchwoman, whom Charlotte increasingly saw as a model of genuine piety. 'My Darling if I were like you I should have my face Zion-ward', she declared, '... but I am not like you. If you knew my thoughts; the dreams that absorb me; and the fiery imagination that at times eats me up and makes me feel Society as it is, wretchedly insipid, you would pity and I dare say despise me.'[90]

How could Charlotte reconcile her idolatry of that eminent sinner, the god-like but adulterous Zamorna, with the precepts of her religion? 'What am I compared to you', she asked Ellen, who had never had an original thought and was utterly without poetry or imagination. 'I feel my own utter worthlessness when I make the comparison. I'm a very coarse, commonplace wretch!'[91]

Ellen Nussey bears a heavy responsibility for encouraging these traits in Charlotte. She was herself of an unusually masochistic turn of mind. From the earliest days of their friendship, she had been constantly self-critical, even seeking a list of her defects from Charlotte. Nor had she hesitated to assess her friend and offer her advice on how to reform her character.[92] Then Charlotte had been able to laugh at her but now, eaten up with frustration and resentment because the fulfilment of her duty brought her no personal satisfaction, she was vulnerable. Ellen's genuine affection for her and frequently offered kindnesses made it all the more difficult to reject her religion. Charlotte therefore accepted all Ellen's little schemes, such as the plan to pray for each other every night at ten o'clock and the constant measuring themselves against an unattainable goal of Christian perfection. Her sense of self-worth was gradually worn away.

I keep trying to do right, checking wrong feelings, repressing wrong thoughts – but still – every instant I find – myself going astray – I have a constant tendency to scorn people who are far better than I am – A horror at the idea of becoming one of a certain set – a dread lest if I made the slightest profession I should sink at once into 'Phariseeism', merge wholly into the ranks of the self-righteous.[93]

In this increasingly unhealthy state of mind, which her father would certainly have deplored, Charlotte clung even closer to Ellen. Nearly all her
letters contain pleas for a visit, and when one was prevented she immediately
believed it to be a sign from God: 'I am not good enough for you, and you
must be kept from the contamination of too intimate society.'[94] When Ellen
announced in February 1837 that she was going on a prolonged visit to her
brother John, the court physician, at his new house in Cleveland Row in
London, Charlotte was overcome with despair. 'Why are we to be divided?'
she cried. 'Surely, Ellen, it must be because we are in danger of loving each
other too well – of losing sight of the <u>Creator</u> in idolatry of the <u>creature</u>.'[95]
Ellen, who shared Charlotte's new brand of piety without being distressed
by it, now found herself the gratified object of Charlotte's ardent affection.

If I could always live with you and daily \read/ the bible with you, if your lips and
mine could at the same time, drink the same draught from the same pure fountain
of Mercy – I hope, I trust, I might one day become better, far better, than my evil
wandering thoughts, my corrupt heart, cold to the spirit, and warm to the flesh will
now permit me to be. I often plan the pleasant life which we might lead to-gether,
strengthening each other in that power of self-denial, that hallowed and glowing
devotion, which the first Saints of God often attained to – My eyes fill with tears
when I contrast the bliss of such a state brightened by hopes of the future with the
melancholy state I now live in, uncertain that I have ever felt true contrition,
wandering in thought and deed, longing for holiness which I shall <u>never, never</u>
obtain – smitten at times to the heart with the conviction that your Ghastly
Calvinistic doctrines are true – darkened in short by the very shadows of Spiritual
Death![96]

The last sentence of this passage contains the key to Charlotte's religious
crisis: her desperate yearning to achieve that perfection of faith which would
ensure her salvation, undermined by the fear that the battle was already
useless if she was not predestined for salvation or had been cast off by God
because she was a hardened sinner. These were what her own father called
'the appaling doctrines of personal Election and Reprobation'.[97] That the
pious and conventional Ellen Nussey, her greatest friend and probably
closest confidante, espoused these Calvinist beliefs must have shaken Charlotte's faith to its core. Ellen herself was not one to branch out into new
ideas or think very deeply, so it is reasonable to infer that she had adopted
her Calvinism from the clergymen who taught her from the local pulpits.
Her own brother the Reverend Henry Nussey held his curacy at Dewsbury
almost exactly contemporaneously with the Brontës' residence at Roe Head.
He had taken up the post in September 1835 and, although he performed his
last official duty as curate on 24 July 1837, he continued to take the occasional
duty there until the following December – precisely the time of Anne's
illness.[98] It is extremely unlikely that Thomas Allbutt would have employed
a curate whose beliefs differed fundamentally from his own, so it can be

assumed that he too shared at least some of the Calvinist beliefs which so distressed Charlotte. 'I abhor myself – ', she told Ellen in another letter, 'I despise myself – if the Doctrine of Calvin be true I am already an outcast.'[99] These sentiments would appear to be precisely those that troubled Anne. James de la Trobe perceived her problem as being that she saw the 'main truths of the Bible respecting our salvation ... more through the law than the gospel, more as a requirement from God than His gift in His Son'.[100] This, in itself, was a virtual definition of Calvinism.

At Roe Head both Anne and Charlotte, particularly the latter, were exposed to a double dose of Calvinism: from the pulpit of the Dewsbury circle of clergymen and, more insidiously, through Ellen Nussey. It is not surprising that both sisters underwent a religious crisis. What is surprising, and is perhaps a reflection of the influence Ellen had gained over Charlotte's mind at this time, is that, despite their supposed closeness, the sisters appear to have been unaware that they shared the same doubts.

It is ironic, though it was also fortunate, that Anne had turned to a Moravian minister for succour, when her own father was such a hostile opponent of Calvinism. Had she been at home, he would undoubtedly have dispelled her fears at once, but away at school Anne had no confidante and no comforter. Charlotte, the natural person to turn to, was herself in no state to advise her. In any case, she seems to have virtually ignored Anne at Roe Head. Charlotte always regarded Anne as a baby sister and was continually surprised when she showed any sign of adult behaviour or feelings, so Anne might not have expected a sympathetic hearing from her. Among her fellow pupils there was no one she could talk to: even Ann Cook was too young to be made a confidante of doubts of this kind.

Once at home and safely removed from the stern moral climate of Roe Head, Anne recovered rapidly from her physical illness. She did not shed her religious depression so easily, for although she eventually became convinced that salvation was open to all through the merits and passion of Christ,[101] a streak of melancholy and sense of personal worthlessness ran through all her religious poetry thereafter. Anne's experience at Roe Head, though not a direct result of the school itself, was to leave as profound a mark upon her character as Charlotte's much earlier experience at Cowan Bridge.

Chapter Eleven

SLAVERY

For the second Christmas in a row, the Brontës had an invalid in their household to nurse back to health. Tabby, though left with a pronounced limp, was fully active about the house again. But Anne's delicate state of health was a cause of concern, so much so that it was decided she should not return to Roe Head at the beginning of the new term in 1838. Charlotte would return alone to resume her teaching duties with Miss Wooler.

Charlotte spent her holiday, as usual, in writing an Angrian story which she completed on Anne's eighteenth birthday, 17 January. Though effectively only an episode, the story was unusually well thought out, with all its incidents closely interwoven to form a single drama. Just as a heroine, Mary Percy, had inspired one of her earlier best efforts, Mina Laury caught Charlotte's imagination this time. Though Charlotte had not yet recognized the fact, it was already becoming apparent that her forte lay with female characters, rather than her preferred male personae, from Zamorna himself to Charles Townshend. The story combines the tale of Lord Hartford's unrequited love for Zamorna's mistress, Mina Laury, with an escapade in which Zamorna lies his way out of a compromising position when his wife catches him visiting his mistress. Interestingly, Hartford's feelings and sufferings are described much more acutely and realistically than Mina Laury's unpleasantly servile devotion to Zamorna. Mina, like Charlotte herself, suffered from Zamorna-blindness:

Miss Laury belonged to the Duke of Zamorna – She was indisputably his property as much as the Lodge of Rivaux or the stately woods of Hawkscliffe ... She had but one idea – Zamorna, Zamorna –! it had grown up with her – become a part of her nature – Absence – Coldness – total neglect – for long periods together – went for nothing – she could no more feel alienation from him than she could from herself.[1]

It is a sign of how far Charlotte and Branwell had already drifted apart that, for a second time, she defied him by reviving Mary Percy, Zamorna's wife. This time she made no attempt to explain away the fact that Branwell had definitely killed her off over a year before, but simply stuck to her own version of events in which Mary had recovered from her illness with the return of Zamorna.[2]

The day before she left home, Charlotte wrote a poem to rally her own and her family's spirits.

> There's no use in weeping,
> Though we are condemned to part;
> There's such a thing as keeping
> A remembrance in one's heart...
>
> We can burst the bonds which chain us,
> Which cold human hands have wrought
> And where none shall dare restrain us
> We can meet again, in thought.[3]

On 30 January 1838, Charlotte set off from Haworth through some of the worst weather the winter had yet seen, heavy snows having fallen continuously throughout the week on top of ground already frozen hard.[4] It is possible that she returned, not to Roe Head but to a much smaller house where the Misses Wooler removed the school some time before Easter of that year. Roe Head had only been taken on a lease and the small number of boarding pupils at the school must have made it difficult to justify the expense of such a large house with its huge grounds. Miss Wooler's own family circumstances were changing: her father, who lived in Dewsbury at the family home, Rouse Mill, had been ill for some time and she was increasingly called upon to visit him. A house nearer Dewsbury therefore seemed a sensible idea.

Exactly when the move took place is not known. The Christmas holiday seems the most likely time, as it would have been complicated to move during term-time. The school had certainly relocated by the Easter holidays, when Mr Wooler actually died.[5] Heald's House, at Dewsbury Moor, was a very different, though no less attractive building, some three or four miles away from Roe Head. A pleasant, low-built, two-storey eighteenth-century gentleman's house of red brick, it had belonged to the Reverend William Margetson Heald, vicar of Birstall. It stood on a hill above the town of Dewsbury, well out of the range of the smoke of the mills, surrounded by ample gardens. Today, the area has been heavily built up and the house is overshadowed by the ugly utilitarian blocks of Dewsbury Hospital, but even so it retains an air of shabby gentility in the quiet backwater of a wide and leafy street. Though it is on a less high and exposed site than Roe Head, it is difficult to see why Mrs Gaskell considered the situation 'low and damp' and the air conducive to bad health.[6] In all probability it was her explanation for the fact that Charlotte fell ill at Heald's House. This was not the result of the relocation of the school, but rather an almost inevitable breakdown caused by Charlotte's overwrought state of mind. The monotony and sheer grind of the daily routine undermined her physical health, while her frustration and gloomy religious outlook poisoned her spirits. Added to this was an increasing sense of isolation. Anne, however little contact she had had with her while she had been at school, was now at home. Ellen Nussey was still in London, so Charlotte no longer had the prospect of her visits to enliven the dull round of teaching. Even Miss Wooler was no longer a constant companion. On one occasion during the Easter holidays, when she should have been at home but had been recalled to take charge after Mr Wooler's death, Charlotte was left completely on her own for sixteen days in a row.[7] The solitary life did not agree with her; she soon became prey to morbid thoughts and what she herself called 'hypochondria'. Many years later, she looked back on this period with anguish, recalling 'the tyranny of Hypochondria' and telling Miss Wooler:

I endured it but a year – and assuredly I can never forget the concentrated anguish of certain insufferable moments and the heavy gloom of many long hours – besides the preternatural horror which seemed to clothe existence and Nature – and which made Life a continual waking Night-mare – Under such circumstances the morbid Nerves can know neither peace nor enjoyment – whatever touches – pierces them – sensation for them is all suffering – A weary burden nervous patients consequently become to those about them – they know this and it infuses a new gall – corrosive in its extreme acritude, into their bitter cup – When I was at Dewsbury-Moor – I could have been no better company for you than a stalking ghost – and I remember I felt my incapacity to < impar > impart pleasure fully as much as my powerlessness to receive it –[8]

The long period on her own seems to have brought Charlotte to breaking point. Within a few weeks she had given up the unequal battle, writing to Ellen Nussey on 9 June 1838:

I ought to be at Dewsbury-Moor you know – but I stayed as long as I was able and at length I neither could nor dared stay any longer. My health and spirits had utterly failed me and the medical man whom I consulted enjoined me if I valued my life to go home. So home I went, the change has at once roused and soothed me – and I am now I trust fairly in the way to be myself again – A calm and even mind like yours Ellen cannot conceive the feelings of the shattered wretch who is now writing to you when after weeks of mental and bodily anguish not to be described something like tranquillity and ease began to dawn again.[9]

Miss Wooler, recognizing that Charlotte had come to the end of the road, presented her with a particularly thoughtful gift, a copy of Walter Scott's poems *The Vision of Don Roderick* and *Rokeby*, on 23 May 1838, presumably the day she left.[10]

That Charlotte's illness was principally in the mind was obvious from the swiftness of her recovery once she was back in the bosom of her family. She was encouraged in this by Mary and Martha Taylor, her lively friends from her own schooldays at Roe Head. They came to stay for a few days at the beginning of June, defeating Charlotte's attempt to write to Ellen.

They are making such a noise about me I can not write any more. Mary is playing on the piano. Martha is chattering as fast as her little tongue can run < as > and Branwell is standing before her laughing at her vivacity.[11]

Despite the reviving gaiety at home, Charlotte was still a prey to morbid sensitivity, noting with alarm that Mary appeared far from well and that her symptoms reminded her forcibly of the consumption that had killed Maria and Elizabeth thirteen years earlier.[12] Charlotte was obsessed with consumption at this time, believing first of all that Anne had fallen victim to it and then, some six months later, that Mary Taylor was a sufferer. Perhaps, in her highly nervous state at Dewsbury Moor, she had talked herself into believing that she, too, had the fatal symptoms – the cough, the pain in the chest or side and the feverishness were all common enough complaints which could easily seem signs of more deadly disease.

The imaginations of Branwell and her sisters had been more productively engaged. Emily and Anne between them produced a whole stream of poems describing the captivity of Alexandrina Zenobia, her misery at her separation from her lover and the faithlessness of her former friends. Emily was also immersed in classical studies, translating Virgil's *Aeneid* and writing notes on the Greek tragedies of Euripides and Aeschylus.[13] Anne, too, undoubtedly pursued her lessons at home.

Branwell, as usual, had several ventures on hand at once. While still continuing his story about the unfortunate Henry Hastings and the vicious circle of debauchees, led by George Ellen, into which he had fallen, Branwell had also embarked on a new project, a life of Warner Howard Warner whom he described as

one whose has been foremost in all our troubles past and whom I may call the greatest Creation of the Storm. All our other \Cheif/ Leaders had been of some account before he alone in our eyes has been born in it and lived in it and < surv > gloriously survived it.[14]

As in his earlier 'Life of Alexander Percy', Branwell gave Warner a distinguished pedigree which set him firmly in his own locality. The family lived near Pendle Hill, the famous haunt of witches which lay just across the moors from Haworth. To the founder of the line in the seventeenth century he gave the resonant name Haworth Currer Warner, which may have been the source of Charlotte's last and most famous pseudonym, Currer Bell.[15] The family emigrated to Africa in 1780, where General Warner conquered the province of Angria from the Ashantee, Warner Howard Warner being his great-grandchild. Though the story was abandoned as Branwell's circumstances changed, it is interesting to see that a scenario similar to Lowood School was envisaged. The six-year-old Warner, a sickly child, was to be sent to Dr Moray's Hawkscliffe Academy, despite the fact that his mother opposed the plan, 'pointing out the probable results from her Sons Unbending spirit and want of power to < ded > assert its rights'.[16]

Once she had recovered her equilibrium, Charlotte added her contribution to the literary activity, writing two long stories in a month. The first, beginning with the now almost obligatory skit on a Methodist service in an Ebenezer chapel, was again a series of loosely connected scenes and kaleidoscopic events featuring Charles Townshend, Charlotte's favourite narrator, and William Percy, estranged son of Northangerland, who plays an increasingly important role in the juvenilia. She introduced a new heroine, who foreshadows the predatory and beautiful Blanche Ingram of *Jane Eyre.* Jane Moore is a dazzling beauty, daughter of an Angrian lawyer, who has ambitions to marry a nobleman and, having set her sights on Lord Hartford, proceeds to court him with ruthless ability. Another interesting episode, irrelevant to the story, is a description of Viscount Macara Lofty, who is discovered recovering from an opium-induced stupor. His ecstatic smiles grow less frequent and his 'almost sensual look of intense gratification & absorption gave place to an air of fatigue'. With throbbing head and shaking hands, he defends his use of opium to the disapproving Townshend:

I was in a state of mind which I will not mock you by endeavouring to describe – but the gloom the despair became unendurable – dread forebodings rushed upon me – whose power I could not withstand – I felt myself on the brink of some hideous disaster & a vague influence ever & anon pushed me over – till clinging wildly to life & reason – I almost lost consciousness in the faintness of mortal terror. Now Townshend – so suffering – how far did I err – when I had recource, to the sovereign specific which a simple narcotic drug offered me?[17]

Though Charlotte later denied that she had ever taken opium,[18] the circumstances in which Lofty resorted to the drug were very similar to her own experiences at Dewsbury Moor.

Having finished this story on 28 June, Charlotte promptly began another which, in a method totally new to her but which would be used by all the sisters in their published novels, told the story through the medium of letters. Curiously, the subject she chose this time was Augusta di Segovia, Alexander Percy's first wife, whom she wilfully transformed into his mistress. Perhaps because Branwell had already covered the ground so well in his first volume of 'The Life of Alexander Percy', Charlotte could make no headway. At the beginning of her eighth chapter she admitted:

One cannot live always in solitude. One cannot continually keep one's feelings wound up to the pitch of romance and reverie. I began this work with the intention of writing something high and pathetic.

She had intended to describe the deathbed of Augusta, poisoned by Robert King, alias Sdeath, and dying alone in agony.

But reader, why should I pursue this subject? All this has been told you before in far higher language than I can use! Revenons à nos moutons! Let it suffice to say that I found this pitch far too high for me. I could not keep it up. I was forced to descend a peg ... I grew weary of heroics and longed for some chat with men of common clay.[19]

Far from being 'men of common clay', the conversationalists were Sir William Percy, Lord Hartford and the inevitable Zamorna, and their 'chat' turned on Percy's appointment to delicate secret diplomatic negotiations in Paris. Charlotte thus fell back on developing the story she had begun in her previous work.

While Charlotte tried to forget Dewsbury Moor by burying herself in her writing, Branwell was preparing to embark on his chosen profession. Any plans to go to the Royal Academy or on a continental tour had now been dropped completely and Branwell's first foray into the world was distinctly less glamorous. Under the patronage of Patrick's old friend and relative by marriage, the Reverend William Morgan, he set up as a professional portrait painter in a studio in Bradford. The actual date of his removal to Bradford is not known. He was certainly at home when the Taylors came to stay in the first week of June. On 22 July 1838, William Morgan paid a rare visit to Haworth to give the afternoon sermon in aid of the church Sunday school and it seems logical that Branwell should have taken advantage of his visit to return to Bradford with him. In any event, he was established in Bradford by 31 July, and living in lodgings only a stone's throw from Morgan's Christ Church.[20]

The house was a modest one, in the middle of a stone-built terrace which lay at right angles to the top of Darley Street, a busy thoroughfare leading to the heart of the town. It was well placed for businessmen seeking their own or their families' portraits, though it was in a residential area rather than in a commercial centre. Branwell's 'Genteel & Comfortable lodgings ... suitable for a Single Gentleman, or a Lady & Gentleman without incumbrance', were at No. 2, Fountain Street where the owner, Isaac Kirby, lived with his wife and two children. Kirby advertised himself as a 'dealer in London & Dublin, Double XX Stout, Porter etc', which he sold from his commercial premises opposite the Rawson Arms in Market Street.[21] It is surely evidence of the fact that Branwell was not yet a confirmed drinker that his father and William Morgan allowed him to lodge with a dealer in beer in his first foray away from home.

The Kirbys and their niece, Margaret Hartley, were among those who sat to their lodger, but Branwell was also able to cultivate the much wealthier clerical circle surrounding his extremely influential patron, William Morgan. He is known to have painted Morgan himself and even the vicar of Bradford, Henry Heap.[22] Though his portrait of Mrs Kirby is unflattering in the extreme, with its sharply angled face and Pinocchio-esque nose, other portraits of the period show that Branwell was a perfectly competent, though not a great, artist. As he settled into his new lodgings, he had every prospect of making at least a modest success of his chosen career.

Though the fact that Branwell was now in a way to earn his own living eased the financial pressures on the rest of his family, it was still an absolute necessity that his sisters should be able to support themselves. Patrick was sixty-one and still working as hard as ever, since he had been without a curate for over a year. His continued good health, let alone his continued existence, could not be relied upon. Charlotte had little option, therefore, but to revoke her decision not to return to Dewsbury Moor after her extended summer holiday ended. On 24 August 1838, she wrote to Ellen Nussey, who had moved on from one brother in London to stay with another, Joshua, in Bath.

I am again at Dewsbury-Moor engaged in the old business teach – teach – teach ... When will you come home? Make haste you have been at Bath long enough for all purposes – by this time you have acquired polish enough I am sure – if the varnish is laid on much thicker I am afraid the good wood underneath will be quite concealed and your old Yorkshire friends won't stand that – Come – Come I am getting really tired of your absence. Saturday after Saturday comes round and I can have no hope of hearing your knock at the door and then being told that 'Miss Ellen Nussey is come.' O dear in this monotonous life of mine that was a pleasant event.[23]

Charlotte, as usual, exaggerated her plight. She was still in touch with Mary and Martha Taylor, who were about to take a tour in Wales, and she had had 'seen a great deal' of one of her former pupils, Ann Cook. It is a measure of Charlotte's changing mood that a girl whom she had once described as one of the 'fat-headed oafs' at Roe Head was now transformed into someone who was 'still the same warm-hearted – affectionate – prejudiced – handsome girl as ever' whom Charlotte did not think at all altered 'except that her carriage &c. is improved'.[24] Of events or gossip in the neighbourhood, Charlotte could only say, 'I have nothing at all to tell you' – this despite the fact that in the previous two weeks Dewsbury had been torn apart by some of the worst riots in its history. The new Poor Law guardians had recently held their first meetings in the town, causing the Radicals to hold a protest rally: the mob went on the rampage, physically attacking the guardians, who had to call out the troops to protect themselves. Only four days before Charlotte wrote her letter, there had been a second anti-Poor Law riot in Dewsbury even though troops were now stationed in the town to keep the populace in order.[25] Of these dramatic events, despite her once-vaunted interest in politics, Charlotte remained oblivious, wrapped up in her own little world at Heald's House.

Charlotte was not alone in returning to the teaching profession. In September, Emily, who was now twenty years old, sought paid employment for the first time. Miss Wooler could not afford to employ another teacher at Dewsbury Moor, so Emily had to look elsewhere and found herself a post at Law Hill, a girls' school at Southowram on the outskirts of Halifax.

Law Hill is little changed today. It stands in glorious isolation high on a hillside with panoramic views across miles of open moor and farmland. To the north lie Queensbury and Shelf, to the southeast, across the wooded grounds of Kirklees Hall, are the familiar landmarks of the tower of Patrick's old church at Hartshead and the site of Roe Head. On a clear day, the view extends far into the heart of the East Riding. Below the house, the hillside falls away steeply into the beautiful wooded Shibden Valley; the village of Southowram is a good half mile further down the hill and its church, which the ladies of Law Hill attended, is another half mile beyond the village.

The house itself had once belonged to a gentleman farmer and it reflects that comparative wealth and solidity. Built of blackened sandstone, the house is square and austere, three storeys high with large sash windows, one on each side of the door and three on each of the upper floors. At the front is a small garden and to the side, across a large cobbled yard with a stone mounting block, was a big stone barn which had been converted into the schoolroom. Out of sight, behind the hill, lay the wealthy and highly cultured town of Halifax. Besides giving the girls an enviable proximity to exhibitions and museums, Halifax attracted eminent musicians from all over Europe. During Emily's residence, there was a concert by Johann Strauss and his waltz band, who performed to great applause in the Halifax theatre. In terms of location, therefore, Law Hill had everything to please Emily.[26]

The school was well established and had been run for many years by Elizabeth and Maria Patchett, sisters of a Halifax banker. The younger sister, who was described as 'very gentle', had got married and gone to live in Dewsbury almost exactly a year before Emily's appointment. It was possibly through her that Emily found out about the situation, for her husband was Titus Senior Brooke. Patrick knew the Brookes from his days as a curate in Dewsbury and Leah and Maria Brooke had both been at school with Charlotte. Though the post may have come to Emily's notice by word of mouth from the Dewsbury district, it is just as likely that she responded to an advertisement in the local press.[27]

Opinion was divided about Elizabeth Patchett, the forty-two-year-old spinster who remained in charge of the school. According to her former pupils, she was a very beautiful woman, who wore her hair in long curls and was a skilful rider. She was fond of teaching, a kind schoolmistress and the daily walks in her company were much prized. On the other hand, a contemporary who lived near the school in the winter of 1836–7 described her as 'stately and austere. We always understood she knew how to keep things in order'.[28] This seems to have been the Brontë view of the school. Even Charlotte was forced to admit that Emily's lot was harder than her own.

My sister Emily is gone into a situation as teacher in a large school of near forty pupils, near Halifax. I have had one letter from her since her departure; it gives an appalling account of her duties – hard labour from six in the morning until near eleven at night, with only one half-hour of exercise between. This is slavery. I fear she will never stand it.[29]

Of the forty-odd pupils at the school, all aged between eleven and fifteen, approximately half were boarders, hence the lateness of the hours Emily had to work. Despite its size, Miss Patchett ran her school with just two other teachers, so Emily's workload would inevitably have been greater than Charlotte's.[30]

Emily did not stand the 'slavery' of Law Hill for long. As had happened before at Roe Head, her health broke down under the strain of living in the disciplined and demanding atmosphere of a boarding school. This was a fairly gradual process; Emily's first term does not appear to have been particularly unhappy. According to several old pupils who remembered her, she was not unpopular 'though she could not easily associate with others, and her work was hard because she had not the faculty of doing it quickly'. The only recorded incident concerning her which survives from this time is typical: one schoolgirl remembered that Emily was devoted to the house dog and once told her class that it was dearer to her than any of them were.[31]

Like Charlotte, Emily took refuge from the harsh realities and fatigue of the daily grind in poetry. The large number of poems she wrote in the three months of her first term suggests that, despite the length of the hours she had to work, she still found leisure for her own writing. As some of the poems are dramatic incidents in the Gondal saga, such as the suicide of Ferdinand de Samara, who has been deceived and abandoned by his former lover, Augusta Almeda,[32] it is even possible that Emily was able to spend time on her prose tales while at Law Hill. Gondal was certainly not forgotten, nor put to one side. In this autumn of 1838 she also wrote three outstanding poems which expressed her personal misery and homesickness. The most clearly autobiographical of these, written on 4 December 1838, is worth quoting in full because it so exquisitely encapsulates Emily's dilemma: would a snatched hour of leisure be better spent in dreams of her beloved home, graphically described even to the path overgrown with weeds, or of Gondal, that 'other clime'?

> A little while, a little while,
> The noisy crowd are barred away;
> And I can sing and I can smile –
> A little while I've holyday!
>
> Where wilt thou go my harassed heart?
> Full many a land invites thee now;
> And places near, and far apart
> Have rest for thee, my weary brow –
>
> There is a spot mid barren hills
> Where winter howls and driving rain
> But if the dreary tempest chills
> There is a light that warms again
>
> The house is old, the trees are bare
> And moonless bends the misty dome
> But what on earth is half so dear –
> So longed for as the hearth of home?
>
> The mute bird sitting on the stone,
> The dank moss< y > dripping from the wall,
> The garden-walk with weeds o'e'r-grown
> I love them – how I love them all!
>
> Shall I go there? or shall I seek
> Another clime, another sky –
> Where tongues familiar music speak
> In accents dear to memory?
>
> Yes, as I mused, the naked room,
> The flickering firelight died away
> And from the midst of cheerless gloom
> I passed to bright, unclouded day –
>
> A little and a lone green lane
> That opened on a common wide

A distant, dreamy, dim blue chain
Of mountains circling every side –

A heaven so clear, an earth so calm,
So sweet, so soft, so hushed an air
And, deepening still the dreamlike charm,
Wild moor-sheep feeding everywhere –

That was the scene – I knew it well
I knew the path-ways far and near
That winding o'er each billowy swell –
Marked out the tracks of wandering deer

Could I have lingered but an hour
It well had paid a week of toil
But truth has banished fancys power
I hear my dungeon bars recoil –

Even as I stood with raptured eye
Absorbed in bliss so deep and dear
My hour of rest had fleeted by
And given me back to weary care[33]

Both the other poems, written in the gloom and snow of November and December at Law Hill, yearned for the transformation that spring and summer would bring to the moors.

For the moors, for the moors where the short grass
Like velvet beneath us should lie!
For the moors, for the moors where each high pass
Rose sunny against the clear sky!

For the moors, where the linnet was trilling
Its song on the old granite stone. –
Where the lark – the wild sky-lark was filling
Every breast with delight like its own –[34]

The third poem, written just before Emily's return home for the Christmas holidays, was an elegy for the harebell, whose delicate flower breathes 'a calm and softening spell', soothing as well as stirring up her longing for the return of summer.[35] Even if being away from home did little for Emily's spirits, it was clearly a stimulus to poetic impulse, as the poems she produced this autumn included some of the best she ever wrote.

The family reunited for the Christmas holidays at the end of 1838, but joy at being home was mixed with concern at Patrick's evidently deteriorating state of health. He had been under considerable stress all year. The annual battle over church rates had been fought and lost but this time the confrontation had been taken a stage further. James Greenwood, the most prominent and well-respected of the Haworth Dissenters, had been prosecuted in the Bradford courts for refusing to pay his church rate. As he was also Chief Constable of Haworth, responsible for much of the parish administration, relations between him and Patrick must have been strained. When Greenwood pleaded that the rate had been levied illegally, the magistrates declared they had no jurisdiction in the matter and 'wished the parties joy of the ecclesiastical courts'. A number of other people in the chapelry were later successfully prosecuted for failure to pay their tithes, a move which can only have further alienated the Dissenters.[36]

In the autumn of 1838 Patrick was driven to consult the up and coming young surgeon from Keighley, John Milligan, about his dyspepsia. Milligan apparently recommended a glass of wine or spirits should be taken with his main meal, a prescription which Patrick found effective but open to misinterpretation. One could well imagine the gleeful reaction of John Winterbotham to news that the rector, one of the founder members of the Haworth Temperance Society, was to be seen imbibing wine. For this reason, Patrick was careful to get Milligan's signature to the prescription, but even that did not quash rumours that the parson had taken to the bottle.[37]

The strain he was under also prompted Patrick to initiate a more vigorous search for a new curate. On 10 January 1839 he wrote to several of his clergyman friends, including James Clarke Franks, requesting them to exert themselves on his behalf. 'I am no Bigot –', he told Franks, but he did not want a Calvinist.

I could not feel comfortable with a coadjutor, who would deem it his duty to preach the appaling Doctrines of Personal Election and Reprobation. As I should consider these, decidedly derogatory to the Attributes of God – so, also I should be fearful of evil consequences to the hearers, from the enforcement of final perseverance, as an essential Article of belief … I want, for this region, a plain, rather than an able – preacher; a zealous, but at the same time a judicious man – One, not fond of innovation, but desirous of proceeding <u>on the good old plan</u> – which, alas! has <u>often</u> been <u>mar'd</u>, but <u>never improved</u>.[38]

Whether Patrick wished it or not, major changes were on the horizon. On 17 January 1839, Henry Heap, vicar of Bradford for the last twenty-two years, died after a long illness.[39] Taking advantage of this situation, the Bishop of Ripon announced that he intended to separate the chapelry of Haworth from Bradford and make it a parish in its own right. Though the proposal was widely welcomed in Haworth, where it would have ended at a stroke the injustice of the township having to pay two sets of church rates and dues, it met with fierce opposition in Bradford. The Simeon trustees, who had just purchased the right to appoint a new vicar of Bradford and who included the Reverend William Carus Wilson, pointed out that the vicar would lose a fifth of his income if Haworth was separated from Bradford. In the meantime, the trustees found themselves with the difficult task of trying to appoint a vicar in a parish where his rights would undoubtedly be challenged in every quarter.[40]

Patrick at least had the comfort of learning from Branwell and Emily that they were both doing as well as could be expected in their first employment. The shock must therefore have been all the greater when Charlotte announced that she had finally given her notice to Miss Wooler and would not be returning to Dewsbury Moor after the Christmas holidays. As she had been on the brink of giving up at least twice before, her family might have thought that this was simply another futile gesture, but Charlotte stuck to her resolve. Though ill health does not seem to have played its part this time, Charlotte was at the limit of her endurance. In addition to her teaching duties she had found herself called upon to play nursemaid to little Edward Carter and his baby sister, Miss Wooler's nephew and niece.[41] The main catalyst, however, seems to have been Miss Wooler's declared intention of giving up the school at Christmas in favour of her sister, Eliza. The sense of personal obligation and friendship for Miss Wooler herself, which had kept Charlotte at Dewsbury Moor for so long, was removed. She owed no such duties to Eliza Wooler. Another reason was that although Miss Wooler intended to continue living in Heald's House, she would also have her own, recently widowed, mother in residence. No doubt Charlotte foresaw that she would be increasingly called upon to give up her precious hours of leisure to the uncongenial task of looking after all the elderly and juvenile members of the extensive Wooler family.[42] Charlotte had therefore taken a formal leave of all her acquaintance in the Dewsbury area and, having done the deed, returned to Haworth in an unusually bright and cheerful frame of mind.

Writing on 20 January 1839 to Ellen Nussey, who had at long last returned from Bath, Charlotte had so far recovered her spirits as to be able to tease her friend.

My dear, kind Ellen
I can hardly help laughing when I reckon up the number of urgent invitations I have received from you during the last three months – had I accepted all, or even half of them – the Birstallians would certainly have concluded that I had come to make Brookroyd my permanent residence – When you set your mind upon a thing you have a peculiar way of hedging one in with a circle of dilemmas so that they hardly know how to refuse you – however I shall take a running leap and clear them all – Frankly my dear Ellen I cannot come – Reflect for yourself a moment – do you see nothing absurd in the idea of a person Coming again into a neighbourhood within a month after they have taken a solemn and formal leave of all their acquaintance – ? … Angry though you are I will venture to sign myself as usual (no not as usual, but as suits circumstances)

Yours under a cloud
C Brontë[43]

Charlotte's gaiety at her release from Dewsbury Moor was reflected in her plans. The day after she wrote her letter, she was due to go to Lascelles Hall on a visit to Amelia Walker – a treat which she regarded with mixed feelings. Something she could look forward to with unmixed pleasure was a visit to Haworth by Mary and Martha Taylor in February, which Charlotte tried to improve further by urging Ellen to join them as well.[44]

Charlotte now also had the time to gratify her writing instincts to the full, an opportunity of which she took advantage in an Angrian story of unusual length. Apart from the usual inconsequential and irrelevant forays into Zamorna's domestic life, her story was principally concerned with a new heroine, Elizabeth Hastings, sister of Branwell's creation, Henry Hastings, the Angrian soldier and writer turned debauched and disgraced outlaw.[45] As so often in the past, Charlotte's story was sparked off by a story Branwell was writing about the efforts of Zamorna's men to round up all the proscribed rebels who had aided Northangerland. Hastings had been reduced to leading sorties of Ashantee and French troops against the Angrians and then, in desperation, had come to Verdopolis in disguise as a 'Richard Wilson' to attempt an assassination of Zamorna. Though the attempt failed, news of Zamorna's 'death' had been spread by the French before anyone became aware of the attempt on his life. Their complicity in the assassination plot was therefore obvious, though the populace continued to blame Northangerland.[46]

Charlotte's story picked up this theme from the point of view of Hastings' loyal sister, who sheltered him while he was on the run, tried to prevent his capture by Sir William Percy and, when he was captured and condemned to death for the assassination attempt, interceded on his behalf with the Duchess of Zamorna. For the first and last time in many years, Charlotte and Branwell were working on the same story at the same time.

Charlotte's story is interesting chiefly because its central character is not a languorous aristocratic Angrian beauty or an infatuated mistress of Zamorna but a much more life-like and original character who is a forerunner of Jane Eyre. Like Jane, and Charlotte herself, Elizabeth Hastings is physically small and insignificant: Townshend calls her a 'pale undersized young woman dressed as plainly as a Quakeress in grey'. The plain exterior belied a loyal soul and a lively wit. When quizzed by Townshend as to why she does not fall into raptures at the very name of Zamorna, she replies, 'I make a point of never speaking in raptures, especially in a stage-coach.'[47]

Just as she was later to do with Jane Eyre, Charlotte endowed Elizabeth with many of her own characteristics. Elizabeth, for example, feels very deeply her own lack of personal attraction. In the presence of the acknowledged beauty, Mary Percy, Duchess of Zamorna, she experiences 'a new feeling – & her heart confessed, as it had a thousand times done before, the Dazzling omnipotence of beauty – the Degradation of personal insignificance'.[48] One hears also Charlotte's own voice in Elizabeth's decision to set up her own school for older girls,

not wearily toiling to impart the dry rudiments of knowledge to yawning, obstinate children – a thing she hated & for which her sharp-irritable temper rendered her wholly unfit – but instructing those who had already mastered the elements of education – reading, commenting, explaining, leaving it to them to listen – if they failed, comfortably conscious that the blame would rest on her pupils, not herself.[49]

Like Charlotte, too, Elizabeth longed for love. Though she becomes respected and admired for her diligence and success in establishing her school,

still the exclusive proud being thought she had not met with a single individual equal to herself in mind, & therefore not one whom she could love ... she was always burning for warmer, closer attachment – she couldn't live without it – but the feeling never woke & never was reciprocated –[50]

When eventually she does fall in love, with William Percy, she is as arch and pert with him as Jane was to be with Mr Rochester. When he seeks compliments, she provokes him by not replying, simply looking down and smiling. And when, like Rochester, he proposes to make her his mistress, she refuses not just because she fears the world's opinion but because she has respect for herself. Though her very soul cries out to give in to his pleas, she answers him, 'I could not without incurring the miseries of self-hatred.' She leaves him, thinking it to be for ever, with the words 'If I stay another moment God knows what I shall say or do ... Good-bye Sir William – I implore you not to follow me – the night is light – I am afraid of nothing but myself.'[51]

The story, which was originally written in three volumes, took Charlotte a full month to complete. It proved once again that her obsession with Zamorna was a major handicap: if she could only shake off his shackles she was capable of creating a spirited and lively heroine and developing a dramatic storyline.

Charlotte began this story with two people both searching for love, William Percy looking for a woman in whom mind and feeling predominated and Elizabeth Hastings for her own equal in intellect and passion. It was therefore a curious coincidence that Charlotte herself was offered love, of a sort, at the very same time. At the beginning of March 1839, she received a marriage proposal out of the blue. The Reverend Henry Nussey, Ellen's brother, the former curate of Dewsbury, was now settled in a new curacy at Donnington in Suffolk and, at twenty-seven years of age, had decided that it was time he should marry. He set about finding a bride with characteristic coolness and efficiency. The first young lady he approached was Mary Lutwidge, the sister of his former vicar, whom he described in his diary as 'a steady, intelligent, sensible, and, I trust, good girl'. That these were her sole attractions and that his own affections were not at all engaged was obvious from his response to her refusal: 'received a decisive reply fm M. A. L.'s papa. A loss, but I trust a providential one. Believe not her will, but her father's. All right. God knows best what is good for us, for his Church, & for his own Glory ... Wrote to a Yorkse friend, C. B. Brothers John & George also'.[52]

Though Henry's proposal to Charlotte is not extant, we have Charlotte's own summary of it in a letter she wrote to his sister on 12 March.

You ask me my dear Ellen whether I have received a letter from Henry – I have about a week since – The Contents I confess did a little surprise me, but I kept them to myself and unless you had questioned me on the subject I would never have adverted to it – Henry says he is comfortably settled at Donnington that his health is much improved & that it is his intention to take pupils after Easter – he then intimates that in due time he shall want a Wife to take care of his pupils and frankly asks me to be that Wife. Altogether the letter is written without cant or flattery & in a common-sense style which does credit to his judgement –[53]

The unromantic nature of the proposal appealed to Charlotte's sense of honesty and there were positive advantages to accepting. She would no longer have to worry about provision for her future. She could forget the idea of having to return to the dreary round of teaching and look forward to the prospect of conducting her own school, safe in the knowledge that her husband could support her financially. Henry was a perfectly eligible bachelor, four years older than herself and a clergyman in her own church. The thought that Ellen could come and live with them was also a 'strong temptation' – had she not once told Ellen how she longed 'for a cottage and a competency of our own' so that they could live together without being dependent on anyone else for their happiness?[54] The problem was that Charlotte, like Elizabeth Hastings and Jane Eyre, had the romantic notion that she should love her husband. 'I asked myself two questions –', Charlotte told Ellen.

Do I love Henry Nussey as much as a woman ought to love the man her husband? Am I the person best qualified to make him happy? – Alas Ellen my conscience answered '<u>no</u>' to both these questions. I felt that though I esteemed Henry though I had a kindly leaning towards him because he is an amiable – well-disposed man yet I had not, and never could have that intense attachment which would make me willing to die for him – and if ever I marry it must be in that light of adoration that I will regard my Husband[55]

The difficult letter of refusal had to be written. Charlotte was careful to avoid wounding what feelings Henry Nussey possessed, but her answer was as decided as Mary Lutwidge's.

My dear Sir

Before answering your letter, I might have spent a long time in consideration of its subject; but as from the first moment of its reception and perusal I determined on which course to pursue, it seemed to me that delay was wholly unnecessary.

You are aware that I have many reasons to feel grateful to your family, that I have peculiar reasons for affection towards one at least of your Sisters, and also that I highly esteem yourself. do not therefore accuse me of wrong motives when I say that my answer to your proposal must be a <u>decided negative</u>. In forming this decision – I trust I have listened to the dictates of conscience more than to those [of] inclination; I have no personal repugnance to the idea of a union with you – but I feel convinced that mine is not the sort of disposition calculated to form the happiness of a man like you. It has always been my habit to study the characters of those amongst whom I chance to be thrown, and I think I know yours and can imagine what description of woman would suit you for a wife. Her character should not be too marked, ardent and original – her temper should be mild, her piety undoubted, her [spirits] even and cheerful, and her '<u>personal attractions</u>' sufficient to please your eye and gratify your just pride. As for me you do not know me, I am not the serious, grave, cool-headed individual you suppose – you would think me romantic and [eccentric – you would] say I was satirical and [severe – however I scorn] deceit and I will never for the sake of attaining the distinction of matrimony and escaping the stigma of an old maid take a worthy man whom I am conscious I cannot render happy.[56]

With these brave and considered words the twenty-three-year-old Charlotte turned down what she acknowledged was likely to be the only marriage proposal she would ever get.[57] The whole episode was later to prove fruitful material for her writing. The third volume of her story about Elizabeth Hastings, written immediately after she had turned Henry Nussey down, introduced just that passion which was so lacking in Henry's proposal. Ultimately, too, it would form the basis for St John Rivers' proposal to Jane Eyre, he, like Henry, needing a wife to support him in his work. If the character of St John Rivers is also drawn from that of Henry Nussey, then Charlotte was indeed wise not to marry him. That this was the case is suggested by the *sang-froid* with which the rejected suitor recorded in his diary on 9 March, 'Received an unfavourable reply fm C. B. The will of the Lord be done.'[58]

Branwell had also taken a decisive step in determining his future. The hard reality of trying to earn his living by painting portraits had finally put paid to his dreams of becoming a great artist. He is usually assumed to have given up his studio in Bradford some time in May 1839, having been established there for little under a year, but it is likely that he came back to Haworth as early as the third week in February. Between 21 and 23 February, he wrote a long chapter in his new work on Angria which he clearly dated at the end from Haworth.[59] At the beginning of March he began to reread his father's precious prize volume of the works of Horace, noting in the margin that he had read the first nine odes of Book II by 5 March and that he had completed the book four days later. As Patrick did not allow Branwell to borrow his Horace when he needed it as a tutor in the classics, it seems extremely unlikely that he would have allowed him to take it to Bradford when Branwell was supposed to be painting for a living.[60] Finally, in a letter dated 17 May to a friend from Bradford, J. H. Thompson, Branwell began by telling him that in response to Thompson's 'last' communication he had resolved to visit Bradford 'for certainly this train of Misconceptions and delays must at last be put a stop to'.[61] Branwell must have already been home for some time if he had exchanged more than one letter with Thompson and a 'train' of misconceptions had built up since his departure.

Branwell had come to the end of his career as a portrait painter. Despite William Morgan's patronage, he had failed to make any great impact. Though he had had a number of commissions, probably enough to just about pay for his lodgings, his keep and his professional expenses, he was not earning enough to live upon comfortably or to give him a secure future. As his friend Francis Leyland pointed out, it was scarcely to be expected that he should succeed in competition with the older, more experienced and well-established artists of the neighbourhood. The 1843 directory lists twenty painters for Bradford alone and any man wealthy enough to commission his portrait would also have been able to afford to travel to the better-known artists based in Halifax or Leeds.[62] The difficulty of earning a living in this field, even for someone endowed with considerable talents, had been forcibly illustrated the previous autumn by the sudden death of Branwell's tutor, William Robinson, at the early age of thirty-nine. Robinson's obituary starkly pointed out the contrast between his artistic and his financial success:

His eminent success, as a portrait painter, introduced him at one period of his life to the highest circles, and the exquisite specimens of his pencil, which adorn the walls of the Royal Palace and the residences of many of the principal nobility, bear testimony to his superior talents. His powers continued unimpaired to the last, and his latest productions show the same high state of finish and beauty. We are sorry to add that he has left a widow and six children totally unprovided for.[63]

If Robinson, a Royal Academician and pupil of Thomas Lawrence, with all his talent and all his contacts, could leave his family destitute, dependent on a charitable subscription for their survival, what hope had Branwell of success? Given the odds against him, his failure was predictable. Nor can his lack of commitment have helped. Given the choice, he would have far preferred to follow his literary bent, and his writing, which he kept up throughout his time in Bradford, must have been a constant distraction from seeking clients and executing commissions.

Most biographers of Branwell would have us believe that he spent his time in Bradford in wild dissipation and that he returned to Haworth a drunkard and an opium-eater, in debt and in disgrace.[64] That there were some elements of truth in this seems likely, but the degree to which Branwell so abased himself is very much open to question. In a letter to J. H. Thompson, written some months after he returned home, Branwell confessed he had incurred 'several Depts' of which his father and aunt had no knowledge.[65] These were clearly not debts due to his landlady, whose only concern after Branwell's departure was that he should return to 'finish' some of her pictures. This Branwell viewed in a poor light: 'I am astonished at Mrs Kirby – I have no pictures of hers to finish But I said that if I returned there I would varnish 3 for her and I do not understand people who look on a kindness as a duty'. Mrs Kirby's pictures remained unvarnished, though she was still sending messages about them through Thompson three months later.[66]

The debts, then, if not to Branwell's landlady and not the sort which could be mentioned to the elders of the Brontë household, may well have been incurred by drinking. However, it is worth bearing in mind the comments of one of Branwell's contemporaries, Anthony Trollope, who spent seven years in London working for the Post Office on an annual salary of ninety pounds rising to one hundred and forty. During the whole period, he was 'hopelessly in debt', apart from two brief intervals when he lived with his mother, and he was twice arrested for debt by sheriffs' officers. Looking back, from a respectable and comfortable old age, he asked himself whether his youth had been very wicked and whether there had been any reason to expect good from him.

When I reached London no mode of life was prepared for me, – no advice ever given to me. I went into lodgings, and then had to dispose of my time. I belonged to no club, and knew very few friends who would receive me into their houses. In such a condition of life a young man should no doubt go home after his work, and spend the long hours of the evening in reading good books and drinking tea ... It seems to me that in such circumstances the temptations of loose life will almost certainly prevail with a young man. Of course if the mind be strong enough, and the general stuff knitted together of sufficiently stern material, the temptations will not prevail. But such minds and such material are, I think, uncommon. The temptation at any rate prevailed with me.

Trollope concludes his account by pondering, 'I wonder how many young men fall utterly to pieces from being turned loose into London after the same fashion.'[67] One can see similarities with Branwell's first taste of freedom, albeit in the less glamorous surroundings of Bradford.

In Bradford Branwell was actively involved in a circle of artistic friends, many of them young and struggling like himself. Some of them were already known to him, like John Hunter Thompson, who had been a fellow pupil of William Robinson at Leeds and was now working as a professional painter from the premises of Mr Aglen, a carver and gilder.[68] Others were established artists in Bradford such as the well-known landscape painter, John Wilson Anderson, who had exhibited through the Northern Society for the Encouragement of the Fine Arts in Leeds, Richard Waller, the portrait painter, and William Geller, an engraver whose work was mainly done in London. Branwell also made the acquaintance of the Halifax sculptor, Joseph Bentley Leyland, a young man of dazzling talent who had taken both Leeds and London by storm in the last few years. Leyland was to become probably Branwell's closest friend, sharing his literary tastes as well as his artistic inclinations. Like Branwell, too, his spectacular early promise went unfulfilled and he died an early death, only three years after Branwell, but already on intimate terms with the debtor's prison.[69] Branwell was introduced as well to a number of local writers, some of whom enjoyed comparatively wide success. Among these were Robert Story, the poet of Gargrave in the Yorkshire Dales, who was widely published in the local press and already had at least two volumes of poems to his name, and John James, a local antiquarian who was later to publish a definitive history of Bradford.[70]

In the company of men such as these, Branwell was undoubtedly in his element. Intelligent, witty and mostly young, the circle met regularly at the George Hotel in Bradford, where drink as well as conversation flowed freely. Branwell, ever anxious to please and probably flattered by the attentions of established writers and artists, would not have held back in paying for the bowls of whisky punch which circulated all evening. Like many another headstrong young man launching out into the world on his own for the first time, he probably did drink too much with his newly found and congenial companions. However, whatever debts he had incurred were all paid off before the end of August – and that without recourse to his father and aunt.[71] Margaret Hartley, the niece of his landlady, Mrs Kirby, who lived with the family in Fountain Street while Branwell was a lodger there, recalled him quite vividly.

He was low in stature, about 5ft 3 inches high, and slight in build, though well proportioned. Very few people, except sitters, came to visit him; but I remember one, a Mr Thompson, a painter also. I remember his sister Charlotte coming and I remember her sisterly ways. She stayed a day, and I believe that was her only visit. They left the house together, and he saw her off by the Keighley coach. I am not aware that his other sisters or that his father, the Rev. Patrick Brontë ever came to Mr Kirby's. It was young Mr Brontë's practice to go home at each weekend, and I remember that while sometimes he took the coach for Keighley, he on other occasions walked to Haworth across the moors. He was a very steady young gentleman, his conduct was exemplary, and we liked him very much.[72]

Whatever excesses Branwell may or may not have got up to in Bradford, they did not impinge on those with whom he lodged. It seems inherently unlikely, too, that he can have had much opportunity for debauchery if, as Margaret Hartley says, he went home every weekend. Her evidence is supported by Leyland, who seems to be quoting Thompson, when he says that Branwell 'certainly was not a drunkard; and that, if he took anything at all, it was but occasionally, and then no more than the commonest custom would permit'.[73]

When Branwell gave up his studio in Bradford, he did not return home in disgrace or even deeply chastened by his experience. He had tried, but failed, to earn his living as an artist and though this could not be anything but a disappointment to his family's ambitions for him, Branwell was unperturbed. Though the years of financial outlay on his artistic training with Bradley and Robinson had turned out to be wasted, at least there had not been the additional, crippling expense of the Royal Academy or a European tour. Even more important, Branwell had not struggled on in the profession to a point beyond which it would be impossible to retreat. It was undoubtedly a wise decision to cut his losses after a trial period and return home to work out an alternative plan for his future.

Branwell's return to Haworth was followed, almost immediately, by that of Emily, and Patrick once more found himself with four adult and dependent children on his hands. Emily had gone back to Law Hill after the Christmas holidays but her resolution to endure began to falter as the school year stretched out endlessly before her. The winter months would inevitably curtail the amount of time she was able to spend outside, walking on her own or in the company of her pupils, and probably brought the usual colds and coughs, often combined with asthmatic attacks, which so frequently afflicted the Brontës at that time of year. To add to her troubles, she seems to have found herself unable to write. After the plethora of poems she had written in the autumn, there is only a single extant poem for the new year – and that was written in the holidays.[74] Between 12 January and 27 March 1839, she apparently wrote nothing, indicating a depression of mind that made writing impossible. This, in its turn, could only have added to her misery for if she had no poetry, she had no means of expressing her unhappiness and obtaining relief. Deprived of the time to indulge in Gondal fantasies by the rigidity and all-pervasive nature of boarding school life and deprived of the power to write by her homesickness and unhappiness, Emily broke down. In a repeat of her brief days as a schoolgirl at Roe Head, her health gave way and she was obliged to return home to Haworth. Though the exact date of her return is not known, it must have been some time in March or early April. Her six short months as a teacher at Law Hill were to be her first and last experiment in earning her own living.[75]

It must have been a matter of considerable concern to Patrick that within three months all three of his children who had ventured out into the world had given up their employment, two of them having succumbed to ill health. Nevertheless, he showed a quite remarkable leniency and did not push them into seeking new posts: rather the reverse. By the second week in March, Charlotte had two options before her. Henry Nussey had informed her of a school in his parish at Donnington in Suffolk which she could take over but, as she regretfully told him, she had not the necessary capital to make a success of it.[76] More realistically, she had the prospect of going as a private governess into the family of Thomas Brooke at Huddersfield, and though she felt it was time she should take up employment again, it was Patrick who urged her to stay at home a little longer.[77] The offer from Mrs Brooke never materialized and in the meantime it was Anne who, in her customary quiet, efficient way, set about making her contribution to the family coffers. At the beginning of March she found herself her first post as a governess with the Ingham family at Blake Hall, near Mirfield. She left home on 8 April and, at her own request, went alone by coach to Mirfield 'as she thought she could manage better and summon more courage if thrown entirely upon her own resources'.[78] If her picture of the young Agnes Grey also leaving home for the first time to be a governess is a true portrait of her own feelings at the time, she did not go unwillingly.

How delightful it would be to be a governess! To go out into the world; to enter upon a new life; to act for myself; to exercise my unused faculties; to try my unknown powers; to earn my own maintenance, and something to comfort and help my father, mother, and sister, besides exonerating them from the provision of my food and clothing; to show papa what his little Agnes could do; to convince mamma and Mary that I was not quite the helpless, thoughtless being they supposed.[79]

Charlotte, too, needed some convincing that her nineteen-year-old sister was capable of holding a post as governess.

Blake Hall was a splendid mansion, far more aristocratic than anything the Brontës had ever had contact with before. Three storeys high, it had an imposing eighteenth-century frontage.[80] Though only a few miles from Roe Head, it did not enjoy such an elevated position, lying in the Calder Valley just beyond Mirfield. A small wooded park separated it from the busy main road between Dewsbury and Huddersfield, giving it an air of rural seclusion. Anne may even have seen the house before when, as a pupil at Roe Head, she attended services at Mirfield Church, which lay only a quarter of a mile away on an elevation overlooking Blake Hall park.

The Inghams of Blake Hall were an old and wealthy family, well known in the Mirfield area. Joshua Ingham, a Justice of the Peace, was thirty-seven and had connections with the Nussey family, his second cousin, Mary, having married Ellen's brother John, the court physician. Mary Nussey was on close terms with her relations at Blake Hall and had stayed with them there. It was possibly through this connection that Anne first heard of the post, though the Inghams were also well known to the Woolers and the rest of the Dewsbury circle. Interestingly, Mrs Ingham was the daughter of Ellis Cunliffe Lister, the reforming Member of Parliament for the relatively new borough of Bradford, and her sister Harriet was the 'clever but refractory' Miss Lister who had so plagued Charlotte at Roe Head.[81]

The family at Blake Hall were all young. Mrs Ingham, 'an amiable conventional woman', was ten years younger than her husband and had already produced five of her eventual thirteen children. The eldest, a six-year-old boy, Cunliffe, and his five-year-old sister, Mary, were the only ones in Anne's care: the younger girls, Martha, Emily and Harriet, were still in the nursery and were not her responsibility.[82] Within a few days of her arrival, Anne had correctly assessed the situation and its problems in a letter home to her sisters. Charlotte, as usual finding it difficult to see her youngest sister in any other terms than as a 'poor child', was 'astonished to see what a sensible, clever letter she writes'. Amazingly and unjustifiably, too, she suggested that Anne's intense reserve might be misinterpreted, adding 'it is only the talking part, that I fear – but I do seriously apprehend that Mrs Ingham will \sometimes/ conclude that she has a natural impediment of speech'. Charlotte relayed Anne's news back to Ellen.

We have had one letter from her since she went – she expresses herself very well satisfied – and says that Mrs Ingham is extremely kind ... both her pupils are desperate little dunces – neither of them can read and sometimes they even profess a profound ignorance of their Alphabet – the worst of it is the little monkies are excessively indulged and she is not empowered to inflict any punishment she is requested when they misbehave themselves to inform their Mamma – which she says is utterly out of the question as in that case she might be making complaints from morning till night – 'So she alternately scolds, coaxes and threatens – sticks always to her first word and gets on as well as she can'.[83]

The problem of discipline was one which was to haunt Anne at Blake Hall. The monstrous Bloomfield children she depicted in *Agnes Grey* may well have been drawn from life. If so, the little Inghams were spoilt, wild and virtually uncontrollable, tormenting their governess by refusing to do as she bid them, defying her authority and continually running to their parents to complain if she made any attempt to discipline them. How far the picture was an accurate portrayal of Anne's experiences and how much a fictional improvement is difficult to assess, but there are strong parallels. The three Bloomfield children were roughly the same age as the Inghams and it is possible that the next child, Martha, was also assigned to Anne's care during her time there. The incident in the book when the three children, having raided and spat in Agnes' workbag and thrown her writing desk out of the window, then go on the rampage in the snow without their hats, coats or gloves, incurring Mr Bloomfield's fury, is strongly reminiscent of a genuine episode told by a descendant of the Inghams. A parcel of scarlet native cloaks arrived at Blake Hall from South America. The young Inghams immediately seized upon them and ran out into the park screaming that they were devils and would not return to their lessons. Anne, reduced to tears, was obliged to go to Mrs Ingham and confess that the children were beyond her control. On another occasion, Mrs Ingham walked into the schoolroom to find that Anne had tied the two children to a table leg in a desperate attempt to keep them at their lessons.[84]

While Anne settled in to her difficult post at Blake Hall, Charlotte jokingly wrote to Ellen on 15 April:

I am as yet 'wanting a situation – like a housemaid out of place' – by the bye Ellen I've lately discovered that I've quite a talent for cleaning – sweeping up hearths dusting rooms – making beds &c. so if everything else fails – I can turn my hand to that – if anybody will give me good wages, for little labour. I won't be a cook – I hate cooking – I won't be a nursery-maid – nor a lady's maid far less a lady's companion – or a mantua-maker – or a straw-bonnet maker or a taker-in of plain-work – I will be nothing but a house-maid.[85]

Anne's departure for Blake Hall, however, had goaded Charlotte into making an effort to find a place for herself as a governess. It was hardly right that only the youngest of the Brontë children should be out earning her own living. Within a month she had found herself an acceptable place only ten or twelve miles away from Haworth as the crow flies, between Colne and Skipton. The Sidgwick family, who lived during the winter months at the gatehouse of Skipton Castle and in the summer at Stonegappe at Lothersdale, needed a temporary governess.[86]

The post had every advantage to offer Charlotte. It was not far from home, it was only temporary and, most important of all, she knew the wife of her new employer by report, if not personally. Mrs Sidgwick was the daughter of John Greenwood, a wealthy manufacturer who lived at the Knowle, one of the grandest houses in Keighley. She had married John Benson Sidgwick in 1827, the ceremony being performed by Patrick's old friend, Hammond Roberson.[87] Her sister, Anne, was married to another old friend of Patrick's, the Reverend Theodore Dury, rector of Keighley. It was probably through Theodore Dury and his curate, John Collins, whose wife was on friendly, visiting terms with the Brontës, that Charlotte first heard of the post.[88]

Some time in May, Charlotte set off for Lothersdale, where the Sidgwicks were in residence, to her first posting as a private governess. Stonegappe is a huge imposing house, three storeys high with a central, square-built bay running the whole height of its frontage. The house is set high on a hillside, surrounded by its own woodland and looking out over a panorama of lower hills and valleys towards the wide flood valley of the River Aire in the distance. The countryside is marked by scattered farmhouses set in lush green pasture, with wooded riverbanks and moorland crowning the higher, uncultivated reaches of the hills. Charlotte herself described the country, the house and the grounds as 'divine'.[89] About a mile away, down a steep and winding hill, was the pretty new church and, beyond that, in the valley bottom, the village of Lothersdale. Just across the fields was Lower Leys Farm where the Reverend Edward Nicholls Carter lived with his wife, the former Susan Wooler, and their three children, while a parsonage house was built for them. The church day and Sunday schools were also temporarily housed in the gardener's cottage at Stonegappe.[90]

In such surroundings, one would have thought Charlotte could have been happy. However, from the very start she did not get on with Mrs Sidgwick. The fact that Charlotte was already known to her did not mean that Mrs Sidgwick treated her with the familiarity and respect Charlotte evidently anticipated. Always swift to see a slight, whether intended or not, Charlotte remarked bitterly to Emily, 'I said in my last letter that Mrs Sidgwick did not know me. I now begin to find that she does not intend to know me.'[91]

Like Anne at Blake Hall, Charlotte found her two charges, the youngest children, Mathilda, aged seven, and John Benson, aged four, beyond her control.

The children are constantly with me, and more riotous, perverse, unmanageable cubs never grew. As for correcting them, I soon quickly found that was entirely out of the question: they are to do as they like. A complaint to Mrs Sidgwick brings only black looks upon oneself, and unjust, partial excuses to screen the children.

Like Anne, too, Charlotte was expected not simply to teach her charges but, to her infinite disgust, 'to wipe the children's smutty noses or tie their shoes or fetch their pinafores or set them a chair'. What Charlotte found most galling of all, however, was the amount of sewing she had to do, a menial task which she felt beneath her. Mrs Sidgwick, she told Emily,

cares nothing in the world about me except to contrive how the greatest possible quantity of labour may be squeezed out of me, and to that end she overwhelms me with oceans of needlework, yards of cambric to hem, muslin nightcaps to make, and, above all things, dolls to dress.

Any illusions about the difference between being a schoolteacher and a private governess rapidly evaporated.

I see now more clearly than I have ever done before that a private governess has no existence, is not considered as a living and rational being except as connected with the wearisome duties she has to fulfil. While she is teaching the children, working for them, amusing them, it is all right. If she steals a moment for herself she is a nuisance.

It was a measure of her discontent that Charlotte discovered she was 'getting quite to have a regard for the Carter family. At home I should not care for them, but here they are friends'. Aware that it would appear at home that nothing suited her and that she was always complaining, she warned Emily not to show her letter to either their father or aunt, only to Branwell, who was likely to be more sympathetic.[92]

In June, the Sidgwicks left Stonegappe to stay at Swarcliffe, a summer residence belonging to Mrs Sidgwick's father, John Greenwood, at Birstwith, three miles from Ripon. Swarcliffe was a large, stately and rambling house on the hill top overlooking the pretty hamlet of Birstwith, which is built round a bridge over the River Nidd. Like Stonegappe, it enjoyed long views over lovely rolling countryside, the flat river valley below, heavily wooded hills and rich agricultural land all around. The move did not lessen Charlotte's trials, though they were now of a different kind. On 30 June she wrote to Ellen Nussey – using a pencil because she could not get ink without going among the company in the drawing-room. She was tempted to pour out 'the long history of a Private Governesses' trials and crosses in her first Situation' to her old friend.

imagine the miseries of a reserved wretch like me – thrown at once into the midst of a large Family – proud as peacocks & wealthy as Jews – at a time when they were particularly gay – when the house was filled with Company – all Strangers people whose faces I had never seen before – in this state of things having the charge given me of a set of pampered spoilt & turbulent children – whom I was expected constantly to amuse as well as instruct – I soon found that the constant demand on my stock of Animal spirits reduced them to the lowest state of exhaustion – at times I felt and I suppose seemed depressed – to my astonishment I was taken to task on the subject by Mrs Sidgwick with a sterness of manner & a harshness of language scarcely credible – like a fool I cried most bitterly – I could not help it – my spirits quite failed me at first. I thought I had done my best – strained every nerve to please her – and to be treated in that way merely because I was shy – and sometimes melancholy was too bad. at first I was for giving all up and going home – But after a little reflection I determined – to summon what energy I had and to weather the Storm –[93]

Charlotte may have told rather less than the truth when she described her sole failings as being 'shy and sometimes melancholy'. According to Mrs Sidgwick, 'Miss Brontë often went to bed all day and left her to look after the children at a time when she was much occupied with her invalid father, Mr Greenwood, at Swarcliffe'. As Mrs Sidgwick was also into the last few weeks of her fifth pregnancy, she had every right to remonstrate with her recalcitrant governess.[94]

The Sidgwicks' account of their governess differs little from Charlotte's version of events in fact, but much in interpretation. 'Mrs Sidgwick told me that Miss Brontë had a most unhappy difficult, temper, and that she took offence where no offence was meant.' 'My cousin [John] Benson Sidgwick, now vicar of Ashby Parva, certainly on one occasion threw a Bible at Miss Brontë! and all that another cousin can recollect of her is that if she was invited to walk to church with them, she thought she was being ordered about like a slave; if she was not invited, she imagined she was excluded from the family circle.'[95] Habits of subservience did not come naturally to Charlotte and one can well imagine that her resentment at being treated as a servant would be readily apparent to her employers.

Though Charlotte was clearly an awkward person to deal with, she had much to put up with in her role as governess. She later told Mrs Gaskell of an incident that had occurred in the stableyard where her pupil John had been lured by his older brother, against the express prohibition of his parents. Egged on by his brother, the boy began throwing stones at Charlotte as she tried to make him leave. One of them hit her so hard on the temple that the boys were frightened into obedience. The next day, when Mrs Sidgwick asked her what had caused the mark on her forehead, Charlotte simply said, 'An accident, ma'am.' The boys, relieved that she had not 'told tales', proved more tractable thereafter and Charlotte, as she herself admitted, began to find them 'a little more manageable' than at first.[96] The most infamous incident, however, again reported by Mrs Gaskell, happened one day at dinner when little John Sidgwick put his hand into Charlotte's and said, 'I love 'ou, Miss Brontë.' 'Whereupon, the mother exclaimed, before all the children, "Love the *governess*, my dear!"'[97]

Such public humiliations from Mrs Sidgwick burnt deep into Charlotte's soul. Her attitude to Mr Sidgwick was much less critical. 'One of the pleasantest afternoons' she spent at Stonegappe was when Mr Sidgwick went out walking with his children 'and I had orders to follow a little behind'. For once, apparently, this did not pique her pride, for the snobbish element in her character took pleasure in the sight of Mr Sidgwick: 'As he strolled on through his fields with his magnificent Newfoundland dog at his side, he looked very like what a frank, wealthy, Conservative gentleman ought to be'.[98]

Charlotte's sufferings with the Sidgwicks were fortunately of short duration. The engagement was only to last until the permanent governess returned and so, by the middle of July, she was back at home, probably to the relief of all concerned. No doubt in the mood for celebration, it was appropriate that she was just in time for a grand concert in Haworth Church. On Tuesday, 23 July 1839, John Frobisher, the leading light in Halifax musical circles, conducted a selection of sacred music: the principal singers were Haworth's own Thomas Parker and Miss Milnes, a well-known Yorkshire performer.[99] The 'oratorio' met with universal approval, though it did not even merit a mention from Charlotte. She had a new scheme to occupy her mind. On her return, she had been 'almost driven ... "clean daft"' by a proposal from Ellen Nussey that the two of them should go off to Cleethorpes for a holiday. Ellen suggested three weeks, but Charlotte found it impossible to offer more than a week. The plan came to nothing, to Charlotte's intense frustration, because Patrick and Aunt Branwell had decided that the whole family should take their first ever holiday together. This was probably a response to all the ill health which had plagued the younger members of the family while away from home and an attempt to give a treat to Anne, who was on her annual leave from Blake Hall. A holiday was not only desirable, from every point of view, but was now a practical possibility as Patrick had a new curate coming to assist him in a few weeks' time. Aunt Branwell insisted that Charlotte should give up the Cleethorpes scheme, but suggested that Ellen should accompany them to Liverpool.[100]

By 4 August, there was still no sign of the Brontës going to Liverpool. 'The Liverpool journey is yet a matter of talk a sort of castle in the air –', Charlotte told Ellen,

but between you and I, I fancy it is very doubtful whether it will ever assume a more solid shape – Aunt – like many other elderly people – likes to <u>talk</u> of such things but when it comes to putting them into actual practice she rather falls off.[101]

In the end, Branwell got tired of waiting for the elders to decide and took himself off to Liverpool in the more congenial company of his old boyhood friend, Michael Merrall. There, at his father's request, he went to St Jude's Church to take notes on a sermon given by the renowned Evangelical preacher, the Reverend H. McNeile. In the first recorded instance of Branwell's taking opium, Leyland reported that Branwell resorted to the drug to alleviate an attack of tic, a severe form of neuralgia and muscular spasm in the face. Later, while wandering through the town, he saw a copy of one of his favourite oratorios, Handel's *Samson*, displayed in a shop window and begged the wealthy Michael Merrall to buy it and the sheet music for several other oratorios and masses.[102] Doubtless, he also took the boat trips from Liverpool across the Irish Sea to the Isle of Man and along the north coast of Wales, which were one of the chief reasons for visiting the country's second largest and busiest port.

Charlotte, in the meantime, reverted with some relief to her original plan. Instead of Cleethorpes, however, on the recommendation of Mary Taylor, they chose to go to Bridlington on the east Yorkshire coast. Charlotte did not care where they went, so long as she could get her first glimpse of the sea: 'the idea of seeing the Sea – of being near it – watching its changes by sunrise, Sunset – moonlight – & noonday – in calm – perhaps in storm – fills & satisfies my mind', she told Ellen, 'I shall be discontented at nothing –.'[103]

While the plans were yet evolving, Charlotte had an adventure which, as she laughingly told Ellen Nussey, more nearly resembled one of the pert and pretty Martha Taylor's than her own. The Reverend William Hodgson, Patrick's first curate, had come over from Colne to spend the day at the parsonage and he brought with him his own curate, a young Irish clergyman, fresh from Dublin University, called Mr Pryce. He proved to be witty, lively, ardent and clever too; he quickly made himself at home and evidently found the company congenial.

at home you know Ellen I talk with ease and am never shy – never weighed down & oppressed by that miserable mauvaise honte which torments & constrains me elsewhere – so I conversed with this Irishman & laughed at his jests – & though I saw faults in his character excused them because of the amusement his originality afforded.[104]

A few days later, Charlotte received a letter addressed in a mysterious hand which turned out to be a proposal of marriage from young Mr Pryce: 'well thought I – I've heard of love at first sight but this beats all. I leave you to guess what my answer would be –', she told Ellen, 'convinced that you will not do me the injustice of guessing wrong.' It was perhaps fortunate that Charlotte's interest had not been awakened, for less than six months later poor Mr Pryce was dead. 'Though I knew so little of him, and of course could not be deeply or permanently interested in < his > what concerned him – I confess when I suddenly heard he was dead, I felt both shocked and saddened. it was no shame to feel so, was it?'[105]

Charlotte's second adventure, her holiday with Ellen, was beset with setbacks and difficulties. She could not get herself over to Leeds in time for the day Ellen first proposed and then, when another had been fixed and all seemed settled, she discovered that the only gig let out on hire in Haworth was in Harrogate and she had no means of getting to Birstall for the next two weeks. Her father, quite rightly, objected to her travelling by coach and walking to Birstall and her aunt 'exclaims against the weather and the roads and the four winds of Heaven'. Now that there was a real difficulty in getting there, the elders were more decidedly opposed to a trip of which they had never really approved.

Papa indeed would willingly indulge me, but this very kindness of his makes me doubt whether I ought to draw upon it – & though I could battle out Aunt's discontent I yield to Papa's indulgence – He does not say so but I know he would rather I stayed at home[106]

In the end, and to the surprise of everyone concerned, Ellen acted with uncharacteristic determination and carried the day. She borrowed her bro-

ther's carriage, drove over to Haworth and arrived on the parsonage doorstep, ready to carry Charlotte off. Branwell praised Ellen's courage: 'it was a
brave defeat', he declared, 'that the doubters were fairly taken aback'.[107]

The journey to Bridlington did not pass without incident, justifying
her father's and aunt's concern about two unaccompanied young ladies
travelling by public transport. The first part of the journey, from Leeds to
York, was by railway – Charlotte's first experience of this new mode of
transport – but the rest of the way had to be travelled by stagecoach.
Unfortunately the coach was full, and though Ellen and Charlotte were sent
on in an open fly, Mr and Mrs Hudson, friends of Henry Nussey who were
waiting to meet them, missed them. They therefore left orders at the hotel
where the fly was due to arrive that the two young ladies should be sent on
in a post chaise to their own home, Easton Farm, which lay two or three
miles from Bridlington. To their intense frustration, Charlotte and Ellen
found themselves being driven away from the seaside, the principal object
of their holiday, to the Hudsons' farm where they were 'detained' for a whole
month. Though hospitably entertained and being held as 'captive guests'
from the best possible motives, their chagrin was immense. Two days after
their arrival, they walked to the coast and there Charlotte had her first
glimpse of the sea. The emotion of this longed-for moment overpowered
her, rendering her speechless and reducing her to tears.[108] Weeks later, she
still fed on the vision:

Have you forgot the Sea by this time Ellen? is it grown dim in your mind? or you
can still see it dark blue and green and foam-white and hear it – roaring roughly
when the wind is high or rushing softly when it is calm?[109]

Even when writing to Henry Nussey, to congratulate him on his having at
last secured a bride, she could not resist dwelling on the thought of the sea.

I will not tell you what I thought of the Sea – because I should fall into my besetting
sin of enthusiasm. I may however say that its glorious changes – its ebb and flow –
the sound of its restless waves – formed a subject for Contemplation that never
wearied either the eye the ear or the mind.[110]

The month at Easton Farm passed pleasantly enough, with long walks
through Harlequin Wood, to Boynton and the sea. Charlotte even whiled
away part of the time by painting a watercolour of the Hudsons sitting in
front of Easton Farm.[111]

This was all very well, but it was not what Charlotte and Ellen had
intended; they were anxious to be independent and they wanted to be by
the sea. Eventually they managed to persuade their over-zealous hosts to
let them go into lodgings for a week in Bridlington. The rooms they chose
were in Garrison Street at Bridlington Quay, 'a neat handsome little town'
about a mile from Bridlington itself. The Quay enjoyed direct access to the

harbour, its northernmost pier commanded beautiful views of Flamborough Head and its mineral springs were highly regarded for their health-giving properties. It was the ideal place 'for persons who have a taste for the peaceful and sequestered scenes of life'.[112] They soon learnt the hard way how well they had been looked after at Easton Farm. Despite daily visits from the Hudsons, bearing gifts from their dairy, the bill for only a week's lodgings used up their entire stock of funds. Nevertheless, this part of the holiday lived up to all their expectations. The sea was on hand for endless contemplation and Charlotte also took great pleasure in watching the seaside visitors. The evening ritual of the promenade greatly amused her, as so many people crowded on to the little pier that they had to march round in regular file in order to be able to walk at all. Typically, too, when they returned to their lodgings one evening and heard a Ranters' meeting in full flow in the chapel opposite, Charlotte was 'wild' to go in and see what they were about. She was only restrained by the reflection, probably uttered by the more prudent Ellen, that it was wrong to criticize or ridicule people acting on a religious impulse.[113]

Charlotte returned to Haworth in mid-October, invigorated by her holiday and 'very fat', her usual description for being in good health.[114] The rest of the autumn she passed quietly enough, like Emily, deeply absorbed in her writing. Emily had written prolifically throughout the year, developing particularly her interest in the doomed Byronic characters which prefigured the creation of Heathcliff.

> I am the only being whose doom
> No tongue would ask no < heart > eye would mourn
> I've never caused a thought of gloom
> A smile of joy since I was born
>
> In secret pleasure – secret tears
> This changeful life has slipped away
> As friendless after 18 years
> As lone as on my natal day[115]

Another vivid poem describes how the cheerful welcome a shepherd family gives to a stranger fades into gloom, their 'hospitable joy' frozen by his cold manner and his 'basilisk' gaze.

> … there was something in his face
> Some nameless thing they could not trace
> And something in his voices tone
> Which turned their blood as chill as stone
> The ringlets of his long black hair
> Fell o'er a cheek most ghastly fair
> Youthful he seemed – but worn as they
> Who spend too soon their youthful day

When his glance drooped 'twas hard to quell
Unbidden feelings sudden swell
And pity scarce her tears could hide
So sweet that brow with all its pride
But when upraised his eye would dart
An icey shudder through the heart
Compassion changed to horror then
And fear to meet that gaze again[116]

One other poem deserves special notice, not least because it is frequently cited as an expression of Emily's attitude towards her brother, 'proving' that she was more tolerant of his faults than her sisters.

Do I despise the timid deer
Because his limbs are fleet with fear?
Or would I mock the wolf's death-howl
Because his form is gaunt and foul?
Or hear with joy the leverets cry
Because it cannot bravely die?

No – then above his memory
Let pity's < eye > heart as tender be
Say 'Earth, lie lightly on that breast,
'And Kind Heaven, grant that spirit rest!'[117]

Quite apart from the fact that it precedes Branwell's downfall by some six years, the poem has an obvious Gondal context and one should never make the mistake of assuming that sentiments expressed by Gondal characters are inevitably those of the author.

While Emily and Charlotte buried themselves in their imaginary worlds, Patrick was having to face up to unpleasant realities. In July the Simeon trustees had announced the appointment of the Reverend Dr Scoresby, an eminent scientist and Arctic explorer from Whitby in North Yorkshire, as the new vicar of Bradford.[118] Dr Scoresby did not take up residence in Bradford until October, but his arrival heralded a new era of change and confrontation in the parish. His first vestry meeting to lay a church rate set the pattern for the future. The Dissenters had brought in their champion, John Winterbotham, who denounced the new vicar for oppressing the poor of Haworth and abused the practice as 'the old dirty path of the Catholic Church'.[119] The Dissenters triumphantly forced the church rate to be voted down and Scoresby had his first taste of the problems Patrick had faced for so long in Haworth.

Scoresby was a different man from Patrick or his own predecessor, Henry Heap, however, a stickler for his rights who would not go down without a fight. The bishop's scheme for Haworth to be separated from the parish of Bradford was now effectively scotched and, within six months of taking office, Scoresby had drawn up a new plan to reorganize his parish into smaller districts, based on a population of about 3,000 each, with plans to build three new churches immediately and six more in future. This was all very well for the vicar of Bradford, who reserved the right of marriage to himself alone and ensured that his own income remained adequate, but it met with immense opposition. Clergymen such as William Morgan, who by the beginning of January 1840 was not even on speaking terms with his vicar, found that their cures would be arbitrarily divided with a subsequent loss of income to themselves.[120] A similar prospect faced Patrick, whose own chapelry, one of the largest in the whole parish, now extended to over 6,000 souls. The only bright spot in an otherwise gloomy prospect was that Patrick had at last secured the services of a curate, William Weightman, who promised to fulfil all Patrick's hopes for his assistant.[121]

The year 1839 drew to a rather depressing close. At the end of November, the Brontës' faithful old servant, Tabby Aykroyd, had at last been obliged to leave them. The leg she had broken three years before had become so badly ulcerated that she was too lame to work. She had bought a little house with her sister, Susanna Wood, and retired there very comfortably on her savings.[122] Apart from a servant girl, Martha Brown, the eleven-year-old daughter of the Haworth sexton who ran errands for them, the whole work of the household devolved on Charlotte and Emily.

I manage the ironing and keep the rooms clean – Emily does the baking and attends to the Kitchen – We are such odd animals that we prefer this mode of contrivance to having a new face among us. Besides we do not despair of Tabby's return and she shall not be supplanted by a stranger in her absence.

I excited Aunt's wrath very much by burning the clothes the first time I attempted to iron but I do better now. Human feelings are queer things – I < would prefer > am much happier black-leading the stoves – making the beds and sweeping the floors at home, than I should be living like a fine lady anywhere else.[123]

Assistance arrived from an unexpected quarter. Anne returned home from Blake Hall for her Christmas holidays only to report that she had been dismissed. Despite having done her best to instil some order and learning into her charges, the Inghams had found no visible improvement in them and held Anne responsible.[124] Christmas 1839 therefore saw the whole Brontë family reunited in Haworth, all four children having failed to hold a job and all four now unemployed.

Chapter Twelve

PATRICK BOANERGES

TUITION. – WANTED, in a small Town in the Neighbourhood of the Lakes, A PRIVATE TUTOR, competent to instruct Two Boys, Ten & Eleven Years old, in a general Course of Education, including the Classics, with the strictest attention to Grammar. Apply to MR STEPHEN SOULBY, Bookseller, Ulverston. Dec 20, 1839.[1]

This advertisement must have leapt off the front page of the *Leeds Intelligencer* when Branwell picked up the newspaper on 21 December. Here, surely, was the ideal job for him, with its emphasis on the classics and its location in that haven of poets and writers, the Lake District. Though he had had no luck in finding a place since his return from Bradford, he had embarked on a reading scheme with his father the previous summer in anticipation of just such an appointment. Patrick had drawn up a plan of action on the fly leaves of his little concordance to the Holy Scriptures.

In June 1839 – I agreed with Branwell, that, under Providence, we should thoroughly read together, the following classics, in the following order only –

1st the first 6 Books of the Aeneid – and the four Gospels – in Greek.
& 2ndly the first 3 < Books > or 6 – Books of Homer's Iliad –
and some of the first Odes of Horace, and the Art of Poetry – besides – translating some English into Latin – The progress of the reading, is to be reguraly set down in this, and the following pages. B.[2]

This was not, as one might suspect, an attempt to brush up Branwell's classical education, for Branwell had never abandoned his Latin and Greek, which had remained a consuming passion. A year earlier, for instance, he had been translating Horace's *Odes* simply for pleasure.[3] It was, however, an attempt to study the classics in a systematic way and its benefit was apparent when Branwell wrote for and immediately obtained the post.

His sisters were flung into a frenzy of activity, shirt-making and collar-stitching ready for his departure on 31 December. Charlotte, having experienced the difficulties of private tutoring at first hand, expressed her own reservations about Branwell's suitability for the post to Ellen.

How he will like, or settle remains yet to be seen, at present he is full of Hope and resolution.
I who know his variable nature, and his strong turn for active life, dare not be too sanguine.[4]

Branwell had already paid his last – and only – visit of that year to the Three Graces Lodge on 16 December 1839.[5] All that remained was for him to say goodbye to his family and set off on the coach from Keighley to Kendal, where, as he later told his friend John Brown, he spent the last night of the old year in a riotous drinking session.

I took a half years farewell of old friend whisky at Kendal on the night after I left – there was a party of gentlemen at the Royal Hotel, and I joined them, we ordered in Supper and whisky-toddy as 'hot as hell!'. They thought I was a P[h]ysician! and put me into the chair – I gave some stiffish toasts – [lacuna] sort, they gave c[un]t & pill[oc]k &c washing [it] down at the same time till the room spun round and the candles danced in our eyes. One of the guests was a respectable old Gentleman with powdered head, rosy cheeks, fat paunch, and ringed fingers – I gave 'may the front door of women ever be open, & the porter Roger ever at his post' after which he brayed off with a speech and in two minutes, in the middle of a grand sentence he stopped, wiped his head, looked wildly round, stammered, coughed, stopped again and called for his slippers. The waiter helped him to bed. Next a tall Irish squire and a native of the land of Israel began to quarrel about their countries and in the warmth of argument, discharged their glasses each at his neighbours throat instead of his own. I recommended purging and bleeding, but they administered each other a real 'Jem Warder', so I flung my tumbler on the floor and swore I'd join 'Old Ireland!' A regular rumpus ensued – but we were tamed at last. I found myself in bed next morning with a bottle of porter, a glass, and a corkscrew beside me. Since then I have not tasted anything stronger than milk-and-water, nor, I hope, shall, till I return at Midsummer; when we shall see about it.[6]

No doubt in bragging about his exploits, the twenty-year-old Branwell exaggerated them a little to suit the older and more worldly John Brown. Nevertheless, it is instructive to see that, despite his relatively sheltered parsonage upbringing, Branwell could indulge in sexual innuendo and the occasional binge just like any other young man of his age.

Branwell probably exaggerated the amount he had drunk as he is unlikely to have wished to travel the last tortuous twenty miles of the mountainous southern Lakeland road between Kendal and Ulverston in a stagecoach with a hangover. At the end of that journey he had still a further ten miles to travel before he came face to face with his new employer in Broughton-in-Furness, a small market town on the River Duddon estuary.

His new employer, Robert Postlethwaite, was about fifty years old, 'a retired County magistrate, a large landowner, and of a right hearty and generous disposition'. Though not of an old-established county family, he was the second largest landowner in the area. His father, a successful merchant who had risen to the office of deputy lieutenant of Cumberland, had built Broughton House in the centre of the town in 1780 and his son continued to live there. From being shipbuilders and timber merchants the family had progressed to partnership in the banking firm of Petty and Postlethwaite in Ulverston and they retained substantial business interests in the town. Robert Postlethwaite's wife, Agnes, was 'a quiet, silent, and amiable woman' and her two sons, his charges, John and William, 'two fine, spirited lads'.[7]

Broughton today is still recognizably the Broughton of Branwell's day. Hidden just below the brow of High Duddon and barely visible from any approach, it is a neat and compact little town which has grown up round the three main roads which meet there. Most of the houses date from the seventeenth and eighteenth centuries when the town was a prosperous centre of the hand loom weaving trade.[8] Virtually all are built in distinctive Lakeland blue-grey stone, though some have been colour-washed and the surrounds of their square sash windows picked out in contrasting colours. Most are only two storeys high and built in terraces straight on to the narrow streets. Round the incongruously large market square, with its obelisk to commemorate the golden jubilee of George III, the cottages are three storeys high but only a single room in width. Above the market square and across a protective belt of parkland is Broughton Tower, a fourteenth-century pele tower which then belonged to the Sawrey family who were lords of the manor.

The main part of the town lies below the market square, down the gentle incline of Griffin Street. At the bottom of the street, on a corner facing the Old King's Head, a splendid seventeenth-century inn, lies the solid and impressive mass of Broughton House. Having only a narrow strip of garden to separate it from the road and being hemmed in by cottages on all sides, the house stands out only because of its exceptional size. Turning the corner, the road winds up a steep hill, past cottages and farmhouses, before opening out into fields. Close to the brow of the hill and virtually the last house in the village is High Syke House, a long low farmhouse with small, cramped rooms, built in 1753. This was where Branwell took lodgings with the family of Edward Fish. His landlord was one of the two town surgeons and Branwell described him as being 'two days out of every seven ... as drunk as a lord'. His wife, Ann Fish, 'is a bustling, chattering, kind-hearted soul' and he had a decidedly pretty eighteen-year-old daughter, Margaret, of whom Branwell could only say 'oh! death and damnation'. There were two younger children also, whom Branwell did not mention, the twelve-year-old John Hardy Fish and his nine-year-old sister, Harriet.[9]

From the windows of High Syke House Branwell could look down across the fields below to the sprawling church of St Mary Magdalene, which stood isolated, a little way off from the town, in the valley bottom. Beyond the church, the valley opens out into the Duddon estuary, giving distant glimpses of the sea. It was this view of the church, looking towards the sea, that Branwell drew in an idle moment while at Broughton.[10]

For Branwell, the chief attraction of Broughton-in-Furness was not the town itself but its location. Perhaps a hundred yards above his lodgings was the brow of High Duddon, which gave him spectacular views across the flat sands of the estuary and the pretty River Duddon, rising to the magnificent, louring mass of Black Combe beyond. William Wordsworth had celebrated both the river and the mountain in his verse.[11] From High Duddon, too, Branwell could look across the fells right into the heart of the Lake District where the soon-to-be Poet Laureate still lived at Rydal Mount. Though physically only on its fringes, spiritually Branwell could feel himself to be in the heart of the Lake Poets' country.

With such incentives to do well, Branwell quickly settled down at Brough-ton-in-Furness, determined to make a good impression on his employers. On 13 March 1840 he wrote to his friend John Brown, the sexton of Haworth and Master of the Three Graces Lodge, whom he addressed as 'Old Knave of Trumps'. Anxious not to appear too conventional and hardworking, Branwell deliberately 'spun him a yarn'. There was more to him than met the eye: like Northangerland, Branwell declared that he cloaked his evil designs under a semblance of piety and civility.

If you saw me now, you would not know me, and you would laugh to hear the character the people give me. Oh, the falsehood and hypocrisy of this world! ... Well, what am I? That is, what do they think I am? A most calm, sedate, sober, abstemious, patient, mild-hearted, virtuous, gentlemanly philospher, – the picture of good works, and the treasure house of righteous thoughts – Cards are shuffled under the table-cloth, glasses are thrust into the cupboard, if I enter the room. I take neither spirits, wine nor malt liquors, I dress in black and smile like a saint or martyr. Everybody says 'what a good young Gentleman is Mr Postlethwaite's tutor!'

... I am getting as fat as Prince William at Springhead and as godly as his friend, Parson Winterbotham – my hand shakes no longer. I ride to the banker's at Ulverston with Mr Postlethwaites and sit drinking tea and talking scandal with old ladies – as to the young ones! – I have one sitting by me just now – fair-faced, blue eyes, dark haired sweet eighteen – she little thinks the devil is so near her![12]

As if to reiterate the difference between the perfection of character he had assumed at Broughton and his supposedly real, macho self, he proceeded to level a stream of schoolboy obscenities at his 'friends' in Haworth.

I was delighted to see your note old squire but I do not understand one sentence – you will perhaps know what I mean – you say something about having got a cock & hens – I know you have got a cock & jolly good one too by < God > Jupiter. How are all about you, I long to hear and see them again. How is the 'Devil's Thumb', whom men call Enoch Thomas, and the 'Devil in Mourning' whom they call Wm Hartley how are [lacuna] and Billy Brown and the Doctor and him who will be used as the tongs of Hell – him whose eyes Satan looks out of, as from windows – I mean [lacuna] esquire? How are little [lacuna] 'Longshanks', [lacuna], and the rest of them? Are they married, buried, devilled and damned? When I come I'll give them a good squeeze of the hand; till then I am too godly for them to think of. And that bow-legged fellow who was always asking me – does your p[ric]k stand? – how is his going on or has he lost it altogether? Beelzebub means to make a walking stick of yours. Keep to thy teetotalism, old squire, till I return; that will mend that old body of yours, till I come back, when we will have a puff & a stiffener.[13]

He signed this letter, 'The Philosopher'. In stark contrast to his insouciant man-of-the-world image which he was so anxious to impress upon John Brown, Branwell added that he meant to continue in the good opinion of the Postlethwaites and their circle at Broughton and, even more tellingly, 'Of course you won't show this letter; and, for Heaven's sake, blot out all the lines scored with red ink.'[14]

While Branwell adapted his character to suit his circumstances, with evident success at Broughton, his sisters had put the failures of the last year behind them and were enjoying a holiday. After the usual series of mishaps and delays, caused in part by Aunt Branwell's sudden determination not to have any visitors during the winter months and then relenting, Ellen Nussey came over to join them for three weeks in February. Though Charlotte regretted Branwell's absence because he had always enlivened Ellen's visits, his place was more than adequately filled by William Weightman, Patrick's new curate.[15]

Weightman has become something of a legend in the Brontë story, a ray of light in the doom and gloom which is supposed to have enveloped the tragic family. It has become an accepted part of the Brontë canon that Anne was in love with him and that his early death was a tragedy from which she never recovered.[16] There is no evidence at all to prove that this was the case and the few 'facts' which are usually cited in its support are, at the very least, open to another interpretation.

William Weightman was twenty-six years old and came from the beautiful old Westmorland market town of Appleby.[17] From Appleby Grammar School he had gone to the newly founded University of Durham where, according to Patrick Brontë, he obtained 'both fame and favour', displayed 'classical attainments of the first order' and graduated as a Bachelor and Master of Arts. Though Patrick was certainly qualified to judge his curate's academic ability, he seems to have been mistaken about his qualifications. According to the university records, William Weightman only spent two years there. His name appears in the examination pass lists for 1838 and 1839 as 'unclassified' and in the graduation lists of June 1839 as a Licentiate of Theology and 'Reverend'. There is no record of his obtaining a higher degree, even after he left the university.[18]

Patrick had applied to the Bishop of Ripon for a curate and William Weightman had been recommended. He therefore came straight from university to his first curacy at Haworth. Although not yet fully ordained, being only a deacon, he began his duties appropriately enough with a baptism and a burial on 19 August 1839.[19]

From the very first he won the admiration and liking of Patrick, his family and the people of Haworth. Charming, good-looking and possessing both a sense of humour and a natural but unobtrusive sympathy, he carried all before him. Patrick was later to say of him:

His character wore well; the surest proof of real worth. He had, it is true, some peculiar advantages. Agreeable in person and manners, and constitutionally cheerful, his first introduction was prepossessing. But what he gained at first, he did not lose afterwards. He had those qualities which enabled him rather to gain ground.[20]

The exceptional nature of William Weightman's qualities was manifested by the ease with which he rapidly gained a place in the Brontë household. Like his predecessor he lodged at Cook Gate with the Ogden family, but unlike poor William Hodgson, he was soon on unusually intimate terms with all the family. What is more, his attentions caused a flutter in more than one female heart at the parsonage. This was particularly obvious while Ellen was staying, when he made 'frequent and agreeable visits' and took the lead in entertaining the younger members of the family.[21]

That February he was invited to give a lecture on the classics to the Keighley Mechanics' Institute and he was determined that the young ladies should come to hear him. With his habitual discretion, he arranged for a married clergyman in Keighley, possibly John Collins, to send them an invitation to tea and offer himself as an escort to and from the parsonage. Even with this correct guardianship, it was feared that Patrick and Aunt Branwell would withhold their permission, but the arrangements were judged acceptable and the party set off in high glee for Keighley. The evening out was only marred by its end: it was midnight before they returned to the parsonage, having walked the four miles each way. Aunt Branwell had prepared hot coffee for the four young ladies but, with a surprising lack of foresight, had not made enough for their two escorts.

Poor Miss Branwell lost her temper, Charlotte was troubled, and Mr Weightman, who enjoyed teazing the old lady, was very thirsty. The great spirits of the walking party had a trying suppression, but twinkling fun sustained some of them.[22]

On 14 February there was excitement of a different kind when Charlotte, Emily, Anne and Ellen each received her very first Valentine in the morning's post. Again, this was William Weightman's doing. He had discovered that none of them had ever had one before so he set to and wrote verses for each of them. Only the titles of three of them are known, but they give an indication of the general tone of each Valentine: 'Fair Ellen, Fair Ellen', 'Away fond Love' and 'Soul divine'. In order to escape detection by the elders, he had then walked ten miles, presumably to Bradford, to post them.[23] The intended kindness was typical of the man, as were the lengths to which he went to ensure that his generous gesture was effective. The girls had no difficulty in detecting his hand in the verses and, evidently touched as well as delighted, replied in kind.

> A Rowland for your Oliver
>   We think you've justly earned;
> You sent us each a valentine,
>   Your gift is now returned.
>
> We cannot write or talk like you;
>   We're plain folks every one;
> You've played a clever trick on us,
>   We thank you for the fun.
>
> Believe us when we frankly say
>   (Our words, though blunt are true),
> At home, abroad, by night or day,
>   We all wish well to you.
>
> And never may a cloud come o'er
>   The sunshine of your mind;
> Kind friends, warm hearts, and happy hours,
>   Through life we trust you'll find.
>
> Where'er you go, however far
>   In future years you stray,
> There shall not want our earnest prayer
>   To speed you on your way...[24]

The return Valentine was careful to adopt a safely bantering tone, which accepted Weightman's verses as flattering but insincere. However, despite the popular belief that it was Anne who fell in love with the new curate, there is considerable evidence to suggest that it was actually Charlotte who fell for his charms. Weightman had just that combination of good looks, humour and intellect which would have appealed to the woman who had rejected Henry Nussey because 'I could not sit all day long making a grave face before my husband – I would laugh and satirize and say whatever came into my head first'.[25] Charlotte certainly bestowed more than ordinary attention on him. It was she, not Anne, who decided to paint his portrait.

The sittings became alarming for length of time required, and the guest had to adopt the gown, which the owner was very proud to exhibit, amusing the party with his critical remarks on the materials used, and pointing out the adornments, silk velvet, etc.[26]

Though the finished portrait does not appear to have survived, there is a delightful pencil drawing by Charlotte which would appear to be a preparatory study for it. It shows a good-looking young man in profile, with a straight nose and generous mouth, long side-burns almost reaching to his chin and hair swept forward in the style of the day which Branwell also adopted. He is wearing an academic gown and beside him there is a pile of carefully placed ecclesiastical books, indicating his clerical status. Later, Charlotte was to take the trouble to paint another portrait, this time of Agnes Walton, a lady in Appleby with whom Weightman gave it to be understood that he was in love.[27]

In addition to these unusual attentions, Charlotte's letters from this period are full of Weightman's sayings and doings, even though such things had never merited her notice when performed by her father, brother or Mr Hodgson. 'Little Haworth has been all in a bustle about Church-rates since you were here –', she told Ellen, describing a meeting on 26 March 1840:

we had a most stormy meeting in the School-room – Papa took the chair and Mr Collins and Mr Weightman < sup > acted as his supporters one on each side – There was violent opposition which set Mr Collins' Irish blood in a ferment and if Papa had not kept him quiet partly by persuasion, and partly by compulsion he would have given the Dissenters their Kail through the reek (a Scotch proverb which I'll explain another time – He and Mr Weightman both bottled up their wrath for that time but it was only to explode with redoubled force at a future period – We had two sermons on Dissent and its consequences preached last Sunday one in the afternoon by Mr Weightman and one in the evening by Mr Collins – < Miss Celia Amelia del > all the Dissenters were invited to come and hear and they actually shut up their chapels and came in a body; of course the church was crowded. Miss Celia Amelia [Weightman] delivered a noble, eloquent high-Church, Apostolical succession discourse – in which he banged the Dissenters most fearlessly and unflinchingly – I thought they had got enough for one while, but it was nothing to the dose that was thrust down their throats in the evening – a keener, cleverer, bolder and more heart-stirring harangue I never heard than that which Mr Collins delivered from Haworth Pulpit last Sunday Evening – he did not rant, he did not cant he did not whine, he did not snivel, he just got up and spoke with the boldness of a man who is impressed with the truth of what he is saying who has no fear of his enemies and no dread of consequences – his sermon lasted an hour yet I was sorry when it was done ... Mr Weightman has given another lecture at the Keighley Mechanic's Institute, and Papa has also given a lecture – both are spoken of very highly in the Newspaper and it is mentioned as a matter of wonder that such displays of intellect should emanate from the village of Haworth 'situated amongst the bogs and mountains and until very lately supposed to be in a state of semi-barbarism' such are the words of the newspaper.[28]

Charlotte's sudden interest in church rates seems to have owed rather more to their current champion than to the actual importance of an issue which had now plagued her father for over six years.

It is undoubtedly significant that Charlotte chose to refer to William Weightman by the nickname 'Miss Celia Amelia',[29] as pseudonyms had always played an important part in her writing. From being a very young girl she herself had almost invariably adopted a masculine persona which freed her from the constraints of female society and conventions. Now, she perversely chose to give Weightman – who was as ardent an example of male heterosexuality as an infatuated spinster could wish – a girlish name which, at the very least, suggested he was effeminate. This would seem to be a deliberate emasculation, a symbolic removal of the danger which this charming, unmarried young man posed to a susceptible and romantic single woman. Treated as if he were a girl, the curate could be admitted into the presence and confidence of herself and her sisters without impropriety; it became possible to enjoy a flirtation with him without having to admit to herself that she had fallen victim to his soon-to-be legendary charm.

That such was indeed the case was frequently suggested by Ellen Nussey, who persisted in dropping hints not only in her letters but also, to Charlotte's infinite annoyance, to Mary and Martha Taylor. Martha, as she was well aware, would not rest until she had found out all there was to know and disseminated the gossip amongst all her acquaintance. Charlotte responded to Ellen's hints by returning them in kind. She asked William Weightman his opinion of Ellen, 'a fine-looking girl and a very good girl into the bargain', and reported it back portentously to her friend; she called her 'Mrs Menelaus', suggesting she was the beautiful Helen for whom the Trojan wars were fought, and warned her not to set her heart on him. She even nicknamed Emily 'the Major' for her supposed tenacity in defending Ellen from Weightman's attentions.[30]

Though there can be little doubt that Weightman treated all the ladies with an unusual degree of familiarity and good-humoured courtesy; there is nothing to suggest that Ellen was particularly susceptible to his charms. She was, in fact, at this very time being courted by a Mr Vincent and, with the support of her family, was seriously considering marriage to him.[31] When she wrote to ask Charlotte's opinion on the subject, her friend responded with unusually pragmatic advice which was totally at odds with the view she had so forcibly expressed when Henry Nussey had sought her own hand in marriage.

Do not be over-persuaded to marry a man you can never respect – I do not say love, because, I think, if you can respect a person before marriage, moderate love at least will come after; and as to intense passion, I am convinced that that is no desirable feeling. In the first place, it seldom or never meets with a requital; and, in the second place, if it did, the feeling would be only temporary: it would last the honeymoon, and then, perhaps, give place to disgust, or indifference, worse perhaps than disgust. Certainly this would be the case on the man's part; and on the woman's – God help her, if she is left to love passionately and alone.

Rather wistfully, Charlotte added, 'I am tolerably well convinced that I shall never marry at all. Reason tells me so, and I am not so utterly the slave of feeling but that I can occasionally hear her voice.'[32] Despite her partiality for William Weightman, she entertained – or wanted to convince herself that she entertained – no hopes or expectations in that direction.

Though the air was full of talk of love and marriage, at least for Charlotte and Ellen who had the time to indulge in such pleasantries, Patrick and William Weightman were hard at work. Contrary to the impression of idleness given by Charlotte, they were deeply involved in trying to relieve the increasing distress in the township. Throughout the winter trade had been greatly depressed, leading to falling wages and rising unemployment. The weather had also been particularly harsh and the hardship had been compounded by the almost total failure of the peat crop, due to the unusually wet summer the previous year, which meant that the poor were deprived of their main source of fuel. They were unable to afford to keep themselves and their children either warm or well fed. The growing discontent manifested itself in a petition from Haworth to Parliament seeking the repeal of the Corn Laws, which kept the price of grain artificially high. The suffering could only be alleviated by charity, administered by Patrick and the Dissenting ministers of the chapelry. The bulk of the work fell on Patrick and his curate – and there was a great deal to do. The sum of £260 was raised by subscription and gifts, including £150 from the London Committee for the Relief of the Distressed Manufacturers. This money was used to purchase 1,800 yards of cotton shirting, 180 pairs of blankets, thirty to forty loads of oatmeal and sixty or seventy loads of potatoes, which then had to be distributed according to need.[33] Despite the additional duties which the depression in trade forced upon him, including an inevitable increase in sick-visiting, and the now customary row over the imposition of a church rate, Patrick still found time for other activities. In April he gave both a lecture to the Keighley Mechanics' Institute and the afternoon sermon in aid of the Sunday schools at William Morgan's Christ Church in Bradford.³⁴

Anne, too, had gone back to work after allowing herself only the briefest of holidays after her dismissal from Blake Hall. This was in stark contrast to Charlotte, who had been unemployed since July 1839 and still showed a marked reluctance to find a new post. She had dithered over an offer to be governess to relatives of her father's old friends, the Halliley family, but, despite Mrs Halliley's best endeavours, had ultimately decided against it.³⁵ The new-found attractions of Haworth, with an attentive and amusing curate in residence, overpowered any sense of duty which demanded that she ought to return to work. As if to prove that lack of will alone stood in the way of Charlotte obtaining a new post, Anne, though less well qualified, had found herself a new place without any difficulty. Had she really been in love with William Weightman, she would no doubt have been as reluctant to leave Haworth as Charlotte.

Anne was now to be governess to four of the five children of the Reverend Edmund Robinson, a wealthy clergyman of independent means, who lived at Thorp Green, near York. This was the furthest away from home that any of the girls had gone as governess. It was also the most prestigious appointment that any of them had ever held. The Robinsons lived in grand style. Their house lay in the centre of a great estate in the rich agricultural triangle of the Vale of York between York, Ripon and Harrogate. Set in acres of parkland, half a mile from the banks of the River Ouse, the house must have been a mansion of some size as the Robinsons employed three male and seven female servants, as well as a governess, all of whom lived in. This was the second-largest establishment in the area, more than double the size of Blake Hall where Anne had previously been a governess. Edmund Robinson was lord of the manor of the nearest village, Little Ouseburn, and owned most of the land round Thorpe Underwoods; twenty-five years later the whole estate would be sold for the enormous sum of £116,750.³⁶ Apart from the Thompsons at nearby Kirkby Hall and the craftsmen in Little Ouseburn and the hamlet of Thorpe Underwoods, virtually all their neighbours were wealthy farmers.³⁷ The nearest settlement of any size – and that smaller than Haworth – was the ancient and busy market town of Boroughbridge, which lay six miles to the northwest of Thorp Green on the Great North Road.

Anne went to take up her post in this quiet rural retreat in May 1840.³⁸ Her own first impressions of the place and her new employers have not survived and Charlotte was too wrapped up in William Weightman even to mention her youngest sister in her correspondence. We know, however, that the Reverend Edmund Robinson was about forty-four years old and a chronic invalid who rarely officiated as a clergyman. His wife, Lydia, the daughter of the Reverend Thomas Gisborne, was four years younger, a dark-haired, vivacious woman whose portrait does not suggest she possessed any extraordinary good looks.[39] The Robinsons had five children: Lydia, aged fourteen, Elizabeth, aged thirteen, Mary, aged twelve, Edmund, the only son, aged eight, and the baby, Georgiana Jane, aged eighteen months, who was to die within the year.[40] Like the Inghams, Anne's new charges were pampered and demanding, but at least they were old enough for her to escape the nursery duties of dressing and feeding them and keeping them clean.

While Anne set to work with a will, determined to overcome her undoubted homesickness and make a success of her new post, Branwell found himself rather too comfortable in his position at Broughton-in-Furness. Unlike Anne, who had to live in the house at Thorp Green and was therefore with her charges day and night, Branwell had only to put in a certain number of hours a day teaching the two Postlethwaite boys and then he was free to do as he wished. Lodging at High Syke House, his comings and goings were not as noticeable as they would have been had he had to live with his employers. Branwell took full advantage of his freedom.

Always a keen walker, he embarked on many excursions in and around the southern lakes. On one such expedition, he unexpectedly fell in with an acquaintance from his days in William Robinson's studio who was driving round the area. In order to prolong their conversation, Branwell drove some ten miles further on the road with him, regardless of the long walk he would have back to Broughton-in-Furness.[41] More productively, he explored the length of the River Duddon, his copy of Wordsworth's sonnets in his hand. At least four years later, he looked back with such affection on this journey or series of journeys that he purchased a copy of James Thorne's *Rambles by Rivers*, which he annotated with his own observations. From these we learn that Branwell enjoyed 'a happy day' at the public house at Ulpha – not because he was able to indulge his propensity for drink but because 'the late Landlord was a character – he knew Greek very respectably and was a proficient in Latin.' He evidently attended divine service at Seathwaite Chapel, adding to Thorne's comments on Robert Walker, the incumbent for sixty-seven years who had died in 1802, that the present incumbent 'Priest Tyson' had had the cure for forty years, 'so that two men have held it for the unexampled time of 105 years!' Thorne's remark that there were now several Methodists and two or three Baptists at Seathwaite roused Branwell's wrath. 'This is since I left –', he wrote in the margin, 'I am sorry for it – the pests!' He also corrected the author's remarks on the tameness of the Duddon between Ulpha and the sands: 'He evidently never passed that part of the valley, where the Scenery is most delightful and it does there possess what he says it does not – A Gentlemans house – Duddon Grove the seat of Miss

Miller – now very likely Mrs Sawrey of Broughton Tower.'[42]

If Wordsworth's sonnets inspired Branwell to explore the Duddon, they also encouraged him to put pen to paper. In what is possibly his only original composition while at Broughton, he wrote a sonnet to Black Combe, the mountain across the Duddon estuary which dominated the surrounding country.

> Far off, and half revealed, 'mid shade and light,
>   Blackcomb half smiles, half frowns; his mighty form
> Scarce bending in to peace; – more formed to fight
>   A thousand years of struggles with a storm
>   Than bask one hour, subdued by sunshine warm
> To bright and breezeless rest; yet even *his* height
> Towers not o'er this world's sympathies – he smiles,
> While many a human heart to pleasure's wiles
>   Can bear to bend, and still forget to rise;
> As though he, huge and heath clad, on our sight
>   Again rejoices in his stormy skies,
>   Man loses vigour in unstable joys.
> Thus tempests find Blackcomb invincible,
> While we are lost, who should know life so well![43]

His proximity to the Lake Poets clearly inspired him to further poetic effort and, despite the failure of his previous efforts to obtain critical comments on his work, he determined to try again. On 15 April he re-edited and made a neat transcription of the long poem he had written two summers ago in Bradford, calling it 'Sir Henry Tunstall'. The name, which he used for the first time, may have been suggested by his journey to Broughton when he had passed the old Clergy Daughters' School at Cowan Bridge and seen the signs to Tunstall where the Reverend William Carus Wilson was still the vicar. The poem, though over-long at 540 lines, was decidedly the best of the narrative genre which Branwell had so frequently adopted over the last few years. It depicted, in typical Angrian terms, the longed-for return to his ancestral home of Henry Tunstall, after sixteen years spent as a soldier in India. The family joy turns rapidly to disillusionment as Tunstall finds himself unable to pick up the threads of his old life:

> They fancied, when they saw me home returning,
> That all my soul to meet with them was yearning,
> That every wave I'de bless which bore me hither;
> They thought my spring of life could never wither,
> That in the dry the green leaf I could keep,
> As pliable as youth to laugh or weep;
> They did not think how oft my eyesight turned
> Toward the skies where Indian Sunshine burned,
> That I had perhaps left an associate band,

That I had farewells even for that wild Land;
They did not think my head and heart were older,
My strength more broken, and my < spri > feelings colder,
That spring was hastning into autumn sere –
And leafless trees make loveliest prospects drear –
That sixteen years the same ground travel oer
Till each wears out the mark which each has left before.[44]

Branwell sent the fair copy of this poem and five of his translations from Book I of Horace's *Odes* to Thomas De Quincey, one of the early contributors to *Blackwood's Magazine*, who now resided at Wordsworth's old home, Dove Cottage at Grasmere. A note to the text of the translations reveals not only Branwell's love for but also his knowledge of the *Odes*: 'There are doubtless many mistakes of sense and language – except the first – I had not when I < un > translated them, a Horace at hand, so was forced to rely on memory. P B Brontë.'[45] Unfortunately for Branwell, he had chosen a bad time to write to De Quincey, who was then prostrate with illness. In all probability he never replied to Branwell's letter; if he did, the correspondence, including Branwell's original letter, is lost. Nevertheless, the fact that De Quincey saw fit to preserve the manuscripts of the poems suggests that he saw at least some merit in them.[46]

Five days after writing to De Quincey, Branwell addressed another Lake Poet, Hartley Coleridge, the eldest son of Samuel Taylor Coleridge, who lived at Nab Cottage on Rydal Water. Branwell's letter reveals how much he had matured since the days of his intemperate demands on the editor of *Blackwood's Magazine* and Wordsworth.

Sir,
It is with much reluctance that I venture to request, for the perusal of the following lines, a portion of the time of one upon whom I can have no claim, and should not dare to intrude; but ... I could not resist my longing to ask a man from whose judgement there would be little hope of appeal.

Since my childhood I have been wont to devote the hours I could spare from other and very different employments to efforts at literary composition, always keeping the results to myself, nor have they in more than two or three instances been seen by any other. But I am about to enter active life, and prudence tells me not to waste the time which must make my independence; yet, sir, I love writing too well to fling aside the practice of it without an effort to ascertain whether I could turn it to account, not in <u>wholly</u> maintaining myself, but in <u>aiding</u> my maintenance, for I do not sigh after fame and am not ignorant of the folly or the fate of those who, without ability, would depend for their lives upon their pens; but I seek to know, and venture, though with shame, to ask from one whose word I must respect: whether, by periodical or other writing, I could please myself with writing, and make it subservient to living.[47]

With this letter, Branwell enclosed a poem of over 300 lines, 'At dead of

Elizabeth Branwell, Mrs Brontë's sister, who lived with the family at Haworth from 1821 until her death in 1842.

Maria, mother of the Brontë children, who died in 1821.

The Clergy Daughters' School at Cowan Bridge; the classroom and dormitory were in a converted mill which stood at right angles to this building and has since been demolished.

The Church of St Michael and All Angels at Haworth, where Patrick Brontë was perpetual curate from 1821 until 1861; it was demolished in 1879.

A nineteenth-century view of Haworth Main Street.

An ambrotype photograph of Haworth Parsonage, taken before Patrick's death in 1861.

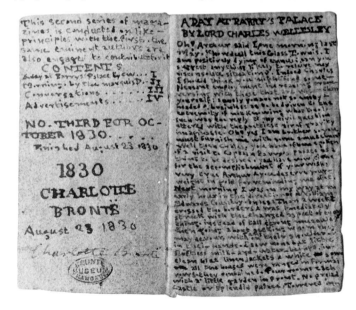

One of the 'Young Men's Magazines', written by Charlotte in 1830 when she was fourteen years old. Reproduced larger than the actual size, which is 6.4 cm × 5.2 cm.

The Miss Woolers' school at Roe Head, Mirfield, where Charlotte, Emily and Anne were pupils and Charlotte later became a teacher.

LEFT Miss Margaret Wooler, headmistress of Roe Head School, who later became a close friend of Charlotte.

CENTRE Ellen Nussey, Charlotte's schoolfellow and lifelong friend, in old age.

RIGHT Mary Taylor, Charlotte's other lifelong friend from Roe Head, photographed in old age. She emigrated to New Zealand in 1845.

Emily's diary paper of 26 June 1837, reproduced actual size. The
sketch shows Emily and Anne sitting at the dining-room table
with the tin box in which they stored the diary papers.

Blake Hall, Mirfield, where Anne held her first post as governess to the Ingham family.

Charlotte's pencil drawing of the Reverend William Weightman, the curate of Haworth, who died in 1842.

Mrs Lydia Robinson, wife of the Reverend Edmund Robinson of Thorp Green, near York. Branwell Brontë's affair with her led to his dismissal from his post as tutor.

...roughton-in-Furness, where Branwell was ...tor to the Postlethwaite boys in 1840. In the ...stance, across the Duddon sands, lies Black ...ombe.

...nwell's poem, 'Real Rest', published in the *...lifax Guardian* on 8 November 1846, under ... pseudonym 'Northangerland'.

POETRY.

REAL REST.

[For the HALIFAX GUARDIAN.]

I see a corpse upon the waters lie,
With eyes turned, swelled and sightless, to the sky,
And arms outstretched, to move as wave on wave
Upbears it in its boundless billowy grave.
Not Time, but Ocean thins its flowing hair;
Decay, not sorrow, lays its forehead bare;
Its members move, but not in thankless toil,
For seas are milder than this world's turmoil;
Corruption robs its lips and cheeks of red,
But wounded vanity grieves not the dead;
And, though those members hasten to decay,
No pang of suffering takes their strength away;
With untormented eye, and heart, and brain,
Through calm and storm it floats across the main:
Though love and joy have perished long ago,
Its bosom suffers not one pang of woe;
Though weeds and worms its cherished beauty hide,
It feels not wounded vanity or pride;
Though journeying towards some far off shore,
It needs no care or purse to float it oer;
Though launched in voyage for Eternity
It need not think upon what is *to be*;
Though naked, helpless, and companionless,
It feels not poverty or knows distress.
   Oh corpse! If thou could'st tell my aching mind
What scenes of sorrow thou hast left behind;
How sad the life which, breathing, thou hast led;
How free from strife thy sojourn with the dead;
I could assume thy place—could long to be
A world-wide wanderer oer the waves with thee!
   I have a misery where thou hast none;
My heart beats bursting while thine lies like stone;
My veins throb wild while thine are dead and dry;
And woes, not waters, dim my restless eye:
Thou longest not with one well loved to be,
And absence does not break a chain with thee:
No sudden agonies dart through thy breast;
Though hast what all men covet, REAL REST.
   I have an outward frame unlike to thine,
Warm with young life—not cold in death's decline;
An eye that sees the sunny light of heaven—
A heart by pleasure thrilled—by anguish riven—
But in exchange for thy untroubled calm,
Thy gift of cold oblivions healing balm,
I'd give my youth—my health—my life to come,
And share thy slumbers in thy ocean tomb.
                              NORTHANGERLAND.

ΛΥΔΙΑ ΓΙΣΒΟΡΝΕ.

June 1st 1846.

Lydia Gisborne
Lydia — G—

On Ouse's grassy banks - last Whitsuntide,
I sat, with fears and pleasures in my soul
Commingled, as "it roamed without controul,"
Oer present hours and through a future wide
Where love, methought, should keep, my heart beside
Her, whose own prison home I looked upon:
But, as I looked, descended summer's sun,
And did not its descent my hopes deride?
The sky though blue was soon to change to grey —
I, on that day, next year must own no smile —
And as those waves, to Humber far away,
Were gliding - so, through that hour might beguile
My Hopes, they too, to woes far deeper sea,
Were passing —
Rolled past the shores of Joy's now dim and distant isle.

MEMORIA.

The manuscript of Branwell's poem to Mrs Robinson, 'Lydia Gisborne', written on 1 June 1846.

midnight – drearily –'. Like 'Sir Henry Tunstall', this was a poem he had written some time ago: the first version had been written in July 1837, the second on 14 May 1838 and this, his third revision, on 20 April 1840.[48] Branwell was thus setting the pattern he was to continue with most of the poems he later sent for publication, taking a piece he had written in the 1830s and reworking it in the 1840s. He described it to Hartley Coleridge as 'the sequel of one striving to depict the fall from unguided passion into neglect, despair, and death. It ought to show an hour too near those of pleasure, for repentance, and too near death for hope'. With the poem Branwell enclosed two of the translations he had sent to De Quincey. They were given, Branwell said, 'to assist an answer to the question – would it be possible to obtain remuneration for translations for such as these from that or any other classic author?'[49]

Having sent out so many letters of this nature over the past few years, without eliciting a response, one can only imagine Branwell's wild delight when he received a reply from Coleridge. Though the letter has not survived, it must have expressed some approbation, for it also contained an invitation to visit Nab Cottage.

The moment he received Coleridge's letter, Branwell must have dropped everything and hurried over to Rydal Water, on the outskirts of Ambleside. He spent the whole of May Day there with Coleridge and, though no account of the visit survives, the two certainly discussed and read to each other their own translations. Branwell was sufficiently encouraged to embark on a complete translation of the first book of Horace's *Odes*, which Coleridge promised to read upon its completion.[50]

Less than two months after the excitement of his meeting with Coleridge, which had seemed to demonstrate that a poetic career was at last within his grasp, Branwell was suddenly brought sharply down to earth again. Mr Postlethwaite dismissed him from his post as tutor to his sons. The reasons for his dismissal are obscure. According to one tradition, Branwell followed Coleridge's advice to pursue his literary efforts to the extent that he neglected his pupils. Another has it that when he did not return to Broughton House as expected one day, William Postlethwaite was sent off to find him and brought him back 'visibly the worse for drink'.[51] These explanations seem odd, given that Branwell was well aware of his need to keep his job at least until he had established his poetic reputation.

A recently discovered source offers another, totally new, explanation which puts the dismissal in a very different light. In October 1859, a friend of Mrs Gaskell's, Richard Monckton Milnes, then Lord Houghton, visited William Brown, the sexton of Haworth, and was shown a number of letters written by Branwell to William's brother, John Brown. Among them was the letter addressed to 'Old Knave of Trumps' from Broughton, which Brown had clearly not censored as Branwell had requested and which Houghton was therefore able to partially transcribe. Beneath his transcript, Houghton noted that Branwell 'left Mr Postlethwaites with a natural child by one of the daughters or servants – which died'.[52]

This revelation, which Houghton gleaned either from other letters or verbally from William Brown, is almost impossible to verify but is not unlikely. On 3 April 1846, Branwell wrote a poem entitled 'Epistle from a Father on Earth to his Child in her Grave'. All the evidence points to this being an autobiographical poem rather than an imaginative or Angrian one.[53]

Branwell was nearly twenty-three years old and possessed considerable charms: though he wore glasses, he was good-looking, with a shock of red hair brushed forward over his high forehead, long side-burns and a straight and prominent nose. Vivacious and witty, he excelled at conversation and was impressively erudite. A writer and a poet, too, he was quite capable of sweeping a young girl off her feet. It is only surprising, perhaps, given the moral climate of the day which allowed young men considerable licence, that this would appear to have been his first sexual experience.[54]

There are a number of possible candidates for the mother of Branwell's child. The most obvious is Margaret Fish, the eighteen-year-old daughter of his landlord at High Syke House, whose beauty Branwell had already admired in his letter to John Brown. However, unless she had a child which died, unbaptized, at birth, or it was taken away from her and fostered, this is most unlikely. She was still living, unmarried and childless, with her family at High Syke House in June 1841 when the population census was taken.[55] The Postlethwaites had no daughter, so we are left with only servants as a possibility. Three women in the parish of Broughton-in-Furness gave birth to illegitimate children in the relevant period, any of whom could have been fathered by Branwell. Robert Pearson, assistant curate, baptized all three: James, son of Eleanor Nelson, 'single woman', on 2 August 1840, Frances, daughter of Frances Atkinson, 'single woman', on 9 December 1840 and Mary, daughter of Agnes Riley, 'spinster', on 21 March 1841.[56]

The census returns for June 1841, almost a year after Branwell left, give us some further clues. Eleanor Nelson was then nineteen and lived at Syke-house, the cottages between Broughton House and High Syke House. She is likely to have been a Postlethwaite servant as the census reveals that her brother, John, was a sixteen-year-old male servant at Broughton House, a post he retained ten years later. As an unmarried mother, she would, of course, have been automatically expelled from her employment when her condition became obvious, which may explain why she was living at home with her parents and her son. However, for James Nelson to have been Branwell's child he would have had to be conceived almost immediately upon Branwell's arrival and even then, presuming he was baptized immediately which was not usual practice, he would have been a seven-month baby. Eleanor married Thomas Armer, a farmer from Cartmel, on 2 October 1841 and though she had more children, her first-born, James, was apparently dead when the next census was taken in 1851.[57]

Frances Atkinson is more promising. In June 1841 she was seventeen, with a six-month-old daughter, living with her family on the road running between Broughton House and High Syke House. Tantalizingly, her occupation is given as female servant, though she clearly did not live in the house of her employers, who are not named. Again, given her address, she is likely to have been a servant of the Postlethwaites or the Fishes. Her daughter, Frances, however, was still living with her grandparents in 1851, though she died at the age of thirteen and was buried on 2 April 1854.[58] This would seem to be too late a date for Branwell's child, as Houghton's statement implies that the child died not long after its birth and certainly before Branwell himself.

The final possibility is Agnes Riley, the twenty-six-year-old daughter of an agricultural labourer who lived at Sunny Bank, which was also in Broughton West. In 1841 her employment was not listed but she lived with her parents and her daughter was said to be four months old. According to her birth certificate, Mary Riley was born on 20 February 1841, so she must have been conceived in May of the previous year while Branwell was living at Broughton. If the pair were not caught *in flagrante*, this would still have given time for the pregnancy to be confirmed, if not obvious, before Branwell was dismissed towards the end of June. The baby was named Mary, and although she may simply have been named after her grandmother, it is significant that this was one of Branwell's favourite names, which he used repeatedly in his juvenilia. Unfortunately, the Rileys appear to have moved from Broughton before the 1851 census so we cannot trace what became of the baby or her mother.[59]

The mother of Branwell's child would have had a claim on him for its maintenance and, if he refused to pay, could have taken bastardy proceedings against him to compel him to do so. Though the maintenance can have been little enough, it would nevertheless have been an additional drain on Branwell's already slight resources. He does not appear to have ever returned to Broughton to visit his child and there is no evidence of any contact with her mother.

Branwell was dismissed at midsummer 1840,[60] having kept his post as a tutor for only six months. He returned to Haworth but whether he told his family the reason for his dismissal can only be conjectured. For him, the fact that he had lost his job paled into insignificance beside the fact that a professional literary career was now opening out before him. Within a few days of his return, he had polished up his translations of the first two books of Horace's *Odes* and sent the first on to Hartley Coleridge for approval. His letter was an odd mixture of self-deprecation and egotism. 'You will, perhaps, have forgotten me,' he told Coleridge, 'but it will be long before I forget my first conversation with a man of real intellect, in my first visit to the classic lakes of Westmoreland.' He went on to request Coleridge's opinion of his translation:

you might tell me whether it was worth further notice or better fit for the fire ... and will you, sir, stretch your past kindness by telling me whether I should amend and pursue the work or let it rest in peace? ... I dared not have attempted Horace but that I saw the utter worthlessness of all former translations, and thought that a better one, by whomsoever executed, might meet with some little encouragement. I long to clear up my doubts by the judgement of one whose opinion I should revere, and – but I suppose I am dreaming – one to whom I should be proud indeed to inscribe anything of mine which any publisher would look at, unless, as is likely enough, the work would disgrace the name as much as the name would honour the work.

Amount of remuneration I should not look to – as anything would be everything – and whatever it might be, let me say that my bones would have no rest unless by written agreement a division should be made of the profits (little or much) between myself and him through whom alone I could hope to obtain a hearing with that formidable personage, a London bookseller.

Branwell evidently had second thoughts about his naive proposal to share the profits of his translation with Coleridge, for he rather touchingly added a footnote: 'If anything in this note should displease you, lay it, sir, to the account of inexperience and <u>not</u> impudence.'[61]

The translations, substantially revised over the last three months, were among the best work Branwell had ever produced and would probably have had a ready market at the time.[62] It is perhaps the most tragic irony of Branwell's life that Coleridge never seems to have got round to sending him a reply, though towards the end of the year, on 30 November or 1 December, Coleridge set out his opinions in a draft letter. It is worth quoting this draft, if only to answer those who believe Branwell to have been a worthless individual and an even more worthless poet.

You are by no means the first or the only person who has applied to me for judgement upon their writings. I smile to think that so small an asteroid as myself should have satellites ... Howbeit, you are – with one exception – the only young Poet in whom I could find merit enough to comment without flattery – on stuff enough to be worth finding fault with. I think, I told you how much I was struck with the power and energy of the lines you sent before I had the pleasure of seeing you. Your translation of Horace is a work of much greater promise, and though I do not counsel a publication of the whole – I think many odes might appear with very little alteration. Your versification is often masterly – and you have shown skill in great variety of measures – There is a racy english in your language which is rarely to be found even in the original – that is to say – untranslated, and certainly untranslateable effusions of many of our juveniles, which considering how thorough[ly] Latin Horace is in his turns of phrase, and collocation of words – is a proof of sound scholarship – and command of both languages –[63]

Coleridge intended to discuss the translation of each ode individually, but evidently ran out of time. Even the draft letter was never completed.

While Branwell waited hopefully for a reply, he undoubtedly told his family of Coleridge's interest in him. This seems to have encouraged Charlotte to contact him herself. She had, as usual, been busy with her writing. Some time in the spring of 1840, or possibly earlier, she completed a new story about Caroline Vernon, the illegitimate daughter of Northangerland by the opera singer, Louisa Vernon.[64] The story was the usual tiresome tale of a young and beautiful girl falling love with Zamorna but it was given an added twist by having Caroline's realization of her feelings dawn only slowly. A new flavour was also added with the introduction of a French theme: Louisa has a French maid, with whom she converses in the vernacular, and Caroline herself is brought out into Parisian society. This was undoubtedly the result of Charlotte's latest reading, for the Taylors had been inundating her with French novels throughout the year: 'I have got another bale of French books from Gomersal –', she told Ellen in August,

containing upwards of 40 volumes – I have read about half – they are like the rest clever wicked sophistical and immoral – the best of it is they give one a thorough idea of France and Paris – and are the best substitute for French Conversation I have met with.[65]

It was not her French story which she decided to send to Coleridge, however, but the beginning of another tale, which she carefully disguised to hide its Angrian origins. Set in the West Riding, it featured Alexander Percy, his daughter Mary, and of course Zamorna under a new name, Arthur Ripley West.[66] Using a pseudonym herself, 'C. T.', which stood for Charles Townshend, one of the narrators she used most often in her Angrian writing, Charlotte sent the manuscript to Coleridge for his comments. Like Southey, he seems to have responded with cautionary advice, though not entirely disapprovingly. The correspondence has not survived but Charlotte's extraordinary letter thanking him for his reply has been preserved in draft form, written on the wrapper in which Coleridge returned the manuscript. It is clear that Charlotte herself now recognized the truth of the advice given her so long ago by both her father and Robert Southey: constant indulgence of the imagination did not make living in the real world any easier.

Authors are generally very tenacious of their productions but I am not so attached to this production but that I can give it up without much distress. You say the affair is begun on the scale of a three volume novel.

I assure you Sir you calculate very moderately – for I had materials in my head I daresay for half a dozen – No doubt, if I had gone on I should have made quite a < Sir Charles Grandison > Richardsonian Concern of it. Mr West should have been my Sir Charles Grandison – Percy my Mr B – and the ladies < you > should have represented Pamela, Clarissa Harriet Byron, &c. Of course it is with considerable regret I relinquish any scheme so charming as the one I have sketched – it is very edifying and profitable to create a little world out of your own brains – and people it with inhabitants who are < like > so many Melchisedecs & have no father nor mother but your own imagination – by daily conversation with these individuals – by interesting yourself in their family affairs and enquiring into their histories you acquire a tone of mind admirably calculated to ennable you to cut a solid & respectable figure in practical life. The ideal and the actual are no longer distinct notions in your mind but amalgamate in an interesting medley from whence result books, thoughts and manners bordering on the idiotic.

As if to prove that her manners now bordered on the idiotic, Charlotte continued the letter in a flippant and frivolous tone which verged on disrespect.

The idea of applying to a regular Novel-publisher and seeing Mr West and Mr Percy at full length in three vols is very tempting – but I think on the whole \from what you say/ I had better lock up this precious manuscript – wait patiently till I meet with some Maecenas who shall discern and encourage my rising talent – & Meantime bind myself apprentice to a chemist & druggist if I am a young gentleman or to [a] Mantua maker & milliner if I am a young lady … I am pleased that you cannot quite decide whether I am \of the soft or the hard sex/ an attorney's clerk or a novel-reading dress-maker. I will not help you at all in the discovery and as to my handwriting < you > or the ladylike touches in my style and imagery you must not draw any conclusion from that. Several young gentlemen curl their hair and wear corsets – and several young ladies are excellent whips and by no means despicable jockies – besides I may employ an amanuensis.[67]

Charlotte seems to have got a *frisson* from the fact that Coleridge was unable to identify her gender. This liberation from the constraint of her femininity and the social conventions imposed on women was a heady potion but one which was later to leave a bitter taste in her mouth.

For Charlotte, still 'wanting a situation', June was a month of social pleasures, despite the bombshell of Branwell's dismissal. On 10 June she travelled over to Gomersal to stay at the Red House with the Taylors, moving on after a few days to stay at Brookroyd with Ellen Nussey. Before the end of the month, Mary Taylor had returned the visit and come to stay at Haworth. The hours passed very pleasantly, the obliging Mr Weightman entertaining their guest with several games of chess 'which generally terminated in a species of mock hostility'.[68] Branwell, on his return home, cast no cloud over the party and enlivened it by paying court to Mary, who was his own age and an acknowledged beauty. Perhaps because of his recent experience at Broughton, however, Branwell was unwilling to be drawn into anything more serious and immediately backed off when he found that Mary responded to his attentions. Writing later in the year to Ellen, Charlotte asked:

Did I not once tell you of an instance of a Relative of mine who cared for a young lady till he began to suspect that she cared more for him and then instantly conceived a sort of contempt for her –? You know to what I allude – never as you value your ears mention the circumstance … Mary is my study – for the contempt, the remorse the misconstruction which follow the development of feelings in themselves noble, warm – generous – devoted and profound – but which being too freely revealed too frankly bestowed – are not estimated at their real value. God bless her – I never hope to see in this world a character more truly noble – she would <u>die</u> willingly for one she loved – her intellect and her attainments are of the very highest standard … yet I doubt whether Mary will ever marry.[69]

If Charlotte viewed her brother's behaviour towards Mary Taylor with distaste, she was also growing rapidly disillusioned with William Weightman. His conduct had not changed, but Charlotte's perception of it had; she realized that his attentions, which had seemed so personal, were freely and equally offered to all the young ladies of his acquaintance. Piqued that she had allowed herself to interpret them otherwise and fearing that she might have appeared foolish, she turned against him with sudden venom. She denounced him to Ellen as 'a thorough male-flirt', listing among his victims an 'inamorata' from Swansea, whose letters he had just sent back, Sarah Sugden of Keighley who was 'quite smitten' and Caroline Dury, Theodore Dury's daughter, to whom he had just despatched 'a most passionate copy of verses'.[70] No doubt observing Weightman behaving in just the same way towards all these ladies as he had towards herself, her sisters and Ellen and seeing their equally rapturous reception of his attentions, Charlotte rather regretted her own infatuation.

Her embarrassment was relatively short-lived, however, for in July they were temporarily deprived of William Weightman's company. He left Haworth on 14 July for Ripon where the bishop, Charles Longley, had announced his intention of holding an ordination ceremony on 19 July. Having passed the bishop's customary oral examinations, Weightman was ordained priest with thirteen other candidates in the magnificent twelfth-century surroundings of Ripon Cathedral.[71] He then went home to Appleby for a holiday before resuming his duties as a fully fledged clergyman in Haworth in September. In Appleby he spent part of the time staying with Agnes Walton and her father, where he seems to have been an accepted suitor for her hand and wrote to Branwell in high glee to describe the balls at which he had figured and speaking 'rapturously' of Agnes herself. Even so, he did not forget his friends in Haworth: the Brontës were overwhelmed with gifts of game, a large salmon and a brace each of wild ducks, black grouse, partridges, snipe and curlew. Nor was Ellen Nussey forgotten: she too received a brace of duck. Charlotte's sour – and unjust – response was to tell Ellen

It is my devout belief that his Reverence left Haworth with the fixed intention of never returning – If he does return it will be because he has not been able to get a living – Haworth is not the place for him, he requires < novelty > a change of faces – difficulties to be overcome. He pleases so easily that he soon gets weary of pleasing at all. He ought not to have been a parson. certainly he ought not.[72]

How prejudiced Charlotte was in her judgement of the young curate, she was soon to find out. She overheard her father asking Weightman why he seemed in such low spirits one evening and his reply that he had been to visit Susan Bland, 'a poor young girl, who, I'm afraid, is dying'. Though Susan Bland was Charlotte's oldest and best scholar in the Sunday school, Charlotte was unaware that she was even ill. Two days later she called to visit the girl and found her

seemingly far on her way to that bourne whence no traveller returns. After sitting with her some time, I happened to ask her mother if she thought a little port wine would do her good. She replied that the doctor had recommended it, and that when Mr Weightman was last there he had sent them a bottle of wine and a jar of preserves. She added that he was always good to poor folks, and seemed to have a deal of feeling and kind-heartedness about him.[73]

It is unfortunate that it is Charlotte's image of William Weightman as a flighty, flirtatious socialite which has been perpetuated when there was clearly a very different and much deeper side to his nature. Others also testified to his assiduous attention to his pastoral duties – which eventually resulted in him catching a fatal dose of cholera. The church registers, too, provide a worthy, if dull, record of the extent to which he relieved Patrick of the round of baptisms, marriages and burials: unlike his predecessor, William Hodgson, he performed almost all the duties, Patrick retaining only the less arduous and less frequent marriage services.[74] Patrick himself, who was best-placed to know, testified to his curate's piety and dedication to his clerical duties:

He thought it better, and more scriptural, to make the love of God, rather than the fear of hell, the ruling motive for obedience. He did not see why true believers, having the promise of the life that now is, as well as that which is to come, should create unto themselves artificial sorrows, and disfigure the garment of gospel peace with the garb of sighing and sadness. Pondering on, and rejoicing in the glad tidings of salvation, he wished others to rejoice from the same principles, and though he preached the necessity of sincere repentance, and heart-felt sorrow for sin, he believed that the convert, in his freedom from its thraldom, should rejoice evermore in the glorious liberty of the gospel ... in the Sunday School, especially, he was useful in more than an ordinary degree. He had the rare art of communicating information with diligence and strictness, without austerity, so as to render instruction, even to the youngest and most giddy, a pleasure, and not a task.[75]

The priest who could win such accolades from so stern a judge as Patrick

Brontë hardly conforms to Charlotte's jaundiced image of a man who 'ought not to have been a parson'.

Patrick's good fortune in possessing a curate of Weightman's abilities was underlined in the autumn of 1840 by the upheavals taking place within the parish of Bradford. The vicar, Dr Scoresby, in his efforts to increase the number of churches within the parish without diminishing his own income, had insisted on his right to retain half the fees due to their incumbents for performance of church offices. This had led to a tremendous clash of wills, particularly in those churches where Henry Heap had never enforced his claims. Prominent among those in the losing battle against Scoresby were Patrick's friends, William Morgan and George Bull. The latter, known in the local press as the 'pugnacious parson' and 'the Factory Child's Friend', was so incensed that, to the infinite loss of the parish, he tendered his resignation. Where Patrick's sympathies lay is virtually impossible to ascertain, though he is likely to have sided with his colleagues against the vicar. Certainly he was prominent in supporting George Bull, being the first to sign a testimonial on his behalf which was publicly presented to him before his departure for Birmingham in September. Another, newer friend, James Bardsley, who had nearly been Patrick's first curate, was also driven to resign when Scoresby refused to nominate him to the newly built church at Bowling, a post which had been promised to him.[76]

There were troubles in Keighley, too. After twenty-six years as vicar, the much-loved and respected Theodore Dury had decided to give up his rapidly expanding, industrial parish in favour of a smaller, rural one in his native Hertfordshire. Patrick had therefore to say goodbye to an old and valued friend whom he had known and worked with for over twenty years. In his place came William Busfeild, like Scoresby a disciple of the new and abrasive school of clergymen, who had wealthy and powerful connections with the Ferrand family of Harden Grange, near Bingley.[77] His arrival coincided with two scandals in Keighley, though Busfeild appears to have been unaware of the second. On 31 August, James Robinson, the parish clerk, a man of dissipated habits who secretly indulged in excessive drinking, committed suicide.[78] Less than three months later, Patrick had a visit from Mrs Collins, wife of Busfeild's curate in Keighley, who had been on friendly terms with the Brontës. She had a terrible tale to tell

of her wretched husband's drunken, extravagant, profligate habits. She asked papa's advice; there was nothing, she said, but ruin before them. They owed debts which they could never pay. She expected Mr C's instant dismissal from his curacy; she knew, from bitter experience, that his vices were utterly hopeless. He treated her and her child savagely; with much more to the same effect. Papa advised her to leave him for ever, and go home, if she had a home to go to. She said this was what she had long resolved to do; and she would leave him directly, as soon as Mr B dismissed him.[79]

Mrs Collins does not appear to have followed Patrick's unequivocal and startlingly unconventional advice, perhaps because her resolve weakened when Busfeild failed to recognize the depravity of his curate and dismiss him.[80] The story had an interesting sequel when, six and a half years later, in April 1847, the Brontës had an unexpected visitor at the parsonage. 'Do you remember my telling you or did I ever tell you about that wretched and most criminal Mr Collins', she asked Ellen then,

– after running an infamous career of vice both in England and France – abandoning his wife to disease and total destitution in Manchester – with two children and without a farthing in a strange lodging-house? Yesterday evening Martha came up stairs to say – that a woman – 'rather lady-like' as she said wished to speak to me in the kitchen – I went down – there stood Mrs Collins pale and worn but still interesting looking and cleanly and neatly dressed as was her little girl who was with her – I kissed her heartily – I could almost have cryed to see her for I had pitied her with my whole soul – when I heard of her undeserved sufferings, agonies and physical degradation – She took tea with us stayed about two hours and entered frankly into the narrative of her appalling distresses – her constitution has triumphed over the hideous disease and her excellent sense – her activity and perseverance have enabled her to regain a decent position in society and to procure a respectable maintenance for herself and her children – She keeps a lodging-house in a very eligible part of the suburbs of Manchester (which I know) and is doing very well – she does not know where Mr Collins is and of course can never more endure to see him – She is now staying for a few days at Eastwood House with the Sugdens who I believe have been all along very kind to her – and the circumstance is greatly to their credit –[81]

Mrs Collins' terrible ordeal at the hands of her husband, which seems to have included his giving her venereal disease, appears to have inspired Anne Brontë's second novel, *The Tenant of Wildfell Hall*, which similarly dealt with a woman's flight from her debauched husband. At the time of Mrs Collins' first visit, though, Anne was still away from home at Thorp Green, where she was struggling against homesickness and finding some relief in poetry.

In one poem, 'The Bluebell', the poet sees a solitary harebell, growing on a grassy bank, which reminds her poignantly of home.

> Whence came that rising in my throat
> That dimness in my eyes?
> Why did those burning drops distill –
> Those bitter feelings rise?
>
> O, that < Bluebell > lone flower recalled to me
> My happy childhood's hours
> When blue bells < were as > seemed like fairy gifts
> A prize among the flowers

Those sunny days of merriment
When heart and soul were free
And when I dwelt with kindred hearts
That loved and cared for me

I had not then mid heartless crowds
To spend a thank[l]ess life
In seeking after others' weal
With anxious toil and strife

'Sad wanderer weep those blissful times
That never may return!'
The lovely floweret seemed to say
And thus it made me mourn[82]

Another poem, written six days later, on 28 August, was more succinct.

O! I am very weary < though >
Though tears no longer flow
My eyes are tired of weeping
My heart is sick of wo[e]

My life is very lonely
My days pass heavily
I'm weary of repining
Wilt thou not come to me?

Oh didst thou know my longings
For thee from day to day.
My hopes so often blighted
Thou wouldst not thus delay[83]

Though it is the accepted view that these poems are autobiographical, a cautionary note should be sounded. Both poems are typical of Gondal, expressing the usual longings of exiled characters who have been torn from their families. 'The Bluebell', with its allusions to the sea, is usually taken to be a reference to Anne's first visit to Scarborough with the Robinsons, but there is actually no evidence that the Robinsons began to take their annual holidays there until the following year.[84] Nor can one presume that the absent loved one, who is urged to hasten to the poet's side, was indeed the curate of Haworth. Again, this is a typical Gondal scenario, so much so that Emily, comfortably ensconced at home, had written a similar poem with the same title, 'Appeal', only three months before.

If greif for greif can touch thee,
If answering woe for woe,
If any ruth can melt thee
Come to me now!

> I cannot be more lonley,
> More drear I cannot be!
> My worn heart throbs so wildly
> 'Twill break for thee –
>
> And when the world despises –
> When Heaven repells my prayer
> Will not mine angel comfort?
> Mine idol hear?
>
> Yes by the tears I've poured,
> By all my hours of pain
> O I shall surely win thee
> Beloved, again![85]

The strong likelihood is that Anne's two poems were not strictly auto-biographical. At most, all one can say is that the choice of subject probably reflected her own undoubted sense of isolation and unhappiness at Thorp Green.

Charlotte, still seeking a post, had had an offer from Mrs Thomas Brooke of Huddersfield, apparently through Miss Wooler, and there followed an interchange of letters.

She expressed herself pleased with the style of my application – with its candour, etc. (I took care to tell her that if she wanted a showy, elegant, fashionable personage, I was not the man for her), but she wants music and singing. I can't give her music and singing, so of course the negotiation is null and void.[86]

Charlotte seemed more troubled by the fact that she was unable to assist Miss Wooler in securing more pupils for her school, which was 'in a consumptive state', than about her own failure to secure a job once more.[87] In fact, she seems to have been rather too comfortable at home, as the cheerful, gossipy tone of her letters to Ellen suggests. She had, too, since the arrival of William Weightman, fallen into the habit of using jocose nicknames for herself and others. As well as calling William Weightman 'Celia Amelia', Ellen 'Mrs Menelaus' and Emily 'The Major', she now took to signing herself off under various, sometimes telling pseudonyms. In March, when Ellen annoyed her by telling Martha Taylor about the Weightman Valentines, she was 'Charivari', an unpleasant cacophany of sound used to deride unpopular weddings and people in France, which was also the name of a satirical French journal. In June, telling Ellen about Weightman's lady friends, she was 'Ça ira', the title of a French revolutionary song suggesting that the aristocrats should go to the guillotine. Most revealing of all, in August, when she despaired of Weightman's return, she became 'Caliban', the misshapen and ill-natured monster enslaved by Prospero in Shakespeare's play *The Tempest*.[88]

Apart from the endless material to be got from William Weightman, there was an interesting diversion from the usual routine when the Brontës received a visit from what Ellen punningly called their 'August relations'. In one of the very rare recorded instances of contact with Mrs Brontë's family, her cousin John Branwell Williams, his wife and daughter arrived in Haworth to spend a day at the parsonage. They were actually staying for a month with John Fennell, Mrs Brontë's uncle, at Cross-stone, just across the moors in the Calder Valley. Charlotte was unimpressed, considering that they gave themselves airs and lambasting them with her sarcasm.

They reckon to be very grand folks indeed – and talk largely – I thought assumingly. I cannot say I much admired them – To my eyes there seemed to be an attempt to play the great Mogul down in Yorkshire – Mr Williams himself was much less assuming than the womenites – he seemed a frank, sagacious kind of man – very tall and vigorous with a keen active look – the moment he saw me he explained that I was the very image of my Aunt Charlotte. Mrs Williams sets up for being a woman of great talents, tact and accomplishment – I thought there was much more noise than work, my Cousin Eliza is a young lady intended by nature to be a bouncing good-looking girl. Art has trained her to be a languishing affected piece of goods.[89]

Despite her acid comments, such entertainment was grist to Charlotte's mill. She had no incentive at all to leave home and seemed to be happy to sit back and wait for Miss Wooler to find her a new post.

It was, in fact, Branwell who had once more gone out in search of employment and found it in a totally new field. For the last two years, work had been progressing on a new railway which would link the West Riding town of Leeds with the Lancashire town of Manchester. At the end of August 1840, it was announced that the twenty-seven-mile section of the railway from Leeds to Hebden Bridge would open on 5 October, leaving only the difficult trans-Pennine connection between Hebden Bridge and Littleborough still to be completed.[90] Branwell had apparently been taking a great interest in the construction of the railway and leapt at the opportunity to work on it. It may seem strange today that anyone should have found the prospect of working on the railways exciting, but it is forgotten what an immense and pioneering project it was. The building of the Summit Tunnel under Blackstone Edge, between Hebden Bridge and Littleborough, was a major feat of engineering and would mark yet another pinnacle of technical achievement. No doubt it was in these terms that Branwell had to defend his new job against his sister's sarcasms. Keeping up the habit she had recently begun of using nicknames, she referred to Branwell as 'Boanerges', the title, meaning 'sons of Thunder', given by Jesus to his disciples, James and John: the name 'Brontë', of course, itself meant 'Thunder' in Greek. Tadmor, continuing the biblical allusion, was a city built in the wilderness by Solomon. In these mockingly grandiose terms she informed Ellen of Branwell's appointment.

A distant relation of mine, one Patrick Boanerges, has set off to seek his fortune in the wild, wandering, adventurous, romantic, knight-errant-like capacity of clerk on the Leeds and Manchester Railroad. Leeds and Manchester, where are they? Cities in a wilderness – like Tadmor, alias Palmyra – are they not?[91]

Despite Charlotte's derision, Branwell had at least secured a job. He was to begin in the employment of the Leeds and Manchester Railway as the 'assistant clerk-in-charge' at the new station of Sowerby Bridge, a small textile town four miles outside Halifax. His appointment was confirmed at a board meeting at Hunt's Bank, Manchester on 31 August, when his annual salary was fixed at £75, rising by ten pounds per year to a maximum of £105. Though Branwell's starting salary was rather less than he could expect to earn as a private tutor, his prospects, assuming promotion, were much better. The confidence his family had in him was reflected in the fact that both Patrick and Aunt Branwell were prepared to stand surety for him for the vast sum of £210, which was considerably more than Patrick's annual income.[92]

Branwell was at his post in time for the official grand opening of the railway on 5 October 1840. The excitement aroused by this event was attested by the thousands of spectators who lined the tracks waiting for a view of the first train. The crowds waved flags and banners, bunting decorated the new stations and at Sowerby Bridge, the second to last station on the line and still based in temporary buildings, 'an immense number of persons were congregated'. A few months later, on 16 December, the last brick was laid to complete the Summit Tunnel, a project which had taken two and a quarter years and cost a number of lives, in a torch-lit ceremony performed by Barnard Dickinson, the resident engineer, before a large crowd of ladies and gentlemen. While they then proceeded to dine at the Summit Inn, the workmen 'were regaled' within the tunnel itself. This was followed, on 1 March 1841, by a visit from George Stephenson, the great railway pioneer himself, who with some of the shareholders took a special trip along the length of the line from Manchester to Normanton to observe the Summit Tunnel, the train passing through Sowerby Bridge both ways.[93]

After the excitement of the official openings, things quietened down in Sowerby Bridge, but not to the extent so often suggested by biographers. It is true that only three trains ran daily each way along the line at the beginning, but by 1 March 1841, when the Summit Tunnel was open and that part of the journey no longer had to be made by omnibus, this had increased to twelve trains each way, a total of twenty-four passing through Sowerby Bridge every day.[94] The clerk and his assistant were therefore kept busy logging the trains and their cargoes, organizing and co-ordinating the loading and unloading of waggons and supervising the safety of passengers. As Sowerby Bridge was the nearest station to Halifax, this was a not inconsiderable task. The *Halifax Guardian* complained that

Since the opening of the Railway, Sowerby Bridge has been one continued scene of battle occasioned by the passing and re-passing of the Omnibuses etc. Opposition has already commenced, and the public may now have a cheap ride to or from that place.[95]

The dangers of horse-drawn omnibuses racing each other up and down the perilously steep hill between the competing inns of Halifax and Sowerby Bridge in an attempt to be the first and cheapest service to get their passengers to the station, added to the bustle and excitement in Sowerby Bridge. The town was already a thriving industrial centre of about 5,000 inhabitants, which owed its wealth to its position, four miles southwest of Halifax, at a crossing of the River Calder at the foot of the Pennines. The precipitous hills surrounding the town provided a plentiful supply of water to run a large number of cotton, woollen, worsted and corn mills in the valley bottom. The Rochdale canal, built in the late eighteenth century, added to the town's prosperity and now extended along the length of the Aire and Calder Navigation to the heartlands of the industrial West Riding and Lancashire and, in the extreme east, to the flourishing port of Goole. Sowerby Bridge had therefore developed long and busy wharves to deal with the canal traffic and a gas works, chemical works and iron foundries had grown up along the banks of the canal.[96]

According to local tradition, Branwell lodged at the Pear Tree Inn in Sowerby Street, overlooking the railway. This seems inherently unlikely. In 1841, there was no Pear Tree Inn in Sowerby Bridge and the site was occupied by a beer house, the lowest form of drinking establishment.[97] However great his supposed propensity for alcohol, Branwell was still a gentleman and a comparatively well paid one at that. No gentleman would have been seen lodging in a beer house: he might possibly have lodged at any one of the six inns in the town, but he is more likely to have rented a suite of rooms with a respectable family as he had already done in Bradford and Broughton and was to do at Luddenden.

For Branwell the chief merit of his new job was his proximity to the literary, artistic and musical circles of Halifax, a town long renowned for its culture. John Frobisher, the organist at Halifax Parish Church, was a prolific organizer of concerts for the Quarterly Choral Society; there were regular, if sometimes bizarre, lectures in the town and, in December, a newly refurbished and reorganized Halifax Theatre opened, offering two different plays every night of the week.[98] In addition, Branwell had old friends in the town. Within a few weeks of his arrival he had already had at least one visit from Joseph Bentley Leyland, the sculptor, who had his studio and marble works at The Square in Halifax town centre. He brought with him his brother, Francis, an antiquarian who ran a bookshop and circulating library from his father's premises, Roberts Leyland & Son, at 15 Cornmarket, again in the centre of Halifax. Francis Leyland's first impressions of Branwell are instructive.

The young railway clerk was of gentleman-like appearance, and seemed to be qualified for a much better position than the one he had chosen. In stature he was a little below the middle height; not 'almost insignificantly small,' as Mr Grundy states, nor had he 'a downcast look;' neither was he 'a plain specimen of humanity.' He was slim and agile in figure, yet of well-formed outline. His complexion was clear and ruddy, and the expression of his face, at the time, lightsome and cheerful. His voice had a ringing sweetness, and the utterance and use of his English were perfect. Branwell appeared to be in excellent spirits, and showed none of those traces of intemperance with which some writers have unjustly credited him about this period of his life.

My brother had often spoken to me of Branwell's poetical abilities, his conversational powers, and the polish of his education; and, on a personal acquaintance, I found nothing to question in this estimate of his mental gifts, and of his literary attainments.[99]

In this hopeful mood, with the real possibility of literary success before him, Branwell ended the year 1840 in a new career on the railway at Sowerby Bridge.

Chapter Thirteen

❧

A WISH FOR WINGS

The new year of 1841 opened with bad news from Gomersal. Joshua Taylor, father of Mary and Martha, had died at Christmas after a long illness. The consequence of his death, as Charlotte anticipated, was to be 'a dissolution and dispersion of the family perhaps not immediately but in the course of a year, or two –'.¹ The Taylor family problems did not interest Charlotte as much as Ellen's: her suitor, Mr Vincent, could not be persuaded to make a proposal in due form. He had written numerous 'sentimental and love-sick' letters to Ellen's brother, Henry, but had not yet declared himself to the object of his attentions. Charlotte lost all patience.

In the name of St Chrysostom, St Simeon and St Jude, why does not that amiable young gentleman come forward like a man and say all that he has to say to yourself personally – instead of trifling with kinsmen and kinswomen?

At Ellen's request, she gave her friend further advice on what she should do, once more setting her a very different standard from herself.

From what I know of your character – and I think I know it pretty well – I should say you will never <u>love before marriage</u> – After that ceremony is over, and after you have had some months to settle down, and to get accustomed to the creature you have taken for your worse half – you will probably make a most affectionate and happy wife – ... Such being the case Nell I hope you will not have the romantic folly to wait for the awakening of what the French call '<u>Une grande passion</u>' – My good girl 'une grande passion' is '<u>une grande folie</u>'. I have told you so before and I tell it you again – Mediocrity in all things is wisdom mediocrity in the sensations is superlative wisdom ... all I have to say may be comprised in a very brief sentence. On one hand don't < marry > accept if you are certain you cannot <u>tolerate</u> the man on the other hand don't refuse because you cannot <u>adore</u> him.²

Ellen seems to have taken Charlotte's advice in rather poor part, suspecting that she was in league with Henry and the rest of her family in trying to persuade her to accept Mr Vincent.³ In fact, Charlotte was in touch with Henry, but attempting to convince him that he ought to rely on Ellen's own judgement in the matter. Rather curiously for a man who was engaged to another woman, Henry had been in fairly regular correspondence with Charlotte since she turned him down. On one occasion she was vastly amused when he asked her to write

in a regular literary way to you on some particular topic – I cannot do it at all – do you think I am a Blue-stocking? I feel half inclined to laugh at you for the idea, but perhaps you would be angry what was the topic to be – Chemistry? or Astronomy? or Mechanics? or Chonchology or Entomology or what other ology? I know nothing at all about any of these –⁴

Now he sent her a poem and asked her to return the gift in kind, provoking an equally satirical reply.

How do you know that I have it in my power to comply with that request? Once indeed I was very poetical, when I was sixteen, seventeen eighteen and nineteen years old – but I am now twenty-four approaching twenty-five – and the inter-mediate years are those which begin to rob life of some of its superfluous colouring. At this age it is time that the imagination should be pruned and trimmed – that the judgement should be cultivated – and a <u>few</u> at least, of the countless illusions of early youth should be cleared away. I have not written poetry for a long while⁵

This was indeed the case. It would seem that the golden dream of Angria had at long last begun to pall. She had written nothing, either poetry or prose, since the beginning of the story she had sent to Hartley Coleridge the previous winter. In telling Henry that 'the judgement should be cul-tivated' she perhaps indicated that she now spent her leisure hours in reading, rather than writing. The old passion for self-improvement, stimu-lated by the gift of the bales of French novels from Gomersal, had sprung to life once more. The hot-house attractions of Angria were now beginning to be replaced by the less exotic but equally potent and foreign attractions of France.

Now, too, she had a new occupation for, after a break of more than eighteen months, she had at last found herself a job. Some time towards the end of February, she accepted the post of governess in the family of John White of Upperwood House at Rawdon, travelling there to take up residence on 2 March 1841. By a singular coincidence, she thus found herself situated within a stone's throw of Woodhouse Grove School, where her parents had met and courted so long ago. Upperwood House was Georgian, 'not very large, but exceedingly comfortable and well regulated', set in its own grounds on the wooded hillside above the lovely Aire Valley. Rural in outlook, it was only a few miles from both Bradford and Leeds and, as Charlotte was swift to point out to Ellen, only nine miles from Brookroyd.

In taking the place I have made a large sacrifice in the way of salary, in the hope of securing comfort – by which word I do not mean to express good eating and drinking, or warm fire, or a soft bed, but the society of cheerful faces, and minds and hearts not dug out of a lead mine, or cut from a marble quarry.[6]

Charlotte's salary was indeed low, a mere twenty pounds per annum, out of which approximately four pounds was to be deducted for her laundry. This was exactly half the sum Anne was earning at Thorp Green, despite the fact that she was younger and less experienced than her sister.[7]

Charlotte's new employer, John White, was a Bradford merchant who, with his brother, had inherited Upperwood from a wealthy uncle in 1818. He and his wife, Jane, were a devoted couple, with three children, Sarah, aged eight, and Jasper, aged six, who were Charlotte's pupils, and Arthur, the baby of the family who was only two and still in the nursery.[8]

Though Charlotte set out determined to do her best, it was probably inevitable that she would encounter difficulties – as she herself was the first to recognize.

no one but myself can tell how hard a governess's work is to me – for no one but myself is aware how utterly averse my whole mind and nature are to the employment. Do not think that I fail to blame myself for this, or that I leave any means unemployed to conquer this feeling. Some of my greatest difficulties lie in things that would appear to you comparatively trivial. I find it so hard to repel the rude familiarity of children. I find it so difficult to ask either servants or mistress for anything I want, however much I want it. It is less pain to me to endure the greatest inconvenience than to request its removal. I am a fool. Heaven knows I cannot help it!⁹[9]

A few years later, writing to advise a friend whose daughters were contemplating the prospect of becoming governesses, Charlotte further analysed her failure: 'the one great qualification necessary to the task', she argued with a passion that spoke from experience, was

the faculty, not merely of <u>acquiring</u> but of <u>imparting</u> knowledge; the power of influencing young minds; that natural fondness for – that innate sympathy with children ... He or She who possesses this faculty, this sympathy – though perhaps not otherwise highly accomplished – need never fear failure in the career of instruction. Children will be docile with them, will improve under them; parents will consequently repose in them confidence; their task will be comparatively light, their path comparatively smooth. If the faculty be absent, the life of a teacher will be a struggle from beginning to end ... she may earn and doubly earn her scanty salary; as a daily governess, or a school-teacher she may succeed, but as a resident governess she will never (except under peculiar and exceptional circumstances) be happy. Her deficiency will harass her not so much in school-time as in play-hours; the moments that would be rest and recreation to the governess who understood and could adapt herself to children, will be almost torture to her who has not that power; many a time, when her charge turns unruly on her hands, when the responsibility which she would wish to discharge faithfully and perfectly, becomes unmanageable to her, she will wish herself a housemaid or kitchen-girl, rather than a baited, trampled, desolate, distracted governess.

Charlotte could not restrain the bitterness that this sense of inadequacy engendered.

I have seen an ignorant nursery-maid who could scarcely read or write – by dint of an excellent, serviceable sanguine – phlegmatic temperament which made her at once cheerful and unmovable; of a robust constitution and steady, unimpressionable nerves which kept her firm under shocks, and unharassed under annoyances – manage with comparative ease a large family of spoilt children, while their Govern-ess lived amongst them a life of inexpressible misery; tyrannized over, finding her efforts to please and teach utterly vain, chagrined, distressed, worried – so badgered so trodden-on, that she ceased almost at last to know herself, and wondered in what despicable, trembling frame her oppressed mind was prisoned – and could not realize the idea of evermore being treated with respect and regarded with affection – till she finally resigned her situation and went away quite broken in spirit and reduced to the verge of decline in health.[10]

The nursery maid with the cheerful disposition and way with children was employed at Upperwood House.[11]

Three weeks into her new post, Charlotte was able to write fairly cheer-fully to Ellen, though complaining of the amount of sewing she was expected to do and which, because the children occupied her fully during the day, she was obliged to do in the evening.

this place is better than Stonegappe but God knows I have enough to do to keep a good heart on the matter – ... Home-sickness afflicts me sorely – I like Mr White extremely – respecting Mrs White I am for the present silent – I am trying hard to like her. The children are not such little devils incarnate as the Sidgwicks – but < at times > they are over-indulged & at times hard to manage

Charlotte begged Ellen to visit her 'if it be a breach of etiquette never mind – if you can only stop an hour, come –'. She concluded her letter by sending

Ellen the 'precious' Valentine William Weightman had sent her this year. 'Make much of it', she told Ellen,

remember the writer's blue eyes, auburn hair & rosy cheeks – you may consider the concern addressed to yourself – for I have no doubt he intended it to suit any-body –[12]

Ellen evidently decided that a visit might not be appropriate, writing instead to offer Charlotte the use of her brother George's gig to bring her over to Brookroyd for a short visit. The invitation inspired Charlotte with unwonted courage.

as soon as I had read your shabby little note – I gathered up my spirits directly – walked on the impulse of the moment into Mrs White's presence – popped the question – and for two minutes received no answer – will she refuse me when I work so hard for her? thought I. Ye-es-es, drawled Madam – in a reluctant cold tone – thank you Ma'am said I with extreme cordiality and was marching from the room – when she recalled me with – 'You'd better go on Saturday afternoon then – when the children have holiday – & if you return in time for them to have all their lessons on Monday morning – I don't see that much will be lost' you <u>are</u> a genuine Turk thought I but again I assented & so the bargain was struck –[13]

While at Brookroyd Charlotte learnt that Mary Taylor had decided to emigrate with her brother, Waring, to Port Nicholson in the North Island of New Zealand. Unlike Charlotte, she was not prepared to buckle down to repellent and subservient employment and she did not lack the courage for the adventure of emigration. Her decision was typically matter of fact and pragmatic.

Mary has made up her mind she can not and will not be a governess, a teacher, a milliner, a bonnet-maker nor housemaid. She sees no means of obtaining employ-ment she would like in England, so she is leaving it.[14]

Charlotte was undoubtedly envious of Mary's independence of spirit and the manner in which she refused to accept the conventional employments open to young women. The contrast with Charlotte's own circumstances seems to have aggravated her burgeoning sense of injustice at having to be at the beck and call of her employers. On her return from Brookroyd, she became markedly more truculent and less willing to please. Just as had happened with the Sidgwicks, she reserved most of her spleen for the lady of the house, to whom she was directly responsible and with whom she was in most contact. This was evident in the differing motives she ascribed to the Whites' displeasure that George Nussey, a 'gentleman', had simply dropped Charlotte off at the gates and not brought her up to the house – 'for which omission of his Mrs W was very near blowing me up – She went quite red in the face with vexation ... for she is very touchy in the matter of opinion'. Mr White's reaction she ascribed, more charitably, to 'regret ... from more hospitable and kindly motives'.[15]

Writing to Ellen nearly a month after her visit, Charlotte expressed her dissatisfaction in a scornful and snobbish attack on her employers' right to be her superiors. Conveniently, she overlooked the fact that she herself was the granddaughter of an Irish farmer and a Cornish shopkeeper and merchant.

During the last three weeks that hideous operation called 'A Thorough Clean' has been going on in the house – it is now nearly completed. for which I thank my stars – as during its progress I have fulfilled the twofold character of Nurse and Governess – while the nurse has been transmuted into Cook & housemaid. That nurse by the bye is the prettiest lass you ever saw & when dressed has much more the air of a lady than her Mistress. Well can I believe that Mrs W has been an exciseman's daughter – and I am convinced that Mr W's extraction is very low – yet Mrs W— talks in an amusing strain of pomposity about his & her family & connexions & affects to look down with wondrous hauteur on the whole race of 'Tradesfolk' as she terms men of business – I was beginning to think Mrs W— a good sort of body in spite of all her bouncing, and boasting – her bad grammar and worse orthography – but I have had experience of one little trait in her character which condemns her a long way with me – After treating a person on the the most familiar terms of equality for a long time – ... If any little thing goes wrong she does not scruple to give way to anger in a very coarse unladylike manner – though in justice no blame could be attached where she ascribed it all – I think passion is the true test of vulgarity or refinement – Mrs W— when put out of her way is highly offensive – She must not give me any more of the same sort – or I shall ask for my wages & go.[16]

Charlotte obviously found some comfort for her own wounded pride in attacking the supposed vulgarity of her employers, but she was being extremely unjust to them. The Whites went out of their way to make her happy. They expressed themselves 'well satisfied' with their children's progress in learning since Charlotte's arrival. She was allowed at least one and possibly two trips to Brookroyd and Ellen was invited to come to Upperwood to visit Charlotte there.[17] Mr White even wrote to Haworth 'entreating' Patrick to spend a week at Upperwood. This was an unheard-of kindness to a governess, which Charlotte ungratefully took it into her head to resent: 'I don't at all wish papa to come – it would be like incurring an obligation –'[18] The fact that her job grew easier with time – to her evident surprise – wrung no concessions from her.

Somehow I have managed to get a good deal more control over the children lately – this makes my life a good deal easier – Also by dint of nursing the fat baby it has got to know me & be fond of me – occasionally I suspect myself of growing rather fond of it – but this suspicion clears away the moment its mamma takes it & makes a fool of it – from a bonny, rosy little morsel – it sinks in my estimation into a small, petted nuisance – Ditto with regard to the other children.[19]

Seemingly determined not to be pleased by her post, Charlotte made ineffectual attempts to find another. Like Jane Eyre, she was apparently offered a position in Ireland which, astonishingly, given her reluctance to be away from home and her refusal to be satisfied with a family as kind and well-meaning as the Whites, she seriously considered accepting.[20]

At the end of June, Charlotte again prevailed over Mrs White, persuading her to extend the holiday she was about to take from a week or ten days to a full three weeks. She arrived in Haworth on the evening of 30 June, only to discover that she had missed Anne who, having spent her own three weeks' holiday at home, had 'gone back to "the Land of Egypt and the House of Bondage"'. Charlotte wasted no time in inviting Ellen over to stay, delaying the visit only when Aunt Branwell decided to go over to Cross-stone to nurse John Fennell, who was seriously ill. On the day Ellen had promised to come Charlotte and Emily 'waited long – and anxiously' for her and Charlotte 'quite wearied my eyes with watching from the window – eye-glass in hand and sometimes spectacles on nose'. Belatedly, they dis-covered that she had gone to stay with her brother, Henry, at Earnley and her visit to Haworth had been cancelled.[21] This was a disappointment but it did not spoil the pleasure of being back at home and learning all the family news.

Patrick had had a fraught spring. He had been summoned to a meeting at the vicarage in Bradford on 1 January, together with the other clergymen of the parish. Though the object of the meeting was not stated, it clearly augured further confrontation. Patrick took the opportunity to present a petition, addressed to Joseph Shackleton, Scoresby's collector of Easter dues in Haworth, acknowledging the vicar's right to the dues but appealing to his forbearance:

in consequence of the hard times & want of sufficient employment, we pray the Vicar to take our case into his kind consideration & if he pleases to remit, for this year what is due from us, we conscientiously declaring that we are at present unable to pay the same.[22]

One hundred and sixty names then followed, each of them owing between 5/5d. and 9/5d., a sum which, in many cases, would be equivalent to a whole week's wages. The distress and poverty also gave John Winterbotham and his cohorts a good excuse to oppose the granting of a church rate in Bradford, which they did to great effect.[23] A few weeks later, on hearing of the somewhat equivocal judgement in the Braintree case of contested church rates, which had been taken to the highest courts in the land, Patrick was prompted to write to the *Leeds Intelligencer.* While taking the opportunity to attack the

Dissenters for what he considered their hidden agenda, the ultimate destruction of the Established Church, he made a heart-felt plea for new legislation:

well defined laws, which in their execution, would admit of but little or no grounds for litigation ... Any law that brings or that would bring, the clergyman and his differing parishioners into annual collision, would be detrimental and wrong; and any law that would have a contrary effect, would be so far right.[24]

Less than two months later, he wrote again on the subject, this time to the *Bradford Observer*. For the first time, Patrick publicly aligned himself with the opposition to Dr Scoresby in Bradford. Though this was undoubtedly a result of his own, strongly held beliefs, he may have been influenced by William Morgan, whose relations with the vicar had deteriorated to such an extent that he refused even to reply to Scoresby's letters and announced his intention to follow the example of George Bull and James Bardsley and resign his living. He was dissuaded by his parishioners, who 'earnestly solicited' his continued ministrations and presented him with a silver service in recognition of their appreciation.[25] Against this background of controversy and bitter exchanges, Patrick took his stand.

it appears to me, that when a new church is built in a large parish, and has, as it ought to have, a district assigned to it, there should be absolute independency there – so that, in no one instance, the parishioners should be answerable for any rate, but that which should be requisite for the repairs of their own church. As for the laying on two or three rates annually on any one district, to keep in repairs churches, it has nothing to do with; this is unreasonable and preposterous, and if there be laws which require it, they should, for the general good, be altered and amended, as soon as possible.[26]

Patrick had more cause than most to know the cost of this policy. For historic, rather than equitable reasons, a fifth of Bradford's church rates came from Haworth – and the chapelry had to levy further rates to support its own church. Patrick declared once more his own decided opposition to the present method of laying church rates, suggesting that commutation was the obvious answer, but he also attacked the Dissenters' claim that compulsory church rates were a violation of conscience. He illustrated his point with a neat little anecdote.

Not long since, I met with a man who objected to the payment of Church-rates, under the plea that to do so would violate the dictates of his conscience. Well knowing his circumstances, I said to him, 'James, do you pay your rents without any such religious scruple?' 'Yes,' said he, 'I do, and why not?' 'Do you know,' I observed, 'that part of these rents go towards keeping beer shops, and part, I fear, towards upholding a gambling house?' 'Yes,' he observed, with rather a downcast countenance, conjecturing, as I suppose, what I was after. 'Well,' I remarked, 'how can you conscientiously do this; do you really think, that even, according to your way of thinking, Church-rates would go to so bad a purpose?' He only observed – 'I have been wrong, but I trust that, by Divine grace, I shall be right for the future, and that no one shall ever mislead me any more by false arguments.' He went home and I heard no more of his opposition to Church-rates.[27]

John Winterbotham was less easily convinced, but he agreed with Patrick's stance against the imposition of a parish rate in the chapelry. At the next church rate meeting in Bradford a few days later, he denounced the vicar and churchwardens for 'the awful fact that they oppress and rob the poor of Haworth to furnish the Lord's Table at Bradford'. This was, he declared, an 'act of religious delinquency' for which they 'ought all to be deeply humbled before God'. Scoresby's answer was legally to enforce the collection of a rate by securing a requisition from the Ecclesiastical Court overturning the Haworth poll; the official document demanding payment of £76 12s. 10d. in church rates to Bradford was backed by the threat of imprisonment for failure to pay.[28]

This time, he faced a united front of opposition. To impose the rate demanded would have placed a tax of almost a pound on every cottage and farm in the township at a time when the poor rate in Haworth was being levied at seven or eight shillings in the pound and many families were still totally dependent on charitable relief. Patrick ran through the formality of chairing a church rate meeting, but he made his own views very obvious from the outset. The meeting was not to make or lay a rate, he declared, but 'to consider a demand' by the churchwardens of Bradford. 'To bring the business into a moveable position' he urged John Brown and John Dean, sexton and constable of the chapelry, formally to propose the rate and then gave John Winterbotham the floor. His motion that no church rate for the parish of Bradford be granted was carried, Patrick gave his thanks and 'the meeting separated with good temper and cordiality'.[29]

After this excitement, the general election of July 1841 was something of an anticlimax. Haworth was favoured with visits from both sets of candidates. The Liberals, Lords Morpeth and Milton, arrived in pouring rain and found little enthusiasm despite the fact that their mill-owning supporters had forced their workmen to wear yellow cards in their hats and form a token crowd of welcome. The Blues, Mr Wortley and Mr Denison, fared a little better. The Liberal 'rent-a-mob' turned out again and tried to drown their speeches from the hustings, but they were countered by a growing band of Chartists, who sided with the Tories in their attacks on the new Poor Law. There was the usual near-riot and much bad feeling, though neither side seems to have emerged with much credit.[30]

Emily, totally absorbed in her imaginary world as usual, appears to have let all the excitements in Haworth wash over her. On 30 July, her twenty-third birthday, she wrote a diary paper, prefixing it with two tiny ink sketches of herself writing by the fire and standing looking out of the window.

A Paper to be opened
when Anne is
25 years old
or my next birthday after –
if
– all be well –

Emily Jane Brontë July the 30th 1841

It is Friday evening – near 9 o'clock – wild rainy weather. I am seated in the dining room \alone/ having just concluded tidying our desk-boxes – writing this document. Papa is in the parlour. Aunt upstairs in her room – she has < just > been reading Blackwood's Magazine to papa – Victoria and Adelaide are ensconced in the peat-house – Keeper is in the Kitchen – Nero in his cage – We are all stout and hearty as I hope is the case with Charlotte, Branwell, and Anne, of whom the first is at Mr White Esqre Upperwood House Rawden The second is at Luddenden foot and the third is I beleive at Scarborough – enditing perhaps a paper corresponding to this –

< Ther > A Scheme is at present in agitation for setting us up in a school of our own as yet nothing is determined but I hope and trust it may go on and prosper and answer our highest expectations – this day 4 – years I wonder whether we shall still be dragging on in our present condition or established to our hearts' content Time will show –

I guess that at the time appointed for the opening of this paper – we (ie) Charlotte, Anne and I – < will shall > shall be all merrily seated in our own sitting-room in some pleasant < part? > and flourishing seminary having just gathered in for the midsummer holydays our debts will be paid off and we shall have c< h >ash in hand to a considerable amount. papa Aunt and Branwell will either have been or be coming to visit us – it will be a fine warm summer evening very different from this bleak look-out [and] Anne and I will perchance slip out into the garden [for a] few minutes to peruse our papers. I hope either this [or] some thing better will be the case –

The Gondalians < are > are at present in a threatening state but there is no open rupture as yet – all the princes and princesses of the [Royal?] royalty are at the palace of Instruction – I have a good many books on hand – but I am sorry to say that as usual I make small progress with any – however I have just made a new regularity paper! and I mean – verb sap – to do great things – and now I close sending from far an ex[hortation] of courage < corag? > courage to exiled and harassed Anne wishing she was here.[31]

In sharp contrast to Emily's obvious contentment in her life at home and her good-humoured optimism about the future, Anne's diary paper is a sad little catalogue of past failures and pessimism. She had had an all too brief holiday of three weeks in June, which she had spent quietly at home with Emily, her father and Aunt Branwell. Just before Charlotte's return, Anne left to join the Robinsons at Scarborough for their annual holiday. The

Robinsons had taken up residence in the prestigious Wood's Lodgings. The house, part of a splendid Georgian terrace, occupied a prime site on the cliff top overlooking the wide sandy beaches of South Bay, with views across to the castle on the headland. No. 2, The Cliff consisted of a drawing room, a dining room, eight bedrooms, a housekeeper's room and a kitchen, so it was large enough for the Robinsons to share with Mr Robinson's mother and sister.[32] It was here that Anne wrote her diary paper.

July the 30th, A.D. 1841.

This is Emily's birthday. She has now completed her 23rd year, and is, I believe, at home. Charlotte is a governess in the family of Mr White. Branwell is a clerk in the railroad station at Luddenden Foot, and I am a governess in the family of Mr Robinson. I dislike the situation and wish to change it for another. I am now at Scarborough. My pupils are gone to bed and I am hastening to finish this before I follow them.

We are thinking of setting up a school of our own, but nothing definite is settled about it yet, and we do not know whether we shall be able to or not. I hope we shall. And I wonder what will be our condition and how or where we shall all be on this day four years hence; at which time, if all be well, I shall be 25 years and 6 months old, Emily will be 27 years old, Branwell 28 years and 1 month, and Charlotte 29 years and a quarter. We are now all separate and not likely to meet again for many a weary week, but we are none of us ill that I know of, and all are doing something for our own livelihood except Emily, who, however, is as busy as any of us, and in reality earns her food and raiment as much as we do.

How little know we what we are
How less what we may be!

Four years ago I was at school. Since then I have been a governess at Blake Hall, left it, come to Thorp Green, and seen the sea and York Minster. Emily has been a teacher at Miss Patchet's school, and left it. Charlotte has left Miss Wooler's, been a governess at Mrs Sidgwick's, left her, and gone to Mrs White's. Branwell has given up painting, been a tutor in Cumberland, left it, and became a clerk on the railroad. Tabby has left us, Martha Brown has come in her place. We have got Keeper, got a sweet little cat and lost it, and also got a hawk. Got a wild goose which has flown away, and three tame ones, one of which has been killed. All these diversities, with many others, are things we did not expect or foresee in the July of 1837. What will the next four years bring forth? Providence only knows. But we ourselves have sustained very little alteration since that time. I have the same faults that I had then, only I have more wisdom and experience, and a little more self-possession than I then enjoyed. How will it be when we open this paper and the one Emily has written? I wonder whether the Gondalians will still be flourishing, and what will be their condition. I am now engaged in writing the fourth volume of Solala Vernon's Life.

For some time I have looked upon 25 as a sort of era in my existence. It may prove a true presentiment, or it may be only a superstitious fancy; the latter seems most likely, but time will show.

Anne Brontë.[33]

The only prospect which seemed to offer Anne any escape was the school scheme. The idea of setting up their own school had been floating in the air for some time now, but over the summer, when first Anne and then Charlotte was at home to discuss the idea with the family, a definite plan had begun to emerge. Writing to Ellen on 19 July, Charlotte told her

> there is a project hatching in this house – which both Emily and I anxiously wished to discuss with you – The project is yet in its infancy – hardly peeping from its shell – and whether it will ever come out – a fine, full-fledged chicken – or will turn addle and die before it cheeps, is one of those considerations that are but dimly revealed by the oracles of futurity Now dear Nell don't be nonplussed by all this metaphorical mystery ... To come to the point – Papa and Aunt talk by fits & starts of our – id est – Emily Anne & myself commencing a School! I have often you know said how much I wished such a thing – but I never could conceive where the capital was to come from for making such a speculation – I was well aware indeed, that Aunt <u>had</u> money – but I always considered that she was the last person who would offer a loan for the purpose in question – A loan however she <u>has</u> offered or rather intimates that she perhaps <u>will</u> offer in case pupils can be secured, an eligible situation obtained &c.[34]

Charlotte's response to Aunt Branwell's generous offer was not one of unmitigated delight. She did not think her aunt would be willing to risk more than £150 on the venture – '& would it be possible to establish a <u>respectable</u> (not by any means a <u>shewy</u> school – and to commence house-keeping with a capital of <u>only</u> that amount?' Ellen was commissioned to seek the opinion of her elder sister, Ann, on whether the finances were viable as the Brontës had no wish to get into debt. 'We do not care how modest – how humble our commencement be so it be made on sure grounds & have a safe foundation', she told Ellen, adding almost as an afterthought, 'Can events be so turned so that you shall be included as an associate in our projects? This is a question I have not at present the means to answer.'[35]

Unable, even now, to leave William Weightman out of her letters, she concluded her important news about the school scheme with a spiteful account of his latest doings.

> I must not conclude this note without even mentioning the name of our reverend friend William Weightman – He is quite as bonny pleasant, light hearted – good-tempered – generous, careless, crafty fickle & unclerical as ever. he keeps up his correspondence with Agnes Walton – During the last Spring he went to Appleby & stayed upwards of a month – in the interim he wrote to Papa several times & from

his letters – which I have seen – he appears to have a fixed design of obtaining Miss Walton's hand & if she can be won by a handsome face – by a cheerful & frank disposition & highly cultivated talents – if she can be satisfied with these things & will not expect further the pride of a sensitive mind & the delicacy of a feeling one – < with > in this case he will doubtless prove successful –[36]

The curate had now become a side issue, however, as Charlotte bent all her energies to achieving the dream of a school of her own. There is no doubt that she was the driving force, though Emily and Anne were willing partners. It was Charlotte who made the plans and conducted the negotiations, while her sisters simply acquiesced in her arrangements. At first she considered siting the school at Bridlington: her own memories of the place were pleasant and, more importantly, she thought that only one other school had been established there.[37] Two months later, an unexpected proposal from Miss Wooler forced a change of plan. Her sister had given up the school at Dewsbury Moor and Miss Wooler suggested that Charlotte should take it over and attempt to revive its flagging fortunes. In return for her own board, Miss Wooler offered Charlotte the use of her furniture, which would be a considerable saving in the initial outlay. This offer had much to recommend it. They would be taking over an established school, with a good reputation, in an area where they themselves were widely known. But by the time Charlotte had organized a loan of £100 from Aunt Branwell, her own enthusiasm for the scheme had dwindled away to nothing. In its place 'a fire was kindled in my very heart which I could not quench'.[38]

The fire had been kindled by Mary Taylor who, instead of emigrating to New Zealand, had gone on a continental tour with her brother, John, and had written to tell Charlotte of her experiences.

Mary's letter spoke of some of the pictures & cathedrals she had seen – pictures the most exquisite – & cathedrals the most venerable – I hardly know what swelled to my throat as I read her letter – such a vehement impatience of restraint & steady work. such a strong wish for wings – wings such as wealth can furnish – such an urgent thirst to see – to know to learn – something internal seemed to expand boldly for a minute. I was tantalized with the consciousness of faculties unexercised – then all collapsed and I despaired[39]

Charlotte had always been the one with a taste for the exotic. Where Mary Taylor's plans for emigration had simply left her cold, the possibility of following her and Martha to Brussels set her imagination alight and she could not let the idea drop. Mary and the Whites, no doubt prompted by Charlotte when she discussed the matter with them, all supported her proposal that she ought to spend some time in a Brussels school. Hiding behind their 'advice', Charlotte took the bull by the horns and wrote to Aunt Branwell.

My friends recommend me, if I desire to secure permanent success, to delay commencing the school for six months longer, and by all means to contrive, by hook or by crook, to spend the intervening time in some school on the Continent. They say schools in England are so numerous, competition so great, that without some such step towards attaining superiority we shall probably have a very hard struggle, and may fail in the end.

Charlotte suggested that as Miss Wooler proposed to lend them her furniture, they would only need half the sum of one hundred pounds which Aunt Branwell had offered them to help set up their school. The remaining fifty pounds, Charlotte argued, would be well employed in giving herself and Emily the chance to spend six months in a foreign school.

I would not go to France or to Paris. I would go to Brussels, in Belgium. The cost of the journey there, at the dearest rate of travelling, would be £5; living is there little more than half as dear as it is in England, and the facilities for education are equal or superior to any other place in Europe. In half a year, I could acquire a thorough familiarity with French. I could improve greatly in Italian, and even get a dash of German, i.e. providing my health continued as good as it is now.

With Mary and Martha Taylor already established in Brussels, Charlotte continued, she would have every opportunity of seeing them, their cousins, the Dixons, who lived in the city and, through them, 'I should probably in time be introduced to connections far more improving, polished, and cultivated, than any I have yet known.' Having marshalled every argument she could muster to convince Aunt Branwell of the advantages of her plan, Charlotte ended her letter with an impassioned plea.

Papa will perhaps think it a wild and ambitious scheme; but who ever rose in the world without ambition? When he left Ireland to go to Cambridge University, he was as ambitious as I am now. I want us all to go on. I know we have talents, and I want them to be turned to account. I look to you, aunt, to help us. I think you will not refuse. I know, if you consent, it shall not be my fault if you ever repent your kindness.[40]

Charlotte did not tell her aunt quite all the truth. Far from simply putting off the plan to take over Miss Wooler's school, it seems it had been abandoned altogether. A few weeks later she told Ellen:

Dewsbury Moor is relinquished perhaps fortunately so it is an obscure & dreary place – not adapted for a school – In my secret soul I believe there is no cause to regret it – My plans for the future are bounded to this intention if I once get to Brussels – & if my health is spared I will do my best to make the utmost of every advantage that shall come within my reach – when the half year is expired I will do what I can –[41]

Only to Emily did Charlotte confide the full extent of her plan:

Before our half-year in Brussels is completed, you and I will have to seek employment abroad. It is not my intention to retrace my steps home till twelve months, if all continues well and we and those at home retain good health.[42]

One can only wonder what Emily's response was to this idea. For someone who had not survived more than six months away from home without becoming physically ill, the prospect of a year among strangers in a foreign land must have been truly intimidating. Anne was surely more likely to benefit from a Brussels education. Nevertheless, Charlotte was ruthless in her plan. She had determined she would get to Brussels 'by hook or by crook' and she knew that the elders were more likely to agree if she did not go alone. Emily was the only practical candidate to accompany her as the alternative meant Anne giving up her job, losing her salary and becoming a third burden on the family finances. Emily's removal would only mean an inconvenience in the running of the household, so Emily it had to be. It was only now that Charlotte revealed to her that the Dewsbury Moor scheme had been intended for herself alone. 'Grieve not over Dewsbury Moor', she told Emily. 'You were cut out there to all intents and purposes, so in fact was Anne; Miss Wooler would hear of neither for the first half-year.'[43]

Charlotte pursued her plans with a single-mindedness which reflected both selfishness and a determination to succeed. She gave her notice to the Whites and assisted in the selection of a new governess to replace her.[44] Aunt Branwell had been persuaded to fund the Brussels scheme. Now it only remained to find an appropriate school. The Château de Koekelberg, where Mary and Martha Taylor were established, was too expensive but she had recommended another, cheaper school in Brussels. Charlotte was still waiting for a second opinion from Mr Jenkins, the episcopal clergyman in Brussels who was, coincidentally, the brother of Patrick's old colleague at Dewsbury, David Jenkins, when her employment came to an end.

I got home on Christmas Eve. The parting scene between me and my late employers was such as to efface the memory of much that annoyed me while I was there, but indeed, during the whole of the last six months they only made too much of me.[45]

Charlotte's attitude alone had been responsible for her unhappiness as a private governess. Once she could see a desirable escape route, she spent less energy finding fault in her circumstances and found her place almost congenial.

Both her sisters were at home when Charlotte returned. Emily had been happy enough running the household but living in the imaginary world of her own creation. Though she had written only ten surviving poems throughout the year, their high narrative content suggests that they were part of the 'good many books' she had on hand when writing her diary paper in July.[46] Among them was one of her finest poems, written in May 1841.

Shall Earth no more inspire thee,
Thou lonely dreamer now?
Since passion may not fire thee
Shall Nature cease to bow?

Thy mind is ever moving
In regions dark to thee;
Recall its usless roving –
Come back and dwell with me –

I know my mountain breezes
Enchant and soothe thee still –
I know my sunshine pleases
Despite thy wayward will –

When day with evening blending
Sinks from the summer sky,
I've seen thy spirit bending
In fond idolatry –

I've watched thee every hour –
I know my mighty sway –
I know my magic power
To drive thy greifs away –

Few hearts to mortals given
On earth so wildly pine
Yet none would ask a< n > Heaven
More like the Earth than thine –

Then let my winds caress thee –
Thy comrade let me be –
Since naught beside can bless thee
Return and dwell with me –[47]

Though the lines undoubtedly expressed Emily's own passionate love for the natural world, it is almost certainly a Gondal poem. It contained an important idea that was to recur in later poetry and also in *Wuthering Heights*: a longing for death that rejected conventional views of Heaven in favour of a Paradise that was as like earth as possible. This idea was taken a stage further in another Gondal poem, written in July, by two mourners at their mother's grave.

We would not leave our native home
For <u>any</u> world beyond the Tomb
No – rather on thy kindly breast
Let us be laid in lasting rest
Or wake – but to share with thee
A mutual immortality –[48]

This is to anticipate Catherine's dream in *Wuthering Heights* by at least five years. 'If I were in heaven, Nelly, I should be extremely miserable', she told Nelly Dean,

I dreamt, once, that I was there … heaven did not seem to be my home; and I broke my heart with weeping to come back to earth; and the angels were so angry that they flung me out, into the middle of the heath on the top of Wuthering Heights; where I woke sobbing for joy.[49]

Another theme of the poems of this year was a familiar one, that of imprisonment, but the emphasis had changed from lamentation and despair at separation to a *cri de coeur* for liberty. A captive bird makes a passionate plea:

> Give we the hills our equal prayer:
> Earth's breezy hills and heaven's blue sea;
> We ask for nothing further here
> But our own hearts and liberty.[50]

In another poem a Gondal character is similarly defiant.

> Riches I hold in light esteem
> And Love I laugh to scorn
> And Lust of Fame was but a dream
> That vanished with the morn –
>
> And if I pray – the only prayer
> That moves my lips for me
> Is – 'Leave the heart that now I bear
> 'And give me liberty' –
>
> Yes – as my swift days near their goal
> 'Tis all that I implore –
> Through life and death, a chainless soul
> With courage to endure! –[51]

It was ironic that Emily was about to exchange the liberty of her life at Haworth for the prison of schooling in Brussels. Deprived of the freedom to pursue her own thoughts and inclinations, she would have neither the time nor the necessary equanimity of spirit to be able to write poetry.

The imminent departure of her sisters to Brussels had given Anne much food for thought. At first she toyed with the idea of giving up her post at Thorp Green in order to take Emily's place in the household, but she had made herself so indispensable that the Robinsons positively pleaded with her to return.[52] Had she really been in love with William Weightman, this would have been the one time when she could have legitimately seized the opportunity to stay at home. Coincidentally, this is also the time when Charlotte made her famous remarks upon which the whole castle in the air has been built. 'He sits opposite to Anne at Church sighing softly – & looking out of the corners of his eyes to win her attention – & Anne is so quiet, her look so downcast – they are a picture –'.[53] The last phrase, 'they are a picture', has been taken to imply that Anne was personally involved and returned Weightman's supposed affection. However, Charlotte was keen to suggest that Weightman was in love with every girl in the neighbourhood and Anne's modest reaction was surely the only one suitable in the circumstances. Had Weightman carried the flirtation any further, making similar overtures at the parsonage, Charlotte would have been the first to comment on it. Moreover, Charlotte's concluding sentence is surely proof that she did not consider Anne's affections were involved. She told Ellen, 'He would be the better of a comfortable wife like you to settle him you would settle him I believe – nobody else would.'[54]

Although there can be no doubt that Anne would have preferred to remain at home – with or without the supposed attentions of the curate – she decided it would be best if she continued in her present employment. After her Christmas holidays, therefore, she returned to Thorp Green not knowing when she would see her sisters again, or even where they were going. Mr and Mrs Jenkins had finally replied with an unfavourable account of the French schools in Brussels, 'representing them as of an inferior caste in many respects'. With less than three weeks to go before their proposed departure, their plans were suddenly changed completely. Baptist Noel, a friend of Patrick's from his days in Thornton, and other clergymen whom Patrick consulted, suggested a school in Lille in northern France. The terms were more expensive – fifty pounds each for board and French alone – but included an extra sum for a private room, a luxury which Aunt Branwell generously agreed to fund.[55] Charlotte regretted the imposed change from Brussels to Lille 'on many accounts' but in the end she got her own way. Mr Jenkins finally found a school of which he approved in Brussels, the plans were changed once more and Charlotte and Emily were plunged into preparation for their immediate departure.

I have lots of chemises – night gowns – pocket handkerchiefs & pockets to make – besides clothes to repair – & I have been every week since I came home expecting to see Branwell & he has never been able to get over yet – we fully expect him however next Saturday.[56]

It had been six months since Charlotte had last seen Branwell,[57] who was still working on the Leeds and Manchester Railway over in Calderdale. In the meantime he had confounded her scepticism by doing well in his new job. Shortly after the grand opening of the Summit Tunnel, Branwell was promoted from his post at Sowerby Bridge. On 1 April 1841 he transferred to the next station further up the line at Luddenden Foot, where he was made clerk-in-charge on a much higher salary of £130 a year. Charlotte, who had hoped that her brother would be a great artist or poet, remained unimpressed, her only comment to Emily being, 'It is to be hoped that his removal to another station will turn out for the best. As you say, it <u>looks</u> like getting on at any rate.'[58]

Luddenden Foot is a small village which, as its name implies, was then only a scattering of houses at the foot of the spectacularly beautiful Luddenden Valley, where it opens out into the Calder Valley. At this point the valley bottom is narrow so that the hills rise sheer on each side of the river and the road and railway which run beside it. Heavily wooded, its floor and hillsides a carpet of bluebells in spring, the valley gives way to steeply shelving pastureland and, on the hill tops, glorious stretches of wild moorland. Branwell took new lodgings in one of Calderdale's many splendid seventeenth-century houses, built by yeoman farmers from the wealth accrued from the wool trade, though by that time simply a working farm. Brearley Hall was only half a mile away across the fields from the new station, though it was perched high above the valley bottom. Branwell's new landlords were a wealthy farmer, James Clayton and his wife, Rachel, who lived there with their two sons, Jonas and Henry, and their respective families. Branwell was their only lodger.[59]

Francis Grundy, a young railway engineer, first made Branwell's acquaintance at this time and painted a dismal portrait of the place.

When I first met him, he was station-master at a small roadside place on the Manchester and Leeds Railway, Luddendenfoot by name. The line was only just opened. This station was a rude wooden hut, and there was no village near at hand. Had a position been chosen for this strange creature for the express purpose of driving him several steps to the bad, this must have been it. Alone in the wilds of Yorkshire, with few books, little to do, no prospects, and wretched pay, with no society congenial to his better tastes, but plenty of wild, rollicking, hard-headed, half-educated manufacturers, who would welcome him to their houses, and drink with him as often as he chose to come, – what was this morbid man, who couldn't bear to be alone, to do?[60]

This colourful, if grim, picture of Branwell's ruin at Luddenden Foot has been accepted unquestioningly by biographers. This period, it is said, proved his downfall. Branwell spent his time in the pubs of the Calder Valley, neglected his job, doodled in the margins of the company ledgers and, as Grundy would have it, went thoroughly to the bad. In support of this view a passage from one of Branwell's letters to Grundy is always quoted:

I would rather give my hand than undergo again the grovelling carelessness, the malignant yet cold debauchery, the determination to find how far mind could carry body without both being chucked into hell, which too often marked my conduct when there[61]

But Grundy, writing nearly forty years later, is an extremely unreliable witness, misdating Branwell's letters to him by several years, delighting in wild exaggeration and having the doubtful benefit of being able to bend his memories to suit Mrs Gaskell's portrait of the black sheep of the Brontë family.[62]

It was simply not true, for instance, that there was no village near at hand. About half a mile from the station was the ancient and pretty village of Luddenden, a thriving centre of the textile trade where stuff-weaving was still carried on in the tall, many-windowed houses and in the larger premises of the new mills. As a railway employee Branwell was allowed to travel free of charge and, by simply getting on the train, he could be in Sowerby Bridge or Hebden Bridge in a matter of minutes or even in Leeds or Manchester in under two hours. He is known to have visited Manchester on at least one occasion, returning full of enthusiasm at the 'lightsome' beauty of the parish church which he described in detail to Sutcliffe Sowden, a young clergyman friend. Nor did he have 'no prospects, and wretched pay'.[63] His promotion within six months of starting work on the railway had shown that he could rise rapidly if his work gave satisfaction. His salary was better than anything he had ever earned before and was almost a third more than William Weightman, for instance, earned as curate of Haworth.[64]

Branwell's personal notebook – not the company ledgers – was indeed a strange mix of notes on railway affairs, poetry and sketches, but it also gives a brief glimpse into the sort of life he led at the time. He noted a concert by the Halifax Quarterly Choral Society at the Old Assembly Rooms in the Talbot Inn, Halifax, for instance, when a selection of sacred music – including one of his favourites, Haydn's *Creation* – was to be performed on 11 November 1840. He also seems to have sent a subscription to the Motet Society, who were based in London, and, from the numerous inscriptions of 'HOLY IESU', 'IESU' and 'SALVATOR' which abound in the notebook,[65] we can presume that he attended other concerts of sacred music in Halifax. The Halifax Quarterly Choral Society performed regularly, including an annual Christmas recital of another of Branwell's favourites, Handel's *Messiah*. Branwell is also unlikely to have missed the opportunity of seeing and hearing a rare performance in Halifax by the virtuoso pianist and 'modern musical wonder', Franz Liszt. His brilliant playing captivated the discerning Halifax audiences and he brought the house down with an impromptu set of variations on the National Anthem. Even the normally staid *Halifax Guardian* was swept away: 'We never remember a concert which was marked by so much enthusiasm, or so many rapturous encores as that of last night.'[66]

Despite Grundy's claims, Branwell also had access to plenty of books. Tradition has it that he was a member of the Luddenden Library, a large private collection of books housed in the upper chamber of the Lord Nelson Inn. This seems unlikely as there is no record of his name in the membership or receipt books and there were strict rules against admitting non-members to meetings.[67] There were, however, a number of much larger libraries in Halifax, including a circulating library run by the Leylands at their shop in Cornmarket and a newly opened subscription library, containing 1,900 volumes and taking in fifteen periodicals, at the Old Cock Inn.[68] In his notebook Branwell noted down new titles that interested him: *Manhood – the cause of its premature decline* by J. I. Curtis, his old passion *Blackwood's Magazine*, and the shortly to be published *Wakefield's Miscellany*. As he also copied out the addresses and directions to the Manchester warehouses of Mr Pearson and Mr Warburton, he presumably found his way there in pursuit of the second-hand books they advertised.[69]

Nor was it the case that Branwell was continually in bad company at Luddenden Foot, as Grundy claimed, and the drunken Irish labourers introduced by later biographers simply did not exist at the time.[70] However, there were incidents to suggest Branwell was occasionally quarrelsome, possibly as the result of drink. He recorded in his notebook, for instance, that he had spent the previous evening with several men – including George Thompson, a Luddenden corn dealer and maltster, James Titterington, a worsted manufacturer, and Henry Killiner, the railway porter. Branwell notes that he had 'quarrelled with J T about going but after a wrestle met him on the road and became friends – Quarrelled almost on the subject with G Thompson <u>Will have no more of it</u>. P. B. B.'[71] Grundy himself, though piously suggesting that 'I did him so much good that he recovered himself of his habits there after my advent', seems to have been an influence for the bad. On one occasion, Branwell thought Grundy had treated him distantly at a party and responded by leaving in a temper and then sending him a set of reproving verses:

> However mean a man may be,
> Know man <u>is</u> man as well as thee;
> However high thy gentle line,
> Know he who writes can rank with thine;
> And though his frame be worn and dead,
> Some light still glitters round his head.[72]

Grundy also accompanied Branwell on several jaunts back to Haworth to consult a well known fortune teller, something which Patrick would have heartily disapproved of.[73]

In fact, Branwell enjoyed some very respectable company at Luddenden Foot. A frequent visitor to his station offices, for instance, was the Reverend Sutcliffe Sowden, a young clergyman who was newly ordained and had only taken up his first appointment as incumbent of St James' Church at Mytholmroyd on 1 May 1841, moving to Hebden Bridge later that year. The two had much in common, being about the same age and sharing a love of the wild beauty of the Calderdale scenery. Sowden was a great walker and noted geologist and Branwell spent many happy hours exploring the countryside with him. Branwell was also well known among the local manufacturers, drawing sketches of two of them, John Murgatroyd and George Richardson, in his notebook.[74] Significantly, it was the 'merchants and mill-owners' of the Upper Calder Valley who raised and put their names to a petition on Branwell's behalf when he was dismissed from the railway, so he must have had many friends among this class.[75] He was not simply mixing with the weavers and factory hands who formed the bulk of the population.

In Halifax, too, Branwell was able to enjoy the company of some of the most respected Yorkshire musicians, artists and writers of the day. Prominent among the first was John Frobisher, who had a finger in every musical pie in the district and had organized Liszt's triumphant concert. Joseph Bentley Leyland, the sculptor, was already an old friend and John Wilson Anderson, an artist Branwell knew from his days in Bradford, was a regular visitor.[76] Among the writers were also old friends and new: William Dearden, for instance, a native of Hebden Bridge and an old family friend, who had known him as a child. Dearden was now based in Huddersfield, where he was principal of the King Street Academy, but he was a poet in his own right, known as the 'Bard of Caldene', and had had his poetry published in the local press. John Nicholson, too, 'The Airedale Poet', whom Branwell had probably met in Bradford, was a regular contributor to the Halifax and Leeds papers. Branwell must also have been introduced to the Halifax-based Thomas Crossley, the 'Bard of Ovenden', who was a mainstay of the poetry columns of Yorkshire newspapers.[77] Another, minor poet who certainly did meet Branwell was William Heaton, who later produced a volume of poems entitled *Flowers of Caldervale*. Heaton, like Anderson and Dearden, was part of the Leyland circle and, like them, an admirer of Branwell Brontë.

He was blithe and gay, but at times appeared downcast and sad; yet, if the subject were some topic that he was acquainted with, or some author he loved, he would rise from his seat, and, in beautiful language, describe the author's character, with a zeal and fluency I had never heard equalled. His talents were of a very exalted kind. I have heard him quote pieces from the bard of Avon, from Shelley, Wordsworth, and Byron, as well as from Butler's 'Hudibras', in such a manner as often made me wish I had been a scholar, as he was. At that time I was just beginning to write verses. It is true I had written many pieces, but they had never seen the light; and, on a certain occasion, I showed him one, which he pronounced very good. He lent me books which I had never seen before, and was ever ready to give me information. His temper was always mild towards me. I shall never forget his love for the sublime and beautiful works of Nature, nor how he would tell of the lovely flowers and rare plants he had observed by the mountain stream and woodland rill. All these had excellencies for him; and I have often heard him dilate on the sweet strains of the nightingale, and on the thoughts that bewitched him the first time he heard one.[78]

In the company of friends such as these, Branwell received encouragement and helpful criticism. They formed a sort of informal society, meeting in the George Hotel in Market Street, Bradford, the Anchor and Shuttle at Luddenden Foot, the Lord Nelson at Luddenden and the Broad Tree, Union Cross, Talbot and Old Cock in Halifax. They even ventured out into Branwell's home territory, occasionally meeting at the Black Bull in Haworth and the Cross Roads, between Haworth and Keighley. The object of the meetings was not simply conviviality: those who were writers read aloud to the group the manuscripts of their latest books and poems for criticism by the other members.[79]

Branwell clearly took the advice of these friends to heart. His work at this period shows constant revisions, suggesting a painstaking search for the perfect turn of phrase which he had been too impatient to achieve in his juvenile work. Equally important, their example encouraged him to pursue again his lifelong ambition to see his poems in print. Within a month of taking up his post at Luddenden Foot, Branwell had his first poem published in the *Halifax Guardian* – some five years before his sisters achieved publication. It is often suggested that Branwell only got his poems in print through the offices of J. B. Leyland and that newspaper publication hardly qualifies as a recognition of talent. This is both churlish and unlikely. Though Roberts Leyland had been the publisher and printer of the *Halifax Guardian* until 1837, there is no evidence to suggest that the Leylands had any influence with its current publisher, James Uriah Walker. More conclusively, Francis Leyland, in his biography of the Brontës, seems unaware that Branwell was actually published in the local press.[80]

The *Halifax Guardian* was justly proud of its poetry columns, welcoming gifts of 'Original Poetry' but also publishing pieces by all the famous poets of the day. Nor did it hesitate to reject material which it considered beneath the high standards of which it openly boasted. The little editorial column addressed 'To our Readers and Correspondents' frequently contained a stinging rebuke to some poor soul who had presumed to send his 'feeble' verses for publication. On the other hand, it gave particular encouragement to poetry written specially for the *Halifax Guardian*, so that its poetry columns were usually fresher, more original and often of a higher standard that the conventional gushings from the likes of Mrs Hemans and Caroline Norton, which were reproduced in the Leeds and Yorkshire papers.

It was therefore a real achievement when Branwell had his first poem printed in the *Halifax Guardian*. There is no doubt that he sent the poem in himself, not through Leyland. A note appeared in the 'To the Readers and Correspondents' section on 22 May 1841 stating that the editor could not find room for certain items sent that week and addressing 'P. B. B.' in particular, adding, 'The Poetry must for the above reason, stand over for a week.'[81] It was in fact a further two weeks before Branwell's poem, 'Heaven and Earth' by 'Northangerland', appeared under the banner of 'Original Poetry (For the Halifax Guardian)'. Perhaps surprisingly, the poem was an affirmation of religious faith, contrasting the 'circumscribed ... scene' of human life with the infinity of Heaven.

> On *Earth* we see our own abode,
> A smoky town, a dusty road,
>   A neighbouring hill, or grove;
> In *Heaven* a thousand worlds of light
> Revolving through the gloom of night
>   O'er endless pathways rove.
>
> While daylight shows this little Earth
>   It hides that mighty Heaven,
> And, but by night, a visible birth
>   To all its stars is given;
> And, fast as fades departing day,
> When silent marsh or moorland grey
>   Mid evening's mist declines,
> Then, slowly stealing, star on star,
> As night sweeps forward, from afar,
>   More clear and countless shines.[82]

This was the first of thirteen poems by Branwell which the *Halifax Guardian* published over the next six years. Eight of them, including this one, were revisions of pieces written 1837–8; two more drew on Angrian themes and probably also dated from that period. All but two were published by Branwell under his favourite pseudonym, Northangerland, suggesting that despite his confidence in his ability he was diffident when it came to publicly acknowledging his authorship.[83]

The only poem which Branwell published under his own initials, 'P. B. B.', was an eight-line squib 'On the Melbourne Ministry', which appeared in the *Halifax Guardian* on 14 August 1841. Necessarily a composition of the moment, it celebrated the fall of the Whig Government after the July elections and the return to power of Sir Robert Peel and the Conservatives. No doubt Branwell, who had been excluded from the election activities at Haworth, attended the celebratory tea parties at the Murgatroyd Arms and the Lord Nelson in Luddenden.[84]

Though these two poems were the only ones to be published while Branwell was still at Luddenden Foot, his notebooks reveal that he was constantly employed in new poetic composition as well as revision of the old. The sheer quantity and quality of this poetry gives the lie to claims that his year on the railway at Luddenden Foot was simply a period of debauchery and defeatism. Interestingly, too, these poems were the most overtly autobiographical he had yet written, suggesting a new and reflective maturity. There is some evidence to indicate that Branwell felt he had not made the most of his talents. In a poem written from his lodgings at Brearley Hall on 8 August 1841, he wrote:

> When I look back on former life
>   I scarcely know what I have been
> So swift the change from strife to strife
>   That passes oer the wildering scene
>
> I only feel that every power –
>   And thou hadst given much to me
> Was spent upon the present hour
>   Was never turned My God to thee[85]

Similarly, on 19 December, a visit to Luddenden Church brought him to the realization that he was losing his sense of direction for the future because of his preoccupation with and absorption in the present.

> O God! while I in pleasures wiles
>   Count hours and years as one
> And deem that wrapt in pleasure smil[e]s
>   My joys can neer be done
>
> Give me the stern < perpetu? > sustaining power
>   To look into the past
> < To see > And see the darkly shadowed hour
>   Which \I/ must meet at last[86]

Such sentiments were the exception to the rule, however, for most of Branwell's poems written at Luddenden Foot were charged with ambition, energy and optimism. Though Charlotte's evident scorn at the lowliness of his position may have stung his pride, Branwell felt that his present, comparatively humble, station in life was no impediment to future greatness. The voice of ambition continued to call:

> Amid the worlds wide din around
> I hear from far a solemn Sound
>   That says "Remember Me!"...
>
> I when I heard it sat amid
>   The bustle of a Town like room
> Neath skies, < by > with smoke stain'd vapours hid,
>   By windows, made to show their gloom –
> The desk that held my Ledger book
> Beneath the thundering rattle shook
>   Of Engines passing by
> The bustle of the approaching train

> Was all I hoped to rouse the brain
> Or startle apathy[87]

Branwell evidently took comfort in comparing his own lowly position with that of men who had gone on to achieve greatness. The storms of a typically grim December day,

> The desolate earth – The Wintry Sky –
> The ceas[e]less rain showers driving by –
> The farewell of the year

did not depress him but rather inspired him to remember the victories of mankind in the face of adversity. Citing Galileo, Tasso, Milton, Johnson, Cowper and Burns – all except Galileo, significantly, writers – he went on to consider how each of them had overcome poverty, low birth, imprisonment, even physical disability, to achieve immortality. Similarly, in the autumn of 1841 he wrote the first of three versions of a long poem about Horatio Nelson, which was evidently inspired by 'Nelsoni Mors', a poem by his father's Cambridge friend, Henry Kirke White. The poem followed Nelson from his unpromising childhood to his glorious death at Trafalgar. In choosing Nelson as his subject, Branwell must have been aware of the similarities in their backgrounds: Nelson, too, was a parsonage child and had lost his mother at an early age.[88]

In writing these poems, Branwell had an eye to publication. He may even have intended to write a whole series of poems on great men of the past, as he twice drew up a list of potential subjects, in each case marking off the ones he had covered.[89] Clearly he had no shortage of inspiration and, though he may have suffered periodic bouts of depression, his literary output and the achievement of his ambition to publish suggests that he had everything to look forward to.

It was therefore a severe blow to his self-esteem when he was summarily dismissed from the Leeds and Manchester Railway. A company audit of the Luddenden Foot ledgers at the end of March 1842 revealed that there was a serious discrepancy in the accounts. The sum of £11 1s. 7d. was unaccounted for and Branwell, though not suspected of theft or fraud, was held responsible. According to Grundy, he was 'convicted of constant and culpable carelessness', the result of his wandering off on rambles round the hills leaving only his porter in charge. According to Leyland, it was to Mr Woolven, his 'fellow-assistant', that Branwell entrusted the running of the station.[90] There are problems with both these claims. Branwell took his duties at Luddenden Foot seriously enough to forgo the pleasure of returning home over Christmas, for instance, even though he must have known that Charlotte and Emily were about to go abroad. Equally, there was no Mr Woolven living in or near Luddenden Foot to whom Branwell could have delegated his duties. Branwell's clerk would appear to have been the twenty-five-year-old William Spence, who lived, like Branwell, at Brearley.[91] It would therefore appear that if Branwell did neglect his duties, he left the station in the charge of either William Spence or Henry Killiner, the thirty-year-old railway porter.

Whatever the rights and wrongs of the matter, Branwell was responsible, morally and officially, for the missing money. The sum was deducted from his quarter's salary, his dismissal was confirmed by a meeting of the board of directors on 4 March, and Branwell found himself unemployed once more.[92] Though dismissal in such circumstances was deeply humiliating and discreditable, there is evidence to suggest the affair was not as serious as it appears at first sight. The Leeds and Manchester Railway was famous for taking an unusually hard line with its staff. Any employee whose neglect, however unintentional, caused an accident could expect instant arrest and prosecution for dereliction of duty. As accidents happened frequently on the new line, this was not a rare event. Likewise, drunkenness was regarded as an extremely serious offence: one engine driver who reported for duty in a state of inebriation was not only prosecuted but sentenced to two months' hard labour.[93] Had Branwell been suspected of either fraud or dereliction of duty, he would undoubtedly have been prosecuted. In fact, a petition in his favour was got up by the merchants and mill owners of the district and presented to the board. Though this did not change the board's mind, it suggests that Branwell's offence can only have been a minor one. Similarly, the facts that, within two months of his dismissal, Branwell sought Grundy's help in obtaining a new post on the same railway and that, four years later, it was intimated to him that he might be considered for one, suggest that his crime was not serious enough to disqualify him from ever working for the company again.[94]

Perhaps fortunately, by the time Branwell returned to Haworth at the beginning of April only his father and aunt were at home. Anne was at Thorp Green and Charlotte and Emily were in their school in Brussels. They had been escorted there by their father who, despite a disinclination to leave home which had grown stronger over the years, determined that his daughters should have his protection for their first trip outside the north of England. The journey came at a time of considerable inconvenience to himself. On 7 January 1842, the Bradford churchwardens had again pressed their demand for a church rate of £76 12s. 10d. to be laid in the chapelry. While Patrick had supported the opponents in their resistance to the previous demand, he was now outspoken in his denunciation of the Bradford churchwardens. He opened the meeting by declaring from the chair that

the rate now demanded, had not, according to his opinion, the sanction of either law or custom, having been laid in quite an unusual way, contrary to the vote and voice of a great majority of the rate payers ... He entreated the body of the rate-payers then before him to consider the dilemma in which the chapelwardens of Haworth were placed, by having such a heavy demand pressed upon them at this time when even the poor's rate could only with the greatest difficulty be obtained and hoped that all parties, both Whigs, Radicals, Tories, Dissenters, Methodists, and Churchmen would unite heartily to save them from the jeopardy and peril to which they are exposed by the strange and unprecedented proceedings of the Bradford churchwardens ... The Rev. gentleman then told the people that his mind was quite made up never more to attempt a compulsory Church Rate either for Bradford or Haworth so long as the law stood as it does.[95]

The meeting had avoided confrontation by using the time-honoured tactic of adjourning the discussion to a future date, but it also agreed to a Dissenting proposal that any legal costs which might be incurred by the Haworth churchwardens in their opposition to Bradford should be indemnified by the vestry. Three weeks later, Patrick wrote to the *Bradford Observer*, defending his stance and, in a side-swipe at Dr Scoresby, pointing out that 'The mainspring of all this may, in some measure, be traced to the anomalous circumstance of having a parish within a parish.'[96]

The suffering in Haworth township had reached new levels as the winter progressed and trade showed no sign of recovery. Again, Patrick was deeply involved in trying to alleviate the hardship of his parishioners. A general subscription was set up among the gentlemen and tradesmen of the chapelry which raised 'large amounts' to augment a further grant of £200 from the London Committee for the Relief of the Distressed Manufacturers. The money was again put to good practical use in the purchase of shirting and coating, sheets and bed coverlets, fifty pairs of clogs, twenty packs of best oatmeal and 200 loads of coal for the most destitute.[97]

It was, therefore, neither a good nor a tactful time for the parson to absent himself on a jaunt to foreign parts. Nevertheless, Patrick's duty to his daughters spoke more loudly than his duty to his parish. In a conscientious effort to do the best he could for his children, he drew up a little notebook of handy French phrases to use on the journey, noting at the beginning:

The following conversational terms, Suited to a traveller, in France, or any part of the Continent of Europe – are taken from Surenne's. New French Manual – for 1840

. . . .

And \with those in my pocket book/ will be sufficient, for me – And must be fully mastered, and ready – Semper – All these, must be kept semper. There are first the French – 2 – the < Englis > right pronunciation – and lastly the English. –

. . . .

Revd. P. B. A. B. –, Haworth, near Bradford – Yorkshire.[98]

Most of the useful phrases (often misspelt) were concerned with food and drink, accommodation and travelling by diligence. They show the age-old traveller's concerns from 'Les draps sont ils sees? = La dra sontil see? = Are the sheets air'd?' to 'S'il vous plait montrez moi le priver = Sil voo play montray moa la priva = If you please shew me the < pri > privy' – the last, curiously, entered under the heading 'Post Office'.[99]

Patrick, Charlotte and Emily set off for Brussels on 8 February 1842.[100] The plan was that they would be accompanied by Mary and Joe Taylor, who had both done the journey several times before. They travelled together by train from Leeds to London, arriving at Euston Station late in the evening after a journey of eleven hours. Despite having seasoned travellers with them, it was apparently Patrick who determined their choice of hotel. In his student days at Cambridge and later, when curate of Wethersfield, he had sometimes stayed at the Chapter Coffee House in Paternoster Row. Once the haunt of the eighteenth-century literati, a place to see and be seen, it had become a sort of gentleman's club where university students and clergymen could spend a few days in London. It was hardly an appropriate place for three young ladies to stay, but they could have done worse. The Chapter Coffee House lay in the heart of the City, within the shadow of St Paul's; Paternoster Row was barred to all but pedestrian traffic, making it a haven of peace in the bustling confusion that filled the surrounding streets. Though the writers and poets had long since moved on to more fashionable areas, it retained its bookish air with wholesale stationers, booksellers and publishers lining each side of the narrow flagged street.[101]

The Chapter Coffee House made an ideal base for forays into the city and Charlotte was determined that see it they would. Since childhood and her creation of the Great Glasstown, she had been obsessed with the very idea of the metropolis. Now, on the dawn of her great adventure, she found herself in London with time to spare before the Ostend packet sailed for Belgium. Into three short days, she crammed a lifetime's ambition to see and experience the sights and sounds of the city. The rest of the party was bullied or cajoled into accompanying her on an orgy of culture. Mary Taylor, rather wearily, reported later to Mrs Gaskell:

she seemed to think our business was, and ought to be, to see all the pictures and statues we could. She knew the artists, and knew where other productions of theirs were to be found. I don't remember what we saw except St Paul's. Emily was like her in these habits of mind, but certainly never took her opinion, but always had one to offer.[102]

Many years later Charlotte was to look back on the experience and, somewhat unfairly, blame Joe Taylor for the frenetic bout of sightseeing. Learning of the 'travelling – and tugging and fagging about and getting drenched and mudded', all on only two meals a day, to which Joe had subjected his bride on her honeymoon, Charlotte remarked 'it all reminds me too sharply of the few days I spent with Joe in London nearly 10 years since – when I was many a time fit to drop with the fever and faintness resulting from long fasting and excessive fatigue'.[103]

If Mary did not recall anything except St Paul's, Charlotte drank in and absorbed every new sight with the greed of one long deprived. Like Lucy Snowe in her novel *Villette*, she first heard the 'colossal hum and trembling knell' of St Paul's as she lay in her bed in the Chapter Coffee House. The next morning, she looked out of the window and saw the cathedral for the first time.

Above my head, above the house-tops, co-elevate almost with the clouds, I saw a solemn, orbed mass, dark-blue and dim – THE DOME. While I looked, my inner self moved; my spirit shook its always-fettered wings half loose; I had a sudden feeling as if I, who had never yet truly lived, were at last about to taste life: in that morning my soul grew as fast as Jonah's gourd ... Prodigious was the amount of life I lived that morning.[104]

It was no coincidence that this passage echoed her own passionate 'longing for wings' which she had so eloquently described to Ellen when reading Mary's descriptions of the pictures and cathedrals she had seen. No doubt, too, Lucy Snowe's words echoed her own feelings. 'I like the spirit of this great London which I feel around me. Who but a coward would pass his whole life in hamlets, and for ever abandon his faculties to the eating rust of obscurity?'[105]

After St Paul's, there was Westminster Abbey to visit, the galleries of the British Museum and the pictures in the National Gallery. There was also the more mundane business of their travel arrangements. They had to purchase their passports, a transaction which the thrifty Patrick later recorded with quiet satisfaction in his notebook had cost them only five shillings each at the Belgian consul's office, half the amount charged by the French consul.[106]

Early on the morning of Saturday, 12 February, the little party made its way down to London Bridge Wharf and boarded the Ostend packet, a small steam ship which made the twice weekly voyage carrying mail and passengers between England and the Continent. The voyage took nearly fourteen hours, so the Brontës and the Taylors would have arrived in Ostend late on Saturday night. Perhaps in deference to Mr Brontë's age, or perhaps because the next day was a Sunday, they decided to stay in Ostend and only set off for Brussels on Monday morning.[107] As the new railway line between Ostend and Brussels had not yet fully opened, they took the more cumbersome and much slower diligence, a public stagecoach which, as Mr Brontë recorded in his notebook, passed through the ancient town of Ghent (pronounced 'Gong', he noted).[108]

The long, slow journey of nearly seventy miles would have been a trial to most travellers, anxious to reach their destination, but Charlotte savoured every moment of her first experience of a foreign country. Later, in *The Professor*, she recalled her own first impressions of Belgium through the eyes of her narrator, William Crimsworth.

This is Belgium, reader – look! Don't call the picture a flat or a dull one – it was neither flat nor dull to me when I first beheld it. When I left Ostend on a mild February Morning and found myself on the road to Brussels, nothing could look vapid to me. My sense of enjoyment possessed an edge whetted to the finest, untouched, keen, exquisite ... I gazed often, and always with delight from the window of the diligence ... Well! and what did I see? I will tell you faithfully. Green, reedy swamps, fields fertile but flat, cultivated in patches that made them look like magnified kitchen-gardens; belts of cut trees, formal as pollard willows, skirting the horizon; narrow canals, gliding slow by the roadside, painted Flemish farm-houses, some very dirty hovels, a grey, dead sky, wet road, wet fields, wet house-tops; not a beautiful, scarcely a picturesque object met my eye along the whole route, yet to me, all was beautiful, all was more than picturesque.[109]

By the time the Brontës and Taylors arrived in Brussels, it was too dark to see anything but the lights of the city. They retired for the night to the Hotel d'Hollande which was conveniently near the diligence terminus.[110] The next morning, the English Episcopal clergyman who had assisted them in their choice of school, Mr Jenkins, arrived with his wife at the hotel to escort them there.

The Pensionnat Heger advertised itself as a 'Maison d'éducation pour les jeunes Demoiselles'. It was situated in the ancient quarter, close to the central park which had been a landmark in the city since at least the seventeenth century. Many of the houses in the area dated from the same period, though the Pensionnat Heger itself was only forty years old. It stood in the Rue d'Isabelle, a straight but narrow street, at the foot of a flight of steps leading up to the park entrance. From the statue of General Belliard at the park gates it was possible to look down on the chimneys of the Rue d'Isabelle below. Halfway along and standing straight on the street was the Pensionnat Heger, a long, low, rather stark building, two storeys high with a regimented row of large, rectangular windows on each floor. The unpromising bleakness of the exterior belied the charms of the interior. Somewhat unexpectedly for a school in the centre of the city, the Pensionnat Heger had a delightful garden, lined with ancient fruit trees. This was to be a haven of peace and rest in the noisy bustle of school life.

The turf was verdant, the gravelled walks were white; sun-bright nasturtiums clustered beautiful about the roots of the doddered orchard giants. There was a large *berceau*, above which spread the shade of an acacia; there was a smaller, more sequestered bower, nestled in the vines which ran all along a high and gray wall, and gathered their tendrils in a knot of beauty, and hung their clusters in loving profusion about the favoured spot where jasmine and ivy met and married them.'''

On one side of the garden ran the 'Allée défendue', a narrow walk overlooked by the windows of the Athénée Royal, the neighbouring boys' school. For that reason it was out of bounds to the pupils of the Pensionnat Heger, though the boys would have had to have had extremely sharp eyes to pierce the thick, tangled foliage of the trees and shrubs which grew over the alleyway. Hardly the pleasantest spot in the garden because of its dense shade, it acquired an air of mystery because it was forbidden – an air that Charlotte was to exploit to the full in both her novels set in Brussels.

The two schoolrooms were large, pleasant and airy, with the teacher's desk set on a dais at one end. Above them ran the long dormitory containing about twenty beds; there was also a long, narrow *réfectoire* where the girls dined, prepared their evening lessons and attended their daily mass. Monsieur and Madame Heger, with their three small daughters, lived on the school premises.[112]

Madame Claire Zoë Heger, who was thirty-eight years old, was the directrice of the school. Her husband, Constantin Georges Romain Heger, was five years younger and, at thirty-three, had already an eminent reputation as a teacher at the Athénée Royal; he also gave literature lessons to his wife's pupils.[113] Madame Heger's terms were comparatively expensive: 650 francs a year for board and an education, 'based on Religion', which included the French language, history, arithmetic, geography, scripture and 'all the needlework that a well-brought up young lady should know'. An additional thirty-four francs was required if the pupil could not provide her own bedding and there were extra charges for lessons in music and languages other than French. Altogether, without the expense of travel, clothing, books and other personal effects, the total cost of six months' schooling for both Charlotte and Emily would have come to around 1055 francs or forty-two pounds.[114] This came within the budget set by Aunt Branwell, but left little room for manoeuvre or for unexpected crises. Charlotte had therefore written anxiously beforehand to enquire about the exact cost of all the 'extras'. The Hegers were struck by the simple, earnest tone of her letter, and agreed between themselves that

These are the daughters of an English pastor, of moderate means, anxious to learn with an ulterior view of instructing others, and to whom the risk of additional expense is of great consequence. Let us name a specific sum, within which all expenses shall be included.[115]

The Hegers' kindness towards their English pupils further extended to permitting them to be absent from the daily mass and even to providing them with a curtained-off recess at the end of the school dormitory, so that they could enjoy at least a measure of privacy.

In handing over his daughters into Madame Heger's care, Patrick must have felt a certain satisfaction in the arrangements that had been made. Charlotte and Emily would enjoy the full benefit of a continental education at a reasonable cost. With his own eyes he had seen that the school fulfilled its claims to be situated in one of the healthiest parts of the town and that the wellbeing of pupils was an object of active concern.[116] He knew that the Taylors were close at hand in the Château de Koekelberg and their cousins, the Dixons, even closer in lodgings in the Rue de la Régence. Mr and Mrs Jenkins had not only promised to keep an eye on the girls but had also given them an open invitation to spend their Sundays and half-holidays at their house in the Chaussée d'Ixelles, just outside the ancient part of the city.[117]

Patrick remained in Brussels for about a week longer, moving out of his hotel to stay with Mr and Mrs Jenkins at their invitation. He used his time to see the sights of the city, visit his daughters to ensure that they were settling in and to achieve what must surely have been his ultimate goal, a trip to Waterloo. For years afterwards, he would regale the parishioners of Haworth with his recollections of the battlefield where the fate of Europe had been decided.[118] Then, and only then, did he set off for home, travelling down through Flanders and northern France before crossing the Channel at Calais and returning to Haworth, via London. Now, with the satisfaction of a seasoned traveller, he could record in his notebook:

I went to Brussels, Lille, Dunkirk, & Calais, in Feby 1842 = and found, the expenses of travelling, under all circumstance generally, to be neither below, nor above one fifth less there, than in England

. . . .

1842. B—

I was only between 2 and 3 weeks away — And the whole expenses of my journey, amounted to about < not more? > £23–10–0, not more = [119]

Chapter Fourteen

❧

ISOLATED IN THE MIDST OF NUMBERS

Charlotte and Emily did not fit easily into their new life at the Pensionnat Heger. In many ways they were already marked out as different from their fellow pupils. Unlike the Château de Koekelberg, where most of the girls were English or German, the Pensionnat Heger catered expressly for Belgians. Lessons were taught exclusively in French and no concessions were expected or sought for the fact that the Brontës were as yet not fluent in the language. They were also almost unique in being Protestant; all the other residents were Catholic except for one other pupil and Madame Heger's English nursery maid. At twenty-five and twenty-four, Charlotte and Emily were considerably older than their classmates and this, combined with their foreign ways and religion, made them seem remote to their fellow pupils. There was, Charlotte noted, without any sense of regret, 'a broad line of demarcation between us and all the rest. We are completely isolated in the midst of numbers'.[1]

Despite the odds stacked against them, the Brontës not only survived but flourished. They made no effort to win friends among their fellow pupils and concentrated on their work to the exclusion of all else. For Emily, the difference between her old, self-regulated life in her quiet home in a moorland township and her new life in a large school in the midst of a foreign city must have been alarming. Apart from the six months of lessons she had had at Roe Head, the only French she knew was what Charlotte had passed on and what she herself had learnt from her reading. To be compelled not only to speak and write French all day every day, but also to have her lessons taught in it, must have been a severe trial. She had so much catching up to do before she could even begin to make sense of her lessons that there was no time for Gondal fantasy.[2] Charlotte was more proficient in French than her sister and therefore adapted more easily. For her, the difficulties of her new position paled into insignificance compared to the bondage of governessing. At the beginning of May, after nearly three months in Brussels, she wrote to Ellen:

I was twenty-six years old a week or two since, and at this ripe time of life I am a schoolgirl, a complete schoolgirl, and, on the whole, very happy in that capacity. It felt very strange at first to submit to authority instead of exercising it – to obey orders instead of giving them; but I like that state of things. I returned to it with the same avidity that a cow, that has long been kept on dry hay, returns to fresh grass. Don't laugh at my simile. It is natural to me to submit, and very unnatural to command.[3]

Charlotte had never lost her passion for acquiring knowledge and now, for the first time in ten years, she had a legitimate reason to submerge herself in an entirely selfish pursuit of learning. Describing the Pensionnat Heger to Ellen Nussey as a large school of forty day-pupils and twelve boarders, she drew analogies with Roe Head. Madame Heger reminded her of Catherine Wooler – she had 'precisely the same cast of mind, degree of cultivation, and quality of intellect' though her 'severe points' were softened because she was a married lady. The three teachers, Mesdemoiselles Blanche, Sophie and Marie, she dismissed as an old maid, a potential one and a talented and original lady whose manners were so repulsive and arbitrary that she had alienated all the pupils except the Brontës. Seven masters also came in to teach the seven branches of learning: French, drawing, music, singing, writing, arithmetic and German.[4] One person alone had already made an outstanding impression upon Charlotte and that was Monsieur Heger, who taught the girls French literature.

There is one individual of whom I have not yet spoken – M Heger, the husband of Madame. He is professor of rhetoric, a man of power as to mind, but very choleric and irritable as to temperament; a little black ugly being, with a face that varies in expression. Sometimes he borrows the lineaments of an insane tom-cat, sometimes those of a delirious hyena; occasionally, but very seldom, he discards these perilous attractions and assumes an air not above 100 degrees removed from mild and gentleman-like. He is very angry with me just at present, because I have written a translation which he chose to stigmatise as *peu correcte*. He did not tell me so, but wrote the accusation on the margin of my book, and asked in brief, stern phrase, how it happened that my compositions were always better than my translations? adding that the thing seemed to him inexplicable. The fact is, some weeks ago, in a high-flown humour, he forbade me to use either dictionary or grammar in translating the most difficult English compositions into French. This makes the task rather arduous, and compels me now and then to introduce an English word, which nearly plucks the eyes out of his head when he sees it. Emily and he don't draw well together at all. When he is very ferocious with me I cry; that sets all things straight. Emily works like a horse, and she has had great difficulties to contend with, far greater than I have had. Indeed, those who come to a French school for instruction ought previously to have acquired a considerable knowledge of the French language, otherwise they will lose a great deal of time, for the course of instruction is adapted to natives and not foreigners; and in these large establishments they will not change their ordinary course for one or two strangers. The few private lessons M Heger has vouchsafed to give us are, I suppose, to be considered a great favour, and I can perceive they have already excited much spite and jealousy in the school.[5]

If Charlotte quickly recognized extraordinary powers in Monsieur Heger, he was not slow to realize the ability of his new pupils. They had begun their education on the usual system, preparing grammatical and syntactical exercises, taking down dictation and extending their vocabulary by copying and translating words and phrases. Having quietly observed their progress, Monsieur Heger decided that they were capable of something more advanced. He proposed to do what he had sometimes done with other older and abler pupils: read them some of the finest passages from French literature, discuss and analyse them together and then get the sisters to reproduce their own thoughts in a similar style. His suggestion was received less than graciously. Emily gave it short shrift, saying she saw no good to be derived from the plan, which would result only in them losing all originality of thought and expression. Charlotte, less belligerently, also doubted the benefits of the scheme but was prepared to try it out simply because she felt bound to obey her teacher.[6] In this unpromising way began the lessons which were to have such a tremendous influence on the Brontës. They subjected Charlotte, in particular, to a new and not unwelcome discipline which was ultimately to transform the whole way she was accustomed to write, releasing her from the verbiage of Angria and setting her firmly on the road to spare and elegant prose.

Frederika Macdonald, who was a pupil at the Pensionnat Heger nineteen years after Charlotte, described Monsieur Heger's method in greater detail.

He would read aloud some eloquent, pathetic, or amusing passage from a classical French author. He would then analyse this passage, and signalise its beauties or criticise its defects. Afterwards he would either himself suggest, or allow his pupils to select, a subject for composition, attuned to the same key, either grave or gay, of the model of excellence he had given; but of a sufficiently different character to make anything resembling unintelligent imitation impossible … The pupil was supposed to write in her own note-book a rough copy of the composition, leaving a wide margin for corrections. The fair copy of the exercise given Monsieur Héger was also to have a wide margin … when the corrected exercise was returned the pupil was held to verify the remarks made, and to re-write the composition, for her own benefit only, with the improvements suggested.

Frequently the exercises would be discussed and criticized in class, the writer being called upon to defend her opinions or a particular choice of phrase. An exercise which met with Monsieur Heger's favour would have to be copied out again and presented to him to keep.[7]

This method of teaching can be seen working in practice in the essays Charlotte and Emily wrote throughout the summer of 1842. Around two dozen have survived, slightly less than half of them by Emily. At least three of Charlotte's earliest compositions can be traced back to their source pieces, which Charlotte transcribed into one of her notebooks. 'The Sick Girl', written on 18 April, was based on Alexandre Soumet's poem, 'La Pauvre Fille', which her essay followed closely, opening with the same observation that sleep is a stranger to the bed of sickness and using the same images of the sun's rays on the mountain and the child's exclusion from the play of her friends; at the end, however, she departed from her original source and allowed the girl to recover.[8]

'Evening Prayer in a Camp', written on 26 April, was more adventurous. The stimulus for this piece was the concept of the incongruity of Christian prayers being said on board ship in the middle of a vast ocean which was taken from Chateaubriand's 'Prière du Soir à bord d'un vaisseau'. Charlotte transposed the scene to an Egyptian desert, added to the power of the image by turning those at prayer into soldiers on the eve of battle and strengthened the contrast by placing them in the confines of a heathen temple.[9]

The third essay, 'Anne Askew', written on 2 June, was an 'Imitation' and therefore the closest of all to its source, 'Eudore. Moeurs Chrétiennes IV Siècle', also by Chateaubriand. The story of Eudore told how this early Christian was faced with being thrown to the lions for his faith; on the evening before his death he received a letter saying that his fiancée had been condemned to be the mistress of another man but would be restored to him undefiled if he sacrificed to the gods. Urged by his companions to make the sacrifice, Eudore went to do so but at the last minute dashed down the libations and declared, 'I am a Christian.' Charlotte again gave the story a different twist, making the central figure Anne Askew, the English Protestant martyr, who was burnt at the stake during the reign of the Catholic Queen Mary. Charlotte began in almost exactly the same words as Chateaubriand: 'In the reign of Mary, Queen of England, a young girl named Anne Askew was about to be put to the rack.' Like Eudore, Anne receives a letter, in her case from the Bishop of Winchester, Stephen Gardiner, offering her a pardon if she will recant. Half dazed by the torture and tempted to end her sufferings, Anne begins to sign the letter but, remembering that only the body can die, she returns voluntarily to the rack, declaring 'I am a Protestant.'[10] One can only wonder what Monsieur Heger, a devout Catholic, thought of his pupil's choice of subject and her defiant conversion of a universal Christian martyr into a specifically Protestant one.

At other times, the passages chosen by Monsieur Heger for study would only be allowed to suggest a subject. One such example was Victor Hugo's account of Mirabeau at the Tribune, in which he pointed out both the faulty 'exaggeration in conception' and the successful nuances of expression. Monsieur Heger then left his pupils to choose their own topic because, he said, 'it is necessary, before sitting down to write on a subject, to have thoughts and feelings about it. I cannot tell on what subject your heart and mind have been excited.'[11] On this particular occasion, Charlotte opted for Peter the Hermit, the preacher who had galvanized Europe into taking up the Crusade, while Emily chose King Harold of England on the eve of the Battle of Hastings. Charlotte's version exalted the spirit of the man, that fire within him which would always compel him to rise above the mundane. Clearly she identified with him herself, returning to the theme of physical beauty which had haunted her since childhood.

Peter the Hermit's strength was not merely physical strength for Nature, or rather, God, is impartial in the distribution of gifts, giving one grace, beauty, bodily perfection, another spirit and moral greatness. Peter was a little man and not good-looking; but he had that courage, that steadfastness, that enthusiasm, that emotional energy which crushes all opposition and makes the will of one man become the law of a whole nation.[12]

Emily, on the other hand, set out to prove that a man could rise to the occasion. To do this she contrasted Harold, the king, in peace time and Harold, the hero, in war.

Harold united in himself all the energy, the power, all the hopes of one nation. Now he was no longer a king, he was a hero. The situation had transformed him; in peace he had undoubtedly been like all other princes occupying a peaceful throne: a miserable slave in his palace, wearied with pleasure, deceived by flatterers, knowing, for he was not a complete fool, that he was the least free of all his people … Harold on the field of battle, without his palace, without his ministers, without his courtesans, without his splendour, without his luxury, having only his country's sky above him and, beneath his feet, that land which his ancestors had held and which he would not abandon except with life; and Harold, surrounded by devoted hearts, who had entrusted him with their safety, their freedom, their existence – what a difference! A divine spirit shone in his eyes, visible to men as well as to his Creator –

a multitude of human passions rising in him at the same time were exalted, sanctified, nearly deified. His courage had no element of rashness, his pride of arrogance, his indignation of injustice, that assurance of presumption. He was inwardly convinced that no mortal power could defeat him. Death, alone, could snatch victory from his arms – and Harold is ready to submit to her because the touch of her hand is to heroes what the blow striking off his shackles is to the slave.[13]

Mrs Gaskell rightly considered Emily's essay superior in both power and imagination to Charlotte's,[14] though her command of French vocabulary and idiom did not yet rival that of her elder sister. Indeed, both girls had had only four months' tuition at this stage, so their achievement was already remarkable.

In some of the exercises, it is possible to make a direct comparison between Charlotte's and Emily's version of the same piece. Both sisters wrote an undated piece, for instance, on the siege of Oudenarde. Charlotte's, as befitted someone who had worshipped military heroes from childhood, concentrates on Simon de Lalaing, the heroic captain of the besieged town, who inspires courage and endurance in his defenders. When his two sons are captured by the enemy, Simon is forced to choose between seeing them executed before his eyes or handing over the keys of the town.

A terrible struggle tore apart his heart – for several minutes he said not a word – he covered his eyes with his hand and leant his brow against the battlemented wall. Soon he rose – his face pale and his lips bloodless – and replied in a firm loud voice, 'If my children die, God will take them to his breast, I have only a duty to fulfil, which is to remain faithful to my country – Men of Ghent, I am not defeated, take yourselves off.'[15]

In the event, the men of Ghent refused to commit such an atrocity and the town was relieved. Then, obviously following her original source, Charlotte ended by stating that there was no more noble example from ancient history.

Marcus Curtius, throwing himself into the gaping fissure which had opened in the middle of the Forum was not moved by a courage more sublime than the commander of Oudenarde, sacrificing his feelings as a father to his principles as a patriot.[16]

Emily's version of the same story takes a much less high-flown view of the events. She gives no prominence to Simon de Lalaing as the inspiration in the city's defence but simply talks of the overwhelming numbers facing the besieged. Interestingly, too, where Charlotte gives the women her customary passive role by simply saying that they supported their commander and that Madame de Lalaing especially had shown herself worthy to be a soldier's wife, Emily typically gives them a much more active part. 'Even the women – that class condemned by the laws of society to be a heavy burden in every instance of action or danger, on this occasion put aside their degrading privileges and played a distinguished role in the defence.'[17] Though Simon de Lalaing had been a much less important figure in her account, his terrible choice loses none of its dramatic force.

> The commander looked at his sons who implored his aid with eyes full of tears; at their side he saw the soldiers, armed with swords, who would put them to death; he hesitated one moment, nature struggling hard against honour – his breast filled with overpowering emotion. But finally the patriot subdued the father and he turned to the men of Ghent saying 'Take the life of these poor children, I cannot put it in the balance against the liberty of my country. I commend their souls to God. My sentence is delivered'.[18]

Emily, too, drew the comparison with Marcus Curtius, but gave it a totally different emphasis: 'there are more men who can leap with Marcus Curtius into a living tomb than can sacrifice, like Lalaing, the tenderest affections of the heart for love of their country'.[19] While Charlotte had considered the individuals involved, believing Lalaing's courage to surpass that of Marcus Curtius, Emily had turned the example into a general observation on mankind. Men are more often motivated to self-sacrifice by brute, unthinking courage than by a deliberate denial of the heart's best feelings.

This air of cynicism is not one which runs through all Emily's French exercises; her misanthropy – and her lack of conventional religious faith – have been vastly over-stated by her biographers. On 15 May, for example, she wrote an essay in defence of cats, attributing their commonly acknowledged bad qualities – hypocrisy, cruelty and ingratitude – to their close resemblance to humans. The cat playing with a mouse is no worse than the man who hunts a fox to the verge of death then throws it to the dogs, or the boy who crushes a butterfly in his hand. The cat's hypocrisy is what humans call politeness 'and anyone who does not employ it to disguise his true feelings would soon be driven out of society'. Even the cat's notorious ingratitude is only another name for its penetration: it sees the motives of those who would bestow favours and judges them for what they are worth. The whole point of the essay, however, as Emily states emphatically at the beginning, is, 'I can truthfully say that I like cats.' 'A cat is the animal who has more human feelings than nearly any other animal', she tells us, yet their vices do not make her hate people any more than she hates cats. It is worth pointing out, too, that Charlotte also seems to have written an essay on the subject, now lost, which espoused exactly the same sentiments.[20]

'Filial Love', another essay, written on 5 August, is also often quoted as an illustration of Emily's jaundiced view of mankind. Only men, she claims, require the threat of the commandment 'Honour your father and mother if you wish to live' to enforce their obedience.

> It is a principle of nature that parents love their children; the doe does not fear the dogs when her little one is in danger, the bird dies on its nest; this instinct is a part of the divine spirit which we share with every animal which exists – and has not

God put a similar sentiment in the heart of children? Something of it, certainly, and yet the voice of thunder cries 'Honour your father and mother or you will die!'[21]

However, what the essay goes on to point out is that the vast majority of children do love their parents quite naturally: those who do not are instinctively shunned by the moral majority. Emily's argument is that, while shunning such 'monsters', we should pity not condemn them.

The hour will come when conscience will awake, then there will be a terrible retribution; what mediator will then plead for the criminal? It is God who accuses him; What power can save the miserable man? It is God who condemns him. He has rejected happiness in his mortal life only to ensure torment in the eternal life. Let angels and men weep for his fate – he was their brother.[22]

A few days after this exercise, both sisters wrote on the subject of the caterpillar. For Charlotte it was an opportunity to compare God's greatest creation, mankind, with his lowliest, a worm: the caterpillar 'lives a crude, materialistic life: it eats and crawls today; it ate and crawled yesterday; it will eat and crawl tomorrow'. It is a symbol of Man's grosser, earthly appetites and just as it apparently dies as a chrysalis only to be reborn as a butterfly, so the human dies in the body to achieve a purified rebirth in the resurrection.[23] Emily took a much more imaginative approach in her essay. Walking through a forest, she questions why everything in the natural world tends to destruction:

Nature is an inexplicable problem; it exists on a principle of destruction; everything must be a tireless instrument of death to others or else cease to live itself; and in the meantime we celebrate the day of our birth and praise God for having entered into such a world.[24]

As if to justify this view she pauses to admire a beautiful flower, only to find that its heart has been eaten out by a caterpillar, which, in disgust, she crushes beneath her foot. A moment later a brilliant butterfly flutters past and realization dawns.

The created should not judge his Creator, here is a symbol of the world to come. Just as the ugly caterpillar is the origin of the splendid butterfly, so this world is the embryo of a new heaven and a new earth whose poorest beauty will infinitely exceed mortal imagination; and when you see the magnificent outcome of what seems so humble to you now, you will despise your blind presumption in accusing Omniscience for not destroying nature in its infancy.[25]

This could hardly be a more eloquent statement of Christian belief; Emily's optimism is reflected in the fact that she chose to call her essay 'The Butterfly', while Charlotte called hers 'The Caterpillar'.

Two months later, in October, Emily and her sister each wrote an essay entitled 'The Palace of Death'. Both followed their original source quite closely, describing a scene where Death, tired of the golden time when men died only of old age, chooses a new minister. Rejecting the claims of Ambition and War (or, in Emily's case, Fanaticism), with their attendant trains of Rage and Vengeance, Envy and Treason, Famine, Pestilence, Sloth and Avarice, Death chooses Intemperance. In Charlotte's case the choice is made because 'War and Ambition are only your children; all the demons which damn mankind are born of you.'[26] Emily, also compelled to choose Intemperance by her source, gave her a stirring speech to justify her candidature to Death:

I have a friend before whom all this assembly will be forced to give way; she is called Civilisation: in a few years time she will come to inhabit this earth with us and every age will augment her power and in the end she will turn Ambition out of your service, she will harness Anger with the law; she will snatch the weapons from the hands of Fanaticism; she will chase Famine out among the savages; I alone will grow and flourish under her reign.[27]

Death, recognizing the truth of this statement, makes Intemperance her Vice-Roy. An apparent belief in the power of civilization to tame the savageries of mankind, which was not uncommon in the nineteenth century, is thus given a cynical twist: Intemperance becomes the vice particularly associated with civilization, flourishing outside the state of nature, and it alone will continue to kill.

If Emily's Brussels essays give us a unique insight into her beliefs, Charlotte's are equally revealing. Their most obvious feature, as Mrs Gaskell observed, was their faith – something which contemporaries believed to be sadly lacking in her letters and her published novels.[28] The emphasis on faith may have owed something to the air of religion which pervaded the Pensionnat Heger. The prospectus had nailed its colours to the mast: 'The course of instruction', it declared, was 'based on Religion.' Monsieur Heger, in particular, was held to be 'profoundly and openly religious', expressing the zeal of his piety in his membership of the Society of St Vincent de Paul, through which he devoted his leisure hours to teaching the poor and the sick.[29] Charlotte was not, however, simply trying to please her master. Monsieur Heger himself recognized that she 'was brought up on the Bible'[30] and there was nothing sycophantic in her defiantly Protestant stance in a Catholic school. Many of her essays were overtly on religious topics; 'Anne Askew', 'Evening prayer in a camp', 'The death of Moses', 'Portrait of Peter the Hermit' and 'The Caterpillar', all written in 1842, fall into this class.

On the other hand, many of the essays apparently on unrelated subjects were coloured by Charlotte's obvious Christian faith. Her description of the ritual immolation of a Hindustani widow is an excuse to attack every aspect of a barbaric practice: the widow, going voluntarily to her death, is upheld as much by pride as religion; the funeral procession is a savage, noisy and pagan display; all the wealth of the Hindustanis, she declares, is not worth a single ray from that star of Bethlehem which the Magi once saw in the East. A sick girl recovers her health in response to fervent prayer and even the sight of a normally timid bird defending its eggs on its nest is a symbol of God's presence in his works.[31]

Monsieur Heger was a ruthless critic, attacking not only technical mistakes, such as incorrect sentence structure and clumsy translations, but also trying to stamp upon his pupils the importance of adopting a style. He was a man with an eye for detail: a single infelicitous word or phrase merited vicious underlining and he was pitiless in his paring away of unnecessary verbiage. This was something that Charlotte, especially, needed greatly; though the Angrian obsession had implanted a love of writing in her blood, she had not yet learnt to control her runaway imagination or to impose discipline on her pen. Monsieur Heger was the first person to offer her objective criticism of her style and suggest ways of improving it. At the end of an early essay, 'The Nest', written on 30 April, he appended a piece of advice:

How very much importance you must give to your details as you unfold your subject! You must sacrifice, underline(without pity), everything that does not contribute to clarity, verisimilitude and effect. Look with great suspicion on everything which sets off the main thought, so that the impression you give is highly coloured, graphic; It is sufficient if the rest remain underline(in its place but in the background). This is what gives to prose style, as to painting, unity, perspective, and underline(effect). underline(Read) the fourteenth Harmonie of Lamartine: underline(The Infinite). We will analyse it together underline(from the point of view of its details).

> May 4   C Heger[32]

Most of the time, Monsieur Heger confined his advice to stringently critical remarks. A good example occurs in Charlotte's exercise on 'Peter the Hermit', written on 31 July. Woolly phrases are tightened up: men 'destined to be' instruments of great change become 'predestined'; an irrelevant phrase incurs a marginal note 'why this expression?'; when she refers to 'Picardy in France', he writes 'unnecessary when you are writing in French'; an adjectival phrase about an illusion 'which he could never attain' is cut with the words 'unnecessary, when you say underline(illusion)'; an elaborate metaphor about the nature of certain men who, like Samson, can break the cords that bind them even when sleeping, is also cut, this time with the forceful comment 'you have begun to talk about Peter, you are into the subject, go straight to the end'.[33] Under such rigorous criticism of her every word and phrase, Charlotte soon learnt the importance of craft and began to appreciate that mere flow of words – her worst fault since childhood – was not enough.

It is difficult to tell what effect Monsieur Heger's criticism had on Emily's writing since there now exists so little of her prose from either before or after Brussels to compare. Most of his annotations on her essays were confined to picking her up on her grammar and underlining or scoring through her literal translation of English words and phrases. There are remarkably few comments on her style. This may suggest that Emily had not yet advanced beyond the point at which her faults in language became less important than her argument, but it is more likely that it actually indicated she had fewer problems in this area. Her essays, like her surviving poems,[34] were more concise and direct in their approach than Charlotte's and, whatever her faults of translation, Monsieur Heger found much to admire in her power of reasoning and expression. He later confided to Mrs Gaskell that he rated Emily's genius as 'something even higher' than Charlotte's. She had, he said, 'a head for logic, and a capability of argument, unusual in a man, and rare indeed in a woman'. The force of this gift, however, he believed to be much impaired by her 'stubborn tenacity of will, which rendered her obtuse to all reasoning where her own wishes, or her own sense of right, was concerned.' His assessment of her character was both penetrating and revealing.

She should have been a man – a great navigator. Her powerful reason would have deduced new spheres of discovery from the knowledge of the old; and her strong, imperious will would never have been daunted by opposition or difficulty; never have given way but with life.

Monsieur Heger also believed that her imaginative powers would have been best displayed in writing history, where 'her view of scenes and characters would have been so vivid, and so powerfully expressed, and supported by such a show of argument, that it would have dominated over the reader, whatever might have been his previous opinions, or his cooler perceptions of its truth'.[35] Charlotte seems to have shared this opinion, later telling her publisher that she considered 'Ellis Bell', her sister's pseudonym, 'somewhat of a theorist'.

now and then he broaches ideas which strike my sense as much more daring and original than practical; his reason may be in advance of mine, but certainly it often travels a different road. I should say Ellis will not be seen in his full strength till he is seen as an essayist.[36]

As we are almost totally dependent on Charlotte's pen for a portrait of Emily, it is interesting to see that Monsieur Heger's assessment of her character seems to have been shared by the few people she came in contact with in Brussels. She not only seems to have set out with absolutely no intention of making friends, but was so uncompromisingly self-centred that she incurred positive dislike. For some months after their arrival in Brussels, the sisters were regularly invited to the Jenkins' house for Sundays and half-holidays. Eventually, however, Mrs Jenkins stopped asking them as it obviously gave them more pain than pleasure to be invited. Her two sons, John and Edward, who were given the task of escorting the Brontës to the Chaussée d'Ixelles, found them awkward and shy and hardly exchanged a word with them during the journey. Once in her home, Mrs Jenkins found them equally difficult.

Emily hardly ever uttered more than a monosyllable, and Charlotte was sometimes excited sufficiently to speak eloquently and well – on certain subjects – but, before her tongue was thus loosed, she had a habit of gradually wheeling round on her chair, so as almost to conceal her face from the person to whom she was speaking.[37]

Charlotte, though willing enough to repay the kindness of her hosts by making an effort at conversation, was afflicted by that 'mauvaise honte' of which she had complained to Ellen Nussey. Emily simply had no wish to please and no interest in doing so. She was quite capable of eloquence when the mood took her: when Monsieur Heger proposed his reading plan to the sisters he had to cut short Emily's protest – she 'would have entered into an argument on the subject'.[38] When her interests were threatened or excited she would defend herself with vigour, but social intercourse she considered a waste of time.

Charlotte was prepared to make other concessions for the sake of harmony. She despised her fellow pupils as much as Emily did, telling Ellen:

If the national character of the Belgians is to be measured by the character of most of the girls in this school, it is a character singularly cold, selfish, animal and inferior – they are besides very mutinous and difficult for the teachers to manage – and their principles are rotten to the core – we avoid them – which is not difficult to do – as we have the brand of Protestantism and Anglicism upon us.[39]

She was, however, prepared to learn from them. It was evidently in Brussels that Charlotte learnt to adapt her dress to suit her tiny figure. She abandoned her old-fashioned dresses with their high waists and large sleeves and collars and began to wear plainer clothes, neatly waisted with narrow sleeves and small, contrasting, embroidered collars. In this she was clearly imitating the Belgian girls and her future heroines, from Frances Henri to Lucy Snowe, would all win approval for the neatness and plain simplicity of their dress even if they lacked the advantages of personal beauty. By contrast, Emily obstinately refused to abandon her old style of dress, persisting in wearing leg-of-mutton sleeves, which had long gone out of fashion and which did not suit her tall, ungainly frame. Her petticoats too, lacking fullness, made her skirts cling to her legs, accentuating her height and thinness. The oddity of her figure and dress brought taunts from her school-fellows, bringing the angry response, 'I wish to be as God made me.'[40]

Despite her defiant stance, Emily made rapid progress in French, German, music and drawing at the Pensionnat Heger. 'Monsieur & Madame Heger begin to recognize the valuable points of her character under her singularities',[41] Charlotte told Ellen thankfully, so the most difficult part of Charlotte's original plan could now be put into practice. Their half year in Brussels was almost exhausted, but she seems to have persuaded Madame Heger to keep them on as pupils in return for some teaching duties. No doubt she told Patrick and Aunt Branwell, as she told Ellen, that the offer had originated from Madame Heger, but the suggestion – so neatly fulfilling her plans for extending their foreign residence – almost certainly came from Charlotte herself.

Madame Heger has made a proposal for both me and Emily to stay another half year – offering to dismiss her English master and take me as English teacher – also to employ Emily some part of each day < as > in teaching music to a certain number of the pupils – for these services we are to be allowed to continue our < devoirs? > studies in French and German – and to have board without paying for it – no salaries however are offered – the proposal is kind and in a great selfish city like Brussels and a great selfish school containing nearly ninety pupils (boarders & day-pupils included) implies a degree of interest which demands gratitude in return – I am inclined to accept it –[42]

Charlotte can have had no real hesitation in staying. Though she was occasionally homesick, on the whole she was thoroughly happy, indulging her natural bent for acquiring knowledge to the full. How happy Emily was cannot be judged, nor whether the prospect of remaining six more months in Brussels filled her with dread or delight. She had certainly suffered at first, just as she had at Roe Head. 'Once more she seemed sinking,' Charlotte observed, 'but this time she rallied through the mere force of resolution: with inward remorse and shame she looked back on her former failure, and resolved to conquer in this second ordeal. She did conquer: but the victory cost her dear.' It was not only force of character that carried Emily through. Somehow she managed to find time for her lifeline, Gondal, writing three poems whose titles and content suggest that they were part of a longer, prose Gondal story.[43]

Madame Heger appears to have decided to break her new teachers in gently. They took up their duties in August, at the beginning of the two month long 'grandes vacances'. Only six or eight boarders, beside the Brontës, remained at the school, though their numbers were supplemented by the five daughters of Dr Thomas Wheelwright, an English surgeon who, when his eyesight failed, had given up his London practice to come to Brussels in July 1842. The Wheelwrights had taken up residence in a flat in the Hotel Olusyenaar, in the Rue Royale, only ten minutes' walk from the Pensionnat Heger. Being newly arrived, the doctor was anxious that his daughters, who were aged six to fourteen, should use the school holidays to prepare themselves for the forthcoming term.[44] They were the Brontës' first pupils in Brussels.

Emily taught music to the three youngest girls, Fanny, Sarah Ann and Julia, thereby earning their everlasting dislike. Their eldest sister, Laetitia, who was later to become one of Charlotte's friends, shared her sisters' antipathy.

I am afraid my recollections of Emily Brontë will not aid you much. I simply disliked her from the first ... She taught my three youngest sisters music for four months to my annoyance, as she would only take them in their play hours, so as not to curtail her own school hours, naturally causing many tears to small children, the eldest ten, the youngest not seven.

Again Emily displayed that self-centredness which allowed her to ride rough-shod over her young pupils' feelings. Such was the young Wheelwrights' loathing of Emily that they refused to invite the sisters to their home, even though they liked Charlotte and found her invariably kind and friendly. Nor could they invite one without the other: 'Charlotte was so devotedly attached to her, and thought so highly of her talents' that it would only have caused offence to exclude her sister.[45]

Only one person seems to have had a good word to say about Emily and that was Louise de Bassompierre, a sixteen-year-old Belgian girl, who was in the first class with the Brontës. Because there were only about a dozen pupils in this class, she got to know both of them quite well. In sharp contrast to the prevailing opinion, she preferred Emily to Charlotte, finding her more sympathetic, kinder and more approachable. That a friendship did exist between the two, however unlikely it may seem, is borne out by the fact that Emily presented her with a signed drawing, a dramatic and detailed pencil study of a storm-damaged pine tree.[46]

Having won the consent of their father and aunt to remain a further six months in Brussels, Charlotte and Emily seem to have settled quickly into their new teaching roles. At the end of September Mary Taylor could report quite truthfully to Ellen Nussey:

Charlotte & Emily are well; not only in health but in mind & hope. They are content with their present position & even gay & I think they do quite right not to return to England though one of them at < leest > least could earn more at the beautiful town of Bradford than she is now doing.[47]

While everything was going better than could have been expected for Charlotte and Emily in Brussels, affairs were proceeding less smoothly at home. Patrick had returned from the Continent to find Haworth in a very depressed condition. It was an indication of the terrible state of trade and the depth of personal suffering caused that one of the most respected cotton spinners in the township, Thomas Lister, of Hollings Mill near Stanbury, committed suicide at the end of April.[48] A few days later, one of Patrick's oldest friends, Thomas Andrew, who had been the Haworth surgeon for the past twenty-four years, died. His funeral, conducted by Patrick on 3 May, was a remarkable manifestation of the esteem and affection in which he was held. So many people came to pay their last respects that the corpse had to be taken out of his house and displayed in the public street: Patrick led the procession of mourners to the church and conducted the burial service. What made Andrew's loss even greater was the fact that he had been particularly skilled in treating the typhus fevers which were endemic among the poor. 'His kindness to the poor was almost unexampled', declared one eulogist, for he had treated hundreds of people over the years, charging them a pittance for his services and often nothing at all.[49] His death at the height of the worst depression in trade that anyone could remember was a particular loss to the suffering poor and it was decided that a memorial should be erected in Haworth Church to his memory. Branwell, still at home and glad to do an old friend a favour, suggested that J. B. Leyland should be commissioned to produce the memorial. It was a good excuse to invite Leyland to dine at the parsonage and, in the evening, he appeared before the monument committee. Later Branwell felt compelled to admit:

I have not often felt more heartily ashamed than when you left the committee at Haworth; but I did not like to speak on the subject then, and I trusted that you would make that allowance which you have perhaps often ere now had to do, for gothic ignorance and ill breeding; and one or two of the persons present, afterwards felt that they had left by no means an enviable impression on your mind.

Branwell was commissioned to draw up the inscription for the monument: 'It is not such an one as would have best pleased myself,' he told Leyland, 'but I was compelled to frame it so as to please others; as to whose taste and judgement you will some time since have formed a tolerably correct opinion.'[50]

Leyland returned in July with the sculpted marble tablet which John Brown, under his watchful eye, then lettered. The inscription, which catalogued Andrew's career, ended with a generous tribute: 'This Tablet was erected by those who knew his worth, & who feel that, while in his death the neighbourhood has lost an honourable & upright man, the poor have lost an able adviser in their calamities, & a generous friend in their need.'[51]

As if the problems in the township were not already overwhelming, Patrick had also to face an outright battle with the vicar of Bradford. In a further effort to enforce a church rate in Haworth, which the chapelry still refused to pay, the churchwardens of Bradford applied to the Court of Queen's Bench for a writ against their fellow officers in Haworth. Fortunately, after a cliff-hanging adjournment, the judges at last decided that they could not issue the writ and the case was dropped.[52] The first stage in an important battle of principle had been won.

Perhaps feeling that he should retire in his moment of triumph, the

Reverend John Winterbotham took this opportunity to announce his resignation from Haworth. He had been offered a post in a Baptist chapel in Upper Canada and, like many of the poor in the township, had decided to emigrate to the more promising New World. As a grand finale, he orchestrated the opposition at his last church rate meeting in Bradford at the beginning of July and then, laden with gifts from grateful Dissenters in the area, he, his wife and five children and two other families from Haworth set sail for Canada on the appropriately named *Nemesis*.[53] Though their relations had been more cordial of late, it must still have been a relief to Patrick to see the last of this belligerent and often unpleasant man who had done so much to stir up hostility to his church.

Branwell, in the meantime, had soon bounced back from the misery into which he had been cast by his dismissal from the Leeds and Manchester Railway. By the middle of May he was cheerful enough to write to J. B. Leyland enclosing a sketch of a half-buried tombstone bearing the legend 'Resurgam', 'I will rise again'.[54] A week later, on 22 May, he wrote along the same lines to Francis Grundy, exaggerating his situation as usual.

I cannot avoid the temptation to cheer my spirits by scribbling a few lines to you while I sit here alone – all the household being at church – the sole occupant of an ancient parsonage among lonely hills, which probably will never hear the whistle of an engine till I am in my grave.

After experiencing, since my return home, extreme pain and illness, with mental depression worse than either, I have at length acquired health and strength and soundness of mind, far superior, I trust, to anything shown by that miserable wreck you used to know under my name. I can now speak cheerfully and enjoy the company of another without the stimulus of six glasses of whisky; I can write, think, and act with some apparent approach to resolution, and I only want a motive for exertion to be happier than I have been for years. But I feel my recovery from <u>almost insanity</u> to be retarded by having nothing to listen to except the wind moaning among old chimneys and older ash trees, nothing to look at except heathery hills walked over when life had all to hope for and nothing to regret with me – no one to speak to except crabbed old Greeks and Romans who have been dust the last five thousand years.[55]

The letter was clearly intended to win Grundy's sympathy, but it was far from the truth. Branwell may have been ill on his return home – from anxiety as to his father and aunt's reaction as much as anything else – but he had been fully occupied since then. He had been deeply involved in the memorial committee and had seen Leyland and two of his friends only two days before he wrote this letter. Though his sisters were all away from home, he had not lacked company. Indeed, without them, he was in a position to enjoy the undivided attention of 'one of my dearest friends', William Weightman. His sister Anne, too, was due home shortly for her annual summer holiday before going on to Scarborough where she would spend six weeks at No. 15, The Cliff, with the Robinsons.[56]

An even more telling argument against Branwell's supposed depression of spirits was the fact that, since his dismissal from Luddenden Foot, he had enjoyed his greatest ever literary success. Before a month had passed, he had seen his first poem published in the newly established Tory newspaper, the *Bradford Herald*. The poem was an entirely new one, a sonnet inspired by Landseer's painting 'The Old Shepherd's Chief Mourner', which he had written at Luddenden Foot. A week later he had a second sonnet, 'On the callousness produced by cares', published simultaneously in the *Bradford Herald* and the *Halifax Guardian*. This was a revision of a poem first written in 1837. On the same day it appeared in the *Halifax Guardian*, Branwell had another new poem published in yet another paper, the *Leeds Intelligencer*. 'The Afghan War', which Branwell seems to have written only twelve days before its publication, was on the entirely topical subject of the disastrous British retreat from Kabul a few months before.[57] A week later again and another sonnet, 'On peaceful death and painful life', appeared in both the *Bradford Herald* and the *Halifax Guardian*. This was also originally written in 1837 but substantially revised and improved.[58] The sheer volume of his material appearing in the local press throughout the month of May suggests that Branwell's mood must have been more optimistic than his letter to Grundy suggests. He must also have been kept extremely busy, writing, revising and sending the poems off for publication.

Branwell kept up this extraordinary momentum throughout the year. 'Caroline's Prayer: on the change from childhood to womanhood' appeared in the *Bradford Herald* and the *Halifax Guardian* at the beginning of June 1842; the same papers both published his 'Song' a week later, his 'An Epicurean's Song' the next month and 'On Caroline' a week after that. All were revisions of earlier Angrian poems.[59]

Branwell was clearly contemplating a literary career once again. He appears to have sent some of these poems to James Montgomery, a poet based in Sheffield, whose works were widely published in the provincial papers. Branwell told Grundy that Montgomery

and another literary gentleman, who have lately seen some thing of my 'head work', wish me to turn some attention to literature, sending me, along with their advice, plenty of puff and praise; and this may be all very well; but I have little conceit of myself, and great desire for activity.[60]

In pursuit of greater 'activity', Branwell had sought Grundy's advice about obtaining another post on the railways, which is surely an indication that he had actually enjoyed his job at Sowerby Bridge and Luddenden Foot. Grundy had answered discouragingly, causing Branwell to reply:

I should have been a fool to entertain, under present circumstances, any very sanguine hopes respecting situations connected with Railways; since I could not but be aware of the great glut in that market.

Branwell's ambitions did not extend simply to gaining a similar post to his previous one. Evidently jealous of his sisters' adventures in Belgium, he had decided that he too should enjoy the benefit of working on the Continent.

I had only < p > hoped that, from the few who are generally found willing \to take them,/ and from so many Railways being contemplated, in France &c., situations abroad would be more attainable.
    You ask me, Sir; why I don't turn my attention in another direction? and so I would but that most of my relations, and more immediate connections, are Clergymen, or, by a private life, somewhat removed from this busy world – And, as for the Church, I have not one mental quality – except perhaps hypocrisy – whi[c]h would make me < p > cut a figure in its pulpits.[61]

His enquiries through Grundy having failed, and nothing else suitable appearing on the horizon, Branwell applied himself to his poetry with renewed zeal. Not all his output was simply reworkings of earlier poems. In the summer of 1842, he responded to a challenge from William Dearden:

Bronté and I agreed that each should write a drama or a poem, the principal character in which was to have a real or imaginary existence before the Deluge; and that, in a month's time, we should meet at the Cross Roads Inn, which is about half-way between Keighley and Haworth, and produce the result of our lucubrations.[62]

Dearden produced his 'Demon Queen', Branwell a long poem in several parts entitled 'Azrael. or the Eve of Destruction'. Dearden, who was not a totally partial critic, believed that if the poem had been published, as Branwell intended, it would 'fully bear out my opinion, and prove to the world that Branwell was not inferior in genius and power to the gifted Currer Bell'.[63] Though the claim was exaggerated, the poem was one of Branwell's best, a dramatic depiction of the confrontation over Methuselah's grave between Noah, the patriarch prophesying God's anger and the flood, and Azrael, the Jewish and Islamic angel of death, who denies God's existence and urges defiance. 'I know', Azrael tells the crowds,

> That Human life revolts to think
> It ever stands on nothing's brink,
> That Human pride recoils to see
> The Heap of dust tis doomed to be! –...
> So when the shadow of TO COME
> Surrounds the Heart with boding gloom
> Nature abhorrs to look at naught
> And frames for ease a world of thought. –
> So – when the Sickman lies to die
> He gasps for Hope in Agony

And as the Earth yeilds none to save
He makes a Hope beyond the grave! –
    Thus Heaven is but an < Mortal > Earthly dream,
Tis Man makes God – not God makes him! –

Azrael's eventual overthrow is presaged in his dying wife's dream in which she sees God on his eternal throne and is called to die before the flood, 'The last on earth who may to heaven attain!'[64]

Though not all the poem was published – and indeed only the first part may have been written – Branwell rewrote the first forty-eight lines and submitted them as 'Noah's Warning over Methuselah's Grave. (From an unpublished poem)' to the *Bradford Herald*, where they appeared on 25 August.[65] Twelve days later, Branwell wrote modestly and diplomatically to *Blackwood's Magazine*, offering them his latest revision of 'Sir Henry Tunstall'. The letter is a model of its kind and eloquently reveals how Branwell's earlier arrogance had been crushed out of him by his repeated failure to achieve a hearing.

Sir,
I beg most respectfully to offer the accompanying lines, for insertion in Blackwoods Edinburgh Magazine.
    They endeavour – feebly enough, I fear – to describe the harsh contrast between a mind, changed by long absence from home, and the feelings still alive in those who have never wandered; and who < f > vainly expect the absent to return with a heart as warm as when they bade him fare well.
    The kind advice and encouragement of Mrs Southey has alone emboldened me to make this offering; and, if you should cast a favourable eye upon it, I shall remain with more of thankfulness than vanity,

Your most obdt Servt,
Patrick. B. Bronté[66]

The lessons learnt from his circle of Halifax friends had also made their mark. Branwell had drafted the letter first before making a fair copy of it to send to the editor; consequently it was neatly written and to the point, unlike his previous efforts. The fact that Branwell had sent the lines to Robert Southey's wife, Caroline Bowles, a poet in her own right, was again an indication of his yearning for approval and his desperation to achieve some sort of opening into the larger world of publishing beyond the provincial press. Despite his newly acquired maturity and the quality of his lines – better than many of the outpourings of more famous authors appearing in *Blackwood's Magazine* at the time – Branwell failed once more to win a response.

Another poem, begun at Luddenden Foot and revised this autumn, was Branwell's epic 'The Triumph of mind over body', a redrafting of his poem on Lord Nelson.[67] Undoubtedly this, too, was intended for publication. It was written up in a fair copy and sent to Francis Grundy – not because he had any literary skills but because he had connections, through his father, with the Martineau family. James Martineau, a Unitarian minister in Liverpool and professor of mental and moral philosophy at Manchester New College since 1840, had been a colleague of Grundy's father and had taught Grundy himself for a year or two. His sister, Harriet Martineau, whom Grundy had also met, was even more famous as the author of novels and works on political economy. They were not the only eminent literary figures to whom the work was sent: through Grundy, Branwell also approached Leigh Hunt, the essayist and poet who was also editor of *The Examiner.* According to Grundy, it was at Branwell's 'special request' that he submitted it for criticism to Leigh Hunt, Miss Martineau 'and others'; 'All spoke in high terms of it.'[68] Of James Martineau's response, Branwell himself indicated that he intended to write 'gratefully and sincerely acknowledging the receipt of his most kindly and truthful criticism – at least in advice, though too generous far in praise'.[69]

While Branwell made an all-out assault on the bastions of contemporary English literature, events in Haworth were moving towards a crisis. In August, the pent-up despair of the famished and fever-stricken unemployed erupted in violence. Led by Chartist activists, thousands of factory workers took up makeshift arms and marched on the northern industrial towns. There they stopped the mills by persuasion or, if necessary, by coercion. There were riots, with violent consequences, in Halifax, Huddersfield, Bradford, Todmorden, Bingley, Skipton and Keighley and, on 14 August, it was estimated that 10,000 Chartists were gathered on Lees Moor, within sight and sound of Haworth.[70] They were joined by malcontents from Haworth, though Patrick, who had lived through the Luddite riots thirty years before, undoubtedly urged on them the futility of doing so. The military were called out to arrest and, in some instances, shoot the rioters. Some order had been restored by 19 August, when most of the Keighley mills were working again, but there was a scare the following Sunday morning. It appeared that the Chartists were starting to assemble again on Lees Moor and parts of the moor were observed to be on fire. Fearing another attack, the bells of Keighley Parish Church were rung to raise the alarm. A party of the 17th Lancers who were stationed in the town and a troop of Yorkshire Hussars, headed by Edward Ferrand, 'the Hero of Harden Grange', as he was dubbed by the local press, set out to encounter them, aided by 300 civilians who were hurriedly gathered from the places of religious worship and armed with staves. By the time the forces had reached Lees Moor, the rioters had dispersed and only a party of Ranters was discovered. Though the outcome had been peaceful there had been genuine cause for alarm in both Keighley and Haworth, where a repetition of events of the previous week had been feared.[71]

A couple of weeks later there was another serious alarm as disgruntled mill workers sabotaged their employers' machinery by removing the plugs from the boilers which powered the looms. The magistrates came to the Black Bull in Haworth to swear in special constables to form an 'Anti-Plug Dragoon Regiment'. Most of the more substantial householders were sworn in, together with servants from the larger establishments. One of them, the son of a manufacturer, reported seeing a light in Matty Wood one evening, the alarm was given and between forty and fifty of the 'regiment' assembled. The 'Plug-Dragoons' were captured and brought back to the Black Bull, where it was discovered that the prisoners were a fisherman, an idiot and a party of children 'engaged in the patriotic exploit of storming a wasp's nest'. Edgy and primed to respond to the serious threat of riot, the Haworth special constables had overreacted. One can well imagine that Branwell was one of the volunteer constables; in after years, the landlord of the Black Bull remembered how Branwell had offered to go in during a mill riot and thrash a dozen fellows 'any one of whom could have put him in his pocket and carried him off at a minute's notice'.[72] Patrick, though too old for such active duty, was no doubt grateful for the pistols he had preserved since the days of the Luddite riots. Certainly, writing to thank John White of Upperwood House for his kind enquiries as to his daughters' progress in Brussels, Patrick was grateful that the Conservatives were now in government and had the situation under control.

In regard to politics, it must now appear to all rational and unprejudiced men, that, had the poor, unprincipled, temporizing Whigs, remain'd much longer in power, we should have been utterly ruined, as a nation, in respect, to both the worlds – < My > May the Most High, enable the Conservatives to do their duty, and protect them from all the evil designs of their enemies! –[73]

While the district was caught up in the alarms and dangers of Chartist rioters, Patrick suffered a personal blow which affected him far more deeply than the current political strife. William Weightman, his curate for the last three years, fell ill with cholera, the scourge of the poor, while out visiting the sick. The disease was invariably fatal and despite the best medical and nursing attentions available, there was little anyone could do to relieve his acute sufferings. He seems to have been taken ill during the third week in August and, as he lingered painfully over several weeks, he was visited regularly by a distraught Branwell and a more stoical Patrick. 'During his illness', Patrick later reported,

I generally visited him twice a day, joined with him in prayer, heard his request for the prayers of this congregation, listened to him whilst he expressed his entire dependence on the merits of the Saviour, heard of his pious admonitions to his attendants, and saw him in tranquility close his eyes on this bustling, vain, selfish world; so that I may truly say, his end was peace, and his hope glory.[74]

William Weightman was just twenty-eight, his death requiring all Patrick's eloquence and faith to explain as the will of the God whom he had served so well. He died on 6 September and was buried four days later in Haworth Church by Patrick himself.[75] As was then customary, Patrick preached a funeral sermon in his memory on the afternoon of Sunday, 2 October. Such was his grief that he was unable to follow his usual practice of preaching ex-tempore and he prepared his sermon in advance, opening it with the words: 'For more than twenty years, during which time I have ministered amongst you, this will be the first sermon I shall have read to this congregation, and it may be the last.' He went on to praise not only his curate's pious end but, more especially, his life, giving way to rare public emotion only when he declared 'we were always like father and son'. It was right to mourn his death, but not without hope, for his salvation was assured. In words which could have been intended for his own son, Branwell, whose poems had often dwelt on the fear of death, he offered understanding and comfort:

There is more of scepticism in man's creed than he is wont to think of. Else, why does the pious youth fear to die? perhaps, that he may live well, perhaps not – or for what reason does the good old man wish to protract his weary existence, till he becomes a burthen to himself, and an incumbrance to others ... that the followers of Christ should tremble at the last step of their journey, which will introduce them into His presence and His glory, can only be accounted for by the weakness of their faith, and the remains of sin...[76]

The tributes to Weightman flooded in. Patrick had his sermon published privately so that it could reach a larger audience; the *Leeds Intelligencer* eulogized Weightman's 'talents, worth, and amiable character' and the inhabitants of Haworth raised a subscription to pay for a monument to their curate. The wording may again have been drawn up by Branwell.

He was three years curate of Haworth and by the congregation, and parishioners in general, was greatly respected, for his orthodox principles, active zeal, moral habits, learning, mildness and affability: his useful labours will long be gratefully remem-bered, by the members of the congregation; and Sunday school teachers, and scholars.[77]

Patrick and Branwell scarcely had time to inform Charlotte, Emily and Anne of Weightman's death and recover from their grief when another blow struck. Aunt Branwell, who had always enjoyed uniformly good health, fell ill. It soon became obvious that she, too, was about to die. Branwell, reeling under the shock, could only write to Grundy, who had protested at his friend's failure to reply to his letters.

There is no misunderstanding. I have had a long attendance at the death-bed of the

Rev. Mr Weightman, one of my dearest friends, and now I am attending at the death-bed of my aunt, who has been for twenty years as my mother. I expect her to die in a few hours.[78]

In fact, it was four more days before Aunt Branwell died, an internal obstruction of her bowel reducing her to helpless agony. Writing to Grundy again on the day she died, Branwell was almost beside himself.

As I don't want to lose a <u>real</u> friend, I write in deprecation of the tone of your letter. Death only has made me neglectful of your kindness, and I have lately had so much experience with him, that your sister would not <u>now</u> blame me for indulging in gloomy visions either of this world or another. I am incoherent, I fear, but I have been waking two nights witnessing such agonising suffering as I would not wish my worst enemy to endure; and I have now lost the guide and director of all the happy days connected with my childhood.[79]

If ever there was a corrective to the usual view of Aunt Branwell as a despotic, unpleasant and narrow-minded spinster who made the Brontë children's lives a misery, Branwell's unsolicited testimonial is it.

Letters had been immediately despatched to Charlotte and Emily in Brussels and to Anne at Thorp Green as soon as Aunt Branwell's death was imminent. The news of her illness did not reach Brussels until 2 November and although Charlotte and Emily made plans for their immediate departure, the next morning's post brought them news of her death. Aunt Branwell was actually buried that day by the Reverend James Chesterton Bradley, curate of Oakworth. As she had wished, her remains were deposited in the church 'as near as convenient to the remains of my dear sister'.[80] Anne arrived home in time for the funeral and was permitted by the Robinsons to spend a few weeks with her family before returning to Thorp Green. This was an absolute necessity as, without Aunt Branwell, the whole burden of running the household would otherwise have fallen on the only servant, twelve-year-old Martha Brown.

Although they were too late to pay their last respects to their aunt, Charlotte and Emily decided it was their duty to return home. They travelled to Antwerp, where they sailed for England on 6 November, arriving in Haworth on the morning of Tuesday, 8 November.[81] They brought with them a letter from Monsieur Heger, addressed to their father, and further bad news. Martha Taylor, Mary's bright, cheerful and flighty younger sister, had died in Brussels only a few days before Aunt Branwell; like William Weightman she had succumbed to cholera and had been devotedly nursed by Mary who had proved 'more than a Mother – more than a Sister watching – nursing – cherishing her – so < more > tenderly, so unweariedly'. Charlotte had rushed over to the Château Koekelberg as soon as she heard the news, but had arrived only to find Martha had died in the night. Mary was taken away to stay with her cousins, the Dixons, in Brussels and on 30 October, the Brontës had visited her. They had walked together to the Protestant cemetery outside Brussels where Martha was buried and had then returned for a pleasant evening at the Dixons'. Charlotte especially returned home in low spirits, writing mournfully to Ellen, 'Aunt – Martha – Taylor – Mr Weightman \are now/ all gone – how dreary & void everything seems –.'[82]

There was some comfort not only in being reunited at home, however, but in the glowing terms of Monsieur Heger's letter to their father. 'I have not the honour of knowing you personally', he told Patrick,

and yet I have a feeling of profound admiration for you, for in judging the father of a family by his children one cannot be mistaken and in this respect the education and sentiments that we have found in your daughters can only give us a very high idea of your worth and of your character. You will undoubtedly learn with pleasure that your children have made extra-ordinary progress in all the branches of learning, and that this progress is entirely due to their love of work and their perseverance. With pupils like this we had very little to do; their progress is more your work than ours. We did not have to teach them the value of time and instruction, they had learnt all this in their paternal home; and we have only had, on our part, the slight merit of directing their efforts and providing suitable material for the praiseworthy activity which your daughters have drawn from your example and your lessons.[83]

Monsieur Heger went on to praise the improvement the girls had shown in their studies. Emily, having received music lessons from the best teacher in Belgium, was now teaching the piano herself and losing the last traces of her crippling shyness. Charlotte had begun to give lessons in French and had already acquired that 'assurance and aplomb' so necessary to teachers. Had they been able to stay, the Hegers would have been able to offer at least one of them a position entirely suited to her tastes and giving her a much coveted independence. Though he did not wish to interfere, Monsieur Heger nevertheless made an indirect appeal to Patrick to allow the girls to return to Brussels.

You must believe, sir, this is not a question of personal interest with us, it is a question of affection. You will pardon me if we speak of your children, if we interest ourselves in their welfare, as if they were part of our own family; their personal qualities, their good will, their extreme zeal are the only reasons which compel us to risk your displeasure.[84]

Charlotte had already determined that she would return to Brussels but, for the moment at least, she had to remain at home. The Brontës were expected to go into mourning for their aunt and did so, though it did not take Charlotte long to arrange to meet Ellen. As her brother, George, was ill at home, Ellen did not wish to leave Brookroyd. Instead, she proposed that Charlotte should visit her there for a week, an invitation which Charlotte snapped up, despite having doubts as to how convenient her presence would be.[85]

Charlotte went to Brookroyd the day after Anne returned to Thorp

Green. Anne had been quite happy to resign the household duties to Emily and had spent at least part of her precious time at home in writing two poems. In view of the fact that this was less than two months after William Weightman's death, it is worth pointing out that neither poem bore any relation to him or even expressed grief or suffering. The first completed a poem begun at Thorp Green in February, 'In memory of a happy day in February'.

> Blessed be Thou for all the Joy
> My soul has felt today!
> O < be > let its memory stay with me
> And never pass away!

The poem celebrated the quiet religious joy she had experienced when she had been given 'a glimpse of truths divine':

> I knew there was a God on high
> By whom all things were made.
> I saw his wisdom and his power
> In all his works desplayed
>
> But most through out the moral world
> I saw his glory shine
> I saw his wisdom infinite
> His mercy all devine.
>
> Deep secrets of his providence
> In darkness long co[n]cealed
> Were brought to my delighted eyes
> And graciously revealed[86]

This poem was completed on 10 November, the same day she began another addressed to the religious poet, William Cowper. The mood of this composition, though appropriately melancholic, was again optimistic. Recalling how she had read Cowper's poems since childhood and in them traced her own sins and sorrows, hopes and fears, she reflected that she had not then known of the poet's real torments. Now, his years of suffering were ended, his 'gentle soul' was in the bosom of his God and had found its home at last.

> It must be so if < as > God is love,
> And < if he > answers fervent prayer;
> Then surely thou shalt dwell on high
> And I may < hope to > meet thee there...
>
> Yet should thy < blackest > darkest fears be true
> If Heaven< 's decree > be so severe
> That such a soul as thine is lost
> O! how < my God > shall I appear?[87]

The question in the last verse was surely hypothetical. It is clear from the rest of the poem that Anne had no doubts as to Cowper's salvation, though she may have feared for her own. In this quietly introspective mood, Anne returned to Thorp Green on 28 November, to recommence her uncongenial duties.[88]

It was while she was at Thorp Green in December that Anne wrote the only poem which can justifiably be attributed to William Weightman's death. It is worth quoting in full, if only because it is often produced as the trump card, 'proving' Anne's unrequited passion for the curate.

> I will not mourn thee, lovely one,
>   Though thou art torn away.
> < They > 'Tis said that if the morning sun
>   Arize with dazzling ray
>
> And shed a bright and burning beam,
>   Athwart the glittering main,
> E< r >re noon shall fade that laughing gleam
>   Enlulphed in clouds and rain.
>
> And if thy life as transient proved
>   It hath been full as bright,
> For thou wert hopeful and beloved;
>   Thy spirit knew no blight.
>
> If few and short the joys of life
>   That thou on earth couldst know
> Little thou knew'st of sin and strife
>   Nor much of pain and wo
>
> < And yet I cannot check my sighs >
> If vain thy earthly hopes did prove
>   Thou canst not mourn their flight
> Thy brightest hopes were fixed above
>   And they shall know no blight.
>
> And yet I cannot check my sighs
>   Thou wert so young and fair
> More bright than Summer morning < skies > skies,
>   But stern Death would not spare
>
> He would not pass our darling bye
>   Nor grant one hour's delay
> But rudely closed his shining eye
>   And frowned his smile away
>
> That Angel smile that late so much,
>   Could my fond heart rejoice,
> And he has silenced by his touch,
>   The music of thy voice,

> I'll weep no more thine early doom
> But O I still must mourn –
> The pleasures buried in thy tomb
> For they will not return![89]

For a poem supposed to represent the depth of Anne's love for William Weightman, cruelly torn from her in her absence and in the prime of his life, the lines are surprisingly calm and resigned. If anything, they reflect the reaction of Patrick as expressed in his 'Funeral Sermon', rather than someone devastated by the loss of the great love of her life. The poem expresses fondness and regret, rather than the desolation and despair one would expect in such circumstances. The strongest expression of affection she uses is qualified by the fact that he is 'our darling' and not 'my darling'. Anne was perfectly capable of writing passionate love poetry for the characters in Gondal and in her novels.[90] In her own religious poetry, too, she plumbs the depths of a heartfelt emotion which is totally absent from this poem, so one cannot argue that her autobiographical poetry lacked the passion of her purely fictional work. The most one can deduce from this poem, granted that it is about William Weightman, is that Anne shared the family affection for him and, like all who came in contact with him, regretted his early death.

The year 1842 drew to a close in a flurry of activity in Haworth. There were two lectures in the village, held in the Forester's Hall: one by a local man, John Townend, on the subject of phrenology, followed a week later by one from a Manchester professor of elocution 'on the present crisis, faction & its influence, origin of the late fearful commotions, university of opinion with respect to reform, necessity of union, how to effect the same and restore the human family to comfort and independence'.[91] Having put the world to rights, Haworth celebrated the end of the year, appropriately enough, with high culture and comedy. A vocal and instrumental concert was held in the church Sunday school, featuring Thomas Parker, the Haworth tenor, and Mrs Boocock, from the Halifax concerts. The orchestra of Haworth players was led for the occasion by Mr G. F. Hoffman,

the celebrated ... German violinist, who astonished a numerous audience by his extra-ordinary abilities as a musician, especially by his performance on the violin-cello, entitled 'The Farmyard' ... all was performed with first rate ability amidst unbounded applause.[92]

Though they were in mourning for their aunt, it seems probable that the Brontës would have attended such a musical treat, especially as it was held under the auspices of the church.

The comedy was provided at Stanbury by the ex-churchwardens of Haworth who, having quarrelled about their office, decided to settle the dispute in the time-honoured fashion.

We are not certain whether the gentlemen were armed with hair-trigger pistols or common blunder-busses, but have been positively informed that the weapons were loaded with cinders, instead of ball. The distance of the gentlemen was 20 paces. They fired & lo! the whole matter ended in smoke, but the gentlemen were satisfied.[93]

With the death of Aunt Branwell, the girls, together with their cousin in Penzance, Eliza Kingston, each inherited an equal share in their aunt's estate. She had left each of the Brontë children – including Branwell – a personal memento, but she chose to leave her money to the four nieces who stood most in need of it.[94] Probate and administration was granted in December and, according to an inventory of the residue of Aunt Branwell's property, the girls could expect to get just under £300 each.[95] Most of the money was invested in shares in the York and North Midland Railway, but as the youngest niece, Anne, had already passed her twenty-first birthday, they could be cashed in. Though not a sum which would transform their lives, the Brontë girls now had at least the benefit of a cushion against immediate financial hardship should their father die.

There was clearly much to be sorted out over the Christmas holidays, but the solutions seem to have come easily. Charlotte was in high spirits; she had been the least close to her aunt and so felt her death less keenly than the other members of her family. She was determined to return to Brussels and there was no one to oppose her, her aunt being the only person who could have exerted sufficient pressure. Aunt Branwell would certainly have moved heaven and earth to prevent Charlotte travelling alone across England and Belgium, as she intended, because she could not find a suitable escort. It is a measure of Charlotte's influence over Patrick that he was persuaded to agree to such an ill-advised plan. Despite her success in Brussels, Emily had no wish to return. She gave up her place at the Pensionnat Heger willingly, almost, one senses, with a feeling of relief, and agreed to resume her old role as the family housekeeper. Anne, who had now spent nearly two years with the Robinsons, was clearly appreciated by them – so much so that, young Edmund Robinson having outgrown her care, they were prepared to accept her suggestion that her brother should be appointed his tutor. At the end of the Christmas holidays, Branwell would join her at Thorp Green. With all her family gainfully employed, Charlotte had nothing to restrain her. She could and would return to Brussels.

In the meantime, she indulged in a little gaiety. Her visit to Ellen was reciprocated in January, and Charlotte teased her friend mercilessly about her current suitors, John and Joe Taylor, and her past one, Mr Vincent. 'There exists a tragedy intitled the "Rival Brothers"', she told Ellen,

I have addressed you in this note as plain Ellen – for though I know it will soon be Mrs J Taylor – I can't for the life of me tell whether the initial J stands for John or

Joe. It is a complete enigma. When I have time I mean to write Mr Vincent's elegy. Poor man! the manufacturers are beating him hollow.[96]

On 27 January 1843, Charlotte left home, catching the nine o'clock train from Leeds to London. Arriving at Euston thirteen hours later, she took a cab to London Bridge Wharf and, despite the late hour, boarded the packet immediately.[97] If, as seems likely, Charlotte used this adventure in her novel *Villette*, she had a frightening experience which would have fully justified her aunt's concerns about the impropriety of a young woman travelling alone. The cabman

offered me up as an oblation, served me as a dripping roast, making me alight in the midst of a throng of watermen.

This was an uncomfortable crisis. It was a dark night. The coachman instantly drove off as soon as he had got his fare; the watermen commenced a struggle for me and my trunk. Their oaths I hear at this moment: they shook my philosophy more than did the night, or the isolation, or the strangeness of the scene.[98]

The packet at first refused let her on board, saying it did not take passengers overnight, but eventually someone took pity on her plight and she was allowed on the boat.[99] They sailed early the next morning, arriving in Ostend at nine in the evening. Next day, Charlotte took the train at midday and arrived at the Pensionnat Heger at seven o'clock on the Sunday evening. 'Mde Heger received me with great kindness', she told Ellen and, omitting to tell her about the incident on London Bridge Wharf, which would undoubtedly have outraged her friend's sensibilities, she airily dismissed the adventure with the comment, 'I had no accident – but of course some anxiety –'.[100]

Charlotte returned to the Pensionnat Heger as a teacher on a salary of sixteen pounds a year, out of which she had only to pay for her own German lessons. As befitted her new status, the Hegers gave orders that in future she was to be called 'Mademoiselle Charlotte' and she took charge of the small but brightest group of pupils in the First Class.[101] Almost immediately upon her arrival she had a visit from Mary Dixon, Mary Taylor's cousin, and was invited to spend the first of many Sundays at their house. By 6 March she could write quite cheerfully to Ellen to describe her life in Brussels.

I am settled by this time of course – I am not too much overloaded with occupation and besides teaching English I have time to improve myself in German. I ought to consider myself well off and to be thankful for my good fortune – I hope I am thankful – and if I could always keep up my spirits – and never feel lonely or long for companionship or friendship or whatever they call it, I should do very well – As I told you before Msieur and Mde Heger are the only two persons in the house for whom I really experience regard and esteem and of course I cannot always be with them nor even often – They told me when I first returned that I was to consider their sitting-room my sitting-room also and to go there whenever I was not engaged in the school-room – this however I cannot < room > do – in the day-time it is a public-room – where music masters and mistresses are constantly passing in and out and in the evening I will not and ought not to intrude on Mr & Mde Heger & their children – thus I am a good deal by myself out of school-hours – but that does not signify –[102]

Though Charlotte made light of her loneliness, it did indeed signify. In following her desire to return to Brussels she had not reckoned on the consequences of being alone, without the constant companionship of Emily which had made her first residence there not only bearable but happy. Then it had not mattered that there was a self-erected barrier between the Brontës and their fellow pupils. Now, however, when she stood in great need of friends, she had few resources to call upon. Mary Taylor had pursued her self-appointed plan of going to Germany as a teacher; Martha was lying in the Protestant cemetery; even the Dixons, the kind, gay and closely knit family with whom she spent so many pleasant hours, were soon to leave Brussels, their father having failed to sell his latest invention to the Belgian government.[103] It was no wonder that Charlotte ended her letter to Ellen on a wistful note.

Good-bye to you dear Nell when I say so – it seems to me that you will hardly hear me – all the < heaving > waves of the Channel, heaving & roaring between must deaden the sound –

Go-o-d – b-y-e
CB[104]

Chapter Fifteen

MONSIEUR HEGER

P ossibly the greatest single influence on Charlotte, both as a person and as a writer, was the time she spent in Brussels; on Emily it is almost impossible to see any effect, however subtle. She seems to have picked up the threads of her old life without a pang of regret, plunging back into her Gondal poetry with an enthusiasm that suggests she had felt its deprivation in Brussels. The only noticeable difference is a slight increase in narrative poetry, charting the siege and fall of Zalona and the death of Rodric Lesley, suggesting that Emily had returned to chronicling the histories of Gondal and Gaaldine on a large scale. Otherwise, her preoccupations, as always, were with the partings and deaths of lovers and lamentations over the graves of loved ones.[1] Monsieur Heger's teaching certainly had no influence on her poetic style, which remained as terse, evocative and simply phrased as ever.

Even Emily's friends were sceptical of the effect Brussels had had upon her. Mary Taylor, writing to Ellen Nussey from Germany, where she was now supporting herself by teaching, enquired curiously:

Tell me something about Emily Brontë. I can't imagine how the newly acquired qualities can <u>fit in</u>, in the same head & heart that is occupied by the old ones. Imagine Emily turning over prints or 'taking wine' with any stupid fop & preserving her temper & politeness!²

Mary clearly considered that Emily's advantages in Brussels had been purely social, rather than academic. This may have been a recognition of her obstinate resistance to Monsieur Heger's teaching practices, but it failed to take into account the fact that the Pensionnat Heger had immeasurably improved her French as well as her German and her music. If nothing else, she had at least gained access to a whole new world of German literature which, with its dramatic qualities and stern tone, would appeal more to the creator of *Wuthering Heights* than the comparatively frivolous French novels Charlotte read so avidly. Ellen Nussey's graphic picture of Emily in the kitchen at the parsonage kneading bread with a German book propped open before her is testimony to her continuing interest.³

In Brussels, Charlotte, too, was making progress in German, having resumed her lessons with Madame Muhl, who, to her consternation, continued to charge as much for teaching one pupil as she had for two. Charlotte simply could not afford these fees, on top of all her other expenses, out of her salary of sixteen pounds. It is a measure of the importance she attached to learning German that she actually wrote home to ask her father for extra money.⁴ From Charlotte's surviving exercise books, we can see that she began with translations of German poetry into English, favouring Schiller, whose works she also translated into French for Monsieur Heger. Her translations from English into German seem to have made little progress, either because she considered the exercise less valuable, or because she did not consider her work worth preserving.⁵

The emphasis on poetry in her German studies was matched by a new move towards translation of poetry in her French lessons with Monsieur Heger. Again, this worked both ways. She translated some stanzas from Walter Scott's *Lady of the Lake* and Byron's *Childe Harold's Pilgrimage* into French, for instance, but also translated Louis Belmontet's 'Les Orphelins' and Auguste Barbier's 'Napoleon' into English.⁶ In both instances, she rendered the originals into verse, rather than taking the easy option of translating them into prose. Though Charlotte considered this work good enough to offer her translation of 'Les Orphelins' for publication in the *Manchester Athenaeum Album* in 1850,⁷ the essays she continued to write for Monsieur Heger throughout this year were immeasurably more valuable in terms of her personal development.

Charlotte had returned to Brussels knowing that Monsieur Heger held her in the highest regard as one of his star pupils. This was the first time that someone outside her family, capable of informed judgement and himself of an intellect equal, if not superior, to her own, had recognized and encouraged her talent. It is not surprising, therefore, that in at least three of the essays she wrote this year she raised the question of the nature of genius.[8] She had done this once before, in her essay on 'Peter the Hermit', identifying herself with him because she saw that the spiritual flame within him overcame his physical insignificance.[9] That essay had been written when her command of French was comparatively weak and, as her powers grew, she returned to the subject again and again with a tenacity of purpose which suggests that she was not only seeking to define genius for herself but demanding recognition from Monsieur Heger. In the light of his comments, her own opinions were radically changed.

In an analysis of Millevoye's poem, 'La Chute des Feuilles', Charlotte wandered far from her subject in attempting to identify the poet's inspiration. Starting from the impressions Millevoye's poem evokes, she posed the question of how deliberately he then executed his intention.

Having prepared his canvas in this way and traced the first rough outlines of his sketch, has he not carefully sought out the details, assembled the images appropriate for making his principal idea stand out? Has he not weighed each thought carefully, considered thoroughly each secondary thought, minutely measured and adjusted each part of the great Whole in such a way that their union will not sin against the master-principle of composition, the principle of Unity? Is this really the procedure Millevoye followed? Is this the method followed by all great poets?

'Souls made of fire and children of the Sun!'

Alas! I do not know: the great souls alone can reply, but there is one thing I do know for sure because the certainty of it depends more on reason than on genius, that is that, for novices in literature, for those who wish to imitate the great masters, this method is the only one that can lead them to an even remotely desirable end; perhaps in following it they will never find anything except lead in their crucibles, perhaps, though, if the sleeping spark of genius bursts into flame during the operation, a new light will illuminate their souls, the true secret of Alchemy will be revealed and their lead will transmute into gold.[10]

Charlotte's allowances for 'novices in literature' showed that she still had reservations about Monsieur Heger's method of teaching by imitation. Having found the courage to question this, she now launched into an explicit defence of her position, that genius was innate and inspirational.

I believe that genius ... has no need to seek out details, that it never pauses for reflection, that it does not think about unity: I believe that details come naturally without the poet having to seek them, that inspiration takes the place of reflection and as for unity, I think that there is no unity more perfect than that which results from a heart filled with a single idea ... The nature of genius is like that of instinct; its operation is at the same time both simple and marvellous; the man of genius produces, without labour and as if by a single effort, results which men without genius, however knowledgeable, however persevering, could never attain.[11]

In literature, if not in religion, Charlotte was a Calvinist: she had no doubt that she was one of the elect who possessed genius and that those who did not, no matter how hard they tried, could never achieve greatness. This was a passionate defence of her own method of writing, so obvious from the juvenilia and her diary fragments, where an inspirational moment or vision leads to uncontrolled outpourings in which her pen can scarcely keep pace with her thoughts. Though Monsieur Heger wrote frequent approving remarks in the margins of this essay, he took issue with Charlotte's main thesis to such an extent that he wrote half a page of 'Observation' at the end. His argument is worth quoting in full, not only because it was put with equal force to Charlotte's own, but also because it eventually won Charlotte round to his way of thinking.

Work does not make a poet: man does not make his own genius, he receives it from heaven – that is indisputable.

Machinery does not create force: it rules its employment, it multiplies its effect a hundredfold.

Man does not know what genius is, it is a gift from heaven, it is something one might call divine. It is the same as force. But imagine two men of the same strength, one without a lever, the other with a lever. The first will lift a thousand pounds, the second, in making the same effort, will uproot a plane tree.

Is a lever worth nothing?

Without a voice there is no singer – undoubtedly – but there will be no singer either without art, without study, without imitation.

Nature makes a painter – but what would he be without study of perspective – of the art of colour. – C. H.

Though he evidently intended to end his comments here, signing his initials, Monsieur Heger was unable to relinquish the subject and returned to the attack.

How much would his pictures be worth, how much would they be desired.

Without study there is no art; without art, there is no effect on men, since art is the epitome of all that the centuries bequeath us, of all that man has found beautiful, of that which has had an effect on man, of all that he has found worthy of saving from oblivion.

Genius without study and without art, without the knowledge of that which has already been done, is Force without a lever, it is Demosthenes, a sublime orator, who stammers and makes himself booed; it is the soul which sings inside and which cannot express its interior songs except in a rough and uneducated voice; it is the sublime musician, finally, who has only an out of tune piano to make the world hear the sweet melodies which he hears ringing out inside him.

Certainly the gem-carver does not make the diamond, but without him the most beautiful diamond is a pebble.

Poet or not, you should study form – if you are a Poet you will be more powerful – your works will live – if not, you will not produce poetry, but you will savour its merit and charm.[12]

Two months after this essay, Charlotte returned to the subject of genius in 'The death of Napoleon'. Again, it was a major digression from the theme of the essay, taking up a quarter of the first draft submitted to Monsieur Heger, and it was completely excised from the final revision. The result was undoubtedly a more concise and structured piece of work, but some of Charlotte's thoughts on genius were thereby lost. In the original version, Charlotte had begun by asking whether anyone without genius could rightly judge and appreciate the quality in someone else.

Has an ordinary individual the right to express his feelings on the life and death of Bonaparte? Does he know how to judge him? Yes; however insignificant he may be he has the right to form an opinion and even to express it: neither king nor emperor has the authority to silence that inner voice that every man hears speaking in his heart and which approves or condemns not only his own actions but the actions of those around him. So one cannot deny to mediocrity her right to judge genius but it does not follow that her judgement is always just.[13]

According to Charlotte, the distinctive quality of mediocrity is moderation, which is the antithesis of genius.

Mediocrity can see the faults of genius, its imprudence, its recklessness, its ambition, but she is too cold, too limited, too self-centred to understand its struggles, its sufferings, its sacrifices; she is also envious and even its virtues appear to her under a false and tarnished light.[14]

Though she never actually makes the claim, it is implicit throughout Charlotte's essay that she aligns herself with 'passionate, misunderstood genius'[15] and she has no reluctance in weighing Napoleon's genius against that of his conqueror, her childhood hero, the Duke of Wellington. From a somewhat half-hearted defence of Napoleon, the essay turns into a eulogy of the duke.

I have said that this man is the equal of Napoleon; in genius, yes: in rectitude of character, in loftiness of aim he is neither his equal nor his superior, he is of another species. Napoleon Bonaparte clung to his reputation and loved celebrity; Arthur Wellesley cares neither for the one nor the other. Public opinion had great value for Napoleon, for Wellington public opinion is an idea, a nonentity which the breath of his powerful will can make disappear, like a soap bubble. Napoleon flattered the people and sought their applause; Wellington spurns it; if his own conscience approves, that is enough, all other praise irritates him … In spite of his pride he is modest; he shrinks from eulogy, he rejects panegyric, he never speaks of himself and never allows anyone else to speak of him; his character equals in grandeur and surpasses in truth that of all other heroes, ancient or modern.[16]

Curiously enough, the very qualities Charlotte praised in Wellington as making his genius superior to Napoleon's were precisely those she had ascribed to the much despised mediocrity: self-control, balance, disdain for passionate excess, and resistance to the claims of all but conscience.[17] This contradiction was removed in the excision of the early passages relating to genius.

Charlotte's final essay on the subject of genius is one of her most interesting. 'Letter from a Poor Painter to a Great Lord', written on 17 October 1843, shows how far she had come to accept Monsieur Heger's doctrine that genius needs discipline and self-control to achieve its potential. Charlotte seems to have had Branwell very much in mind when she wrote this essay. The poor painter assumes the belligerent and self-confident tone which Branwell had himself adopted in his earliest efforts to obtain publication in *Blackwood's Magazine.* Though he is seeking a patron, he does not flatter the great lord or beat about the bush, but addresses him with direct honesty.

My Lord, I believe that I have talent. Do not be indignant at my presumption, do not accuse me of arrogance, I do not know that feeble feeling, the child of vanity; but I know well another feeling, Respect for myself, a feeling born of independence and integrity. My Lord I believe that I have Genius. This declaration shocks you; you find it arrogant, I find it perfectly simple. It is not universally recognised that without genius no artist can succeed? Would it not then be sheer stupidity to devote oneself to the arts without being sure that one has this indispensible quality?[18]

In describing the poor artist's early difficulties, however, Charlotte spoke with the voice of bitter personal experience.

Throughout all my early youth the difference which existed between me and most of the people who surrounded me, was an embarrassing enigma to me which I did not know how to resolve; I thought myself inferior to everyone and it distressed me. I thought it was my duty to follow the example set by the majority of my acquaintances, an example sanctioned by the approbation of prudent and legitimate mediocrity, and yet I felt myself incapable of feeling and behaving as that majority felt and behaved ... There was always excess in what I did; I was either too excited or too despondent; without wanting to I allowed everything that passed through my heart to be seen and sometimes there were storms passing through it; in vain I tried to imitate the sweet gaiety, the serene and equable spirits which I saw in the faces of my companions and which I found so worthy of admiration; all my efforts were useless; I could not restrain the ebb and flow of blood in my arteries and that ebb and flow always showed itself in my face and in my hard and unattractive features. I wept in secret.[19]

This, as Monsieur Heger could not fail to recognize, was a *cri de coeur* from his pupil; it was not the poor painter speaking but the Charlotte Brontë who had told Ellen Nussey, 'I am not <u>like</u> you', and who had longed to be more like her conventional friend. Once again, but this time explicitly, she utterly rejected the idea that she was 'mediocre' and demanded recognition of the genius which made her stand out from the crowd. The difference now was that she accepted the need to hone her talents. Her poor painter spent four years in Italy learning the technicalities of his art. Echoing the words

Monsieur Heger had written at the bottom of her essay on 'La Chute des Feuilles', she wrote:

I suffered much in Florence, Venice and Rome and there I gained what I wanted to possess; an intimate knowledge of all the mechanical mysteries of Painting, a taste cultivated according to the rules of art. As for natural genius, neither Titian, nor Raphael nor Michaelangelo would have known how to give me that which comes from God alone; the little I have, I have got from my Creator...[20]

Only a month before she wrote this essay, Monsieur Heger had presented Charlotte with a copy of his speech at the annual prizegiving at the Athénée Royal.[21] In it, he had stoutly defended the importance of encouraging pupils to strive to emulate the best in everything they did; emulation was the key to self-improvement. The speech had obviously struck a chord in Charlotte's nature as she drew on it in her essay; having left his country and gone abroad, the poor painter declared:

I lacked neither courage nor fortitude, I set to work immediately; sometimes, it is true, despair overwhelmed me for an instant, for when I saw the works of the great masters of my art, I felt myself truly despicable; but the fever of emulation came to drive away that momentary demoralisation and from that profound consciousness of inferiority, I drew new strength for work – it aroused in me a fixed resolution – 'I wish to do all, to suffer all, in order to win all'[22]

Through the medium of her poor painter addressing his patron, Charlotte, the writer, could speak out far more boldly to her tutor than she could in the flesh. Essays like this one were the key elements in Charlotte's relationship with Monsieur Heger, as her later novels make abundantly clear. Three out of Charlotte's four novels contain an essay written by a pupil for her teacher, *Jane Eyre* being the only exception. In each case the essay serves as the midwife of love, the means by which the hero is brought to a recognition of the intellectual powers and emotional depth hidden beneath the otherwise unexceptional exterior of an apparently conventional young woman. William Crimsworth, in *The Professor*, for instance, receives a *devoir* from his Anglo-Swiss pupil, Frances Henri, on the subject of King Alfred.

'Now,' thought I, 'I shall see a glimpse of what she really is; I shall get an idea of the nature and extent of her powers; not that she can be expected to express herself well in a foreign tongue, but still, if she has any mind, here will be a reflection of it.' ... There were errors of orthography, there were foreign idioms, there were some faults of construction, there were verbs irregular transformed into verbs regular; it was mostly made up, as the above example shews, of short and somewhat rude sentences, and the style stood in great need of polish and sustained dignity; yet such as it was, I had hitherto seen nothing like it in the course of my professorial experience.[23]

Lucy Snowe in *Villette* also produces essays for her teacher, Monsieur Paul

Emanuel, which he rates highly enough to compel her to reproduce them before two examiners to prove her exceptional ability. In *Shirley*, Louis Moore is so struck that he is able to recite from memory the whole of Shirley's *devoir* on 'The First Blue-Stocking' years after she has written it.[24] Significantly, in each case, greater prominence is given to the teacher's reaction to the essay than to the pupil's production of it. Clearly Charlotte, consciously or subconsciously, had hoped to win more than simple intellectual admiration from Monsieur Heger.

The vexed question of Charlotte's relationship with Monsieur Heger has haunted Brontë scholars since the revelation, at the beginning of this century, of the letters she wrote to him after her return to England. Their passionate and frank admissions of attachment might suggest that there was even an adulterous affair, particularly as Monsieur Heger's side of the correspondence is missing. One of his surviving letters, written to another former pupil several decades later, suggests otherwise. Though this relationship was beyond all doubt entirely proper, the letter breathes an intimacy and sensuality which a susceptible woman would find deeply erotic. 'I only have to think of you to see you', he told the lady in question.

I often give myself the pleasure when my duties are over, when the light fades. I postpone lighting the gas lamp in my library, I sit down, smoking my cigar, and with a hearty will I evoke your image – and you come (without wishing to, I dare say) but I see you, I talk with you – you, with that little air, affectionate undoubtedly, but independent and resolute, firmly determined not to allow any opinion without being previously convinced, demanding to be convinced before allowing yourself to submit – in fact, just as I knew you, my dear L—, and as I have esteemed and loved you[25]

This could be Mr Rochester talking to Jane Eyre. It was hardly surprising that Charlotte was seduced – mentally and morally, if not physically. 'He made much of her, & drew her out, & petted her, & won her love', a friend of the Hegers wrote in 1870, long before Charlotte's passion had become public knowledge.

There was no such fore-gone intention on his part, – that was his practise with all his wife's most intellectual pupils, & let me hasten to add, there was no illicit affection on his part either. – He was a worshipper of intellect & he worshipped Charlotte Bronte thus far & no further.[26]

Lonely, vulnerable and acutely aware that the mental powers which estranged her from most people made her special in Monsieur Heger's eyes, Charlotte was easily won. During the course of 1843 she gradually slipped from normal feelings of respect and esteem for her teacher into an unhealthy and obsessive dependency on Monsieur Heger's every expression of approval.

After her return to Brussels at the beginning of the year, Charlotte had begun to give English lessons to him and Monsieur Chapelle, his brother-in-law. 'If you could see and hear the efforts I make to teach them to pronounce like Englishmen and their unavailing attempts to imitate,' she told Ellen Nussey in March, 'you would laugh to all eternity.' Monsieur Heger had taken her and another pupil, presumably also a foreigner, out into Brussels to see the Carnival celebrations before Lent: though she dismissed the experience as 'nothing but masking and mum[m]ery', it was later to provide valuable material for *Villette*.[27]

The optimism with which Charlotte had returned to Brussels gradually wore away. 'We have entered upon the gloom and abstinence of Lent', she told Ellen, '– the first day of Lent we had coffee without milk for breakfast – vinegar & vegetables with a very little salt-fish for dinner and bread for supper –'.[28] The hardship of the diet was increased by a prolonged season of harsh weather. February had already been bitterly cold and this continued throughout most of March. Though Charlotte had hoped that Ellen might be able to join her in Brussels, she was now glad that her friend was safe at home in England.

If I had seen you shivering as I shivered myself – if I had seen your hands and feet as red and swelled as mine were – my discomfort would just have been doubled – I can do very well under this sort of thing – it does not fret me – it only makes me numb and silent – but if you were to pass a winter in Belgium you would be ill –[29]

Even though better weather was on the way and the Lenten diet was coming to an end, Charlotte still did not press her friend to join her in Brussels: 'there are privations & humiliations to submit to – there is monotony and uniformity of life – and above all there is a constant sense of solitude in the midst of numbers'.[30] Though Charlotte still found her employment at the Pensionnat Heger infinitely preferable to her earlier posts as a teacher at Roe Head and as a private governess, she was already complaining of the monotony and sense of exclusion which had brought her to breaking point in her previous careers. Indeed, the whole progress of her career in Brussels had begun to follow a now familiar pattern. By the beginning of May she was telling Branwell of her increasing distaste for her pupils.

the people here are no go whatsoever – amongst 120 persons, which compose the \daily/ population of this house I can discern only 1 or 2 who deserve anything like regard – This is not \owing/ to foolish fastidiousness on my part – but to the absence of decent qualities on theirs – they have not intellect or politeness or good-nature or good-feeling – they are nothing – I don't hate them – hatred would be too warm a feeling – They have no sensations themselves and they excite none – but one wear< y >ies from day to day of caring nothing, fearing nothing, liking nothing hating nothing – being nothing, doing nothing – yes, I teach & sometimes get red-in-the face with impatience at their stupidity – but don't think I ever scold or fly into a passion – if I spoke warmly, as warmly as I sometimes used to do at Roe-Head they would think me mad – nobody ever gets into a passion here – such a thing is not known – the phlegm that thickens their blood is too gluey to boil.[31]

Monsieur Heger was the only exception to this rule, though Charlotte had little contact with him now that her formal lessons had ceased. 'I am still indebted to him for all the pleasure or amusement I have', she declared. He loaded her with books and, even as Charlotte was writing to Branwell, called in to present her with a little German Testament, no doubt in an attempt to encourage her studies of that language. Charlotte ended her letter with a confession which she could probably have made to no one but Branwell.

It is a curious metaphysical fact that always in the evening when I am in the great Dormitory alone – having no other company than a number of beds with white curtains I always recur as fanatically as ever to the old ideas the old faces & the old scenes in the world below[32]

A resumption of Angrian imaginings was probably the last thing Charlotte needed at this juncture. It was a sign not only that the novelty of her continental education had well and truly worn off but also that she was no longer finding intellectual fulfilment in it.

Charlotte's disillusionment was also reflected in a significant shift in her attitude towards Madame Heger, repeating the familiar pattern of her relationships with previous employers. From being grateful and appreciative of her kindness, Charlotte had now begun actively to dislike her – but, typically, blamed it on Madame Heger's attitude towards herself. 'I am convinced that she does not like me', Charlotte wrote to Emily at the end of May, '– why, I can't tell, nor do I think she herself has any definite reason for the aversion.'[33] As Charlotte herself pointed out, though, Madame Heger could not understand why her new teacher refused to socialize with her fellow teachers. The obvious contempt with which Charlotte regarded them and her pupils cannot have helped to make relations easy in a boarding school of such small proportions. This must have been a matter of concern to Madame Heger, particularly as Charlotte was not even on speaking terms with Mademoiselle Blanche, one of the three schoolmistresses.[34] Nor can it have escaped Madame Heger's notice that her husband was the one person excepted from Charlotte's general condemnatory attitude. As she was the *directrice* of the school, it was too easy for Charlotte to lay the blame for all her own problems at Madame Heger's door. Just as she had done at the Sidgwicks' and the Whites', Charlotte directed all her venom at the mistress and found every excuse for the master.

M Heger is wondrously influenced by Madame, and I should not wonder if he disapproves very much of my unamiable want of sociability. He has already given me a brief lecture on universal <u>bienveillance</u>, and, perceiving that I don't improve

in consequence, I fancy he has taken to considering me as a person to be let alone –
left to the error of her ways; and consequently he has in a great measure withdrawn
the light of his countenance, and I get on from day to day in a Robinson-Crusoe-
like condition – very lonely.[35]

A few weeks later, she poured out her misery to Ellen.

To-day the weather is gloomy and I am stupefied with a bad cold and a headache.
I have nothing to tell you my dear Ellen one day is like another in this place – I
know you, living in the country, can hardly believe that it is possible life can be
monotonous in the centre of a brilliant capital like Brussels – but so it is – I feel it
most on the holidays – when all the girls and teachers go out to visit – and it
sometimes happens that I am left during several hours quite alone – with 4 great
desolate schoolrooms at my disposition – I try to read, I try to write but in vain. I
then wander about from room to room – but the silence and loneliness of all the
house weighs down one's spirits like lead – you will hardly believe it when I tell
you that Mde Heger (good & kind as I have described her) never comes near me
on these occasions – she is a reasonable and calm woman but Nelly as to warm
heartedness She has as much of that article as Mrs Allbutt – I own I was astonished
the first time I was left alone thus – when everybody else was enjoying the pleasures
of a fête-day with their friends – and she <u>knew</u> I was quite by myself and never took
the least notice of me – Yet I understand she praises me very much to everybody
and says what excellent lessons I give &c. – She is not colder to me than she is to
the other teachers – but they are less dependent on her than I am – they have
relations & acquaintances in Bruxelles. You remember the letter she wrote me when
I was in England how kind and affectionate it was – is it not odd –? I fancy I begin
to perceive the reason of this mighty distance & reserve it sometimes makes me
laugh & at other times nearly cry –. When I am sure of it I will tell you.[36]

If Charlotte thought Madame Heger was estranged from her because she
had uncovered her guilty secret, then one can only sympathize with Madame
Heger. However, it seems more likely that Charlotte's uneasy conscience
simply misinterpreted what she herself described as Madame Heger's habitual reserve with all the teachers. Significantly, too, Monsieur Heger's implied
neglect met with no complaints from his besotted pupil.

Charlotte's loneliness – which one cannot help feeling was largely self-
imposed – was compounded by the removal of the Dixon and the Jenkins
families from Brussels. Mary Dixon, Mary Taylor's cousin and Charlotte's
closest friend in the family, had already left for Germany earlier in the year.
By the middle of August, Abraham Dixon had given up his house in the
Rue de la Régence and removed, with the rest of the family, to cheaper
accommodation in Ostend. Mr Jenkins, the Episcopal clergyman in Brussels
who had been so kind to the Brontës on their first arrival, was away for the
best part of the summer. Shortly after his return from a visit to England he
fell seriously ill of a brain fever; though he recovered, he seems to have
spent the rest of the summer convalescing in Ostend and then England.[37]

Only the five Wheelwright girls remained out of all Charlotte's English friends in Brussels, but even they went away on holiday in the latter part of August. For the two other English girls now at the Pensionnat Heger, Charlotte had little time or sympathy: Susanna Mills made no impression upon her at all and Maria Miller she considered selfish, worldly and sly.[38]

It was therefore no wonder that Charlotte dreaded the prospect of the long vacation. Writing to Ellen on 6 August, she told her:

I forewarn you that I am in low spirits and that Earth and Heaven seem dreary and empty to me at this moment – In a few days our vacations will begin – everybody is joyous and animated at the prospect because everybody is to go home – I know that I am to stay here during the 5 weeks that the holidays last and that I shall be much alone and consequently get downcast and find both days & nights of a weary length – It is the first time in my life that I have really dreaded the vacation ... Alas I can hardly write, I have such a dreary weight at my heart – and I do so wish to go home – is not this childish? Pardon me Nell, I cannot help it[39]

Being on her own at Roe Head for a few weeks over Easter in 1838 had reduced Charlotte to mental and physical breakdown. Three weeks into this vacation, therefore, Charlotte could write with some relief to Emily that 'more than half the holidays are now past, and rather better than I expected'. She had, she said, spent much of the time wandering rather aimlessly through the streets of Brussels but one incident showed just how low her morale had sunk. She related her little adventure to Emily with a casualness deliberately designed to play down its startling unorthodoxy. After a walk to visit Martha Taylor's grave in the Protestant cemetery outside Brussels, she had returned to the city and almost accidentally found herself in the great Cathedral of Ste Gudule where vespers was taking place. She sat through the service but then could not find the will to leave.

An odd whim came into my head. In a solitary part of the Cathedral six or seven people still remained kneeling by the confessionals. In two confessionals I saw a priest. I felt as if I did not care what I did, provided it was not absolutely wrong, and that it served to vary my life and yield a moment's interest. I took a fancy to change myself into a Catholic and go and make a real confession to see what it was like. Knowing me as you do, you will think this odd, but when people are by themselves they have singular fancies ... a little wooden door inside the grating opened, and I saw the priest leaning his ear towards me. I was obliged to begin, and yet I did not know a word of the formula with which they always commence their confessions. It was a funny position. I felt precisely as I did when alone on the Thames at midnight. I commenced with saying I was a foreigner and had been brought up a Protestant. The priest asked if I was a Protestant then. I somehow could not tell a lie, and said 'yes'. He replied that in that case I could not 'jouir du bonheur de la confesse'; but I was determined to confess, and at last he said he would allow me because it might be the first step towards returning to the true church. I actually did confess – a real confession. When I had done he told me his address, and said that every morning I was to go to the rue du Parc – to his house – and he would reason with me and try to convince me of the error and enormity of being a Protestant!!! I promised faithfully to go. Of course, however, the adventure stops there, and I hope I shall never see the priest again.[40]

That Charlotte should not only have been driven to visit a hated Catholic priest but also that she should have made 'a real confession' to him is an indication of her desperate state of mind. All her instincts told her that her growing obsession with a married man was totally reprehensible and she obviously needed to talk to someone, if only to get the guilty secret off her chest. With no one close at hand in whom she could confide, the anonymity of the Catholic confessional suddenly had an unexpected appeal. Standing condemned in her own eyes, Charlotte could not bring herself to make a similar 'real confession', even to Emily, to whom she gave no indication at all of what she had actually said to the priest. Though the confession must in itself have provided some relief, Charlotte's immediate reaction was a sense of shame. Almost as an afterword, she told Emily, 'I think you had better not tell papa of this. He will not understand that it was only a freak, and will perhaps think I am going to turn Catholic.'[41]

The incident was to be replicated in almost exactly the same terms in *Villette*, the most autobiographical of Charlotte's novels. These are Lucy Snowe's reasons for visiting the confessional:

I said, I was perishing for a word of advice or an accent of comfort. I had been living for some weeks quite alone; I had been ill; I had a pressure of affliction on my mind of which it would hardly any longer endure the weight.[42]

Lucy Snowe, like Charlotte herself, had no intention of taking up the priest's suggestion that she should visit him. Interestingly, the reason for this was that she feared that his sympathy and comfort might really have tempted her to turn Catholic.

The probabilities are that had I visited Numéro 3, Rue des Mages, at the hour and day appointed, I might just now, instead of writing this heretic narrative, be counting my beads in the cell of a certain Carmelite convent on the Boulevard of Crécy, in Villette.

If Charlotte herself came so close to conversion in her hour of need, this might explain her subsequent virulent antipathy to everything Catholic and particularly her abhorrence of the Catholic priesthood. Hers was the hatred of one who had been severely shocked by her own receptiveness to temptation and, as the years went by, it became easier to blame the tempter than her own weakness in being tempted. At the time, however, Charlotte, like Lucy Snowe, was grateful to the priest. 'He was kind when I needed kindness; he did me good. May Heaven bless him!'[43]

What no one but Charlotte herself could decide was what she ought to do. Morally, there was no doubt that she ought to remove herself from the Pensionnat Heger, but she could not do so without admitting that the Brussels experiment had been a failure. It had not lived up to her expectations; it had not become a dramatic escape route from her earlier career though she could now place a higher price on her teaching services. Her dilemma was summed up in a letter to Emily at the beginning of October.

I should like uncommonly to be in the dining-room at home, or in the kitchen, or in the back kitchen. I should like even to be cutting up the hash, with the clerk and some register people at the other table, and you standing by, watching that I put enough flour, and not too much pepper, and, above all, that I save the best pieces of the leg of mutton for Tiger and Keeper, the first of which personages would be jumping about the dish and carving-knife, and the latter standing like a devouring flame on the kitchen floor. To complete the picture, Tabby blowing the fire, in order to boil the potatoes to a sort of vegetable glue! How divine are these recollections to me at this moment! Yet I have no thought of coming home just now. I lack a real pretext for doing so; it is true this place is dismal to me, but I cannot go home without a fixed prospect when I get there; and this prospect must not be a situation; that would be jumping out of the frying-pan into the fire.

Rather wistfully, Charlotte asked Emily if she and their father really wanted her very much to come home: 'I have an idea that I should be of no use there – a sort of aged person upon the parish.'[44] If Charlotte had hoped that her dilemma would be resolved for her by a summons back home, she was mistaken. Her family could not or would not take the decision for her. So she tried, somewhat half-heartedly, to give her notice to Madame Heger:

If it had depended on her I should certainly have soon been at liberty but Monsieur Heger – having heard of what was in agitation – sent for me the day after – and pronounced with vehemence his decision that I should not leave –[45]

Charlotte could not overlook so decided an intervention: at the very least it was proof that Monsieur Heger still held her in high regard and that was more important to her at this juncture than her personal pride or inclination. Perhaps thinking that he had neglected his former pupil, Monsieur Heger renewed his lessons with her. Discovering, from a chance remark, that her knowledge of arithmetic 'would have disgraced a charity-schoolboy', he started her on a course in the subject.[46] If Charlotte's experience reflected that of Lucy Snowe, it was not an altogether happy one, her master becoming increasingly severe and sarcastic as her abilities improved. The intention was to provoke her to greater effort but, in Charlotte's low state of mind, the effect was simply to discourage her and the lessons were soon given up. She was still producing the occasional essay for Monsieur Heger, but even this seems to have been a declining interest, her last surviving one dating from 6 October 1843.[47]

Charlotte's loathing of Madame Heger increased as she felt herself apparently losing her husband's goodwill. 'Madame Heger is a polite – plausible and interested person – I no longer trust to her', she told Ellen, adding in a note written the day after in her *General Atlas of Modern Geography*,

Brussels – Saturday Morning Octbr 14th.1843, – First class – I am very cold – there is no fire – I wish I were at home with Papa – Branwell – Emily – Anne & Tabby – I am tired of being amongst foreigners it is a dreary life – especially as there is only one person in this house worthy of being liked – also another who seems a rosy sugar-plum but I know her to be coloured chalk.[48]

In this increasingly fraught and unpleasant situation, the only person who seems to have been prepared to offer Charlotte unequivocal advice was Mary Taylor. She repeatedly told her that she should leave Brussels, suggesting that she should join her in Germany and even offering to share her pupils with Charlotte so that she could be guaranteed a living. Though Charlotte claimed that she could not possibly take advantage of Mary's 'disinterested generosity, quite peculiar to herself', the real reason she refused seems to have been an aversion to teaching boys; 'opinion & custom run so strongly against what she does ... if her pupils had been girls, it would be all well – the fact of their being boys (or rather young men) is the stumbling block'.[49]

Even though Charlotte would not join her, Mary Taylor persisted in urging her to leave Brussels. By the end of the year even Charlotte had become convinced that this was a necessity. On 19 December she wrote a short and businesslike note to Emily which revealed nothing of what the decision had cost her.

Dear E. J.
I have taken my determination. I hope to be at home the day after New Year's Day. I have told Mme Heger. But in order to come home I shall be obliged to draw on my cash for another £5. I have only £3 at present, and as there are several little things I should like to buy before I leave Brussels – which you know cannot be got as well in England – £3 would not suffice. Low spirits have afflicted me much lately, but I hope all will be well when I get home – about all, if I find papa and you and B. and A. well. I am not ill in body. It is only the mind which is a trifle shaken – for want of comfort.
    I shall try to cheer up now. – Good-bye.

C. B.[50]

Charlotte's desperation can be measured by the fact that she made no excuses for returning home and, more significantly, that she had no prospective employment lined up in England.

The task of saying goodbye to her few friends in Brussels was soon accomplished. Laetitia Wheelwright was given a scrap of paper inscribed in

Flemish and French, 'Think of me and I will always think of you.' On Christmas Day Charlotte dined for the last time with the Jenkins family, where she was also able to say her farewells to Abraham Dixon, Mary Taylor's uncle and father of her own friend, Mary.[51] The most difficult leave-taking was the last: saying goodbye to the Hegers for what all knew would be a final separation. Charlotte later told Ellen:

I think however long I live I shall not forget what the parting with Monsieur Heger cost me – it grieved me so much to grieve him who has been so true and kind and disinterested a friend –[52]

Monsieur Heger gave Charlotte a diploma, sealed with the seal of the Athénée Royal, testifying to her teaching abilities. He also suggested that she should take one of his daughters to England as a pupil, an offer Charlotte refused 'as I knew it would not be agreeable to Madame –'.[53]

Her low opinion of the phlegmatic nature of her Belgian pupils was somewhat confounded by the degree of regret they expressed at her departure – a feeling she did not reciprocate.[54] On Sunday, 31 December, the last day of the old year, Charlotte took her final leave of Brussels. The experiences of the last two years, both intellectually and emotionally, had marked her for life. She had successfully undergone the rigours of an academic discipline imposed by Monsieur Heger, emerging as a better and more powerful writer. And she had fallen in love for the first time – with a man who was the antithesis of everything that she had previously valued. Monsieur Heger was as far removed as it was possible to be from Zamorna: small, ugly, short-tempered and, above all, Catholic, he shared only his married state with the hero who had dominated Charlotte's imagination for so long. Her unrequited passion for him was to alter permanently and radically her vision of what the male hero should be. The future creator of Mr Rochester and Paul Emanuel was born.

In Haworth, the parsonage household was being capably run by Emily. Though she had nominal assistance from Tabby Aykroyd, who had returned in Charlotte's absence, the bulk of the work fell on her shoulders. Tabby was too old and lame to be of much practical use, but she was company for Emily while Patrick was busy.[55] And busy he certainly was. Since William Weightman's death he had been without a curate, giving added piquancy to the fact that he had to deliver the annual sermon in aid of the Church Pastoral Aid Society himself. A few days later, however, the Reverend James William Smith, MA, arrived in Haworth, taking up his first duties on 12 March 1843.[56] Smith was an Irishman who shared the fiery temper and illiberal sentiments of his predecessor, William Hodgson, but added to them an avaricious and unscrupulous temperament. Patrick, though undoubtedly grateful for any assistance, soon found that he had little in common with his new curate and that Mr Smith would be no replacement for William Weightman.

On 14 March Patrick and Smith were undoubtedly among the many neighbouring clergy who attended the consecration of St John's Church in Keighley, a ceremony performed by the Bishop of Ripon.[57] The Reverend William Busfeild had raised £2,000 for the building of this new church, aided by grants from various societies, as part of his aggressive campaign against the Dissenters in his parish. His attitude was the antithesis of Patrick's, attempting to bludgeon his parishioners into submission over the church rate question. Patrick, meanwhile, put his own declared principles into action by collecting a voluntary subscription towards the upkeep of his church from his congregation, instead of imposing a church rate on the chapelry.[58]

He was also actively campaigning on wider issues. On 20 May he wrote an anguished letter to the *Leeds Intelligencer*, deploring the attempts to raise rebellion in Ireland and attributing this to the Established Church's loss of precedence there. Famine, poverty and nationalism were combining to produce a potent and explosive situation, culminating in a movement to repeal the 1801 Act of Union. 'I am no bigot', wrote Patrick,

I am a friend to liberty of conscience and political liberty; but I am an open and avowed enemy to hypocrisy, false zeal, revolutionary principles, and all those motives and movements which can have for their end only what is doubtful, or extremely exceptionable and bad.[59]

A month later he expanded his views in a letter 'on the ominous and dangerous vagaries of the times' to the *Halifax Guardian*, apparently in response to a personal request from the editor.

The insane, but fearful project of the repeal of the Union, in the Emerald Isle, the sensitive, senseless and serious secession from the Kirk of Scotia, the selfish corn-law agitation in Albion, and the Rebecca movement in Wales, are all of the same family, where the father is the prince of the power of the air, and the different members, his willing agents...

Notwithstanding the nineteenth century's advances in science, true religion and sound principles were in decline. All the present agitation, he declared, was the result of 'a restless disposition for change, an untoward ambition, a recklessness of consequences, and a struggle for power and predominance'.[60] Patrick's fears about the political instability of the realm, particularly in Ireland, intensified as the year progressed. By November he was convinced that civil war was imminent in Ireland and wrote for the first time in many years to his brother, Hugh Brontë, at Ballinaskeagh. The letter reveals just how seriously he regarded the Catholic threat, even to the point of considering that forceful resistance would be legitimate.

Dear Brother,

I wish to know, how you are all doing, in these turbulent times, As I learn from the Newspapers, Ireland, is at present, in a very precarious situation, and circumstances there must, I should think – lead to civil war – Which, in its consequences, is the worst of all wars – I hope, that the Protestants, (of <u>all</u> denominations, are, by arming themselves, and laying down, proper plans, of orginazation, duly, on their guard –. Otherwise, they may be taken by surprize, and murder'd by their insidious, and malignant enemies – As the Army cannot be every where. All the Protestants in Ireland, ought to remember, what a few determined men, did at the seige of Derry – But, whatever, in these cases, be done, should be in strict accordance with the Laws – If all the Protestants in Ireland, were rightly armed and organized, they need not – owing to their good cause, and their superior intellects, and wealth, fear their opponents – Should the Romanists gain their ends, they will destroy, and utterly exterminate, <u>both Churchmen, and Dissenters</u> – and, I hope, that both Dissenters, and Churchmen, see this, and will act, accordingly. I like not war, but Christ has said, in reference to a case of necessity, like this, 'let him who has no sword, sell his Garments and buy one.' –

Yet, whilst I say these things, I would admonish you, and all my Brothers, and Friends, not to be rash, and neither to break the Laws of God, or Man – And I would say, let prudence, and justice, be joined to courage – and due precaution –[61]

One can understand Charlotte's insistence that Emily should not tell Patrick of her 'freak' Catholic confession in Brussels.

Other subjects also preoccupied Patrick during the summer months. On the morning of 1 July 1843, Colonel David Fawcett was shot dead by Lieutenant Alexander Munro in a duel at Camden Town. The sheer waste of life in pursuit of 'Honour, [which] understood in this sense, is a mere ignis fatuis', prompted Patrick to write to the *Leeds Mercury*. In his denunciation of duelling on both scriptural and practical grounds, Patrick revealed his own interest in the subject.

I remember, that once when in London, and at another time when in Brussels, I heard professed duellists speak on the subject, in which their hands were stained with blood. From what I could gather, I should say that their minds were ill at ease, and that some of them would have given up all pretensions to their false notions of honour, in order to have restored the dead to life.[62]

In this letter and another on the same subject to the *Leeds Intelligencer* a couple of months later, Patrick recommended that an Act of Parliament should be passed which would make it an offence punishable by transportation for life to give or accept a challenge.[63]

Another subject close to his heart was national education. He was swift to condemn the Dissenters whose opposition to and defeat of a parliamentary bill had deprived the manufacturing districts of a centralized and standardized education system. Their arguments, he complained to the *Leeds Intelligencer*, were all utterly inconclusive, and ... dictated by party spirit, or sectarian prejudice. Divested of all the rhetorical flourishes and sophistry ... the naked truth only amounted to this, – the Church of England must be thwarted[64]

Even if national education could not be achieved, Patrick fought hard to improve schooling in his locality. He was a founder member of the Bradford Church Institution which was set up in July 1843 to encourage the building of Anglican schools.[65] On 4 August, he wrote an impassioned letter to the National Society, seeking a grant towards a new school in Haworth and painting a grim picture of the state of education in the township.

I have resided in Yorkshire above 30 years and have preached and visited in different parishes – I have also been in Lancashire and from my reading, personal observation and experience I do not hesitate to say that the populace in general, are either ignorant, or wicked, and in most cases where they have a little learning it is either of a skismatical, vainly philosophical or treacherously political nature. Some exceptions no doubt there are, but they are few and far between. I live in the midst of these delusions and though Mr Smith my able and faithful clerical coadjutor in Godly zeal – heartily joins with me in all our Apostolical labours of love, we have more, far more, than enough to do.[66]

Patrick also enlisted the support of the vicar of Bradford in his campaign. Towards the end of October, Dr Scoresby, himself an enthusiastic promoter of education, visited Haworth to view potential sites for building 'as speedily as possible' a new church day schoolroom and schoolhouse.[67]

On 2 January 1844, a new National School was officially opened in Haworth under the auspices of the church. The master was Ebenezer Rand, who had been trained at the National Society's Central School in London; the problem of providing a mistress for the girls was solved by the appointment of his wife. At a nominal charge of twopence per week, irrespective of age or proficiency, the pupils were taught everything from the three 'Rs' to singing and had their books, slates and pencils provided free of charge. Special evening classes were also held for the factory children who could not attend school during the day. The benefits of the scheme were recognized immediately and, within a month of opening, the school already had 170 pupils.[68] Its continued success was not assured, however, as the National Society only donated twenty pounds a year towards the salaries of the Rands and the fees were not enough to cover the shortfall. At the end of January Patrick was compelled to write round to all the principal inhabitants of Haworth, urging them to make a liberal donation to ensure the school's survival.[69] Later in the year he was able to report with satisfaction to the National Society that the school had brought immediate benefits to the local children.

The little creatures also find that the way to wisdom is the road to pleasure and go on in their work for the acquisition of knowledge with alacrity and delight. This is,

I conceive, as it ought to be, for 'wisdom's ways are ways of pleasantness, and all her paths are peace'.[70]

The establishing of the National School obviously owed at least something to the vicar of Bradford's interest in education and his earlier visit to Haworth. His intervention on another educational matter caused Patrick some personal anguish and great controversy in the township. For more than six years, the Free Grammar School near Oxenhope had been run by a Mr Ramsbottom, a local Wesleyan Methodist preacher, though the seventeenth-century foundation required that the master should be a graduate of Oxford or Cambridge – a condition which effectively excluded all Dissenters. On 4 January, Dr Scoresby wrote to Patrick pointing out this irregularity and suggesting that he should call a meeting of the trustees to dismiss Ramsbottom and appoint 'a proper master' with his assistance. The letter was offensively phrased, implying that Patrick, as the supervising clergyman, and the trustees had been culpably negligent in their duties, lecturing them on 'the course which is plainly their duty to pursue' and threatening them with an application to the Lord Chancellor if they failed to carry out his 'suggestions'. The trustees had little option but to give the present master notice to quit at midsummer,[71] but the Dissenters responded by attacking Patrick. The *Bradford Observer* carried a sarcastic little report that Patrick had announced in his sermon that he would no longer perform the burial service over anyone not baptized into the Church of England. This was a malicious distortion of the truth, as Patrick was quick to point out in a letter the following week. His refusal to bury the unbaptized was not aimed at Dissenters but at his own parishioners who fulfilled their secular duty in registering their children's births with the district registrar but failed in their divine duty to have the religious rite performed.[72]

As if he had not enough to do, Patrick also wrote to the papers on a matter which had always been a personal obsession of his – the dangers of fire. Prompted by the recent condemnation of the Hindu practice of suttee, or widow-burning, he wrote to point out that parental negligence frequently led to children being burnt to death. In particular, he drew attention to the fact that linen and cotton clothing was especially inflammable and recommended that children and women (who, with their long skirts, were also vulnerable) should be encouraged to wear silk or woollen clothing. As a graphic illustration of his argument he explained that in his twenty years at Haworth he had buried between ninety and a hundred children who were burnt to death after their clothes caught fire.[73]

Charlotte was shocked on her return to Haworth at the beginning of 1844 to discover that, despite his activity, her father's health had deteriorated rapidly in her absence. He was now sixty-six years of age: his eyesight was failing rapidly and he had to face the prospect that he might soon go blind. Various schemes to reduce his duties to a more manageable level by dividing his chapelry into two or even three separate districts had all come to nothing and he was increasingly obliged to rely on his curate, James Smith, and old friends, such as Thomas Brooksbank Charnock and Thomas Crowther, for assistance.[74] Ill-natured gossip in the village did nothing to improve his plight: the lotion he was using on his eyes seems to have been alcohol-based, giving rise to more rumours that the parson had taken to drink. Patrick was so distressed by the slander that he even considered prosecuting those responsible.[75] The fact that Charlotte had been unaware of her father's difficulties was an additional burden of guilt to shoulder with those of her raw emotions concerning Monsieur Heger and her sense of failure. Writing at the end of January to Ellen Nussey, who was on a visit to her brother Henry at Earnley, she was full of gloom.

I do not know whether you feel as I do Ellen – but there are times now when it appears to me as if all my ideas and feelings except a few friendships and affections are changed from what they used to be – something in me which used to be enthusiasm is tamed down and broken – I have fewer illusions – what I wish for now is active exertion – a stake in life – Haworth seems such a lonely, quiet spot, buried away from the world – I no longer regard myself as young, indeed, I shall soon be 28 and it seems as if I ought to be working and braving the rough realities of the world as other people do – It is however my duty to restrain this feeling at present and I will endeavour to do so.[76]

Charlotte claimed that it was her wish to commence a school, as indeed everyone now expected her to do. She had sufficient money and qualifications for the undertaking but, she asserted, there was now an insuperable barrier to her attaining the objective for which she had striven so long: her father's health.

I have felt for some months that I ought not to be away from him – and I feel now that it would be too selfish to leave him (at least so long as Branwell and Anne are absent) in order to pursue selfish interests of my own –[77]

Though this argument was accepted by Charlotte's friends and biographers, it was disingenuous. It would obviously have been a greater comfort to Patrick to know that his children were all well placed to earn their livings for the foreseeable future than to have them unemployed at home and dependent on his own inadequate salary. The parsonage was comfortably run with the assistance of two loyal and reliable servants, Tabby Aykroyd and Martha Brown; more importantly, he had Emily to act as his housekeeper and, when necessary, as his amanuensis. There was no need for Charlotte to remain at home. Her father's ill health was simply a convenient excuse for her own depression of spirits and resultant lethargy which were the real reasons for her reluctance to make a new start.

There was then a tinge of envy in Charlotte's remark that Branwell and Anne, who had just returned to Thorp Green after the Christmas holidays, were both 'wondrously valued' in their situations.[78] In both cases, this had been achieved by hard work and at considerable personal cost. Branwell had found it extremely difficult to adapt to being a tutor again after the comparative independence of his post on the railway. On 30 March 1843, a few months into his new job, he had written a poem into his old Luddenden Foot notebook.

I sit this evening far away
  From all I used to know
And \nought reminds my soul to/ day
  < The hours gone >\Of happy/ long ago

\Unwelcome/ cares \unthought of/ fears
  Around my room arise
I seek for suns of former years,
  But clouds oercast my skies

< I seek for what has smiled one hour >
  < And in the next has flown >

Yes – Memory where\fore/ does thy voice
  Bring old times back to view
As Thou wouldst bid me not rejoice
  In < scenes >\thoughts/ and prospects new[79]

Branwell's uncertainties and unhappiness were probably compounded by the fact that he was in a new and strange place, cut off from all his old friends in Halifax. He was not even living under the same roof as his sister, having taken lodgings at the Old Hall, a seventeenth-century red brick house with a Dutch-style roof which seems to have been part of a working farm. The building was attractive enough for Branwell to draw it in pen and ink later that year.[80] Initially, at least, Branwell was so miserable that he became ill. Patrick was deeply concerned and took the extraordinary step of visiting his son in March, when he had to be in York himself to give evidence at the Assizes in a notorious forgery case.[81] Gradually, however, Branwell seems to have settled, helped, no doubt, by the Robinsons' obvious appreciation of his talents.

Anne, too, had had her difficulties which Branwell's proximity seems, in some measure, to have allayed. At the end of May she wrote a confident poem which forcefully rejected Calvinist dogma as uncharitable and irreligious and asserted her own belief in the then unfashionable idea of universal salvation.

You may rejoice to think yourselves secure
You may be grateful for the gift divine
That grace unsought which made your black hearts pure
And fits your earthborn souls in Heaven to shine

But is it sweet to look around and view
Thousands excluded from that happiness
Which they deserve at least as much as you
Their faults not greater nor their virtues less?[82]

Anne spent her holiday at home in June preparing a book of her favourite music to take back with her to Thorp Green. Significantly, her choice was dominated by religious pieces which she seems to have chosen as much for their sentiments as their tunes. Anne copied out words and music to thirty-two items, eight of them ballads, mostly of the 'Ye banks and braes' variety, but seventeen were hymns and a further seven were sacred songs.[83] The month of July she again spent in Scarborough with the Robinsons, lodging this time at No. 14, The Cliff, while her employer's mother lodged at No. 4.[84]

Returning to Thorp Green at the beginning of August she seems to have been afflicted with religious uncertainty and loneliness once more. On 10 September 1843 she wrote an impassioned plea for stronger faith and the removal of the doubts which plagued her.[85] This was followed by several poems reflecting her own homesickness. In 'The Captive Dove', echoing a subject Emily had already treated, she took a totally different stance from her sister, begging not for freedom but for companionship in captivity. Though the poem almost certainly belongs to the Gondal cycle, it is interesting because it undoubtedly reflects Anne's own character: unlike Emily, who was selfish and single-minded in the pursuit of her liberty, Anne was prepared to accept her duty, however uncongenial, though she too longed for freedom.[86] In November, as the Christmas holidays gradually came within sight, Anne was overwhelmed with homesickness. Well aware of the physical beauties and comforts of her residence, Anne still rejected them in favour of

> my barren hills
> Where colder breezes rise;
>
> Where scarce the scattered, stunted trees
>   Can yield an answering swell,
> But where a wilderness of heath
>   Returns the sound as well...
>
> Restore to me that little spot,
>   With grey walls compassed round,
> Where knotted grass neglected lies,
>   And weeds usurp the ground.

> Though all around this mansion high
> Invites the foot to roam,
> And though its halls are fair within –
> Oh, give me back my HOME![87]

The Christmas holidays were a brief but welcome break in the now well-established routine of teaching at Thorp Green and there was the added pleasure of seeing Charlotte for the first time for over a year, though her depressed state of mind cannot have passed unnoticed. Anne wrote a joyful poem on Christmas morning, celebrating the birth of Christ and the sound of bells floating on the breeze which heralded it.[88] Returning to Thorp Green at the end of January, she again took up the Gondal story which seems to have preoccupied her during the previous autumn and inspired the poems of that period. She was also expanding her own academic horizons, apparently beginning to teach both German and elementary Latin to her pupils.[89]

Emily, too, was mentally absorbed in Gondal. In February 1844, she began to collect her poems together, extracting them from their prose tales going as far back as March 1837 and copying them out into one notebook which she entitled 'Gondal Poems' and another which she left untitled. In fact, there was no hard and fast distinction between the two, for Emily does not appear to have stuck to her intention to include only personal poems in the second notebook.[90] She would continue to copy her poems into the volumes until May 1848, suggesting that her obsession with Gondal continued right through the publication of *Poems* with her sisters in 1846 and *Wuthering Heights* in 1847.

Throughout 1844 she continued to produce a steady stream of poems following the fortunes of her imaginary heroes and heroines. The same characters continued to entrance her, from the unloved and embittered 'foster-child of sore distress' who had featured in her earlier poems, to the wilful but greatly loved Augusta. Even the same subjects provided inspiration, particularly the parting of loved ones either by death or by finding themselves on opposing sides in war.[91] Though she may have been stuck in a rut, it was a fruitful one, inspiring some of her most lyrical poetry. The elegy by 'E. W.' at the grave of Augusta is a typical example.

> The linnet in the rocky dells,
> The moor-lark in the air,
> The bee among the heather bells
> That hide my lady fair –
>
> The wilddeer browse above her breast;
> The wildbirds raise their brood,
> And they, her smiles of love carest,
> Have left her solitude!

I ween, that when the graves dark wall
Did first her form retain
They thought their hearts could ne'er recall
The light of joy again –

They thought the tide of greif would flow
Unchecked through future years
But where is all their anguish now,
And where are all their tears?

Well, let them fight for Honour's breath
Or Pleasure's shade pursue –
The Dweller< s > in the land of Death
< Are >\Is/ changed and carless too –

And if their eyes should watch and weep
Till sorrows' source were dry
She would not in her tranquil sleep
Return a single sigh –

Blow, west wind, by the lonely mound
And murmer, summer streams,
There is no need of other sounds
To soothe my Lady's dreams –[92]

Emily's dependence on Gondal had never faltered and even now, when there was nothing to disturb the equilibrium of her existence, when she was secure in her home and free to control her own destiny, she retreated into her imagination. Unlike Charlotte or Anne, for whom there was a certain desperation in clinging to Angrian and Gondal fantasy, for Emily it was neither a relief from, nor a frustration of, the daily routine: it was a necessary part of life. Emily's hymn to the imagination was an eloquent exposition of her own thoughts and feelings.

> thou art ever there to bring
> The hovering visions back and breathe
> New glories o'er the blighted spring
> And call a lov[e]lier life from death
> And whisper with a voice divine
> Of < other > real worlds as bright as thine
>
> I trust not to thy phantom bliss
> Yet still in evenings quiet hour
> With Never < dying > failing thankfulness
> I welcome thee benignant power
> Sure solacer of human cares
> And brighter hope when hope despairs –[93]

Though Emily lived in a world of her own there was, as usual, plenty going on in the township, with public performances of Haydn's *Creation* and Handel's *Samson* and *Judas Maccabeus* by the Haworth Quarterly Choral Society and lectures on every subject from medical botany to Chartism. One misfortune which must have affected the Brontës was the closing of Haworth subscription library, the sale of which was advertised by placard to take place on Easter Monday, 1844.[94] July was a particularly busy month. On Friday, 19 July, before breaking up for the summer holidays, the pupils of the new Church National School were publicly examined in the Scriptures, history, geography, English grammar and arithmetic to the credit of their teachers and the general satisfaction of their patrons and parents. The Rands and some of the church trustees were invited to a celebratory tea at the parsonage afterwards.[95] It was also announced that a new headmaster had been appointed for the Free Grammar School near Oxenhope: the Reverend Joseph Brett Grant, BA, an Oxford graduate, would replace the unfortunate Wesleyan, Mr Ramsbottom.[96] An added benefit of the appointment as far as Patrick was concerned was that he would then have another clergyman in the township to call on when he needed assistance.

The Sunday after the public examinations, the Reverend Samuel Redhead, making his first visit to Haworth since he had been so rudely ejected over twenty years before, came to give the afternoon and evening sermons on behalf of the Church Sunday school. Redhead was accompanied by his son-in-law, the Reverend J. Hodgson Ramsbotham, and the pair would undoubtedly have had to be entertained and put up for the night at the parsonage before their return home to Calverley.[97] On more secular affairs, Patrick chaired a meeting to discuss the growing problem of the scarcity of water in the township. It was agreed to set up a committee to look into the feasibility of bringing water from the only effective source of supply, a spring at West End on the common. As far as Patrick was concerned, this was the start of a fourteen-year battle to improve the water supply and sanitary arrangements in Haworth. No doubt he was also involved in the meetings which were held to promote and investigate a possible railway link from Keighley up to Haworth, which would have made a considerable difference to the trade of the township.[98]

Throughout all this activity, Charlotte remained almost stupefied by low spirits. Only Ellen seemed able to rouse her to anything like her old self, inviting her over to Brookroyd for a couple of weeks in March, where she was pampered into feeling somewhat more lively. She returned bearing a gift of Sicilian Pea and crimson cornflower seeds from Ellen to Emily, only to find her sister grieving over the death of the family cat – an animal so pampered that it seemed to have lost a cat's nature and subsided into luxurious amiability and contentment. The sisters made the most of a spell of good weather by walking out frequently on the moors 'to the great damage of our shoes but I hope to the benefit of our health'.[99]

In June, Anne and Branwell came home for their holiday, an occasion which seems to have been marked by a trip out to Bolton Bridge, a local beauty spot, close to the picturesque ruins of Bolton Abbey.[100] Though one might have thought that her brother and sister would have welcomed the chance to relax at home without company, Charlotte lost little time in inviting Ellen over for a visit. In the end, she was only able to share the last week of their holiday before they departed to join the Robinsons at Scarborough. Nevertheless, they had an enjoyable time walking on the moors and paying visits. There was 'plenty of fun & fatigue' with the Heatons at Ponden Hall, a walk 'under umbrellas' in the Greenwoods' garden at Oxenhope and even a trip to Bradford. Ellen was also gratified to hear Samuel Redhead preach and Tom Parker sing on her last Sunday at Haworth.[101] Just as there had been in the days of William Weightman, flirtation was in the air. To the girls' evident amusement, the new curate, Mr Smith, was particularly attentive to Ellen, arousing semi-serious expectations about his intentions. For the first and only time in his life, Patrick intervened in the family's affairs of the heart and expressed his views on his curate quite forcibly.

Papa has two or three times expressed a fear that since Mr Smith paid you so much attention he will perhaps have made too great an impression on your mind which will interfere with your comfort I tell him I think not as I believe you to be mistress of yourself in those matters. Still he keeps saying that I am to write to you and dissuade you from thinking of him I never saw papa make himself so uneasy about a thing of the kind before – he is usually very sarcastic on such subjects.

Patrick's unflattering opinion of his curate seems to have been justified, as Charlotte was swift to inform Ellen.

Mr Smith has not mentioned your name since you left – except once when papa said you were a nice girl – he said – 'Yes – she is a nice girl – rather quiet – – – I suppose she has no money' – and that is all I think the words speak volumes – they do not prejudice one in favour of Mr Smith I can well believe what papa has often affirmed – and continues to affirm – i.e. that Mr Smith is a very fickle man – that if he marries he will soon get tired of his wife – and consider her as a burden – also that money will be a principal consideration with him in marrying.[102]

Mr Smith's departure for the curacy of Keighley in the middle of October seems to have been felt as a general relief all round. Patrick had been anxious to find an early replacement and seems to have welcomed his departure, despite the additional duties which then devolved on him as a result of the seven-month vacancy.[103] Charlotte would later lampoon him mercilessly in her novel, *Shirley*, as the obnoxious and pugnacious Mr Malone whose father 'termed himself a gentleman: he was poor and in debt, and besottedly arrogant; and his son was like him'.[104] Like another of Patrick's colleagues, Mr Collins, Smith would end his clerical career ignominiously, absconding four years later to Canada without the knowledge of his friends and family and leaving behind a mass of debts, including money that he had been given for charitable purposes but had appropriated for his own use.[105] The curates in *Shirley* were milksops compared to the real ones of Charlotte's experience.

The family gathering in the summer prompted some discussions about the Brontës' future and an important decision was taken. Teaching was really the only option and, as Charlotte had pointed out, everyone expected her to open a school on her return from Brussels. Unwilling to leave home again, Charlotte now settled on a slightly different plan. She would open her school in the parsonage, beginning with five or six girls who would board in the rooms vacated by Anne and Branwell. The new scheme had some obvious advantages which allowed Patrick to give it his full support. It would avoid the problem of an initial expensive outlay in buying or renting a property and fitting it out and, if it failed, there would be no great financial loss. The housekeeping duties could be taken on by Emily, who would not have to leave their father unattended and could easily expand her present role to care for a small number of girls with the assistance of tried and trusted servants. 'Emily does not like teaching much', Charlotte told Monsieur Heger, 'but she would always do the housekeeping and, although she is a little reclusive, she has too good a heart not to do everything for the well-being of the children.'[106] On the other hand, there were two great disadvantages. Should Patrick die, the school would be evicted from the parsonage, either to close or relocate elsewhere. Perhaps more importantly, Haworth was too far from any centre of population for the school to be able to draw on the day pupils which would make all the difference to its finances.

Charlotte stirred herself into activity, writing round to old contacts in the hope of securing pupils. The Whites of Upperwood had unfortunately just committed their eldest daughter to Miss Cockhill's school at Batley, though they indicated that they would have quite happily sent her to Haworth. In view of her family and social connections, Charlotte also wrote to Mrs Busfeild, wife of the present vicar of Keighley, sending her the precious diploma from Monsieur Heger as evidence of her capabilities. Mrs Busfeild's reaction to the school scheme was typical of that of nearly everyone Charlotte approached: she thought it a praiseworthy idea, that the fees were moderate especially in view of the quality of education offered and that the limited number of pupils was an advantage in that it would ensure more individual attention. She feared, however, that the disadvantage of the 'retired situation' would outweigh all the benefits and that the Brontës would find it extremely difficult to attract pupils.[107]

In fact, the fees were actually quite high compared to similar establishments in the area. The Brontës proposed to offer board and a general education, comprising writing, arithmetic, history, grammar, geography and needlework, at a standard rate of thirty-five pounds a year. In addition, pupils could have lessons in French, German, Latin, music and drawing for an extra guinea per subject per quarter. A small charge of five shillings a quarter would be made for the use of the piano and a further fifteen shillings a quarter for laundry. Each young lady was to be provided with one pair of sheets, pillow cases, four towels, a dessert spoon and a teaspoon. Charlotte had some cards of terms printed, advertising 'The Misses Bronte's Establishment', and sent copies to Ellen to circulate around the Dewsbury area.[108]

Despite Ellen's best efforts, it soon became obvious that the school scheme was getting nowhere. By the beginning of October Charlotte had to write to Ellen to confess as much.

I – Emily & Anne are truly obliged to you for the efforts you have made in our behalf – and if you have not been successful you are only like ourselves – every one wishes us well – but there are no pupils to be had – We have no present intention however of breaking our hearts on the subject – still less of feeling mortified at defeat – The effort must be beneficial whatever the result may be – because it teaches us experience and an additional knowledge of the world[109]

Ellen continued to dispense cards of terms despite Charlotte's dire warnings: 'depend upon it Ellen if you were to persuade a mamma to bring her child to Haworth – the aspect of the place would frighten her and she would probably take the dear thing back with her instanter'.[110]

The school scheme was abandoned with little regret. Patrick and Emily were no doubt relieved that their privacy was not to be invaded by strangers, however few and ladylike the pupils might have been. Anne and Branwell had, of necessity, been excluded, at least in the initial stages, so they too had lost nothing by the school's failure. Even Charlotte, who had most to lose and gain by the plan, seems to have been little more than perfunctory in attempting to ensure its success. Compared with her single-minded determination to get to Brussels, for instance, her efforts on behalf of the school scheme were desultory. All her drive and enthusiasm had deserted her, all her passion was directed into a futile correspondence with Monsieur Heger and a self-destructive longing to return to Brussels to see him once more. 'Oh it is certain that I shall see you again one day –', she wrote to him, 'it must be – for as soon as I have earned enough money to go to Brussels I will go there – and I will see you again even if it is only for a moment.' In preparation for that forlorn hope she still learnt half a page of French by heart each day so that she did not forget the language and so that she would not have to remain dumb before him when they next met.[111] To Monsieur Heger alone Charlotte confided the pain of her depressed spirits and the consequent lethargy which afflicted her.

I would not know this lethargy if I could write – in the past I could spend days, weeks, whole months writing and not without reward – for Southey and Coleridge – two of our best authors to whom I had sent certain manuscripts were good enough to show their approbation of them – but at present my sight is too weak to write – if I write much I will go blind. This weakness of sight is a terrible privation for me – without it do you know what I would do Monsieur? – I would write a book and I would dedicate it to my literature master – to the only master I have ever had – to you Monsieur. I have often told you in French how much I respect you – how much I am indebted to your goodness, to your advice, I would like to say it once in English – it cannot be – it must not be thought of – the career of letters is closed to me – that of teaching alone is open to me – it does not offer me the same attractions – it does not matter, I will enter it and if I do not go far it will not be for lack of diligence.[112]

The fact that she was writing in French seems to have broken down the natural reticence and modesty which would once have held Charlotte back from declaring her feelings for any man so openly. It was almost as if the constraints of writing in a foreign language actually liberated her: she could put into French what she could not say in English because she did not have to face up to the hard truth of what she had said. She wrote frequently to Monsieur Heger throughout 1844, though he seems to have destroyed her more excessive outpourings, and even those letters which have survived were torn into pieces and later painstakingly reconstructed.[113]

The failing eyesight of which Charlotte complained seems to have been a purely imaginary affliction, symptomatic of her depressed state of mind. Her letters to Monsieur Heger and Ellen Nussey show no sign of any difficulty with her eyes: the writing is as tiny, neat and meticulous as ever and, on occasion, a long letter is packed into a half sheet of paper divided into four pages. This is in stark contrast to Patrick, whose approaching blindness is fully borne out by his increasingly large and untidy writing, uncharacteristically marked with blots and heavily punctuated as he paused, pen in hand, to peer at what he had written. This was a return of Charlotte's morbid depression and resulting hypochondria in the late spring of 1838, which drove her into resignation from Roe Head. Then she had convinced herself that she was suffering from consumption, as she imagined her sister, Anne, and her friend, Mary Taylor, to be. Now, she persuaded herself that she was going blind, like her father. It was certainly a good excuse for not writing a book but, had it been true, it would have made her intention of setting up school totally impractical. Charlotte was simply wallowing in misery and self-pity, unable to shake off her prostration of spirits and afraid to venture out beyond the safe haven of her home. It would take a major crisis to force her to take up the threads of her life again.

Chapter Sixteen

MRS ROBINSON

A crisis was indeed brewing: one that would explode on the unsuspecting Brontë family in the summer of 1845. For the first few months of the new year, however, those at Haworth remained unaware of incipient trouble at Thorp Green. Patrick toiled away, refusing to make any concessions to his fast-failing vision. Charlotte, writing to Ellen, described how

his sight diminishes weekly and can it be wondered at – that as he sees the most precious of his faculties leaving him, his spirits sometimes sink? It is so hard to feel that his few and scanty pleasures must all soon go – he now has the greatest difficulty in either reading or writing – and then he dreads the state of dependence to which blindness will inevitably reduce him – He fears that he will be nothing in his parish –[1]

Despite being 'anxious and dejected', Patrick remained a force to be reckoned with. Though he had once been an outspoken critic of Dr Scoresby's policies, he also appreciated the good he had done, particularly in the field of education. Dr Scoresby was now threatening to resign because of the weight of parochial opposition to him. Though unable to get to

Bradford to attend a meeting to dissuade the vicar from his purpose, Patrick nevertheless sent a strongly worded letter of support.

should the Address you speak of, be one to thank Dr Scoresby, the vicar of Bradford, for his past, able and faithful services, or to < request > entreat him to continue in his present most important, but difficult situation, I request and authorise you to affix my name.[2]

He also lent his beleaguered vicar a show of practical support, inviting him to Haworth to deliver the annual Sunday school sermon in the church.[3]

Patrick had at long last secured a replacement curate in the place of the unsatisfactory Mr Smith. The Reverend Arthur Bell Nicholls had much in common with his new parson. He was an Irishman, like Patrick, born in January 1819 near Belfast in Northern Ireland. His father, William Nicholls, seems to have been a poor farmer, like Hugh Brontë, but Arthur was orphaned at an early age. From the age of seven he had been brought up and educated by his maternal uncle, Dr Alan Bell, who was headmaster of the renowned Royal School at Banagher in the south of Ireland. Dr Bell seems to have continued his financial support of his nephew, sending him up to Trinity College, Dublin as a fee-paying pensioner in July 1836. He matriculated the following year, in January 1837, when he would have been just eighteen, and he graduated as a Bachelor of Arts almost exactly seven years later, in February 1844.[4] When he came to Haworth, he was a young man, twenty-six years old, fresh from his ordination as a deacon at Ripon on 18 May 1845. He took his first duty the following Sunday, 25 May, followed by his first marriage on 28 May and his first burial the following day. Charlotte's earliest impressions were unusually favourable: 'he appears a respectable young man, reads well, and I hope will give satisfaction'.[5] Within a few months of his arrival he had almost completely taken over all the official duties – a sign not only of Patrick's failing sight, but also of the fact that the new curate enjoyed his parson's full confidence.

The final innovations of this spring were also pleasant ones. On 29 April Patrick convened a meeting in the church vestry to consider raising a subscription to replace the three church bells with a peal of six. The response was enthusiastic and in just over two months enough money had been raised to enable him to place an order for the casting of the bells with Mr Mears of London. By the end of October, the new bells were in place, enabling the team of ringers to join in the new fashion for change-ringing competitions.[6] Of greater significance was the building of the first church in the newly created parish of Oakworth, which lay between Haworth and Keighley. This marked the beginning of a more realistic demarcation of the Haworth chapelry borders, belatedly taking into account the population changes over the last few decades. Patrick and Arthur Nicholls were undoubtedly among the clergy who attended the public ceremony on 28 July to lay the foundation stone of the new church.[7]

Charlotte, meanwhile, moped about at home, unable to forget Monsieur Heger but doing little to help herself to do so. Despite an expense she could ill afford, for instance, she had all the books he had given her bound and took delight in contemplating her 'little library'.[8] When Joe Taylor had announced the previous autumn that he was going to Brussels she seized the opportunity to write to Monsieur Heger, from whom she had heard nothing for over six months. She awaited Joe's return in the new year with eager anticipation, sure that he would at last bring her a letter. Her disappointment was doubly bitter when he returned empty-handed. In anger and sorrow she wrote reproachfully to Monsieur Heger yet again. 'Mr Taylor has returned, I asked him if he had a letter for me – "No, nothing". "Patience" said I – his sister will return soon. Miss Taylor has returned "I have nothing for you from Monsieur Heger" says she "neither a letter nor a message." ' Unable to contain herself any longer, she burst out in uncontrollable pain and despair.

Day and night I find neither rest nor peace – if I sleep I have tortured dreams in which I see you always severe, always gloomy and annoyed with me –

Forgive me then Monsieur if I take the course of writing to you again – How can I endure life if I make no effort to alleviate my sufferings?

I know that you will be impatient when you read this letter – you will say again that I am over-excited – that I have black thoughts &c. It may be so Monsieur – I do not seek to justify myself, I submit to every kind of reproach – all that I know – is that I cannot – that I will not resign myself to lose the friendship of my master completely – I would rather undergo the greatest physical sufferings than always have my heart torn apart by bitter regrets.

If my master withdraws his friendship entirely from me I will be completely without hope – if he gives me a little – very little – I will be content – happy, I will have a reason for living – for working –

Monsieur, the poor do not need much to live – they only ask for the crumbs of bread which fall from the rich man's table – but if one refuses them these crumbs of bread – they die of hunger – Nor do I need much affection from those I love – I would not know what to do with an absolute and complete friendship – I am not used to such a thing – but you once showed me a <u>little</u> interest when I was your pupil in Brussels – and I cling on to preserving that <u>little</u> interest – I cling on to it as I cling to life.[9]

One cannot but feel sorry for Monsieur Heger, a married man whose character and morals were above reproach. If he replied to his highly-strung former pupil, it merely encouraged her to write again. If he did not reply, in the hope that she might forget him, she brooded on his supposed neglect and became even more hysterical and obsessive. His own letters to her, infrequent as they seem to have been, contained nothing more than kindly advice about her character, her studies and her mode of life. He clearly had nothing to be ashamed of in his side of the correspondence, actually encouraging Mrs Gaskell to search for his own letters, which he was sure Charlotte would have preserved.[10]

Fortunately for Charlotte, Monsieur Heger was no Zamorna; he had no wish to take advantage of her passion for him. Even after she was dead and rumours about him were rife, he refused to allow publication of Charlotte's letters to him as he had no wish to harm her reputation.[11] In them, Charlotte showed all the servile and self-debasing devotion which her heroine, Mina Laury, had once displayed for Zamorna. Unlike Jane Eyre, Charlotte had no wish to be Monsieur Heger's equal: she wanted to be his inferior – even his slave – and she took a masochistic pleasure in desiring his dominance over her. Her poetry at this time also explored this type of relationship and, in at least one instance, seems to have drawn directly on her own experience.

> At first I did attention give
> Observance – deep esteem
> His frown I failed not to forgive
> His smile – a boon to deem
>
> Attention rose to interest soon
> Respect to homage changed
> The smile became a valued boon
> The frown like grief estranged
>
> The interest ceased not with his voice
>   The homage tracked him near
> Obedience was my heart's free choice
>   Whatere his word severe
>
> His praise unfrequent – favour rare
>   Unduly precious grew
> And too much power – a haunting fear
>   Around his anger threw –
>
> His coming was my hope each day
>   His parting was my pain!
> The chance that did his steps delay
>   Was ice in every vein
>
> I gave entire affection now
>   I gave devotion sure
> And strongly took root and fast did grow
>   One mighty feeling more
>
> The truest love that ever heart
>   Felt at its kindled core
> Through every vein with quickened start
>   A tide of life did pour[12]

It was not as if Charlotte did not have distractions to divert her from her unhealthy obsession. In the new year Mary Taylor came to stay for a few days at Haworth,[13] a visit which Charlotte returned in February. After Mr Taylor's death the family had moved from Red House to the rather less salubrious Hunsworth House, which was right next to the Taylor mills in Cleckheaton. The visit had a sad purpose. After many delays and changes of plan, Mary had at last determined to emigrate to New Zealand with her brother. The imminent departure of one of her closest friends to the other side of the world did nothing to lift Charlotte's gloom. On her return she wrote to Ellen Nussey who was in Bridlington, nursing her brother George.

I spent a week at Hunsworth not very pleasantly; headache, sickliness, and flatness of spirits made me a poor companion, a sad drag on the vivacious and loquacious gaiety of all the other inmates of the house. I never was fortunate enough to be able to rally, for as much as a single hour, while I was there. I am sure all, with the exception perhaps of Mary, were very glad when I took my departure.[14]

Mary, with typical forthrightness, had tried to tackle Charlotte about her depression and lack of motivation for the future which contrasted so strongly with her own ability to determine her fate. She described to Mrs Gaskell how they had talked over what Charlotte should do:

she told me she had quite decided to stay at home. She owned she did not like it. Her health was weak. She said she would like any change at first, as she had liked Brussels at first, and she thought that there must be some possibility for some people of having a life of more variety and more communion with human kind, but she saw none for her. I told her very warmly that she ought not to stay at home; that to spend the next five years at home, in solitude and weak health, would ruin her; that she would never recover it. Such a dark shadow came over her face when I said, 'Think of what you'll be five years hence!' that I stopped, and said, 'Don't cry, Charlotte!' She did not cry, but went on walking up and down the room, and said in a little while, 'But I intend to stay, Polly'.[15]

Charlotte was well aware of her failings at this time, telling Ellen, 'I begin to perceive that I have too little life in me, nowadays, to be fit company for any except very quiet people. Is it age, or what else, that changes one so?'[16] Even Joe Taylor fell victim to her increasingly bitter state of mind.

I saw his lordship in a new light last time I was at Hunsworth – sometimes I could scarcely believe my ears when I heard the stress he laid on wealth – Appearance Family – and all those advantages which are the acknowledged idols of the world – His conversation on Marriage – (and he talked much about it) differed in no degree from that of any hackneyed Fortune-Hunter – except that with his own peculiar and native audacity he avowed views & principles which more timid individuals conceal. Of course I raised no argument against anything he said I listened and laughed inwardly to think how indignant I should have been 8 years since if any one had accused Joe Taylor of being a worshipper of Mam[m]on and of Interest.

Indeed I still believe that the Joe Taylor of 10 years ago is not the Joe Taylor of to-day – the world with its hardness and selfishness has utterly changed him – He thinks himself grown wiser than the wisest – in a worldly sense he is wise, his feelings have gone through a process of petrification which will prevent them from ever warring against his interest – but Ichabod! all glory of principle and much elevation of character is gone![7]

Ellen's account of having mistaken a bachelor doctor in Bridlington for a married man and therefore having treated him with unwonted civility also made Charlotte consider the changes that time had wrought upon her. Ten years ago she would have laughed heartily at the tale and wondered how Ellen could possibly regret having been civil to a decent individual merely because he was unmarried. Now, however, she was able to see the common-sense behind such protocol. If women wished to avoid the stigma of husband-seeking,

they must act & look like marble or clay – cold – expressionless, bloodless – for every appearance of feeling of joy – sorrow – friendliness, antipathy, admiration – disgust are alike construed by the world into an attempt to hook in a husband –[18]

If she truly believed this, one can only wonder what Charlotte thought she was doing in writing her impassioned letters to Monsieur Heger.

Charlotte's condemnation of the worldly attitude of her friends and society in general at this time seems to have owed at least something to her own obsession with money, or rather the lack of it. Mary Taylor, with her usual acute perceptiveness, was well aware that most of Charlotte's problems stemmed from her financial straits, describing her life as a 'waking nightmare of "poverty and self-suppression"'. She herself had frequently urged on Charlotte the importance of earning money. 'It seems to me hard indeed that you who would succeed better than anyone in making friends and keeping them should be condemned to solitude from you[r] poverty', Mary would write in 1850.

To no one would money bring more happiness, for no one would use it better than you would. – For me with my headlong selfindulgent habits I am perhaps better without it, but I am convinced it would give you great and noble pleasures. Look out then for success in writing. You ought to care as much for that as you do for going to Heaven.[19]

In Brussels Charlotte had encountered a terrifying vision of her own possible future: a teacher, ten years older than herself, who used her male relatives to bear notes to unmarried men in the hope that one of them could be persuaded to marry her and save her from becoming a sister of charity if and when her present employment failed. Mary had then attempted to comfort her.

I promised her a better destiny than to go begging any one to marry her, or to lose her natural feelings as a sister of charity. She said, 'My youth is leaving me; I can never do better than I have done, and I have done nothing yet.' At such times she seemed to think that most human beings were destined by the pressure of worldly interests to lose one faculty and feeling after another 'till they went dead altogether. I hope I shall be put in my grave as soon as I'm dead; I don't want to walk about so.' Here we always differed! I thought the degradation of nature she feared was a consequence of poverty, and that she should give her attention to earning money. Sometimes she admitted this, but could find no means of earning money. At others she seemed afraid of letting her thoughts dwell on the subject, saying it brought on the worst palsy of all. Indeed, in her position, nothing less than entire constant absorption in petty money matters could have scraped together a provision ... She used very inconsistently to rail at money and money-getting, and then wish she was able to visit all the large towns in Europe, see all the sights, and know all the celebrities.[20]

The whole concept of the Brontës' poverty has been greatly exaggerated, as much by Mary Taylor and Mrs Gaskell as by Charlotte herself. Her education and inclination both led her to want a life of leisured luxury in which she could pursue her reading and writing at will. The necessity of earning her own living thus produced a gnawing resentment which had poisoned her relations with her employers in the past and embittered her future prospects. She seems to have been unable to appreciate the advantages she had, including that of a comfortable home. By comparison with most of her father's parishioners, the Brontës enjoyed enormous wealth; in contrast to their homes, where large families of six, seven or more lived cramped in one or two rooms, the parsonage must have seemed a palace. Patrick's income, too, though not large in the general scale of clergy earnings, was at least three or four times that of the majority of his parishioners and, unlike theirs, it was secure and not dependent on the vagaries of trade.

The sort of wealth which Charlotte wanted would have given her the leisure and financial freedom to indulge her artistic preferences and travel widely: unless she married a man with a fortune, it was out of the question. Her prospects of marriage were also fast receding with each passing year. An actuaries' table, published in the local press some five years earlier, had pointed out that two-thirds of women who did marry had done so before the age of twenty-five. By the age of thirty, this figure had risen to eighty-five per cent so that the chances of marrying later in life were extraordinarily slim.[21] By these calculations, even Anne, the youngest Brontë, had passed the age at which she was likeliest to marry, and all three sisters were faced with almost certain spinsterhood.

Charlotte's preoccupation with money and future financial security was not therefore entirely unjustified, even if her inclinations were at odds with her earning capabilities. On 23 April, just two days after her twenty-ninth birthday, she wrote to Miss Wooler to thank her for her advice on purchasing an annuity. She and Emily had written to Miss Wooler's contact but he could only offer them a four and a half per cent return on their capital invested at the age of twenty-five, rising to five per cent if invested at the age of thirty. As none of the sisters had yet reached thirty, they decided to defer the decision on transferring their small capital for a year. Then they could decide whether to go for a five per cent annuity or purchase one which would give them an annual return of ten per cent if the paying out of the annuity was deferred for a further twelve years. Despite the greater reward, as Charlotte appreciated, this would be to take a huge risk, tying up their finances without return until each of them was forty-two years old. With favourable circumstances and moderate economy, they would be able to save the difference out of the interest.[22] For the moment, then, the sisters' money remained where it was, in the original investments Aunt Branwell had made in the York and North Midland Railway and the Reeth Consolidated Mining Company.

Probably by default, in the absence of her sisters in Brussels and at Thorp Green, Emily had assumed responsibility for managing their small inheritance. Charlotte told Miss Wooler:

Emily has made herself mistress of the necessary degree of knowledge for conducting the matter, by dint of carefully reading every paragraph & every advertisement in the news-papers that related to rail-roads and as we have abstained from all gambling, all \mere/ speculative buying-in & selling-out – we have got on very decently.[23]

This praise for Emily's handling of the investment is often taken as evidence of her financial acumen, particularly as she was able to boast of a 'degree of success' in the unstable and uncertain boom-and-bust market of railway shares. However, Emily's management seems to have consisted solely in leaving the money where it was; she made no attempt to spread the investment or put money into new ventures or different companies. By the time she and Anne died, their capital was still invested exactly as it had been when Aunt Branwell first left it to them.[24]

Charlotte was increasingly discontented with her present lot. Mary Taylor had sailed for her great adventure in New Zealand in March; even Ellen was away in Bridlington and shortly to go to Hathersage. Only Charlotte remained stranded at home, feeling herself imprisoned in Haworth. Despite all that the locality had to offer in the way of music and lectures, it could not compete with the imagined glories and glamour of travel. Charlotte was left to contrast her friends' experiences with her own increasingly miserable existence.

I can hardly tell you how time gets on here at Haworth – There is no event whatever to mark its progress – one day resembles another – and all have heavy, lifeless physiognomies – Sunday – baking-day and Saturday are the only ones that bear the slightest distinctive mark – meantime life wears away – I shall soon be 30 – and I have done nothing yet – Sometimes I get melancholy – at the prospect before and behind me – yet it is wrong and foolish to repine – and undoubtedly my duty directs me to stay at home for the present – There was a time when Haworth was a very pleasant place to me, it is not so now – I feel as if we were all buried here – I long to travel – to work to live a life of action –[25]

She was even contemplating the possibility of going to Paris as a governess, the glamour of the situation outweighing the drudgery of the employment.[26]

The opportunity to get out of Haworth, at least temporarily, soon presented itself. Ellen invited Charlotte to join her at Hathersage, a small village in the Derbyshire Peak District, not far from Sheffield, where she was supervising alterations to the vicarage in preparation for her brother Henry's forthcoming marriage to Emily Prescott. Henry had at last found a bride who fitted his criteria, including that of possessing a small fortune. Once the marriage had taken place at the end of May 1845, Ellen felt free to ask Charlotte to join her. At first Charlotte refused, thinking it would be wrong to leave her father for any length of time when his eyesight was so poor and his spirits so low. In the middle of June, however, circumstances changed. Branwell and Anne came home for their annual summer holiday and Anne dropped her bombshell. She had handed in her resignation and did not intend to return to Thorp Green. Her reasons for doing so would only become clear later. Branwell was only home for a week and then had to return before taking the rest of his holiday while the Robinsons were at Scarborough. Anne's presence at home freed Charlotte to accept Ellen's invitation.[27]

The visit to Hathersage proved difficult to arrange, partly because of the problems of travelling in unfamiliar country and partly because Emily and Anne had plans for their own amusement. They had decided to celebrate Anne's release from the bondage of teaching by taking a short holiday together. Their first idea was to go to Scarborough, a place which Anne loved but Emily had never visited. They would take advantage of the opening of a new railway from York to Scarborough which would make the trip much easier. When the opening of the railway was delayed until 7 July, however, they were obliged to change their plans. A two-day visit to Ilkley, some fifteen miles from Haworth, was contemplated, but in the end they settled on the more exciting prospect of a trip to York.[28]

Emily and Anne left home on 30 June, travelling on the newly opened Keighley line to Bradford, where they changed trains for Leeds then York. Emily's description of the holiday, which she included in her diary paper written a month later on her twenty-seventh birthday, is a fascinating revelation of her priorities.

Anne and I went our first long Journey by ourselves \together/ – leaving Home on the 30th of June – monday – sleeping at York – returning to Keighley Tuesday evening sleeping there and walking home on wednesday morning – though the weather was broken, we enjoyed ourselves very much except during a few hours at Bradford and during our excursion we were Ronald Macelgin, Henry Angora, Juliet Augusteena, Rosobelle Esraldan, Ella and Julian Egramont Catherine Navarre and Cordelia Fitzaphnold escaping from the Palaces of Instruction to join the Royalists who are hard driven at present by the victorious Republicans –[29]

While Anne had been so moved by her first glimpse of York Minster that she had recorded it in her diary paper four years earlier, Emily mentions none of the sights she had seen for the first time. Clearly, the opportunity to indulge in a Gondal 'play' with Anne meant more to her than anything else she had seen or done on their brief trip. Though it was at least thirteen years since the creation of their imaginary world, Emily, at almost twenty-seven, had lost none of her enthusiasm for Gondal, acting out the roles of its heroes and heroines with as much gusto as when a child.

The day after her sisters returned from their jaunt, Charlotte set off for Hathersage. The Reverend Henry Nussey had been appointed curate there in April 1844 and four months later the Duke of Devonshire, in whose gift the living lay, preferred him to the vicarage.[30] The village was much like Haworth: a cluster of stone cottages lining either side of a steeply climbing road, with the church and vicarage on an eminence at the top end and a number of needle factories, which gave the village its principal industry, in the valley bottoms. From its vantage point on the hillside, Hathersage looks out over a magnificent prospect of undulating hills, covered with pasture and woodland, rising to the greater heights of the surrounding moors. The landscape is on a larger scale than that of Haworth: the valleys are wider, the hills are higher and the skylines, where menacing ridges of exposed and weather-beaten rock thrust stark against the clouds, are more dramatic.

Though Charlotte was to stay only a brief three weeks at Hathersage, the visit was to be a major influence in shaping *Jane Eyre*. It is possible that she was already turning over in her mind the various elements of the later part of the story when she arrived in Hathersage. In 'The Missionary', an undated poem which probably belongs to this time, she describes the agonies suffered by a man who gives up the woman he loves in order to become a missionary overseas. This scenario was to be developed more fully in *Jane Eyre*, where St John Rivers loves Rosamund Oliver but refuses to ask her to share his own destiny as a missionary in India because he knows she will not be able to adapt to its hardships. It is unlikely to be coincidental that the poem and the St John Rivers episode seem to have been conceived while Charlotte was staying in the home of Henry Nussey. Not only had he once proposed to Charlotte in the same business-like and unemotional way as St John Rivers did to Jane Eyre, but since then he had himself toyed with the idea of becoming a missionary.[31] It was not unnatural that Charlotte should recall these things while living in the house which she and his sister were preparing to receive his bride.

Whether or not Charlotte was consciously seeking material for the story that, a year later, was to become *Jane Eyre*, the village of Hathersage and its setting were to feature prominently in her novel. Even the name of its heroine seems to have been adopted from the four splendid medieval brasses of the Eyre family in the church.[32] The fifteenth-century Eyre home, North Lees Hall, which lay two miles from Hathersage, may also have provided Charlotte with material for her description of Rochester's Thornfield Hall. Charlotte's own journey across the flat moorlands between Sheffield and Hathersage, where the desolation is broken only by scattered outcrops of rock, was to provide an appropriate setting for Jane's flight from Rochester, and Hathersage itself became the fictional village of Morton.[33]

Charlotte's arrival was much less traumatic than Jane Eyre's: Ellen met her off the omnibus in Sheffield and brought her safely back to her brother's new home.[34] The vicarage was a pleasant eighteenth-century house, built of local stone, and not dissimilar in appearance to Charlotte's own home. Like Haworth Parsonage, it too was bounded on at least one side by the churchyard, but took full advantage of its elevated situation to drink in the magnificent views across the surrounding valleys toward the moors. In preparation for his marriage, Henry Nussey had undertaken a major extension to the house, adding a bay windowed sitting room and two new bedrooms.[35] Ellen had been left to supervise the completion of the work and the refurnishing of the house. Charlotte's visit therefore provided her with some welcome moral support in a task made more difficult by the fact that Henry's bride, Emily Prescott, was a virtual stranger whose tastes were, as yet, unknown.

Charlotte had made it a condition of coming to stay that she should be left to enjoy Ellen's company in peace and not be dragged out 'a visiting'. This was not to be, of course, with the gregarious Ellen as a companion. There were two or three visits to the Wright family at North Lees Hall, which Miss Wright returned, and the architect called in daily, despite the fact that the builders no longer required his presence.[36] Writing to her friend, Mary Gorham, on 22 July, Ellen revealed that they had also taken a trip along the valley to Castleton to see the famous caverns where the semiprecious mineral Blue John was mined and worked into jewellery and ornaments.

We have been to Castleton & the Miss Halls accompanied us through the caverns & were very lively & noisy – another party came in soon after – a gentleman & lady – they crossed the river [clinging?] together to our great amusement we could not discover whether they were – brother & sister or what but the lady was very sweet looking & the gentleman twice addressed a word or two to me once when we passed them in the caverns & to say good morning when they left ... Charlotte was very much pleased with the caverns but the mirth of [the] Miss Halls was rather displeasing to her –[37]

For Charlotte, who liked to contemplate the beauties of nature in silence, Ellen's choice of companions was extraordinarily insensitive; it was not surprising that she found their silly behaviour displeasing. At least, however, she had had the opportunity to see the caverns and, because they had borrowed a pony, they were able to drive a little further up the dale and view the dramatic sight of Peveril Castle clinging precariously to the spectacular cliffs above Peak Cavern. For Charlotte the trip must have been made twice as exciting by the knowledge that this was where Sir Walter Scott, one of the greatest influences on her juvenile writings, had set his novel *Peveril of the Peak*.

All in all, despite minor irritations, Charlotte's visit to Hathersage was such a success in lifting her spirits that Ellen had little difficulty in persuading her to stay on for a third week. With her usual cunning, Ellen had written to Emily beforehand to obviate any protests from Charlotte that she was needed at home. This had elicited one of Emily's rare letters, a cheerful if brief note giving her approval to the plan.

Dear Miss Ellen,
   If you have set your heart on Charlotte staying another week she has our united consent; I for one will take everything easy on Sunday – I'm glad she is enjoying herself: let her make the most of the next seven days & return stout and hearty – Love to her and you from Anne & myself and tell her all are well at home.

Yours affecty –
E J Brontë[38]

The concern which Ellen had evidently expressed about Sunday was because this was one of the most important days of the Haworth Church calendar, the annual Sunday school services, when the preacher was a visiting clergyman. This year the Reverend P. Eggleston of Heptonstall was coming to preach the afternoon sermon and no less a figure than the vicar of Bradford, Dr Scoresby, was preaching in the evening.[39] The arrangements for hospitality at the parsonage would therefore have been more important than usual.

   Emily's cheerfulness reflected both her contentment in her role as housekeeper and, more importantly, her fulfilment as a writer. From the volume of her poetry one can deduce that she had been working steadily since the new year, producing a number of poems, including five which she herself judged worthy of publication the following year.[40] This is confirmed by her diary paper, written for her twenty-seventh birthday, 30 July 1845:

The Gondals still flo[u]rish bright as ever I am at present writing a work on the

First Wars – Anne has been writing some articles on this and a book by Henry Sophona – We intend sticking firm by the rascals as long as they delight us which I am glad to say they do at present –[41]

Emily seems to have been completely unaware that Anne no longer shared her own unabated enthusiasm for Gondal. In her last half year at Thorp Green Anne's poetry had grown progressively more autobiographical and more unhappy in tone, even when it retained its Gondal context.[42] She had still been able to find some solace in the imaginary world as a retreat from reality when she wrote this poem on 24 January:

> Call me away; there's nothing here,
>   That wins my soul to stay;
> Then let me leave this prospect drear;
>   And hasten far away.
>
> To our belovèd land I'll flee,
>   Our land of thought and soul,
> Where I have roved so oft with thee,
>   Beyond the Worlds controll.[43]

Though it may be reading too much into what may be written in Gondal character, by 1 June she had moved into a state of depression and self-loathing which only piety could cure.

> Oppressed with sin and wo,
> A burdened heart I bear,
> Opposed by many a mighty foe:
> But I will not despair.
>
> With this polluted heart,
> I dare to come to Thee,
> < Devine > Holy and Mighty as Thou art:
> For Thou wilt pardon me.[44]

In her diary paper, which she wrote on Thursday, 31 July, 'sitting in the Dining Room in the Rocking Chair before the fire with my feet on the fender', Anne's disillusionment with Gondal is quite clearly spelt out.

Emily is engeaged in writing < the > the Emperor Julius's life She has read some of it and I very much want to hear the rest – She is writing some poetry too I wonder what it is about – I < am writing > have begun the third volume of passages in the life of an Individual, I wish I had < finnish > finished it – ... We have not yet finished our Gondal chronicles that we began three years and a half ago when will they be done? – The Gondals are at present in a sad state the Republicans are uppermost but the Royalists are not quite overcome – the young sovereigns with their brothers and sisters are still at the palace of Instruction – The Unique Society < we > above half a year ago were wrecked on a dezart Island < du > as they were returning from Garldin – they are still there but we have not played at them much

[454]

yet – The Gondals in general are not in first rate playing condition – will they improve?[45]

The railway trip to York with Emily a month earlier had obviously done little to stimulate Anne's interest in Gondal, even though she had joined in playing at the characters.

Anne's diary paper, in sharp contrast to Emily's, reveals a depression that extends beyond the disappointment with Gondal. This was perhaps inevitable given the uncertainty of her future, now that she had finally resigned her post at Thorp Green; it is likely, too, that she was worried about what had already happened there and apprehensive about what might happen in her absence.

Yesterday was Emily's birthday and the time when we should have opened our 1845[sic: should be 1841] paper but by mistake we opened it to day instead – How many things have happened since it was written – some pleasant some far otherwise – Yet I was then at Thorp Green and now I am only just escaped from it – I was wishing to leave [?it] then and if I had known that I had four years longer to stay how wretched I should have been – < then too. I was writing the fourth volume of Sophala – > but during my stay I have had some very unpleasant and undreamt of experience of human < nature > nature – ... I wonder how we shall all be and where and how situated < when we open this pap > on the thirtyeth of July 1848 When if we are all alive Emily will be just < thirty > 30 I shall be in my 29th year Charlotte in her 33rd and Branwell in his 32nd and what changes shall we have seen and known and shall we be much changed ourselves? I hope not – for the worse at least – I for my part cannot well be <u>flatter</u> or older in mind than I am now –[46]

Despite their closeness, Emily seems to have had little sympathy with Anne's low spirits. Indeed, it is curious that Emily should ever have gained the reputation of being the most sympathetic of the Brontës, particularly in her dealings with Branwell,[47] as all the evidence points to the fact that she was so absorbed in herself and her literary creations that she had little time for the genuine suffering of her family. Her attitude at this time seems to have been brusque to the point of heartlessness. This is understandable where Charlotte was concerned, since her problems were largely self-inflicted, but it is surprising to find Emily equally unsympathetic towards Anne, who was the victim of circumstances beyond her control. Her impatience with her siblings is evident in her diary paper.

I should have mentioned that last summer the school scheme was revived in full vigor – we had prospectuses printed despatched letters to all aquaintances imparting our plans and did our little all – but it was found no go – now I dont desire a school at all and none of us have any great longing for it – we have cash enough for our present wants with a prospect of accumolation – we are all in decent health – only that papa has a complaint in his eyes and with the exception of B[ranwell] who I hope will be better and do better, hereafter. I am quite contented for myself – not as idle as formerly, altogether as hearty and having learnt to make the most of the present and hope for the future with less fidgetiness that I cannot do all I wish – seldom or [n]ever troubled with nothing to do < illegible > and merely desiring that every body could be as comfortable as myself and as undesponding and then we should have a very tolerable world of it –

It was all very well for Emily to feel irritation at the rest of her family's despondency, but her place was secure and she was no longer expected to go out into the world to earn her living like them. Her preoccupations are neatly summed up at the end of her paper.

Tabby has just been teasing me to turn as formerly to 'pilloputate' – Anne and I should have picked the black currants if it had been fine and sunshiny – I must hurry off now to my turning and ironing I have plenty of work on hands and writing and am altogether full of business with best wishes for the whole house till 1848 – July 30th and as much longer as may be I conclude E J Brontë[48]

The diary papers are as interesting for what they omit as for what they include. The one subject which must have been foremost in every member of the Brontë family's mind was barely touched upon. Emily's entry was cryptic in its brevity.

Anne left her situation at Thorp Green of her own accord – June 1845
Branwell left – July 1845 [49]

That there was a world of difference between the two departures was merely suggested by the omission in Branwell's case of those four all-important words 'of [his] own accord'. Anne's diary note was equally unforthcoming, not even mentioning the fact that her brother had left Thorp Green.

Branwell has left Luddenden foot and been a Tutor at Thorp Green and had much tribulation and ill health he was very ill on Tuesday but he went with John Brown to Liverpool where he now is I suppose and we hope he will be better and do better in future – [50]

This unnatural reticence on a subject which was to have such a devastating and far-reaching effect on all the family has haunted Brontë scholars ever since, particularly as the Robinsons themselves refused to offer any public explanation. Was there a mystery about Branwell's sudden dismissal from Thorp Green? Did he genuinely have an affair with his Mrs Robinson, as he claimed? Or was there a more sinister reason? Every possible explanation has been put forward, from Branwell's having used his undoubted skills in handwriting to forge his employer's signature to the suggestion that he corrupted and seduced the young Edmund Robinson who was alone in his care.[51] Though Branwell sank very low, he did not sink into criminality: had he forged documents or made homosexual advances to his pupil there was no need for the Robinsons themselves to suppress the evidence, rather a positive duty to expose and prosecute their former tutor. On the whole it has been generally accepted that Branwell's story was substantially true: he did have an affair with Mrs Robinson, as he claimed and as his family and Mrs Gaskell undoubtedly believed. What has remained in doubt is Mrs Robinson's complicity: was she simply the innocent object of a young man's fantasies or was she 'that bad woman who corrupted Branwell Brontë'?[52] Fortunately, new evidence has come to light which allows us to make a more informed judgement on the causes of Branwell's dismissal.

The first account of what had happened was given by Charlotte to Ellen Nussey. She had arrived home from Hathersage at ten o'clock on Saturday night, 26 July, totally unprepared for what was to follow.

I found Branwell ill – he is so very often owing to his own fault – I was not therefore shocked at first – but when Anne informed me of the immediate cause of his present illness I was greatly shocked. he had last Thursday received a note from Mr Robinson sternly dismissing him < from > intimating that he had discovered his proceedings which he characterised as bad beyond expression and charging him on pain of exposure to break off instantly and for ever all communication with every member of his family – [53]

This sounds as though Charlotte was quoting directly from Mr Robinson's letter, though she gives no indication of what Branwell's fault had been. The fact that Branwell was threatened with 'exposure' suggests that his employer did not suspect any collusion with members of his family who would similarly be 'exposed' by any revelations about Branwell. On the other hand, the fact that he was forbidden to communicate with *every* member of the Robinson family might suggest that one of them was equally implicated in Branwell's transgression. This, too, is the only conclusion one can draw from the silence of Mrs Robinson and her children when Mrs Gaskell published her *Life of Charlotte Brontë*, which all but named Mrs Robinson as the 'depraved woman' who had tempted Branwell into 'the deep disgrace of deadly crime'.[54] It is true that Mrs Robinson, now Lady Scott, sought and published a legal retraction of Mrs Gaskell's accusations but one would have thought that the simplest and most obvious method of disproving the story was for the Robinsons to set forth the real reasons for Branwell's dismissal. Yet they conspicuously failed to do this, which suggests that there was at least some element of truth in the charges.

This possibility finds some support in a dispassionate review of the whole situation by George Smith, Mrs Gaskell's publisher. With the threat of legal action hanging over him and Mrs Gaskell uncontactable on the Continent, the author's and publisher's solicitors held a conference:

it was determined to employ detectives in order to ascertain what evidence was available to justify the alleged libel. Much gossip, it was found, existed; but it was gossip of the kind which is apt to dissolve into mere vapour when tested in a court of law. The following Memorandum will show the sort of information which the Rev. Patrick Brontë, Branwell's father, regarded as 'evidence' in this case, I am not much of a lawyer but I think I can conceive the opinion a lawyer would have of such 'evidence' – Branwell constantly received letters from Mrs — but Mr Bronte himself never saw them; could not say whether they were signed with her name; he 'understood' that the letters showed guilt; often remonstrated with Branwell, but he would keep up the correspondence. After his death (Branwell's) 'the children' made the letters into a bundle and burnt them. A servant who went by the name of 'Cherry' was privy, he believed, to a good deal. A gardener – whose name he did not know – had definite proofs of guilt and had informed, as he understood, Mrs —'s husband. A surgeon who attended the family, he had been told, was cognizant of the intimacy. His conversations with his son, who frequently spoke freely with him, left no doubt as to the nature of the intimacy, etc., etc. All this, of course, was mere unverifiable gossip, quite insufficient to justify a public accusation.[55]

Though there was not enough hard evidence to rely on in a court of law, there was clearly much talk about Branwell's relationship with Mrs Robinson, both in Haworth and at Thorp Green. Mr Brontë's claims may have been legally unverifiable, but they were supported in other contemporary testimonies.

In the October after his dismissal Branwell himself gave a succinct account of his time at Thorp Green to Francis Grundy, his old friend from the railway days.

I fear you will burn my present letter on recognising the handwriting; but if you will read it through, you will perhaps rather pity than spurn the distress of mind which could prompt my communication, after a silence of nearly three (to me) eventful years ... In a letter begun in the spring of 1848 [sic], and never finished owing to incessant attacks of illness, I tried to tell you that I was tutor to the son of [the Reverend Edmund Robinson], a wealthy gentleman whose wife is sister to the wife of [William Evans], M. P. for the county of [Derbyshire], and the cousin of Lord [?Trevelyan]. This lady (though her husband detested me) showed me a degree of kindness which, when I was deeply grieved one day at her husband's conduct, ripened into declarations of more than ordinary feeling. My admiration of her mental and personal attractions, my knowledge of her unselfish sincerity, her sweet temper, and unwearied care for others, with but unrequited return where most should have been given, ... although she is seventeen years my senior, all combined to an attachment on my part, and led to reciprocations which I had little looked for. During nearly three years I had daily 'troubled pleasure, soon chastised by fear'. Three months since I received a furious letter from my employer, threatening to shoot me if I returned from my vacation, which I was passing at home; and letters from her lady's-maid and physician informed me of the outbreak, only checked by her firm courage and resolution that whatever harm came to her, none should come to me...[56]

Some scholars have suspected that this story of an affair with Mrs Robinson was simply concocted to give a romantic hue to the more mundane or possibly more heinous crime that had caused his dismissal. It is true that Branwell had had a fascination with adultery and seduction from childhood, his *alter ego*, Northangerland, being a consummate practitioner of those arts. Even Branwell, however, could not have been so foolhardy as to think that his sisters and, above all, his clergyman father, would find adultery with his employer's wife a more acceptable reason for dismissal than simple debauchery, debt, theft or fraud. Citing the 'fact' that Branwell's version of events was not told to his friends until the autumn after his dismissal as proof that he had made up the story in the interval is misconceived.[57] It was only to Grundy, with whom he had lost contact for nearly three years, that Branwell was obliged to tell his story in full. No such explanation was necessary for J. B. Leyland, the other correspondent who kept some of Branwell's letters, because he was probably told the whole sorry tale as it unfolded. This was certainly true of John Brown, the Haworth sexton and stonemason, who had long been Branwell's confidant despite the disparity in their ages and social standing.

One of the most exciting pieces of new evidence to emerge is the revelation that Branwell wrote to John Brown from Thorp Green, telling him of the progression of his affair with Mrs Robinson. Brown preserved these letters and I suspect that their existence was known to Mrs Gaskell when she was researching her *Life of Charlotte Brontë*. As she could not be contacted when the libel action was threatened, they were not available as evidence to support her stance. That she might have known of them, however, is suggested by the fact that it was her friend and fellow admirer of Charlotte, Richard Monckton Milnes, who saw the letters on a visit to Haworth in October 1859 and noted some of their contents in his commonplace book.

The letters show that Branwell's affair with Mrs Robinson began surprisingly early, within a few months of his arrival at Thorp Green in January 1843. Though he had been melancholy and homesick when he wrote his poem 'Thorp Green' at the end of March, by May he was writing in the highest of spirits to John Brown:

to say he is living in a palace, with a delightful pupil – 'I curl my hair & scent my handkerchief like a Squire – I am the favourite of all the household – my master is generous – but my mistress is DAMNABLY TOO FOND OF ME* He asks his friend seriously to advise him what to do – tells him to consult two other grave men, who will understand him. is it worth-while for him to go on to extremities, which she evidently desires – the husband is sick and emaciated – she is always making him presents, talking to his sister (the governess) about him – telling him she does not care a farthing for him – asking him if he loves her & so on, – that bull-headed & beastly-hearted fellow [name omitted] has written me a letter tht may do me a gt deal of harm: he [prays?] counsel – 'don't care about the spelling, but say wht you think' he signs this 'Jacob the son of Joseph'.
*She is a pretty woman, about 37, with a darkish skin & bright glancing eyes. –[58]

This letter bears all the hallmarks of Branwell's style: his curious mix of boastfulness and indecisiveness, his humour and his fondness for writing in capital letters. There can be no doubt as to its authenticity even though the original appears not to have survived. It therefore raises some important points. Mrs Robinson, by Branwell's account, seems to have made all the running in the affair – as one would expect given their relative social positions and the seventeen-year difference in their ages. Had Branwell simply been living an Angrian fantasy and imagining himself into Northangerland's shoes, this could not have happened: Northangerland was emphatically always the seducer, never the seduced. Though Branwell clearly enjoyed the attentions he was receiving and being able to brag about them to his friends, it would have been a much bigger feather in his cap if he could have boasted that it was he who had swept the lady of the house off her feet. The fact that he was the one being seduced therefore lends credence to his story. Mrs Robinson's gifts to him and her continual questioning of Anne seem to have been regarded by Anne simply as evidence of the high regard in which her brother was held. At this point she cannot have suspected anything improper in their relationship and was able to report with entire truth to her sister at the end of the year that they were 'both wondrously valued in their situations'.[59]

That Branwell should have sought John Brown's advice on whether he should risk a sexual relationship with Mrs Robinson seems surprising, though perhaps it was because Brown seems to have had a reputation for philandering.[60] Branwell himself was no innocent, having apparently already fathered a child at Broughton-in-Furness, and he had no difficulty in recognizing that Mrs Robinson wished him to 'go on to extremities'. He clearly saw that Mrs Robinson was sexually frustrated: her husband's ill health may have rendered him impotent and Branwell was an athletic and good-looking young man, dependent on her for his place as tutor to her son, whose daily presence in the house would not be questioned. No doubt, too, it was a boost to her vanity that at forty-three years of age she was still capable of seducing a young man of twenty-eight, despite the competing attractions of her three teenage daughters. Mrs Gaskell was later to suggest, on the authority of the lady's own cousins, that this was neither the first nor the last time that Mrs Robinson had taken a lover and that her own relations had been obliged to drop her acquaintance because she had been 'a bad heartless woman for long & long'.[61] Though this was not entirely true, as Mrs Robinson found staunch defenders among her family and friends, such as Sir James Stephens, the behaviour of her own daughters suggests that their mother was not a model of rectitude. Only three months after Branwell's dismissal Lydia, the eldest, was to cause a public scandal by running off with the Scarborough actor, Henry Roxby, and marrying him at Gretna Green even though she was only just twenty years old and therefore under age for marrying without parental consent. Her second daughter, Elizabeth, also committed an indiscretion serious enough to jeopardize her prospects of making a good marriage, by having an affair with a Mr Milner who threatened to publish her love letters in the York press and sue her for breach of promise when she refused to marry him. He had to be bought off at a cost of over £150, which suggests that he had some justice in his claim. Even the youngest daughter, Mary, seems to have been something of a flirt. In 1848 Charlotte commented that she and Elizabeth were 'both now engaged to different gentlemen – and if they do not change their minds – which they have done already two or three times – will probably be married in a few months'.[62] For all three daughters to have so flown in the face of convention in their dealings with the opposite sex suggests that their mother's influence, if not her actual example, had not been of the best.

Branwell's choice of pseudonym in his letter to John Brown was significant: both men had been brought up on the Bible and would know that the name Jacob meant 'the supplanter' in Hebrew.[63] The name was therefore a shared joke indicating that Branwell had taken the husband's place in Mrs Robinson's affections. How soon the affair became adulterous cannot be determined but, if Branwell's own testimony is to be believed, it would appear that he was sleeping with Mrs Robinson before the end of his first year at Thorp Green. Again, Lord Houghton's commonplace book provides us with a tantalizing extract from Branwell's letters to John Brown.

In Novr 1843 he writes regretting tht he has not seen some Haworth friends – 'I know you think I drink, but the time is past when I could hold out against you all. I take no wine & brandy & water only once in the day – that is, before breakfast to enable me to face the AGONY of the day' 'My little lady grows thinner every day – she is full of spirit & courage, except in the thought of parting with me.' He abuses a Methodist Preacher, who is told if he says anythg to damage him (B. B.) he shall be ruined & Miss Anne Marshall saw him do enough to hang him. He sends his friend a 'lock of <u>her</u> hair, wch has lain < at night > on his breast – wd to God it could do so <u>legally</u>!' he ends in great depression – without signature.[64]

The reference to the 'Methodist Preacher' remains a mystery. Ann Marshall was Mrs Robinson's lady's-maid and confidante. Thirty-four years old when Branwell came to Thorp Green, she had graduated from children's nurse to lady's-maid and was therefore well placed to learn the secrets of the household. As Winifred Gérin has pointed out, there is an unexplained oddity in her dealings with the Robinson family. Between 4 July 1843 and 19 March 1845 Mr Robinson signed promissory notes over to her to the value of £520; these were not a mere formality as interest on them was paid and the total capital sum was repaid in full in 1846.[65] It seems unlikely that she would have loaned such a sum to her employers in the first place as she earned only £12 a year and would not have needed to work at all if the capital sum had been available to her. The fact that the promissory notes only relate to the period of Branwell's residence at Thorp Green inevitably gives rise to speculation that the two things were connected. However, it seems highly unlikely that such a large sum was Ann's price for spying on her mistress, as Gérin suggests, and there were other people – including at least three others who were probably servants – to whom Mr Robinson also gave promissory notes.[66] It may simply be that these were a form of investment by Mr Robinson to secure pensions for the future benefit of servants who had given long and faithful service.

In addition to Ann Marshall, Branwell had another confidant at Thorp Green. His fund of anecdotes, entertaining manner of relating stories and musical skills, had rapidly won him a circle of friends in the locality. Among these was Dr John Crosby, a surgeon in his mid-forties, who was the Robinson family physician and therefore in constant attendance on the ailing Mr Robinson. He was apparently a widower, living along with his fifteen-year-old son, William, and a female servant in the village of Great Ouseburn.[67] Like Ann Marshall, Dr Crosby had unquestioned access to the house and, as Patrick Brontë later claimed, he was cognizant of the affair. Again like Ann Marshall, he was to keep in touch with Branwell after his dismissal and to be a main source of information about Thorp Green.

At this distance it is impossible to chart the progress of Branwell's affair with Mrs Robinson. Mrs Gaskell says of him that

He was so beguiled by this mature and wicked woman, that he went home for his holidays reluctantly, stayed there as short a time as possible, perplexing and distressing them by all his extra-ordinary conduct – at one time in the highest spirits, at another, in the deepest depression – accusing himself of blackest guilt and treachery, without specifying what they were; and altogether evincing an irritability of disposition bordering on insanity.[68]

This is borne out by the swings of mood also apparent in his letters to John Brown and by Charlotte, who thankfully told Ellen after the Christmas holidays of 1844–5 that Branwell had been 'quieter and less irritable on the whole this time than he was in summer'. The previous October, too, she had reported to Monsieur Heger that 'my poor brother is always ill'.[69]

Branwell's highly pitched emotional state did not prevent him writing poetry, however, and there is evidence to show that he was still honing his skills and experimenting with form and metre. Very little survives from his days at Thorp Green, but this is not because his obsession with Mrs Robinson precluded all literary activity. Recent research has shown that there was a Thorp Green notebook, just as there had been a Luddenden Foot notebook.[70] Only a few scattered pages are now extant but they are of the greatest importance in providing an insight into Branwell's happiness at Thorp Green. One of the poems, based on Wordsworth's 'View from the Top of

Black Comb', reveals that he continued to take great pleasure in making excursions into the surrounding countryside. From Grafton Hill, an eminence between Thorp Green and Boroughbridge, Branwell could enjoy a panoramic view across Yorkshire which, as he describes it, no doubt reminded him of the landscape of Angria. Surveying the Vale of York, with the towers of York Minster and Ripon Cathedral both clearly visible, it was the ruins of Fountains Abbey which brought him to his usual theme.

> And girt by Studley's woods the walls that now
> Like sunbeams shining upon winter snow
> Mock with their ruin < happiness > splendours long since gone
> And say one fate awaits on flesh and stone"

Despite its gloomy conclusion, the poem is remarkable for its serenity and obvious enjoyment of the scene, suggesting it was written during the summer of 1843 or 1844.

Another poem, written at about the same time, is even more autobiographical and seems to have arisen directly out of an incident with Mrs Robinson. As was perhaps natural once the Robinsons knew that Branwell had trained as a portrait painter, he seems to have given the ladies tuition in painting and drawing and, on this particular occasion, Mrs Robinson had shown him her self-portrait.

> Her \effort/ shews a < creature > picture made
>   To contradict its meaning
> Where \should be/ sunshine < should be painting > painting shade,
>   And smile with sadness screening;
> Where God has given a cheerful < heart > view
>   A < groundless sorrow > gloomy vista showing
> Where heart and < countenance both are > face, are fair and true
>   A shade of doubt bestowing
>
> Ah Lady if to me you give
>   The power your sketch to < amend > adorn
> How little of it shall I leave
>   Save smiles that shine like morn.
> Ide keep the hue of < youth demure > happy light
>   That shines from summer skies
> Ide drive the shades from smiles so bright
>   And dry such shining eyes
>
> Ide give a calm to one whose heart
>   has banished calm from mine
> Ide brighten up Gods work of art
>   Where thou hast dimmed its shine
> And all ask[sic] the wages I should ask
>   For such a happy toil

Ill name them – < worthy of > far beyond my task –
THY PRESENCE AND THY SMILE[72]

Though the poem exists only in draft form, scribbled in pencil on a page from the missing notebook, it was undoubtedly intended for presentation to Mrs Robinson. One can well imagine her gratification on receiving poetic tributes of this kind from her son's young tutor – though she might not have appreciated his tactful removal of the reference to her own 'youth demure'!

It is not impossible that it was the discovery of poems like this, addressed to Mrs Robinson, that brought about Branwell's downfall. Even if the poems were not signed or attributed to Northangerland, Mr Robinson must have been able to recognize Branwell's distinctive handwriting. He certainly knew of Branwell's poetic efforts and ambitions, which Mrs Robinson encouraged but which he dismissed with contempt. Mrs Robinson was herself distantly related to Thomas Babington Macaulay whose *Lays of Ancient Rome* had been published to great acclaim in 1842, the year before Branwell's appointment to Thorp Green. It was undoubtedly through her that Branwell gained access to Macaulay, much to Mr Robinson's disgust: 'my late unhappy employer shrunk from the bare idea of my being able to write anything, and had a day's sickness after hearing that Macaulay had sent me a complimentary letter'.[73]

Branwell also claimed that Mr Robinson would not recognize his poetic pseudonym 'Northangerland', in which case it seems unlikely that he was aware that his son's tutor was actually publishing poems under his very nose in the *Yorkshire Gazette*. This was a newspaper produced in York by Henry Bellerby, a bookseller and stationer who also ran one of York's two public libraries from his shop at No. 13, Stonegate. The Robinsons had an account with Bellerby and Branwell, like the rest of the family, borrowed books from his library.[74] As Branwell was undoubtedly a regular visitor at the shop and library it is only surprising that his contact with Bellerby did not result in his poems being published by the *Yorkshire Gazette* much earlier. As it is, the paper published only four poems by Branwell, all of them within ten weeks of his dismissal.

On 10 May 1845 the *Yorkshire Gazette* carried two sonnets by 'Northangerland', 'Blackcomb' and 'On Landseer's Picture – "The Shepherd's Chief Mourner" – a dog watching alone by his master's grave'. They were both old poems. The first had been written five years earlier, when Branwell was a tutor at Broughton-in-Furness, the second, which had already appeared in the *Bradford Herald* in 1842, dated back to at least 1841.[75] The fact that he had at last got an *entrée* to a new newspaper seems to have encouraged Branwell. Sixteen days later he made a fair copy of a pair of new sonnets called 'The Emigrant', which were duly published in the *Yorkshire Gazette* on 7 June. The subject was topical as the newspapers were full of the recent spate of emigrations prompted by the hardships endured by the poor in England and Ireland in 'the hungry forties'. Many unemployed working-class families, as well as those, like Mary Taylor, seeking to earn their own living in a less censorious society, had left for the new worlds of Canada, Australia and New Zealand. Branwell's first sonnet gives the story of the departing emigrant a new twist.

> When sink from sight the landmarks of our home,
>   And – all the bitterness of farewells o'er –
> We yield our spirit unto ocean's foam,
>   And, in the new-born life which lies before,
>   On far Columbian or Australian shore,
> Strive to exchange time past for time to come;
>   How melancholy then – if morn restore
> (Less welcome than the night's forgetful gloom)
>   Old England's blue hills to our sight again;
> When we, our thoughts seemed weaning from her sky,
>   That *pang*, which wakes the almost silenced pain!
> Thus, when the sick man lies, resigned to die,
>   A well-loved voice, a well-remembered strain,
> Lets time break harshly in upon eternity.[76]

The second sonnet is less innovative and less successful, describing how the emigrant, now settled in his new home, finds comfort and calm in memories of the old.

At the beginning of June 1845 everything seemed to be going well for Branwell. He still enjoyed his lady's favours, his tutorial post was not arduous and left him plenty of time for his own pursuits, and his recent poetic efforts had been crowned with the accolade of publication in a widely respected journal. Neither he nor the Robinsons seem to have had the faintest inkling of the crisis that was about to burst upon them, though it must have been about this time that Anne Brontë handed in her resignation. Her reasons for doing so were never explicitly stated. Even her diary paper, written shortly after Branwell's dismissal, only hints at general dissatisfaction. Rereading her diary paper of 1841, she recalled:

How many things have happened since it was written – some pleasant some far otherwise – Yet I was then at Thorp Green and now I am only < just > escaped from it – I was wishing to leave < it > then and if I had known that I had four years longer to stay how wretched I should have been ... but during my stay I have had some very unpleasant and undreamt of experience of human < nature > nature –[77]

This suggests that Anne was aware of the relationship between her brother and Mrs Robinson, though not necessarily that it was about to be exposed. As she must have served out her notice, her resignation would seem to have been prompted by a growing sense of disgust with Mrs Robinson and her children rather than fear of a scandal involving her brother. Five years with the Robinsons had brought her to the end of her endurance.

On 3 June, anticipating some hours of leisure ahead, Branwell compiled and sent off a list of books he would like to borrow from Mr Bellerby's library.[78] A week later, on 11 June, Mr Robinson paid Anne the £3 10s. which was owed to her since the payment of her last quarter's salary of £10 on 11 May. On the same day, 11 June, he also advanced Branwell his quarter's salary of £20, which was not due until 21 July. Mr Robinson's reasons for taking this unusual step are not clear. It cannot have been an effective dismissal or the payment would have been only for that proportion of the salary which had been earned, as Anne's had been. Even though Mr Robinson may have been anticipating the fact that Branwell was about to go home for a week's holiday, it still seems odd that he should have advanced the salary so early. The Robinsons themselves were to leave for Scarborough on 4 July but Branwell would be back at Thorp Green with them for at least two weeks before they set off – giving ample time for the salary to be paid then.[79] Though it is tempting to see something sinister in this early payment, the reason may simply be that Branwell needed the money for his travel arrangements and that Mr Robinson tidied up his accounts with the Brontës by paying both on the same day before they left for home. Whatever the explanation, it is clear that even at this late date Mr Robinson had no cause for dissatisfaction with Branwell, or he would not have advanced his salary.

Though their salaries were paid on 11 June the Brontës probably did not leave Thorp Green till the following Saturday, 14 June. Charlotte does not mention Anne or Branwell in her letter to Ellen written on 13 June, but they were certainly at home by 18 June when their presence enabled Charlotte to write in high glee to accept Ellen Nussey's invitation to Hathersage. By 27 June Branwell had gone again: 'Branwell only stayed a week with us', Charlotte told Ellen, 'but he is to come home again when the family go to Scarbro'.'[80] Though Branwell's comings and goings at this time also seem strange, it is unlikely that he lied to his family about his orders to return to Thorp Green, as Anne would have been able to contradict him.

Much has been made of the fact that when the Robinsons set off for Scarborough on 4 July, they left Edmund behind in his tutor's care. This is seen as the catalyst for Branwell's subsequent dismissal; both Winifred Gerin and Daphne du Maurier, for instance, suggest that Edmund revealed something about his tutor when he rejoined the family in Scarborough on 17 July which caused his outraged father to write that very day to dismiss Branwell.[81] Unfortunately, the assumption that Edmund was left behind is based solely on the unreliable and contradictory evidence of the visitor lists published in the weekly Scarborough newspapers. Even if we do accept that he might have travelled separately and that his belated appearances in the listings of the *Scarborough Record* and *Scarborough Herald* are significant, the newspapers offer conflicting dates for his arrival and both place it after the accepted date of 17 July.[82] As the two papers were sister publications, the likeliest explanation is that Edmund's name was simply omitted by accident and that, in attempting to rectify the mistake, an apparent mystery was created.

The fact that Edmund travelled with the rest of his family is indirectly confirmed by other, more reliable, sources. The journal of George Whitehead, who lived at Little Ouseburn, notes that the Robinsons set off for Scarborough on Friday, 4 July; though he seems to have been well informed about the family, he does not mention that Edmund was left behind.[83] This same date is confirmed by Mr Robinson himself, who recorded his travelling expenses to Scarborough in his cash book the following day. Of great significance is the fact that among those expenses is 17s. for the purchase of a whip for Edmund; as provision was made for five horses, Edmund was presumably riding one of these rather than with his family in the coach. Another gift to him of 12/6d. is recorded on 16 July.[84] It therefore seems most likely that Edmund actually went to Scarborough with his family, as he had done in previous years, and that he was not left behind in Branwell's care. As Charlotte had told Ellen, Branwell would return home to Haworth when the family went to Scarborough.

If Branwell did linger at all it would have been to observe the grand opening of the York and Scarborough Railway, which took place on Monday, 7 July,[85] three days after the Robinsons left Thorp Green. Given Branwell's past career on the railway and his continuing interest in the subject, one could well imagine that he would wish to see the celebrations, which were marked by processions and speeches.

The Robinsons had been at Scarborough – and Branwell at Haworth – for almost two weeks before Branwell received his letter of instant dismissal. The gossip in Haworth, recounted many years later by the sister of Nancy Garrs, was that the gardener at Thorp Green had surprised Branwell and Mrs Robinson together in the boathouse and had informed the lady's husband. This story was certainly current in 1856 when George Smith's detectives were told by Patrick Brontë himself that 'A gardener – whose name he did not know – had definite proofs of guilt and had informed, as he understood, Mrs —'s husband.' This seems as good an explanation as any for the suddenness of the blow which befell Branwell. It is highly probable that he would have had an assignation with Mrs Robinson on the eve of their separation for the holiday, and there may have been a boathouse on the banks of the Ouse, just over half a mile from the house and therefore eminently suitable for a clandestine meeting. Perhaps, after conducting a secret affair undiscovered for two years, they had grown careless and did not notice that they were observed. It is more likely, however, that the assignation took place in the boathouse on the shore at Scarborough, just below the Robinsons' lodgings at The Cliff.[86] This would explain the delay between the Robinsons' departure for Scarborough and the sending of the letter of dismissal. If Branwell was supposed to be at home, but had indiscreetly followed his mistress to Scarborough and was recognized by the family servant, then discovery of the affair was almost inevitable.

The identity of the gardener lends some support to this story. He was a Robert Pottage and his wife also worked for the Robinsons. Despite his job, Pottage seems to have accompanied the Robinsons to Scarborough, perhaps to assist the groom, William Allison, with the horses and luggage on the journey. On 5 July, among the expenses for the journey, Mr Robinson records a payment of £1 10s. to 'Pottage and to band'. While the coupling of the two items suggests that the payment was regarded by Mr Robinson as of trifling importance, it is just possible that it might have been a gratuity for information given. It is not clear whether Pottage remained in Scarborough or returned immediately to Thorp Green. If he had not already divulged his secret in person, he then had a much-needed opportunity to mull over his predicament – he was certain to incur Mrs Robinson's wrath if he betrayed her to her husband, but equally he would fall foul of Mr Robinson if the affair came to light by other means. Having decided that he owed his loyalty to his employer, he may then have revealed what he had seen in a letter to Mr Robinson. Though it may be pure coincidence, Pottage did not last long in the Robinsons' employment: he 'left and finish'd all up' at Thorp Green on 13 February 1846 and left Little Ouseburn altogether on 23 March, only two months before Mr Robinson died.[87] As Mr Robinson's rapidly failing health had been evident to all and his death was now imminent, one cannot help wondering whether Pottage decided to leave before the management of the estate fell entirely into the hands of his vengeful widow.

Mr Robinson's letter certainly sounds like the immediate reaction of a betrayed husband; his language was strong, though he may not have gone so far as to threaten to shoot his former tutor if he returned to Thorp Green as Branwell claimed.[88] What is surprising is that – as far as one can tell – the revelation of the affair led to no breach with his wife. He remained as open-handed with her as he had always been, even during the holiday in Scarborough when he must have taken his decision to sack Branwell,[89] and, though he cut his eldest daughter out of his will for making her runaway match, his erring wife suffered no such hardship. This suggests that Mrs Robinson was able to divert her husband's anger onto Branwell and depict herself as the innocent and unwilling recipient of his attentions. The alternative, that there really was no affair and that Branwell was dismissed for some other reason, does not square with the rest of the evidence.

Perhaps the most damning indications of Mrs Robinson's guilt came after the dismissal. There seems to be no other explanation for the large sums of money Branwell received from Thorp Green or the visit of Mrs Robinson's coachman, apparently sent by her;[90] nor indeed for the continuing corres-

pondence with both Ann Marshall and Dr Crosby, who relayed information about Mrs Robinson while also conveniently keeping him at a distance.

Branwell's first reaction to his dismissal was characteristically dramatic,
as Charlotte reported to Ellen:

We have had sad work with Branwell since – he thought of nothing but stunning
< his > or drowning his distress of mind – no one in the house could have rest –
and at last we have been obliged to send him from home for a week with some one
to look after him –⁹¹

Though Branwell had over-indulged many times before, he did not become
a habitual drinker until the abrupt ending of his affair with Mrs Robinson.⁹²
Charlotte's use of the word 'stunning' as well as 'drowning' his distress also
suggests that Branwell may have tried opiates as well as alcohol in an attempt
to find relief in oblivion. At this stage, however, he was still capable of
pulling himself together, at least temporarily. He had been despatched, in
the company of John Brown, to the west coast, from where he wrote on 31
July to a sceptical Charlotte:

[he] expresses some sense of contrition for his frantic folly – he promises amendment
on his return – but so long as he remains at home I scarce dare hope for peace in
the house We must all I fear prepare for a season of distress and disquietude –⁹³

In fact, Branwell's brief trip from home does seem to have had the effect
of calming him down. Though Liverpool may seem a strange choice of
destination it was immensely popular with holidaymakers from the West
Riding, who could travel there cheaply and quickly on the Manchester and
Leeds Railway. Liverpool was then the starting point for taking pleasure
steamers along the beautiful coast of North Wales and to the Isle of Man
and across the Mersey to the new town of Birkenhead. Branwell and John
Brown certainly took the trip along the Welsh coast, for Branwell not only
sketched Penmaenmawr mountain from the sea but also later wrote a poem
inspired by it.⁹⁴ Even during the steamer trip he seems to have found some
relief in poetry, writing at least one poem, titled 'Lydia Gisborne' in Greek
letters, which gives an insight into his agitated state.

> Cannot my soul depart < How i.w. I ? die >
>   Where will it fly?
> Asks my tormented heart,
>   Willing to die.
> When will this restlessness
> Tossing in sleeplessness –
> Stranger to happiness –
>   Slumbering lie.
>
> Cannot I < pass > chase away
>   Life in my tomb

Rather than pass away
  Lifetime in gloom,
With sorrows employing
Their < powers > arts in destroying
The power of enjoying
  The comforts of home?

Home it < it > is not < to > with me
  Bright as of yore
Joys are forgot with me
  \Taught to deplore/
  < Happy no more >
<u>My</u> home has ta'en its rest
<u>In</u> an afflicted breast
That I have often pressed
But – may <u>no more</u>.[95]

By the end of his short holiday Branwell had recovered enough of his former spirits to be able to write with black humour to his old friend, the Halifax sculptor, J. B. Leyland:

> I returned yesterday from a week's journey to Liverpool and North Wales, but I found during my absence that wherever I went a certain woman robed in black, and calling herself 'MISERY' walked by my side, and leant on my arm as affectionately as if she were my legal wife.
>   Like some other husbands, I could have spared her presence.[96]

It was scarcely surprising that Branwell should find his home no longer 'Bright as of yore' on his return. Though the full weight of the Brontës' wrath was to fall on Mrs Robinson, the 'diabolical seducer' as Patrick called her,[97] the atmosphere at the parsonage was undoubtedly disapproving. It was not simply that Branwell had committed mortal sin in breaking the seventh commandment, but that he was unwilling or unable to disentangle himself from the relationship: his only wish, amounting almost to monomania, was to return to Mrs Robinson. Patrick was unremittingly stern with his son; Emily simply seems to have found him irritating.[98] But it was Charlotte – who had always been the closest to him and who, having fallen in love with a married man herself, should have been the most sympathetic to his plight – who proved to be his harshest critic. Her hostility to him seems to have been inflamed by her always burning sense of injustice. She had had to bear her suffering in silence and exert a rigid self-control to prevent herself giving way to her abiding sense of desolation and loss. Branwell, on the other hand, was totally self-indulgent in his pain, telling his story to anyone who would listen. While her love for Monsieur Heger remained a closely guarded secret for over seventy years, known or guessed by only a few people, Branwell's passion for Mrs Robinson was immediately common knowledge throughout the township.

Charlotte's bitterness and contempt for Branwell were voiced in her letters to Ellen Nussey, who lent a more than usually sympathetic ear. Her own brother, George, had had a mental breakdown at the beginning of the year and by the summer his condition had deteriorated to the point that he had had to be sent to Dr Belcombe's private asylum at York for treatment. Another brother, Joseph, was an alcoholic whose behaviour paralleled that of Branwell. The two friends commiserated with one another:

You say well in speaking of Branwell that no sufferings are so awful as those brought on by dissipation – alas! I see the truth of this observation daily proved – Ann and Mercy must have a weary and burdensome life of it – in waiting upon their unhappy brother – it seems grievous indeed that those who have not sinned should suffer so largely.[99]

There is a palpable sense of personal injury here which is a subcurrent throughout Charlotte's complaints about her brother. It was not so much Branwell's self-pity and attempts to seek oblivion in drink which grated, but the fact that he inflicted them on his family and Charlotte herself. It has to be said that she aggravated her own sense of martyrdom by refusing either to take up Ellen's invitations to Brookroyd or to allow Ellen to visit Haworth: 'Branwell makes no effort to seek a situation –', she reported angrily, 'and while he is at home I will invite no one to come and share our discomfort.' Again she told Ellen, 'Branwell offers no prospect of hope – he professes to be too ill to think of seeking for employment – he makes comfort scant at home.'[100] Charlotte even complained to her old schoolmistress, Margaret Wooler:

You ask about Branwell; he never thinks of seeking employment and I begin to fear that he has rendered himself incapable of filling any respectable station in life, besides, if money were at his disposal he would use it only to his own injury – the faculty of self-government is, I fear almost destroyed in him[101]

There is a double standard here, as in all Charlotte's remarks on Branwell's misdoings at this time. She accuses him of failing to look for employment yet she herself had been unemployed for two years, effectively allowing herself to be kept by her father and Anne. It was no excuse that she was needed at home, however much she might have comforted herself with the thought, as Emily was clearly a perfectly competent housekeeper who could manage without her assistance, as she had done while Charlotte was in Brussels. Although she had formed a rather wild ambition to go to Paris in search of a situation,[102] she had done nothing concrete to find herself a post. Similarly, she criticized Branwell's lack of self-control, with its devastating effect on the family, yet, despite the rigorous suppression of her own emotions and refusal to make scenes or voice her unhappiness, as Branwell did, her deep depression had similarly been inflicted on family and friends alike. Her only outlet for her pent-up feelings was her correspondence with Monsieur Heger, which was becoming increasingly uninhibited and anguished even as she became more censorious of her brother's conduct.

I tell you frankly ... that I have tried to forget you, for the remembrance of a person whom one believes one must never see again and whom, nevertheless, one greatly respects, exhausts the spirit too much and when one has suffered that kind of anxiety for one or two years, one is ready to do anything to recover peace of mind. I have done everything, I have sought out occupation, I have absolutely forbidden myself the pleasure of speaking of you – even to Emily but I cannot conquer either my regrets or my impatience – this is humiliating – not to know how to be master of one's own thoughts, to be slave to a regret, a memory, slave to a dominating and fixed idea which tyrannizes one's spirit.[103]

It is not surprising that Charlotte had no sympathy to spare for her brother when her own suffering, from the identical cause, was so extreme. It must have been doubly galling to be forced to witness his extravagant and very public displays of grief when her own pride forbade her to find relief in such indulgence.

While it is easy to empathize with Charlotte because we see events through her eyes, it is important to redress the balance in Branwell's favour. Her claims, for instance, that he had given no thought to finding employment are patently untrue. Rather surprisingly, Branwell contemplated a return to the railways. A new line had been proposed, commencing at Hebden Bridge, running through a tunnel under Cock Hill to Oxenhope and then on to Keighley via Haworth and Oakworth. The scheme had the great commercial advantage of linking up the Manchester and Liverpool Railway with the Leeds and Bradford Railway and there is no doubt that, had it been carried out, it would have transformed the prosperity of Haworth. For this reason, Patrick Brontë and most of the principal inhabitants of Haworth lent their names as promoters of the plan and Joseph Greenwood of Spring Head took a place on the provisional board of directors. Applications for shares were advertised in the *Leeds Intelligencer* on 11 October 1845 and, at about the same time, Branwell himself applied for the post of Secretary to the new Railway, blithely declaring, 'I trust to be able to produce full testimonials as to my qualifications and Securities, if required, to any probable amount.'[104]

Despite any influence his father may have had with the board, Branwell's prospective employers were clearly unimpressed with the fact that he had lost his previous post on the railways for failing to keep proper accounts. As Charlotte remarked bitterly to Ellen:

the place (a Secretaryship to a Railroad Committee) is given to another person Branwell still remains at home and while <u>he</u> is here – <u>you</u> shall not come – I am more confirmed in that resolution the more I know of him – I wish I could say one word to you in his favour – but I cannot – therefore I will hold my tongue.[105]

In fact, had Branwell secured the position, he would not have held it for long. The proposal to build the railway coincided with the 'Railway Panic' when large numbers of schemes folded and investors lost heavily in the process: the plan was abandoned and Haworth had to wait another twenty-two years for its rail link.

This failure does not seem to have deterred Branwell, for he continued to badger Francis Grundy with requests for employment on the railways and even considered the possibility of going to the Continent when he saw no openings in Britain. In the meantime, he busied himself with acting as a go-between for his old friend J. B. Leyland, and John Brown, the latter being responsible for lettering and erecting a memorial in Haworth Church to Joseph Midgeley of Oldfield which Leyland had carved.[106] The renewal of this particular friendship led to a revival of Branwell's spirits; though still harping upon his disappointment, his letters became increasingly chatty and irreverent in tone and were frequently illustrated with hastily sketched and wittily captioned vignettes.

More importantly, Leyland encouraged him to take up his writing again in earnest. Branwell had two new poems published in the *Halifax Guardian* in the early winter of 1845, both of them inspired by the abrupt ending of his liaison with Mrs Robinson. The first of these, 'Real Rest', published on 8 November, pictures a corpse floating on the water and envies its peace in death.

> I have an outward frame unlike to thine,
> Warm with young life – not cold in death's decline;
> An eye that sees the sunny light of heaven –
> A heart by pleasure thrilled – by anguish riven –
> But in exchange for thy untroubled calm,
> Thy gift of cold oblivions healing balm,
> I'd give my youth – my health – my life to come,
> And share thy slumbers in thy ocean tomb.[107]

The second, 'Penmaenmawr', which was published on 20 December, was much more overt in its references to Mrs Robinson – intentionally so, as Branwell told Leyland in a covering letter enclosing a copy of the poem.

I ought to tell you why I wish anything of so personal a nature to appear in print.

I have no other way, not pregnant with danger, of communicating with one whom I cannot help loving. < these > Printed lines with my usual signature 'Nor-thangerland' would excite no suspicion ... I sent through a private channel one letter of comfort in her great and agonizing present afflictions, but I recalled it through dread of the consequences of a discovery.

Though written in November, the poem harked back to his voyage on the steamer from Liverpool along the coast of North Wales. 'These lines only have one merit', he told Leyland,

– that of < tru > really expressing my feelings while sailing under the Welsh mountain – When the band on board the steamer struck up 'Ye banks and braes' – and God knows that, for many different reasons, those feelings were far enough from pleasure.[108]

Had Branwell seriously intended Mrs Robinson to see the poem he would surely have submitted it to the *Yorkshire Gazette*, which he knew the family read, but this was possibly too great a risk. Even if Henry Bellerby had been willing to print a poem by the recently disgraced and dismissed Robinson tutor, anyone at Thorp Green familiar with Branwell's poetic aspirations would have recognized his Northangerland pseudonym. While Branwell may have fondly believed Mr Robinson was ignorant of his pen name, the poem contained lines which would undoubtedly have raised his former employer's suspicions.

> I knew a flower whose leaves were meant to bloom
> Till Death should snatch it to adorn the tomb,
> Now, blanching 'neath the blight of hopeless grief
> With never blooming and yet living leaf;
> A flower on which my mind would wish to shine,
> If but one beam could break from mind like mine:
> I had an ear which could on accents dwell
> That might as well say 'perish' as 'farewell' –
> An eye which saw, far off, a tender form
> Beaten, unsheltered, by affliction's storm –
> An arm – a lip – that trembled to embrace
> My Angel's gentle breast and sorrowing face –
> A mind that clung to Ouse's fertile side
> While tossing – objectless – on Menai's tide![109]

If Mrs Robinson did get to see the *Halifax Guardian*, then these lines must have caused her great alarm. While it might be amusing to have a young man writing her ardent love poetry in private, it was a different thing to have him blazoning his passion across the pages of the local newspapers in progressively more indiscreet verse. It is therefore a matter for speculation whether the sums of money which Mrs Robinson sent Branwell over the next few years were an attempt to buy his silence and persuade him not to publish further poems which might lead to a public discovery of their affair. Certainly it is the case that this was the last of Branwell's published poems to have any bearing on his relationship with Mrs Robinson.

The measured tones and carefully worked lines of 'Penmaenmawr' are in stark contrast to the hastily scribbled verses Branwell had poured out in the first frantic reaction to his dismissal. Even so, the poem ends with a plea for peace of mind that was still proving elusive.

> Oh soul! that draw'st yon mighty hill and me
> Into communion of vague unity,
> Tell me, can I obtain the stony brow
> That fronts the storm, as much unbroken now
> As when it once upheld the fortress proud,
> Now gone, like its own morning cap of cloud?
> Its breast is stone. Can I have one of steel,
> T'endure – inflict – defend – yet never feel?
> It stood as firm when haughty Edward's word
> Gave hill and dale to England's fire and sword,
> As when white sails and steam-smoke tracked the sea,
> And all the world breathed peace, but waves and me.
> Let me, like it, arise o'er mortal care;
> All evils bear, yet never know despair;
> Unshrinking face the griefs I now deplore,
> And stand, through storm and shine, like moveless
> PENMAENMAWR.[110]

In addition to his efforts for the *Halifax Guardian*, Branwell even seems to have contemplated yet another assault on *Blackwood's Magazine*, sending Leyland a copy of his lines for his prior approval.[111]

Branwell had not merely occupied himself with poetry, but had also embarked on a major new project. Just as he had always done, from the days of their childhood when he had been the innovator in their juvenile writings to the publishing of his poetry in more recent years, Branwell was the first member of his family to tread a new path, in seeing the potential of the novel as a marketable commodity and setting about writing one for publication. He explained the inception of his book to Leyland.

I have, since I saw you at Halifax, devoted my hours of time snatched from downright illness, to the composition of a three volume <u>Novel</u> – one volume of which < has > is completed – and along with the two forthcoming ones, has been really the < work > result of half a dozen by past years of thoughts about, and experience in, this crooked path of life.

I felt that I must rouse myself to attempt some-thing while < labouring under > roasting daily and nightly over a slow fire – to wile away my torment and I knew that in the present state of the publishing and reading world a Novel is the most saleable article so that where ten pounds would be offered for < the > a work the production of which would require the utmost stretch of a man's intellect – two hundred pounds would be a refused offer for three volumes whose composition would require the smoking of a cigar and the humming of a tune.

My Novel is the result of years of thought and if it gives a vivid picture of human feelings for good and evil – veiled by the cloak of deceit which must enwrap man and woman – If it records as faithfully as the pages that unveil man's heart in Hamlet or Lear < I shall be > the conflicting feelings and clashing pursuits in our uncertain path through life I shall be as much gratified (and as much astonished) as I should be if in betting that I could jump over the Mersey I jumped over the Irish Sea. It would not be more pleasant to light on Dublin instead of Birkenhead than to leap from the present bathos of fictitious literature on to the firmly fixed rock honourd by the foot of a Smollet or Feilding.

That jump I expect to take when I can model a rival to your noble Theseus who haunted my dreams when I slept after seeing him – but meanwhile I can try my utmost to rouse from almost killing cares, and that alone will be its own reward.[112]

Branwell's 'Novel' was indeed the result of years of thought, for it appears that it was a reworking of an Angrian story he had written as early as December 1837. His choice of this particular story and his treatment of it were obviously influenced by his affair with Mrs Robinson. The story was that of Maria, the beautiful wife of the dissolute William Thurston, and her seduction by Alexander Percy, Earl of Northangerland.

In the original, Maria was drawn to Percy's romantic character, 'that strange union ... of debauched profligacy and impassioned feeling and restless ambition, and which then was but beginning to be overclouded by his after embittered melancholy' and her interest was stimulated by 'the story of his life, its ceaseless wanderings and rumoured crimes'. In common with Percy's other conquests she is already half in love with him before she meets him and is a ready and willing victim; Percy wins her over simply because he is Percy and irresistible to women.[113] In the new version, which Branwell titled 'And the Weary are at Rest', Maria Thurston is a virtuous woman driven into Percy's arms, despite herself, because she is a neglected wife who longs for love.

Mrs Maria Thurston had known enough of Sorrow, and God had intended her to both know and feel enough of love. She had before her a man capable of exciting every feeling that a woman can know – She had, as the possessor of her own person, a man, if I can write him down as such, who could not gain more than momentarily her feelings, and who never could feel hers at all. She had lost thoughts of him \except/ in her ideas of dread < at > of him and so many years had elapsed since he had bestowed on her even one moment of, I fear, selfish fondness, that the rem\em/brance of her bridal days caused the astonishment which one feels < at having > when thinking that ones childhood took for truth the gibberish of a nursery tale.[114]

Maria Thurston had thus become a portrait of Mrs Robinson, who had herself attracted Branwell's sympathy by her claims of marital neglect. Maria is pious, like Mrs Robinson, and is thus deeply torn by the conflict of her faith and her illicit love. When she finally succumbs to Percy's attentions she falls weeping to her knees and offers a 'scarcely coherent prayer':

O God forgive me if thou can'st! I do not know how much I have angered thee – I do not know whether or not I sin in daring to pray to thee – I only know that I cannot help myself, that I am going whither my every feeling leads me, and that, come what may, into thy hands I must fall. The world will now judge ill of me – My sisterhood will shun me – snares will surround me – my life will be endangered, < and > a long dark future may be preparing for me and Hell itself may rise to meet me at my coming; But how can I shake off what my heart clings to? How can I vow to thee that I will forget him who seems all I have hoped for and never obtained? How can I return to silent submission under heartless tyranny and keep any promise to hate the name of love?"[115]

Though Maria Thurston had become Mrs Robinson, Percy did not become Branwell Brontë, except in so far as he embodied all Branwell's wish-fulfilment. They shared a love of intellectual pursuits, music and poetry, a bravado, passion and natural eloquence, but there was always a naivety about Branwell which was not reflected in the cynical and manipulative Percy, who was effortlessly master of every situation.

Writing his novel had at least the benefit of employing Branwell's time and deflecting his mind from his emotional problems. Though it remained unfinished, the simple act of creativity was a comfort. His career and his personal life lay in ruins; literature was now his only resource.

Chapter Seventeen

THE BOOK
OF RHYMES

Branwell's declared intention of writing a novel for publication set Charlotte thinking. 'We had very early cherished the dream of one day becoming authors', she was later to write; the dream had never been relinquished but the necessity of earning a living had always intervened.' But what if the two could be combined? What if the compulsion to write, which had so often frustrated the effort to work at less congenial tasks, could be turned into a means of livelihood? Charlotte's chance discovery of a notebook of Emily's poems at this time must have seemed like the answer to a prayer. She described that momentous find five years later in an account which, though deliberately low key, could not suppress the thrill of excitement.

One day, in the autumn of 1845, I accidentally lighted on a MS. volume of verse in my sister Emily's handwriting. Of course, I was not surprised, knowing that she could and did write verse: I looked it over, and something more than surprise seized me, – a deep conviction that these were not common effusions, nor at all like the poetry women generally write. I thought them condensed and terse, vigorous and genuine. To my ear, they had also a peculiar music – wild, melancholy, and elevating.
   My sister Emily was not a person of demonstrative character, nor one, on the

recesses of whose mind and feelings, even those nearest and dearest to her could, with impunity, intrude unlicensed; it took hours to reconcile her to the discovery I had made, and days to persuade her that such poems merited publication. I knew, however, that a mind like hers could not be without some latent spark of honourable ambition, and refused to be discouraged in my attempts to fan that spark to flame.

Meantime, my younger sister quietly produced some of her own compositions, intimating that since Emily's had given me pleasure, I might like to look at hers. I could not but be a partial judge, yet I thought that these verses too had a sweet sincere pathos of their own.[2]

Emily's rage was entirely understandable. Though she had long been accustomed to read her Gondal stories and poems to Anne, Charlotte had been excluded because her partnership had been with Branwell. That partnership had effectively ended by about 1840 when brother and sister were continually separated by the demands of their employment. Whether or not Charlotte was aware that Emily and Anne still continued their Gondal sagas, she should not have intruded uninvited into their world. It was a violation of that secrecy which was an integral part of Gondal to have read the poems herself, but then to demand that they should be published was an unforgivable offence.

It was therefore all the more surprising that Emily was eventually won round, even if it did take some time. Anne's part in the quarrel and Charlotte's reaction to it were typical: Anne played the part of peacemaker by voluntarily sacrificing her own private poems, and Charlotte, patronizing as ever towards her youngest sister – whom she does not even name in her account – praised her verse in terms which made it clear she thought they were nothing out of the ordinary.

Charlotte claimed both the discovery and the inspiration to publish as her own; she was undoubtedly the driving force behind the publication. Even so, she had to make two important concessions to her sister: the Gondal origins of her verse would be disguised by judicious emendation of the text and, more importantly, the poems would be published under pseudonyms and their authors' true identity was to remain a secret. The decision to adopt pseudonyms was one that Emily and Anne forced upon Charlotte as a *sine qua non* of publication. Though Charlotte would always rather regret being bound by this promise, she soon came to see the advantages of their assumed names.[3]

Averse to personal publicity, we veiled our own names under those of Currer, Ellis, and Acton Bell; the ambiguous choice being dictated by a sort of conscientious scruple at assuming Christian names positively masculine, while we did not like to declare ourselves women, because – without at that time suspecting that our mode of writing and thinking was not what is called 'feminine' – we had a vague impression that authoresses are liable to be looked on with prejudice; we had noticed how critics sometimes use for their chastisement the weapon of personality, and for their reward, a flattery which is not true praise.[4]

The actual choice of pseudonyms has been the subject of much debate and speculation. The name 'Currer' was familiar to the Brontës as that of the philanthropist Frances Richardson Currer, who was a benefactor of many local institutions, including the Clergy Daughters' School at Cowan Bridge and the Keighley Mechanics' Institute. It was also a name that Branwell had used in his 'Life of Warner Howard Warner' written in February 1838: an ancestor of the protagonist had been called 'Haworth Currer Warner'. Ellis, too, was a well-known name in the West Riding. The Ellis family were the main mill owners in Bingley, a few miles from Haworth, and their deeds were frequently reported in the local newspapers. In addition, Ellis Cunliffe Lister-Kay was the Liberal Member of Parliament who had been elected to represent Bradford after the Reform Bill. The name 'Acton' was probably familiar to Anne from her days at Thorp Green. The 'Bell' surname may have been suggested by Patrick's curate's middle name, Arthur Bell Nicholls, or by the simple fact that Haworth Church had just acquired a new peal of bells.[5] In each case the girls retained their own initials beneath the cover of their new identities.

The autumn months were spent in choosing the poems to be included in the publication. The final selection provides a fascinating indication of the turn that the Brontës' literary lives had taken since adulthood. Charlotte, the driving force in rushing into print, contributed nineteen poems: of these, thirteen had been written as long ago as 1837, when she had enjoyed an immensely productive year at Roe Head, and three in 1838, 1839 and 1841 respectively. The remaining three poems, for which there are no extant manuscripts, were probably more recent compositions.[6] Out of the nineteen, only one, 'The Teacher's Monologue', was definitely autobiographical. Three, 'Pilate's Wife's Dream', 'Winter Stores' and 'The Missionary', seem to stand alone as story-poems in their own right, but the remaining fifteen all owed their origins to Angria. Clearly, then, Charlotte herself considered that her best work had been produced in the golden years of the Angrian chronicles; since then – and probably really since Brussels when Monsieur Heger had so influenced her style – she had virtually abandoned poetry as a vehicle for her imagination.

Charlotte was later to look back on her contribution with a feeling akin to shame, saying that she would view the possibility of a reprint with unmixed pleasure only if her own work was omitted. 'Let me warn you', she wrote to a Miss Alexander who had sent her a fan letter and wished to buy *Poems*,

that it is scarcely worth your while to send for it. It is a collection of short fugitive pieces; my own share are chiefly juvenile productions written several years ago, before taste was chastened or judgement matured – accordingly they now appear to me very crude.[7]

To Mrs Gaskell she was even more blunt:

I do not like my own share of the work, nor care that it should be read:... Mine are chiefly juvenile productions; the restless effervescence of a mind that would not be still. In those days, the sea too often 'wrought and was tempestuous' and weed, sand, shingle – all turned up in the tumult. This image is much too magniloquent for the subject, but you will pardon it.[8]

In sharp contrast to Charlotte, both Emily and Anne contributed poems of much more recent date. Anne selected twenty-one poems, all of them written since 1840 and all, bar one, since her appointment to Thorp Green; seventeen of them had been written in the last three years, the highest proportion in 1845.[9] Although it is particularly difficult to distinguish between Anne's personal and Gondal poetry, it would appear that around half of the poems were either autobiographical or religious, and so not from the Gondal sagas. Anne had to trawl through at least five different copybooks to find poems which she considered worthy of publication.

Emily also contributed twenty-one poems, the two earliest written in 1839 but the vast majority, fourteen in all, in the last two years. All the poems were chosen from two notebooks, six from one and fifteen from the other,[10] which suggests that the latter was the manuscript Charlotte had found and surreptitiously read. Since both were written in the minute, cramped hand which clearly signalled the private world of Gondal, it must have required both persistence and effort on Charlotte's part to decipher her sister's poems; she may have made the original discovery by chance but it was a deliberate choice to read on. Emily's outrage at Charlotte's 'unwarrantable liberty'[11] is therefore all the more understandable.

Emily was careful to edit out any references in the poems she selected which might alert a reader to the Gondal subtext. This was most obvious in the poems written earlier in 1845. 'Angora's shore', for example, in Emily's elegiac lament 'Cold in the earth – and the deep snow piled above thee!', was changed to the less exotic 'northern shore'.[12] Even more dramatically, the published version of 'The Prisoner' was composed of two sections of a much longer poem cobbled together to omit the Gondal storyline and given a new ending with a specially composed last verse. As the beginning of this poem is dated 9 October 1845 in its original manuscript form, Emily must either have only just finished it or even have been still working on it when Charlotte suggested that they should publish. The poem is rightly one of Emily's most famous, as it includes the powerful and intensely emotional description of the captive's vision.

'He comes with western winds, with evening's wandering airs,
With that clear dusk of heaven that brings the thickest stars;
Winds take a pensive tone and stars a tender fire
And visions rise and change which kill me with desire –

Desire for nothing known in my maturer years
When joy grew mad with awe, at counting future tears;
When, if my spirit's sky was full of flashes warm,
I knew not whence they came from sun or thunder storm;

But first a hush of peace, a soundless calm descends;
The struggle of distress and feirce impatience ends;
Mute music sooths my breast – unuttered harmony
That I could never dream till earth was lost to me.

Then dawns the Invisible; the Unseen its truth reveals;
My outward sense is gone, my inward essence feels –
Its wings are almost free, its home, its harbour found;
Measuring the gulf, it stoops and dares the final bound –

O, dreadful is the check – intense the agony
When the ear begins to hear and the eye begins to see;
When the pulse begins to throb, the brain to think again,
The soul to feel the flesh and the flesh to feel the chain.

Yet I would lose no sting, would wish no torture less;
The more that anguish racks the earlier it will bless;
And robed in fires of Hell, or bright with heavenly shine
If it but herald Death, the vision is divine –"[3]

These lines are frequently cited to prove that Emily was a mystic, undergoing the same sort of personal revelation as St John of the Cross or St Teresa of Avila. Though she may use the same sort of ecstatic religious terminology in describing the vision, their experience is essentially different in that it is centred on union with God. For Emily, speaking through her Gondal characters, the vision is a visitation of a 'Benignant Power' which she characterizes here, and indeed elsewhere, as a personification of hope or imagination. One is reminded of Charlotte's equally powerful and emotional experiences of Angrian visions, which she described so vividly at Roe Head.[4] Like her older sister, Emily externalized her imagination; her poems and stories did not seem to her to inhabit her head but were played out before her as if they were creations independent of her control. She was simply a passive spectator who could visualize so strongly that she only wrote what she actually saw. The fact that she externalizes and personifies imagination as a visitant 'God of Visions' does not make her a mystic, particularly as the recipients of the visions in her poems are usually defeated or imprisoned Gondals. Their wish for death, as the end of suffering, finds no echo in Emily herself though it recalls Branwell's extravagant poetic demands for 'real rest'. Another of Emily's poems, written in February 1845 and included in the final selection, is illustrative of this. 'The philosopher' is unable to reconcile the warring elements in his own breast or to find the spirit of harmony that will harness them.

> – 'And even for that Spirit, Seer,
> I've whached and sought my life time long
> Sought Him in Heaven, Hell, Earth, and Air
> An endless search – and always wrong!
>
> Had I but seen his glorious eye,
> <u>Once</u> light the clouds that wilder me,
> I ne'er had raised this coward cry
> To cease to think and cease to be –
> I neer had called oblivion blest
> Nor stretching eager hands to Death
> Implored to change for lifeless rest
> This sentient soul, this living breath
>
> < But > O let me die – that power and will
> Their cruel strife may close
> And vanquished Good victorious Ill
> Be lost in one repose[15]

In direct contrast to this plea for oblivion is Emily's last great poem which, though a defiant rejection of conventional organized religion, is also a triumphant declaration of faith. Since this is the only statement of its kind in all Emily's extant writings, one cannot assume that it is necessarily an expression of her own belief, particularly as it was transcribed into a notebook containing many Gondal poems. Nevertheless, one can understand why Charlotte was happy to believe that these were the last lines Emily ever wrote, rather than the mediocre and tedious Gondal verses which actually had that dubious distinction.[16]

> No coward soul is mine
> No trembler in < the > the world's storm-troubled sphere
> I see Heaven's glories shine
> And Faith shines equal arming me from fear
>
> O God within my breast
> Almighty ever-present Deity
> Life, that in me hast rest
> As I Undying Life, have < strength > power in thee
>
> Vain are the thousand creeds
> That move men's hearts, unutterably vain,
> Worthless as withered weeds
> Or idlest froth amid the boundless main

To waken doubt in one
Holding so fast by thy infinity
So surely anchored on
The steadfast rock of Immortality

With wide-embracing love
Thy spirit animates eternal years
Pervades and broods above,
Changes, sustains, dissolves, creates and rears

Though Earth and moon were gone
And suns and universes ceased to < shine > be
And thou wert left alone
Every Existence would exist in < thine > thee

There is not room for Death
Nor atom that his might could render void
Since thou art Being and Breath
And what thou art may never be destroyed.[7]

This poem, written on 25 January 1846, was to be the last that Emily considered worth transcribing into her fair copy notebooks.[8] Though she did not altogether abandon poetry, her efforts in future would be principally channelled into prose. One cannot regret the creation of *Wuthering Heights*, but there must be a lingering sense of frustration that Emily's poetic career was ended so abruptly. The sustained quality and increased philosophical depth of the poems she had produced over the previous eighteen months prove that Emily was at the very height of her poetic powers when Charlotte proposed publication. Though she was then a lone voice crying in the wilderness, few now would disagree with Charlotte's assessment of Emily's gifts:

I know – no woman that ever lived – ever wrote such poetry before – Condensed energy, clearness, finish – strange, strong pathos are their characteristics – utterly different from the weak diffusiveness – the laboured yet most feeble wordiness < of > which dilute the writings of even very popular poetesses.[9]

Charlotte's discovery of Emily's poems was the catalyst she needed to pull herself out of the apathy she had suffered since returning from Brussels. At last she had a renewed sense of purpose in life and she set about the problem of publication with her old determination, sweeping aside her sisters' doubts and writing round to prospective publishers. At first, she made as little headway as Branwell had in his efforts to publish in *Blackwood's Magazine*. Undeterred, she wrote to William and Robert Chambers of Edinburgh, publishers of one of the Brontës' favourite periodicals, *Chambers's Edinburgh Journal*, seeking their advice: 'they may have forgotten the circumstance,' Charlotte wrote warmly some years later, 'but *I* have not, for from them I received a brief and business-like but, civil and sensible reply.'[20] Charlotte's gratitude suggests that their advice – which has not survived – bore fruit.

One can therefore presume that it was as a result of this advice that she wrote the following equally 'brief and business-like' letter to Aylott & Jones, a small publishing house at No. 8, Paternoster Row, London.

Jany – 28th – /46

Gentlemen

May I request to be informed whether you would undertake the publication of a Collection of short poems in 1 vol. oct[avo] –

If you object to publishing the work at your own risk – would you undertake it on the Author's account? –

I am Gentlemen
Your obdt hmble Servt
C Brontë

Address
Revd P. Brontë
Haworth Bradford – Yorkshire[21]

Aylott & Jones must have replied positively by return of post, for on 31 January Charlotte was writing to them again asking for an estimate of the cost of printing '200 to 250 pages' of an octavo volume 'of the same quality of paper and size of type as Moxon's last edition of Wordsworth'. On 6 February she posted them the manuscript, being obliged to divide it into two parcels on account of the weight, and following it with several anxious enquiries as to the safe arrival of both parcels.[22]

The plan to model the book of poems on Moxon's edition of Wordsworth had to be abandoned almost immediately for Charlotte's inexperience had led her to substantially overestimate the published size of the completed manuscript. 'The M.S. will certainly form a thinner vol – than I had anticipated', she admitted, before suggesting a reduction in size to a duodecimo format and specifying a long primer type. On 3 March, less than five weeks after her initial enquiry, Charlotte sent a banker's draft for £31 10s. so that printing could commence.[23] The fact that the sisters were able to scrape together such a large sum – just over three quarter's of Anne's annual salary at Thorp Green – is an indication of Charlotte's ambition to get into print at whatever cost.

As the prospect of achieving her goal grew closer, Charlotte's spirits rose. Her sense of duty was always stricter and more oppressive when she was miserable but, as soon as she had a purpose in life, it was flung aside. Now, busy and happy for the first time in three years, she suddenly abandoned her resolution to neither go away nor invite her friends to stay while Branwell remained at home and agreed to visit Ellen at Brookroyd. She left home on

18 February[24] with the intention of staying for a week or nine days but Ellen, with her usual tenacity, soon undermined this resolution. As she had done when they were staying together at Hathersage, Ellen sought Emily's permission for a longer stay. The answer came back as laconic as ever.

Dear Miss Ellen,
    I fancy this note will be too late to decide one way or the other with respect to Charlotte's stay – yours only came this morning (Wedensday) and < I > unless mine travels faster you will not receive it till Friday – Papa, of course misses C and will be glad to have her back. Anne and I ditto – but as she goes from home so seldom you may keep her a day or two longer if your eloquence is equal to the task of persuading her – that is if she be still with you when you get this permission
Yours truly E J Brontë[25]

As an afterthought, she added 'love from Anne'.[25]

    In the event, Charlotte was able to justify a longer absence from home. One of Ellen's cousins had married William Carr, 'an experienced surgeon' who practised in Gomersal and Charlotte took the opportunity to consult him about her father's increasing blindness. His advice was that an operation could be performed and would be successful in restoring his sight but that it should be delayed until the cataract which was causing the problem had hardened enough to be removable.

    Returning home on 2 March, Charlotte reported Mr Carr's opinion to Patrick who was 'much cheered ... but I could perceive he caught gladly at the idea of deferring the operation a few months longer'.[26] Less happily, she had a confrontation with Branwell, who had spent the day at the White Horse Tavern on the pretext of organizing a shooting match.

I went into the room where Branwell was to speak to him about an hour after I got home – it was very forced work to address him – I might have spared myself the trouble as he took no notice & made no reply – he was stupified – My fears were not vain Emily tells me that he got a sovereign from Papa while I have been away under pretence of paying a pressing debt – he went immediately & changed it at a public-house – and has employed it as was to be expected – she concluded her account with saying he was 'a hopeless being' – it is too true – In his present state it is scarcely possible to stay in the room where he is – what the future has in store – I do not know –[27]

Charlotte could almost have added that she did not care for she had a far more absorbing prospect on hand. She had sent the money to Aylott & Jones the day after her return from Brookroyd and within a week she was viewing sample proof sheets. This threw her into some alarm about the competence of the proofreader – 'such a mistake for instance as <u>tumbling</u> stars instead of <u>trembling</u> would suffice to throw an air of absurdity over a whole poem', she complained. Curbing her impatience to see the book in print, she decided that the authors would have to do the proofreading themselves, despite the delay it would cause. 'You need not enclose the M.S.', she told Aylott & Jones, 'as they can correct the errors from memory.'[28]

Up to this point the sisters seem to have been successful in keeping their authorship secret. Everyone at the parsonage had been kept in ignorance, as had Ellen Nussey. Even in her correspondence with Aylott & Jones Charlotte had scrupulously referred to the authors in the third person though it required no massive intellect to guess that the 'C Brontë' who wrote their letters was likely to be one of the 'three persons – relatives' who had contributed some of the poems.[29] The comings and goings of large packets of proofs, however, did not escape attention and Charlotte was obliged to write again to her publishers.

Gentlemen

As the proofs have hitherto always come safe to hand under the direction of C. Brontë esqre – I have not thought it necessary to request you to change it, but a little mistake having occurred yesterday – I think it will be better to send them to me in future under my <u>real</u> address which is

Miss Brontë
Revd P. Brontë's &c.

I am Gentlemen Yrs trly
CB—

March 28th/46[30]

The 'little mistake' would appear to have been that the parcel of proofs was delivered to one of the male members of the household. As Patrick was now so blind that he was unable to write his own letters and had to use Charlotte as his amanuensis,[31] it seems most probable that Branwell was the accidental recipient. Though Charlotte was later to assert that he never knew that his sisters had published a line, this seems unlikely. Initially, of course, his sisters' pseudonyms would have meant nothing to him, but even if he did not suspect that they were preparing manuscripts for publication, he could not have failed to see the numerous advance copies of their books in the house. He had only to dip into *Poems* to find verses familiar to him from the days when he and Charlotte had worked together on Angria and it needed little imagination to work out that Currer, Ellis and Acton Bell were Charlotte, Emily and Anne Brontë. His friends, with more partisan spirit than accuracy, were later to claim that he boasted of his sister's success with *Jane Eyre* and even that he was the real author of *Wuthering Heights*.[32]

If the parcel of proofs was delivered to Branwell by mistake, it is not surprising that his curiosity should have been aroused and that he made further investigations. Though it is pure supposition, another odd incident may possibly be laid at his door. On 7 May Charlotte told Aylott & Jones, 'I have to mention that your three last communications and the parcel had all been opened – where or by whom, I cannot discover; the paper covering the parcel was torn in pieces and the books were brought in loose.'[33]

It has to be said that Charlotte herself clearly did not suspect Branwell or she would not have told her publishers about the mishap. There were, too, other occasions long after Branwell's death on which parcels and letters from London to Haworth went astray.[34] What makes it possible that Branwell was the culprit this time is that a letter he wrote to J. B. Leyland on 28 April closely reflects the contents of one of the damaged letters from Aylott & Jones. This was a reply to a letter from Charlotte requesting very specific information on how to set about finding a publisher for works of fiction. 'It is evident', Charlotte had written,

that unknown authors have great difficulties to contend with before they can succeed in bringing their works before the public, can you give me any hint as to the way in which these difficulties are best met. For instance, in the present case, where a work of fiction is in question, in what form would a publisher be most likely to accept the M.S. –? whether offered as a work of 3 vols or as tales which might be published in numbers or as contributions to a periodical?

< Is it usual to writ > What publishers would be most likely to receive favourably a proposal of this nature?

Would it suffice to <u>write</u> to a publisher on the subject or would it be necessary to have recourse to a personal interview?

Your opinion and advice on these three points or on any other which your experience may suggest as important – would be esteemed by us a favour[35]

Only a fortnight after this was written, Branwell wrote miserably to J. B. Leyland bemoaning 'the quietude of home, and the inability to make my family aware of the nature of most of my sufferings'.

Literary exertion would seem a resourse, but the depression attendant on it, and the almost hopelessness of bursting through the barriers of literary < cliques > circles, and getting a hearing among publishers, make me disheartened and indifferent; for I cannot write what would be thrown, unread, in to a library fire: Otherwise I have the materials for a respectably sized volume, and if I were in London personally I might perhaps try Henry Moxon – a patronizer of the sons of rhyme; though I dare say the poor man often smarts for his liberality in publishing hideous trash.

As I know that, while here, I might send a manuscript to London, and say goodbye to it I feel it < useless to > folly to feed the flames of a printers fire.

So much for egotism![36]

This letter certainly sounds as if Branwell had read Aylott & Jones' reply to Charlotte and the reference to Moxon, whose edition of Wordsworth's poems had been the original model for his sisters' publication, may be more than coincidental.

If Branwell was aware of the publishing plans going on under his nose at the parsonage then one can understand his increasing alienation from his family. Having once been acknowledged as the pre-eminent poet and the unquestioned leader in all their literary endeavours, he was now reduced to such an object of contempt in his sisters' eyes that they do not seem to have even considered asking him to contribute to their volume. There is no better summary of their attitude to him at this time than the reason Charlotte gave for keeping their publishing ventures a secret from him: 'we could not tell him of our efforts for fear of causing him too deep a pang of remorse for his own time misspent, and talents misapplied'.[37]

In fact, Branwell, though still unemployed, was not without occupation. He had been inspired to write a poem on 'the recent stirring events in India', where the British had nearly been overwhelmed by a Sikh uprising, their commander Sir Robert Sale had been killed and their position only retrieved through the skill of Sir Henry Hardinge. (Curiously enough, the same events inspired Charlotte to make an appropriate adaptation of one of her Angrian poems for publication.) Branwell had intended to set his poem to music and he had in mind one of his favourite tunes, Gluck's 'Mater divinae gratiae'. Recalling an acquaintance from his days on the railways, Branwell wrote to John Frobisher, the organist of Halifax Parish Church, who was also the leader of the Halifax Quarterly Choral Society. 'I dare say you have forgotten both myself and a conversation in which, some years ago, I alluded to a favourite air', he began, before suggesting that Frobisher might like to look the lines over and publish them either as 'Gluck's air adapted to English words by myself' or as his own arrangement. 'I Only chose Gluck's air as a musical accompaniment to the words', he later told Frobisher, 'from a love of the mingled majesty and tenderness of the composition, and not at all from any idea that my rhymes were worthy of the great German composer.'[38]

Branwell may have followed up his letter with a personal visit to Frobisher, for he was in Halifax at the beginning of April. 'I cannot, without a smile at myself, think of my stay for three days in Halifax on a business which need not have occupied three hours', he told Leyland, 'but in truth when I fall back <u>on</u> myself I suffer so much wretchedness that I cannot withstand any temptations to get <u>out</u> of myself.' Branwell's 'business' seems to have included a visit to the *Halifax Guardian* offices where, still vainly searching for employment despite his sister's jibes, he placed an advertisement for a situation that would take him abroad.[39]

He also handed in a poem, 'Letter from a Father on Earth to his Child in her Grave', written on 3 April, which the paper duly published on 18 April 1846. On first glance, this appears to be simply another Angrian poem, particularly as it is signed 'Northangerland' and relates to the death of the writer's daughter. However, unlike all the other Angrian poems Branwell submitted for publication, this one has no precedent dating from the 1830s. It is actually firmly rooted in the present, with topical references to 'April showers' and to 'India's wildest wars'. The subject of the poem is treated in a markedly different fashion from the Angrian poems about death: this is no wild lament for the loss of a loved one which leaves the living desolate. Instead, the grief is calm and measured, tempered by the knowledge that death has at least prevented suffering in future life. As in Branwell's recent poems, like 'Real Rest', it is the living who suffer most. Another curious feature is the frequent and almost irrelevant digression into the author's own feelings.

> I write words to thee which thou wilt not read,
> For thou wilt slumber on howe'er may bleed
> The heart, which many think a worthless stone,
> But which oft aches for its beloved one;

Or again:

> If, then, thoud'st seen, upon a summer sea
> One, once in features, as in blood like thee
> On skies of azure blue and waters green
> Commingled in the mist of summer's sheen,
> Hopelessly gazing – ever hesitating
> 'Twixt miseries, every hour fresh fears creating
> And joys – whate'er they cost – still doubly dear –
> Those 'troubled pleasures soon chastised by fear' –
> If thou hadst seen him thou wouldst ne'er believe
> That thou hadst yet known what it was to live.[40]

This sounds remarkably like the genuine voice of Branwell Brontë describing his affair with Mrs Robinson – even to the point of quoting the same line he had used in his account to Grundy – and it is therefore tempting to regard the poem as autobiographical. If this is the case, then here we have further evidence for the existence of Branwell's illegitimate child and an indication of the possible period of her death. The fact that Branwell can have barely known her and was, in any case, far more preoccupied with his enforced separation from Mrs Robinson, perhaps explains the absence of any great feeling of grief.

> ... thou hadst beauty, innocence and smiles,
> And now hast rest from this world's woes and wiles,
> While I have a restlessness and worrying care,
> So, sure thy lot is brighter – happier – far!
> So may it prove – and, though thy ears may never
> Hear these words sound beyond Death's darksome river
> Not vainly, from the confines of despair
> May rise a voice of joy that THOU art freed from care![41]

In addition to these poems, Branwell had embarked on a major new project which was instigated by J. B. Leyland. This was intended to be an epic poem, relating the history of Morley Hall in Lancashire, which had once belonged to Leyland's ancestors. The two men had made a 'friendly compact' that Branwell would write the poem and Leyland would model a medallion portrait of his friend. Unfortunately, Branwell seems never to have completed his side of the bargain though he was inordinately proud of Leyland's medallion, which made him look like a Roman emperor.[42]

Branwell's output over these months suggests that he was certainly capable of contributing to his sisters' little book of poems and their action in excluding him seems rather petty and mean. He could not afford to pay for the publication of his own work because, unlike them, he had no legacy on which to draw.

On 7 May 1846 the first three copies of *Poems* by Currer, Ellis and Acton Bell arrived at the parsonage. At only 165 pages of text, the little books were even thinner than they had been led to expect and the paper was not the good quality Charlotte had ordered. An errata slip noting four misprints that had slipped through the proofs – all, incidentally, in Charlotte's poems – had had to be included and there were typographical inconsistencies in the contents page. The price, which Charlotte had originally suggested should be five shillings, was set at four shillings and was prominently displayed in gilt letters on the front cover under the title and their names. The thrill of seeing their first book in print must have more than compensated for these minor disappointments. This was no home-made effort like their juvenilia, written by hand and carefully stitched into paper covers, but a properly printed volume, handsomely bound in bottle green cloth with a geometrical design on the front.[43] Here at last was the solid reality resulting from all those years of fevered imagination and frantic scribbling, the culmination of a life's dream.

For Charlotte, however, it was not enough simply to have got into print. What she craved was recognition and the very day that the sisters received their advance copies she wrote to Aylott & Jones requesting them to send copies and advertisements 'as early as possible' to ten leading periodicals and newspapers, including, of course, *Blackwood's Magazine*.[44] 'I should think the success of a work depends more on the notice it receives from periodicals than on the quantity of advertisements', Charlotte told her publishers, and stipulated that they should spend no more than two pounds on advertising. She requested that they would send her copies of any reviews which appeared and only if they were favourable would she consider any further expenditure.[45]

Charlotte had to curb her impatience for nearly two months before the reviewers at last turned their attention to *Poems*, but in the meantime a catastrophe hit the Brontë household which must have driven all thoughts of literary fame from the sisters' minds. It began with an innocent enough announcement in the local York papers: the Reverend Edmund Robinson of Thorp Green had died on Tuesday, 26 May 1846, at the age of forty-six. 'He died as he lived', claimed the obituary, 'in firm & humble trust in his Saviour.'[46] It seems likely that Branwell did not see the notice, for on 1 June he wrote a sonnet which he again titled, in Greek lettering, 'Lydia Gisborne' – Mrs Robinson's maiden name. Ironically, the poem was a calm and reflective piece looking back to his last days at Thorp Green with sorrow rather than hectic grief.

> On Ouse's grassy banks – last Whitsuntide,
>   I sat, with fears and pleasures, in my < mind > soul
>   Commingled, as 'it roamed without controul',
> Oer present hours and through a future wide
> Where love, me thought, should keep, my heart beside
>   Her, whose < own > own prison home I looked upon:
>   But, as I looked, descended summer's sun,
> And did not its descent my hopes deride?
> The sky though blue was soon to change to grey –
> I, on that day, next year must own no smile –
> And as those waves, to Humber far away,
>   Were gliding – so, though that hour might beguile
> My Hopes, they too, < were > to woe's far deeper sea,
> < were passing – passed by, bequeathing tears instead >
> Rolled past the shores of Joy's now dim and distant isle.

Beneath the sonnet he sketched himself, a lonely figure with top hat and cane, standing beneath trees on a hill top looking out across the River Ouse and Vale of York towards Thorp Green. In each of the bottom corners he drew a tombstone, one inscribed 'MEMORIA', memories, and the other 'EHEU', alas. More significantly, like any young man in love, he had toyed with the name of his beloved, rejecting her current name as if he could pretend that her marriage did not exist and writing in the margin in an idle moment 'Lydia Gisborne' and, beneath it, 'Lydia – B—'.[47] As he did so he little imagined that his lover's husband was now dead and that it was now possible for Lydia Gisborne/Robinson to become Lydia Brontë.

When the news eventually filtered through to Haworth, Branwell went almost wild with joy at the prospect of a legitimate union with Mrs Robinson. 'I had reason to hope that ere \very/ long I should be the husband of a Lady whom I loved best in the world', he later told Leyland, 'and with whom, in more than competence, I might live at leisure to try to make myself a name in the world of posterity, without being pestered by the small < by > but countless botherments, which like mosquitoes sting us in the world of workday toil.'[48] To marry the woman he loved and in the process become a gentleman at leisure would, at one stroke, justify all his sufferings and restore him to the good opinion of his family. It was no wonder that he was unable to conceal his glee. Confident that Mrs Robinson loved him as much as he loved her, he waited for her summons to Thorp Green. When the blow fell, therefore, it hit Branwell all the harder because it was so totally unexpected. Charlotte gave a sardonic account of her brother's troubles to Ellen Nussey.

We – I am sorry to say – have been somewhat more harassed than usual lately – The death of Mr Robinson – which took place about three weeks or a month ago – served Branwell for a pretext to throw all about him into hubbub and confusion with his emotions, &c. &c. Shortly after came news from all hands that Mr Robinson had altered his will before he died and effectually prevented all chance of a marriage between his widow and Branwell by stipulating that she should not have a shilling if she ever ventured to reopen any communication with him – Of course he then became intolerable – to papa he allows rest neither day nor night – and he is continualy screwing money out of him sometimes threatening that he will kill himself if it is withheld from him – He says Mrs R— is now insane – that her mind is a complete wreck – owing to remorse for her conduct towards Mr R— (whose end it appears was hastened by distress of mind) – And grief for having lost him. I do not know how much to believe of what he says but I fear she is very ill –[49]

Though Charlotte clearly doubted the truth of Branwell's account, he told the same story consistently to his friends and it seems indisputable that he was merely repeating what he himself had been told by his informants at Thorp Green. Suspicion arises because it was simply not true that Mr Robinson had altered his will to ensure that his widow would get nothing if she 'reopened communication' with Branwell.

Mr Robinson had indeed made a new will, on 2 January 1846, but it was not because he felt his own death was imminent or because he wanted to prevent his widow remarrying. Branwell's name was not even mentioned. Mr Robinson's purpose was actually to punish his eldest daughter, Lydia, for her rash elopement and marriage to the actor Henry Roxby, by cutting her out of his will. The original intention had been that all three daughters, Lydia, Elizabeth and Mary, should benefit from the £6,000 settled by each side of the family on their parents when they married in 1824. The new will treated Lydia as if she did not exist, dividing the Gisborne settlement equally between Elizabeth and Mary on their mother's death and the Robinson money between Elizabeth and Mary, who were to receive £1,000 each, and Edmund junior who was to receive the remaining £4,000. This was the only change made to Mr Robinson's will which, as in the earlier versions of 1825 and 1831, left all his property, valued at some £60,000, in trust for his son. Mrs Robinson herself was appointed a trustee and executor of the will and guardian of the children, together with her brothers-in-law, the Venerable Archdeacon Charles Thorpe and the Member of Parliament William Evans, and the family solicitor, Henry Newton. As was usual in financial settlements of this kind, Mrs Robinson was to have an income from the residue of her husband's estate after his debts had been paid off until she died or until she married again. On remarriage she would also cease to be a trustee, executor or guardian.[50] Such provisions were perfectly normal in the days before the Married Women's Property Act and were intended to protect the inheritance of a son and heir against the interests of a stepfather. It was not their purpose to prevent a widow remarrying, but this was undoubtedly an interpretation that could be put on them in Mr Robinson's case.

The question then arises as to who invented this interpretation. Most authors have been inclined to think that Branwell himself was responsible, arguing that he did so because he needed an excuse for being unable to marry Mrs Robinson, whose romance with him existed solely in his imagination.[51] There can now be little doubt that there was a relationship between them and, equally, it seems much more likely that Mrs Robinson herself would use the will as an excuse for keeping Branwell at arm's length. Her reaction to her daughter's runaway marriage with a penniless actor was to endorse her husband's decision by cutting Lydia out of her own will, so there was little likelihood that Mrs Robinson herself would throw away all for love. Though she had complete control over her father's marriage settlement of £6,000, the income on such a sum would not be sufficient to keep her in the style to which she was accustomed: a pampered woman who could fritter away more than thirty pounds on brooches, shawls and the like in just a single month[52] was not likely to wish to remarry unless her second husband was a man of substance. However captivated by Branwell's attractions, Mrs Robinson was not prepared to risk her comfortable style of life and incur the amusement and contempt of society by marrying a penniless tutor seventeen years her junior.

However obvious this may seem to the modern commentator, it is a measure of the spell she had cast over Branwell that the idea never even occurred to him. It was, however, perfectly clear to Mrs Robinson that it was more important than ever to keep Branwell at a distance and that he must be restrained from doing anything rash that might compromise her. To forestall any act of folly, she therefore took the extraordinary step of sending her coachman, William Allison, to Haworth to give Branwell 'the statement of her case'.[53] If anything points to her guilt in the affair it is surely the fact that she involved so many people as her messengers and go-betweens. She seems to have made confidants not just of her personal maid, Ann Marshall, which might be expected, but also of her medical attendant, Dr Crosby, and, most surprisingly of all, her coachman. William Allison was clearly loyal, however, and was rewarded for his services by being one of the few Thorp Green servants to remain with the family after the household was broken up.[54]

His visit to Haworth was surprisingly indiscreet – indeed, he seems to have almost courted publicity. Instead of calling quietly at the parsonage, he stopped at the Black Bull and sent a messenger to fetch Branwell to him. To the intense interest of the local gossips, the two were closeted together for some time, then Allison paid his bill and left. Nothing was seen or heard of Branwell until about an hour later when a noise 'like the bleating of a calf' was heard; when the curious came to investigate they found Branwell lying 'in a kind of fit', literally prostrated by the unexpected blow to his pride and prospects.[55]

The next day he had recovered sufficiently to send an agonized letter to Leyland: the 'wretched scrawl', so different from Branwell's usual neat hand, covered with crossings out, smudges and ink blots, was eloquent testimony to his distress.

Mr Robinson of Thorp Green is <u>dead</u>, and he has left his widow in a dreadful state of health. She sent the Coachman over to me yesterday, and the account which he gave of her sufferings was enough to burst my heart.

Through the will she is left quite powerless, and her eldest daughter who married imprudently, is cut off without a shilling.

The Executing Trustees detest me, and one declares that if he sees me he will shoot me.

These things I do not care about, but I do care for the life of the one who suffers even more than I do. Her Coachman said it was a pity to see her, for she was only able to kneel in her bedroom in bitter tears and prayers. She has worn herself out in attendance on him, and his conduct during the few days before his death, was exceedingly mild and repentant, but that only distressed her doubly. Her conscience has helped to agonize her, and that misery I am saved from.[56]

Though it defies belief that Mrs Robinson should have admitted her coachman to her bedroom to witness her sufferings, she was clever enough to portray herself in the way most calculated to appeal to Branwell. Stoicism might have earned his respect but extravagant grief struck a chord in his own nature. Just in case Branwell might be tempted to return to Thorp Green to comfort her, Mrs Robinson piled on the agony by staging an interview with Dr Crosby, the details of which she knew he would pass on. 'Well, my dear Sir,' Branwell wrote to Leyland,

I have got my finishing stroke at last – and I feel stunned into marble by the blow.

I have this morning recieved a long, kind and faithful letter from the medical gentleman who attended Mr R. in his last illness and who has \since/ had an interview with one whom I can never forget.

He knows me <u>well</u>, and he pities my case most sincerely – for he declares that though used to the rough ups and downs of this weary world, he shed tears from his heart when he saw the state of that lady and knew what I should feel.

When he mentioned my name she stared at him and fainted. When she recovered she in turns dwelt on her inextinguishable love for me – her horror at having been the first to delude me into wretchedness, and her agony at having been the cause of the death of her husband, who, in his last hours, bitterly repented of his treatment of her.

Her sensitive mind was totally wrecked. She wandered into talking of entering a nunnery; and the Doctor fairly debars me from hope in the future.[57]

While Mrs Robinson cast herself in the role of tragic heroine, threatening madness and retreat into a nunnery, Branwell was genuinely driven to the edge of insanity. He had neither eaten for three days nor slept for four nights after the news of Mr Robinson's death reached him: he had reached such a pitch of anticipation that the dashing of his hopes left him a physical and mental wreck. 'My appetite is lost,' he told Leyland, 'my nights are dreadful, and having nothing to do makes me dwell on past scenes – on her own self, her voice – her person – her thoughts – till I could be glad if God would take me. In the next world I could not be worse than I am in this.'[58] Again, aptly summarizing his plight for the remaining two years of his life, he complained:

What I shall <u>do</u> I know not – I am too hard to die, and too wretched to live. My wretchedness is not about castles in the air, but about stern realities; my hardihood < lit > lies in bodily vigour; but; Dear Sir, my mind sees only a dreary future which I as little wish to enter on, as could a martyr to be bound to the stake.[59]

What he famously did, of course, was to resort to drink in an attempt to drown his sorrows. His exasperated sister complained to Ellen that 'he neither can nor will do anything for himself – good situations have been offered more than once – for which by a fortnight's work he might have qualified himself – but he will do nothing – except drink, and make us all wretched'. One of the 'good situations' was the offer of a place on the Leeds and Manchester Railway, where he had been formerly employed, 'if he would behave more steadily'; but, she declared bitterly, 'he refuses to make an effort, he will not work – and at home he is a drain on every resource – an impediment to all happiness'.[60] As usual she was being unfair to her brother. Even in the midst of telling Francis Grundy of his woes, he did not fail to ask his friend to exert himself on his behalf and help him find employment.[61]

While the attention of the whole household was necessarily fixed on Branwell and his complete collapse, the little book of *Poems* had been doing the rounds of the journals. Two frustrating months of silence had passed since its publication and then suddenly, on 4 July, two anonymous reviews appeared on the same day. Irritatingly, both seemed almost as much exercised by the identity of the mysterious Bells as by the quality of their verse – a problem that was to return with a vengeance to haunt the Brontës when they published their novels. 'No preface introduces these poems to the reader', the *Critic* declared.

Who are Currer, Ellis, and Acton Bell, we are nowhere informed. Whether the triumvirate have published in concert, or if their association be the work of an editor, viewing them as kindred spirits, is not recorded. If the poets be of a past or of the present age, if living or dead, whether English or American, where born, or where dwelling, what their ages or station – nay, what their Christian names, the publishers have not thought fit to reveal to the curious reader.[62]

In attempting to conceal their identity and sex, therefore, the Brontës had unwittingly stimulated the curiosity of the reviewers and created a mystery where none was intended. The reviewer of the *Critic* did at least have the perception to recognize why they had sought anonymity.

Perhaps they desired that the poems should be tried and judged upon their own merits alone, apart from all extraneous circumstances, and if such was their intent, they have certainly displayed excellent taste in the selection of compositions that will endure the difficult ordeal.[63]

Sydney Dobell, writing anonymously in the *Athenaeum*, simply assumed that the Bells were brothers, but he did have the discernment to note the superiority of Ellis' contribution.

The second book on our list furnishes another example of a family in whom appears to run the instinct of song. It is shared, however, by the three brothers – as we suppose them to be – in very unequal proportions; requiring in the case of Acton Bell, the indulgences of affection ... and rising, in that of Ellis, into an inspiration, which may yet find an audience in the outer world. A fine quaint spirit has the latter, which may have things to speak that men will be glad to hear, – and an evident power of wing that may reach heights not here attempted.[64]

The reviewer in the *Critic* was less discriminating and far more fulsome in his praise, delivering as favourable a review of *Poems* as the Brontës could have wished.

... it is long since we have enjoyed a volume of such genuine poetry as this. Amid the heaps of trash and trumpery in the shape of verses, which lumber the table of the literary journalist, this small book of some 170 pages only has come like a ray of sunshine, gladdening the eye with present glory, and the heart with promise of bright hours in store. Here we have good, wholesome, refreshing, vigorous poetry – no sickly affectations, no namby-pamby, no tedious imitations of familiar strains, but original thoughts, expressed in the true language of poetry ... The triumvirate have not disdained sometimes to model after great masters, but then they are *in the manner* only, and not servile copies. We see, for instance, here and there traces of an admirer of Wordsworth, and perhaps of Tennyson; but for the most part the three poets are themselves alone; they have chosen subjects that have freshness in them, and their handling is after a fashion of their own.

While recognizing that the poems were unconventional in form and would not have universal appeal, the reviewer was unstinting in his own praise.

they in whose hearts are chords strung by nature to sympathize with the beautiful and the true in the world without, and their embodiments by the gifted among their fellow men, will recognize in the compositions of Currer, Ellis and Acton Bell, the presence of more genius than it was supposed this utilitarian age had devoted to the loftier exercises of the intellect.[65]

This 'unexpectedly and generously eulogistic' commendation, justifying Charlotte's insistence on publication in the face of her sisters' opposition, clearly went to her head. She wrote hastily to Aylott & Jones authorizing them to spend a further ten pounds on advertisements which were all to quote this passage from the *Critic*'s review and requesting that copies of *Poems* should be sent to a further four journals.[66] If she had hoped that this would stimulate a flow of similarly favourable reviews, she was sadly mistaken. Not a single notice appeared in the press until 10 October, when the *Halifax Guardian*, which must also have been a recipient of a review copy, published Emily's 'Death Scene' in its poetry section, attributing it to 'Ellis's Poems' but without any critical comment.[67] The same month, the *Dublin University Magazine* published the third and last review of *Poems*; again the notice was favourable though not to an extent calculated to make the public rush out and buy the book. The critic, William Archer Butler, Professor of Moral Philosophy at the university, was 'disposed to approve' of the poems, which he characterized with startling inappropriateness as 'uniform in a sort of Cowperian amiability and sweetness'; they were, he declared, 'full of unobtrusive feeling; and their tone of thought seems unaffected and sincere'.[68] By the time this review appeared, however, Charlotte was so grateful for any critical attention whatsoever that she wrote to thank the editor for its inclusion. 'I thank you in my own name and that of my brothers, Ellis and Acton, for the indulgent notice that appeared in your last number of our first, humble efforts in literature', she wrote, before adding her own fulsome tribute to the magazine:

but I thank you far more for the essay on Modern Poetry which preceded that Notice – an essay in which seems to me to be condensed the very spirit of truth and beauty; if all or half your other readers shall have derived from its perusal the delight it afforded to myself and my brothers – your labours have produced a rich result.

After such criticism an author may indeed be smitten at first by a sense of his own insignificance – as we were – but on a second and a third perusal he finds a power and beauty therein which stirs him to a desire to do more and better things – it fulfils the right end of criticism – without absolutely crushing – it corrects and rouses – I again thank you heartily and beg to subscribe myself

Your Constant and grateful reader
Currer Bell.[69]

If *Poems* caused little stir among the critics, it sank without trace as far as readers were concerned. A year after its publication, only two copies had been sold and the sisters took the decision to present some to the authors they admired. In her accompanying letter to J. G. Lockhart, Walter Scott's son-in-law and biographer, Charlotte adopted a satirical tone to conceal the disappointment that its failure had caused.

My relatives Ellis & Acton Bell and myself, heedless of the repeated warnings of various respectable publishers, have committed the rash act of printing a volume of poems.

The consequences predicted have, of course, overtaken us; our book is found to be a drug; no man needs it or heeds it; in the space of a year our publisher has disposed but of two copies and by what painful efforts he succeeded in getting rid of those two – himself only knows.

Before transferring the edition to the Trunk-makers, we have decided on distributing as presents a few copies of what we cannot sell. We beg to offer you one in acknowledgement of the pleasure and profit we have often and long derived from your works.[70]

Similar letters were sent to Alfred Tennyson, Thomas De Quincey and Ebenezer Elliott.[71] Some comfort could be derived from the fact that the few who read *Poems* enjoyed it; in addition to the praise of the reviewers, the sisters also received an unsolicited testimonial from Frederick Enoch, of Cornmarket, Warwick, who was one of the two purchasers of the volume. He wrote to them through Aylott & Jones asking for their autographs and received in reply the unique slip of paper which bears the signatures of Currer, Ellis and Acton Bell.[72]

The complete commercial failure of *Poems* was in many ways an irrelevance to Charlotte. Unlike Emily and Anne, she no longer wrote poetry, so the world's judgement was not something she needed to take to heart. The mechanics of steering the book through the press, which had been entirely Charlotte's domain, had given her a new object in life. As she herself wrote, 'the mere effort to succeed had given a wonderful zest to existence; it must be pursued'.[73] Producing *Poems* had taught valuable lessons: poetry did not sell and it was not economic to pay for the publication of one's own work: if they seriously intended to attempt to earn a living from their writing, then they would have to be a lot more hard-headed about the whole business. The first decision, to write novels, which, as Branwell had pointed out, were the most saleable articles in the current state of the publishing and reading world,[74] was taken long before *Poems* appeared in print. As early as 6 April 1846, Charlotte had been able to tell Aylott & Jones that 'C. E & A Bell are now preparing for the Press a work of fiction – consisting of three distinct and unconnected tales which may be published either together as a work of 3 vols. of the ordinary novel-size, or separately as single vols. –'. By 27 June Charlotte had completed the fair copy of her novel, *The Professor*, and on 4

July she wrote to Henry Colburn, one of the leading London publishers of fiction, offering him 'three tales, each occupying a volume and capable of being published together or separately, as thought most advisable'. 'The authors of these tales', she added with pride, 'have already appeared before the public.'[75]

The 'three tales', over which the sisters had laboured throughout the winter and spring, were *The Professor, Wuthering Heights* and *Agnes Grey*. Returning to the habits of their childhood, the sisters wrote their books in close collaboration, reading passages aloud to each other and discussing the handling of their plots and their characters as they walked round and round the dining-room table each evening.[76] In their choice of subject and in their handling of it, both Charlotte and Emily drew heavily on Angria and Gondal. In Charlotte's case especially, this was a mistake. Contrary to her own belief that the juvenilia had been a valuable apprenticeship in writing, in fact they had trained her in habits which would eventually become anathema to the mature novelist. As she later claimed in a preface to the work, 'in many a crude effort destroyed almost as soon as composed I had got over any such taste as I might once have had for the ornamented and redundant in composition – and had come to prefer what was plain and homely'.

I said to myself that my hero should work his way through life as I had seen real living men work theirs – that he should never get a shilling he had not earned – that no sudden turns should lift him in a moment to wealth and high station – that whatever small competency he might gain should be won by the sweat of his brow … that he should not even marry a beautiful nor a rich wife, nor a lady of rank – As Adam's Son he should share Adam's doom – Labour throughout life and a mixed and moderate cup of enjoyment.[77]

This determination to put Angria behind her and write about the real and the ordinary was somewhat marred in the execution. Indeed, the early chapters – which are the most flawed – with their heavy-handed caricatures of the feuding Crimsworth brothers, set in a Yorkshire mill counting-house, were simply an adaptation of Branwell's Angrian tale, 'The Wool is Rising', written when he was a mere seventeen.[78] Unable to shake off the shackles of Angria, Charlotte fell into her old bad habits of Gothic exaggeration. Edward Crimsworth, for instance, is a crudely drawn character who even resorts to the horsewhip in his perversely vicious behaviour towards his brother. Once she had broken from Branwell's original Angrian scenario and transported her protagonist to Belgium, where she could draw on her own experiences of life as a teacher in a Brussels school, the novel begins to gain a life of its own and the latent power of her writing begins to emerge. As a novelist she was always at her best – her most vivid, energetic and sincere – when she drew on personal experience. It was therefore also a major error to adopt a masculine narrator for *The Professor*. Charlotte was a quintessentially feminine writer: her talents for describing repressed emotion and for accurate observation of the minutiae of daily life were those of the passive observer, a role pre-eminently that of the nineteenth-century woman. Since childhood, however, she had adopted a masculine persona and she was unable to break the habit now: William Crimsworth was simply the Angrian Charles Townshend under another name. Unable to write convincingly as a man, Charlotte retreated behind the comforting familiarity of the sarcastic and frequently flippant shell. In so doing, she destroyed the heart of the novel, for her central character is unreal. In her last novel, *Villette*, Charlotte was to prove that it was possible to have an embittered and uncharismatic but realistic first-person narrator without losing the interest or sympathy of the reader. Whether it was Charlotte herself who finally realized that a female voice was best suited to her talents, or whether this was pointed out to her by her discerning publishers, *The Professor* was the last of her writings to have a male protagonist.

Despite her best intentions, Charlotte was unable to throw off the dead hand of Angria. For Emily, it would seem, there was no such conflict, for without Gondal there was no writing. *Wuthering Heights*, which, ironically, is regarded as the archetypal Yorkshire novel, was actually Gondal through and through and therefore owed as much, if not more, to Walter Scott's Border country as to Emily's beloved moorlands of home. Echoes of his novel *Rob Roy*, for instance, are to be found throughout the book.[79] In *Wuthering Heights* one is irresistibly reminded of *Rob Roy*'s setting in the wilds of Northumberland, among the uncouth and quarrelsome squirearchical Osbaldistones, who spend their time drinking and gambling. The spirited and wilful Cathy has strong similarities with Diana Vernon, who is equally out of place among her boorish relations. Heathcliff, whose unusual name recalls that of the surly Thorncliff, mimics Rashleigh Osbaldistone in his sinister hold over the Earnshaws and Lintons and his attempts to seize their inheritances.

Familiar characters from the juvenilia appear throughout the novel. The fact that many of them seem to be drawn from Angria, as well as Gondal, would appear to suggest the common source of inspiration which lay behind them both. Heathcliff, for example, is a re-creation of the dark, brooding outlaw, Douglas, whose origins were shrouded in mystery and who was doomed from birth to be blighted by fate; sadistic and cruel, Douglas' sole redeeming feature was his passionate love for the ambitious and beautiful queen of Gondal. Cathy, too, is prefigured in the Gondal poetry as the bright-haired, wilful darling of fortune but she also owes much to Branwell's creation, Mary Henrietta Percy, 'with manners – So unsophisticated so natural yet so < generaly? > curiously capricious < and > reserved \and proud/'. The passion and often physical violence of their relationship had been anticipated in Alexander Percy's treatment of his equally spirited wives, Augusta, in Branwell's 'Life' of his hero, and Zenobia, in Charlotte's story 'The Foundling'.[80] The dour, hypocritical manservant, Joseph, is likewise based on Percy's evil genius, Sdeath, who, after numerous transformations, adopts the Yorkshire dialect and canting Calvinism which characterize Joseph.[81] Many of the themes and incidents in the story can be traced back to the Brontës' juvenile writings, from the death-defying love of Heathcliff and Catherine to Heathcliff's deliberate ruin of the Earnshaw and Linton families.[82]

Having spent so much of her life at home, Emily had always been the one most dedicated to, and involved in, her imaginary world. There was no perceivable break between her Gondal writings and her novel; indeed, it seems likely that she went straight from writing her long Gondal poem, 'The Prisoner', to *Wuthering Heights*. Despite its precise use of dates, *Wuthering Heights* is set in an indistinct past and in an imprecise location: though entirely accurate in its depiction of Yorkshire dialect, customs and life, these are also features of the Gondal world. All the things which so shocked the critics when the novel was published were typical of both Gondal and Angria, from the amoral tone to the scenes of drunken debauchery, casual cruelty and passionate love. Like *Poems*, *Wuthering Heights* was presented to an uncomprehending public without preface, introduction or explanation and it was left to Charlotte, ever her sister's apologist, to insist that it was simply a tale of the 'wild moors of the north of England' produced by a 'homebred country girl'.[83] The wilder and darker world of Gondal which had actually bred the novel must remain a secret.

The obvious conclusion is that, unlike her sisters, Emily made no attempt to break with the world of her imagination. Charlotte and Anne, on the other hand, had had their literary efforts continually interrupted and constrained by the demands of earning a living. Anne, in her attempt to write a publishable novel, found inspiration not in the hothouse world of Gondal but in her own quiet and unremarkable life as a governess. Anne seems to have shared Charlotte's belief that her novel should portray the real but, unlike *The Professor*, with its lurid opening chapters, *Agnes Grey* really did portray 'Adam's Son sharing Adam's doom'. Alone of the sisters, Anne chose a female first-person narrator, which was in itself a break with juvenile tradition. How closely she allowed life to dictate art in her depictions of the trials of governess life it is impossible to assess, but the monstrous Bloomfield and Murray households, with their spoilt, tyrannical and malicious children, seem to owe much to Anne's experiences with the Inghams of Blake Hall and the Robinsons of Thorp Green. Unlike Emily, Anne set out her stall with the opening words of her novel: 'All true histories contain instruction', she wrote, before proceeding with her simple tale of virtue rewarded.[84]

Though overshadowed by her sisters' much more dramatic novels – and completely ignored by Charlotte who did not consider it worthy of comment in either her biographical or editorial prefaces to the 1850 reissue of *Wuthering Heights & Agnes Grey* – Anne's first novel had many strengths of its own. Enlivened by a quiet humour, it is a far deadlier exposé of the trials of being a governess than her sister's more famous *Jane Eyre*. It is also the first novel to have a plain and ordinary woman as its heroine. Charlotte is usually credited with this innovation in *Jane Eyre*, which, she told her friends, was written to prove to her sisters that a heroine 'as plain and as small as myself' could be as interesting as their conventionally beautiful ones.[85] Once again Charlotte ignores the fact that in Agnes, Anne had already created just such a heroine.

> I could discover no beauty in those marked features, that pale hollow cheek, and ordinary dark brown hair; there might be intellect in the forehead, there might be expression in the dark grey eyes: but what of that?

To this harsh appraisal of her own appearance, Agnes adds the somewhat bitter corollary:

> It is foolish to wish for beauty. Sensible people never either desire it for themselves or care about it in others. If the mind be but well cultivated, and the heart well disposed, no one ever cares for the exterior.
> So said the teachers of our childhood; and so say we to the children of the present day. All very judicious and proper no doubt; but are such assertions supported by actual experience?[86]

In creating her plain and unassuming heroine, Anne was breaking new ground, but in giving her to the curate, Mr Weston, a man of her own age and station in life, she was more realistic than her sister, who allowed Jane Eyre to win her wealthy employer who was twice her age.

As Charlotte had made clear from the start, the three novels were intended to be published either together, in the three-volume set which was then the standard method of marketing fiction, or as individual volumes. The brown paper parcel containing the novels began 'plodding its weary round in London'[87] at the beginning of July 1846, but it was to be a full year before a publisher expressed any interest. The difficulty of getting published for the first time was compounded by the fact that the Brontës expected to be paid for their work. Emily had also unwittingly contributed to their problems by producing a manuscript which was far too long for either of the proposed formats. *Wuthering Heights* on its own filled two volumes, making a three-volume set impractical unless one of the other two novels was dropped. Though it is possible she may have originally intended to write *Wuthering Heights* in one volume,[88] the complex structure and neat resolution of the plot suggest that she simply miscalculated the conversion of manuscript pages to print, as had happened with *Poems*. For the moment, however, the sisters could derive satisfaction from the fact that they had each completed a novel, as they waited with anxious anticipation to discover how they were received.

The possibility of earning a living from writing had become more important over the last few months as Patrick's health declined and it became increasingly obvious that Branwell was unlikely ever to be in a position where he could keep his sisters. Patrick was now almost totally blind. Though he could still deliver sermons which lasted exactly half an hour, he had to be led to the pulpit and had been compelled to delegate virtually all his pastoral duties to his curate.[89] Fortunately, in Arthur Bell Nicholls he had a willing and able assistant on whom he could rely completely. His frequent visits to the parsonage to consult with his rector did not go unnoticed in the village, however, and Charlotte was indignant to find that she had to defend herself to Ellen Nussey.

Who gravely asked you whether Miss Brontë was not going to be married to her papa's Curate'? I scarcely need say that never was rumour more unfounded – it puzzles me to think how it could possibly have originated – A cold, far-away sort of civility are the only terms on which I have ever been with Mr Nicholls – I could by no means think of mentioning such a rumour to him even as a joke – it would make me the laughing-stock of himself and his fellow-curates for half a year to come – They regard me as an old maid, and I regard them, one and all, as highly uninteresting, narrow and unattractive specimens of the 'coarser sex'.

In the same letter, Charlotte was called upon to advise her friend on whether she should leave home to earn her bread by 'Governess drudgery' or stay there to look after her aged mother, thereby 'neglecting <u>for the present</u> every prospect of independency for yourself and putting up with daily inconvenience – sometimes even with privations'. In an interesting commentary on her own situation, Charlotte wrote:

The right path is that which necessitates the greatest sacrifice of self-interest – which implies the greatest good to others – and this path steadily followed will lead <u>I believe</u> in time to prosperity and to happiness though it may seem at the outset to tend quite in a contrary direction – Your Mother is both old and infirm; old and infirm people have few sources of happiness – fewer almost than the comparatively young and healthy can conceive – to deprive them of one of these is cruel – If your Mother is more composed when you are with her – stay with her – If she would be unhappy in case you left her – stay with her – It will not apparently, as far [as] shortsighted humanity can see – be for your advantage to remain at Brookroyd – nor will you be praised and admired for remaining at home to comfort your Mother – Yet probably your own Conscience will approve you and if it does – stay with her. I recommend you to do – what I am trying to do myself.[90]

Though this advice was somewhat disingenuous, in that the problems of living at home could never exceed the privations of being a governess for Charlotte, there is no doubt that she was offering a candid opinion and that she genuinely believed that she was making a sacrifice in staying at Haworth. Ever an active man, both physically and mentally, Patrick's increasing disablement must have made him not only depressed but also difficult and demanding. When he could no longer read or write for himself, nor even walk down the street to his church without assistance, it is not surprising that he needed more of his daughters' time. His sense of helplessness could only have been compounded by his physical inability to exert any sort of control over Branwell, whose complete moral and mental breakdown must have caused his father untold anguish. There was frustration, too, that he could not play his full part in the parish. At the beginning of the year there had been a subscription fund to organize in favour of the Quarter of a Million League Fund and a new headmaster to appoint to Haworth Free Grammar School. The long-awaited new peal of bells for the church had arrived and, on 10 March, their installation was celebrated with a change ringing competition and a dinner at the Black Bull in the evening.[91] On Whit Monday Patrick had delivered his annual sermon to the Sunday school teachers and children, but had been obliged to forgo the customary processional walk through the village; in the afternoon his place was taken by the Reverend James Cheadle, vicar of Bingley, who preached to 230 members of the Oddfellows in Haworth Church. Again, a couple of weeks later, he was obliged to miss the ceremonial laying of the foundation stone for a new National School at Oxenhope, though this was a project that had been very dear to his heart.[92] His pastoral duties were also severely curtailed at just the time when they were most needed: though not as bad as during the terrible years early in the decade, the poor state of trade and the consequent decline in wages was a source of misery and privation in the township. Many of his parishioners were unable to pay their rates and, when summoned before the Keighley magistrates, could only plead absolute poverty. One woman had only 4/6d. – only marginally more than the price of the sisters' volume of *Poems* – on which to support herself, her husband and two children each week.[93]

On a more positive note, however, Patrick was able to join in the celebrations at the beginning of Haworth Rush-Bearing week. His old Evangelical friend, the Reverend Thomas Crowther, returned to Haworth to give the annual Sunday school sermons on 19 July, raising over twenty-five pounds through the collections, and he stayed overnight in order to attend an oratorio in the church the following day. The oratorio was held for the benefit of Thomas Parker, the celebrated Haworth tenor, who sang with Mrs Sunderland from the Halifax concerts and a great variety of instrumental and choral performers. It was a sad commentary on the bigotry now so rampant in Haworth that the concert was boycotted by all the Puseyite clergy of the district – including, apparently, Patrick's curate, Arthur Bell Nicholls – because Parker was a Baptist. For this reason alone it was gratifying that the church was 'crowded to suffocation' and Patrick, 'the venerable incumbent ... who is now totally blind', made a point of sitting prominently in the west gallery with his like-minded clerical friends, Thomas Crowther and Thomas Brooksbank Charnock, and the head of his church trustees, Joseph Greenwood, J. P.[94] Though not mentioned in the newspaper reports of the occasion it seems likely that Charlotte, Branwell, Emily and Anne were also present for they would not have missed an oratorio on their own doorstep. On the Tuesday, 21 July, Patrick had also the gratification of hearing the half-yearly public examination of scholars in the National School at Haworth which furnished proof of the flourishing state of the school he had established. A week later, however, he was a prominent absentee from the Sunday school anniversary celebrations at Newsholme, a tiny hamlet near Oakworth, where the neighbouring clergy, including Arthur Bell Nicholls, Mr Grant of Oxenhope, the vicar of Keighley and his curate, Mr Egglestone, turned out in force.[95]

Compelled to absent himself from so many of the activities in the chapelry, these were indeed 'mournful days – when Papa's vision was wholly obscured – when he could do nothing for himself and sat all day-long in darkness and inertion'. Patrick's blindness was now so far advanced that an operation had become a necessity and, with this in mind, Charlotte and Emily 'made a pilgrimage' to Manchester at the beginning of August to find a suitable surgeon.[96] The operation was too delicate to be entrusted to a general surgeon like William Carr, whom Charlotte had consulted in Gomersal earlier in the year, or one of Patrick's old physician friends in Bradford or Leeds. Manchester had not only a pioneering and nationally famous infirmary, but also flourishing medical schools and a specialist eye hospital. Charlotte and Emily seem to have made their way there and, more by good fortune than choice, they were referred to William James Wilson, a founder of the eye hospital, former President of the Manchester Medical Society and recently elected Honorary Fellow of the Royal College of Surgeons.[97] They could not have fallen into better hands. Mr Wilson was associated with both the infirmary in Piccadilly and the eye hospital in St Mary's, but he also had a 'large and highly respectable' practice in the town. As Patrick was not admitted to either hospital, he must have consulted Mr Wilson privately in his rooms at No. 72, Mosley Street. Not surprisingly, Mr Wilson refused to commit himself to surgery until he had examined Patrick's eyes for himself, and Charlotte promised to return in about three weeks' time with her father.[98]

Charlotte and Patrick arrived in Manchester on Wednesday, 19 August, and saw Mr Wilson immediately; he pronounced Patrick's eyes 'quite ready' for the operation, fixed it for the following Monday and considerably cheered his patient by offering a very favourable prognosis. The first night was spent in a hotel, but the next day they moved into lodgings recommended by Mr Wilson at No. 83, Mount Pleasant, Boundary Street, off the Oxford Road, which were to be their home for at least the next month. The lodgings were kept by an old servant of his but she was away in the country recuperating from a serious illness and, to her consternation, Charlotte found herself in charge of all their boarding arrangements. Though she had helped around the parsonage, particularly with the ironing and bedmaking, she had always been content to leave all the catering to Emily. In a panic she wrote to Ellen for advice.

I find myself excessively ignorant – I can't tell what the deuce to order in the way of meat – &c I wish you or your Sister Ann could give me some hints about how to manage – For ourselves < we > I could < man > contrive papa's diet is so very simple – but there will be a nurse coming in a day or two – and I am afraid of not having things good enough for her – Papa requires nothing you know but plain beef & mutton, tea and bread and butter but a nurse will probably expect to live much better – give me some hints if you can –[99]

If Patrick was apprehensive, he did not show it. On the day of the operation Mr Wilson and the two surgeons who assisted him 'seemed surprised' at his 'extraordinary patience and firmness', Charlotte told Ellen.[100] Just how extraordinary that patience and firmness were can only be appreciated when one knows that the whole operation, which lasted a quarter of an hour and involved the complete extraction of the left lens, was conducted without anaesthetic. The courageous old man, nearly seventy years of age, not only endured the physical pain without flinching or complaint, but even took such an interest in the proceedings that he later made notes in the margin of his copy of Graham's *Modern Domestic Medicine*.

Belladonna a virulent poison – was first applied, twice, in order to expand the pupil – this occasioned very acute pains for only about five seconds – The feeling, under the operation – which lasted fifteen minutes, was of a burning nature – but not intolerable – as I have read is generally the case, in surgical operations. My lens was <u>extracted</u> so that cataract can < not > never return in that eye –[101]

'Mr Wilson entirely disapproves of couching', Charlotte wrote sternly to Ellen, as if rebuking her for her surgeon cousin's advice to remove only the cataract.[102] Mr Wilson had also explained that he would only perform the operation on one eye in case infection set in and completely destroyed the sight. The greatest care was taken to avoid this.

I was confined on my back – a month in a dark room, with bandages over my eyes for the greater part of the time – and had a careful nurse, to attend me both night, & day – I was bled with 8 leeches, at one time, & 6, on another, (these caused but little pain) in order to prevent, inflammation –

In a marginal note Patrick added, 'Leeches must be put on the <u>temples</u>, and not on the <u>eyelids</u>.'[103]

While Patrick lay quietly in his darkened room waiting and praying for the restoration of his sight, Charlotte found herself with time on her hands. The nurse was efficient and, despite her previous fears about the housekeeping, there was little for Charlotte to do; she could not even cheer her father by talking to him, for initially Patrick was to speak and be spoken to as little as possible. She herself was suffering from a raging toothache which had troubled her on and off for over a month; it flared up again as soon as she got to Manchester and added sleepless nights to her already long and wearisome days.[104] Charlotte took refuge, as she had always done, in her imagination. She began to write *Jane Eyre*.

Chapter Eighteen

THREE TALES

*Cur
Bell*

Ellis Bell

Acton Bell

Though it is tempting to see *Jane Eyre* as the result of some inspirational flash of genius, in fact the ideas for the novel had been floating around in Charlotte's head for some time. Gateshead Hall and the St John Rivers scenario had been the subject of manuscript fragments she had written as long ago as 1844 and Rochester himself, with his pride and sarcastic wit, his string of past mistresses, illegitimate child and overwhelming attractiveness to women was a re-creation of her childhood hero, Zamorna, in all but his physical appearance. A single new element came into play, however, which was to transform this unpromising rehash of Angrian material into one of the greatest novels ever written in the English language. Perhaps learning from her Brussels chapters in *The Professor,* Charlotte began to draw on personal experience to flesh out her characters and scenes. Jane Eyre's childhood sufferings at Lowood School at the hands of Mr Brocklehurst were a searing and immediately recognizable indictment of Carus Wilson's Clergy Daughters' School. In the saintly Helen Burns, too, she drew from life, taking as a model her eldest sister, Maria. Ironically, this was the one character the reviewers were to find fault with, considering her too good to be true, though Charlotte staunchly defended her. 'You are right in having faith in the reality of Helen Burns's character:' she told William Smith Williams, 'she was real enough: I have exaggerated nothing there: I abstained from recording much that I remember respecting her, lest the narrative should sound incredible."

Because the novel began with such an intensely personal re-creation of Charlotte's deeply harrowing days at the Clergy Daughters' School, bound up as it was with a reliving of the terrible anger and grief caused by her sisters' deaths, *Jane Eyre* opened with a passion that had been totally absent from all her earlier literary efforts. It was an emotion that was to sweep through the entire novel, from the young Jane's violent denunciations of the injustices inflicted on her to the adult's equally spirited declaration of her own self-worth:

Do you think I can stay to become nothing to you? Do you think I am an automaton? – a machine without feelings? and can bear to have my morsel of bread snatched from my lips, and my drop of living water dashed from my cup? Do you think, because I am poor, obscure, plain, and little, I am soulless and heartless? – You think wrong! – I have as much soul as you, – and full as much heart! And if God had gifted me with some beauty, and much wealth, I should have made it as hard for you to leave me, as it is now for me to leave you. I am not talking to you now through the medium of custom, conventionalities, nor even of mortal flesh:– it is my spirit that addresses your spirit; just as if both had passed through the grave, and we stood at God's feet, equal, – as we are!²

Through the medium of her creation, Charlotte was at last able to articulate all the pent-up emotion which had been fermenting in her soul for the last four or five years. She could not declare her love for Monsieur Heger in such shameless terms, but her heroine could and would. Like Monsieur Heger, Mr Rochester was married, and Jane, like Charlotte, would take the moral line and flee from temptation; but Jane, unlike Charlotte, would eventually win her man. In the essential morality of the tale – so unlike Charlotte's Angrian writing – whereby the heroine unwittingly sins by falling in love with a married man, suffers in separating from him and is redeemed and rewarded in the end – it was almost as if Charlotte was trying to prove to herself and Branwell that she had taken the right path. The alternative to tearing oneself away from a married lover was to subject oneself to 'a constant phantom, or rather two – Sin and Suffering':³ in Branwell she had an object lesson of her own fate had she given in to her inclinations.

In the uncongenial surroundings of the narrow, red-brick terraces of urban Manchester, Charlotte began the first draft of her new novel in her customary fashion, using a pencil to write in little square paper books which she had to hold close to her eyes because of her shortsightedness.⁴ She wrote steadily for the five weeks she remained in Manchester, her work providing a welcome relief from anxiety about her father's slow progress. Mr Wilson had expressed confidence from the start, however, and five days after the operation Patrick's bandages were removed. He could only see dimly but 'Mr Wilson seemed perfectly satisfied, and said all was right.' Two weeks later Patrick's sight was still weak and his eyes sore, but he was able to sit up for most of the day in his darkened room. By 22 September, after agitating for over three weeks, Charlotte was finally given permission by Mr Wilson to dismiss the nurse, whom she had found 'too obsequious &c. and not I should think to be much trusted'.[5] Within a week they were at home, their release hastened by Mr Wilson's departure for Scotland. Once on familiar territory, Patrick rapidly regained his strength and, to his infinite joy, gradually recovered his sight. 'Through divine mercy, and the skill of the surgeon, as well as my Dr Ch's attention, and the assiduity of the nurse –', he recorded in the margin of his *Modern Domestic Medicine*, 'after a year of nearly total < blindness > blindness – I was so far restored to sight, as to be able to read, and write, and find my way, without a guide –'. When he totted up the expenses of the whole operation he discovered it had cost him nearly fifty pounds, a quarter of his annual salary. This was despite the fact that Mr Wilson had generously remitted most of his fee, charging him only ten pounds instead of his usual twenty or thirty. The rooms had cost £1.5s. a week, the nurse 15/- a week and there had been their own and her board to find as well.[6] From every point of view, however, the expense had been fully justified. By November he was so far recovered that Arthur Bell Nicholls was able to return home to Ireland for a well-earned three-week holiday, leaving Patrick to perform all three Sunday services and conduct the baptisms and burials which occurred in his absence.[7]

Once at home – and relieved to find that there had been no crisis with Branwell in her absence – Charlotte pressed on with her novel. As the work progressed, her interest grew and by the time she had got Jane to Thornfield Hall, she could not stop writing. Harriet Martineau, repeating what Charlotte herself had told her, described how she was completely caught up in the story.

On she went, writing incessantly for three weeks; by which time she had carried her heroine away from Thornfield, and was herself in a fever, which compelled her to pause. The rest was written with less vehemence, and with more anxious care. The world adds, with less vigour and interest.[8]

Remembering that her previous attempt to make her hero a son of Adam, sharing Adam's doom, had signally failed to attract a publisher's attention, she deliberately reverted to 'the wild wonderful and thrilling – the strange, startling and harrowing'.[9] The inspiration for Rochester's mad wife, locked up in the attics of Thornfield Hall, came from a number of sources, including a local story of a house on the borders of the parishes of Haworth and Oakworth where, according to the Oakworth curate, James Chesterton Bradley, the insane wife of the owner was kept incarcerated. Her depiction of the nature of Bertha's madness, with its venom and violence directed chiefly against her husband, seems to have owed at least something to Ellen Nussey's confidences about her brother George. Recently confined in a private asylum near York run by the enlightened Dr Belcombe, George's condition varied considerably. He was visited by Ellen just at the time Charlotte was writing the Thornfield chapters and her account of his behaviour obviously intrigued Charlotte: '[h]is delusion is one of the most painful kind for his relations. How strange that in his eye affection should be transformed into hatred. It is as if the mental vision were inverted and such is no doubt the case. The change in his brain distorts all impressions.'[10] Henry Nussey's pragmatic offer of marriage provided the model for St John Rivers' proposal, from which Jane was only saved by the magical intervention, in the truest tradition of Charlotte's Angrian tales, of Rochester's spirit calling aloud to hers across the miles that separated them.

While Charlotte continued to write at white heat, Emily and Anne seem to have been less than enthusiastic about writing a second novel in the face of the general rejection of their first. Both retreated into the comfortable privacy of Gondal where no one but themselves could read and judge their efforts. Anne wrote several long poems after sending off her manuscript and it is clear from their content that she was engaged in a prose narrative to which they belonged. The poems were on familiar themes: the prisoner mourning the loss of his freedom and his love; childhood friends torn apart by politics to become bitter enemies; the disconsolate lover.[11] Emily, too, seems to have turned back with relief to Gondal. Her only surviving poem from this period is a long companion piece to one by Anne, written on the same day and on the same subject. Emily's poem depicts the remorse of the captor who has killed his prisoner's infant daughter and taunted him as he lay dying only to have him return good for evil by saving the life of the captor's only son.[12] Though there was undoubtedly solace in going back to Gondal, neither sister seems to have recaptured the quality of verse which they had so markedly achieved prior to their attempts at publication.

If Emily and Anne seem to have rather lost their way in the autumn of 1846, this was doubly true of Branwell. Utterly crushed by the removal of his last hopes regarding Mrs Robinson, he seems to have given himself up to drink. Aware of the disapproval at home and possibly wishing to spare his recuperating father, Branwell seems to have spent much of his time in Halifax with J. B. Leyland.[13] He even briefly took up residence at a public house, the Ovenden Cross, just outside Halifax on the Keighley road. The innkeeper, John Walton, had nine children and the eldest of these, twenty-year-old Mary, obviously fell for Branwell's charms. Though she was later to call him 'an inveterate drunkard' and a 'lamentable instance of what a man becomes who trusts for happiness in earthly things alone', at the time she appears to have sought out his company and got him to write and sketch entries in the commonplace book she kept.[14]

As Mary Walton pointed out, Branwell's contribution reflected his distempered state of mind. Beneath his sonnet 'Why hold young eyes the fullest fount of tears' he drew a haggard and gloomy man's face which he labelled 'The results of Sorrow'. He also copied out a more recent sonnet, 'When all our cheerful hours seem gone for ever', which he had first sent to Leyland on 28 April 1846. Below it he sketched a churchyard with a tombstone in the foreground on which he had drawn a skull and crossbones and written 'I IMPLORE FOR REST'. Interestingly, he was to quote the same lines in Latin a few weeks later in a letter to Leyland, where he described them as being an Italian epitaph.[15] On another page he sketched a head and shoulders portrait of 'Alexander Percy Esqr M.P.', quoting below it the lines from Lord Byron,

> No more – no more – Oh never more on me
> The freshness of the heart shall fall like dew,
> Which, out of all the lovely things we see
> Extracts emotions beautiful and new![16]

Branwell, unlike his sisters, had never had any reluctance to share his imaginary world with his friends and acquaintances and one can well imagine that the sketch of Percy was done to explain his own use of the Northangerland pseudonym to the assembled crowd in the taproom. Branwell's final entry in the book was a profile sketch of himself, looking grimmer and more gaunt than his earlier self-portraits, above the lines

> Think not that life is happiness,
> But deem it <u>duty</u> joined with <u>care</u>.
> Implore for <u>Hope</u> in your distress,
> And for your answer get <u>Despair</u>.
> Yet travel on, for Life's rough road
> May end, at last, in rest with GOD.
>
> Northangerland.[17]

Below this poem he drew a man kneeling on a rock, shielding his eyes from the sight of a sinking ship. Next to Branwell's manuscript entries, Mary stuck in several newspaper cuttings, including ones of his most recently published poems, 'Penmaenmawr' and 'Letter from a Father on Earth to his Child in her Grave'.[18] Clearly, Mary Walton admired the talents of her visitor then, even if in later life she felt obliged to adopt a more prim and pious line.

Branwell's habit of mixing verse and sketches was becoming more pronounced as he slipped further into alcoholic excess. Some of his letters to Leyland at this time are virtually incomprehensible as he flits from topic to topic, illustrating his witticisms with appropriate little pen and ink sketches.

Constant and unavoidable depression of mind and body sadly shackle me in even <u>trying</u> to go on with any mental effort which might rescue me from the fate of a dry toast soaked six hours in a glass of cold water, and intended to be given to an old Maid's squeamish Cat.
Is there really such a thing as the 'Risus Sardonicus' – the Sardonic laugh.? Did a man ever laugh the morning he was \to be/ hanged – ?[19]

The drinking could not go on, however, if only because Branwell could not finance what had now become a habit. Even his friends and the accommodating landlords of what he called 'the ensnaring town of Halifax'[20] could not supply him with drinks for nothing or on credit for ever and in the end there had to be a reckoning. It came at the beginning of December, as Charlotte reported with heavy sarcasm to Ellen, who was staying with her brother Joshua at Oundle.

You say I am 'to tell you plenty'. What would you have me to say – nothing happens at Haworth – nothing at least of a pleasant kind – one little incident indeed occurred about a week ago to sting us to life – but if it gives no more pleasure for you to hear than it did for us to witness – you will scarcely thank < you > me for adverting to it –
It was merely the arrival of a Sheriff's Officer on a visit to Branwell – inviting him either to pay his debts or to take a trip to York – Of course his debts had to be paid – it is not agreeable to lose money time after time in this way but it is ten times worse – to witness the shabbiness of his behaviour on such occasions – But where is the use of dwelling on this subject – it will make him no better.[21]

Charlotte's bitterness was, for once, entirely understandable, though one gets the impression that she thought a spell in the debtor's prison at York might be just what Branwell needed to bring him back to his senses. That was a public humiliation which the parson and his family could not afford, however often they had to bail out the errant black sheep.
Certainly Charlotte was right to think that Branwell could not now reform. Within a few weeks of the visit from the Sheriff's Officer, Branwell was already expressing concern about his unpaid bills at the Old Cock in Halifax and mysteriously promising that 'the moment that I recieve my outlaid cash, or any sum which may fall into my hands through the hands of one whom I may never see again, I shall settle it'.[22] The undoubted inference of this remark is that Branwell had applied directly or indirectly to Mrs Robinson for financial aid. This is borne out by a long and rambling letter to Leyland written in the new year of 1847.

This last week an honest and kindly friend has warned me that concealed hopes about one lady < may > \should/ be given up let the effort to do so cost what it may. He is the Family medical attendant, and was commanded by Mr Evans M.P for North Derbyshire to return me, unopened, a letter which I addressed to Throp[sic] Green and which the Lady was not permitted to see.[23]

It surely cannot be coincidence that Dr Crosby's letter was followed almost immediately by one from Ann Marshall; it appears that Mrs Robinson was making doubly sure that Branwell heard what she wanted him to hear and that he was kept away from her by fair means or foul. The receipt of Ann Marshall's letter, while he was actually writing to Leyland, was enough to tip Branwell over from bitter self-pity into hysteria: even his handwriting changes dramatically from his usual neat, rounded script to an increasingly untidy and illegible scrawl.

I have recieved to day, since I begun my scrawl – a note from her maid Miss Ann Marshall and I <u>know</u> from it that she has been terrified by vows which she was forced to swear to, on her husband's deathbed, (with every < ghastly > addition of terror which the ghastly dying eye could inflict upon a keenly sensitive and almost <u>worried</u> woman's mind) a complete severance from him in whom lay her whole hearts feelings – When that husband was scarce cold in his grave her relations, who controlled the whole property overwhelmed her with their tongues, and I am <u>quite</u> <u>conscious</u> that she has succumbed in terror, to what they have said.[24]

It is a measure of how well Mrs Robinson knew Branwell that – even at second-hand – she was able to manipulate him so completely. Once more she had been able to avert the possible disaster which his unsolicited letter might have provoked by playing her role as the put-upon widow, distracted by grief and conscience. The least she could do in such circumstances was secretly to send money to her former lover and it seems that this was one occasion on which Branwell received, through Dr Crosby's hands, the sum of twenty pounds.[25]

The realization now finally dawned on Branwell that whatever hopes he might have clung to regarding Mrs Robinson, their separation was final and irrevocable. He had to face some unpleasant home truths.

I have been in truth too much petted through life, and in my last situation I was so much master, and gave myself so much up to enjoyment that now when the cloud of ill health and adversity has come upon me it will be a disheartning job to work myself up again through a new lifes battle, from the position of five years ago to which I have been compelled to retreat with heavy loss and no gain. My army stands now where it did then, but mourning the slaughter of Youth, Health, Hope and both mental and physical elasticity.

The last two losses are indeed important to one who once built his hopes of rising in the world < to > on the possession of them. Noble writings, works of art, music or poetry now instead of rousing my imagination, cause a whirlwind of blighting

Sorrow that sweeps over my mind with unspeakable dreariness, and if I sit down and try to write all ideas that used to come clothed in sunlight now press round me in funeral black; for really every pleasureable excitement that I used to know has changed to insipidity or pain.

I shall never be able to realize the too sanguine hopes of my friends, for at 28 I am a thouroghly <u>old man</u> – mentally and bodily – Far more so indeed than I am willing to express…

My rude rough aquaintances here ascribe my unhappiness solely to causes produced by my sometimes irregular life, because they have known no other pains than those resulting from excess or want of ready cash – They do not know that I would rather want a shirt than want a springy mind, and that my < my > total want of happiness, were I to step into York Minster now, would be far, far worse than their want of an hundred pounds when they might happen to need it; and that if a dozen glasses or a bottle of wine drives off their cares, such cures only make me outwardly passable in company but <u>never</u> drive off mine.

He summed up his despair in haunting words that could well serve as an epitaph for his last two years of life.

<u>I</u> know, only that it is time for me to be something when I am nothing. That My father cannot have long to live, and that when he dies my evening, which is already twilight, will become night – That I shall then have a constitution still so strong that it will keep me years in torture and despair when I should every hour pray that I might die.[26]

Armed with Mrs Robinson's money and desperate to escape the censorious atmosphere of the parsonage, Branwell set about the wilful destruction of his bodily health in the inns of Haworth and Halifax. Though he believed that, like Northangerland, his constitution could withstand any excess, the onset of dependence on alcohol and opiates signalled his slow decline into terminal illness.

Forced to watch Branwell slipping into the abyss created by his inability to control himself, Charlotte fought even harder against her own propensity to excessive emotion and self-indulgence. She recognized also that his depression, like hers, was as much a physical as a mental illness; however, as she told Mary Taylor, knowing the cause did not remove the feeling.[27] In the face of her rebellious spirit, she clung to the two rocks of duty and conscience. Obliged to turn down an offer from Ellen Nussey to set up a school together, she explained:

if I <u>could</u> leave home Ellen – I should not be at Haworth now – I know life is passing away and I am doing nothing – earning nothing a very bitter knowledge it is at moments – but I see no way out of the mist – More than one very favourable opportunity has now offered which I have been obliged to put aside – probably when I am free to leave home I shall neither be able to find place nor employment – perhaps too I shall be quite past the prime of life – my faculties will be rusted – and my few acquirements in a great measure forgotten – These ideas sting me keenly sometimes – but whenever I consult my Conscience it affirms that I am doing right in staying at home – and bitter are its upbraidings when I yield to an eager desire for release – I returned to Brussels after Aunt's death against my conscience – prompted by what then seemed an irresistible impulse – I was punished for my selfish folly by a total withdrawal for more than two years of happiness and peace of mind – I could hardly expect success if I were to err again in the same way –

Echoing her brother's words a few months later, in a way that confirms the affinity they had shared since childhood, she told Ellen:

I shall be 31 next birthday – My Youth is gone like a dream – and very little use have I ever made of it – What have I done these last thirty years –? Precious little –[28]

The weather, which had been unusually mild all year, turned savage at its close. Writing to Ellen on 13 December 1846, Charlotte complained:

the cold here is dreadful I do not remember such a series of North-Pole-days – England might really have taken a slide up into the Arctic Zone – the sky looks like ice – the earth is frozen, the wind is as keen as a two-edged blade – I cannot keep myself warm –[29]

A consequence of the change in the weather was that all the Brontës caught severe colds and coughs, deteriorating in Patrick's case into influenza and Anne's into asthma. Unaware that this was merely a poignant foretaste of what was to come, Charlotte sympathetically described Anne's sufferings:

she had two nights last week when her cough and difficulty of breathing were painful indeed to hear and witness and must have been most distressing to suffer – she bore it as she does all affliction – without one complaint – only sighing now and then when nearly worn out – she has an extraordinary heroism of endurance, I admire but I certainly could not imitate her.[30]

In Haworth, too, there was great hardship. Wages had been low all year in consequence of the depression in trade and yet the price of bread and potatoes, the staple diet of the poor, was unusually high. By August, the powerloom workers and wool-combers of the district were coming out on strike but, as demand was so low, the manufacturers were able to hold out for over three months. The long and bitter strike was only brought to a close at the end of November through the mediation of Frederick Greenwood of Rishworth Hall and, even then, the wool-combers were obliged to continue supplying at their old prices with only the promise of an increase in the new year if there was a general improvement in trade. The consequences of the strike – in which Patrick is said to have supported the men against their masters[31] – were manifold: in Haworth and Stanbury a Wool-combers' Protective Society was formed to give the cottage industry a united front in its dealings with the manufacturers, and there was a revival of agitation for a

Ten Hours Bill and a repeal of the Corn Laws, with public meetings addressed by Richard Oastler in Keighley and petitions to Parliament.[32]

Of the greatest consequence for the Brontës, however, was a general decline in health caused by the poverty of the mill-hands and wool-combers, the poor quality of their home and working conditions and the high price of provisions. Such was the concern in Keighley about the rising mortality rates that, after much lobbying by John Milligan, the surgeon, supported by the local wool-combers, the rector and his curate began an investigation into the sanitary conditions of the town. It seems likely, now that his sight was restored and given his interest in medical matters, his concern for the poor and his friendship with the pioneering surgeon, that Patrick attended Milligan's three lectures to the Keighley Mechanics' Institute in February and March 1847 on the subject of public health and sanitary conditions in large towns. Among other startling statistics, Milligan revealed that the average age at death in Keighley varied considerably according to class and occupation, rising from a mere nineteen for wool-combers to thirty-eight for widows and spinsters. It was a symptom of the times that an effort to raise a public subscription for the distressed poor in Keighley failed because it was generally felt that relief should be given from public rates and not private charity.[33]

The restoration of Patrick's sight had given him a new lease of life, though he declined to attend a farewell tea in Bradford for Dr Scoresby, whose ill health had compelled him to resign. The new vicar, John Burnett, was to be a less abrasive and controversial figure but, on the other hand, he did not have his predecessor's energy and commitment to reform. A bad cold prevented him reading himself in and officially taking up office for over a month.[34] Perhaps for this reason, when Scoresby's plan for the division of the parish finally obtained Parliamentary approval and Oxenhope became a separate parish in its own right, it was Archdeacon Musgrove from Halifax who preached at the opening service held in the newly built National School and not the Reverend John Burnett. Patrick himself came the following week to preach the afternoon service in support of his former curate, Joseph Grant, now the incumbent of the new parish.[35]

Patrick returned with quiet pleasure to his former preoccupation of writing to the press. On 23 March 1847, he took up his pen in support of the Government's plan for a system of compulsory national education; his letter, published in the *Leeds Intelligencer*, called for an end to the sectarian opposition to the teaching of religion, which threatened to undermine the whole scheme. If this course of opposition was pursued

it will be recorded in men's minds and the imperishable pages of history, that a class of professing Christians, in highly favoured England, in the nineteenth century, opposed with all their might the best plan ever devised, or that could be devised, for the universal spread of divine knowledge, and useful science.[36]

Education had always been close to Patrick's heart, but two months later he wrote to the *Leeds Mercury* in defence of a new scientific discovery which clearly fascinated him. He made marginal notes on the subject in his copy of Graham's *Modern Domestic Medicine*.

As was discovered, in 1847 – Sulphuric < Ether > ether, inhaled, through a suitable apparatus, destroys – for some minutes, all consciousness – < without any bad results > – so that all surgical operations, may \now/ be effected without any sense of pain – < P. B. > Limbs have been amputated, teeth extracted, and persons have been operated on for hernia and the stone, without their having any knowledge whatever, of what had been done – The liquid, must not be swallowed, < B. > Drs Jackson & Morton, Americans, were the discoverers. < B. > care must be taken not to bring the flame of a candle near the operator, otherwise there might be a destructive explosion.[37]

Aware of what a difference ether could have made during his own operation of the year before, Patrick stoutly defended its use against those who spread fears about its consequences. 'Every friend to humanity ought to cry "all hail" to such a messenger of good tidings', he declared enthusiastically, before adding, more soberly:

Having read both sides of the question, and judging from the opinions of some of the most learned, able, and humane of the faculty, it appears to me to be evident, that as it regards the inhalation of the vapour of ether, a great, a useful, and important discovery has been made, and one that ought to be patronized by every friend to humanity.[38]

On 20 September, Patrick wrote to the *Leeds Intelligencer* on a subject about which he had always felt strongly: the promotion of pious young men within the Church. In his letter, he supported the Bishop of Ripon's recent initiative in appointing subdeacons to assist in performing all the clerical duties except administering the sacrament, but he pointed out how essential it was to ensure that the candidates, though well educated, were not expected to have Latin and Greek like the ordained clergy. This would be raising the standards too high and defeat the object of the exercise. It was also, he argued, equally important to ensure that the subdeacons should have an adequate salary. 'It cannot be supposed that these could properly fulfil their spiritual duties, were they to be under the necessity of carrying on some shop-keeping or mechanical employment', he claimed, adding that well-educated parish clerks and some schoolmasters would make ideal candidates.[39]

On an altogether lighter note a couple of months later, Patrick wrote a poem celebrating his curate's victory over the washerwomen of Haworth. It had long been the custom in the township to spread wet sheets and laundry out to dry over the tombstones in the churchyard. This deeply offended

Arthur Bell Nicholls' sense of propriety and, after a long struggle, he secured their eviction. Patrick was evidently greatly amused by the furore.

> In Haworth, a parish of ancient renown,
> Some preach in their surplice, and others their gown,
> And some with due hatred of tower and steeple,
> Without surplice, or gown, hold forth to the people;
> And High Church, and Low Church, and <u>No Church at all</u> –
> Would puzzle the brains of St Peter and Paul –
> The Parson, an< d > old man, but hotter than cold,
> Of late in reforming, has grown very bold,
> And in his fierce zeal, as report loudly tells,
> Through legal resort, has reformed the bells –
> His Curate, who follows – with all due regard –
> Though Foild by the Church, has reform'd the Churchyard.

Patrick's affection for his curate was obvious in the teasing flourish at the end of the poem.

> The females all routed have fled with their clothes
> To stackyards, and backyards, and where noone knows,
> And loudly \have sworn/ < declare > by the suds which they swim in,
> They'll wring off his head, for his warring <u>with women</u>.
> Whilst their husbands combine & roar out in their fury,
> They'll <u>Lynch</u> him at once, without trial by Jury.
> But saddest of all, the fair maidens declare,
> < In > Of marriage or love, \he/ must ever despair.[40]

While Patrick took simple pleasure in his renewed ability to read and write, Charlotte was growing increasingly discontented as her enthusiasm for her new book waned. 'Do you ever get dissatisfied with your own temper Nell when you are long fixed to one place, in one scene subjected to one monotonous species of annoyance?' she asked Ellen. 'I do; I am now in that unenviable frame of mind – my humour I think is too soon overthrown – too sore – too demonstrative and vehement –'.[41] The darkness of her mood was increased by Ellen's reports from Northamptonshire, where she was mixing unhappily in the more elevated social circles of her brother Joshua, vicar of Oundle. 'I used to say and to think in former times that you would certainly be married –', Charlotte told Ellen,

I am not so sanguine on that point now – It will never suit you to accept a husband you cannot love or at least respect – and it appears there are many chances against your meeting with such a one under favourable circumstances – besides from all I can hear and see Money seems to be regarded as almost the Alpha and Omega of requisites in a wife –

Moving on to consider 'Society', Charlotte aired all the prejudices which made her portrayal of Blanche Ingram and her peers so unconvincing in *Jane Eyre*.

As to Society < it see > I don't understand much about it – but from the few glimpses I have had of its machinery it seems to me to be a very strange, complicated affair indeed – wherein Nature is turned upside down – Your well-bred people appear to me figuratively speaking to walk on their heads – to see everything the wrong way up – a lie is with them truth – truth a lie – eternal and tedious botheration is their notion of happiness – sensible pursuits their ennui … if I was called upon to <u>swop</u> (you know the word I suppose?) to swop tastes and ideas and feelings with Mrs Joshua Nussey for instance – I should prefer walking into a good Yorkshire kitchen fire – and concluding the bargain at once by an act of voluntary combustion –

Mrs Nussey's neglect of Ellen provoked a further dose of Charlotte's vitriol: 'Is she a frog or a fish –? She is certainly a specimen of some kind of cold-blooded animal –'.[42]

Once returned to Brookroyd at the end of January, Ellen began to pester Charlotte with invitations to stay. Perhaps even more conscious of Ellen's social superiority after her visit to her grand relations, Charlotte refused even to consider accepting until Ellen had taken her turn in accepting the Brontës' hospitality at Haworth: 'it is natural and right that I should have this wish –', she declaimed, 'to keep friendship in proper order the balance of good offices must be preserved – otherwise a disquieting and anxious feeling creeps in and destroys mutual comfort'. The visit would have to be deferred till the summer, however, when they could 'be more independent of the house and of one room'. This elliptical remark was Charlotte's way of saying that her guest would be spared the necessity of Branwell's presence if they were not confined to the dining room by the weather. Branwell, she explained, had been conducting himself very badly of late: 'I expect from the extravagance of his behaviour and from mysterious hints he drops – < that > (for he never will speak out plainly) that we shall be hearing news of fresh debts contracted by him soon –'.[43]

If Branwell had his secrets, his sisters also had theirs – one which they took 'special care' to ensure he did not discover. Elizabeth and Mary Robinson, Anne's former pupils at Thorp Green, had suddenly recommenced their correspondence with her after a silence of six months dating back to their father's death.[44] Why they should have stopped writing and why they began again, flooding Anne with daily letters for a fortnight 'crammed with warm protestations of endless esteem and gratitude', is a mystery. One can only guess that perhaps Mrs Robinson had intervened, prohibiting the correspondence while there was a danger that Branwell might return to Thorp Green to make trouble and allowing it again once he had accepted that there was no hope of his becoming her husband. It is possibly relevant, too, that the family were on the point of leaving Thorp Green for Birmingham, where they were to live at Great Barr Hall with Sir Edward Scott, a distant relative, who was soon to be Mrs Robinson's second husband.[45] There was even less risk that Branwell would pursue his former lover once she was away from the familiar territory of Thorp Green. It is even possible that Mrs Robinson herself had encouraged the resumption of their contact with Anne in an effort to counteract Branwell's side of the story. If this was her tactic then she succeeded, for the Brontës were deeply puzzled by the letters, particularly as the girls spoke with great affection of their mother and 'never make any allusion intimating acquaintance with her errors – It is to be hoped they are and always will remain in ignorance on that point – especially since – I think – she has bitterly repented them'.[46]

Ellen Nussey's long-awaited visit to Haworth had been arranged for the third week in May. Charlotte had long ago given up her prohibition on visitors while Branwell was at home since it was clear that there was no likelihood of him leaving for the foreseeable future. Nevertheless, she felt obliged to warn Ellen what to expect.

Branwell is quieter now – and for a good reason – he has got to the end of a considerable sum of money of which he became possessed in the Spring – and consequently is obliged to restrict himself in some degree – you must expect to find him weaker in mind and the complet[e] rake in appearance – I have no apprehension of his being at all uncivil to you – on the contrary he will be as smooth as oil[47]

Now that Charlotte was getting her own way and the visit was arranged, she was in high glee. Ellen would take advantage of the new railway line from Bradford to Keighley, which had opened on 16 March, to travel from Birstall by train.

if you can arrive at Keighley by about 4 o'clock in the afternoon Emily, Anne & I will all three meet you at the Station – we can take tea jovially together at the Devonshire Arms and walk home in the cool of the evening – this, with fine weather will I think be a much better arrangement than fagging through four miles in the heat of noon.[48]

A few days later, Charlotte wrote again. 'I *do* trust nothing will now arise to prevent your coming. I shall be anxious about the weather on that day; if it rains, I shall cry.' In answer to a query from the ever punctilious Ellen, Charlotte responded 'Come in black, blue, pink, white, or scarlet, as you like. Come shabby or smart; neither the colour nor the condition signifies; provided only the dress contain Ellen Nussey, all will be right: *à bientôt.*'[49]

Having looked forward with such excitement to Ellen's visit for so many weeks, it was a terrible blow when it was called off only the day before she was due to arrive. Ellen's sister Ann had also received an invitation to go from home, so Ellen had to forgo her visit. Still smarting from her disappointment and resentful of what appeared to her to be a slight to her family, Charlotte wrote a stinging letter to her friend.

I can not blame you – for I know it was not your fault – but I must say I do not altogether exempt your sister Anne from reproach – I do not think she considers it of the least consequence whether little people like us of Haworth are disappointed or not, provided great nobs like the Briar Hall gentry are accommodated – this is bitter, but I feel bitter –

As to going to Brookroyd – it is absurd – I will not go near the place till you have been to Haworth –

My respects to all and sundry accompanied with a large amount of wormwood and gall – from the effusion of which you and your Mother alone are excepted –

CB

Charlotte could not quite contain her anger against Ellen herself, adding in a postscript scribbled at right angles to the rest of her page, 'I thought I had arranged your visit tolerably comfortably for you this time – I may find it more difficult on another occasion.'[50]

Though Charlotte later had the grace to apologize for her sharp words, her feeling that Ellen's visit had been cancelled because something better had been offered continued to niggle and she could not resist the occasional snide remark. Hearing that George's fiancée, Amelia Ringrose, was proposing to stay at Brookroyd prompted a bitter rejoinder: 'you would find her … a better household companion than me – more handy – more even-humoured, more amiable in short' and Ann was deliberately omitted from the 'sincere love' and 'best love' that Charlotte sent her sister Mercy and Mrs Nussey.[51]

Branwell's chastened mood was not entirely due to the fact that he had spent all the money Mrs Robinson had sent him in the spring. The excesses in which he had indulged had brought on 'a fit of horror inexpressible, and violent palpitation of the heart', which seems to indicate the onset of *delirium tremens*. Since then he had been obliged to take greater care of himself physically, though, as he complained to Leyland, 'The best health will not kill <u>acute</u>, and <u>not ideal</u>, mental agony.'[52]

As an alternative to drink, he tried to find refuge from his misery in writing but his every effort was so coloured by his mood that, instead of taking him out of himself, writing simply reinforced his unhappiness. Like Emily and Anne, he had reverted to the imaginary world of his childhood but the obsession with his flawed hero, Northangerland, which had dominated all his Angrian writings, now returned to haunt him. With the dismal ending of all his own ambitions, Branwell could no longer summon enthusiasm for Northangerland's machinations to achieve power; instead, it was the figure of Northangerland, defeated, debauched and disgraced, with which he identified most closely.

In searching through his old notebooks, he came across a poem he had written on 15 December 1837, on the death of Mary Percy, Northangerland's wife. The subject had obvious affinities for Branwell. He copied the poem out, taking great care to redraft clumsily phrased lines and improve the scansion, and sent it to the *Halifax Guardian*. It was published on 5 June 1847, where it appeared under the title 'The End of All'; ironically, it was to be his last work to appear in print.

> In that unpitying winter's night,
>   When my own wife – my Mary – died,
> I, by my fire's declining light,
>   Sat comfortless, and silent sighed.
>   While burst unchecked, grief's bitter tide,
> As I, methought, when she was gone,
>   Not hours, but years like this must bide,
> And wake, and weep, and watch alone...
>
> I could not bear the thoughts which rose,
>   Of what *had* been and what *must* be,
> But still the dark night would disclose
>   Its sorrow-pictured prophecy:
>   Still saw I – miserable me,
> Long – long nights else – in lonely gloom,
>   With time-bleached locks and trembling knee,
> Walk aidless – hopeless – to my tomb.[53]

Rereading these lines, ten years after he had first written them, Branwell must have been startled to find himself fulfilling their uncannily prophetic vision of his own future which had then seemed so brilliant. His own life was imitating that of his creation to an extent he could not then have dreamt possible. The only glimmer of hope in the thick pall of gloom which hung over him was that, as this poem had proved, his work was still worth publishing.

The final removal of any hopes Branwell had cherished concerning Mrs Robinson absolutely prostrated him. He sought comfort in the oblivion of drink and abandoned all serious attempts at writing. His few remaining extant poems for the period 1847 to 1848 are simply unfinished reworkings of old material.[54] Man and boy he had always been an innovator, eager to try out new forms and new ideas, his inspiration fed by his ambition to appear in print and his delight in Angria. Now his only hope of publication lay in the poems he had written as a teenager and Angria had become a morass from which he could not extricate himself.

Charlotte must have thought that she was finished as a publishable writer. *Poems*, which had been her brainchild, had sold only two copies and the manuscript of her novel *The Professor* was still doing the dreary round of the publishers' offices. *Wuthering Heights* and *Agnes Grey* had fared little better. They had been accepted for publication, but not on the terms that the sisters had wished. Emily and Anne were, in effect, to pay for their publication as a three-volume set, just as they had paid for *Poems*. The terms were, as Charlotte described them, 'somewhat impoverishing to the two authors'; they were to advance fifty pounds, which would be refunded if and when their novels sold sufficient copies to cover the sum.[55] It is not clear whether Thomas Cautley Newby, the publisher, had actually rejected *The Professor* altogether or whether Charlotte had simply refused to pay for its publication. Tenacious to the end, Charlotte prepared to send her manuscript for the seventh time to a 'forlorn hope', the small publishing house of Smith, Elder & Co. of 65, Cornhill, London. Having written so often, only to be rejected, she simply wrote a bald, business-like accompanying note – very different from the first one she had sent to Henry Colburn almost exactly a year before.

Gentlemen
   I beg to submit to your consideration the accompanying Manuscript – I should be glad to learn whether it be such as you approve and would undertake to publish – at as early a period as possible. Address – Mr Currer Bell Under cover to Miss Brontë Haworth Bradford Yorkshire

July 15th /47

Messrs Smith & Elder Cornhill[56]

So low were her expectations that she did not even bother to parcel up the manuscript in new paper, simply crossing out the last address and writing in the new. As George Smith later commented, 'This was not calculated to prepossess us in favour of the MS. It was clear that we were offered what had been already rejected elsewhere'. It must have come as no surprise to Charlotte when she received no reply, but after an anxious wait of three weeks she was concerned enough to write again to check that the manuscript had arrived safely and to enclose a stamped addressed envelope for Smith, Elder & Co.'s answer.[57]

   What Charlotte could not know was that William Smith Williams, the firm's reader, had recognized the 'great literary power' of *The Professor*, but did not believe it would sell. He consulted the young proprieter of the firm, George Smith, and they agreed to send a letter of 'appreciative criticism' declining the work but expressing the opinion that Currer Bell was capable of producing a book which would command success.[58] Three days after sending her stamped addressed envelope, Charlotte was astonished to receive a reply. Opening it, 'in the dreary expectation of finding two hard hopeless lines, intimating that Messrs. Smith and Elder "were not disposed to publish the MS." ', she found instead a two-page letter which she read in trembling excitement.

It declined, indeed, to publish that tale, for business reasons, but it discussed its merits and demerits so courteously, so considerately, in a spirit so rational, with a discrimination so enlightened, that this very refusal cheered the author better than a vulgarly-expressed acceptance would have done. It was added, that a work in three volumes would meet with careful attention.[59]

Still reluctant to abandon her cherished first novel, Charlotte wrote back to plead again for *The Professor.*

Your objection to the want of varied interest in the tale is, I am aware, not without grounds – yet it appears to me that it might be published without serious risk if its appearance were speedily followed up by another work from the same pen of a more striking and exciting character. The first work might serve as an introduction and accustom the public to the author's name, the success of the second might thereby be rendered more probable.[60]

Smith, Elder & Co. declined to accept this specious argument and politely rejected *The Professor* once more while expressing their willingness to see Charlotte's new work – a 'narrative in 3 vols. now in progress and nearly completed, to which I have endeavoured to impart a more vivid interest than belongs to the Professor'.[61] Charlotte estimated that it would take her about a month to complete *Jane Eyre,* but the tantalizing prospect of an interested publisher spurred her faster. The fair copy of the manuscript was finished in just over two weeks and posted off by rail from Keighley on 24 August. The new station would not accept a prepaid parcel, so Charlotte asked Smith, Elder & Co. to let her know the cost so that she could reimburse them in postage stamps. Her naive suspicion regarding the 'excessive parsimony of London publishers in regard to postage stamps' seems to have both touched and amused the gentlemen of Smith, Elder & Co., but, to their credit, it did not lead them to underrate their potential new author.[62]

While Charlotte spent an anxious fortnight awaiting their judgement, the readers at Smith, Elder & Co. were united in their opinion of *Jane Eyre.* One young reader was so 'powerfully struck' by the tale that his enthusiasm caused merriment: 'You seem to have been so enchanted, that I do not know how to believe you', George Smith laughingly declared. When William Smith Williams, who was a more clear-headed judge of literary matters, confessed that he had sat up half the night to finish the manuscript, George Smith was intrigued and, at Williams' behest, read it for himself.

He brought it to me on a Saturday, and said that he would like me to read it. There were no Saturday half-holidays in those days, and, as was usual, I did not reach home until late. I had made an appointment with a friend for Sunday morning; I was to meet him about twelve o'clock, at a place some two or three miles from our house, and ride with him into the country.

After breakfast on Sunday morning I took the MS. of 'Jane Eyre' to my little study, and began to read it. The story quickly took me captive. Before twelve o'clock my horse came to the door, but I could not put the book down. I scribbled two or three lines to my friend, saying I was very sorry that circumstances had arisen to prevent my meeting him, sent the note off by my groom, and went on reading the MS. Presently the servant came to tell me that luncheon was ready; I asked him to bring me a sandwich and a glass of wine, and still went on with 'Jane Eyre.' Dinner came; for me the meal was a very hasty one, and before I went to bed that night I had finished reading the manuscript.[63]

In the subsequent light of *Jane Eyre*'s phenomenal success, George Smith always gave the impression that his firm had instantly recognized the novel's potential and accepted it with unqualified enthusiasm. In fact, events at the time suggest a rather different story. Though it may be true that George Smith accepted the book for publication the day after he read the manuscript, he was nevertheless a hard-headed man of business and did not let his enthusiasm run away with him. The terms on which it was to be published were not overly generous, even for a first-time author. 'Currer Bell' was offered one hundred pounds for the copyright on condition that Smith, Elder & Co. had first right of refusal on 'his' next two books, for which 'he' was also to receive one hundred pounds each. In the event, with further editions and foreign rights, the actual payments were in the region of five hundred pounds per novel; even so, by comparison with, for instance, the eight hundred pounds paid to Mrs Gaskell for the English copyright alone of her two-volume biography of Charlotte, the money on offer was poor.[64] Though Charlotte remained loyal to Smith, Elder & Co. because the firm had been the first to recognize her talent, the issue of her remuneration was always to be a touchy subject.

Charlotte was no fool and was well aware that the contract offered by Smith, Elder & Co. would not guarantee her the capability of earning her living solely from writing. Given the temptation to accept the offer of publication on any terms that did not actually impoverish her, Charlotte proved to be less naive than the firm might have expected. 'In accepting your terms, I trust much to your equity and sense of justice', she told them, before adding:

One hundred pounds is a small sum for a year's intellectual labour, nor would circumstances justify me in devoting my time and attention to literary pursuits with so narrow a prospect of advantage did I not feel convinced that in case the ultimate result of my efforts should prove more successful than you now anticipate, you would make some proportionate addition to the remuneration you at present offer. On this ground of confidence in your generosity and honour, I accept your conditions.[65]

While Charlotte was prepared to give way on the subject of payment, she was completely intransigent on the question of making further alterations to her manuscript. She might doubt her own financial acumen but never her literary judgement. Interestingly, since they never admitted to this publicly, her publishers seem to have had considerable doubts about the chapters on Jane Eyre's childhood and, in particular, on Lowood School, suggesting that she should rewrite them. Charlotte thanked the firm for their 'judicious remarks and sound advice', but then added with more firmness than truth:

I am not however in a position to follow the advice; my engagements will not permit me to revise 'Jane Eyre' a third time, and perhaps there is little to regret in the circumstance; you probably know from personal experience that an author never writes well till he has got into the full spirit of his work, and were I to retrench, to alter and to add now when I am uninterested and cold, I know I should only further injure what may be already defective. Perhaps too the first part of 'Jane Eyre' may suit the public taste better than you anticipate – for it is true and Truth has a severe charm of its own. Had I told <u>all</u> the truth, I might indeed have made it far more exquisitely painful – but I deemed it advisable to soften and retrench many particulars lest the narrative should rather displease than attract.[66]

Perhaps feeling that she had been a little too uncompromising in defence of *Jane Eyre*, Charlotte tried to take a more emollient line on the next book, which she was now committed to writing.

I shall be happy ... to receive any advice you can give me as to choice of subject or style of treatment in my next effort – and if you can point out any works peculiarly remarkable for the qualities in which I am deficient, I would study them carefully and endeavour to remedy my errors.
   Allow me in conclusion to express my sense of the punctuality, straightforwardness and intelligence which have hitherto marked your dealings with me.
                                                            And believe me Gentlemen
                                                                  Yours respectfully
                                                                        C Bell.
Since you have no use for 'the Professor', I shall be obliged if you will return the MS.S. Address as usual to Miss Brontë &c.[67]

At this juncture, clearly not appreciating how fast Smith, Elder & Co. would act, Charlotte went off to Brookroyd to have a short holiday with Ellen Nussey. Within six days of accepting their terms, she had not only received the first proof pages, which her sisters forwarded to her, but also marked the few errors they contained and returned them to 65, Cornhill. Of necessity, this had to be done under Ellen's nose. Charlotte was still bound by her vow to Emily and Anne to keep their authorship secret, so the fact that she did her proofreading openly in front of her friend was the closest she could come to confiding in Ellen without breaking the letter of her agreement with her sisters. The spirit of that agreement was clearly broken, but fortunately Ellen was canny enough to recognize that she must maintain the conspiracy of silence; she never even hinted to Emily and Anne that she was aware of the sisters' secret.[68]

Charlotte returned home on 24 September, missing her connection at Leeds and so having to 'cool my heels at the station for 2 hours' till the next train to Keighley and then having a 'very wet, windy walk' back to Haworth. Her boxes arrived the next day, having been surreptitiously packed with presents by Ellen: Patrick sent his thanks for a useful firescreen and Tabby Aykroyd 'was charmed' with her cap, declaring 'she never thought of naught o' t' sort as Miss Nussey sending her aught –'. There were gifts for Anne, whose health was still delicate after the coughs and colds of the winter and spring, and Emily too. 'I was infuriated on finding a jar in my trunk', Charlotte scolded her friend:

– at first I hoped it was empty but when I found it heavy and replete I could have hurled it all the way back to Birstal – however the inscription A— B— softened me much – it was at once kind and villa[i]nous in you to send it – you ought first to be tenderly kissed and then afterwards as tenderly whipped – Emily is just now sitting on the floor of the bed-room where I am writing, looking at her apples – she smiled when I gave < that > them and the collar to her as your presents with an expression at once well-pleased and slightly surprised – Anne thanks you much – All send their love –[69]

Ten days later, Anne wrote a rare letter to Ellen, thanking her for the jar of medicinal crab-cheese which 'is excellent, and likely to be very useful, but I don't intend to need it' and for her 'unexpected and welcome epistle'. Charlotte had evidently complained at length to Ellen and expressed her fears about the prevailing east wind, which always brought sickness in its wake: she had felt its influence 'as usual'. Anne, too, had suffered from its ill effects

in some degree, as I always do, more or less; but this time, it brought me no reinforcement of colds and coughs which is what I dread the most. Emily considers it a 'dry uninteresting wind', but it does not affect her nervous system ... I have no news to tell you except that Mr Nicholl's begged a holiday and went to Ireland three or four weeks ago, and is not expected back till Saturday – but that I dare say is no news at all.[70]

Poor Mr Nicholls, who was so uninteresting even to the normally kind and gentle Anne, attracted nothing but vituperation from Charlotte, who seems to have regarded him with utter contempt. 'Mr Nicholls is not yet returned but is expected next week', she told Ellen in her turn.

I am sorry to say that many of the parishioners express a desire that he should not trouble himself to re-cross the channel but should remain quietly where he is – This is not the feeling that ought to exist between shepherd and flock – it is not such as is prevalent at Birstal – it is not such as poor Mr W[e]ightman excited.[71]

Charlotte's hostility may have owed something to the fact that rumours were still afloat that she was 'about to be married to her papa's Curate'. Certainly, she herself had been expecting his imminent removal to a new parish earlier in the summer and the fact that he seems not to have sought any promotion away from Haworth may have encouraged gossip about his intentions towards Charlotte. Ellen, too, was no doubt teasing her friend by praising the young curate in her letters, provoking a sharp retort from Charlotte: 'I cannot for my life see those interesting germs of goodness in him you discovered. his narrowness of mind always strikes me chiefly – I fear he is indebted to your imagination for his hidden treasures.'[72]

Anne's somewhat disingenuous claim that she had no news to tell Ellen concealed the facts that she also was about to have a novel published and was now working on a second novel herself. It is not possible to discover exactly when she began it, but the likelihood is that it had been prompted by the unexpected visit to the parsonage in April of Mrs Collins, the long-suffering wife of the former curate of Keighley. Her 'frank ... narrative of her appalling distresses', which included a description of the 'infamous career of vice' run by her husband, his abandoning of her and their two children, absolutely penniless, 'to disease and total destitution' in Manchester and her slow fight back to health and respectability, had taken two hours in the telling and won the horrified sympathy and admiration of the Brontës.[73] Anne seems to have been especially fascinated by the fact that Mrs Collins had not only survived the physical and mental degradation of her marriage but emerged as an independent and morally strong woman – and in doing so had saved her children from corruption at the hands of their father. This idea was to be the basis of Anne's second novel, a book which was to be so profoundly disturbing to contemporary ideas of decency that it was to sink without trace for almost 150 years after its conception. In Helen Graham she created a heroine who would rise above the depravity of her husband and his circle, have the courage to leave him and earn her own living and yet have the compassion to go back to comfort him as he lay dying. In Arthur Huntingdon, she created a fallible and not entirely unlikeable sinner, whose gradual decline into drunkenness and vice is more the result of moral weakness than actual criminality: her model for this character, famously, was her brother Branwell.

With her usual patronizing attitude towards her youngest sister, Charlotte dismissed *The Tenant of Wildfell Hall* out of hand. 'The choice of subject was an entire mistake. Nothing less congruous with the writer's nature could be conceived.'[74] Yet Charlotte could not argue with the central thesis of the book, which expressed a view she had herself expounded in connection with her brother. Writing to her old headmistress, Miss Wooler, at the beginning of the previous year Charlotte had commented:

You ask me if I do not think that men are strange beings – I do indeed, I have often thought so – and I think too that the mode of bringing them up is strange, they are not half sufficiently guarded from temptation – Girls are protected as if they were something very frail and silly indeed while boys are turned loose on the world as if they – of all beings in existence, were the wisest and the least liable to be led astray.[75]

This question of the differences in the education of boys and girls had obviously been much discussed at the parsonage, where Branwell's freedom to pursue his own interests as a young man had contrasted so sharply with the enforced subjection to discipline and duty which had ruled his sisters' lives. The fact that Branwell had failed to fulfil his early talents was daily impressed on them as he drank himself insensible or wallowed in self-pity and depression. It was no wonder, then, that Anne saw it as her duty to expose the fallacy of current education in a series of passionate arguments, attacking the idea that girls were hothouse plants to be guarded against every evil, and boys were hardy trees capable of withstanding every assault on their morals.

You would have us encourage our sons to prove all things by their own experience, while our daughters must not even profit by the experience of others. Now I would have both so to benefit by the experience of others, and the precepts of a higher authority, that they should know beforehand to refuse the evil and choose the good, and require no experimental proofs to teach them the evil of transgression. I would not send a poor girl into the world, unarmed against her foes, and ignorant of the snares that beset her path: nor would I watch and guard her, till, deprived of self-respect and self-reliance, she lost the power, or the will to watch and guard herself; – and as for my son – if I thought he would grow up to be what you call a man of the world – one that has '*seen life,*' and glories in his experience, even though he should so far profit by it, as to sober down, at length, into a useful and respected member of society – I would rather that he died to-morrow! – rather a thousand times![76]

Anne herself declared that her book had not been written in vain if it deterred one young man from following in Huntingdon's footsteps or prevented one thoughtless girl from falling into 'the very natural error' of her heroine.[77] Charlotte, always more conventional than her youngest sister, felt it necessary to apologize for Anne's 'pure, but, I think, slightly morbid' motives in choosing her subject:

She had, in the course of her life, been called on to contemplate, near at hand and for a long time, the terrible effects of talents misused and faculties abused; hers was naturally a sensitive, reserved, and dejected nature; what she saw sank very deeply into her mind; it did her harm. She brooded over it till she believed it to be a duty to reproduce every detail (of course with fictitious characters, incidents, and situations) as a warning to others. She hated her work, but would pursue it. When reasoned with on the subject, she regarded such reasonings as a temptation to self-indulgence. She must be honest; she must not varnish, soften, or conceal.[78]

Anne herself took a much more robust view of her purpose in writing the book, setting forth her views without apology in her preface to the second edition.

My object in writing the following pages, was not simply to amuse the Reader, neither was it to gratify my own taste, nor yet to ingratiate myself with the Press and the Public: I wished to tell the truth, for truth always conveys its own moral to those who are able to receive it.

She also took a much stronger stance on the necessity of portraying her scenes of debauchery realistically, fighting her corner with an energy and intelligence for which Charlotte was incapable of giving her credit.

when we have to do with vice and vicious characters, I maintain it is better to depict them as they really are than as they would wish to appear. To represent a bad thing in its least offensive light, is doubtless the most agreeable course for a writer of fiction to pursue; but is it the most honest, or the safest? Is it better to reveal the snares and pitfalls of life to the young and thoughtless traveller, or to cover them with branches and flowers? O Reader! if there were less of this delicate concealment of facts – this whispering 'Peace, peace,' when there is no peace, there would be less of sin and misery to the young of both sexes who are left to wring their bitter knowledge from experience.[79]

Though Charlotte suggested that Anne wrote her book out of a sense of duty, and a distasteful one at that, the tone of much of *The Tenant of Wildfell Hall* belies this. The scenes with Gilbert Markham's family in particular are full of teasing good humour and are an eminently successful attempt to portray a cheerful and normal family whose preoccupation with the every-day is in complete contrast to the sordid mystery of Helen Graham's life. Like Charlotte herself when writing *Jane Eyre*, Anne seems to have got caught up in her story to the exclusion of all else and to the detriment of her health. 'I would fain hope that her health is a little stronger than it was – and her spirits a little better –', Charlotte wrote to Ellen in the October, 'but she leads much too sedentary a life, and is continually sitting stooping either over a book or over her desk – it is with difficulty one can prevail on her to take a walk or induce her to converse.'[80]

The fact that Emily, unlike her sisters, did not produce a second novel has caused much argument. Some claim that *Wuthering Heights* is such an astonishing and powerful novel that Emily exhausted all her genius in writing it. Others, that its poor reviews led her to scorn the very idea of setting another work before an uncomprehending public. Though widely accepted, both views are wrong. There can be little doubt that Emily did embark on a second novel. 'Neither Ellis nor Acton allowed herself for one moment to sink under want of encouragement', Charlotte claimed; 'energy nerved the one, and endurance upheld the other. They were both prepared to try again.'[81] Certainly, despite the singularity of *Wuthering Heights*, Emily was not short of material for a new novel and could have effectively plundered Gondal again for further inspiration. Nor would poor reviews have discouraged her, for if she had began her next work before her first was published, as both Charlotte and Anne did, there was no reason for her to expect a critical savaging. The almost complete absence of manuscript material for the last two years of her life suggests that she was working on another project, channelling all her energies into this just as she had done when writing *Wuthering Heights*. Though the evidence is admittedly inconclusive, further weight is lent to the argument by the existence of a letter from her publisher, Thomas Cautley Newby, addressed to Ellis Bell.

Dear Sir,

I am much obliged by your kind note & shall have great pleasure in making arrangements for your next novel. I would not hurry its completion, for I think you are quite right not to let it go before the world until well satisfied with it, for much depends on your new work if it be an improvement on your first you will have established yourself as a first rate novelist, but if it fall short the Critics will be too apt to say that you have expended your talent in your first novel. I shall therefore, have pleasure in accepting it upon the understanding that its completion be at your own time.

> Believe me
> My dear Sir
> Yrs sincerely
> T C Newby

Feb. 15. 1848[82]

It has been suggested that this letter was actually intended for Anne and referred to *The Tenant of Wildfell Hall*. Though Newby notoriously confused Ellis and Acton Bell in an advertisement in *The Examiner* the previous month, describing *Wuthering Heights* as 'Acton Bell's successful new novel', this does not automatically mean that he was confused about the identity of his correspondent. The content of his letter is undoubtedly more applicable to Ellis than Acton Bell, for though the reviewers were hardly enthusiastic about *Wuthering Heights*, they gave it far more coverage than *Agnes Grey*, which was virtually ignored. Newby's letter, indeed, reflects the comment in a review which appeared in that very same issue of *The Examiner*: 'If this book be, as we apprehend it is the first work of the author, we hope that he will produce a second, – giving himself more time in its composition than in the present case.'[83] What could be more natural than that, having read this encouraging comment, Emily should write to Newby offering him her second novel but requesting that she should be given time to complete and revise it?

If, then, as seems almost certain, Emily did begin a second novel, we are faced with the problem of what became of the manuscript, why it was never published and why it is never mentioned in extant correspondence. The most obvious solution is that the novel was never completed and was therefore destroyed. The reviews of *Wuthering Heights* had not been so damning that its author might feel disinclined to complete or publish a second novel, but it is possible that, as the person with responsibility for running the parsonage household, Emily found it increasingly difficult to find time for the dull and time-consuming task of revision as first Branwell and then she herself fell ill. Given that Emily fought to the very end against her consumption and refused to make any physical concessions, it is unlikely that she had the mental energy to complete the book after September 1848. Similarly, as she did not accept that her death was inevitable, there is no reason to suppose that she made plans for that contingency and destroyed the unfinished manuscript herself.

The likelihood, therefore, is that this was done by Charlotte after Emily's death, a possibility that would also explain Charlotte's silence on the subject of Emily's second novel. There are two good reasons why Charlotte should have been the perpetrator of this act of wilful destruction. Firstly, as her reaction to *The Tenant of Wildfell Hall* shows, Charlotte believed very strongly that there were certain subjects which were not suitable for novelistic treatment. If Emily's novel was a second dipping into the murky waters of Gondal then Charlotte could well have felt that its subject 'was an entire mistake' and that it should not go to press – especially if it was incomplete. Secondly, Charlotte was immensely protective of her sister's reputation. Admiring yet also fearing her 'unbending' spirit, Charlotte believed that 'an interpreter ought always to have stood between her and the world' and appointed herself to that task. Just as she had an unalterable image in her mind of Anne as timid, gentle and unoriginal, so she had a mirror image of Emily as the stern, inflexible and yet innocent possessor of a 'secret power and fire'. If the second novel would have merely reinforced the criticisms which had been expressed, sometimes with extreme savagery, about *Wuthering Heights*, then Charlotte may have felt it her duty to protect her sister from its consequences. 'Whether it is right or advisable to create beings like Heathcliff, I do not know', Charlotte wrote in 1850, adding, 'I scarcely think it is.'[84] If the central character of Emily's second novel was similarly unredeemed, Charlotte had her justification for preventing its publication. To destroy the manuscript would be to leave the world with the impression that Emily was indeed a 'giant' and a 'baby god' whom death had cut off in her prime before she could fully develop the powers within her. If that was her intention, then she succeeded beyond her wildest dreams.

While Emily and Anne laboured over their manuscripts, Charlotte was putting the finishing touches to the proofs of *Jane Eyre*. She was grateful to Smith, Elder & Co. for relieving her of the burden of punctuation, 'as I found the task very puzzling – and besides I consider your mode of punctuation a great deal more correct and rational than my own'.[85] There would be no preface to *Jane Eyre*, she decided, no doubt because it would be impossible to write one without some allusion to the sex and circumstances of the author; ironically, in accepting her publisher's suggestion that 'an auto-biography' should be added as a subtitle, she inadvertently contributed to the speculation.[86] On the morning of 19 October 1847, Charlotte received the first six copies of her new novel, printed in three volumes and bound in cloth covers. 'You have given the work every advantage which good paper, clear type and a seemly outside can supply –', she told her publishers: 'if it fails – the fault will lie with the author – you are exempt.'[87] She then possessed her soul with patience and braced herself for the reviews.

The first wave of newspaper notices were somewhat disappointing: Charlotte felt that the one in the *Literary Gazette* had been 'indited in rather a flat mood' and that in the *Athenaeum* had 'a style of its own which I respect, but cannot exactly relish'. She reconciled herself to their muted praise by recognizing 'that journals of that standing have a dignity to maintain which would be deranged by a too cordial recognition of the claims of an obscure author', adding rather wistfully, '– I suppose there is every reason to be satisfied – Meantime a brisk sale would be an effectual support under the hauteur of lofty critics'.[88] Hard on the heels of these reviews, however, came praise of a type and from a source which thrilled Charlotte. Her greatest literary hero, William Makepeace Thackeray, had been sent a pre-publication copy of the book, prompting a reply which William Smith Williams passed on to Charlotte.

I wish you had not sent me Jane Eyre. It interested me so much that I have lost (or won if you like) a whole day in reading it at the busiest period, with the printers I know waiting for copy. Who the author can be I can't guess – if a woman she knows her language better than most ladies do, or has had a 'classical' education. It is a fine book though – the man & woman capital – the style very generous and upright so to speak … Some of the love passages made me cry – to the astonishment of John who came in with the coals. St John the Missionary is a failure I think but a good failure there are parts excellent I dont know why I tell you this but that I have been exceedingly moved & pleased by Jane Eyre. It is a womans writing, but whose? Give my respects and thanks to the author – whose novel is the first English one (& the French are only romances now) that I've been able to read for many a day.[89]

Though this was praise and recognition of the sort Charlotte had longed for all her life, she seems to have been determined to keep her expectations low. Ruthlessly crushing her gratification, Charlotte drafted a careful reply back to Mr Williams, telling him with deliberate understatement that his letter had been 'very pleasant to me to read ... very cheering to reflect on'. 'I feel honoured in being approved by Mr Thackeray because I approve Mr Thackeray', she explained. 'One good word from such a man is worth pages of praise from ordinary judges.'[90]

The 'ordinary judges', who Charlotte had feared would find nothing to approve in her 'mere domestic novel', were soon to fall over themselves in their eagerness to praise what one critic called 'decidedly the best novel of the season'.[91] The *Critic* congratulated itself on its perspicacity in noting Currer Bell's earlier work, *Poems*, and described *Jane Eyre* as 'a story of surpassing interest' and one which 'we can cordially recommend ... to our readers, as a novel to be placed at the top of the list to be borrowed, and to the circulating-library keeper, as one which he may safely order. It is sure to be in demand.' 'There can be no question but that *Jane Eyre* is a very clever book. Indeed it is a book of decided power', trumpeted *The Examiner*. The *Era* went one better:

This is an extraordinary book. Although a work of fiction, it is no mere novel, for there is nothing but nature and truth about it, and its interest is entirely domestic; neither is it like your familiar writings, that are too close to reality. There is nothing morbid, nothing vague, nothing improbable about the story of Jane Eyre; at the same time it lacks neither the odour of romance nor the hue of sentiment ... The story is, therefore, unlike all that we have read, with very few exceptions; and for power of thought and expression, we do not know its rival among modern productions ... all the serious novel writers of the day lose in comparison with Currer Bell.[92]

Reading the litany of critical commendations sent to her with meticulous care by William Smith Williams, Charlotte was almost dazed. 'There are moments when I can hardly credit that anything I have done should < hard > be found worthy to give even transitory pleasure to such men as Mr Thackeray, Sir John Herschel, Mr Fonblanque, Leigh Hunt and Mr Lewes – that my humble efforts should have had such a result is a noble reward.'[93]

Most reviewers managed to find the 'obvious moral' in the tale: 'that laws, both human and divine, approved in our calmer moments, are not to be disobeyed when our time of trial comes, however singular the "circumstances" under which we are tempted to disregard them'. The only dissonant note came from the *Spectator*, which criticized the 'low tone of behaviour (rather than of morality) in the book'. Charlotte, who hardly dared trust to the critics' approval, panicked at this. 'The way to detraction has been pointed out and will probably be pursued', she explained with a perception that was to be justified by later reviews; 'I fear this turn of opinion will not improve the demand for the book – but time will shew; if "Jane Eyre" has any solid worth in it – it ought to weather a gust of unfavourable wind.'[94]

In fact, demand for *Jane Eyre* was almost unprecedented. The first edition of, probably, some 2,500 copies, was published on 16 October 1847; it had sold out within three months and the book was to be reprinted again in January and the following April.[95] By any standard, *Jane Eyre* was a resounding success.

The same could not be said of *Wuthering Heights* and *Agnes Grey*. Though Newby had agreed to their publication long before Charlotte had even finished writing *Jane Eyre*, he had not sent out the first proof-sheets until the beginning of August. While *Jane Eyre* was completed, typeset, bound, published and getting its earliest reviews, they still languished at Mr Newby's. Sensible of the contrast between her own treatment and that of her sisters, Charlotte wrote to ask Mr Williams if Mr Newby often acted in this way, or whether this was simply an exceptional instance of his methods.

Mr Newby … does not do business like Messrs Smith & Elder; a different spirit seems to preside at 172 Mortimer Street to that which guides the helm at 65 Cornhill. Mr Newby shuffles, gives his word and breaks it; Messrs Smith & Elders performance is always better than their promise. My relatives have suffered from exhausting delay and procrastination, while I have to acknowledge the benefits of a management at once businesslike and gentlemanlike, energetic and considerate.[96]

It is worth pointing out at this stage that Smith, Elder & Co. was a relatively new firm which had been founded in 1816 by two Scots, George Smith, senior, and Alexander Elder. Their publishing list was not particularly impressive, the most popular work being a fourteen-year run of the periodical *Friendship's Offering* and their most prestigious some distinguished scientific works, including Sir Humphry Davy's collected *Works* in nine volumes and Charles Darwin's *Zoology of the Voyage of the Beagle* in five volumes. More recently they had published Sir John Herschel's *Results of Astronomical Observations made during the years 1834–8 at the Cape of Good Hope*, R. H. Horne's *The New Spirit of the Age* and John Ruskin's first work, *Modern Painters*. Both of the latter works had been published under the aegis of George Smith, junior, who had joined the firm at the age of fourteen and, on his father's death in 1846, had taken over the management of its publishing concerns. In 1847, when he accepted *Jane Eyre*, he was still only twenty-three years old and had yet to transform the firm into the highly respected and financially successful concern that it became.[97] Despite his youth, he was astute both as a businessman and as a judge of character. He had spotted William Smith Williams wasting his remarkable literary gifts as a book keeper to a firm of lithographers and, on discovering that he hated his employment and spent his spare time working as a theatre critic for the *Spectator,* invited him to join Smith, Elder & Co. as his own literary assistant and general manager of the publishing department. Williams, too, had only taken up his post with the firm in the year before Charlotte submitted *The Professor* and, as the author of her courteous and discriminating letter of rejection, was directly responsible for attracting one of its most famous and best-selling authors to Smith, Elder & Co.[98] In later years, particularly after the deaths of her brother and sisters, Charlotte was to rely increasingly on his shrewd literary judgement and his friendship for moral support.

In sharp contrast to the newly dynamic Smith, Elder & Co., Thomas Cautley Newby was a sole operator who had set himself up as a publisher in Mortimer Street off Cavendish Square in 1820. Though he ran a varied list, ranging from novels to travel books and manuals, he had published nothing of any note over the years; *Wuthering Heights, Agnes Grey, The Tenant of Wildfell Hall* and Anthony Trollope's first novel, *The Macdermots of Ballycloran,* were his only claims to fame in later years.[99] In view of his poor treatment of Emily and Anne, it is worth comparing their experience with that, in exactly the same year, of Anthony Trollope, whose mother, one of the most popular novelists of the day, secured the best deal she could on his behalf: Newby was to print the book at his own expense and give its author half its profits. 'Many a young author expects much from such an undertaking', Trollope later wrote in his autobiography,

I can with truth declare that I expected nothing. And I got nothing ... I was sure that the book would fail, and it did fail most absolutely ... I have Mr Newby's agreement with me, in duplicate, and one or two preliminary notes; but beyond that I did not have a word from Mr Newby. I am sure that he did not wrong me in that he paid me nothing. It is probable that he did not sell fifty copies of the work; – but of what he did sell he gave me no account.[100]

Despite his low expectations, Trollope nevertheless felt that he had been ill served by Newby and, the following year, he took his next book elsewhere.[101]

Charlotte's complaints about Newby's dilatory behaviour led William Smith Williams to offer to take over the publication of *Wuthering Heights* and *Agnes Grey,* but Emily and Anne were obstinate in their determination to go their own way. By the middle of November they had received the final proof-sheets, so publication at last seemed imminent.[102] Though Emily and Anne's desire to achieve success independently of their sister was laudable, it was somewhat misguided. Newby had only begun to give serious attention to the publication of their novels when he realized that there was reflected glory – not to mention money – to be made from the magical name of Bell. The mystery surrounding the sex and identity of Currer Bell would fuel interest in his own publication of works by Ellis and Acton Bell and, as circumstances would swiftly prove, he was not averse to manipulating the truth in order to gain maximum publicity and sales.

At the beginning of December 1847, *Wuthering Heights* and *Agnes Grey* were finally published – or so their authors were obliged to deduce from the fact that they received their six publication copies. Despite the length of time the books had been in the press, Emily and Anne were mortified to discover that almost all the errors that they had so painstakingly corrected in the proof-sheets appeared unchanged in the final copies.[103]

If, in sticking with Newby, Emily and Anne had hoped to assert their mental and literary independence from Charlotte, they were soon to be disillusioned. The reviewers, aided by Newby's judicious advertising, were not slow to realize the connection between the three Bells and to draw comparisons between their works. The appearance of *Wuthering Heights* and *Agnes Grey* only reinforced what was gradually becoming a consensus of critical opinion on the 'low tone of behaviour' in the Bells' books. Unfortunately, one of the earliest reviews was in the *Spectator*, which had first raised the question in reviewing *Jane Eyre* and now returned to the attack. The reviewer disapprovingly drew particular attention to the affinity between the writers: 'In each, there is the autobiographical form of writing; a choice of subjects that are peculiar without being either probable or pleasing; and considerable executive ability, but insufficient to overcome the injudicious selection of the theme and matter.' The *Athenaeum* soon followed with its own sour comment: 'The Bells seem to affect painful and exceptional subjects: – the misdeeds and oppressions of tyranny – the eccentricities of "woman's fantasy".'[104]

Wuthering Heights, as the more dramatic of the two new works, attracted by far the greater proportion of comment and the same criticisms recur again and again. Some of these were justified. The *Atlas*, for instance, was not alone in declaring that the book 'sadly wants relief', but then went on to overstate its case: 'There is not in the entire *dramatis personae* a single character which is not utterly hateful or thoroughly contemptible.'[105] There was a constant litany of complaint about the brutality and violence of some of the scenes and about the use of expletives, which, contrary to custom, Emily had written out in full rather than indicated by a dash.[106] The reviewers searched in vain for a moral to the story, the most charitable judgement being that in the *Britannia*: 'We do not know whether the author writes with any purpose; but we can speak of one effect of his production. It strongly shows the brutalizing influence of unchecked passion.'[107]

Despite the baffled reaction of some of the critics, there was still much to encourage Emily in their reviews. The *Britannia* offered the perceptive comment that Ellis Bell's creations 'strike us as proceeding from a mind of limited experience, but of original energy, and of a singular and distinctive cast'. At least two critics were enthralled almost against their will. An American reviewer wrote in the *Literary World*:

Fascinated by strange magic we read what we dislike, we become interested in characters which are most revolting to our feelings, and are made subject to the immense power, of the book ... we are spell-bound, we cannot choose but read.[108]

The critic in *Douglas Jerrold's Weekly Newspaper* concurred.

Wuthering Heights is a strange sort of book, – baffling all regular criticism; yet, it is impossible to begin and not finish it; and quite as impossible to lay it aside afterwards and say nothing about it ... We strongly recommend all our readers who love novelty to get this story, for we can promise them that they never have read anything like it before.

Though, 'very puzzled and very interested' by a book which he finally left to his readers to decide upon, this critic nevertheless foresaw a great future for the author. 'We are quite confident that the writer of *Wuthering Heights* wants but the practised skill to make a great artist; perhaps, a great dramatic artist.' Even the fault-finding G. W. Peck, who characterized it as 'a coarse, original, powerful book', was obliged to concede that 'if the rank of a work of fiction is to depend solely on its naked imaginative power, then this is one of the greatest novels in the language'.[109]

Though most reviewers seem to have been intrigued by *Wuthering Heights* and, even when overtly hostile, dedicated many column inches to its discussion, they tended completely to overlook *Agnes Grey*. The few who referred to it did so only to remark on the fact that it lacked the power of *Wuthering Heights* and was 'more agreeable' in subject matter and treatment. Generally, however, the notices were dismissive. 'Some characters and scenes are nicely sketched in it', observed the *Britannia*, 'but it has nothing to call for special notice.' The *Atlas* was even worse, describing *Agnes Grey* as 'a somewhat coarse imitation of one of Miss Austin's [sic] charming stories ... It leaves no painful impression on the mind – some may think it leaves no impression at all.'[110]

With such reviews the Brontë sisters had to be content. On the whole, despite the adverse comments, their first forays into novel writing had attracted more attention and been better received than they might have expected.

As for *Jane Eyre*, its runaway success must have seemed barely credible. Early in December Charlotte was 'glad and proud' to receive a bank bill for one hundred pounds from Smith, Elder & Co.[111] with the prospect of more to come as she was already having to prepare a second edition of the novel for the press, a mere two months after publication of the first. Apart from some minor emendations, Charlotte wanted to take the opportunity of a new edition to add a preface acknowledging her thanks to the public, 'the select Reviewers … who have encouraged me as only large-hearted and high-minded men know how to encourage a struggling stranger' and her publishers. Nevertheless, and this was undoubtedly the real reason for writing a preface, she could not resist answering those 'timorous or carping' critics who had designated *Jane Eyre* an 'improper' book. 'I would remind them of certain simple truths', she began.

Conventionality is not morality. Self-righteousness is not religion. To attack the first is not to assail the last. To pluck the mask from the face of the Pharisee, is not to lift an impious hand to the Crown of Thorns.
    These things and deeds are diametrically opposed: they are as distinct as is vice from virtue. Men too often confound them; they should not be confounded: appearance should not be mistaken for truth; narrow human doctrines, that only tend to elate and magnify a few, should not be substituted for the world-redeeming creed of Christ. There is – I repeat it – a difference; and it is a good, and not a bad action to mark broadly and clearly the line of separation between them.[12]

Though the writing of the preface might have eased Charlotte's 'heart-ache' at hearing the novel called 'godless' and 'pernicious', it would perhaps have been wiser to have simply ignored the critics; certainly Charlotte later regretted its enthusiastic tone and wished she had written it in a cooler mood.[13] Indeed, it is surprising that Smith, Elder & Co. allowed Charlotte to betray her naivety in this way. One can only assume that in the rush to bring out a second edition before the first was sold out, her publishers did not pay much attention to the preface. In so doing they allowed her to commit a cardinal error – one which was to expose her to even more malicious gossip and critical unpleasantness. They allowed her to dedicate the second edition of *Jane Eyre* to her literary hero, William Makepeace Thackeray.[14] What those in London knew, but Charlotte could not know, was the tragedy of Thackeray's life: in 1840, after only four years of marriage, his wife had gone insane and had to be incarcerated for her own safety. The parallels with Mr Rochester were obvious and made all the more pronounced because in *Vanity Fair*, which was then making its first appearance in serial form, Thackeray had created the scheming, ambitious and heartless Becky Sharp who, like Jane Eyre, had begun life as a humble governess and raised herself by marriage with her employer. The dedication in *Jane Eyre* therefore lent credence to speculation already rife in London that 'Currer Bell' had been a governess in Thackeray's family and that the novel was based upon the truth. Charlotte was mortified when she discovered her mistake, particularly when Thackeray himself wrote to inform her and yet thanked her for 'the greatest compliment I have ever received in my life':

Well may it be said that Fact is often stranger than Fiction! … Of course I knew nothing whatever of Mr Thackeray's domestic concerns: he existed for me only as an author: ... I am <u>very, very</u> sorry that my inadvertent blunder should have made his name and affairs a subject for common gossip.

The very fact of his not complaining at all – and addressing me with such kindness – notwithstanding the pain and annoyance I must have caused him – increases my chagrin. I could not half express my regret to him in my answer, for I was restrained by the consciousness that that regret was just worth nothing at all – quite valueless for healing the mischief I had done."[5]

Despite the acute misery caused by the fact that her intended compliment had gone so badly awry, there was much to look forward to in the coming year. *Jane Eyre* was going into its second edition and her publishers were anxiously waiting for her to decide on her next book. Emily and Anne had got their first books in print and were both working on a second novel. With every prospect that they would in future be able to earn their livings in the only way that had ever been congenial, the Brontë sisters could face the new year with equanimity.

Chapter Nineteen

⌘

THE SHADOW
IN THE HOUSE

The year 1848 dawned inauspiciously with a prevailing easterly wind, which always brought illness to the Brontë household. 'We are all cut up by this cruel east wind', Anne wrote to Ellen Nussey, 'most of us, e.i. Charlotte, Emily, and I, have had the inf[l]uenza, or a bad cold instead, twice over within the space of a few weeks; Papa has had it once. Tabby has hitherto escaped it altogether.' Excusing her 'shabby little note', Anne explained, 'I have no news to tell you, for we have been nowhere, seen no one, and done nothing (to <u>speak</u> of) since you were here – and yet we contrive to be busy from morning to night.'

Though Anne could write cheerfully enough, her father was in low spirits. He had had a particularly grim few months with Branwell, who had been 'more than ordinarily troublesome and annoying of late – he leads papa a wretched life'. Branwell had 'contrived by some means to get more money from the old quarter' and had plunged back into his dissolute habits. In this he seems to have been ably assisted by J. B. Leyland, who had been commissioned to carve decorations for the new church being built at Oxenhope.[2] This work no doubt provided an excuse for Branwell to visit Leyland

[543]

in the company of John Brown, who worked closely with the sculptor. The three were soon spending Branwell's money in the Halifax inns. Writing apologetically to Leyland in early January, Branwell struggled unconvincingly to justify his conduct. 'I was <u>really</u> far enough from well when I saw you last week at Halifax', he protested:

I was not intoxicated when I saw you last, Dear Sir, but I was so much broken down and embittered in heart that it did not need much extra stimulus to make me experience the fainting fit I had, after you left, at the Talbot, and another, more severe at < the Co > Mr Crowthers – the Commercial Inn near the Northgate.[3]

The accompanying sketch of 'The rescue of the < Talb > Punch bowl. a scene in the Talbot' belied Branwell's words, depicting John Brown ('St John in the Wilderness') spilling the punchbowl and scattering glasses as he wrestled the table away from Branwell ('St Patrick – alias Lord Peter'), Leyland ('Phidias'), Daniel Sugden ('Sugdeniensis', the landlord) and 'Draco the Fire Drake'. Confirming the morbidity of his mood, he drew a self-portrait above this sketch in which he depicted himself naked with a noose around his neck, in the guise of '<u>Patrick</u> Reid', the notorious Mirfield murderer who was hanged at York on 9 January 1848.[4]

Branwell's 'fainting fits' were almost certainly brought on by his excessive drinking and may have been a symptom of *delirium tremens*. Writing to Ellen at about the same time, Charlotte complained, 'he is always sick, has two or three times fallen down in fits'. On one notorious occasion, Branwell even managed to set his bedclothes on fire while lying in a drunken stupor. Fortunately, Anne happened to be passing his open door and, realizing the danger, tried to rouse him. When she could not do so she ran to get Emily, who unceremoniously dragged her brother out of his bed, flung him into the corner and the blazing bedclothes into the middle of the room, dashed to the kitchen for a large can of water and doused the flames.[5] When his children were small, Patrick had been deeply concerned about the dangers of fire, with candles, oil lamps and open fires in constant use in the house; now, with his son an irresponsible alcoholic, he insisted that in future Branwell should sleep in the same room as himself. In doing this, the seventy-year-old Patrick was making a rod for his own back: he was 'harassed night and day' by Branwell's 'intolerable conduct'. As Mrs Gaskell melodramatically described it, possibly on the authority of Martha Brown, the Brontës' servant:

he had attacks of delirium tremens of the most frightful character; he slept in his father's room, and he would sometimes declare that either he or his father should be dead before morning. The trembling sisters, sick with fright, would implore their father not to expose himself to this danger; but Mr Brontë is no timid man, and perhaps he felt that he could possibly influence his son to some self-restraint, more by showing trust in him than by showing fear … In the mornings young Brontë would saunter out, saying, with a drunkard's incontinence of speech, 'The poor old man and I have had a terrible night of it; he does his best – the poor old man! but it's all over with me;' (whimpering) 'it's *her* fault, *her* fault.'[6]

More prosaic, and infinitely more touching, is Patrick's note in the margin of his copy of Graham's *Modern Domestic Medicine*. Marking the section on 'Insanity, or Mental Derangement' with an asterisk, he wrote: 'there is also "delirium tremens", brought on, sometimes, by intoxication – "the patient thinks himself haunted; by demons, sees luminous [?substans?], in his imagination, has frequent tremors of the limbs, If intox—n, be left off – this madness, will in general, gradually diminish &c.' Reading the text, he obviously recognized his son's symptoms: 'unrestrained behaviour … an irritability which urges on the patient in an extravagant pursuit of something real or imaginary, to the ruin of himself, or annoyance of his friends; and ultimately leads him, if opposed in his disordered wishes, to acts of extreme violence'. Under the causes of insanity, Patrick could not fail to notice that the first of the 'passions and emotions most productive of this complaint' was love. Poignantly, however, and as if taking at least some of the responsibility for his son's mental and physical breakdown on himself, the cause Patrick underlined was 'hereditary disposition'. All he could do now was pray for his son and repeat Charlotte's hopeless comment: 'what will be the ultimate end God knows –'.[7]

As if it was not enough to watch his only son killing himself through drink, Patrick had recently had to face a shocking tragedy involving one of his oldest friends, the Reverend Thomas Brooksbank Charnock, son of the former minister of Haworth. After taking a Master of Arts degree at Oxford, Charnock had returned to reside in the area and, having no parish of his own and being of independent means, he had frequently assisted Patrick by taking duties for him. At the end of October 1847, aged only forty-seven, he committed suicide by hanging himself in his dressing room. Though his reasons for doing so were not discovered, it was particularly distressing that a clergyman, whose faith in God alone should have given him hope, had been driven to such straits of desperation. Though it was too late to do anything for his old friend now, Patrick did what he could to preserve his dignity in death, taking the burial service in Haworth Church himself instead of delegating it to his curate.[8]

In the circumstances, it was not surprising that Patrick's spirits were low at the beginning of 1848. Perhaps with the view of cheering him up, Emily and Anne persuaded Charlotte that it was now time to tell their father of her literary success. Reluctant at first, a small incident made up her mind for her: she overheard the postman asking Patrick where one Currer Bell could be living and his reply that there was no such person in the parish. Charlotte wrote in haste to Smith, Elder & Co., informing them that in future it would be better 'not to put the name of Currer Bell on the outside of communications; if directed simply to Miss Brontë they will be more likely to reach their destination safely. Currer Bell is not known in this district and I have no wish that he should become known.'⁹ Then, taking a copy of *Jane Eyre*, some newspaper reviews and her courage into her hands, she 'marched into his study' and had the following conversation with him:

'Papa I've been writing a book.' 'Have you my dear?' and he went on reading. 'But Papa I want you to look at it.' 'I can't be troubled to read MS.' 'But it is printed.' 'I hope you have not been involving yourself in any such silly expense.' 'I think I shall gain some money by it. May I read you some reviews.'¹⁰

In this matter-of-fact way, Patrick learnt that his quiet, reclusive, thirty-one-year-old daughter was 'Currer Bell', the literary sensation of London. As Mrs Gaskell reported it to a friend after hearing the story directly from Charlotte herself, Patrick's reaction was equally subdued. He invited his daughters to tea the same afternoon and informed them: 'Children, Charlotte has been writing a book – and I think it is a better one than I expected.'¹¹ Though Patrick may not have immediately recognized the brilliance of *Jane Eyre*, there is manifold evidence of his pride and joy in Charlotte's achievement which was to be the comfort of his declining years. Displaying his quiet sense of humour, he may even have passed on the book to one of his clerical friends whose daughters had been at the Clergy Daughters' School, for Charlotte reported to Smith Williams:

I saw an elderly clergyman reading it the other day, and had the satisfaction of hearing him exclaim 'Why – they have got — school, and Mr — here, I declare! and Miss —' (naming the original of Lowood, Mr Brocklehurst and Miss Temple) He had known them all: I wondered whether he would recognize the portrait, and was gratified to find that he did and that moreover he pronounced them faithful and just – he said too that Mr — (Brocklehurst) 'deserved the chastisement he had got'¹²

The 'elderly clergyman' is likely to have been Thomas Crowther, vicar of Cragg Vale, who had sent his daughters to the Clergy Daughters' School in the early 1830s and later made 'disparaging remarks' about it to Arthur Nicholls. With barely concealed glee, Charlotte noted that though her 'elderly clergyman' had recognized her characters, he had not recognized 'Currer Bell': 'What author would be without the advantage of being able to walk invisible?' she declared with no small satisfaction. 'One is thereby enabled to keep such a quiet mind.'¹³

Charlotte was well aware that she could not afford to rest on her laurels for long, however, and for some time had been pondering the problem of her next work. Wisely, in view of her preferred method of writing through numerous drafts, she rejected her publishers' suggestion of a serial and decided on 'another venture in the 3 vol: novel form'.¹⁴ Finding a subject was more difficult and she discussed the problem at length with both William Smith Williams and George Henry Lewes, an author and reviewer who, somewhat self-importantly, had written to Currer Bell to say that he intended to review *Jane Eyre*. In so doing, he had warned her to 'beware of Melodrama' and 'adhere to the real', suggesting that she ought not to 'stray far from the ground of experience'. Charlotte had replied by telling him the cautionary tale of *The Professor*, which was declared by all to be 'original, faithful to Nature' but was rejected seven times on the grounds that 'such a work would not sell'. The experience had taught her the importance of allowing the imagination free rein: 'is not the real experience of each individual very limited?' she demanded:

and if a writer dwells upon that solely or principally is he not in danger of repeating himself, and also of becoming an egoist?

Then too, Imagination is a strong, restless faculty which claims to be heard and exercised, are we to be quite deaf to her cry and insensate to her struggles?[15]

Having read Lewes' reviews of *Jane Eyre*, Charlotte wrote to thank him for his generous treatment, adding an explanation for her defence of the imaginative over the real.

I mean to observe your warning about being careful how I undertake new works: my stock of materials is not abundant but very slender, and besides neither my experience, my acquirements, nor my powers are sufficiently varied to justify my ever becoming a frequent writer...

If I ever <u>do</u> write another book, I think I will have nothing of what you call 'melodrama'; I <u>think</u> so, but I am not sure. I <u>think</u> too I will endeavour to follow the counsel which shines out of Miss Austen's 'mild eyes'; 'to finish more, and be more subdued'; but neither am I sure of that. When authors write best, or at least, when they write most fluently, an influence seems to waken in them which becomes their master, which will have its own way, putting out of view all behests but its own, dictating certain words, and insisting on their being used, whether vehement or measured in their nature; new moulding characters, giving unthought-of turns to incidents, rejecting carefully elaborated old ideas, and suddenly creating and adopting new ones. Is it not so? And should we try to counteract this influence? Can we indeed counteract it?[16]

The acclaimed author of *Jane Eyre* was still at heart the same girl who had once written, 'I'm just going to write because I cannot help it', and whose Angrian dreams had been so vivid and compulsive that they had appeared more real than her Roe Head surroundings. Curiously, until Lewes suggested it, Charlotte had never read any Jane Austen. She then read *Pride and Prejudice*, famously declaring it

An accurate daguerreotyped portrait of a common-place face; a carefully-fenced, highly cultivated garden with neat borders and delicate flowers – but no glance of a bright vivid physiognomy – no open country – no fresh air – no blue hill – no bonny beck. I should hardly like to live with her ladies and gentlemen in their elegant but confined houses.[7]

While Charlotte realized, as Lewes did not, that Jane Austen's style and tone were the absolute antithesis of her own, she nevertheless also recognized his criticism of her tendency to melodrama and her 'untrue' pictures of high society. It was, after all, what many of the reviewers had found fault with and Smith Williams himself advised her to avoid. Thanking him for his literary advice, Charlotte told Smith Williams that she kept his letters and referred 'not unfrequently' to them. 'Circumstances may render it impracticable for me to act up to the letter of what you counsel,' she told him,

but I think I comprehend the spirit of your precepts – and trust I shall be able to profit thereby. Details – Situations which I do not understand, and cannot personally inspect, I would not for the world meddle with, lest I should make even a more ridiculous mess of the matter than < poor > Mrs Trollope did in her 'Factory Boy' – besides – not one feeling, on any subject, public or private, will I ever affect that I do not really experience –[18]

Trying hard to learn from all the criticism proffered by reviewers and newly found literary friends alike, Charlotte searched with increasing desperation for a suitable subject. Three times she began a new novel, only to be dissatisfied and abandon the results almost at once. Searching through her papers for inspiration she came across the manuscript of her much-rejected first novel. It still occupied a soft spot in her heart and she wrote to Smith Williams to plead on its behalf.

A few days since I looked over 'the Professor.' I found the beginning very feeble, the whole narrative deficient in incident and in general attractiveness; yet the middle and latter portion of the work, all that relates to Brussels, the Belgian school &c. is as good as I can write; it contains more pith, more substance, more reality, in my judgement, than much of 'Jane Eyre.' It gives, I think, a new view of a grade, an occupation, and a class of characters – all very common-place, very insignificant in themselves, but not more so than the materials composing that portion of 'Jane Eyre' which seems to please most generally –.

My wish is to recast 'the Professor', add as well as I can, what is deficient, retrench some parts, develop others – and make of it a 3 vol. work; no easy task, I know, yet I trust not an impracticable one.[19]

Smith Williams, with more sense than sentiment, swiftly stamped on the idea and Charlotte was obliged to look elsewhere, eventually finding her inspiration for *Shirley* in an unfinished Angrian tale she had written some years before.[20]

Despite Charlotte's forebodings, the second edition of *Jane Eyre* was selling as well as the first. Indeed, such was the book's popularity that an enterprising dramatist, John Courtney, adapted it for the stage; by the beginning of February 1848 *Jane Eyre*, subtitled *The Secrets of Thornfield Manor*, was in production at the Victoria Theatre in London. Drawing this somewhat startling information to Charlotte's attention, the erstwhile theatre critic of the *Spectator*, Smith Williams, offered to attend and send her his report if 'Currer Bell' was unable to go in person. Though curious to know what the play would be like, Charlotte refused to influence his decision on whether to go or not, though declining that possibility for herself.

A representation of 'Jane Eyre' at a Minor Theatre would no doubt be a rather afflicting spectacle to the author of that work: I suppose all would be woefully exaggerated and painfully vulgarised by the actors and actresses on such a stage. What – I cannot help asking myself – would they make of Mr Rochester? And the picture my fancy conjures up by way of reply is a somewhat humiliating one. What would they make of Jane Eyre? I see something very pert and very affected as an answer to that query.[21]

Smith Williams decided to try the play and duly reported back with a vivid description: 'you have raised the veil from a corner of your great world – your London –', Charlotte wrote in response, 'and have shewn me a glimpse of what I might call – <u>loathsome</u>, but which I prefer calling <u>strange</u>. Such then is a sample of what amuses the Metropolitan populace! ... You must try now to forget entirely what you saw'. Hot on the heels of the play came further proof of *Jane Eyre*'s popularity: a French lady wrote to ask its author's consent to a French translation and, more solidly, Smith, Elder & Co. sent a further remittance of one hundred pounds.[22]

The success of *Jane Eyre* had opened up a whole new world for Charlotte, a world that contrasted sharply with her life at home in Haworth. 'I cannot thank you sufficiently for your letters,' she wrote to Smith Williams, 'and I can give you but a faint idea of the pleasure they afford me; they seem to introduce such light and life to the torpid retirement where we live like dormice.'[23] In addition to her regular correspondence with Smith Williams, Charlotte had had letters from her fellow novelists George Henry Lewes, William Thackeray and Julia Kavanagh. With the last, Charlotte felt a strong empathy, partly because she detected in her letters 'a slight, pleasant echo of the Irish accent, as well as to feel the warmth of an Irish heart' and partly because Miss Kavanagh lived alone with her aged mother, whom she supported by her writing.[24] Charlotte had also begun to receive complimentary copies of books. Some, like R. H. Horne's 'very real, very sweet' poem *Orion*, were gifts from other Smith, Elder & Co. authors but most, like Leigh Hunt's *A Jar of Honey from Mount Hybla*, were the latest works issuing from the press and were from the publishers themselves.[25] This kindness was worth more than the simple monetary value of the books to the Brontës; for the first time in their lives they were able to see and read the newest books as they were published instead of having to wait for them to be available in the circulating and subscription libraries. Not only were they kept abreast of contemporary literature but also, because Charlotte felt under an obligation to repay the gifts with some sort of critical comment, her letters are full of her analyses of the new publications. Charlotte thus developed her own critical powers while also creating a lifeline to the literary society and conversation she so craved.

Emily and Anne benefited as much as Charlotte from Smith, Elder & Co.'s munificence but, despite her efforts to persuade them otherwise, they refused to change their publisher. Having tried and failed the previous November, Charlotte returned to the attack in the spring. 'If Mr Newby always does business in this way,' she had told Smith Williams, 'few authors would like to have him for their publisher a second time.'[26] Smith Williams had, of course, again responded by offering to publish Ellis and Acton Bell's next works but Emily and Anne had no intention of coming to Smith, Elder & Co. under Charlotte's patronage. Mr Newby reported that *Wuthering Heights* was selling well, so there was every prospect of Emily and Anne recovering their initial deposit; 'consequently', Charlotte reported in a miffed tone, 'Mr Newby is getting into marvellously good tune with his authors.' So much so, that Emily and Anne both did exactly what Charlotte had prophesied they would not, and offered him their second novels. This left Charlotte in the embarrassing predicament of having to turn down the offer which she herself had extracted from Smith, Elder & Co.: 'their present engagements to Mr Newby are such as to prevent their consulting freely their own inclinations and interests',[27] she lied, knowing that her sisters had deliberately renewed their contracts even while she was negotiating on their behalf. For once, she would not be able to organize her sisters' lives.

In all the excitement of her new career as an author, Charlotte had somewhat overlooked her old friendship with Ellen Nussey. Their letters had become infrequent over the winter months: Charlotte had more interesting correspondents in London and Ellen was preoccupied with a visit from Amelia Ringrose, her brother George's fiancée, whom Charlotte had not yet met. Once – and that not long ago – Charlotte would have been glad that Ellen had persuaded Amelia to write to her, pitying Amelia's plight in her unhappy home and equally unhappy engagement to a man whose sanity seemed increasingly unlikely to return. Now, however, she could scarcely conceal her impatience. 'You must excuse the brevity of this note,' she told Amelia in response to her first letter, 'I do not possess your fluent pen in correspondence.' She did not even bother to reply to Amelia's second letter, telling Ellen, 'I really had nothing to say worth saying or which could interest her – I might indeed have sat down and concocted something elaborate – but where is the use of scribbling letters of that sort? It is merely time thrown away.'[28] As Charlotte was bound by her vow to Emily not to discuss the most important and interesting part of her life, her letters to

Ellen were simply a series of responses to things Ellen had told her, combined with apologies for her lengthy silences. 'I meant to have written to you by to-day's post – but two or three little things have occurred to hinder me and I am afraid now I shall be too late', she wrote at last on 28 January, omitting to tell her friend that the 'two or three little things' were the receipt of Thackeray's letter thanking her for the dedication of *Jane Eyre* and her own appalled letter to Smith Williams on discovering Thackeray's secret.[29] The only news she then had to impart related to the Robinsons of Thorp Green. Elizabeth and Mary 'still amaze me by the continued frequency and constancy of their correspondence –', she told Ellen, neglecting to mention the even more astonishing fact of their indiscretion regarding their mother.

poor girls – they still complain of their Mother's proceedings – that woman is a hapless being; calculated to bring a curse wherever she goes by the mixture of weakness, perversion & deceit in her nature. Sir Edward Scott's wife is said to be dying – if she goes I suppose they will marry – that is if Mrs R. can marry – She affirmed her husband's will bound her to remain single – but I do not believe anything she says.[30]

A full six months before Lady Scott died, and only nine months before Mrs Robinson succeeded in marrying the widower, the Brontës were informed of her plans by her daughters: if nothing else, this confirms Mrs Robinson's immorality in pursuing the husband of a dying woman and her ruthlessness in carrying out her plans. Branwell would not be allowed to disturb those plans and the sums of money by which she financed his habit continued to flow. As late as June 1848 Branwell was still applying to her for money with which to pay his debts at the Old Cock and Talbot inns at Halifax, staving off his creditors by telling them that 'my receipt of money on asking, through Dr Crosby, is morally certain'.[31]

Branwell's problems were becoming an increasing irrelevance to Charlotte, who was happily absorbed in her challenging new role as an author. A third edition of *Jane Eyre* being now in prospect, Smith Williams offered her the chance to illustrate her book. Ironically, in view of the many hours she had spent on her 'nimini-pimini' copies of engravings in the hope that she might one day be a professional artist, Charlotte knew that she would have to reject the offer. 'It is not enough to have the artist's eye; one must also have the artist's hand to turn the first gift to practical account', she told Smith Williams.

I have, in my day, wasted a certain quantity of Bristol board and drawing-paper, crayons and cakes of colour, but when I examine the contents of my portfolio now, it seems as if during the years it has been lying closed, some fairy had changed what I once thought sterling coin into dry leaves, and I feel much inclined to consign the whole collection of drawings to the fire; I see they have no value.

As so often these days, she compared her lack of artistic talent with one who had it in abundance, her hero Thackeray. 'How he can render with a few black lines and dots, shades of expression so fine, so real; traits of character so minute, so subtle, so difficult to seize and fix – I cannot tell; I can only wonder and admire.'[32]

Though she refused to illustrate *Jane Eyre*, she did agree to append a second preface, or rather a note, to the third edition, disclaiming the authorship of any other work of fiction: 'my claim to the title of novelist rests on this one work alone'.[33] Though intended to quash doubts about the separate identity of the Bells, whom the reviewers persisted in regarding as a single author, the note was neither prominent nor informative enough to prevent further speculation.

In fact, the publication of the third edition prompted a confrontation with Ellen Nussey. Rumours surrounding its authorship had begun to take definite shape in the Birstall and Gomersal area, where Charlotte's literary ambitions and connections with the Clergy Daughters' School were well known. Ellen, aware that the rumours could well be correct, wrote immediately to hint that her friend had been identified as 'Currer Bell'. If she had hoped for a confidence, she was wrong: Charlotte snapped back at her with a sharp 'Write another letter and explain that last note of yours distinctly.' When Ellen elaborated, she received an equally imperious and hostile response.

I have given <u>no one</u> a right either to affirm, or hint, in the most distant manner, that I am 'publishing' – (humbug!) Whoever has said it – if any one has, which I doubt – is no friend of mine. Though twenty books were ascribed to me, I should own none. I scout the idea utterly. Whoever, after I have distinctly rejected the charge, urges it upon me, will do an unkind and an ill-bred thing. The most profound obscurity is infinitely preferable to vulgar notoriety; and that notoriety I neither seek nor will have. If then any Birstallian or Gomersallian should presume to bore you on the subject, – to ask you what 'novel' Miss Brontë has been 'publishing,' – you can just say, with the distinct firmness of which you are perfect mistress, when you choose, that you are authorised by Miss Brontë to say, that she repels and disowns every accusation of the kind. You may add, if you please, that if any one has her confidence, you believe you have, and she has made no drivelling confessions to you on the subject.[34]

Charlotte was in an impossible position, being bound by her promise to Emily to keep the secret of their authorship and yet, in so doing, putting Ellen in the invidious position of spreading a lie. Though written as if dashed off in a rage, Charlotte's letter shows signs of being carefully thought out. She never actually denies her authorship, only refuses to acknowledge it; and it was certainly true that she had made no 'drivelling confession' of it to Ellen. Nevertheless, there is an undeniable cruelty in her unnecessary insistence on Ellen's having her confidence and yet using her to deny the truth. If the secret ever did get out, then Ellen would be publicly humiliated for taking such a firm stance against the truth, especially when a simple denial of knowledge would have sufficed.

This deceit was especially unkind as Charlotte seems to have taken her other great friend, Mary Taylor, completely into her confidence. She, of course, was in New Zealand, but her family and circle were still in Gomersal so it would not have been impossible for the news to have leaked out through her. Writing at the end of June 1848, Mary noted that she had received a copy of *Jane Eyre* 'about a month since', but as the mailings took six months to travel from England to New Zealand, Charlotte must have sent her the book in January 1848 at the latest. 'It seemed to me incredible that you had actually written a book', Mary confessed to Charlotte. 'Such events did not happen while I was in England.' It is possible that Charlotte had Emily's permission to exempt Mary Taylor from the general prohibition, for Mary seems to have received copies of *Wuthering Heights* and *Agnes Grey* at the same time. Comparing the three books, Mary, who was writing a book herself, commented:

You are very different from me in having no doctrine to preach. It is impossible to squeeze a moral out of your production ... You have done wisely in choosing to imagine a high class of readers. You never stop to explain or defend anything & never seem bothered with the idea – if Mrs Fairfax or any other well intentioned fool gets hold of this what will she think? And yet you know the world is made up of such, & worse. Once more, how have you written through 3 vols. without declaring war to the knife against a few dozen absurd do[ct]rines each of which is supported by 'a large & respectable class of readers'? Emily seems to have had such a class in her eye when she wrote that strange thing Wuthering Heights. Ann too stops repeatedly to preach commonplace truths. She has had a still lower class in her mind's eye. Emily seems to have followed the[e b]ookseller's advice.

Not only did Mary have copies of the sisters' books and know exactly who had written what, but also she was in full possession of all the details of their publication. 'As to the price you got it [was] certainly Jewish ... If I were in your place the idea of being bound in the sale of 2! more would prevent from ever writing again ... I exceedingly regret having burnt your letters in a fit of caution, & I've forgotten all the names. Was the reader Albert Smith? What do they all think of you?'[35] Though we can only regret that Mary had seen fit to burn Charlotte's letters telling of her literary adventures, this in itself was an indication that Charlotte's trust in her friend's discretion was not misplaced.[36]

Charlotte could talk to Mary Taylor in a way that she could not to Ellen. The same was true of her correspondence with William Smith Williams, which had opened up a whole new world of literary and political discussion for Charlotte. The French Revolution of February 1848, in which Louis

Philippe, the 'Citizen King', was forced to abdicate and flee to England, was a subject of the deepest interest to Charlotte and she found a fellow enthusiast in Smith Williams. In letter after letter she discussed the 'unhappy and sordid old man!', 'Mean, dishonest Guizot', his chief minister whose dismissal had brought about the king's own downfall, and 'brilliant, unprincipled Thiers' who 'writes as if the Shade of Bonaparte were walking to and fro in the room behind him, and dictating every line he pens'. She warned Smith Williams against putting too much faith in the Republicans: there were too few men of rational intellect amongst them and too many Radicals demanding universal suffrage.[37]

While Charlotte retained her arguments for Smith Williams, she shared her feelings on the subject with her old headmistress, Miss Wooler. Recalling her youthful, ardently partisan obsession with the Napoleonic wars, she wrote, rather ruefully:

I remember well wishing my lot had been cast in the troubled times of the late war, and seeing in its < ?stimulating > exciting incidents a kind of stimulating charm which it made my pulses beat fast only to think of ... I have now outlived youth; and, though I dare not say that I have outlived all its illusions – that the romance is quite gone from Life, the veil fallen from Truth, and that I see both in naked reality – yet certainly many things are not to me what they were ten years ago; and amongst the rest, 'the pomp and circumstance of war' have quite lost in my eyes their factitious glitter –

The girl who had once idolized Wellington as the personification of military glory was now a woman who saw more clearly the suffering war brought in its wake.

it appears to me that insurrections and battles are the acute diseases of nations, and that their tendency is to exhaust by their violence the vital energies of the countries where they occur. That England may be spared the spasms, cramps and frenzy-fits now contorting the Continent and threatening Ireland, I earnestly pray!

With the French and Irish, I have no sympathy. With the Germans and Italians I think the case is different: as different as the love of Freedom is from the lust of License.[38]

Charlotte's nervousness about the spread of revolution from the Continent to the United Kingdom was compounded by the presence in her locality of so many English Radicals. The French Revolution had sparked off a huge revival of the Chartist movement and their mass meetings, often several thousand strong, were being held uncomfortably close to Haworth. Only days before Charlotte's letter to Miss Wooler, there was one such gathering at Gilstead Moor above Bingley; the following week 8,000 met on Farnhill Moor near Kildwick, where they were addressed by the Haworth Chartist, Abraham Lighton, and between four and five thousand met the day after in Keighley market place. At the end of May there were serious riots in

Bradford where 5,500 men, including many heads of families, were on relief; a further 7,000 in the outlying districts were in the same position and the poor rate was running at seven shillings in the pound to support them. Extra regiments were drafted into the town from Colne, just across the Lancashire border, and Manchester, to keep the populace under control.[39]

Charlotte was able to write about the Chartists with greater detachment than she had written about the French. 'Your remarks concerning the Chartists seem to me truly sensible', she congratulated Smith Williams:

their grievances should not indeed 'be neglected, nor the existence of their sufferings ignored'. It would now be the right time, when an ill-advised movement has been judiciously repressed to examine carefully into their causes of complaint and make such concessions as justice and humanity dictate. If Government would act so, how much good might be done by the removal of ill-feeling and the substitution of mutual kindliness in its place![40]

This curious lack of involvement in the struggles of the Chartists, which were taking place literally before her eyes, was characteristic also of the passages she was then currently writing in *Shirley*. It is extraordinary that a writer with such a reputation for realism, truth and feeling did not allow the contemporary sufferings of the Chartists to inform her portrayal of the Luddites. Conditions in the 1840s were very similar to those in the early decades of the century: a prolonged slump in the textile trade brought in its wake high unemployment and abysmally low wages; the price of bread was high and disease made rapid inroads on the working population; the consequence at this time, as it had been then, was that the mill workers took refuge in Radical politics. Charlotte could not have stepped out of the front door of her home without seeing the suffering all around her and, as the rector's daughter, she could not have avoided some parish-visiting among the poor. Nevertheless, she might as well have lived on a rural estate in the south of England for all the effect that her personal experience brought to her book. While one cannot criticize an author for choosing to write about the middle rather than the working classes, one can surely question the lack of heart in dealing with the Luddites themselves when their activities are central to the plot. The only working man whose character is at all fleshed out, Joe Scott, is not only a cut above his fellows because of his education and position as foreman, but also is on the side of the authorities. It is ironic that despite Charlotte's abundant opportunities to observe the sufferings of the poor during periods of distress, she relied instead on her reading, conscientiously consulting the files of the *Leeds Mercury* 'in order to understand the spirit of those eventful times'.[41] For a novelist whose stated objective was to write only about details and situations she could understand, *Shirley* was a missed opportunity: the starving and desperate Luddites are merely incidental to her plot, their cause effectively seen only from the point of view of those in authority, and depicted with less realism and sympathy than in those reports she had read in the *Leeds Mercury*.

Discussing her new work with Smith Williams, Charlotte declared her intention of avoiding the subject of governesses because she did not wish the book to resemble *Jane Eyre*. However, almost despite herself, a theme was gradually emerging. 'I often wish to say something about the "condition of women" question', she told Smith Williams,

– but it is one respecting which so much 'cant' has been talked, that one feels a sort of repugnance to approach it. It is true enough that the present market for female labour is quite overstocked – but where or how could another be opened? Many say that the professions now filled only by men should be open to women also – but are not their present occupants and candidates more than numerous enough to answer every demand? Is there any room for female lawyers, female doctors, female engravers, for more female artists, more authoresses? One can see where the evil lies – but who can point out the remedy? When a woman has a little family to rear and educate and a household to conduct, her hands are full, her vocation is evident – when her destiny isolates her – I suppose she must do what she can – live as she can – complain as little – bear as much – work as well as possible. This is not high theory – but I believe it is sound practice –[42]

This was a subject to which Charlotte would return again and again, it being one of obvious relevance to her own situation. One cannot escape the conclusion that her intellectual engagement with the subject arose purely and simply as a result of her own unhappiness. If she had been financially independent, 'the condition of women' would not have mattered to her. She could not write about a cause for ideological reasons, out of empathy or even altruism, though she admired those, like Mrs Gaskell or Harriet Beecher Stowe, who could. Personal experience alone could engage her interest. 'I have always been accustomed to think that the necessity of earning< s > one's subsistence is not in itself an evil;' she explained in a later letter:

but I feel it may become a heavy evil if health fails, if employment lacks; if the demand upon our efforts made by the weakness of others dependent upon us, becomes greater than our strength suffices to answer ... I think you speak excellent sense when you say that girls without fortune should be brought up and accustomed to support themselves; and that if they marry poor men, it should be with a prospect of being able to help their partners. If all parents thought so, girls would not be reared on speculation with a view to their making mercenary marriages – and consequently women would not be so piteously degraded as they now too often are.[43]

In taking up 'the "condition of women" question', Charlotte was making her 'protest against the world's absurdities' which Mary Taylor had sought but failed to find in *Jane Eyre*; *Shirley*, unlike her first published novel, would have a 'doctrine to preach'.[44]

While Charlotte struggled to recapture the white heat of intensity with which she had written *Jane Eyre*, Anne was putting the finishing touches to *The Tenant of Wildfell Hall*. The new work was soon being advertised by Thomas Cautley Newby with what Charlotte described as 'a certain tricky turn in its wording which I do not admire', and was published in the last week of June 1848. With characteristic ingenuity and an audacity he had not yet dared reveal in London, Newby had also sold the first sheets of the book to an American publisher as the latest work by Currer Bell, extracting a high price for the privilege. Smith, Elder & Co.'s American correspondent, learning that a rival had received the book, wrote indignantly to complain of foul play, enclosing a letter from Newby, 'affirming that "to the best of his belief 'Jane Eyre' 'Wuthering Heights' – 'Agnes Grey' – and 'The Tenant of Wildfell Hall' (the new work) were all the production of one writer"'. 'This was a lie', Charlotte declared furiously to Mary Taylor, 'as Newby had been told repeatedly that they were the productions of 3 different authors – but the fact was he wanted to make a dishonest move in the game'.[45]

Smith, Elder & Co.'s response, undoubtedly prompted by the thought that Charlotte had somehow managed to find a publisher for *The Professor*, was a letter to their author 'all in alarm, suspicion and wrath' demanding an explanation.[46] There was only one way of proving to everyone's satisfaction that the Bells were three separate persons and that was to provide ocular proof. Though they no doubt attempted to persuade her to accompany them, Emily flatly refused to go to London: the insistence on anonymity had been her *sine qua non* for publishing and she had no intention of coming forward at this late stage. Besides, she could argue that the whole matter was simply Charlotte and Anne's problem, as it had arisen over Anne's book and Charlotte's name. If it was really necessary to go to the publishers in person, then two authors would do as well as three – there was no need to involve her. The argument probably raged for most of the day, for though the letter arrived in the morning post on 7 July, Charlotte and Anne did not set out until the late afternoon. Even then, though Charlotte would have liked to have used the opportunity to abandon her pseudonym, Emily insisted that only the two publishers should be let into their secret. 'The upshot of it', Charlotte later told Mary Taylor,

was that on the very day I received Smith & Elder's letter – Anne and I packed up a small box, sent it down to Keighley – set out ourselves after tea – walked through a thunderstorm to the station, got to Leeds and whirled up by the night train to London – with the view of proving our separate identity to Smith & Elder and confronting Newby with his lie –[47]

Though they had travelled by second-class ticket from Keighley to Leeds, they changed to a first-class carriage for the night train to London, arriving about eight o'clock the next morning at the Chapter Coffee House in

Paternoster Row – 'our old place Polly', Charlotte told Mary, 'we did not well know where else to go'. They washed themselves, had some breakfast, sat for a few minutes and then set off to 65, Cornhill 'in queer, inward excitement'.

We found 65 – to be a large bookseller's shop in a street almost as bustling as the Strand – we went in – walked up to the counter – there were a great many young men and lads here and there – I said to the first I could accost – 'May I see Mr Smith –?' – he hesitated, looking a little surprised – but went to fetch him – We sat down and waited awhile – looking a[t] some books on the counter – publications of theirs well known to us – many of which they had sent us copies as presents.[48]

Saturday being a full working day, George Smith was already in his office, but he was busy and anxious not to be disturbed. When the clerk came with the message that two ladies wished to see him, Smith sent out to ask for their names which the Brontës declined to give, saying they had come on a private matter. Ever courteous, Smith concealed his impatience and went out to meet the two 'rather quaintly dressed little ladies, pale-faced and anxious-looking' who were waiting for him.[49] An amused Charlotte later reported their first meeting.

somebody came up and said dubiously
'Did you wish to see me, Ma'am?' 'Is it Mr Smith?' I said looking up through my spectacles at a young, tall, gentlemanly man. 'It is.'
  I then put his own letter into his hand directed to 'Currer Bell.' He looked at it – then at me – again – yet again – I laughed at his queer perplexity – a recognition took place – I gave my real name – 'Miss Brontë' – We were both hurried from the shop into a little back room – ceiled with a great skylight and only large enough to hold 3 chairs and a desk – and there explanations were rapidly gone into – Mr Newby being anathematized, I fear with undue vehemence. Smith hurried out and returned quickly with one whom he introduced as Mr Williams – a pale, mild, stooping man of fifty – very much like a faded Tom Dixon – Another recognition – a long, nervous shaking of hands – Then followed talk – talk – talk – Mr Williams being silent – Mr Smith loquacious –
  'Allow me to introduce you to my mother & sisters – How long do you stay in Town? You must make the most of the time – to-night you must go to the Italian opera – you must see the Exhibition – Mr Thackeray would be pleased to see you – If Mr Lewes knew "Currer Bell" was in town – he would have to be shut up – I will ask them both to dinner at my house &c.'[50]

At this point Charlotte was obliged to stop the flow with 'a grave explanation'. Their publishers alone were to be admitted to the secret of their identity; to the rest of the world they must remain 'gentlemen'. With that intuition which made him such a sympathetic correspondent, Smith Williams 'understood me directly'. George Smith, who relished the prospect of the sensation that the two tiny provincial ladies would make in a London which characterized them as the 'coarse Bell brothers', 'comprehended by slower degrees – he did not like the quiet plan – he would have liked some excitement, eclat &c.' He tried another tack, urging them to attend a literary party incognito as his 'Country Cousins', but Charlotte was obliged to veto this plan too when she learnt that men like Thackeray could not be invited without a hint as to whom they would meet, even though the desire to see some of the people Smith mentioned 'kindled in me very strongly'. 'I declined even this – I felt it would have ended in our being made a show of – a thing I have ever resolved to avoid.' Smith made a last-ditch attempt to persuade the sisters to stay at his house, but this too they declined. As they parted, Smith told them that he would bring his own sisters to meet them that evening, a courtesy Charlotte had not the heart to refuse again. Having dropped their bombshell, Charlotte and Anne retired to the quiet obscurity of the Chapter Coffee House, where Charlotte 'paid for the excitement of the interview by a thundering head-ache & harrassing sickness'.[51]

It is difficult to believe that, prior to this interview, neither George Smith nor William Smith Williams had guessed that 'Currer Bell' was one and the same as the 'Miss Brontë' to whom they had addressed 'his' correspondence. Smith later claimed that, for his own part, he had never had much doubt on the subject of the writer's sex – 'but then I had the advantage over the general public of having the handwriting of the author before me. There were qualities of style, too, and turns of expression, which satisfied me that "Currer Bell" was a woman, an opinion in which Mr Williams concurred.' George Smith's observation of Charlotte's appearance and character, informed by later and better acquaintance, was equally perceptive:

I must confess that my first impression of Charlotte Brontë's personal appearance was that it was interesting rather than attractive. She was very small, and had a quaint old-fashioned look. Her head seemed too large for her body. She had fine eyes, but her face was marred by the shape of the mouth and by the complexion. There was but little feminine charm about her; and of this fact she herself was uneasily and perpetually conscious. It may seem strange that the possession of genius did not lift her above the weakness of an excessive anxiety about her personal appearance. But I believe that she would have given all her genius and her fame to have been beautiful. Perhaps few women ever existed more anxious to be pretty than she, or more angrily conscious of the circumstance that she was *not* pretty.[52]

George Smith was equally sensitive in his assessment of Anne Brontë, though this was the only occasion on which he ever saw her. 'She was a gentle, quiet, rather subdued person, by no means pretty, yet of a pleasing appearance. Her manner was curiously expressive of a wish for protection and encouragement, a kind of constant appeal which invited sympathy.'[53] Charlotte's first impressions of George Smith were more favourable.

Mr Smith made himself very pleasant – he is a firm, intelligent man of business though so young – bent on getting on – and I think desirous to make his way by fair, honourable means – he is enterprising – but likewise cool & cautious. Mr Smith is a practical man –[54]

He was also, she might have added, extremely good-looking: twenty-five years old, dark-eyed and dark-haired, with a clear pale face and an athletic figure kept in trim by his daily habit of riding. By contrast, William Smith Williams – the 'pale, mild, stooping man of fifty' – was more of a kindred spirit to Charlotte and Anne, a man who was 'altogether of the contemplative, theorizing order ... [who] lives too much in abstractions':

he was so quiet but so sincere in his attentions – one could not but have a most friendly leaning towards him – he has a nervous hesitation in speech and a difficulty in finding appropriate language in which to express himself – which throws him into the background in conversation – but I had been his correspondent – and therefore knew with what intelligence he could write – so that I was not in danger of underrating him.[55]

On the Saturday evening, 8 July, after their eventful first meeting in the morning, Charlotte was unable to throw off her headache and nausea, despite a strong dose of sal volatile. She was, therefore, still in 'grievous bodily case' when the Smiths were announced and found the sisters clinging together on the most remote window-seat of the long, low dingy room where the elderly waiter, touched by their plight, had given them refuge.

They came in two elegant, young ladies in full dress – prepared for the Opera – Smith himself in evening costume – white gloves, &c a distinguished, handsome fellow enough – We had by no means understood that it was settled that we were to go to the Opera – and were not ready – Moreover we had no fine, elegant dresses either with us or in the world – However on brief rumination, I though[t] it would be wise to make no objections – I put my headache in my pocket – we attired ourselves in the plain – high-made, country garments we possessed – and went with them to their carriage – where we found Williams likewise in full dress. They must have thought us queer, quizzical-looking beings, especially me with my spectacles – I smiled inwardly at the contrast which must have been apparent between me and Mr Smith as I walked with him up the crimson carpeted staircase of the Opera House and stood amongst a brilliant throng at the box-door – which was not yet open. Fine ladies & gentlemen glanced at us with a slight, graceful superciliousness quite warranted by the circumstances – Still I felt pleasurably excited – in spite of headache and sickness & conscious clownishness; and I saw Anne was calm and gentle – which she always is –

The performance was Rosini's opera of the 'Barber of Seville' – very brilliant though I fancy there are things I should like better – We got home after one o'clock – we had never been in bed the night before – had been in constant excitement for 24 hours – you may imagine we were tired.[56]

Smith later told Mrs Gaskell about a touching incident at the opera. As they had climbed the grand staircase, Charlotte, overcome by the splendour of her surroundings, had involuntarily pressed his arm and confided in a whisper, 'You know I am not accustomed to this sort of thing.'[57]

Charlotte may have nipped in the bud George Smith's plans to show her off as his trophy author but she could not prevent him devising schemes for her entertainment. The day after they had attended the opera, the Brontë sisters were escorted to morning service at St Stephen's, Walbrook by Smith Williams but, to their disappointment, Dr Croly, whom they had wished to hear, did not preach.[58] In the afternoon George Smith arrived with his mother in their carriage to carry them off for dinner. Throughout the ordeal of the opera and the less public but equally trying dinner with the Smiths, who had not been told who their visitors really were, Charlotte was buoyed up by her sense of the ridiculous: nothing could be more incongruous than to see the 'elegant, handsome' man about town, George Smith, 'treating with scrupulous politeness these insignificant spinsters' – 'a couple of odd-looking country-women'.[59] She had, too, the secret satisfaction of knowing that all these fine ladies and gentlemen who had looked down so super-ciliously on herself and her sister would have fallen over themselves to meet the author of *Jane Eyre*.

At the Smiths' grand residence in Westbourne Place, Bishop's Road, Paddington, the Brontës were given a fine dinner 'which neither Anne nor I had appetite to eat – and were glad when it was over'. 'I always feel under awkward constraint at table', Charlotte confided in Mary Taylor. 'Dining out would be a hideous bore to me.'[60] The following day, Monday, Mrs Smith called on the sisters but, to their relief, left them to make their own way round the exhibitions at the Royal Academy and the National Gallery. They dined again at the Smiths' but spent the evening with Smith Williams and his family in the more congenial surroundings of his '\comparatively/ humble but neat residence'. There, no doubt to the Brontës' gratification, they met a daughter of Leigh Hunt, who was Smith Williams' friend: 'she sang some little Italian airs which she had picked up among the peasantry in Tuscany, in a manner that charmed me – for herself she was a rattling good-natured personage enough –'.

On Tuesday Morning we left London – laden with books Mr Smith had given us – and got safely home. A more jaded wretch than I looked when I returned, it would be difficult to conceive – I was thin when I went but was meagre indeed when I returned; my face looked grey & very old – with strange deep lines plough[ed] in it – my eyes stared unnaturally – I was weak and yet restless. In a while however these bad effects of excitement went off and I regained my normal condition.[61]

Having exhausted herself reliving the excitement of the whirlwind trip to London, Charlotte ended her long account to Mary Taylor with the news that she and Anne had also visited Newby. Frustratingly, she deferred the description of what must have been another momentous meeting to a later letter, which she seems never to have written.⁶² One small surviving record of the 'pop visit', as Mary Taylor termed it, gives a touching insight into the Brontës' arrangements. In the tiny notebook in which she also jotted down George Smith's address and directions to his house, Charlotte noted the expenses of the journey and their stay. Their second-class tickets from Keighley to Leeds had cost five shillings and their first-class tickets on the train to London £4 9s.; on their return journey, they economized by travelling second class from Euston at a cost of only £3 4s. Their embarrassment at their inadequate country clothing is indicated by the purchase of new gloves and parasols (five shillings and sixteen shillings respectively) and they paid two shillings to get into the Academy exhibition. Three nights at the Chapter Coffee House cost them £2 5s., somewhat more than the inn at Leeds where they stayed overnight on their return for a mere nine shillings. They came home bearing presents for their sister and the servants – a twelve-shilling copy of Tennyson's *Poems* for Emily and books for Martha Brown and Tabby Aykroyd – but, curiously, nothing for either Patrick or Branwell. The whole trip, including tips to porters and the cost of cabs in London, had cost Charlotte and Anne exactly fourteen pounds – nearly three-quarters of their annual salary as governesses.⁶³

The fact that two publishers were now aware that the brothers Bell were actually three sisters made little or no immediate difference to the Brontës; apart from their father, Mary Taylor and possibly Branwell no one else knew. Ellen's suspicions about Charlotte, however, had received unexpected confirmation. Less than a month before the 'pop visit', Ellen herself had gone to London to stay in Cleveland Row with her brother John, the court physician. She had found 'quite a *fureur*' about the authorship of *Jane Eyre* on her arrival and, having obtained a copy, read the first half page aloud. 'It was as though Charlotte Brontë herself was present in every word, her voice and spirit thrilling through and through', Ellen later declared.⁶⁴ Persistent as ever, she wrote to her friend, only to receive yet another putdown: 'Your naïveté in gravely enquiring my opinion of the "last new novel" amuses me: we do not subscribe to a circulating library at Haworth and consequently "new novels" rarely indeed come in our way, and consequently \again/ we are not qualified to give opinions thereon.'⁶⁵

Ellen was clearly not the only one to suspect her friend's authorship – indeed, anyone who knew the fate of Maria and Elizabeth Brontë could hardly fail to recognize the portrait of the Clergy Daughters' School. It was not surprising, then, that a man as intelligent and well read as Joe Taylor, Mary's brother, was one of the first to put two and two together. Early in June he had taken the unusual step of making an expedition to Haworth with his cousin, Henry Taylor, and Henry's cousin, Jane Mossman, despite a 'pouring wet and windy day'. The ostensible purpose of the visit was to make enquiries about Madame Heger's school on behalf of Henry's sister, Ellen Taylor, but Charlotte clearly suspected an ulterior motive. 'Nothing of importance in any way was said the whole time – it was all rattle – rattle of which I should have great difficulty now in recalling the substance ... The visit strikes me as an odd whim: I consider it quite a caprice, prompted probably by curiosity.'[66] Charlotte clearly knew that the astute Joe Taylor had guessed her secret though she did not – could not, because of her promise to Emily – gratify him by confessing it.

The intense alarm with which Emily herself viewed any divulgence of the sisters' authorship was graphically illustrated after the visit to London. In one of his letters, Smith Williams alluded to Charlotte's sisters, bringing down an explosion of wrath upon Charlotte's head. She wrote back hastily and apologetically:

Permit me to caution you not to speak of my Sisters when you write to me – I mean do not use the word in the plural. 'Ellis Bell' will not endure to be alluded to under any other appellation than the 'nom de plume.' I committed a grand error in betraying < her > his identity to you and Mr Smith – it was inadvertent – the words 'we are three Sisters' escaped me before I was aware – I regretted the avowal the moment I had made it; I regret it bitterly now, for I find it is against every feeling and intention of 'Ellis Bell.'[67]

Perhaps surprisingly, given the concerns about the confusion of the identity of the 'Bells', the first reviews of *The Tenant of Wildfell Hall* were clear that Acton Bell was different from Currer, though obviously related to him. These reviews appeared on 8 July, the very day that Charlotte and Anne confronted George Smith at 65, Cornhill. Despite the fact that the *Athenaeum* gave 'our honest recommendation of *Wildfell Hall* as the most interesting novel which we have read for a month past', the general tone of the reviews reflected the increasingly critical view of the Bells. 'The Bells must be warned against their fancy for dwelling upon what is disagreeable', warned the *Athenaeum*.[68] The *Spectator* was even more explicit.

The Tenant of Wildfell Hall, like its predecessor, suggests the idea of considerable abilities ill applied. There is power, effect, and even nature, though of an extreme kind, in its pages; but there seems in the writer a morbid love for the coarse, not to say the brutal; so that his level subjects are not very attractive, and the more forcible are displeasing or repulsive, from their gross, physical, or profligate substratum ... There is a coarseness of tone throughout the writing of all these Bells, that puts an offensive subject in its worst point of view, and which generally contrives to dash indifferent things.[69]

'I wish my Sister felt the unfavourable [notices] less keenly', Charlotte confessed to Smith Williams. 'She does not say much, for she is of a remarkably taciturn, still, thoughtful nature, reserved even with her nearest of kin, but I cannot avoid seeing that her spirits are depressed sometimes'.[70]

Despite – or possibly because of – the reviews, *The Tenant of Wildfell Hall* sold extremely well; a second edition was in preparation before the end of July and published during the second week in August, just six weeks after the first. Stung by the remarks in the *Spectator*, Anne was goaded out of her usual reserve. She took the unprecedented step of adding a preface which castigated her critics for being 'more bitter than just' and stoutly defended her decision to depict vice so graphically. She also took issue with the continuing speculation about her sex.

I am satisfied that if a book is a good one, it is so whatever the sex of the author may be. All novels are or should be written for both men and women to read, and I am at a loss to conceive how a man should permit himself to write anything that would be really disgraceful to a woman, or why a woman should be censured for writing anything that would be proper and becoming for a man.[71]

The immense popularity of the Bells and the number of column inches devoted to discussion of their works in the press reminded Aylott & Jones that they still had virtually an entire print run of *Poems* by Currer, Ellis and Acton Bell sitting unsold on their shelves. They wrote to ask what should now be done with them, prompting Charlotte to get in touch with George Smith. 'I wished much to ask your advice about the disposal of the remaining copies, when in London', she told him, 'but was withheld by the consciousness that "the Trade" are not very fond of hearing about <u>Poetry</u>'. Blaming the 'limited sale' on the fact that *Poems* had not been widely advertised, Charlotte hinted that Smith, Elder & Co. might like to take the book over and remedy the deficiency. It was with some delight she learnt that her suggestion had been acted upon and that *Poems* was likely to be reissued by her own publishers.[72]

Happily looking forward to this, enjoying her literary discussions with Smith Williams and gratified by an invitation from the directors of the Manchester Athenaeum to their annual *soirée* which, naturally, she turned down,[73] Charlotte was completely oblivious to the impending tragedy which was about to engulf her family.

Branwell's health had worsened so imperceptibly over the last eighteen months that no one had noticed how ill he had become. So often drunk or hung over, it could only be expected that his constitution would be affected. Since at least the beginning of the year he had been suffering from fainting fits and *delirium tremens*; presumably, too, he had not escaped the bouts of influenza which had afflicted the entire household in the spring and summer. What no one yet realized was that these illnesses masked the symptoms of the tuberculosis which now had Branwell in its grip.

In the middle of June he had written to J. B. Leyland in the hope of fending off his creditors. Thomas Nicholson, landlord of the Old Cock Inn at Halifax, was threatening a court summons and had written to Patrick demanding settlement of Branwell's bills. Sending ten shillings with John Brown and promising to pay the rest as soon as he obtained an advance from Dr Crosby, Branwell wrote in panic: 'If he refuses my offer and presses me with law I am RUINED. I have had five months of such utter sleeplessness violent cough and frightful agony of mind that jail would destroy me for ever – '. Pathetically he added that he had long intended to write a letter of five or six pages 'but intolerable mental wretchedness and corporeal weakness have utterly prevented me'.[74] No doubt Leyland, like the Brontë family, simply thought Branwell was crying wolf once more. 'Branwell is the same in conduct as ever –', Charlotte complained to Ellen at the end of July, 'his constitution seems much shattered – Papa – and sometimes all of us have sad nights with him – he sleeps most of the day, and consequently will lie awake at night –'[75] Any sympathy Charlotte might have felt for her brother had long evaporated; now he simply irritated her.

Certainly Branwell did little to court his family's approval. Not only was he hopelessly entangled in debt but also he was driven to the abuser's extremes of duplicity in his desperation to feed his habit. Mrs Gaskell describes how he would steal out of the house while all the family were at church to cajole the village druggist out of a lump of opium.[76] His last extant letter provides sad confirmation of this. Dated only 'Sunday. Noon', when the household would indeed be at church, it was addressed to his old friend and drinking companion, John Brown.

> Sunday. Noon.
>
> Dear John,
>
> I shall feel very much obliged to you if [you] can contrive to get me Five pence worth of Gin in a proper measure
>
> Should it be speedily got I could perhaps take it from you or Billy at the lane < it > top or what would be quite as well, sent out for, to you.
>
> I anxiously ask the favour because I know the < favour > good it will do me.
>
> Punctualy at Half-past Nine in the morning you \will/ be paid the 5d out of a shilling given me then. Yours,
>
> P.B.B.[77]

Nothing could have illuminated Branwell's decline so clearly as this pitifully ill-written, ill-spelt, confused begging letter with its pathetic disclosures that he was dependent on his father's charity for the gift of a shilling and reduced to drinking gin.

During the third week in September, Branwell had an unexpected visitor, Francis Grundy, his friend from happier days on the railway at Luddenden Foot. Grundy ordered dinner for two in a private room at the Black Bull and then sent up to the parsonage for Branwell. While he waited, he was surprised to receive a visitor himself: touched by the kindness Grundy was showing to his son, Patrick Brontë had come down to see him and warn him to be prepared for a dramatic change in Branwell's appearance. 'Much of the Rector's old stiffness of manner was gone', Grundy noted:

He spoke of Branwell with more affection than I had ever heretofore heard him express, but he also spoke almost hopelessly. He said that when my message came, Branwell was in bed, and had been almost too weak for the last few days to leave it; nevertheless, he had insisted upon coming, and would be there immediately.[78]

Despite Patrick's warning, Grundy was nevertheless deeply shocked when his friend at last made his appearance.

Presently the door opened cautiously, and a head appeared. It was a mass of red, unkempt, uncut hair, wildly floating round a great, gaunt forehead; the cheeks yellow and hollow, the mouth fallen, the thin white lips not trembling but shaking, the sunken eyes, once small, now glaring with the light of madness, – all told the sad tale but too surely.[79]

Grundy hid his surprise, greeted his guest 'in my gayest manner, as I knew he best liked' and forced a stiff glass of hot brandy upon him. 'Under its influence, and that of the bright, cheerful surroundings, he looked frightened – frightened of himself. He glanced at me a moment, and muttered something of leaving a warm bed to come out into the cold night.' Gradually, however, with another glass of brandy inside him, 'something like the Brontë of old' returned, though he remained grave throughout the evening. 'He described himself as waiting anxiously for death – indeed, longing for it, and happy, in these his sane moments, to think that it was so near' and declared that his death would be solely due to his disastrous relationship with Mrs Robinson. As Grundy reluctantly took his leave, Branwell pulled a carving knife from his sleeve and confessed that, having given up hope of ever seeing Grundy again, he had imagined his message was a call from Satan. He had armed himself with the knife, which he had long kept hidden, and come to the inn determined to rush into the room and stab its occupant. Only the sound of Grundy's voice and his manner had 'brought him home to himself' as Branwell described it. 'I left him standing bare-headed in the road', Grundy remembered, 'with bowed form and dropping tears. A few days afterwards he died.'[80]

Though Branwell had long been obsessed with death and had increasingly shown a preoccupation with epitaphs and images of death, his conversation with Grundy revealed that he knew he had not long to live. The end came so suddenly, however, after all the months of slow decline, that it caught everyone, including the doctor who had attended him all summer, by surprise. Charlotte was later to be comforted by the fact that a 'most propitious change marked the few last days of poor Branwell's life', a change which, with hindsight, she recognized as being a portent of death: 'his demeanour, his language, his sentiments were all singularly altered and softened', she wrote, 'the calm of better feelings' filled his mind and 'a return of natural affection marked his last moments'.[81]

Two days before his death, Branwell was well enough to walk down the lane into the village. As he returned to the parsonage, he was overcome by faintness and shortness of breath and had to be helped home by William Brown, the sexton's brother. Their faltering progress was observed by Tabitha, William's thirteen-year-old niece. Sixty years later, she still vividly recalled the incident. 'There was a low step to mount and I can always remember seeing him catch hold to the door side – it seemed such hard work for him. I believe that was the last time he was ever out.'[82]

The next day, Branwell was unable to get up from his bed. John Wheelhouse, the Haworth doctor, was sent for and told the shocked family that his patient was close to death. In an agony of distress, the anguished father who had had such high hopes for this, his only son, knelt in prayer by his bedside and wrestled for his soul. Though he had attended untold deathbeds, including those of his dearly beloved wife, sister-in-law and William Weightman, he had done so in the safe and sure knowledge that the dying had all had faith in their eternal future. It was the bitterest pill of all that only his most precious son had rejected the comforts of his religion and refused to repent of his manifold sins. In this, his darkest hour, and with who knows what desolation in his heart, Patrick begged his son to seek salvation with all the urgency that approaching death could instil. Gradually, perhaps through mere force of will, he brought Branwell to a recognition of his vices and the repentance of them. The chimera of Mrs Robinson was finally driven away. Throughout this, his last night, Branwell talked of his 'misspent life, his wasted youth, and his shame, with compunction'. Some time before the end, John Brown came and was left alone with the dying man. Branwell, looking back over his past excesses – in which Brown had so often shared – made no mention of the woman for whom he had destroyed himself. Calm and self-possessed, he seemed 'unconscious that he had ever loved any but the members of his family, for the depth and tenderness of which affection he could find no language to express'. Seizing John Brown's hand, he cried, 'Oh, John, I am dying!' and then, as if speaking to himself, he murmured, 'In all my past life I have done nothing either great or good.'[83]

At about nine o'clock on the morning of Sunday, 24 September, the Brontë family gathered round Branwell's bed to witness his life drawing to its close. He remained perfectly conscious to the end: 'I myself, with painful, mournful joy, heard him praying softly in his dying moments', Charlotte told Smith Williams, 'and to the last prayer which my father offered up at his bedside, he added "amen". How unusual that word appeared from his lips – of course you who did not know him, cannot conceive'. After a struggle of twenty minutes, which must have seemed an eternity to his distressed family, Branwell started convulsively, almost to his feet, and fell back dead into his father's arms. He was thirty-one years old.[84] Watching this, the first death she had ever witnessed,[85] Charlotte felt the dawnings of pity for her brother:

When the struggle was over – and a marble calm began to succeed the last dread agony – I felt as I had never felt before that there was peace and forgiveness for him in Heaven. All his errors – to speak plainly – all his vices seemed nothing to me in that moment; every wrong he had done, every pain he had caused, vanished; his sufferings only were remembered; the wrench to the natural affections only was felt ... – He is at rest – and that comforts us all long before he quitted this world – Life had not happiness for him.[86]

Though she now felt able to forgive her impetuous brother's sins, Charlotte was not able to forget them. There was a bitterness about his life – if not his death – that she could not put aside. Writing to Smith Williams a week after Branwell's untimely end she revealed how deep the rift had grown between the once inseparable pair.

the removal of our only brother must necessarily be regarded by us rather in the light of a mercy than a chastisement: Branwell was his Father's and his Sisters' pride and hope in boyhood, but since Manhood, the case has been otherwise. It has been our lot to see him take a wrong bent; to hope, expect, wait his return to the right path; to know the sickness of hope deferred, the dismay of prayer baffled, to experience despair at last; and now to behold the sudden early obscure close of what might have been a noble career.

I do not weep from a sense of bereavement – there is no prop withdrawn, no consolation torn away, no dear companion lost – but for the wreck of talent, the ruin of promise, the untimely dreary extinction of what might have been a burning and a shining light. My brother was a year my junior; I had aspirations and ambitions for him once – long ago – they have perished mournfully – nothing remains of him but a memory of errors and sufferings – There is such a bitterness of pity for his life and death – such a yearning for the emptiness of his whole existence as I cannot describe – I trust time will allay these feelings.[87]

In thus writing his obituary, Charlotte revealed the poison which had eaten away at her relationship with her brother until it had eventually destroyed the love she had once had for him; he had committed the unforgivable sin of not living up to her expectations of him. Despite her measured cadences, all the force of her emotion was concentrated on that one word 'obscure': while the rest of her letter is written in her usual neat and even script that one word stands out, its letters crushed together as if written in a spasm of barely suppressed savagery.

Patrick's reaction to his son's death was both more natural and more charitable, though it was reported by Charlotte with all the jealousy of the well-behaved sibling seeing a father's love of the prodigal son.

My poor Father naturally thought more of his <u>only</u> Son than of his daughters, and much and long as he had suffered on his account – he cried out for his loss like David for that of Absalom – my Son! my Son! And refused at first to be comforted –[88]

'It was my fate to sink at the crisis when I should have collected my strength', Charlotte told Ellen. The stress or what she called 'the awe and trouble of the death-scene' brought on a headache and nausea on the day itself, followed by internal pain, loss of appetite and bilious fever.[89] No doubt her extreme reaction was caused not just by the sudden loss of the brother who had once been so close to her, but also by the recognition that she could so easily have succumbed to the same fate. Had she given in just a little more to her feelings about Monsieur Heger, perhaps she too would have been tipped over the edge. Charlotte took to her bed for a week while the rest of the family struggled to come to terms with their loss and make preparations for the funeral. The burden of performing the last intimate rites for their brother, as well as preparing the customary burial tea, purchasing mourning clothes and stationery and organizing the printing and distribution of funeral cards therefore fell on Emily and Anne, who set about their tasks with their usual calm efficiency. Anne even had to write to Smith Williams on Charlotte's behalf to thank him for his letters, which she was too indisposed to answer.[90]

It was not to be expected that Patrick would perform the burial service for his son but, rather than simply pass the duty on to his curate, he called on his old friend, Branwell's godfather, William Morgan. On Thursday, 28 September, Branwell's body was carried the short distance from his home to his father's church, where it was interred in the family vault next to the remains of his mother, aunt and sisters.[91] John Brown, performing a more respectable service for him than he had so often done in the past, added Branwell's name to the family monument on the wall in the church. His death was registered by the village doctor, John Wheelhouse, who certified the cause as 'Chronic bronchitis – Marasmus', though the symptoms and subsequent events suggest that the deterioration in Branwell's lungs and his wasting away were actually due to consumption, which was rife in the village.[92] Whatever the technical causes of his death, his family and friends had no doubt whatsoever about the real reason:

Patrick Branwell Brontë was no domestic demon – he was just a man moving in a mist, who lost his way. More sinned against, mayhap, than sinning, *at least* he proved the reality of his sorrows. They killed him…[93]

Chapter Twenty

STRIPPED AND BEREAVED

' "We have buried our dead out of our sight" ', Charlotte wrote to William Smith Williams at the beginning of October 1848,[1] little knowing that Branwell's death was only the beginning of her troubles. Suffering 'terrible' nights and 'impressions experienced on waking ... such as we do not put into language',[2] Charlotte was at first too preoccupied with her own misery and psychosomatic illness to notice her sisters' indisposition. In response to anxious queries from Ellen and Smith Williams, Charlotte painted a miserable portrait of herself 'sitting muffled at the fireside, shrinking before the east wind (which for some days has been blowing wild and keen over our cold hills), and incapable of lifting a pen for any more formidable task than that of writing a few lines to an indulgent friend'.[3] All the family had suffered 'harassing coughs & colds' in the wake of the changeable weather and dreaded cold easterly winds but it was not until the end of October that Charlotte began to suspect something more serious was amiss. 'I feel much more uneasy about my sisters than myself just now', she told Ellen.

Emily's cold and cough are very obstinate; I fear she has pain in the chest – and I sometimes catch a shortness in her breathing when she has moved at all quickly – She looks very, very thin and pale. Her reserved nature occasions one great uneasiness of mind – it is useless to question her – you get no answers – it is still more useless to recommend remedies – they are never adopted.

Nor can I shut my eyes to the fact of Anne's great delicacy of constitution. The late sad event has I feel made me more apprehensive than common – I cannot help feeling much depressed sometimes – I try to leave all in God's hands, and to trust in his goodness – but faith and resignation are difficult to practise under some circumstances.[4]

It was a mark of their extraordinary esteem for and kindness towards their authoress, that Smith, Elder & Co. did everything in their power to assist her in these dark days. Smith Williams sent letters written expressly to divert her; George Smith sent her a hundred pounds, proof that the third edition of *Jane Eyre* was selling well; more importantly, a large parcel of books arrived, unsolicited, for the sisters to read and return at leisure. As George Smith refused to accept their thanks, Charlotte wrote to tell him that the loan of the books was indeed well timed: 'no more acceptable benefit could have been conferred on my dear sister Emily who is at present too ill to occupy herself with writing, or indeed with anything but reading. She smiled when I told her Mr Smith was going to send some more books – she was pleased.' The opening of the parcel and examination of the books had cheered Emily; their perusal was to occupy her for many a weary day.[5]

The terrible realization that there was something seriously amiss with Emily shook Charlotte out of her own hypochondria and self-pity: 'the tie of sister is near and dear indeed,' she wrote, 'and I think a certain harshness in her powerful, \and/ peculiar character only makes me cling to her more'.[6] Those ties were to be stretched to the limit as Emily stubbornly refused to answer enquiries about her health, let alone accept any offers of assistance. Clinging to hope as a lifeline, Charlotte wrote to Smith Williams on 2 November:

I would fain hope that Emily is a little better this evening, but it is difficult to ascertain this: she is a real stoic in illness, she neither seeks nor will accept sympathy; to put any question, to offer any aid is to annoy; she will not yield a step before pain or sickness till forced; not one of her ordinary avocations will she voluntarily renounce: you must look on, and see her do what she is unfit to do, and not dare to say a word; a painful necessity for those to whom her < life > health and existence are as precious as the life in their veins.[7]

Emily had refused all medicine and medical advice; nothing could induce her to see a physician. The problem of how to help someone who would not be helped clearly exercised William Smith Williams, as well as Emily's family, and he wrote to suggest that she should try homoeopathy. Charlotte gave his letter into Emily's hands, carefully refraining from endorsing its suggestions: 'it is best usually < not > to leave her to form her own judgement', she confided to Smith Williams, 'and <u>especially</u> not to advocate the side you wish her to favour; if you do she is sure to lean in the opposite direction, and ten to one will argue herself into non-compliance.' Emily read the letter, pronounced Smith Williams' intention 'kind and good' but declared him to be under a delusion – 'Homoeopathy was only another form of quackery'.[8]

Having clutched at the straw of homoeopathy, only to have it fly from her grasp, Charlotte wrote to Ellen in absolute despair.

I told you Emily was ill in my last letter – she has not rallied yet – she is <u>very</u> ill: I believe if you were to see her your impression would be that there is no hope: a more hollow, wasted pallid aspect I have not beheld. The deep tight cough continues; the breathing after the least exertion is a rapid pant – and these symptoms are accompanied by pain in the chest and side. Her pulse, the only time she allowed it to be felt, was found to be at 115 per minute. In this state she resolutely refuses to see a doctor; she will give no explanation of her feelings, she will scarcely allow her illness to be alluded to.[9]

Repeating the words she had once spoken of Branwell, she confessed, 'God only knows how all this is to terminate.' In her heart, however, she was all too well aware: 'More than once I have been forced boldly to regard the terrible event of her loss as possible and even probable. But Nature shrinks from such thoughts.' As Emily marched inexorably towards death, Charlotte clung to her with even greater desperation: 'I think Emily seems the nearest thing to my heart in this world', she declared to Ellen.[10]

Charlotte's closest friends did all they could to assist her. Ellen offered to come and stay, but Emily could not contemplate the upset and refused to have her. Smith Williams sent a book on homoeopathy in a further attempt to persuade Emily to accept some treatment; she read it but remained intractable. Smith Williams and George Smith together offered to seek medical advice anonymously on Emily's behalf from 'an eminent London physician', Dr Epps: Charlotte prepared a statement of her sister's symptoms and sent it to him through them: the reply, when it came, was too late and too obscurely worded to be of use and, in any case, Emily refused to take the medicine he sent.[11]

Observing even the smallest change in her sister's condition, Charlotte alternated between despair and self-deluding hope. Unlike his volatile daughter, Patrick could not be sanguine. 'My Father is very despondent about her', Charlotte reported to Smith Williams. 'Anne and I cherish hope as well as we can ... but my father shakes his head and speaks of others of our family once similarly afflicted, for whom he likewise persisted in hoping against hope, and who are now removed where hope and fear fluctuate no more.' If Patrick had thought to prepare his daughters for Emily's death, he failed. Charlotte clutched at the 'important differences' between their case and Emily's: 'I <u>must</u> cling to the expectation of her recovery; I <u>cannot</u> renounce it', she cried, as if, in repeating this mantra, she could ward off the inevitable.[12]

Unable to prevent or halt Emily's decline, Charlotte could think of little else but her sister. Distractions only added to the bitterness which was threatening to overwhelm her. Throughout the year Anne had continued to hear almost daily from her former pupils, Elizabeth and Mary Robinson. In the summer they had both announced that they were engaged to be married – not for the first time, as Charlotte cynically noted.

Not one spark of love does either of them profess for her future husband – one of them openly declares that interest alone guides her – and the other, poor thing! is acting according< s > to her mother's wish, and is utterly indifferent herself to the man chosen for her. The lighter-headed of the two sisters takes pleasure in the spectacle of her fine wedding-dresses and costly bridal presents – the more thought-ful can derive no gratification from these things and is much depressed at the contemplation of her future lot – Anne does her best to cheer and counsel \her/ – and she seems to cling to her quiet, former governess as her only true friend.[13]

What was to be increasingly distressing, however, was the news they reported of their mother. 'Of Mrs R— I have not patience to speak', Charlotte informed Ellen, '– a worse mother a worse woman, I may say, I believe hardly exists – the more I hear of her the more deeply she revolts me.' Apparently quoting the Robinsons' letters to Anne, Charlotte revealed that the girls expected to be 'sacrificed' in the course of a few months.

the unhappy Lady Scott is dead – after long suffering both mental and physical, I imagine, she expired two or three weeks ago. The Misses R— say that their mother does not care in the least what becomes of them; she is only anxious to get them husbands of any kind that they may be off her hands, and that she may be free to marry Sir. E. Scott – whose infatuated slave, it would appear, she is. They assert that she does not appear to have the least affection for them now – formerly she professed a great deal, and was even servilely submissive to them – but now she treats them quite harshly – and they are often afraid to speak to her.[14]

On 8 November, a mere six weeks after Branwell's death – an event of which she was almost certainly as ignorant as she was careless – Mrs Robinson achieved her ambition and married Sir Edward Scott. All Charlotte could bring herself to say on the subject was 'She is now Lady Scott – her daughters say she is in the highest spirits.'[15]

That there was some justification in the daughters' complaints is suggested by the fact that shortly before her mother's remarriage, Mary Robinson had been married off to Henry Clapham, even though both the young people were still legally minors. Henry Clapham was a manufacturer, residing at Aireworth House just outside Keighley, and a relative of both the Sugdens and the Greenwoods of Haworth. 'A low match for her –', Charlotte declared to Ellen, 'she feels it so'; Mary later complained to Anne that her husband had deceived them with his account of his fortune, establishment and connections.[16] The new Mrs Clapham, not even professing to be happy in her letters to Anne, had evidently decided to respond by cutting 'a prodigious dash' in Keighley and was infuriating the local gentry by her pride and assumption of superiority.

She & her sister threaten to pay us a visit – they have written to ask if they can bring the carriage up to the house – we have < lit > told them 'yes', as we think if they bring it once through those breakneck turnings – they will not be in a hurry to try the experiment \again/ –[17]

In the end the visit turned out better than expected, despite the fact that the Brontës were in no mood for such guests. The Robinsons came at the beginning of December and Charlotte reported back to Ellen that they were 'attractive and stylish looking girls'. To their hosts' evident bemusement 'they seemed overjoyed to see Anne; when I went into the room they were clinging round her like two children – she, meantime, looking perfectly quiet and passive. Their manner evinced more levity and giddiness than pretension or pomposity.'[18]

This unwelcome intimacy with the Robinsons was a continual and painful reminder of Branwell's sufferings. Another irritant, even more hurtful because it reflected on Charlotte and her sisters, was the increasingly disparaging tone of the reviews. The appearance of *The Tenant of Wildfell Hall*, so soon after *Jane Eyre*, *Wuthering Heights* and *Agnes Grey*, had only confirmed the critics in their belief that the Bells were obsessed with the coarse and brutal. The reviewer in *Sharpe's London Magazine*, for instance, declared his intention of noticing *The Tenant of Wildfell Hall* simply to warn his readers, especially his lady readers, against being tempted to peruse it. Preferring to believe that this was the work of a man, rather than a woman, he lambasted the 'profane expressions, inconceivably coarse language, and revolting scenes and descriptions by which its pages are disfigured'.[19] Most reviewers seized the opportunity of Acton Bell's new publication to return to the attack on *Jane Eyre* and *Wuthering Heights*. The critic in the *Rambler* was typical: describing the religious sentiments of Acton's characters as either false or bad, he prefaced his remarks by declaring that *The Tenant of Wildfell Hall* shared the same faults as *Jane Eyre*, 'one of the coarsest books which we ever perused', and condemning the author's 'perpetual *tendency* to relapse into that class of ideas, expressions, and circumstances, which is most connected with the grosser and more animal portion of our nature'.[20] The *North American Review* described Ellis Bell as 'a spendthrift of malice and profanity', Heathcliff as 'the epitome of brutality' and concluded by saying that the power evinced in *Wuthering Heights* was power thrown away – 'Nightmares

and dreams, through which devils dance and wolves howl, make bad novels.'
It was this review that Charlotte read to her sisters late in November, hoping
to amuse them.

As I sat between them at our quiet but now somewhat melancholy fireside, I studied
the two ferocious authors. Ellis the 'man of uncommon talents but dogged, brutal
and morose,' sat leaning back in his easy chair drawing his impeded breath as he
best could, and looking, alas! piteously pale and wasted – it is not his wont to laugh –
but he smiled half-amused and half in scorn as he listened – Acton was sewing, no
emotion ever stirs him to loquacity, so he only smiled too, dropping at the same
time a single word of calm amazement to hear his character so darkly portrayed. I
wonder what the Reviewer would have thought of his own sagacity, could he have
beheld the pair, as I did. Vainly too might he have looked round for the masculine
partner in the firm of 'Bell & Co.' How I laugh in my sleeve when I read the solemn
assertions that 'Jane Eyre' was written in partnership, and that it 'bears the marks
of more than one mind, and one sex'.[21]

Sitting together at home, it was comparatively easy for the sisters to overlook
the more barbed comments of their critics and find amusement in their
wilder speculations about the identity and sex of the 'Bells'. The fact that
their authorship was such a close-guarded secret was a form of empowerment, just as it had been in the long-gone days of childhood 'scribblemania':
it was the three of them against the world. Once her sisters were gone,
however, and there was no one to share the conspiracy of silence, Charlotte
found that the secret lost all its zest. Not only could she no longer take
pleasure in wrong-footing the critics but also, brooding alone on the severer
reviews, she came to see their attacks on her sisters as a defilement of their
memory. The injustice of the fact that these hostile reviews were to be the
last that her sisters would read, and that no one recognized their talents as
she thought they ought to be recognized, was to be an increasingly bitter
pill for Charlotte.

Emily was now in the final stages of consumption, though neither she nor
her family apparently suspected how close she was to death. Though the
pain in her side and chest had improved, her cough, shortness of breath and
extreme emaciation had not; to add to her troubles, she began to suffer from
diarrhoea, though she remained adamant that 'no poisoning doctor' should
come near her.[22] 'Never in all her life had she lingered over any task that
lay before her, and she did not linger now', Charlotte later wrote of her
sister.

She sank rapidly. She made haste to leave us. Yet, while physically she perished,
mentally, she grew stronger than we had yet known her. Day by day, when I saw
with what a front she met suffering, I looked on her with an anguish of wonder and
love. I have seen nothing like it; but, indeed, I have never seen her parallel in
anything. Stronger than a man, simpler than a child, her nature stood alone. The

awful point was, that, while full of ruth for others, on herself she had no pity; the spirit was inexorable to the flesh; from the trembling hand, the unnerved limbs, the faded eyes, the same service was exacted as they had rendered in health. To stand by and witness this, and not dare to remonstrate, was a pain no words can render.[23]

The evening before her death, she insisted on feeding the dogs, Keeper and Flossy, as she had always done. As she stepped from the warmth of the kitchen into the cold air of the damp, stone-flagged passage, she staggered and almost fell against the wall. Charlotte and Anne, rushing to help her, were brushed aside and, recovering herself, she went on to give the dogs their dinner. Mrs Gaskell reported how Charlotte shivered recalling the pang she had felt when, having searched over the bleak December moors for a single sprig of heather to take in to Emily, she realized that her sister had not even recognized her favourite flower.[24] On the morning of Tuesday, 19 December 1848, she insisted on rising at seven as was her habit. Combing her hair before the fire, the comb slipped from her fingers and fell into the hearth: she was too weak to pick it up, and before Martha Brown arrived and retrieved it for her, a large part of it had been burnt away by the flames.[25] Neither Martha nor Charlotte dared to offer assistance as Emily slowly dressed herself and made her way downstairs. Still struggling to keep up an appearance of normality, she even attempted to pick up her sewing. Watching her laboured breathing, Charlotte scribbled a brief note to Ellen: 'I should have written to you before if I had had one word of hope to say – but I have not – She grows daily weaker ... Moments so dark as these I have never known – I pray for God's support to us all. Hitherto he has granted it.'[26]

By midday, Emily was worse. Her unbending spirit finally broken, she whispered between gasps for breath, 'If you will send for a doctor, I will see him now.' Dr Wheelhouse was summoned immediately but, of course, it was too late: there was nothing he could do.[27] Tradition has it that Emily refused to the last to retire to bed, dying, as unconventionally as she had lived, on the sofa in the parsonage dining room. This seems unlikely, as there is no contemporary source for the story and Charlotte later movingly described how Emily's dog, Keeper, 'lay at the side of her dying-bed'. In all probability, therefore, Emily was carried upstairs to her own little room over the hall, which had once been the 'children's study'. Unlike Branwell, she fought death to the end. And it was a bitter end. There was no time for consolatory words or acceptance of the inevitable. After 'a hard, short conflict', Emily was torn from the world, 'turning her dying eyes reluctantly from the pleasant sun'. At two o'clock in the afternoon, aged thirty, she died: the relentless conflict between strangely strong spirit and fragile frame was over.[28]

At this crisis, Charlotte turned, not to Ellen Nussey, her friend since childhood and the only person outside the Brontë household who had ever got close to Emily, but to William Smith Williams. She wrote to him the day after Emily's death, a letter that was all the more poignant for its brevity and simple dignity.

My dear Sir

When I wrote in such haste to Dr Epps, disease was making rapid strides, nor has it lingered since, the galloping consumption has merited its name – neither physician nor medicine are needed more. Tuesday night and morning saw the last hours, the last agonies, proudly endured till the end. Yesterday Emily Jane Brontë died in the arms of those who loved her.

Thus the strange dispensation is completed – it is incomprehensible as yet to mortal intelligence. The last thre[e] months – ever since my brother's death seem to us like a long, terrible dream. We look for support to God – and thus far he mercifully enables us to maintain our self-control in the midst of affliction whose bitterness none could have calculated on

Believe me yours sincerely
C Brontë
Wednesday[29]

The following day Smith Williams wrote back in shock and sorrow to offer his comfort. This appears to be his only extant letter to Charlotte, and it reveals clearly why she turned to him for sympathy and encouragement at this point and at other crises in her life.

London 21st Dec /48

How to address you, my Dear Madam, on this distressing occasion I know not. To describe the astonishment & pain that the mournful intelligence has caused me, & the deep concern at the loss to her family & to the world of your gifted sister Emily, which Mr Smith shares with me, is beyond my power. We feel for you & your surviving – oh! what a world of sadness there is in that word! – your only sister, & for your bereaved father, & would fain shew our sympathy in other ways than words, if we knew how...

To mitigate your grief for such a loss, the only way is to think of the gain to her who has been taken from you, & of the duties that now devolve upon you to support your bereaved father & comfort your sister & be comforted by her. But how superfluous it is of me to remind you of the duties that your strong sense of rectitude & energy of will prompt you to perform, and which only bodily weakness – and may God give you strength to bear this heavy affliction! – can prevent you from fulfilling. And when after the first dread shock of losing one who was your other self has passed off, & left your mind calm enough to reflect with serene sorrowful contemplation on the great and good qualities of her who is now a memory of the past and a hope for the future, you cannot but find sweet consolation in recalling those noble traits of character & high intelligence for which she was distinguished: for she being dead yet liveth & speaketh. It has often occurred to me that if it were possible for us to think of our departed relatives & friends \only/ as if they were only removed to a brighter world and a purer sphere, and could dwell upon < them > our recollections of them without the disturbing medium of grief, how much more grateful & vivid, & ennobling would our regard & esteem for them be...

Great griefs are life-lasting 'tis true; but their influences are as refreshing and beneficial to the soul as the night to the earth, & sleep to the body. May your night of sorrow be brief & relieved by the blessed rays of consolation that no grief is devoid of, and may the morning of peace & resignation dawn upon you both with the refreshing serenity of hopeful and affectionate feelings. You and your sister must be more & more endeared to each other now that you are left alone on earth, and having the same hopes, & sorrows, & pursuits, your sympathies will be more & more \closely/ entwined.

God Bless & comfort you both, my dear friends, is the devout prayer of

Your sincere & attached
Wm Smith Williams.[30]

Charlotte was surely right in describing this letter as 'eloquent in its sincerity'.[31]

Though Emily had been far closer to her than Branwell in recent years, Charlotte did not give way this time. Instead of taking to her bed, she became a pillar of strength to her father and sister, who were both far from well. 'My father says to me almost hourly, "Charlotte, you must bear up – I shall sink if you fail me." These words – you can conceive are a stimulus to nature. The sight too of my sister Anne's very still but deep sorrow wakens in me such fear for her that I dare not falter. Somebody <u>must</u> cheer the rest."[32]

Emily would surely have approved of the way the arrangements for her funeral were carried out with the minimum of fuss and show. Obituary notices were sent out to the local papers and funeral cards printed for circulation among friends and relatives; white funeral gloves were purchased for the mourners and Emily's hair was cut to provide mourning jewellery.[33] The burial service, held on 22 December, was simple and quiet: this time Patrick did not send for Morgan but gratefully put the obsequies in the capable hands of his curate, Arthur Bell Nicholls. It was surely appropriate that the small funeral procession was headed by the bereaved father, mourning his 'beloved daughter', and Keeper, Emily's faithful dog, 'walking first side by side'. They were followed by Charlotte and Anne and then, in their turn, by Tabby and Martha. As Charlotte was later to recall with sad pride, Keeper also followed Emily's coffin to the vault where she was buried, lay in the family pew at their feet while the burial service was being read and then took up his forlorn station outside the door of Emily's room, where he howled pitifully for many days.[34]

The day after the burial, Charlotte at last wrote to tell Ellen. 'She died on Tuesday, the very day I wrote to you. I thought it very possible then she might be with us still for weeks and a few hours afterwards she was in

Eternity.' Inviting Ellen to come to Haworth to provide the consolation of a friend's presence, Charlotte reassured her:

We are very calm at present. why should we be otherwise? – the anguish of seeing her suffer is over – the spectacle of the pains of Death is gone by – the funeral day is past – we feel she is at peace – no need now to tremble for the hard frost and keen wind – Emily does not feel them She has died in a time of promise – we saw her taken from life in its prime –[35]

For Charlotte, this was to become a litany: Branwell was forever to be an example of promise betrayed, Emily one of promise unfulfilled. 'I will not now ask why Emily was torn from us in the fulness of our attachment', Charlotte wrote to Smith Williams on Christmas Day 1848,

rooted up in the prime of her own days, in the promise of her powers – why her existence now lies like a field of green corn trodden down – like a tree in full bearing – struck at the root; I will only say, sweet is rest after labour and calm after tempest, and repeat again and again that Emily knows that now.[36]

Curiously, Emily's publisher, Thomas Cautley Newby, had announced at the beginning of December that he was to publish another work by Ellis and Acton Bell. After receiving only twenty-five pounds for the copyright of *The Tenant of Wildfell Hall*, despite its good sales, Anne had already said that she would not use him again and would offer any new work to Smith, Elder & Co.[37] This leaves only the intriguing possibility that Emily had informed Newby that her next book was almost complete, not anticipating that her own rapid decline in health would prevent her finishing it to her satisfaction. Had Newby ever received the manuscript he would undoubtedly have published it, so the obvious inference is again that Charlotte, finding and reading Emily's second novel, decided that its subject, too, was 'an entire mistake' and would not improve 'Ellis Bell's' reputation. In such circumstances, she must have felt justified in destroying the manuscript.

The subject of Emily's second novel is a matter for speculation only; however, despite the traumas in the Brontë household, the publications continued. Smith, Elder & Co. had reissued *Poems* by Currer, Ellis and Acton Bell in November 1848; even with their backing and the newly found reputation of the authors, however, the book had only slow and disappointing sales. The critics, too, were obtuse in discerning talent only in the poems of Currer Bell, fulfilling their own prophecy that the author of *Jane Eyre*, the best of the Bell novels, would also be the best poet.[38] Ironically, however, it was Anne who was enjoying a quiet success with her poems. *Fraser's Magazine* had published her long poem, 'The Three Guides', written on 11 August

1848, in their issue of that month. In December they carried another of her poems, printed under her pseudonym, Acton Bell. Coming as it did at such a bleak time, this was particularly gratifying to Anne. Ellen Nussey, who had answered her friend's call and come straight over to Haworth at the end of December, observed a slow smile stealing over Anne's face as they sat before the fire one evening. When she asked her why, Anne replied, 'Only because I see they have inserted one of my poems.'[39] This was the first formal admission of their publishing that any of the Brontës had made to Ellen. It occurred only after Emily's death.

The poem was one Anne had written earlier in the year, in April, but its verses had greater resonance in the wake of the deaths of Branwell and Emily.

> Believe not those who say
>   The upward path is smooth,
> Lest thou shouldst stumble in the way,
>   And faint before the truth.

Though unintentional, the poem was also an answer to those of her critics who had attacked Anne's motives in writing *The Tenant of Wildfell Hall*:

> What matters who should whisper blame,
>   Or who should scorn or slight? –
> What matters – if thy God approve,
>   And if, within thy breast,
> Thou feel the comfort of His love,
>   The earnest of His rest![40]

On the same day she learnt of the publication of 'The Narrow Way', Anne replied to a letter she had received from the Reverend David Thom of Liverpool. He had written Acton Bell an enthusiastic and flattering letter, expressing the pleasure he had derived from the 'Bells'' novels but especially congratulating her on her espousal of the doctrine of universal salvation in *The Tenant of Wildfell Hall*. This had, in fact, been noticed and condemned by certain critics. The very idea that there was no such thing as eternal damnation and that, after a period of purifying purgatory, all men, however wicked, could attain heaven is 'alike repugnant to Scripture, and in direct opposition to the teaching of the Anglican Church', *Sharpe's London Magazine* had thundered. Thom's letter of support, whether in response to the novel or the review, was undoubtedly welcome to Anne: she had cherished the idea from childhood, she told him,

with a trembling hope at first, and afterwards with a firm and glad conviction of its truth. I drew it secretly from my own heart and from the word of God before I knew that any other held it. And since then it has ever been a source of true delight to me to find the same views either timidly suggested or boldly advocated by benevolent and thoughtful minds;

In *The Tenant of Wildfell Hall*, Anne confessed to Thom, 'I have given as many hints in support of the doctrine as I could venture to introduce into a work of that description. They are however *mere* suggestions, and as such I trust you will receive them.'[41]

Anne's own faith was about to be put to its severest test of all. Since at least the beginning of December she had been too delicate to do much and, ominously, had complained of frequent pains in the side.[42] Her profound grief at Emily's death and the unbearable strain her illness had caused over the last few months, combined to reduce Anne's health still further. Over Christmas and New Year, as it became apparent that she was not recovering as she should, she fell victim to a further bout of influenza. Alarmed and concerned that Dr Wheelhouse was out of his depth, Patrick decided that Anne should see a specialist. On 5 January 1849, Mr Teale, a respected Leeds physician experienced in cases of consumption, came to the parsonage to examine her. Ellen Nussey, who was still staying with the Brontës, recalled how Anne was 'looking sweetly pretty and flushed and in capital spirits for an invalid', even though she was fully aware of the importance of the diagnosis.

While consultations were going on in Mr Brontë's study, Anne was very lively in conversation, walking round the room supported by me. Mr Brontë joined us after Dr Teale's departure and, seating himself on the couch, he drew Anne towards him and said, 'My *dear* little Anne.' That was all – but it was understood.[43]

Only three days before this, Charlotte had told Smith Williams that Anne, and her father, were suffering from 'severe influenza colds'. Now she knew that Anne, too, had tubercular consumption and that it was only a matter of time until she lost her last remaining sister: the only hope Mr Teale could offer was for a 'truce or arrest' to the progress of the disease if Anne followed a strict regimen of quiet and rest and took the codliver oil and carbonate of iron he prescribed for her.[44]

Anne's cheerful show of bravery, not only during Mr Teale's visit but also throughout the ensuing months, was all the more remarkable and poignant because it was assumed. Knowing how much her father and sister had suffered from seeing Emily refuse medical treatment, she submitted to all the revolting, painful and ultimately useless remedies suggested by the doctors. Within days of Mr Teale's visit she was having blisters – hot compresses intended to draw the disease to the surface – applied to her side and taking doses of codliver oil which she graphically described as smelling and tasting like train oil; the effect of these treatments was to weaken her further with nausea.[45] Nevertheless, she appeared calm and stoical to her family: 'Anne is very patient in her illness', Charlotte told Smith Williams, '– as patient as Emily was unflinching. I recall one sister and look at the other with a sort of reverence as well as affection – under the test of suffering neither have faltered.'[46] Had Charlotte but known it, Anne's outward passivity was a shell, masking an all too natural panic and despair. The religious doubts which had haunted her in the past returned. Two days after Mr Teale's visit, Anne poured out in a poem her private anguish on hearing her death sentence

> A dreadful darkness closes in
>   On my bewildered mind
> O let me suffer & not sin
>   Be tortured yet resigned
>
> Through all this world of whelming mist
>   Still let me look to thee
> And give me courage to resist
>   The Tempter till he flee
>
> Weary I am – O give me strength
>   And leave me not to faint
> Say thou wilt Comfort me at length
>   And pity my complaint
>
> I've begged to serve thee heart & soul
>   To sacrifice to thee
> No niggard portion but the whole
>   Of my identity
>
> I hoped amid the brave & strong
>   My < given > portioned task might lie
> To toil amid the labouring throng
>   With purpose Keen & high
>
> But thou hast fixed another part
>   And thou hast fixed it well
> I said so with my bleeding heart
>   When first the anguish fell
>
> O thou hast taken my delight
>   & hope of life away
> And bid me watch the painful night
>   & wait the weary day
>
> The hope & the delight were thine
>   I bless thee for their loan
> I gave thee while I deemed them mine
>   Too little thanks I own[47]

It was not simply the thought of death itself that instilled such despair into Anne, but rather the fact that she had achieved so little. Her life, like Branwell's and Emily's, was to be the story of ambition and potential unfulfilled. Three weeks later, having had time to reflect on her fate and come to terms with it, Anne returned to the poem and added a further nine verses. Less desperate in tone, they show Anne's determination to find some value in the suffering which, she knew all too well, she would have to endure.

> These weary hours will not be lost
>   These days of passive misery
> These nights of darkness anguish-tost
>   If I can fix my heart on thee...
>
> ... That secret labour to sustain
>   With humble patience every blow
> To gather fortitude from Pain
>   And hope & holiness from Wo
>
> Thus let me serve thee from my heart
>   Whate'er my written fate
> Whether thus early to depart
>   Or yet awhile to wait
>
> If thou shouldst bring me back to life
>   More humbled I should be
> More Wise more strengthened for the strife
>   More apt to lean on thee
>
> Should Death be standing at the gate
>   Thus should I Keep my vow
> But Lord whate'er my future fate
>   So let me serve thee now[48]

While Anne kept her innermost thoughts and sufferings to herself, Charlotte could not be so self-contained, especially once Ellen had returned to Brookroyd. 'In sitting down to write to you', she told Smith Williams,

I feel as if I were doing a wrong and a selfish thing; I believe I ought to discontinue my correspondence with you till times change and the tide of calamity which of late days has set so strongly in against us, takes a turn. But the fact is, sometimes I feel it absolutely necessary to unburden my mind. To papa I must only speak cheeringly, to Anne only encouragingly, to you I may give some hint of the dreary truth.[49]

That dreary truth was soon told: 'Anne cannot study now, she can scarcely read; she occupies Emily's chair – she does not get well.' What could not be told so quickly was the anguish Charlotte herself was suffering.

When we lost Emily I thought we had drained the very dregs of our cup of trial but now when I hear Anne cough as Emily coughed, I tremble lest there should be exquisite bitterness yet to taste. However I must not look forwards, nor must I look backwards. Too often I feel like one crossing an abyss on a narrow plank – a glance round might quite unnerve...

All the days of this winter have gone by darkly and heavily like a funeral train; since September sickness has not quitted the house – it is strange – it did not use to be so – but I suspect now all this has been coming on for years: unused any of us to the possession of robust health, we have not noticed the gradual approaches of decay; we did not know its symptoms; the little cough, the small appetite, the tendency to take cold at every variation of atmosphere have been regarded as things of course – I see them in another light now.[50]

In the circumstances, and given Charlotte's tendency to hypochondria at times of stress or crisis, it is not surprising that she herself now developed the symptoms of consumption. Even though, at Mr Teale's recommendation, she no longer shared a bed with Anne, Charlotte had pains in her chest and back, her voice was hoarse and her throat sore. She treated herself with pitch plasters, bran tea and applications of hot vinegar and, when Ellen sent a present of cork soles which retained warmth against the cold, stone-flagged parsonage floors for the genuine invalid, Charlotte commissioned her to buy a pair for herself.[51]

Charlotte was fortunate in having good friends. Ellen Nussey gave practical assistance, not only sending the cork soles but also recommending and purchasing a respirator to ease Anne's breathing; Smith Williams offered moral support, an ever-sympathetic ear and another parcel of carefully chosen books.[52] George Smith suggested that Dr John Forbes, a personal friend who was also editor of the *Medical Review*, physician to the Queen's household and, most importantly, one of the first authorities in England on consumptive cases, should visit Haworth and examine Anne for himself. Charlotte, clutching at straws, ran to her father with this last proposal only to be bitterly disappointed when he rejected it. More realistic than his daughter, he could not see that anything would be achieved by dragging a physician, however eminent, all the way from London when Anne was already in the care of Mr Teale. 'Notwithstanding his habitual reluctance to place himself under obligations', Charlotte informed George Smith that Patrick would 'unhesitatingly accept an offer so delicately made ... did he think any really useful end could be answered by a visit from Dr Forbes'. It is a measure of Charlotte's desperation that she then went behind her father's back and requested that Dr Forbes would at least comment on Mr Teale's diagnosis and course of treatment. Dr Forbes replied with a speed and kindness that Charlotte was long to remember. He knew Mr Teale well and thought highly of him; his course of treatment was just what he would himself have recommended, but he warned against entertaining sanguine hopes of recovery. Disappointed once more, Charlotte reported his verdict to Ellen, adding, 'There is some feeble consolation in thinking we are doing the very best that can be done – the agony of forced, total neglect is not now felt as during Emily's illness.'[53]

By the beginning of February, the worst of Anne's symptoms had abated; she was less feverish and her cough was less troublesome. Suddenly hopeful that the remedies might be working and that Anne might gain a lasting reprieve, Charlotte began to give some thought to the writing she had neglected for so long. 'My literary character is effaced for the time –', Charlotte had written to Smith Williams only two weeks before. 'Should Anne get better, I think I could rally and become Currer Bell once more – but if otherwise – I look no farther – sufficient for the day is the evil thereof.'[54] Though new composition had been next to impossible in recent weeks, she had occupied her spare moments in making a fair copy of the first volume of her new book, *Shirley*. It was therefore with a sense of dismay that Charlotte read *Mary Barton*, the recently published first novel by Mrs Gaskell, which was a powerful indictment of contemporary Manchester life. Set during the terrible distress of the industrial slump of 1842–3, the plot centred on the murder of one of the mill owners by his desperate workmen. Though in feeling, tone and sympathy *Mary Barton* was a world away from *Shirley*, Charlotte could not escape the conclusion that to a certain extent she had been pre-empted in both subject and incident: her novel, too, was set in the north of England during industrial troubles and involved an assassination attempt on a mill owner. The similarity was enough to prompt her to submit the manuscript of her first volume to Smith, Elder & Co., even though this went against the grain: 'remember', she warned Smith Williams,

if I shew it to you – it is on two conditions. The first that you give me a faithful opinion – I do not promise to be swayed by it but I should like to have it – the second that you shew it and speak of it to <u>none</u> but Mr Smith. I have always a great horror of premature announcements – they may do harm and can never do good.[55]

Discovering a few days later that Smith Williams and George Smith had an informal evening chat each day with James Taylor, the manager in charge of the staff of clerks at 65, Cornhill, Charlotte felt that Taylor's exclusion might seem invidious and therefore exempted him also from her general prohibition. Desperately anxious not to produce a second novel inferior to her first, Charlotte declared, 'I court the keenest criticism', before exhorting them, 'Be honest therefore all three of you – If you think this book promises less favourably than "Jane Eyre" – say so: it is but trying again.'[56]

It was to be nearly a month before Charlotte heard Smith, Elder & Co.'s verdict on *Shirley*. The passage of time probably reflected the difficulty facing her friends at the firm: they were undoubtedly sensitive to Charlotte's vulnerability at this time and, though an honest opinion had been sought, it was not possible to foresee the consequences if it was given. In the end, they settled for a general approbation which would encourage their author while expressing reservations on only one or two issues. Both Smith Williams and James Taylor, for instance, complained of a lack of distinctness and impressiveness in *Shirley*'s male characters – a criticism which Charlotte acknowledged as being probably just: 'When I write about women I am sure of my ground', she told Taylor, '– in the other case, I am not so sure.'[57]

The main criticism, however, was reserved for the first chapter with its boisterous and unflattering portrayal of the 'shower of curates'. Both George Smith and Smith Williams were of the opinion that this was a misjudgement so serious that it warranted complete removal and the substitution of a new beginning. Charlotte, however, displayed her customary stubbornness. Promising that their advice would be 'duly weighed', she nevertheless defended it on the same grounds as she had defended the 'Lowood' portion of *Jane Eyre*: '– it is true', she wrote emphatically, 'the curates and their ongoings are merely photographed from the life'.[58]

There was certainly little love lost between Charlotte and the curates who had passed through Haworth Parsonage in recent years. As long ago as the summer of 1845 she had written sharply to Ellen:

I have no desire at all to see your medical-clerical curate – I think he must be like all the other curates I have seen – and they seem to me a self-seeking, vain, empty race. At this blessed moment we have no less than three of them in Haworth Parish – and God knows there is not one to mend another.

The other day they all three – accompanied by Mr Smidt (of whom by and bye I have grievous things to tell you) dropped or rather rushed in unexpectedly to tea. It was Monday and I was hot & tired – still if they had behaved quietly and decently – I would have served them out their tea in peace – but they began glorifying themselves and abusing Dissenters in such a manner – that my temper lost its balance and I pronounced a few sentences sharply & rapidly which struck them all dumb – Papa was greatly horrified also – I don't regret it.[59]

Charlotte's vitriolic pen had spared none of them. James Smith was savagely indicted as Mr Malone, but at least there was some justice in the portrayal; James Bradley, the curate of Oakworth, and Joseph Grant, the incumbent of Oxenhope, suffered less severely but had their every failing exposed with more accuracy than charity. To their intense mortification – and the great glee of their parishioners – they were each instantly recognizable, an eventuality Charlotte had not foreseen.

Nevertheless, she did not regret her portrayal of the curates in *Shirley*. She questioned Smith Williams relentlessly as to why he disliked the opening chapter: 'is it because you think this chapter will render the work liable to severe handling by the press? Is it because knowing as you now do the identity of "Currer Bell" – this scene strikes you as unfeminine –? Is it because it is intrinsically defective and inferior –? I am afraid the two first reasons would not weigh with me – the last would.' When he and James Taylor replied in unison that the subject required a more artistic treatment, Charlotte rounded on them:

Say what you will – gentlemen – say it as ably as you will – Truth is better than Art. Burns' Songs are better than Bulwer's Epics. Thackeray's rude, careless sketches are preferable to thousands of carefully finished paintings. Ignorant as I am, I dare to hold and maintain that doctrine.⁶⁰

When she later came to end her novel with a brief résumé of the subsequent careers of her curates, she could not resist a sly dig at Smith Williams and Taylor: 'Were I to give the catastrophe of your life and conversation', she declared of Malone, ' "Impossible!" would be pronounced here: "untrue!" would be responded there. "Inartistic!" would be solemnly decided. Note well! Whenever you present the actual, simple truth, it is, somehow, always denounced as a lie.'⁶¹

Charlotte's sudden burst of enthusiasm for her writing was to be as short-lived as the reprieve on Anne's failing health. By the middle of March she was in decline again, a gradual and fluctuating decline but nevertheless inexorable. Both Charlotte and Patrick found it an almost unbearable duty to answer correspondence, particularly when Anne was going through a bad period and the unspoken thought that her death was imminent coloured every waking moment. Charlotte was compelled to answer a letter from Laetitia Wheelwright, one of her Brussels friends, who complained of her silence since her last letter. As that had been written on 14 September, only ten days before the unimagined horror of the train of events was set in motion, Charlotte's reply was a painful recitation of recurrent death and illness. 'God has hitherto supported me in some sort through all these bitter calamities', she claimed, 'but there have been hours – days – weeks of inexpressible anguish to undergo – and the cloud of impending distress still lowers dark and sullen above< s > us.'⁶²

Patrick, similarly, had to reply to anxious enquiries from the Rands, the former teachers of the Haworth National School, who had moved to Stalybridge. 'I have indeed had my ample share of trouble –', he told Mr Rand. 'But it has been the Lord's will – and it is my duty, to resign – My only son has died, and soon after him, a beloved daughter, died also – For these things we may weep, since Christ himself wept over his dead freind … Yet, whilst we grieve, it should not be without hope.' He ended his letter, eloquent in its brevity, with kind regards from 'All my Family that remain'.⁶³

Towards the end of March Ellen wrote with a kind offer to relieve Charlotte of some of the burden of nursing her sister: Anne was invited to Brookroyd, where she would be looked after by Ellen and her sisters. Anne was touched by the proposal but felt it would not be appropriate to quarter an invalid on the already overcrowded Nussey household. She had, instead, a proposal of her own to make which she relayed through Charlotte: if Patrick could not be persuaded to leave home and Charlotte was obliged to remain with him at Haworth, would Ellen consider accompanying her to the seaside or an inland watering place, whichever the doctor recommended? In putting forward this plan, Charlotte expressed her own, very strong, reservations.

Papa says her state is most precarious – she may be spared for some time – or a sudden alteration might remove her ere we were aware – were such an alteration to take place while she was \far/ from home and alone with you – it would be too terrible – the idea of it distresses me inexpressibly, and I tremble whenever she alludes to the project of a journey. In short I wish we could gain time and see how she gets on –[64]

In an effort to gain that time, which Anne was all too well aware that she did not have, Charlotte persuaded Ellen to 'write such an answer to this note as I can shew Anne – you can write any additional remarks to me on a separate piece of paper'. Ellen obliged, expressing her willingness to go with Anne but saying that 'her friends' were reluctant for her to undertake the responsibility of accompanying an invalid; besides, she added, repeating Charlotte's argument that May was generally a bad month for weather, it would be better to go in June or even July, when they could be assured of warmer, drier days.[65]

No doubt realizing that Charlotte, as usual, was trying to organize her life and had influenced Ellen's decision, Anne decided, with characteristically patient perseverance, to write to Ellen herself. It was at least two months since she had last put pen to paper, but seeing the beautifully neat, even handwriting, clear and easy to read despite the fact that each page is crossed, it is easy to forget the physical and mental effort which that letter must have cost Anne. If Charlotte would not act the part of honest broker, Anne must act for herself. 'I do not think there would be any great responsibility in the matter', she earnestly informed Ellen, adding, with great dignity,

I know, and everybody knows that you would be as kind and helpful as any one could possibly be; and I hope I should not be very troublesome. It would be as a companion not as a nurse that I should wish for your company; otherwise, I should not venture to ask it.

Laboriously, she countered Ellen's arguments one by one, undoubtedly using the same reasoning she had already used on Charlotte. 'You say May is a trying month, and so say others', Anne declared, tacitly pointing out that she had recognized her sister's hand in framing Ellen's reply.

The earlier part is often cold enough I acknowledge, but, according to my experience, we are almost certain of some fine warm days in the latter half when the laburnams and lilacs are in bloom; whereas June is often cold and July gener[a]lly wet.

Dismissing Ellen's arguments as the feeble excuses that they were, Anne appealed to her common sense.

But I have a more serious reason than this for my impatience of delay: the doctors say that change of air or removal to a better climate would hardly ever fail of success <if> in consumptive cases if \the remedy <be> were/ taken in <u>time</u>, but the reason why there are so many disappointments is, that it is generally deferred till it is too late. Now I would not commit this error; and to say the truth, thouhg I suffer much less from pain and fever than I did when you were with us, I am decidedly weaker and very much thinner my cough still troubles me a good deal, especially in the night, and, what seems worse than all, I am subject to great shortness of breath on going up stairs or any slight exertion. Under these circumstances I think there is no time to be lost.

Unlike Charlotte, who could not even bring herself to mention the word in her letter to Ellen, Anne now faced the prospect of her own death with calm courage.

I have no horror of death: if I thought it inevitable I think I could quietly resign myself to the prospect, in the hope that you, dear Miss Nussy, would give < as much > as much of your company as you possibly could to Charlotte and be a sister to her in my stead. But I wish it would please God to spare me not only for Papa's and Charlotte's sakes, but because I long to do some good in the world before I leave it. I have many schemes in my head for future practise – humble and limited indeed – but still I should not like them all to come to nothing, and myself < th > to have lived to so little purpose. But God's will be done.[66]

Anne's schemes, which remain shrouded in mystery, would indeed come to nothing, as would her attempt to foil her sister's conspiracy. Ellen enclosed her letter in one of her own to Charlotte: having read it Charlotte's only comment was 'it was touching enough – as you say'. Just as obdurate in her own way as Emily, Charlotte chose to ignore Anne's own wishes and persisted in doing what she herself considered best, confessing to Ellen that she was glad her mother and sisters had also objected to Anne's plan, and that, even if they had consented, she never could: 'it would never do'.[67]

In the battle to prevent Anne going away, Charlotte had tried to enlist the support of Mr Teale, but, contrary to her expectation, he had no objections to the scheme and actually recommended Scarborough, which was Anne's own first choice of destination. His advice, carefully recorded by Patrick in the margins of his Graham's *Modern Domestic Medicine*, only confirmed what Anne herself had said: 'change of place & climate, could prove beneficial, only in the early stage of consumption – that afterwards, the excitement caused by change of scenes, and beds, and strange company, did harm –'. Mr Teale was also quite happy for Anne to go in May, as she wished.[68]

Charlotte's last defence against the plan, her often-stated comment that her father would not leave home and could not be left alone, finally gave way when Patrick himself intervened: it was his express wish that Charlotte should accompany Anne – he would be perfectly satisfied to be left in the care of their two faithful servants, Tabby Aykroyd and Martha Brown.[69] In all conscience, Charlotte could not now oppose Anne's wishes and, dragging her heels in the process, she began to make the necessary arrangements.

Though one may sympathize with her predicament, it is not easy to understand Charlotte's reluctance to take Anne to Scarborough. It was certainly not the fear that the journey would be too much for her sister, because the advice had always been the earlier the better, and the longer it was put off, the greater the risk to the invalid. The likeliest explanation seems to be that Charlotte, watching her last remaining sister fade before her eyes, could not bring herself to face the idea that she was about to die. At this time, Charlotte was increasingly haunted by her memories of Emily's shocking death. 'I cannot forget Emily's death-day;' she told Ellen on 12 April, 'it becomes a more fixed – a darker, a more frequently recurring idea in my mind than ever: it was very terrible, she was torn conscious, panting, reluctant though resolute out of a happy life. But it will not do to dwell on these things –'.[70] To add to the terror of facing yet another death scene, which, like Branwell's and Emily's, might fall suddenly and unexpectedly, Charlotte was undoubtedly afraid that this would occur among strangers. At least if it happened at home she would have the comfort of supporting and being supported by her father.

By 1 May, Charlotte was still hoping to put off the journey for another two or three weeks. Writing to Ellen, whose offer to accompany them to Scarborough had been gratefully accepted, Charlotte found further cause for delay in Anne's sudden relapse.

The change to finer weather has not proved beneficial so far; she has sometimes been so weak and suffered so much from pain in her side during the last few days – that I have not known what to think. It may however be only a temporary aggravation of symptoms; she may rally again and be much better – but there must be some improvement before I can feel justified in taking her away from home.

Not surprisingly, as Charlotte was aware, Anne was feeling increasingly resentful of the delay, though she did not voice her reproaches.

Yet to delay is painful – for as is always the case I believe under her circumstances – she seems herself but half conscious of the necessity for such delay: she wonders I believe why I do not talk more about the journey: it grieves me to think she may even be hurt by my seeming tardiness. She is very much emaciated – far more so than when you were here – her arms are no thicker than a little child's. The least exertion brings a shortness of breath – she goes out a little every day – but we creep rather than walk.[71]

By the middle of May, Anne's persistence paid off and Charlotte at last capitulated. They booked rooms in Wood's Lodgings at No. 2, The Cliff, where Anne had previously stayed with the Robinsons and which she declared to be one of the best situations in the town. They were to have a good-sized sitting room and an airy, double-bedded lodging room over-looking the sea, all for thirty shillings a week. The money was to come from a fortuitously timed legacy of £200 from Anne's godmother, Fanny Outhwaite, who had died in February; as Charlotte pointed out, it could not be better employed than in an attempt to prolong if not restore Anne's life.[72] Margaret Wooler, who had a house in the bleaker North Bay at Scarborough, wrote to offer her assistance, but everything was in hand. The journey was finally fixed for Wednesday, 23 May, though in the event it was put off to the following day. Even up to the last minute Charlotte had her misgivings about the wisdom of going, but she could no longer gainsay her sister who had 'a fixed impression that the sea-air will give her a chance of regaining strength – that chance therefore she must have'.[73]

Ellen Nussey came to stay the night before so that they could all set off together, Charlotte having warned her not to be shocked – or rather, not to betray her shock – at Anne's appearance.[74] Around noon on the Thursday, Patrick, Tabby and Martha gathered to say goodbye to Anne: there was little that could be said so the farewells were doubtless fairly muted. Another painful ceremony had also to be undergone before she could depart: she had to give a last caress to Emily's dog, Keeper, and her own faithful spaniel, Flossy, neither of whom would comprehend the finality of this parting.

Patrick had firmly rejected all Charlotte's attempts to organize him in her absence and had refused even the solace of Mr Nicholls' company.[75] One can only guess his feelings as he watched his youngest child being carried away from home. He and the servants were resigned to the knowledge that this was likely to be the last time they would ever see her on earth.

Anne, Charlotte and Ellen travelled down to Keighley where they caught the 1.30 p.m. train to Leeds. There they readily found assistance in helping the invalid across the lines and in and out of carriages.[76] They journeyed on by rail as far as York that day, staying overnight at the George Hotel, a coaching inn in Coney Street. After a rest and dinner there, Anne was so far revived as to be able to go out in a bathchair. Like most tourists and holidaymakers, they had some shopping to do. Neither Anne nor Charlotte had a wardrobe appropriate to a fashionable seaside resort, so Charlotte had drawn up a list of the things they needed to purchase in York – bonnets, combs, black silk stockings, dresses, gloves and a ribbon for the neck. They then had to go through the 'dreary mockery' of wandering round the shops to find the items, a task that evidently proved too much for Anne, as they only bought the essential bonnets and gloves.[77]

Before they left York the next day, at Anne's especial request, they paid a visit to York Minster, which had always impressed her as it had Branwell: gazing up at its fluid heights, the massive stonework contrasting with the delicacy of the tracery and sculpture, Anne was moved to say, 'If finite power can do this what is the …', before emotion stayed further speech. Anne's happy mood sustained her throughout the train journey to Scarborough, during which she delightedly pointed out all the best views to her companions. Arriving in Scarborough itself, she was again revived by her joy at seeing the sweeping sandy bay and the glorious stretch of sea once more.[78]

Anne was determined not to lose a single moment of her stay; equally, she had decided that Charlotte and Ellen should not be held back by her weakness but should explore the place for themselves. The morning after their arrival, Saturday, Anne insisted on going to the baths and being left there with only the attendant in charge. She later paid for her stubbornness in walking back alone to their lodgings when, overcome with exhaustion, she fell at the garden gate. Typically, Anne kept her accident from Charlotte and Ellen, who only heard about it some time afterwards. In the afternoon, she drove herself in a donkey cart on the beach for an hour. She had taken over the reins herself, fearing that the boy would force the donkey to go faster than she or it wished. Like all her family, Anne had always been fond of animals and could not bear to see them ill treated. When Ellen joined her she was just giving the boy a lecture on treating the animal well.[79]

Anne devised plans for Charlotte and Ellen in the hope that they would learn to love Scarborough as much as she did. She even insisted on taking them along the famous bridge across the ravine in the middle of the bay, which afforded a glorious prospect of the cliffs and sands with the sea beyond. Apart from this extravagance, their expenses were meagre: two shillings for dandelion coffee, three pennies for a glass of lemonade, four for half a dozen oranges.[80]

On Sunday, 27 May, Anne wanted to go to church, but was dissuaded by Charlotte and Ellen, who also refused to go themselves because it would have meant leaving her unattended. While Charlotte occupied herself in writing to Smith Williams, Anne sat at the window of their 'pleasant' lodgings looking down on a sea as calm as glass. As she drew her pitifully impeded breath, Charlotte implored Smith Williams, 'Write to me. In this strange place your letters will come like the visits of a friend.'[81] In the afternoon Anne took her customary short walk but, overcome by exhaustion, she asked to be left alone to enjoy the view from a comfortable seat near the beach while her companions went on to the saloon which they had not yet visited. In the evening, Anne tried and failed again to persuade Charlotte and Ellen to leave her and go to church. They did allow her to sit quietly by the window, however, watching with rapt expression a particularly splendid sunset over the sea. It was clear to them all that she had not long to live. As the last rays of the sun sank beyond the horizon, Anne returned to the fireside and, with that practical concern for others that was a hallmark of her character, discussed with Charlotte the propriety of them returning home: she did not wish to do so for her own sake, she said, but because she thought others might suffer more if she died in Scarborough.⁸²

The discussion was unresolved. Anne passed a reasonable night, rose and dressed herself before seven o'clock the following morning and was ready to go downstairs before the rest of her little party. As she reached the top of the stairs, she was overcome with faintness and, smiling, informed her concerned sister and friend that she was afraid to descend. Ellen immediately offered to try to carry her, a suggestion which pleased Anne as much as it angered and distressed Charlotte. An argument ensued in which Ellen emerged triumphant and Charlotte was persuaded to go back to her room so that she did not have to witness the spectacle. Ellen, going down a couple of steps below Anne, told her to put her arms around her neck saying, 'I will carry you like a baby', and promising to put her down if she was too heavy. More by determination than physical strength, Ellen succeeded in carrying the prostrate Anne downstairs. At the very bottom, however, Anne's head suddenly fell forward like a leaden weight on top of Ellen's: shocked by the blow and by the thought that only death could have caused it, Ellen staggered to Anne's easy chair and, dropping her into it, fell on her knees in front of the invalid. Despite being shaken, Anne put out her arms to comfort her friend and said, 'It could not be helped, you did your best.'⁸³

Anne had her breakfast of boiled milk, prepared especially for her, and all seemed well until about eleven o'clock, when she suddenly announced that she felt a change. Believing that she had not long to live, she again asked whether it would be possible to return home in time. Unable to give an answer, Charlotte summoned a doctor and Anne asked him 'how long he thought she might live – not to fear speaking the truth, for she was not afraid to die'. The doctor admitted that death was close at hand, she thanked him for his truthfulness and he left, returning two or three times in the next few hours to check on his patient.

For some time Anne continued to sit in her easy chair, looking, as Ellen later described her, 'so serene & reliant' as she prayed quietly, invoking blessings on her sister and her friend and enjoining Ellen: 'Be a sister in my stead. Give Charlotte as much of your company as you can.' When she became restless as death approached, she was carried across to the sofa. On being asked if she were easier, she replied, 'It is not <u>you</u> who can give me ease, but soon all will be well through the merits of our Redeemer.'⁸⁴ The doctor, 'a stranger' as Charlotte bitterly remarked, 'wondered at her fixed tranquillity of spirit and settled longing to be gone': in all his experience, he told them, he had never seen such a deathbed and it gave evidence of no common mind. Even while she lay dying, her thought was for others: seeing Charlotte barely able to restrain her grief, Anne whispered, 'Take courage,

Charlotte; take courage.'[85] Conscious to the last, Anne died, very calmly and gently, at about two o'clock in the afternoon on Monday, 28 May 1849.

Her passing was so quiet that no one in the house, except the mourners at her side, was aware of it: dinner was announced through the half-open door even as Charlotte leaned over to close the eyes of her dead sister. The 'dreary mockery' of the intrusion of daily life at such a moment was enough to send Charlotte into paroxysms of weeping. All the force of the grief, frustration and bitterness she had kept in check over so many long months now overwhelmed her. For the remainder of the day she was in a state of nervous collapse and it was not until the next day that she was able to recover some semblance of calm and set about the duties required of her. Then, in a state of feverish exhaustion, she wrote brief notes to her father, anxiously waiting alone in Haworth, and to Smith Williams.[86] It was Ellen who had to go into town for the unpleasant duty of registering the death, giving as its cause 'Consumption six months'. It was probably Ellen, too, who got in touch with Margaret Wooler, to tell her of Anne's death. Though living in the town and aware of the Brontës' impending visit, Miss Wooler seems to have kept a tactful distance until her sympathy and practical assistance were required in the aftermath of Anne's death.[87] No doubt she and Ellen were responsible for sending the obituary notice to the local papers. By a strange irony, it appeared in the same issue of the *Scarborough Gazette* as a front page advertisement for the Scarborough Circulating Library which put *Jane Eyre* at the top of its list of new popular novels.[88]

The funeral arrangements were complex. To take Anne's body back to Haworth would be a devastating experience for both Charlotte, who would have to accompany the coffin, and her seventy-two-year-old father, who would have to be present at the burial of his third child in nine months. Though it may have seemed morally wrong to lay Anne apart from the rest of the family, Charlotte had the excuse that her sister had always loved Scarborough and would have been happy to have found her resting place there. She therefore determined to bury Anne in the town where she had died, but she had to make the arrangements quickly to prevent her father making the long and difficult journey from Haworth to Scarborough to attend the funeral. In her letter written the day after Anne's death, Charlotte informed her father that she had planned the funeral for the next day, Wednesday, 30 May: as he would not have received the letter until the very morning of the funeral, there would be no way in which he could possibly get to Scarborough in time.[89] He therefore had to accept Charlotte's *fait accompli* and, alone in his study at Haworth, pray for his daughter's soul while her body was interred seventy miles away.

It was an additional distress to the mourners that the parish church of St Mary at Scarborough, where Anne was to be buried, was undergoing extensive rebuilding. The funeral service had to be held in the daughter church of Christ Church, virtually next door to Wood's Lodgings, and then the little cortège had to wind slowly up the steep, narrow streets to St Mary's churchyard where the burial took place in the midst of the rebuilding work. There, on the headland, just below the dramatic ruins of the castle on the cliff top and looking out across the bay she had always loved, Anne Brontë was laid to rest.[90] The doctor's kind offer to attend her funeral had been turned down so that her only official mourners were her sister and Ellen Nussey. At the church, however, they were unexpectedly joined by Margaret Wooler, who had come to give Charlotte her support by her kind and unobtrusive presence.[91]

Once the first desperate agony of grief had passed, Charlotte grew calmer and was able to reflect more positively on her sister's death. Describing it to Smith Williams a few days later, she was able to take comfort from the contrast of Anne's gentle passing with Emily's last violent struggles for life:

she died without severe struggle – resigned – trusting in God – thankful for release from a suffering life – deeply assured that a better existence lay before her – She believed – she hoped, and declared her belief and hope with her last breath. – Her quiet – Christian death did not rend my heart as Emily's stern, simple, unde-monstrative end did – I let Anne go to God and felt He had a right to her I could hardly let Emily go – I wanted to hold her back then – and I want her back hourly now – Anne, from her childhood seemed preparing for an early death – Emily's spirit seemed strong enough to bear her to fulness of years – They are both gone – and so is poor Branwell – and Papa has now me only – the weakest – puniest – least promising of his six children – Consumption has taken the whole five.[92]

The passage of even such a short time had altered Charlotte's perceptions of Anne's death: her own outburst of grief had become a resigned 'letting go', her declaration the day after Anne's death that 'I did not think it would be so soon' had become an expectation of her early death since childhood. Charlotte even persuaded herself that she had known from the moment of their departure that Anne would die in Scarborough and that she herself had acquiesced in the plan because 'I wanted her to die where she would be happiest.'[93] Curiously, too, Charlotte seems to have formed the odd impression that Anne was glad to die. 'Anne had had enough of life such as it was – in her twenty-eighth year she laid it down as a burden. I hardly know whether it is sadder to think of that than of Emily turning her dying eyes reluctantly from the pleasant sun.'[94] Such an impression was totally at odds with all the 'humble and limited' schemes for future practice which Anne had still cherished only weeks before her death; it suggests a total misunderstanding of Anne's resignation at the end which was not due to a disillusionment with life but merely an acceptance of the inevitable and a firm belief in life after death. However often Anne might have trembled in the past at the seeming magnitude of her sins, her precious doctrine of universal salvation had offered her sanctuary and security at the end. Charlotte's belief that Anne was ready to die can only be explained by her low opinion of Anne's talents: to Charlotte, Anne's early death was not as tragic as Emily's, or even Branwell's, because there was not the same sense of unfulfilled promise. As Charlotte could not admit to having this feeling, even to herself, she found acceptance of Anne's death in believing that her sister was glad to die.

Deeply aware that she, the eldest of the Brontë children who reached adulthood, was now the sole survivor, Charlotte could not suppress an anguished questioning of her fate: 'Why life is so blank, brief and bitter I do not know – Why younger and far better than I are snatched from it with projects unfulfilled I cannot comprehend', she wrote to Smith Williams, repeating a week later that 'life seems bitter, brief – blank'.[95] There was some comfort in the kindness of her friends: Martha Brown, who had written to assure Charlotte that all was well at home in her absence so that she did not feel obliged to return at once; Ellen, 'a calm, steady girl – not brilliant, but good and true', whose presence was a solace that stood between her and total isolation; Smith Williams, upon whom she had no claim but who wrote to her constantly 'in the strain best tending to consolation'.[96] Her father, too, deeply concerned by her own poor health and the effect of the unremitting stress of the last nine months, wrote and 'ordered' her to remain at the seaside, thereby defying her often-expressed belief in his inability to manage without her.[97]

Charlotte could not bear the gaiety of Scarborough, with its now painful associations, so about a week after Anne's death she and Ellen moved ten miles down the east coast to the smaller, less fashionable resort of Filey. There they again engaged cliff-top lodgings, this time not in the centre, but at the southern-most edge of the town, where they were most likely to find the peace and quiet Charlotte so needed. Cliff House, which was kept by Mrs Smith, widow of the land agent who had built it, looked straight out on to the sea and Charlotte found consolation in viewing the 'wild rocky coast' and 'very solitary' sands, which suited her desolate mood.[98]

Shortly after her arrival she wrote to her father to tell him her new address and the arrangements she had made in Scarborough. She had paid all the expenses for Anne's funeral out of the money Anne had taken with her and had ordered a stone to be erected over her grave. The inscription was to be plain and simple: 'Here lie the remains of Anne Brontë, daughter of the Revd. P. Brontë, Incumbent of Haworth, Yorkshire. She died, Aged 28, May 28th 1849'.[99] A week later, Charlotte found time to write sadly to Smith Williams 'because I feel in the mood to do so without, I trust, paining you'. She now found some consolation for her sisters' deaths in contemplating the fact that they had left her a noble legacy in her memories of them:

Were I quite solitary in the world – bereft even of Papa – there is something in the past I can love intensely and honour deeply – and it is something which cannot change – which cannot decay – which immortality guarantees from corruption.

They have died comparatively young – but their short lives were spotless – their brief career was honourable – their untimely death befel amidst all associations < which > that can hallow, and not one that can desecrate.

The searing sorrows of the last nine months, which had deprived her of a brother and two sisters, had left her emotionally drained and, without the religious faith which had sustained her, would just as surely have destroyed her too.

A year ago – had a prophet warned me how I should stand in June 1849 – how stripped and bereaved – had he foretold the autumn, the winter, the spring of sickness and suffering to be gone through – I should have thought – this can never be endured. It is over. Branwell – Emily – Anne are gone like dreams – gone as Maria and Elizabeth went twenty years ago. One by one I have watched them fall asleep on my arm – and closed their glazed eyes – I have seen them buried one by one – and – thus far – God has upheld me. from my heart I thank Him.[100]

Charlotte would have preferred to stay at Filey but Ellen, perhaps finding the strain of coping alone with her grieving friend too much, insisted that they should move on to Bridlington and spend a week with the Hudsons at Easton Farm. The move was not a happy one and even though Charlotte deferred her return home for a day to fit in with the carrier's arrangements, they did not spend a full week there.[101]

The return to Haworth Parsonage had to be faced and on 20 June Charlotte and Ellen packed their bags and set out for home. 'I got home a little before eight o'clock', Charlotte later told her friend.

All was clean and bright waiting for me – Papa and the servants were well – and all received me with an affection which should have consoled. The dogs seemed in strange ecstasy. I am certain they regarded me as the harbinger of others – the dumb creatures thought that as I was returned – those who had been so long absent were not far behind.

I left Papa soon and went into the dining-room – I shut the door – I tried to be glad that I was come home – I have always been glad before – except once – even then I was cheered but this time joy was not to be the sensation. I felt that the house was all silent – the rooms were all empty – I remembered where the three were laid – in what narrow dark dwellings – never were they to reappear on earth. So the sense of desolation and bitterness took possession of me – the agony that <u>was to be undergone</u> – and <u>was not</u> to be avoided came on – I underwent it & passed a dreary evening and night and a mournful morrow – to-day I am better.[102]

On the 'mournful morrow' Charlotte attempted to find some relief for her overcharged feelings in writing a poem on her sister's death. The unfinished lines were eloquent testimony to her later comment on Tennyson's *In Memoriam*: 'bitter sorrow, while recent, does not flow out in verse'.¹⁰³

The daily routine of the house went on as usual, despite the fact that three of its inhabitants were now dead. 'The great trial', as Charlotte confessed to Ellen, 'is when evening closes and night approaches – At that hour we used to assemble in the dining-room – we used to talk – Now I sit by myself – necessarily I am silent.'¹⁰⁴ Perhaps surprisingly, she was not afflicted by the same suffocating oppression of the spirits she had suffered after her return from Brussels. Now that she had a real and terrible grief to bear, it was a sense of Jane Eyre-ish rage at the injustice of her threefold loss which attacked her at these moments. This she preferred to confide in the less shockable ear of Smith Williams.

In the day-time effort and occupation aid me – but when evening darkens something in my heart revolts against the burden of solitude – the sense of loss and want grows almost too much for me. I am not good or amiable in such moments – I am rebellious – and it is only the thought of my dear Father in the next room, or of the kind servants in the kitchen – or some caress from the poor dogs which restores me to softer sentiments and more rational views. As to the night – could I do without bed – I would never seek it – waking – I think – sleeping – I dream of them – and I cannot recall them as they were in health – still they appear to me in sickness and suffering –¹⁰⁵

That anger against her fate which had, in the past, pricked on her ambition to succeed as a writer was now to be her saving grace, preventing her relapsing into morbidity. Even so, it was to be a continual fight. The sound of the clock ticking loud through the still house was a constant reminder of what had been. The sight of Keeper making his daily visit to Emily's bedroom or Flossy looking wistfully round for Anne would wring her heart. The pleasure of receiving another parcel of books from Cornhill was to be poisoned by the memory that Emily was just beginning to be ill when the first such parcel had arrived, that Charlotte had read one of Emerson's essays to her the night before she died, reading on until she found that her sister was not listening. 'I thought to recommence next day –', Charlotte told Smith Williams, adding, with her peculiar gift for reinventing the past where her sisters were concerned, 'Next day, the first glance at her face told me what would happen before night-fall.'¹⁰⁶

'My life is what I expected it to be –', Charlotte confessed to Ellen,

sometimes when I wake in the morning – and < to > know that Solitude, Remembrance and Longing are to be almost my sole companions all day through – that at night I shall go to bed with them, that they will long keep me sleepless – that next morning I shall wake to them again – Sometimes – Nell – I have a heavy heart of it.

But crushed I am not – yet: nor robbed of elasticity nor of hope nor quite of endeavour – Still I have some strength to fight the battle of life. I am aware and can acknowledge I have many comforts – many mercies – still I can get on.[107]

Among those mercies were the friendship of Ellen and Smith Williams, both of whom wrote continually to her to buoy up her spirits. The latter even had a practical suggestion to make – why not get a cheerful young companion to ease her loneliness? Charlotte acknowledged that it was a good idea in some respects,

but there are two people whom it would not suit – and not the least incommoded of these would be the young person whom I might request to come and bury herself in the hills of Haworth – to take a church and stony churchyard for her prospect – the dead silence of a village parsonage – in which the tick of the clock is heard all day long – for her atmosphere – and a grave, silent spinster for her companion. I should not like to see youth thus immured.

Echoing the words of one of her most damning notices, in the *Quarterly Review*, and thereby revealing how much the barbed comments had festered in her mind, she added:

For society – long seclusion has in a great measure unfitted me – I doubt whether I should enjoy it if I might have it.

Sometimes I think I should, and I thirst for it – but at other times I doubt my capability of pleasing or deriving pleasure. The prisoner in solitary confinement – the toad in the block of marble – all in time shape themselves to their lot.[108]

There was, as Charlotte recognized, only one cure for her grief and loneliness. Recalling Shakespeare's lines from *Macbeth*, Charlotte took her courage in both hands and declared to Smith Williams, 'Labour must be the cure, not sympathy – Labour is the only radical cure for rooted sorrow.'[109] 'The fact is,' she later confided, rather less grandiloquently, 'my work is my best companion – hereafter I look for no great earthly comfort except what congenial occupation can give –.'[110]

Chapter Twenty-One

❧

NO LONGER INVISIBLE

Charlotte's 'radical cure for rooted sorrow' was to return to *Shirley*, the book she had begun with such high hopes when her brother and sisters were still alive. She had written almost two-thirds of it when Branwell had been struck down; since then she had lost both Emily and Anne and the manuscript had been laid aside, virtually forgotten. Now, in unaccustomed isolation, she began to write again, but her mood had changed irrevocably. Her loss permeated the remainder of the novel. She opened the third volume with a chapter entitled 'The Valley of the Shadow' and with words that were wrung from her own heart.

The future sometimes seems to sob a low warning of the events it is bringing us, like some gathering though yet remote storm, which, in tones of the wind, in flushings of the firmament, in clouds strangely torn, announces a blast strong to strew the sea with wrecks ... At other times this Future bursts suddenly, as if a rock had rent, and in it a grave had opened, whence issues the body of one that slept. Ere you are aware, you stand face to face with a shrouded and unthought-of Calamity – a new Lazarus.'

Over that future, Charlotte had had no control, but in her book she wielded the powers of life and death over her characters, just like the Genius Tallii of long ago. In her first chapter since her sisters' deaths, she felled Caroline Helstone with a sudden fever and brought her to the very threshold of death. Kinder than God had been in her own life, Charlotte saved her heroine and miraculously restored her to health through the discovery that her nurse was actually her long-lost mother. The plot was as improbable as Charlotte's juvenile efforts at resurrection, but her descriptions of the mother's sufferings as she 'wrestled with God in earnest prayer' at the bedside of her dying daughter were as real and searing as anything she had written.

Not always do those who dare such divine conflict prevail. Night after night the sweat of agony may burst dark on the forehead; the supplicant may cry for mercy with that soundless voice the soul utters when its appeal is to the Invisible. 'Spare my beloved,' it may implore. 'Heal my life's life. Rend not from me what long affection entwines with my whole nature. God of heaven – bend – hear – be clement!' And after this cry and strife, the sun may rise and see him worsted ... Then the watcher approaches the patient's pillow, and sees a new and strange moulding of the familiar features, feels at once that the insufferable moment draws nigh, knows that it is God's will his idol shall be broken, and bends his head, and subdues his soul to the sentence he cannot avert, and scarce can bear.[2]

Reading these lines before she knew anything about Charlotte Brontë, Mrs Gaskell, who had recently lost her own beloved baby son, recognized and empathized with the suffering which had inspired them.[3] For Charlotte there was a catharsis in living through her characters and allowing them a gentler fate than her own; even so, she never lost sight of the fact that her writing was now her profession. Taking up what she had developed as one of the main themes of *Shirley*, she passionately defended the right of women to work in a letter to Smith Williams.

Lonely as I am – how should I be if Providence had never given me courage to adopt a career – perseverance to plead through two long, weary years with publishers till they admitted me? – How should I be with youth past – sisters lost – a resident in a moorland parish where there is not a single educated family? In that case I should have no world at all: the raven, weary of surveying the deluge and without an ark to return to, would be my type. As it is, something like a hope and motive sustains me still. I wish all your daughters – I wish every woman in England had also a hope and motive: Alas! there are many old maids who have neither.[4]

Smith Williams' daughter, Louisa, was attempting to secure a place at the Queen's College, an establishment connected with the Governess Institution which offered four years of training to potential governesses. Charlotte had had her reservations about the Governess Institution from the start. It seemed to her 'both absurd and cruel' to raise the standard of governesses' acquirements still higher, when they were already not half nor a quarter paid for what they taught and, in most instances, not a half nor a quarter of their attainments were required by their pupils. 'It is true the world demands a brilliant list of accomplishments; for £20 per ann. it expects in one woman the attainments of several professors', but, Charlotte had argued, good health, steady unimpressionable nerves and an ability to impart information, rather than acquire it, were far more important qualities in a governess.[5] Now, however, when she had been forced by the events of the last year to realize that her mind and her work were her only resources, Charlotte urged Smith Williams to consider the priceless advantage of the education his daughter would gain.

Come what may – it is a step towards independency – and one great curse of a single female life is its dependency … Believe me – teachers may be hard-worked, ill-paid and despised – but the girl who stays at home doing nothing is worse off than the hardest-wrought and worst-paid drudge of a school. Whenever I have seen, not merely in humble, but in affluent homes – families of daughters sitting waiting to be married, I have pitied them from my heart. It is doubtless well – very well – if Fate decrees them a happy marriage – but if otherwise – give their existence some object – their time some occupation – or the peevishness of disappointment and the listlessness of idleness will infallibly degrade their nature.[6]

No doubt among those families of daughters sitting waiting to be married Charlotte had in mind the Nusseys: Ann, who at the grand age of fifty-three had at last secured a husband and was now fluttering about making preparations for her wedding as if she were a schoolgirl bride; Mercy, forty-one years old and so jealous of her elder sister's good fortune that she threatened the happiness of the whole household; Ellen herself, already thirty-two, for so long the subject of Charlotte's teasing about her suitors and earnest advice on the sort of man she should marry and now, like Charlotte, as they both admitted, facing a future as an old maid.[7]

What that future was likely to be Charlotte painted with grim realism in her portraits of the despised and misunderstood 'old maids', Miss Mann and Miss Ainley, in *Shirley*. Miss Mann, who had 'passed alone through pro-tracted scenes of suffering, exercised rigid self-denial, made large sacrifices of time, money, health for those who had repaid her only by ingratitude', had become a censorious, morose and deeply lonely woman. Miss Ainley, who would watch by any sickbed, feared no disease, would nurse the poorest whom no one else would nurse and was serene, humble, kind, and equable throughout, was yet despised for being repellently ugly and barely thanked for her services, which had come to be expected. It was hardly right that the world should demand only one thing of unmarried women: a life of self-sacrifice, requited only by a distant praise for their devotion and virtue. 'Is this enough? Is it to live?' Charlotte made Caroline Helstone cry as she faced the prospect of spinsterhood:

Is there not a terrible hollowness, mockery, want, craving, in that existence which is given away to others, for want of something of your own to bestow it on? I suspect there is. Does virtue lie in abnegation of self? I do not believe it. Undue humility makes tyranny; weak concession creates selfishness ... Each human being has his share of rights. I suspect it would conduce to the happiness and welfare of all, if each knew his allotment, and held to it as tenaciously as the martyr to his creed.[8]

Charlotte always claimed that she could not write books on matters of public interest nor for a moral or philanthropic purpose. Though she was to prove this emphatically by what she omitted from *Shirley* on the question of the rights and sufferings of mill workers, the whole story was an exploration of the 'Woman Question' which so exercised educated minds at this time. Again, however, despite her fiercely argued case for women to have an independent and valued existence outside marriage, Charlotte lacked the courage of her convictions and ended her book in the conventional manner by providing both her heroines with a husband.[9]

Charlotte worked long and hard at her book throughout the summer after Anne's death. Inevitably it was a struggle, not least because her unhappiness manifested itself as usual in ill health. Not surprisingly, after three sudden deaths in the family, she could not help seeing in every cough or cold the first sign of something worse. She had returned from 'that dismal Easton' with the seeds of a cold that she could not throw off and when she developed a sore throat, cough and pain between her shoulders, she was extremely alarmed. 'Say nothing about it –', she ordered Ellen, 'for I confess I am too much disposed to be nervous.' A month later she was still complaining of cold, but a recurrence of her father's bronchitis threw her into near panic: 'I feel too keenly that he is the last, the only near and dear relation I have in the world.'[10]

Floundering in the depths of hypochondria, which was not helped by an outbreak of English cholera in Haworth, Charlotte commissioned Ellen to buy her a fur boa and cuffs (in July!) and a shower-bath.[11] The emotional milestone of the first anniversary of Branwell's death found her in despair. Both the servants were ill in bed, Martha in a critical condition with a serious inflammation and Tabby, whose lame leg had broken out in ulcers, having had a bad fall from her kitchen chair. Depressed with headache and sickness herself, Charlotte 'fairly broke down for ten minutes – sat & cried like a fool'. The crisis passed, however. Martha recovered, her mother and sister came to assist in the house and, a couple of days later, a 'huge Monster-package' arrived from Leeds containing the shower-bath which Ellen had at last managed to find.[12]

Throughout these traumas, Charlotte's writing provided her with a life-line to sanity. By the end of August, the fair copy of the manuscript was complete and ready to go to the publishers. Charlotte found herself unable to decide whether it was better or worse than *Jane Eyre*, but, as she owned to Smith Williams, 'Whatever now becomes of the work – the occupation of writing it has been a boon to me – it took me out of dark and desolate reality to an unreal but happier region.' After toying with 'Hollows Mill' and 'Fieldhead' as the title, she finally settled on *Shirley*, 'without any explanation or addition – the simpler and briefer, the better'.[13]

Though she was anxious to send the manuscript off to Cornhill as soon as possible, James Taylor, her newest correspondent at the firm, had offered to call and collect it in person on his return from a holiday in Scotland. Charlotte was somewhat alarmed at this proposal, particularly as she could not remember meeting Taylor at Cornhill and perhaps suspected his motives in wishing to beard 'Currer Bell' in his den. The idea that she might be a peep-show for the curious appalled her, but it was difficult to turn down the offer. Instead, while appearing to welcome the prospect of his visit, she tried to put Taylor off with a long recital of the difficulties of actually getting to 'a strange uncivilized little place' such as Haworth – 'he must remember that at a station called Shipley the carriages are changed – otherwise they will take him on to Skipton or Colne, or I know not where'. For good measure, she warned him that he could only call for the day because she could not entertain him for longer: ignoring the fact that Arthur Bell Nicholls would gladly have made himself available, she told Taylor she had neither father nor brother to walk the moors with him or show him the neighbourhood. And, like many a child before and since, she blamed her elderly parent for her lack of hospitality. It was irksome to him to give much of his time to a stranger, she claimed, blaming 'the peculiar retirement of papa's habits'; 'without being in the least misanthropical or sour-natured – papa habitually prefers solitude to society, and Custom is a tyrant whose fetters it would now be impossible for him to break'.[14] It was no wonder that Patrick gained a reputation at Cornhill for being a fierce, solitary eccentric when his own daughter described him thus.

When James Taylor did eventually call, on 8 September, the visit did not go well. Charlotte took an immediate personal dislike to him. 'He is not ugly – but very peculiar', Charlotte later told Ellen privately, 'the lines in his face show an inflexibility and – I must add – a hardness of character which do not attract.' When he looked at her 'in his keen way', she actually recoiled before him and, even though he was clearly both excited and nervous at meeting 'Currer Bell' for the first time, his stern, abrupt manner only added to his physical repugnance in her eyes. Patrick, too, did not get on well with his guest, who seems to have been unaware of the impression he had made on the Brontës. Certainly he reported favourably back to Cornhill, compelling Charlotte to reciprocate with more politeness than truth that the pleasure had been mutual and that she and her father had enjoyed the hour or two of conversation with him exceedingly.[15] When Taylor wrote to her a few days after his visit, Charlotte did not reply for a week, excusing herself on the grounds that she had had a clergyman staying, though she had found time in the interval for at least two letters to Smith Williams.[16]

It was an immense relief to Charlotte to get the manuscript of *Shirley* off her hands at last, particularly when Smith Williams wrote back expressing a favourable opinion. 'Your letter gave me great pleasure', she declared.

An author who has shewn his book to none, held no consultation about plan, subject, characters or incidents, asked and had no opinon from one living being, but fabricated it darkly in the silent workshop of his own brain – such an author awaits with a singular feeling the report of the first impression produced by his creation in a quarter where he places confidence[17]

The unspoken thought was implicit in every line – this was not how Charlotte had been accustomed to write.

Despite her apparent deference to the gentlemen of Smith, Elder & Co., Charlotte was quite capable of standing her own ground and defying them. She had already refused to replace the first chapter. Now, when Smith Williams added his weight to James Taylor's criticisms of the episode of Shirley's nervousness after she had been bitten by a supposedly mad dog, Charlotte admitted the justice of their remarks: 'the thing is badly managed – and I bend my head and expect in resignation what, <u>here</u>, I know I deserve – the lash of criticism', but added, 'I <u>cannot</u> alter now. It sounds absurd but so it is.' 'I can work indefatigably at the correction of a work before it leaves my hands,' she told Smith Williams, 'but when once I have looked on it as completed and submitted to the inspection of others, it becomes next to impossible to alter or amend.'[18] The only major concession she made was to substitute a translation for the French *devoir* she had written as a specimen of Shirley's work for Louis Moore. Since this alteration had not been specifically requested, though Smith Williams had observed that the French in *Shirley* might be cavilled at, Charlotte seems to have decided on it unilaterally fearing it might be thought pretentious.[19]

On only one point did Charlotte and Cornhill lock horns, and that was over the preface Charlotte had written for the work. It was an answer to the unsigned notice of *Jane Eyre* by Elizabeth Rigby in the *Quarterly Review* of December 1848. When it appeared, Charlotte was still numb from the shock and grief of Emily's sudden death: 'the lash of the Quarterly, however severely applied, cannot sting', she had then written.[20] Over the succeeding months, however, Charlotte had brooded on the review and eventually decided to answer her critic, just as Anne had answered hers in her preface to the third edition of *The Tenant of Wildfell Hall*. Anne's preface had been a dignified and reasonable, though passionately argued, defence of the realism of her scenes of debauchery and attack on the critics' assumption that her sex made a difference to the correctness of her approach as a writer. Charlotte, in contrast, let fly in one of her most bitingly sarcastic moods, addressing her critic as if in a letter. Having first checked with Smith Williams that the *Quarterly's* reviewer was indeed a woman, Charlotte mocked her by echoing her own phrases on the sex of 'Currer Bell': 'he feels assured – his heart tells him that the individual who did him the honour of a small notice in the "Quarterly" – if not a woman, properly so called – is that yet more venerable character – an Old Woman'.[21] As Currer Bell, Charlotte then went on to treat Miss Rigby's main points, dismissing most of them in a taunting yet flippant way strongly reminiscent of her juvenile writings as Charles Towns-hend and her ill-advised letter to Hartley Coleridge written all those years ago.

To the most hurtful criticism, that, if a woman, 'Currer Bell' must have long forfeited the society of her own sex 'for some sufficient reason', Charlotte responded:

You should see – Ma'am, the figure Currer Bell can cut at a small party: you should watch him assisting at a tea-table; you should behold him holding skeins of silk or Berlin wool for the young ladies about whom he innocuously philanders, and who, in return, knit him comforters for winter-wear, or work him slippers for his invalid- < foot >\member/ (he considers that rather an elegant expression – a nice substitute for – gouty foot; it was manufactured exp\r/essly for your refinement) you should <u>see</u> these things, for seeing is believing. Currer Bell forfeit the society of the better half of the human race? Heaven avert such a < cla > calamity –!

Swinging from heavy-handed sarcasm to positive libel, Charlotte attacked 'The idea by you propagated, if not by you conceived' that 'Currer Bell' had been Thackeray's governess. The inhabitants of Mayfair clearly had nothing better to do than to tell or hear some new thing: 'Who invents the new things for their consumption?' Charlotte demanded. 'Who manufactures fictions to supply their cravings? I need not ask who vends them: you, Madam, are an active sales-woman; the pages of your "Quarterly" form a notable advertising medium.' Charlotte ended her 'letter' with a long and flippant discourse on the accuracy of 'Currer Bell's' descriptions of ladies' dresses and fabrics and closed with a vitriolic flourish.

What a nice, pleasant gossip you and I have had together, Madam. How agreeable it is to twaddle at < our > \ones/ ease unmolested by a too fastidious public! Hoping to meet you one day again – and offering you such platonic homage as it becomes an old bachelor to pay

I am yours very devotedly
Currer Bell

As an afterthought she added a postscript in which the anger and hurt could not be hidden under a frivolous tone and were exposed, naked, for all to see.

N.B. I read all you said about governesses. My dear Madam – just turn out and be a governess yourself for a couple of years: the experiment would do you good: a little irksome toil – a little unpitied suffering – two years of uncheered solitude might perhaps teach you that to be callous, harsh and unsympathizing is not to be firm, superior and magnanimous.

Recognizing the abruptness of her change in tone, Charlotte added a final rejoinder: 'It was a twinge of the gout which dictated that postscript.'[22]

There can be no doubt that Smith, Elder & Co. were right to reject this preface: it did not answer any of the criticisms made, its sarcastic flippancy could easily be mistaken for simple frivolity and, in publicly assuming the role of a crusty 'old bachelor', Charlotte was simply laying herself open to future criticisms as and when her true sex and identity became known. Both Smith Williams and George Smith urged her to replace her 'Word to the "Quarterly"' with a biographical preface which would be a far more effective answer to the critic once the tragedies of the last year were revealed. Charlotte refused. 'I cannot change my preface. I can shed no tears before the public, nor utter any groan in the public ear.' Her life was irrelevant to her book, she declared, pointing out that it was not 'C. Brontë' who had been attacked by the *Quarterly*: 'it is "Currer Bell" who was insulted – he must reply'. Equally, she refused to offer a properly argued defence of her book, declaring to George Smith that she could not condescend to be serious with the *Quarterly*, 'it is too silly for solemnity'. In the face of Charlotte's intransigence, Smith, Elder & Co. were left with no option but to refuse to publish the preface. Charlotte was deeply annoyed and brusquely declined to replace it with another.[23]

By fair means or foul, however, Charlotte contrived to get her chance of 'a little word' to her critic on the subject of governesses in the pages of the novel itself. When Mrs Pryor attempts to dissuade Caroline Helstone from becoming a governess, she describes the misery of her own previous employment in that capacity with the Hardman family. Relaying Miss Hardman's pronouncements on governesses, 'a bore to almost any gentleman, as a tabooed woman, to whom he is interdicted from granting the usual privileges of the sex, and yet who is perpetually crossing his path', a woman who should be kept 'in a sort of isolation' in order to maintain 'that distance which the reserve of English manners and the decorum of English families exact', Mrs Pryor was actually quoting verbatim from the *Quarterly Review*.[24] By putting these remarks into this context, Charlotte invited her readers to condemn them, though few, if any, can have recognized their source. The rejection of her more overt attack on Elizabeth Rigby was a keen disappointment, particularly as Charlotte was gradually coming to realize the insidious effect of the review on potential readers. She herself had kept it from her father, as she knew it would have worried him, but she learnt that Miss Heald, sister of the vicar of Birstall, relying solely on the authority of the *Quarterly* had declared *Jane Eyre* to be 'a wicked book' – 'an expression which – coming from her – I will here confess – struck somewhat deep'.[25]

With the publication of her second book, the question of her sex and her identity, which had been so virulently attacked in the *Quarterly*, came up for renewed discussion. Smith, Elder & Co., anxious on her behalf to deflect further speculation and unnecessary comment in the reviews – and probably also with an eye to the sensation that the unmasking of 'Currer Bell' would cause – suggested that she should abandon her pseudonym. Now that her sisters were dead, her obligation to preserve their secret had come to an end and there was no real need for her to maintain the pretence. It was tempting to reveal her true identity so that she could meet famous authors and take her place in a society made accessible by her literary success. But she had learnt the benefits of anonymity and was now reluctant to lose it. The most obvious one was also the most practical. 'I think if a good fairy were to offer me the choice of a gift, I would say – grant me the power to walk invisible', Charlotte once told George Smith, 'though certainly I would add – accompany it by the grace never to abuse the privilege.'[26] In *Jane Eyre* Charlotte had been able to get away with her portraits from the life, even in the case of William Carus Wilson and the Clergy Daughters' School, because the events had happened long ago. In *Shirley*, however, though the story was set in the past, the characters were drawn on people who were not only still alive but also nearly all living in the small communities of Birstall and Gomersal, where everyone knew everyone else and most were related by marriage if not birth. It was inevitable that readers of the novel would recognize not only the setting of the novel in that area but also themselves and their neighbours.

Charlotte seems to have been blissfully unaware of this, answering Smith Williams' query as to whether she thought she would escape identification in Yorkshire with a cheerful 'I am so little known, that I think I shall.' Blithely describing how she had managed her characters, she declared, 'Besides the book is far less founded on the Real – than perhaps appears.' Instancing Mr Helstone, Caroline's uncle and rector of Briarfield, Charlotte explained:

If this character had an original, it was in the person of a clergyman who died some years since at the advanced age of eighty. I never saw him except once – at the Consecration of a Church – when I was a child of ten years old. I was then struck with his appearance and stern, martial air. At a subsequent period I heard him talked about in the neighbourhood where he had resided – some mentioned him with enthusiasm – others with detestation – I listened to various anecdotes, balanced evidence against evidence and drew an inference.[27]

Remarkably, even though Charlotte had analysed and reproduced Hammond Roberson's character so minutely, it seems never to have occurred to her that others would recognize his portrait. Similarly, in depicting the Reverend William Margetson Heald, vicar of Birstall, as Mr Hall, rector of Nunnely, Charlotte underestimated the accuracy of her own portrait and the perspicacity of her subject: 'he knows me slightly,' she conceded, 'but he would as soon think I had closely observed him or taken him for a character – he would as soon, indeed, suspect me of writing a book – a novel – as he would his dog – Prince'.[28]

Just how wrong she was in her assumptions Charlotte was soon to discover. Rumours were clearly rife. In London, Smith, Elder & Co. were actively fielding enquiries about her identity: the name 'Charlotte Brontë' had obviously been whispered about, possibly by Thomas Cautley Newby, her sisters' publisher, though as yet it meant nothing to the curious. In Keighley, where the 'gossiping inquisitiveness of small towns is rife', her envelopes of proofs were, Charlotte suspected, being opened and examined by those curious to find out why she received so many letters and packages from London.[29] The real damage came from Birstall and Gomersal, however, and that even before *Shirley* had come into the district.

On 24 October, two days before the novel was due to be published, Charlotte went to Birstall to stay with Ellen Nussey, calling in at the dentist in Leeds on the way.[30] Ellen had at last been formally admitted to the secret of the Brontës' authorship, Charlotte having presented her with a copy of *Wuthering Heights* during her visit to Haworth after Emily's death. Mary Taylor had known for even longer, but it was her brother Joe, whose suspicions had prompted him to visit the previous summer, who finally made Charlotte's secret an open one. Evidently believing him to be more trustworthy than he proved, and fearing that the realism of her portraits of the Taylor family as the Yorkes in *Shirley* might offend, Charlotte had sent him copies of those chapters in which they featured. With remarkable equanimity for someone who had just discovered his sister's friend to be the notorious 'Currer Bell' and himself and his family to have been 'daguerreotyped' as characters in her next novel, Joe Taylor simply remarked that 'she had not drawn them strong enough'.[31]

The day after her return home, Charlotte wrote to Smith Williams in considerable chagrin.

During my \late/ visit I have too often had reason – sometimes in a pleasant – sometimes in a painful form < to be glad > to fear that I no longer walk invisible – 'Jane Eyre' – it appears has been read all over the district – a fact of which I never dreamt – a circumstance of which the possibility never occurred to me – I met sometimes with new deference, with augmented kindness – old schoolfellows and old teachers too, greeted me with generous warmth – and again – ecclesiastical brows lowered thunder on me. When I confronted one or two large-made priests I longed for the battle to come on – I wish they would speak out plainly.[32]

The implicit criticism in the attitude of some of her Birstall acquaintances who suspected her of being 'Currer Bell' was soon to be replaced by the more overt criticism of the reviewers. *Shirley*, a novel in three volumes by Currer Bell, was published on 26 October 1846. The first review appeared five days later in the *Daily News*. 'Let me speak the truth – when I read it my heart sickened over it … On the whole I am glad a decidedly bad notice has come first – a notice whose inexpressible ignorance first stuns and then stirs me.' The reviewer had declared the opening chapter 'vulgar … unnecessary … disgusting', and, ironically, given the reaction in Birstall and Gomersal, 'Not one of its men are genuine. There are no such men. There are no *Mr Helstones*, *Mr Yorkes*, or *Mr Moores*. They are all as unreal as Madame Tussaud's waxworks.' 'Are there no such men as the Helstones and Yorkes?' Charlotte demanded furiously of Smith Williams. '<u>Yes there are</u> Is the first chapter disgusting or vulgar? <u>It is not: it is real.</u>' 'As for the praise of such a critic –', she added, 'I find it silly and nauseous – and I scorn it.' The praise, which so stuck in Charlotte's throat, was particularly obnoxious to her because it all centred on the fact that the reviewer had divined that '*Shirley* is the anatomy of the female heart' and that 'Currer Bell is petticoated'.[33]

In some respects, the review in the *Daily News* set the tone for the rest. The critics were, without exception, unanimous in deciding that *Shirley* proved 'Currer Bell' was a woman: 'There is woman stamped on every page', declared the *Atlas*, and the *Critic*, more acutely, pointed out that 'The female heart is here anatomized with a minuteness of knowledge of its most delicate fibres, which could only be obtained by one who had her own heart under inspection. The emotions so wondrously described were never *imagined*: they must have been *felt*.' The reviewer in *Fraser's Magazine* was even prepared to bet 'a trifle' that 'Currer Bell' was not only a woman – 'She knows women by their brains and hearts, men by their foreheads and chests'! – but a Yorkshire woman and one who had been a governess.[34]

On the whole, however, and with one notable exception, the fact that Charlotte's sex had been 'outed' did not influence the tone of the reviews in the way that she had feared. The criticisms were virtually uniform and mostly just, though put with varying degrees of force and perspicacity. Though Charlotte would often reject such criticisms out of hand when she considered the reviewer to be 'to the last degree incompetent, ignorant, flippant', as in the *Daily News*, she would accept quite meekly the same points made more thoughtfully and intelligently. The notice in *The Examiner* was typical in its criticisms, though untypical in the fact that Charlotte recognized its author as Albany Fonblanque, a man whose power and discernment she admired: 'I bend to his censorship, I am grateful for his praise; his blame deserves consideration; when he approves, I permit myself a moderate emotion of pride'.[35]

Fonblanque was equal in his praise and blame, though meting out both with greater enthusiasm than most of his contemporaries. He acknowledged that *Shirley* evinced the same 'peculiar power' as *Jane Eyre*, but felt that the story, the characters and the theme all bore too strong a resemblance to the earlier work.

While we thus freely indicate the defects of *Shirley*, let us at the same time express, what we very strongly feel, that the freshness and lively interest which the author has contrived to impart to a repetition of the same sort of figures, grouped in nearly the same social relations, as in her former work, is really wonderful. It is the proof of genius.

The book possessed deep interest, an irresistible grasp of reality, a marvellous vividness and distinction of conception and an intense power of graphic delineation and expression. 'There are scenes which for strength and delicacy of emotion are not transcended in the range of English fiction', he declared, but the faults were manifold. 'Story there is none in *Shirley*.' 'The expression of motive by means of dialogue is...indulged to such minute and tedious extremes, that what ought to be developments of character in the speaker become mere exercitations of will and intellect of the author.' The characters are 'created by intellect, and are creatures of intellect. Habits, actions, conduct are attributed to them, such as we really witness in human beings; but the reflections and language which accompany these actions, are those of intelligence fully developed, and entirely self-conscious ... in real men and women such clear knowledge of self is rarely developed at all'; 'even in the children ... we find the intellectual predominant and supreme. The young Yorkes, ranging from twelve years down to six, talk like Scotch professors of metaphysics.' The old criticism of *Jane Eyre* reared its ugly head again: there was 'an excess of the repulsive qualities not seldom rather coarsely indulged ... She has a manifest pleasure in dwelling ... on the purely repulsive in human character.'

Fonblanque had also one or two telling criticisms to make which were unique to his review but revealed his perspicacity in reading the character of his author from her work.

There is a hankering, not to be suppressed, after the fleshpots of Egypt – a strong sympathy with Toryism and High Church. The writer sees clearly that they are things of the past, but cannot help regretting them. The tone assumed to the dissenters and the manufacturers is hardly fair. Their high qualities are not denied, but there is a disposition to deepen the shadows in delineating them. There is cordiality when the foibles of rectors and squires are laughed at, but when the defects of the commercial class are touched there is bitterness.[36]

In pointing out her snobbery, Fonblanque had recognized one of the most unattractive of Charlotte's traits and one that contributed most to her discontent and unhappiness both at Haworth, where Dissenters and manufacturers were in the majority, and as a governess, where an English gentleman like Mr Sidgwick had been excused the same sins for which the exciseman's daughter, Mrs White, was lambasted.

The only constantly reiterated complaint which Fonblanque did not make was the lack of focus in *Shirley*. Unlike *Jane Eyre*, which had been written in the first person and thus had a single point of view, *Shirley* was written in the third person and had a multiplicity of characters, many of whom, as the critics were swift to point out, did nothing to advance or enhance the story. More importantly, there was a significant shift in the book's interest from Caroline Helstone to Shirley Keeldar, who was only introduced at the end of the first volume.[37] What the critics could not know, but Charlotte later divulged to Mrs Gaskell, was that Shirley was a tribute to her sister's memory, a portrayal of Emily as she might have been had she been placed in health and prosperity. It was, inevitably, a romanticized portrait. The externals were all there – her studiousness, her lack of ceremony, her habit of sitting on the floor, her devotion to her huge dog Tartar, even the incident where she had been bitten by a suspected mad dog and secretly cauterized the wound herself – but the heart was missing.

Even Ellen Nussey did not recognize the supposed original of Shirley, despite her familiarity with Emily's outward traits.[38] As Emily herself failed in health and was snatched so suddenly from life, the importance of her fictional counterpart grew in Charlotte's mind. By the time it came to naming the book, for Charlotte the interest had shifted from Caroline, Robert Moore and Hollows Mill to Shirley and Fieldhead, though most reviewers still seemed to think Caroline the heroine of the novel.

The general consensus of critical opinion was that *Shirley* was better written than *Jane Eyre* but lacked the earlier novel's fire and originality: a worthy successor but not one that would further Currer Bell's reputation. Charlotte aptly summed it up in her comment that those who were most charmed with *Jane Eyre* were the least pleased with *Shirley*, while those who had spoken disparagingly of *Jane Eyre* liked *Shirley* a little better than its predecessor.[39]

Even though some reviews, like that in *The Times*, were openly hostile and sarcastic in their treatment of *Shirley*, only one cut Charlotte to the quick. The reasons that it did so were twofold: first and foremost, it did the unforgivable in judging *Shirley* almost entirely on the sex of its author; second, it was written by George Henry Lewes, the only person outside Cornhill whom Charlotte had admitted to anything like a literary friendship and whose betrayal was therefore all the more hurtful. Throughout their correspondence in the months following the publication of *Jane Eyre*, Charlotte had maintained her pseudonym and sent her replies through Smith, Elder & Co. to avoid the postmarks which might betray her locality. Grateful for his favourable review of her first novel, she had submitted to his rather bombastic lecturings in his private letters, but ably defended her corner against his insistence on realism and drawing from personal experience. On the publication of *Shirley* he had written to her again, expressing his dislike of the first chapter which in his review he would describe as 'offensive, uninstructive and unamusing', and his conviction that Currer Bell was a woman. This prompted a sharp response from Charlotte.

I wish you did not think me a woman: I wish all reviewers believed 'Currer Bell' to be a man – they would be more just to him. You will – I know – keep measuring me by some standard of what you deem becoming to my sex – where I am not what you consider graceful – you will condemn me ... Come what will – I cannot when I write think always of myself – and of what is elegant and charming in femininity – it is not on those terms or with such ideas I ever took pen in hand; and if it is only on such terms my writing will be tolerated – I shall pass away from the public and trouble it no more. Out of obscurity I came – to obscurity I can easily return.[40]

In the light of this letter, Lewes' subsequent treatment of 'Currer Bell' in the *Edinburgh Review* was little short of disgraceful. What was almost worse, throughout the review Lewes took every opportunity to gloat over the fact that he was privy to the secret of 'Currer Bell' and suggest that he was on intimate terms with her.

In fact, Lewes had just discovered Charlotte's true identity. Either by persistent enquiry or by pure accident, he had met a former schoolfellow of hers who had recognized the Clergy Daughters' School in 'Lowood' and Charlotte Brontë in 'Currer Bell'. Smith Williams had written at the beginning of November to warn her that the discovery had been made, though Charlotte was at a loss to identify his informant. It could not have been one of the Cowan Bridge girls, she insisted, because none of them could possibly have remembered her. 'I cannot conceive that I left a trace behind me', she told Smith Williams. 'My career was a very quiet one. I was plodding and industrious, perhaps I was very grave, for I suffered to see my sisters perishing, but I think I was remarkable for nothing.'[41] As Charlotte suspected, it seems most likely that it was a Roe Head girl who recognized her, particularly as the discovery came within two weeks of the publication of *Shirley*, which would have confirmed any suspicions aroused by *Jane Eyre*.

Whoever his mysterious informant was, Lewes not only made use of his newly acquired knowledge, but positively boasted of it. He alluded unnecessarily to the *Quarterly Review*'s conclusion that the author of *Jane Eyre* was 'a heathen educated among heathens' merely so that he could add with a revelatory flourish, '– the fact being, that the authoress is the daughter of a clergyman!' 'She must learn also to sacrifice a little of her Yorkshire roughness to the demands of good taste', he pontificated, making it clear he knew where she lived, 'neither saturating her writings with such rudeness and offensive harshness, nor suffering her style to wander into such vulgarities as would be inexcusable – even in a man.' He revealed her spinsterhood in a particularly callous and cruel way, by criticizing the unnatural way in which Mrs Pryor had parted with her baby: 'Currer Bell! if under your heart had ever stirred a child, if to your bosom a babe had ever been pressed … never could you have imagined such a falsehood as that!' The peculiar nastiness of this remark can only be appreciated by realizing that Lewes had begun his review with the grandiloquent statement that 'The grand function of woman … is, and ever must be, maternity.'[42] Currer Bell had failed not only as a writer but also as a woman.

'I have received and perused the "Edinburgh Review"', Charlotte wrote to Smith Williams, adding, with quiet dignity,

– it is very brutal and savage. I am not angry with Lewes – but I wish in future he would let me alone – and not write again what makes me feel so cold and sick as I am feeling just now –[43]

To Lewes himself she sent 'but one little word': 'I can be on my guard against my enemies, but God deliver me from my friends!'[44] Too self-important to understand the hurt he had caused, Lewes wrote demanding an explanation, and received a longer but still dignified reply.

I will tell you why I was so hurt by that review … not because its criticism was keen or its blame sometimes severe; not because its praise was stinted (for indeed I think you give me quite as much praise as I deserve) but because, after I had said earnestly that I wished critics would judge me as an <u>author</u> not as a woman, you so roughly – I even thought – so cruelly handled the question of sex …

With a magnanimity which Lewes surely did not deserve and which Charlotte would not have granted to a lesser personage, she told him that she bore him no malice.

I imagine you are both enthusiastic and implacable, as you are at once sagacious and careless. You know much and discover much, but you are in such a hurry to tell it all, you never give yourself time to think how your reckless eloquence may affect others, and, what is more, if you knew how it did affect them you would not much care.

Ending her letter with implicit reproof, she signed herself 'yours with a certain respect and some chagrin Currer Bell'.[45] If Lewes had thought his sagacity in uncovering her identity had earned him the right to a letter from Charlotte Brontë, he was sadly mistaken: Currer Bell had been insulted, Currer Bell would reply.

Lewes' tactless and cruel behaviour was in sharp contrast to that of Mrs Gaskell. Like him, she had been consumed with curiosity to find out the identity of 'Currer Bell' and had asked her friend, Eliza Fox, to make enquiries of Dr Epps, whose contact with Charlotte had become public knowledge.[46] By the middle of November Mrs Gaskell was privy to at least some information about Charlotte and, struck by the passages on watching at Caroline's sickbed in *Shirley*, which had been sent to her with the author's compliments, wrote privately to her through Smith, Elder & Co. to express her sympathy. 'She said I was not to answer it', Charlotte told Smith Williams, 'but I cannot help doing so. Her note brought the tears to my eyes: she is a good – she is a great woman – proud am I that I can touch a chord of sympathy in souls so noble.'[47] Though Charlotte gave away little in her reply, writing impersonally as 'Currer Bell', she admitted Mrs Gaskell so far into her confidence as to own her sex – the first time she had done so in writing as 'Currer Bell'.

Currer Bell <u>must</u> answer Mrs Gaskell's letter – whether forbidden to do so or not – and She must acknowledge its kind, generous sympathy with all her heart.

Yet Mrs Gaskell must not pity Currer Bell too much: there are thousands who suffer more than she: dark days she has known; the worst, perhaps, were days of bereavement, but though CB. is the survivor of most that were dear to her, she has one near relative still left, and therefore cannot be said to be quite alone.

Currer Bell will avow to Mrs Gaskell that her chief reason for maintaining an incognito is the fear that if she relinquished it, strength and courage would leave her, and she should ever after shrink – from writing the plain truth.[48]

Mrs Gaskell could not resist a triumphant note to Catherine Winkworth, 'Currer Bell (aha! what will you give me for a secret?) She's a she – that I will tell you – who has sent me *Shirley*', but otherwise respected Charlotte's confidence.[49] She and Harriet Martineau were both recipients of *Shirley*, not simply because Charlotte admired them but also because she was morbidly inclined to see in them a resemblance to her dead sister. 'In Mrs Gaskell's nature – it mournfully pleases me to fancy a remote affinity to my sister Emily – in Miss Martineau's mind I have always felt the same – though there are wide differences –'.[50]

Charlotte's postbag now regularly included letters from her admirers. These ranged from the great and good, like Mrs Gaskell, Harriet Martineau and, more surprisingly, Sir John Herschel, the famous astronomer, to the humble and eccentric. One 'not quite an old maid, but nearly one, she says', sent Charlotte an enthusiastic letter declaring that if 'Currer Bell' were a gentleman and like his heroes, she suspected she would fall in love with him. Half-laughing, half-crying, Charlotte retorted to Smith Williams, 'You and Mr Smith would not let me announce myself as a single gentleman of mature age in my preface – but if you had permitted it, a great many elderly spinsters would have been pleased.'[51] Another letter was alarming not just in its excessive enthusiasm for *Shirley* but because the writer announced his 'fixed, deliberate resolution to institute a search after "Currer Bell" and sooner or later to find him out'. 'It almost makes me feel like a Wizard who has raised a spirit he may find it difficult to lay', Charlotte confessed to Smith Williams. 'But I shall not think about it. His sort of fervour often foams itself away in words.'[52]

Charlotte's anonymity and with it her ability to 'walk invisible' was gradually being whittled away. Lewes had started the process in London, Joe Taylor in Gomersal: the news would soon spread to the papers and it was simply a matter of time until the truth became public knowledge.

Aware of this, and that she had at least tried to live up to Emily's insistence on anonymity even after her sister's death had removed the necessity for it, Charlotte began to toy with the idea of going to London as the acknowledged author of *Jane Eyre* and *Shirley*. Smith Williams had been pressing the idea upon her for over a year, but her brother and sisters' illnesses and deaths had made it impossible; afterwards she had been reluctant to go out into society. Looking back over that period, Charlotte had admitted 'there have been intervals when I have ceased to care about literature and critics and fame – when I have lost sight of whatever was prominent in my thoughts at the first publication of "Jane Eyre" – but now I want these things to come back – vividly –'.⁵³ Ambition was reborn.

'I am trying by degrees to inure myself to the thought of \some day/ stepping over to Keighley, taking the train to Leeds – thence to London – and once more venturing to set foot in the strange, busy whirl of the Strand and Cornhill', she wrote to Smith Williams on 15 November. 'I want to talk to you a little and hear by word of mouth how matters are progressing – Whenever I come – I must come quietly and but for a short time – I should be unhappy to leave Papa longer than a fortnight.'⁵⁴ Charlotte could now consider leaving her father alone with the servants for two weeks, without even a second thought, when it suited her own plans.

Her original idea was to take up a long-standing invitation from the Wheelwrights, her Brussels friends, who now lived at 29, Phillimore Place in Kensington: that was until something better turned up. Hearing that she intended to come to London, George Smith himself wrote to her, suggesting that she should stay with him and making his mother write to second the offer. Charlotte leapt at the chance. Somewhat disingenuously telling Smith that at first she had thought she would have to decline because of her prior invitation, she then went on to declare:

these friends only know me as Miss Brontë, and they are of the class, perfectly worthy but in no sort remarkable – to whom I should feel it quite superfluous to introduce Currer Bell; I know they would not understand the author. Under these circumstances my movements would have been very much restrained, and in fact this consideration formed a difficulty in the way of my coming to London at all. I think however I might conscientiously spend part of the time with you and part with my other friends.⁵⁵

She was even prepared to defer her visit to the Wheelwrights in order to come at a more convenient time for the Smiths. In the meantime, she sent for a dressmaker and had her prepare a whole new wardrobe of clothes, from dresses down to underclothes: this time, even though she was still obliged to wear mourning, she would not be caught going to the opera in her 'plain – high-made, country garments'.[56]

Charlotte's eagerness to stay with the Smiths in London was a manifestation of what Mary Taylor called her 'notion of literary fame – a passport to the society of clever people'.[57] It was also a sign of her growing friendship with George Smith. Although most of her correspondence with Smith, Elder & Co. had been with Smith Williams, she had been favourably disposed towards its young head since she first met him during the 'pop visit' with Anne. Over the last few months, however, their friendship had burgeoned over the unlikely matter of Charlotte's seeking George Smith's advice on her investments. Writing to thank him for the £500 he had sent her on the completion of *Shirley*, she told him she felt both pleased and proud of the amount she had earned. 'I should like to take care of this money:' she informed him earnestly, 'it is Papa's great wish that I should realize a small independency if you could give me a word of advice respecting the wisest and safest manner of investing this £500, I should be very much obliged to you.' She could not, of course, apply to her 'ordinary acquaintances' for information, as this would naturally lead to speculation about the source of her new-found fortune. George Smith advised Charlotte to place her money in the Funds, where it would earn an unspectacular but safe dividend, and offered to make all the necessary arrangements on her behalf.[58] He also, at her request, investigated the value of her shares in the York & North Midland Railway in the wake of the recent crash in prices. She was shocked to learn that her holding was now virtually worthless: 'In fact', she told him,

the little railway property I possessed, according to original prices – formed already a small competency for one with my views and habits, now – scarcely any portion of it can with security be calculated on. I must open this view of the case to my father by degrees, and meantime wait patiently until I see how affairs are likely to turn. Some of the local papers strenuously advise against selling just now; they affirm that the market is far more depressed than it otherwise would be, by the fact of shareholders hurrying to sell, in a panic.[59]

There was a kindness in George Smith's attentions and a comfort in placing her financial affairs in his obviously capable hands for Charlotte, who was feeling increasingly isolated at Haworth. She knew she was assured of his protection in London and, judging by his reaction to her first visit, that she could rely on him to entertain her.

Retracing the steps of the 'pop visit', but this time alone, Charlotte travelled by train to London on Thursday, 29 November 1849, and was taken to the Smiths' house in Westbourne Place, Paddington. Her publisher's family had now been admitted into the secret of their guest's true identity.

[617]

'Mrs Smith received me at first like one who has had the strictest orders to be scrupulously attentive –', Charlotte told Ellen,

I had fire in my bedroom evening and morning – two wax candles – &c. &c. and Mrs S & her daughters seemed to look on me with a mixture of respect and alarm – but all this is changed – that is to say the attention and politeness continue as great as ever – but the alarm and estrangement are quite gone – she treats me as if she liked me and I begin to like her much – kindness is a potent heart winner.[60]

Of George Smith himself, Charlotte would only say 'he pleases me much: I like him better even as a son and brother than as a man of business', a comment that instantly drove Ellen to romantic speculations which Charlotte just as quickly quashed.[61] The first four or five days in the 'big Babylon', as Charlotte termed London, passed in 'a sort of whirl ... for changes, scenes and stimulus which would be a trifle to others, are much to me'. Her days were spent in sightseeing, her evenings 'in society', an arrangement which swiftly wore down her slender stock of animal spirits. 'Nothing charmed me more during my stay in Town', she later wrote to Miss Wooler, 'than the pictures I saw – one or two private collections of Turner's best water-colour drawings were indeed a treat: his later oil-paintings are strange things – things that baffle description.'[62]

She was also taken to see the great actor, William Charles Macready, whose performances in Shakespearean tragedy were the talk of London. Charlotte saw him twice, in *Macbeth* and *Othello*, and was not impressed. 'I astounded a dinner-party by honestly saying I did not like him', she told Miss Wooler with the quiet satisfaction of one who was proud of her dissent. 'It is the fashion to rave about his splendid acting – anything more false and artificial – less genuinely impressive than his whole style I could scarcely have imagined.' She had added to the general consternation by attacking the stage system itself: actors could manage farce well enough but they knew nothing about tragedy or Shakespeare and the theatre was therefore a failure. 'I said so – and by so saying produced a blank silence – a mute consternation.'[63]

Smith Williams took her on a tour of the new Houses of Parliament and later invited her for a quiet evening at his home, where she was at last introduced to his wife, who had been ill on her previous visit, and renewed her acquaintance with his daughters.[64] The Wheelwrights, too, though Charlotte seems to have abandoned her plans to stay with them, invited her to lunch at their home.[65] Though grateful for these kindnesses, her first meetings with the stars of the literary firmament meant far more to Charlotte than the renewing of old friendships.

The highlight of her stay was the Smiths' dinner party on the evening of 4 December when, for the first time, she came face to face with her hero, Thackeray. She had spent the whole day in a mixture of dread and anticipation, too nervous even to eat. By the time Thackeray was announced at seven in the evening, she had been fasting since breakfast, and was faint from hunger. 'Excitement and exhaustion together made savage work of me that evening', she told Ellen miserably. Recalling that meeting later, it seemed unreal: 'when Mr Thackeray was announced and I saw him enter, looked up at his tall figure, heard his voice the whole incident was truly dream-like – I was only certain it was true because I became miserably destitute of self-possession ... Had I not been obliged to speak, I could have managed well, but it behoved me to answer when addressed and the effort was torture – I spoke stupidly'.[66] Thackeray himself seems to have been touched by Charlotte's evident nervousness, her vulnerability emphasized by her tiny size compared to his own great height and bulk. What he remembered was 'the trembling little frame, the little hand, the great honest eyes', declaring that 'An impetuous honesty seemed to me to characterize the woman.'[67] He was later to be a victim of that honesty but, on this occasion, Charlotte was so overawed by her 'Titan's' presence that she remained subdued and silent. Writing to her father the next day, she gave him a graphic account of that evening.

yesterday I saw Mr Thackeray. He dined here with some other gentlemen. He is a very tall man – above six feet high, with a peculiar face – not handsome – very ugly indeed – generally somewhat satirical and stern in expression, but capable also of a kind look. He was not told who I was – he was not introduced to me – but I soon saw him looking at me through his spectacles and when we all rose to go down to dinner – he just stept quietly up and said 'Shake hands' so I shook hands – He spoke very few words to me – but when he went away he shook hands again in a very kind way.[68]

Thackeray's satirical conversation both fascinated and baffled Charlotte, who found it almost impossible to tell when her hero was joking. When the gentlemen entered the drawing room, for instance, he asked her 'if she had perceived the secret of their cigars'. Charlotte answered literally and then realized, as several people smiled, that Thackeray had been alluding to a passage in *Jane Eyre*. 'It is better – I should think to have him for a friend than an enemy –', she told her father, 'for he is a most formidable looking personage. I listened to him as he conversed with the other gentlemen – all he says is most simple, but often cynical, harsh, and contradictory.'[69]

Five days later, on Sunday, 9 December, Charlotte paid a visit to another of the great and equally formidable literary figures of the day, Harriet Martineau, a novelist and author of essays on political economy. Charlotte herself seems to have requested the interview on learning that Miss Martineau was staying with her cousins, Richard and Lucy Martineau, in Westbourne Street, just round the corner from the Smiths' residence. Charlotte had long admired Miss Martineau, chiefly on account of her novel

Deerbrook. In the letter accompanying the copy of *Shirley* she had sent her, Charlotte had inadvertently referred to herself as 'she' but crossed this out and replaced it with 'he'. This mistake only confirmed Miss Martineau in her belief that 'a certain passage in "Jane Eyre", about sewing on brass rings, could have been written only by a woman or an upholsterer'. She had therefore responded by addressing her reply externally to 'Currer Bell Esqre' but had begun her letter 'Madam'. Charlotte had not reciprocated by admitting Miss Martineau to her confidence as she had Mrs Gaskell, so when 'Currer Bell's' note arrived the Martineaus were still no wiser. The note expressed 'a very strong wish to see you' and declared, 'Do not think this request springs from mere curiosity. I hope it has its origin in a better feeling. It would grieve me to lose this chance of seeing one whose works have so often made her the subject of my thoughts.'[70]

In great excitement, the Martineaus invited 'Currer Bell' to join them for an early tea at six o'clock and spent the interval trying to guess what their visitor would be like. Harriet Martineau, who was very deaf and relied on an ear trumpet, insisted that her cousins should shout the name to her when the visitor was announced so that she was not left in doubt a moment longer than necessary. Lucy Martineau described Charlotte's entrance in a letter to her son the next day:

I lighted plenty of candles that we might see what manner of man or womankind it was, & we sat in wondering expectation ... The hand pointed to 5 minutes past six, & we said it is a hoax after all! When lo! a carriage stopped at the door, the bell rung, and Yelland flung open the door announcing —— ! & in came a neat little woman, a <u>very</u> little sprite of a creature nicely dressed; & with nice tidy bright hair – Tho' the cat was out of the bag here, we are bound not to tell her name, for she does not wish it to be made generally known, sooner than it of necessity will be – & that will not be long I expect. Her voice and way of speaking, somehow in the upper part of her nose, is <u>extremely</u> like the Miss Mitchells...[71]

Harriet Martineau herself thought Charlotte 'the smallest creature I had ever seen (except at a fair) and her eyes blazed'. Like Lewes, and possibly through him, the Martineaus had heard the gossip identifying 'Currer Bell' as Charlotte Brontë and therefore, when her name was announced, they already knew something of her history. What Harriet Martineau had not anticipated was a moment she graphically described in her *Autobiography*.

When she was seated by me on the sofa, she cast up at me such a look, – so loving, so appealing, – that, in connexion with her deep mourning dress, and the knowledge that she was the sole survivor of her family, I could with the utmost difficulty return her smile, or keep my composure. I should have been heartily glad to cry.[72]

After tea, the two authoresses were left alone together and discussed the reviews of Charlotte's books, 'the little sprite' going 'red all over with pleasure' when Miss Martineau declared *Jane Eyre* to be a first-rate book.

Their hosts rejoined them a couple of hours later, Lucy Martineau reporting that 'she was so pleasant & so naive, that is to say so innocent and un Londony that we were quite charmed with her ... Her age we imagined to be about 32, some of us think younger, some older.'[73]

The news that 'Currer Bell' had visited Harriet Martineau spread like wildfire. Lucy Martineau's already exaggerated version of Charlotte's life – 'This is her 1st visit to London, & she lives in a most retired part of England, never seeing <u>any</u> body, & her Father has not slept out of his \own/ house for the last 20 years' – was further garbled in the telling, though at least the Martineaus preserved the secret of Charlotte's name. Thackeray, however, despite the delicate discretion he had shown at their first meeting, did not and so Charlotte Brontë was unmasked before the literary coteries of London.[74]

'I get on quietly –', Charlotte told her father, 'most people know me I think, but they are far too well-bred to shew that they know me – so that there is none of that bustle or that sense of publicity I dislike.'[75] On the last night of her visit, the Smiths held another dinner party in her honour to which they invited seven gentlemen, including the five literary critics of *The Times, Athenaeum, Examiner, Spectator* and *Atlas.* Charlotte had fortified herself morally and physically for the occasion by lunching with the Wheelwrights so that she was able to await the eight o'clock dinner with resignation. Nevertheless, when it came to actually facing the 'literary Rhadamanthi ... men more dreaded in the world of letters than you can conceive' over dinner, she abandoned the prominent place set for her at the bottom of the table and went to sit next to the comforting and protective Mrs Smith.[76]

Among the eminent critics present were John Forster, editor of *The Examiner,* and Henry Chorley, the literary and musical reviewer of the *Athenaeum,* but it was the presence of someone from *The Times* which must have caused Charlotte most anguish. *The Times* had published its review on 7 December, while she was in London, and it was one of the most overtly hostile she had received. Describing *Shirley* as 'very clever, as a matter of course', the reviewer had then gone on to lambast the story as 'commonplace and puerile', the characters as 'creatures of the author's brain – certainly not of our every-day world' and the dialogue as 'such as no mortal lovers ever spoke, or, we trust, ever will speak in Miss Currer Bell's books again'. At the end of an extremely sarcastic notice, the critic had dismissed the book as 'at once the most high flown and the stalest of fictions'. Not surprisingly, the morning that this review appeared *The Times* unaccountably disappeared from the Smiths' morning room. Charlotte was not to be fooled, and quietly insisted that Mrs Smith should show her the paper. Mrs Smith took up her work while Charlotte read the review, but she could not help observing the tears stealing down her guest's face and falling into her lap.[77] Later, telling Miss Wooler about her dinner with the critics, Charlotte remarked with something like contempt, 'some of them had been very bitter foes in print but they were prodigiously civil face to face – these gentlemen seemed infinitely grander, more pompous, dashing, shewy than the few authors I saw ...'[78] She liked John Forster, who would later, and without her knowledge, play such an important part in her life, but described the distance between his 'loud swagger' and Thackeray's 'simple port' as being like the distance between Shakespeare's writing and Macready's acting. It was Henry Chorley, however, who fascinated her: he was a 'peculiar specimen' and she was unsure whether to react to him with utter contempt and aversion or, for the sake of latent good, to forgive his obvious evil. 'One could well pardon his unpleasant features, his strange voice, even his very foppery and grimace – if one found these disadvantages connected with living talent and any spark of genuine goodness – If there is nothing more than acquirement, smartness and the affectation of philanthropy –', she added sardonically, 'Chorley is a fine creature.'[79]

One of the good things to emerge from this meeting with her critics was that Charlotte lost her awe of them. Having met them, observed their own failings and found them to be mortal after all, she would in future no longer feel any obligation to be bound by their judgement. The evening passed off better than she had expected. She was able to endure the unaccustomed length of the dinner 'quite courageously' and was not too overwrought to converse. It was only when she got to bed and was unable to sleep that she discovered how much their presence and conversation had excited her. Next day she was so worn out that, having said her farewells to the Smiths and set off for home, she was obliged to break her journey overnight at Derby and spend the night at an inn.[80] She reached home on Saturday afternoon, 15 December, to find her father and the servants all well. On the Monday morning she wrote her thank-you letters to Laetitia Wheelwright, Mrs Smith and, most especially, George Smith. After telling him how much his mother's 'considerate attention and goodness' had enhanced her visit, she added:

As to yourself – what can I say? Nothing. And it is as well: words are not at all needed: very easy is it to discover that with you to gratify others is to gratify yourself; to serve others is to afford yourself a pleasure. I hope this may long be the case, and I wish the Leigh Hunts and the Jameses may never spoil your nature. I suppose you will experience your share of ingratitude and encroachment – but do not let them alter you. Happily they are the less likely to do this because you are half a Scotchman and therefore must have inherited a fair share of prudence to qualify your generosity, and of caution to protect your benevolence. Currer Bell bids you farewell for the present

CB—[81]

This curiously formal letter, so different in style and tone from the ones sent to his mother and Laetitia Wheelwright, was obviously carefully drafted before being sent and is all the more revealing for that, suggesting an anxiety to please and impress. The use of her 'Currer Bell' pseudonym was significant too, for, as we shall see, George Smith was the only one of her correspondents with whom she used it consistently. The masculine *nom-de-plume* freed her from the constraints that would normally be expected in letters between a young unmarried man and woman and enabled her to write in a flirtatious way wholly inappropriate to the spinster daughter of a clergyman.

The easy and teasing relationship that had developed between George Smith and his authoress during her fortnight in London was amply illustrated in the letters which followed. On 26 December, for instance, she wrote:

My dear Sir,
   Your note reminded me of the 'cross portrait'; it is exceedingly wayward. You shall have the full benefit of the character you give of yourself; I am willing to look on you as a 'hard-headed and close-fisted man of business', only – remember – your conduct must be consistent with the claim you prefer to these epithets; if you are 'close-fisted', shut your hand against Currer Bell, give him no more books...[82]

George Smith's 'man of business' image was to be a shared joke which would recur frequently in future correspondence. The whole basis of their new intimacy was revealed in the same letter: 'one should study human Nature under all aspects', Charlotte told her publisher, 'one should see one's friends for instance, in Cornhill as well as in Westbourne-Place; one should hear them discuss "discounts" and "per-centages" as well as converse at their own fireside'. As a sample of this intimacy, she gave him a tongue-in-cheek description of the proceedings of what she archly called a group of gentlemen commissioned to choose ladies' bonnets for East Indian exportation.

You do not know the anecdote, but it is quite authentic, and the little circumstance to which it refers took place < it > in the City – not far from C—h—ll. The bonnets were carefully chosen, and subsequently – with a conscientious desire to have all right – they were <u>tried on</u>, and judgement duly passed as to their merits. Imagination cannot resist the impulse to picture this scene – it rises before her, and she looks at it with delighted eyes. She sees a back-room crowded with bonnet-boxes; she sees three umpires whom she knows well; P— stands in the back-ground waiting to pack. Opinions vary and tastes differ just sufficiently to give interest to the discussion. A gentianella blue satin is found most becoming to Mr T—y—r; Mr W—m's artist's eye finds a \special/ charm in the rich tint of a 'chapeau grenat' (anglice a garnet-coloured velvet bonnet) while Mr G—e S—th divides his preference between the prettiest little pink drawn-silk and the neatest white chip with a single drooping ostrich feather.
   Here ensues the packing scene – P— is now the principal figure – and he is

beheld – not without anguish – applying to fabrics of satin, velvet, chip and straw those principles of compression and compactness on which he acts with such skill and success in the stowage of books and stationary.

There is a third scene – the unpacking at Calcutta or elsewhere – but from hence Imagination turns her face with dismay and covers her eyes with her wings[83]

Writing again to George Smith on 15 January, Charlotte teasingly forbore to thank him for sending a replacement copy of a book that had been lost in the post. 'I leave the correction of such proceedings to the "man-of-business" within you', she told him, 'on the "close-fisted" Head of the Establishment in Cornhill devolves the duty of reprimanding Mr G—e S—th; they may settle accounts between themselves – while Currer Bell looks on and wonders but keeps out of the melée.' Assuring him that Caroline Helstone had no original and was 'a native of Dreamland, and as such can have neither voice nor presence except for the fancy', she added, 'N.B. that last sentence is not to be read by the "Man of business"; it sounds much too bookish.'[84] Clearly the relationship with George Smith, even when conducted only by letter, added a much-needed sparkle to Charlotte's life.

The return from London inevitably brought on a depression of spirits, not least because it fell only a few days before the first anniversary of Emily's death. In the past Charlotte had always doubled her pleasure from excursions into society by faithfully describing all she had seen and heard to Emily.[85] That pleasure was now denied her, but she had seen and done so much that she needed a receptive female companion to whom she could confide her impressions and opinions, relive her experiences and chat inconsequentially. She therefore turned to Ellen, asking her to come over to Haworth as soon as possible and offering to send the Haworth gig to collect her from Keighley station so that she need not walk the final four miles.[86]

The day before Charlotte wrote to Ellen, Patrick, whose thoughts must also have been preoccupied with the anniversary of his daughter's death on the morrow, wrote a hymn affirming his faith in God and His Church. Though the Christmas message of new life and hope must have been peculiarly poignant in the light of his recent bereavements, Patrick's faith never wavered:

> Then welcome with pleasures profound
> The joys which the season commands.
>
> Let Christ and His love be our theme,
> Let earth with its cares pass away,
> Let heavenly thoughts be our dreams,
> And practice our duty by day.

Patrick had the first five verses of the hymn printed for use in the Christmas services at church and also sent a complete copy to the *Leeds Intelligencer,* where the lines were published under his initials on 22 December.[87]

Ellen arrived five days later for a stay of three weeks.[88] The friends had much to talk about, for as well as all the excitement of Charlotte's London visit there was the distinct prospect of a marriage between mutual friends, Joe Taylor and Amelia Ringrose. Amelia's original engagement to Ellen's brother, George, had been reluctantly broken off when it became evident that he was unlikely either to regain his sanity or to return from Dr Belcombe's asylum near York. For the last two months, Joe Taylor had been paying her an increasing amount of attention, much to Charlotte's amusement. 'Take notice – you will see more of Mr Joe', she had written in one of her brief letters to Amelia, without disclosing that Joe had actually written to her asking her opinion of Miss Ringrose. She had replied with a 'faithful opinion', but had refrained from asking why he wanted it. 'I said she was what I called truly amiable, actively useful – genuinely good-natured – sufficiently sensible – neither unobservant nor without discrimination \but/ Not highly intellectual, brilliant or profound.' Whether Charlotte's opinion carried any weight or not, the two had become informally engaged by the beginning of December, leading Charlotte to say, 'I do not like to think about it; I shudder sometimes.'[89] She was therefore extremely put out when, virtually unannounced, Joe Taylor arrived for dinner one day shortly after her return from London. The ostensible purpose of his visit was to invite Charlotte to spend Christmas in Birmingham with the Dixons, the Taylors' cousins who had befriended Charlotte in Brussels. In fact he was about to go to Hull to ask Amelia's father formally for his consent to their marriage and, knowing that Mr Ringrose was a notoriously difficult character, he wanted Charlotte's advice on how to proceed. As he left he promised to return while Ellen was staying at Haworth to let them know the outcome of his visit.[90]

Writing to Smith Williams on 3 January 1850, Charlotte apologized for her tardy response to his letter: 'just now I am enjoying the treat of my friend Ellen's society and she makes me indolent and negligent – I am too busy talking to her all day to do anything else'. 'When I first saw Ellen I did not care for her –', Charlotte confessed to Smith Williams,

we were schoolfellows – in the course of time we learnt each others faults and good points – we were contrasts – still we suited – affection was first a germ, then a sapling – then a strong tree: now – no new friend, however lofty or profound in intellect < could be to me what Ellen is > – not even Miss Martineau herself – could be to me what Ellen is, yet she is no more than a conscientious, observant, calm, well-bred Yorkshire girl. She is without romance – if she attempts to read poetry – or poetic prose aloud – I am irritated and deprive her of the book – if she talks of it I stop my ears – but she is good – she is true – she is faithful and I love her.[91]

While Ellen's friendship was undoubtedly genuine and based on many years' standing, Charlotte's new-found fame as an author allowed Ellen to bask in reflected glory. The deaths of her sisters had deprived Charlotte of her most intimate companions and Ellen now willingly filled their place, gaining a higher level of Charlotte's affection and confidence than might otherwise have been the case.

An early indication of Ellen's newly acquired status came during her visit to Charlotte, when she received a letter from the vicar of Birstall. 'Fame says you are on a visit with the renowned Currer Bell', William Margetson Heald had written, before asking her to get Charlotte to identify all the originals of the characters in *Shirley*. He had just discovered that he himself featured in the novel as Mr Hall, admitting 'in that Mr Hall is represented as black, bilious & of dismal aspect, stooping a trifle & indulging a little now & then in the indigenous dialect, – this seems to sit very well on your humble servant'. Mr Heald himself had recognized many of the characters in the book, though he defended Hammond Roberson against his unflattering portrayal as Mr Helstone, declaring that Charlotte had evidently got her impressions of him through an unfriendly medium and did not understand the full value of 'one of the most admirable characters I ever knew or expect to know'. As he had become part of 'Currer Bell's' stock-in-trade himself, 'tho' I had no idea that I should ever be made a means to amuse the public', Mr Heald thought he had 'an equitable claim to this intelligence by way of my dividend'. Fortunately, he took the whole affair in good part, ending his letter with the comment, 'One had need "walk ... warily in these dangerous days" when as Burns (is it not he?) says "A chield's among you taking notes and faith he'll prent it" –'.[92]

Someone else who took his portrayal in *Shirley* in remarkably good part was Arthur Bell Nicholls, the curate of Haworth. He got to know about the novels earlier than anyone else in Haworth and, as Charlotte herself was unlikely to have confided in him, it was probably Patrick who, unable to contain his pride in his daughter's reception among the London literati, had told her secret to his curate. He immediately got hold of *Jane Eyre* and, having read it, was soon 'crying out for the "other book"' – 'much good may it do him', Charlotte commented truculently.[93] Her description of his reaction to *Shirley* is deservedly famous, though it is rarely pointed out that it gives a much more attractive portrait of Mr Nicholls than the dour, doctrinaire one of Brontë legend.

Mr Nicholls has finished reading 'Shirley' he \is/ delighted with it – John Brown's wife seriously thought he had gone wrong in the head as she heard him giving vent to roars of laughter as he sat alone – clapping his hands and stamping on the floor. He would read all the scenes about the curates aloud to papa – he triumphed in his own character.

What Mr Grant will say is another question. No matter.[94]

Perhaps encouraged by Mr Nicholls' reaction, Patrick had also informed his old friend, William Morgan, that his daughter was the acclaimed author of *Jane Eyre*. Much to Charlotte's surprise, since she regarded him as a stuffy and bombastic pedant, he too reacted favourably, writing to her 'not in blame but in the highest strain of eulogy – ! he says it thoroughly fascinated and enchained him – &c. &c. &c.'[95]

What little remained of Charlotte's secret was finally blown away at the beginning of February. She glumly reported the circumstance to Ellen, who was now back at Brookroyd.

Martha came in yesterday – puffing and blowing and much excited – 'I've heard sich news' she began – 'What about?' 'Please ma'am you've been and written two books – the grandest books that ever was seen – My Father has heard it at Halifax and Mr George Taylor and Mr Greenwood and Mr Merrall at Bradford – and they are going to have a meeting at the Mechanics' Institute and to settle about ordering them.' 'Hold your tongue, Martha, and be off.' I fell into a cold sweat. 'Jane Eyre' will be read by John Brown by Mrs Taylor and Betty – God help keep & deliver me![96]

The news spread like wildfire throughout the township and soon all Haworth was clamouring to read Miss Brontë's clever books. 'The Haworth People have been making great fools of themselves about "Shirley" –', Charlotte told Ellen,

they take it in an enthusiastic light – when they got the vols. at the Mech— Instn all the members wanted them – they cast lots for the whole three – and whoever got a vol. was only allowed to keep it two days and to be fined a shilling per diem for longer detention – It would be mere nonsense and vanity to tell you what they say.[97]

Though Charlotte pretended to scoff at the reaction of her neighbours to the discovery that their parson's daughter was a famous author, she was nevertheless grateful for their enthusiasm and for their pride in her books, not least because it was a source of 'reviving pleasure' to her father in his old age. She was particularly touched by the 'artless and earnest, genuine and generous' testimony of one of the poor working men of the township. A Dissenter whom she had not spoken to above two or three times in her life, he had a mind 'too keen for his frame' and could barely support his large family. After reading *Jane Eyre* he had written a record of his feelings, and this, by fair means or foul and without his knowledge, had come into Charlotte's hands. He had not dared give it to her himself, saying 'Miss Brontë, if she knew he had written it would scorn him', but Charlotte considered it 'one of the highest, because one of the most truthful and artless tributes her work has yet received'; 'I value it more than testimonies from higher sources', she told Smith Williams.[98]

Another working man who had read *Jane Eyre* and *Shirley* was prompted to write to his local paper when his suspicions that he knew the author were confirmed by articles in the press. As he was 'a factory boy' who had emigrated from Haworth and now lived in Spencer, Massachusetts, his letter had peculiar interest for Charlotte, who was sent a copy by Smith, Elder & Co. As she said, it was a 'curious mixture of truth and inaccuracy', vividly recalling Patrick's features, hearing him preach, his failing sight and his cataract operation, but having 'no very particular recollection' of his children. Indeed, the writer only remembered the son who 'came home a year or two ago, having just finished his education. He was thought to be an able artist', and two daughters 'who lived in Bradford ... although they have made the tour of Europe'. Oddly, his most enduring image of the sisters – and one which occurs again and again in contemporary recollections – is that of the sisters taking their daily walk with their favourite dog.[99]

Though it might be expected that local people would be proud of Charlotte Brontë's success, it was surprising that this seems to have extended even to those who should have been mortified by their own portrayal in *Shirley*.

The very Curates – poor fellows! shew no resentment; each characteristically finds solace for his own wounds in crowing over his brethren. Mr Donne was – at first a little disturbed; for a week or two He fidgetted about the neighbourhood in some disquietude – but he is now soothed down, only yesterday I had the pleasure of making him a comfortable cup of tea and seeing him sip it with revived complacency. It is a curious fact that since he read 'Shirley' he has come to the house oftener than ever and been remarkably meek and assiduous to please – Some people's natures are veritable enigmas – I quite expected to have one good scene at the least with him, but as yet nothing of the sort has occurred – and if the other curates do not tease him into irritation, he will remain quiet now.[100]

As if the local furore were not enough, Charlotte's 'anchorite seclusion' at Haworth was also under threat. 'One or two curiosity-hunters have made their way to Haworth Parsonage', she reported to Smith Williams, adding somewhat optimistically, '– but our rude hills and rugged neighbourhood will I doubt not form a sufficient barrier to the frequent repetition of such visits'.[101]

Among those who braved the hills was the Reverend Andrew Cassels, who arrived unannounced just after dinner one afternoon, demanded to see Mr Brontë and was shown into the parlour where he talked for an hour 'in a loud vulgar key'. Consumed with curiosity, Charlotte interrogated Martha as to who the visitor was: 'Some mak' of a tradesman', she had replied, 'he's not a gentleman I'm sure'. When Charlotte took her tea with her father, she discovered that the caller was the vicar of Batley though Martha, with her usual forthrightness, declared he looked no more like a vicar than she did. Even Patrick had to admit that he was 'rather shabby-looking' and amused Charlotte by telling her that Cassels had tried to induce him to dine at the

Black Bull that evening by offering him 'two or three bottles of the best wine Haworth could afford!' Though he professed to have come to view the scenery, the real purpose of his visit was to invite Patrick to Batley, telling him, by way of a corollary, to bring his daughter with him.[102]

Any lingering hopes that it might be possible to retain at least some measure of local anonymity were soon to be dashed. On 28 February 1850, the *Bradford Observer* trumpeted:

It is understood that the only daughter of the Rev P Brontë, incumbent of Haworth is the authoress of *Jane Eyre* and *Shirley*, two of the most popular novels of the day, which have appeared under the name of 'Currer Bell'.[103]

The power to walk invisible had finally been withdrawn.

Chapter Twenty-Two

THE SOCIETY OF CLEVER PEOPLE

While Ellen Nussey stayed at Haworth, Charlotte had managed to keep reasonably cheerful. Once she had gone, depression began to creep in. Anxious to keep it at bay, and remembering how her work had been her saviour through the dark days of the previous year, Charlotte attempted to make a start on her next novel. Without her almost visionary imaginative power to aid her, however, the words, the characters, the scenes would not come and she abandoned the effort after two or three attempts.[1]

Charlotte's gloom was not helped by an unaccountable silence from Smith, Elder & Co. Now that the publication of *Shirley* was out of the way and her visit was over, there was really no need for a continuation of the correspondence except as a token of friendship. The complete absence of letters for over a month was therefore both galling and distressing and Charlotte was very much ashamed to discover how dependent upon their stimulus she had become. Day after day she waited for the post with rising expectation, only to have her hopes dashed once more. 'This is a stupid, disgraceful, unmeaning state of things –', she wrote angrily to Ellen, 'I feel bitterly enraged at my own dependence and folly – It is so bad for the mind to be quite alone – to have none with whom to talk over little crosses and disappointments and laugh them away. If I could write I daresay I should be better but I cannot write a line.'²

In this mood, Charlotte took violent exception to a well-meaning letter from poor Miss Wooler, who had written to assure her former pupil that 'in spite of all I had gone and done in the writing line – I still retained a place in her esteem'. Charlotte wrote her a crushing reply.

You seem to think that I had feared some loss in your esteem owing to my being the reputed Author of this book [*Jane Eyre*] – such a fear – one so unjust to both you and myself, never crossed my mind. When I was in London – a woman whose celebrity is not wider than her moral standing is elevated – and in each point she has no living superior – said to me 'I have ever observed that it is to the coarse-minded alone – "Jane Eyre" is coarse.' This < observ > remark tallied with what I had myself noticed; I felt its truth … I own when I hear of any one making an exaggerated outcry against 'Jane Eyre' immediately in my own mind I come to no very complimentary conclusion respecting the natural quality of that persons tastes and propensities.³

Charlotte's omission of her defender's name was deliberate: Harriet Martineau, however renowned and morally elevated, was also an avowed atheist whose arguments would carry no weight with readers of the conservative *Quarterly Review*.

Patrick was deeply concerned to see Charlotte's growing despondency and, in his own quiet way, did what he could to relieve it. 'A few days since a little incident happened which curiously touched me', Charlotte told Ellen,

Papa put into my hands a little packet of letters and papers – telling me that they were Mamma's and that I might read them – I did read them in a frame of mind I cannot describe – the papers were yellow with time all having been written before I was born – it was strange to peruse now for the first time the records of a mind whence my own sprang – and most strange – and at once sad and sweet to find that mind of a truly fine, pure and elevated order. They were written to papa before they were married – there is a rectitude, a refinement, a constancy, a modesty, a sense – a gentleness about them indescribable. I wished She had lived and that I had known her.⁴

Patrick's sensitive and delicate gesture was probably prompted by his recent reading of *Shirley*, in which he recognized in Caroline's longing for her mother something of the depth of loss Charlotte herself had sustained when her own mother had died so young.

Having seen the beneficial effects of Charlotte's visit to London, Patrick was also keen to ensure his daughter took another trip from home. Since the New Year, she had had at least two invitations to Gawthorpe Hall, the home of Sir James and Lady Kay Shuttleworth, which lay just across the moors over the Lancashire border at Padiham near Burnley. Sir James was a medical doctor who had taken an active and pioneering role as Secretary to the Committee of the Council on Education; ill health, brought on by over-work, had compelled him to resign the secretaryship the previous year and he had then been made a baronet. Now, fretting in the provinces, he had had the immense good fortune to find the literary sensation of the decade living on his doorstep and he was determined to take 'Currer Bell' under his wing. When Charlotte declined his first invitation, he declared his in-tention to call on her instead. Charlotte could hardly refuse to receive him but her reply was ungracious to say the least: 'my only regret and scruple', she told Lady Kay Shuttleworth, in whose name the letter had been written, 'is that it should be so little worth your while to undertake such a journey'.[5]

Sir James was not one to be put off by the reluctance of a potential literary trophy, however, and, though the visit had to be put off because of his ill health, he 'persisted in coming' and eventually came 'boring to Haworth' on 1 March. Charlotte's impressions of him were no more favourable on meeting him. 'The baronet looks in vigorous health', she remarked sar-donically to Ellen, adding that he looked thirty-five rather than his forty-four years. 'Sir James is very courtly, fine-looking; I wish he may be as sincere as he is polished. He shows his white teeth with too frequent a smile; but', she airily concluded, having done exactly that, 'I will not prejudge him.' During the visit, the Kay Shuttleworths had renewed their invitation to Charlotte in her father's presence and, to her infinite dismay, Patrick took their side at once. Her best excuse had been unceremoniously rendered useless. Charlotte miserably admitted 'this left me without plea or defence'. She flatly refused to go with them there and then, but reluctantly agreed to go the next day.[6]

Charlotte travelled by train from Keighley to Burnley, where she found Sir James waiting for her. A drive of about three miles brought them to the gates of Gawthorpe where the long drive up a 'somewhat desolate avenue' did not prepare Charlotte for her first stunning view of the hall towering 'grey, antique, castellated and stately before me'.[7] Built at the turn of the seventeenth century, three storeys high with a central tower, graced with mullioned windows and lacy stone balustrades, Gawthorpe Hall is still the 'model of old English architecture' Charlotte saw; surrounded by woods on three sides, it opens out on the fourth giving picturesque prospects across the fields and valleys towards the mist-shrouded summit of louring Pendle Hill. Inside, it is as grand as it is beautiful, with intricate plaster ceilings and oak-panelled rooms all bearing the Shuttleworth family crest. It was no wonder that Charlotte was impressed: Gawthorpe Hall was the embodiment of those Angrian mansions Branwell had so loved to describe.

'On the whole' Charlotte decided she got on very well with Sir James, admiring his clear intellect, highly cultivated mind and polished manners. Nevertheless, the nicest thing she could think of to say about him was that 'the dialogues (perhaps I should rather say monologues for I listened far more than I talked) by the fireside in his antique oak-panelled drawing-room, while they suited him, did not too much oppress and exhaust me –'. His wife, to whom the house and ancient family actually belonged, was less aristocratic in manner than her husband: frank, good-humoured and active, she was the perfect foil to her politician husband whose illness had fretted his nerves to the point of irritability. Their four children were all fine 'in their way', but the person whom Charlotte instinctively liked better than anyone else in the house was the governess, a quiet, intelligent young German girl, who also took an immediate liking to Charlotte. 'She is very well treated for a governess –', Charlotte told Ellen, 'but wore the usual pale, despondent look of her class – She told me she was home-sick – and she looked so.'[8]

The 'quiet drives to old ruins and old halls situated amongst older hills and woods' were the best part of her visit. Writing to thank Lady Kay Shuttleworth on her return, Charlotte said:

My visit to Gawthorpe Hall has left me certain images – certain pictures pleasant to contemplate: your grey, stately hall fills one page of my mental sketch book, Whalley Abbey another, Mytton Hall a third, the tombs of the Sherburns a fourth and old Pendle dwells in every background.[9]

Once the visit was over, Charlotte was 'as usual, glad I have been', and she acknowledged the wisdom of Patrick's insistence that she should go when she confessed to Ellen:

The brief absence from home – though in some respects trying and painful in itself – has I think given a better tone to my spirits – All through the month of Feby – I had a crushing time of it – I could not escape from or rise above certain most mournful recollections – the last days – the sufferings – the remembered words – most sorrowful to me – of those who – Faith assures me – are now happy. At evening – and bed-time such thoughts would haunt me – bringing a weary heart-ache.

On her return, Charlotte found a pile of letters waiting for her, positive proof that she had not been forgotten by her friends. As well as a parcel from Ellen, there were letters from Laetitia Wheelwright and Amelia Ringrose, from two people she had never met, Thornton Hunt and Miss Alexander, and, to her great joy, from Smith Williams and George Smith.[10]

Thornton Hunt, the journalist son of Leigh Hunt, had sent a note requesting Charlotte to write for the new journal, the *Leader*, which he was just setting up with G. H. Lewes. Charlotte declined the offer, as she did all serial writing, knowing that she could not write to journalistic deadlines. Thornton Hunt's strictures on 'Art', expressed in his letter, had puzzled Charlotte: 'There is a certain jargon in use amongst critics on this point, through which it is physically and morally impossible for me to see day-light', she told George Smith.

One thing however I see plainly enough, and that is Mr Currer Bell needs improvement and ought to strive after it – and this (D. V.) he honestly intends to do – taking his time, however – and following as his guides Nature and Truth; if these lead to what the Critics call 'Art' it < will all come right in the end > is all very well – but if not – that grand desideratum has no chance of being run after or caught.

She also told George Smith of an observation that had been made to her on her visit to Gawthorpe Hall which had struck her by its truth: 'while the people in the South object to my delineation of Northern life and manners, the people of Yorkshire and Lancashire approve: they say it is precisely that contrast of rough nature with highly artificial cultivation which forms one of < our > their main characteristics'. From this, she deduced, 'the question arises whether do the London Critics or the old Northern Squires understand the matter best?', leaving one in no doubt as to her own conclusion.[11]

In replying to Miss Alexander, Charlotte revealed the difference that a few short weeks had made to her position. Miss Alexander, daughter of a Wakefield doctor, had written to her directly, instead of through Smith, Elder & Co., at the end of January. Charlotte had not replied because at that point she was still hoping that she might yet remain anonymous. Indeed, only a few days afterwards, she had written a peremptory note in answer to a query from a Mr Lovejoy 'respectfully suggesting' that 'as "Currer Bell" is the only name which has been acknowledged in connection with the authorship of "Jane Eyre" and "Shirley" that name alone can with propriety be printed in a Library Catalogue'. She had added darkly, 'Rumour must at all times be regarded as an unsafe guide.' Now, however, there was little point in maintaining the façade, so Miss Alexander received an acknowledgement of her second letter.[12]

Another pleasure was a new parcel of twenty books from Smith, Elder & Co., ranging from weighty tomes such as the three-volume *Life of Southey* by his son, Hazlitt's *Essays* and Charles Lamb's *Letters*, to novels such as Jane Austen's *Sense and Sensibility* and Meinhold's *Amber Witch*. Smith Williams and James Taylor had included several books on feminine issues: Julia Kavanagh's *Women in France during the Eighteenth Century*, Alexander Scott's *Suggestions on Female Education* and the ominously titled *Woman's Friendship* and *Woman and her Master*. 'I wonder how you can choose so well', Charlotte told Smith Williams, 'on no account would I forestall the choice.'[13] Writing a few weeks later when she had read Jane Austen's *Emma*, she anatomized the vast gulf that lay between their different styles of writing.

She does her business of delineating the surface of the lives of genteel English people curiously well; there is a Chinese fidelity, a miniature delicacy in the painting: she ruffles her reader by nothing vehement, disturbs him by nothing profound: the Passions are perfectly unknown to her ... Her business is not half so much with the human heart as with the human eyes < eyes >, mouth, hands and feet; what sees keenly, speaks aptly, moves flexibly, it suits her to study, but what throbs fast and full, though hidden, what the blood rushes through, < what > what is the unseen seat of Life and the sentient target of Death – this Miss Austen ignores ... Jane Austen was a complete and most sensible lady, but a very incomplete, and rather insensible (not senseless) woman, \if/ this is heresy – I cannot help it.[14]

The arrival of a new parcel of books was particularly welcome because the keen frosts and dreaded cold easterly winds which ushered in the month of April as usual brought illness in their wake. 'Low fever', which was rife in the township, also made its way into the parsonage, affecting Charlotte, Patrick and Martha.[15] This was an opportune moment for Benjamin Herschel Babbage, an inspector commissioned by the General Board of Health in London, to arrive in Haworth to investigate the water supply and sanitary conditions. Patrick had campaigned long and hard to get this inspection: he and Arthur Nicholls, with the local surgeons, Mr Hall and Mr Wheelhouse, had headed a petition to the General Board of Health for assistance in procuring a better water supply on 29 August 1849.[16] On 5 February 1850 he had written to complain that 'Having long since petitioned for an authorized Agent, to come and look into our situation, with regard to a sufficient supply of pure water, we are much disappointed, at not having seen any such Agent, nor having got any satisfactory answer to our petition.' Babbage eventually turned up on 4 April, producing a damning report which fully justified all Patrick's concerns about the poor state of health in Haworth. As Patrick had all too good a reason to know, the mortality rate was ten and a half per cent higher than that laid down in law as being so unhealthy as to require special remedies. The report, when it was eventually printed, recommended the installation of sewers, a piped-water supply and at least one water closet for every three houses, the setting up of a public slaughterhouse and the immediate closure of the churchyard.[17]

The general malaise was not confined to Haworth for, at this juncture, Ellen Nussey too fell seriously ill.[18] Contending against colds, headaches, loss of appetite and her anxiety about Ellen, Charlotte's spirits sank again. Having complained when there were no letters from London, she now complained that there were too many, including 'some very bothering ones from people who want opinions about their books'. Unconscious of the irony that she herself had once been an aspiring author who had persistently sought the opinions of the literary giants of the day and waited in desperation for a reply, she now abused those who turned to her: 'they are most difficult to answer, put off and appease without offending – for such characters are excessively touchy and when affronted turn malignant. Their books are too often deplorable.'[19]

One small bright spot – which Charlotte evidently did not consider worth reporting even to Ellen – was the second anniversary soirée of the Haworth Mechanics' Institute, which took place on the evening of 1 April. Michael Merrall, Branwell's childhood friend, was Treasurer of the Institute and had invited speeches from Patrick, Joseph Grant from Oxenhope and William Armstrong, a surgeon from Kirkby Malzeard, who had been a prime mover in setting up the institute. Patrick's speech was, 'as usual, characterised by the sterling good sense which his great experience as an observer of human nature, and his general tact in delineating the workings of the mind so fully capacitate him for'; Grant 'spoke ably on the advantages of knowledge' as did William Armstrong, but it was the last who brought the house down. 'His complimentary observations on the writings of the author of "Shirley" were responded to by the most enthusiastic applause, which would no doubt be very gratifying to Miss Brontë.'[20] Charlotte may not have liked the public nature of this acclamation, but she could not fail to appreciate the spirit which had prompted it.

She dreaded the prospect of another journey to London for the same reason. Sir James Kay Shuttleworth was determined that she should go in his company and that he would 'introduce' her to society. He had begun his campaign to persuade her during her visit to Gawthorpe Hall, but knowing full well that he intended to parade her as his prize, she had then 'given notice' that she would not be 'lionized'. Sir James was not to be denied. He bombarded her with invitations, ignoring her obvious reluctance and overriding all her objections. The parties would only be small, he declared, and she ought to regard the visit strictly in the light of a lesson which would inform her future writing. Her father, pleased at this attention and anxious that she should not allow herself to sink into depression and apathy at Haworth, was 'eager and restless' for her to go; 'the idea of a refusal quite hurt him'.[21] In the face of such overwhelming odds, Charlotte capitulated and agreed to go at the beginning of May.

Circumstances were to work against her, however. Ellen's illness took a more serious turn and her symptoms, relayed by letter, sounded alarmingly like Anne's. Charlotte urged her to consult Mr Teale instead of her cousin, Mr Carr, in whom Charlotte had lost all confidence since the business with Patrick's cataracts; 'as to trifling with serious illness, the thought makes one sick –'. Learning of Mr Carr's prescriptions, she remarked in disgust, 'I abhor and distrust their "strong medicines." He is not dealing with a horse or an elephant.'[22] When Ellen did not improve, Charlotte panicked and, deciding that her friend must be at death's door, she dropped everything and rushed over to Brookroyd to see the invalid for herself. Her fears had been unnecessary for, after six days, when Charlotte had to go to Leeds for a 'dentist-operation', Ellen was well enough to accompany her.[23]

Charlotte returned home to find her father ill with a bad cold which threatened to develop into bronchitis. While he was still in bed the following day, Joe Taylor arrived on another of his capricious visits and treated Charlotte to a four-hour diatribe on the subject of his plans to marry Amelia Ringrose. He arrived in an 'odious humour' and within ten minutes was abusing 'old Ringrose', who kept putting difficulties in his way. Charlotte sat quietly, 'minding her sewing' and trying to keep her patience, but the fact was she had long since lost any sympathy with Joe Taylor's marital ambitions. After his visit to Tranby to meet Mr Ringrose in the new year, Charlotte had noticed with dismay that his attitude towards the whole affair was increasingly selfish and imbued with 'a sort of unmanly absence of true value for the woman whose hand he seeks'. Charlotte grew 'more and more convinced that his state of mind approximates that which was so appallingly exhibited in < Bran > poor Branwell during the last few years of his life'. If such was the case, she predicted only 'hopeless misery' for the woman he married.'4

Amelia, whom she had never met but with whom she had occasionally corresponded, seemed to be the only pure thing involved: 'she stands between her coarse father and cold unloving suitor like innocence between a pair of world-hardened knaves', Charlotte told Ellen. What really infuriated her was the financial bargaining that was going on behind the scenes, particularly as Joe Taylor had been less than candid in telling Amelia about his prospects. 'If J. T. has no means of keeping a wife – if he does not possess a sixpence he is sure of, how can he think of marrying a woman from whom he cannot expect she should work to keep herself?' she demanded angrily, then, working herself up into a passion, she continued:

After all J. T. is perhaps only like the majority of men: certainly those men who lead a gay life in their youth and arrive at middle age with feelings blunted and passions exhausted can have but one aim in marriage – the selfish advancement of their interest; And to think that such men take as < wife > wives – as second selves – women young, modest, sincere – pure in heart and life, with feelings all fresh and emotions all unworn, and bind such virtue and vitality to their own withered existence – such sincerity to their own hollowness – such disinterestedness to their own haggard avarice – to think this – troubles the soul to its inmost depths. Nature and Justice forbid the banns of such wedlock.

Conscious that she had hardly been discreet, Charlotte added, 'Burn this note the minute you have read it – it is written under excitement', an injunction which Ellen ignored.'5 Though Charlotte expressed herself freely to Ellen, she could hardly do the same to Amelia, who constantly solicited her advice. 'Be cautious but not timid, watchful but not suspicious' was the only opinion she would give, a Delphic utterance which, not unnaturally, threw Amelia into a panic. Charlotte refused to be drawn any further, contenting herself – if not Amelia – by saying that the pair should be left to manage their own affairs and neither matchmaker nor match-marrer should step between.[26] Even as Joe Taylor visited her, Charlotte was still being inundated with notes, letters and gifts from his prospective bride. 'I sometimes find it difficult to answer her letters – but am always touched by their amiability', Charlotte told Ellen, though yet another missive prompted the sour comment, 'when she is married she must take care to be more sparing of her love to her spouse than she is of epistles to her friends'.[27]

It was perhaps an indication of the general irritation which the Taylor–Ringrose marriage inspired in her that Charlotte, somewhat unfairly, blamed Joe for the fact that all the household fell sick shortly after his visit: 'he seemed to bring a lot of illness with him into the house', she remarked darkly. She herself had a bad cold and stubborn sore throat, Martha had sickness, fever and the tic-douloureux, a severe form of facial neuralgia which brought on muscular spasms, Patrick was still bronchitic and only Tabby escaped unscathed.[28]

The general state of ill health at least provided Charlotte with an excuse to cry off her trip to London with the Kay Shuttleworths. 'I cannot say that I regret having missed this ordeal', Charlotte wrote of Sir James' plan to spend a week travelling down to London via the houses of his friends and relations. 'I would as lief have walked amongst red-hot ploughshares.' The only thing she did regret was the missed opportunity to attend the Royal Literary Fund Society Dinner. As a woman she was ineligible to attend the actual dinner, but through the kindness of John Driver, a friend of her father's, she had obtained a ticket for the Ladies' Gallery, where she would have been able to hear the after-dinner speeches of the great literati and artists, including Thackeray and Dickens. 'I don't think all London can afford another sight to me so interesting', Charlotte sighed to Ellen.[29]

By the middle of May, Patrick was well enough to be left and was insistent that Charlotte should not defer her visit any longer. Reluctantly, therefore, she arranged to travel down to London on 23 May but, at the last minute, was reprieved again by a sudden and severe relapse in Sir James' health. Terrified that his literary prize might escape him, Sir James wrote two notes to Charlotte from his sickbed claiming a promise from her that she would wait till he was better and not allow anyone else ' "to introduce me," as he says, "into the Oceanic life of London." ' The promise was willingly given but Charlotte gratefully seized on the fact that his doctors had prohibited company and conversation as an excuse for avoiding the visit altogether. She wrote to Lady Kay Shuttleworth, a less formidable and more tractable person than her husband, to tell her that 'My visit – I have decided in my own mind – must be postponed indefinitely;' adding, as if to forestall argument, 'I feel sure that in this decision I shall have your concurrence.'[30]

Once more then I settle myself down in the quietude of Haworth Parsonage, with books for my household companions, and an occasional letter for a visitor – a mute society but neither quarrelsome, nor vulgarizing nor unimproving.[31]

If there was relief in avoiding the Kay Shuttleworths and their introduction to London society, there was also inevitably disappointment and the threat of encroaching depression. A letter from James Taylor, complaining of being chained to his desk at Cornhill during the warm spring days, prompted a sad reply.

It is a pity to think of you all toiling at your desks in such genial weather as this. For my part I am free to walk on the moors – but when I go out there alone – everything reminds me of the times when others were with me and then the moors seem a wilderness, featureless, solitary, saddening – My sister Emily had a particular love for them, and there is not a knoll of heather, not a branch of fern, not a young bilberry leaf not a fluttering lark or linnet but reminds me of her. The distant prospects were Anne's delight, and when I look round, she is in the blue tints, the pale mists, the waves and shadows of the horizon. In the hill-country silence their poetry comes by lines and stanzas into \my/ mind: once I loved it – now I dare not read it – and am driven often to wish I could taste one draught of oblivion and forget much that, while mind remains, I never shall forget. Many people seem to recall their departed relatives with a sort of melancholy complacency – but I think these have not watched them through lingering sickness nor witnessed their last moments – it is these reminiscences that stand by your bedside at night and < stand > rise at your pillow in the morning At the end of all, however, there exists the great hope – Eternal Life is theirs now.[32]

In such a mood, it was fortunate that Charlotte still had her friends at Smith, Elder & Co. Learning from Smith Williams and James Taylor that Charlotte had had to cancel her London visit, George Smith persuaded his mother to invite her to stay with them at their new home at No. 76, Gloucester Terrace in Hyde Park Gardens. There was a world of difference between the prospect of staying with the Smiths, where she would be comfortably protected and allowed to do as she wished, and staying with the Kay Shuttleworths who only wanted to show her off to London society. Having given her promise to Sir James, however, Charlotte had great difficulty in keeping faith. Writing to Mrs Smith on 25 May, she explained her predicament but said that if she did go to the Kay Shuttleworths she would only do so for a few days and then would be 'excessively disposed, and probably profoundly thankful to subside into any quiet corner of your drawing-room, where I might find a chair of suitable height'. Enclosing a pair of white knitted baby-socks, which she had begun during her last visit and only just finished, Charlotte remarked, 'I am sorry you have changed your residence as I shall now again lose my way in going up and down stairs, and stand in great tribulation, contemplating several doors, and not knowing which to open.'[33]

Despite telling Mrs Smith she could not make any plans for at least a fortnight or three weeks, only five days later Charlotte was comfortably ensconced in Gloucester Terrace. The day before setting off she had written to Lady Kay Shuttleworth to make her excuses for going back on her promise.

'I am summoned to London to-morrow', she declared, as though she had been compelled to go, 'on a little business which it seems cannot well be deferred.' She would be staying with her publisher, whose address she gave, 'on condition of being allowed to be very quiet, and not taken into company', and she would call on the Kay Shuttleworths before she returned to Yorkshire.[34] If she had hoped to escape Sir James' clutches, she was mistaken. Before she had been three full days in London, Sir James had called twice and his wife once: to Charlotte's 'great horror' he talked of taking her to Hampton Court and Windsor – 'God knows how I shall get on –', Charlotte wrote in despair to Ellen, 'I perfectly dread it.'[35]

Charlotte's 'little matters of business to transact', it need hardly be said, were simply a convenient excuse and had not really required her presence; she had her dividends on her money in the Funds to sort out at the bank and a power of attorney to arrange so that she would not be required to do this in person in future. The only other business which could lay claim to her attention was the publication of the first cheap edition of *Jane Eyre* which Smith, Elder & Co. had launched in a single volume at the beginning of May. Charlotte had seen and approved an early copy then, so there was nothing to be done in relation to this 'business' either.[36]

Nor was the visit as quiet as Charlotte suggested. In the first three days alone she went to the opera, where she was evidently more impressed by the elegant dresses of the lords and ladies in the audience than by the music, to the exhibition at the Royal Academy, where she particularly admired Landseer's portrait of Wellington on the field of Waterloo and 'The Last Man', 'a grand, wonderful picture' by her childhood favourite, John Martin, and to the Zoological Gardens, for which the secretary had sent her an honorary ticket of admission. This last excursion seems to have interested her more than the others, for she gave her father a detailed account of the 'inexpressible noises' made by the American birds, the great Ceylon toads 'not much smaller than Flossy' and a cobra with 'the eyes and face of a fiend'.[37]

There were plenty of other outings which George Smith, with his customary good humour and perception, organized to please his visitor. On one occasion he took her to the Ladies' Gallery of the House of Commons so that she could indulge her lifelong interest in politics. Unable to sit with her, he arranged that she had only to look at him when she got tired and he would come up and fetch her away. George Smith waited and waited for a signal: 'There were many eyes, they all seemed to be flashing signals to me, but much as I admired Miss Brontë's eyes I could not distinguish them from the others.' Eventually, fearing that he must have missed the signal and realizing that he was probably causing quite a stir by staring into the Ladies' Gallery, he went round to collect her and apologized for keeping her waiting. Charlotte replied, 'I made no signal, I did not wish to come away', and, knowing her handsome host's liking for a pretty face, added, 'Perhaps there were other signals from the Gallery.'[38]

On Sunday, 9 July, George Smith took her to the Chapel Royal, where he could be fairly sure that she would catch sight of her hero, the Duke of Wellington. As luck would have it, he was there and Charlotte was able to see in the flesh the man whose exploits had inspired her childhood writings and, indirectly, been the cause of her presence in London as an author. Somewhat tamely, all she had to say of him was that 'he is a real grand old man', even though her escort had indulged her to the extent of following the duke out of the chapel and so arranging their walk that she met him twice on his way back to Apsley House. Another Sunday was spent less successfully at a Friends' Meeting House where, displaying that intolerance and sense of the absurd which had marked her perception of Dissenting worship since childhood, she was afforded more amusement than edification. Her host apparently had the good grace to be embarrassed.[39]

Charlotte was also reintroduced to literary society. G. H. Lewes was invited to lunch one day, having missed the dinner on Charlotte's previous visit. This was the first occasion when George Smith witnessed 'the fire concealed beneath her mildness'. Lewes, displaying that complete lack of understanding which had characterized his review of *Shirley*, had the indiscretion to say across the table, 'There ought to be a bond of sympathy between us, Miss Brontë; for we have both written naughty books!' 'This fired the train with a vengeance, and an explosion followed', George Smith remembered many years later. 'I listened with mingled admiration and alarm to the indignant eloquence with which that impertinent remark was answered.' When they parted at the end of the evening, they shook hands and Charlotte remarked, 'We are friends now, are we not?' alluding for the first time to Lewes' shameful review of *Shirley*. 'Were we not always, then?' Lewes asked, still impervious to her feelings on that subject; 'No! not always', Charlotte replied significantly and without elaboration.[40]

To Ellen, Charlotte was more forthcoming, describing Lewes as 'a man with both weaknesses and sins; but unless I err greatly the foundation of his nature is not bad'. Curiously – one might even say incomprehensibly – it was his appearance which told in his favour: 'the aspect of Lewes' face almost moves me to tears –', she told Ellen, 'it is so wonderfully like Emily – her eyes, her features – the very nose, the somewhat prominent mouth, the forehead – even at moments the expression'.[41] Lewes' own cruelly dismissive description of Charlotte was worthy of the man who had been unable to see beyond the fact that the author of *Shirley* was a woman: 'a little, plain, provincial, sickly-looking old maid'.[42]

Another author whom Charlotte met on this visit was Julia Kavanagh, the twenty-five-year-old protégée of Smith Williams, who supported herself and her mother by her writings. One cannot help wondering whether Charlotte herself perceived the strange reversal of roles that was now thrust upon her: whereas she had been the tiny trembling stranger looking up, physically and mentally, to Thackeray and Martineau, here she was, the grand literary lady, meeting the 'little, almost dwarfish figure to which even I had to look down – not deformed – that is – not hunchbacked but long-armed and with a large head and (at first sight) a strange face. She met me half-frankly, half tremblingly.' As they sat and talked in Julia Kavanagh's 'poor but clean and neat little lodging', Charlotte was once again struck by a resemblance to the dead: 'it was Martha Taylor in every lineament'.[43]

Smith Williams, who had made the introduction at Miss Kavanagh's request, saw a lot more of Charlotte during this visit than he had during her last. He attended a ball given by Mrs Smith at Gloucester Terrace with one of his sons and three of his daughters, the five of them creating something of a sensation with their good looks and graceful manners.[44] But the highlight of the visit was, once again, a meeting with Thackeray. This time he made a private morning call at Gloucester Terrace and stayed above two hours alone with Charlotte and George Smith, who was an amused and perceptive witness of the 'queer scene' that occurred. 'I was moved to speak to him of some of his short-comings (literary of course) one by one the faults came into my mind and one by one I brought them out and sought some explanation or defence – He did defend himself like a great Turk and heathen – that is to say, the excuses were often worse than the crime itself.' 'She was angry with her favourites if their conduct or conversation fell below her ideal', Thackeray acknowledged ruefully, while refusing to treat the subject with the seriousness Charlotte thought it deserved. 'The truth is,' George Smith declared,

Charlotte Brontë's heroics roused Thackeray's antagonism. He declined to pose on a pedestal for her admiration, and with characteristic contrariety of nature he seemed to be tempted to say the very things that set Charlotte Brontë's teeth, so to speak, on edge, and affronted all her ideals. He insisted on discussing his books very much as a clerk in a bank would discuss the ledgers he had to keep for a salary. But all this was, on Thackeray's part, an affectation: an affectation into which he was provoked by what he considered Charlotte Brontë's high falutin'. Miss Brontë wanted to persuade him that he was a great man with a 'mission;' and Thackeray, with many wicked jests, declined to recognise the 'mission.'[45]

The confrontation ended in 'decent amity' and on 12 June, Charlotte was invited to dinner at Thackeray's house in Young Street. The momentousness of the occasion was felt by everyone present, from Thackeray himself, anxiously pacing the floor before Charlotte's arrival, to his young daughters in a frenzy of excitement at the thought of meeting 'Jane Eyre' herself. Thackeray had invited a brood of women novelists to meet the literary lioness: Mrs Crowe, who specialized in writing on the supernatural, Mrs

Proctor, wife of the poet 'Barry Cornwall' and mother of the poetess Adelaide Proctor, who was also present.[46]

Anne Thackeray, then only a girl, described how they watched the carriage arrive, Thackeray himself go out into the hall to welcome his guests, the door opening wide, his re-entrance with George Smith and, between them, 'a tiny, delicate, serious, little lady, pale, with fair straight hair, and steady eyes. She may be a little over thirty; she is dressed in a little *barège* dress, with a pattern of faint green moss. She enters in mittens, in silence, in seriousness.'[47] Mrs Brookfield, a society hostess of less romantic inclinations, noted that Charlotte, 'a timid little woman with a firm mouth, did not possess a large enough quantity of hair to enable her to form a plait, so therefore wore a very obvious crown of brown silk'. The hairpiece was a new one which Charlotte had commissioned Ellen Nussey to buy in April in preparation for the London trip: though it might have seemed a good idea at the time, it did not create the desired effect.[48]

The hairpiece was but one source of amusement for the gathering at Thackeray's. After the solemnity and breathless excitement of Charlotte's entrance, the announcement of dinner came as a relief: 'we all smile as my father stoops to offer his arm', Anne Thackeray reported, 'for, though genius she may be, Miss Brontë can barely reach his elbow'. As they walked out together, Thackeray unwisely addressed her as 'Currer Bell'. Charlotte's response was typically prickly. 'She tossed her head and said "She believed there were books being published by a person named Currer Bell ... but the person he was talking to was Miss Brontë – and she saw no connection between the two"'.[49]

Throughout the dinner Charlotte sat gazing at Thackeray 'with kindling eyes of interest, lighting up with a sort of illumination every now and then as she answered him'. Afterwards, the ladies left the gentlemen to their port and returned to the drawing room, where everyone waited for the brilliant conversation that never began at all. Charlotte herself, without George Smith or Thackeray himself to guard her, retreated into a corner of the study and sat on the sofa exchanging a low word now and then with the only person with whom she felt comfortable, Miss Truelock, the governess. Eventually, realizing that brilliance was not to be forthcoming, Mrs Brookfield leant forward with a little commonplace and asked, 'Do you like London, Miss Brontë?' There was a short silence while Charlotte considered the question, then, 'very gravely', she replied, 'Yes and No.'

That put the seal on the evening. The disappointed ladies grew bored and restless. Thackeray himself, oppressed by the gloom and silence, could scarcely contain his discomfort and, as Charlotte left, he quietly crept out of the room, out of the house and retired to the masculine comforts of his club. As George Smith later commented, the failure of the evening was a singular illustration of Charlotte's want of social gifts and Thackeray's impatience of social discomfort.[50] Though the ladies who had spent 'one of the dullest evenings of their lives' made much capital out of relating the anecdote for years afterwards at Charlotte's expense, it has to be said that Thackeray's choice of guests showed a remarkable insensitivity to Charlotte's character and feelings. Having read her books and met her several times, he knew her to be hypersensitive about her appearance, her lack of social graces and her provincialism. He also knew that she was painfully shy in company and was only moved to speak on intellectual subjects or on her own high-flown ideas about the writer's calling. Nevertheless, he exposed her to a group of society women, mere dabblers in the world of literature, whose interests and lives had nothing in common with her own. The failure of the dinner party was therefore as much his fault as Charlotte's.

On the way home from Thackeray's, Charlotte proved that she had kept her eyes open even if she had not said much, by suddenly leaning forward, placing her hands on George Smith's knees and saying, 'She would make you a very nice wife.' 'Whom do you mean?' asked George Smith. 'Oh! you know whom I mean', Charlotte replied. She had noticed that he had been very taken with the charms of Adelaide Proctor and she knew her companion well enough to know that he was merely bluffing when he pretended not to know what she meant.[51]

The day after Thackeray's dinner party, Charlotte had to undergo another ordeal. George Smith had persuaded her that she ought to have her portrait painted and had undertaken to pay for sittings with George Richmond, the celebrated society artist. A former pupil of Henry Fuessli, whose pictures Charlotte had copied with such care and detail as a girl, Richmond enjoyed a busy practice, taking four sitters a day, many of them the leading literary figures of the time. His style was pre-eminently suited to Charlotte, as his standard portraits were simple, quiet and subtly flattering likenesses in a mix of coloured chalks, chiefly black, white and red.[52]

It is a measure of George Smith's persuasive charm and Charlotte's liking for him that she allowed him to overcome her initial reluctance towards having a portrait made of what, she was all too well aware, were neither beautiful nor attractive features. When she arrived at the studio, she was in a state of heightened nerves and great anxiety. It needed little to push her over the brink and that little was the wretched hairpiece. George Richmond was puzzled when she removed her hat to see what he took to be a pad of brown merino on her head and, unable to imagine what its purpose was, asked her to remove it. Not surprisingly, Charlotte burst into tears of mortification.[53] Richmond took this to be a symptom of his famous sitter's overwrought state, and Charlotte was prohibited from seeing the portrait until it was complete. When she was finally allowed to see the finished work, she again burst into tears, exclaiming that it was so like her sister Anne.[54] For once, there was some justice in this remark. Since living in Belgium,

Charlotte had abandoned her fussy, ringleted hairstyle, which had not suited the plainness of her features. Now she wore her hair parted down the centre and swept back simply over her ears into a chignon at the back, the effect being to slim down the broadness of her face and forehead; the artist himself supplied the fullness which she lacked in reality and which the hairpiece had so signally failed to redress. Richmond captured the beauty of her large hazel eyes, her one redeeming feature, and played down the size of her prominent nose and mouth. With subtle shadowing, too, and by turning her face slightly to one side, he reduced the squareness of her lower jaw. The resulting portrait was like and not like, a faithful reproduction of the separate features but a more harmonious rendering of the whole. As Mary Taylor was later to comment on seeing the portrait reproduced in Mrs Gaskell's *Life of Charlotte Brontë*, 'It must upset most people's notions of beauty to be told that the portrait at the beginning is that of an ugly woman. I do not altogether like the idea of publishing a flattered likeness. I had rather the mouth and eyes had been nearer together, and shown the veritable square face and large disproportionate nose.'[55]

However nerve-racking for Charlotte the sessions with George Richmond had been, at least they pre-empted further demands for her portrait. She was able to turn down an offer from John Everett Millais, for instance, on the grounds that she was engaged to Richmond. Her attraction for Millais, apart from her remarkably fine eyes, was that she fulfilled his idea of what a woman of genius should look like: she 'looked tired with her own brains' he commented, memorably.[56] Though it was undoubtedly a relief to Charlotte not to have to undergo the intense personal scrutiny of a portrait painter again, one cannot help wondering what the Pre-Raphaelite painter of romantic beauties would have made of Charlotte Brontë.

Charlotte's supposedly short trip to London had been so extended that it was now nearly a month since she had left home. 'My London visit has much surpassed my expectations this time', Charlotte told Ellen, 'I have suffered less and enjoyed more than before.'[57] Just how much she had enjoyed her visit, and the company of George Smith in particular, Charlotte rather shamefacedly had to reveal to Ellen. Originally, she had agreed to go on to Brookroyd at the end of her stay in London. Now she had to explain that her visit to Ellen would be cut in half by an excursion with George Smith to Edinburgh. Knowing that Ellen would be shocked to the core that Charlotte could even consider so offending propriety by travelling in the company of an eligible young bachelor and that she already had her suspicions about the relationship between her friend and the publisher, Charlotte went to great lengths to explain away her decision. George Smith had to fetch his youngest brother home from school in Scotland for the vacation. One evening he had announced his intention of taking his sister with him and then, the next evening, he proposed that Charlotte should meet them in

Edinburgh to be shown the sights. 'I concluded he was joking – laughed and declined – however it seems he was in earnest; being always accustomed to have his will, he brooks opposition ill. The thing appearing to me perfectly out of the question – I still refused – Mrs Smith did not at all favour it –'.[58] Mrs Smith, it would seem, had also begun to suspect that there was a little too much friendliness between her precious eldest son and his prize authoress. Her benign surveillance, which Charlotte had once found so comforting when she was exposed to the presence of other gentleman, had already been turned to 'her cherished and valued son' and she would actively discourage any increase in their intimacy.[59]

Mrs Smith may have been mistress of the house but George Smith was master of his mother. Having emphatically sided with Charlotte in opposing the plan, she was now persuaded to argue his case for him – or so Charlotte led Ellen to believe. Without explicitly denying the fact, or mentioning the word 'marriage', she suggested to Ellen that there was nothing between herself and George Smith.

Now I believe that George and I understand each other very well – and respect each other very sincerely – we both know the wide breach time has made between us – we do not embarrass each other, or very rarely – my six or eight years of seniority, to say nothing of lack of all pretension to beauty &c. are a perfect safeguard – I should not in the least fear to go with him to China –[60]

The very fact that she called her publisher by his Christian name must have rung alarm bells with both Ellen and Mrs Smith. The difference in their ages – it was actually almost exactly eight years – and Charlotte's lack of conventional beauty were not impediments to their intimacy; George Smith himself referred constantly to her fine eyes and his delight in her quick and clear intelligence.[61] She, for her part, could not fail to be touched and flattered by the evident admiration of a handsome and clever young man who was one of the most eligible bachelors in literary London. Their correspondence over the past six months shows that they had fallen into a habit of easy raillery which was a convenient cover for any deeper emotions.

Charlotte left London and arrived safely at Brookroyd on 25 June. Writing to thank Mrs Smith for having had her as a guest for a month, Charlotte told her, quite truthfully, 'I never remember to have enjoyed myself more in the same length of time.'[62] Charlotte stayed with Ellen a bare week before leaving to join George and Eliza Smith in Scotland. The original plan had been that Charlotte would meet them in Glasgow and accompany them on a tour that would take them from Tarbet on Loch Lomond to Oban at the mouth of Loch Linnhe and then back through a portion of the Highlands to Edinburgh. However, after what one can only presume to have been two days of relentless pressure from Ellen Nussey, Charlotte regretfully agreed to give up the more adventurous part of the journey and simply join the

Smiths for two days in the more civilized surroundings of Edinburgh.[63]

For the brief duration of Charlotte's visit, George Smith had hired a driver 'who knew every interesting nook and corner in Edinburgh, who was better read in Scottish history and the Waverley Novels than I was, and whose dry humour exactly suited Miss Brontë'. The visit became a homage to Walter Scott, whose works had been such an influence on the young Brontës. There were excursions to his house at Abbotsford and the ruined abbey he had restored at Melrose, and in Edinburgh to Scott's monument as well as to Arthur's Seat and the historic parts of the city. 'I always liked Scotland as an idea', Charlotte told Smith Williams on her return, 'but now, as a reality, I like it far better; it furnished me with some hours as happy almost as any I ever spent.'[64] Writing to Laetitia Wheelwright ten days later, Charlotte was still in danger of falling into her besetting sin of enthusiasm: 'though the time was brief, and the view of objects limited, I found such a charm of situation, association and circumstance that I think the enjoyment experienced in that little space equalled in degree and excelled in kind all which London yielded during a month's sojourn. Edinburgh compared to London is like a vivid page of history compared to a huge dull treatise on Political Economy – and as to Melrose and Abbotsford the very names possess music and magic.'[65]

On the return journey, Charlotte parted from the Smiths at York railway station, taking the next train to Leeds and going back to stay with Ellen Nussey at Brookroyd.[66] It was now over five weeks since she had left Haworth or seen her father, who, understandably, was growing anxious for her return. She had, in fact, left at an extremely inconvenient time for, in her absence, the parsonage was being reroofed and major repairs undertaken. Writing to Ellen a full month after the work had begun, Patrick informed her that 'after a host of labour amidst, decayed laths and rafters, < and > and broken lime plaster, and busy carpenters, Masons, and repairers of various descriptions, we have at length, got our house put into order'. His liberal sentiments compelled him to add:

amidst all this bustle, both workmen, and servants, as well, as the more important Trustees – have acted in good will, fidelity, and harmony – I have often thought, that when it has been otherwise, it has been as much owing to the Employers, as the Employed – In general people can be more easily, led than driven, and respect, has a far more prevailing influence than fear –

Patrick discovered that one of the workmen was a Catholic. Instead of expressing disapproval, Patrick simply told him to keep up to his faith and he would be all right at the last.[67]

For someone who had so often insisted on the necessity of staying at home with her father, even when her sisters and brother were alive, Charlotte's absence when her presence was so needed is difficult to explain. It was not simply that she was running away from her memories of her sisters which haunted her at home; it would seem that, despite herself, Charlotte was more than a little in love with George Smith. Having spent just three days travelling in his company, away from the duennaship of his mother, Charlotte returned in a state of almost total nervous collapse and took to her bed. The news, relayed by Ellen, threw Patrick into a panic. 'It may be that she is labouring under one of her usual bilious attacks, and if so, she will I trust, through a merciful providence, speedily recover –', he replied, adding urgently, 'Should you see any feverish symptoms, call in the ablest medical advice, for the expenses of which, I will be answerable – And lose no time – And write to me, soon, as soon as you can –'.[68]

In fact, it may well have been that Ellen exaggerated Charlotte's illness; certainly she was at home within three days of receiving her father's letter and was considerably annoyed to find all the household worked up into a 'sad pitch of nervous excitement and alarm' about her. At the foot of Bridge-house Lane she had encountered John Greenwood, the Haworth stationer, staff in hand, about to set off to Brookroyd on Patrick's orders to discover in person how Charlotte was. 'I can't deny but I was annoyed;', Charlotte crisply informed Ellen, 'there really being small cause for it all.' She was soon to discover what really lay at the bottom of the panic. 'I have recently found that Papa's great discomposure had its origin in two sources – the vague fear of my being somehow about to be married to somebody – having "received some overtures" as he expressed himself – as well as in apprehension of illness.'[69] There was an implicit reproof in these words. Only one person could have frightened Patrick into thinking either that Charlotte was on the point of marriage or that she was ill. It would seem that Ellen, in one of her devious manoeuvres, had hinted in her letter to Patrick that something more momentous lay behind the impropriety of Charlotte's trip with George Smith. This would also explain Patrick's ellip-tical message in his reply: 'Tell Charlotte to keep up her spirits – When, once more, she breathes the free exhilirating air of Haworth, it will blow the dust and smoke, and impure malaria of London, out of < hea > her <u>head, and heart</u> –'.[70]

Inevitably, Charlotte was miserable on her return, contrasting the whirl of excitement in which the last six weeks had passed with the lonely mon-otony of life in Haworth. 'I am beginning to get settled at home – but the solitude seems heavy as yet', Charlotte told Ellen, admitting too that she had put off writing to London to inform her friends of her return because she no longer had faith in the power of temporary excitement to do real good. 'My present endeavours are directed towards recalling my thoughts, cropping their wings drilling them into correct discipline and forcing them to settle to some useful work.' she informed Smith Williams a couple of days later, 'they are idle and keep taking the train down to London or making a foray over the Border, especially are they prone to perpetrate that last excursion –'. To George Smith himself she wrote a short note, refraining from a longer and more discursive letter because she was, somewhat mysteriously, 'mindful of the "fitness of things" and of the effect of locality' – perhaps an allusion to the perceived impropriety of their friendship.[71]

Her chastened mood did not outlast the month. At the end of July two boxes arrived at the parsonage. The larger one, addressed to Patrick, contained Richmond's portrait of Charlotte, the smaller one contained a framed portrait of the Duke of Wellington for Charlotte. Patrick's first reaction was to think that Charlotte's portrait made her look too old, though he acknowledged that the expression was 'wonderfully good and life-like'. Writing to thank George Smith, however, he confessed that the picture improved upon acquaintance: 'Without ostentatious display, with admirable tact and delicacy, he has produced a correct, likeness, and succeeded, in a graphic representation of mind, as well as matter ... I may be partial, and perhaps, somewhat enthusiastic, in this case', he declared with pride, 'but in looking on the picture ... I fancy I see strong indications, of the Genius, of the Author, of "Shirley", and "Jane Eyre".'[72] Only one person actually disapproved of the portrait and that was old Tabby, who tenaciously maintained that it was not like and was too old-looking, 'but, as she, with equal tenacity, asserts that the Duke of Wellington's picture is a portrait of "the Master" (meaning papa), I am afraid not much weight is to be ascribed to her opinion', Charlotte laughingly told George Smith.[73]

The portrait of Wellington was equally welcome at the parsonage, since father and daughter both hero-worshipped the original. 'I esteem it a treasure', Charlotte pronounced, while Patrick affirmed that it came the nearest of all portraits he had seen 'to my preconceived idea of that great man'. Patrick promised to keep the two portraits amongst his most highly valued treasures, regretting only 'that some are missing, who, with better taste and skill, than I have, would have fully partaken of my joy'.[74] Branwell's father, unlike his sister, could still remember his abilities affectionately and without linking them to his faults.

George Smith had refused to accept any thanks for the pictures, so Charlotte had signed her letter, 'I am yours very thanklessly (according to desire)' and had received a mock-stern rebuke in reply pointing out that it was merely good business sense to keep his authors happy. Charlotte was unable to let this pass.

The manner of doing a kind – or – if you will – merely a just action, the degree of pleasure that manner imparts, the amount of happiness derived from a given source – these things cannot indeed be handled, paid away and bartered for material possessions as many can, but they colour our thoughts and leaven our feelings – just as the sunshine of a warm day, or the impressions of delight left by fine scenery might do. We may owe as deep a debt for golden moments as can ever be incurred for golden coin.[75]

For the most part, Charlotte was able to keep her correspondence with George Smith light-hearted, though she was coming under increasing pressure from her father and Ellen, both of whom seem to have been expecting that George Smith would propose. In some anguish, Charlotte wrote to Ellen begging her not to broach the subject any more.

> It is the undisguised and most harassing anxiety of others that has fixed in my mind thoughts and expectations which must canker wherever they take root ... I have had to entreat Papa's consideration on this point – indeed I have had to <u>command</u> it – my nervous system is soon wrought on – I should wish to keep it in rational strength and coolness – but to do so I must determinedly resist the kindly meant, but too irksome expression of an apprehension for the realization or defeat of which I have no possible power to be responsible.[76]

The reaction which set in following the excitement of her visits to London, Brookroyd and Edinburgh soon became an oppressive gloom. 'I cannot describe what a time of it I had after my return from London – Scotland &c.', Charlotte later told Ellen, 'there was a reaction that sunk me to the earth – the deadly silence solitude, desolation were awful – the craving for companionship – the hopelessness of relief – were what I should dread to feel again.'[77]

About this time, Charlotte received an unexpected visit from a party of grandees. She had just declined an invitation to Harden Grange, the Bingley home of Busfeild Ferrand, a wealthy landowner, Justice of the Peace and Member of Parliament for Knaresborough. Two or three days later Mrs Ferrand turned up at the parsonage with a large party of ladies and gentlemen, including two members of the Young England party in the House of Commons, Lord John Manners, 'tall, stately – black-haired and whiskered', who bore a timely gift of a brace of pheasants for Patrick, and George Smythe, 'not so distinguished-looking – shy and a little queer –'.[78] Both Manners and Smythe had literary pretensions, but the visit seems to have been prompted as much by curiosity to see 'Currer Bell' in her own home as by a desire to meet the author herself.

Though such a visit was flattering, it was scarcely welcome. Nor was yet another invitation from the Kay Shuttleworths, though at least this time there was no threat of being shown off round the drawing rooms and public places of London. The Kay Shuttleworths had taken a house on the shores of Lake Windermere for the autumn and winter, which was the reason for the invitation. Though Charlotte was reluctant to accept, the thought of paying her first visit to the land of the Lake Poets was attractive. Patrick, concerned about her health and perhaps anxious that she should meet new people outside George Smith's circle, urged her to go.[79]

She set off on 19 August, arriving at eight o'clock in the evening after a tedious journey during which she had to change carriages three times and wait an hour and a half at Lancaster. Sir James was waiting for her at Windermere station and there was a pleasant drive along the wooded banks of the lake edge to Low-wood, then a steep climb up a narrow lane to Briery Close. 'This place is exquisitely beautiful', Charlotte wrote to her father the day after her arrival, 'though the weather is cloudy misty and stormy – but the sun bursts out occasionally and shews the hills and the lake.'[80] On the subject of Sir James she remained silent, but she found an instant ally and friend in Mrs Gaskell, who arrived later that same evening. Even at this, their first meeting, Charlotte had none of the tortured shyness which usually afflicted her: remembering Mrs Gaskell's kind and sympathetic letter on the publication of *Shirley*, Charlotte came straight up to her the moment she arrived and shook her by the hand. Later, during tea, Mrs Gaskell had the opportunity for a closer observation of the 'little lady in black silk gown'. 'She is (as she calls herself) <u>undeveloped</u>;' she told Catherine Winkworth,

thin and more than $\frac{1}{2}$ a head shorter than I, soft brown hair, not so dark as mine; eyes (very good and expressive looking straight & open at you) of the same colour, a reddish face; large mouth & many teeth gone; altogether <u>plain</u>; the forehead square, broad, and <u>rather</u> overhanging. She has a very sweet voice, rather hesitates in choosing her expressions, but when chosen they seem without an effort, <u>admirable</u> and <u>just</u> befitting the occasion.[81]

Lady Kay Shuttleworth, ill with a cold, was confined to the house, but she still took the opportunity to gossip with Mrs Gaskell, giving her a highly romanticized view of Charlotte's home and background, full of half-truths and downright untruths, and portraying Patrick as 'the strange half-mad husband' who drove his wife to an early death, sawed up chairs and burnt hearth rugs in fits of temper. All of which, while it increased Mrs Gaskell's sympathy for Charlotte Brontë, was also to irreparably prejudice her against Patrick.[82]

Charlotte's own confidences to Mrs Gaskell were much less dramatic: she talked about the Clergy Daughters' School, where the pain she had suffered from hunger was not to be told, about her father's reaction to reading *Jane Eyre* and about her own prospect of a lonely death.[83] 'She is quiet sensible unaffected with high noble aims', Mrs Gaskell enthused. 'She is sterling and true; and if she is a little bitter she checks herself, and speaks kindly and hopefully of things and people directly; the wonder to me is how she can have kept heart and power alive in her life of desolation.' Charlotte's own impressions of Mrs Gaskell, who was six years her senior, were equally favourable, if more subdued. 'I was truly glad of her companionship She is a woman of the most genuine talent – of cheerful, pleasing and cordial manners and – I believe – of a kind and good heart.'[84]

The morning after Mrs Gaskell's arrival, Sir James took the two ladies and a Mr Moseley, an inspector of schools, who had joined them for breakfast, out on the lake. There Charlotte and Mrs Gaskell discovered a mutual liking for Francis Newman, the controversial free thinker, brother of the more famous Catholic convert, and for John Ruskin; they later quarrelled in friendly fashion, over politics and Tennyson, whom Charlotte loathed. After dinner they actually set off to drive to Coniston to visit the Tennysons, who were staying in the area, but to the wordless fury of Mrs Gaskell, Sir James decided to turn back when it began to rain.[85]

An evening visit to the home of another famous writer, Thomas Arnold, did materialize, though Charlotte was so nervous at the thought of going there that she was afflicted with an acute headache all day. She had not then read the *Life of Dr Arnold*, but she had formed a highly idealized impression of the former headmaster of Rugby and Regius Professor of History at Oxford, who had died eight years previously. It was, therefore, an intense disappointment to meet his widow and daughters at Fox How, the holiday home he had built above Rydal Water. The journey there, through Ambleside and along the beautiful riverside of the valley winding up the back of Loughrigg Fell, past the houses where Thomas De Quincey had lived and Dora Wordsworth after her marriage to Edward Quillinan, was to linger long in Charlotte's memory. Even though it was almost dark when they reached the unpretentious Lakeland stone house, magnificently situated at the head of the little valley, Charlotte could still perceive that the situation was 'exquisitely lovely': 'the house looked like a nest half-buried in flowers and creepers – and, dusk as it was, I could <u>feel</u> that the valley and the hills round were beautiful as imagination could dream'.[86] Mrs Arnold, an amiable woman who had once been very pretty, greeted Charlotte in what Sir James and Mrs Gaskell both afterwards assured her was a 'conventional manner', but which she found 'lacking that genuineness and simplicity one seemed to have a right to expect in the chosen life-companion of Dr Arnold'. Neither she nor her daughters were intellectual and, though impressed by the show of family unity they presented, Charlotte thought their opinions were imitative rather than original, sentimental rather than sound.[87]

Most of the time, however, was taken up with driving about in a carriage to show Charlotte the glorious Westmorland scenery: 'could I have wandered about amongst those hills <u>alone</u> – I could have drank in all their beauty –', Charlotte sighed. 'I longed to slip out unseen, and to run away by myself in amongst the hills and dales. Erratic and vagrant instincts tormented me, and these I was obliged to control, or rather, suppress – for fear of growing in any degree enthusiastic, and thus drawing attention to the "lioness" the authoress – the She-Artist.'[88] In fact, the one fly in the ointment throughout a visit which would otherwise have been most congenial to Charlotte was Sir James Kay Shuttleworth himself. To their frustration and amusement he persisted in lecturing his lady authors on 'Art' and 'bringing ourselves down to a lower level' and 'the beauty of expediency' – this, as Mrs Gaskell pointed out, from a man 'who has never indulged in the exercise of any talent which could not bring him a tangible and speedy return'. Charlotte, who was forced to accept Sir James' 'advice' with a show of 'calm resignation', felt more bitterly towards their host than Mrs Gaskell. 'I honour his intellect – with his heart – I believe I shall never have sympathy ... To Authors as a class (the imaginative portion of them) he has a natural antipathy, their virtues give him no pleasure – their faults are wormwood and gall in his soul.' Acknowledging his kindness to her and Mrs Gaskell's belief that he had a sincere and strong friendship for her, Charlotte nevertheless 'scarcely desired a continuation of the interest he professes in me – were he to forget me – I could not feel regret –'.[89]

As usual, once her visit was over, Charlotte was glad that she had been, though she had had no wish to prolong it beyond a week.[90] A few days later, she sat down to write to her new-found friend.

Papa and I have just had tea; he is sitting quietly in his room, and I in mine; 'storms of rain' are sweeping over the garden and churchyard: as to the moors, they are hidden in thick fog. Though alone I am not unhappy; I have a thousand things to be thankful for, and, amongst the rest, that this morning I received a letter from you, and that this evening I have the privilege of answering it.[91]

She was equally cheerful with Ellen, who seems to have been depressed following a visit to Tranby, where both Amelia Ringrose and her sister, Rosy, were deep in preparations for their weddings. 'Cheer up dear Nell – and try not to stagnate', she urged Ellen. 'Humanity cannot escape its fate which is to drink a mixed cup – Let us believe that the gall and the vinegar are salutary.' Even a visit from Joe Taylor failed to throw her: she was able to listen to him with equanimity, not least because, now that his marriage was arranged, he looked forward to it with quiet satisfaction. Having seen all he wanted to see of life, he was now prepared to settle.[92]

All in all, Charlotte's life seemed to have taken a turn for the better. Her health had benefited from her excursion to the Lakes and her father's appetite and spirits had improved since her return. James Taylor, after a long silence, had resumed his correspondence and was sending the *Athenaeum* to her. In addition, a notice of the kind 'over which an author rejoices with trembling' had appeared in the *Palladium*.[93] This anonymous review was the first to enthuse seriously about *Wuthering Heights*, though its author, Sydney Dobell, refused to believe that it was not an early work by Currer Bell. 'Not a subordinate place or person in this novel, but bears more or less the stamp of high genius', Dobell had declared. 'It is the unformed writing of a giant's hand; the "large utterance" of a baby god.' *Jane Eyre* exhibited all the same qualities brought to maturity. These were also evident in *Shirley*, but 'labouring on an exhausted soil. Israel is at work, indeed; but there is a grievous want of straw, and the groan of the people is perceptible'. *Shirley*, he accurately perceived, was written by an artist not spoilt but maimed and disabled by criticism. He urged 'Currer Bell', in her next novel, to ignore the critics and remember as far as possible the frame of mind in which she had sat down to write *Wuthering Heights*; maturity would prevent her making the mistakes which had marred her earliest work.[94]

The appearance of this review seems to have prompted William Smith Williams to suggest that Smith, Elder & Co. should reprint *Wuthering Heights* and *Agnes Grey* in their new cheap, single-volume format. Charlotte leapt at the chance, offering to write a preface and explanatory notice of the authors, but, significantly, in the light of what happened to Emily's second novel, declining to add any other compositions by them 'as I would not offer a line to the publication of which my sisters themselves would have objected'. Her opinion of Anne's second novel is also illuminating:

'Wildfell Hall' it hardly appears to me desirable to preserve. The choice of subject in that work is a mistake – it was too little consonant with the character – tastes and ideas of the gentle, retiring, inexperienced writer. She wrote it under a strange, conscientious, half-ascetic notion of accomplishing a painful penance and a severe duty. Blameless in deed and almost in thought – there was from her very childhood a tinge of religious melancholy in her mind – this I ever suspected – and I have found amongst her papers, mournful proofs that such was the case.[95]

Charlotte, it appears, was prepared to consign her sister's novel to oblivion because she considered its subject at odds with her own perception of what Anne's character was and ought to have been.

Charlotte was fortunate in being able to leave the complicated negotiations for permission to reprint her sisters' books in the competent – and ruthless – hands of George Smith. While Newby made himself 'scarce as violets at Christmas', evading all attempts to pin him down to a meeting 'like a Publisher metamorphosed into a Rainbow',[96] Charlotte set to work on a biographical notice of her sisters that would, once and for all, establish the separate identities of Currer, Ellis and Acton Bell. Giving a brief outline of their lives from the point at which they had assumed authorship, and omitting all mention of the rest of their family or their place of residence, Charlotte went on to describe her sisters' characters. Her words, because of their persuasive power, have ever since been taken to be written on tablets of stone, handed down from the Great Author; absolute and unquestionable truths. Yet, as Charlotte herself confessed in her concluding sentence, they were written with only one purpose in mind, and that was to answer the critics who had complained of 'Ellis' and 'Acton's' love of the coarse, brutal and degrading. Every word was carefully chosen to nail the lies and assumptions which lay behind the reviews. Instead, Charlotte built the edifice under which the Brontës have sheltered ever since, portraying them as children of nature, whose inexperience, innocence and sense of truth led them to portray life as they saw it, in ignorance of the sensibilities of a more sophisticated reading public. To that end she had to pretend that they were uneducated and wrote purely from 'the dictates of intuition'.

In externals, they were two unobtrusive women; a perfectly secluded life gave them retiring manners and habits. In Emily's nature the extremes of vigour and simplicity seemed to meet. Under an unsophisticated culture, inartificial tastes, and an unpre-tending outside, lay a secret power and fire that might have informed the brain and kindled the veins of a hero; but she had no worldly wisdom; her powers were unadapted to the practical business of life; she would fail to defend her most manifest rights, to consult her most legitimate advantage. An interpreter ought always to have stood between her and the world. Her will was not very flexible, and it generally opposed her interest. Her temper was magnanimous, but warm and sudden; her spirit altogether unbending.

Anne's character was milder and more subdued; she wanted the power, the fire, the originality of her sister, but was well-endowed with quiet virtues of her own. Long-suffering, self-denying, reflective, and intelligent, a constitutional reserve and taciturnity placed and kept her in the shade, and covered her mind, and especially her feelings, with a sort of nun-like veil, which was rarely lifted. Neither Emily nor Anne was learned; they had no thought of filling their pitchers at the well-spring of other minds; they always wrote from the impulse of nature, the dictates of intuition, and from such stores of observation as their limited experience had enabled them to amass. I may sum up all by saying, that for strangers they were nothing, for superficial observers less than nothing; but for those who had known them all their lives in the intimacy of close relationship, they were genuinely good and truly great.

This notice has been written, because I felt it a sacred duty to wipe the dust off their gravestones, and leave their dear names free from soil.[97]

If writing the preface was painful, the task of going through her sisters' papers was exquisitely so. She had decided that she would, after all, add a selection of her sisters' poems to the new edition. In the light of her earlier statement that she 'would not offer a line to the publication of which my sisters themselves would have objected', her editorial policy on the poems was curious in the extreme. She selected seven of Anne's poems and eighteen of Emily's, seventeen of them from her fair copy books, but in virtually every one she made substantial editorial changes. In some cases these were undoubtedly what her sisters would have wanted, as for instance substituting 'sister' instead of 'Gerald' or 'sheep' instead of 'deer', to hide the Gondal origins of the poems.[98] Others were purely technical, correcting faults in metre or rhyme, which again were uncontroversial. But there were a large number of 'corrections' which were not demanded by the texts and which were simply Charlotte's 'improvements'. Some of these were unnecessary and capricious: in a line by Emily describing cornfields as 'emerald and scarlet and gold', Charlotte changed 'scarlet' to 'vermeil', a pretentious word which would not have been in her sister's poetic vocabulary. In another poem, which she entitled 'The Night-Wind', Charlotte changed the tenses in the last verse, creating a much more awkward last line, and substituted 'church-aisle' for 'church-yard'. These can only have been dictated by the fact that Emily herself had been buried in the church vaults rather than the churchyard – a fact irrelevant to the poem.[99] To four poems, two of which were short extracts from longer originals, Charlotte actually added between four and eight lines of her own composition, usually to bring the poem to an end. In one case, 'Silent is the House – all are laid asleep', this meant that out of twenty lines, only the first twelve were by Emily, the remainder of the poem being by Charlotte.[100] None of this, of course, was indicated in either the text or Charlotte's accompanying notes.

Charlotte treated Anne's poems in an even more cavalier fashion. Her careful choice of only seven poems, of which six were entirely religious in theme, was dictated partly by her own perception of Anne as Emily's inferior – therefore Anne would not be allowed to speak on the same subjects as Emily – and partly by her desire to prove Anne's piety to her critics. Ignoring the large body of Gondal verse, Charlotte therefore selected poems which, in the main, depicted their author as a despondent but faithful Christian, struggling under the burden of her own sense of unworthiness. Again, however, she made substantial alterations to the manuscript originals, nearly always to tone down Anne's more despairing expressions. In 'I have gone backward in the work', for instance, she removed one verse entirely and altered the last line from 'And hear a wretch's prayer' to 'Christ, hear my humble prayer!'[101] In another, where the poet expresses a longing 'To see the glories of his face', Charlotte unnecessarily substituted her own line 'Like Moses, I would see his face.' Similarly, in a hymn where the refrain of one verse was 'I know my heart will fall away', Charlotte changed the line to 'Thy suppliant is a castaway.'[102]

The poem which suffered most from Charlotte's editorial policy was one which it is surprising she felt able to include at all, her sister's last lines on learning that she had consumption. Out of the original seventeen verses, Charlotte selected only eight for publication, thereby omitting all Anne's stronger expressions of grief and despair and creating a false impression of calm resignation to the inevitable. In one verse, she perversely altered Anne's meaning: for Anne's original, referring to her own sufferings,

> O thou hast taken my delight
> & hope of life away
> And bid me watch the painful night
> & wait the weary day

Charlotte substituted

> Thou, God, hast taken our delight
> Our treasured hope away.
> Thou bidst us now weep through the night
> And sorrow through the day.[103]

Charlotte's version would seem to suggest that she thought the verse referred to Anne's grief at the death of Emily, and therefore she wished to associate herself with it by changing the pronouns from 'my' to 'our'. The resulting substitution is therefore not only a clumsier alternative but also a mis-interpretation of the original.

One can well imagine that both her sisters would have been infuriated by Charlotte's unwarranted interference in their work: it was on a par with her many attempts to organize them during their lives. Nevertheless, Charlotte clearly believed that she was performing her 'sacred duty' in her self-appointed role as her sisters' interpreter to the world and the task had not been pleasant.

The reading over of papers, the renewal of remembrances brought back the pang of bereavement and occasioned a depression of spirits well nigh intolerable – for one or two nights I scarcely knew how to get on till morning – and when morning came I was still haunted with a sense of sickening distress –

Confessing this to Ellen, she added apologetically, 'I < th > tell you these things – because it is absolutely necessary to me to have some relief – You will forgive me – and < to > not to trouble yourself – or imagine that I am one whit worse than I say.'[104] So deep had her depression become that Charlotte even began to consider the possibility of leaving home again. 'I feel to my deep sorrow – to my humiliation – that it is not in my power to bear the canker of constant solitude –', she told Smith Williams, explaining why she had been unable to make a real start on her next book,

I had calculated that when shut out from every enjoyment – from every stimulus but what could be derived from intellectual exertion, my mind would rouse itself perforce – It is not so: even intellect – even imagination will not dispense with the ray of domestic cheerfulness – with the gentle spur of family discussion – Late in the evenings and all through the nights – I fall into a condition of mind which turns entirely to the Past – to memory, and memory is both sad and relentless. This will never do –[105]

Chapter Twenty-Three

⁊

RUNNING AWAY
FROM HOME

The ability to write would normally have provided Charlotte with a much-needed escape from the cloud of depression that threatened to overwhelm her, but the nature of her work over the previous few months had only added to her misery. Writing a biographical notice and an introduction to *Wuthering Heights* and editing her sisters' poems had only impressed upon her the loss she had suffered and the desolation of her present existence. The approach of winter, too, could only make things worse: as the days grew shorter and the light failed earlier, her evenings became interminable. Her eyesight was not good enough to permit her to read or write by artificial light and her father and the servants always retired to bed punctually at nine o'clock. Unable to occupy either her mind or her hands in the long hours she had once spent so happily with her sisters, the burden of her solitude became unbearable.

Visitors did come regularly, but they were not of Charlotte's seeking. In September 1850, William Forster, a wool merchant from Bradford who was later to become a distinguished statesman, and his wife Jane, the eldest daughter of Thomas Arnold, called unexpectedly and were shown into 'the little bare parlour' by Martha Brown. Patrick himself, preceded by Keeper, Emily's 'superannuated mastiff', came to welcome them and then went out to get his daughter. She arrived after 'a long interval', which was probably spent in rushing around trying to make herself look presentable for her august guests. She stayed and talked for a while, Patrick popping in again to give Mr Forster a newspaper, then she disappeared 'for an age' to prepare the dinner, leaving her guests alone with Flossy, 'a fat curly-haired dog'. Her reappearance, with Martha Brown and dinner, was greeted with relief and the Forsters finally departed in the middle of the afternoon, having extracted a promise that Charlotte would visit them in the spring. 'Miss Brontë put me so in mind of her own "Jane Eyre"', Mrs Forster wrote to her friend Mrs Gaskell. 'She looked smaller than ever, and moved about so quietly, and noiselessly, just like a little bird ... barring that all birds are joyous."

The Forsters were followed by a more sentimental visitor, John Stores Smith, a young man of twenty-two who belonged to the literary circles of Halifax. Despite his youth he had already written two striking books, *Mirabeau* and *Social Aspects*, published in 1848 and 1850 respectively, which he had sent to Charlotte earlier in the year. His reasons for doing so were not entirely altruistic: having heard the rumours that Currer Bell was Charlotte Brontë, his friends had persuaded him to send *Mirabeau* to Charlotte at Haworth; her reply, though signed 'Currer Bell', was a tacit admission of her authorship. A few Sundays later, a couple of his friends had taken the opportunity to attend Haworth Church so that they could ogle the authoress, but Smith had declined to accompany them. Instead, he sent her *Social Aspects* on its publication and was rewarded with a second letter, signed 'CBrontë', offering her 'sincere congratulations on the marked – the important progress made by the author'.[2] Encouraged by her kindness, he had presumed to write again and, surprisingly, received an invitation to dinner. His arrival was scarcely propitious, for his dog attracted the attention of Keeper who had been lying asleep on the doorstep and, by the time he came face to face with Charlotte, he had his own terrier barking furiously under his arm and Keeper growling at his calves. Charlotte, suppressing a quiet smile, told him she had half an hour's writing to do before dinner and took him into her father's study. This was, of course, simply an excuse to give herself time to assist Martha in preparing the dinner.

Patrick was, in Smith's eyes, 'the ruin of what had been a striking and singularly handsome man. He was tall, strongly built, and even then perfectly erect. His hair was nearly white, but his eyebrows were still black ... He was dressed very carelessly, in almost worn out clothes, had no proper necktie, and was in slippers.' Smith spent an uncomfortable hour with Patrick before being summoned in to dinner with Charlotte, when he had an opportunity to scrutinize his hostess for the first time.

She was diminutive in height, and extremely fragile in figure. Her hand was one of the smallest I have ever grasped. She had no pretensions to being considered beautiful, and was as far removed from being plain. She had rather light brown hair, somewhat thin, and drawn plainly over her brow. Her complexion had no trace of colour in it, and her lips were pallid also; but she had a most sweet smile, with a touch of tender melancholy in it. Altogether she was as unpretending, undemonstrative, quiet a little lady as you could well meet.

Like most men, Smith was transfixed by her eyes: 'they looked you through and through – and you felt they were forming an opinion of you ... by a subtle penetration into the very marrow of your mind, and the innermost core of your soul'. After an equally uncomfortable dinner, Smith spent an unexpectedly happy two hours in conversation with his hostess. Reticent about herself, she was nevertheless voluble in describing London literary life, speaking with contempt of 'the minor Guerillas and Bohemians of Letters' and with distaste of Charles Dickens, whose ostentatious extravagance she disliked. Without expressly trying to dissuade Smith from his intention of giving up commerce and going to London to earn his living as a writer, she made it clear that she thought he would fail: 'she seemed to think the tamest Haworth life was preferable to the turning of the pen into a literary tight-rope-dancing machine for gold'. They parted with Charlotte's 'maternal' words of warning ringing in his ears: 'seek out and gain the friendship of the highest and best in literature ... but as for the general body of those who call themselves literary men avoid them as a moral pestilence'.[3]

Other admirers also forced themselves on Charlotte's attention. One, signing himself 'K. T.', offered to give Charlotte a copy of the record he had kept of his friends' opinions on *Jane Eyre*; she declined this but said she would be interested to learn the first impressions *Shirley* had made on unbiased minds. ' "Shirley", it would seem – has not been a general favourite; of the reason for its comparative failure, I have not sufficiently clear idea, and any information tending to enlighten me on that point, I should esteem a boon.'[4] Despite his irritatingly verbose style, 'K. T.' had some profound thoughts on *Shirley* which he diffidently proffered to its author: it had too many characters, the interest was not sufficiently sustained and was too scattered, he had difficulty in understanding the motives of the characters and little sympathy with their natures; most importantly, it was a book 'founded upon and curbed by actual appearances and real people'. Her 'obligation to the literal' had hampered and tied up her writer's powers. Interestingly, too, he guessed that Charlotte's own preference for *Shirley* lay in the fact that she had laboured over it and that in the superiority of the descriptive powers she had employed there, she had mistaken 'the satisfaction of the artist for the merit of the book'. Writing to thank him, Charlotte, much to her amusement, astounded 'K. T.' by displaying her extraordinary powers of analysis and divining that he was young, an Irishman and an artist. 'Why should it annoy you that I discovered your Country?' she asked him. 'Is Ireland then a Nazareth a Galilee < f > from which no prophet or good thing can come?'⁵

Charlotte's ability to analyse character sometimes gave her an almost prophetic ability to foresee the future, as John Stores Smith had discovered when she warned him that he would not be able to earn his living as a writer in London and as Joe Taylor was soon to discover. His marriage to Amelia Ringrose had finally taken place in October and Charlotte had received a happy letter from Amelia expressing 'wondrous faith in her husband's intellectual powers and acquirements'. 'Joe's illusion will soon be over –', Charlotte muttered darkly, 'but Amelia's will not – and therein she is happier than he –'. Even before their marriage, Charlotte had correctly foreseen that Amelia's affection would soon cease to find a response in Joe Taylor and that her overtures would meet only chilly silence. 'I fancy – however – this is the fate of most feeling women – and when they find there is no remedy for the inevitable – they submit to circumstances – and take resignation as a substitute for content', was her cynical comment to Ellen. 'Amelia will do this, but not yet – nor for two or three years will it be required of her. You will see her happy for that time – nor <u>after that time</u> will she admit herself to be otherwise than happy – indeed if children come – the mother will well support the wife: the bridal interest lost – maternal interest will replace it.'⁶

Apart from her correspondence and occasional visitors, Charlotte had only her books to divert her. G. H. Lewes had lent her some French novels during her London visit, which she now found time to read, disliking Balzac and preferring the 'Fantastic, fanatical, unpractical enthusiast', George Sand.⁷ Altogether more to her taste were the books from Smith, Elder & Co., which included *The Roman*, a long poem by Sydney Dobell, the *Palladium* reviewer, and, at her request, A. P. Stanley's *Life of Thomas Arnold*. This latter book interested her deeply and she found much to admire in both the man and his work. 'I was struck too by the almost unbroken happiness of his life;' she told Smith Williams, rather wistfully, 'owing partly to a singular exemption from those deep and bitter griefs which most human beings are called on to endure ... One feels thankful to know that it has been permitted to any man to live such a life.'⁸

Thomas Arnold was to become almost a heroic figure to her. 'Oh! I wish Dr Arnold were yet living or that a second Dr Arnold could be found', Charlotte declared to Smith Williams. 'Were there but ten such men amongst the Hierarchs of the Church of England – she might bid defiance to all the scarlet hats and stockings in the Pope's gift –'.⁹ This outburst was prompted by the Pope's appointment of Nicholas Wiseman as Cardinal and Archbishop of Westminster. As it was the first such appointment since the Elizabethan Reformation, it caused an hysterical reaction among

Protestants, particularly Anglicans, who saw the creation of Roman Catholic bishoprics in England as papal aggression. Wiseman himself was especially feared and loathed because of his influence on the Oxford Movement and his active role in winning over Puseyites to the Church of Rome – he had confirmed John Henry Newman into the Catholic faith himself. Now there were rumours that he had aspirations to the Papacy and that, if successful, he would abolish the celibacy of the Catholic priesthood and thus remove the last obstacle to reunion with the Church of England. Patrick Brontë himself had been moved to write 'A Tract for the Times' for the *Leeds Intelligencer*, pointing out, more in sorrow than anger, that 'the whole fabric of our establishment is shaken to its very centre, and threatens to fall. The people in general no longer look on our establishment as the bulwark of Protestantism, but a Romish nursery – whilst true churchmen are overwhelmed with confusion and sorrow.' The Catholics and other dissenters shculd be warned, he added, that if they overthrew the Church of England, all religion would be overthrown and people would look instead to the Goddess of Reason as they had done during the French Revolution.[10]

The clergy of the archdeaconry of Craven, to which Haworth belonged, sent a long letter to the same paper demanding a meeting to discuss the papal aggression. This was held in Leeds on 27 November and, although Patrick himself was not well enough to undertake the journey, Arthur Bell Nicholls was one of the 250 clergymen who put their names to the resulting resolution condemning the Pope for dishonouring the Queen, ignoring the existence of the Church of England and sowing the seeds of strife throughout the land.[11]

Charlotte's loathing of Catholicism, which had been deepened by her own susceptibility to it in Brussels, was fanned to a white heat by these events. Writing to George Smith, she could not resist a sardonic portrayal of her publishers setting up an oratory in the small backroom at Cornhill, 'with a saint in a niche – two candles always burning, a "prie-dieu" and a handsomely bound Missal; also a Confessional Chair – very comfortable, for the Priest – and a square of carpet or – better – the bare boards for the penitent'. Messrs Taylor, Williams and Smith would daily tell their beads and sign themselves with holy water, once a month making confession and receiving absolution. 'The ease this will give to your now never-disburthened heretic consciences – words can but feebly express'. The alternative, if they resisted, was martyrdom at Smithfield, 'some First Sunday in Advent (1860)'. 'Forgive all the nonsense of this letter –', Charlotte asked George Smith, 'there is such a pleasure and relief either in writing or talking a little nonsense sometimes to anybody who is sensible enough to understand and good-natured enough to pardon it.'[12]

The necessity of finding some escape from the oppression of the monotony and silence of her daily life at last drove Charlotte from home again.

Anxious to see the new edition of *Wuthering Heights & Agnes Grey* through the press, she had turned down invitations to stay with Ellen, the newly married Taylors, Sir James Kay Shuttleworth and, reluctantly, Mrs Gaskell, though she clung to the hope that a visit to her might be arranged in January. As the second anniversary of Emily's death loomed, Charlotte could no longer bear the 'intolerably poignant' memories which had haunted her for the past three months. She accepted an invitation to stay with Harriet Martineau for 'a <u>cosy</u> winter visit' at Ambleside in the Lake District.[13]

Charlotte arrived on 16 December at The Knoll, Miss Martineau's pleasant and unpretentious Lakeland stone villa built on a slight rise in the plain at the northern end of Lake Windermere. Standing at the foot of Loughrigg Fell, it was surrounded by mountains at the rear and looked out towards the lake at the front.[14] Harriet Martineau was something of an eccentric. She had designed the house herself and was undertaking experiments in self-sufficiency by keeping her own livestock and growing her own food. A tall and large-built woman of forty-eight, she enjoyed a robust health which neither her intellectual pursuits nor the handicap of her deafness had undermined: 'her powers of labour – of exercise and social cheerfulness are beyond my comprehension', Charlotte reported to her father with awe.

Her visitors enjoy the most perfect liberty; what she claims for herself she allows them. I rise at my own hour, breakfast alone – (she is up at five, takes a cold bath and a walk by starlight and has finished breakfast and got to work by 7 o'clock) I pass the morning in the drawing-room – she in her study. At 2 o'clock we meet, work, talk and walk together till 5 – her dinner hour – spend the evening together – when she converses fluently, abundantly and with the most complete frankness – I go to my own room soon after ten – she sits up writing letters till twelve.[15]

For Charlotte the week of her visit passed quickly and enjoyably. She could not entirely avoid the Kay Shuttleworths, who were still at Briery Close, but as they were both unwell she was not obliged to see as much of them as might otherwise have been the case. Nevertheless, Sir James called almost daily to take her out in his carriage and Harriet Martineau had arranged plenty of other visits for her.[16] One evening they dined at the house of Edward Quillinan, Wordsworth's son-in-law, where Charlotte met Matthew Arnold, the only other guest, for the first time. He described her as 'past thirty and plain, with expressive gray eyes though' and said he talked to her 'of her curates, of French novels, and her education in a school at Brussels'. Charlotte's first impressions were unfavourable: though 'Striking and pre-possessing in appearance – his manner displeases from its seeming foppery', and she thought 'the Shade of Dr Arnold seemed to me to frown on his young representative'. However, she soon discovered that, like his mother, he improved upon acquaintance: 'erelong a real modesty appeared under his assumed conceit, and some genuine intellectual aspirations as well as high educational acquirements displaced superficial affectations'.[17]

After an early dinner, which Miss Martineau had made a condition of the visit so that she could get her delicate guest home before nightfall, the ladies returned to The Knoll where the proofs of Miss Martineau's new book had just arrived. This was her *Letters on the Law of Man's Social Nature and Development*, which she had co-written with Henry Atkinson, and it was the first exposition of 'avowed Atheism and Materialism' Charlotte had ever read. Miss Martineau read some of the *Letters* to Charlotte, and though she strongly disagreed with their doctrine, she was impressed with 'the tone of calm power' in the writing. Her view of the completed book, given privately to James Taylor, was one of instinctive horror. To one who had lost so many members of her family, the 'unequivocal declaration of disbelief in the existence of God or a Future Life' was a prospect not to be borne. 'The strangest thing is that we are called on to rejoice over this hopeless blank – to receive this bitter bereavement as great gain – to welcome this unutterable desolation as a state of pleasant freedom. Who <u>could</u> do this if he would? Who <u>would</u> do it if he could?'[18]

It was hardly surprising that Charlotte felt Miss Martineau had lost her way in writing this sort of book, or that she urged her to return to novel-writing and to produce another *Deerbrook*. On another occasion, Miss Martineau read the opening chapter of her *Introduction to the History of the Peace* out loud to her guest. Its subject was Wellington and the Peninsular War and, after two or three pages, Miss Martineau was amazed when Charlotte looked up at her, stole her hand into hers and said, with tears running down her cheeks, 'Oh! I do thank you! Oh! we are of one mind! Oh! I thank you for this justice to the man.' As Miss Martineau remarked, 'I saw at once there was a touch of idolatry in the case, but it was a charming enthusiasm.'[19]

On the evening before her departure, Charlotte finally persuaded Miss Martineau to try the experiment of mesmerizing her. Harriet Martineau was one of the most vocal exponents of this nineteenth-century fashion for relieving mental and physical illness through hypnotism, but even she was reluctant to try its effects on Charlotte, in whose nerves she had no confidence. Charlotte was 'strangely pertinacious', however, and on that final Sunday, when Miss Martineau could no longer plead her own tiredness as an excuse, she insisted that the experiment should be made. They began the process, but at the moment when Charlotte cried out that she was under the influence, Miss Martineau's own nerve failed her and she abandoned the attempt, softening the blow to Charlotte by telling her that in time she might prove to be an excellent subject.[20]

The visit passed off remarkably well, considering the disparate natures of the two literary lions. 'I trust to have derived benefit from my visit to Miss Martineau', Charlotte wrote to Smith Williams, on her return, 'a visit more interesting I certainly never paid: if self-sustaining strength can be acquired by example, I ought to have got good – but my nature is not hers – I could not make it so though I were to submit it seventy times seven to the furnace of affliction and discipline it for an age under the hammer and anvil of toil and self-sacrifice.'[21] However much she had enjoyed her visit, Charlotte had no wish to extend it beyond a week: Miss Martineau had relatives and friends coming for Christmas so there would be no more delightful *tête-à-têtes* by the fireside, Miss Martineau talking and Charlotte sitting mute. The Kay Shuttleworths pressed her to stay with them, but Charlotte made her excuses and went instead to Birstall and the more congenial company of Ellen Nussey, leaving her father to spend Christmas alone at Haworth.[22]

Charlotte returned home on Boxing Day, relieved to find her father well, but already beginning to be oppressed with sickness and headache herself as she struggled to come to terms with the unaccustomed silence of the house. Two packets 'directed in two well-known hands' from Cornhill were waiting for her and provided a much-needed distraction; '– you are all very – very good', she wrote gratefully to Smith Williams. Even so, it was an indication of her depressed spirits that it took her nearly a week to steel herself to write her replies.[23] In one of the packets was a small pile of newspaper reviews of the cheap edition of *Wuthering Heights & Agnes Grey*, which had been published on 10 December. The general tone of the reviews was remarkably similar: all were more interested in the Biographical Notice than in the reprinted novels and many of them, quite rightly, took exception to Charlotte's blanket assertion that the critics had failed to do her sisters' novels justice, quoting their own earlier reviews to prove the point.[24]

On 1 January 1851, Charlotte seems to have given herself a mental shaking and made a New Year's resolution to reply to all her letters. Smith Williams and James Taylor each received a measured appreciation of her visit to Miss Martineau, and Mrs Gaskell a letter of thanks for sending Charlotte a copy of her Christmas book, *The Moorland Cottage*, 'which I find to be as sweet, as pure, as fresh as an unopened morning daisy'.[25] A humorous letter from George Smith, bemoaning his difficulties with Thackeray, who was still promising 'really to set about writing' the Christmas book whose publication had already been officially announced, prompted a longer response in like vein. 'Allow me to suggest an appropriate revenge', Charlotte told him:

Put out of your head the cherub-vision of the 'innocent and happy Publishers' sitting on clouds in Heaven and thence regarding with mild complacency the tortures of perjured authors – descend from this height – turn author yourself and write 'The Lion's History of the Man' or 'A Revelation of the crimes of popular A— th—rs by a spirited P—b—sh—r.' Here is an idea which, properly handled, might 'mark an epoch in the history of Modern Literature'.[26]

As had become a habit over the last year, Charlotte sent George Smith's original letter to Ellen Nussey, telling her to read it 'because it gives a very fine notion both of his temper and mind'. Ellen, of course, immediately perceived the undercurrent of affection beneath the easy badinage, prompting Charlotte once again to have to deny that she was about to marry her publisher. In so doing, however, she tacitly admitted that she must have contemplated the prospect. 'Were there no vast barrier of age, fortune &c. there is perhaps enough personal regard to make things possible which now are impossible', she told Ellen. 'Meantime I am content to have him as a friend and pray God to continue to me the commonsense to look on one so young so rising and so hopeful in no other light.'[27]

Ellen herself was now being pursued by John Taylor, who, as Charlotte had predicted, had suddenly discovered that he, too, wanted a wife when his brother Joe had married Amelia Ringrose. Charlotte 'loudly applauded' Ellen's resolution not to let herself be fooled by his attentions: 'All you say about John T— is written with capital sense – stick to it – if he fails to come on like a man – he is not in the slightest degree worthy of you – and therefore not to be regretted.'[28] At nearly thirty-five, both friends were enjoying an unexpected renaissance of the flirtations of their youth.

Charlotte's circle of correspondents had now far outgrown the usual letters from Cornhill, Ellen Nussey and Laetitia Wheelwright. A notice in the *Bradford Observer* that Miss Brontë had lately been on a visit to Miss Martineau at Ambleside prompted her old schoolfellow, Amelia Walker, to get in touch. She had recently returned from the Continent and was now at Torquay, from where she wrote 'a longish letter – full of claptrap sentiment and humbugging attempts at fine writing – in each production the old trading spirit peeps out – she asks for autographs – ... specimens of [Miss Martineau's] handwriting and Wordsworth's & Southey's and my own –'.[29]

Other correspondents were complete strangers. One, signing himself 'A Mountaineer of the Wild West', had gathered from her Biographical Notice that she had decided not to republish *The Tenant of Wildfell Hall* and urged her to reconsider. 'It may be quite true that the subject was not of natural growth in Acton Bell's mind; of this you alone can judge ... – but it is none the less true that the book throughout tells of a mind whose productions we cannot afford to lose.' The book, he declared, 'bears the stamp of great genius', its close was 'instinct with deep feeling' and it was 'full of a quiet reflective power, that the titanic energy of Ellis Bell did not admit of'.[30] By a curious coincidence, another man describing himself as a 'mountaineer', John Abbott of McGill College, Montreal, wrote to Charlotte from Canada in February. All the tales of the moors and mountains by the Bells had been his special favourites long before he had discovered the identity of the authors, he declared, before revealing that he was 'intimately acquainted with both your father and mother with the latter more especially < the latter > as I lived for some months in the same house with her before she was married'. Recounting his nocturnal meeting with the band of Luddites on their way to attack Rawfolds Mill, he recalled how frightened Maria Branwell had been and how the incident had then found its way into *Shirley*.[31]

The problem of her next book was weighing heavily on Charlotte's conscience. She had still made no real start on it, more than a year after the publication of *Shirley*, and was haunted by the fear that her dilatoriness disappointed both her father and Cornhill. In an attempt to appease them both, therefore, she suggested yet again that a revision of *The Professor* might serve. Smith Williams gently rejected the proposal once more, adding that Smith, Elder & Co. were quite prepared to wait as long as it took for her new book. His 'kind and friendly letter' gave Charlotte both 'heartfelt satisfaction – and such a feeling of relief as it would be difficult to express in words'.[32] The sincerity of this brief note was in marked contrast to the flippant tone in which she wrote to George Smith, explaining that *The Professor* had now had the honour of being rejected nine times by the trade, three of the rejections going to his own share. Comparing her own affection for it to that of 'a doting parent towards an idiot child', she refused to allow George Smith to take the manuscript into his custody. 'Ah – No!' she exclaimed:

His modest merit shrinks at the thought of going alone and unbefriended to a spirited Publisher. Perhaps with slips of him you might light an occasional cigar – or you might remember to lose him some day – and a Cornhill functionary would gather him up and consign him to the repositories of waste paper, and thus he would prematurely find his way to the 'buttermen' and trunkmakers. No – I have put him by and locked him up – not indeed in my desk, where I could not tolerate the monotony of his demure quaker countenance, but in a cupboard by himself.[33]

George Smith, like Smith Williams, was understanding and encouraging about Charlotte's inability to take up her work again. He offered her two invitations for the summer, one to accompany him on a trip down the Rhine and the other to stay with him in London. The very hint of the continental trip had been enough to throw Charlotte into a fever, but she was wise enough to see that it was unlikely to come about: 'all London would gabble like a countless host of geese' and Smith's mother and sisters would certainly step in to prevent it.[34] The London invitation was a more practical proposition, but, as Charlotte pointed out from the bitterness of experience, 'one can lay no plans three or four months beforehand'. 'Besides –', she added in a lighter vein,

I don't deserve to go to London; nobody merits a treat or a change less. I secretly think, on the contrary, I ought to be put in prison and kept on bread and water in solitary confinement without even a letter from Cornhill – till I had written a book.

The result of such treatment, she suggested, would either be a three-volume manuscript or else she would be in 'a condition of intellect that would exempt me ever after from literary efforts and expectations'.[35]

In the light of her subsequent portrayal of George Smith and his mother in *Villette*, it is interesting that it was Smith himself who suggested to Charlotte that she might find a subject for her novel at his firm. 'Do you know that the first part of your note is most dangerously suggestive?' she asked him.

What a rich field of subject you point out in your allusions to Cornhill &c. – a field at which I myself should only have ventured to glance like the Serpent at Paradise; but when Adam himself opens the gates and shews the way in what can the honest Snake do but bend its crest in token of gratitude and glide rejoicingly through the aperture?

But – no: don't be alarmed. You are all safe from Currer Bell – safe from his satire – safer from his eulogium. We cannot (or at least I cannot) write of our acquaintance with the consciousness that others will recognize their portraits, or that they themselves will know the hand which has sketched them.[36]

For the moment, however, Charlotte could not write at all and, nothing else being in prospect, she invited Ellen to Haworth in the second week of March to stay 'just so long as you could comfortably bear the monotony'.[37] A week into Ellen's visit, Charlotte had a letter from Mrs Gaskell inviting her to stay in Manchester. Reluctantly turning the invitation down, Charlotte expressed the hope that Ellen would not leave her for some weeks: 'her attentions – her affection – her very presence give me a sort of new life – a support and repose for which I cannot be too thankful. Then it does me good to have to look after her comfort in return, to be called on to amuse her and make her happy; my rest at night has been calmer and more continuous since she came; she benefits me indeed in many ways.'[38]

During Ellen's stay, Charlotte received an overture of friendship from Sydney Dobell, the twenty-seven-year-old poet, author of *The Roman*, who had reviewed the Brontës' novels in the *Palladium* the previous year. In view of his appreciation of *Wuthering Heights*, Charlotte had requested that he should be sent a copy of the new single-volume edition when it was published in December. The book and Charlotte's covering letter took three months to arrive, causing Dobell to write in frustration and anxiety lest his unavoidable failure to reply had caused offence. 'Surely we are marked out for friendship', Dobell had stated, pointing out that they were both young, that as unknowns they had both achieved success with their first literary works and that much was expected of them in future. 'Friendship … among those who share the same gifts, responsibilities and dangers becomes almost a duty of self-preservation', he announced, adding an invitation to visit him in Gloucestershire, where the serenity and mildness of the countryside might restore her health. Apologizing for seeming over-familiar in a letter, he urged her to remember, 'I have long been a brother to you in my thoughts', and that his words unconsciously betrayed him.[39] Charlotte's response was cool but not unfriendly. 'I feel sure you must be some years my junior, because it is evident you still view life from a point I have long out-travelled. I believe there is a morning light for you on the world ... I am a journeyer at noon-tide.' If ever they met, he must regard her as 'a grave sort of elder sister'. Dobell replied with the gallant comment, 'That you are not "young" I cannot believe, even on your own testimony. The heart of Jane Eyre will never grow old.'[40]

Another friendship which had been almost entirely nourished by correspondence was that with James Taylor, the managing clerk of Smith, Elder & Co. Out of the blue, however, Charlotte learnt from George Smith that Taylor was going out to India to take charge of the firm's interests in Bombay. Charlotte's opinion of Taylor had always been equivocal. His letters had been a source of interest and amusement which she had missed when deprived of them, but Taylor himself she had instinctively found repulsive. As early as December 1849 she had complained to Ellen that he was 'of the Helstone order of men – rigid, despotic and self-willed ... he has a determined, dreadful nose in the middle of his face which when poked into my countenance cuts into my soul like iron.' In January of this year, 1851, Charlotte had defended herself against Ellen's charge that George Smith might propose to her by declaring that there was more likelihood of her marrying 'the little man', as she always referred to Taylor, 'if "matches" were at all in question, which <u>they are not</u>'. 'He still sends his little newspaper', she told Ellen,

– and the other day there came a letter of a bulk, volume, pith, judgement and knowledge, worthy to have been the product of a giant. You may laugh as much and as wickedly as you please – but the fact is there is a quiet constancy about this, my diminutive \and red-haired/ friend, which adds a foot to his stature – turns his sandy locks, dark and altogether dignifies him a good deal in my estimation[41]

As soon as she learnt of his going abroad, Charlotte wrote to wish him health and prosperity in his undertaking, but her letter crossed in the post with one from him requesting permission to call at Haworth on 4 April, on his return journey from Scotland.[42]

As her earlier comments had indicated, Charlotte was well aware that the reason for this visit was to make her a formal offer of marriage, the third she had received. It was one she could not accept.

An absence of five years – a< n > dividing expanse of three oceans – the wide difference between a man's active career and a woman's passive existence – these things are almost equivalent to an eternal separation – But there is another thing which forms a barrier more difficult to pass than any of these. Would Mr T— and I ever suit –? could I ever feel for him enough love to accept of him as a husband? Friendship – gratitude – esteem – I have – but each moment he came near me –

and that I could see his eyes fastened on me – my veins ran ice.[43]

The very things which Charlotte had tried so many times to convince Ellen were all that were necessary for a happy marriage were not enough for Charlotte herself. It was not simply that she did not and could not love James Taylor, but that she had an overpowering aversion to him physically. It would have been strange for a woman so sensitive to her own plainness to reject a man purely on the grounds of his appearance: what lay at the bottom of that aversion was deeply revealing. Small in stature, red-headed, with his 'determined, dreadful nose', James Taylor reminded her irresistibly of Branwell. It says much about Charlotte's relationship with her brother that this was the only occasion on which a resemblance to one of her dead siblings did not predispose Charlotte in that person's favour but had the opposite effect. 'I saw him very near and once through my glass –', she wrote to Ellen on the evening of Taylor's visit, 'the resemblance to Branwell struck me forcibly – it is marked.'[44] As a reason for rejecting Taylor, Charlotte could not even admit this to herself, let alone anyone else. A couple of weeks later, when she had had time to consider her response more fully, she offered Ellen another explanation.

I am sure he has estimable and sterling qualities – but with every disposition – with every wish – with every intention even to look on him in the most favourable point of view at his last visit – it was impossible to me in my inmost heart to < look up > think of him as one that might one day be acceptable as a husband. It would sound harsh were I to tell even <u>you</u> the estimate I felt compelled to form respecting him; dear Nell – I looked for something of the gentleman – something I mean of the <u>natural</u> gentleman – you know I can dispense with acquired polish – and for looks – I know myself too well to think that I have any right to be exacting on that point – I could not find one gleam – I could not see one passing glimpse of true good-breeding – it is hard to say – but it is <u>true</u>. In mind too; – though clever, – he is second-rate; – thoroughly second-rate. One does not like to say these things – but one had better be honest – Were I to marry him – my heart would bleed – in pain and humiliation – I could not – <u>could</u> not look up to him – No – if Mr T— be the only husband Fate offers to me – single I must always remain.[45]

Interestingly, Patrick took James Taylor's part against his daughter.

I discover with some surprise that Papa has taken a decided liking to Mr Taylor. The marked kindness of his manner to the little man when he bid him good bye – exhorting him to be 'true to himself his Country and his God' and wishing him all good wishes – struck me with some astonishment at the time – and whenever he has alluded to him since it has been with significant eulogy. When I alleged that he was 'no gentleman' – he seemed out of patience with me for the objection.[46]

Neither his daughter nor her suitor had offered him an explanation for Taylor's sudden visit to Haworth but, with his usual penetration in such matters, Patrick had seen its purpose. 'I have told him nothing – yet he seems to be au fait to the whole business', Charlotte complained. 'I could think at some moments – his guesses go farther than mine. I believe he thinks a prospective union, deferred for 5 years, with such a decorous reliable personage would be a very proper and advisable affair –'. Only the previous autumn, Charlotte had dismissed gossip about her imminent marriage as 'twaddle', alleging that her father found 'the least allusion' to the idea of her marrying 'most offensive'.⁴⁷ His reaction to a genuine offer of marriage belies this statement. Clearly he was still concerned about his daughter's future: in five years' time he would probably be dead and it would be a comfort to him in the meantime to know that when Taylor returned from India, his daughter would be provided with a decent home, income and husband. The prospect held no fears for him and he had no intention of standing in the way of her making an advantageous marriage. He even told Charlotte that if she married and left him he would give up housekeeping and go into lodgings. As his daughter refused to confide in him, he could only guess her intentions and hint his approbation. 'I ask no questions and he asks me none,' Charlotte told Ellen, adding rather petulantly, 'and if he did, I should have nothing to tell him – nor he me for he & Mr T— were never long enough alone together to have had any communication on the matter –'.⁴⁸

James Taylor gave Charlotte a book at parting, requesting that she would keep it for his sake and adding that he hoped she would continue to write to him in India: 'your letters <u>have</u> been and <u>will</u> be a greater refreshment than you can think or I can tell', he had told her sadly as he left. 'And so < H > he is gone, and stern and abrupt little man as he is – too often jarring as are his manners – his absence and the exclusion of his idea from my mind – leave me certainly with less support and in deeper solitude than before.'⁴⁹

As if to emphasize the fact that in turning down James Taylor's offer of marriage Charlotte had committed herself to a lonely and uncertain future, on the very evening of his departure, Patrick was struck down with a sudden sickness and she had to put him to bed early. When he at last fell into a doze, she left him: 'I came down to the dining-room with a sense of weight, fear and desolation hard to express and harder to endure.' 'A wish that you were with me <u>did</u> cross my mind', she told Ellen, 'but I repulsed it as a most selfish wish – ... to think that < you are > one is burdening and racking others – makes all worse.' Though far away in New Zealand, Mary Taylor spoke truly when she said, 'It must be gloomy indeed for Charlotte to see her Father's health declining. It is frightful< l > to see death coming to take the last, & one can scarcely calculate the effects on a weakened painstruck mind like Charlotte's.'⁵⁰

Patrick continued unwell for some time, feeling feverish and sickly and, unusually for him, not getting up for breakfast. It was only when it became clear that the illness was an inflammation of the stomach, rather than a recurrence of his dreaded bronchitis, that Charlotte's anxiety receded a little.[51] That her fears were understandably exaggerated is suggested by the fact that Patrick himself was still campaigning vigorously on several fronts. On 12 February 1851 he had written to the General Board of Health, pointing out that it was long since he had first applied for assistance in gaining a supply of pure water for the township: 'We are greatly surprized and grieved that nothing has yet been done towards the furtherance of this desirable end', he complained. It was not simply that London was being dilatory, however, for opposition to the inspector's recommendations had been quietly gathering momentum. In response to a public meeting at the end of March, Patrick had to request the removal from the scheme of several outlying farms because the expense of supplying them with piped water was too high and that the churchyard should not be closed until a new burial ground had been found to replace it.[52]

If Patrick had hoped to unite the people of Haworth behind him by making these concessions, he failed signally. Within days of the meeting, several of the wealthiest and most powerful people in Haworth – most of them members of Patrick's own congregation – were writing behind his back to seek exemption from the new water rate which would have to be imposed to pay for the reforms. Patrick, ever the champion of the underdog, was almost driven to despair. 'There has already been long, and tedious delay –', he thundered,

there has been a deal of sickness amongst us, and there is now a great want of pure water, which ills might have been prevented, or palliated, had the remedial measures we hope for, been duly applied. A few interested individuals, might try to throw difficulties in the way, but by the large majority, consisting chiefly of the working people, there is an anxious desire that the work should on the earliest opportunity be done –

He closed his letter with a peremptory 'Please to send me an early answer.'[53]

Patrick was also at loggerheads with the Church Pastoral Aid Society which had effectively paid for him to have a curate since 1838. Despite numerous letters, however, they had not confirmed the grant for the forth-coming year and Patrick was deeply concerned. Without the grant he could not pay Arthur Bell Nicholls' salary and without him he could not perform his parish duties. It was to be nearly two months more, causing Patrick 'long, and powerful suspense', before he finally heard that his grant had been renewed. Even then, it seems it was largely owing to the intervention of the Reverend A. P. Irwine, the district secretary based in Manchester. Writing to thank him on 15 April, Patrick announced that he had taken heart from the renewal of his grant and had also applied for a lay reader with the object of rooting out reactionary High Church Puseyism in the chapelry. Displaying all his old energy and vigour, he declared:

I thoroughly detest it both root and branch, Yea, in all its bearings and habits, whether under the pretence, of decency, it appears in formal dresses, or with the plea of conscience, it talks of <u>carrying out the Liturgy</u> (in order that it may carry in the <u>Breviary</u>) or whether it, may shew itself in candles or in crosses or in vigils or in fastings, whatever colour or form it may assume, it is equally odious to me –

Patrick was therefore seeking 'a judicious, pious, Evangelical young man' who, 'by entering into every house and doing his best, might, under providence, be an instrument of much good, and no evil'. Though he still took two services every Sunday himself, 'I am unable to run over these hills, as I once did – And my Curate though an active and diligent young man, cannot do all that ought to be done.'⁵⁴ Though Patrick's health might be failing in this, his seventy-fifth year, his spirit was as strong as ever.

Charlotte, on the other hand, was becoming more and more miserable at home. On 12 April, she turned down an invitation to stay at Hunsworth with Joe and Amelia Taylor on the grounds that 'I don't like to carry low spirits from home'. As this had been her main excuse for travelling away from Haworth in the past, it seems more likely that Charlotte simply could not face the prospect of staying with Amelia who, after a fraught pregnancy, was not far off her confinement. The fuss and concern over every little alteration in Amelia's condition was more than Charlotte could bear and she had once or twice been provoked to a sharp retort in private to Ellen.⁵⁵ This suspicion is confirmed by Charlotte's positively joyful acceptance of an invitation from Mrs Smith only five days later.

Before I received your note, I was nursing a comfortable and complacent conviction that I had quite made up my mind not to go to London this year: the Great Exhibition was nothing – only a series of bazaars under a magnified hot-house – and I myself was in a pharisaical state of superiority to temptation. But Pride had its fall. I read your invitation and immediately felt a great wish to descend from my stilts. Not to conceal the truth – I should like to come and see you extremely well.⁵⁶

Writing to inform George Smith of her 'somewhat egregious failure' to stay at home until she had written her next book, she confessed, 'One can't help it. One does not profess to be made out of granite.' She also admitted to being somewhat nettled – even a little pained – by Mrs Gaskell's and Harriet Martineau's insistence on treating her like an invalid and securing her invitations to stay in the milder climate of southern counties with 'kind but misled strangers'. 'Why may not I be well like other people?' Charlotte asked him. 'I think I am reasonably well; not strong or capable of much continuous exertion, (which I do not remember that I ever was) and apt no doubt to look haggard if over-fatigued – but otherwise I have no ailment and I maintain that I am well, and hope (D. V.) to continue so awhile.' Despite her constant exhortations to the gentlemen of Smith, Elder & Co. that they should only write when they had time, Charlotte could not resist a sally that revealed just how dependent she was on their letters: 'Please to tell Mr Williams that I dare on no account come to London till he is friends with me, which I am sure he cannot be, as I have never heard from him for nearly three months.'[57]

In preparation for her London visit Charlotte again renewed her wardrobe. On her next trip to Leeds, Ellen was commissioned to ask in the stores for a selection of black and white lace cloaks and some small size chemisettes for every day and best wear to be sent to Haworth so that she could make her choice in the privacy of her own home. Having chosen a black lace shawl, however, she discovered that when she wore it against her black satin dress the beauty of the lace was lost and it looked brown and rusty. She therefore wrote to Mr Stocks, the storekeeper, who obligingly sent to London for a white replacement. 'The price is less – being but < one > 1£ 14s. it is pretty – neat and light – looks well on black – and upon reasoning the matter over, I came to the philosophic conclusion that it would be no shame for a person of my means to wear a cheaper thing – so I think I shall take it: and if you ever see it – and call it "trumpery" so much the worse.'[58] As this attempt to buy on her behalf had turned out so disastrously, Charlotte herself took a trip to Leeds at the beginning of May. At Hunt and Halls, she chose a bonnet 'which seemed grave and quiet there amongst all the splendours – but now it looks infinitely too gay with its pink lining – I saw some beautiful silks of pale sweet colours but had not the spirit or the means to launch out at the rate of 5s per yd and went and bought a black silk at 3s after all – I rather regret this – because Papa< s > says he would have lent me a sovereign if he had known. I believe if you had been there you would have forced me to to get into \debt/.'[59]

In view of her extensive preparations, it was therefore in an ironic mood that she told George Smith, 'Of course I am not in the least looking forwards to going to London – nor reckoning on it – nor allowing the matter to take any particular place in my thoughts: no: I am very sedulously cool and nonchalant.'[60] Even though the visit was again to be 'quiet and obscure as usual (any other style of procedure disagreeing with me mentally and corporeally)', Charlotte was suffering from extremities of nerves which manifested themselves in headaches and occasional sickness.[61]

Charlotte's visit to London was fixed for Thursday, 29 May – just nine days after James Taylor's departure for India. He had written requesting a last interview in London, but Charlotte had refused, saying that her visit was already fixed for June 'and therefore in all human probability we shall see each other no more'.[62] Nevertheless, rumours were rife that Charlotte was going to London to get engaged or even married – rumours to which even Patrick, Martha and Tabby subscribed, much to her irritation.

In the event, Charlotte travelled to London on Wednesday, the day before she had originally planned, arriving at ten p.m. at Euston station where

George Smith and his mother were waiting for her. The alteration in the plans had been made so that the next day she could attend one of Thackeray's lectures on 'The English Humorists of the Eighteenth Century'.[63]

The lecture proved to be one of the high points of Charlotte's visit. She wrote enthusiastically to both her father and Ellen, describing the experience in unusual detail. The very saloon in which the lecture was held was splendid: 'the walls were all painted and gilded the benches were sofas stuffed and cushioned and covered with blue damask, the audience was composed of the very elite of London Society – Duchesses were there by the score –'. 'I did not at all expect that the great Lecturer would know me or notice me under these circumstances – with admiring Duchesses and Countesses seated in rows before him – but he met me as I entered – shook hands – took me to his Mother whom I had not seen before and introduced me.'[64] What Charlotte did not tell her father or Ellen was that the introduction had caused her immense embarrassment and anger. With his usual high spirits and thoughtlessness, Thackeray had said in a loud voice 'audible over half the room', 'Mother, you must allow me to introduce you to Jane Eyre.' Naturally, heads had turned in every row and everyone stared at the 'disconcerted little lady' who grew confused and angry when she realized every eye was upon her. During the lecture itself Charlotte was too absorbed to notice the attention she herself was receiving; amidst all his grand surroundings, Thackeray 'just got up and spoke with as much simplicity and ease as if he had been speaking to a few friends by his own fireside'. The lecture was 'truly good', painstakingly compiled, finished without being studied and enlivened with quiet humour and graphic force.[65]

At its close, Charlotte's ordeal began. Someone came up behind her, leaned over and said, 'Will you permit me, as a Yorkshireman to introduce myself to you?' After a moment's hesitation Charlotte recognized the Earl of Carlisle, who had the courtesy to enquire after her father, recalling the time they had shared an election platform at Haworth back in 1834, and begging to be remembered to him. Moments later, Richard Monckton Milnes, a writer, friend of Mrs Gaskell and Yorkshire Member of Parliament, introduced himself on the same grounds. He was followed by Dr Forbes, the London doctor whom Charlotte had consulted about Anne's symptoms and who had sent her copies of his books: this was their first meeting, but, given their previous contacts, Charlotte could truthfully say he was someone 'whom I was sincerely glad to see'. Thackeray himself accosted Charlotte again, demanding to know her opinion of the lecture, a request which left her tongue-tied with embarrassment. Mrs Smith, who had accompanied Charlotte to the lecture, was making her customary surveillance on her guest's behalf and was aware that while they talked the audience were gradually forming into two lines on each side of the aisle to the door. Realizing that the longer they delayed the worse the ordeal would become,

Mrs Smith put her arm through Charlotte's to steady her nerves and swept her, trembling, from the room.[66]

The next day Thackeray paid an afternoon call at 76, Gloucester Terrace. 'I had a long talk with \him/ and I think he knows me now a little better than he did', Charlotte airily told Ellen. George Smith's description of the visit was somewhat different. He had arrived home from work shortly after Thackeray was announced and entered the drawing room to discover a scene in full progress.

Thackeray was standing on the hearthrug, looking anything but happy. Charlotte Brontë stood close to him, with head thrown back and face white with anger. The first words I heard were, 'No, Sir! If you had come to our part of the country in Yorkshire, what would you have thought of me if I had introduced you to my father, before a mixed company of strangers, as "Mr Warrington"?' Thackeray replied, 'No, you mean "Arthur Pendennis." ' 'No, I don't mean Arthur Pendennis!' retorted Miss Brontë; 'I mean Mr Warrington, and Mr Warrington would not have behaved as you behaved to me yesterday.' The spectacle of this little woman, hardly reaching to Thackeray's elbow, but, somehow, looking stronger and fiercer than himself, and casting her incisive words at his head, resembled the dropping of shells into a fortress.

George Smith eventually recovered his presence of mind and interposed; Thackeray made the necessary, 'half-humorous' apologies and the parting was a friendly one. As Smith commented, Thackeray had roused the hidden fire in Charlotte's soul and was badly scorched himself as a result.[67]

The same day, Charlotte paid her first visit to the Crystal Palace, Sir Joseph Paxton's enormous glass edifice in Hyde Park, housing the first international 'Great Exhibition' which had been opened to the public by Queen Victoria on 1 May. Writing to her father, Charlotte described it as 'a mighty Vanity Fair... It was very fine – gorgeous – animated – bewildering – but I liked Thackeray's lecture better'. On Saturday, Charlotte went to see the exhibition at Somerset House, which proved something of a disappointment: 'about half a dozen of the pictures are good and interesting – the rest of little worth'. The following day, Sunday, she went to hear an afternoon sermon by the great Swiss Protestant preacher, Jean Henri Merle d'Aubigné: 'it was pleasant – half sweet – half sad – and strangely suggestive to hear the French language once more.'[68] This flurry of activity during the first few days of Charlotte's trip to London was hardly the 'quiet and obscure' visit she had described to Mrs Gaskell. Nevertheless, it set the pattern for what was to become the busiest and most public of all Charlotte's visits.

There were four further visits to the Great Exhibition. The second, a week after the first, impressed Charlotte more profoundly. 'Its grandeur does not consist in one thing', she told her father, 'but in the unique assemblage of all things – Whatever human industry has created – you find there'. The display of manufactured goods was so vast and so varied that it recalled the *Arabian Nights* or even her own Angrian creations to mind.

It may be called a Bazaar or a Fair – but it is such a Bazaar or Fair as eastern Genii might have created. It seems as if magic only could have gathered this mass of wealth from all the ends of the Earth – as if none but supernatural hands could have arranged it thus – with such a blaze and contrast of colours and marvellous power of effect.

Thirty thousand people visited the exhibition that day and Charlotte herself spent three hours there, returning to Gloucester Terrace 'very sufficiently bleached and broken in bits' by the experience.[69]

Another visit was remarkable only for the fact that Charlotte saw the ex-royal family of France there, and another for the kind attentions of her escort, Sir David Brewster, the Scottish physicist who had invented the kaleidoscope and was one of the foremost scientists of the day. Though Charlotte had rather dreaded his scientific explanations, he spent two hours pointing out the most remarkable curiosities on display and giving information kindly and simply without being asked.[70] Charlotte was privileged to be able to visit the Great Exhibition so many times and in such company but in retrospect she decided it was not much to her taste. 'I never was able to get up any raptures < about what I saw > on the subject', she later told Miss Wooler, adding, 'It is an excessively bustling place – and after all its wonders appeal too exclusively to the eye and rarely touch the heart or head.'[71]

Appealing more to Charlotte's heart, and therefore being more to her taste, were two visits to the theatre. Previously she had seen only opera, which left her cold, and the mannered acting of Macready, which she despised. This time, however, she went to the French Theatre to hear and see 'Rachel', the thirty-one-year-old actress, Elisa Félix, who was the most famous French actress of the day. On the first occasion, Rachel was taking the title role in *Adrienne Lecouvreur* by Gabriel Legouvé and Augustin Scribe. 'I have seen Rachel', Charlotte wrote in awed tones to Amelia Taylor, '– her acting was something apart from any other acting it has come in my way to witness – her soul was in it – and a strange soul she has – I shall not discuss it.' Two weeks later, Charlotte saw Rachel again, this time in one of her most famous roles, as the tragic heroine Camilla in Corneille's classic play, *Horace*: 'a wonderful sight –', she told Ellen,

terrible as if the earth had cracked deep at your feet and revealed a glimpse of hell["] – I shall never forget it – she made me shudder to the < p > marrow of my bones: in her some fiend has certainly taken up an incarnate home. She is not a woman – she is a snake – she is the —.[72]

In that character, Charlotte declared, 'I shall *never* forget her – she will come to me in sleepless nights again and yet again.' She would also provide rich material for *Villette* where Charlotte would portray her as the actress Vashti, 'Hate and Murder and Madness incarnate'. 'She and Thackeray are the two living things that have a spell for me in this great London', Charlotte told Amelia Taylor, '– and one of these is sold to the Great Ladies – and the other – I fear – to Beelzebub.'[73]

Charlotte's irritation with Thackeray grew more marked over the period of her stay. She was particularly put out when he deferred his next lecture because 'the Duchesses and Marchionesses have petitioned him to put it off on account of Ascot Races – wearisome selfish seraphim that they are'. It was anathema to her that she should be deprived of the treat of hearing him lecture again simply on the whim of the women of fashion. Likewise, she was not impressed when he was invited to dine at the Smiths' and left early because the Duchess of Norfolk, the Marchioness of Londonderry, Lady Chesterfield and Lady Clanricarde were going to the Queen's fancy dress ball and wanted 'their pet and darling' to see them in their costumes. Nevertheless, Charlotte still prolonged her visit to the last possible minute in order to hear one more lecture from Thackeray: 'Nor was I disappointed; on the theme of Fielding – he put forth his great strength – and though I could not <u>agree</u>, I was forced to <u>admire</u>.'[74]

On 16 June, Charlotte went to hear another lecture which also fulfilled her expectations, Cardinal Wiseman addressing the Roman Catholic Society of St Vincent de Paul. All her prejudices came to the fore as she gleefully described the cardinal to her father.

He is a big portly man something of the shape of Mr Morgan; he has not merely a double but a treble and quadruple chin; he has a very large mouth with oily lips, and looks as if he would relish a good dinner with a bottle of wine after it. He came swimming into the room smiling, simpering, and bowing like a fat old lady, and sat down very demure in his chair, and looked the picture of a sleek hypocrite ... The Cardinal spoke in a smooth whining manner, just like a canting Methodist preacher. The audience seemed to look up to him as to a god.

Even the 'bevy of inferior priests' surrounding him were 'very dark-looking and sinister men' and the speeches, naturally, all turned on the necessity of straining every nerve to make converts to Popery.[75] Given her reaction to this meeting, it was perhaps surprising that Charlotte later attended the Spanish Ambassador's Chapel to observe Cardinal Wiseman holding a confirmation. Having gone to be disgusted and outraged she was not disappointed: 'The whole scene was impiously theatrical', she wrote with scorn.[76]

The strain of all the excitement and activity began to tell. After two weeks in London, Charlotte began to suffer a series of debilitating nervous headaches. Writing to Ellen one morning in 'an inexpressibly flat state' she complained of two days of continuous headache 'which grew at last rampant and violent – ended with excessive sickness – and this morning I am better but quite weak and washy. I hoped to leave my headaches behind me at Haworth – but it seems I brought them carefully packed in my trunk and very much have they been in my way since I came.'

I cannot boast that London has agreed with me well this time – the oppression of frequent head-ache – sickness and a low tone of spirits has poisoned many moments which might otherwise have been pleasant – Sometimes I have felt this hard and been tempted to murmur at Fate which condemns me to comparative silence and solitude for eleven months in the year – and in the twelveth while offering social enjoyment takes away the vigour and cheerfulness which should turn it to account.[77]

In such a mood, Charlotte had seen no reason to further spoil her pleasure by announcing her arrival to the Kay Shuttleworths who were also in London for the season. Nevertheless, Sir James soon tracked her down and at first was 'disposed to be much hurt' that Charlotte had not told him or visited him. With characteristic energy, he tried to sweep her off at once to stay at his house, but he met his match in Mrs Smith who recounted Charlotte's engagements and made it clear that such a move was out of the question. Charlotte thought she had 'got off' with a promise to visit for a day, but was soon proved wrong. 'Since Sir J. K. S. discovered that I was in London', she wrote wearily to Ellen, 'I have had precious little time to myself.'[78]

One Monday in particular left her absolutely drained and exhausted. She was summoned to breakfast at ten o'clock with Samuel Rogers, the eighty-eight-year-old 'patriarch poet', who had been a friend of Wordsworth, Scott and Byron. This was 'a most calm refined and intellectual treat' for though Rogers held regular breakfasts for celebrities, he never invited more than three guests. On this occasion Charlotte shared the honours with a relation of Lady Kay Shuttleworth, the beautiful Mrs Davenport, and Lord Glenelg. After breakfast, Sir David Brewster arrived to take her to the Great Exhibition and after two hours there, 'when, as you may suppose – I was <u>very</u> tired', she was escorted to Lord Westminster's for a further two-hour private viewing of his splendid art gallery.[79] While such arrangements did credit to Sir James' wish to entertain his unwilling guest, they took little account of her lack of stamina.

It was not surprising, then, that Charlotte turned down a number of invitations while she was in London. Thackeray had two or three times pressed her to allow him to introduce her to his great lady friends, but Charlotte had no inclination to be patronized by society hostesses. The Marquis of Westminster, whose pictures she viewed, invited her to a great party, but this she 'resolutely declined'.[80] Richard Monckton Milnes, whom she had met at Thackeray's lecture, invited her to his house in Pall Mall, but Charlotte declared she had 'laid down for myself the rule of not going out anywhere during my stay in Town' and could not infringe that rule. It must have been something of an embarrassment, therefore, when she met him again at the Kay Shuttleworths' after Sir James bullied her into going to dinner there.[81] Only Mrs Gore, the prolific novelist who had presented Charlotte with a copy of her book *The Hamiltons* the previous year, received a more regretful refusal: 'if the <u>power</u> had been mine to comply ... the <u>will</u> was certainly not wanting'.[82]

Mrs Smith had been Charlotte's constant companion on her many outings because George Smith had been too preoccupied with business to be the assiduous escort he had been on previous occasions. 'Mr S. is somewhat changed in appearance', Charlotte wrote to Ellen:

– he looks a little older, darker and more care-worn – his ordinary manner is graver – but in the evening his spirits flow back to him – Things and circumstances seem here to be as usual – but I fancy there has been some crisis in which his energy and filial affection have sustained them all – this I judge from seeing that Mother and Sisters are more peculiarly bound to him than ever and that his slightest wish is an unquestioned law.[83]

Charlotte's acute sensitivity to atmosphere had not betrayed her. Though she was unaware of the facts, she had suspected from the start that there was more to James Taylor's sudden departure to India than met the eye. What she did not know was that George Smith had been having problems with his quondam senior partner, Patrick Stewart, who ran the firm's foreign agency. In 1848, Smith had discovered that Stewart had been defrauding the firm and had brought it close to bankruptcy. Not wishing to cause a public scandal, Smith had refrained from prosecution and kept Stewart on, but without a partnership or financial responsibility. This unsatisfactory state of affairs had been allowed to drift on until Stewart's friends persuaded him to take a job in Calcutta. Taylor's appointment seems to have been tied in with this as the firm needed someone it could trust to run the lucrative India trade. His departure placed even more pressure on George Smith, however, and more than once during Charlotte's visit he was detained in the office till three in the morning.[84] The occasions when he was free were therefore doubly precious.

Towards the end of Charlotte's stay she had two outings with George Smith, a day in Richmond with his family[85] and, more remarkably, an expedition with him alone to visit a phrenologist in the Strand who pursued the then fashionable vogue for reading character from the bumps and indentations in the cranium. The visit to Dr Browne was paid anonymously, the pair adopting the names of Mr and Miss Fraser, and the resulting analysis of their characters was to provide a fertile subject for future repartee. Like most pseudo-sciences, phrenology had its believers, including Charlotte, who were prepared to overlook the errors in recognizing the truths. Reading

'Mr Fraser's' character when she returned home, Charlotte cried delightedly, 'it is a sort of miracle – like – like – like as the very life itself': Smith himself considered the analysis 'not so happy'.[86]

He is an admirer of the fair sex. He is very kind to children. Is strongly attached to his home. Is of a very affectionate and friendly disposition … Is fond of the ideal and romantic and possesses a strongly developed organ of language. He has a just sense of the value of time, and is not prone to procrastinate. Is active and practical though not hustling or contentious.[87]

Charlotte's character had its share of uncannily accurate assessments – though no more than she herself would have been able to deduce from close observation.

Temperament for the most part nervous … Her attachments are strong and endur-ing – indeed this is a leading element of her character … She is sensitive and is very anxious to succeed in her undertakings, but is not so sanguine as to the probability of success. She is occasionally inclined to take a gloomier view of things than perhaps the facts of the case justify … She has more firmness than self reliance, and her sense of justice is of a very high order … She is endowed with an exalted sense of the beautiful and ideal, and longs for perfection. If not a poet her sentiments are poetical or are at least imbued with that enthusiastic glow which is characteristic of poetical feeling … In its intellectual development this head is very remarkable. The forehead is at once very large and well formed. It bears the stamp of deep thoughtfulness and comprehensive understanding. It is highly philosophical. It exhibits the presence of an intellect at once perspicacious and perspic[u]ous … This Lady possesses a fine organ of language and can … express her sentiments with clearness precision and force –[88]

Of this analysis, Charlotte had 'nothing to say – not a word', and though forbidden to comment further on George Smith's she could not resist saying, 'If I had the right to whisper a word of counsel – it should be merely this. Whatever your present self may be – resolve with all your strength of resolution – never to degenerate thence – Be jealous of a shadow of falling off.'[89]

Having put off her return twice, Charlotte eventually left London on 27 June, but even then she did not go straight home. Mrs Gaskell had invited her to stay with her in Manchester for a few days at the end of her London visit and had proved accommodating throughout Charlotte's changes in plan.[90] In the end, however, Charlotte could spare her only two days – it was nearly five weeks since she had left home and she could not put off the evil moment much longer. 'The visit to Mrs Gaskell on my way home – let me down easily', Charlotte told George Smith.

She lives in a large – cheerful, airy house, quite out of Manchester Smoke – a garden surrounds it, and as in this hot weather, the windows were kept open – a whispering of leaves and perfume of flowers always pervaded the rooms. Mrs Gaskell herself is a woman of whose conversation and company I should not soon tire – She seems to me kind, clever, animated and unaffected – her husband is a good and kind man too.[91]

The Gaskells had had four daughters, Marianne, who was away at school, Meta, Flossy and Julia, the eldest being fifteen, the youngest only five, 'all more or less pretty and intelligent', who filled the house with liveliness and gaiety. Rather to her surprise, Charlotte found the Gaskell girls endearing and was deeply touched by the way they responded to her. The youngest child, Julia, swiftly became an especial favourite. 'Could you manage to convey a small kiss to that dear but dangerous little person – Julia?' Charlotte asked Mrs Gaskell some weeks after her return. 'She surreptitiously possessed herself of a minute fraction of my heart, which has been missing ever since I saw her.'[92]

After the lively Gaskell household, it was quite a contrast when Charlotte returned home on the last day of June, but she was determined to make the best of it: 'even Haworth Parsonage does not look gloomy in this bright summer weather: it is somewhat still – but with the windows open – I can hear a bird or two singing on certain thorn-trees in the garden'.[93] The house had been thoroughly spring cleaned by Martha in her absence, though Charlotte was somewhat shocked to find that Patrick had had the piano removed out of the parlour and taken upstairs into one of the bedrooms; 'there it must necessarily be absurd – and in the Parlour it looked so well – besides being convenient for your books – I wonder why you don't like it –'.[94] It does not seem to have occurred to Charlotte that the presence of the silent piano in the room where Patrick spent most of his time must have been a painful daily reminder of his three children who had all loved to play it.

Knowing how difficult Charlotte always found it to return to Haworth after the gaiety of London, George Smith had been kind enough to send her at least a couple of long cheerful letters, which she seized upon gratefully.

I had made up my mind to tell you that I should expect no letter from Cornhill for three months to come (intending afterwards to extend this abstinence to six months for I am jealous of becoming dependent on this indulgence – you – doubtless cannot see why, because you do not live my life) – Nor shall I now expect a letter – but since you say that you would like to write now and then – I cannot say never write without imposing on my real wishes a falsehood which they reject – and doing to them a violence to which they entirely refuse to submit;

'Tell your Mother', she added at the end of a very long letter, 'I shall try to cultivate good spirits as assiduously as she cultivates her geraniums.'[95] This was easier said than done, however, especially when there was no Emily to whom she could recount all her adventures. As she had to unburden herself to someone she turned once more to her surrogate sister, Ellen Nussey, and invited her to stay. She had also invited Margaret Wooler: 'The pleasures of society – I cannot offer you, nor those of fine scenery, but I place very much at your command the moors – some books – a series of quiet "curling-hair times" – and an old pupil into the bargain.' Miss Wooler was already engaged, however, and offered to come later in the year. 'In truth it was a great piece of extravagance on my part to ask you and Ellen Nussey together,' Charlotte admitted; 'it is much better to divide such good things. To have your visit in <u>prospect</u> will console me when hers is in <u>retrospect</u>.'⁹⁶ Ellen's visit was equally quiet, enlivened only by walks on the moors and the by now customary annual visit of the Reverend Thomas Crowther, vicar of Cragg Vale, who came to preach the two Sunday school sermons on 20 July.⁹⁷ There was also a visit from a 'stiff little chap', Henry Robinson, a manufacturer of Keighley, who had called to enlist Patrick's support over an epitaph for his cousin, but who self-importantly took the opportunity to tell Charlotte he had discovered that she had got the name 'Jane Eyre' from a sign in Kirkby Lonsdale. When he got home his wife had corrected him, telling him the sign read 'J. Eyre' and referred to a James, not a Jane. Much to Charlotte and Ellen's amusement, he wrote an elaborate letter of contrition saying that he regarded Charlotte as 'an Angel borne aloft, hovering and scanning the vicissitudes concomitant to humanity in all her various forms'.⁹⁸

Once Ellen had gone, life at Haworth was quieter than before. Even Mr Nicholls had departed for a holiday in Ireland, having invited himself to take a 'farewell tea' at the parsonage the evening before he left, somewhat to Charlotte's surprise. She was unable to resist the sardonic comment to Ellen that he had 'comported himself somewhat peculiarly for him – being extremely good – mild and uncontentious'.⁹⁹

As the late summer drew to a close, the weather turned unpleasant. Keighley Parish Feast was washed out with heavy rain and there were violent thunderstorms. The rapid changes from hot to cold which took place over the next few weeks brought illness in their wake, the old and the weak being especially affected.¹⁰⁰ Charlotte's own health deteriorated under the strain of her enforced seclusion. 'It is useless to tell you how I live –', Charlotte wrote to Ellen, 'I endure life – but whether I enjoy it or not is another question.'¹⁰¹ Ellen Nussey's mother, too, fell ill, seriously enough for Ellen to call her brother John, the court physician, from London to her bedside. The family bickerings and her mother's own ingratitude for Ellen's patient nursing were all relayed to Charlotte, who doled out sympathy and good advice from the safe distance of Haworth. As Mrs Nussey's death appeared imminent, Charlotte, with her own memories of her brother's and sisters' deaths still raw in her mind, could do no more than tell her friend that 'I well know what you are now going through.'¹⁰² When she unexpectedly recovered after several months of debilitating illness, however, Charlotte was the first to be delighted. 'I am very glad your Mother is so clearly cheating the doctors – I <u>do</u> like to hear of their croakings being at fault', she exulted, adding a little later, 'the Doctors cannot now deny that she has fairly given them the slip – I admire her as a clever old lady'.[103] It was perhaps fortunate that, in her own delicate state of health, Charlotte had the cheering example of Mrs Nussey's recovery before her.

It was not so much her physical weakness that was a trial to Charlotte, however, as her own increasingly morbid mood. This was not helped by her inability to settle to her new novel. Her guilty conscience about this poisoned all her relations with Smith, Elder & Co., though everyone there was remarkably understanding. Perhaps in an effort to galvanize her into writing by offering her a less intimidating prospect than a three-volume novel, George Smith suggested that she should undertake a serial, but Charlotte was adamant. 'My dear Sir – give Currer Bell the experience of a Thackeray or the animal spirits of a Dickens and then repeat the question. Even <u>then</u> he would answer, "I will publish no Serial of which the last number is not written before the first comes out".'[104]

Unable to offer her publishers a novel of her own, Charlotte tried to assuage her guilt by securing them the opportunity to publish Harriet Martineau's next book. She had taken up Charlotte's suggestion that she should return to novel-writing and, believing that she was conferring a favour on both parties, Charlotte acted as broker between Miss Martineau and Smith, Elder & Co. It was agreed that the novel could be published anonymously, though Charlotte soon realized that 'Secret-keeping does not agree with her at all' and began to have qualms about how good the novel might be. She wrote to George Smith:

You must not be <u>too</u> sanguine about the book – for though, it seems to me, there are grounds for anticipating that she will produce something superior to what she has yet written in the same class – yet perhaps the Nature and bent of her genius hardly warrant the expectation of first rate excellence in fiction.[105]

While Harriet Martineau set to work with her usual energy, Charlotte could settle to nothing. She had her excuses in that there was an unusual number of visitors to the parsonage that autumn. At the end of August, William Morgan came to call, arriving in time for a nine o'clock breakfast; 'fat – well and hearty', he brought Charlotte 'a lot of tracts as a present'. Though Charlotte disliked Morgan and was clearly unimpressed with his gift, the gesture showed the same 'latent feeling' which had been roused by his reading of *Shirley* earlier in the year. 'I was especially struck by his remark about the chap. entitled "The Valley of the Shadow &c."' Charlotte had observed to Ellen at the time, 'he must have a true sense of what he read or he could not have made it.'[106] Morgan's visit had a dual purpose: to tell Patrick that his newly built Christ Church day schools, accommodating 600 children and infants, had opened the previous day and, more importantly,

Constantin and Claire Zoë Heger, with their family, painted within a few years of Charlotte's departure from Brussels.

A view of the rue d'Isabelle, Brussels, showing the Pensionnat Heger and its gardens on the left-hand side.

The gateway to the Pensionnat Heger, which is graphically described in *Villette*.

Charlotte's caricature of herself at the bottom of a letter to Ellen Nussey written from Brussels on 6 March 1842. Ellen is the pretty lady on the right with her suitor, Mr Vincent.

A prospectus for the school which Charlotte, Emily and Anne intended to set up at Haworth Parsonage in 1844. As no pupils could be found, the plan had to be abandoned.

The Misses Brontë's Establishment

FOR

THE BOARD AND EDUCATION

OF A LIMITED NUMBER OF

YOUNG LADIES,

THE PARSONAGE, HAWORTH,

NEAR BRADFORD.

Terms.

	£.	s.	d.
BOARD AND EDUCATION, including Writing, Arithmetic, History, Grammar, Geography, and Needle Work, per Annum,	35	0	0
French, German, Latin ... each per Quarter,	1	1	0
Music, Drawing, ... each per Quarter,	1	1	0
Use of Piano Forte, per Quarter,	0	5	0
Washing, per Quarter,	0	15	0

Each Young Lady to be provided with One Pair of Sheets, Pillow Cases, Four Towels, a Dessert and Tea-spoon.

A Quarter's Notice, or a Quarter's Board, is required previous to the Removal of a Pupil.

ABOVE LEFT A portrait of Charlotte Brontë, commissioned by George Smith, her publisher, and drawn in chalk by the society artist George Richmond.

ABOVE George Smith of Smith, Elder & Co., Charlotte's publisher, who became her close friend.

LEFT William Smith Williams, the reader at Smith, Elder & Co. who first recognised the genius of *Jane Eyre* and corresponded regularly with Charlotte.

ABOVE RIGHT Mrs Elizabeth Cleghorn Gaskell, the novelist, who met Charlotte in 1850, became her friend and, after her death, wrote *The Life of Charlotte Brontë*.

RIGHT Arthur Bell Nicholls, curate of Haworth from 1845 to 1861, who married Charlotte in 1854.

FAR RIGHT A letter by Patrick Brontë campaigning against the Poor Law, published in the *Leeds Intelligencer* on 22 April 1837.

LIBERTY OR BONDAGE.

TO THE LABOURERS, MECHANICS, AND PAUPERS OR SLAVES OF ENGLAND.

My dear friends and fellow-creatures, whose best interest I earnestly desire and pray for, in reference to both the worlds, I would take the liberty of addressing to you a few words of advice, in this most important crisis of our affairs. All who know me, are fully aware, that I am a conscientious Conservative, but at the same time, a genuine reformer, and that I regard not *men*, but *measures*. Had it not been for the imperious nature of our affairs, I should not have taken the liberty of saying or writing any thing to you at the present moment. My duty, however, before God and men in general, and myself in particular, is paramount to every other consideration, and therefore, as I would answer at the last day of account for whatever talents may be committed to my charge, I must speak the whole truth and nothing but the truth, as far as shall come within the scope of my knowledge. A law has lately been passed called the Poor Law Amendment Bill; a greater misnomer I never read or heard. It is a monster of iniquity, a horrid and cruel deformity, even in regard to what before was no very shapely or symmetrical representation. I know that a committee is sitting to *amend* the bill—but let me tell you, my dear friends, that it *cannot be amended; it must be repealed altogether.* This deceptive attempt reminds me of a cunning shopkeeper who had a great number of spurious coins, and who placed them in large parcels on his counter, and when any customer called and wanted an odd halfpenny or sixpence, he ordered him to choose it out of these parcels. The ignorant and simple were often thus deceived, but the wise and wary said to themselves, we cannot get anything good out of that which is altogether bad, and consequently escaped the snare that was laid for them. Do you likewise. The whole poor law amendment bill is an assemblage of base metals, therefore resolutely reject it as such, and be not deceived by the cunning craftiness of men, whereby they lie in wait to deceive. We are told in the five books of Moses that *the poor shall never cease from the land,* and are exhorted *to open our hands wide to relieve them.* And the eternal God *says multiply and replenish the earth.* The blessed Saviour, also, follows up these injunctions with still more forcible admonitions. But a set of unfeeling, antiscriptural men, have lately arisen, who, being themselves only paupers on a larger scale— (as they are, in many instances supported by the country, and in a great measure, by the very men whom they wish to oppress)—who, nevertheless, teach doctrines in direct opposition to the *law* and the *gospel.* What, then, my friends are we to do under these circumstances? Why, verily, I see no plan better for us than that adopted by the Apostles, namely, *to obey God, rather than man. We will not* therefore submit to go to their *bastiles. We will not live* on their water gruel, and on their two ounces of cheese, and their fourteen ounces of bread per day. We will not suffer ourselves to be chained by their three *tyrannical commissioners; and we never will endure* the idea, of men rolling in affluence and luxury, prescribing to us the most extreme line which can keep soul and body together. We have religion, reason, justice and humanity, on our side, and by these we are determined to stand or fall. We regard not sophistry, or selfishness—we look to God, to justice, and common sense; and knowing as we very well do, that we constitute the numerical and physical force of the nation, we are fully determined to be *physically supplied;* that is, to have not the luxuries, but the necessaries of life. Thus, my dear friends, in your name and mine, I have briefly written what I conceive to be equitable, perhaps at no small risque. Then let me request you to do *your duty*—petition, remonstrate, and resist *powerfully* but *legally,* and God, the father and friend of the poor, will crown all your efforts with success.

I remain your sincere Friend,

Haworth, April 17, 1837.　　　P. BRONTE.

thumping boy whom its father means to christen Homer a
the least, though the mother suggests that 'poetaster' wo
be more suitable; but that sounds too aristocratic.

Is the medallion cracked that Thorwaldsen executed Of

AUGUSTUS CAESAR. ?

I wish I could see you, and, as Haworth fair is h
on Monday after the ensuing one, your presence then wou
gratify one of the...

FALLEN.

In my own register of transactions during my nights
days I find no matter worthy of extraction for your per
All is yet with me clouds and darkness; I hope yo
have, at least, blue sky and sunshine.

Constant and unavoidable depression of mind

A typical letter from Branwell to his friend, the Halifax sculptor J. B. Leyland. Written in October
1846, this one includes Branwell's self-portrait based on Leyland's medallion likeness of him.

body sadly shackle me in even trying to go on with any mental effort which might rescue me from the fate of a dry toast soaked six hours in a glass of cold water, and intended to be given to an old maid's squeamish cat.

Is there really such a thing as the "Risus Sar-donicus" — the Sardonic laugh.? Did a man ever laugh the morning he was, to be hanged.?

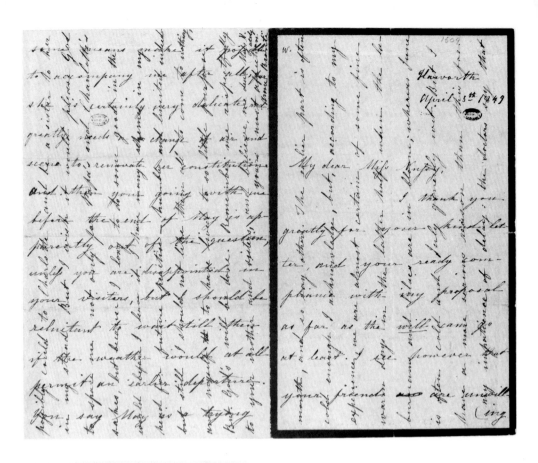

Anne's letter to Ellen Nussey, asking Ellen to accompany her to Scarborough, written on 5 April 1849, several weeks before her death.

Anne's gravestone in the churchyard of St Mary's, beneath the castle wall at Scarborough.

to inform him that he had decided to end his ministry in Bradford. He had been in Bradford for forty years, thirty-six of them as minister of Christ Church, and at the age of sixty-nine, he now felt it was time to hand over his parish to a more active minister and retire to a quieter one where the duties would be within his capabilities. He preached his farewell sermon on 26 October and was presented with twenty pounds by his Sunday school teachers and the magnificent sum of £256 by his parishioners at a soirée the following evening. He then left Bradford for Buckinghamshire, where he had been appointed rector of the quiet rural parish of Hullcott.[107] For Patrick this was the severance of a friendship which had lasted more than forty years. Though his children had always held William Morgan in contempt, he and Patrick had been bound together since they first embarked on the ministry with a shared faith and mission; since then they had forged new and closer links through marriage and over the years they had performed the sacred offices for one another's families. Their parting must have been a source of immense sadness, particularly as both men were well aware that they were unlikely to meet again.

Within a month of parting from his wife's cousin-in-law, Patrick was called upon to meet his wife's nephew for the first time. Thomas Brontë Branwell, the son of Maria's youngest sister, Charlotte, came to visit unexpectedly in the third week of September. His mother had died in 1848 but his father, Mrs Brontë's cousin, had married again and was still alive; Thomas had been born the same year as Branwell Brontë and, given the interchange of patronymics, it seems likely that Thomas was Patrick's godson. This in itself could hardly have been responsible for the visit, though it might have provided an excuse for it. The most probable reason was that the Branwells of Penzance had discovered that their relative was a literary giant and despatched Thomas to investigate and report back; this would explain Charlotte's reluctance to commit her impressions of him to paper.[108]

Charlotte was somewhat peeved at this unexpected disruption to her plans. Thomas Brontë Branwell stayed several days at the parsonage and, as soon as he left, she wrote immediately to Miss Wooler telling her that 'the coast is now clear' and urging her to come before the spell of fine weather ended. She arrived a week later, on 29 September, on her first visit to Haworth. To Charlotte's evident surprise, their former, sometimes prickly relationship had mellowed. 'Miss Wooler is and has been very pleasant', she wrote to Ellen a few days after her guest's arrival.

She is like good wine; I think time improves her – and really – whatever she may be in person – in mind she is younger than when at Roe-Head. Papa and She get on extremely well I have just heard Papa walk into the dining-room and pay her a round compliment on her good sense.[109]

Patrick had always had a penchant for intelligent women, and Miss Wooler was no exception. When she left he sent his best wishes and expressed the hope that they would see her again at Haworth soon. 'He would not say this unless he meant it', Charlotte felt obliged to point out and urged Miss Wooler to return for a fortnight or three weeks instead of the brief ten days she had stayed this time. 'You very kindly refer with pleasure to your brief stay with us', Charlotte wrote some time later. 'My dear Miss Wooler – the visit was an enjoyment to me too – a true enjoyment; your society raised my spirits in a way that surprised myself – and which you could only appreciate by seeing me as I am alone – a spectacle happily not likely to come in your way.' It also came as something of a surprise to Charlotte, who had always regarded her former headmistress as a model of spinsterhood, to learn just how much the visit had meant to Miss Wooler. 'She seems to think so much of a little congenial company – a little attention and kindness – that I am afraid these things are rare to her.'[110]

With Miss Wooler's visit in the past, Charlotte no longer had an excuse to prevent her writing, yet the task was as uncongenial as ever. As the anniversary of her brother's death passed and that of Emily's approached, her spirits altogether failed her. Instead of giving way to her inclination and leaving home, she resolutely turned down every invitation that came her way. 'As to running away from home every time I have a battle of this sort to fight – it would not do', she told Mrs Gaskell, who had offered her one of the invitations. 'Besides the "weird" would follow. As to shaking it off – that cannot be.' Harriet Martineau and Ellen Nussey were also turned down, as were the Forsters, her unwelcome visitors from Bradford, to whom Charlotte, somewhat brusquely, wrote, 'I find it is not in my power to leave home.'[111]

In the deepening gloom that afflicted her, the only ray of light was her correspondence with Smith, Elder & Co., bringing a taste of the world outside Haworth. There were two letters from James Taylor in Bombay, the second of which Charlotte sent to Ellen for her perusal: 'in its way – it has merit – that cannot be denied – abundance of information – talent of a certain kind – alloyed (I think) here and there with errors of taste – He might have spared many of the details of the bath scene – which – for the rest tallies exactly with Mr Thackeray's account of the same process.' It was scarcely honest, therefore, when replying to Taylor, for Charlotte to devote a whole paragraph of her reply to an appreciation of this description, particularly as she prefaced her remarks with the comment, 'The Bath-Scene amused me much.'[112] 'This little man – with all his long letters – remains as much a conundrum to me as ever –', Charlotte had told Ellen. Before replying to his letters, she took the unusual step of writing to Smith Williams to ask for his 'impartial judgement of Mr Taylor's character and disposition' because she did not like to continue the correspondence without further information. His reply praised Taylor's judgement, sense and principle but drew attention to his faults of manner and temper. This merely confirmed what Charlotte herself believed, particularly as she had heard more open complaints about Taylor's irritable temper since his departure for India. Deciding that he was 'a little too harsh, rigid, and unsympathising' to be anything more to her, Charlotte replied to Taylor in 'a calm civil manner' which could not be misinterpreted as offering anything more than simple friendship.'³

Far more important to Charlotte than Taylor's letters were those of George Smith. Uniformly kind, cheerful and encouraging, their bantering tone provided much-needed relief from her own depression, creating a comfortable sense of intimacy and forcing her to reply in kind. 'I will tell you a thing to be noted, often in your letters, and almost always in your conversation –', Charlotte told him,

… I mean an undercurrent of quiet raillery – an inaudible laugh to yourself; a not unkindly but somewhat subtle playing on your correspondent or companion for the time being – in short – a sly touch of a Mephistopheles with the fiend extracted … I by no means mention this as a <u>fault</u> – I merely tell you – you have it. And I can make the accusation with comfortable impunity – guessing pretty surely that you are too busy just now to deny this or any other charge.'⁴

It was perhaps the fear that he had gone too far in one of his letters that prompted George Smith to write a hurried apology for his 'flippancy and impertinent license'. 'Allow me to say that you never need to mention these words because (it seems to me) that your nature has nothing to do with the qualities they represent – nothing in this world', she hastened to assure him.

I do not believe that except perhaps to people who had themselves a good deal of effrontery and hardness – you could be otherwise than kindly and considerate – you are always so to Currer Bell – < you are always so to C > and always have been, which is one chief reason why he has a friendship for you.'⁵

Here again, fearful of overstepping the bounds of propriety, or rather, freed from them to express herself sincerely, Charlotte assumed her masculine pseudonym. She did this again when turning down his suggestion that she should write a serial.

though Currer Bell cannot do this – you are still to think him your friend – and you are still to be <u>his</u> friend. You are to keep a fraction of yourself – if it be only the end of your little finger – for <u>him</u>, and that fraction he will neither let gentleman or lady – author or artist … take possession of – or so much as meddle with. He reduces his claim to a minute point – and that point he monopolizes.

Just how much George Smith's friendship meant to her she further hinted in the same letter, responding to his invitation to come to London for a week before Christmas with a distinct negative.

No – if there were no other objection – (and there are many) there is the pain of that last bidding good-bye – that hopeless shaking hands – yet undulled – and unforgotten. I don't like it. I could not bear its frequent repetition. Do not recur to this plan. Going to London is a mere palliative and stimulant: reaction follows.[116]

Winter, she explained, was a better time for working than summer, because it was less liable to interruption. 'If I could always work – time would not be long – nor hours sad to me – but blank and heavy intervals still occur – when power and will are at variance. This however is talking Greek to an eminent and spirited Publisher. He does not believe in such things.'[117] Only a week after explaining that she had started to write again, she had abandoned her book once more and was obliged to tell George Smith that it would not be ready for publishing next season. 'If my health is spared', she told him,

I shall get on with it as fast as is consistent with its being done – if not <u>well</u> – yet as well as I can do it: <u>Not one whit faster</u>. When the mood leaves me (it has left me now – without vouchsafing so much as a word of a message when it will return) I put by the M.S. and wait till it comes back again; and God knows, I sometimes have to wait long – <u>very</u> long it seems to me.[118]

Charlotte's caveat about her health was to prove all too prophetic. They had been beset with illness at the parsonage throughout October. First Tabby had caught influenza, which she passed to Martha, then Martha suffered two separate attacks of quinsy, a sort of ulcerated inflammation of the throat, and finally Patrick caught cold: 'so far I keep pretty well – and am thankful for it –', Charlotte told Ellen, 'for who else would nurse them all –'.[119]

Towards the end of November, however, the weather grew more severe and Charlotte, out walking one day, was smitten with a sudden pain in her right side. 'I did not think much of it at first – but was not well from that time', she told Mrs Smith two months later. 'Soon after I took cold – the cold struck in, inflammatory action ensued, I had high fever at nights, the pain in my side became very severe – there was a constant burning and aching in my chest.' Not surprisingly, as these were the same symptoms that Emily and Anne had suffered in their final illnesses, Charlotte was unable to sleep and completely lost her appetite. 'My own conclusion', she confessed, 'was that my lungs were affected – but on consulting a medical man – my lungs and chest were pronounced perfectly sound, and it appeared that the inflammation had fallen on the liver.'[120]

With hindsight, Charlotte was able to recognize that the diagnosis was correct but at the time she was unconvinced. 'The doctor speaks encouragingly', she told Ellen gloomily, 'but as yet I don't get better.'[121] Convinced in her own mind that she herself was now suffering from the consumption which had afflicted her sisters at exactly this season three years before, Charlotte did not rally. The death of Keeper, Emily's beloved dog, on 1

December was a further blow, coming as it did less than three weeks before the anniversary of his mistress's death. He was ill for a single night and then 'went gently to sleep' the following morning; 'we laid his old faithful head in the garden', Charlotte told Ellen, adding that Anne's dog, Flossy, was 'dull and misses him'. 'There was something very sad in losing the old dog; yet I am glad he met a natural fate – people kept hinting that he ought to be put away which neither Papa nor I liked to think of.'[122]

Try as she might, Charlotte could not escape the thrall of the past. Two days before the anniversary of Emily's death, she could bear it no longer and wrote to Ellen begging her to come to Haworth, if only for a few days. 'I am well aware myself that extreme and continuous depression of spirits has had much to do with the origin of the illness – and I know a little cheerful society would do me more good than gallons of medicine', she confessed to Ellen, adding, 'If you <u>can</u> come – come on < Thursday > Friday –'.[123] The change in date was significant. On Friday it would be 19 December, exactly three years since Emily was torn from the world. It was an anniversary Charlotte was anxious to forget. The flurry of preparation for her guest's arrival would provide a welcome distraction from painful memories and from the fear that she had contracted the same fatal disease as her sister.

Chapter Twenty-Four

❦

VILLETTE

Ellen responded immediately to Charlotte's summons by coming straight to Haworth, though she did not arrive until the day after the third anniversary of Emily's death. As usual, her presence cheered Charlotte, but she could only stay for a week and, after she left, Charlotte had a sudden relapse: 'my head continued to ache all Monday – and yesterday the white tongue – parched mouth and loss of appetite were returned', Charlotte reported to her friend, '– accordingly I am to take more medicine'.[1] Mr Ruddock, who visited that day, identified the source of Charlotte's illness as her liver and prescribed her a course of 'blue pills', containing a small dose of mercury, which she was to take for a week. Within a few days, however, Charlotte was seriously ill, 'unable to swallow any nourishment except a few teaspoonfuls of liquid per diem, my mouth became sore, my teeth loose, my tongue swelled, raw and ulcerated while water welled continually into my mouth'.[2] These, as Charlotte, unlike her doctor, realized, were the classic symptoms of mercury poisoning. She abandoned the course of pills and was able to dissuade her father, who was going through agonies of anxiety, from calling in Mr Teale, the specialist whom they had consulted over Anne. Charlotte was able to report with a certain grim satisfaction to Ellen that Mr Ruddock was 'sorely flustered when he found what he had done', declaring that 'he never in his whole practice knew the same effect produced by the same dose on man – woman or child – and avows it is owing to an altogether peculiar sensitiveness of constitution'.[3] Suddenly, Emily's apparently wayward and stubborn refusal to be treated by 'poisoning doctors' seemed justified.

Looking back over this period, Charlotte herself recognized that illness alone was not responsible for her suffering.

It cannot be denied that the solitude of my position fearfully aggravated its other evils. Some long, stormy days and nights there were when I felt such a craving for support and companionship as I cannot express. Sleepless – I lay awake night after night – weak and unable to occupy myself – I sat in my chair day after day – the saddest memories my only company. It was a time I shall never forget – but God sent it and it must have been for the best[4]

Now that Charlotte was genuinely ill, she had at least an excuse to avoid visiting local grandees who continued to inundate her with invitations. Previously, she had blamed her father's precarious state of health for her refusal to leave home, prompting William Forster to write to Richard Monckton Milnes that 'there was no use in our trying to get her away from her father ... she will not, I expect can not, leave him'.[5] This gave Monckton Milnes, the Yorkshire MP whom Charlotte had met in London, the bright idea of inviting both Charlotte and her father to his home, Fryston Hall at Ferrybridge. Fortunately for Charlotte, this invitation arrived when she was at her weakest and she was able to hand over the task of writing the refusal to her father with a clear conscience. 'Were I in the habit of going from home, there are few persons, to whom I would give the preference over yourself,' Patrick replied, '– such not being the case, you will permit me to retain my customary rule, unspoken, and kindly accept my excuse.' 'My Daughter,' he added, almost as an afterthought, 'I regret to say, is not well enough to be a visitor anywhere, just now – She has been out of health, for some time, and though now better, requires care, And for the present, I should wish her to stay at home.'[6]

Another person who tried an appeal to Patrick to get Charlotte away from Haworth was Ellen Nussey. Alarmed at the reports of her friend's health, Ellen did what she had frequently done in the past and wrote to Charlotte's family to get permission for a visit to Brookroyd which she knew Charlotte herself would decline. 'I wish you could have seen the coolness with which I captured your letter on its way to Papa', Charlotte informed Ellen, 'and at once conjecturing its tenor, made the contents my own.' For the moment she was too nauseous to travel but, she assured Ellen, the moment she felt well enough to do so, she would come to Brookroyd. In the meantime, she urged her friend, 'Be quiet. Be tranquil.'[7]

It was not until the end of January that Charlotte was strong enough to make the journey to Brookroyd, even then taking the train only as far as Bradford and travelling the rest of the way in Ellen's brother-in-law's gig. She had given strict instructions to her 'dear physician': 'I am to live on the very plainest fare – to take no butter – at present I do not take tea – only milk and water with a little sugar and dry bread – this with an occasional mutton chop is my diet – and I like it better than anything else.'[8] Ellen's companionship soon rallied Charlotte's health and spirits. Ten days after her arrival she was able to respond positively to a kind letter from Mrs Gaskell.

As the date of this letter will shew – I am now from home – and have already benefited greatly by the kind attentions and cheerful society of the friends with whom I am staying – friends who probably do not care for me a pin – as Currer Bell – but who have known me for years as C. Brontë – and by whom I need not fear that my invalid weaknesses (which indeed I am fast overcoming) will be felt as a burden.

Certainly the past Winter has been to me a strange time – had I the prospect before me of living it over again – my prayer must necessarily be – 'Let this cup pass from me.'[9]

She was even well enough to receive a visit from Miss Wooler's sister Eliza, who made a morning call with three of her nieces and a nephew, though an invitation to dinner at the family home, Rouse Mill, had to be cancelled when the weather proved too severe.[10]

Charlotte returned home on 11 February 1852, but the beneficial effects of her fortnight's holiday were to prove all too transitory. She was particularly chagrined that her brief excursion had caused her to miss George Smith who, on the spur of the moment, had made a detour on his trip to Scotland and called unexpectedly at the parsonage. 'I do wish now I had delayed my departure from home a few days longer', she wrote wistfully to him, 'that I might have shared with my Father the true pleasure of receiving you at Haworth Parsonage. Such a pleasure your visit would have been as I have sometimes dimly imagined but never ventured to realize.'[11]

The reason for George Smith's sudden visit to Haworth was never properly explained. Undoubtedly he was worried about Charlotte's state of health and her admitted inability to produce her next novel: perhaps he simply wanted to see for himself whether she really was on the verge of death as London gossip constantly suggested. He may also have been concerned that his recent rejection of Harriet Martineau's latest novel, 'Oliver Weld', might have been taken to heart by Charlotte, who had not only persuaded Miss Martineau to write her first novel in many years but had acted as broker between author and publisher to secure the book for Smith, Elder & Co. What all had hoped would turn out to be another *Deerbrook* was in fact a thinly disguised and badly written political and religious polemic which put everyone concerned in a difficult position.[12] George Smith was anxious not to offend Charlotte, but the book was unacceptable from both a literary and a commercial point of view. Charlotte herself, who had gone to the trouble of suggesting pseudonyms for the author and had actually read the first volume of the book in manuscript before sending it on to Smith, Elder & Co., was embarrassed by the fact that the golden prize she had hoped to bring to her publishers had turned out to be mere counterfeit. She had admitted her doubts to George Smith in her covering letter when sending the manuscript but, unwilling to hurt or alienate her other friend, had written 'gloriously' about it to her. Harriet Martineau, after a long silence which Charlotte feared meant that she had taken permanent offence, eventually admitted that the novel had been 'a foolish prank' but was scornful of George Smith's timidity in refusing to publish a pro-Catholic book.[13] Though Charlotte had reassured George Smith that the whole sorry episode had not in any way diminished her own regard for him, he may have felt it necessary to discuss the matter face to face.

Whatever George Smith's motives in coming to Haworth were, Patrick must have been able to reassure him, for he did not take up Charlotte's invitation to come to her at Brookroyd and never repeated his visit to her home. His frequent expressions of goodwill continued. He persuaded his mother to invite Charlotte to London again in the hope that a change of air and scene would do her good. This Charlotte regretfully rejected. 'A treat must be <u>earned</u> before it can be <u>enjoyed</u> and the treat which a visit to you affords me is yet unearned, and must so remain for a time – how long I do not know.'[14] More remarkably, knowing Charlotte's enthusiasm for Thackeray, George Smith sent her the manuscript of the as yet unpublished first volume of *The History of Henry Esmond Esquire*. This, as Charlotte gratefully acknowledged, was a rare and special pleasure. As usual, Thackeray's work filled her with a mixture of admiration and irritation.

In the first half of the work what chiefly struck me was the wonderful manner in which the author throws himself into the spirit and letter of the times whereof he treats ... No second-rate imitator can write in this way; no coarse scene-painter can charm us with an allusion so delicate and perfect. But what bitter satire – what relentless dissection of diseased subjects! Well – and this too is right – or would be right if the savage surgeon did not seem so fiercely pleased with his work. Thackeray likes to discover an ulcer or an aneurism; he has pleasure in putting his cruel knife or probe into quivering, living flesh. Thackeray would not like all the world to be good; no great satirist would like Society to be perfect.

As usual – he is unjust to women – quite unjust: there is hardly any punishment he does not deserve for making Lady Castlewood peep through a key-hole, listen at a door and be jealous of a boy and a milkmaid.

Many other things I noticed that – for my part – grieved and exasperated me as

I read – but then again came passages so true – so deeply thought – so tenderly felt – one could not help forgiving and admiring.

Interestingly, in the light of her own reluctance to treat social issues in her novels, Charlotte added a cautionary note. 'I wish he could be told not to care so much for dwelling on the political or religious intrigues of the times. Thackeray, in his heart, does not value political or religious intrigue of any age or date."[15] Charlotte had made the same criticism of Harriet Martineau's *Oliver Weld* – 'I wish she had kept off theology' – and this seems to reflect her own disillusionment with politics. The girl who had once written with breathless fervour about the emancipation of Catholics was now a cynical and uninterested observer, telling Ellen Nussey, 'I am amused at the interest you take in politics – don't expect to rouse me – to me all ministries and all oppositions seem to be pretty much alike D'Israeli was factious as Leader of the Opposition – Lord J Russel[l] is going to be factious now that he has stepped into D'I's shoes – Confound them all."[16] Perhaps as a result of her disillusionment with Branwell, Charlotte's childhood enthusiasm for politics had gone the same way as her childhood enthusiasm for war.

Despite everyone's efforts on her behalf, Charlotte did not get better. She had hoped to slip home from Brookroyd without informing the Haworth doctor, but someone had seen her arrive at Keighley station and told Mr Ruddock who promptly 'came blustering in' and 'was actually cross' that she had not written to him immediately. He tried to insist on her resuming a course of quinine tonics which she was convinced disagreed with her and then, just as suddenly, contradicted himself and prescribed something else. It was no wonder that Charlotte wrote despairingly to Ellen, 'I wish I knew better what to think of this man's skill. He seems to stick like a leech: I thought I should have done with him when I came home."[17] Ellen tried to persuade her to come with her on an extended visit to Sussex where her friend, Mary Gorham, was about to be married, but Charlotte was adamant. 'I tell you now that unless \want of/ health should absolutely compel me to give up work and leave home (which I trust and hope will not be the case) I certainly shall not think of going.' Besides, she added, somewhat bitterly, 'You can never want me less than when in Sussex surrounded by amusement and friends."[18] Miss Wooler added her own invitation, but Charlotte was equally firm: 'Your kind note holds out a strong temptation, but one that must be resisted', she told her, adding by way of explanation,

From home I must not go unless health or some cause equally imperative render a change necessary. For nearly four months now (i.e. since I first became ill) I have not put pen to paper – my work has been lying untouched and my faculties have been rusting for want of exercise; further relaxation is out of the question and I will not permit myself to think of it.

It was a useful excuse but somewhat unfair to the remarkably patient George

Smith to add, 'My publisher groans over my long delays; I am sometimes provoked to check the expression of his impatience with short and crusty answers.'[19]

Charlotte set to with a will and by 29 March 1852, six weeks after her return from Brookroyd, she had completed her draft of the first volume of *Villette* and began to make a fair copy of it for her publishers. The manuscript bears striking evidence of her state of mind during its composition. The first three chapters, which concern the child Paulina and had been conceived possibly as long ago as January 1850, were written up with scarcely any revision. The remainder of the volume, written in fits and starts but mainly since Charlotte's visit to London in the summer of 1851, contains an average of three emendations per page. This suggests that Charlotte had toiled over the rough drafts, working and reworking them until she was satisfied before copying them up; it confirms the slowness of her rate of composition and the fact that, unlike with *Jane Eyre*, or even sections of *Shirley*, she had not been caught up and driven by her imagination. Only the last chapter, describing the nightmare long vacation Lucy Snowe spends virtually alone in the school at Villette, bears evidence of considerable revision.[20] Here Charlotte was drawing on her own experience of the summer vacation at the Pensionnat Heger in 1843, which, as in the novel, drove her to a Catholic church where she made a confession; but more painfully, it impressed upon her the solitude of her current existence.

My heart almost died within me; miserable longings strained its chords. How long were the September days! How silent, how lifeless! How vast and void seemed the desolate premises! How gloomy the forsaken garden – gray now with the dust of a town-summer departed. Looking forward at the commencement of those eight weeks, I hardly knew how I was to live to the end. My spirits had long been gradually sinking; now that the prop of employment was withdrawn, they went down fast. Even to look forward was not to hope: the dumb future spoke no comfort, offered no promise, gave no inducement to bear present evil in reliance on future good.[21]

For a while Charlotte stuck to her task. More invitations to go from home were received and declined with firmness. Mrs Gaskell was hoping for a visit to Manchester some time in the late spring or summer and Mrs Gore, the novelist who had tried so hard to meet Charlotte during her visit to London the previous June, wrote to enquire if she was coming up to Town again this year.[22] Both were told that she had no intention of leaving home until her book was completed, but the summer months stretched before her like an abyss. No visits from home, at her own insistence; a reduction in contact with Ellen, who departed for Sussex at the end of May and did not return till the beginning of October; silence from India where James Taylor, nursing his rejection like a festering wound, could not resume correspondence on terms of friendship alone; worst of all, a falling off in the number of letters from Cornhill, where George Smith and William Smith Williams, overwhelmed by work, were unaware that Charlotte would interpret their failure to write regularly as an expression of their 'bitter disappointment ... at my having no work ready for this season'.[23]

At home there was little to distract her. The Easter celebrations in Haworth passed her by unremarked though they must have increased her domestic duties. The Reverend William Cartman, Headmaster of the Grammar School at Skipton, came to preach two sermons on Easter Sunday which helped to raise funds for the recent improvements and repairs to the church which Patrick had carried out. In the afternoon there was an unusual funeral in the church when the brethren of the Keighley District of the Ancient Order of Foresters turned out in force to accompany the body of James Greenwood, the constable of Morton, to its final resting place in the churchyard. The following day, Easter Monday, was the fourth annual meeting of the Haworth Mechanics' Institute, held in the National School room, where, ironically, one of the greatest novelists of the day was probably one of the anonymous ladies who were thanked for providing the excellent repast.[24]

Try as she might Charlotte could not settle down into a regular habit of writing. As always, this had the effect of bringing on the vicious cycle of depression and consequent poor health. Mary Taylor, though far away in New Zealand and several months behind with all the news from home, nevertheless had her finger on Charlotte's pulse when she wrote that April. 'It is really melancholy that now, in the prime of life in the flush of your hard earned prosperity you can't be well! Did not Miss Martineau improve you? If she did why not try her & her plan again? But I suppose if you had hope & energy to try, you wd be well.'[25] Charlotte was indeed bereft of both hope and energy; without them, writing was a chore. While Mary was penning this letter, Charlotte was just receiving her previous one, which informed her of the death from consumption, on 27 December 1851, of Mary's cousin and close companion, Ellen, with whom she had set up shop in Wellington. Charlotte read Mary's letter with searing pain: it 'wrung my heart so – in its simple strong, truthful emotion – I have only ventured to read it once. It ripped up half-scarred wounds with terrible force – the death-bed was just the same – breath failing &c.' Almost worse than this was Mary's voicing of one of Charlotte's greatest fears for herself, that she should 'in her dreary solitude become "a stern, harsh, selfish woman" – this fear struck home – again and again I have felt it for myself – and what is my position – to Mary's?'[26]

In the end, Charlotte gave up the unequal struggle and decided to take a short holiday away from home. She had two excuses for breaking her self-imposed prohibition. Mr Ruddock had obligingly pronounced that a trip southwards (to Sussex, for instance) might be enervating, but recommended a visit to Scarborough or Bridlington as being likely to brace and strengthen his patient; and she had persuaded herself that she had 'a sad duty' to perform in visiting Anne's grave at Scarborough for the first time in the three years that had passed since her death.[27] The idea of staying in Scarborough itself was altogether too painful to contemplate, so Charlotte decided to return to the lodgings at Filey, where she had stayed with Ellen after Anne's death. Knowing that Ellen would be annoyed that she had chosen the east Yorkshire coast in preference to Sussex, she waited till Ellen set off on her travels before making her own way to Filey, arriving within a day or two of the anniversary of Anne's death. From there she wrote defensively to Ellen. 'I am at Filey utterly alone. Do not be angry. The step is right.'[28]

To her father, Charlotte wrote a long and altogether more chatty letter. He had just recovered from his annual spring bout of bronchitis and Charlotte was anxious to put on a brave front for him and write a cheerful letter to keep up his spirits. 'On the whole I get on very well here –', she told him,

but I have not bathed yet as I am told it is much too cold and too early in the season. The Sea is very grand. Yesterday it was a somewhat unusually high tide – and I stood about an hour on the cliffs yesterday afternoon – watching the tumbling in of great tawny turbid waves – that made the whole shore white with foam and filled the air with a sound hollower and deeper than thunder. There are so very few visitors at Filey yet – that I and a few sea-birds and fishing-boats have often the whole expanse of sea, shore and cliff to ourselves – When the tide is out – the sands are wide – long and smooth and very pleasant to walk on. When the high tides are in – not a vestige of sand remains. I saw a great dog rush into the sea yesterday – and swim and bear up against the waves like a seal – I wonder what Flossy would say to that.

On Sunday afternoon I went to a church which I should like Mr Nicholls to see. It was certainly not more than thrice the length and breadth of our passage – floored with brick – the walls green with mould – the pews painted white but the paint almost all worn off with time and decay – at one end there is a little gallery for the singers – and when these personages stood up to perform – they all turned their backs upon the congregation – and the congregation turned <u>their</u> backs on the pulpit and parson – The < ludi > effect of this manoeuvre was so ludicrous – I could hardly help laughing – had Mr Nicholls been there – he certainly would have laughed out.[29]

Charlotte also made one of her exceptionally rare comments on local affairs, knowing that it was a matter that would interest her father deeply. Richard Shackleton Butterfield, a hard-nosed Liberal Free-trader from Keighley, had taken a mill in Haworth where he employed his weavers at the lowest possible rates and obliged them to work the two-loom system, whereby one weaver had to run two looms simultaneously and, though doing the work of two men, still received only single wages. On 18 May his weavers had walked out and Richard Butterfield had taken the unusual and provocative step of applying to the magistrates' clerk at Bradford for warrants to compel them to work his system. When they refused, eight men were arrested and brought before the bench. Two of them were committed to two months hard labour at Wakefield prison for breaking their contracts before the third, Robert Redman, announced that he could prove that Butterfield regularly lowered their wages in the middle of a warp, without notice, and that weavers had been discharged in the middle of a warp for refusing to attend a second loom. When Butterfield admitted that this was true, the bench reversed its decision, discharged all the prisoners and ordered him to pay them 3/6d. each for their day's wages, declaring that the contract could not be binding on the men if it was not also binding on the master. Charlotte's famous sense of justice did not exactly rejoice on the weavers' behalf. 'I cannot help enjoying Mr Butterfield's defeat –', she told her father, 'and yet in one sense this is a bad state of things – calculated to make working-people both discontented and insubordinate.'[30]

The cheerful façade of her letter to her father hid a more unhappy truth, as she freely confessed to Miss Wooler.

The first week or ten days – I greatly feared the sea-side would not suit me – for I suffered almost constantly from head-ache and other harassing ailments; the weather too was dark, stormy and excessively – <u>bitterly</u> cold; my Solitude, under such circumstances, partook of the character of Desolation; I had some dreary evening-hours and night-vigils.[31]

To Ellen, who took a deep interest in ailments of every kind and was – with less reason – more of a hypochondriac than herself, Charlotte gave a still more detailed account of her sufferings. The 'first week or ten days' had now grown to a fortnight, during which Charlotte had 'constantly recurring pain in the right side – the right hip – just in the middle of the chest – burning and aching between the shoulders – and sick headache into the bargain –'. The real reason for her afflictions soon became clear. 'My spirits at the same time were cruelly depressed – prostrated sometimes – I feared the misery and the sufferings of last winter were all returning –'.[32]

Ellen Nussey had told her that William Wooler, Miss Wooler's eldest brother, who was a physician in Derby, recommended walking three or four hours each day for people suffering from liver complaints: 'accordingly I have walked as much as I could since I came here, and look almost as sunburnt and weather-beaten as a fisherman or a bathing-woman with being out in the open air'. On one such occasion, she had set off to walk to Filey Brig but had been frightened back by two cows; on another she had braved the elements and been sea-bathing – 'it seemed to do me good'.[33] Her most important task, which probably accounted for her poor spirits and health at the beginning of her holiday, was completed within a few days of her arrival.

On 4 June she travelled over to Scarborough to visit Anne's grave. The trauma of the visit was somewhat lessened by her irritation on discovering that there were five errors in the inscription on the gravestone. The fact that she had to order the stone to be refaced and relettered was a justification for the unhappy pilgrimage – one that Charlotte never repeated.[34]

Almost despite herself, the change of air and scene at Filey did Charlotte good. During the last two weeks her health improved dramatically and she seems to have thrown off the last of the lingering ill effects of the mercury poisoning. Consequently her spirits also improved, though her work 'stood obstinately still': 'certainly a torpid liver makes torpid brains:' she told Miss Wooler, 'no spirit moves me'. She had, however, learnt to be philosophical. 'My labours as you call them', she informed Ellen who was also anxiously enquiring as to her progress, 'stand in abeyance and I cannot hurry them – I must take my own time – however long that time may be.'[35]

She returned home at the end of June to find that Martha had carried out the annual spring clean in her absence and that the local painter, John Hudson, had painted all the windows, gates, doors, waterspouts and watertubs:[36] the parsonage therefore looked bright and clean inside and out. Everyone was well and there was even an amusing letter from Miss Martineau waiting for her which described how she had received a visitation from Joe Taylor and his family at Ambleside under the plea of being Charlotte's friends. Charlotte could not decide whether to be annoyed at Joe Taylor's presumption and inconsistency – he having railed against Lord John Manners and Mr Smythe for their 'insolence' in calling on Charlotte on a similar plea – or to laugh at Harriet Martineau's assessment of the little party. 'She terms A. "a tranquil little Dutchwoman."', Charlotte relayed to Ellen. 'Joe's organ of combativeness and contradiction amused and amazed her: she liked the baby best of the lot.'[37]

The little girl, Emily Martha, born the previous autumn, had been the subject of immense parental anxiety as she had been weak and sickly from birth. Perhaps because she cried at every new face, she was known as 'Tim', short for 'Timon', the misanthrope.[38] Charlotte's sympathy had been stretched to breaking point by Amelia's understandable obsession with her child and her frequent outpourings of woe on its behalf. Exasperation – 'I have had many little notes (whereof I answer about 1 in three) ... Self & child the sole all absorbing topics' – was mingled with sarcasm: 'I don't know what that dear Mrs Joe T— will make of \her/ little one in the end: between port-wine and calomel and Mr Bennet and Mr Anderson – I should not like to be in its socks.'[39] When the baby was subjected to a rigorous water treatment to restore its health, even Patrick was driven to comment that 'if that child dies, its parents ought to be tried for infanticide'![40] All this provided fruitful material for *Villette*: Ginevra Fanshawe (whose name had been changed from Amelia in the manuscript) became an obsessive mother, her letters on the subject of her son's childhood illnesses a 'perfect shout of affliction' containing the accusation that Lucy Snowe did not know 'what it was to be a mother'. These echoed Amelia's own cry to Ellen: '<u>You</u> never were a Mother', which Charlotte tartly described as 'really theatrical and entirely superfluous'.[41] However irritating Amelia's weakness might be in real life, it provided splendid fodder for Charlotte's fiction.

For a couple of weeks after her return, Charlotte worked steadily at the second volume of *Villette*, but before she could get fully into the flow of writing again, Patrick suffered a minor stroke.

He was suddenly attacked with acute inflammation of the eye. Mr Ruddock was sent for and after he had examined him – he called me into another room, and said that Papa's pulse was bounding at 150 per minute – that there was a strong pressure of blood on the brain – that in short the symptoms were decidedly apoplectic –

'Active measures' were taken and, by the next day, Patrick's pulse had been reduced to ninety. The partial paralysis which had also afflicted him disappeared completely within a couple of days, but his eye remained badly inflamed for nearly a month. This was a cause of acute anxiety to him as his worst fear was that he might again lose his sight. His spirits varied, sinking badly whenever he suffered any sort of relapse, and then he became short-tempered and irritable.[42]

The stroke could hardly have come at a worse time from Patrick's point of view, occurring only a few days before the arrival in Haworth of William Ranger, another inspector from the General Board of Health. He had been sent in response to a petition, got up by Richard Shackleton Butterfield, and signed by the leading inhabitants and property owners in the township, alleging malpractice in the elections to the local Board of Health, which had recommended the improvements to the water supply. Confined to bed, Patrick could not make his representations to the inspector, who, falling prey to the self-interest of the agitators, recommended that the property qualification for election to the local board should be raised from five to ten pounds – a move that, as Patrick pointed out – would disenfranchise all but ten houses in the township, five of them inns. It would also, of course, prevent the improvements being carried through, as the property owners were unwilling to bear the extra costs on their water rates. It was not surprising that Patrick and Charlotte had been pleased at Butterfield's defeat in the courts over his striking workmen.[43] The whole sorry saga would drag on and the poor would continue to die of preventable disease for a further six years.

The stress of this affair had probably contributed to Patrick's stroke. Once again, Charlotte found herself trying to write a book while nursing her father. Not surprisingly, the 'severe shock' and anxiety caused by this sudden and unexpected proof of her father's frailty brought on a bout of Charlotte's sick headaches. Nevertheless, she managed, with the help of Martha in the house and Arthur Bell Nicholls in the parish. By the end of August Patrick's excellent constitution had prevailed and he was looking forward to taking up his duties once more.[44]

The second volume of *Villette* progressed slowly. A solicitous letter from George Smith, enquiring after her father's health and sending a copy of the new single-volume edition of *Shirley*, produced an unusually subdued response. Without any of the flippant references to the 'Man-of-business' which she would once have made, she somewhat wearily lectured him on over-working. On the new edition she could only manage an elliptical ' "Shirley" looks very respectable in her new attire', instead of her usual profuse wishes for her publishers to profit by its success.[45]

Only a guarded letter from Ellen, who was still in Sussex and, as usual, reading more into the attentions of Mary Gorham's brother than was probably intended, succeeded in provoking Charlotte to a passionate outburst.

Perhaps you think that as I generally write with some reserve – you ought to do the same. My reserve, however, has its foundation not in design, but in necessity – I am silent because I have literally nothing to say. I might indeed repeat over and over again that my life is a pale blank and often a very weary burden – and that the Future sometimes appals me – but what end could be answered by such repetition except to weary you and enervate myself?

The evils that now and then wring a groan from my heart – lie in position – not that I am a single woman and likely to remain a single woman – but because I am a lonely woman and likely to be lonely. But it cannot be helped and therefore imperatively must be borne – and borne too with as few words about it as may be.[46]

A month later, on the fourth anniversary of Branwell's death, she wrote miserably to Ellen, wishing that she could invite her to Haworth but knowing that she should not do so until her work was finished: 'But oh Nell! I don't get on – I feel fettered – incapable – sometimes very low.' Her liver was playing her up again, 'it hinders me in working – depresses both power and tone of feeling', and even the death of the family hero, the Duke of Wellington, at the grand old age of eighty-three, failed to rouse her to any expression of grief.[47]

Despite the fact that her depression was gradually bringing her work to a grinding halt, Charlotte persevered in her refusal to go from home. Miss Wooler had written in response to a suggestion from Charlotte earlier in the year that she might join her former headmistress at Scarborough in the autumn. 'It would be pleasant at the seaside this fine warm weather,' Charlotte replied wistfully, 'and I should dearly like to be there with you; to such a treat, however, I do not now look forward at all.'[48] A month later, William

Forster and his wife 'made another of their sudden calls here', bringing with them a Miss Dixon, who turned out to be a distant relative of Charlotte's friends from Brussels. They tried to carry Charlotte back with them to Rawdon but this was one invitation she had no difficulty in refusing.[49]

At the beginning of October, Ellen returned home, having spent over four months with the Gorhams in Sussex, more than half that time after the marriage and departure on honeymoon of her friend. If, as seems likely from mysterious allusions such as to her visit bringing 'future benefit in more ways than one', Ellen had hoped that Mary's brother would propose to her, she was once again to be disappointed.[50] Hers was a classic case of always the bridesmaid, never the blushing bride.

Ellen's return to Yorkshire after such a long absence made it impossible for Charlotte to resist her longing to see her old friend again. Fortunately, her father was so concerned about her ailing health and spirits that he urged her to invite Ellen to stay, so she was able to lay the blame for breaking her resolution squarely on him. 'Papa expresses so strong a wish that I should ask you to come', she began her letter to Ellen, 'and I feel some little refreshment so absolutely necessary myself that I really must beg you to come to Haworth for one single week.' Somewhat ruefully, she added, 'I thought I would persist in denying myself till I had done my work – but I find it won't do – the matter refuses to progress – and this excessive solitude presses too heavily – So let me see your dear face Nell just for one reviving week.'[51]

Ellen arrived at Haworth on 15 October and stayed, as Charlotte had insisted, 'one little week'. She brought with her a good-sized parcel from Miss Wooler which, on opening, Charlotte was delighted to find contained some winter chemises. The gift could not have been more opportune, as Charlotte stood in urgent need of them and had been too preoccupied with her work to buy or make new ones herself. The immediate lifting of her spirits which Ellen's companionship always brought was apparent in her chatty letter to Miss Wooler thanking her for the gift. Nevertheless, she pointed out, she had not allowed Ellen to stay longer than was necessary. 'I would not have her any longer – for I am disgusted with myself and my delays – and consider it was a weak yielding to temptation in me to send for her at all – but in truth my spirits were getting low – prostrate sometimes and she has done me inexpressible good.'[52]

That good was self-evident. The day after Ellen's departure, Charlotte 'fell to business' and cracked on with her work. Three days later, with 'the welcome mood still ... decently existent, and my eyes consequently excessively tired with scribbling', she scrawled a note to Ellen and another to Smith Williams. The latter was so unusually brief and almost peremptory in tone that it is worth quoting in full.

Octbr 26 1852

My dear Sir

In sending a return-box of books to Cornhill – I take the opportunity of enclosing 2 Vols. of M.S. the third Vol. is now so near completion that I trust, if all be well, I may calculate on its being ready in the course of two or three weeks. My wish is that the book should be published without Author's name.

I shall feel obliged if you will intimate the safe arrival of the manuscript –

Believe me
Yours Sincerely
C Brontë

W. S. Williams Esqr.[53]

The abruptness of this note cannot simply be explained away by the fact that Charlotte was tired after several days of continuous writing – she had, after all, managed a lengthier and inconsequential letter to Ellen the same day. The absence of all her former friendliness and, indeed, sense of intimacy, suggests rather that Charlotte had taken offence at Smith Williams' long silence. Unless the letters are missing, it would seem he had not written to her since July, and then only in response to a letter from her asking him questions which needed replies. Prior to that, Charlotte's last letters written in her old friendly style dated as far back as the beginning of April. Charlotte seems to have persuaded herself that the cessation of the correspondence was an expression of Cornhill's 'bitter disappointment' at her failure to produce a new book that season.[54]

Charlotte's haughty demand for anonymity in the publication of her next work was astonishingly naive. Smith, Elder & Co. might have been prepared to offer this to Harriet Martineau, who had not published a novel for over twelve years, but it was hardly to be expected that they would do the same for the eagerly awaited new work by Currer Bell. Indeed, they were counting on the announcements to achieve large sales. Smith Williams was concerned enough about this request to take the letter to his employer and it was George Smith himself who replied to Charlotte, forcefully putting the publisher's point of view. To him, Charlotte was prepared to be more conciliatory and to reveal the anxiety which lay behind her request.

As to the anonymous publication – I have this to say. If the with-holding of the author's name should tend materially to injure the publisher's interest – to interfere with booksellers' orders, &c. I would not press the point; but if no such detriment is contingent – I should be most thankful for the sheltering shadow of an incognito. I seem to dread the advertisements – the large lettered 'Currer Bell's New Novel' or 'New Work by the Author of "Jane Eyre." ' These, however, I feel well enough are the transcendentalisms of a retired wretch – and must not be intruded in the way of solid considerations; so you must speak frankly.[55]

An unspoken consideration, which must have weighed just as heavily as fear of disappointing the critics, was that this would be Charlotte's first novel to appear before a public to whom her true identity and much of the circumstances of her life had been revealed. Everyone would know exactly who had written *Villette*: the work would be judged by what people knew of her and, if the reaction to *Shirley* was anything to go by, it would be examined with an eye to identifying the originals of her characters. This would be a major embarrassment to her, for it was not difficult to recognize Charlotte herself in the lonely, watchful and caustic Lucy Snowe or, more importantly, George Smith in the handsome Dr John Graham Bretton.

Several years before, when Ellen Nussey had claimed to recognize all the characters in *Shirley*, except the two heroines, Charlotte had written a crushing response.

You are not to suppose any of the characters in Shirley intended as literal portraits – it would not suit the rules of Art – nor my own feelings to write in that style – we only suffer reality to <u>suggest</u> – never to <u>dictate</u> – the heroines are abstractions and the heros also –[56]

From her own references to, for instance, the curates, by their fictitious names, however, it is clear that Charlotte herself did not believe this statement, though it came as an immense surprise to her that the originals of her characters in *Shirley* should be so easily identifiable. Undoubtedly, the fear that George Smith would recognize his own portrayal and, more importantly, Charlotte's own feelings for him as expressed in the fiction, had been at least partially responsible for the paralysis which had seized her so often when writing *Villette*. There was, too, the difficulty of resolving the relationship. Should Lucy Snowe, like Jane Eyre, triumph over her richer and more beautiful rivals for Dr John's affections? If she did, would this, in effect, be a declaration of Charlotte's own hopes for her relationship with George Smith?

By the time Charlotte completed the fair copy of the first two volumes of *Villette* she had decided that this was not possible: realism must conquer fancy in fiction as it must in life. Towards the close of the second volume, therefore, she made Lucy Snowe bury Dr John's precious letters to her in the school garden, thereby symbolically declaring the end of that relationship.[57] Though she knew that Lucy and Dr John were not destined for each other, the reader – in this case George Smith himself – was left with no such certainty. Charlotte's trepidation in sending the manuscript was even more intense than usual: would George Smith recognize himself and, if he did, what would he make of the fictitious life Charlotte had planned for him? She had gone to greater pains than ever before to disguise the character's origins, his being the only instance in all her work of one whose fictional occupation differed from his genuine one. 'You must notify honestly what you think of "Villette" when you have read it', Charlotte anxiously asked him,

I can hardly tell you how much I hunger to have some opinion besides my own, and how I have sometimes desponded and almost despaired because there was no one to whom to read a line – or of whom to ask a counsel. 'Jane Eyre' was not written under such circumstances, nor were two-thirds of 'Shirley'. I got so miserable about it, I could bear no allusion to the book – < and ha > it is not finished yet, but now – I hope.

As an afterthought, she added, 'Remember to be an honest critic of "Villette" and tell Mr Williams to be unsparing – not that I am likely to alter anything – but I want to know his impressions and yours.'[58]

There can be no doubt that George Smith immediately recognized his own portrait. Had he not discovered his own character, there was plenty of other material to point it out to him: his own mother appearing as Mrs Bretton, the actress Rachel as Vashti, even the incident when he had calmly escorted his party to safety when a fire broke out in the theatre, which he had described in a letter to Charlotte, was faithfully reproduced. 'Currer Bell's' visits to his home in London had proved even more fruitful than he had expected.

Charlotte did not have long to wait for Cornhill's reaction to the first two volumes of *Villette*. Like most of her other victims, though perhaps with greater cause, George Smith was not displeased to have been made fodder for her fiction. Within a week of receiving the manuscript he had read it and expressed his approval, prompting a relieved response from Charlotte. 'I feel in some degree authorized to rely on your favourable impressions', she added, 'because you are quite right where you hint disapprobation.' Charlotte was so pleased that George Smith not only approved of the book so far but had also not taken his own portrayal amiss, that something of the old gaiety which had so long been missing from her letters to him returned. Knowing that he was wise to the secret, she could play on the new pseudonyms as she had once with her own 'Currer Bell'. George Smith had evidently enquired what was to be the fate of Dr John. 'Lucy must not marry Dr John;' she declared,

he is far too youthful, handsome, bright-spirited and sweet-tempered; he is a 'curled darling' of Nature and of Fortune; he must draw a prize in Life's Lottery; his wife must be young, rich and pretty; he must be made very happy indeed. If Lucy marries anybody – it must be the Professor – a man in whom there is much to forgive – much to 'put up with.' But I am not leniently disposed towards Miss Frost – from the beginning I never intended to appoint her lines in pleasant places.[59]

The change in Lucy's surname she explained in a letter to Smith Williams.

I can hardly express what subtility of thought made me decide upon giving her a cold name; but – at first – I called her 'Lucy Snowe' (spelt with an 'e') which 'Snowe' I afterwards changed to 'Frost.' Subsequently – I rather regretted the change and wished it 'Snowe' again … A <u>cold</u> name she must have – partly – perhaps – on the 'lucus a non lucendo' – principle – partly on that of the 'fitness of things' – for she has about her an external coldness.

This letter to Smith Williams, written in response to his criticisms of *Villette*, was very different from her jocular letter to his superior, again reflecting her estrangement from a man who had once been her closest confidant. Where she had freely admitted George Smith's criticisms, she stubbornly stood her ground against Smith Williams. 'The 3rd vol. may perhaps do away with some of the objections – others will remain in force', she told him.

I do not think the interest of the story culminates anywhere to the degree you would wish. What climax there is – does not come on till near the conclusion – and even then – I doubt whether the regular novel-reader will consider 'the agony piled sufficiently high' – (as the Americans say) or the colours dashed on to the Canvass with the proper amount of daring. Still – I fear they must be satisfied with what is offered: my palette affords no brighter tints – were I to attempt to deepen the reds or burnish the yellows – I should but botch.

Unless I am mistaken – the emotion of the book will be found to be kept throughout in tolerable subjection.[60]

One of Smith Williams' strongest objections was to the character of Lucy Snowe. Aware that it would be seen as a self-portrait of the author, he perhaps sought to soften the criticism he anticipated in the reviews by suggesting that she should give further details of Lucy's early life to explain why her nature was so warped and create greater sympathy for her. (This was, it should be remembered, on the same lines as his recommendation to Charlotte on publishing *Shirley*, when he had suggested that she should prefix a biographical notice to deflect the reviewers from personal comment which he knew would hurt her.) He received no thanks for his concern, merely a tart response.

You say that she may be thought morbid and weak unless the history of her life be more fully given. I consider that she <u>is</u> both morbid and weak at times – the character sets up no pretensions to unmixed strength – and anybody living her life would necessarily become morbid. It was no impetus of healthy feeling which urged her to the confessional for instance – it was the semi-delirium of solitary \grief and/ sickness. If, however, the book does not express all this – there must be a great fault somewhere. I might explain away a few other points but it would be too much like drawing a picture and then writing underneath the name of the object intended to be represented. We know what sort of a pencil that is which needs an ally in the pen.[61]

The example Charlotte had picked to illustrate her point, one of the most painfully autobiographical incidents in the whole novel, revealed she could be as severe to herself as she was to her fictional creations. Interestingly, one of the objects of her revision of the manuscript before sending it to Cornhill had been to remove hints as to the unhappiness of Lucy's early life. Among the deleted passages were a reference to her 'residence with kinsfolk – I do not call it <u>home</u>', a lament for 'lost affections' and a sentence beginning 'Many a solitary struggle have I had in life'.[62] Perhaps Charlotte, turning Smith Williams' point upon its head, had feared that any allusions to Lucy's early life might be taken to be purely autobiographical by the reviewers and decided that they should therefore be avoided.

The reaction at Cornhill was such as to cheer Charlotte and encourage her to proceed apace with the third volume. She even submitted 'under protest, and with a kind of ostrich-longing for concealment' to 'the advertisements and large letters', and allowed the long-delayed single-volume edition of *Shirley*, which had been printed in August with endpapers carrying notices of her new work, to be issued.[63] On 10 November, she was able to write confidently to George Smith telling him that 'should I be able to proceed with the 3rd vol. at my average rate of composition, and with no more than the average amount of interruptions – I should hope to have it ready in about three weeks'. Since she had made the same prediction two weeks earlier and had not fulfilled it, she left it to her publishers to decide whether they should begin typesetting the first two volumes before they received the third.[64]

In the event, Charlotte finished the third volume and its transcription only ten days later, sending it to George Smith on 20 November with the admonition to 'speak, as before, frankly'. The unprecedented speed with which she completed *Villette* seems to have had two causes: her knowledge that the earlier part had met with approval, even though it drew on her own relationship with George Smith, and her belief that the last volume, in which Dr John was happily married off to Paulina and Lucy Snowe was partnered with the 'crabbed Professor', could not cause offence. Having completed the task which had hung over her with such appalling effect on her health and spirits for nearly three years, she laid down her pen with quiet confidence. 'Now that "Villette" is off my hands –', she told George Smith, 'I mean to try to wait the result with calm. Conscience – if she be just – will not reproach me, for I have tried to do my best.'[65]

Four days later, Charlotte packed her bags and set off for a well-earned visit to Ellen, intending to go on from Brookroyd to spend a week at Ambleside with Harriet Martineau.[66] An invitation from Mrs Smith to stay in London, which arrived just as she was setting off, was politely deferred: 'it pleases me to have it in prospect, it is something to look forward to and to anticipate; I keep it, < something > on the principle of the school-boy who hoards his choicest piece of cake'. Her father had suggested another, more cogent, reason. It might be better to learn the fate of *Villette* at the hands of the reviewers before travelling to London. 'I would rather undergo that infliction at Haworth', Charlotte confessed, 'than in London.'[67] Another, equally compelling reason for not immediately accepting the invitation was that, as yet, there had been no response from Cornhill to the third volume of *Villette*.

Ten days after she sent off the manuscript, there was still no word. This was unheard of in all Charlotte's dealings with Smith, Elder & Co. On Wednesday, 1 December, she could contain herself no longer and wrote a brief note to George Smith. 'I am afraid – as you do not write – that the 3rd Vol. has occasioned some disappointment. It is best, however, to speak plainly about it, if it be so. I would rather at once know the worst than be kept longer in suspense.'[68] The letter prompted a response, but not the one Charlotte had expected. A bank bill arrived, containing £500 for the copyright of the novel. This in itself signified her publisher's acceptance of the work, but there was no covering note – not a single line expressing approval or disapproval. By now Charlotte was panic-stricken. She made up her mind to take the next available train to London 'to see what was the matter and what had struck my publisher mute'. Fortunately, the next morning brought a letter from George Smith: 'you have thus been spared the visitation of the unannounced and unsummoned apparition of Currer Bell in Cornhill', she told him, adding a little lecture which did not half reveal the state of anxiety to which she had been wrought. 'Inexplicable delays should be avoided when possible, for they are apt to urge those subjected to their harrassment to sudden and impulsive steps.'[69]

The reason for George Smith's silence now became apparent. He *was* unhappy with the third volume, though not enough to turn down the manuscript or demand a rewrite. What he objected to was the fact that his own character, Dr John, had almost completely dropped out of sight and that the story now pursued the growing relationship between Lucy Snowe and Monsieur Paul Emanuel. 'I must pronounce you right again, in your complaint of the transfer of interest in the 3rd vol – from one set of characters to another', Charlotte replied. 'It is not pleasant, and will probably be found as unwelcome to the reader, as it was, in a sense, compulsory upon the writer.' It would not have been possible for Charlotte to have united Lucy Snowe and Dr John in marriage: even under the apparently safe mantle of fiction there were bounds beyond which she dared not step. 'The spirit of Romance would have indicated another course, far more flowery and inviting ... but this would have been unlike Real Life, inconsistent with Truth – at variance with Probability.'[70]

George Smith, it seems, would have preferred the romantic solution. Though he undoubtedly had a sound literary case in arguing that the transfer of interest was too sudden and unexpected, there seems to have been a much more personal reason behind his disappointment. Though he continued to 'make a mystery of his "reason" ', it was clear that 'something in the third volume sticks confoundedly in his throat', so much so that nearly three weeks after the manuscript had been sent to Cornhill, Smith Williams had still not been permitted to read it. In a second letter, which Charlotte withheld from Ellen allegedly because 'so many words are scarcely legible, you would have no pleasure in reading it', George Smith made it clear that he thought the alliance between Dr John and Pauline misjudged. 'She is an odd, fascinating little puss,' he had told Charlotte in response to her question, but added 'crabbedly' that he was 'not in love with her'.[71] Was this, one cannot help wondering, a subtle suggestion that George Smith himself was in love with Charlotte Brontë? Or, at the very least, that he would have preferred her to any of the society beauties whom Charlotte was always pointing out as appropriate brides for him? Even Charlotte admitted that the fictional bride she had given him was a failure. She had aimed at making Paulina's character 'the most beautiful' in the book but she had turned out to be the weakest, 'and if this be the case – the fault lies in its wanting the germ of the <u>real</u>, in its being purely imaginary'. Was this a covert suggestion that the ideal bride for George Smith was equally illusory? The correspondence was clearly getting too near the bone for George Smith. 'He tells me … that he will answer no more questions about "Villette" ', Charlotte was obliged to tell Ellen.[72]

On 8 December, Charlotte returned home from Brookroyd. The brief visit had, as usual, proved beneficial to her though it resulted in her abandoning her plan to go on to Ambleside. Miss Wooler had also come to stay and she had joined Ellen in arguing that it was quite wrong of Charlotte to go to the house of a self-declared atheist. Under their combined pressure, she gave way, 'both my Father and my friends in this neighbourhood being so much opposed to the visit – that without giving them pain – I could not please Miss Martineau'.[73] It was her friends' opposition, however, that proved more potent than her father's. Nevertheless, even to them, Charlotte remained stout in Miss Martineau's defence. 'My dear Miss Wooler –', she wrote to her former headmistress who had returned to the attack,

I read attentively all you say about Miss Martineau: the sincerity and constancy of your solicitude touche<s> me very much; I should grieve to neglect or oppose your advice, and yet I do not feel that it would be right to give Miss Martineau up entirely … To speak the truth – my dear Miss Wooler – I believe if you were in my place, and knew Miss Martineau as I do – if you had shared with me the proofs of her rough but genuine kindliness, and had seen how she secretly suffers from abandonment, you would be the last to give her up; you would separate the sinner from the sin, and feel as if the right lay rather in quietly adhering to her in her strait – while that adherence is unfashionable and unpopular – than in turning on her your back when the world sets the example. I believe she is one of those whom opposition and desertion make obstinate in error; while patience and tolerance touch her deeply and keenly, and incline her to ask of her own heart whether the course she has been pursuing may not possibly be a faulty course.[74]

Charlotte's laudable loyalty, which may have been strengthened by fellow feeling because she herself had been ostracized by certain circles in Birstall and Dewsbury after the condemnation of *Jane Eyre*, was not to be rewarded. Miss Martineau, highly affronted that Charlotte had suggested she lost friends by publishing her infamous Atkinson letters, demanded the excision of this letter from Mrs Gaskell's biography.[75]

With no prospect of an early visit to Ambleside, Charlotte determined to accept Mrs Smith's invitation and go to London after Christmas.[76] Before she could do so, however, a domestic crisis turned her whole world upside down. On 13 December, Arthur Bell Nicholls, her father's curate for the past seven and a half years, asked her to marry him. The proposal was not entirely unexpected. 'I know not whether you have ever observed him specially – when staying here –', Charlotte wrote to Ellen,

your perception in these matters is generally quick enough – <u>too</u> quick – I have sometimes thought – yet as you never said anything – I restrained my own dim misgivings – which could not claim the sure guide of vision. What Papa has seen or guessed – I will not inquire – though I may conjecture. He has minutely noticed all Mr Nicholls's low spirits – all his threats of expatriation – all his symptoms of impaired health – noticed them with little sympathy and much indirect sarcasm. On Monday evening – Mr N was here to tea. I vaguely felt – without clearly seeing – as without seeing, I have felt for some time – the meaning of his constant looks – and strange, feverish restraint. After tea – I withdrew to the dining-room as usual. As usual – Mr N sat with Papa till between eight & nine o'clock. I then heard him open the parlour door as if going. I expected the clash of the front-door – He stopped in the passage: he tapped: like lightning it flashed on me what was coming. He entered – he stood before me. What his words were – you can guess, his manner – you can hardly realize – nor can I forget it – Shaking from head to foot, looking deadly pale, speaking low, vehemently yet with difficulty – he made me for the first time feel what it costs a man to declare affection where he doubts response. The spectacle of one ordinarily so statue-like – thus trembling, stirred, and overcome gave me a kind of < shock > strange shock. He spoke of sufferings he had borne for months – of sufferings he could endure no longer – and craved leave for some hope. I could only entreat him to leave me then and promise a reply on the morrow. I asked him if he had spoken to Papa. He said – he dared not – I think I half-led, half put him out of the room. When he was gone I immediately went to Papa – and told him what had taken place. Agitation and Anger disproportionate to the occasion ensued – if I had <u>loved</u> Mr N and heard such epithets applied to him as were used – it would have transported me past my patience – as it was – my blood boiled with a sense of injustice – but Papa worked himself into a state not to be trifled with – the veins on his temples started up like whip-cord – and his eyes became suddenly blood-shot – I made haste to promise that Mr Nicholls should on the morrow have a distinct refusal.

I wrote yesterday and got this note. There is no need to add to this statement any comment – Papa's vehement antipathy to the bare thought of any one thinking of me as a wife – and Mr Nicholls' distress – both give me pain. Attachment to Mr N— you are aware I never entertained – but the poignant pity inspired by his state on Monday evening – by the hurried revelation of his sufferings for many months – is something galling and irksome. That he cared something for me – and wanted me to care for him – I have long suspected – but I did not know the degree or strength of his feelings.[77]

Charlotte's relations with Mr Nicholls had undergone a sea-change in recent times. From holding him in cold contempt, making little distinction between him and the other curates whom she had so viciously lampooned in *Shirley*, she had begun to refer to him in a more kindly fashion. The previous summer, in 1851, on the eve of his departure for a holiday in Ireland, he had invited himself to tea and behaved 'somewhat peculiarly for him – being extremely good – mild and uncontentious'.[78] This summer, for the first time, she had included good wishes to Mr Nicholls, as well as to Tabby and Martha, in her letters from Filey to Patrick, suggesting that she was beginning to see him as a member of the household circle. Her comments on the little church at Filey, which she would have liked him to see and which would have made him laugh out loud, indicate that their earlier 'cold, far-away sort of civility' had given way to a friendlier relationship.[79] No doubt, too, his willing assumption of Patrick's duties after his stroke had made a favourable impression and led to increased intimacy.

Arthur Bell Nicholls is a shadowy figure, not least because he deliberately sought retirement. In itself, Charlotte's fame meant nothing to him: it was the woman he loved, not the authoress. It was typical of his often overlooked sensitivity, however, that he waited until she had finished *Villette* before declaring the passion which, he knew, would throw the parsonage into disarray. A big, tall man, with a strong square face, framed by dark hair and formidably long side whiskers, Arthur Nicholls had something of the Rochester physique. Like Rochester, too, he was a man of hidden depths, as his emotional outburst proved. Though frequently portrayed as something of a bigot in religious matters and stern, harsh and unbending in person, there are glimpses of him which show him in a much more favourable light. A former pupil at the church school in Stanbury, which had been his particular responsibility, remembered how he used to visit the school twice a week, accompanied by his brown retriever and always bringing sweets for the children. Another little girl recalled how he would place her on the back of the dog, Plato, which was a cross between a Newfoundland bitch and a water spaniel, and ride her across the fields, to her home, from the parsonage. An even more delightful picture is conjured up by the Haworth man who regularly accompanied Mr Nicholls up on to the moors for trout-tickling expeditions: 'he was fearful fond of going to Smith Bank', the sportsman recounted, 'and we gate mony a lot. We'd no rods or lines … but just put our hands under them as they lay under the stones in the pools and laiked [played] with them, and when we gate hod on them we threw them as far as we could into t'field'.[80]

The fact that Mr Nicholls had the common touch did him no favours in Patrick's eyes. He was furious with his curate, not only because he had not sought Patrick's permission before proposing, which suggested subterfuge on Mr Nicholls' part, but also for his presumption in daring to propose to Charlotte. 'I am afraid also that Papa thinks a little too much about his want of money; he says the match would be a degradation – that I should be throwing myself away – that he expects me, if I marry at all – to do very differently; in short – his manner of viewing the subject – is – on the whole, far from being one in which I can sympathize.' Patrick could not bear the thought that his brilliant and successful daughter, who might, with his approval, have had James Taylor, should succumb to the common lot of clergymen's daughters and marry her father's curate. He treated Mr Nicholls with 'a hardness not to be bent – and a contempt not to be propitiated', refusing even to speak to him and communicating with him only by letter.[81]

Patrick's overreaction to the whole situation was perhaps the one thing calculated to drive Charlotte into Mr Nicholls' arms. Her sense of justice would not allow her suitor's motives and character to be unfairly impugned. When Patrick wrote 'a most cruel note' to his curate, who was horrifying his landlady, Martha Brown's mother, by refusing his meals, Charlotte 'felt that the blow must be parried, and I thought it right to accompany the pitiless despatch by a line to the effect that – while Mr N. must never expect me to reciprocate the feeling he had expressed – yet at the same time – I wished to disclaim participation in sentiments calculated to give him pain'. She also 'exhorted him to maintain his courage and spirits', an expression which Mr Nicholls may have interpreted as evidence that all was not yet lost. In any event, having offered his resignation, he then attempted to take it back again. This Patrick would not allow, unless he had a written promise 'never again to broach the obnoxious subject either to him or to me'.[82] Torn between wanting to stay so that he would not lose touch with Charlotte and refusing to give a promise he could not keep, Mr Nicholls found himself in an impossible situation. As everyone lined up behind Patrick in condemning and vilifying the curate, Charlotte was increasingly drawn to his defence: 'but I am sorry for one other person whom nobody pities but me', she told Ellen,

Martha is bitter against him: John Brown says he should like to shoot him. They don't understand the nature of his feelings – but I see now what they are. Mr N is one of those who attach themselves to very few whose sensations are close and deep – like an underground stream, running strong but in a narrow channel. He continues restless and ill – he carefully performs the occasional duty – but does not come near the church, procuring a substitute every Sunday.[83]

Mistreated and misunderstood, Mr Nicholls was suddenly a much more interesting person to Charlotte than the quiet clergyman conscientiously but unremarkably performing his parish duties.

With passions in Church Lane running so high and the situation apparently irresolvable, Charlotte was glad to have the opportunity to run away and allow events to unfold in her absence. Gratefully taking up Mrs Smith's invitation to stay at Gloucester Terrace, Charlotte left Haworth early in the morning on 5 January 1853, and arrived in Euston Square at quarter past four that afternoon.[84]

It says something for the state of affairs at home that Charlotte could find sanctuary with George Smith and his mother, despite her anxieties about their reaction to their portrayals in *Villette*. Having come to some sort of an understanding with George Smith by letter, it was his mother whom Charlotte found most difficulty in facing. Her kind letter inviting Charlotte to London had provoked a regretful comment: 'I almost wish I could still look on that kindness just as I used to do: it was very pleasant to me once.'[85] The feeling which had gradually crept over her during the last year, that the kindness of her friends at Cornhill was not personal but merely a business arrangement to encourage her to produce another book, had extended to include Mrs Smith, her publisher's partisan mother.

Writing to Ellen almost a week after her arrival, Charlotte announced, 'I have not much to tell you – nor is it likely I shall have – I do not mean to go out much or see many people.' Sir James Kay Shuttleworth had been as insistent as usual that he should be informed when she was in town so that he could escort her round, but she had no intention of letting him know that she was there until she was nearly at the end of her stay. 'I really so much dread the sort of excited fuss into which he puts himself – that I only wish to see just as much of him as civility exacts.' Mrs Smith and her daughters appeared 'pretty much as usual', but Charlotte was both startled and concerned to see the change in George Smith:

hard work is telling early – both his complexion, his countenance and the very lines of his features are altered – it is rather the remembrance of what he was than the fact of what he is which can warrant the picture I have been accustomed to give of him. One feels pained to see a physical alteration of this kind – yet I feel glad and thankful that it is <u>merely</u> physical: as far as I can judge mind and manners have undergone no deterioration – rather, I think, the contrary.[86]

During Charlotte's visit, she was to witness him going through one of his periodic stints of excessive work, and was later to look back on 'that week of over-work which occurred when I was in London' as 'a thing not to be forgotten'.[87]

From the Smiths Charlotte was at last able to glean some news of James Taylor. They reported that he was getting on well in India, where his probity and usefulness were held in esteem, but that the hot climate was playing havoc with his temper and nerves: 'it seems he is bad to live with – I never catch a pleasant word about him', she reported to Ellen, no doubt privately blessing the providence that had broken off their relationship.[88]

During this visit to London, which was to last a month, Charlotte passed her time very quietly, having the excuse of needing to correct the proofs of *Villette* to turn down invitations. She did make some excursions, however, and the fact that these were chosen by herself, rather than her hosts, accounted for their unusual nature. 'Being allowed to have my own choice of sights this time –', she told Ellen, 'I selected rather the <u>real</u> than the <u>decorative</u> side of Life.' She visited two prisons, the modern Pentonville and the ancient Newgate, where she got into trouble with the warders for taking pity on and talking to a poor girl 'with an interesting face, and an expression of the deepest misery' who had killed her illegitimate child. She was also taken to see the financial centres of the City, the Bank of England and the Exchange, to the General Post Office and the offices of *The Times* newspaper and to both the Foundling Hospital for orphans and Bethlehem Hospital, better known as Bedlam, the institution for the insane. 'Mrs S— and her daughters are – I believe – a little amazed at my gloomy tastes', Charlotte told Ellen with some amusement, 'but I take no notice.'[89]

Charlotte's sudden and unprecedented interest in matters of social welfare may have been prompted by a nagging feeling of guilt. The 'social novel' was very much in vogue, as Charlotte had recognized when sending George Smith the manuscript of *Villette*, telling him, somewhat apologetically:

You will see that 'Villette' touches on no matter of public interest. I cannot write books handling the topics of the day – it is of no use trying. Nor can I write a book for its moral – Nor can I take up a philanthropic scheme though I honour Philanthropy – And voluntarily and sincerely veil my face before such a mighty subject as that handled in Mrs Beecher Stowe's work – 'Uncle Tom's Cabin'. To manage these great matters rightly they must be long and practically studied – their bearings known intimately and their evils felt genuinely – they must not be taken up as a business-matter and a trading-speculation.[90]

She took up a similar theme in her reply to Mrs Gaskell, whose work was imbued with her concern for the social evils of the day. Mrs Gaskell had written to plead for a delay in the publication of *Villette*, so that it would not come out at exactly the same time as her own new novel, *Ruth*, and attract invidious comparisons in the reviews. Charlotte readily persuaded George Smith to defer the publication, adding, ' "Villette" has indeed no right to push itself before "Ruth". There is a goodness, a philanthropic purpose – a social use in the latter, to which the former cannot for an instant pretend'.[91] Charlotte's visits to the prisons and hospitals were perhaps an attempt to remedy what she obviously saw as an omission in her work.

The publication of *Villette* was deferred until 28 January 1853. 'I daresay – arrange as we may – we shall not be able wholly to prevent comparisons', Charlotte had written to Mrs Gaskell, 'it is the nature of some critics to be invidious: but we need not care: we can set them at defiance: they <u>shall</u> not make us foes: they <u>shall</u> not mingle with our mutual feelings one taint of jealousy: there is my hand on that: I know you will give clasp for clasp.'[92] On the day before and the day of publication, Charlotte busied herself in sending out inscribed copies to various friends. Ellen Nussey received one, as did Miss Wooler, inscribed 'from her affectionate pupil'. John Forbes, the expert on consumptive diseases who had advised her on Anne's illness and had just escorted her round the Bethlehem Hospital, was also given a copy inscribed 'in acknowledgment of Kindness'.[93] Another recipient was Sir James Kay Shuttleworth, whom she had been unable to avoid and who had been in constant attendance during the last week of her visit. 'I believe the gift perplexed him a little', Charlotte reported with malicious glee to Mrs Gaskell,

it seemed to imply that of course he would read the book. He took great pains to put into words a neat apology for not giving himself that specially congenial pleasure. I hope some kind-hearted domestic has long ere this 'sided' the volumes out of his reach – thus enabling him to sink into oblivion of their existence.[94]

Five days after the publication, before the first reviews appeared, Charlotte returned home. The visit had been as quiet as she could have wished and yet there was a lingering sense of disappointment. 'My visit has on the whole passed pleasantly enough with some sorrowful impressions', she enigmatically reported to Ellen. One can only surmise that *Villette* had erected a barely perceptible but nevertheless insuperable barrier between herself and the Smiths. The knowledge that they had unwittingly provided the raw material for her novel inevitably created a feeling of mutual unease. Perhaps the long hours George Smith spent in his office were an attempt to avoid seeing too much of her.[95]

It was hardly surprising that Charlotte was unable to face the prospect of returning home alone. In her absence, events had gradually come to a head. Patrick had written her two vitriolic letters, pouring out his venom on the unfortunate Mr Nicholls and hinting obliquely that he held her partly responsible for encouraging his curate's attentions.

You may wish to know, how we have been getting on here especially in respect to < man, and > <u>master</u>; and <u>man</u>, On yesterday, I preached twice, but my man, was every way, very queer – He shun'd me, as if I had been a cobra de Capello – turning his head from the quarter, where I was, and hustling away amongst the crowd, to avoid contact – It required no Lavater to see, that his countenance was strongly indicative of mortified pride, and malevolent resentment – People < have > have begun to notice these things, and various conjectures are afloat – You thought me too severe – but I was not candid enough – His conduct might have been excus'd by the world, in a confirmed rake – or unprincipled army officer, but in a <u>clergyman</u>, it is justly chargeable, with base design \and/ inconsistency, < and dangerous designs > – I earnestly wish that he had another and better situation – As I can never trust him any more, in things of importance – I wish him no ill – but rather good, and wish that every woman may avoid him forever, unless she should be determined on her own misery – All the produce of the Australian <u>Diggins</u> would \not/ make him and any wife he might have, happy –[96]

In his second letter, Patrick reverted to a formula he had used to pleasanter effect as a young man, writing to his daughter in the character of Anne's dog, Flossy. Though the letter was intended to be humorous, it was too savage and too insidious in its denigration of Mr Nicholls to be funny.

You have condescendingly sent your respects to me, for which I am very grateful, and in token of my gratitude, I struck the ground three times with my tail – But let me tell \to you/ my affairs … As many things are done before me, which would not be done, if I could speak, (well for us dogs that we cannot speak) so, I see a good deal of human nature, that is hid from those who have the gift of language. I observe these manuoevres, and am permitted to observe many of them, which if I could speak, would never be done before me – I see people cheating one another, and yet appearing to be friends – many are the disagreeable discoveries, which I make, which \you/ could hardly believe if I were to tell them – One thing I have lately seen, which I wish to mention – No one takes me out to walk now, the weather is too cold, or \too/ wet for my master to walk in, and my former travelling companion, has lost all his apparent kindness, scolds me, and looks black upon me –[97]

Patrick's relentless campaign of vilification evidently extended to Mr Nicholls' failure to walk the parsonage dog. In these circumstances, it is hardly surprising that the curate at last gave up and, in an uncharacteristically dramatic gesture, offered himself to the Society for the Propagation of the Gospel as a missionary to the Australian Colonies of Sydney, Melbourne or Adelaide. On the standard application form he was sent to fill in, he gave his reason for wanting to be a missionary as, 'I have for some time felt a strong inclination to assist in ministering to the thousands of of [sic] our fellow Countrymen, who by Emigration have been in a great measure deprived of the means of grace.'[98] 'Disappointment in love' was hardly the sort of motivation likely to appeal to the society.

On the form he listed six referees, all of whom were required to submit letters on his behalf. Their tributes were all more or less fulsome. Sutcliffe Sowden, the vicar of Hebden Bridge and a friend of eight years' standing, declared, 'His character & conduct are above all reproach. His abilities are certainly more than average', and expressed his regret that if Nicholls succeeded in gaining the appointment, Sowden himself would lose by it 'one of my most esteemed & respected neighbours'.[99] Joseph Grant, incumbent of Oxenhope, took pains to point out how the church at Haworth had prospered since Nicholls' appointment: the National School had increased its scholars from sixty to between two and three hundred, church attendance had increased sixfold and in Stanbury he had been personally responsible for building a schoolroom used by both weekday and Sunday schools and as a place of worship where he took the Sunday service.[100] William Cartman, Headmaster of the Grammar School at Skipton, in a long and generous tribute, expressed the general feeling.

for uprightness & steadiness of Conduct, Activity in the prosecution of his pastoral labours, Zeal & devotion to his ministrations, & \specially/ successful management of < in > the Parochial Schools in his Parish, there is not to [be] found his equal.

In the whole Course of my ministerial Career for the last 30 years, (& I do indeed speak advisedly) I never met with a young man whom in every respect as to his general demeanour & personal Qualities I so much admired.

Perhaps fearing that Patrick might do his curate less than justice in his reference, Cartman made a point of informing the society that 'Mr Brontè has often detailed to me his invaluable services, & has frequently said, that shd. he leave him, he should not know how to supply his place'.[101] He need not have worried. Though Patrick could not work himself up into the enthusiastic tones of his fellow clergymen, neither could he be less than fair to the curate who had served him so well for the last eight years. During that time, Nicholls had

behaved himself, wisely, soberly, and piously – He has greatly promoted the interest of the National, and Sunday Schools; he is a man of good abilities, and strong constitution – He is very discreet, is under no pecuniary embarrassment, that I am aware of, nor is he, I think, likely to be so, since, in all pecuniary and other matters, as far as I have been able to discover, he is wary, and prudent – In principles, he is sound and orthodox – and would I think, under Providence, make an excellent Missionary.[102]

By the time Charlotte returned home from London, the die had been cast. Nicholls had sent off his application form and given the society notice that his 'present engagement', as curate of Haworth, would be concluded at the end of May.[103]

Whether she knew of these developments or not, Charlotte obviously dreaded her reception in Haworth and wrote from London asking Ellen Nussey to meet her at Keighley and accompany her on the final stage of her journey home.[104] No doubt eager enough to learn the state of affairs in Haworth, Ellen agreed to lend the moral support of her presence and came to stay for a fortnight. Together, the two friends awaited the critics' verdict on *Villette*. 'The book, I think, will not be considered pretentious – nor is it of a character to excite hostility', Charlotte had averred as she completed the manuscript.[105] This time she was to be proved right.

The reviews were almost unanimously favourable, though they seem to have been infected by the subdued tones of the book. The *Examiner* declared that *Villette* 'amply sustains the fame of the author of *Jane Eyre* and *Shirley*', while the *Literary Gazette*, praising as 'infinitely delightful' its 'charm of freshness', went further:

This book would have made her famous, had she not been so already. It retrieves all the ground she lost in *Shirley*, and it will engage a wider circle of admirers than *Jane Eyre*, for it has all the best qualities of that remarkable book, untarnished, or but slightly so, by its defects.[106]

The criticisms, on the whole, were minor but justified. There were complaints about the transfer of interest from Paulina – a character whom, despite Charlotte's reservations, most critics seemed to think was one of the most attractive and successful in the book – to Lucy; and some reviewers were disgruntled by the lack of plot, though even the most hostile admitted the veracity and excellence of her characters.[107] The largest number of complaints, however, were about the character of Lucy Snowe. In an otherwise entirely favourable review, the critic of the *Spectator* argued that 'this book, far more than *Jane Eyre*, sounds like a bitter complaint against the destiny of those women whom circumstances reduce to a necessity of working for their living'.[108] The *Guardian* complained of the 'somewhat cynical and bitter spirit' in which 'Currer Bell' conceived her tales, excusing this on the grounds that 'It may be the world has dealt hardly with her; it may be that in her writings we gather the honest and truthful impressions of a powerful but ill-used nature; that they are the result of affections thrown back upon themselves, and harshly denied their proper scope and objects.' Though Charlotte would never admit it, this was fair comment. Nevertheless, the reviewer spoilt his case by arguing from it that one should reject an acquaintance with Jane Eyre, Lucy Snowe and the creator of whom they were manifestations. Smith Williams considered this an 'unmanly insult', but Charlotte was simply contemptuous of the 'poor Guardian critic' and his 'right to lisp his opinion that Currer Bell's female characters do not realize his notion of ladyhood'.[109]

The *Guardian*'s point that the book was steeped in bitterness was made most tellingly in the review that Charlotte took most to heart. It was not simply that the *Daily News* review made criticisms which hurt her deeply, but the fact that it was written by a woman she had considered to be her friend, Harriet Martineau. Just as G. H. Lewes had once presumed upon his personal acquaintance with Charlotte in his review of *Shirley*, so Harriet Martineau allowed her intimate knowledge of the author to infuse her critique of *Villette*.

the book is almost intolerably painful … An atmosphere of pain hangs about the whole, forbidding that repose which we hold to be essential to the true presentment of any large portion of life and experience. In this pervading pain, the book reminds us of Balzac; and so it does in the prevalence of one tendency, or one idea, throughout the whole conception and action. All the female characters, in all their thoughts and lives, are full of one thing, or are regarded by the reader in the light of that one thought – love. It begins with the child of six years old, at the opening – a charming picture – and it closes with it at the last page; and, so dominant is this idea – so incessant is the writer's tendency to describe the need of being loved, that the heroine, who tells her own story, leaves the reader at last under the uncomfortable impression of her having either entertained a double love, or allowed one to supersede another without notification of the transition. It is not thus in real life. There are substantial, heartfelt interests for women of all ages, and under ordinary circumstances, quite apart from love:

Miss Martineau also criticized the way Charlotte had gone 'out of her way to express a passionate hatred of Romanism' which she found a 'striking peculiarity' in 'one so large and liberal, so removed from ordinary social prejudices as we have been accustomed to think "Currer Bell" '.[110] She reiterated her disapproval in a personal letter: 'I do deeply regret the reason given to suppose your mind full of one passion – love – I think there is unconscionably too much of it (giving an untrue picture of life) &, speaking with the frankness you desire, I do not like its kind – I anticipate a renewal of the sort of objection which you mentioned to me as inexplicable to you, the first evening we met; & this time, I think it will not be wholly unfounded.'[111] This brought an angry response from Charlotte: 'I know what *love* is as I understand it; and if man or woman should be ashamed of feeling such love, then is there nothing right, noble, faithful, truthful, unselfish in this earth, as I comprehend rectitude, nobleness, fidelity, truth, and dis-interestedness.'[112]

It was perhaps fortunate that Charlotte did not learn Thackeray's opinion of *Villette* which, while coinciding with Miss Martineau's, at least had the merit of being expressed privately.

it amuses me to read the author's naive confession of being in love with 2 men at the same time; and her readiness to fall in love at any time. The poor little woman of genius! the fiery little eager brave tremulous homely-faced creature! I can read a great deal of her life as I fancy in her book, and see that rather than have fame, rather than any other earthly good or mayhap heavenly one she wants some Tomkins or another to love her and be in love with. But you see she is a little bit of a creature without a penny worth of good looks, thirty years old I should think, buried in the country, and eating up her own heart there, and no Tomkins will come. You girls with pretty faces and red boots (and what not) will get dozens of young fellows fluttering about you – whereas here is one a genius, a noble heart longing to mate itself and destined to wither away into old maidenhood with no chance to fulfil the burning desire.'[113]

One wonders what Thackeray would have made of the fact that Charlotte had received four proposals of marriage – though he was certainly right in that these had all been turned down because Charlotte felt no reciprocal passion.

Well might Charlotte cry again, 'I can be on my guard against my enemies, but God deliver me from my friends!'[114] She had taken such offence at Miss Martineau's comments that there was now an irreparable rift between them. Having shown her friend loyalty when she was under attack for the Atkinson letters, Charlotte now felt doubly betrayed. 'You express surprise that Miss Martineau should apply to <u>you</u> for news of <u>me</u>'. she wrote to George Smith towards the end of March;

The fact is I have never written to her since a letter I received from her about eight weeks ago – just after she had read 'Villette'. What is more – I do not know when I can bring myself to write again. The differences of feeling between Miss M. and myself are very strong and marked; very wide and irreconcilable ... In short she has hurt me a good deal, and at present it appears very plain to me that she and I had better not try to be close friends; my wish indeed is that she should quietly forget me.[115]

For a few more weeks Charlotte brooded on the quarrel, then gathered courage to write to Miss Martineau herself to tell her that she no longer wished to have any communication with her.[116] The unlikely alliance between two 'literary lions' was at an end.

Chapter Twenty-Five

༄

TOMKINS TRIUMPHANT

*V*illette had fully justified Charlotte's expectation that it would cause less controversy and be better received than its two predecessors. Writing to Ellen, who had returned to Brookroyd after a brief fortnight at Haworth, Charlotte owned that 'the import of all the notices is such as to make my heart swell with thankfulness to Him who takes note both of suffering and work and motives – Papa is pleased too'.[1]

Patrick had taken a disproportionate amount of interest and pride in *Villette* as if to compensate for his unbending and vitriolic treatment of Mr Nicholls: perhaps he thought to divert his daughter's thoughts from marriage to her career. Not only had he closely followed the book's critical reception, but he had also intervened to secure a review in the provincial press. He wrote to George Smith requesting that a copy should be sent to the *Leeds Mercury*, which 'enjoys a wide circulation and considerable influence in the North of England', and also wrote to its editor, Edward Baines, stating that 'Already, several able, and just reviews, have appeared in the London papers – but from what I know of your critical taste and talents, I have a strong desire to < know > learn your opinion.' The *Leeds Mercury* no longer reviewed books in its columns, but a long and highly appreciative notice of *Villette* did appear in the *Leeds Intelligencer*, which cordially commended the book to the paper's readers.[2]

Such was Patrick's pride that he even sent a copy of the single-volume edition of *Jane Eyre* to his brothers and sisters back in Ireland, inscribing it with a justifiably boastful note.

To Mr Hugh Brontè, Ballinasceaugh, near Rathfriland Ireland – This is the first work, published by my Daughter – under the fictitious name of Currer Bell – which is the < usal > usual way – at first, by Authors, but her real name, is everywhere known – She sold the copyright of this, and her other two works for fifteen hundred pounds – so that she has to pay for the books she gets, the same as others – Her other two books, are in six volumes, and would cost nearly four pounds – This was formerly in three volumes – In two years hence, when all shall be published in a cheaper form, if all be well, I may send them – You can let my brothers and sisters, read this – P. Brontë, A. B. Incumbent of Haworth near Keighley. Jany.20th.1853 –[3]

Though Charlotte may have cringed at her father's actions, she took considerable pleasure in the fact that he was enjoying her success. She was less happy about the assiduity with which some of her so-called friends brought the bad notices to his attention. Mr Grant, for instance, who had been lampooned in *Shirley* and was probably taking a quiet revenge, was the first to bring the *Guardian* review, that 'choice little morsel for foes'. 'For my own part I can only record this significant fact', Charlotte told Smith Williams who was responsible for sending her the reviews,

I am indebted to my publishers for all I know of the favourable notices of 'Villette'. The hostile notices have been the care of my friends. When I revolve this consideration it makes me smile. My friend are very good – very. I thank some of them for the pains < I ta > they take to enlighten me. My publishers on the other hand are extremely vexatious – they excite a tendency to chiding and expostulation – but to speak truth – I like them no worse for provoking as they are – I feel they mean kindly. But seriously – they must please to remember that I would far rather receive unpleasant news through their medium than that of any other. The book is in one sense theirs as much as it is mine; and I know they are not glad to hear it cried down.[4]

With the acknowledged success of *Villette*, something of the old spirit of her correspondence with George Smith revived. 'On the whole the critique I like best yet is one I got at an early stage of the work, before it had undergone the "Old Bailey"; being the observations of a respected amateur critic – one A. Frazer Esqre.', she wrote to him, teasing him with the name he had assumed for their visit to the phrenologist in 1851. 'I am bound to admit however that this gentleman confined his approving remarks to the 2 first vols., tacitly condemning the 3rd by the severity of a prolonged silence.'[5]

Towards the end of February a parcel arrived from Cornhill containing a framed engraving of Samuel Lawrence's portrait of Thackeray, the original of which Mrs Smith had taken Charlotte to see in the artist's studio the previous month. It was a typically thoughtful gift from the young publisher, but knowing his distaste for effusive thanks, Charlotte gave him what she knew he would appreciate most, a spirited account of its receipt. 'At a late hour yesterday evening —', she told him, in mock-grandiose terms, 'I had the honour of receiving at Haworth Parsonage a distinguished guest – none other than W. M. Thackeray Esqre. Mindful of the rites of hospitality – I hung him in state this morning. He looks superb in his beautiful, tasteful gilded gibbet.'[6]

Another letter, requesting information as to the fate of Monsieur Paul Emanuel, prompted an equally satirical reply. Every reader should settle the catastrophe for himself, Charlotte firmly told George Smith:

(Drowning and Matrimony are the fearful alternatives) The Merciful – like Miss Mulock, Mr Williams, Lady Harriet St Clair and Mr Alexander Frazer – will of course choose the former and milder doom – drown him to put him out of pain. The cruel-hearted will on the contrary pitilessly impale him on the second horn of the dilemma – marrying him without ruth or compunction to that – person – that – that – individual – 'Lucy Snowe'.[7]

The question was one that had intrigued many of *Villette*'s readers and Charlotte had received several requests for a definitive answer. 'You see how much the ladies think of this little man whom you none of you like', she playfully accused Smith Williams.

I had a letter the other day announcing that a lady of some note who had always determined that whenever she married, her elect should be the counterpart of Mr Knightley in Miss Austen's 'Emma' – had now changed her mind and vowed that she would either find the duplicate of Professor Emanuel or remain for ever single!!![8]

Charlotte herself told Mrs Gaskell that her original intention was that Paul Emanuel should drown at sea on his way back to marry Lucy Snowe; like Charlotte herself, Lucy would not get her man. However, her father (to whom she must have been reading the manuscript) had pleaded so anxiously for a 'happy ending' because he disliked books that left a melancholy impression on the mind, that she had felt obliged to defer at least in part to his wishes. Unable to alter her own vision of his fate, she had veiled it in the oracular terms which so fascinated her readers. To their anxious queries, she responded equally enigmatically. 'Since the little puzzle amuses the < lady > ladies it would be a pity to spoil their sport by giving them the key', she told Smith Williams.[9] In the general bonhomie that accompanied the publication of *Villette*, Charlotte's relations with Smith Williams had also undergone something of a restoration to their former state. His task of sending her the reviews had given them a subject for discussion, and for the first time in well over a year she wrote at length and in a friendly fashion to him.[10]

Had it not been for the increasingly difficult and unhappy situation at Haworth, Charlotte could well have rested on her laurels and got on with her life. As it was, the strain was becoming obvious even to outsiders. At the beginning of March, the township was graced with a rare visit from Dr Charles Longley, the diocesan bishop, who stayed overnight with the Brontës at the parsonage. 'He is certainly a most charming little Bishop –', Charlotte reported of this future Archbishop of Canterbury, 'the most benignant little gentleman that ever put on lawn sleeves – yet stately too, and quite competent to check encroachments.'[11] This skill had been displayed during the evening when the curates, who had all been invited to tea and supper, began to 'upbraid' Charlotte in their characteristically heavy-handed way for 'putting them into a book'. Always anxious to keep her personal and authorial lives separate, Charlotte had been embarrassed and appealed to the bishop as to whether it was fair to drive her into a corner in this way. Impressed with her gentle and unassuming manners, Dr Longley had apparently rescued his hostess and put the curates in their place.[12]

Inevitably, Arthur Nicholls was heavily involved in the arrangements and, with the other local parsons, was a constant presence in the house. Perhaps inevitably, too, flustered by the extra work and anxious that every-thing should go well, Charlotte was irritated by his hang-dog appearance. 'Mr Nicholls demeaned himself not quite pleasantly –', she announced tartly to Ellen,

I thought he made no effort to struggle with his dejection but gave way to it in a manner to draw notice; the Bishop was obviously puzzled by it. Mr N also shewed temper once or twice in speaking to Papa. Martha was beginning to tell me of certain 'flaysome' looks also – but I desired not to hear of them ... He dogged me up the lane after the evening service in no pleasant manner – he stopped also in the passage after the Bishop and the other clergy were gone into the room – and it was because I drew away and went upstairs that he gave that look which filled Martha's soul with horror. She – it seems – meantime, was making it her business to watch him from the kitchen-door –

When Mr Nicholls also got into a needless quarrel with the school inspector who followed hard on the bishop's heels, Charlotte lost all patience. 'The fact is I shall be most thankful when he is well away – I pity him – but I don't like that dark gloom of his ... If Mr N be a good man at bottom – it is a sad thing that Nature has not given him the faculty to put goodness into a more attractive form.'[13] To his eternal credit, the bishop soon perceived the cause of the curate's dejection and, sympathizing with his very evident misery, made a point of pressing his hand and speaking kindly to him on parting. Despite Mr Nicholls, the visit passed off 'capitally well', the bishop declaring himself 'thoroughly gratified with all he had seen' and Charlotte's reactive headache and bilious attack politely awaiting his departure before putting in their appearance.[14]

For several weeks after the bishop's visit, the parsonage was in constant turmoil with a stream of visitors. William Morgan made a welcome return to Bradford to preach at his old church, but his threatened visit to Haworth – 'the infliction' as Charlotte called it – did not materialize.[15] Nevertheless, in his next letter he informed the Brontës that he had 'lately found his way to Cornhill'.

He writes that he had a 'long and interesting conversation' with one of my publishers, but does not say whether it was Mr Williams or Mr Smith – and that it was suggested that the 'French phrases' in 'Villette' – about which the worthy old gentleman has already several times expressed himself a good deal disturbed) shall be translated in foot-notes in a new edition.[16]

Reporting this back to Smith Williams, Charlotte sardonically remarked, 'I can't say that < say that > this suggestion quite meets my ideas', but as the future editions of *Villette* were printed untranslated, one can only presume that Mr Morgan heard what he wanted to hear.

At Easter, Charlotte was too busy with parish affairs to consider a visit to Brookroyd; there were 'Sermons to be preached, parsons to be entertained. Mechanics' Institute Meetings and tea-drinkings to be solemnized'. William Cartman came over from Skipton to preach the afternoon and evening sermons on Easter Sunday. The following day it was the annual soirée of the Haworth Mechanics' Institute; there was the usual 'respectable tea-party' in the church schoolroom, at which the guests were entertained by the Haworth Choral Society, and Patrick gave one of the speeches.[17]

The bustle and activity in Haworth failed to revive Mr Nicholls' spirits. His uncertainty as to Charlotte's feelings towards him, which had been so evident during the bishop's visit, had finally led him to abandon the idea of becoming a missionary. Emigrating to Australia was simply too final a solution and one which would pre-empt any possibility of a change in Charlotte's attitude towards him. On 1 April 1853, he withdrew his application, citing his continuing rheumatic problems as his justification, and sought another curacy instead.[18] Charlotte was almost in despair about him when she wrote to Ellen Nussey a few days later.

He & Papa never speak. He seems to pass a desolate life. He has allowed late circumstances so to act on him as to freeze up his manner and overcast his countenance not only to those immediately concerned but to every one. He sits drearily in his rooms – If Mr Cartman or Mr Grant or any other clergyman calls to see and as they think to cheer him – he scarcely speaks – I find he tells them nothing – seeks no confidant – rebuffs all attempts to penetrate his mind – I own I respect him for this – He still lets Flossy go to his rooms and takes him to walk – He still goes over to see Mr Sowden some times – and, poor fellow – that is all. He looks ill and miserable. I think and trust in Heaven that he will be better as soon as he fairly gets away from Haworth. I pity him inexpressibly. We never meet nor speak – nor dare I look at him – silent pity is just all I can give him – and as he knows nothing about that – it does not comfort. He is now grown so gloomy and reserved – that nobody seems to like him – his fellow-curates shun trouble in that shape – the lower orders dislike it – Papa has a perfect antipathy to him – and he – I fear – to Papa – Martha hates him – I think he might almost be <u>dying</u> and they would not speak a friendly word to or of him.

How much of all this he deserves I can't tell – certainly he never was agreeable or amiable – and is less so now than ever – and alas! I do not know him well enough to be sure there is truth and true affection – or only rancour and corroding disappointment at the bottom of his chagrin. In this state of things I must be and I am – <u>entirely passive</u>. < I know if I were near him > I may be losing the purest gem – and to me far the most precious – life can give – genuine attachment – or I may be escaping the yoke of a morose temper – In this doubt conscience will not suffer me to take one step in opposition to Papa's will – blended as that will is with the most bitter and unreasonable prejudices. So I just leave the matter where we must leave all important matters.[19]

Faced with the prospect of two more months of Mr Nicholls' unremitting gloom before his employment terminated and he could leave Haworth, Charlotte fled. She had had a standing invitation to visit the Gaskells at Manchester since February and this she now accepted, arriving by train in the early evening of 22 April.[20]

The visit was not an entire success. Even before she arrived, she had been stricken with nerves at the thought of meeting the Gaskell children again. 'Whenever I see Florence & Julia again – I shall feel like a fond but bashful suitor who views at a distance the fair personage to whom – in his clownish awe – he does not risk a near approach', she had written to Mrs Gaskell the previous year. 'Such is the clearest idea I can give you of < the > my feeling towards children I like but to whom I am a stranger – and to what children am I not a stranger?'[21] It was a shock to discover that there was a genuine stranger, a young lady, staying with the Gaskells, a fact which reduced her (and the other guest) to an uncomfortable silence. Matters were made worse when Charlotte retired to her room and found a letter from Ellen Nussey, repeating a lurid story about a ghost which was supposed to haunt a house she was about to visit. The story so preyed on Charlotte's mind that she spent a sleepless night and paid for this, and her nerves, with one of her sick headaches the following day.[22]

Mrs Gaskell tried hard to please her difficult guest. She invited a group of friends one evening, among them the Winkworth sisters, who sang Scottish ballads 'exquisitely'.

Miss Brontë had been sitting quiet and constrained till they began 'The Bonnie

House of Airlie,' but the effect of that and 'Carlisle Yetts,' which followed, was as irresistible as the playing of the Piper of Hamelin. The beautiful clear light came into her eyes; her lips quivered with emotion; she forgot herself, rose, and crossed the room to the piano, where she asked eagerly for song after song. The sisters begged her to come and see them the next morning, when they would sing as long as ever she liked; and she promised gladly and thankfully. But on reaching the house her courage failed. We walked some time up and down the street; she upbraiding herself all the while for folly, and trying to dwell on the sweet echoes in her memory rather than on the thought of a third sister who would have to be faced if we went in. But it was of no use...[23]

Mrs Gaskell was obliged to make their excuses for her non-appearance as best she could and they left without achieving the object of their visit. Mrs Gaskell ascribed Charlotte's paranoia on encountering strangers to what Charlotte herself described as her 'almost repulsive' plainness. 'I notice that after a stranger has once looked at my face, he is careful not to let his eyes wander to that part of the room again!' 'A more untrue idea never entered into any one's head', Mrs Gaskell commented, going on to describe how Charlotte's 'pleasant countenance, sweet voice, and gentle, timid manners' had won over at least one of her male guests who had a preconceived dislike of her because of her work.[24]

Another evening, two gentlemen were invited to dinner in the anticipation that they and Charlotte would get on well together. Unfortunately, Charlotte's response to yet more strangers was to draw into her shell, answering their questions in monosyllables, until they gave up the unequal task and talked to Mrs Gaskell instead. During their conversation, however, they began to discuss Thackeray's lectures, which he had recently repeated in Manchester, and Charlotte again forgot herself and entered warmly into the argument. 'She gave Mr Thackeray the benefit of some of her piercingly keen observation', Mrs Gaskell later told a friend. 'My word! he had reason when he said he was afraid of her.' Speaking with all the bitterness of one who had watched a much-loved and revered brother destroy himself, she had attacked Thackeray's light-hearted treatment of the novelist Henry Fielding's character and vices. 'Had Thackeray owned a son grown or growing up, – a son brilliant but reckless – would he of [sic] spoken in that light way of courses that lead to disgrace and the grave? ... I believe if only once the spectacle of a promising life blasted in the outset by wild ways – had passed close under his eyes – he never <u>could</u> have spoken with such levity of what led to its piteous destruction.'[25]

On Monday evening, 25 April, the Gaskells took Charlotte to the Theatre Royal where the 'Manchester Shakspearian Society' were putting on a production of *Twelfth Night* for the benefit of the Manchester Free Library. Charlotte's discreet silence on the subject is perhaps explained by the lambasting that the production received in the local press: Orsino was 'too boisterous and loud, with an artificial pitch of voice', Antonio 'couldn't be heard' and Olivia 'merely walked through her part'. As was the usual practice at the time, the play had been heavily cut and the text bowdlerized, so the evening had to be filled out with an opening address (on 'The Emancipation of Knowledge') and a closing farce, *Raising the Wind*.[26]

Though Mrs Gaskell clearly felt that the visit was a failure in some respects, Charlotte had actually thoroughly enjoyed herself. They parted on more than friendly terms: 'she is so true, she wins respect, deep respect, from the very first – and then comes hearty liking, – and last of all comes love', Mrs Gaskell told a friend. 'I thoroughly loved her before she left.'[27] Charlotte, too, looked back on the visit as one cementing their friendship. 'The week I spent in Manchester has impressed me as the very brightest and healthiest I have known for these five years past', she wrote to her kind hostess, signing another letter, 'Yours, with true attachment'. Before she left, she extracted a promise that, at her father's 'particular desire', Mrs Gaskell would visit her at Haworth before the summer was out.[28]

Charlotte's visit to the Gaskells had lasted a bare week. She returned home from Manchester via Brookroyd, where she spent a few days with Ellen Nussey who was feeling low and miserable about her own future. After many months of indecision and prevarication, she had at last decided to pay a visit to the Reverend Francis Upjohn, the sixty-six-year-old vicar of Gorleston in Suffolk, and his wife, Sarah, who may have been a distant relation. Their proposal, which Charlotte described as 'peculiar' and Patrick as 'not delicately expressed', was that Ellen should 'go and spend some time with them on a sort of experiment visit – that if the result were mutually satisfactory – they would wish in a sense to adopt you – with the prospect of leaving you property – amount of course indefinite'.[29] Mary Taylor took a typically robust view of the proposal, writing a 'reply' on Ellen's behalf:

Your coarseness of feeling that allows you to [pay] me the greater part of my wages only after your death, your evident dishonesty in leaving the < eg > engagement so indefinite that I might do < th > two women's work for twenty years to come & then have no \legal/ claim either on you or your heirs, yr evident notion that an expensive dress & diet is to compensate for the absence of money wages, all make me think that your feelings, principles & pleasures are very different to mine, and there could be no companionship in the case.[30]

Always afraid that her financial future looked bleak, especially when her mother died, Ellen had not wished to dismiss the prospect of a comfortable home out of hand. Charlotte's visit bolstered her confidence, which had quailed even further at the thought of staying in a haunted house, and at the end of May she set off for Great Yarmouth to pay her 'experiment visit'. Before her month was up, however, Ellen had had such a 'hard time of it and some rough experience' with 'these strange, unhappy people', that she sought sanctuary at her brother Joshua's rectory at Oundle.[31]

For Charlotte, the return to Haworth could not be a happy one. Mr Nicholls had still a month to go before he came to the end of his engagement and his presence was a continual source of strain and reproach. Sunday, 15 May, was an ordeal not to be forgotten. 'It seems as if I were to be punished for my doubts about the nature and truth of poor Mr N—'s regard', Charlotte wrote to Ellen.

Having ventured on Whitsunday to stay the sacrament – I got a lesson not to be repeated. He struggled – faltered – then lost command over himself – stood before my eyes and in the sight of all the communicants white, shaking, voiceless – Papa was not there – thank God! Joseph Redman spoke some words to him – he made a great effort – but could only with difficulty whisper and falter through the service. I suppose he thought; this would be the last time; he goes either this week or the next. I heard the women sobbing round – and I could not quite check my own tears.
    What had happened was reported to Papa either by Joseph Redman or John Brown – it excited only anger – and such expressions as 'unmanly driveller.' Compassion or relenting is no more to be looked for than sap from firewood.

Charlotte felt 'somewhat sick physically, and not very blithe morally' as she recounted this misadventure to Ellen the next day. She could no longer doubt either the strength of Mr Nicholls' devotion or his own efforts to conceal it; there must have been born, too, a sense of fellow feeling with him. She had once thought that they had no congenial tastes and feelings: she could no longer doubt that they at least shared the capacity for suffering in the face of unrequited love. In handwriting that showed all too vividly the evident distress she felt, Charlotte added:

I never saw a battle more sternly fought with the feelings than Mr N— fights with his – and when he yields momentarily – you are almost sickened by the sense of strain upon him. However he is to go – and I cannot speak to him or look at him or comfort him a whit – and I must submit. Providence is over all – that is the only consolation[32]

A few days later there was a certain satisfaction in discovering that a subscription was being raised in the township to offer a testimonial of respect to the departing curate. There was much curiosity as to the reasons for the departure, which had never been made public. Obviously, gossip had been rife since Mr Nicholls had broken down so publicly during the communion service, but the curate neither expected nor sought sympathy. The church-wardens felt obliged to interrogate him, putting the question plainly to him, 'Why was he going? Was it Mr Brontë's fault or his own? His own – he answered. Did he blame Mr Brontë? ["]No: he did not: if anybody was wrong it was himself." Was he willing to go? "No: it gave him great pain." '[33] With more loyalty and generosity of spirit than truth, Mr Nicholls maintained this point to the end of his life, telling Clement Shorter forty years later that there was never 'any quarrel between Mr Brontë & myself – an unkind or angry word never passed between us – we parted as friends when I left Haworth – my leaving was solely on my own account – I was not driven away by him – I always felt that he was perfectly justified in his objections to my union with his daughter.'[34]

While lauding Mr Nicholls' sense of honour and feeling, Charlotte could not ignore his obstinacy and sullenness. Patrick had spoken to him 'with <u>constrained</u> civility, but still with <u>civility</u>' at the Whitsuntide tea-drinkings, only to be cut short by his curate. 'This sort of treatment offered in public is what Papa never will forget or forgive –', Charlotte wrote despairingly to Ellen, 'it inspires him with a silent bitterness not to be expressed.'[35]

The long ordeal was now drawing to a close. On the evening of 25 May, a deputation of the local gentry and some of the neighbouring clergy gathered in the National School room where Michael Merrall, on behalf of the congregation, teachers and scholars of the church and its Sunday schools, presented Mr Nicholls with a handsome, inscribed gold watch.[36] Conveniently, Patrick was not very well, so Charlotte advised him to stay away. The following evening Mr Nicholls called at the parsonage to hand over the deeds of the National School, which had been his pride and joy, and to say goodbye.

They were busy cleaning – washing the paint &c. in the dining-room so he did not find me there. I would not go into the parlour to speak to him in Papa's presence. He went out thinking he was not to see me – And indeed till the very last moment – I thought it best not – But perceiving that he stayed long before going out at the gate – and remembering his long grief I took courage and went out trembling and miserable. I found him leaning against the garden-door in a paroxysm of anguish – sobbing as women never sob. Of course I went straight to him. Very few words were interchanged – those few barely articulate: several things I should have liked to ask him were swept entirely from my memory. Poor fellow! but he wanted such hope and such encouragement as I <u>could</u> not give him. Still I trust he must know now that I am not cruelly blind and indifferent to his constancy and grief … However he is gone – gone – and there's an end of it.[37]

In the emotion of the moment Charlotte had not even asked Mr Nicholls where he was taking up his next post, so the chances of her learning about his future fate were remote. He left Haworth quietly at six o'clock the following morning: it is possible that he did so without even a new job in prospect, for he was not appointed to the curacy of the little village of Kirk Smeaton, near Pontefract, until August.[38] He had performed his duties in Haworth faithfully to the end, taking the services in church the preceding Sunday – 'it was a cruel struggle' – and his last duty, appropriately enough a burial, two days before his departure. His successor, the unlucky George de Renzy, had already been appointed and performed his first duties two days later on 29 May.[39]

Racked by misery and guilt, Charlotte tried to find consolation, as she had always done, in occupation. Though she had apparently told Mrs Gaskell that she was 'not going to write again for some time', she began the rough draft of a new story, 'Willie Ellin', hoping to lose herself in her imagination.[40] Reading, too, was a refuge and on the evening of Mr Nicholls' departure a new box of books arrived from Cornhill, a gift which could hardly have been better timed. With it came a letter from a Mrs Holland which touched Charlotte deeply. She had read *Villette* and found in it a consolation for her own poignant and bitter grief. 'This hope sustained me while I wrote –', Charlotte replied the next day, 'that while many of the prosperous or very young might turn distastefully from the rather sad page – some – tested by what you well term "the pitiless trials of life" – might hear in it no harsh and unsympathetic voice.' Writing with the scorching memory of Mr Nicholls' great unhappiness still new upon her, Charlotte poignantly commented that 'One assurance that we have done good; one testimony that we have assuaged pain – ... comes more healingly to the heart than all the eulogiums on intellect that ever were uttered'.[41]

More than ever at this time Charlotte needed the companionship of someone of her own age and sex. Ellen Nussey was still at Oundle and unlikely to return for at least another month, so Charlotte applied to Mrs Gaskell, even though it was such a short time since her own visit to Manchester. She was extremely sensitive about the contrast between that visit and what she had to offer her friend. 'When you take leave of the domestic circle and turn your back on Plymouth Grove to come to Haworth', she warned Mrs Gaskell, 'you must do it in the spirit which might sustain you in case you were setting out on a brief trip to the backwoods of America. Leaving behind your husband, children, and civilization, you must come out to barbarism, loneliness, and liberty. The change will perhaps do good, if not too prolonged...'[42]

Before Mrs Gaskell could arrive, Charlotte's health, which had been remarkably good since she had completed *Villette*, gave way under the intolerable stress of the last month. She caught a cold which developed into severe influenza, compelling her to take to her bed for ten days, and obliging Patrick to write on her behalf to postpone Mrs Gaskell's visit indefinitely. By 12 June, she was well enough to write a brief note to George Smith 'lest my silence should be misunderstood', though still suffering from acutely painful headaches.[43]

The stress also told on Patrick, not least because he must have been aware that his daughter's illness was a manifestation of an unhappiness for which he was personally responsible. The very thing happened that Charlotte had feared most and which had persuaded her to reject Mr Nicholls in such uncompromising terms. Her father had a second stroke which, for a time, brought on complete blindness: he could not even distinguish between night and day. Though Charlotte was filled with alarm and feared the worst, he gradually recovered some vision but his sight was never fully restored to its former state. 'I think him very patient with the apprehension of what, to him would be the greatest of privations, hanging over his head', Charlotte told George Smith a month later, 'I can but earnestly hope that what remains of sight may be spared him to the end.'[44] Out of this evil some good was to come. More than ever dependent on his daughter and his curate for the smooth running of the parish and its many institutions, Patrick was to become increasingly aware of what he had lost in the efficient and hard-working Mr Nicholls.

The sudden deterioration in his sight obliged Patrick to abandon a some-what startling half-formed project of his to go to London for a few days in the summer.[45] As Patrick's last expedition from home had been when he escorted his daughters to Brussels in 1842, and he had, since then, turned down invitations from local men as eminent as Richard Monckton Milnes on the grounds that he did not go from home, the scale of the plan is astonishing. It can only have been conceived as a rather pathetic attempt on Patrick's part to divert Charlotte's attention from Mr Nicholls' sorrows and give her pleasure. That he was prepared at the age of seventy-six to undergo the long and difficult railway journeys which would have been involved, not to mention the turmoil and disruption to his quiet home life which a visit to London would entail, is a measure of his love for his daughter and his anxiety to 'make it up' to her.

Though she had dutifully submitted to her father's wishes, Charlotte had left Patrick in no doubt as to her own views: that he had been unjust and unnecessarily cruel to Nicholls. If she had been left to decide for herself, however, it is not easy to perceive what line she would have taken. One can only guess that she would perhaps have allowed Nicholls to court her so that she could have got to know him better and then taken a more informed decision. The strong suspicion remains, however, that had her father not so overreacted to the proposal and driven Mr Nicholls to such uncharacteristic displays of emotion, she would never have looked further than the 'statue-like' exterior and seen the heart of the man.

As it was, Charlotte's sense of injustice and pity had made her suddenly far more favourable to Mr Nicholls than she would otherwise have been. His departure brought home to her once again the solitude of her existence and Patrick's seizure, following so close on its heels, was yet another reminder of his mortality and the horror of an existence as the last survivor of a closely knit family which his death would bring her.

Miserable and unwell, Charlotte brooded on her wrongs and became touchy and sensitive even with well-meaning friends. A letter from George Smith, who was himself ill and overwrought with work, prompted a sym-pathetic response with a sting in its tail.

What you now feel is always I believe felt at some time of life or other by those [who] have much to do or suffer – whose lot it is to bear heavy responsibilities, or undergo severe anxieties, and in whose moral constitution there is that degree of elaborateness which will result in sensitive feeling.

Notwithstanding your aged sensations – you are far too young to despair for a moment. You will be better: I know you will be better, but in care, in mental rest and moderate physical exercise lie the means of cure. Let no influence, let no exigency, if possible, impose on you the spur or the goad: I am sure you do not need them, nor ever did in your life, not even when you turn with distaste from the task of answering a friendly letter; and let me just say, though I say it not without pain, a correspondence which has not interest enough in itself to sustain life – <u>ought</u> to die.[46]

In her present bitter and unhappy state, Charlotte had once again persuaded herself that her publisher's friendliness was purely business-motivated; though his letters were a lifeline to her, she could not believe that he considered the correspondence anything other than a troublesome necessity to keep his author sweet. There was a certain misanthropic sense of the fitness of things and a savage pleasure in her suggestion that it should end.

Charlotte's sense of isolation and deprivation had grown overwhelming in the wake of Arthur Nicholls' departure. She temporarily lost all sense of proportion and, for the first time – and without consulting Smith, Elder & Co. – answered one of her critics in the press. The *Christian Remembrancer* had carried an anonymous review of *Villette* by Anne Mozley, sister of the editor, in April. As an organ of the Church of England, it carried considerable weight with Charlotte's closest friends, Ellen Nussey and Miss Wooler, and with her domestic circle. Though she had ignored its partisan attacks on her before, in the three months since the publication of this review she had allowed one particular passage to fester in her mind. Still protesting against the 'outrages on decorum, the moral perversity, the toleration of, nay, indifference to vice which deform her first powerful picture of a desolate woman's trials and sufferings' in *Jane Eyre*, the reviewer concluded that the intervening years had brought the author

a little happiness and success, for in many important moral points *Villette* is an improvement on its predecessors. The author has gained both in amiability and propriety since she first presented herself to the world, – soured, coarse, and grumbling; an alien, it might seem, from society, and amenable to none of its laws.[47]

Apart from the hurtful but excusable ignorance of the devastation which the intervening years had actually wrought on Charlotte, it was the last sentence which particularly stuck in her throat. To her it seemed like a repetition of that insidious suggestion in the *Quarterly Review* notice of *Jane Eyre* that 'Currer Bell', if a woman, had 'for some sufficient reason, long forfeited the society of her own sex'.[48] That insult, published when Charlotte's true identity was not yet known, had provoked her to a bitingly sarcastic response which Smith, Elder & Co. had wisely declined to publish. Now, her veil of anonymity cast aside and her sense of isolation hard upon her, she read into the *Christian Remembrancer* review an insinuation that there was 'some disadvantageous occult motive for a retired life'. Once again, she took up her pen in her own name to defend herself, this time offering 'a few words of temperate explanation'.

Providence so regulated my destiny that I was born and have been reared in the seclusion of a country parsonage. I have never been rich enough to go out into the world as a participator in its gaieties, though it early became my duty to leave home in order partly to diminish the many calls on a limited income. That income is lightened of claims in another sense now, for of a family of six I am the only survivor.

My father is now in his seventy-seventh year; his mind is clear as it ever was, and he is not infirm, but he suffers from partial privation and threatened loss of sight; and his general health is also delicate, he cannot be left often or long: my place consequently is at home.[49]

The October issue of the periodical carried a notice from the editor acknowledging Charlotte's letter 'which claims at once our respect and sympathy'. 'We wrote in entire ignorance of the author's private history, and with no wish to pry into it', he hastened to assure her, adding, 'We now learn with pleasure, but not with surprise, that the main motive for this seclusion is devotion to the purest and most sacred of domestic ties.'[50]

In the past Charlotte had liked to use the excuse of those 'domestic ties' to avoid uncongenial employment or visiting, and Patrick had neither interfered with nor attempted to command her. Now, however, when for once he had laid down the law and stuck rigidly to it, her 'domestic ties' had become bonds against which she chafed. She tried to find relief in her writing but 'Willie Ellin' did not progress as it should. It seems to have been a reworking of those elements of *The Professor* left out of *Villette*. Again, it concerned two strikingly contrasted brothers: Edward Ellin, a grossly abusive and violent manufacturer, given to horsewhipping his brother, who is recognizably the same as his prototype in the earlier novel, Edward Crimsworth; and William Ellin, the gentle and gentlemanly younger son, impoverished and reluctantly dependent on his loathed half-brother. Though the characters – even to their Christian names – had been lifted straight from *The Professor* and could therefore claim an ancestry all the way back to Branwell's juvenile story, 'The Wool is Rising', Charlotte added poignancy by making the victimized younger brother a ten-year-old child.[51] Though she continued with the story in June, she seems to have abandoned it the following month, perhaps feeling that she was simply retreading already well-worn ground or, more likely, fearing that the critics would not take kindly to Edward Ellin, another 'vulgar' and 'profane' creation from the pen of 'Currer Bell'.

Without the solace of writing, Charlotte was driven to her usual expedient when miserable – temporary flight from home. Having fulfilled her duties at home by entertaining the Reverend W.R. Smith, William Morgan's replacement at Christ Church in Bradford, who came to give the annual Sunday school sermons at the end of July, and the Reverend William Bus-feild, vicar of Keighley, who preached for the Oddfellows the following day,[52] she felt free to leave.

It is an indication of the impression her previous visit to Scotland had left on her memory that she chose to go there again in the uncongenial company of Joe Taylor and his family, rather than visit Ellen at Brookroyd or Miss Wooler who had taken a house at Hornsea for the summer. Ellen may have paid a brief visit to Haworth on her return from Oundle[53] but the friends were rapidly falling out over the question of Mr Nicholls. Ellen entirely disapproved not only of Mr Nicholls himself but also, and more especially, of Charlotte's increasingly obvious change in attitude towards him.

Some time in July, Mr Nicholls had returned to Haworth (without Patrick's knowledge, it has to be assumed), staying at Oxenhope with Mr Grant. By fair means or foul he had contrived to get in touch with Charlotte and had persuaded her to permit him at least to correspond with her.[54] Ellen, it seems, disapproved of this clandestine correspondence. On 12 August she wrote to Mary Taylor, expecting her support in the battle to keep Charlotte out of Mr Nicholls' clutches. Instead, she received a round condemnation herself.

You talk wonderful nonsense abt C Brontë in yr letter. What do you mean about 'bearing her position so long, & enduring to the end'? & still better – 'bearing our lot whatever it is'. If its C's lot to be married shd n't she bear that too? or does your strange morality mean that she shd refuse to ameliorate her lot when it lies in her power. How wd she be inconsistent with herself in marrying? Because she considers her own pleasure? If this is so new for her to do, it is high time she began to make it more common. It is an outrageous exaction to expect her to give up her choice in a matter so important, & I think her to blame in having been hitherto so yielding that her friends can think of making such an impudent demand.[55]

Ellen's attitude was particularly offensive to Charlotte in that it was so two-faced. Only a few months before, she had been in high hopes that she would secure a husband for herself in Mary Gorham's brother. Now, when Charlotte had the possibility of marrying, she turned all sniffily moralistic and insisted on the duty of spinsterhood. There is no doubt that jealousy and fear were responsible. Since the deaths of Emily and Anne, Ellen had (she thought) made herself indispensable to Charlotte as her friend, her surrogate sister and her confidante. Ellen took immense pride and satisfaction in this role, more especially, it has to be said, since Charlotte had become famous as 'Currer Bell'. After Charlotte's death, it was to become her *raison d'être*. A husband threatened all that. Charlotte would naturally confide in him and, however important her friendship with Ellen remained, it could never be as intimate as it was before her husband came between them.

Exactly when the disagreement between Charlotte and Ellen became an open quarrel is not clear, but it is surely significant that there are no extant letters from Charlotte between 20 June 1853 and 1 March 1854.[56] Ellen may, of course, have destroyed some which, as the quarrel grew more bitter, put her in a bad light or contained harsh words from Charlotte. Certainly, at some point, they not only stopped visiting each other but also stopped writing, maintaining a frigid silence that spoke more of the breakdown in their friendship than any volume of words could have done. In December Miss Wooler tried to intervene but in vain: 'Do not think that your kind wish respecting E. Nussey and myself does not touch or influence me; it does both;' Charlotte responded, 'yet I hardly know how to take the step you recommend'.[57] Towards the end of February 1854, when Patrick had finally been persuaded to sanction Mr Nicholls' letters and visits and events were moving towards their inevitable conclusion, Charlotte found the necessary nerve and forgiveness to put an end to the quarrel. Ellen had been ill and this provided an excuse for a reconciliation. Ellen grasped the olive branch willingly: a friendship diminished in intimacy by the intervention of a husband was better than no friendship at all. She could not resist pouring out her woes to Mary Gorham, now Mrs Hewitt, and how one-sided that account was is evident from Mary's response.

I was glad to receive your second letter telling me you had heard from Miss Brontë – glad for her as well as you – for it seemed unnatural that she could so throw off all her old friendship that she did not evince some little return of it when you were ill – I was very glad she did – it must have comforted you very much and you had suffered so much pain about her evidently. Now you are ready to forget all I can see – and that is kind and right – but she will not quite forget I hope – but will remember enough to see how your true friendship was shown in it – and be guided by you – her thoughts – and affections must really need control. It is an example of the dangerous gift such a mind as hers must be, and I trust it <u>will</u> overcome temptations, and shine out brightly at last – That will be a happiness to you indeed.[58]

Evidently Mr Nicholls' name had not been mentioned in the reconciliation. Indeed, it was not until 11 April 1854, when Charlotte wrote to tell Ellen that she was engaged to be married, that the full story of the intervening months of his courtship was revealed. Charlotte began her account with the words 'Matters have progressed thus since last July'.[59] One can only assume that the quarrel dated back to then and to Mr Nicholls' first secret visit to Haworth.

This also explains the fact that Charlotte did not visit Brookroyd again that year and decided to go with the Taylors to Scotland in August – a choice she was rather to regret. What had appealed to Charlotte was the plan to take up residence at Kirkcudbright or some other watering-place on the Solway Firth. Rather surprisingly, given her previous acid comments on the subject, she had reckoned without little 'Tim' and her ailments. No sooner had they reached the Solway Firth and stayed but a single night than the baby, 'that rather despotic member of modern households', developed diarrhoea. 'To my unskilled perception its ailments appeared very slight – nowise interfering with its appetite or spirits, but parental eyes saw the matter in a different light', Charlotte reported sardonically to Miss Wooler. To her immense frustration it was decided that the air of Scotland was 'unpropitious' for the child and that they should return to the safety of Yorkshire. The only lasting memory of Scotland which Charlotte was to garner on this visit was of the thirty-mile journey through richly cultivated and well-wooded scenery between Dumfries and Kirkcudbright, which was spent on the outside of a stagecoach.[60]

The Taylors resolved to go to Ilkley, a fashionable spa town on the edge of the Yorkshire Dales, not far from Haworth. Unfortunately for Charlotte, though she was very taken with the town, she was obliged to cut short her stay after only three days because her box, containing her clothes, had been mislaid in the hurry of changing trains. Having come to terms with her disappointment at losing the chance to stay in Scotland for such a frivolous reason, Charlotte was able to look back on her week away with pleasure. Nevertheless, it had entirely confirmed her view of the unhealthy state of baby-worship in the Taylor household. 'The world does not revolve round the Sun – that is a mistake;' she remarked sarcastically,

certain babies – I plainly perceive – are the important centre of all things. The Papa and Mama could only take their meals, rest and exercise at such times and in such measure as the despotic infant permitted. While Mrs J. eat her dinner, Mr J. relieved guard as nurse. A nominal nurse indeed accompanied the party, but her place was a sort of anxious, waiting sinecure, as the child did not fancy her attendance.[61]

She returned home to find Patrick complaining, rather pathetically, of weakness and depressed spirits, so she felt obliged to turn down an invitation from Miss Wooler to join her at Hornsea on the Yorkshire coast.[62] A letter from Mrs Gaskell a few days later, proposing to make her long-deferred visit to Haworth within the next few weeks, was a bright spot on the horizon, but when she had still not arrived at the end of the second week in September, Charlotte could stand it no longer and left home again. Her change of mind seems to have been dictated partly by her own irritation at Patrick's implacable hostility to Mr Nicholls and his efforts to claim her sympathy for his poor state of health. No doubt, too, her own feelings of guilt were partially responsible, for she was concealing from her father the fact that Mr Nicholls had made another visit to Haworth since her return from Scotland, during which he seems to have met Charlotte, and that their correspondence was continuing.[63]

Such were the pressures at home that Charlotte accepted Miss Wooler's invitation, agreeing to meet her at Ilkley for a few days rather than travelling further afield to Hornsea.[64] In writing to tell Miss Wooler about her Scottish expedition, Charlotte had said she liked Ilkley exceedingly and longed to revisit it, so this was a happy choice of location for the visit. The two friends could wander the wide, tree-lined streets, admire the grand new hotels, visit the mineral water spa on the hillside above the town and walk up to the moors where the skyline was dominated by the sombre outline of the Cow and Calf rocks. No doubt Charlotte took the opportunity to unburden her mind on the subject of her breach with Ellen and the problem with Mr Nicholls; certainly, while her friendship with Ellen lay in tatters, her liking for and intimacy with Miss Wooler increased.[65]

As luck would have it, during the two or three days she was away a letter arrived from Mrs Gaskell. Perhaps suspecting from her large, masculine handwriting that it was from Mr Nicholls, Patrick opened the letter and found that Mrs Gaskell intended to come in four days' time. Writing to tell her that Charlotte should be back by then and that her visit was welcome, Patrick made it clear how much he hoped for from Mrs Gaskell's visit.

As far as I am able to discover from what my Daughter has told me, and from my perusal of your able, moral, and interesting literary works –, I think that you, and she are congenial spirits, and that a little intercourse between you, might, under the strange vicissitudes, and frequent trials of this mortal life – under providence – be productive of pleasure and profit to you both – We are gregarious beings, and cannot always be comfortable, if alone – and a faithful, and intellectual friend – when such an one can be found – is often productive of pleasure and profit – and needed by us, next to that Greatest, and Best of All Friends – who sticketh closer than a brother –

Clearly, a little moral feminine company might reinforce Charlotte's sense of duty to her father as well as providing her with the distraction of suitable amusement. He ended his letter with words which strangely echoed Charlotte's own invitation to Mrs Gaskell: 'We can promise you nothing here but a hearty welcome, and peaceful seclusion – nevertheless, this may not be without its use – for a season –'.[66]

In fact his letter was unnecessary, for Charlotte arrived home the next day and was able to answer for herself.[67] Annoyance at her father's having opened her letter probably added to the already frosty atmosphere at the parsonage. Mrs Gaskell arrived at Keighley station in the early afternoon of Monday, 19 September 1853, to be met by a cab which carried her the four miles to Haworth. Like many a tourist after her, Mrs Gaskell was gratified to find the 'lead-coloured' day lent just the right gloomy aspect to her first impressions of the place and admirably fulfilled all her preconceptions about it. The houses, factories, even the landscape looked 'dull' and 'grey' to a Mancunian used to the warmer colours of red brick: even the moors, which should have been a blaze of purple, were brown and dull – a fact which she curiously attributed to a thunderstorm a few days previously rather than the simple fact that the brief heather season was over.[68]

At the parsonage gate she was 'half-blown back by the wild vehemence of the wind which swept along the narrow gravel walk' and on the steps she encountered 'a ruddy tired-looking man of no great refinement' who was just leaving. This turned out to be Francis Bennoch, a self-styled 'patron of Authors and literature' from London who had arrived shortly before, despite having had a letter from Charlotte declining the visit. He had produced a manuscript dedication of a work by the writer Mary Mitford as 'a sort of portable certificate of his merits' and, having 'captivated' Patrick, obtained his desired interview with a reluctant Charlotte through him. Perhaps fearing that Mr Bennoch would also importune Mrs Gaskell if he realized who she was, Charlotte hastily swept her invited guest inside the house. Discussing the visit later, Patrick 'abused us both for "a couple of proud minxes" when we said we would rather be without individual patronage if it was to subject us to individual impertinence': 'Oh, please burn this letter as soon as you have read it', Mrs Gaskell added, alarmed at her indiscretion.[69]

Charlotte gave Mrs Gaskell 'the kindest welcome' and if she had feared that her guest might find her home poor and humble after the wealth and style of Plymouth Grove, she was soon set right. Mrs Gaskell enthused about everything: the dining room

looked the perfection of warmth, snugness & comfort, crimson predominating in the furniture, wch did well with the bleak cold colours without. Everything in her department has been new within the last few years; and every thing, furniture, appointments, &c. is admirable for its consistency. all simple, good, sufficient for every possible reasonable want, & of the most delicate and scrupulous cleanliness. She is so neat herself I got quite ashamed of any touches of untidiness – a chair out of its place – work left on the table were all of them, I could see, annoyances to her habitual sense of order; not annoyances to her temper in the least – you understand the difference.

Mrs Gaskell had been given Aunt Branwell's old bedroom, the largest in the house, and she tried hard to find something favourable to say about it, finally lighting on the fact that the view (directly over the 'pestiferous' churchyard to the moors beyond) was 'beautiful in certain lights', adding with uncon-scious irony, 'moon-light especially'.[70]

During the four days of her visit, Mrs Gaskell came to recognize the set routine at the parsonage which, in most respects, had not changed since Charlotte's childhood. They breakfasted together with Patrick in his room at nine, then left to await the post in the dining room. About noon they went for a walk, returning to dine at two – 'Mr Brontë having his dinner sent to him in his sitting-room according to his <u>invariable</u> custom'; another walk at four o'clock preceded tea at six, when they were joined again by Patrick, which Mrs Gaskell (wrongly) considered unusual. After tea Patrick retired to his study to smoke a clay pipe, leaving Charlotte and Mrs Gaskell to chat before the fire in the dining room. At half-past eight the whole household, including Tabby and Martha, gathered for prayers, and by nine o'clock everyone except Charlotte and her guest was in bed. They sat up for at least another hour, Mrs Gaskell drawing out of Charlotte stories about her past life and how they had influenced her work, before finally retiring to bed. 'Monotonous enough in sound,' Mrs Gaskell said of this routine, 'but not a bit in reality.'

The long walks on the moors were particularly memorable, Charlotte pointing out 'in the gloom of the distant hollows ... a dark grey dwelling – to the Scotch firs growing near them often – & told me such wild tales of the ungovernable families who lived or had lived therein that Wuthering Heights even seemed tame comparatively'. The novelist in Mrs Gaskell was fascinated by these tales of 'dare-devil people' and she could not resist a typical exaggeration in summing them up: 'These people build grand houses, & live in the kitchens, own hundreds of thousands of pounds & yet bring up their sons with only just enough learning to qualify them for over-lookers during their father's lifetime & greedy grasping money-hunters after his death.' Though she did not say so, she obviously considered Charlotte quite justified in not 'visiting' with any of them.[71]

Irrepressibly curious, and longing insatiably for more lurid details about her friend's family, Mrs Gaskell even interrogated Martha Brown. One day they 'stole out' while Charlotte was busy and Martha took her to see the memorial tablet in the church. Once started, the garrulous Martha could not be stopped, relaying the dramatic details with morbid relish, from Emily's last morning with 'the rattle in her throat while she <u>would</u> dress herself', to Anne's gentle lament, 'Oh, if it was but Spring and I could go to the sea – Oh if it was but Spring.' It was Martha who told Mrs Gaskell about the Brontës' habit of walking round the table each evening.

For as long as I can remember – Tabby says since they were little bairns Miss Brontë & Miss Emily & Miss Anne used to put away their sewing after prayers, & walk all three one after the other round the table in the parlour till near eleven o'clock. Miss Emily walked as long as she could; & when she died Miss Anne & Miss Brontë took it up, – and now my heart aches to hear Miss Brontë walking, walking on alone.

Mrs Gaskell then learnt that after she had escorted her to bed each evening Charlotte would return downstairs to her solitary walk: 'She says she could not sleep without it – that she & her sisters talked over the plans & projects of their whole lives at such times.' The poignancy of this routine did not fail to strike Mrs Gaskell: 'I am sure I should fancy I heard the steps of the dead following me.'[72]

The visit was clearly a great success: Mrs Gaskell was ready and willing to be pleased by any and everything and Charlotte, warmed by her companionship, unburdened herself to her friend. The whole sad story of Mr Nicholls was revealed, together with Charlotte's own fatalistic views on its likely termination. She told Mrs Gaskell that she believed some people were appointed beforehand to sorrow and much disappointment and that it was well for those who had rougher paths to perceive that it was God's will and therefore moderate their expectations, abandon hope and cultivate patience and resignation.[73] This was not how Charlotte herself was actually handling the question of Mr Nicholls, but Mrs Gaskell was impressed with the passivity and hopelessness of the statement. She allowed it to colour and inform her opinion of Patrick Brontë – the way, for instance, that 'He never seemed quite to have lost the feeling that Charlotte was a child to be guided and ruled'; and though he was invariably polite and agreeable to her, she was 'sadly afraid of him in my inmost soul; for I caught a glare of his stern eyes over his spectacles at Miss Brontë once or twice which made me know my man; and he talked at her sometimes'. Her views of him already poisoned by Lady Kay Shuttleworth's gossip, it was unfortunate that Mrs Gaskell met Patrick at the one time when he had exercised his paternal authority and, as a result, his relationship with his daughter was at its lowest point ever. She went away with the indelible impression that Patrick was a domestic tyrant, a man who 'ought never to have married' or had children and one whose selfish love of solitude had condemned his daughter to a life of isolation even in her own home. Its legacy was to be the travesty of a portrait which appeared in *The Life of Charlotte Brontë*.[74]

A more positive outcome of the visit was that Mrs Gaskell, her romantic heart all aquiver with sympathy for the thwarted lovers, determined to do a little matchmaking on their behalf. A month after her visit she wrote in triumph to her friend, Richard Monckton Milnes. 'With skilful diplomacy, for which I admire myself extremely, I have obtained the address we want', she announced. She had sworn Monckton Milnes to secrecy, for 'if my well-meant treachery becomes known to her I shall lose her friendship, which I prize most highly', but she needed his help because, as a powerful, influential and wealthy patron of the arts, he had access to the funds of various charitable institutions. 'I have been thinking over little bits of the conversation we had relating to a pension', she told him, adding with a sure instinct,

I do not think she would take it; and I am quite sure than *one* hundred a year given as acknowledgement of his merits, as a good faithful clergyman would give her ten times the pleasure that *two* hundred a year would do, if bestowed upon her in < a > her capacity as a writer. I am sure he is a thoroughly good hard-working, self-denying curate … Her father's only reason for his violent & virulent opposition is Mr Nicholls's utter want of money, or friends to help him to any professional advancement.[75]

Having set the wheels in motion for an Anglican clergyman to receive a pension for services rendered, the Dissenter Mrs Gaskell sat back and waited to see the result of her plotting.

Her departure had left Charlotte feeling even more isolated and unhappy than usual. 'After you left, the house felt very much as if the shutters had been suddenly closed and the blinds let down. One was sensible during the remainder of the day of a depressing silence, shadow, loss, and want'.[76] She found some occupation in writing to Francis Bennoch, her would-be patron, who had called just before Mrs Gaskell arrived. Turning down his invitation to stay with him in London, she added that she would very much like to call on him, 'though at present I see little prospect of events calling me there'. The following Sunday she had two clergymen to entertain, William Cartman, who gave the afternoon sermon at Stanbury, and John Burnett, the vicar of Bradford, who preached in the evening at Haworth.[77]

Having performed these duties, Charlotte left home again, seeking refuge with Miss Wooler, this time at Hornsea, a quiet seaside town between the more fashionable resorts of Scarborough and Bridlington. Charlotte spent a pleasant week, despite the mishap of a child being sick into her lap on the coach journey home.[78] At Haworth, another dreary month passed by with nothing to relieve the strained relations between father and daughter except the occasional visiting clergyman who came to assist with the services.[79]

In the middle of November, Charlotte suddenly decided to go to London. There was an element of mystery about this visit from the start. Charlotte told Mrs Gaskell:

Now – I believe – it will be necessary for me to go up to London erelong on a little matter of business (no-thing relating to literature or publishing, as I hardly need say – but wholly and solely touching my small income) and I want to know if you could suggest to me where I could get quiet and respectable lodgings for a few days … I might of course apply to Mr Smith – but then he would ask me to stay at his Mother's which I would rather avoid. I merely wish to go quietly – to get my business done and to come home.[80]

If Charlotte's explanation was genuine, the 'business' is likely to have been connected with her capital which George Smith had invested for her in the Funds and which paid her a regular dividend through his hands. She had not heard from George Smith since the middle of July, a fact which, combined with her earlier disappointment at receiving only five hundred pounds for the copyright of *Villette,* instead of the seven hundred for which she had hoped, may have made her decide to end his power of attorney and take her financial affairs back into her own control.[81] Alternatively, as Mr Nicholls persisted in his courtship, she may simply have wished to discover how much she was worth and whether she had enough money to enable them to marry in defiance of her father. If she was contemplating even the possibility of marrying, however half-heartedly, it is understandable that she would not wish to confide in George Smith. A more likely possibility, in the light of subsequent events, is that Charlotte, concerned at her publisher's long silence, simply intended to make the sort of 'visitation of the unannounced and unsummoned apparition of Currer Bell in Cornhill' she had threatened once before.[82]

On 21 November, she wrote to Mrs Shaen, one of the Winkworth sisters who were close friends of Mrs Gaskell, and asked her to book lodgings that she had recommended in Bedford Place for a week from 24 November.[83] By a curious twist of fate, however, on the same day she received an unexpected letter from George Smith, which caused her great consternation: 'tho' brief and not explicit' it 'seemed indicative of a good deal of uneasiness & disturbance of mind'. Charlotte's suspicions were immediately aroused and she wrote not to him, but to his mother, for an explanation. 'What ails him?' she demanded. 'Do you feel uneasy about him, or do you think he will soon be better? If he is going to take an important step in life – as some of his expressions would seem to imply – is it one likely to conduce to his happiness and welfare?'[84] Clearly she found it as impossible to ask George Smith himself if he was to be married as he found it to tell her.

Poor Mrs Smith was left with the uncomfortable task of telling Charlotte that her son was indeed about to announce his engagement to Elizabeth Blakeway, the beautiful daughter of a wealthy London wine merchant, whom he had met in April and fallen in love with at first sight. Ironically, she was just the sort of bride Charlotte had predicted would suit George Smith, and, naturally, far more eligible than Charlotte Brontë. Mrs Smith struggled for words as she drafted the unpalatable news.

I shall answer you[r] kind enquiries about my Son with a great deal of pleasure – he is quite well and very happy – < there is every prospect > he is thinking of < his > taking a very important step in Life the most important and \I think/ with every prospect of happiness. I am very thankful and pleased about it – I am sure he will as soon as it is quite settled enter < fully > into all the particulars with you – it is not < fully > so yet tho' I have no doubt in my own mind all will be as his best Friends could wish and you will \soon/ hear < soon > from him again...[85]

As Mrs Smith intended, this letter left no room for doubt. George Smith was about to be engaged to be married, his choice had the full weight of his family's approval and his 'best Friends' could not wish it otherwise. Any lingering hopes Charlotte may have cherished in that direction herself were absolutely crushed. Lucy should not marry Dr John.

Just how hurt Charlotte was by this news was manifest in her reactions. She immediately cancelled her trip to London with a laconic 'Man <u>proposes</u> but Another <u>disposes</u>', announcing that 'circumstances have taken a turn which will prevent my intended journey to London'.[86] She packed up and returned to Cornhill a box of their books, following it with a curt note to Smith Williams: 'Do not trouble yourself to select or send any more books. These courtesies must cease some day – and I would rather give them up than wear them out.'[87] When the letter she dreaded finally arrived bearing the official tidings of George Smith's engagement, she wrote him an even more brusque and savage reply.

Decbr 10th 1853

My dear Sir

In great happiness, as in great grief – words of sympathy should be few. Accept my meed of congratulation – and believe me

Sincerely yours
C. Brontë

George Smith Esqre[88]

The proffered congratulations provided but a thin veil against the scorching intensity of Charlotte's pain; George Smith could be left in no doubt that he had caused the bitterest hurt and deepest offence. The relationship between Currer Bell and Smith, Elder & Co., Charlotte Brontë and George Smith, lay in smouldering ruins.

Abandoned by the two people she cared for most, George Smith and Ellen Nussey, Charlotte's sense of isolation grew intense. 'I wonder how you are spending these long winter evenings', she wrote to Miss Wooler. 'Alone – probably – like me.' To Mrs Gaskell she explained how living 'a very still lonely life', when the post brought a friendly letter it was an immediate stimulus to reply. 'You put it away, saying in about three days I shall reply. The three days pass; you happen to be a little downcast; it seems to you that you have nothing to say worth saying. It may be very pleasant to you to <u>receive</u> letters, but what can <u>you</u> write worth < worth > imparting?'[89]

It was not surprising, feeling both isolated and betrayed by her closest friends, that Charlotte finally turned to the one person who had loved her consistently and unconditionally, Arthur Bell Nicholls. She decided to give him a fair chance and to that end she had to inform her father that they had been writing to each other for the last six months. There was a certain relief from guilt in making the confession.

The correspondence pressed on my mind. I grew very miserable in keeping it from

Papa. At last sheer pain made me gather courage to break it – I told all. It was very hard and rough work at the time – but the issue after a few days was that I obtained leave to continue the communication.[90]

More importantly, she demanded the right to become better acquainted with her suitor. This was a complete volte face: from complete deference to her father's wishes, she was now setting out the agenda and demanding his compliance with her wishes. It may be unfair to Arthur Nicholls, but one cannot avoid the suspicion that Patrick's implacable opposition to the match had been a useful excuse for Charlotte to turn him down. Despite Mrs Gaskell's impressions of dutiful and unhappy resignation to paternal duty, Charlotte had not been certain in her own mind that she should marry Mr Nicholls. She had always used Patrick's ill health as an excuse for preventing her leaving home; that excuse served again while she remained undecided about Mr Nicholls; it was to be dropped just as unceremoniously when it no longer coincided with her wishes. With the dream of a more brilliant destiny as the wife of George Smith finally shattered, with her Cornhill connections severed and her lifelong friendship with Ellen apparently at an end, the love of a good and worthy, if ordinary, man suddenly seemed more precious. Even if the feeling was not mutual, no one could doubt that he cared for her: he offered her security, affection and loyalty. The dawning of this realization marked the end of Charlotte's dutiful obedience; she would fight tooth and nail for the right to a chance of happiness.

Patrick had never been able to gainsay his daughter when she decided something and he now, reluctantly and with bad grace, conceded that Charlotte and her suitor should be allowed to meet. Mr Grant was once more pressed into service and in January 1854, Mr Nicholls spent ten days at Oxenhope vicarage. This time the meetings were all open and above board. Charlotte had the 'opportunity to become better acquainted' she had demanded of her father with the result that 'all I learnt inclined me to esteem and, if not love – at least affection'. Patrick, though still 'very – <u>very</u> hostile – bitterly unjust', was compelled not only to acquiesce in the meetings but also to receive his prospective son-in-law at the parsonage, a task which he performed 'not pleasantly'.[91]

Though his prospects were so suddenly and unexpectedly improved, Mr Nicholls still did not have an easy time of it. Even the weather was against him, heavy snowfalls in the new year having been followed by severe frosts which froze the snow to a depth of three feet or more.[92] Before he left, Charlotte warned him that he still had great obstacles in his way, so he returned to Kirk Smeaton comforted but by no means confident. Soon after his return he had an interview with Richard Monckton Milnes who had, at Mrs Gaskell's behest, exerted his influence on his behalf. 'I must tell you that I made Mr Nicholls' acquaintance in Yorkshire', he reported back:

He is a strong-built, somewhat hard-featured man, with a good deal of Celtic sentiment about his manner & voice – quite of the type of the northern Irishman.

He seemed sadly broken in health & spirits & declined two cures, which Dr. Hook enabled me to offer him – one in Lancashire of considerable interest, [but?] requiring much energy – another in Scotland, requiring none at all. He gave me the impression of a man whose ardour was burnt out. I was amused at his surprise at the interest I took in him & I carefully avoided any mention of you. He spoke with great respect of Mr Bronte's abilities & character & of her simply & unreservedly …[93]

It was hardly surprising that Mr Nicholls should decline the posts offered to him: it was more essential than ever that he should be near Haworth so that he did not lose the little advantage he had already gained. His remarkable lack of bitterness towards Patrick was consistent with his attitude throughout the affair – and wholly admirable.

Now that Mr Nicholls was accepted (however reluctantly) as a suitor for Charlotte's hand, the atmosphere at the parsonage gradually returned to normality. Patrick busied himself with parish affairs: the extreme hardship caused by a three-month-long strike at Merralls' mill; the dispute between Bradford and Keighley over plans to draw water from the Worth River, which would have put paid to Patrick's own schemes for Haworth; an invitation to attend a Church Pastoral Aid Society meeting in Bradford.[94] Two dramatic incidents, occurring within a fortnight of each other, must also have claimed his attention and exercised his pastoral care. Feelings were still running high after the prolonged strikes of the winter over the introduction of the two-loom system and someone discharged a gun into the houses of two weavers who were working the system at Butterfield's mill, breaking windows and damaging property but not causing injury or loss of life. A fifty-pound reward was offered for the conviction of the offenders. The second incident caused even greater excitement: the body of a newborn boy was discovered buried in a field. The inquest established that he was the child of an unmarried mother, Susey Sunderland, who had kept her pregnancy secret and delivered herself some six to eight weeks previously. Anxious to avoid scandal and to keep her job, she had not sought medical attention and had missed only half a day's work at the mill. As it could not be proved that she had murdered the child, the inquest simply recorded a verdict that he had been 'found dead in a field'.[95]

Despite the human tragedy behind both these stories, which must have interested the novelist in Charlotte, she made no reference to either of them in her letters. She was absorbed in her literary correspondence and making tentative plans for the future. She accepted an invitation to stay with Francis Bennoch and his wife in London in May with the proviso that

I will trust you for not '<u>lionizing</u>' me – indeed I should suppose I am now too far out of date to make an eligible 'lion' or 'lioness' – but at any rate – you will I know spare me that vulgarizing process to which I have ever felt an insurmountable repugnance. It would not answer with me, for I could not \always/ 'roar' when I was bid – I am afraid I should sometimes disappoint my shew-men.[96]

She wrote to thank Sydney Dobell for the gift of his second book, *Balder,* a dramatic poem of lurid and morbid colouring. Recognizing that it would not be as popular as his first work, she offered a sympathy born of her own experience: 'How is it that while the first-born of genius often brings honour the second almost as often proves a source of depression and care? I could almost prophesy that your third will atone for any anxiety inflicted by this his immediate predecessor.'[97]

Literary criticism was also sought from her from an altogether different quarter. Not for the first time, a hopeful author presumed upon family acquaintance to ask her opinion of his work.[98] Henry Garrs, a younger brother of Nancy and Sarah Garrs, the Brontës' nurserymaids, sought her advice on publishing some poems he had written. Charlotte made it clear that 'any opinion I may give is intended merely for your <u>private</u> satisfaction – not for <u>public</u> use', but took the trouble to go through the manuscript with great care, marking 'prominent errors' in spelling and rhythm. After careful revision and provided he could get sufficient subscribers, she thought that he would be justified in publishing his poems – though warning him of the fate of *Poems* by Currer, Ellis and Acton Bell. 'Should you decide on pub-lishing, you may put down my < own > father's name and my own as subscribers for a copy each. Be very cautious however not to commit yourself to pecuniary risk. Printers and Publishers are hazardous men to deal with: it is seldom an author comes off without loss.'[99]

It was ironic that on the very day she wrote this advice to Henry Garrs she unexpectedly received a cheque for ninety pounds from the 'shuffling scamp' himself, Thomas Cautley Newby.[100] It had taken him the best part of four years to produce the money he owed for her sisters' publications.

Charlotte had also resumed her correspondence with Ellen Nussey. Her first few letters were non-committal and avoided all mention of the burning issue which had been responsible for their quarrel in the first place.[101] Ellen remained unaware of how matters had progressed until, towards the end of March, Charlotte accidentally put letters to Mr Nicholls and Ellen in the wrong envelopes and thus inadvertently revealed to her friend that she was not only in correspondence with Arthur Nicholls but also about to welcome him on a visit to the parsonage. Evidently flustered, Charlotte tried to gloss over the importance of the visit and make amends by inviting Ellen to Haworth as well.

I wish you <u>could</u> come about Easter rather than at another time \for this reason/ – Mr Nicholls – if not prevented – proposes coming over then – I suppose he will stay at Mr Grant's, as he has done two or three times before – but he will be frequently coming here – which would enliven your visit a little – perhaps too – he might take a walk with us occasionally – altogether it would be a little change for you such as – you know – I could not always offer.[102]

Ellen had no wish for 'a little change' or to have her visit 'enlivened' by the presence of the loathed Mr Nicholls: she declined to come at Easter though she did not break the fragile peace by giving her true reasons. As it happened, Charlotte's 'little plans' were 'deranged' by the news that Mr Nicholls had decided to come a fortnight early: this was inconvenient, for Patrick was suffering from his usual spring attack of bronchitis but, with characteristic persistence, Mr Nicholls refused to be put off.[103]

He arrived on Monday, 3 April 1854 and stayed till the Friday. Whether his illness had left Patrick too weak to argue, or whether, in the face of his daughter's determination, he could no longer maintain his opposition, he was at last persuaded to sanction the marriage. Charlotte left him little choice, laying down the law both to him and to her suitor with customary bossiness: she would marry; she would not leave her father; Mr Nicholls would return to Haworth as curate; he would live in the parsonage with them.[104] There was nothing left for them to do but bury their grievances and acquiesce in her arrangements.

Chapter Twenty-Six

❧

SO HAPPY

On Friday, 7 April 1854, Arthur Nicholls returned to Kirk Smeaton to celebrate Palm Sunday in an appropriate mood of triumph. It was not until the following Monday that Charlotte gathered sufficient courage to begin the task of informing her friends. What should have been joyous and excited letters were actually subdued and rather forlorn. The most difficult to write was the first, which had to be to Ellen. For the first time Charlotte gave her a bare recital of how matters had progressed since their quarrel last July, ending with the announcement, 'In fact, dear Ellen, I am engaged.' Struggling for words to convey her feelings, she could only report:

I am still very calm – <u>very</u> – inexpectant. What I taste of happiness is of the soberest order. I trust to love my husband – I am grateful for his tender love to me – I believe him to be an affectionate – a conscientious – a high-principled man – and if with all this, I should yield to regrets – that fine talents, congenial < views > tastes and thoughts are not addded – it seems to me I should be most presumptuous and thankless.

Providence offers me this destiny. Doubtless then it is the best for me – …

The marriage would take place in the summer, probably July, and Charlotte hoped that Ellen would be her bridesmaid. Aware that she hardly sounded like a joyful bride, Charlotte added, 'There is a strange – half-sad feeling in making these announcements – The whole thing is something other than imagination paints it beforehand: cares – fears – come mixed inextricably with hopes."

The same apologetic tone pervaded her letter to Miss Wooler the next day. 'The destiny which Providence in His goodness and wisdom seems to offer me will not – I am aware – be generally regarded as brilliant – but I trust < it > I see in it some germs of real happiness." This was a theme she was to touch on more than once. Most of the time she blamed her father: 'The feeling which had been disappointed in Papa – was <u>ambition</u> – paternal <u>pride</u> ever a restless feeling – as we all know', she told Ellen. To Mrs Gaskell, she confessed, 'I could almost cry sometimes that in this important action in my life I cannot better satisfy papa's perhaps natural pride. My destiny will not be brilliant, certainly, but Mr Nicholls is conscientious, affectionate, pure in heart and life. He offers a most constant and tried attachment – I am very grateful to him ...' Writing to Ellen at the end of the month, Charlotte returned to the theme again: 'I trust the illusions of Ambition are quite dissipated – and that he really sees it is better to relieve a suffering and faithful heart – to secure in its fidelity < and > a solid good – than unfeelingly to abandon one who is truly attached to his interests as well as mine – and pursue some vain empty Shadow –'.³ One is left with the uncomfortable feeling that Charlotte was trying to convince herself, as much as her father and her friends, that Mr Nicholls' virtues compensated for the humble station in life he offered her.

The one undeniable cause for satisfaction in all this was the knowledge that the marriage would ensure her father a comfortable old age; his son-in-law's salary, however meagre, would be a useful addition to the family income and, more importantly, as Patrick's health failed, he was assured of willing and able help in the parish. 'My hope is that in the end this arrangement will turn out more truly to Papa's advantage – than any other it was in my power to achieve. Mr N— only in his last letter – refers touchingly to his earnest desire to prove his gratitude to Papa by offering support and consolation to his declining age. This will not be mere <u>talk</u> with him – he is no talker – no dealer in professions.' Patrick himself, realizing the benefits of the arrangements, had come round with surprising rapidity. 'Papa's mind seems wholly changed about this matter;' Charlotte happily informed Ellen. 'And he has said both to me and when I was not there – how much happier he feels since he allowed all to be settled. It is a wonderful relief for me to hear him treat the thing rationally – and quietly and amicably to talk over with him themes on which, once I dared not touch.'⁴

The necessity of having someone reliable in the parish had been forcibly brought home to Patrick by his own continuing ill health. His bronchitis lingered ominously: he had been unable to preach for some time and on Easter Monday he was still too unwell to attend the annual soirée of the Haworth Mechanics' Institute.[5] An invitation to join James Cheadle, vicar of Bingley, in meeting Dr Longley, the Bishop of Ripon, also had to be turned down, despite the fact that Patrick had received a kind and cordial letter from the 'good and dear' bishop, expressing his approval of Mr Nicholls' return and pleasure at the ensuing 'domestic arrangements'.[6]

Now that the matter was decided, both Patrick and Mr Nicholls were anxious to hasten events. Charlotte, however, dragged her feet. She had much to arrange: her proffered visit to Francis Bennoch had to be cancelled and arrangements made for a brief bride-visit to Mrs Gaskell, the Taylors and the Nusseys.[7] There were alterations to be made at the parsonage to accommodate its new inmate. Charlotte had promised her father that the 'plan of residence ... should maintain his seclusion and convenience uninvaded' and to that end the little pantry behind the dining room had to be converted into a study for Mr Nicholls. The workmen were called in and Charlotte herself was busy stitching: 'the little new room is got into order now and the green and white curtains are up – they exactly suit the papering – and look neat and clean enough'.[8]

There were also business arrangements to be made. Reluctantly, Charlotte realized she would have to write to George Smith since he had managed all her investments on her behalf. That she had still not forgiven him for getting engaged (he had married in the meantime) was more than apparent. This was how she announced her own engagement to the man who had once been her most intimate male friend:

My dear Sir
　It having become necessary that my Stock in the Funds should be transferred to another name, I have empowered Mr Metcalfe – my Solicitor – the Bearer of this note – to ask such particulars as are required to fill up the Power of Attorney for a transfer...

Listing all the sums she believed she had invested, totalling £1,684 7s. 6d., she ended her letter with a brusque, 'Apologising for the unavoidable trouble thus given I am, my dear Sir Yours sincerely C Brontë'.[9] No word of explanation; no enquiry after or good wishes for himself or his family; no point of personal reference at all. They might have been total strangers.

George Smith was too acute not to realize the implications of the letter and he wrote a long and friendly reply which Charlotte could not ignore. Grudgingly, and with many a barbed comment that revealed the soreness she still felt, Charlotte accepted his congratulations and good wishes on her forthcoming marriage. 'It gave me also sincere pleasure to be assured of your own happiness –', she told him, 'though of that I never doubted – I have faith also in its permanent character – provided Mrs George Smith is – what it pleases me to fancy her to be.' Giving him a brief résumé of her courtship, she added, 'My expectations, however, are very subdued – very different – I dare say – to what <u>yours</u> were before you were married.' Even now she could not bear to include his wife in the good wishes she felt obliged to send the Smith family: 'I hardly know in what form of greeting to include your wife's name – as I have never seen her – say to her whatever may seem to you most appropriate – and most expressive of good-will.' That was the nearest she could get to magnanimity towards the woman who had succeeded where she had failed. She ended her letter with a sad comment that nevertheless bore a sting in its tail. 'In the course of the year that is gone – Cornhill and London have receded a long way from me – the links of communication have waxed very frail and few. It must be so in this world. All things considered – I don't wish it otherwise.'[10]

There was a sense of coming to the end of an era in all this which was intensified by the visits Charlotte paid to the friends of her maiden days at the beginning of May. Writing to Mrs Gaskell, appropriately enough on 26 April which had been designated a Day of National Humiliation and Prayer on account of the war against Russia, Charlotte revealed that she had not passed on her invitation to Mr Nicholls because she did not want to 'unsettle him' by letting him accompany her.[11] As Mrs Gaskell correctly suspected, however, Charlotte was more concerned about how Mr Nicholls, whom she termed 'a Puseyite and very stiff', would react to her Unitarian friends. 'I had a little talk with him about <u>my</u> "latitudinarianism" and <u>his</u> opposite quality', she told Mrs Gaskell,

He did not bristle up at all – nor feel stiff and unmanageable – he only groaned a little over something in 'Shirley' touching 'baptismal regeneration and a wash-hand basin.' Yet if he is indulgent to some points in me – I shall have carefully to respect certain reverse points in him. I don't mean to trifle with matters deep-rooted and delicate of conscience and principle. I know that when once married I shall often have to hold my tongue on topics which heretofore have rarely failed to set that unruly member in tolerably facile motion. But I <u>will not</u> be a bigot – My heart will always turn to the good of every sect and class.[12]

Invitations for Mr Nicholls to visit Hunsworth and Brookroyd were also forthcoming, but were turned down on his behalf because Mr Cator, his rector, was away in London till June 'and he always stipulates that his Curate shall remain at Kirk-Smeaton while he is away'.[13] This, as we shall see, did not prevent Mr Nicholls visiting his fiancée at Haworth in his vicar's absence.

On 1 May, Charlotte set out for Manchester. Her visit to Plymouth Grove was to last an all too brief four days, but it passed off extremely well. Mrs Gaskell was all agog to learn the details of Charlotte's romance and relayed the gossip with all possible speed to her friends. Allowing for her incorrigible embroidering, the description is nevertheless a dramatic insight into the clash of wills between father and daughter.

To hear her description of the conversation with her father when she quietly insisted on her right to see something more of Mr Nicholls was really fine. Her father thought that she had a chance of some body higher or at least farther removed from poverty. She said 'Father I am not a young girl, not a young woman even – I never was pretty. I now am ugly. At your death I shall have 300£ besides the little I have earned myself – do you think there are many men who would serve seven years for me?' And again when he renewed the conversation and asked her if she would marry a curate? – 'Yes I must marry a curate if I marry at all; not merely a curate but *your* curate; not merely *your* curate but he must live in the house with you, for I cannot leave you'. The sightless old man stood up & said solemnly 'Never. I will never have another man in this house', and stalked out of the room. For a week he never spoke to her. She had not made up her mind to accept Mr Nicholls & the worry on both sides made her ill – then the old servant interfered, and asked him, sitting blind & alone, 'if he wished to kill his daughter?;' and went up to her and abused Mr Nicholls for not having 'more brass.' And so it has ended where it has done.'[4]

Mrs Gaskell positively hugged herself with glee at the knowledge that she had played her own little part in bringing the couple together, sending the letter announcing Charlotte's engagement to Richard Monckton Milnes and John Forster and laughing over her account of Mr Nicholls' puzzlement to account for Mr Milnes' interest in him.[5]

Charlotte also seems to have unburdened herself to Katie Winkworth, a distant relative of Mrs Gaskell's, whose singing of Scottish ballads had so entranced her on a previous visit. They had a long conversation on the merits and demerits of Mr Nicholls. 'I cannot conceal from myself that he is *not* intellectual', she had declared, 'there are many places into which he could not follow me intellectually.' Katie had robustly pointed out that 'if a man had a firm, constant, affectionate, reliable nature, with tolerable practical sense, I should be much better satisfied with him than if he had an intellect far beyond mine, and brilliant gifts without that trustworthiness'. Charlotte's startling response to this was that 'such a character would be far less amusing and interesting than a more impulsive and fickle one; it might be dull!' The conversation, which had begun so seriously, ended in general laughter when Katie observed that such a character would at least enable one to 'do the fickleness required one's self, which would be a relief sometimes'.[16]

By the time Charlotte left Plymouth Grove, her premarital nerves were 'greatly comforted' and both Mrs Gaskell and Katie Winkworth were convinced that Charlotte would be 'much more really happy' with Mr Nicholls, 'than with one who might have made her more in love'. It was Katie, however, who proved the more perceptive when she suggested, 'But I *guess* the true love was Paul Emanuel after all, and is dead; but I don't know, and don't think Lily [Mrs Gaskell] knows…'[17]

From Manchester, Charlotte travelled to Hunsworth to stay with Joe and Amelia Taylor. This visit, too, was curtailed to a mere four days, during which Charlotte, perhaps made more maternal by her approaching marriage, developed a strong attachment to little 'Tim', who was now two and a half years old. Though Charlotte felt herself 'very decent' in health, Amelia declared the opposite: certainly 'Tim' must have thought her old-looking for she called her 'grandmamma', a nickname which Charlotte affectionately adopted in her later correspondence.[18] On Monday, 8 May, Charlotte transferred to Brookroyd: it was almost exactly a year since her last visit and, though no one knew it, it was to be her last. Any lingering awkwardnesses were soon swept away and Ellen was pressed into service helping Charlotte to choose her trousseau in Leeds and Halifax – the bride herself stipulated nothing expensive or extensive and that the bonnets and dresses should all be capable of being 'turned to decent use and worn after the wedding-day'.[19]

Charlotte returned to Haworth on the evening of 13 May to find that arrangements for the wedding were gathering pace. Not surprisingly, George de Renzy, the unfortunate curate who had stepped into Mr Nicholls' shoes and was now surplus to requirements, was feeling aggrieved. Though 'perfectly smooth and fair-spoken' to Patrick, he wrote unpleasantly to Mr Nicholls and had the 'deplorable weakness to go and pour out acrimonious complaints to John Brown, the National Schoolmaster and other subordinates'. His conduct roused Charlotte's bile: 'This only exposes himself to disrespectful comment from those exalted personages', she told Ellen. 'For his own and his office-sake I wish he would be quiet.' He was also making difficulties about the date of his departure, casting all the wedding plans into disarray. 'Mr de R's whole aim is to throw Papa into the dilemma of being without a curate for some weeks', Charlotte wrote angrily to Ellen,

Papa has every legal right to frustrate this at once by telling him he must stay till his quarter is up – but this is just the harsh decided sort of measure which it goes against Papa's nature to adopt and which I can not and will not urge upon him while he is in delicate health. I feel compelled to throw the burden of the contest upon Mr Nicholls who is younger – more pugnacious and can bear it better. The worst of it is Mr N. has not Papa's rights to speak and act or he would do it to purpose –[20]

Patrick had already conceded that his curate should take three weeks of paid leave but Mr de Renzy was now 'moving heaven & earth to get a fortnight more – on pretence of wanting a holiday', Charlotte exploded. It was not until 16 June that matters were finally settled. Charlotte had wanted the wedding deferred till the second week in July, but Patrick had given way and Mr de Renzy had obtained his holiday: he would leave on 25 June. 'This < th > gives rise to much trouble and many difficulties, as you may imagine – and Papa's whole anxiety now is to get the business over – Mr Nicholls – with his usual trustworthiness – takes all the trouble of providing substitutes on his own shoulders.'[21]

Charlotte's annoyance at Mr de Renzy's behaviour was symptomatic of her nerves before the wedding. Even her future husband was causing her considerable irritation – because of his frequent visits! While she had been away, he had been ill with a recurrence of his rheumatic complaint, a fact she seems to have learnt from Mr Grant rather than Arthur himself. Charlotte was thrown into a panic. Was she about to marry a chronic invalid? 'I fear – I fear –', she confessed to Ellen, 'but however I mean to stand by him now whether in weal or woe'. She then revealed – for the first time – that his lack of money had not been Patrick's sole objection to Mr Nicholls: his liability to rheumatic pain had also been 'one of the strong arguments used against the marriage'.[22] One wonders what the other 'strong arguments' were and whether one of them was the danger of pregnancy and childbirth to a woman of delicate health in her late thirties. Though not a subject openly discussed at this period, by the very nature of his job Patrick could not be unaware of the risks.

The reports of Mr Nicholls' illness proved groundless. He came to visit on Monday, 22 May and stayed till the following Saturday. 'At first I was thoroughly frightened by his look ... It was wasted and strange, and his whole manner was nervous', Charlotte told Ellen. 'My worst apprehensions – I thought were in the way of being realized.' When she questioned him, however, she discovered that he had no rheumatic pains and no complaint at all to which he could give a name; he had been to see Mr Teale, who had told him there was nothing whatsoever wrong with him except an overwrought mind.

He was going to die, however, or something like it, I took heart on hearing this – which may seem paradoxical – but you know – dear Nell – when people are really going to die – they don't come a distance of some fifty miles to tell you so ... In short I soon discovered that my business was – instead of sympathizing – to rate him soundly. He had wholesome treatment while he was at Haworth – and went away singularly better.

That Charlotte could now joke about dying, however sardonically, was singular proof of the change in her which Mr Nicholls' devotion had wrought. She was already taking pleasure in affectionate chiding, exclaiming at his impatience in wishing to be married. 'There is not a female child above the age of eight but < would > might rebuke him for the spoilt petulance of his wilful nonsense.'[23]

It was during this visit that Charlotte's marriage settlement was drawn up and signed.[24] This was standard practice in the days before the Married Women's Property Act, because a woman could not own anything in her own right: all her money and estate, whether earned or inherited before or after her marriage, automatically became her husband's property. Fathers wealthy enough to do so would tie up a sum of money in trust for the sole benefit of the daughter and, after her death, her children: this ensured that the daughter would receive an income in the event of widowhood and, if she was marrying a widower with children, or died and her widower remarried, only her own children would benefit from the trust.

Charlotte's marriage settlement was unusual in two respects. Firstly, the money involved, £1,678 9s. 9d., was entirely her own, the sum of her earnings from her writings and what was left of her railway investments, so that she had the entire disposal of it at her command; and secondly, a clause in the settlement determined that, if Charlotte died childless before her husband, the entire value of the trust would revert not to Arthur Nicholls but to Patrick Brontë. Clearly, then, the object of the settlement was to ensure that Mr Nicholls could not touch any of Charlotte's money. During her lifetime the income would be paid out to her 'for her sole and separate use' by Joe Taylor, who was appointed the sole trustee of the fund; if she was widowed, the trust ended and Charlotte regained sole control of the capital and its income. If she died first, it would remain in trust for her children until they came of age, when the capital would be divided among them.[25]

Several factors may account for Charlotte's decision to exclude Mr Nicholls from all control over her money. It was common sense to ensure that, if she was left a widow, her life savings should not be swallowed up in Mr Nicholls' estate and possibly revert to Irish relations, leaving her or her children destitute. Given their respective ages (she was thirty-eight, he was thirty-five), state of health and the risks of childbearing, however, it was much more likely that Charlotte would die, childless, before her husband. As he was comparatively young and still had his career before him, it again made sense that it should be Patrick who would benefit from the money. Had Charlotte not married, the money would inevitably have been his; she was determined that he would not lose financially by the marriage and this was a way of ensuring that he did not do so. It is a measure of Mr Nicholls' love for Charlotte and his determination to 'offer support and consolation' to Patrick's 'declining age' that he willingly acquiesced in an arrangement which would leave him always dependent solely on his meagre curate's income.[26]

The settlement was drawn up by Richard Metcalfe, the Keighley solicitor who had been sent to London to enquire of George Smith about Charlotte's investments, and it was signed and sealed in his presence on 24 May 1854, at Haworth Parsonage by Charlotte, Arthur Nicholls and Joe Taylor; Patrick and Mr Metcalfe acted as witnesses.

The business formalities over, Charlotte hoped for a clear run to complete all the other wedding arrangements. She was 'busy & bothered', trying to finish all her sewing – 'Mr N— hindered me for a full week' – and 'got thoroughly provoked' when 'my worthy acquaintance at Kirk-Smeaton' announced he would be returning to stay at Haworth for another week. She sent him a smart reply that 'he positively should not stay the whole week –

and expostulated with him seriously'.[27] Even the comparatively simple matter of printing wedding cards announcing the marriage was a cause of harassment. Ellen had been commissioned to organize them, but Charlotte proved difficult to please: she had to double her order for cards because Mr Nicholls had 'such a string of clerical acquaintance', she forgot to order white sealing wax, she didn't like the fancy envelopes and demanded a new design and then she did not order enough because there was 'no end to his string of parson-friends'. She even got agitated about the travel arrangements for Miss Wooler and Ellen, the only guests she had invited to the wedding; fearing that Miss Wooler would insist on walking from Keighley and would then arrive 'half-killed' by the heat, she begged Ellen to arrive on the same train so that a cab could be organized to bring them to Haworth.[28]

It must have been a relief to everyone when a wedding date was at last fixed for a few days after Mr de Renzy's departure. Arthur Nicholls took up residence for the last time with the accommodating Mr Grant at Oxenhope and Ellen and Miss Wooler were installed at the parsonage. In accordance with Charlotte's wishes, Mr Nicholls had made all the arrangements for the wedding as secretly as possible so that hardly anyone in the township was aware of what was happening. Early on the morning of Thursday, 29 June 1854, John Robinson, a youth who was favoured with private lessons from Mr Nicholls, was waylaid in Church Lane by John Brown. The sexton told him about the wedding and instructed him to go to the top of the hill and look for the approach of three men, the bridegroom, Joseph Grant and Sutcliffe Sowden, the vicar of Hebden Bridge. As soon as he saw them he was to run to the parsonage and pass on the news. John Robinson did as he was told, and was then sent to fetch Joseph Redman, the old parish clerk, to the church. He came immediately, pausing only to lace his boots against the wall.[29]

As the clock struck eight on 'that dim quiet June Morning', Charlotte entered the church with Ellen and Miss Wooler. She was dressed simply and plainly in a white muslin dress with delicate green embroidery, a lace mantle and a white bonnet, trimmed with lace and a pale band of small flowers and leaves. The few Haworth people who were fortunate enough to catch a glimpse of her thought she looked like a snowdrop.[30] Though Charlotte had declared beforehand that the only people at the ceremony would be Ellen, Miss Wooler and Sutcliffe Sowden, and that the Grants had only been invited to the wedding breakfast afterwards, this was not to be. If John Robinson is correct then Mr Grant accompanied his guests to the church: Joseph Redman, John Brown and John Robinson himself were all there and it seems unlikely that Martha and Tabby would have been excluded from such an important family occasion. The only person of central importance who was missing was Patrick. Mrs Gaskell tells us that he decided the night before that he would not attend, causing consternation, a hurried consultation of the Prayer Book, the discovery that the bride could be given away by her father or a 'friend' and the pressing into service of Miss Wooler as his proxy.[31] It is perhaps not surprising that the seventy-seven-year-old Patrick could not face the prospect of giving away his last remaining child, but Charlotte clearly believed that his plea of ill health was genuine and worried about him constantly on her honeymoon.[32]

The service was brief. Mr Nicholls' friend, Sutcliffe Sowden, officiated, Miss Wooler gave Charlotte away and Ellen Nussey performed her perennial role as bridesmaid. The newly married pair signed the register in the vestry, witnessed by the two ladies, and the little party made its way out of the side door into Church Lane and walked up to the parsonage for the wedding breakfast. Though Charlotte had insisted that there should be no fuss and everything should be kept as quiet as possible, Martha had raided the village gardens to decorate the house with bouquets and Ellen scattered flowers in the bride's honour at the wedding breakfast. Even this ceremony was not prolonged and John Robinson, waiting in the lane before school began, saw a carriage and pair drive up to the parsonage gates ready to carry Mr and Mrs Nicholls off to Keighley station. (As a reward for his services he was called out of school just as lessons began and given breakfast at the parsonage.) Charlotte wore one of her new dresses from Halifax, made from silvery-grey silk with a lavender tinge to it, with large sleeves narrowing to the cuff, a full skirt, tight waist and velvet trimmed neck.[33]

The honeymoon began inauspiciously. Charlotte was already suffering from a cold and, by the time the newly-weds reached their destination in Wales, the weather was wet and wild. From their 'comfortable inn' at Conway Charlotte scribbled a hasty note to Ellen and, one presumes, to her father, to announce their safe arrival.[34] What Charlotte made of her wedding night, which was undoubtedly her first sexual experience, one can only guess: though she did not love Mr Nicholls when she married him, she had never found him physically repugnant like the unfortunate James Taylor, and her honeymoon letters, full of affectionate references to 'my dear husband', suggest a growing and happy intimacy.

Despite the unfavourable weather, the first few days of the honeymoon were spent exploring the dramatic North Wales coast from Conway to Bangor and driving through the spectacular valleys of Snowdonia. Charlotte was enthralled: 'one drive indeed from Llanberis to Beddgelert surpassed anything I remember of the English Lakes'.[35] One wonders whether the sight of Penmaenmawr, looming over the coast above Conway, reminded her of her unfortunate brother and the poetry it had inspired in him.

On 4 July, they travelled across Anglesey and caught the packet steamer to Dublin. They were fortunate to have a calm day and therefore a good passage. Charlotte's cold had got worse so the two days that they spent in Dublin were restricted to driving around the city, Arthur obviously taking pride in showing his bride his old student haunts, including the library, museum and chapel of his *alma mater*, Trinity College. In many ways the whole honeymoon was to be dedicated to an exploration and discovery of Arthur Bell Nicholls' past. In Dublin they were joined by his brother, manager of the Grand Canal from Dublin to their home town, Banagher, who was 'a sagacious well-informed and courteous man', a cousin, who was studying at the university and another cousin, 'a pretty lady-like girl with gentle English manners'. Quite what sort of barbarians Charlotte had expected her husband's Irish relations to be is not clear – but she was constantly surprised and pleased by their 'Englishness', by which she meant their gentility. The male members of his family all turned out to be 'thoroughly educated gentlemen'; Mrs Bell, the aunt who had brought him up, 'is like an English or Scotch Matron quiet, kind and well-bred', the apparent explanation for this peculiarity being explained by Charlotte's next comment: 'It seems she was brought up in London.'[36]

Arthur's brother and cousins escorted the newly-weds the eighty-odd miles from Dublin to Banagher, where Charlotte was equally surprised and gratified by her husband's former home. 'I cannot help feeling singularly interested in all about the place', she wrote to Miss Wooler. 'In this house Mr Nicholls was brought up by his uncle Dr Bell – It is very large and looks externally like a gentleman's country-seat – within most of the rooms are lofty and spacious and some – the drawing-room – dining-room &c. handsomely and commodiously furnished.' Having thought that she was taking a step down in the world in marrying a humble curate, Charlotte was being forced to revise her opinions. 'My dear husband too appears in a new light here in his own country', she admitted, adding proudly, 'More than once I have had deep pleasure in hearing his praises on all sides. Some of the old servants and followers of the family tell me I am a most fortunate person for that I have got one of the best gentlemen in the country. His Aunt too speaks of him with a mixture of affection and respect most gratifying to hear.' Feeling thankful that she had made the right choice in her husband, she now added another laudatory adjective to her mental list of his virtues, 'unboastful'.[37] Significantly, there was no suggestion that he should be taken to be introduced to her Irish relatives: she was all too well aware that they were of a totally different class from the refined and comparatively wealthy Bells.

After a week at Banagher, during which Mrs Bell kindly nursed Charlotte back to health ('fatigue and excitement had nearly knocked me up – and my cough was become very bad'), the newly-weds travelled along the banks of the Shannon and Lough Derg to Limerick and then cut across to Kilkee on the West Coast – 'such a wild, iron-bound coast – with such an ocean-view as I had not yet seen – and such battling of waves with rocks as I had never imagined'.[38] Restored to health, unexpectedly pleased with and proud of her new relations and, most of all, her new husband, Charlotte's happiness shines out of her letters. 'I had heard a great deal about Irish negligence &c. I own that till I came to Kilkee – I saw little of it', she told Catherine Wooler.

Here at our Inn – splendidly designated 'the West-End Hotel' – there is a good deal to carp at if one were in a carping humour – but we laugh instead of grumbling – for out of doors there is much indeed to compensate for any indoor short-comings; so magnificent an ocean – so bold and grand a coast – I never yet saw. My husband calls me – Give my love to all who care to have it…[39]

It was a long time since Charlotte had written anything so light-hearted as this careless valediction or, indeed, enjoyed the intimacy of shared humour.

At Kilkee yet another of Charlotte's reservations about her marriage was dispelled. Writing to Katie Winkworth, to whom she had confided her 'grand doubts' about 'congenial tastes' before her marriage, she explained:

The first morning we went out on to the cliffs and saw the Atlantic coming in all white foam, I did not know whether I should get leave or time to take the matter in my own way. I did not want to talk – but I did want to look and be silent. Having hinted a petition, licence was not refused – covered with a rug to keep off the spray I was allowed to sit where I chose – and he only interrupted me when he thought I crept too near the edge of the cliff. So far he is always good in this way – and this protection which does not interfere \or pretend –/ is I believe a thousand times better than any half sort of pseudo sympathy.[40]

From Kilkee they spent nearly a fortnight touring the southwest corner of Ireland: they took in all the most famous beauty spots, Tarbert, on the mouth of the Shannon, Tralee, Killarney (did she think of her father's story?), Glengarriff on Bantry Bay, ending up in Cork. Charlotte was literally speech-less. 'I shall make no effort to describe the scenery through which we have passed', she told Ellen. 'Some parts have exceeded all I ever imagined.'[41] The tour was marred by a single, terrifying incident. Charlotte had ignored their guide's advice to dismount from her horse on a particularly broken and dangerous section of path through the Gap of Dunloe near Killarney. The horse panicked, rearing and plunging, and, while her husband was pre-occupied trying to calm it, it threw Charlotte to the ground. Charlotte 'saw and felt' the horse kicking, plunging and trampling round: 'I had my thoughts about the moment – its consequences – my husband – my father –'. The moment he realized what had happened, Arthur released the horse, which sprang over her, leaving her shocked but unhurt. 'Of course the only feeling left was gratitude for more sakes than my own.'[42] It is an interesting indication of how much Charlotte's priorities had changed in the past month that her first thought was for her husband, not her father.

Nevertheless, it was in some ways a relief to reach Dublin and know that they would soon be home. Patrick had been ill and Charlotte was anxious to see him again, knowing that nothing would cheer him like her presence. They returned to Haworth in the early evening of Tuesday, 1 August, having been away for almost exactly a month.[43]

They were immediately plunged straight into the routine of parish life. 'Since I came home I have not had an unemployed moment,' Charlotte declared with satisfaction,

my life is changed indeed – to be wanted continually – to be constantly called for and occupied seems so strange: yet it is a marvellously good thing. As yet I don't quite understand how some wives grow so selfish – As far as my experience of matrimony goes – I think it tends to draw you out of, and away from yourself.

In this same letter Charlotte also made some rather odd comments which are often taken out of context and used to suggest that she still had deep reservations about her marriage, particularly the sexual side.

Dear Nell – during the last 6 weeks – the colour of my thoughts is a good deal changed: I know more of the realities of life than I once did. I think many false ideas are propagated perhaps unintentionally. I think those married women who indiscriminately urge their acquaintance to marry – much to blame. For my part – I can only say with deeper sincerity and fuller significance – what I always said in theory – Wait God's will. Indeed – indeed Nell – – it is a solemn and strange and perilous thing for a woman to become a wife. Man's lot is far – far different.

These enigmatic words would appear to mean that, as someone accustomed to exercising her own judgement and making her own decisions, Charlotte found the change to a dependent existence very difficult, but it does not necessarily follow that she regretted or was unhappy in her marriage. Indeed, exactly the opposite was the case. Had she had serious reservations about married life she would hardly have made playful references to Sutcliffe Sowden, the eligible bachelor who had married them, which suggest that she was already matchmaking between her own and her husband's best friends. And she ended the letter with a glowing postscript: 'Have I told you how much better Mr Nicholls is? He looks quite strong and hale – he gained 12 lbs during the 4 weeks we were in Ireland. To see this improvement in him has been a main source of happiness to me; and to speak truth – a subject of wonder too.'[44]

Charlotte, too, was blossoming in her new married life. Patrick was unwell when they returned but under Charlotte's solicitous care he soon recovered and was preaching again before the month was out. Arthur had started as he meant to go on and since their return he had taken over all the duties from Patrick: 'each time I see Mr Nicholls put on gown or surplice – I feel comforted to think that this marriage has secured Papa good aid in his old age', Charlotte told Miss Wooler gratefully.[45] Every morning he was in the National School by nine o'clock where he taught religious instruction till ten thirty; almost every afternoon he spent visiting among the poor: 'Of course he often finds a little work for his wife to do, and I hope she is not sorry to help him'.[46]

They were inundated with visitors and wellwishers. Among the first were Sutcliffe Sowden, who came over from Hebden Bridge for the day with a friend, and Mr and Mrs Grant who joined them for tea.[47] So many parishioners called that the newly-weds decided to show their appreciation by inviting the scholars and teachers of the Sunday and day schools, the church bellringers and singers *et al.*, to a tea and supper in the schoolroom in Church Lane. Five hundred people attended, as Charlotte proudly told Miss Wooler:

They seemed to enjoy it much, and it was very pleasant to see their happiness. One of the villagers in proposing my husband's health described him as 'a consistent Christian and a kind gentleman.' I own the words touched me – and I thought – (as I know you would have thought – had you been present) – that to merit and win such a character was better than to earn either Wealth or Fame or Power. I am disposed to echo that high but simple eulogium now. If I can do so with sincerity and conviction seven years – or even a year hence – I shall esteem myself a happy woman.[48]

The same thought, that a happy marriage was better than anything success as a novelist had to offer, was echoed a month later in another letter to Miss Wooler.

You ask what visitors we have had? – A good many amongst the clergy &c. in the neighbourhood, but none of note from a distance. Haworth is – as you say – a very quiet place; it is also difficult of access, and unless under the stimulus of necessity or that of strong curiosity – or finally that of true and tried friendship – few take courage to penetrate to so remote a nook. Besides, now that I am married I do not expect to be an object of much general interest. Ladies who have won some prominence (call it either notoriety or celebrity) in their single life – often fall quite into the background when they change their names; but if true domestic happiness replace Fame – the exchange will indeed be for the better.[49]

The extraordinary thing is not that Charlotte was so very happy in her married life but that she was so busy. It was not as if her domestic role had changed dramatically: the parson's daughter had simply become the curate's wife. It was still the same round of entertaining visiting clergy, organizing parish tea-drinkings, teaching in the schools and visiting the poor. The only difference was that in the past these duties had been performed unwillingly and had been so uninteresting to her that they barely merited a mention in her correspondence. Now, they assumed such importance in her life that she could fill a whole letter recounting them.[50] As the parson's daughter she had been expected to do them; as the curate's wife she wanted to do them to please her husband. Suddenly she discovered that there was a social life in Haworth after all.

Despite her absorption in her married life, Charlotte did not forget her friends. Ellen was invited to the parsonage early in September, though she was unable to come until the twenty-first of the month;[51] she seems to have stayed a fortnight, during which Charlotte and her husband tried to foster the apparent liking between her and Sutcliffe Sowden. Arthur had earlier announced his intention of taking 'sundry rather long walks' during Ellen's stay 'and as he should have his wife to look after – and she was trouble enough – it would be quite necessary to have a guardian for the other lady. Mr S— seemed perfectly acquiescent'. Mr Sowden did not take the bait: future letters from him proved 'uninteresting', a sure sign that they contained no reference to Ellen.[52]

Even while Ellen was still at Haworth, Charlotte was busy inviting Mrs Gaskell and her husband to stay: 'Come to Haworth as soon as you can find a fitting time –', she pleaded. 'My Father – all in this house who have once seen you, wish to see you again. My husband does not know you yet, but when he <u>does</u> know you, he will feel as others feel; besides I want you to see him.' To her everlasting regret, Mrs Gaskell did not take up the invitation, citing 'some little obstacle', which, in fact, was her new enthusiasm for Florence Nightingale, whose family she stayed with twice in October.[53]

Hard on Ellen's heels, the Taylors visited Haworth. They came for a day on 10 October in order to arrange a more prolonged visit. Arthur's first meeting with Amelia was not auspicious. She was currently 'worshipping' and 'assiduously cultivating' one of her husband's former flames which Charlotte thought 'strained – odd – unnatural'. Arthur, however, was 'very strong upon it – much out of patience with Amelia. I don't know whether I shall be able to keep him at home now whenever she does come. He threatens to bolt.'[54] He did not have time to do so for, only a week later, Joe escorted his family over and left them to stay at the parsonage for a few days. 'We got on with them better than I expected', Charlotte reported to Ellen, little 'Tim', in particular, captivating the Brontë household.

Tim behaved capitally on the whole. She amused Papa very much – chattering away to him very funnily – his white hair took her fancy – She announced a decided preference for it over Arthur's black hair – and coolly advised the latter to 'go to the barber, and get his whiskers cut off.' Papa says she speaks as I did when I was a child – says the same odd unexpected things. Neither Arthur nor Papa liked A's look at first – but she improved on them – I think.

It was Charlotte's unguarded comments in this letter that sparked off the old animosity between Ellen and Arthur again.

Arthur has just been glancing over this note – He thinks I have written too freely about Amelia &c. Men don't seem to understand making letters a vehicle of communication – they always seem to think us incautious. I'm sure I don't think I have said anything rash – however, you must <u>burn</u> it when read. Arthur says such letters as mine never ought to be kept – they are dangerous as lucifer matches – so be sure to follow a recommendation he has just given 'fire them' – or 'there will be no more.' such is his resolve. I can't help laughing – this seems to me so funny. Arthur however says he is quite 'serious' and looks it, I assure you – he is bending over the desk with his eyes full of concern.[55]

Ellen took an equally serious view of the matter, particularly when Arthur pressed the point a few days later.

Dear Ellen – Arthur complains that you do not distinctly promise to burn my letters as you receive them. He says you must give him a plain pledge to that effect – or he will read every line I write and elect himself censor of our correspondence.

He says women are most rash in letter-writing – they think only of the trust-worthiness of their immediate friend – and do not look to contingencies – a letter may fall into any hand. You must give the promise – I believe – at least he says so, with his best regards – or else you will get such notes as he writes to Mr Sowden – plain, brief statements of facts without the adornment of a single flourish – with no comment on the character < of > or peculiarities of any human being – and if a phrase of sensibility or affection steals in – it seems to come on tiptoe – looking ashamed of itself – blushing 'pea-green' as he says – and holding both its shy hands before its face. Write him out his promise on a separate slip of paper, in a <u>legible</u> hand – and send it in your next.[56]

Charlotte clearly saw no difficulty in this: she seems to have regarded her letters to Ellen as personal and ephemeral and therefore not worth keeping. The fact that none of Ellen's letters to her are extant suggests that Charlotte did not keep them,[57] which perhaps explains her lack of concern over whether her own were destroyed or not. Ellen, however, was furious. She had carefully hoarded all Charlotte's letters over the years and, as her friend had become famous, regarded them as doubly precious. Arthur placed her on the horns of a dilemma. She could give the promise and be forced to destroy all Charlotte's future letters or she could refuse and, with Arthur as self-elected censor, be deprived of all the intimate details which made her friend's correspondence so individual and so much fun. Doubtlessly cursing Arthur with every word, she wrote out her promise: 'My dear Mr Nicholls, As you seem to hold in great horror the *ardentia verba* of feminine epistles, I pledge myself to the destruction of Charlotte's epistles, henceforth, if you pledge yourself to <u>no</u> censorship in the matter communicated – Yours very truly, E Nussey.' The Jesuitical phrasing of the promise was deliberate. Ellen had no intention of burning Charlotte's letters, and (to take a kindly view) convinced herself that Arthur censored his wife's future letters. She later wrote upon the note when it was returned to her, 'Mr N. continued his censorship so the pledge was void.'[58]

Completely unaware that Ellen had no intention of destroying his wife's letters, Arthur accepted the note at face value. 'Arthur thanks you for the promise', Charlotte told her, '... on my asking him whether he would give the pledge required in return – he says "yes we may now write any dangerous stuff we please to each other – it is not "<u>old friends</u>" he mistrusts, but the chances of war – the accidental passing of letters into hands and under eyes for which they were never written'.[59]

The flurry of visits to Haworth Parsonage continued. Early in November, Sutcliffe Sowden came over again, bringing his younger brother, George, who was also in clerical orders. They stayed the night, and Charlotte was careful to pass on that 'Mr S asked after "Miss Nussey".'[60] A few days later, Sir James Kay Shuttleworth and an unnamed friend descended and stayed the weekend. There was a reason for the visit. Unable to patronize 'Currer Bell' as he wished, he was now trying to patronize her husband. He had built a grand new church on his doorstep at Padiham and hoped that Arthur would accept the living, which was worth £200 a year, double his current salary. Had there been no other reason – and one cannot imagine that Charlotte could have borne the dependency implied in such an arrangement – the fact that Arthur had promised not to leave Haworth during Patrick's lifetime would have prevented him accepting the offer.[61] Sir James then asked Arthur – somewhat half-heartedly, one feels, having not gained his real object – to recommend another clergyman for the post. Not unnaturally, Arthur thought of Sutcliffe Sowden, for whom the increase in income would be particularly welcome, but the transparency of Sir James' dealings soon became clear as obstacles were suddenly raised and the post was eventually offered elsewhere.[62]

The happiness of Charlotte's married life had transformed her health. Writing to Miss Wooler in the middle of November, a time when, since the death of her sisters, she had always been ill, she claimed that 'for my own part – it is long since I have known such comparative immunity from headache, sickness and indigestion, as during the last three months'. 'My life is different to what it used to be', she added. 'May God make me thankful for it! I have a good, kind, attached husband, and every day makes my own attachment to him stronger.'[63]

Though he could not accompany her because of his duties in Haworth, Arthur had agreed that Charlotte should go on a visit to the Nusseys and the Taylors in November. This had to be deferred, ironically, because there was serious illness at both Brookroyd and Hunsworth. The first delay was caused by Joe Taylor falling ill of a gastric fever and being carried off to Scarborough on medical advice.[64] Charlotte had several distraught letters from Amelia and, as Joe was patently dangerously ill, she replied as comfortingly as she could. 'You never were more thoroughly right in your thoughts than when you believed I cared for yourself and Joe – <u>that</u> I do with my whole heart', she declared.

I have known Joe above twenty years and differed from him and been enraged with him and liked him and cared for him as long – and <u>you</u> dear Amelia – well – I will just say this – I can now realize how Joe will appreciate the value of a nature genuinely affectionate – which will adhere to him the closer and love him the better because there is something to be done for him – In high health – there might have been women who would give life more brilliancy, in sickness – no wife could be better than Joe's own actual wife.'[65]

Scarborough had no effect and the Taylors returned to Hunsworth, where Joe began to make preparations for his death. Amelia was in despair. Again Charlotte wrote to comfort her: she was convinced that his recovery was not only likely but probable. She warned Amelia not to let Joe 'quit his hold upon life in thought nor entirely relax his <u>will</u> to live', explaining that 'A mental tendency inherited from his Mother will dispose him to do this too soon. He must remember it is better for his wife, better for his child – better for many that he should live. <u>He</u> may feel that he can already lie down serene and fearless by his Father and Grandfather – but others may find it too difficult and dreary to live on after he has left them.'[66]

Charlotte had put off going to Brookroyd because she had wanted to go on to Hunsworth on the same trip from home. Then came news that Mercy Nussey was also ill. Ellen reported that she was suffering from a low fever; Arthur was not happy at the idea of Charlotte being exposed to any contagion, 'fever – you know is a formidable word', though she herself was unconcerned. Fortunately, before she had fixed her plans to go to Brookroyd, a letter came from Miss Wooler warning them that Mercy's fever was actually the deadly typhus. 'I thank you very much for your truly kind warning', Charlotte responded, '– and I believe my husband thanks you still more.'[67] There was now absolutely no possibility of Charlotte going to Brookroyd, but she had difficulty making her excuses. It was not clear whether Ellen was actually aware that her sister had typhus and, if she did not know, then Charlotte had no wish to alarm her. She therefore wrote to defer the visit on the grounds that it was her husband's wish that she should do so. 'I shall not get leave to go to Brookroyd before Christmas now – so do not expect me', she told Ellen, adding, without mentioning the fearful word 'typhus':

For my own part I really should have no fear – and if it just depended on me – I should come – but these matters are not quite in my power now – another must be consulted – and where his wish and judgment have a decided bias to a particular course – I make no stir, but just adopt it. Arthur is sorry to disappoint both you and me, but it is his fixed wish that a few weeks should be allowed yet to elapse before we meet –

By making the decision appear to be simply a dictatorial whim on her husband's part, Charlotte unintentionally fanned the flames of her friend's hatred for Arthur. Ellen would never forgive him for depriving her of Charlotte's last visit to Brookroyd. Nor did Charlotte help matters by referring to her husband as 'my dear boy' and ending her letter with a comment that made it clear to Ellen that her own place as Charlotte's most intimate friend had been usurped.

I am writing in haste – It is almost inexplicable to me that I seem so often hurried now – but the fact is whenever Arthur is in, I must have occupations in which he can share, or which will not at least divert my attention from him – Thus a multitude of little matters get put off till he goes out – and then I am quite busy.[68]

Ellen's role in Charlotte's life had been reduced to a 'little matter' over which Arthur's smallest desires took precedence.

The year seemed to be drawing to a gloomy close. Almost exactly three years to the day after the death of Keeper, Anne's dog Flossy died. 'Did I tell you that our poor little Flossy is dead?' Charlotte asked Ellen. 'He drooped for a single day – and died quietly in the night without pain. The loss even of a dog was very saddening – yet perhaps no dog ever had a happier life or an easier death.' Tabby, too, was ill, suffering from an attack of diarrhoea so severe that even though the Haworth doctor, Mr Ingham, was ill himself, Charlotte wrote to ask him to prescribe her some medicine.[69]

Events outside Haworth, too, could not fail to impinge on the household. The news from the Crimea was appalling. Though the British had succeeded in repulsing two Russian attacks at Balaclava and Inkerman, their casualties (including, most famously, the victims of the Charge of the Light Brigade) had been immense and they had failed to take Sebastopol. Devastated by disease, without the resources or medical supplies to sustain a winter campaign and their lines of provision cut off by the hostile weather, the soldiers were dying in their hundreds. Any lingering illusions about the glory of war which Charlotte had once cherished had long since been crushed. 'I say nothing about the War', she told Miss Wooler,

– but when I read of its horrors – I cannot help thinking that it is one of the greatest curses that can fall upon mankind. I trust it may not last long – for it really seems to me that no glory to be gained can compensate for the sufferings which must be endured. This tone may seem a little ignoble and unpatriotic – but I think that as we advance towards middle age – nobleness and patriotism bear a different sig-nification to us to that which we accept while young.[70]

In response to the sufferings, a national Patriotic Fund had been established to raise voluntary subscriptions for the benefit of the wounded and the widows and orphans of the dead. With typical concern, Patrick convened a meeting in the National School on 16 December to raise a subscription in the township; as his eyesight was so poor, however, it was Charlotte and her husband who wrote out the circulars to the leading members of the community inviting their attendance.[71]

Despite the almost universal gloom and the fact that this was normally her most unhappy time of year, Charlotte remained resolutely cheerful.

Marriage had clearly eclipsed the painful memories of her sisters' deaths which had so overshadowed previous winters. Writing to Ellen on Boxing Day 1854, she ended her letter like any other new bride.

Arthur joins me in sincere good wishes for a happy Christmas & many of them to you and yours. He is well – thank God – and so am I – and he is 'my dear boy' certainly – dearer now than he was six months ago – in three days we shall actually have been married that length of time!⁷²

The new year began well enough. Charles Dickens came to Bradford on 28 December to give one of his celebrated public readings of *A Christmas Carol* at St George's Hall; he was followed, on 11 January, by the Earl of Carlisle, who gave a lecture on the poetry of Thomas Gray.⁷³ As Charlotte had met both men, one wonders whether she was in the audience for either or both occasions, or whether they were now as remote to her as Cornhill. Her own literary exertions had virtually ceased, though this was more a result of circumstance than decision; her thoughts sometimes reverted to her writing. 'One Evening at the close of 1854', Arthur later told George Smith,

as we sat by the fire listening to the howling of the wind around the house my poor wife suddenly said, 'If you had not been with me I must have been writing now' – She then ran upstairs, brought down & read aloud the beginning of her New Tale – When she had finished I remarked, 'The Critics will accuse you of repetition, as you have again introduced a school' – She replied, 'O I shall alter that – I always begin two or three times before I can please myself' – But, it was not to be –⁷⁴

The two chapters which Charlotte read to her husband were a reworking of 'Willie Ellin', the story she had begun in the late spring of 1853. This time, the fragment, which became known as 'Emma', introduced a sensitive young girl, Matilda Fitzgibbon, who, though personally unpopular because of her unpromising looks and depressed spirits, is nevertheless petted and fêted by her headmistress because of her apparent wealth and aristocratic pretensions. She is then exposed as an impostor whose father's title and estate do not exist; as the headmistress turns on her in vindictive spite she finds a new and unexpected protector in William Ellin.⁷⁵ Even this fragment, however, was over a year old, having been written the previous November. Probably she had written nothing since.

Whether she wished to do so or not, Charlotte was not given the chance to develop her story. In the second week of January, she and her husband were invited to Gawthorpe Hall as the guests of Sir James Kay Shuttleworth. The baronet evidently had some thoughts of persuading Arthur to change his mind about the living of Padiham but was rather thwarted by his persistent refusal and the current incumbent's withdrawal of his resignation.⁷⁶ According to Mrs Gaskell, Charlotte returned from Gawthorpe Hall feeling unwell, having aggravated a cold she had caught at the end of November by walking in thin shoes on damp ground. This seems unlikely, though Charlotte had complained of a chill after she had been caught in the rain while walking on the moors above Haworth to see the snow-swollen waterfall on Sladen Beck. This was proffered as a partial excuse for not going to Brookroyd in December. But Charlotte had declared herself to be well in her next extant letter and there is nothing to suggest the 'lingering cold' which Mrs Gaskell describes.[77]

The real cause of Charlotte's sudden poor health was the fact that, at thirty-eight years old, she was pregnant. She hinted as much to Ellen in a letter describing the classic symptoms of what is misleadingly known as morning sickness.

My health has been really very good ever since my return from Ireland till about ten days ago, when the stomach seemed quite suddenly to lose its tone – indigestion and continual faint sickness have been my portion ever since. Don't conjecture – dear Nell – for it is too soon yet – though I certainly never before felt as I have done lately. But keep the matter wholly to yourself – for I can come to no decided opinion at present.[78]

At first the nausea was not bad enough to prevent her fulfilling her normal round of duties. After their return from Gawthorpe Hall, one of Arthur's cousins, the Reverend James Adamson Bell, came to stay briefly: 'the visit was a real treat', Charlotte told Amelia, '– He is a cultivated, thoroughly educated man with a mind stored with information gathered from books and travel – and what is far rarer – with the art of conversing appropriately and quietly and never pushing his superiority upon you.'[79] She was also well enough to be making plans for visiting Hunsworth and Brookroyd at the end of January, though assuring Amelia that she would not intrude if Joe was still too ill to derive benefit from her coming: she knew, from 'sorrowful experience', she told Amelia, 'that visits even from dear friends are rarely advisable during serious sickness. Ellen Nussey used, with a good intention enough, to volunteer her presence when my sisters were ill; it was impossible for me to do with her –'.[80]

Within a few days of making her tentative plans, however, Charlotte herself was compelled to take to her bed. She was too ill even to answer a letter from Ellen, obliging her husband to write one of his 'plain, brief statements of fact' on her behalf. Though she still held out hope of going to Brookroyd on 31 January, Arthur added, 'I should say that unless she improve very rapidly, it will not be advisable for her to leave home even then –'. By 29 January, Arthur was so concerned about his wife's deteriorating condition that he sent to Bradford for Dr MacTurk 'as I wish to have better advice than Haworth affords –'. Dr MacTurk came the next day: 'His opinion was that her illness would be of some duration – but that there was no immediate danger –'.[81]

This opinion was echoed by Patrick in a letter to Sir James Kay Shuttle-worth.

Owing to my Dear Daughter's indisposition, she has desired me to answer your kind letter, by return of post – for several days past, she has been confin'd to her bed, where she still lies, oppress'd with nausea, sickness, irritation, & a slow feverish feeling – and a consequent want of appetite and digestion. < indigestion > – her village, surgeon, visits her daily, & we have had a visit from Dr. Macturk of Brad-ford – who, both think her sickness is symptomatic – and that after a few weeks they hope her health, will again return – nevertheless the trying circumstance gives much uneasiness in our little family circle – where till lately, considering our respective ages, we have all been, in good health & spirits –[82]

A fortnight later there was still no improvement. In answer to an avalanche of anxious letters from Ellen, who seems to have believed that Arthur was forbidding Charlotte to write, he painfully inscribed a few lines. 'It is difficult to write to friends about my wife's illness, as its cause is yet uncertain –', he wrote, 'at present she is completely prostrated with weakness & sickness & frequent fever – all may turn out well in the end, & I hope it will; if you saw [her] you would perceive that she can maintain no correspondence –'.[83] Clearly he was beginning to have his doubts about the probability of Char-lotte's recovery.

This thought must have occurred to Charlotte too, for three days later, on 17 February, she made her will. The brief legal disposition of her property spoke volumes about her marriage and the unexpected happiness it had brought her. Overturning the careful arrangements of her marriage settle-ment, the will left everything to Arthur Bell Nicholls, 'to be his absolutely and entirely'. There was no provision at all for Patrick, whose name appears only with that of Martha Brown as a witness to Charlotte's shaky signature. The will was a declaration of Charlotte's absolute faith in her husband's integrity; she now knew that he did not require a legal obligation to compel him to look after her father.[84]

As if the strain was not already unbearable, on the very day that Charlotte made her will, Tabby Aykroyd died. She was eighty-four years old and had been the Brontës' servant in weal and woe for over thirty years. It fell to Arthur to bury her in Haworth churchyard, just beyond the parsonage garden wall and within sight of the room where his own wife lay dying.[85] Too weak to write anything but the briefest of pencilled notes to her closest friends, Charlotte nevertheless made the effort to sing her husband's praises in every one. 'I am not going to talk about my sufferings, it would be useless and painful –', she told Ellen. 'I want to give you an assurance which I know will comfort you – and that is that I find in my husband the tenderest nurse, the kindest support – the best earthly comfort that ever woman had. His patience never fails and it is tried by sad days and Broken nights.'[86] A few days later, when Ellen had sent on a cheering letter from Mary Hewitt describing how she had suffered similar weakness and emaciation before being safely delivered of her child, Charlotte responded pathetically: 'In much her case was wonderfully like mine – but I am reduced to greater weakness – the skeleton emaciation is the same &c., &c. &c. I cannot talk – even to < to > my dear patient constant Arthur I can say but few words at once.'[87] To Amelia, Charlotte wrote:

Let me speak the plain truth – my sufferings are very great – my nights inde-scribable – sickness with scarce a reprieve – I strain until what I vomit is mixed with blood. Medicine I have quite discontinued – If you <u>can</u> send me anything that will do good – <u>do</u>.

As to my husband – my heart is knit to him – he is so tender, so good, helpful, patient.

Poor Joe! long has he to suffer. May God soon send him, you, all of us health strength – comfort.[88]

Amelia sent medicines but they had no perceptible effect; Charlotte refused to allow her husband to send for the doctor Amelia recommended: 'I know it would be wholly useless.' 'Oh for happier times!' she could not help crying. 'My little Grandchild – when shall I see her again?' When Martha tried to cheer her by telling her to look forward to her own baby that was coming, Charlotte could only sigh, 'I dare say I shall be glad some time, but I am so ill – so weary –'.[89]

Though she had days when she revived a little and was able to swallow 'beef-tea – spoonsful of wine & water – a mouthful of light pudding at different times –',[90] Charlotte grew inexorably weaker and closer to death. By the second week in March she could no longer even hold a pencil to write and her husband had to answer her letters for her. He, too, had to break the 'awful & painful' news to Charlotte that Ellen's brother-in-law, Robert Clapham, had suddenly died and, though he did it as gently as he could, it was still a great shock. 'These seem troubled times, my dear Miss Nussey.', he wrote. 'May God support you through them –'.[91] A week later, Charlotte was no longer fully conscious, having slipped into a 'low wan-dering delirium' during which she constantly craved food and drink. Mrs Gaskell describes how 'Wakening for an instant from this stupor of intel-ligence, she saw her husband's woe-worn face, and caught the sound of some murmured words of prayer that God would spare her. "Oh!" she whispered forth, "I am not going to die, am I? He will not separate us, we have been so happy".'[92]

Throughout his tender and ceaseless care of his wife, Arthur Nicholls had not failed to do his parochial duties; with terrible irony it even fell to him to conduct the prayers and services on 21 March, which had been declared another Day of National Humiliation and Prayer because of the war in Russia. Towards the end of March, however, even his strength and courage failed him: he abandoned his duties to his old friend, Joseph Grant, and maintained a constant vigil at his wife's bedside.[93] In this crisis, it was Patrick Brontë, now seventy-eight years old and nearly the sole survivor of his large family, who rose to the occasion with dignity and grace. 'My Dear Madam', he wrote to Ellen Nussey on 30 March 1855:

We are all in great trouble, and Mr Nicholls so much so, that he is not so sufficiently strong, and composed as to be able to write – I therefore devote a few moments, to tell you, that my dear Daughter is very ill, and apparently on the verge of the grave – If she could speak, she would no doubt dictate to us whilst answering your kind letter, but we are left to ourselves, to give what answer we can – The Doctors have no hope of her case, and fondly as we a long time, cherished hope, that hope is now gone, and we [have] only to look forward to the solemn event, with prayer to God, that he will give us grace and strength sufficient unto our day –

Will you be so kind as to write to Miss Wooler, and Mrs Joe Taylor, and inform them that we requested you to do so – telling them of our present condition Ever truly and respectfully Yours,

P. Brontë[94]

Early on Saturday morning, 31 March 1855, Charlotte died, just three weeks before her thirty-ninth birthday. 'Mr Brontè's letter would prepare you for the sad intelligence I have to communicate', Arthur wrote to Ellen. '– Our dear Charlotte is no more – She died last night of Exhaustion. For the last two or three weeks we had become very uneasy about her, but it was not until Sunday Evening that it became apparent that her sojourn with us was likely to be short – We intend to bury her on Wednesday morng.' 'On [the] whole she had not much suffering –', he wrote to Mary Hewitt soon afterwards, 'she spoke little during the last few days, but continued quite conscious.'[95] Mr Ingham, the Haworth surgeon who had attended Charlotte throughout her last illness, certified the cause of death as 'Phthisis', indicating a progressive wasting disease. There seems little doubt that it was the pregnancy and its consequent violent nausea which had worn her down; the baby, of course, died with her.[96] Despite their prolific ancestry, there would be no descendants of the Brontës of Haworth.

United in their grief, Charlotte's father and husband were not to be left to mourn in peace and privacy for long. Only hours after her death the first intrusions began. Ellen Nussey arrived on the doorstep, having taken the first available train after receiving Patrick's note telling her of Charlotte's imminent demise. 'I had begged to go before', Ellen later wrote in anguish, 'but Mr Brontë and Mr Nicholls objected, fearing the excitement of a meeting for poor Charlotte.' It was undoubtedly even more impossible for them 'to do with her' than it had been for Charlotte when Ellen had tried to volunteer her presence during her sisters' illnesses. Not surprisingly, Patrick did not come down to welcome the unwelcome visitor but, as courtesy demanded, he sent a message inviting Ellen to stay until the funeral. It was Martha Brown who escorted Ellen upstairs to the bedchamber to see her friend's body laid out in death, and it was also Martha who invited Ellen to perform the funeral obsequies: 'her death chamber is in vivid remembrance,' Ellen told George Smith five years later,

I last saw her in death. Her maid Martha brought me a tray full of evergreens & such flowers as she could procure to place on the lifeless form – My first feeling was, no, I <u>cannot cannot</u> do it – next I was grateful to the maid for giving me the tender office – what made it impossible at first was the rushing recollection of the flowers I spread in her honour at her wedding breakfast and <u>how</u> she admired the disposal of the gathering brought by Martha from the village gardens...[97]

On Wednesday, 4 April 1855, the small funeral cortège accompanied Charlotte's coffin the few hundred yards from her home to her final resting place. The church and churchyard were crowded with parishioners, rich and poor alike, who had come to pay their last respects to the woman who had, so unexpectedly, made Haworth eternally famous. Among them, as Patrick was touched to notice, was a poor blind girl from Stanbury who had insisted on being led the four miles to Haworth Church so that she could attend the funeral of the woman who had been kind to her.[98] Sutcliffe Sowden, who only nine months before had married her to Arthur Nicholls, now performed the burial service over her and committed her body to the family vault beneath the church aisle.[99] Having outlived all his six children, as well as his wife and sister-in-law, all but one of whom lay in the same vault, Patrick returned alone to the parsonage with the son-in-law whose marriage he had so bitterly opposed and who was now to be the sole remaining prop of his declining years. 'It is an hourly happiness to me dear Amelia', Charlotte had written some weeks before her death, 'to see how well Arthur and my Father get on together now – there has never been a misunderstanding or wrong word.'[100] Though her own happiness had been all too brief, her marriage had secured her father lasting comfort.

Ellen Nussey returned home an hour after the funeral, nursing her grievances against Charlotte's father and, more especially, her widower. Bitterly resentful of her exclusion during Charlotte's last illness, Ellen's dislike of Arthur was now so intense it must have been palpable. Spitting with venom, she later recalled how, on 'The very day of my arrival', he had said to her, 'Any letters you may have of Charlotte's you will not shew to others & in course of time you will destroy them.'[101] Ellen had been unable to refuse, though she reneged on this promise as she had on her earlier one. If Arthur thought he could keep his wife's life a private matter, he was sadly mistaken, underestimating not only Ellen's desire to play a public role as 'the friend of Charlotte Brontë', but also that of people whose contacts with her had only been slight.

Even before she was buried, another self-important busybody had got to work. John Greenwood was the Haworth stationer. Earlier in life he had been a wool-comber but he had been unable to support his large family because of his ill health. Selling paper as a sideline, he had been encouraged by the patronage of the Brontë family (who must have singlehandedly kept him in business), and Charlotte, in particular, had gone out of her way to help him extend into the bookselling trade by ensuring that her publishers supplied him with the cheap editions of her books to sell.[102] Clearly he knew the family, though no better than many others in the township, but he had literary pretensions himself and therefore highly prized his connections with 'Currer Bell'.

It was John Greenwood who took it upon himself to inform Charlotte's famous friends of her death, taking care to portray himself as one of her intimate circle. Mrs Gaskell responded in shock and dismay.

I can not tell you how VERY sad your note has made me. My dear dear friend that I shall never see again on earth! I did not even know she was ill ... You may well say you have lost your best friend; strangers might know her by her great fame, but we loved her dearly for her goodness, truth, and kindness, & those lovely qualities she carried with her where she is gone.[103]

Not knowing it was the very day of Charlotte's funeral, she wrote immediately to Patrick offering her sympathy, only to receive somewhat of a rebuff.

I thank you for your kind sympathy – My Daughter, is indeed, dead, and the solemn truth presses upon her worthy, and affectionate \Husband/ and me, with great, and, it may be with unusual weight – But, others, also, have, or shall have their sorrows, and we feel our own the most – The marriage that took place, seem'd to hold forth, long, and bright prospects of happiness, but in the inscrutable providence of God, all our hopes have ended in disappointment, and our joy < ended > in mourning – May we resign to the will of the Most High – After three months of sickness, a tranquil death closed the scene. But our loss we trust is her gain – But why should I trouble \you/ longer with our < sorry > sorrows. 'The heart knoweth its own bitterness' – and we ought to bear with fortitude our own grievances, & not to bring others – into our sufferings - ...

In a touching postscript Patrick added, 'Excuse this scrawl, I am not fit, at present, to write much – nor to write satisfactorily.'[104] Interestingly, having asked John Greenwood for further details and discovered that her friend had died in pregnancy, Mrs Gaskell regretted even more that she had not kept in touch. 'How I wish I had known! ... it is no use regretting what is past; but I do fancy that if I had come, I could have induced her, – even though they had all felt angry with me at first, – to do what was so absolutely necessary, for her very life!'[105] If the thought of abortion had occurred to

Mrs Gaskell, had it occurred to Charlotte, her father or her husband?

Another of Charlotte's famous friends whom John Greenwood contacted before she had even been laid in the family vault was Harriet Martineau. Despite having had no contact with Charlotte since their quarrel over *Villette*, Miss Martineau responded in private and in public with generous tributes. To Greenwood himself she wrote:

I am indebted to you for your kindness in informing me of my poor friend's departure. It is seldom that I use the word 'poor', which has now slipped from my pen; but she so loved life, her lot was so singular in surviving so many of her family, and I trust so happy at last in having formed new ties, that I did hope for longer life for her, though I often feared it could hardly be ... Vast as was her genius, and infinitely as I admired it, I honoured yet more her integrity and unspoiled upright-ness, simplicity, and sense. She was a noble woman, such as society ill can spare.[106]

Like Mrs Gaskell, she sought further details of Charlotte's life from the more than willing John Greenwood, but then she proceeded to blazon the story across the pages of the *Daily News*. In a tribute which began with the dramatic opening line ' "Currer Bell" is dead!', Harriet Martineau drew on Charlotte's Biographical Notice of her sisters, John Greenwood's infor-mation and her own memories, to draw the outline of a picture that Mrs Gaskell would embellish and which would become part of the Brontë legend. Most of the half-truths, misconceptions and downright untruths which would give such lurid colouring to the story of Charlotte's life were already evident here: a father who was 'simple and unworldly' and 'too much absorbed in his studies to notice her occupations'; an only brother 'a young man of once splendid promise which was early blighted'; a home among the 'wild Yorkshire hills ... in a place where newspapers were never seen'. Against all the odds, Charlotte had triumphed.

From her feeble constitution of body, her sufferings by the death of her whole family, and the secluded and monotonous life she led, she became morbidly sensitive in some respects; but in her high vocation, she had, in addition to the deep intuitions of a gifted woman, the strength of a man, the patience of a hero, and the con-scientiousness of a saint.

Having suffered herself from criticism of her 'masculine' occupation as a writer, Harriet Martineau was anxious to dispel the view that there was anything unnatural or unfeminine in Charlotte's profession.

There was something inexpressibly affecting in the aspect of the frail little creature who had done such wonderful things, and who was able to bear up, with so bright an eye and so composed a countenance, under such a weight of sorrow, and such a prospect of solitude. In her deep mourning dress (neat as a quaker's), with her beautiful hair, smooth and brown, her fine eyes blazing with meaning, and her sensible face indicating a habit of self-control, if not of silence, she seemed a perfect household image – irresistibly recalling Wordsworth's description of that domestic treasure. And she was this. She was as able at the needle as the pen. The household knew the excellence of her cookery before they heard of that of her books. In so utter a seclusion as she lived in – in those dreary wilds, where she was not strong enough to roam over the hills, in that retreat where her studious father rarely broke the silence – and there was no one else to do it; in that forlorn house, planted on the very clay of the churchyard, where the graves of her sisters were before her window; in such a living sepulchre her mind could not [but] prey upon itself; and how it did suffer, we see in the more painful portions of her last novel – 'Villette.'"[07]

The myth of Charlotte Brontë was born.

Chapter Twenty-Seven

൏

SAINTLINESS, TREASON AND PLOT

Charlotte had died at the beginning of Holy Week, one of the busiest times of the church year. It was an indication of the measure of their grief that neither Patrick nor Arthur, both strong and conscientious men, could perform their duties. Sutcliffe Sowden proved a good friend, taking not only Charlotte's burial service but four more during the week; J. H. Mitchell, the incumbent of Cullingworth, also lent assistance by preaching the sermons on Easter Day and taking Patrick's place in addressing the Haworth Mechanics' Institute the following day.[1] Michael Merrall, Chairman of the Institute, deeply impressed the gathering in his opening speech

by a brief but touching and pathetic reference to the mournful death of the Institute's most distinguished member and patroness, 'Currer Bell'. The talented authoress was a life member of the Institution, and from its commencement down to the latest period of her life, ever evinced a deep interest in its welfare and prosperity. Copies of all her valuable works she presented to its library; and at its soirée of 1854, as also on several previous occasions, she presided at one of the tea tables, and honoured the meeting with her presence.[2]

Letters of sympathy continued to flood in as the news of Charlotte's death spread; they came from all kinds of people, from friends of friends, like Mary Hewitt, to one-time intimates, like George Smith. Though somewhat late in offering his condolences, his letter prompted a moving and dignified response from Patrick:

My Dear Sir,

   I thank you for your kind sympathy. Having heard my Dear Daughter speak so much about you and your family, your letter seem'd to be one from an Old Friend. Her Husband's sorrow and mine, < are > is indeed very great – We mourn the loss of one, whose like, we hope not, ever to see again – and as you justly state we do not mourn alone – That you may never experimentally know, sorrow such as ours, and that when trouble does come, you may receive, due aid from Heaven, is the sincere wish and ardent prayer, of Yours, very

respectfully & truly,
P. Brontë[3]

The private eulogies of Charlotte were both a comfort and a sad pleasure, but neither Patrick nor Arthur could take much satisfaction from the increasingly prurient and speculative notices which appeared in the press. The trend had begun with Harriet Martineau's well-meant but highly coloured obituary. This inspired at least one genuine tribute, Matthew Arnold's poem, 'Haworth Churchyard', which appeared in the May issue of *Fraser's Magazine.*

Strew with roses the grave
Of the early-dying. Alas!
Early she goes on the path
To the Silent Country, and leaves
Half her laurels unwon,
Dying too soon: yet green
Laurels she had, and a course
Short, yet redoubled by Fame.[4]

Though labouring under the delusion that Charlotte and her family lay in the open churchyard at Haworth – and very cross to discover that her actual resting place did not suit his artistic notions – Arnold had at least treated the subject with the tact due to her living relations.[5]

   This was not the case with the newspapers and magazines which, almost universally, carried extracts from Harriet Martineau's obituary and, with equal unanimity, homed in on its most extraordinary aspects: the harshness of the school which killed her sisters and stunted her own growth, her father's remoteness and the isolation of her own life at Haworth.[6] The public appetite for Brontë scandal was whetted and there were plenty of people waiting in the wings to keep up the supply. One disloyal and, not surprisingly, anonymous informant wrote to the *Literary Gazette* with further gossip.

Mr Brontë is the incumbent of Haworth, & the father of the 'three sisters'; two had already died when Mr Nicholls, the curate, wished to marry his last sole hope. To this Mr Brontë objected, as it might deprive him of his only child; & though they were much attached, the connexion was so far broken that Mr Nicholls was to leave. Then the vicar of Bradford interposed, by offering to secure Mr Nicholls the incumbency after Mr Brontë's death. This obviated all objections, & last summer a new study was built to the parsonage, and the lovers were married, remaining under the father's roof. But alas! in 3 months the bride's lungs were attacked, & in 3 more the father & husband committed their loved one to the grave! Is it not a sad reality in which the romance ends? May God comfort the two mourners!⁷

Again the story was picked up and reprinted by the national and local papers, this time with more damaging and lasting effect. The completely untrue assertion about the intervention of the vicar of Bradford was never to be forgotten in Haworth and after Patrick's death it was undoubtedly one of the reasons why the trustees, ever suspicious of any attempt by Bradford to overturn or undermine their authority, refused to accept his son-in-law in his stead.⁸ Arthur already had his detractors in Haworth, who resented his refusal to see his wife as anything but the woman he loved: John Greenwood, for instance, within a month of Charlotte's death, was already agitating for daguerreotypes of Richmond's portrait of her to be published and for a marble tablet to be erected to her memory in the church.⁹

Forced to be aware of the insatiable appetite for information about his wife, Arthur's natural inclination was to maintain a dignified silence and ignore the printed gossip and innuendo. Nevertheless, he was also well aware that Charlotte's lack of discretion in writing to her friends had placed potentially explosive material in the hands of others who did not share his wish to keep her private life private. In sorting through his wife's papers after her death, he realized that there were confidences made before her marriage which she had not shared with him. The one that most upset him was the discovery that James Taylor had proposed to her and that Charlotte had seriously considered accepting him. His first reaction was to go over to Brookroyd to ask Ellen for further information; she was not at home but at least, he believed, he had her promise not to let anyone read Charlotte's letters and to destroy them in due course. He therefore wrote to Miss Wooler, who, unlike Ellen, shared his concern and entered fully into his wishes. With her customary discretion, she had already – albeit reluctantly – destroyed the letter containing Charlotte's confidences about James Taylor on learning of her engagement to her future husband. 'Your letter did not surprise me & required no apology', she told him.

… There is something peculiarly revolting in the bare idea of those communications being laid open to the public gaze, which were intended only for the eye of a confidential & sympathizing friend … I hope soon to be able to collect & look over the letters I have preserved & you may rest assured my dear Sir, that I will retain none that contain anything which might give pain to any individual, much less to you, who are so deeply interested in all that relates to one, whose memory I shall ever cherish – her loss I must ever regret, but what is it compared with yours?'[10]

Ellen's reaction was as hysterical and resentful as Miss Wooler's had been calm and supportive. Fourteen years later she could still write venomously of how, having failed to find her at Brookroyd, Arthur had tried 'to get me into his neighbourhood to stay with some intimate friends of his, which I decidedly declined', the implication being that he had sought to obtain the information by underhand means. Using the emotive language of which she was an absolute mistress, she could also declare sanctimoniously that 'it was a great shock to me discovering that he had been ransacking his wife's things so speedily after losing her'.[11]

It was Ellen who finally pushed Charlotte's father and widower, against their better judgement and to their lasting regret, into answering the scandalmongers in the press. At the beginning of June a gossipy article appeared in *Sharpe's London Magazine*, which, with salacious glee, related a series of lurid anecdotes about Charlotte's life and gave a grim portrayal of her home and father.[12] With the same haste with which she had always brought bad reviews of Charlotte's books to her attention, Ellen wrote to Arthur expressing her concern. 'I am sure both you and Mr Brontë will feel acutely the misrepresentations and the malignant spirit which characterises it. Will you suffer the article to pass current without any refutations?' she demanded.

The writer merits the contempt of silence, but there will be readers and believers. Shall such be left to imbibe a tissue of malignant falsehoods, or shall an attempt be made to do justice to one who so highly deserved justice, whose very name those who best knew her but speak with reverence and affection? Should not her aged father be defended from the reproach the writer coarsely attempts to bring upon him?

Having urged Arthur to do his duty, Ellen then proceeded to tell him how to do it, neatly asserting her own superior knowledge of Charlotte's life in the process.

I wish Mrs Gaskell, who is every way capable, would undertake a reply, and would give a sound castigation to the writer. Her personal acquaintance with Haworth, the Parsonage, and its inmates, fits her for the task, and if on other subjects she lacked information I would gladly supply her with facts sufficient to set aside much that is asserted, if you yourself are not provided with all the information that is needed on the subjects produced.[13]

The great irony – and one that has passed unrecognized to the present day – is that Mrs Gaskell was actually responsible for the article, which quoted extensively from the two letters she had written from the Lake District in 1850 after her first meeting with Charlotte. As we have seen, these were largely based on Lady Kay Shuttleworth's gossip, itself drawn from the only servant ever to be dismissed from the Brontë household.[14] Ellen was certainly right to feel indignation at the 'misrepresentations' and 'tissue of malignant falsehoods' in the article, but in nominating Mrs Gaskell as her friend's champion she was unwittingly appointing the very person who had made them public knowledge.

Sharpe's London Magazine was not normally seen at the parsonage, so it was duly ordered and read. Arthur then replied with a letter that was as patient with Ellen as it was charitable towards the article. While agreeing that the writer had made many mistakes, he pointed out that he did not do so from any unkind motive but merely 'to gratify the curiosity of the multitude in reference to one who had made such a sensation in the literary world'. He went on:

But even if the article had been of a less harmless character, we should not have felt inclined to take any notice of it, as by doing so we should have given it an importance which it would not otherwise have obtained. Charlotte herself would have acted thus; and her character stands too high to be injured by the statements in a magazine of small circulation and little influence – statements which the writer prefaces with the remark that he does not vouch for their accuracy. The many laudatory notices of Charlotte and her works which appeared since her death may well make us indifferent to the detractions of a few envious or malignant persons, as there ever will be such.

The remarks about Patrick, far from giving him pain, had simply made him laugh – 'indeed, I have not seen him laugh as much for some months as he did while I was reading the article to him'. He ended his letter with the sad little comment: 'We are both well in health, but lonely and desolate.'[15]

Arthur seems to have been a little premature in rejecting Ellen's suggestion out of hand. Patrick's first reaction may have been to laugh, but when he thought the matter over, the idea of an authorized biography of his daughter, written by one of her own friends, herself a celebrated author, not unnaturally appealed to his paternal pride. Perhaps Ellen wrote to him too, hoping that he might be persuaded where Arthur could not and pointing out that it was only a matter of time until someone less well qualified and less sympathetic than Mrs Gaskell produced a biography of his daughter. There must have been considerable argument between the two men but in the end Arthur bowed to Patrick's wishes. Only five days after his son-in-law had turned the idea down flat, Patrick himself wrote to Mrs Gaskell.

Finding that a great many scribblers, as well as some clever and truthful writers, have published articles, in Newspapers, and tracts – respecting my Dear Daughter Charlotte, since her death – and seeing that many things that have been stated, are true, but more false – and having reason to \think/ that, some may venture to write her life, who will be ill qualified for the undertaking, I can see no better plan, under these circumstances, than to apply to some established Author, to write a brief account of her life – and to make some remarks on her works – You, seem to me, to be the best qualified, for doing what I wish should be done – If therefore, you will be so kind as to publish a long or short account of her life and works, just as you may deem expedient & proper – Mr Nicholls, and I, will give you, such information, as you may require –

I should expect, and request that you would affix your name, < and > so that the work might obtain a wide circulation, and be handed down to the latest times – Whatever profits might arise from the sale, would of course, belong to you – You, are the first to whom I have applied – Mr Nicholls, approves of the step I have taken, and could my Daughter speak from the tomb, I feel certain, she would laud our choice –[16]

Curiously enough, the idea of writing a memoir of her friend had already occurred to Mrs Gaskell. Thinking over her last visit to Haworth in the September of 1853 and realizing how much of what Charlotte told her then she had already forgotten, she had decided to spend the summer writing down her personal recollections of Charlotte from the time of their first meeting in the Lake District and here and there 'copying out characteristic extracts from her letters'. Originally, she had thought to do this simply for her daughters to read, but in confiding the idea to George Smith, and in telling him that 'the time may come when her wild sad life, and the beautiful character that grew out of it may be made public', she was clearly staking her claim to any future biography. Even so, she admitted that 'this sort of record of her could not be made public at present without giving pain'.[17]

She was therefore both surprised and delighted to receive Patrick's letter inviting her to undertake precisely this sort of memoir and promising her every cooperation. 'I have taken some time to consider the request', Mrs Gaskell wrote to George Smith only the day after she received Patrick's letter, '... but I have consented to write it, *as well as I can*.' Mrs Gaskell was well aware of the problems she would face, not least because she had already formed unfavourable notions about Patrick which she believed had considerable bearing on the formation of his daughter's character: such details would now have to be omitted or 'merely indicated' during Patrick's lifetime.[18] The news that Mrs Gaskell had accepted the commission 'has broken in like a ray of light on our gloomy solitude', Patrick wrote, enclosing for her assistance a rough outline of his own and his children's lives. He also paid his own handsome tribute to his daughter: 'I never knew one, less selfish than she was, or more disposed to suffer, herself – to save others from suffering –'.[19]

It was not until 23 July 1855, some five weeks later, that Mrs Gaskell at last found time in her busy schedule to pay a visit to Haworth. Obviously feeling that she would need moral support in facing her friend's fearsome father again, she took Katie Winkworth with her. They arrived in 'broiling heat' about one o'clock in the afternoon. The normally loquacious Mrs Gaskell was reduced to an unusually terse description of the few hours she spent at the parsonage. 'It was a most painful visit. Both Mr Brontë & Mr Nicholls cried sadly. I like Mr Nicholls.'[20] Though frequently accused of not caring about his children, the depth of Patrick's emotion can perhaps be gauged by the fact that, a full year after his daughter's death, he could still confess that 'my grief is so deep and lasting, that I cannot long dwell on my sad privation – I try to look to God, for consolation, and pray that he will give me grace, and strength equal to my day – and resignation to his will.'[21]

No one could doubt Mrs Gaskell's sensibility and it was with the kindest of motives, leavened with a not unnatural reluctance to repeat the exercise, that she left Haworth determined not to seek future information from the two people who had been closest of all to the subject of her biography. Instead, she would rely on friends and acquaintances, some of whom had their own axe to grind. Far from saving Patrick and Arthur from future grief, she was unintentionally to inflict further trauma upon them.

The day after her visit, both Mrs Gaskell and Arthur Nicholls wrote to Ellen Nussey, requesting that she would make her letters available for the biography. Mrs Gaskell made it clear that both men had agreed to her suggestion that the book should make Charlotte's 'most unusual character (as taken separately from her genius,)' known to her readers who would 'expect to be informed as to the circumstances which made her what she was'. Despite their agreement, Mrs Gaskell was shrewd enough to realize that Patrick did not fully appreciate the scale of interest felt by strangers in his daughter's personal history. He wanted her life to be written, and written by Mrs Gaskell, his last words being, 'No quailing, Mrs Gaskell! no drawing back!' 'Mr Nicholls was far more aware of the kind of particulars which people would look for; and saw how they had snatched at every gossiping account of her, and how desirable it was to have a full and authorized < account >\history/ of her life if it were done at all. His feeling was against it's being written; but he yielded to Mr Brontë's impetuous wish ...' He had presented her with a dozen of Charlotte's letters addressed principally to Emily, one or two to her father and brother and one to her aunt, all dating from 1839–43, and had suggested that she should contact Ellen for earlier correspondence.[22]

Arthur's letter echoed Mrs Gaskell's but it is clear that he expected to be consulted about the material that was to be used in the book.

The greatest difficulty seems to be in obtaining materials to shew the development of Charlotte's Character – For this reason Mrs G. is anxious to see any of her letters – Especially those of an early date – I think I understood you to say that you had some – if so – we should feel obliged by your letting us have any, that you may think proper – not for publication, but merely to give the writer an insight into her mode of thought – Of course they will be returned after a little time –

I confess that the course most consonant with my own feelings would be to take no steps in the matter but I do not think it right to offer any opposition to Mr Brontè's wishes – We have the same object in view, but should differ in our mode of proceeding –[23]

Ellen was actually staying with Miss Wooler in Ilkley when Mrs Gaskell's letter was forwarded to her: it was an indication of their respective attitudes towards the biography that Ellen wished very much to invite Mrs Gaskell to join them but that Miss Wooler refused to allow her to do so.[24] On her return home Ellen went through all her letters from Charlotte, carefully reading over every one, erasing names of persons and places, and putting them into date order. From 500 letters, she selected some 300 for Mrs Gaskell's perusal, handing them over to her in person when she called at Brookroyd in the middle of August.[25] 'They give one a very beautiful idea of her character', Mrs Gaskell wrote after she had read them, adding, 'I am sure the more fully she, Charlotte Brontë – the *friend* the *daughter* the *sister* the *wife* is known – and known where need be in her own words – the more highly will she be appreciated.'[26] Through Ellen's offices, Mrs Gaskell eventually secured an interview with the reluctant Miss Wooler at Brookroyd and impressed her sufficiently to persuade her to part with her letters: 'I hardly know how it is,' she told Miss Wooler, 'but I like them better than any other series of letters of hers that I have seen.'[27]

Not surprisingly, George Smith proved equally reluctant to part with his letters. After an increasingly irate set of missives from Mrs Gaskell, he finally lent her about twenty letters, some of them only fragments, principally concerned with the Newby transactions and Charlotte's criticisms of Thackeray. Forewarned by Ellen Nussey, Mrs Gaskell knew that this was only the tip of the iceberg and refused to be put off. 'The remainder', Mr Smith suavely announced, 'contain matter of too purely personal a nature to be generally interesting.' He offered to lend them on condition that they were returned: 'He is very civil, more civil than satisfactory', Mrs Gaskell observed darkly to Ellen, who advised her that an unannounced visit to Cornhill might prove more productive. Smith Williams, too, was persuaded to part with his letters, which Mrs Gaskell again liked better than any others she had seen apart from those to Miss Wooler: by this time she had gathered enough material to notice that 'it is curious how much the spirit in which she wrote varies according to the correspondent whom she was addressing'.[28]

In addition to Charlotte's own letters, Mrs Gaskell was assiduous in contacting people who might be able to help her. John Greenwood was set to work transcribing the Brontë memorial tablet in the church; another friend was deployed to find books about the 'peculiar \customs &c–/ character of the population' of Haworth; a chance meeting with Dr Scoresby at a house party provided an opportunity to pump him for 'many curious anecdotes about the extraordinary character of the people round Haworth'.[29]

Above all, however, it was Ellen Nussey who provided information, stories and contacts. Unlike Charlotte's husband, she was a willing, even eager, participant in the exercise and, perhaps inevitably, Mrs Gaskell absorbed many of her opinions and prejudices without questioning them. Inevitably, too, Patrick and Arthur came out badly and, since it was easier and less painful to accept Ellen's versions of events than to interrogate Charlotte's father and widower, Mrs Gaskell made no attempt to counterbalance the evidence she was building up.

Unaware of the direction the biography was taking, Patrick and Arthur had resumed the threads of their normal life as far as was possible in the wake of Charlotte's death. A fortnight after that event, Patrick had bought a dog of mixed Newfoundland and retriever ancestry from Mr Summerscale, the national schoolmaster. He named it Cato, after the classical orator, and though it was clearly intended for companionship, a note in his account book that 'My Dr Dtr Ch.tte, greatly admired him' suggests another reason for the purchase. A couple of months later, Patrick bought another dog, this time a cross between a Newfoundland and a water spaniel, from Mr Summerscale, which was named Plato in honour of the classical phil-osopher.[30] There were other changes in the household too. Martha Brown, worn out after her labours running the house singlehandedly while nursing Tabby and Charlotte, had herself fallen ill. She could not be cared for at the parsonage and, as her father was terminally ill, there was no place for her at home: she was therefore sent to Leeds to Mrs Dean's alms-houses, where she was gradually restored to health. In her absence, the household duties devolved on her younger sister, Eliza, who Patrick hastened to reassure her was 'very steady, and does her work very well'.[31]

Other old and faithful servants were also in touch again as news of Charlotte's death spread. Nancy Garrs had come back to Haworth, possibly to attend Charlotte's funeral, and her sister, Sarah, who had emigrated to the States, wrote to Patrick from Iowa. Replying with a brief sketch of the family's history since her departure, he added, with justifiable pride, 'You probably, little thought, that the children you nursed on your knees, would have been so much noticed by the world – as they have been – Emily and Anne, wrote and published Clever Books – and Charlotte's writings, and fame, are known in all parts where Genius, and learning are held in due estimation.' Referring to the 'happy union' between his daughter and Arthur Nicholls, 'a very worthy and respectable Clergyman', he described how 'her loving Husband, and, I, < hav > are left to mourn her irreparable loss'.[32] Despite the bitterness of their former quarrel, the two men were now totally reconciled. There was no higher proof of this than when on 20 June 1855 Patrick made his own will. He left two specific bequests: forty pounds to his brother, Hugh Brontë, 'to be equally divided amongst all my Brothers and Sisters to whom I gave considerable sums in times past' and almost as much again, thirty pounds, to Martha Brown 'as a token of regard for long and faithful services to me and my children'. Everything else he left, without reservation, to his 'beloved and esteemed Son-in-Law...for his own absolute benefit'.[33]

Though Patrick continued to preach at least once and often twice every Sunday, he had effectively handed over all the responsibility for taking duties to Arthur, performing only one or two burials and baptisms a year. It therefore fell to Arthur's lot to perform the burial service for John Brown, Martha's father, Branwell's friend and sexton of Haworth, on 13 August 1855.[34]

Throughout the autumn Mrs Gaskell was busy in her search for materials. She visited Brookroyd twice, once on her way to stay with the Kay Shuttleworths at Gawthorpe Hall in August and again in early October, when Ellen had arranged for Miss Wooler to be staying there. Mrs Gaskell did not gain much '*direct* information' from Miss Wooler, but Ellen supplied that deficiency with a will. She wrote her own account of Anne's last days at Scarborough, copying out and embellishing notes she had made at the time in her pocketbook. She also sent extracts from Charlotte's letters, which she suggested should be included in the memoir. One of these was Charlotte's commentary on the death of Anne's schoolfriend, Ann Cook, Ellen's reason for including it being 'I think the young lady's friends would most probably be gratified if dear C.'s comments on her decease were inserted – they are monied and influential people in this neighbourhood, some of them not very friendly to Currer Bell's emanations. Would they not be won by her kindly thought of one of their own?'[35]

Ellen was even employed as an intermediary in securing Mrs Brontë's letters to Patrick, since Mrs Gaskell 'dare not' ask him herself. Patrick had sent her four letters containing a mixture of facts and anecdote to assist her, but otherwise there was no communication between them.[36] Partly this was due to Mrs Gaskell's reluctance to revive painful memories and partly to Arthur Nicholls' unwillingness to give the biographer anything more than he was absolutely required to do. Nevertheless, both he and Patrick had been concerned by the silence: 'We have neither heard nor seen anything of Mrs Gaskell –', he wrote to Ellen Nussey in December. 'I have every confidence that she will do ample justice to Charlotte – but I am quite sensible that she has undertaken a very difficult task with only slender material.'[37] His sentiments were echoed by Patrick in a letter to Mrs Gaskell herself on 23 January 1856. 'You will find herewith, a letter, and verses, which I have received from a Lady with whom I have no acquaintance –', he told her,

You will exercise your own judgement, in reference to them, and all other concerns, connected with the arduous, and < sad > responsible task you have kindly undertaken. Mr Nicholls, and I often think of what you < so > have so obligingly < undertaken > enter'd on, of what the public, will expect from you, on whatever subject you may write; and of the few facts, and incidents, you have of a biographical nature, – we so frequently talk over, and meditate on these things, that we are forced at last, to solve the difficulty, by saying that you must draw largely on the resources of your own mind – My Daughter had that to do, in no small degree, in the works which she gave to the world – ... I often think that if you would write a running critique on her <u>works</u>, as well as her <u>life</u> – it would be highly popular, and render your task easier, by an accession of subject matter – But I must have done – an oppressive sadness comes over my heart, when I reflect that my Dear Daughter is forever gone –[38]

What neither Patrick nor Arthur realized was the vast number of Charlotte's letters to which Mrs Gaskell now had access nor, more importantly, the extent to which she was planning to quote from them.

She had begun to write in February 1856, but was continually frustrated and forced to rewrite as new material came to light. Enquiries to Mary Taylor in New Zealand had revealed that Mary had destroyed all her letters from Charlotte, a fact she now bitterly regretted. 'They would have been much better evidence than my imperfect recollection & infinitely more interesting.' Mary did respond with a lively account of their schooldays at Roe Head, however, from which Mrs Gaskell was to quote extensively in her biography.[39] Mrs Gaskell had also unearthed the Wheelwrights and, more importantly, the Hegers. Charlotte had been reluctant to sanction the translation of *Villette* into French and had tried to prevent its publication in Belgium, fearing that the portrait of the Pensionnat Heger and its principals was all too easily recognizable. Inevitably, the book had made its way to Brussels and the Hegers had been made aware of their unconscious contribution to English literature. There were even rumours that the Pensionnat Heger had suffered a loss of pupils as a result.[40] Certainly, Madame Heger had taken justifiable umbrage at her portrait in the novel and when Mrs Gaskell travelled over to Brussels in the early summer of 1856 she flatly refused to see her. Constantin Heger, however, more aware of his former pupil's genius and more sympathetic to her sufferings, was quite prepared to assist her biographer. He sent her examples of both Emily's and Charlotte's *devoirs*, described his teaching methods and transcribed carefully selected extracts from Charlotte's letters to him for Mrs Gaskell's edification. When she came to Brussels, he not only agreed to see her, but swiftly won both her liking and her respect, not least because he had refused to defend himself by publishing Charlotte's letters to him. Displaying a tact that was not evident elsewhere in her biography, Mrs Gaskell protected Monsieur Heger (and Charlotte's reputation) as best she could by deliberately glossing over the reasons for Charlotte's estrangement from his wife and her eventual departure from Brussels.[41]

By the middle of July, Mrs Gaskell had completed a considerable portion of her biography. George Smith had urged her to take her time: 'There is no hurry; there would be a great cry of indelicacy if it were published too soon. Do it well, and never fear that the public interest in her will die away.' However, he had already expressed reservations about her portrayal of Patrick Brontë. Mrs Gaskell was affronted. 'Now I thought that I carefully preserved the reader's respect for Mr Brontë, while truth and the desire of doing justice to her compelled me to state the domestic peculiarities of her childhood, which (as in all cases) contributed so much to make her what she was.' She appealed to Ellen, to whom she had read the same section of the manuscript, and received a stout defence: 'I do not wish anything you have said suppressed only I think your readers will have to be taught to think kindly of Mr B–'.[42]

Mrs Gaskell also sought Ellen's advice on her next visit to Haworth. 'I still want one or two things to complete my materials', she informed her, 'and I am very doubtful if I can get them – at any rate, I think they will necessitate my going to Haworth again, and I am literally *afraid* of that.' She wanted Monsieur Heger's letters to Charlotte, the manuscripts of *The Professor* and Charlotte's last, unfinished story and Charlotte's 'long, constant, and minute' letters to her father from London. How should she best proceed in trying to prise these things from Mr Nicholls, she asked Ellen, and would it be better to let them know she was coming or 'take them unawares'?[43] Ellen's reply was not particularly helpful.

I think Mr N. ought to have no reserve with you, his very affection should make him see it is wisest, best, and kindest to tell the whole truth to you in everything that regards her literary life or her domestic virtues – I wish I could talk to him half an hour and convince him that the more she is known the more highly will she shine and be the means of good to the readers of her Memoir.

She did, however, offer one practical piece of advice: 'I think you may win him by your own heartiness in the work – at any rate you will Mr B., and for a quiet life Mr N. will have to yield where Mr B. is urgent and impatient.'[44]

In the end, Mrs Gaskell compromised. She reminded Charlotte's father and widower of her existence by persuading her husband to send Patrick a printed copy of the sermon he had preached on 4 May which had been a Day of National Thanksgiving for the peace with Russia. The sermon had defended both the war and the peace as honourable and drew a sharp distinction between 'the peace of mere compulsion', which was simple slavery, and 'the peace of the gospel', which was 'the fellowship of free agents'. Writing to thank him, Patrick could say quite sincerely, 'The principles, and practices, which, it so ably advocates, are perfectly in accordance with my, own on the great subjects of peace, and war', adding, with unspoken reproach, 'We often wonder here, how Mrs Gaskell, is getting on, with Her mournful, but interesting < Task > Task.'[45]

He was soon to find out. The day after he wrote the letter, when he himself was confined to bed with rheumatism and Martha was away, so that there was only the 'little girl' Eliza to run the house, Mrs Gaskell arrived on his doorstep in the company of Sir James Kay Shuttleworth.[46] This was a master stroke on Mrs Gaskell's part. The unexpected arrival of such important guests threw the whole household into chaos, particularly as Patrick insisted on getting up; there was therefore no time for dreaming up arguments or excuses. Both clergymen looked up to Sir James and he was shameless in using his influence and authority over them. Mrs Gaskell reported to George Smith that Sir James was 'not prevented by the fear of giving pain from asking in a peremptory manner for whatever he thinks desirable. He was extremely kind in forwarding all my objects; and coolly took actual possession of many things while Mr Nicholls was saying he could not possibly part with them'. Mrs Gaskell was anxious to have a photograph taken of the Richmond portrait, but greatly to her annoyance, her previous applications had met with a decided refusal, even when made through George Smith. Here Sir James proved his worth again.

Sir J. P K S coolly introduced the subject of the portrait, as if he had known nothing of Mr Nicholls' reluctance, asked Mr Brontë's leave to have it photographed, whh was readily granted with a reference to Mr Nicholls for an ultimate decision, so then Sir James said 'Oh! I know Mr Nicholls will grant it – and we will trust to Mrs Gaskell to send over a photographer from Manchester, for I dare say he would not like to part with the portrait, –' & he so completely took it for granted that Mr Nicholls had no time to object. But I can not feel quite comfortable in absolutely wresting things from him by mere force of words.[47]

In material terms the visit was a great success. Mrs Gaskell and Sir James carried off the manuscripts of *The Professor* and the last unfinished story; completely unexpectedly, and 'by far the most extraordinary of all', there was a packet 'about the size of a lady's travelling writing case', full of the little books written in childhood. Mrs Gaskell described this find in great excitement to George Smith: 'they are the wildest & most incoherent things, as far as we have examined them, *all* purporting to be written, or addressed to some member of the Wellesley family. They give one the idea of creative power carried to the verge of insanity.'[48]

Having involved Sir James Kay Shuttleworth, it now proved impossible to shake him off. Though the manuscripts (like the letters) had only been lent on the understanding that they would give Mrs Gaskell a better idea of Charlotte's literary development, Sir James took it into his head that *The Professor* must be published. Mrs Gaskell was alarmed, fearing that the novel (which she had not yet read) might relate even more closely to the Hegers than *Villette* and might provoke Monsieur Heger into publishing Charlotte's letters to him. 'I can not tell you how I should deprecate anything leading to the publication of those letters', she told George Smith anxiously, adding gloomily, 'I foresee, if Sir James has set his will upon it, *it is* to be published whatever may be the consequences. He over-rides all wishes, feelings, and delicacy. I saw that in his way of carrying everything before him at Haworth, deaf to remonstrance and entreaty.'[49]

Sir James had determined that he himself would edit the manuscript, but this time he was to be thwarted by the more subtle machinations of Mrs Gaskell. Having read so many of Charlotte's letters she knew that her friend 'would have especially disliked *him* to meddle with her writings', and that his sole reason for wishing to do so was 'to appear to the world in intimate connexion with her': she hinted these things while forwarding Sir James' proposal to George Smith and Arthur Nicholls. Having read the novel she was not anxious to see it published, feeling that it would not add to Charlotte's reputation as Sir James claimed and that it would simply give further fuel to the critics: 'there are one or two remarkable portraits – the most charming *woman* she ever drew, and a glimpse of that woman as a mother – very lovely; otherwise little or no story; & disfigured by more coarseness, – & profanity in quoting texts of Scripture disagreeably than in any of her other works.' Not wishing to associate herself with the book she declined to edit it personally on the grounds that she was too busy: instead, she recommended Smith Williams, whom she believed Charlotte herself would have chosen.[50]

In the event, Arthur himself proved unexpectedly firm and refused to bow to Sir James' wishes, privately telling Mrs Gaskell that he feared Sir James would be hurt but 'knowing his wife's opinion on the subject, he could not allow any such revisal'. To George Smith, who was now eager to publish the manuscript which he had rejected three times in its author's lifetime, Arthur wrote with equal decision.

It appears from Sir James Kay Shuttleworth's note to Mrs Gaskell that there are some passages in it that he would wish to extirpate. I could not consent to any revisal of the work; at the same time I should not wish to gave [sic] occasion for malignant criticism – If therefore < any > it should appear to < Mr & Mr > Mr Brontè & myself, that any such result would be likely to accrue, we should hesitate before giving < it > the work to the public –[51]

A month later, on 20 September 1856, he wrote again to George Smith.

I have read 'The Professor' over to Mr Brontè. Our opinion is, that with the exception of two or three strong expressions which might be open to misinterpretation, no revision of the MS is necessary. Indeed if any extensive alteration had been requisite we could not have consented to the publication of the tale. We have erased the few seemingly objectionable phrases.[52]

Ellen Nussey always claimed that Charlotte's husband cared nothing for her as an author, 'literally groaning' when she expressed a wish to write and once declaring that 'Currer Bell could fly up to heaven for all he cared'.[53] Her malicious comments seem to have gained general acceptance because

Arthur made no secret of the fact that he loved the woman, rather than the authoress. Nevertheless, this did not preclude a pride in his wife's work. Arthur not only consented to the publication of this and other work by his wife but also was absolutely painstaking in his efforts to preserve its integrity; clearly he knew how she had refused to alter the opening chapter of *Shirley* and the closing chapter of *Villette*. Indeed, his desire to ensure that his wife's wishes were carried out overrode any other considerations and he left in passages, such as Hunsden Yorke's blasphemies, which must have been offensive to him personally as a clergyman. Unlike Sir James, he had no wish to see his own name appear as the editor of the work, but he did the job conscientiously, asking to see proofs as it was printed. On Mrs Gaskell's advice, the payment for the book was worked out on the basis of its length, and Arthur, having meticulously counted the pages of both *Villette* and *The Professor* and done his computation, asked for and received £220 from Smith, Elder & Co.[54]

Arthur's editorial policy left Mrs Gaskell and George Smith in something of a quandary: 'oh! I wish Mr Nicholls wd have altered more!' she exclaimed to the publisher. 'I fear from what you say he has left many little things you would & I would have taken out, as < both not > \neither/ essential to the characters or the story, & as likely to make her misunderstood. For I would not, if I could help it, have another syllable that could be called coarse to be associated with her name.'[55] The problem was that if the novel came out before the biography it would reinforce all the criticisms which had been made in the past. The solution, suggested by George Smith, was to publish the biography first: this would confound the critics by explaining the reasons for Charlotte's apparent coarseness and brutality and convert repugnance into sympathy. *The Professor* would then be viewed more tolerantly by the press. Mrs Gaskell grasped at this suggestion and, fortunately, there was no opposition from Haworth:

I beg to assure you that neither Mr Brontè nor myself could for one moment think of interfering with you in arranging the details of the publication of 'The Professor'. The period of its appearance is a matter entirely for your consideration ... Our only anxiety, as I am sure your's also, is that no step may be taken, which could possibly prove prejudicial to the fame of the author —[56]

Though the problem of *The Professor* had been so neatly solved, the difficulties over the biography were not so easily to be overcome. Apart from her two visits to Haworth, almost a year apart, and the few letters from Patrick to Mrs Gaskell, there had been no contact between the biographer and the family of her subject. In the meantime, Patrick had perhaps grown a little uneasy. A new pamphlet, which Patrick described as a 'strange compound of truth and error' had appeared. He sent Mrs Gaskell a copy, denouncing its account of his marriage as 'entirely wrong' and seeking to explain the 'eccentricity' which had been credited to him. He made an interesting defence which, incidentally, reveals him to have been a reader of Mrs Gaskell's novels and to have shared his children's delight in satire.

The Book-making gentry whose little works I have seen, appear to make me a somewhat extraordinary and eccentrick personage I have no great objection to this, admitting they can make a penny by it. But the truth of the matter is – that I am, in some respects, a kindred likeness to the father of Margaret, in 'North and South.' peacable, feeling, sometimes thoughtful – and generally well-meaning. Yet unlike him, in one thing – by occasionally getting into a satirical vein – when I am disposed to dissect, and analyze human character, and human nature, studying closely its simples and compounds, like a curious surgeon – And being in early life thrown on my own resources – and consequently obliged, under Providence, to depend on my own judgement, and exertions, I may not be so ready as some are, to be a follower of any man, or a worshipper of conventionalities or forms, which may possibly to superficial observers, acquire me the character, of a little exccentricity. Thus freely have I spoken to you – in order that in your work, you may insert such facts, as may counteract, < and >\any/ false statements, that may have been made, or might be made, respecting me, or mine.

From what has already transpired, I think you will see the prudence of < my > our choice, and request, in reference to your undertaking to write the life of 'Currer Bell'.[57]

Patrick's confidence in Mrs Gaskell's impartiality was to be sadly misplaced: she, like all the other scandalmongers, would simply repeat the malicious anecdotes she had heard without having the courage to question their supposed perpetrator about their authenticity. Of this Patrick was completely unaware. Though even now he did not actually request to see the manuscript before it was published, Patrick was obviously concerned that this privilege should not be accorded to others.

We begin, now to long for seeing your work in print – And doubt not, you will see the propriety of shewing your Manuscript to none, except Mr Gaskell, your Family, and the Publisher, and compositor. Much harm has often been done, by an opposite line of conduct, Authors, have been fetter'd, bias'd, and made to appear in other lights than their own – Genius has often been crush'd, and fame mar'd, by officious critics, and familiar Friends.[58]

It seems that the person Patrick had in mind was Sir James Kay Shuttleworth, whose overbearing conduct on his recent visit to Haworth and attempts to appropriate the editorship of *The Professor* evidently made Patrick fear that he would also exert his influence over Mrs Gaskell. What neither Patrick nor Arthur seems to have suspected was the extent to which Ellen Nussey had been involved in preparing the biography: they seem to have presumed that she, like them, had simply supplied her letters and left Mrs Gaskell to make up her own mind. Mrs Gaskell leapt to the quite wrong conclusion that Patrick's prohibition on her showing the manuscript to others was aimed at Ellen. 'There is some little jealousy (the nearest word, but not the right one) of Miss Nussey on Mr Brontë's part, and he especially forbids my showing the MS of my biography to her', she told George Smith, revealing how much she had herself been influenced by Ellen's view of things. The prohibition placed Mrs Gaskell in a difficult position because 'she is about the only person who would care to see it in MS, because she wants to know what extracts I have taken from all her letters; and she has a right to know this, if she wishes'. With typical determination, Mrs Gaskell decided to circumvent the prohibition by inviting Ellen to Manchester and reading the entire manuscript aloud to her. Ellen was thus the only person in Charlotte's circle to know what the biography contained before it was published: not surprisingly, since she had been the source for so much of the material, Mrs Gaskell was 'gratified to hear her repeatedly say how completely the life at the Parsonage appeared to her reproduced'.[59]

The cosy relationship between Mrs Gaskell and Ellen Nussey meant that the former guarded the latter's rights jealously; it never seems to have occurred to her that Charlotte's husband and father had equal, if not greater rights than her friend. Her treatment of them was downright shabby. To her they were simply an embarrassment and an irritation, mere obstacles to be circumvented. In her use of Charlotte's letters she was little short of dishonest with them.

From the very start of the undertaking, Patrick, Arthur and Ellen had all been united in expecting Mrs Gaskell to use Charlotte's letters for information only: none of them expected her to quote from them in her biography.[60] Mrs Gaskell was well aware of this but was understandably seduced by the power of Charlotte's writing. As early as August 1856, when she was about halfway through the biography, George Smith suggested that her extensive use of Charlotte's letters should be indicated somewhere in the title or advertising. This was an idea that Mrs Gaskell was swift to crush for fear that Arthur would be alerted.

I do not wish the letters to assume a prominent form in the title or printing; as Mr Nicholls has a strong objection to letters being printed at all; and wished to have all her letters (to Miss Nussey & every one else) burned. Now I am very careful what extracts I make; but still her language, where it can be used, is so powerful & living, that it would be a shame not to express everything tha[t] can be, in her own words. And yet I don't want to alarm Mr Nicholls' prejudices.[61]

Clearly she hoped to get round this problem by simply not revealing how much she had quoted. Arthur might object once the book was published but by then it would be too late. In the middle of November, however, Mrs Gaskell made a discovery which appalled her. Henry Chorley, the literary critic of the *Athenaeum*, having learnt that she was intending to quote

Charlotte's correspondence, wrote to warn her: 'Remember correspondent's permission to publish goes for nothing; the legal power over any deceased person's papers lies with the executors ... and thus Mr Nicholls <u>may</u>, if he likes turn sharp round on you, and not merely protest, but <u>prohibit</u>'. She wrote in a panic to George Smith.

Now I did <u>not</u> know all this; and Mr Nicholls is a terribly tickle person to have to do with; if I asked him for leave \to make large extracts from her letters as I am doing/, he would, ten to one, refuse it, – if I did not ask him, but went on, as I am doing, I <u>think</u> he would sigh & submit; but I could not feel sure ... what shall I do if Mr N were to prohibit all I have written from appearing[?]

George Smith was just as alive to the problem as Mrs Gaskell. The letters gave the memoir much of its life and originality: without them it would be a much poorer work. 'I am <u>most</u> careful to put nothing in from Miss Brontë's letters that can in any way implicate others', she declared. 'I conceal in some cases the names of the persons she is writing to.'[62] She seems to have been impervious to the fact that Arthur himself was unmistakably revealed to the world making his trembling proposal of marriage and being accepted as a less than brilliant destiny by his future wife.

Publisher and author put their heads together and came up with a scheme to outwit Charlotte's husband. They decided that George Smith would send him a 'business form of application' which would transfer the copyright of the 'materials of the biography' into Mrs Gaskell's hands: this seems to have been passed off as standard practice – a simple precaution to obviate any future financial claims on the biographer by Charlotte's executors.[63] Though completely unused to the workings of the publishing world, Arthur was not to be fooled by the small print. He declined to sign, 'not because I have, or ever had the slightest intention of making any pecuniary claim on Mrs Gaskell on account of the work on which she is engaged; but simply because, if I did so, I should be thereby precluded from making any further use of the MS. referred to –'. Patiently explaining his own reluctant involvement in commissioning the biography– 'if such a work was undertaken at all I would rather she did it than anyone else, as I knew her kindly feelings toward my wife'– he nevertheless pointed out that his only role had been to forward manuscripts to her 'but never with any idea of giving < over > the exclusive right to them'.[64]

George Smith, 'the man-of-business' as Charlotte had so often teasingly called him, now showed the steel that underlay his genial manner. Though his side of the correspondence is missing, he seems to have accused Arthur of reneging on his agreement with Mrs Gaskell. To a man of such transparent honesty, such an accusation was unbearable: 'I never authorized her to publish a single line of my wife's MS & correspondence', he wrote indignantly, 'such a thing was never mentioned – in fact until the receipt of your note I was not even aware that it was contemplated –'.[65] Arthur bowed to the pressure and did as he was required, but not without considerable bitterness at the way he had been outmanoeuvred. 'I have signed the enclosed document,' he told George Smith,

as it seems to be taken for granted that I am to do so, tho' why it should, I know not, as I never entered into any arrangement with Mrs Gaskell to convey to her the copyright of any of my wife's MS. for the purposes of the Memoir or any other – I trust I shall not be required to do anything more in a matter, which from beginning to end has been a source of pain and annoyance to me; as I have been dragged into sanctioning a proceeding utterly repugnant to my feelings – Indeed nothing but an unwillingness to thwart Mr Brontè's wishes could have induced me to acquiesce in a project, which in my eyes is little short of desecration –[66]

As Arthur Nicholls retired hurt, George Smith reported his triumph to Mrs Gaskell. 'I am so glad that it was you, and not I, that had "the fierce correspondence" with Mr Nicholls', she replied. 'I shd have been daunted at once.'[67] Grateful that even now Arthur had not demanded to see a copy of the book before it was published, Mrs Gaskell hastened to complete her arrangements. A photographer, Mr Stewart, was sent over to Haworth to take the Richmond portrait and, like Mrs Gaskell herself, was so enraptured that he overstepped his brief and took views of the village, church and parsonage, all of which he offered to Cornhill for engraving and inclusion in the book.[68] The manuscript, still in a very disorganized state with additions and emendations interleaved and letters copied so hastily that names and sensitive passages had not been deleted, was sent to Smith, Elder & Co. in December 1856 and the proofs began to appear in early January.[69] Recognizing the extraordinary expenses – such as the visit to Brussels – to which the biography had put her, George Smith paid Mrs Gaskell £800 for the English copyright, allowing her to negotiate further sums for German, French and American editions. She obviously had a guilty conscience about her treatment of Arthur, for in thanking George Smith for his generosity, she informed him, 'I < want > \mean/ to send 100£ to Mr Nicholls for the parish of Haworth – I shd like a village pump[;] they are terribly off for water –'.[70]

Despite some last-minute hitches, including insertions of new material at proof stage and the substitution of Mrs Gaskell's bad drawing of the parsonage and church for Mr Stewart's unengravable photographs, the book was completed by 7 February 1857. 'And please to remember I am just the reverse of Miss Brontè;' she wrote to George Smith. 'I never want to see or hear of any reviews; when I have done with a book I want to shake off the recollection thereof forever.'[71] With that, Mrs Gaskell packed her bags and departed for Italy, leaving her book to its fate.

The *Life of Charlotte Brontë* was published by Smith, Elder & Co. on 25

March 1857, in a two-volume set. Two thousand and twenty-one copies were printed, the odd number being accounted for by the complimentary copies Mrs Gaskell had promised to those who had assisted her in the project. Given the level of interest in Charlotte Brontë and the unusually high costs of publishing the book, it was a surprisingly small print run and a further 1,500 copies had to be printed on 22 April, followed by a further 700 on 4 May.[72]

The book created a sensation comparable to the first publication of *Jane Eyre*. It was seized upon and avidly read by everyone, from London literati to provincial novel readers, all of whom were intrigued to discover how and why a woman as retired as Charlotte Brontë had produced some of the most passionate and explosive fiction the world had yet seen. The success of Mrs Gaskell's decision to vindicate her friend by blaming her family and her upbringing in Haworth for all the critical condemnation of her writing was amply vindicated by the reviews. 'A strange childhood! – out of which, through various schools and other harsh experiences, the Brontës grew up to man and woman's estate, and which explains a good deal in their subsequent history', declared *Fraser's Magazine*.[73] Charlotte's old foe, the *Christian Remembrancer*, was even more explicit.

Charlotte Brontë's small glimpse of the world showed her but an indifferent part of it, and her home held a monster whom the strong ties of an inordinate family affection constrained her to love and care for and find excuses for. Whatever extenuation can be found for want of refinement – for grosser outrages on propriety than this expression indicates – the home and the neighbourhood of Charlotte Brontë certainly furnish; she wrote in ignorance of offending public opinion.[74]

The *North American Review*, which had so violently castigated the ferocious Bells and their appalling books, was similarly compelled to admit that the *Life of Charlotte Brontë* explained and excused the faults it had once condemned:

the knowledge that the authors painted life as it lay around them in their daily path is sufficient refutation of the charge, that they revelled in coarseness for coarseness' sake, and drew pictures of vice in accordance with their own inherent depravity ... there are several points wherein our present knowledge of the author decidedly modifies, and others in which it totally changes, opinions passed upon it in the absence of such knowledge.[75]

The extraordinary way in which the biography completely changed the opinions of even Charlotte's most bigoted critics was epitomized by Charles Kingsley, author of *Westward Ho!* and *The Water Babies*, in a private letter to Mrs Gaskell. '*Shirley* disgusted me at the opening: and I gave up the writer and her books with the notion that she was a person who liked coarseness. How I misjudged her! and how thankful I am that I never put a word of my misconceptions into print, or recorded my misjudgements of one who is a whole heaven above me.'[76]

In the general chorus of breast-beating, only one reviewer had the courage to question the whole idea that the author's life should be used to vindicate the perceived faults of her fiction. William Roscoe, writing in the *National Review*, took issue with Mrs Gaskell's emotive denunciation of the 'thought-less critics' who had not realized that the 'sad and gloomy views of life' in the Brontës' novels were 'wrung out of them by the living recollection of the long agony they suffered'. 'A living author is known to the world by his works only, or, if not so, it is with his works alone the public are concerned,' he pointed out,

and he has no cause of complaint if he is fairly judged by them without any allowance for the private conditions under which they were produced. On the other hand, he has the corresponding right to demand that personal considerations and private information shall not be dragged in as elements of literary judgement, and that his publicity as an artist shall not give pretext for invading the seclusion of his private life…[77]

One cannot help feeling that the Brontë sisters themselves would have added a fervent amen to this statement. It was, after all, the very reason why they had chosen to appear before the public under pseudonyms in the first place: so that their work should be judged on its merits alone and not by the circumstances of their sex or personal life. Mrs Gaskell had turned their stand for anonymity on its head: their lives were now the excuse for their works and henceforward it would be impossible to judge the two separately.

William Roscoe was also one of the very few reviewers to protest that the essentially private nature of Charlotte's life, passed effectively within the walls of one household and not on the public stage, rendered a biography so soon after her death peculiarly invasive. In so doing he unwittingly pinpointed the difference between Patrick and Arthur's expectations of Mrs Gaskell's work and what she actually produced.

The biographer who has to deal with such a life must choose between a mode of treatment which reduces his field to the limits of a memoir, and scarcely allows him to do justice to his task, or one which, on the other hand, is sure in its wider scope to do some injury to the rights and susceptibilities of others. Mrs Gaskell made her choice, and has unflinchingly acted upon it … Frankly we will state our conviction, that she was mistaken.[78]

Roscoe was virtually alone in his protest, however, the general tenor of the reviews being acclamation for Mrs Gaskell and sympathy for her subject: the school of 'poor Charlotte' biography had been born. Indeed, one might go so far as to say that it was the birth of a school of hagiography, for a disconcerting tendency to view Charlotte as a martyr to her sufferings was already apparent. G. H. Lewes, for example, foresaw that the book would create 'a deep & painful impression; for it ... presents a vivid picture of a life noble and sad, full of encouragement & healthy teaching, a lesson in duty & self-reliance', and Charles Kingsley declared that Mrs Gaskell had given the world a picture of 'a valiant woman made perfect by sufferings'. Even Sir James Kay Shuttleworth, who had had the benefit of knowing Charlotte personally, added his paeon of praise and expressed the hope that Arthur Nicholls would 'learn to rejoice that his wife will be known as a Christian heroine, who could bear her cross with the firmness of a martyr saint'.[79] The *Spectator* carried into print the view that 'Mrs Gaskell's account of Charlotte Brontë and her family [is] one of the profoundest tragedies of modern life, if tragedy be, as we believe it to be, the contest of humanity with inexorable fate – the anguish and the strife through which the spirit nerves itself for a grander sphere – the martyr's pang and the saint's victory.'[80]

Mrs Gaskell's *Life of Charlotte Brontë* was, as G. H. Lewes claimed, 'a triumph for you' and 'a monument for your friend'.[81] She had set out to vindicate Charlotte's reputation and had succeeded beyond her wildest dreams. Unfortunately, her path was littered with casualties, not the least being the two men who had entrusted her with the task in the first place. Their different reactions were equally characteristic. Patrick wrote first to the publisher and then to the biographer herself. He had read the books 'with a high degree of melancholy interest,' he told George Smith, 'and consider them amongst the ablest, most interesting and best works of the kind. Mrs Gaskell – though moveing in, to Her \what/ was a new line, a somewhat critical matter – has done Herself great credit, by this Bio-graphical Work, which I doubt not will place Her higher in literary fame, even than She stood before –'. To Mrs Gaskell he confessed that if she had not agreed to write the biography, in the final instance he would have undertaken the task himself. 'But the work is now done, and done rightly, as I wish'd it to be, and in its completion, has afforded me, more satisfaction, than I have felt, during many years of a life, in which has been examplified the saying that "man is born to trouble as the sparks fly upwards["].' Pro-claiming the portraits of his family 'full of truth and life', he singled out that of Branwell for special praise: 'The picture of my brilliant and unhappy son, and his diabolical seducer, are masterpieces.' It was almost as an afterthought that he added, 'There are a few trifling mistakes, which should it be deem'd necessary, may be corrected in the Second Edition.'[82] To be able to speak so dismissively of his own caricature speaks volumes for Patrick's selfless pride and generosity, which would not let him diminish his daughter's portrait in order to set the record straight on himself.

Arthur was not as fulsome in his praise, perhaps because he was more aware than Patrick of the wider implications of some of Mrs Gaskell's personal revelations about the Brontës. He was, however, scrupulously fair.

'I have read the work with inexpressible pain', he told George Smith, '– Mrs Gaskell has done justice to her subject – she has however fallen into many errors; but fewer perhaps than might have been expected. She has moreover inserted some things, which ought never to have been published – It was not without reason that I instinctively shrank from the proposal of a Biography – But I suppose, it matters not, provided the curiosity of the Publick be gratified –'.[83] Arthur had more reason than most to regret Mrs Gaskell's lack of discretion in her quotation from Charlotte's letters. It must have been a terrible mortification for this sensitive and intensely private man to have his wife's description of his emotional proposal of marriage and her unenthusiastic acceptance of it become public property – not least because the local papers gleefully seized upon this section and printed it for the edification of all his parishioners and clerical friends.[84]

Indeed, the local papers showed an even more remarkable insensitivity to the feelings of Charlotte's father and widower than Mrs Gaskell herself. Where she had merely hinted or indicated that Patrick's eccentricities had been largely responsible for his daughter's unhappiness, they laid the blame fairly and squarely on his shoulders. One reporter from the *Bradford Observer* was prompted by the *Life of Charlotte Brontë* to make what he called 'a pilgrimage to Haworth'. With more poetic licence than accuracy he described the parsonage as 'grim, solitary, neglected, and wretched-looking' and then, blithely indifferent to the pain his remarks would cause, continued: 'as we looked at that weatherbeaten house, and thought of the stern old man, left childless and alone, we could not help feeling for his troubles, although they had in a great measure been brought about by his own discipline and mode of life'. The reviewer in the *Leeds Intelligencer* was more charitable, but still condemnatory, describing Patrick as 'one who yet lives, bereft of all his children, in age, and we fear infirmity, which nevertheless has not availed to purchase for him a little forbearance from some who have reviewed his daughter's memoirs. After all, the whole that can be said is that he may have made some mistakes in bringing up a family of girls...'[85]

In the light of comments such as these, it is not surprising that when pressed by William Gaskell, who was acting on his wife's behalf in her absence abroad, Patrick requested some changes to the second edition, which was published on 22 April.

The principal mistake in the memoir – which I wish to mention, is that which states that I laid my Daughters under restriction with regard to their diet, obliging them to live chiefly on vegetable food. This I never did. After their Aunts death, with regard to housekeeping affairs they had all their own way. Thinking their constitutions to be delicate, the advice, I repeatedly gave them was that they should wear flannel, eat as much wholesome animal food as they could digest, take air and exercise in moderation, and not devote too much time and attention to study and composition.

As a postscript – and not as a firm request – he added with admirable mildness of manner, 'The Eccentrick Movements ascribed to me, at pages 51 & 52, Vol. I. – have no foundation in fact –'.[86]

Though Patrick had been reluctant to cast doubt on the general veracity of the book by insisting on alterations, others were not so reticent. Everyone, it seemed, had a complaint to make. G. H. Lewes asked that a phrase should be inserted pointing out that his article in the *Edinburgh Review* was not disrespectful to women as Charlotte had suggested. Samuel Redhead's son-in-law wrote to Mrs Gaskell and the *Leeds Intelligencer* disputing Scoresby's highly coloured account of Redhead's rejection by Haworth Church in 1819 and offering his father-in-law's diary as proof of what really happened. Harriet Martineau, who could be a vitriolic correspondent when her blood was up, wrote 'sheet upon sheet regarding the quarrel? misunderstanding? between her & Miss Brontë'.[87] Most damaging of all, Mrs Gaskell was threatened with two suits for libel, one from the former Mrs Robinson, now Lady Scott, and one from William Carus Wilson.

Curiously enough, Mrs Gaskell herself had foreseen this problem. 'Do you mind the law of libel', she had asked George Smith the previous autumn. 'I have three people I want to libel – Lady Scott (that bad woman who corrupted Branwell Brontë) Mr Newby, & Lady Eastlake, the < two > first \& last/ not to be named by name, the mean publisher to be gibbetted.'[88] When she submitted her manuscript, George Smith immediately raised objections to her treatment of both Lady Scott and Thomas Newby. Mrs Gaskell, somewhat disingenuously, declared herself unaware that she had indicated Lady Scott's identity so obviously: 'The part where I point her out most clearly seems to me to be "Lady— in May-Fair." I thought when I wrote this that she lived in May-Fair, – I have since learnt that she does not, – but certainly there are plenty of "Lady—",s in May Fair, though we will hope not so many as bad as she is.' To this she added, with the novelist's disregard for historical accuracy, 'I put that in as I have said, to point the contrast of her life, & Branwell's death.' 'About Newby', she freely admitted, 'I was quite aware that, as you saw the MS, my expressions were actionable … I should like to warn others off trusting to him as much as I cd.'[89]

George Smith was able to dissuade her from the libellous statements about Newby, but on Lady Scott she was immoveable. 'I see you think me merciless', she told him, but she had heard so many corroborative accounts of Lady Scott's bad behaviour from her cousin and another relation, Lady Trevelyan, she felt sure of her ground. Nor did she believe that Lady Scott would risk bringing an action that would only further damage her reputation. Had Mrs Gaskell been at home when Lady Scott threatened legal action, it is not necessarily a foregone conclusion that she would have submitted to the publication of the uncontested retraction which her husband and lawyers concocted in her absence and without her knowledge. The retraction of 'every statement ... which imputes to a widowed lady ... any breach of her conjugal, of her maternal, or of her social duties, and more especially of the statements ... which impute to the lady in question a guilty intercourse with the late Branwell Brontë' appeared in *The Times* on 30 May 1857, together with a letter from Newton & Robinson, Lady Scott's solicitors, acknowledging that Mrs Gaskell had acted in reliance on information she believed to be well founded.⁹⁰

Mrs Gaskell herself arrived home in the midst of this crisis to find Lady Scott's action settled, but another one threatened by William Carus Wilson's son. This, however, she was determined to resist, not least because in this instance a fierce correspondence was being carried out in the press which, albeit on one side only, fully justified her comments about conditions at the Clergy Daughters' School. Unfortunately for him, Arthur had been provoked into defending his wife in what was to become an increasingly acrimonious and vituperative correspondence. 'I do think Mrs Gaskell has been rash;' he had declared in reference to Lady Scott's action, 'she seems to have forgotten that she was dealing with living persons – I shall ever regret that I did not ask to see the MS. as I think I could have convinced her of the injudiciousness of some things in it.'

Nevertheless, he too felt confident that 'she has only done justice in that case – Mr Wilson says that he is told it is actionable – I do not however think that there is much danger in that quarter – He and his friends have been most industrious in circulating through the press & privately an adverse review, containing an attempt at refutation of the statements regarding Cowan Bridge; and making a vile attack on my poor wife – I was so provoked that I wrote an answer, which has appeared in the Manchester papers & some others.' Mr Wilson's supporters had even sent copies of their 'vile attack' to Patrick anonymously through the post, an action which further incensed his son-in-law.⁹¹

For almost three months the controversy raged in the press, the local papers being particularly assiduous in printing allegation and counter-allegation. Unwisely, Arthur could not allow the derogatory remarks about his wife and the veracity of her portrayal of Cowan Bridge to pass unchallenged. He, too, took to copying his replies to the *Leeds Intelligencer, Leeds Mercury* and *Halifax Guardian*, answering his opponents point by point with increasing irritation and anguish. When the Wilson camp carried the campaign into *The Times*, Arthur sent a copy of his reply there too, telling George Smith that if the paper refused to print it, Patrick 'seems determined to have it inserted as an advertisement'.⁹² This was the course of action they decided to take when confronted by a pamphlet refuting the charges against the school which the Wilsons had printed and circulated. Only George Smith himself, whom they had asked to insert the advertisement as 'we really do not know any other person in town', was able to dissuade them. It was Patrick who replied, Arthur having gone to Ireland for a few weeks of well-deserved holiday. 'Owing to what you have said we have made up our minds, <u>not</u> to advertise in the "Times" ', he wrote, 'Enough has been written, to justify "Currer Bells" intimations, in regard to what has been stated, under the garb of fiction, in "Jane Eyre".' There was a condition attached to this withdrawal from the combat, however, which made it clear how much Charlotte's family regretted the public retraction over the Lady Scott affair.

I hope, therefore, that Mrs Gaskell, having strong proofs on her side, will, make <u>no concessions</u> to Messrs Shepherd, and Wilson, whether they cajole, or threaten. There ought to be <u>no more concessions</u> – Errors may be legitimately corrected, but nothing more should be done by Authors.[93]

In a letter to George Smith a few days later, he commented, 'Mrs Gaskell, in her third Edition, of the "Memoir", will require, the full exercise, of her talents, taste, and <u>judgement</u>.' Patrick clearly regarded the last as fallible for he added, 'I hope, that you will put in a word, now and then –'.[94]

If Arthur had hoped that the controversy would die away in his absence, he was singularly mistaken. Another combatant had entered the fray, reaching new heights of personal invective, for she was an acquaintance, if not a personal friend. Sarah Baldwin, wife of the incumbent of Mytholmroyd, was also the daughter of Thomas Crowther, the vicar of Cragg Vale, who had preached so often in Haworth Church and was a friend of both Patrick and Arthur. Though she had been a pupil at Cowan Bridge, she had not, as Arthur wearily and repeatedly pointed out, been there at the same time as Charlotte and had completely escaped the troubles of the early years.[95] As a vociferous defender of the school, she was particularly upset when Arthur said that her own father had made disparaging remarks about it when he had withdrawn his youngest daughter. After an exchange of some half dozen increasingly vituperative letters, the editor of the *Halifax Guardian* intervened. He wrote to Patrick, securing his consent to drop 'this interminable, and not very pleasant, controversy' and, with the judgement of Solomon, ably summed up the arguments:

There *were* certain hardships and irregularities at the Cowan Bridge School when Miss Brontë was there, which were remedied as soon as they became known to its Reverend and benevolent promoter. Miss Brontë made a novelist's use of this incident of her life, in which, as always occurs with minds that brood silently on their wrongs, the shadows had been deepened and darkened by reflection. Mrs Gaskell, in that spirit of hero-worship with which modern biographers are infected, accepted the exaggerated caricature for the reality; and hence the controversy in which so much warmth has been displayed, and so many hard words exchanged.[96]

Sarah Baldwin was not to be deprived of the last word, however, and the following week inserted a lengthy letter as an advertisement.[97] The editor, whose sympathies appear to have lain with Charlotte's family, allowed Arthur to insert one last response on 8 August. Repeating once again that the whole question revolved around the state of the school '*during the time that Miss Brontè was there*', Arthur closed his letter with stiff dignity. 'I have discharged a painful but necessary duty.' he declared. 'Henceforth Charlotte Brontè's assailants may growl and snarl over her grave undisturbed by me.' Sarah Baldwin had prepared another response, 'much stronger than any previous one', but a private letter from Arthur to her husband, containing 'one or two explanatory remarks' and a 'candid tribute to Mr Crowther's character', persuaded her to let the matter rest.[98]

Arthur's relief was to be short-lived. The very day that William Baldwin wrote to accept the ending of the Cowan Bridge controversy, a letter appeared in the *Bradford Observer* which raised a fresh and equally bitter dispute. The letter was from William Dearden, an old friend of the Brontë family, who had visited Patrick with Joseph Leyland's brother, Francis, on 8 July. They had, inevitably, discussed Mrs Gaskell's *Life of Charlotte Brontë*, which Patrick had praised while also complaining of the ridiculous anecdotes purporting to illustrate his character and of his treatment by the reviewers.

There was nothing unusual in this, for Patrick was accustomed to disown the anecdotes to all his visitors, and had written to both Mrs Gaskell and George Smith telling them that 'I never was subject to those explosions of passion ascribed to me, and never perpetrated those eccentric and ridiculous movements, which I am ashamed to mention.'[99] He himself had deliberately refrained from public comment on these issues because he was reluctant to cast further doubt on Mrs Gaskell's veracity in the wake of the Lady Scott libel threat and the Cowan Bridge controversy; he had simply asked Mrs Gaskell to remove them from the forthcoming third edition, which she agreed to do. His letter to her, written on 30 July, is a model of its kind, revealing not only his self-deprecating sense of humour but also his remarkable forbearance.

I may have been troublesome to you … but, I was roused a little, by the impertinent remarks, of a set of pennyaliner, hungry, pedantic, and generally ignorant reviewers. – No, one, despises them, and their productions more than I do; but the misfortune is, that the multitude, see not as we see, and not judging for themselves are often misled, by the false judgement of others. I do not deny that I am somewhat excentrick. Had I been numbered amongst the calm, sedate, <u>concentric</u> men of the world, I should not have been as I now am, and I should, in all probability, never have had such children as mine have been. I have no objection, whatever to your representing me as a <u>little</u> exccentric, since you, and other learned friends will have it so; only don't set me on, in my fury to burning hearthrugs, sawing the backs of chairs, and tearing my wife's silk gown … It is dangerous, to give credence hastily, to informants – some may tell the truth, whilst others from various motives may greedily, invent and propagate falsehoods ... I am not, in the least offended, at your telling me that I have faults! I have many – and being a Daughter of Eve, I doubt not, that you also have some. Let us both try to be wiser and better, as Time recedes, and Eternity advances.'[100]

William Dearden, however, took it into his head that Mrs Gaskell had traduced his old friend and that he should be publicly vindicated in the press. He therefore wrote to the *Bradford Observer* twice, furiously attacking Mrs Gaskell for her calumny of 'this venerable clergyman, now on the verge of the grave' whom she had 'tarred and feathered by the malice of an ignorant country gossip'. He castigated her for giving credence to a sacked nurse instead of the long-serving and faithful servants, Martha Brown and Nancy Garrs, denounced her portrayal as a travesty of the truth and, worst of all, quoted Patrick himself as saying, 'I did not know that I had an enemy in the world; much less one who would traduce me before my death. Everything in that book ... which relates to my conduct to my family, is either false or distorted.'[101]

Patrick wrote immediately to Mrs Gaskell to set the record straight:

with this article, I had nothing whatever to, do – I knew nothing of it till I saw it in print, and was much displeased when I saw it there. Though hard press'd by some ruthless critics, as well as Mr Wilson and his party, I held both my tongue and my pen – believing, that you were a friend to my Daughter Charlotte, and no enemy to me, and feeling confident that whatever you found to be mistakes, you would willingly correct in the third Edition.[102]

The matter might and should have ended there had not yet another officious 'friend' intervened. Under the pretext of defending Mrs Gaskell from Patrick's supposed accusation that she was an enemy, Harriet Martineau declared that she had seen two of his letters praising the memoir in terms which made it impossible for him to have so completely changed his mind in the interval. The real reason for writing her letter, however, was to vent her spleen about Charlotte's remarks on herself and Mrs Gaskell's portrayal of their quarrel. 'When I find that, in my own case, scarcely one of Miss Brontë's statements about me is altogether true, I cannot be surprised at her biographer having been misled in other cases of more importance.'[103]

Two days after Harriet Martineau's statement in the *Daily News* was copied in the *Bradford Observer*, William Dearden returned to the parsonage in high dudgeon, anxious to take up the cudgels once more on Patrick's behalf. Patrick tried to dissuade him, but there was little he could do to restrain his self-appointed champion. A couple of days later he wrote an eloquent plea for peace which came little short of an express prohibition on further comment.

I trouble you with a few lines merely to state, that I wish nothing more should be written against Mrs Gaskell, in regard to the 'Memoir.' She has already encountered very severe trials, which generally falls to the lot of celebrated authors. She has promised to omit, in the third Edition, the errroneous statements respecting me; which is all, I can now, reasonably expect or desire, as no more, I think, can be safely, or prudently done. As for myself, I wish to live in unnoticed and quiet retirement; setting my mind on things above in heaven, and not on things on the earth beneath, and performing my duty to the utmost of my power; esteeming myself after all, but an unprofitable servant, and resting my hopes for salvation, on the all-prevailing merits of the Saviour of a lost world, and considering, that the passing affairs of this life – which too much occupy the attention of passing mortal man, are but dust and ashes, when compar'd with the concerns of Eternity.

Lest Dearden should be in any doubt, he added a postscript. 'I never thought < otherwise > otherwise of Mrs Gaskell, than that she was a friend of my Daughter, and no enemy to me. In alluding to enemies, I meant false informants, and hostile Critics.'[104] Aware that his pleas were likely to fall on deaf ears, Patrick wrote again to Mrs Gaskell to put the record straight. 'My real, or pretended friends,' he wrote with unaccustomed bitterness, 'seem in their gossiping skill, to have combined, to paint me not as a single but a double Janus, looking, and smiling or frowning, with my four faces, in opposite directions, as may best suit my own selfish convenience. They would please me better, by minding their own affairs, and letting mine alone.'[105]

Dearden, of course, could not let Harriet Martineau's statement pass without comment, and ill-advisedly rushed off a reply to the *Bradford Observer* which wrongly accused Harriet Martineau of not having seen the whole of Patrick's letters.[106] The whole terrible cycle of ill-informed accusation and counter-accusation was about to begin again. Matters were made worse by an article in the *Spectator,* which the *Bradford Observer* obligingly reprinted for the edification of the Brontës' home circles. Pointing out how Mrs Gaskell's accounts of the Clergy Daughters' School, Branwell's affair and now Charlotte's father had all been denounced as untrue, it picked up Harriet Martineau's unpleasantly suggestive comment that 'It is a perilous task to write the history of a singularly imaginative person, during the lifetime of contemporaries.' 'Interpreting this passage in the ordinary way,' declared the *Bradford Observer,* 'we might understand that Charlotte Brontë dealt less in fiction when she was writing "Jane Eyre" and other romances than when she professed to be stating plain facts.'[107]

It says much for Patrick's patience and restraint that he was able to resist the temptation to reply. What seems to have tipped the scale, however, was the continuing circulation of Harriet Martineau's charges against Charlotte combined with the publication in September of the long-awaited third edition of the *Life of Charlotte Brontë*. Mrs Gaskell had done her best to please everyone, despite feeling aggrieved that her version of events had been disputed. 'I *did so try* to *tell the truth*,' she wrote miserably to Ellen Nussey, '& I believe *now* I hit as near the truth as any one *could* do.' To George Smith, she complained more robustly: 'I hate the whole affair, & every thing connected with it.'[108] Nevertheless, she had removed the offending passages about Patrick, Lady Scott and the 'plenty and even waste' in the Brontë household under the Garrs sisters and had toned down references to an easily identifiable Haworth girl who had been seduced. She had even placed a denial from Harriet Martineau alongside Charlotte's statement that she had lost friends by writing the Atkinson letters and allowed her to give her own version of the quarrel between them. It was this that particularly irked Patrick and Arthur, though Patrick had been generous in his praise of the new edition. 'With the work as it now stands, all reasonable persons must be satisfied; since in it, there is much to praise, and little or nothing to blame. It has, I think, arrived at a degree of perfection, which was scarcely attainable, in a first, and second Edition.' He expressed the somewhat forlorn hope that there would now be a period of calm and that there would be no fault-finders, adding, with unfortunately prophetic words:

unless some one like Miss Martineau should arise, determin'd to be hostile, and to put the worst construction, on the best intentions, both in words and actions. Notwithstanding Miss Martineau's strange and unhappy illusions, which mystify, and bewilder, her Atheistical Brain, I had thought she was a Woman, naturally kind, and just and generous, who would not knowingly, or willingly injure the memory of any one, especially that of the dead, who were unable to defend themselves.[109]

He was soon to find out just how wrong he had been. As Harriet Martineau continued to complain loud and long in print that Charlotte's statements about her were not true, Patrick wrote to her privately to remonstrate, pointing out that 'I have ever heard her speak of you, in terms of kindness, and veneration, and when any one spoke of you otherwise, she took your part.' Miss Martineau dashed off a dismissive reply, repeating her accusation with the added sting that Charlotte's remarks about her were 'more like hallucinations< s > than sober statement'. She referred Patrick to the third edition where, she claimed, Mrs Gaskell had 'corrected' his daughter's misstatements.[110]

The letter was gratuitously offensive, prompting Arthur to look through the new edition to see exactly what concessions Mrs Gaskell had made to Charlotte's erstwhile friend. Amongst the new material she had supplied, he found the passage she quoted from Harriet Martineau's letter to Charlotte about the love in *Villette*. 'Your letter is now in my possession', he told her, 'this passage does not occur in it – I shall adopt the same means, that you have, to inform the public that the individual, who accuses my wife of inaccuracies, has herself been guilty of a much graver offence.'[111]

Clearly alarmed, Harriet Martineau wrote a self-justificatory letter, claiming to have supplied the quote from memory and that 'in a spirit of kindness' she had leapt to the defence of Patrick against the unjust imputations of William Dearden; in a desperate bid for sympathy she also told him that she was herself 'deep in my last illness' – as she had been for over two years and was to be until her death in 1876, nineteen years later. Nevertheless, she demanded to see the original of her letter or a certified copy. 'This is the first step', she ominously declared. 'We shall then see what next.'[112]

Arthur sent off a copy of the letter with an understandable but provocative retort.

Your intention in writing to 'the Daily News' may have been very kind: but will you pardon me for saying that your interference was wholly gratuitous? Mr Brontè being quite competent to take care of himself: he would moreover have willingly dispensed with a vindication which was made the occasion of bringing a charge of general untruthfulness against his daughter.[113]

Unable to deny that her supposed quotation was substantially different from her original letter, Harriet Martineau changed tack, accusing him of deliberately deceiving Mrs Gaskell by telling her that he had destroyed all Charlotte's papers when he clearly had not. Aware now that he was dealing with a hysterical woman who might be on her deathbed, Arthur replied more patiently than he might otherwise have done, pointing out that he had claimed only to have destroyed Charlotte's letters to himself. Patrick, too, wrote again, confessing how sorely he still felt his bereavement. 'This it is that makes, both Mr Nicholls and me, feel sensitive, in regard to any prejidices, or misrepresentations, bearing upon the character of my Dear Daughter Charlotte.' Reiterating the advice he had given Mrs Gaskell, he added, 'Beware of the designs, of prejudiced, or reckless Informants.'[114] This was clearly a reference to John Greenwood, who had told Miss Martineau that Arthur had burnt all Charlotte's papers. She had wrongly believed that the statement had come directly from Arthur himself and had used it as further evidence of his duplicity in dealing with Mrs Gaskell. Forwarding a letter from Greenwood himself, in which he abjectly confessed that he only 'believed Mrs Nicholls made it a rule not to keep letters, except those of importance', Arthur could not restrain his anger at uncovering yet another example of unwarranted interference in his affairs. Greenwood's letter showed that he acted 'solely on supposition' and 'His position is not such as would have enabled him to know any thing of Miss Brontè's private affairs, further than what he [might] have learnt by gossiping with servants. His relation to Miss Brontè consisted in being the recipient of her bounty and advice, when in distress from the claims of a large family.'[115]

Responding by return of post to Miss Martineau's demand for all her letters to Charlotte to be sent back to her, Arthur informed her that he had not read any of them, except the ones relevant to the quarrel, and requested her to send Smith, Elder & Co. a revised transcript of her letter on *Villette* for inclusion in a future edition. This she agreed to do.[116] The 'warlike correspondence' which had been carried on at a fast and furious pace – there are twelve extant letters written in only ten days – now came to an end. Arthur evidently sought to extend a hand of friendship at the close but Miss Martineau, taking the somewhat warped view that she had been vindicated by the correspondence, crowed to her friends about her 'victory': 'I fancy these gentlemen (who are <u>not</u> gentlemen, however) have never before been opposed or called to account. In their own parish they reign by fears: and I hope it may be good for them to find they can get wrong.'[117]

Whether it was good for them or not, this was the last occasion on which either Patrick or Arthur ventured personally into Brontë controversy. Clearly there was little to be gained and much to lose by sinking to the level of Charlotte's critics: a dignified silence was the most appropriate response. From now on they would put their faith in the third edition of the *Life of Charlotte Brontë* to defend Charlotte's reputation. As Patrick himself had declared:

my opinion, and the reading world's opinion of the 'Memoir,' is, that it is every \way/ worthy of what one Great Woman, should have written of Another, and that it ought to stand, and will stand in the first rank, of Biographies, till the end of time.[118]

Chapter Twenty-Eight

❧

THE END OF ALL

In the general furore which greeted Mrs Gaskell's *Life of Charlotte Brontë*, the publication of Charlotte's first novel, *The Professor*, slipped by almost unnoticed. Printing began shortly after the biography had appeared but was so slow that Arthur, who meticulously proofread every page, began to fear that he might lose the brief holiday he had planned to take in June. A plea to George Smith produced the desired effect and the book was ready for publication by the third week in May: it appeared as a two-volume set at the beginning of June. Characteristically self-effacing, Arthur only allowed his name to be appended to a brief foreword claiming that he had consented to the publication because 'it has been represented to me that I ought not to withhold "The Professor" from the public'; he made no mention of his own conscientious work as editor and left his wife to speak for herself in the foreword she had written when proposing to revise it as her second publication.[1]

Despite the huge interest in the Brontës' works which the *Life of Charlotte Brontë* had stimulated, only 2,500 copies were printed. Though this was a respectable number for a hardbacked novel, it pales into insignificance when compared to the print runs and sales of the cheap editions of the Brontës' works. Twenty-five thousand copies of *Jane Eyre* were printed in July 1857, with further reprints of 5,000 each six months and a year later; 20,000 copies of *Shirley*, printed in September 1857, had sold out within nine months; 15,000 copies of *Villette* were printed in December 1857 and 5,000 more six months later; even *Wuthering Heights & Agnes Grey*, despite its initial critical mauling, had its sales boosted to the extent that 15,000 had to be printed in March 1858. Though early sales of *The Professor* were not bad, almost two-thirds of the print run being sold within a month, there were still copies on hand five years later and the sales did not warrant the production of a cheap edition until 1860.[2]

The lacklustre sales were mirrored by unenthusiastic reviews. Where the critics condescended to notice it at all, it was generally subsumed in a larger piece on the *Life of Charlotte Brontë*. Opinions ranged from 'the poorest of all Charlotte Brontë's productions' to, in Frances Henri, 'the most attractive female character that ever came from the pen of this author'. Though some reviewers doubted the wisdom of publishing a work which could not add to Charlotte's literary reputation, all were agreed that it was remarkable as a literary curiosity and evidence of how Charlotte's powers had developed in the interval between it and *Villette*.[3] The cool response to *The Professor* did not disappoint Arthur, who had had no great expectations of success: 'The Reviews of the work, which I have seen,' he told George Smith, 'are quite as favourable as I expected.'[4]

The dramatic effect of the *Life of Charlotte Brontë* was not only felt on the sales of the Brontës' novels but also on their home and neighbours. The book itself was in great demand in Haworth. One enterprising bookseller (John Greenwood, perhaps?) had bought a copy on its first issue and then lent it out at the rate of a shilling a week for each volume. Even at that price, those who could not afford to purchase a copy outright were queuing up to borrow the volumes, which were eagerly read and criticized.[5] Arthur found himself being unjustly reviled by the 'charitable folks' in the township, who assumed that he had supplied Mrs Gaskell with her grotesque tales about Haworth and its people, even though he was not aware of some of the stories until he saw them in the book.[6]

The book had placed Haworth firmly on the map. There had been a trickle of tourists ever since the publication of *Shirley* and the identification of 'Currer Bell'; in the wake of Mrs Gaskell's powerful and emotive descriptions of the place, this now became a flood. 'Haworth has been inundated with visitors –', Arthur wrote to George Smith a mere two months after the biography had appeared. 'But with one or two exceptions we have not seen any thing of them – It would be a great nuisance if they were to intrude on us –'[7] By July the local papers had begun to comment. 'The memoir of this lady is producing quite a revolution in the ancient village of Haworth', declared the *Bradford Observer* and the *Leeds Intelligencer*.

Scarcely a day passes that a score of visitors do not make a pilgrimage to the spot where Charlotte Brontë lived and died. The quiet rural inns, where refreshment for man & beast, of a plain but excellent kind, used to be obtainable at a fabulously low price, have raised their tariff to an equality with the most noted hotels in the pathways of tourists, & if they advance their charges much more they will rank among the most costly houses of entertainment in the Queen's dominions. The old proverb, 'make your hay while the sun shines', is diligently obeyed by the bonifaces in this locality.[8]

Tourists walking up the main street were confronted with the first examples of Brontë souvenirs: even the chemist was cashing in on the trend, displaying photographs of Patrick Brontë, the church and the parsonage for sale in his windows. William Brown, who had taken his brother's place as sexton, was similarly milking the tourists for all they were worth, inviting them to see Charlotte's signature in the marriage register and then showing them his own collection of photographs 'with an intimation that they were for sale'.[9] It is difficult to believe that his rector and curate were aware of how he was abusing his position in the church.

'From different parts of this variegated world,' Patrick informed Mrs Gaskell with a mixture of pride and irritation, 'we have in this place \daily/ many strangers, who from various motives, pay a visit to the Church and neighbourhood, and would, if we would let them, pay a gossiping visit to us, in our proper persons.'[10]

Among the 'select few' who were granted the privilege of an interview was the Duke of Devonshire, who stopped for about an hour at the parsonage and invited Arthur and Patrick to visit him at his seat at Bolton Abbey in September.[11] A less illustrious but equally favoured visitor was a correspondent of the *Bradford Observer*, whose complaint has been echoed by every tourist since. 'Our previous conceptions of the locality had been formed entirely from Mrs Gaskell's description and the frontispiece to the "Memoirs of Charlotte Brontë;" and we found all our expectations most gloriously disappointed', he reported.

We had supposed Haworth to be a scattered and straggling hamlet, with a desolate vicarage and a dilapidated church, surrounded and shut out from the world by a wilderness of barren heath, the monotony of the prospect only broken by the tombstones in the adjacent graveyard. Our straggling hamlet we found transformed into a large and flourishing village – not a very enlightened or poetical place certainly, but quaint, compact, and progressive, wherein, by the bye, we observed three large dissenting chapels and two or three well-sized schools.

One of Martha Brown's sisters was a waitress at the White Lion Inn, where the correspondent and his friend took their dinner, and through her they obtained a fifteen-minute interview with Patrick at the parsonage. Their faith in Mrs Gaskell, already undermined, underwent a further diminution during the visit. Patrick so impressed them with his fine physique, despite his eighty years, his courteous and gentlemanly bearing and his obviously sincere feeling, that they deliberately set out to find out what his parishioners thought of him. One and all pronounced him to be held in great affection and respect and all denied knowledge of Mrs Gaskell's pistol-shooting anecdotes.[12]

Another visitor was Edward White Benson, a future Archbishop of Canterbury, but then only a twenty-nine-year-old clergyman, who was granted an interview in January 1858, presumably because he was a cousin of the Sidgwicks of Stonegappe where Charlotte had once been a governess. Naturally they discussed Mrs Gaskell's biography, Patrick revealing that neither he nor his son-in-law had been consulted by Mrs Gaskell and lamenting not only his own caricature but also the 'many unfounded things pertaining to our neighbours' which had appeared in the book: with his usual penetration he also observed that though the third edition was more truthful, 'vulgar readers would always prefer the first'.[13]

With so many tourists of varying degrees of fame coming to Haworth, it was perhaps not surprising that advantage was taken of them in more ways than one. Approaches had been made to the Duke of Devonshire, through Sir Joseph Paxton, seeking financial assistance towards a public subscription in Haworth which was intended to fund the provision of heating in the church and schools. 'This has been done, without our knowledge,' Patrick wrote indignantly to Sir Joseph,

and most assuredly, had we known it, would have met with our strongest opposition. We have no claim on the Duke. His Grace, honour'd us with a visit, in token of his respect for the memory of the Dead, and His liberality and munificence, are well, and widely known, and the mercenary, taking an unfair advantage of these circumstances, have taken a step which both Mr Nicholls, and I utterly regret and condemn.[14]

Though Patrick and Arthur were anxious not to profit financially by the fame which Mrs Gaskell's biography had brought them, Patrick was only too delighted when, having read the book, former friends got in touch again. He wrote anxiously to correct James Cheadle, the incumbent of Bingley, who had told an enquirer that Patrick was a graduate of Trinity College, Dublin, 'since the Inquirer may be some old friend, with whom I shall like to revive half-dead associations. At any age, this is pleasant, but < at > at mine, it is especially so – since many I once knew and esteem'd and loved, are now gone, and but few new ones, have arisen, to take their place –'.[15]

An old colleague at St John's College was one of the first to renew contact. The Reverend John Nunn, Patrick's fellow sizar, was now the rector of Thorndon in Suffolk and, although some five years younger than Patrick, was in a very poor state of health. Clearly he and his wife had derived an alarming picture of the backward state of Haworth from Mrs Gaskell. They offered to send Patrick a newspaper (until he pointed out that he could see any paper he wished through his own subscriptions and the various institutions in the village) and followed this up by offering him a home with them in their large and comfortable rectory. Despite their illusions about the barbarous state of Patrick's neighbourhood, there was much pleasure to be gained from grumbling together about the bad spirit of the present age and the shocking spread of 'Romish idolatry'.[16]

Another old friend who was prompted to write by the biography was the Reverend Robinson Pool, who had been minister of the Dissenting chapel in Thornton during Patrick's incumbency there. His letters brought back memories of a different and more poignant kind. 'I can fancy, almost, that we are still at Thornton, good neighbours, and kind, and sincere friends, and happy with our wives and children', Patrick wrote. 'You have had your trials, both sharp, and severe, but God has given you grace, and strength sufficient unto your day – My trials you have heard of – I feard often, that I should sink under them; but the Lord remembered mercy in judgement, and I am still living.'[17]

The pleasure of renewing old friendships was somewhat marred by sad news from Buckinghamshire: William Morgan, if not Patrick's oldest then certainly his closest friend, had died on 30 March 1858, while on a visit to Bath.[18] Like John Nunn and Robinson Pool, he was several years younger than Patrick himself who, having outlived all his family, now seemed likely to outlive all his friends. That his own death must now be close at hand did not trouble Patrick, however, and he set about making preparations with the calmness of an unquestioning faith. It was at about this time that he ordered a new memorial tablet for his family in Haworth Church. The old one had been so full of names that the letters had had to be made smaller and the lines more cramped together towards the bottom of the tablet. By the time Charlotte died, it was so full that her name could not be added and had to be inscribed on a separate plaque below. The simple and elegant new tablet, sculpted by Mr Greaves of Halifax, was made of Carrara marble and plainly ornamented. The names, ages and dates of death of Mrs Brontë and her six children were inscribed, and space was left for the insertion of Patrick's own name below that of his family. William Brown was entrusted with the task of removing the old tablet, breaking it up and burying it in a corner of the parsonage garden, safe from the prying eyes and hands of souvenir hunters.[19]

For the rest, Patrick lived quietly and simply enough, continuing to preach in his church but, after a severe attack of bronchitis in the spring of 1858, only doing so once each Sunday. James Hoppin, a professor from Yale, heard him preach on a text from Job, 'There the wicked cease from troubling; and there the weary be at rest', about this time. The sermon impressed him both by its delivery – 'the simple extemporaneous talk of an aged pastor to his people, spoken without effort, in short, easy sentences' – and by its obvious personal application – 'he seemed to long for wings like a dove to fly away from this changeful scene, and be at rest'.[20]

As an American, James Hoppin, too, was welcomed to the parsonage, though he had not wished to intrude and had not sought a meeting. Patrick, however, 'thought much of America' and he enjoyed a brief conversation with his guest during which he quizzed him about the great spiritual movements which from time to time passed over America. Interestingly, he expressed the belief that revivalist movements, though real enough, were accompanied by 'too much animal excitement'. 'He struck me as being naturally a very social man,' Hoppin later observed, 'with a mind fond of discussion, and feeding eagerly on new ideas, in spite of his reserve.'[21]

Yet another American, less tactful than Hoppin, was determined not to leave Haworth without seeing Charlotte Brontë's husband and father. Henry Jarvis Raymond, editor of the *New York Times*, called at the parsonage and presented his card. The words 'New York', as Arthur later told him, were sufficient to ensure him a welcome. Like the correspondent of the *Bradford Observer*, this journalist was also forced to conclude that Mrs Gaskell had somewhat overstated her case. 'I remarked ... that I had been agreeably disappointed in the face of the country and the general aspect of the town, that they were less sombre and repulsive than Mrs Gaskell's descriptions led me to expect. Mr Nicholls and Mr Brontë smiled at each other, and the latter remarked: "Well, I think Mrs Gaskell tried to make us all appear as bad as she could".'[22]

The Americans appear to have been amongst Charlotte's greatest admirers, not only making their way to Haworth to visit her home but constantly importuning for her autograph. Arthur, who regarded everything his wife had written as sacrosanct, could not be induced to part with any of her manuscripts and it was left to Patrick to cut up one of the few letters he had retained into small fragments to satisfy the demand.[23]

Life in Haworth, though changed for ever by Mrs Gaskell's *Life of Charlotte Brontë*, gradually resumed an even tenor. Improvements were constantly being made, despite resistance from the town rate-payers. A Haworth Gas Company was established in 1857 which made and stored gas to supply lighting for the streets and those who could afford to light their houses. An unfortunate incident marred the introduction of such an important amenity: an inexperienced workman from the company 'incautiously' applied a light to gas leaking from a pipe in the street, causing a serious explosion in which a passer-by was severely injured. A year later, the new little reservoir above Hall Green, for which Patrick had campaigned so long, was completed, at last providing Haworth with a constant supply of sweet and fresh piped water.[24] The Mechanics' Institute was increasingly prosperous and successful: it had a library, news room and reading room and sponsored a series of lectures for its members and their guests.[25] Music continued to flourish: old Tom Parker was still alive and giving the occasional recital, but Haworth had a new and rising musical star, John Earnshaw, who gave a grand classical concert in the National School room in October 1858. As a pupil of the Keighley violinist, J. T. Carrodus, who was now engaged by the Royal Italian Opera and the Philharmonic Concerts in London, he was able to prevail upon his teacher and the extensive and equally musical Carrodus family to play.[26]

Outside the township, the increasing prosperity and importance of Bradford was reflected in the calibre of literary celebrities who were now being attracted to the place. William Makepeace Thackeray, Charles Dickens and John Ruskin, who had regarded Charlotte's provincialism with varying degrees of scorn, were now frequent visitors to Halifax and Bradford, where they lectured and read to the assembled Yorkshire masses.[27] One of the strangest of all manifestations of nascent Brontë worship also took place in Bradford where, on 4 January 1859, Gerald Massey, the poet of the Chartist and Christian Socialist movements, lectured the members and friends of the Bradford Mechanics' Institute on the subject of 'Charlotte Brontë'. Though his lecture was little short of a eulogy, one cannot help wondering how he justified describing Charlotte's life to an audience which must have contained many who had known the Brontës personally and included at least one, Nancy Garrs, who was in a far better position to tell that story than him. He seems to have been impervious to such considerations – and to the sensitivities of Charlotte's father and husband living so near at hand – because four days later he repeated the lecture at the Mechanics' Institute in Keighley.[28] John Milligan, the Keighley surgeon who chaired the latter meeting, seems to have felt some sense of shame, sending Patrick a modern medical work in what could be construed as a gesture of apology. Even more extraordinary was the fact that Massey actually seized the opportunity to pay a visit to the parsonage. Up to that point, he had relied solely on the first edition of Mrs Gaskell for his information on the Brontës' childhood and their father's supposedly reclusive and explosive temperament. At least he had the intelligence to realize, on meeting Patrick, that Mrs Gaskell's account of him was a travesty and the grace to amend his portrayal of the father of the Brontës for future lectures.[29]

Far from dying away, interest in the Brontës intensified with the passing of time. The fact that they had written so little only seems to have increased the public desire to see more of their work. In August 1859, for example, Abraham Holroyd, a Bradford antiquarian who was friendly with the Garrs family and had once met Charlotte Brontë, reprinted Patrick's little pamphlet *The Cottage in the Wood*.[30] Patrick could not flatter himself that the decision to republish owed anything to the literary or moral merits of the story: it was saleable purely and simply on its curiosity value as a work by the father of Charlotte Brontë.

More importantly, George Smith approached Arthur to inform him that he was planning to start a new periodical, the *Cornhill Magazine*, and suggested that he might like to send the two chapters of Charlotte's last unfinished novel for inclusion. The idea seems to have come indirectly from Mrs Gaskell, who had wanted to add it as an appendix to the new, cheap edition of her *Life of Charlotte Brontë* 'to make the book more attractive, & likely to sell'. George Smith had initially asked her to approach Arthur with the idea of her editing it for the *Cornhill* but she objected: 'I am afraid of Mr Nicholls,' she told him, '& I think you would be more likely to get him to grant you a favour than I; and perhaps even you more likely if you did not name my name.'[31] Accepting the validity of her argument, George Smith wrote to Arthur himself and suggested that Thackeray, Charlotte's hero, should be invited to write an introduction.

Perhaps somewhat to Smith's surprise, Arthur leapt at the proposal and, even more surprisingly, volunteered a vivid description of how Charlotte had read the manuscript to him in the winter of 1854, which Thackeray was to use almost verbatim in his introduction. He transcribed the manuscript himself and posted it off to George Smith three days later, together with a diffidently offered suggestion that the *Cornhill* might be interested in some of the poems by Emily, Anne and Branwell that he had in his possession.[32] A few days later, he reluctantly sent the original manuscript with a wistfully expressed plea that 'If you do not very much wish to retain < it > the MS I should be greatly obliged by your letting me have it again'. When it had not been returned after three weeks, he enquired anxiously as to whether it had been sent and, when it finally arrived safely, wrote immediately to thank George Smith 'very sincerely' for allowing him to have it back again. The touching reason for the fuss he had made then became clear. 'I prize it much as being the last thing of the kind written by the Author', Arthur confessed.[33]

Both he and Patrick were thrilled to receive a letter from Thackeray explaining his new role as editor of the *Cornhill* and his hopes for its future: 'Mr Brontè was wonderfully pleased with the talent & tact displayed in it.' The first issue was equally warmly welcomed, both men finding something to their personal taste in articles on the volunteer movement and microscopic studies.[34] When 'The Last Sketch' had not appeared in the second issue, however, Arthur assumed that Smith, Elder & Co. had decided against publishing it and peremptorily demanded the return of the proofs. A soothing explanation from George Smith produced an apologetic climb-down, 'as I had really no great wish for its publication, I was desirous of giving you an opportunity of reconsidering the propriety of inserting it in your Magazine'.[35] 'The Last Sketch' finally appeared towards the end of March, prefaced by Thackeray's generous and deeply personal tribute to Charlotte. Both Patrick and Arthur were moved to express their gratification: 'what he has written does honour both to his head and heart', pronounced Patrick, while Arthur added, 'Mr Thackeray's introductory remarks to "The Last Sketch" are greatly admired in this neighbourhood; for my own part I feel that I am deeply indebted to him for them.'[36]

The pride and satisfaction which this publication gave Arthur, which was in such strong contrast to his reaction to Mrs Gaskell's biography, led him to offer the *Cornhill* a number of other works by Charlotte and Emily Brontë. The poems were always offered tentatively and humbly: if they were accepted, Arthur read the proofs and submitted willingly to editorial changes; if they were rejected, he at once acquiesced in the decision. Over the next eighteen months two poems by Charlotte and one by Emily were published in the magazine.[37] These were carefully selected, not only for their merit but also for their lack of autobiographical content. Only too well aware of the pain that personal revelation could cause, Arthur was meticulous in avoiding causing hurt or offence to others. For this reason, he submitted nothing by Branwell, despite enquiries about his manuscripts.

In October 1859, for instance, Richard Monckton Milnes who, as well as being a Member of Parliament was also a man of letters, came to Haworth specifically to see Branwell's papers, his curiosity having been aroused when Mrs Gaskell allowed him to look through the material lent to her for her biography. William Brown showed him Branwell's letters to his brother[38] and Arthur evidently consulted him on the propriety of publishing some of Branwell's other work. What this was can only be guessed. Though it may only have been some of his poems to Mrs Robinson, it is more likely that it was part of the vast collection of letters, sketches and poems inherited by Francis Leyland from his brother, Joseph, which he was anxious to publish as a corrective to Mrs Gaskell. Writing to thank Richard Monckton Milnes for his advice, Arthur declared:

Neither Mr Brontè nor I have any intention of publishing them: indeed we had some time ago already refused to allow them to be printed: for leaving their merit as literary Compositions out of the question altogether, we saw plainly that their subject could not fail to give pain to some persons – We are therefore glad to find that your opinion fully demonstrates the propriety of our decision.[39]

Patrick's health was, by this time, beginning to fail. He had performed his last marriage as long ago as February 1857, his second to last baptism two months later and his last burial on 26 October 1858, Arthur having taken over all the duties on his behalf. The only reason he performed his last baptism as late as 14 November 1859 was to save Arthur from dire consequences. John Greenwood, determined to ensure that his claims to friendship with Charlotte should not be forgotten, decided to call his youngest child 'Brontë Greenwood'. Not surprisingly, Arthur, who had been deeply annoyed to discover Greenwood's role as Mrs Gaskell's informant, declared that he would not christen the child with that name. The matter was left unresolved until the child was nine months old; he then started to ail and, fearing that he would not live, Patrick summoned the Greenwoods to the parsonage and privately baptized the child. When Arthur discovered the entry in the register, he was apparently extremely angry and was only appeased when Patrick pointed out how awkward it would have been for him if the little boy had died unchristened.[40]

It was about this time, too, that Patrick had to give up his last and most important role as a clergyman. On 30 October 1859, he preached his last sermon from the pulpit of Haworth Church. The occasion was not a formal leave-taking, it was simply that this was the last occasion on which he was well enough to walk to the church and address the congregation.[41] The winter of 1859 proved to be unusually severe and Patrick was confined to the house with his usual bronchial complaints. He was not actually ill – indeed, at the end of January, Arthur reported that he was 'wonderfully well' even though he was approaching his eighty-third birthday. A month later he confirmed 'Mr Brontè continues pretty well – He has been much confined to the house this winter owing to the very severe frost. I hope that with the return of a milder season he will be able to resume his afternoon Sermon.'[42]

This was not to be, however, for by the beginning of August Patrick was virtually confined to bed. Indeed, he was so much of an invalid that when Dr Longley, the Bishop of Ripon, came to Haworth to conduct the first confirmation in the township since 1824, he was unable to participate in the proceedings. It was therefore left to Arthur to conduct a mass baptism of thirteen young people the day before the actual confirmation service and to host the bishop's visit. With his habitual kindness, 'the good and dear Bishop' made a point of visiting Patrick in his bedroom before he left Haworth.[43] Such a sign of weakness in Patrick was so uncharacteristic that rumours were already flying around that he was on the point of death. Indeed, one local paper even reported that it believed Arthur would become the next incumbent of Haworth, provoking an indignant response that 'he had no expectation of obtaining the appointment'.[44] There was therefore almost a palpable air of disappointment when Patrick recovered enough to be able to take a turn round the garden and, assisted by his son-in-law, even a short walk along the footpath leading to the moor. 'If Mr Brontë continues to improve in the same ratio as he has done of late,' declared the *Bradford Observer*, 'he will preach again, an event which no one in Haworth would have considered possible a few weeks ago.'[45]

The following month he was well enough to write a couple of short notes to Mrs Gaskell,[46] but when she and her daughter, Meta, arrived to visit him on 25 October 1860, he was again confined to bed. Mrs Gaskell had considerable doubts about going to Haworth, not surprisingly being some-what afraid to come face to face again with the man she had so traduced in her biography. Under pressure from Meta, who was anxious to meet the old man, Mrs Gaskell eventually decided that it was better 'to brave his displeasure if there were any, and to please him by the attention if there were none'. When they arrived, having taken a fly from Keighley station, they were obliged to wait a quarter of an hour in the dining room before Martha at last escorted them upstairs. Meta was most favourably impressed:

we were taken into his bedroom; where everything was delicately clean and white, and there he was sitting propped up in bed in a clean nightgown, with a clean towel laid just for his hands to play upon – looking Oh! very different from the stiff scarred face above the white walls of cravat in the photograph – he had a short soft white growth of beard on his chin; and such a gentle, quiet, sweet, half-pitiful expression on his mouth, a good deal of soft white hair, and spectacles on. He shook hands with us, and we sat down, and then said how glad he was to see Mama – and she said how she had hesitated about coming, – feeling as if he might now have unpleasant associations with her – which never seemed to have entered his head – then he asked her how, since he last saw her, she had passed through this weary and varied world – in a sort of half-grandiloquent style – and then interrupting himself he said 'but first tell me how is that young lady, whose friend went to the Massacres in India?' I thought he meant the Ewarts, or something, and was quite surprised (besides other things) when Mama pointed to me, and said I was here, and then he prosecuted his inquiries about the engagement, and its breaking off; and then turned round and told me that he hoped I would forget the past; and would hope – that we ought all to live on hope. –

Patrick told the Gaskells how he had had so many applications for Charlotte's handwriting that he was obliged to cut up her letters into strips of a line each and again averred that 'the <u>Memoir</u> is a book which will hand your name down to posterity'. Harking back, as he always did with visitors, to his own portrayal, he complained that the statement that he had not allowed his children to eat meat had given ammunition to the Wilson camp in their attempts to defend the Clergy Daughters' School. They discussed politics and Thackeray's notice in the *Cornhill* until Patrick dropped a strong hint that it would be desirable for them to leave in the next five minutes or so, which his guests understood to mean that Arthur was due home from school. Though Meta was evidently rather taken with Patrick, her mother was surprisingly unpleasant about him. 'He is touchingly softened by illness;' she told Smith Williams, 'but still talks in his pompous way, and mingles moral remarks and somewhat stale sentiments with his conversation on other subjects.' Clearly she had already forgotten how surprised and pleased she had been by the way he had behaved 'like a brick' when she was under pressure from all sides about the first edition of the biography.[47]

After they left the parsonage, the Gaskells went to pay a visit to John Greenwood, where they were informed, at passionate length, about Arthur's furious reaction to the baptism of young Brontë Greenwood. Mrs Gaskell had evidently still not learnt that John Greenwood was a partial and hostile observer, for she accepted his account without question because it confirmed her own prejudices. 'Mr Nicholls seems to keep him [Patrick] rather *in terrorem*', she announced, misinterpreting Patrick's natural anxiety that his son-in-law should not be upset by an unexpected confrontation with Charlotte's biographer for fear of Arthur's anger. '<u>He</u> is more unpopular in the village than ever; and seems to have even a greater aversion than formerly to any strangers visiting his wife's grave; or, indeed, to any reverence paid to her memory, even by those who knew and loved her for her own sake.' Even Meta seems to have been infected by Greenwood's bile, commenting on the Brontë Greenwood story, 'this is a specimen of Mr N's sullen, obstinate rooted objection to any reverence being paid to Miss B. one might almost say at any rate to people caring to remember her as an authoress'.[48] It was a pity the Gaskells could not have talked to some of the Americans who had been welcomed to the parsonage by Charlotte Brontë's husband.

Though confined to bed, Patrick remained 'on the whole pretty well' throughout the winter of 1860, but as the new year turned he suffered a severe relapse. Though recovery was not expected, his astonishingly tough physique pulled him through yet again.[49] His decline was now steady. So much of Martha's time was now taken up in looking after the invalid that her sister Eliza was hired again on 1 February to assist in running the house.[50] The weather was extremely severe throughout the early months of 1861, the roads between Skipton and Keighley becoming impassable as the snow drifted as high as the tops of the walls. Dr Cartman proved his friendship and showed considerable determination in getting through to Haworth for Patrick's eighty-fourth birthday on 17 March 1861: he also made himself useful by preaching two sermons in the church the same day.[51] On 4 April, Arthur reported to George Smith that 'Mr Brontè continues pretty well – He has been confined to bed for some months, and seems to lose strength very gradually; his mental faculties however remain quite unimpaired –'. About a fortnight later there came sad news from Suffolk: Patrick's old friend John Nunn had died on 16 April, at the age of seventy-nine.[52] Patrick himself was soon to follow.

About six o'clock on the morning of 7 June 1861, Patrick was seized with convulsions: before Arthur could get to him he was unconscious. Even then, death would not come swiftly to take the last Brontë who, of all his family, was the one most glad to die. He lingered, in a state of unconsciousness, with Arthur and Martha in constant attendance, until between two and three o'clock in the afternoon, his spirit went rejoicing to meet its Maker.[53] He had served his God and his church faithfully for fifty-five years, forty-one of them in Haworth. Many of the inhabitants of his far-flung chapelry had known no other incumbent and they came in their hundreds to pay their last respects. On 12 June 1861, the day of the funeral, all the shops in Haworth voluntarily closed, the unaccustomed 'silence and solemnity that reigned around' proving 'the deep estimation in which the venerable incumbent was held'. In the church every pew and available space was taken and several hundred people were forced to remain outside in the churchyard.[54]

In accordance with Patrick's wishes, Arthur had arranged everything with unostentatious simplicity. There was no passing bell and no psalms were sung. The coffin, preceded by Dr Burnett, vicar of Bradford, and William Cartman, who jointly conducted the burial service, was carried from the parsonage to the church and then to the family vault by six of Patrick's closest friends and neighbours, all clergymen: Joseph Grant from Oxenhope, J. H. Mitchell from Cullingworth, H. Taylor from Newsholme, William Fawcett from Morton, John Smith from Oakworth and John Mayne from Keighley. Arthur followed the coffin, accompanied by Martha and Eliza Brown, their mother and Nancy Garrs: Sutcliffe Sowden, too, was among the crowd of mourners. Anyone who might have doubted the personal affection which had arisen between Patrick and his son-in-law had only to observe Arthur's conduct: he was so 'deeply affected' that he had to be physically supported by William Cartman.[55] Patrick's body was placed in the family vault, authority from the Secretary of State having been obtained in consequence of the formal closure of the over-full churchyard in 1856. The last name was then added to the memorial tablet in the church, above the inscription from I Corinthians, Chapter xv, verses 56–7: 'The sting of death is sin, and the strength of sin is the law, but thanks be to God which giveth us the victory through our Lord Jesus Christ.'[56]

For Arthur, however, the sting of death was to be terrible indeed. He was too prostrate with grief to note the fact that the church trustees had held a meeting on the day of Patrick's funeral to decide what course of action they should take over the appointment of a new incumbent. Patrick had outlived all the twelve trustees who had appointed him in 1820 and it was their descendants, at least two of whom were not even resident in the district, who had inherited the right to decide who should replace him. This first meeting was adjourned because it was deemed inappropriate to discuss the subject with the former incumbent not yet cold in his grave.[57]

The deferral several months forward of the next trustees' meeting seemed to confirm the general expectation that this was simply a formality and that Arthur would succeed his father-in-law. He had, after all, been incumbent of the parish in all but name for the previous six years, carrying out all the duties virtually singlehandedly. A few days after Patrick's funeral, Arthur resumed his pastoral role, teaching in the schools, performing the duties and preaching at the Sunday services. He also read the evening prayers 'with great solemnity' on 23 June, when Dr Burnett returned to Haworth to preach Patrick's funeral sermon to a packed church.[58] On 13 August he had to officiate on an even more traumatic occasion: the funeral of his closest friend, Sutcliffe Sowden. His death had been sudden and tragic: coming home from a parish visit at half past ten on the dark and stormy night of 8 August, he had had some sort of a fit, fallen into the canal at Hebden Bridge and drowned. 'Of a quiet and somewhat retiring disposition', he had been universally liked and respected. Almost exactly two months to the day after Patrick's funeral there was a second impressive gathering for the burial of a beloved clergyman. The shops and mills in Hebden Bridge closed for the day, the crowds lined the streets to pay their last respects, the Sunday school teachers and children carried posies of flowers, which they scattered on the coffin in the open grave. Joseph Grant of Oxenhope and William Baldwin, the rector of Mytholmroyd, were among the mourners, but it fell to Arthur, 'between whom and the deceased there had existed a brotherhood of 14 years standing', to read the burial service. Overcome with emotion at this second loss in such a short time, Arthur was 'so deeply affected as to be often wholly inaudible'.[59] He had lost not only a friend but also another precious link with his wife.

One crumb of comfort at this time was that Archdeacon Musgrave, in a gesture that was welcomed as a fitting tribute to Sutcliffe Sowden himself, appointed his younger brother, George, to the incumbency of Hebden Bridge.[60] Such comfort was to be denied Arthur Nicholls at Haworth.

At a second meeting attended by ten of the twelve trustees, his name was put forward for the incumbency. Only four trustees, including the chairman, voted in his favour; five voted against him and one, the Dissenter, abstained. On this narrowest of margins, Arthur effectively lost the appointment. Consultations with Dr Burnett were evidently held for, at a third meeting, when all the trustees were present, his candidate, John Wade, won the vote by seven votes to Arthur's five.[61]

That the candidate of the vicar of Bradford should have been preferred before the man who had been curate of the parish for sixteen years requires some explanation. Two reasons are usually cited: that there was a general antipathy towards him in Haworth, caused by what Mrs Gaskell calls his 'aversion' to having anyone pay reverence to his wife's memory, and that he had antagonized the church trustees by refusing to arrange for the late chairman, Michael Heaton, to be buried with his wife in a part of the churchyard that had been closed.[62] Neither reason stands up to close scrutiny.

There are only three contemporary sources which mention Arthur's unpopularity in the township: Mrs Gaskell, her daughter Meta, and Charles Hale, an American who visited Haworth in November 1861.[63] The Gaskells' source of information was John Greenwood, who seems to have been at loggerheads with Arthur since the latter discovered his unwarranted interference and claims to friendship with Charlotte after her death; the baptizing of his child had simply been the latest in a series of incidents which had given Greenwood good reason to dislike the curate and to interpret his actions as hostility to his wife's literary reputation. The corroborative evidence from Charles Hale proves doubly fallacious. Not only was he a personal friend of Mrs Gaskell, who wrote his account of his visit from her home at Plymouth Grove, but he too quotes the Brontë Greenwood story as evidence, confusing the Greenwoods with the Browns in the process; more importantly, he himself states that he got the story not from the principals involved, but from Mrs Gaskell. 'General aversion', therefore, becomes one parishioner with a grudge and literary contacts who perpetuated his claims.

The overwhelming evidence of all those who wrote accounts of meeting Arthur when they visited Haworth was entirely favourable: he impressed his wife's admirers as quiet, courteous and kind. More significantly, the reminiscences of those who had lived in the chapelry during his curacy, especially those who had been taught by him in the schools, give the impression of a man who was not merely respected but also well liked and whose departure was genuinely regretted.[64]

The story about Michael Heaton is equally bizarre. The fact that he was buried by Joseph Grant is of no significance, for Grant was sometimes called upon to officiate in Arthur's absence. Similarly, the fact that the faculty for his burial was obtained by the family rather than the minister is irrelevant: Arthur's own application on Patrick's behalf was made not in his public but his private capacity as the deceased's son-in-law. Moreover, the fact that the chairman of the trustees was one of those who voted for Arthur rather than John Wade[65] suggests that if there was any truth in the incident at all, the matter had been forgiven and forgotten by those most concerned.

We are therefore left with the problem of finding an explanation for Arthur's rejection. That the margin was as narrow as one on the first occasion and two on the second is an indication that the issue was not clear cut, even in the trustees' minds.

One factor may have been a wish to end the Brontë associations with the church and appoint a minister who would not be a celebrity because of his personal connections. Another may have been the desire to avoid continuing the position in which the new incumbent, like Patrick, was totally dependent on his salary for his income, which meant pressure on the trustees to find funds for extraordinary expenses, such as repairs to the church and parsonage. In both areas, John Wade was a preferable candidate; he was unsympathetic, if not actually hostile, towards the Brontës and possessed of independent means, which enabled him to contribute towards the parish funds rather than be a drain on them. On the other hand he was tainted by being the vicar of Bradford's candidate and, more importantly, by his having been rejected by the Simeon trustees for the incumbency of Girlington only eighteen months before on unspecified grounds about which dark hints were thrown. Dr Burnett had pushed his candidacy for that post too and, when he was rejected, had felt obliged to defend his choice against the Simeon trustees' accusations and offer him a curacy at the parish church until a new vacancy turned up.[66] He was therefore especially anxious to secure Wade a new post and may have suggested that his successful candidacy would ensure that the long-discussed creation of Haworth as an independent parish would meet a favourable reception. This is supposition, but the Orders in Council which eventually gave Haworth its independence from Bradford were finally signed on 30 August 1864, only three years after Wade's appointment.[67]

Ultimately, however, the trustees' choice of John Wade in preference to Arthur Nicholls seems attributable chiefly to that bloody-mindedness which is characteristic of Yorkshiremen and more especially of the people of Haworth. They seem to have wished to assert their own authority in the face of a general expectation that they would prefer the curate. Even Arthur seems to have laboured under this same delusion: from the day he resumed his duties after Patrick's funeral he signed the parish registers as 'Officiating Minister', rather than 'Curate'. This may have been technically correct, but it implied a presumption guaranteed to infuriate the trustees, who were just as sensitive about their right to appoint the incumbent as their forebears. Nor was Arthur's case helped by newspaper reports that his appointment was expected and that the vicar of Bradford had promised him the place on his marriage.[68]

Whatever the rights and wrongs of the trustees' choice, their deliberations were held in secret and their decision was not made public until 18 September, three months after Patrick's funeral. Arthur had reverted to signing himself 'Curate' as early as 4 August, suggesting that he had already been informed by then that his candidacy was unacceptable to the trustees.[69] Having lost his wife, his father-in-law and his closest friend, Arthur was now to be deprived of his home and his employment. Clearly he could not remain as curate when the trustees had so publicly displayed their lack of confidence in him: he handed in his resignation immediately and prepared to vacate the parsonage, which would now have to be handed over to the new incumbent.

Despite the bitterness he must have felt, Arthur maintained a dignified silence and made no public comment. It was left to the editor of the *Bradford Observer*, himself a Dissenter, to denounce the 'shabbiness and heartlessness' of the decision:

the trustees will be asked by the country not whether their choice is a better man, but whether Mr Nicholls is unfit for the incumbency of Haworth? They are responsible, first to the parishioners, and next to all England for an answer. Have they interpreted the feelings of the parishioners correctly? Is it possible that the people of Haworth wished to turn adrift in a thankless manner a gentleman, no longer young, who had been for so many years their teacher in divine things?

The *Bradford Observer*'s advocacy was a two-edged sword, however, its reasons for supporting Arthur being, in all probability, precisely those which had caused his rejection.

It is not many months ago since Patrick Brontë went down to the grave in ripe old age; he was the last of his race, but he wanted not in his latter helpless years the watchful kindness of a son. Mr Nicholls, his curate, & the widowed husband of Charlotte, smoothed the old man's dying bed, and saw his head laid in the grave. He had for many years laboured in every sense as the Pastor of Haworth. His character is above reproach, and his faithful discharge of the duties of his office well known. What was more natural than that the people of Haworth would wish the incumbency to be conferred on the man that had gone out and in before them for such a long time, and who stood in the relation of husband to her that first made their district known to fame. Outsiders never doubted for a moment but that the congregation would do all in their power to perpetuate by the only remaining link the connection that fortune had formed between them and a child of genius. It is therefore with a feeling different from surprise that we now learn the unexpected issue.[70]

Though well-meant, such expressions of support could only rub salt in Arthur's wounds: if the trustees did not see fit to appoint him on his own merits why should they do so solely because he had been briefly married to Charlotte Brontë?

The new incumbent made his presence felt with unseemly haste. Only four days after the announcement of his appointment, he officiated in the church on Sunday and baptized his first Haworth infants.[71] Arthur literally had only days to pack up his belongings and leave the parsonage. Apart from the vault containing the mortal remains of the woman he loved, there was nothing to keep him in Haworth or its neighbourhood. Still raw with grief at his recent bereavements and devastated by his humiliating rejection by the church trustees, he had no one to turn to and nowhere to go. Only his old home in Ireland offered sanctuary. It was impossible for him to take all the contents of the parsonage with him, but he was determined to keep everything of personal or sentimental value: all the family manuscripts, most of the Brontës' signed books, their writing desks, even items of his wife's clothing, he packed up and took with him to Ireland. The larger items of household furniture, the contents of the kitchen, some of the pictures and books had to be left behind. Mr Cragg, the local auctioneer, was called in and over the course of two days, on 1 and 2 October, he sold off 485 lots and raised £115 13s. 11d.[72] To an intensely private man like Arthur Nicholls, the sight of souvenir and bargain hunters going through the Brontës' possessions and the dispersal of the contents of their home, must have been a traumatic experience.

There was no point in lingering. Less than a month after John Wade's appointment, Arthur quietly and without ceremony departed from Haworth.[73] This time there was no public testimonial, no parting gift from a grateful Sunday school and congregation. His departure was not even noticed in the local papers. He was accompanied only by Patrick's dogs, Plato and Cato, and more surprisingly, by Martha Brown. From initial hostility towards the man who had presumed to love her mistress, she had been won to such a pitch of loyalty and devotion that, when Arthur offered her the chance to continue in his employment, she left her home and her family for the unknown and life among strangers in Ireland. By a curious twist of fate, when she died on 19 January 1880, aged fifty-two, she was on a visit to her family in Haworth, so she was buried in the churchyard only a stone's throw from the parsonage.[74]

Arthur returned to Banagher to live with his aunt, Mrs Bell, and her daughter, who had moved from Cuba House, where he had brought Charlotte as a bride, to a somewhat smaller residence on the top of the hill above the town and overlooking the Shannon.[75] Whether he intended his flight to Ireland to be temporary or permanent is not known, but in this quiet rural backwater, far from Haworth and everything to do with the Brontës, Arthur soon settled into the peaceful obscurity which he had always craved. Martha Brown, with her Yorkshire accent and her famous sponge cakes, was more of a celebrity than her master. Well liked and respected by all his neighbours, particularly the children, Arthur became a stalwart of the local community. The only manifestation of his bitterness at his treatment by the Haworth church trustees was that he never again sought or obtained a clerical appointment: in his new life he would be a farmer. The money he had inherited from the Brontës was not enough for him to live on – despite Ellen Nussey's hysterical accusations that he had enriched himself at their expense – and he gradually subsided into genteel poverty.

On 25 August 1864, at the age of forty-five and nearly nine and half years after the death of Charlotte, he married again. His second wife was Mary Bell, his cousin, the 'pretty lady-like girl with gentle English manners' whom Charlotte had met on honeymoon. The marriage was affectionate and companionable but childless, and the second Mrs Nicholls seems to have been under no illusions about her husband's undying devotion to the first. Their house was a shrine to the Brontë family: the parsonage grandfather clock stood on the stairs near Leyland's medallion of Branwell; Patrick's gun and a photograph of Haworth Parsonage hung in the dining room; the drawing room was given over to Richmond's portrait of Charlotte, the engraving of Thackeray and a large number of framed drawings by the Brontës.[76] When he died, on 2 December 1906, a few weeks before his eighty-eighth birthday, Mary had his coffin placed beneath the portrait of Charlotte until it was carried from the house. He was buried in the churchyard at Banagher, surrounded by his Bell relations: over his grave Mary erected a simple marble cross carved with the inscription 'Until the day break and the Shadows flee away' and the legend 'In Loving Memory of The Revd

Arthur Bell Nicholls, formerly Curate of Haworth Yorkshire'.[77]

Desperately short of money, Mary Nicholls reluctantly began to break up the collection of Brontëana which her husband had so lovingly preserved for nearly half a century, selling the manuscripts and books in two large sales at Sotheby's in 1907 and 1914 to a world eager to preserve anything connected with the remarkable Brontë family. She herself died on 27 February 1915 and was buried next to her husband in Banagher churchyard.[78]

By retiring to Ireland, where he was largely forgotten, Arthur effectively protected himself against much of the unpleasantness which was to arise from the pursuit of Brontë fanatics. On the whole, he was able to maintain his dignity to the end and achieve a peace of mind that would not have been possible had he stayed in Haworth or its neighbourhood.[79]

Apart from Mrs Gaskell, who never attempted another biography and died suddenly in 1865,[80] most of Charlotte's friends rivalled her father and husband in their longevity. Of her publishers, James Taylor survived the climate of India till 1874, dying in Bombay, William Smith Williams died the following year and George Smith, who went on to found the *Dictionary of National Biography* and become the grand old man of English publishing, died in 1901.[81] Constantin Heger, unlike his fictional counterpart, Paul Emanuel, enjoyed a long career of outstanding academic success, becoming one of the most eminent professors of the Athénée Royal in Brussels and dying, six years after his wife, in 1896.[82]

Of Charlotte's friends from school, Miss Wooler lived to a ripe old age, dying in her nineties, in 1885. Though spared the worst excesses of Brontë fanatics, to the end of her life she was harassed by Americans who came to interview her about her most famous pupil. 'I cannot refuse to see them', she told her great-nephew. 'It is very trying, but I will do my best.'[83]

Mary Taylor, on the other hand, remained serenely indifferent to the lure of fame as Charlotte Brontë's friend. She returned from New Zealand in 1860, having earned enough money through her shopkeeping in Wellington to build a house for herself, High Royd, at Gomersal, where she lived in sturdy independence till her death in 1893. Unconventional to the end, she published a number of what would now be called feminist articles, defending the right of women to think, work and employ themselves in purposeful activity. These ideas were expanded in her novel, *Miss Miles*, which she was working on while Charlotte was writing *Shirley*. Though their themes were similar, the fact that Mary did not finish and publish her book till 1890, forty years after her friend, meant that the originality of its message was lost. It sank without trace. Nevertheless, Mary continued to live by her own creed, even organizing a ladies' walking tour in Switzerland which culminated in an ascent of Mont Blanc when she was nearly sixty years of age.[84] She and Ellen discovered that age and experience had only widened the gulf between them; they had little in common and their friendship foundered soon after

Mary's return from New Zealand. Like Ellen, she never married, but unlike her former friend, lived a practical, useful and happy life, unburdened by regrets. She was, as Ellen bitterly complained, '<u>dead</u> to any approach on the Brontë subject', wisely refusing to be drawn into the inexhaustible demand for further information, and therefore earning the reputation of being 'peculiar'.[85]

It was Ellen Nussey, however, who was universally recognized as the fount of all knowledge where the Brontës were concerned. Though thinly disguised as 'E' throughout the *Life of Charlotte Brontë*, her role as Mrs Gaskell's informant was immediately and widely known. One can hardly avoid the impression that she had preened herself because Mrs Gaskell turned constantly to her for information, rather than to the hated husband and father; it was her version of events which would be made immortal by Mrs Gaskell's pen. Ellen had expected nothing but praise and gratification for this role and was genuinely shocked and appalled when she incurred considerable censure for supplying Mrs Gaskell with information which, it was suggested, should never have been published. Ironically, the very people whose good opinion she most cared for, the clergymen and her Anglican friends in Birstall and Gomersal, proved to be the most critical.

Alarmed at this unexpected turn of events, Ellen wildly tried to justify herself, mainly by blaming Charlotte's husband and father: she had told them they ought to have oversight of the book, she had only lent her letters because they had insisted, she had supplied information on the sisters '<u>only</u>'. As early as 1860 she was already uttering the complaint she was to reiterate for the rest of her life: 'What I have reaped has not been pay of gold or of praise – It has been neglect from the father whose dying child I bore in my arms down two flights of stairs (when at Scarboro') – Of blame from the husband whose feelings I strove to spare...'[86]

It was Charlotte's husband who bore the brunt of her increasingly hysterical accusations. He had been in 'a savage humour' with her ever since the publication of the *Life of Charlotte Brontë*, though 'he never had any just reason to be so': she had not had a line from him since Mr Brontë died, and then she had only received 'a most ungracious reply'.[87] Judging Arthur's behaviour by her own, she was unable to believe that he had not kept her own letters to Charlotte and frequently denounced him to anyone prepared to listen. Believing that she had been betrayed by Mrs Gaskell, Ellen made several attempts to 'set the record straight', as she saw it, by writing her own biography of Charlotte. Like Mrs Gaskell, however, she discovered to her horror and indignation that she could not quote from Charlotte's letters without her husband's approval, but this she could not bring herself to ask.

The fact that she was thus effectively gagged turned Ellen's hatred towards Arthur into paranoia. Writing to George Smith, for whom she had hoped to produce a *Cornhill* article on Charlotte, she let loose the full venom of her nature: 'it would be wise of him to be civil even at some [cost?] to himself –', she threatened. 'I have a letter respecting him which I would in his place give almost a fortune to possess ... if you think it right you can give him a hint that he has not all the power on his side.'[88] In sharp contrast to Ellen's vitriolic outpourings, Arthur made very few comments on the situation, privately confessing only, 'I find it hard to "forget & forgive" her for her proceedings in reference to my dear Wife.'[89]

Ellen made several attempts to circumvent Arthur and publish her letters from Charlotte but met with little success.[90] In the end, she had to be content with her role as the oracle to be consulted by all who wished to learn more about the Brontës. Ironically, this probably gave her more influence than any account she might have penned as, despite increasingly slender means, she held open house to biographers, reporters and admirers of her friend. Sinking into a querulous, embittered and impoverished old age, her only pleasure became her 'little chats' with visitors who would listen spellbound to the reminiscences of one who had been the friend of Charlotte Brontë.[91] She died at the end of November 1897, aged eighty, and was buried in the churchyard of St Peter's Church at Birstall. Her obituary declared her to have been 'a woman of exceptional intellectual power and personality'.[92] Ellen Nussey had finally become a part of the myth of the Brontës which she had done so much to create and perpetuate.

That the myth has survived is a tribute to the emotive power of Mrs Gaskell's *Life of Charlotte Brontë*, which surely lives up to Patrick's expectation that it 'will stand in the first rank, of Biographies, till the end of time'.[93] It is, however, a flawed masterpiece. Mrs Gaskell was a supreme writer of fiction but she too easily identified what she perceived to be the facts of Charlotte's life with the themes of her own novels: Charlotte and her sisters thus became the dutiful, long-suffering daughters and Branwell the wastrel son of a harsh, unbending father.[94] The portrayal of Charlotte as the martyred heroine of a tragic life, driven by duty and stoically enduring her fate, served its purpose at the time. Charlotte's wicked sense of humour, her sarcasm, her childhood *joie de vivre* which enlivens the juvenilia, are completely ignored. So, too, are her prejudices, her unpleasant habit of always seeing the worst in people, her bossiness against which her sisters rebelled, her flirtations with William Weightman and George Smith and her traumatic love for Monsieur Heger. What remains may be a more perfect human being, but it was not Charlotte Brontë. Mrs Gaskell's Emily, too, reduced to a series of vignettes illustrating her unusual strength of character, betrays nothing of the obsession with Gondal which made her almost incapable of leading a life outside the sanctuary of her home but led her to the creation of the strange and wonderful world of *Wuthering Heights*. Anne is simply a cipher, the youngest child, whose boldness in defying convention by adopting a plain heroine in *Agnes Grey* and advocating startlingly unorthodox religious beliefs and women's rights in *The Tenant of Wildfell Hall* finds no place in Mrs Gaskell's portrait. Most of all, however, it was the men in Charlotte's life who suffered at her biographer's hands. The Patrick Brontë who took such tender care of his young children, campaigned incessantly on behalf of the poor of his parish and espoused unfashionable liberal causes is unrecognizable in her malicious caricature of a selfish and eccentric recluse. Similarly, the Branwell who was his family's pride and joy, the leader and innovator, artist, poet, musician and writer, is barely touched upon, despite the fact that, without him, there would probably have been no Currer, Ellis or Acton Bell.

For all her faults, Mrs Gaskell at least ensured that the lives of the Brontës would be as perennially fascinating to future generations as their novels. The trickle of visitors to Haworth, which began in the 1850s, has now become a mighty flood: hundreds of thousands of Brontë enthusiasts, from every part of the globe, come each year to walk the moors which were such an inspiration to the family and to visit the once obscure parsonage which housed such febrile talent. The very ordinariness of the surroundings makes the Brontës' achievements all the more extraordinary. They had neither wealth nor power and therefore lacked the richness and diversity of experience which these can bring; what they did have was the vicarious experience of books and an irrepressible creativity which more than supplied their place. More than anything else, however, they had each other. As children they had needed no other companions and in the sometimes heated, often intense, but always affectionate rivalry between them, they had each found a place and a voice. Even as adults they tended to exclude others: though self-sufficient as a unit, they were dependent on each other for the mutual support and criticism which underpinned their lives and illumined their literary efforts. Without this intense family relationship, some of the greatest novels in the English language would never have been written.

NOTES

All the notes give a manuscript source, from which any quotation is taken, followed by a reference, where applicable, to a printed source in square brackets. Where there is a manuscript, *ibid.* refers to that rather than the printed source. It should be observed that in many, if not most, cases there are substantial differences between the quotation from the manuscript and the printed source. Differences may range from simple punctuation to major omissions. The printed text is therefore given only as a guide for easy reference to and identification of quotations and sources. Where I have been unable to locate the manuscript this is indicated by 'n.l.' and the quotation is taken from the printed source: occasionally this leads to anomalies, such as the use of the diaeresis on the Brontë name before it was introduced, but this is unavoidable as there is no way of knowing what accent was used. Where the Brontës have titled a manuscript, this name is given; where it is untitled, I have used the first line of the quotation as a reference or, if it has subsequently been given a title which is commonly used, I have given this in square brackets, as in [Roe Head Journal]. Within each note, all references, including page numbers, are given in the order in which they appear in the text, rather than in chronological or numerical sequence.

Abbreviations have been used in the notes to refer to frequently occuring names, manuscript collections and books, as listed on the following pages. The title, date and reference number (where applicable) of each individual manuscript is given in the relevant note. Full bibliographical details of printed sources cited less frequently are collected in the Ancillary Source Information on pp. 977–80. Bibliographical details of all other printed sources, including articles, are given in full in the relevant note.

Unless stated otherwise, references to the Brontës' published novels are based on the Oxford University Press World's Classics editions. This information should not be regarded as a comprehensive bibliography of all sources which are available or have been used in this biography. In particular, I have only cited secondary works whose interpretation of the Brontës' lives or works I have discussed.

ABBREVIATIONS

Names
AB   Anne Brontë
ABN   Reverend Arthur Bell Nicholls, Charlotte's husband
CB   Charlotte Brontë

ECG Mrs Elizabeth Gaskell, Charlotte's biographer
EJB Emily Jane Brontë
EN Ellen Nussey, Charlotte's friend
GS George Smith, Charlotte's publisher
HM Harriet Martineau, Charlotte's friend and fellow writer
MB Maria (Branwell) Brontë
MT Mary Taylor, Charlotte's friend
MW Margaret Wooler, Charlotte's headmistress at Roe Head and friend
PB Reverend Patrick Brontë
PBB [Patrick] Branwell Brontë
WSW William Smith Williams, Charlotte's editor

Manuscript Collections
All Saints', Wellington: All Saints' Parish Church with St Catherine's, Eyton, records available through the archivist, Miss Marjorie McCrea
Beinecke: Beinecke Rare Book & Manuscript Library, Yale University, Connecticut, USA
Berg: The Berg Collection, New York Public Library, New York, USA
BFRL: Barrow in Furness Reference Library, Barrow in Furness, Cumbria
Birmingham: Harriet Martineau Collection, The Library, University of Birmingham
BL: Manuscript Collections, British Library, London
Bodleian: Department of Western Manuscripts, Bodleian Library, Oxford
Borthwick: Borthwick Institute of Historical Research, University of York
Boston: Rare Books & Manuscripts Department, Boston Public Library, Boston, Massachusetts, USA
BPM: The Library, Brontë Parsonage Museum, Haworth, W. Yorkshire
Brotherton: The Brotherton Collection, Brotherton Library, University of Leeds, W. Yorkshire
Brown: John Hay Library, Brown University Library, Providence, Rhode Island, USA
Buffalo: Rare Book Room, Buffalo and Erie County Public Library, Buffalo, New York, USA
CMS: Archives of the Church Missionary Society, University of Birmingham
Columbia: Butler Library, Columbia University in the City of New York, USA
CRO, Barrow in Furness: Cumbrian Record Office (Cumberland archives), Duke Street, Barrow in Furness, Cumbria
CRO, Kendal: Cumbria Record Office (Westmorland archives), County Hall, Kendal, Cumbria
Dixon: Dixon Papers, available through Elizabeth Pirie, Leeds City Museum, Leeds, W. Yorkshire
EN, Reminiscences: Biographical notes on the Brontës made by Ellen Nussey at various times and for various purposes: a manuscript source is indicated where located, otherwise only the printed version is given.
ERO: Essex Record Office, County Hall, Chelmsford, Essex
Eton: The Library, Eton College, Windsor
Fales: Fales Library, New York University, New York, USA
Firth: Elizabeth Firth, entries in her diaries made between 1812 and 1825: MS 58 A (MS Q 091 F), Firth Papers, University of Sheffield
Fitzwilliam: Department of Manuscripts, Fitzwilliam Museum, Cambridge
Guildhall: Manuscripts Section, Guildhall Library, Aldermanbury, London
Halifax: Halifax Reference Library, Halifax, W. Yorkshire
Harrogate: Harrogate Reference Library, Harrogate, N. Yorkshire
Harvard: The Houghton Library, Harvard University, Cambridge, Massachusetts, USA
Haverford: The Quaker Collection, Haverford College Library, Haverford, Pennsylvania, USA
Haworth Census: Census Returns for Haworth Chapelry, 1821–61, Microfilm, Keighley Reference Library
Haworth Church Registers: originals in WYAS, Bradford, photocopy Haworth Church
Huntington: Department of Manuscripts, The Huntington Library, San Marino, California, USA
IGI: International Genealogical Index, microfiche available most reference libraries
Illinois: Rare Books Library, University of Illinois at Urbana-Champaign, Illinois, USA
John Murray: Smith, Elder & Co. archives, John Murray (publishers), London
Keighley: Keighley Reference Library, North Street, Keighley, W. Yorkshire
Kentucky: The Library, University of Kentucky, Lexington, Kentucky, USA
Kirklees: Kirklees Reference Library, The Central Library, Huddersfield, W. Yorkshire
Knox: Seymour Library, Knox College, Galesburg, Illinois, USA
KSC: Hugh Walpole Collection, The Library, King's School, Canterbury, Kent

Law Colln: Large private collection, including many Brontë letters, manuscripts and items of
  memorabilia, which has not been located. Facsimiles of most of the important pieces are available.
Lichfield: Lichfield Record Office, The Friary, Lichfield, Staffordshire
LSL, Dewsbury: Local Studies Library, Dewsbury
LSL, Shrewsbury: Local Studies Library, Castlegates, Shrewsbury
Maine: Manuscripts & Special Collections, Maine Historical Society, Portland, Maine, USA
Manchester: Manuscript Room, Manchester Public Library, St Peter's Square, Manchester
Missouri–Columbia: Ellis Library, University of Missouri–Columbia, Columbia, Missouri, USA
Montague: Montague Collection, New York Public Library, New York, USA
NLS: Department of Manuscripts, National Library of Scotland, Edinburgh
Pennsylvania: Historical Society of Pennsylvania, Locust Street, Philadelphia, Pennsylvania, USA
Penzance: The Library, Morrab Gardens, Penzance, a private subscription library
Pforzheimer: The Carl H. Pforzheimer Collection, New York Public Library, New York, USA
Pierpont Morgan: Department of Autograph Manuscripts, Pierpont Morgan Library, New York, USA
Princeton: Parrish & Taylor Collections, Department of Rare Books & Special Collections, Princeton
  University, Princeton, New Jersey, USA
PRO: Public Record Office, Kew, Richmond, Surrey
Redruth: Redruth Reference Library, Clinton Road, Redruth, Cornwall
Rochester: Department of Rare Books and Manuscripts, University of Rochester, New York, USA
Rosenbach: Rosenbach Museum and Library, Philadelphia, USA
Rutgers: Symington Collection, The Library, Rutgers University, New York, USA
Rylands: John Rylands University Library of Manchester, Deansgate, Manchester
Scarborough: Scarborough Reference Library, Scarborough, N. Yorkshire
Scripps: Ella Strong Denison Library, Scripps College, Claremont, California, USA
Sheffield: Firth Papers, Special Collections, The Library, University of Sheffield
SJC: St John's College, Cambridge; available through The Bursary, St John's College
Skipton: Skipton Reference Library, Skipton, Yorkshire
SUNY: Poetry/Rare Books Collection, University Libraries, State University of New York at Buffalo,
  New York, USA
Swarthmore: Friends Historical Library, Swarthmore College Library, Swarthmore, Pennsylvania, USA
TC Cambridge: The Library, Trinity College, Cambridge
TC Dublin: Manuscripts Department, Trinity College Library, Dublin, Ireland
Texas: Harry Ransom Humanities Research Center, University of Texas at Austin, USA
ULC: University Archives, University Library, Cambridge
USPG: Archives of the United Society for the Propagation of the Gospel, Waterloo Road, London
Wellesley: Special Collections, Margaret Clapp Library, Wellesley College, Massachusetts, USA
Whitby: Scoresby Papers, Archives of the Whitby Literary and Philosophical Society, The Whitby
  Museum, Pannett Park, Whitby, N. Yorkshire
Woodhouse Grove: Woodhouse Grove School, Rawdon, Bradford, W. Yorkshire
Wordsworth Trust: The Wordsworth Trust, Dove Cottage, Ambleside, Cumbria
WYAS: West Yorkshire Archive Service at Canal Road, Bradford; Calderdale, at Central Library,
  Halifax; Kirklees, at Kirklees Central Library, Huddersfield; Chapeltown Road, Sheepscar, Leeds
  and Newstead Road, Wakefield
YMM: The 'Young Men's Magazines', Branwell and Charlotte's miniature books, written as children,
  containing a variety of poems and stories.

Books

Allott	Miriam Allott (ed.), *The Brontës: The Critical Heritage* (London, Routledge & Kegan Paul, 1974)
Brontëana	J. Horsfall Turner (ed.), *Brontëana: The Reverend Patrick Brontë's Collected Works* (Bingley, 1898)
BST	Brontë Society, *Transactions* (Haworth, 1895 to date)
C&P	J. A. V. Chapple & Arthur Pollard (eds), *The Letters of Mrs Gaskell* (Manchester, MUP, 1966)
CA	Christine Alexander, *An Edition of the Early Writings of Charlotte Brontë* (Oxford, Basil Blackwell, Shakespeare Head Press, 1987–91), 2 vols
CA, *EW*	Christine Alexander, *The Early Writings of Charlotte Brontë* (Oxford, Basil Blackwell, 1983)
CB, *Biographical Notice*	Charlotte Brontë, 'Biographical Notice of Ellis & Acton Bell', [1850], EJB, *Wuthering Heights*, pp.359–65

Chadwick Mrs Ellis H. Chadwick, *In the Footsteps of the Brontës* (London, Pitman & Sons, 1914)

Chitham Edward Chitham (ed.), *The Poems of Anne Brontë: a New Text and Commentary* (London, Macmillan, 1979)

Collins Robert Collins (ed.), *The Hand of the Arch-Sinner: two Angrian Chronicles of Branwell Brontë* (Oxford, Clarendon Press, 1993)

Du Maurier Daphne du Maurier, *The Infernal World of Branwell Brontë* (Harmondsworth, Penguin Books, 1972)

ECG, *Life* Mrs Gaskell, *The Life of Charlotte Brontë* (London, J. M. Dent, 1971)

Fraser Rebecca Fraser, *Charlotte Brontë* (London, Methuen, 1988)

Grundy Francis H. Grundy, *Pictures of the Past* (London, Griffith & Farrar, 1879)

Hatfield C. W. Hatfield (ed.), *The Complete Poems of Emily Jane Brontë* (New York, Columbia University Press, 1941)

Hibbs Helier Hibbs (ed.), *Victorian Ouseburn: George Whitehead's Journal* (York, privately printed, 1990)

HM, *Autobiography* Gaby Weiner (ed.), *Harriet Martineau's Autobiography* (London, Virago, 1988; repr. of Smith, Elder & Co. edn in 3 vols, 1877)

JB *SP* Juliet R. V. Barker (ed.), *The Brontës: Selected Poems* (London, J. M. Dent, repr. 1993)

JB *ST* Juliet R. V. Barker (ed.), *Sixty Treasures: the Brontë Parsonage Museum* (Haworth, Brontë Society, 1988)

L&D John Lock and Canon W. T. Dixon, *A Man of Sorrow: the Life, Letters and Times of the Rev Patrick Brontë* (London, Nelson & Sons, 1965)

L&L T. J. Wise and J. A. Symington, *The Lives, Friendships and Correspondence of the Brontë Family* (Oxford, Basil Blackwell, Shakespeare Head Press, 1933), 4 vols

Leyland Francis A. Leyland, *The Brontë Family* (London, Hurst & Blackett, 1886), 2 vols

M&U T. J. Wise and J. Alex Symington (eds), *The Miscellaneous & Unpublished Writings of Charlotte Brontë & Patrick Branwell Brontë* (Oxford, Basil Blackwell, Shakespeare Head Press, 1934), 2 vols

Poems, 1846 *Poems* by Currer, Ellis & Acton Bell (Aylott & Jones, 1846)

Poems of EJB & AB T. J. Wise and J. Alex Symington (eds), *The Poems of Emily Jane Brontë & Anne Brontë* (Oxford, Basil Blackwell, Shakespeare Head Press, 1934)

Ratchford Fannie E. Ratchford, *The Brontës' Web of Childhood* (New York, Columbia University Press, 1941)

Reid T. W. Reid, *Charlotte Brontë: a Monograph* (New York, Scribner, Armstrong & Co., 1877)

Scruton William Scruton, *Thornton & the Brontës* (Bradford, J. Dale & Co., 1898)

Shorter Clement K. Shorter, *Charlotte Brontë & Her Circle* (London, Hodder & Stoughton, 1896)

Smith George Smith, *A Memoir, with some pages of Autobiography* (London, private circulation, 1902)

Stevens Joan Stevens (ed.), *Mary Taylor: Friend of Charlotte Brontë: letters from New Zealand & Elsewhere* (Oxford, OUP, 1972)

Venn J. A. Venn, *Alumni Cantabrigiensis (1752–1900)* (Cambridge, CUP, 1951) 6 vols

VN *CB* Victor Neufeldt (ed.), *The Poems of Charlotte Brontë: a New Text and Commentary* (New York, Garland Publishing, 1985)

VN *PBB* Victor Neufeldt (ed.), *The Poems of Patrick Branwell Brontë: a New Text and Commentary* (New York, Garland Publishing, 1990)

WG *AB* Winifred Gérin, *Anne Brontë* (London, Thomas Nelson, 1959)

WG *CB* Winifred Gérin, *Charlotte Brontë: The Evolution of Genius* (Oxford, OUP, 1967)

WG *EJB* Winifred Gérin, *Emily Brontë* (Oxford, OUP, 1971)

WG *FN* Winifred Gérin, *Five Novelettes* (Folio Press, 1971)

WG *PBB* Winifred Gérin, *Branwell Brontë* (London, Thomas Nelson, 1961)

Whitehead Barbara Whitehead, *Charlotte Brontë & her 'dearest Nell'* (Otley, Smith, Settle, 1993)

CHAPTER ONE

1. Admissions Register 1802–35: MS C4.5 no. 1235, SJC.

2. Residence Register: MS C27.1 no. 2, SJC. James Wood, Patrick's tutor, made a similar mistake and had to alter the name in his list of pupils from 'Brante' to 'Bronte' (MS TU1.1 p.64: SJC). It has been assumed that this was the moment when Patrick 'changed' his name and that he did so in imitation of the title, Duke of Brontë, which had been conferred on Horatio Nelson in 1799 by the King of the Two Sicilies, in recognition of his services in the Mediterranean; Brontë was a village on the slopes of Mount Etna in Sicily: see, for example, Bentley, *The Brontës and their World*, pp.8–9; Jane Gray Nelson, 'Sicily and the Bronte Name', *BST*:16:81:43–5. The Brontës' contemporaries also thought there was a link with Nelson: see CB to WSW, 5 Nov. 1849: MS n.l., [*L&L*, iii, 33].

3. PB to ECG, 20 June 1855: MS EL B121 pp.1–2, Rylands, [*BST*:8:43:8].

4. The fictions of William Wright's *The Brontës in Ireland* seem to have entered Brontë mythology, despite the devastating and unanswerable criticisms of it which appeared within a few years of its publication. Wright's objective was to suggest that Patrick's early career was dependent on the patronage of local Presbyterian ministers, that *Wuthering Heights* was really the story of Hugh Brontë's childhood and that Hugh was the originator of Irish tenant-right theories. Wright effectively destroyed his own case by admitting that 'none of the Irish Brontës knew anything of the early history of the family ... the information they had to communicate was merely an echo from the English biographies'. Even Alice, Patrick's youngest sister, whom Wright claimed as his main informant, 'mixed up different events in a way sometimes that made it difficult to disentangle them': Wright, *The Brontës in Ireland*, p.50. For criticisms of Wright's theories see: Angus Mackay, 'A Crop of Brontë Myths', in the *Westminster Review*, Oct. 1895, pp.424–37; Ramsden, *The Brontë Homeland*; J. Horsfall Turner, 'The Brontës in Ireland', in his *Brontëana*, pp.267–304. Edward Chitham's *The Brontës' Irish Background* is a misguided and unconvincing attempt to rehabilitate Wright.

5. Wright was the originator of the claim that Patrick's mother was a Roman Catholic. Though Patrick's description of the marriage as a 'suitable' one may have been an attempt to gloss over an unpalatable truth in view of the Brontës' hostile reaction to the 'Papal Aggression' of the 1850s, there is no first-hand evidence that Eleanor McClory was ever a Catholic. Hugh Brontë and Eleanor McClory were apparently married in 1776 at the Protestant Magherally Church, though there are no registers for the period to confirm this. Records exist of the baptism of six of their children at the Protestant Drumballyroney Church, there being no registers at the time of Patrick's birth and the registers for the period after 1791, when the three youngest daughters were born, being missing: *Brontëana*, p.284. The family grave was also in Drumballyroney churchyard, on the south side of the church: Ramsden, *The Brontë Homeland*, p.96, quoting an account of the funeral of Alice Brontë, Patrick's youngest sister who died on 15 January 1891, from the *Banbridge Chronicle*.

6. The Drumballyroney parish registers record the name five times as 'Brunty' between 1779 and 1791 and once as 'Bruntee' in 1786: Register of Baptisms, Drumballyroney Church, [*Brontëana*, p.284]. According to a report in the *Belfast Mercury*, which appeared in April 1855, just after Charlotte Brontë's death, the family were locally known as 'Prunty' [*L&L*, iv, 184–5]. Several books said to have belonged to the Irish Brontës contain 'Patrick Prunty' autographs of extremely doubtful authenticity: see Elias Voster, *Arithmetic in Whole and Broken Numbers* (Dublin, Richard Cross, 1789): HAOBP:bb65 p.250, BPM; Abbé Lenglet du Fresnoy, *Geography for Youth* (Dublin, P. Wogan, 1795): HAOBP:bb200 p.129, BPM. Though these are cited as the main evidence for Patrick's having deliberately changed his name, the autographs are inconsistent with genuine examples of Patrick's signatures and appear to me to be blatant forgeries. John and William 'Bronte' were tenants of Henry Stafford Willock of Tullyquilly, near Rathfriland (close to the Brontës' home) in 1780, though there were many variants of the name in the records of County Armagh and County Tyrone (T. G. F. Paterson, 'The Brontës and Co Armagh', in the *Armagh Guardian*, 16 Aug. 1957, p.3). For arguments concerning the origin of the name see *Brontëana*, pp.280–5; Chitham, *The Brontës' Irish Background*, pp.34–6.

7. PB, notes accompanying his letter to ECG, 20 June 1855: MS EL B121 p.2, Rylands, [*BST*:8:43:8]. The birthplace was first identified by William Wright, who reproduced a photograph of it as his frontispiece to *The Brontës in Ireland*, but there is no documentary evidence to support the identification.

8. Patrick's brothers and sisters, with their dates of baptism: William (16 March 1779); Hugh (27 May 1781); James (8 Nov. 1783); Walsh (19 Feb. 1786); Jane (1 Feb. 1789); Mary (1 May 1791). Three more daughters, the twins Rose and Sarah, born about 1793, and Alice, born about 1795, followed, but the relevant baptismal registers are missing. I am grateful to the Revd William Seale, rector of Drumgooland, for checking the entries on my behalf. Sarah, the only one of Patrick's sisters to marry, eloped with Simon Collins and one of her daughters, Rose Ann, after her marriage to David Heslip, came to live in Bradford. There is no evidence of any contact between her and

her cousins at Haworth: 'A Relative of the Bron-
tës', the *Sketch*, 10 Feb. 1897, p.118; William Wright,
'Mrs Heslip and the Brontës in Ireland', the
Sketch, 10 March 1897, p.288.

9. The baptismal registers of Drumballyroney
Church give Lisnacreevy as the birthplace of
Hugh, James, Walsh, Jane and Mary Brontë
between 27 May 1781 and 1 May 1791 but Bal-
lyroney for the second son, William, baptized
on 16 March 1779: *Brontëana*, p.284. The possibility that the Brontës only ever lived at Lisnacreevy and Ballynaskeagh, and that their
location at Emdale was one of Wright's fictions,
cannot be entirely discounted. Wright 'found'
the cottage at Emdale which he identified as
Hugh Brontë's home on one of his later journeys
to the area. The information that Alice Brontë,
the youngest child, who died aged ninety-five
on 15 January 1891, had been born at Ballynaskeagh appears to have come from Alice
herself: *Brontëana*, pp.293–4. The farm at Ballynaskeagh remained the Brontë family home
at least until the death of Hugh junior in 1863
and probably later. There is a photograph of it
in *Brontëana*, opp. p.vi.

10. ECG to John Forster, [Sept. 1853]: [C&P,
p.245].

11. The inference of Patrick's statement to Mrs
Gaskell is that he stayed at school until he was
sixteen: PB to ECG, 20 June 1855: MS EL B121
p.1, Rylands, [*BST*:8:43:8]. This flatly contradicts
Wright's claims that Patrick was apprenticed to
a linen weaver: *The Brontës in Ireland*, pp.227–30.
The story that Patrick helped a local blacksmith
seems more likely, as this is not incompatible
with his farming background or his schooling:
it is told, for instance, in Fraser, p.5.

12. Patrick 'was educated at a school near Glascar'
according to the account of Alice Brontë's
funeral in the *Banbridge Chronicle*, quoted in
Ramsden, *The Brontë Homeland*, p.97.

13. John Lindsay's account book is quoted in Paterson, 'The Brontës and Co Armagh', in the
Armagh Guardian, 16 Aug. 1957, p.3.

14. *Ibid.* Officer posts were only held by gentlemen.

15. Wright, *The Brontës in Ireland*, pp.231ff. again
claimed that Patrick was tutored and promoted
by the local Presbyterian minister, Andrew
Harshaw, but this is at odds with all the evidence, which points to connections solely with
the Episcopalian church at Drumballyroney,
where Thomas Tighe had been the rector since
1778.

16. Hugh took over the family farm, William
apparently set up a public house in later life,
James was a shoemaker and Walsh a road-
builder: *Brontëana*, pp.286–91.

17. Patrick says that he ran his school for 'five or
six years', which would place his appointment
as tutor in 1798 or 1799: PB to ECG, 20 June 1855:
MS EL B121 p.1, Rylands, [*BST*:8:43:8].

18. *Brontëana*, p.286.

19. See below, pp.157–8, 428–9.

20. Venn, pt ii, vi, pp.189–90.

21. Patrick later wrote extensively on this subject.
See, for example, PB, 'On Conversion', *The Pastoral Visitor*, Feb. 1815, pp.11–12; March 1815, pp.21–
2; April 1815, pp.26–9; July 1815, pp.52–4; Sept.
1815, pp.70–1; Oct. 1815, pp.78–9.

22. L & D, p.11.

23. Simeon was perpetual curate of Trinity
Church, Cambridge from 1783 until his death in
1836. For a succinct account of his views and
influence see Pollard & Hennell (eds), *Charles
Simeon (1759–1836)*.

24. *Belfast Mercury*, April 1855, quoted in *L&L*, iv,
185. As the rest of the article is full of inaccuracies, there is no real reason to credit this
story either.

25. There were no other English or Irish universities at this time; Durham was not founded
until the 1830s.

26. Venn, pt ii, vi, pp.189–90.

27. Haig, *The Victorian Clergy*, pp.37–47. The greater
likelihood of obtaining financial assistance was
obviously a major factor in preferring St John's
to Trinity College, Dublin which would otherwise have seemed a more logical choice. Henry
Kirke White, a contemporary of Patrick's at
Cambridge, also chose St John's for financial
reasons, though Trinity, Cambridge would have
suited his purpose better: Kirke White, *Remains*,
i, 160.

28. PB, notes accompanying his letter to ECG, 20
June 1855: MS EL B121 p.2, Rylands. The gap
between his arrival and his admittance to the
college, which is confirmed by Henry Martyn
(see below, note 31), may have been taken up
with reading and preparation for his course.

29. Only two or three Irishmen were admitted
each year over the period of Patrick's residence
in Cambridge; there were seven 'gentlemen-
commoners' and thirty-four pensioners in his
year: Admissions Register 1802–35: MS C4.5,
SJC; University Matriculation Register, 20 Nov.
1759–22 May 1818: MS Matr.4., ULC.

30. Even the pious William Wilberforce, with his
tutor's approval, could waste his days in gambling instead of attending lectures: Pollack, *Wilberforce*, p.7.

31. Henry Martyn to William Wilberforce, 14 Feb.
1804: MS Wilberforce d.14 p.17, Bodleian, [L&
D, p.18].

32. Kirke White, *Remains*, i, 172. Patrick was said to
have acquired a copy of White's poems in which
he wrote on the flyleaf that he had known White
at Cambridge and picked up the book from a
wreck on the Yorkshire coast: J.A. Erskine
Stuart to unknown, 17 Oct. 1896: MS in Brotherton.

33. Kirke White, *Remains*, i, 174. The payments
made by the new occupant to the old one on
taking possession of a college room appear to
relate to the purchase of furnishings; although
his tutor, James Wood, kept a list of room allo-
cations, Patrick's name does not appear so he

must either have shared rooms with another sizar or had garret rooms: James Wood, List of Pupils 1791–1814: MS TU1.1.1, SJC.

34. Scott (ed.), *Admissions to St John's College*, pt iv, pp.568–70.

35. Kirke White, *Remains*, i, 173.

36. Carus, *Memoirs of the Life of Charles Simeon*, Pollard & Hennell (eds), *Charles Simeon (1759–1836)*.

37. *Ibid.*, p.167. When Ellen Nussey offered to lend Patrick Carus' *Life of Simeon*, Charlotte replied, 'I dare say papa would like to see the work very much, as he knew Mr Simeon': CB to EN, 3 May 1848: MS n.l., [*L&L*, ii, 212]. She later commented, 'Papa has been very much interested in reading the book – there is frequent mention made in it of persons and places formerly well known to him – he thanks you for lending it him': CB to EN, 18 Aug. 1848: MS Grolier E13 pp.2–3, BPM, [*L&L*, ii, 246].

38. Sally Stonehouse, 'Cambridge Echoes of the Brontës', *BST*:19:5:211.

39. *Cambridge University Calendar* (Cambridge, 1806), pp.143–5.

40. Kirke White, *Remains*, i, 222. Lemprière's *Bibliotheca Classica*, inscribed on the flyleaf in Patrick's hand 'The gift of Mr Toulmen, pupil – Cambridge, Price 12s.': HAOBP:bb34, BPM. The only Toulmen I have been able to identify, always presuming that this pupil was a member of the university, is one Charles 'Toulmin', who was admitted a pensioner at Caius in September 1800 but then relocated to Christ's within three weeks, where he became a scholar in 1802 and resided till Michaelmas 1803. He was ordained deacon on 25 September 1803 and priest on 16 December 1804; curate of St Mary's Church at King's Lynn, he died in London in December 1805: Venn, pt ii, v, 212.

41. James Wood (1760–1839) was an eminent mathematician, a former grammar school boy from Bury in Lancashire who came to St John's as a sizar in 1778, became a D.D. and Master of the college in 1815 and Vice-Chancellor of the university the following year. A fellow of the Royal Society, his books on algebra, mathematics, mechanics and optics became standard works: *Dictionary of National Biography*, lxii, 359–60; Scott (ed.), *Admissions to St John's College*, iv, Appx i, 568–70. Joshua Smith had been admitted as a sizar to St John's in 1776, was ordained in the Church of England and from 1789 had been joint tutor of the college with James Wood; he had to resign from the college when he married in 1804. Patrick was sent instead to Thomas Catton, also a former sizar, who had been a fellow of the college since 1784 and a tutor since 1787; he had been made a B.D. in 1791. Catton was an eminent astronomer with responsibility for the college observatory, the only one in the university: *ibid.*, iv, Appx i, 481; Venn, pt i, 540.

42. Examination Book: MS C15.6, SJC. I am grateful to Malcolm Underwood, archivist of St John's, for his identification of Beausobre and Dodderidge.

43. Henry Kirke White, who found the mathematics very difficult, complained that 'many men come up with knowledge enough for the highest honours, & how can a man be expected to keep up with them who starts without any previous fund?': Kirke White, *Remains*, i, 169.

44. Examination Book: MS C15.6, SJC.

45. *Ibid.* The college evidence is confirmed by the university records, where Patrick appears as a Prizeman as a Freshman, Junior Sophomore and Senior Sophomore: *Cambridge University Calendars* (1804), p.109; (1805), p.190; (1806), p.216.

46. The books are now preserved in the Bonnell Collection at the Brontë Parsonage Museum, HAOBP:bb207 and bb208, BPM.

47. Charlotte, for example, wrote on her letter from the Poet Laureate 'Southey's Advice To be kept for ever': CB, note on wrapper from Robert Southey, 21 April 1837: MS in private hands, on loan as MS BS 14.5, BPM.

48. Exhibitions Book, 1800–23: MS SB9.14, SJC. My figures are considerably less than those given by Lock & Dixon, p.17; theirs, presumably, are based on Wright, *The Brontës in Ireland*, pp.263–4 which are, in turn, based on the information in the college Admissions Book. The Exhibitions Book is a more accurate guide, as it records the actual sums handed over to each exhibitioner.

49. Venn, pt ii, iv, 347. A Senior Wrangler was a man who had been placed first in the order of merit in the Mathematical Tripos.

50. Henry Martyn to John Sargent, [c.Jan.–Feb. 1804]: MS Wilberforce d.14 p.16, Bodleian. John Sargent was vicar of Graffham, Sussex; he was married to Wilberforce's cousin, [Pollack, *Wilberforce*, p.170].

51. Henry Martyn to William Wilberforce, 14 Feb. 1804: MS Wilberforce d.14 p.17, Bodleian, [L& D, p.18].

52. See notes 50 and 51.

53. See, for example, his letters suggesting alterations to service equipment: PB to Master General of the Ordnance, War Office 29 Nov. 1841 and 4 July 1848: MSS WO44/621, PRO.

54. *Cambridge Chronicle*, 10 Sept. 1803, p.3; 29 Oct. 1803, p.3.

55. *Ibid.*, 25 Feb. 1804, p.4. Of 154 men enlisted, 40 were from Trinity, which had fewer ordained undergraduates than St John's, 35 from St John's, 21 from Jesus, 18 from Caius and single figures from each of the remaining ten colleges and halls.

56. Admissions Register, 1802–35: MS C4.5, SJC.

57. *Cambridge Chronicle*, 2 June 1804, p.4.

58. Stonehouse, 'Cambridge Echoes of the Brontës', *BST*:19:5:211.

59. *Cambridge University Calendar* (1808), pp.253–6. The written questions set for Honours can-

didates sitting for their B.A. in January 1806 are given at pp.258–74.

60. Thomas Tighe, Certification of PB's Age, 30 Dec. 1805: MS 10326/137 no. 6 item no. 6, Guildhall, [L&D, p.21].

61. J. Fawcett, Certification of Attendance at Lectures, 22 March 1806: MS 10326/137 no. 6 item no. 7, Guildhall, [L&D, p.21]. Curiously, though it anticipates Patrick's graduation by a whole month, the certification refers to him as 'Patrick Bronte B.A.'.

62. Subscriptions Register 1803–24: MS in ULC.

63. *Ibid.*; Book of College Supplications to the University, no. 201: ULC.

64. The midsummer accounts for 1806 show that Patrick, who is listed separately from the other twelve graduates, confirming that he took his degree at a slightly later date, received £4: Exhibitions Book 1800–23: MS SB9.14, SJC. Patrick's copy of Walter Scott's *The Lay of the Last Minstrel* (London, Longman & Co., 1806) is MS HAOBP:bb54, BPM.

65. Kirke White, *Remains*, i, 194.

66. *Ibid.*

67. Residence Register: MS C27.1, SJC; *Cambridge University Calendar* (1806), pp.13–14.

68. PB, Nomination to Curacy of Wethersfield, 28 June 1806: MS 10326/137 no. 6 item no. 1, Guildhall.

69. PB, Notice of Candidature for Holy Orders, 29 June 1806: MS 10326/137 no. 6 item no. 3, Guildhall, [L&D, p.22].

70. PB, Letters Testimonial, 2 July 1806: MS 10326/137 no. 6 item no. 8, Guildhall, [L&D, p.22].

71. PB to the Secretary of the Bishop of London, 4 July 1806: MS 10326/137 no. 6. item no. 4, Guildhall, [L&D, p.22].

72. PB, Ordination Papers, 10 Aug. 1806, [L&D, p.23].

73. Bishop of Lichfield's Subscription Book 1805–9: MS B/A/4/41, Lichfield.

74. The evidence for this visit is contradictory. Rose Heslip, Patrick's niece, first of all denied that Patrick had ever returned to Ireland but then remembered her mother telling her that Patrick had preached at Drumballyroney after his ordination: 'A Relative of the Brontës', the *Sketch*, 10 Feb. 1897, p.118; William Wright, 'Mrs Heslip and the Brontës in Ireland', the *Sketch*, 10 March 1897, p.288.

75. The fact that both certificates of Patrick's age were written by his father on 25 September and that one of them adopts the accent that Patrick had only begun to use in his ordination documents suggests that he was with his father when they were drawn up. It is possible, however, that Hugh Brontë simply copied out drafts sent to him by Patrick. The fact that both certificates are written in the same hand as Hugh Brontë's signature, not that of the witness, John Fury, is evidence that Hugh was not illiterate, as is often suggested. Patrick, incidentally, was twenty-nine, not twenty-eight: Hugh Brontë, Cer-

tification of Age, 25 Sept. 1806: MS 10326/137 no. 6 items nos. 2 & 5, Guildhall.

76. Most biographers, relying on Wright, *The Brontës in Ireland*, pp.264–5, repeat that Patrick always sent £20 a year home to his mother in Ireland. This is inconceivable. At Cambridge Patrick's own annual income hardly amounted to £20; at Wethersfield, though he had £60 a year, he now had to find his own board and lodging. By the time he was in a position to be able to afford the sum, as minister at Hartshead, Thornton and then Haworth, he was married, with a growing family to support, and he himself was so short of money that he was writing to various charities for additional income. He undoubtedly sent occasional sums, like the £1 he sent in February 1859 when his sister fell ill, but given the state of his own finances he could not have afforded to send £20 a year to his mother until her death in about 1822. Besides, she remained in the family home and had two unmarried sons, Hugh and James, working and able to support her.

77. Even when Charlotte took her honeymoon in Ireland and visited her husband's relations, she did not use the opportunity to see her own Irish relatives.

78. Copy of the Diocesan Return for Wethersfield for 1801–10, in the Register of Baptisms and Burials, 1801–12, St Mary Magdalene, Wethersfield: Microfilm T/R 132/3, ERO. According to this return, there were 280 families in Wethersfield, 29 employed in agriculture, 165 in labouring jobs and 63 in trade. The population remained static over the ten years, increasing by only 68.

79. 6-inch 2nd edition Ordnance Survey Map, 1898. Most of the buildings marked on this map are still there and are described from my own observations.

80. *The Parish Church of Saint Mary Magdalene: some notes for visitors*, pp.1–2: typescript notes available at the church, Wethersfield.

81. I have been unable to trace any contemporary references to Miss Davy. Henry Dixon, in his memoirs, stated that Jowett had rooms in a house hired by his master (the doctor) and that Patrick occupied these when Jowett was absent: H. N. Dixon, 'Reminiscences of an Essex Country Practitioner a Century Ago', the *Essex Review*, xiv (1915), p.6.

82. *The Parish Church of Saint Mary Magdalene: some notes for visitors*, p.4.

83. *Wethersfield United Reform Church*, 2pp. typescript notes: MS D/NC 31/2, ERO.

84. Dixon, 'Reminiscences of an Essex Country Practitioner a Century Ago', p.6. The parish registers confirm that Jowett only officiated in church between late July and early October each year, unless he was without a curate and was unable to find a local substitute.

85. Register of Marriages, 1754–1812, St Mary Magdalene, Wethersfield: Microfilm T/R 132/3,

ERO. Register of Baptisms and Burials, 1801–12, St Mary Magdalene, Wethersfield: Microfilm T/R 132/3, ERO.

86. *Ibid.*

87. *Ibid.*; Dixon, 'Reminiscences of an Essex Country Practitioner a Century Ago', the *Essex Review,* xiii (1914), p. 195. Patrick's first burial, a twelve-year-old boy, took place on 26 October 1806; thereafter he performed an average of three a month, rising to eight during the typhus epidemic in December: Register of Baptisms and Burials, 1801–12, St Mary Magdalene, Wethersfield: Microfilm T/R 132/3, ERO.

88. There is a board in St Mary Magdalene Church at Wethersfield which records the details of the Dorothy Mott charitable fund which was set up in 1759. Patrick's name does not appear as being present at any of the meetings of vicar and churchwardens regarding the charity lands, distribution of coal etc.: Churchwarden's Books, St Mary Magdalene, Wethersfield: MSS D/P 119/8/5 and D/P 119/8/6, ERO.

89. Dixon, 'Reminiscences of an Essex Country Practitioner a Century Ago', the *Essex Review,* xiii, p.198.

90. Venn, pt ii, iv, 573.

91. Beryl Board, draft for the churches section of the *Victoria County History of Essex,* ix (not yet published). I am grateful to Mrs Board for allowing me to see her typescript prior to publication.

92. Register of Marriages, St Peter's Church, Colchester: Microfilm D/P 178/1/8, ERO. Although only the marriage register of St Peter's contains the officiating minister's name, I have been unable to find any mention of Patrick, though L&D, p.31, say he took duty there. Storry signed the Letters Testimonial which Patrick needed for his promotion to Dewsbury, which are dated 8 May 1810: MS ADM 1810, Borthwick.

93. PB, *Si Quis,* 26 July 1807: MS 10326/138 no. 5 item no. 6, Guildhall, [L&D, p.31]. Joseph Jowett, certificate, 14 July 1807: MS 10326/138 no. 5 item no. 1, Guildhall, [L&D, p.31].

94. PB, Letters Testimonial, n.d.: MS 10326/138 no. 5 item no. 3, Guildhall, [L&D, pp.30–1].

95. Patrick sent the papers expressing the vain hope that 'his Lordship will not look upon it as too late': PB to the Bishop's Secretary, 29 July 1807: MS 10326/138 no. 5 item no. 5, Guildhall, [L&D, pp.31–2].

96. I have been unable to find any references to Mary Burder in contemporary records at this period. For the facts I have therefore followed the account given by Mrs Lowe, Mary's daughter, to Augustine Birrell in his *Life of Charlotte Brontë,* pp.18–23, though I have reservations about its accuracy. It seems extremely unlikely, for instance, that Miss Davy could have been seventy years old if her niece was only eighteen.

97. Birrell, *Life of Charlotte Brontë,* p.20.

98. PB to Mary Burder, 1 Jan. 1824: MS n.l., [L& L, i, 68].

99. PB to Mary Burder, 28 July 1823: MS n.l., [L& L, i, 62].

100. Birrell, *Life of Charlotte Brontë,* pp.22–3.

101. Mary Burder to PB, 8 Aug. 1823: MS n. l., [L& L, i, 65].

102. I am indebted to Mr Donald Hathaway, who lived at Broad Farm until he was eighteen, for the description of the house which was demolished in the 1950s to make way for a now-abandoned American air base. The valuation is from the Wethersfield Tithe Award, 22 Dec. 1842: MS D/CT 393A, lot 791–841, ERO. The amount is a capital valuation of the farm, not an assessment of annual income produced. Haworth Parsonage, by comparison, was revalued at £10 13s. in 1851, having previously been worth only £7: PB, Account Book, c. 1845–61: MS BS 173, p.12, BPM.

103. Wethersfield Tithe Award, 22 Dec. 1842: MS D/CT 393A, lot 766–868, ERO. I am grateful to Mrs Rita Norman of Wethersfield for her assistance in confirming the identification and existence of The Park today.

104. Mary Burder to PB, 8 Aug. 1823: MS n.l., [L& L, i, 64].

105. PB to Mary Burder, 1 Jan. 1824: MS n.l., [L& L, i, 67].

106. Mary Burder to PB, 8 Aug. 1823: MS n.l., [L& L, i, 64].

107. Residence Register: MS C27.1, SJC.

108. PB to Mary Burder, 1 Jan. 1824: MS n.l., [L& L, i, 67].

109. Patrick's absence at Glenfield is suggested by the fact that Joseph Jowett performed the usual church offices throughout the summer but had to get the curate of Finchingfield in to take a marriage on 20 September and a burial on 21 September. Someone else deputized on 11 October, but Patrick was back again performing a burial service on 18 October: Register of Baptisms and Burials, 1801–12 and Register of Marriages, 1754–1812, St Mary Magdalene, Wethersfield: Microfilm T/R 132/3, ERO. Robert Cox was admitted as a sizar at St John's some six months after Patrick, in March 1803, but had transferred to Queens' College on 1 January 1804, graduating from there in 1806. He was ordained in 1807 and was rector of Broughton Astley in Leicestershire: Venn, pt ii, i, 161. John Barnwell Campbell, who came from South Carolina, was admitted as a pensioner at Queens' in 1804 and graduated in 1808: *ibid.,* pt ii, i, 501.

110. PB to Revd Mr Campbell, 12 Nov. 1808: MS p.2, Princeton, [L&D, p.39]. The quotation is from St Paul to the Corinthians, ch. 6, v. 14. Significantly, Patrick used it again in his little book, *The Cottage in the Wood,* written in 1815; his pious cottager, Mary, rejects an atheist's offer of marriage with these words: 'I shall follow the directions of God, and he says, "Be not unequally yoked together with unbelievers: for what fellowship hath righteousness with

unrighteousness? And what communion hath light with darkness? and what concord hath Christ with Belial? or what part hath he that believeth with an infidel?" ... Whatever religious person marries one that is not religious, breaks an express commandment that God will make these labours end well, that have such a bad beginning? Every truly converted character, who would make advances in piety, and become wiser and happier, must have a partner of similar views and feelings, who, at all times, will prove a *help* rather than a *hindrance*': PB, *The Cottage in the Wood*, pp.26–7, [*Brontëana*, pp.111–12]). Campbell was an obvious confidant for Patrick, who remarked in this letter, 'In some things, our lots in life are nearly similar; both as respects our late love affairs, & our voluntary exile from our Dear Homes; though I believe, literally speaking, <I believe it is not necess> it is not voluntary': PB to Revd Mr Campbell, 12 Nov. 1808: MS p.2, Princeton, [L&D, p.39].

111. Although I have not been able to trace her attendance at the Congregational chapel at this time, according to the Essex IGI the many Burders at Great Yeldham, Castle Hedingham and Finchingfield were all Nonconformists and Mary's four daughters, born between 1825 and 1830, were all baptized at Wethersfield Congregational Chapel. Mary herself married the Reverend Peter Sibree, minister of the Congregational Chapel, in 1824, and came to live in the manse only a couple of doors down the village green from St George's House.

112. Mary Burder to PB, 8 Aug. 1823: MS n.l., [L& L, i, 64].

113. PB to Mary Burder, 1 Jan. 1824: MS n.l., [L& L, i, 66].

114. PB to Revd Mr Campbell, 12 Nov. 1808: MS p.2, Princeton, [L&D, p.40].

115. Maria Tipton, John Nunn's niece, told Clement Shorter that she stayed with her uncle in 1857; prompted by hearing her referring to Mrs Gaskell's *Life of Charlotte Brontë*, which she was reading at the time, John Nunn told her, 'Patrick Bronte was once my greatest friend.' The next morning, he brought out a thick bundle of letters, told her that they were from Patrick and referred to his spiritual state and said that he had read them through again and would now destroy them: Shorter (ed.), *The Brontës: Life and Letters*, i, 25 n.2.

116. PB to Mary Burder, 1 Jan. 1824: MS n.l., [L& L, i, 67].

117. PB to Mrs Burder, 21 April 1823: MS n.l., [L& L, i, 61]; PB to Mary Burder, 28 July 1823: MS n.l., [L&L, i, 62].

118. Register of Marriages, 1754–1812 and Register of Baptisms and Burials, 1801–12, St Mary Magdalene, Wethersfield: Microfilm T/R 132/3, ERO. L&D, p.40, confuse the date of the burial with the date of the registration.

119. Pigot & Co, *National Commercial Directory* (1822), pp.378–9; the *Shropshire Gazetteer* (Wem, T. Gregory, 1824), pp.144, 671; Evans, *Wellington*.

120. R. M. Baxter, 'A History of Wellington' (typescript, 1949): typescript in LSL, Shrewsbury.

121. *Shrewsbury Chronicle*, 6 Jan. 1809, p.2.

122. Wellington Presentation papers & deeds: MS B/A/3, Lichfield. In McCrea, *A History of the Parish Church of All Saints Wellington, Shropshire*, pp.3, 23, John Eyton is described as the third son of Robert Eyton, vicar of Ryton [sic], Shifnal, but his entry in Venn, pt ii, ii, 449, describes him as the third son of Thomas Eyton esquire of Wellington. The presentation deeds give his dates at Wellington as 1802–23, not 1803–22, as stated in McCrea.

123. Venn, pt ii, ii, 449; W[illiam] M[organ], 'A Short Account of the late Rev John Eyton, A.M. Vicar of Wellington, Shropshire', *The Cottage Magazine*, April 1823, pp.109–12; Hulbert, *The Manual of Shropshire Biography, Chronology and Antiquities*, p.17. Eyton's 'Sermon preached on the occasion of the late Naval Victory' at Trafalgar was the first publication in 1805 of Edward Houlston, a bookseller and printer based in Wellington: Philip A. Brown, 'Houlstons of Wellington Shropshire – a well known publishing house in early Victorian times', *Shropshire Magazine*, April 1959, p.15.

124. Evans, *Wellington*, p.55.

125. McCrea, *A History of the Parish Church of All Saints Wellington, Shropshire*, and personal observation.

126. W[illiam] M[organ], 'A Short Account of the late Rev John Eyton, A.M. Vicar of Wellington, Shropshire', pp.112–13. Eyton's ill health obliged him to give up his formal duties some time before his death. He died in Portsmouth where he had been sent to spend the winter of 1822–3 for the benefit of his health. Patrick's fellow curate and great friend, William Morgan, wrote an obituary of him from Bradford on 9 February 1823, which was published by John Buckworth in the April issue of *The Cottage Magazine*.

127. Registers of Baptisms and Burials and of Marriages, All Saints' Church, Wellington: MSS at All Saints', Wellington. The accent had now become 'Brontë'.

128. An assessment for the relief of the poor of Eyton, 25 May 1809: MS at St Catherine's Church, Eyton. Three baptisms and ten marriages were performed by John Eyton and William Morgan respectively: I am grateful to Miss McCrea for supplying me with this information from the parish registers at St Catherine's Church, Eyton.

129. *Shrewsbury Chronicle*, 10 Feb. 1809, p.3; 26 May 1809, p.3; 9 June 1809, p.3; 16 June 1809, p.3. The Reverend John Waltham was a leading Evangelical: in a memoir of his life published by John Buckworth in his *Cottage Magazine* it was stated 'if the path of our reverend friend, both as a Christian and a Minister, was as the shining

light; the end of his path was as the perfect day.':John Buckworth (ed.), *The Cottage Magazine* (1815), pp.30–4.

130. *Shrewsbury Chronicle*, 27 Oct. 1809, p.3.

131. *Ibid.*, 3 Nov. 1809, p.3. A Lancasterian school was run along the lines established by the founder, Joseph Lancaster, and employed older pupils to assist the teacher by instructing the younger children.

132. Forrest, *Old Churches of Shrewsbury*, p.101.

133. *Ibid.*, p.101; Charlesworth, *A Choice of Churches*; Hulbert, *The Manual of Shropshire Biography*, p.26.

134. C. A. Hulbert to L. Hainsworth, 20 Aug. 1885: MS BS ix, H p.1, BPM; Kenneth G. Kinrade, 'The Remarkable Career of Charles Hulbert', *Shropshire Magazine*, Nov. 1956, pp.18–20 and Dec. 1956, pp.17–19.

135. Fennell, *A Sermon preached at the Funeral of the Rev. John Crosse*, makes it clear that Fennell supported Crosse's Methodist leanings; prior to his ordination, he was also the first head of the newly established school at Woodhouse Grove, near Bradford, which had been set up specifically for the sons of Methodist ministers: see below, p.48.

136. I have deduced Morgan's appointment from his signatures in the Register of Marriages, All Saints' Church, Wellington: MS, All Saints', Wellington. For Patrick's friendship with Morgan see: C. A. Hulbert to L. Hainsworth, 20 Aug. 1885: MS BS ix, H p.1, BPM.

137. For the facts and anecdotes about John Fletcher I have followed the account given of him in the 'Lives of Eminent Christians' series which appeared in *The Cottage Magazine* (1825), pp.9–18, 289–300, 325–32, 361–9, 397–404 and (1826) pp.1–9, 37–44, 73–81, 109–19. This account itself draws largely on the lives of Fletcher by Gilpin and Cox.

138. *Ibid.*, Nov. 1825, pp.368–9; April 1826, p.115; John Fletcher, *The Portrait of St Paul: or the true model for*

Christians and Pastors, translated from a French manuscript of the late Revd John William de la Flechère, vicar of Madeley, with an account of the author by the Revd Joshua Gilpin (Shrewsbury & London, 1790), 2 vols. Patrick dedicated a poem 'To the Rev J Gilpin, on his improved edition of the *Pilgrim's Progress*' in PB, *Cottage Poems*, pp.87–93, [*Brontëana*, p.87].

139. Morgan, *The Parish Priest*, p.8.

140. *Ibid.*, pp.8–9.

141. W. Matthews, 'Charlotte Brontë', *The Methodist New Connexion Magazine* (London, 1889), p.208; Morgan, *The Parish Priest*, pp.13, 130.

142. Henry Martyn to William Wilberforce, 14 Feb. 1804: MS Wilberforce d.14 p.17, Bodleian, [L&D, p.18].

143. PB to Mrs Burder, 21 April 1823: MS n.l., [*L & L*, i, 61].

144. L&D, p.44, state that Patrick met Buckworth at St Chad's in 1809, but Buckworth's attachment to St Chad's did not take place till 1813: Anon., *Memoir of the Rev. John Buckworth*, pp.117–18, 55.

145. James Wood's Commonplace Book 1808–36, 6 Nov. 1809: MS M1.3 p.214, SJC. I am grateful to Dr Peter Searby for drawing my attention to the entries in Wood's commonplace book.

146. *Ibid.*, pp.219, 223.

147. Register of Marriages, All Saints' Church, Wellington: MS, All Saints', Wellington. Patrick's letters testimonial from Wellington stated that he had resided there till 4 December 1809: MS ADM 1810, Borthwick.

148. Morgan also added two scriptural texts referring to brotherly love beneath his dedication: *Sermons or Homilies appointed to be read in Churches* (Oxford, Clarendon Press, 1802): MS HAOBP:bb57, BPM.

149. PB, Letters testimonial from Wethersfield, n.d.: MS ADM 1810, Borthwick; PB, Letters testimonial from Wellington, 8 Dec. 1809: MS ADM 1810, Borthwick.

CHAPTER TWO

1. Scargill & Lee, *Dewsbury As It Was*, introduction & nos. 30, 36, 46, 47, 49.

2. *Ibid.*, introduction and no.50; Bielby, *Churches and Chapels of Kirklees*, pp.30–2. The church has been rebuilt so many times that it is impossible to visualize it as it was in 1809, though the medieval parts of the interior and the 1767 tower remain.

3. Page (ed.), *Victoria History of the County of York*, iii, 524.

4. Baines, *History, Directory and Gazetteer of the County of York* (Leeds, 1822), i, 161–7; Scargill & Lee, *Dewsbury As It Was*, introduction.

5. *Ibid.* The Moravians were a Protestant sect, originating in Czechoslovakia: they had a strong following in the Gomersal and Pudsey area, where they established Fulneck School. A

Moravian minister, James de la Trobe, was to attend Anne Brontë when she was ill at Roe Head School at the end of 1837: see below, pp.281, 285.

6. Patrick's date of arrival in Dewsbury is given in PB, Letters testimonial from Dewsbury, 12 June 1810: MS ADM 1810, Borthwick. For the figures from the parish registers see: Register of Marriages, 1796–1812, All Saints' Church, Dewsbury: Microfiche D9/19, WYAS, Bradford; Register of Baptisms and Burials, 1796–1812, All Saints' Church, Dewsbury: Microfiche D9/8, WYAS, Bradford. These figures do not include the ones for Ossett, which are recorded separately, but not comprehensively, in the same register. Only the marriage register bears the name of the officiating minister, so it is not possible to ident-

ify what proportion of the baptisms and burials were carried out by Patrick. Judging by the new-format registers, which came into use in 1813 and did give the officiating minister's name, Buckworth relied on his curates to perform the vast majority of the duties.

7. Anon., *Memoir of the Rev. John Buckworth*, pp.178–9.

8. *Ibid.*, pp.52–3.

9. *Ibid.*, pp.114–17. Though Patrick was influenced by Buckworth's example, he never adopted his 'moderate Calvinism': *ibid.*, p.184.

10. Frederick W. Smith, 'Notes Towards a History of Dewsbury' (unpublished typescript, 1967): LSL, Dewsbury; Anon., *Memoir of the Rev. John Buckworth*, pp.17, 195.

11. Mr Senior, quoted in Yates, *The Father of the Brontës*, p.47.

12. Anon., *Memoir of the Rev. John Buckworth*, pp.49–51.

13. Mrs Hepworth, quoted in Revd Thomas Whitby to J. A. Erskine Stuart, 13 Dec. 1886: MS BS xi, 63 p.2, BPM.

14. Yates, *The Father of the Brontës*, pp.31–4.

15. *Ibid.*, p.42, and L&D, p.64, say that it was the vicar's ill health which prevented him attending the procession, but according to Patrick his vicar was in Oxford taking his M.A. only five days before the Whit walks: PB to Thomas Porteus, 6 June 1810: MS ADM 1810, Borthwick, [L&D, pp.68–9].

16. Mr Senior & Miss Wilson, quoted in Yates, *The Father of the Brontës*, pp.42–9. Mr Senior and Miss Wilson were apparently eye-witnesses. See CB, *Shirley*, pp.303–5 for Charlotte's fictionalization of the incident.

17. Joseph Tolson, quoted in Yates, *The Father of the Brontës*, pp.74–7. Yates' source was not Tolson himself, but the latter's daughter-in-law and grandson.

18. Patrick later worked closely with him to free William Nowell: see below, pp.37–8.

19. Marmaduke Fox, quoted in Yates, *The Father of the Brontës*, p.29.

20. *Ibid.*, pp.35–7. Mrs Hepworth, quoted in Revd Thomas Whitby to J. A. Erskine Stuart, 13 Dec. 1886: MS BS xi, 63 pp.2–4, BPM. The way the bell-ringing incident is reported, as if it was an example of Patrick's ill-temper, rather than his faith, is typical of the misrepresentations of him which proliferated after Mrs Gaskell's *Life* appeared.

21. Yates, *The Father of the Brontës*, pp.37–9. This suggestion is also accepted by L&D, p.66, but the *Memoir of the Rev. John Buckworth*, pp.49–52 says that the young men were taught in evening classes twice a week and does not mention residency at the vicarage. I suspect Patrick had to give up his place to David Jenkins, the new curate who was appointed in anticipation of Patrick's preferment to Hartshead.

22. PB to Thomas Porteus, 6 June 1810: MS ADM 1810, Borthwick, [L&D, pp.68–9].

23. Even the letters testimonial are confused in their dating: those from Wethersfield are dated 8 May 1810; those from Wellington are dated 8 May 1809, though they must date from 1810 as they testify to Patrick's having left Wellington on 4 December 1809; those from Dewsbury are dated 12 June 1810: all are in MS ADM 1810, Borthwick.

24. John Buckworth to the Archbishop of York, 19 July 1810: MS ADM 1810, Borthwick.

25. Parish Registers, All Saints' Church, Dewsbury: Microfiches D9/8, D9/19, WYAS, Bradford; Parish Registers, St Peter's Church, Hartshead-cum-Clifton: Microfiche D31/3, WYAS, Kirklees [printed, to the end of 1812 only, in Armytage (ed.), *The Parish Registers of Hartshead*].

26. David Jenkins first signed the Dewsbury marriage register on 6 August, 1810; he carried out nine marriages at Hartshead between 9 August 1810 and 28 March 1811. Joseph Ogden had officiated at all the previous marriages, assisted infrequently at Dewsbury and also occasionally when Patrick was minister at Hartshead. Register of Marriages, 1798–1812, St Peter's Church, Hartshead-cum-Clifton: Microfiche D31/3, WYAS, Kirklees. The fact that Jenkins was officiating as early as August 1810 contradicts the assertion of L&D, p.69, that it was the failure of the new curate to arrive which caused the delay in Patrick's removal to Hartshead. L&D, pp.68–9, 84, 90–1, also gloss over the fact that Patrick's appointment to Hartshead took place in 1810 but he did not commence his duties till the following year.

27. *Leeds Mercury*, 15 Dec. 1810, p.3.

28. *Ibid.*

29. Mary Burder to PB, 8 Aug. 1823: MS n.l., [L & L, i, 64].

30. *Leeds Mercury*, 15 Dec. 1810, p.3. It has usually been assumed, by L&D, pp.74–5, among others, that Patrick actually wrote the long letter about Nowell's case under the pseudonym 'Sydney'. This does not seem to me to fit the facts. There would be no point in going to the trouble of adopting a pseudonym, then giving away the identity by including a letter addressed to the 'Revd. P. Bronte' at the end, unless the pseudonym belonged to someone else. Patrick never used a pseudonym in any of his other correspondence with newspapers, partly because his title gave him the right to comment on public affairs. The letter does not appear to me to have some of the characteristic traits of Patrick's writing, the most obvious omission being quotation from Scripture, nor would Patrick have written 'we Englishmen' as he was always proud of his Irish ancestry. It is therefore my view that Patrick did not write the 'Sydney' letter, though he was clearly heavily involved in the actual case. Incidentally, I have found no evidence that Patrick contributed any articles to either the *Leeds Mercury* or the *Leeds Intelligencer* before

1824, though L&D, p.89, say that he had 'already contributed a number of articles' to them by 1811; the fact that the 'Sydney' letter is the only one before 1824, after which Patrick wrote fairly frequently, confirms my belief that it was not written by him.

31. *Leeds Mercury*, 17 Aug. 1811, p.3. There was an angry correspondence between Mr Dawson and Mr Rylah concerning the correctness of Dawson's behaviour as the examining magistrate afterwards: *ibid.*, 24 Aug. 1811, p.3; 7 Sept. 1811, p.3.

32. See above, p.33.

33. Bielby, *Churches and Chapels of Kirklees*, pp.12–14; ECG, *Life*, p.4.

34. Pobjoy, *The Story of the Ancient Parish of Harts-head-cum-Clifton*, pp.124, 111–12, 75–6. The occupations are cited in the parish registers: Armytage (ed.), *The Parish Registers of Hartshead*, pp.280–3, 292–3, 306–9.

35. The name is spelt 'Armitage' in all the contemporary sources I have consulted, therefore I have adopted that spelling, even though modern sources tend to use 'Armytage'.

36. Wood, *Hartshead & District in Times Past*, pp.11–12.

37. Sarah J. Williams to J. A. Erskine Stuart, [*c*.1886–7]: MS BS xi, 67 p.1, BPM.

38. John Buckworth, *A Series of Discourses Containing a System of Doctrinal Experimental and Practical Religion, Particularly Calculated for the Use of Families, Preached in the Parish Church of Dewsbury Yorkshire* (Wakefield, E. Waller, 1809): MS HAOBP:bb11, BPM. Buckworth added copies of two more recent sermons to the book, a funeral sermon for Joseph Hutchinson, who died on 12 July 1809, and a sermon for the Day of National Humiliation on 28 February 1810.

39. Parish Registers, St Peter's Church, Hartshead: Microfiche D31/3, WYAS, Kirklees [Armytage (ed.), *The Parish Registers of Hartshead*, pp.280, 282–3, 292–3, 306–9].

40. Registers of Marriages, 1798–1812 and 1813–68, St Peter's Church, Hartshead: Microfiche D31/3, WYAS, Kirklees [up to Dec. 1812, Armytage (ed.), *The Parish Registers of Hartshead*, pp.292–3]; Registers of Baptisms, 1798–1812 and 1813–72, St Peter's Church, Hartshead: Microfiche D31/3, WYAS, Kirklees [up to Dec. 1812, Armytage (ed.), *The Parish Registers of Hartshead*, pp.280–3]; Registers of Burials, 1798–1812 and 1813–36, St Peter's Church, Hartshead: Microfiche D31/3, WYAS, Kirklees [up to Dec. 1812, Armytage (ed.), *The Parish Registers of Hartshead*, pp.306–9]. In January 1813, all the parish registers were taken out of the clerk's hands and were filled in by Patrick, so it is possible to see exactly how many services he performed.

41. Register of Marriages, 1796–1812, All Saints' Church, Dewsbury: Microfiche D9/19, WYAS, Bradford. Patrick officiated at marriages, for example, on 20 May, 2 and 16 June, 7 July, 25

September and twice on 25 December 1811, signing the register as 'P Brontë Minister'.

42. W. Matthews, 'Charlotte Brontë', *The Methodist New Connexion Magazine* (London, 1889), p.208; Armytage (ed.), *The Parish Registers of Hartshead*, p.306. All three took occasional duties for Patrick: for David Jenkins see above, note 26; Hammond Roberson performed three baptisms on 28 August 1814 and two baptisms and a burial on 11 September 1814; William Morgan performed three burials on 21 March 1813 and Maria Brontë's christening on 23 April 1814: Parish Registers, St Peter's Church, Hartshead: Microfiche D31/3, WYAS, Kirklees.

43. Sarah J. Williams to J. A. Erskine Stuart, [*c*.1886–7]; MS BS xi, 67 p.1, BPM.

44. [PB], *Winter Evening Thoughts. A Miscellaneous Poem* (London, Longman; Wakefield, J. Hurst, 1810). The poem was printed by E. Waller, who also printed John Buckworth's *A Sermon Preached in the Parish Church of Dewsbury Yorkshire on Wednesday, February 28th 1810, the Day Appointed for the General Fast* (Wakefield, printed by E. Waller & Sold by J. Hurst, [1810]). I have been unable to locate the original of John Nunn's copy which is referred to in L&D, p.56. Though this is Patrick's first identified publication I suspect that he may have published something at Wellington. Edward Houlston, the Shropshire printer and publisher, lived and worked in Wellington and had published work by Patrick's vicar, John Eyton; mixing in highly literate circles at Madeley, it seems likely that Patrick would have been prompted to take up the pen himself.

45. 'Dum, operosa parvus carmina fingo: me quoque, qui facio, judice, digna lini plurima cerno'. The phrase 'operosa parvus carmina fingo' is from Horace, *Odes*, iv. no. 2, ll.31–2; the rest of the sentence was apparently constructed by Patrick himself. [PB], *Winter Evening Thoughts. A Miscellaneous Poem*, [L&D, p.57].

46. The quotation is from St Paul's Letter to the Corinthians, ch. 9, v. 22: it was used again in *The Rural Minstrel* and *The Maid of Killarney*.

47. PB, *Winter Evening Thoughts*, [PB, *Cottage Poems*, p.51].

48. *Ibid.*, [PB, *Cottage Poems*, p.53].

49. PB, *Cottage Poems*, pp.7–8, [*Brontëana*, p.19].

50. *Ibid.*, p.xiv, [*Brontëana*, p.21].

51. *Ibid.*, pp.1–13, 87–93, [*Brontëana*, pp.22–6, 51–3]. The poem to Buckworth rules out any possibility of a rift between Patrick and his vicar, which would have been the natural consequence of the supposed quarrel with John Halliley: see above, pp.35–6.

52. Robert Southey to CB, March 1837: MS n.l., [*L&L*, i, 155].

53. PB, Sermon on the Gospel according to St Matthew, ch. 3, v. 11, [1811]: MS MA 2696 pp. 11–12, Pierpont Morgan.

54. PB, Sermon on the Epistle of Paul to the Romans, ch. 2, vv.28–9, [*c*.1811]: MS BS 150 pp.2–3, 8, 19, BPM.

55. PB to Joseph Buckle, 31 July 1811: MS ADM 1811, Borthwick, [L&D, p.90].
56. PB, Letters testimonial from Dewsbury, 27 Aug. 1811 and John Buckworth nomination letter to Archbishop of York, 30 Aug. 1811: MS ADM 1811, Borthwick.
57. Kipling & Hall, *On the Trail of the Luddites*, p.3.
58. *Ibid.*, p.7. 'A Cottage Writer', who, according to L&D, p.121, may have been Patrick, wrote an article condemning violence and telling the poor to look to God for comfort: 'A Letter to the Labouring Poor, on the Distresses of the Times', John Buckworth (ed.), *The Cottage Magazine* (1816), pp.382–5. Though 'A Cottage Writer' is an Evangelical Irishman with a Yorkshire parish, and one would have expected Patrick to contribute to his vicar's magazine, I remain unconvinced that he is Patrick, principally because of the difference in style from his usual work.
59. Kipling & Hall, *On the Trail of the Luddites*, p.9.
60. The best and most vivid account of the attack is given in the *Leeds Mercury*, 18 April 1812, p.3: Charlotte used this version when writing *Shirley*: see below, p.555. See also Kipling & Hall, *On the Trail of the Luddites*, pp.31–6, 38–42.
61. The Cartwright Testimonial has unfortunately been illegible for many years, so it cannot be proved whether Patrick was one of the twenty-five signatories: 'A Testimonial presented to Mr William Cartwright of Rawfolds by the undersigned Inhabitants of the West Riding of the County of Yorkshire, approving of his conduct in defending his mill on the night of 11th April 1812', 17 May 1813: MS BS ix, C, BPM.
62. Typically, Mrs Gaskell, and those following her, have attributed the firing of the pistol out of the window to Patrick's explosive temper and violent character: ECG, *Life*, pp.31–2. The bullet could not be removed from the barrel of the gun except by discharging it.
63. *Leeds Mercury*, 25 April 1812, p.3.
64. *Ibid.*, 2 May 1812, p.3.
65. Kipling & Hall, *On the Trail of the Luddites*, p.49.
66. Thomas Atkinson, quoted in Yates, *The Father of the Brontës*, pp.91–3.
67. Sarah J. Williams to J. A. Erskine Stuart, [c.1886–7]: MS BS xi, 67 p.3, BPM.
68. Yates, *The Father of the Brontës*, pp.86–7.
69. The *Morning Chronicle*, 25 July 1811, p.1 contains an advertisement for the sale of the property by Mr Teale, surgeon, who was presumably father to the Mr Teale who attended Anne Brontë when she was dying of consumption: see below, pp.581–4.
70. MS Minute Book of the Wesleyan Academy, Woodhouse Grove: MS at Woodhouse Grove School, Rawdon [19 Aug. 1811 and 25 Sept. 1811]. I am grateful to the headmaster of the school for allowing me to see this book and quote from it.
71. *Ibid.*, [July 1812]; Slugg, *Woodhouse Grove School*, p.91; Pritchard, *The Story of Woodhouse Grove School*, pp.16, 20. Patrick is often referred to as

the examiner in the Scriptures at Woodhouse Grove (see, for example, Wilks, *The Brontës*, p.21), but his appointment was as 'examiner in Classical Learning'; the examiner in the Scriptures was a separate appointment, usually made in conjunction with the Wesleyan Conference. L&D, p.147, are also incorrect in supposing Patrick was never invited back as an examiner after the Methodists separated from the Church of England. The Minute Books make it clear that he was appointed again in 1823 and was 'first reserve' the previous year.
72. C. W. Hatfield, 'The Relatives of Maria Branwell', *BST*: 9:49:249–50. According to the 1841 census, the Branwells were still grocers in Market Square and, judging by the size of their establishments, were flourishing: Census Returns for Penzance, 1841: Microfiche, Redruth. See also Pigot & Co., *Directory of Devon and Cornwall* (1830), p.157.
73. Rees, *Old Penzance*, p.105. The 'Nelson Banner', made for a public procession in Penzance to mark the occasion, is still displayed in the old parish church at Madron.
74. S. Richards & L. Oldham, 'The Branwell Home in Penzance', *Old Cornwall*, viii, no. 7, Autumn 1976, pp.324–5; P. A. S. Pool, 'The Branwells of Penzance' (unpublished typescript, 1990), pp.2–3, Penzance.
75. Rees, *Old Penzance*, p.69. Penzance was also one of the five coinage towns in the Duchy of Cornwall where tin was weighed, coined and an impost charged: W. G. Maton, 'Observations on the Western Counties of England [1794–6]' in Pearse Chope (ed.), *Early Tours in Devon and Cornwall*, p.226.
76. Pool, 'The Branwells of Penzance', p.5. When Elizabeth Branwell died in 1842, her money was still invested in Bolitho's Bank; see below, p.913 n.95.
77. Rees, *Old Penzance*, pp.20, 28; Pool, 'The Branwells of Penzance', p.2; The Record Books of the Ladies' Book Club survive but no Branwells appear in the list of presidents; however the club purchased *Jane Eyre*, *Shirley*, *Villette* and *Life of CB* as each was published: MS Record Book of the Ladies' Book Club, 1770–1912: Penzance.
78. Pearce (ed.), *The Wesleys in Cornwall*, esp. pp.165, 166–7, 170.
79. Hatfield, 'The Relatives of Maria Branwell', pp.247, 249; Eanne Oram, 'A Brief for Miss Branwell', *BST*: 14:74:29; Pool, 'The Branwells of Penzance', p.3. Jane was never reconciled to her husband, who was expelled from the Methodist movement for a serious moral lapse, and never regained her older children. She received a life annuity of fifty pounds in her father's will, from which her husband was excluded, and died in Penzance in 1855. For the Branwells' role in building the chapel see: Pool, *The History of the Town and Borough of Penzance*, pp.93–4.
80. *The Universal British Directory, Devon and*

Cornwall (London, 1798), iv, 284; Maton, 'Observations on the Western Counties of England [1794–6]', p.257.

81. Richards & Oldham, 'The Branwell Home in Penzance', pp.324–5; prior to the building of St Mary's Church, the parish church lay at Madron, a steep one and a half mile walk inland.

82. Ivy Holgate, 'The Branwells at Penzance', *BST*:13:70:430; Thomas Branwell, Last Will & Testament, 26 March 1808: MS in Penzance.

83. The disaster, caused by storms, claimed the lives of 850 men on the *St George* and a further 580 on the *Defence*. The loss of the ships was not confirmed till a month after they went down with all hands; Lieutenant Branwell is listed amongst those lost: *West Briton*, 24 Jan. 1811, p.2.

84. The marriage took place at Madron Church on the same day as Patrick and Maria's, 29 December 1812: *Royal Cornwall Gazette*, 9 Jan. 1813, p.3.

85. Elizabeth Branwell's only legatee outside the Brontë family was Jane's daughter, Eliza Kingston, suggesting that she had closer links with this niece than with her brother's children.

86. MB to PB, 26 Aug. 1812: MS n.l., [*L&L*, i, 8–9].

87. *Ibid.*, i, 9.

88. MB to PB, 5 Sept. 1812: MS n.l., [*L&L*, i, 11].

89. *Ibid.*, i, 11.

90. MB to PB, 11 Sept. 1812: MS n.l., [*L&L*, i, 12].

91. John Abbott to CB, 22 Feb. 1851: MS pp.2–3 in private hands.

92. MB to PB, 11 Sept. 1812: MS n.l., [*L&L*, i, 12].

93. MB to PB, 18 Sept. 1812: MS n.l., [*L&L*, i, 13].

94. *Ibid.*, i, 13.

95. *Ibid.* The fact that the Bedfords had come about the blankets is referred to in MB's footnote to her letter of 21 Oct. 1812, [*L&L*, i, 20]. Patrick also acted as an intermediary to secure some carpet: MB to PB, 5 Dec. 1812: MS n.l., [*L&L*, i, 23].

96. MB to PB, 18 Sept. 1812: MS n.l., [*L&L*, i, 14].

97. MB to PB, 23 Sept. 1812: MS n.l., [*L&L*, i, 15–16].

98. MB to PB, 3 Oct. 1812: MS n.l., [*L&L*, i, 17–18].

99. *Ibid.*, i, 18; PB, *Cottage Poems*, pp.63–7 [*Brontëana*, pp.44–5]. L&D, pp.33–4, 95, refer to this poem as Patrick's 'dolorous lines to Mary Burder'. Jane Fennell clearly did not share their opinion of the merit of his verses. I do not think the poem was addressed to Mary Burder: all the other poems were written in 1811, long after he left Wethersfield and long after Mary's eighteenth birthday. The poem also refers to the lady's parents drinking her health on her birthday: Mary's father had died before Patrick came to Wethersfield and, even with poetic licence, Patrick would not have committed such a solecism.

100. MB to PB, 21 Oct. 1812: MS n.l., [*L&L*, i, 18–19].

101. William Morgan (ed.), *The Pastoral Visitor*, ii no. 22, Oct. 1816, p.146. The Bibles had 'no notes or comment' to avoid sectarian clashes over interpretation; the other half of the subscription went to the parent society in London.

102. *Leeds Mercury,* 31 Oct. 1812, p.3. The meeting was held on 28 October 1812.

103. MB to PB, 18 Nov. 1812: MS p.2, Brotherton, [*L&L*, i, 20–2]. This is the only one of Maria's letters for which I have been able to trace an original manuscript.

104. *Ibid.*, pp. 2–3.

105. MB to PB, 5 Dec. 1812: MS n.l., [*L&L*, i, 22–3].

106. *Ibid.*, i, 22–3.

107. Register of Marriages, 1803–12, Guiseley Parish Church: MS p.122, WYAS, Leeds; the story about the veil occurs in the *Bradford Observer*, 14 July 1859, p.6, quoting an extract referring to Mr Brontë's Methodist connections from the recently published life of the Reverend Jabez Bunting. The marriages were reported in the *Leeds Intelligencer*, 4 Jan. 1813, p.3.

108. Hatfield, 'The Relatives of Maria Branwell', p.250.

109. There are no anecdotes about MB in Yates, *The Father of the Brontës*, the main source of contemporary stories; the only reference to her at this period which I have been able to find is that she was in a 'delicate state of health' which was the attributed cause of the Brontës' removal from Hartshead: Sarah J. Williams to J. A. Erskine Stuart, [*c.*1886–7]: BS xi, 67 pp.2–3, BPM.

110. The figure of £62 is quoted in PB to Joseph Buckle, 31 July 1811: MS ADM 1811, Borthwick. Mrs Gaskell, however, says that the living was worth £202: ECG, *Life*, p.205.

111. PB, *The Rural Minstrel: A Miscellany of Descriptive Poems* (Halifax, P. K. Holden, 1813), pp.ix–x, [*Brontëana*, p.71]. An advertisement for the book, describing it as 'just published', costing 3s. and being by the same author as *Cottage Poems*, appeared in the *Leeds Intelligencer*, 27 Sept. 1813, p.2.

112. PB, 'An Elegy' and 'Winter', *The Rural Minstrel*, pp.55–61, 71–6, [*Brontëana*, pp.85–7, 89–91].

113. *The Rural Minstrel*, pp.1–15, 97–108, [*Brontëana*, pp.72–6, 96–9].

114. 'Kirkstall Abbey' is subtitled 'a fragment of a romantic tale', which implies that it was originally part of a longer prose story, like the poetry sections in the *Maid of Killarney*; it may, of course, simply be a literary device: PB, *The Rural Minstrel*, pp.17–33, [*Brontëana*, pp.76–80]. I have been unable to find a contemporary reference to Kirkstall Abbey being the scene of Patrick's proposal to Maria, though it is not unlikely, given the fact that it was a frequent destination on their walks.

115. PB, *The Rural Minstrel*, pp.47–8, [*Brontëana*, p.83].

116. *Ibid.*, pp.77–9, [*Brontëana*, p.91].

117. I have discussed this influence in my article, 'Poetic Justice: the importance of poetry in the lives and literature of the Brontës', *The Brontë*

Society and The Gaskell Society Joint Conference, 1990: Conference Papers (Keighley, The Brontë Society, 1990), pp.7–8.

118. Register of Baptisms, St Peter's Church, Hartshead: Microfiche D31/4, WYAS, Kirklees. Despite Patrick's views on the importance of baptism, his own children do not seem to have been baptized within any specific period of birth: the length of time between birth and baptism varied from 21 days in the case of Emily to 199 days in the case of Elizabeth. No date of birth can therefore be posited for Maria based on her baptismal date alone.

119. MS Minute Book of the Wesleyan Academy, Woodhouse Grove: MS at Woodhouse Grove School, Rawdon [28 April 1813, 3 Dec. 1813, 22 Dec. 1813]; Pritchard, *The Story of Woodhouse Grove School*, pp.20–2. Fennell was given an additional month's salary when he left but it was the end of the year before his expenses had been repaid and his accounts with the school had finally been settled.

120. *Leeds Intelligencer*, 11 July 1814, p.3.

121. Circular for the Bradford Church Missionary Association, enclosed with letter of William Morgan to Revd Josiah Pratt, [pm 21 Oct. 1813]: MS in archives of CMS.

122. William Morgan to Revd Josiah Pratt, [pm 21 Oct. 1813], and enclosed minutes of meeting in Bradford on 11 Oct. 1813 to form a Church of England Missionary Society for Africa and the East: MS in archives of CMS; *Leeds Intelligencer*, 3 Oct. 1814, p.3.

123. *Leeds Mercury*, 22 Oct. 1814, p.2; Morgan (ed.), *The Pastoral Visitor*, ii. no. 22, October 1816, pp.146–9.

124. *Leeds Intelligencer*, 10 April 1815, p.3. Patrick is not mentioned by name but must have been one of the 'large number of clergy' at the meeting.

125. PB to Richard Burn, Secretary to the Governors of the Bounty Office, 27 Jan. 1820: MS ADM 1820, Borthwick, [L&D, p.197]: Patrick complained that the living of Thornton was

usually returned as being worth £140 a year but that realistically it was worth only £127 yearly.

126. G. C. Moore Smith, 'The Brontës at Thornton', *The Bookman*, Oct. 1904, p.18. It is here stated that Elizabeth was named after her other godmother, Elizabeth Firth; this is improbable given the fact that the child would have had to have remained un-named for at least five months before the Brontës met Elizabeth Firth and that all three of the eldest Brontë girls, and indeed the only son, were named after Branwells.

127. Venn, pt ii, i, 95; Yates, *The Father of the Brontës*, p.89. According to Venn, Atkinson, son of the vicar of Kippax, took his B.A. from Magdalene College in 1802 and an M.A. in 1814; he had been perpetual curate of Thornton since his ordination as a priest in 1804. He married Frances Walker and remained at Hartshead until his death in 1866.

128. On 13 March 1815 Patrick signed a document agreeing to pay the accustomed dues to the vicar of Bradford: 20d. per adult burial, 10d. per infant burial and 6d. for every christening or churching. The document refers to the fact that Patrick has been 'nominated and appointed' by John Crosse: PB, Assignation of dues to Bradford, 13 March 1815: MS BS 151, BPM.

129. Parish Registers, St Peter's Church, Hartshead: Microfiche D31/3, WYAS, Kirklees. L&D, p.157, misled by Yates, *The Father of the Brontës*, p.89, state that Patrick's last service was the marriage on 15 May 1815; this was only the last marriage, there were other services afterwards. Incidentally, once the registers had changed to the new format in 1813, one can see that Patrick had shown an unusual level of commitment in his performance of church duties, requiring deputies on only six occasions in 1813 and two (one of them his own daughter's baptism) in 1814. For the Brontës' arrival in Thornton see: Firth, 19 May 1815.

CHAPTER THREE

Title: 'I can fancy, almost, that we are still at Thornton, good neighbours, and kind, and sincere friends, and happy with our wives and children': PB to Revd Robinson Pool, 18 March 1858: MS BS 206 p.1, BPM, [L&D, p.203].

1. Firth, 23 July 1815.
2. *Ibid.*, 18 Jan. 1816.
3. Revd G. Thomas to Revd William Scoresby, 8 Dec. 1840: MS in unsorted bundle, 1840, Whitby. The letter, from the incumbent of Thornton protesting to the vicar of Bradford about the proposed formation of new parishes at Clayton and Denholme, states, 'When I entered on the incumbency of Thornton, by your appointment, it was on the understanding that the incum-

bency included the hamlets of Clayton and Denholme.' The parish registers make it clear that Patrick was ministering regularly to the people of Allerton and Wilsden, the last of which was equidistant from Thornton and Bingley, and therefore divided informally between the two parishes: Old Bell Chapel Registers, Thornton: Microfiche 81D85/8/1, WYAS, Bradford.

4. ECG, *Life*, p.27.
5. Scruton, pp.16, 21–3, 27–30.
6. Baines, *History, Directory and Gazetteer of the County of York* (Leeds, 1822), i, 619; Page (ed.), *Victoria History of the County of York*, iii, 533. My figures do not include Wilsden, which was split between several parishes. The population

figures for 1811, with the 1821 figures in brackets, are as follows: Thornton chapelry, 3,016 (4,100); Allerton township, 1,093 (1,488); Clayton township, 2,469 (3,609); and Wilsden 1,121 (1,711). Patrick quite accurately estimated that the population of the chapelry was 9,000 in 1820: P B to Richard Burn, Secretary to the Governors of the Queen Anne's Bounty Office, 27 Jan. 1820: MS ADM 1820, Borthwick, [L&D, pp. 197–8].

7. Firth, 1812–25: MS 58 A i–xiv (MS Q 091 F), Sheffield. Incomplete and inaccurate transcripts of the diaries are given in Moore Smith, 'The Brontës at Thornton', *The Bookman*, Oct. 1904, p.19; *L&L*, i, 39–45; L&D, pp.158, 166–9, 173–7, 181, 190–1, 196–7, 199, 201–2.

8. PB to Richard Burn, Secretary to the Governors of the Queen Anne's Bounty Office, 27 Jan. 1820: MS ADM 1820, Borthwick, [L&D, pp.197–8]. According to the Thornton Terrier, the parsonage was 'situated in the village of Thornton, consisting of six rooms, three on the ground floor, and three bed-chambers, having a stand for a cow and horse at one end, and a cottage at the other – All built of stone and lime … There is a road round the West End into a garden at the back of the house – which is enclosed by a stone wall': P B, Thornton Terrier, 31 July 1817: MS in Borthwick.

9. Leyland, i, 16–17.

10. Burials at Thornton averaged at fifty-five a year, baptisms at forty-three: Register of Burials, 1813–39 and Register of Baptisms, 1813–27, Old Bell Chapel, Thornton: Microfiche 81D85/8/1, WYAS, Bradford.

11. See, for example, L&D, pp.162ff.; Chitham, *A Life of Emily Brontë*, pp.11–13.

12. Firth, 6, 7, 9, 11 June 1815. Allerton Hall had been built by Elizabeth Firth's uncle, Joshua, who died in 1814; it was then purchased by the Kayes: Holgate, 'The Brontës at Thornton, 1815–1820', *BST*:13:69:330.

13. Firth Family Pedigree: MS 58 C i & E, Sheffield; W. B. Trigg & G. Dent, 'City Fold, Wheatley', *Transactions of the Halifax Antiquarian Society*, 1934, pp.182–4.

14. Firth, 12 June 1815. The diary references almost invariably refer to 'Mrs Bronte', 'Miss Branwell' or 'Mr Bronte's', which I take to be shorthand for 'Mr Bronte's family'; on the rare occasions when Patrick called he is distinguished by his own reference: see, for example, 'Mr & Mrs Bronte', 'Mr & Mrs Bronte & Miss Branwell' and 'Mr & Mrs Bronte's family' on 22 August 1815, 18 June 1816 and 9 May 1817. I have been unable to find a contemporary reference for the assertion in L&D, pp.56–7 that Elizabeth Branwell came to Hartshead in the new year of 1815.

15. Register of Baptisms, 1813–27, Old Bell Chapel, Thornton: Microfiche 81D85/8/1, WYAS, Bradford, [L&D, p.169]; Firth, 26 Aug. 1815.

16. Morgan (ed.), *The Pastoral Visitor*, July 1815, pp.52–3. For Morgan's articles on the subject see

ibid., Feb., March and April 1815, pp.11–12, 21–2, 26–9 respectively; see above, pp.43–4 for Patrick's earlier writings on the subject of conversion.

17. *Ibid.*, July 1815, p.53.

18. *Ibid.*, Sept. 1815, p.71; Oct. 1815, pp.78–9.

19. Patrick's literary approach to 'On Conversion' is discussed in Kate Lawson, 'Patrick Brontë's "On Conversion"', *BST*:19:6:271–2.

20. PB, *The Cottage in the Wood, or the Art of Becoming Rich and Happy* (Bradford, T. Inkersley, 1815), p.5, [*Brontëana*, pp.102–3].

21. Although the diaeresis appears on the title page, it does not appear in any of Patrick's signatures in the registers or in his letters at this time where he was still using 'Brontë'.

22. *Brontëana*, p.100.

23. Morgan (ed.), *The Pastoral Visitor*, August 1816, p.128.

24. J.B.M., 'Things worthy to be considered by all persons who doubt about going to the Holy Sacrament', *The Pastoral Visitor*, July 1815, pp.54–5. 'J.B.M.' are the initials of Jane's full name, 'Jane Branwell Morgan'.

25. MB, 'The Advantages of Poverty, in Religious Concerns', n.d.: MS in Brotherton, [*L&L*, i, 24]. L&D, pp.128–9, date the manuscript to the period of Patrick's courtship of Maria but this seems unlikely; the concerns of the piece, which reflect those of Patrick, the access through William Morgan to his newly founded *The Pastoral Visitor*, and the fact that Jane Morgan had contributed to her husband's magazine, would make an 1815 date more probable.

26. MB, 'The Advantages of Poverty, in Religious Concerns', n.d.: MS pp.1–2, Brotherton, [*L&L*, i, 24–5].

27. *Ibid.*, p.6.

28. *L&L*, i, 24; L&D, p.129. I have been unable to locate a published version of Maria's article but as the manuscript returned to Patrick's hands it seems likely it was rejected.

29. Firth, 6 Sept. 1815.

30. *Ibid.*, 11–13 Oct. 1815; *Leeds Mercury*, 30 Sept. 1815, p.3; 14 Oct. 1815, p.3; 3 Aug. 1816, p.2; 14 Oct. 1815, p.3.

31. *Ibid.*, 14 Oct. 1810, p.3.

32. Subscribers' Lists, Bradford Library & Literary Society, 1815: MS 42D81/1/2/1/3, WYAS, Bradford. Patrick is only listed as a member for 1815; the list covers the period 1815 and 1817–28 but Patrick's name does not appear again. William Morgan and Mr Firth were both members.

33. Firth, 18 Jan. 1816.

34. *Ibid.*, 26 March, 21 April 1816; Register of Baptisms, 1813–27, Old Bell Chapel, Thornton: Microfiche 81D85/7/1, WYAS, Bradford. There was a tradition in the Franks family that the Atkinsons were Charlotte's godparents: *L&L*, i, 33 n.1.

35. Firth, 12 July 1816.

36. *Ibid.*, 25, 28 July 1816.

37. *Ibid.*, 29, 31 July, 1 Aug. 1816.

38. *Bradford Observer*, 29 May 1886, p.7. William

Morgan, Mrs & Miss Fanny Outhwaite and John Crosse were all connected with the Bradford School of Industry.

39. C. A. Binns, 'Brontë Nurses', a letter to *The Dalesman*, August 1986, p.415; the author of this letter was the great-great-great-grandchild of Nancy's sister, Ruth.

40. Venn, pt ii, ii, 189; Scruton, *Pen and Pencil Pictures of Old Bradford*, pp.32–4; Morgan, *The Parish Priest*.

41. *Leeds Mercury,* 3 June 1816, p.3.

42. John Fennell quoted in Morgan, *The Parish Priest*, pp.166–7.

43. John Fennell, *A Sermon Preached at the Funeral of the Rev. John Crosse, A.M. late Vicar of Bradford, on Sunday, the 23rd of June 1816* (Bradford, T. Inkersley, 1816); Morgan, *The Parish Priest*.

44. Scruton, *Pen and Pencil Pictures of Old Bradford*, p.34.

45. Firth, 19 Nov. 1816. L&D, p.175, and L&L, i, p.41, both run the entry for the previous day, 18 November, into that for the 19th, falsely creating the impression that the Firths and Brontës watched the eclipse together over tea at the Brontës'. The *Leeds Mercury,* 9 Nov.1816, p.3, gives the times for the eclipse which make it clear that this occurred on the following day.

46. L&D, p. 176.

47. Kipling & Hall, *On the Trail of the Luddites*, p.51.

48. *Leeds Mercury,* 14 June 1817, p.3; 21 June 1817, p.3.

49. Firth, 18 March 1817. The suggestion that she had come to help with Maria's latest confinement is from L&D, p.177. The only Thomas I have been able to locate is the sixty-year-old lodging house keeper, Nancy Thomas, who in 1841 lived in Chapel Street, Penzance, next door to Jane Branwell, widow of Maria's cousin, Robert (1775–1833): Census Returns for Penzance, 1841: Microfilm, Redruth.

50. Firth, 11,18 May 1817.

51. PB, National Society Questionnaire, [c.1817]: MS Y/A Mic 63, Borthwick. To a question asking what Sunday schools there were in his chapelry, Patrick replied that there were 49 boys and 51 girls in his Sunday school, 70 boys and 60 girls belonging to the Independent Dissenters at the Meeting House in Thornton, 130 boys and 170 girls of the same class of Dissenters in a neighbouring hamlet, 100 boys and 150 girls in the Baptist Sunday school and 40 boys and 50 girls at the Methodist one.

52. *Leeds Mercury,* 17 May 1817, p.3; Firth, 13 May, 12 July 1817. Patrick and Mr Firth stayed with the Haighs at Longlands, a house in Batley: the Haighs were friends of the Firths and the Brontës had dined at least once with Miss Haigh at Kipping House. Charlotte Brontë later went to school at Roe Head with Miss Hannah Haigh who probably belonged to the Longlands family: J. T. M. Nussey, 'Notes on the background of three incidents in the lives of the Brontës', *BST.*15:79: 331–3.

53. Firth, 26, 27 June 1817. Recording his birth,

Elizabeth calls him Branwell Patrick.

54. Register of Baptisms, 1813–27, Old Bell Chapel, Thornton: Microfiche 81D85/7/1, WYAS, Bradford; PB to Mrs Franks, 6 July 1835: MS BS 184 p.1, BPM, [L&L, i, 130] where he refers to Mr & Mrs Firth acting as Branwell's 'sponsors'. It is possible that Maria's sister, Charlotte, or her husband, Joseph Branwell, acted as godparent to Branwell, particularly as their own son, born in the same year, 1817, was named Thomas Bronte Branwell, suggesting that Patrick and Maria were his godparents. L&D, pp.176–7, state that John Fennell, who baptized Branwell, had just been appointed minister of Cross-stone, John Crosse's old church between Hebden Bridge and Todmorden. In fact, Fennell was nominated to Cross-stone by the vicar of Halifax in April 1819 and did not take up the post till that year; at the time of his nomination, he was curate of Christ Church in Bradford: *Leeds Mercury,* 24 April 1819, p.2; Gravestone of Jane and John Fennell, Cross-stone churchyard, now at BPM.

55. *Leeds Mercury,* 8 Nov. 1817, p.2; 15 Nov. 1817, p.3; 22 Nov. 1817, p.3. Elizabeth Firth noted the death and funeral of the 'ever to be lamented Princess Charlotte' in her diary: Firth, 6, 19 Nov. 1817

56. *Ibid.,* 7, 8 Nov. 1817.

57. *Ibid.,* 12 Nov. 1817. James Clarke Franks was to win the Norrisian Prize at the University of Cambridge for the fourth year running in May 1818, which was an outstanding achievement; he became chaplain of Trinity College, Cambridge and was appointed deputy Hulsean Lecturer in 1821: *Leeds Mercury,* 16 May 1818, p.3; 7 April 1821, p.3.

58. Firth, 23 Dec. 1817. There is a photograph of Green House, Mirfield, in Pobjoy, *The Story of the Ancient Parish of Hartshead-cum-Clifton*.

59. *Leeds Mercury,* 7 Feb. 1818, p.3. The festivities began on 3 February, Shrove Tuesday.

60. *Blackwood's Magazine*, iii, April 1818, p.102.

61. PB, *The Maid of Killarney; or, Albion and Flora: a modern tale; in which are interwoven some cursory remarks on Religion and Politics* (London, Baldwin, Cradock & Joy, 1818). The book was printed in Bradford by T. Inkersley, who had previously published Patrick's *The Cottage in the Wood*.

62. PB, *The Maid of Killarney,* p.v, [*Brontëana,* p.133]. The quotations on the title page are taken from two sources: the first three lines are from Horace's *Satires*, bk i, no. i, ll.24–6; the second two lines are from Horace's *Ars Poetica*, ll.343–4. Roughly translated, the first quotation says 'and yet what harm can there be in presenting the truth with humour; as teachers sometimes give children biscuits to coax them into learning their ABC' and the second 'the man who has managed to blend profit with delight wins everyone's approbation, for he gives his reader pleasure at the same time as he instructs him'.

63. *Ibid.,* pp.v–vi, [*Brontëana,* p.133].

64. PB, *Cottage Poems*, p.xiv, [*Brontëana,* p.21].

65. PB, *The Maid of Killarney*, p.121, [*Brontëana*, p.180].
66. *Ibid.*, pp.72–3, 52–5.
67. *Ibid.*, pp.24–6, 19.
68. Patrick is likely to have attended the meeting of West Riding clergymen called at Wakefield on 21 April 1819, to raise a petition to Parliament against granting further immunities to Catholics: *Leeds Mercury*, 24 April 1819, p.2. For Patrick's opinions on Roman Catholic Emancipation see his letters to the *Leeds Intelligencer*, 15 Jan. 1829, p.4, 29 Jan. 1829, p.4., 5 Feb. 1829, p.4. See also below, pp.157–8. Patrick's children were even more prejudiced against Catholicism than their father. Charlotte savagely attacked the 'Romish Religion' and the 'necromancy' of Irish Catholic priests in her Tales of the Islanders, vol. ii, chs iv &v, 21 Nov–2 Dec. 1829: MS in Berg, [CA, i, 108–13].
69. PB, *The Maid of Killarney*, pp.49–50, [*Brontëana*, pp.150–1].
70. PB, letters to the *Leeds Mercury*, 10 Jan. 1829, p.4., 14 Nov. 1829, p.4 and to the *Leeds Intelligencer*, 6 May 1830, p.4..
71. Charlotte's first romantic heroine, Marion Hume, in particular, is almost a carbon copy of Flora, even to the point of playing the harp. For a description of her culled from various manuscripts, see CA *EW*, p.71.
72. Firth, Cash Account May 1818, 20 Oct. 1818; *ibid.*, 19, 22 May 1818.
73. *Ibid.*, 30 July 1818; Register of Baptisms, 1813–27, Old Bell Chapel, Thornton: Microfiche 81D85/7/1, WYAS, Bradford. L&D, p.180 and WG *EJB*, p.1, name Emily's godparents as Jane Branwell Morgan and the Fennells, the latter stating it as one of the two 'facts' known about Emily's infancy, but there is no contemporary source that I can find which identifies them. The christening mug, now in the Brontë Parsonage Museum, was purchased from Arthur Bell Nicholls' niece and would therefore appear to be genuine: HAOBP:H6, BPM, [JB *ST* no. 44].
74. Firth, 19 Aug. 1818.
75. Bins, 'Brontë Nurses', *The Dalesman*, Aug. 1986, p.415.
76. *Leeds Mercury*, 3 Oct. 1818, p.3; Firth, 19 Oct., 9 Nov. 1818.
77. Holgate, 'The Brontës at Thornton', *BST*:13:69:334–6, 327; Churchwardens' Book for the Chapelry of Thornton, 27 Dec. 1817: Microfiche 81D85/12/2, WYAS, Bradford; Firth, 9 Dec. 1818.
78. Firth, 10 Nov., 6 Dec. 1818. Almost £27 had been spent on joinery and interior redecoration by the time the chapel reopened on 6 December; a further £10 8s. 4d. was spent over the following three months: Churchwardens' Book for the Chapelry of Thornton, 28 Dec. 1818, 7 May 1819: Microfiche 81D85/12/2, WYAS, Bradford.
79. Holgate, 'The Brontës in Thornton', *BST*:13:69:336. Holgate speculates that Patrick gave Thomas Driver the name 'Rembrandt', but

the man came from a family of painters and they undoubtedly chose his name, just as Thomas Parker, the singer from Haworth, named his children after famous composers.
80. *Leeds Mercury*, 21 Nov. 1818, p.2; 5 Dec. 1818, pp.2–3. Funeral sermons were preached in the parish church at Bradford and at Christ Church on 2 December, but the Old Bell Chapel did not reopen till 6 December. Official mourning did not end till 29 December: *ibid.*, 2 Jan. 1819, p.3.
81. Firth, 8 Jan. 1819.
82. This anecdote is related in Scruton, p.59. There is clearly some truth in it as the churchwardens' accounts show a payment of 9/10d. for 'treating Abm Sharp and Clerk paid for Children at Bradford when Bishop was on confirmation' in the accounts for 27 December 1819: Churchwardens' Book for the Chapelry of Thornton, 27 Dec. 1819: Microfiche 81D85/12/2, WYAS, Bradford. There are a number of problems, however, not least the fact that Scruton reports the incident taking place in March and the children being caught in a snow storm; if this was the case then the payment should have been approved by the meeting of 7 May 1819. It would seem highly improbable that sixty children could be given a hot meal for less than 2d. each, so a hot drink seems more likely – or the numbers in the party were substantially less than the sixty Scruton quotes. Though both the churchwardens' accounts and Scruton refer to the confirmation being by the 'bishop', in 1819 the parish of Bradford was still directly under the authority of the Archbishop of York, the bishopric of Ripon not being created till 1832. L&D, p.178, with typically fanciful licence, and without a shred of evidence, suggest that Patrick himself downed an Irish whiskey while the young people were eating. Scruton's reliability is extremely suspect: see, for example, his story about Patrick's courtship of Maria, which can be disproved from other sources: Scruton, p.50.
83. *Leeds Mercury*, 24 April 1819, p.2. L&D, p.176, wrongly state that Fennell was appointed in April 1817. See above, note 54.
84. Register of Burials, 1813–36, Haworth Church. Charnock was buried on 31 May 1819.
85. PB to Stephen Taylor, 8 July 1819: MS n.l., [L&D, p.187].
86. Mr Stocks to Mr Greenwood, 1 June 1819: MS BS, ix, S p.1, BPM, [L&D, p.182]. Patrick was later to return the favour by signing a petition testifying to Mr Stocks' good character when the latter was wrongly accused of perjury and perversion of the course of justice and deprived of his magistracy: see below, p.178. L&D, p.182, wrongly describe Mr Stocks as a 'clerical friend' of Patrick's.
87. A photocopy of this deed was kindly made available to me by Mr Jack Wood, Treasurer to the Church Trustees, Haworth, [L&D, pp.210–11].
88. L&D, pp.211–12.

89. Anthony Moss to Revd Edward Ramsden, 15 June 1819: MS RMP 392, WYAS, Calderdale.
90. Henry Heap to the Archbishop of York, 2 June 1819: MS ADM 1820, Borthwick.
91. *Leeds Intelligencer*, 14 June 1819, p.3.
92. Holgate, 'The Brontës at Thornton', *BST*:13:69:330.
93. PB to Stephen Taylor, 8 July 1819: MS n.l., [L&D, pp.187–8]. Patrick is said to have gone to see Stephen Taylor and introduced himself as the new incumbent, upon which Taylor took him on one side and informed him in no uncertain terms that this was not the case: Miss Mariner, quoted in Craven, *A Brontë Moorland Village*, p.58.
94. PB to Stephen Taylor, 8 July 1819: MS n.l., [L&D, p.188].
95. PB to Stephen Taylor, 14 July 1819: MS n.l., [L&D, p.188]. Though Patrick may have come over to Haworth to take one of the three services on 12 July, he was also in Thornton that day to perform two baptisms and William Anderton likewise performed two baptisms on that day in Haworth: Register of Baptisms, 1813–27, Old Bell Chapel, Thornton: Microfiche 81D85/7/1, WYAS, Bradford; Register of Baptisms, 1813–29, Haworth Church.
96. PB to Stephen Taylor, 21 July 1819: MS n.l., [L&D, pp.189–90].
97. *Ibid.*, p.190.
98. *Leeds Mercury*, 23 Oct. 1819, p.2.
99. PB to Stephen Taylor, 9 Oct. 1819: MS n.l., [L&D, p.191].
100. Holgate, 'The Brontës in Thornton', *BST*:13:69:337, quoting 'a record book' in Bradford Cathedral.
101. *Leeds Mercury*, 30 Oct. 1819, p.3.
102. ECG, *Life*, pp.18–20.
103. *Leeds Intelligencer*, 18 April 1857, p.7. With typical obtuseness, Mrs Gaskell complained on receiving this different version of 'the Haworth commotions', 'I don't see any great difference': ECG to EN, 16 June [1857]: [C&P, p.453]. Samuel Redhead preached at the afternoon and evening services on 21 July 1844, which was presumably the occasion on which he was accompanied by his son-in-law to Haworth: *Bradford Observer*, 25 July 1844, p.5; Haworth Church Hymn Sheets, 21 July 1844: MS BS x, H, BPM.
104. *Leeds Intelligencer*, 22 Nov. 1819, p.2.
105. Register of Burials, 1813–36, Register of Baptisms, 1813–29, Register of Marriages, 1813–37, Haworth Church. These were the only recorded occasions when Patrick officiated at Haworth before he took up the perpetual curacy there in April 1820. Samuel Redhead, contrary to Mrs Gaskell's statement that he had assisted the previous incumbent during a long illness, took only one funeral, on 7 November 1819, and

seven baptisms and two marriages, all on 4 November 1819. The bulk of the services during the vacancy at Haworth, and many of those during the eighteen months prior to James Charnock's death, were taken by the Reverend William Anderton.
106. Firth, Nov.–Dec. 1819.
107. *Ibid.*, 17, 18 Jan., 25 March 1820. Anne Brontë's maternal grandmother was Anne Branwell (*née* Carne).
108. PB to Richard Burn, Secretary to the Governors of the Queen Anne's Bounty Office, 27 Jan. 1820: MS ADM 1820, Borthwick, [L&D, pp.197–8].
109. PB to the Archbishop of York, 4 Feb. 1820: MS ADM 1820, Borthwick, [L&D, p.198].
110. Henry Heap to Archbishop of York, 9 Feb. 1820: MS ADM 1820, Borthwick, [L&D, p.200].
111. *Ibid.*
112. PB, Nomination to Haworth, 8 Feb. 1820: MS ADM 1820, Borthwick.
113. PB, Letters testimonial for Haworth, 8 Feb. 1820: MS ADM 1820, Borthwick.
114. PB, Assignation of dues to Bradford, 8 Feb. 1820: MS n.l., [L&D, pp.199–200].
115. PB to Archbishop of York, 9 Feb. 1820: MS ADM 1820, Borthwick, [L&D, p.201]. The licence clearly did state the joint nomination by vicar and trustees as this was how the appointment was reported in the *Leeds Intelligencer*, 13 March 1820, p.2.
116. Henry Heap to Archbishop of York, 9 Feb. 1820: MS ADM 1820, Borthwick, [L&D, p.200].
117. Firth, 25 Feb. 1820.
118. According to the registers, Patrick did not officiate at baptisms, marriages and burials in Haworth between his appointment and taking up residence there; he may have taken some of the Sunday services. For his and his successor's duties in Thornton see: Register of Baptisms, 1813–27, Old Bell Chapel, Thornton: Microfiche 81D85/7/1, WYAS, Bradford; Register of Burials, 1813–39, Old Bell Chapel, Thornton: Microfiche 81D85/8/1, WYAS, Bradford.
119. *Leeds Mercury*, 5 Feb. 1820, p.2; 12 Feb. 1820, p.3.
120. *Ibid.*, Jan.–March 1820, *passim*.
121. Firth, 31 March 1820; J. Firth Franks to G. C. Moore Smith, n.d.: MS 58 (MS Q 091 F), C, vi, Sheffield.
122. Register of Baptisms, 1813–27, Old Bell Chapel, Thornton: Microfiche 81D85/7/1, WYAS, Bradford; Firth, 25 March 1820.
123. *Ibid.*, 5 April 1820; Joyce Eagleton, *The Story Tellers* (Bradford Libraries & Information Services, 1990), p.1, quoting her great-grandfather who was an eye-witness of the Brontës' departure from Thornton.

CHAPTER FOUR

Title: PB to John Buckworth, 27 Nov. 1821: *The Cottage Magazine* (1822), p.245, [*L&L*, i, 58].

1. ECG, *Life*, p.6.
2. (*Jane Eyre*) *Christian Remembrancer*, April 1848; *North American Review*, Oct. 1848; *Quarterly Review*, Dec. 1848, [Allott, pp.89, 98, 111]. (*Wuthering Heights*) *Examiner*, 8 Jan. 1848; *Britannia*, 15 Jan. 1848; *American Review*, June 1848, [Allott, pp.222, 225, 236]. (*The Tenant of Wildfell Hall*) *North American Review*, Aug. 1849: quoted in Lloyd Evans, *Everyman Companion to the Brontës*, p.384.
3. G. H. Lewes, unsigned review in *Leader*, 28 Dec. 1850, [Allott, p.292].
4. CB, *Biographical Notice*, p.359.
5. Thomas Hobbes, *Leviathan* (Harmondsworth, Penguin, 1977), p.186.
6. ECG, *Life*, pp.6–20.
7. Unsigned review, *Christian Remembrancer*, July 1857, [Allott, p.365]: ECG to unknown, 23 Aug. [1855]: [C&P, p.369].
8. Babbage, *Report to the General Board of Health*, p.7.
9. Baines, *History, Directory and Gazetteer of the County of York* (1822), i, 519. Of the thirteen mills in Haworth, three were wool staplers, five worsted manufacturers, two worsted top manufacturers, one a worsted spinner, one a worsted yarn manufacturer and one a cotton spinner and manufacturer.
10. The Babbage Report of 1850 stated that 'Many of the inhabitants of Haworth, pursue the occupation of combing wool for the factories. This business is carried on in their houses. In order to obtain the proper temperature for this operation, iron stoves are fixed in the rooms where it is carried on, which are kept alight day and night, and the windows are seldom, if ever, opened, excepting in the height of summer. In some cases I found that this business was carried on in bed-rooms, which consequently became very close and unhealthy, from the high temperature maintained by the stoves, and the want of ventilation.': Babbage, *Report to the General Board of Health*, p.6.
11. Babbage also noted the 'huge hollows and vast spoil heaps' on the moor round Haworth, marking the extensive workings for flagstones and ashlar blocks: *ibid.*, p.4. The state of the oat crop is annually reported in the local newspapers and the accounts of the Keighley Agriculture Show, which began in 1843, reveal that the Haworth area was renowned for its pigs: see, for example, *Halifax Guardian*, 15 Oct. 1846, p.7. For the trades and professions in Haworth in 1822 see Baines, *History, Directory and Gazetteer of the County of York*, i, 519.
12. L&D, pp.204–6, have a highly romanticized account of the Brontës' arrival at Haworth via Cullingworth and what they call 'Brae' (Brow) moor but there is no evidence that they came this way rather than the more direct route through Denholme. According to the 1771 map

of the area, they could have travelled from Thornton to Denholme Gate, then taken the turnpike road to the Flappit and turned down Brow into Haworth. It is not clear when the road between Denholme and Oxenhope was built; it is not on this map, but is on the 1850 one. Either way, there was no need to detour though Cullingworth: T. Jeffery, *Maps of Yorkshire* (1771); 6-inch Ordnance Survey Map, 1850.

13. ECG to [John Forster], [September 1853]: [C&P, p.244].
14. In my account of Haworth I have drawn from a variety of sources, including personal observation over the last twenty-odd years and information garnered from Haworth residents. For the identification of places in and information on Brontë Haworth I have consulted nineteenth-century photographs in the archives of the BPM and maps in the Keighley Reference Library, particularly the 1850 map drawn up to accompany Babbage's *Report to the General Board of Health*, and also the collection made by Steven Wood of Haworth. In addition, I owe an immense debt to the late Eunice Skirrow of Haworth, a dear friend and Honorary Secretary of the Brontë Society, whose unrivalled knowledge of the history of Haworth was the result of years of research as well as her descent from the family of Martha Brown, the Brontës' servant; she walked me round Haworth tirelessly, pointing out what remains of its Brontë past.
15. Sarah Fermi, 'A "Religious" Family Disgraced', *BST*:20:5:291; CB, wedding card list, June 1854: MS Bon 126, BPM, [*L&L*, iv, 132].
16. Davids & Moore, *Haworth in Times Past*, pp.5, 12, 13, 15, 24–5. Principally a collection of nineteenth-century photographs, this book is an invaluable source of material on old Haworth. See also Babbage, *Report to the General Board of Health*, map and p.16; Haworth Census, 1851. The farmhouse which worked Haworth Fair fields can still be seen, sandwiched between Main Street and the by-pass.
17. West Lane and Back Lane were 'macadamized' as early as 1850: Babbage, *Report to the General Board of Health*, pp.18, 26.
18. *Ibid.*, p.13.
19. Davids & Moore, *Haworth in Times Past*, p.26. 'Brandy Row' and the other houses on the lower side of Main Street have suffered the same fate as those in Changegate: they have been demolished and the land turned into carparks.
20. Babbage, *Report to the General Board of Health*, pp.14–15. A number of houses on West Lane retain their cellar entrances with separate numbering from the door at street level.
21. *Ibid.*, pp.14–18 and illustration.
22. *Ibid.*, pp.12–13.
23. *Ibid.*, p.26. Bad though the mortality figures were, it should be pointed out that Bradford

and Keighley had had similar ones in the past; Haworth was simply late in tackling the problem. According to Babbage's mortality rate tables, at least two of the six Brontë children should have died before they were six; in fact Maria was eleven, Elizabeth ten. The average age at death was twenty-five, so Charlotte at thirty-eight, Branwell at thirty-one, Emily at thirty and Anne at twenty-nine, all exceeded the statistical average.

24. Steven Wood, unpublished map of Haworth correlating the Babbage Report map with the tithe award and census returns: copy in the BPM; Baines, *History, Directory and Gazetteer of the County of Yorkshire* (1822), i, 519.

25. Church of St Michael, Haworth: Plan of graves proposed to be disturbed and covered, 1879: MS RD/AF/2/7/3 Plan F, Ripon Diocesan Archives, WYAS, Leeds. The Brontë vault, containing the bodies of Aunt Branwell and all the Brontës, except Anne, who died and was buried in Scarborough, was in the west corner of the old church. It was sealed over when the new church was built and a brass plaque in the floor near the Brontë Memorial Chapel now marks its site. There was an outcry against the demolition of the old church but sentimental attachment to the 'Brontë church' was no argument against that of building a bigger and better church 'to the greater glory of God'. The Reverend John Wade, who resented his predecessor's fame, which attracted people to the church who only wanted to see the 'Brontë pew', was supported by the Merralls, who gave £5,000 for a new church: Memorials & Petitions to the Bishop of Ripon against the demolition of Haworth Church: MS RD/AF/2/7/3, Ripon Diocesan Archives, WYAS, Leeds; letters and editorials in the *Bradford Observer*, 10 April–21 June 1879. For the closing services at Haworth Church see *ibid.*, 15 Sept. 1879, p.3.

26. The 'intolerable nuisance' was ended in the autumn of 1866 when the buildings were purchased and demolished by the Reverend John Wade; the church gates were reset in the space created. The whole transaction cost Mr Wade £330: MS notes in the front of the Register of Burials, 1854–84, Haworth Church.

27. A number of the pew doors were preserved: HAOBP:C16, 17, 19, 27 & 28, BPM. Some pew receipts are also extant: MS BS x, H, BPM. Abraham Holroyd, quoted in Scruton, pp.113–15; Emily Dowson, 'A Visit to Haworth in 1866', *BST*:15:78:256.

28. [Charles Hale], 'An American Visitor at Haworth, 1861', *BST*:15:77:134. The sounding board was a canopy over the pulpit which projected the parson's voice forward towards his congregation. The text 'To me, to live is Christ, to die is gain' was Grimshaw's favourite and appears in the Wesleyan Methodist chapel he built in Haworth and on what appears to be his own teapot. The teapot, inscribed on one side,

'To Me To live is Christ to die is Gain' and on the other 'Wm. Grimshaw. A. B. Haworth', is in the Brontë Parsonage Museum. It is usually referred to as Aunt Branwell's, under the mistaken impression that she was an out-and-out Methodist and would therefore have welcomed this link with Grimshaw. She was, of course, no more a Methodist than Patrick, and it seems likely that the teapot was handed down from Grimshaw to his successors at the parsonage: [JB *ST*, no.5].

29. EN, Reminiscences: MS pp.63–4, KSC, [*BST*:2:10:81–2].

30. *Ibid.*, p.64; Abraham Holroyd, describing a visit to Haworth in the summer of 1853, says 'he delivered an extempore sermon, devoid of all oratorical display, and remarkable for studied simplicity': Scruton, pp.113–15. PB, *The Maid of Killarney*, p.131, [*Brontëana*, p.185].

31. The plaque over the door of the school read: 'This National Church Sunday School is under the management of trustees of whom the Incumbent for the time being is one. It was erected AD 1832 by Voluntary Subscription and by a grant from the National Society in London. Train up a child in the way he should go and when he is old he will not depart from it. Prov. xxii.6.' The barn is marked on the map accompanying Babbage's *Report to the General Board of Health* and also appears on certain old photographs of Haworth Parsonage.

32. For the closure of the churchyard see below, p.957 n.56; for the planting of trees in November 1864 see MS note at front of the Register of Burials, 1854–84, Haworth Church.

33. ECG to [John Forster], [September 1853]: [C& P, p.243].

34. Plan of Proposed Extension to Haworth Parsonage, 1872–8: MS BS ix, H, BPM. The extension demolished Patrick's back kitchen, turned the kitchen itself into a lobby for the new dining room and caused the realignment of the old garden wall, pushing it further out into Church Lane to accommodate the new wing. Upstairs, the main back bedroom lost its mullioned window, facing out over the moors, as this external wall now became an internal one with a door knocked through to give access to the bedrooms and bathroom created in the new wing. The Reverend John Wade, who carried out these alterations, had a private income as well as his salary and was therefore in a position to carry out the work, unlike Patrick. I am assuming that the parsonage had the same external arrangements as the two houses built on almost identical lines in Haworth, Bridge House, at the foot of Bridgehouse Lane, and the Manor House, at the top of Lord Lane. The existence of narrow mullions is confirmed by the remnants of a mullioned window found in the small back bedroom, identified by Mrs Gaskell as 'the servants' room'. It is possible that there was a room over the back kitchen built on by the Brontës

and the servants may have slept there when there were more people living in the house.

35. The back kitchen is marked in outline on the map accompanying Babbage's *Report to the General Board of Health*; the tall narrow chimney is clearly visible in many old photographs taken before the trees were planted in the churchyard in November 1864. What appears to be a high, two-storey extension at the back of the house may have been the back kitchen or possibly the peat store next to it. The latter is, I believe, the small extension marked on the Babbage map and not the room inside the house, which later became Mr Nicholls' study. Though it is next to impossible to tell for certain, it seems most likely that the peat store was a single-storey lean-to type building in the back yard, whose shape is outlined by ivy on the photographs, and the back kitchen was the two-storey building. The two-seater privy is remembered by older inhabitants of Haworth and the existence of the well is confirmed by a note referring to its being cleaned out in September 1847, when eight decomposing tin cans which had turned the water yellow were removed: PB, Account Book, [c.1845–61]: BS MS 173 p.8, BPM.

36. There is supposed to have been a 'gate of the dead', at the foot of the garden giving access to the churchyard, through which the Brontë coffins were carried to the vault under the church. The evidence for this is unsatisfactory. The wall itself has been rebuilt many times so that, despite the plaque, the outlines visible there are not genuine. It only appears clearly on Mrs Gaskell's notoriously inaccurate drawing of the parsonage and church which appeared in the front of her *Life*. It may appear on one photograph taken from the hilltop beyond the churchyard, which seems to be the basis of Mrs Gaskell's drawing, but this may only be a tall gravestone. It does not appear on any other photographs, though the angle from which they are taken would not make it immediately obvious. Nor does it appear on the map accompanying Babbage's *Report to the General Board of Health*, where, however, the semicircular path in the parsonage garden and the paths across the churchyard are clearly marked; no path to a gate is marked on either side of the wall. The other obvious difficulty about a 'gate of the dead' at that point in the garden wall is that, if used, it would have meant walking across several graves, even in the Brontës' day.

37. ECG, *Life*, pp.3–4; Dowson, 'A Visit to Haworth in 1866', *BST*:15:78:255; CB to EN, 25 March 1844: MS BS 50.8 p.1, BPM, [*L&L*, ii, 5]. There is a memo in Patrick's notebook, 'I will never flag the garden walks – since, Ch[arlotte]e, & M[arth]a, [cum?] dixerunt, ut, it would cost £5 – look worse, be more slippery, in frost – require washing, & produce weeds, between the joinings – B. 1851.': PB, Account Book, [c.1845–61]: MS BS 173 p.12, BPM.

38. ECG, *Life*, p.4.

39. EN, Reminiscences: MS p.59, KSC, [*BST*:2:10:76]. Characteristically, Ellen implies that she was responsible for the innovation of curtains which were adopted by Charlotte, some time after 1849, during one of Ellen's visits: 'it did not please her father, but it was not forbidden'. Patrick's concern to avoid anything inflammable in a house where there were children (later to be short-sighted adults) and open flames because of fires and candles, arose from the high number of fatalities in Haworth caused by burning in domestic accidents. He wrote to the newspapers on the subject in the hope of alerting others to the danger: see PB to *Leeds Mercury*, 16 March 1844, p.6. 'Damask and Muslin Window Hangings' are mentioned in Mr Cragg's advertisement for the sale by auction of the contents of Haworth Parsonage, 1 Oct. 1861: MS BS x, H, BPM.

40. EN, Reminiscences: MS pp.59–60, KSC, [*BST*:2:10:76–9].

41. ECG, *Life*, p.28; ECG to [John Forster], [September 1853]: [C&P, p.243]. Mrs Gaskell describes the sitting room as being larger than the study but this was only effected in 1850 when substantial alterations were made to the house, including moving the interior wall of the sitting room further out into the hall; prior to that, as one can tell from the positioning of the arch in the hall, the two front rooms were the same size. See also map accompanying Babbage's *Report to the General Board of Health*.

42. PB to John Buckworth, 27 Nov. 1821: *The Cottage Magazine* (1822), p.244, [*L&L*, i, 58].

43. Register of Burials, 1813–36, Register of Baptisms, 1813–29, Register of Marriages, 1813–37, Haworth Church. For example, in 1820–3 alone, Patrick baptized 24 children on 24 July 1820, 19 on 16 Oct. 1820, 17 on 25 Dec. 1820, 19 on 24 April 1821, 20 on 15 Oct. 1821 and 20 the following day, 16 on 9 April 1822, 30 on 31 March 1823, 21 on 22 July 1823 and 17 on 14 Oct. 1823. Three children in each of the Hodgson, Ogden and Sugden families were baptized on 15 Oct. 1821 and 15 Sept. 1822. Unmarried mothers seem to appear on virtually every page of the register in certain years.

44. Register of Burials, 1813–36, Haworth Church; Register of Marriages, 1813–37, Haworth Church.

45. James Parker, Petition to the Committee of the Charity at Harrogate for the purpose of enabling the Afflicted and Distressed Poor to receive the Benefit of the Waters at that place, 6 June 1820: MS 94D85/10/1/3, WYAS, Bradford.

46. Firth, 6–7, 21 June, 8, 11–12 Sept., 4–6 Nov. 1820; *Leeds Mercury*, 10 June 1820, p.3. The diary says that Patrick was going to the visitation at Leeds but this must be a mistake as the visitation, held by Archdeacon Markham, took place in Bradford Parish Church.

47. Firth, 13, 21, 22, 27 Dec. 1820.

48. *Ibid.*, 2, 4 Jan. 1821. Patrick stayed a few days to

comfort the bereaved widow and daughter.

49. PB to John Buckworth, 27 Nov. 1821: *The Cottage Magazine* (1822), p.245, [*L&L*, i, 58–9]; ECG, *Life*, p.29. Mrs Gaskell calls it an internal cancer; having given birth to six children in as many years at a comparatively late age, Maria was probably susceptible to uterine cancer.

50. PB, notes in Thomas John Graham, *Modern Domestic Medicine* (London, Simpkin & Marshall et al., 1826), pp.221,220: MS HAOBP:bb210, BPM. In 1846, after discussion with Mr Wilson who removed the cataracts from his eyes, Patrick altered his first note to read: 'As Mr Wilson, surgeon, said, & I have read, and seen, <sometimes> frequently but not always – when <a> cancer, is radically cut out in one part, it breaks out in another – B.': *ibid.*, p.220.

51. PB to John Buckworth, 27 Nov. 1821: *The Cottage Magazine* (1822), p.245, [*L&L*, i, 58–9]; ECG, *Life*, p.30.

52. Register of Burials, 1813–36, Register of Baptisms, 1813–29, Register of Marriages, 1813–37, Haworth Church.

53. PB to John Buckworth, 27 Nov. 1821: *The Cottage Magazine* (1822), p.245, [*L&L*, i, 58].

54. Firth, 9, 21 Feb., 17 April, 26 May, 22 June 1821. Though not mentioned in her diary, her cash account at the end of the book for March shows 3/4d. 'expenses to Haworth'; the postchaise in which she collected Maria and Elizabeth cost 10/- to hire, according to her cash account for May.

55. John Fennell went all the way to London to see William Morgan when his son-in-law fell ill of a bilious fever there in March 1818, so it is inconceivable that he would not have visited Haworth, twelve miles away, when his niece was mortally ill: Elizabeth Wadsworth, 'Diary', *Transactions of the Halifax Antiquarian Society*, 1943, p.130.

56. PB to John Buckworth, 27 Nov. 1821: *The Cottage Magazine* (1822), p.246, [*L&L*, i, 59–60].

57. ECG, *Life*, p.33. The family are identified as the Greenwoods by Sarah Fermi in 'A "Religious" Family Disgraced', *BST*:20:5:294.

58. PB to John Buckworth, 27 Nov. 1821: *The Cottage Magazine* (1822), p.245, [*L&L*, i, 58–60].

59. *Ibid.*

60. *Leeds Mercury*, 18 Aug. 1821, pp.2, 3; Venn, pt ii, vi, 189.

61. PB to John Buckworth, 27 Nov. 1821: *The Cottage Magazine* (1822), p.245–6, [*L&L*, i, 59].

62. ECG to Catherine Winkworth [25 Aug. 1850], [*C&P*, p.124]. The nurse's evidence is extremely unreliable, but the fact that Maria was distressed by the sight of her children during her illness is borne out by the other servants. Nancy Garrs apparently told Mrs Chadwick that 'Mrs Brontë was to the very last interested in her children, though she could only see them at intervals, and one at a time, as it upset her': Chadwick, p.63.

63. L.A. Herbert, 'Charlotte Brontë: Pleasant Interview with the Old French Governess of this Famous Author', Special Correspondence of 'The Post', no.7: typescript of original cutting in the possession of Dr Stull, a descendant of Sarah Garrs, BPM.

64. Register of Baptisms, 1813–29, Register of Burials, 1813–36, Haworth Church. There is no evidence at all to suggest that only Maria and Elizabeth attended the funeral with their father and aunt, as L&D, p.230, state: at this time, when death was a much more everyday occurrence, children were not shielded from either the deathbed or the funeral as they are today.

65. PB to John Buckworth, 27 Nov. 1821: *The Cottage Magazine* (1822), p.246, [*L&L*, i, 59].

66. Patrick started to take the duties again on 29 September with two baptisms and two burials on that day: Register of Baptisms, 1813–29, Register of Burials, 1813–36, Haworth Church. For his financial problems see PB to John Buckworth, 27 Nov. 1821: *The Cottage Magazine* (1822), p.244, [*L&L*, i, 59]. For the annuity see Ivy Holgate, 'The Branwells at Penzance', *BST*:13:70:430. An annuity, by its very nature, ceased on the death of the recipient.

67. PB to John Buckworth, 27 Nov. 1821: *The Cottage Magazine* (1822), p.246, [*L&L*, i, 59–60]. Elizabeth Firth recorded in her cash account for 1821 at the back of her diary for that year that she had given two guineas to the 'Subscription for Mr Bronte'. Though it is likely that Mrs Firth, Dr & Miss Outhwaite and Mrs Atkinson (the former Frances Walker) all joined in the subscription they could not have been the sole contributors to such an enormous sum, as L&D, p.233, suggest. Patrick had plenty of other wealthy friends, including the Rands, the Lamberts, the Tetleys and, of course, his clerical acquaintances.

68. PB to John Buckworth, 27 Nov. 1821: *The Cottage Magazine* (1822), pp.246–7, [*L&L*, i, 60]. For Miss Currer's philanthropy see below, pp.119, 928 n.5.

69. Patrick noted, 'I paid Wm Tetley Esqr no–46– Westcat, Bradford, Yorkshire, the £50:0:0, which I owed him, in 1821, in the presence of Mrs Tetly, & his son, and burnt the note'; as he then goes on to say, 'Mr Tetley made me a present of half a dozen of port, in Augt 1830 =', it seems likely that Patrick was repaying the debt at about this time: PB, Account Book, [*c*.1845–61]: MS BS 173 inside front cover, BPM, [L&D, p.233].

70. Firth, 8–10 Dec. 1821. It was a family tradition, noted by her grandson, that Patrick had asked Elizabeth Firth to marry him: Moore Smith, 'The Brontës at Thornton', *The Bookman*, October 1904, p.18. The sequence of events recorded in her diary, including the unusual noting of a receipt of a letter from Patrick, her writing 'a last letter' to him two days later and the two-year breach which followed, all suggest that a proposal did take place: Firth, 12, 14 Dec. 1821, 4 Oct. 1823.

71. James Clarke Franks actually came to dinner on the night Elizabeth Firth rejected Patrick: *ibid.*, 14 Dec. 1821; Peters, *Unquiet Soul*, p.4, says that Patrick was rejected in 'a friendly but decisive way', but a two-year refusal to have anything to do with him seems anything but 'friendly'. It was not until 4 October 1823 that Patrick called to 'renew acquaintance' with Elizabeth Firth; he was invited to stay for a couple of nights, so presumably the quarrel was patched up at this point: Firth, 4 Oct. 1823.

72. ECG, *Life*, 29–30. The older biographies, without exception, follow her line as does Peters, *Unquiet Soul*, pp.6–8. Chitham, *A Life of Emily Brontë*, pp.19–23, seems to believe all the stories against Patrick and even Fraser, pp.27–9, with some qualifications, accepts the subdued view of life at the parsonage.

73. [Nancy Garrs], *Illustrated Weekly Telegraph*, 10 Jan. 1885, p.1; Nancy had earlier reported that Aunt Branwell was a 'bit of a tyke', keeping the key to the cellar herself and personally dispensing a gill of beer to each of the servants daily: Helen Arnold, 'The Reminiscences of Emma Huidekoper Cortazzo: a friend of Ellen Nussey', [*BST*: 13:68:227].

74. ECG, *Life*, p.30.

75. PB to ECG, 7 April 1857: MS EL B121 p.1, Rylands, [*BST*:8:44:127]; [Nancy Garrs], *Illustrated Weekly Telegraph*, 10 Jan. 1885, p.1; William Dearden to *Bradford Observer*, 20 Aug. 1857, p.8. A meat jack was the mechanism for turning a spit to roast meat.

76. See, for example, EJB, Diary Paper, 24 Nov. 1834: MS Bon 131, BPM, [JB *ST*, no. 11]; CB to EJB, 1 Oct. 1843: MS n.l., [*L&L*, i, 304–5]; EN, Reminiscences: MS p.62, KSC, [*BST*:2:10:81].

77. ECG, *Life*, p.33.

78. *Ibid.*, p.32; PB to ECG, 7 April 1857: MS EL B121 p.3, Rylands, [*BST*:8:44:128]; [Nancy Garrs], *Illustrated Weekly Telegraph*, 10 Jan. 1885, p.1; Lady Kay Shuttleworth, whose home at Gawthorpe Hall was close to Burnley where the dismissed nurse lived, passed on the anecdotes to Mrs Gaskell when she and Charlotte were her guests on a visit to the Lakes in 1850: ECG to Catherine Winkworth, [25 Aug. 1850]: [C&P, pp.124–5].

79. William Dearden to *Bradford Observer*, 20 Aug. 1857, p.8; [Nancy Garrs], *Illustrated Weekly Telegraph*, 10 Jan. 1885, p.1.

80. William Dearden to *Bradford Observer*, 20 Aug. 1857, p.8. Though Mrs Gaskell protested that Charlotte herself had told her the anecdote, Patrick himself totally denied it, telling Mrs Gaskell, 'With respect to tearing my wife's slik [sic] gown, my dear little daughter must have been misinform'd' and pointing out that he always advised his children to wear silk or wool as being less inflammable: PB to ECG, 30 July 1857: MS EL B121 p.2, Rylands, [*BST*:8:44:129].

81. ECG, *Life*, p.33.

82. William Dearden to *Bradford Observer*, 20 Aug. 1857, p.8.

83. William Dearden to *Bradford Observer*, 27 June 1861, p.7.

84. William Dearden quotes an American review of ECG, *Life*, which described Patrick as 'this moody, wretched parson, a man who, like a mad dog, ought to have been shot, or like a victim of its bite, smothered between two feather beds. Society is far too tolerant of these domestic hyenas, who are perpetual glooms upon their households'; Maria is represented as 'this poor, persecuted woman [who] died, a victim to the dogged, gloomy asceticism of the believer in the Thirty-Nine Articles'. Though the review is an extreme one, it represents the popular view of Patrick, derived from Mrs Gaskell, which persists today: William Dearden to *Bradford Observer*, 20 Aug. 1857, p.8.

85. William Dearden to *Bradford Observer*, 27 June 1861, p.7.

86. PB to ECG, 24 July 1855: MS EL B121 pp.2–3, Rylands, [*BST*:8:43:91–2]; ECG, *Life*, pp.35–6.

87. PB to ECG, 30 July 1855: MS EL B121 pp.5–7, Rylands, [*BST*:8:43:94–5]; ECG, *Life*, p.36.

88. Sarah Garrs, quoted in Harland, *Charlotte Brontë at Home*, p.32.

89. *Ibid.*, pp.17–24.

90. Mrs Chadwick, possibly on the authority of Nancy Garrs, says that Patrick 'made a practice of telling them stories to illustrate a geographical or history lesson, and they had to write it out the next morning. Consequently they thought it out in bed – a habit Charlotte continued all her life in connection with her stories': Chadwick, p.63. Dearden also says, 'Mr Brontë was in the habit of giving instruction to his children at stated times during the day, adapted to their respective ages and capacities. He had too high an appreciation of the value of education to neglect his duty in that particular, as a father of a family': William Dearden to *Bradford Observer*, 20 Aug. 1857, p.8.

91. Herbert, 'Charlotte Brontë: Pleasant Interview with the Old French Governess of This Famous Author', special correspondence to 'The Post', n.d.: typescript copy from the scrap book of Mary Stull, BPM.

92. EN, Reminiscences, [*L&L*, i, 97]; ECG, *Life*, p.33.

93. PB to John Buckworth, 27 Nov. 1821: *The Cottage Magazine* (1822), p.245, [*L&L*, i, 60]; ECG, *Life*, pp.38, 50, 124–5.

94. Sarah Garrs, quoted in Harland, *Charlotte Brontë at Home*, pp.31–2. For the Brontës' children's books, see below, p.150.

95. ECG, *Life*, pp.29, 35; Harland, *Charlotte Brontë at Home*, pp.19–20; Peters, *Unquiet Soul*, pp.6–7.

96. In 1829 Charlotte wrote that they took both the *Leeds Intelligencer* (Tory) and the *Leeds Mercury* (Whig) as well as seeing three other papers a week: CB, History of the Year, 12 March 1829: MS Bon 80(11), BPM [CA, i, 4]; ECG, *Life*, p.37.

97. *Leeds Mercury*, 20 July 1822, p.3; the exact date of the death of Patrick's mother is not known

but L&D, p.25, identify if as taking place in 1822.

98. *Leeds Mercury,* 21 Dec. 1822, p.3. The Reverend William Carus Wilson was founder and governor of the Clergy Daughters' School at Cowan Bridge, see below, pp.120ff.

99. *Leeds Mercury,* 8 Feb. 1823, p.3.

100. Isabella Dury to Miss Mariner, 14 Feb. 1823: MS BS ix, D p.1, BPM, [L&D, p.237].

101. PB to Mrs Burder, 21 April 1823: MS n.l., [*L& L*, i, 61].

102. MS Minute Book of the Wesleyan Academy, Woodhouse Grove: MS at Woodhouse Grove

[11 April, July 1823]; Methodist Conference, 30 July 1823: *Minutes of the Methodist Conferences,* (London, Wesleyan Conference Office, 1864), v, 419.

103. PB to Mary Burder, 28 July 1823: MS n.l., [*L& L*, i, 62–3].

104. PB to Mary Burder, 1 Jan. 1824: MS n.l., [*L& L*, i, 67].

105. Mary Burder to PB, 8 Aug. 1823: MS n.l., [*L& L*, i, 65–6].

106. PB to Mary Burder, 1 Jan. 1824: MS n.l., [*L& L*, i, 67].

107. *Ibid.,* i, 68.

CHAPTER FIVE

Title: CB, *Jane Eyre,* p.50.

1. Firth, 4, 6 Oct 1823.

2. Though Florence Nightingale is famous for changing Victorian attitudes to nursing, this was not to happen till the 1850s; in the earlier period nursing was still a despised profession, restricted exclusively to the working classes.

3. PB, *The Maid of Killarney,* p.115, [*Brontëana,* p.178]. In fairness to Patrick it should be pointed out that he qualifies the remark by saying that although, as a general rule, women should not be educated like men, there were honourable exceptions. Nor did Patrick apply this rule to his own daughters, who were encouraged in their pursuit of learning well beyond the standards of the day.

4. Richmal Mangnall, *Historical and Miscellaneous Questions for the Use of Young People* (London, Longman *et al.,* 1813). The Brontës had their own copy of this book, which Charlotte and Anne used at Roe Head: MS HAOBP:bb215, BPM.

5. The information on Richmal Mangnall is garnered from her obituary in the *Leeds Mercury,* 13 May 1820, p.3.

6. Elizabeth Firth, Prize Cards, 11 April 1811, 25 March 1813: MS 58 C5.i & ii, Sheffield.

7. Firth, 1812, 1813.

8. See, for instance, WG *AB,* p.17.

9. PB to ECG, 20 June 1855: MS EL B121 p.4, Rylands, [*BST*:8:43:89].

10. *Leeds Intelligencer,* 4 Dec. 1823, p.1. A pseudo-prospectus, drawn up as a joke, which features a 'Singing and Scourge-Mistress', has unfortunately been accepted at face value by a number of biographers after it was published by the Brontë Society: Edith Weir, 'Cowan Bridge: New Light from Old Documents', *BST*:11:56:20–1; Lane, *The Brontë Story,* pp.55–6; Pollard, *The Landscape of the Brontës,* p.57. The authenticity of the prospectus was first questioned by Myra Curtis, 'Cowan Bridge School: an old prospectus re-examined', *BST*:12:63:187–92.

11. *Leeds Intelligencer,* 4 Dec. 1823, p.1.

12. A typical school of this period like, for example, the Robinsons' Academy for young ladies at

Spring Wood Field near Huddersfield, cost £27 per annum, with an additional one guinea entrance fee and 14/- a quarter charged for laundry: *Leeds Intelligencer,* 1 June 1824, p.1.

13. *Ibid.,* 6 Nov. 1823, p.3.

14. *Ibid.,* 22 Jan. 1824, p.2.

15. Charlotte was at least aware of Charles Dickens' savage indictment of Yorkshire schools in *Nicholas Nickleby,* published in 1838–9; she scrawled 'Dotheboys Hall' and 'Squeers' on the back of one of her manuscripts: CB, 'I have now written a great many books', n.d.: MS Bon 125(1) verso, BPM.

16. *Leeds Intelligencer,* 4 Dec. 1823, p.1.

17. Carus Wilson preached regularly, for instance in Keighley, on behalf of the Bible Society, Society for Promoting Christianity among the Jews, the Keighley National Schools and Sunday Schools: see *Leeds Intelligencer,* 30 Dec. 1822, p.3; 25 Oct. 1827, p.3; *Leeds Mercury,* 21 Oct. 1826, p.3; 28 Oct. 1826, p.3; 25 Oct. 1828, p.3; 30 Oct. 1830, p.3.

18. Theodore Dury, his wife, his sister and his father were all either donors or subscribers to the Clergy Daughters' School by 1827, when their names were included in the lists appended to the Report; by this time Theodore Dury was also one of the trustees of the school: [*Report on the*] *School for Clergymen's Daughters* (Kirkby Lonsdale, 1827), pp.3, 14.

19. See, for example, WG *CB,* pp.1–16; WG *PBB,* pp.9–10; Chitham, *A Life of Emily Brontë,* pp.29–47.

20. ECG, *Life,* p.39.

21. CB to WSW, 4 Jan. 1848: MS HM 26008, Huntington, [*L&L,* ii, 174].

22. ECG, *Life,* p.39.

23. *Ibid.,* pp.38–49.

24. *Ibid.,* p.41; CB, *Jane Eyre,* p.48; This appears to have been common practice; at Woodhouse Grove, as early as 1812, each boy had 'a piece of ground about three yards long and two yards and a half broad for a garden, which we are to cultivate ourselves': John S. Stamp to his father, 29 Feb. 1812, [Slugg, *Woodhouse Grove School,* p.340].

25. See above, pp.53, 54.

26. Charlotte's rebellion against being treated as an object of charity is obvious throughout the Lowood chapters of *Jane Eyre*.

27. [*Report on the*] *School for Clergymen's Daughters*, p.5.

28. *Leeds Intelligencer*, 6 Nov. 1823, p.3; Slugg, *Woodhouse Grove School*, p.165, referring to the period 1822–8 when the boys were provided with a 'sealskin' cap, dark blue cloth jacket and corduroy trousers which had to last the year.

29. Admissions Register, Clergy Daughters' School, 1824–39: MS in CRO, Kendal, hereafter referred to as 'Admissions Register'. Pupil nos. 1–44 inclusive: Charlotte was no. 30, Emily no. 44; Miss Evans, quoted in ECG, *Life*, p.48. Miss Evans was one of the superintendents of the school during the Brontë period.

30. Admissions Register, pupil no. 38; Charlotte Hane, aged 22, is no. 37; PB to ECG, 30 July 1855: MS EL B121 p.1, Rylands, [*BST*:8:43:93]. Mrs Gaskell wrongly states that Mellany Hane was paid for by her brother; according to the Admissions Register, he only paid for her elder sister and Mellany's fees were paid by the Clergy Orphans' Society. Charlotte was not the youngest girl at the school as WG, *CB*, p.9 states: two six-year-olds, Elizabeth Hayes and Martha Thompson, were already there when she came and in less than two months she was joined by the six-year-old Emily and three other eight-year-olds: Admissions Register, pupils nos. 16, 26, 35, 42, 43.

31. CB, *Jane Eyre*, pp.52–3.

32. *Leeds Intelligencer*, 22 Jan. 1824, p.2. At Bowes school, 300 boys washed without running water in a single horse trough and shared two towels between them: *ibid.*, 6 Nov. 1823, p.3; Slugg, *Woodhouse Grove School*, pp.22–3. In the period 1855–61, one boy complained that when the open-air water tank was low, the washing water had 'a number of grubs, worms, and decaying leaves' in it: *Woodhouse Grove School 1812–1962*, p.32.

33. CB, *Jane Eyre*, pp.44–52.

34. Guide Leaflet, Parish Church of St John the Baptist, Tunstall, Cumbria.

35. 'CMR' to ABN, 26 May 1857: MS p.4, in private hands. Part of this letter was quoted, with 'CMR's' permission, by Nicholls in his letter of 29 May 1857 which was published in the *Leeds Mercury*, 2 June 1857, p.1, *Leeds Intelligencer*, 6 June 1857, p.10 and *Halifax Guardian*, 6 June 1857, p.7. I have been unable to identify 'CMR' as there are no girls with those initials, or the initials 'CM' as forenames, in the Admissions Register; she was living in Leeds when she wrote to Arthur Nicholls.

36. 'Clericus' to ABN, July 1857: MS p.3, in private hands. It is worth noting that Charlotte's supporters nearly all use initials or pseudonyms, rather than their own names. As Mrs Gaskell told George Smith, 'many who are now offering me testimony in proof of my correctness are

poor people, – I mean governesses, struggling surgeons' wives, schoolmistresses &c. – who say I *may* make use of their names, if absolutely necessary – but that it may seriously injure them if I do. And of course I must do anything rather than bring them into trouble': ECG to GS, 5 June [1857]: [C&P, p.451].

37. J. S. Stamp to his father, 11 April 1812, [Slugg, *Woodhouse Grove School*, pp.341–2].

38. *Woodhouse Grove School 1812–1962*, pp.19, 23; Slugg, *Woodhouse Grove School*, pp.77, 183; Firth, 1812–13.

39. CB, *Jane Eyre*, pp.46, 51–2.

40. ECG, Note to the Third Edition of *Life*, quoted in CB, *Jane Eyre*, Clarendon edn, Appx ii, p.620; 'Clericus' to ABN, July 1857: MS p.3, in private hands.

41. *Ibid.*, p.2. 'Clericus' was writing on behalf of his wife. When Arthur Nicholls quoted this letter in his own letter to the *Halifax Guardian*, 18 July 1857, p.3, another former pupil, Sarah Baldwin, replied identifying the sisters as the daughters of the vicar of Olney and herself quoted a letter from 'E' stating that after this unfortunate incident, Carus Wilson allowed her bread and milk for breakfast: *Halifax Guardian*, 1 Aug. 1857, p.6. From the school register it is possible to identify the daughters of the vicar of Olney as Elizabeth and Maria Gauntlett, who were admitted to the school on 4 February 1826, aged fifteen and thirteen respectively. They both left on 21 June 1830, Elizabeth, the 'E' of Sarah Baldwin's letter, to a situation as a private governess and Maria, the wife of 'Clericus', as a teacher in a Manchester school: Admissions Register, nos. 81, 82.

42. 'A.H.' to *Littell's Living Age*, 15 Sept. 1855, [*BST*:16:83:210]. Though 'A.H.' is frequently identified as Miss Evans, she was in fact Miss Andrews, a teacher who was temporarily superintendent at the opening of the school until the appointment of Miss Evans. Arthur Bell Nicholls and Mrs Gaskell identified her as the 'Miss Scatcherd' of *Jane Eyre*. She later married a Mr Hill and went to live in the United States. Though she does not appear to have recognized her own portrait in *Jane Eyre*, her son evidently did and was furious. Miss Evans, who, like her fictional character, 'Miss Temple', left the school in 1826 to marry the Reverend J. Connor of Melton Mowbray, died just before the publication of Mrs Gaskell's *Life of Charlotte Brontë*. Brett Harrison, 'The Real "Miss Temple"', *BST*:16:85:361–4; T. J. Winnifrith, 'Miss Scatcherd's Identity', *BST*:16:85:364.; ECG to GS [mid-Aug. 1857], [C&P, p.465].

43. ABN to *Leeds Intelligencer*, 23 May 1857, p.7.

44. 'CMR' to ABN, 26 May 1857: MS pp.1–3, in private hands. These sections of this letter were quoted, with 'CMR's' permission, by Nicholls in his letter of 29 May 1857 which was published in the *Leeds Mercury*, 2 June 1857, p.1, *Leeds Intelligencer*, 6 June 1857, p.10 and *Halifax Guardian*, 6 June 1857, p.7. There was once a rebellion at Woodhouse Grove when the boys refused to eat

for three days after the cook was seen using the porridge ladle in the swill tub: *Woodhouse Grove School 1812–1962*, pp.23–5.

45. 'A. H.' to *Littell's Living Age*, 15 Sept. 1855, [*BST*:16:83:210].

46. Slugg, *Woodhouse Grove School*, p.160. This was still better than the Bowes school, where the boys had meat three times a week, with cakes made of water, meal and potatoes the other days: for tea on Sunday evening they got 'the skimming of the pot' which was usually full of maggots: *Leeds Intelligencer*, 6 Nov. 1823, p.3.

47. Sarah Bicker died at Cowan Bridge on 29 September 1826. The eleven other contemporaries of hers who left school in ill health, six to die shortly afterwards, were (with Admissions Register no., date of departure and any marginal comment): 2, Hannah Bicker, 24 June 1827 (died 1828 'of a consumption'); 8, Mary Chester, 18 Feb. 1825 (left in ill health, died 26 April 1825); 17, Maria Brontë, 14 Feb. 1825 (left in ill health, died 8 May 1825 'Decline'); 18, Elizabeth Brontë, 31 May 1825 (left in ill health, died 15 June 1825 'in decline'); 19, Elizabeth Robinson, 1 March 1825 (left in ill health, died 29 April 1825 'in a decline'); 22, Isabella Whaley, 2 April 1825 (left 'in good health', died 23 April 1825 'Typhus Fever'); 32, Jane Lowry, 3 Sept. 1825 (left in ill health); 39, Ann Dockeray, 8 June 1825 (left 'with bad legs'); 45, Mary Eleanor Lowther, 27 Jan. 1825 (left in ill health 'which incapacitated her for study'); 50, Charlotte Banks, 19 May 1825 (left 'in a spinal case'); 53, Jane Allanson, 30 May 1825 ('went home ill'). The twenty who left Jan.–Sept. 1825 were, in order of their departure: 45, Mary Lowther, 27 Jan. (ill health); 17, Maria Brontë, 14 Feb. (ill health; died 8 May); 8, Mary Chester, 18 Feb. (ill health; died 26 April); 19, Elizabeth Robinson, 1 March (ill health; died 29 April); 21, Ann Whaley, 2 April; 22, Isabella Whaley, 2 April (died of typhus 23 April); [23, Phebe Whaley, [2 April] (see below)]; 50, Charlotte Banks, 19 May (ill health); 46, Clara Parker, 30 May; 53, Jane Allanson, 30 May (ill health); 18, Elizabeth Brontë, 31 May (ill health; died 15 June); 30, Charlotte Brontë, 1 June; 44, Emily Brontë, 1 June; 24, Jane Abbot, 8 June; 39, Ann Dockeray, 8 June (ill health); 34, Eliza Grover, 13 June; 35, Harriet Grover, 13 June; 31, Eliza Goodacre, 14 June; 32, Jane Lowry, 3 Sept. (ill health); 33, Mary Lowry, 3 Sept. The Whaley sisters apparently left school on 2 April, though in both Ann and Isabella's cases this has been crudely altered from 22 April, the confusion arising perhaps from the fact that Isabella died on 23 April. Though no date at all is given for Phebe's removal, it seems likely she left on the same day as her sister.

48. According to the register, two girls died at the school: Mary Tate (no. 79) 'Died of the Typhus Fever' on 14 August 1829 and Emma Tinsley (no. 177) died on 6 June 1831 'in a sure and certain hope of a better resurrection complaint con-

sumption'. Another girl, Mary Anna Clarke (no. 83), died of 'a consumption' on 11 June 1829 and as there is no note of her being sent home, she may also have died at the school. Her sister, Anne (no. 84), *was* sent home from school the day before Mary died. The names of the fifteen others who left the school in ill health, are: 94, Frances Iron, 15 Nov. 1826; 92, Anne King, 27 Dec. 1826; 103, Harriet Iron, 1827; 114, Martha Meadowcroft, 18 June 1828; 131, Mary Allen, 17 Jan. 1829; 130, Maria Forshaw, 26 Sept. 1829 (died 10 Oct.); 110, Thomasin Adin, 5 June 1830 (died 24 June 'consumption'); 135, Mary Anne Hannaford, 8 June 1830 (died 26 June); [121, Rebecca Kenney, 22 June 1830 ('Home since dead')]; [124, Mary Anne Kenney, 22 June 1830 ('Home since dead')]; 238, Maria Overend, July 1830 (died 27 July); 134, Jane Mason, 16 Oct. 1830; 146, Harriet Williams, 10 May 1831; 176, Margaret Jones, 10 May 1831 ('Went home very ill and died'); 99, Mary Hitch, 19 Nov. 1831 (died in Dec. 'consumption'). The two Kenney sisters are not noted as having been sent home in ill health so their subsequent deaths may have been unrelated to the school, particularly as no date of death is recorded. Incidentally, the register's evidence of how many pupils were sent home in ill health to die there shows that W. W. Carus Wilson was being casuistical, at the very least, in his claim that 'For the whole 35 years the school has been in existence there have been but two attacks of fever, which carried off but six pupils': W. W. Carus Wilson to the *Halifax Guardian*, 18 July 1857, p.3.

49. Pritchard, *The Story of Woodhouse Grove School*, pp.118, 123; Sale, *The History of Casterton School*, pp.18, 30.

50. Mrs Gaskell, talking of Aunt Branwell, says that the Brontës were grateful to her for enforcing habits of order, method and neatness upon them which eventually became second nature; in after life they realized the incalculable benefits of her training, for, 'with their impulsive natures, it was positive repose to have learnt implicit obedience to external laws': ECG, *Life*, pp.124–5.

51. Admissions Register, nos. 17, 18; 'A. H.' to *Littell's Living Age*, 15 Sept. 1855, [*BST*:16:83:209]. Miss Andrews said that they had both recently recovered from whooping cough and measles, but the Admissions Register only noted that they had both had whooping cough and scarlet fever. The children had all had scarlet fever in 1821, when their mother was dying: see above, p.103.

52. Admissions Register, nos. 17, 18.

53. See, for example, the lists of acquirements of the daughters of two of Patrick's friends: Margaret Plummer, aged fourteen, 'Reads very badly – Writes badly – Ciphers very little – Works pretty well – Knows nothing of Grammar, Geography, History, French, Music or Drawing'; her sister, Mary, who entered the school in 1828 aged fifteen, 'Reads, spells, &

writes very badly – works badly Knows nothing else'; similarly, ten-year-old Harriet Jenkins 'Reads badly – Writes none – Ciphers none – Works but little – Knows nothing of Grammar, Geography, History or Accomplishments': *ibid.*, nos. 9, 14, 132.

54. 'A.H' to *Littell's Living Age*, 15 Sept. 1855, [*BST*:16:83:209]; Admissions Register, nos. 17, 18; Ledger of the Clergy Daughters' School, 26 Jan. 1825: MS WDS338/1, p.13, CRO, Kendal; PB to ECG, 20 June 1855: MS EL B121 p.4, Rylands, [*BST*:8:43:89].

55. Admissions Register, nos. 9, 14. Thomas Plummer had officiated at baptisms and burials in May 1819 after Charnock's death, and as recently as 23 May 1824 had baptized three children for Patrick: Register of Baptisms, 1813–29, Register of Burials, 1813–36, Haworth Church; he is listed as headmaster of the Free Grammar School in Keighley in Pigot & Co.'s *National Commercial Directory* (1828–9), p.989. A 'small needlework' was given to Miss Dixon's cousin, Margaret, by Maria Brontë when they were both at 'Casterton' (the later name of the Clergy Daughters' School): Miss Dixon to Mr Butler Wood, 21 Oct. 1895: MS DB 28/23, WYAS, Bradford. Margaret Plummer is the only Margaret in the Admissions Register. The present is described as a needlecase in Galloway's *A Descriptive Catalogue of Objects in the Museum of the Brontë Society at Haworth*, p.27.

56. Admissions Register, no. 30; 'A.H.' to *Littell's Living Age*, 15 Sept. 1855, [*BST*:16:83:209]. 'My father and mother called to see them at school at *Casterton* on their wedding tour Sept 1824 and in my mother's account book at that time is entered 3 Miss Brontes 2/6 each': Elizabeth Franks note, n.d.: MS 58 C.1., Sheffield.

57. [*Report of the*] *School for Clergymen's Daughters*, p.5. Five weeks in the summer was standard for boarding schools as parents could not often afford to bring their children long distances home more than once a year: even then, as at Cowan Bridge, some parents had to leave their children in school throughout the annual holiday, for which they were charged a guinea. *Ibid.*, p.5; Slugg, *Woodhouse Grove School*, p.125. The overlooking of the quarterly letter home was also standard practice, *ibid.*, p.168.

58. Admissions Register, no. 30.

59. CB to WSW, 5 Nov. 1849: MS n.l., [*L&L*, iii, 34]; 'A.H.' to *Littell's Living Age*, 15 Sept. 1855, [*BST*:16:83:210].

60. *Ibid.*, p.209. Miss Andrews had, of course, the benefit of hindsight and also a desire to clear the school of any suggestion of mistreatment of its most famous pupil.

61. *Leeds Mercury*, 4 Sept. 1824, p.3.

62. PB, *A Sermon Preached in the Church of Haworth ... in Reference to an Earthquake* (Bradford, T. Inkersley, 1824), pp.5–6, [*Brontëana*, pp.211–12].

63. Mrs H. Rhodes to J. A. Erskine Stuart, [1887]: MS BS xi, 49 pp.1–2, BPM.

64. *Leeds Mercury*, 11 Sept. 1824, p.3.

65. PB, *A Sermon Preached ... in Reference to an Earthquake*, p.11, [*Brontëana*, p.215].

66. *Leeds Intelligencer*, 9 Sept. 1824, p.2; *Leeds Mercury*, 11 Sept. 1824, p.3.

67. *Ibid.*

68. *Leeds Mercury*, 11 Sept. 1824, p.3; *Leeds Intelligencer*, 22 Sept. 1824, p.3, where it states, more conservatively and probably more accurately, that 200 horses passed through the Stanbury toll-bar on Sunday, 12 September on their way to Crow Hill.

69. *Leeds Mercury*, 18 Sept. 1824, p.3. Patrick also wrote again to the *Leeds Intelligencer*, 16 Sept. 1824, p.3, on the same lines but suggesting that the land at Crow Hill was continuing to sink and the cavity was now nearly a mile across.

70. PB, *A Sermon Preached ... in Reference to an Earthquake*, pp.5, 11, [*Brontëana*, pp.211, 218].

71. 'JPJ' to the *Liverpool Mercury*, reprinted in the *Westmoreland Advertiser & Kendal Chronicle*, 25 Sept. 1824, p.4. Patrick's original account in this newspaper on 11 Sept. 1824, p.2. As the *Westmoreland Advertiser & Kendal Chronicle* was the local paper for Cowan Bridge, one wonders whether Carus Wilson also saw Patrick's letter and used it as an 'improving' example to the girls at the school.

72. Thomas Inkersley printed Patrick's *The Cottage in the Wood* and *The Maid of Killarney*. He was also responsible for printing both John Buckworth's *Cottage Magazine* and William Morgan's *Pastoral Visitor* and was much used by Bradford churchmen. There is a story that the young Charlotte accompanied Patrick to Inkersley's and sat correcting the proofs of his work while Patrick talked politics with the printer. This incident, if true, cannot relate to Patrick's earthquake pieces as Charlotte was away at school at the time and Emily was too young to have been able to perform the task: Scruton, pp.66–7.

73. PB, *The Phenomenon or, An Account in Verse, of the Extraordinary Disruption of a Bog* (Bradford, Thomas Inkersley, 1824), p.12, [*Brontëana*, p.208]. It is worth comparing Patrick's benevolent view of divine judgement with William Carus Wilson's terrible and terrifying view; both were writing for children, yet the difference in emphasis is almost irreconcilable. See below, p.136, for one of Carus Wilson's children's stories.

74. Emily's poem 'High waving heather, 'neath stormy blasts bending' is an apocalyptic evocation of a moorland storm and flood, but there is no particular reason to link it with the Crow Hill bog-burst twelve years before: EJB, 'High waving heather, 'neath stormy blasts bending', MS Bon 127 p.18, BPM, [JB *SP*, pp.42, 120–1].

75. PB to Mr Mariner, 10 Nov. 1824: MS n.l., [L& D, p.255].

76. [Nancy Garrs], *Illustrated Weekly Telegraph*, 10 Jan. 1885, p.1.

77. Herbert, 'Charlotte Brontë: Pleasant Interview with the Old French Governess of this Famous

Author', special correspondence of 'The Post': typescript of newspaper cutting from Mary Stull's scrapbook, BPM; the locks of hair, mounted on a board, are HAOBP:J81, BPM. Mrs Brontë's is dark brown, with a tinge of auburn, Branwell's distinctly ginger: Patrick's hair, added in 1861, is white.

78. Admissions Register, no. 44. WG *CB*, p.10 & WG *EJB*, p.7 suggests that Emily travelled alone in the company of the coach guard, like the young Jane Eyre. Apart from the inherent improbability of Patrick consigning his youngest school-age child to the care of a guard when he had personally taken the older girls, the evidence points to the fact that he went himself. On 25 November, the day Emily entered the school, there was a burial and a baptism at Haworth Church. For the first time since July, Patrick did not take either in person, securing instead the services of the Reverend Bernard Greenwood, headmaster of Oxenhope Grammar School. This suggests to me that Patrick was offloading his duties so that he could escort Emily to Cowan Bridge: Register of Burials, 1813–36, Register of Baptisms, 1813–29, Haworth Church.

79. Miss Evans to ECG, quoted in ECG, *Life*, p.48; A. Evans to PB, 23 Sept. 1825: MS p.1, in private hands; Admissions Register, no. 44; Ledger of the Clergy Daughters' School, 26 Nov. 1824: MS WDS/38/1, p.13, CRO, Kendal.

80. CB, *Jane Eyre*, p.60; 'CMR' to ABN, 26 May 1857: MS in private hands. The list of clothes in the Entrance Rules does not include boots, only shoes and pattens; gloves (which Jane Eyre did not have) were also on the list: [*Report on the*] *School for Clergymen's Daughters*, p.5. The attendance at Tunstall Chapel was ended the year after the Brontës left, the girls transferring to the newly refurbished Leck Chapel which was only half a mile from the school: Chadwick, p.80.

81. 'A.H' to *Littell's Living Age*, 15 Sept. 1855, [*BST*:16:83:209]; 'CMR' to ABN, 26 May 1857: MS p.2, in private hands.

82. CB to WSW, 28 Oct. 1847: MS MA 2696 R-V p.2, Pierpont Morgan, [*L&L*, ii, 150]. When Mrs Gaskell visited Charlotte in September 1853, 'We talked over the old times of her childhood; of her elder sister's (Maria's) \death −/ just like that of Helen Burns in "Jane Eyre;" of those strange starved days at school;' ECG to unknown [end Sept. 1853], [C&P, p.249].

83. CB, *Jane Eyre*, p.56.

84. ECG, *Life*, p.45. A 'blister' was an application which literally brought the skin out in blisters; it was intended to draw internal poisons to the body surface and was widely used in consumptive cases.

85. 'CMR' to ABN, 26 May 1857: MS p.3, in private hands. For those who were grateful to Carus Wilson, see Sarah Baldwin to *Halifax Guardian*, 13 June 1857, p.6. The wife of 'Clericus' who complained so much about the food nevertheless

stated that she felt herself 'under great obligations to the School for the sound education she received & the judicious discipline, moral & intellectual, under which the pupils were placed and that she always expresses herself grateful to Mr Wilson for much personal kindness': 'Clericus' to ABN, July 1857: MS p.4, in private hands.

86. As early as 1815, Carus Wilson had been warned by no less a person than Charles Simeon that his views were 'unduly Calvinistic': CB, *Jane Eyre*, Clarendon edn, Appx ii, p.621. He was actually refused ordination on those grounds by the Bishop of Chester: Pollard & Hennell, *Charles Simeon (1759–1836)*, p.164.

87. Carus Wilson, *A Child's First Tales*, p.47. The story is a peculiarly apt one for the rebellious Jane Eyre and her equally passionate creator, Charlotte Brontë. It should be pointed out that exemplary horror stories of this type were not uncommon at the time and are still published today. The Evangelical Tract Distributors of Edmonton in Canada recently published *Awful Death of a Young Infidel*. It is the story of a college student who belittled the Bible and was then mortally wounded in a train crash; on his deathbed he realizes too late the errors of his ways and dies shrieking, 'Mother! I'm lost! **lost!** damned! **damned forever!**'

88. William Carus Wilson, *The Children's Friend*, December 1826.

89. The Cowan Bridge copy of Richard Baxter's *Dying Thoughts, with Meditations from Owen* (London, 1822), inscribed on the flyleaf 'No 15 Library Clergy School 5 March 1825' is MS WDS/38/4, CRO, Kendal.

90. *Hymns for Infant Minds*, by the authors of 'Original Poems', 'Rhymes for the Nursery' &c (London, J. Holdsworth, 1825), inscribed on flyleaf, 'To Miss Turner For attention to Spelling 2nd Class. December 19th 1826': MS HAOBP:bb198, BPM.

91. Admissions Register, no.17. The ledger shows a charge of 8½d. for a letter, recorded under the date 21 February 1825 but presumably dating back to before Maria's removal from the school on 14 February: Ledger of the Clergy Daughters' School, 21 Feb. 1825: MS WDS/338/1, p.13, CRO, Kendal.

92. This quotation from a letter by Patrick is recorded in the margin of the Admissions Register, no. 17.

93. Register of Burials, 1813–36, Haworth Church. Unlike after his wife's death, Patrick did not cease taking duty: he performed burials on 7 and 10 May, between Maria's death and funeral, and the day after her funeral he resumed his ordinary duties with a burial on the 13th: Maria's death is noticed in the *Leeds Mercury*, 14 May 1825, p.3.

94. Mrs Chadwick was given this information by a relative of Carus Wilson: Chadwick, p.78; CB, *Jane Eyre*, Clarendon edn, Appx ii, p.616.

95. Ledger of the Clergy Daughters' School, 31

May 1825: MS WDS/338/1, p.13, CRO, Kendal. Elizabeth's fare cost 16/-. There is no record of any letter, so presumably Patrick was not informed that his daughter was coming home; presumably, too, had he known Elizabeth was coming home he would have arranged for Charlotte and Emily to accompany her instead of having to travel up to fetch them himself the next day.

96. Chadwick, p.78; Admissions Register, nos. 30, 44. Mrs Gaskell believed Patrick had sent Charlotte and Emily back to the school after the deaths of Maria and Elizabeth, which did nothing to improve her already dim view of his parental role: ECG, *Life*, pp.45, 48–9.

97. Admissions Register, no. 18; *Leeds Mercury*, 18 June 1825, p.3, where it says she died of an 'affection[sic] of the lungs'; Register of Burials, 1813–36, Haworth Church.

98. CB, *Shirley*, p.448. Emma's status is not clear; Charlotte originally intended her to be an orphan and Conway FitzGibbon may have proved not to be her father.

99. See, for example, EJB, *Wuthering Heights*, p.242.

100. Her father, an alcoholic, dies in the course of the novel, having shown no interest in her: AB, *Tenant of Wildfell Hall*, p.256.

101. PBB to Editor of *Blackwood's Magazine*, [8] Dec. 1835: MS 4040 pp.1–2, NLS, [*L&L*, i, 133]. Branwell remembered incorrectly: the passage was from 'Christmas Dreams' which appeared in *Blackwood's Magazine* in January 1828, two and

a half years after his sisters' deaths. I suspect Branwell was confusing the timing of the article with that of 'The Twin Sisters', a somewhat turgid poem on the death through consumption of a girl, coincidentally called Maria, whose twin sister Anna, unable to bear life without her, also dies. The poem appeared in the May issue of *Blackwood's Magazine*, xvii, 1825, pp.532–3, so it was published the very month Maria Brontë died. As the Brontës probably did not see the issue immediately, the poem would have been even more appropriate to their situation when Elizabeth was sent home to die at the end of the month.

102. PBB, 'Calm and clear the day declining', n.d.: part in MS BS 130, BPM, [Leyland, i, 218, 221]. The poem belongs to a sequence of poems which includes 'Harriet', 'Caroline' and 'Sir Henry Tunstall': the dead child is golden haired (Maria was dark), was buried in a churchyard (Maria was buried in the vault under the church) and her parents are both still alive (Maria's mother was dead).

103. MT to ECG, 18 Jan. 1856: MS n.l., [Stevens, pp.159–60].

104. CB to WSW, 5 Nov. 1849: MS n.l., [*L&L*, iii, 33–4].

105. Miss Evans, quoted in ECG, *Life*, p.48.

106. Miss Evans to PB, 23 Sept. 1825: MS p.2, in private hands.

107. *Ibid.*, pp.2, 1.

CHAPTER SIX

Title: 'Wiggins might indeed talk of scriblemania if he were to see me just now': CB, 'I'm just going to write because I cannot help it' [Roe Head Journal], c.Oct. 1836: MS Bon 98(7) p.1, BPM.

1. PB to Richard Burns, Secretary to the Governors of Queen Anne's Bounty, 25 Aug. 1825: MS n.l., [*L&D*, p.267].

2. PB to Richard Burns, Secretary to the Governors of Queen Anne's Bounty, 1 Dec. 1825: MS n.l., [*L&D*, p.268].

3. *Bradford & Wakefield Chronicle*, 24 Sept. 1825, p.2.

4. PB to the Secretary, British & Foreign Bible Society, 3 Oct. 1825: MS in archives of Bible Society, ULC.

5. *Leeds Mercury*, 3 Dec. 1825, p.3. In the end, the election was uncontested so two Tories, including Wilson, and two Whigs, were returned to Parliament for the county: *ibid.*, 24 June 1826, p.3.

6. *Bradford & Wakefield Chronicle*, 10 Sept. 1825, p.4; *Leeds Mercury*, 17 Sept. 1825, p.3; 21 Jan. 1826, p.3.

7. *Leeds Mercury*, 20 May 1826, p.3; 22 July 1826, p.2; 13 May 1826, p.3, 20 May 1826, p.3. Haworth would have had a share in the £1,500 sent by the London Committee for the relief of the Distressed Poor for distribution within the parish of Bradford.

8. PB to Mrs Taylor, 12 April 1826: MS RMP 792, WYAS, Calderdale.

9. See, for instance, *Bradford & Wakefield Chronicle*, 6 Aug. 1825, p.4; *Leeds Mercury*, 1 July 1826, p.3. Theodore Dury was a wealthy man in his own right, but was also married to Anne Greenwood, daughter of a Keighley manufacturer. John Buckworth, Patrick's vicar at Dewsbury, was similarly placed, being married to Rachel Halliley whose father, the manufacturer, was rich enough to leave £4,000 to each of his daughters in his will: John Brooke, Renunciation of Probate & Trusteeship, 1 Jan. 1833: MS in WYAS, Bradford. James Clarke Franks, Thomas Atkinson and Hammond Roberson all enjoyed large private incomes and had married moneyed wives. Patrick seems to have been unusual in having only his own salary for income.

10. *Leeds Mercury*, 15 July 1826, p.2; 21 Oct. 1826, p.3; *Leeds Intelligencer*, 25 Oct. 1827, p.3, where Patrick is not listed as being present or giving a speech.

11. *Leeds Mercury*, 8 July 1826, p.2; 28 Oct. 1826, p.3; Register of Burials, 1813–36, Haworth Church; *Leeds Mercury*, 9 Dec. 1826, p.3.

12. *Ibid.*, 16 Dec. 1826, p.3, where the name is given as 'Burran'. It is 'Burwin' in the Register of Burials, 1813–36, Haworth Church, where the burials are

recorded between 16 Sept. and 6 Dec. 1826; *Leeds Mercury*, 17 Feb. 1827, p.3.

13. *Ibid.*, 21 July 1827, p.3.

14. *Leeds Intelligencer*, 26 July 1827, p.3. Haworth Church Hymn Sheet, 22 July 1827: MS x, H, BPM.

15. *Leeds Mercury*, 16 Aug. 1828, p.2. This incident may have inspired, for example, the arrival by balloon at Strathfieldsay of the little king and queens in CB, Tales of the Islanders, vol. ii, 6 Oct. 1829: MS p.3 Berg, [CA, i, 101].

16. Thomas Salmon, *A New Geographical & Historical Grammar* (Edinburgh, Willison & Darling, 1771), MS HAOBP:bb204, BPM; the Brontës' copy of Oliver Goldsmith's *History of England*, heavily annotated by Patrick, was shown to Charles Hale by William Wood on 8 November 1861; Wood had bought it for eighteen pence at the Brontë sale the month before: [Charles Hale], 'An American Visitor at Haworth, 1861', *BST*:15:77:132; Haworth Parsonage Sale Catalogue, 2 Oct. 1861: MS BS x, H, lot 106, BPM; Rollin's *History* (no publication details given) was sold on the second day of the Brontë Sale for 3/6d.: *ibid.*, lot 49; J. Goldsmith, *A Grammar of General Geography* (London, Longman, 1823), MS HAOBP:bb217, BPM. There was at least one other geography book. In her 'History of the Year', written in 1829, Charlotte says she has in front of her an 'old Geography', one hundred and twenty years old, on a blank leaf of which her sister Maria had written 'papa lent me this Book': MS Bon 80(11) p.1, BPM, [CA, i, p.4].

17. Hannah More, *Moral Sketches of Prevailing Opinions and Manners* (London, T. Cadell & W. Davies, 1784); the inscription on the flyleaf has been virtually erased but includes Patrick's signature and the dates '1819' and 'March, 1820': MS HAOBP:bb59, BPM.

18. 'A copy of "Pilgrim's Progress", dated 1743, belonging to the Brontë family' and 'A copy of "The Doctrine of the Passions", 1791, by J Watts, [sic] DD', with Charlotte's autograph, were sold at the Sotheby's sale of the contents of Robinson Brown's Museum of Brontë Relics, on 2 July 1898, lots 58 and 59. The copy of Isaac Watts' *The Doctrine of the Passions* (Berwick, W. Phorson, 1791) is now HS HAOBP:bb66, BPM. John Milton, *Paradise Lost* (Glasgow, J. Robertson & J. Gillies, 1797), with Charlotte's autograph on the title page, is MS HAOBP:bb39, BPM. For their influence on the Brontës, see CA *EW*, pp.18, 118, 132, 283, 296.

19. Thomas à Kempis, *Extract of the Christian's Pattern* (London, T. Cordeux, n.d.); the original flyleaf with Maria's signature is missing, though 'M. Branwell July 1807' has apparently been copied from it on to the inside front cover by someone else: MS HAOBP:bb202, BPM; James Thomson, *The Seasons* (London, W. Suttaby & C. Corrall, 1803), signed 'Maria Branwell 1804 Penzance' inside front cover & 'M. Branwell' on the title page, is MS HAOBP:bb213, BPM;

Thomas Browne, *The Union Dictionary* (London, Wilkie & Robinson, 1806), signed 'M Branwell Feby 9 1808' and 'C Bronte' on title page, is MS HAOBP:bb196, BPM.

20. CB, *Shirley*, p.389.

21. CB to Hartley Coleridge [1840]: MS MA 2696 R–V p.2, Pierpont Morgan, [*BST*:10: 50:17].

22. *Bible* (Oxford, 1825), inscribed on flyleaf 'To Emily Jane Brontë, by her affectionate Father, Feb 13th, 1827': Sotheby's Sale of Arthur Bell Nicholls' Books & Manuscripts, 26 July 1907, lot no. 11; *The Book of Common Prayer* (Oxford, Clarendon Press, 1823) inscribed by Patrick 'Miss Outhwaite, to her God daughter Anne Brontë – Feby. 13th: 1827': MS HAOBP:bb48, BPM. I have not been able to identify why this day was so special. *Bible* (no place of publicn, 1821) inscribed 'To Anne Brontë, with the love and best wishes of her godmother Eliz. Firth, Oct. 1823'. Underneath this, Patrick wrote, 'To read it and keep it for the sake of the donor.': Sotheby's Sale of Arthur Bell Nicholls' Books & Manuscripts, 26 July 1907, lot 12. At the same sale were also sold Charlotte's New Testament (Cambridge, 1823) 'with inscription from Mr and Mrs Morgan' (lot no. 13) and Jane Branwell Morgan's Greek Prayer Book, inscribed 'J. B. Morgan, 1813. A Memorial of Mrs Morgan, presented to Rev P Brontë, B. A. Haworth, Sept 29, 1827; presented by the Rev Wm Morgan, B.D. Oct 2, 1827' (lot no. 5). Jane Branwell Morgan is buried next to her parents in the parish churchyard of Cross-stone which has recently been converted into housing. The gravestones were only just legible when I visited the churchyard during the conversion in 1989; they are now at the BPM. Register of Burials 1813–32, Cross-stone Church: MS p.147 no. 1172 [27 Sept. 1827] (Microfilm), WYAS, Calderdale. For the influence of the Bible on the Brontës' writings see CA *EW*, pp.18, 240–3.

23. [New Testament (publication details missing with title-page)]: MS HAOBP:bb5, BPM. On the first page of the text, for instance, is a note in Branwell's hand 'P B Brontë Began Matthew. Nov 13 1829 in latin'. The date may possibly read '1828'.

24. W. M. Thackeray to WSW, 23 Oct. 1847, [*L & L*, ii, 149].

25. John Dryden, *The Works of Virgil Translated into English Verse* (London, Rivington, 1824): MS HAOBP:bb64, BPM.

26. Three fragments of notes and translations from the Latin by Emily, one of which is dated 13 March 1838, are preserved at King's School, Canterbury. Anne bought R. Valpy's textbook, *Delectus Sententiarum et Historiarum* (London, Longman & Co., 1842) and inscribed it 'Anne Brontë Thorp Green – November 1843': MS HAOBP: bb226, BPM.

27. See, for instance, C. K. Shorter, *The Brontës and their Circle* (London, J. M. Dent, 1914), p.429; WG *CB*, pp.24, 44; WG *EJB*, pp.12, 27, 32; Hewish,

Emily Brontë: a Critical and Biographical Study, pp.34–5. The use of Keighley Mechanics' Institute library was first suggested by Clifford Whone, 'Where the Brontës Borrowed Books', *BST*:11:60:344–58; he prints the 1841 catalogue of books.

28. The Keighley Mechanics' Institute had been inaugurated on 21 March 1825 with a speech by one of the Brontës' heroes, Edward Baines, jr, Editor of the *Leeds Mercury*. *Leeds Mercury*, 26 March 1825, p.3. For examples of lectures see *ibid.*, 17 Sept. 1825, p.3; 26 Nov. 1825, p.3; *Bradford & Wakefield Chronicle*, 10 Dec. 1825, p.2; 17 Dec. 1825, p.2, where it is stated that 'a respectable audience consisting of the principal ladies and gentlemen in this neighbourhood, together with members of the Mechanics' Institute' heard lectures by William West, a chemist from Leeds. The relatively minor role played by Patrick in the Keighley Mechanics' Institute was first pointed out by Ian Dewhirst, 'The Rev Patrick Brontë and the Keighley Mechanics' Institute', *BST*:14:75:35–7. See also, Keighley Mechanics' Institute, Annual Reports, 1833–43, 1847–61: Keighley.

29. *Catalogue of Books Contained in the Library of Ponden Hall* (Keighley, William Weatherhead, n.d.). A copy of this catalogue is in the BPM. I am indebted to an unpublished article by Eddie Flintoff of Leeds University, intended as a preface to an edition of Branwell's translations of the *Odes* of Horace, for this information and most of the references to the Keighley circulating libraries.

30. CB to EN, 26 June 1848: MS HM 24463 p.2, Huntington, [*L&L*, ii, 227]; Winnifrith, *The Brontës and Their Background*, pp.84ff., dismisses the idea of the Brontës using a circulating library but Charlotte's letter to Branwell from Roe Head implicitly suggests they did. She is pleased Aunt Branwell has decided to subscribe to *Fraser's Magazine* as 'there would be no possibility of borrowing, or obtaining a work of that description from a circulating library': CB to PBB, 17 May 1832: MS Grolier A p.3, BPM, [*L&L*, i, 88]. It is worth noting that there was a subscription library in Haworth (though when it was established I have been unable to find out): its sale on Easter Monday, 1844, was described as a 'mad project': *Bradford Observer*, 28 March 1844, p.5.

31. Gordon Bottomley, Memoir of Alfred Bottomley (reprinted from New Church Magazine for Jan. 1932), p.8, Keighley.

32. [Benjamin Binns], 'The Brontës and the Brontë Country: a Chat with One Who Knew Them', *Bradford Observer*, 17 Feb. 1894, p.6; *Keighley & Haworth Argus*, 2 Jan. 1855; 1 April 1855; the newspaper had ceased publishing by November 1855 when the first issue of the *Keighley Advertiser & Airedale Courant* was published to fill the gap caused by its demise. Thos Duckett Hudson of 32 High Street is listed as a bookseller and druggist in White's *History, Gazetteer & Directory of the West Riding of Yorkshire* (1838), i, 685–6.

33. *The Keighley Visitor*, a temperance magazine, was published monthly from October 1853 by Robert Aked, 'stationer', of Low Street, Keighley. He also printed the Haworth Church hymn sheets and Patrick's two pamphlets, *The Signs of the Times* (Keighley, 1835) and *A Brief Treatise on the Best Time and Mode of Baptism* (Keighley, 1836); he is listed as a printer and as having a circulating library in Baines, *History, Directory and Gazetteer of the County of York* (1822), i, 219.

34. CA, i, 4, says that Mr Driver was the local doctor, but I have been unable to trace any doctor of this name in either the local directories for Haworth and Keighley or the Haworth church registers. There was a Reverend Jonas Driver, A.M., of Haworth, who died aged thirty-five and was buried on 22 December 1831: Register of Burials 1813–36, Haworth Church. His death would tie in with the cessation of the loan and Aunt Branwell's decision the following May to subscribe to *Fraser's Magazine*, which Charlotte considered a poor substitute: CB to PBB, 17 May 1832: MS Grolier A p.3, BPM, [*L&L*, i, 88].

35. CB, 'The History of the Year', 12 March 1829: MS Bon 80(11) p.2, BPM, [JB *ST*, no. 56].

36. O'Bronte appears, for instance, in 'Noctes Ambrosianae' in *Blackwood's Magazine*, xxiii, 1828, pp.779, 800; xxix, 1831, p.1.

37. Aesop's *Fables* were the inspiration for the play of 'Our Fellows': CB, 'The History of the Year', 12 March 1829: MS Bon 80(11) p.3, BPM, [JB *ST*, no. 56]. The influence of the *Arabian Nights' Entertainment* is obvious throughout the early juvenilia, see, for example, CB, 'Silence', YMM for Nov. 1830, 26 Aug. 1830: MS BS 12 pp.3–10, BPM, [CA, i, 241–55, wrongly dated to 16 Aug.]. For a discussion of the influence of the *Arabian Nights' Entertainment* and the *Tales of the Genii* see CA *EW*, pp.18, 30, 52, 106. Fables from Dyche's *Spelling Book* are apparently quoted several times in an untraced letter by Patrick Brontë to the *Leeds Intelligencer*, which is in turn quoted by the Reverend John Winterbotham in his letter to the *Leeds Mercury*, 8 March 1834, p.6. Walter Scott's *Tales of a Grandfather*, inscribed 'A New Year's Gift by Miss E.B. to her dear little nephew and nieces, Patrick, Charlotte, Emily, and Anne Brontë, 1828', is referred to in a footnote to ECG, *Life* (London, Smith, Elder & Co., 1905), p.125.

38. See, for example, the Brontë copies of Bewick woodcuts in the Brontë Parsonage Museum: HAOBP:P.Br A3, B2.5, C3.5, C9, E2, BPM. Bewick produced *Select Fables* in 1779 and *Fables of Aesop* in 1818.

39. For Bradley's biography see note to a poem 'Tribute to the memory of the late John Bradley of Keighley' by 'ZZ' of Keighley, published in the *York Courant*, 29 Feb. 1844, p.7 and [no author], *Keighley Past and Present* (London &

Keighley, 1858), p.98; William Dearden to *Bradford Observer*, 27 June 1861, p.7. Branwell's copy of Hogarth's 'Idle Apprentices' was shown to Emma Cortazzo by Martha Brown's brother-in-law in 1882: Helen Arnold (ed.), 'The Reminiscences of Emma Huidekoper Cortazzo', *BST*:13:68:226; it was sold at the Binns's sale of Brontë Relics by Wooller Jennings at Saltaire, *Catalogue of Antique Furniture*, 27 Jan. 1886, lot 385. A copy of this catalogue is in the BPM.

40. Abraham Sunderland was definitely teaching Emily and Anne by 1834 as he is referred to in EJB, Diary Paper, 24 Nov. 1834: MS Bon 131 p.2, BPM [JB *ST*, no. 11], but the fact that Branwell's little book, 'History of the Rebellion in My Fellows', which dates from 1828, is written on music paper suggests that they were having music lessons at this time: PBB, History of the Rebellion in My Fellows, 1828: MS BS 112, BPM. Thomas Plummer is confused with John Bradley by Benjamin Binns, the son of the Haworth tailor, who says Branwell received drawing and painting lessons from him. Plummer may well have tutored Branwell in other subjects, given his position as headmaster of the grammar school: [Benjamin Binns], 'The Brontës and the Brontë Country: a Chat with One Who Knew Them', *Bradford Observer*, 17 Feb. 1894, p.6.

41. Many of the toys are in the Brontë Parsonage Museum: a top HAOBP:H160 and a set of bricks HAOBP:H161 were found under the floorboards in 1949. Other toys at the BPM include the barrel HAOBP:H163(1) and the carved wooden lion HAOBP:H163(2). For the ninepins see notes 42 and 61. The wax-headed dolls in linen and muslin frocks, one with a hat, were sold at the Hodgson Sale of Brontë Relics, 6 July 1933, lot 208. The doll's cradle was shown to Charles Hale in November 1861 by the sexton's wife and sold at Robinson Brown's Sale of Brontë Relics: [Charles Hale], 'An American Visitor to Haworth', *BST*:15:77:128; Sotheby's Sale of Robinson Brown's Collection of Brontë Relics, 2 July 1898, lot 65. The tiny tea service, with the legend 'Ladies all i pray make free And tell me how you like your tea' on the saucers is at the BPM, HAOBP:H167(1–4), as is a children's plate portraying a girl in a cart with the legend 'What pleasure fills my little heart When seated in thy wooden cart To see thee act the horse's part My Brother', HAOBP:H157. The toy iron, which is arbitrarily associated with Emily because she was the one who looked after the household in later life, is also at the BPM: HAOBP:H165.

42. The acquisition of the ninepins and various sets of toy soldiers are recorded in the introduction to Branwell's 'History of the Young Men', 15 Dec. 1830: MS Ashley 2468 p.1, BL, [*M&U*, i, 63].

43. Leyland, i, 63–4.

44. CB, 'The History of the Year', 12 March 1829:

MS Bon 80(11) p.3, BPM, [JB *ST*, no. 56].

45. CB, Tales of the Islanders, vol. i, 30 June 1829: MS pp.2–3, Berg, [*CA*, i, 21–2].

46. CB, Tales of the Islanders, vol. i, 30–1 June 1829; vol. ii, 6 Oct–2 Dec. 1829; vol. iii, 3–8 May 1830; vol. iv, 14–30 July 1830: MSS in Berg, [*CA*, i, 21–33, 99–113, 140–54, 196–211].

47. PBB, 'History of the Rebellion in My Fellows', 1828: MS BS 112, BPM.

48. ECG, *Life*, pp.50–60 introduced this idea and gave it substance by, for example, reproducing a page from Charlotte's 'The Secret', written in November 1833, by which time the juvenile writings were much more substantial in every sense of the word. After quoting Charlotte's 'Catalogue of my Books' written in August 1830, which lists twenty-two volumes, Mrs Gaskell states that the average volume contained 'from sixty to a hundred pages' and was generally larger than the page reproduced. This is simply not the case. The average size of the YMM, for example, was less than 4cm by 6cm, with about twenty written sides (ten leaves) per volume. Mrs Gaskell, like later biographers, including WG *CB*, pp.17–55, conflates the juvenilia. By quoting later works as if they were written before Charlotte went to Roe Head, they create the impression that the childhood writings were much more sophisticated than they actually were. This impression has accidentally been given added weight by the editorial policy of Christine Alexander's otherwise invaluable *Edition of the Early Writings of Charlotte Brontë*, by standardizing and 'correcting' the grammar, punctuation and spelling of the original manuscripts the works appear more carefully written and more perfect than they are in reality.

49. Ruskin, *Praeterita* (Oxford, OUP, 1978), pp.42–8.

50. Shaen (ed.), *Memorials of Two Sisters*, pp.9–10.

51. *Ibid.*, p.10.

52. See above, note 48.

53. EJB, Diary Paper, 30 July 1845: MS p.2, in private hands, [*L&L*, ii, 49–50]. This Gondal play-acting took place less than a year before they began to write their novels, *Wuthering Heights* and *Agnes Grey*.

54. CB, The History of the Year, 12 March 1829: MS Bon 80(11) p.4, BPM, [JB *ST*, no. 56]. Branwell's account gave the story a slightly different emphasis: 'I gave Charlotte <Twm> Twemy (i.e. Wellington) \to Emily/ Pare (Parry) \to Anne/ Trott (Ross) to take care of them though they were to be mine and I to have the disposal of them as I would – shortly after this I gave them to them as their own –': PBB, History of the Young Men, 15 Dec. 1830–7 May 1831: MS Ashley 2468 p.8, BL, [*M&U*, i, 76].

55. *Ibid.*, p.7, BL, [*M&U*, i, 75]. Branwell's description of the taking of the island and the indiscriminate slaughter of the Dutch is very similar to the account of the British expedition against Bladensburgh and Washington in 'Campaigns

of the British Army at Washington, &c' in *Black-wood's Magazine*, x,1821, pp.180–7. This article had already inspired Branwell's 'Battell Book', his first extant manuscript: PBB, Battell Book, 12 March 1827: MS BS 110, BPM. The kingdom of Ashantee appears on the map of West Africa in J. Goldsmith's *Grammar of General Geography* (London, Longman & Co., 1823), opp. p.74: MS HAOBP:bb217, BPM. Branwell's map of the Glasstown Confederacy, which he painted as a frontispiece to his 'History of the Young Men', is clearly based upon this: PBB, History of the Young Men, 15 Dec. 1830–7 May 1831: MS Ashley 2468, frontispiece, BL, [reproduced in CA *EW*, p.33].

56. PBB, History of the Young Men, 15 Dec. 1830–7 May 1831: MS Ashley 2468 pp.7, 9, BL, [*M&U*, i, 76]. A similar but much briefer account of the history of the Twelves was written by Charlotte in April 1829; Branwell drew on, quoted from and expanded this account. He also changed the names of all the Twelves except Arthur Wellesley and Frederick Guelph/Brunswick, Duke of York; in Charlotte's account they have much grander, aristocratic names such as FitzGeorge and de Rothsay: CB, A Romantic Tale, or The Twelve Adventurers, 15–28 April 1829: MS in Law Colln, [CA, i, 7–18].

57. See, for example, 'North-West Passage: Expedition under Captain Ross and Lieutenant Parry', *Blackwood's Magazine*, iv, 1818, pp.339–44; 'Remarks on Captain Parry's Expedition', *ibid.*, viii, 1820, pp.219–23; 'Captain Parry's Voyage', *ibid.*, ix, 1821, pp.289–99.

58. *Blackwood's Magazine*, v, 1819, pp.175–83, 302–10. This seems to have been the source of much of the information used by the Brontës; the kings Sai TooToo and Quamina and the capital of Ashantee, Coomassie, are all described here. One passage, asking why the king of England did not send one of his own sons to the king of Ashantee and why he sent so small a force to Africa, is strongly echoed in PBB, History of the Young Men, 15 Dec. 1830–7 May 1831: MS Ashley 2468 pp.7–8, BL, [*M&U*, i, 74, 76].

59. A map and a census of lands and population appear as unrelated items at the end of CB, 'There was onc[e] a litle girl', n.d.: MS Bon 78 p.9, BPM, [CA, i, 3]. A much more complex map of 'the Glasstown Confederacy' serves as a frontispiece to PBB, History of the Young Men, 15 Dec. 1830–7 May 1831: MS Ashley 2468, BL, [reproduced in CA *EW*, p.33].

60. Dungeons held a peculiar fascination for all the Brontë children. Under the school on Vision Island, for example, there were dungeons for naughty schoolchildren. 'These cells are <arch>\dark, vaulted/ arched and so far down in the earth that the loudest shreik could not be heard by any inhabitant of the upper world and in these as well as the dungeons the most unjust torturing might go on without any fear of detection if it was not that I keep the key of the

dungeon & Emily keeps the key of the cell's …': CB, Tales of the Islanders, vol. i, 30–1 June 1829: MS p.9, Berg, [CA, i, 24].

61. PBB, History of the Young Men, 15 Dec. 1830–7 May 1831: MS Ashley 2468 pp.1, 8, BL, [*M&U*, i, 63, 78]. Only one of the ninepins was still extant by January 1831.

62. A sample, by Parry, goes ' "Hellow! Dear! Oi tee troy bowt's cawming oup tow us" (i.e. – Hello there! I see 3 boats coming up to us)': *ibid.*, p.5, [*M&U*, i, 69]. Charlotte uses the 'old young men tongue' when describing Parry's Land in a way which suggests she saw it as baby talk, rather than simply an attempt to reproduce broad Yorkshire dialect: see below, p.163.

63. PBB, History of the Young Men, 15 Dec. 1830–7 May 1831: MS Ashley 2468 pp.10, 16, BL, [*M&U*, i, 83, 94]. See also below, p.873 n.76.

64. CB, Tales of the Islanders, vol. i, 30–31 June 1829: MS pp.9, 10, Berg [CA, i, 24].

65. EJB, Diary Paper, 24 Nov. 1834: MS Bon 131 p.1, BPM, [*L&L*, i, 124].

66. CB, Tales of the Islanders, vol. ii, 6 Oct.–2 Dec. 1829: MS pp.1–2, Berg, [CA, i, 100].

67. Patrick's three letters were published in the *Leeds Intelligencer*, 15 Jan. 1829, p.4, 29 Jan. 1829, p.4 and 5 Feb. 1829, p.4. Opposing letters from William Morgan and Hammond Roberson were published with Patrick's second letter: 29 Jan. 1829, p.4.

68. *Ibid.*, 15 Jan. 1829, p.3. The phrase was quoted and supported by William Morgan in his letter the following week, despite his virulent attack on Patrick's attribution of the conversion of the Anglo-Saxons to Catholics.

69. PB to *Leeds Intelligencer*, 15 Jan. 1829, p.4.

70. *Ibid.*, 29 Jan. 1829, p.4.

71. *Ibid.*, 5 Feb. 1829, p.4.

72. PB to *Leeds Mercury*, 10 Jan. 1829, p.4.

73. The three extant little books are Branwell's 'History of the Rebellion in My Fellows', written in 1828 (MS BS 112, BPM) and his 'Battell Book', dated 12 March 1827 (MS BS 110, BPM, [JB *ST*, no.35]). The latter is based on a review of *A Narrative of the Campaigns of the British Army at Washington* which appeared in *Black-wood's Magazine*, ix, 1821, pp.180–7. The third book, by Charlotte, is illustrated with tiny watercolours like Branwell's 'Battell Book'; it is an undated short story, probably written for Anne, beginning 'There was onc[e] a litle girl and her name was Ane': MS Bon 78, BPM, [CA, i, 3].

74. PBB, [Branwell's Blackwood's] Magazine for January 1829, [?Jan. 1829]: MS Lowell 1(8), Harvard. Charlotte wrote an account of the foundation of the play of the O'Dears on 12 March 1829 (MS Bon 80(11), BPM) though CA, i, 6 transcribes the name as O Deans and WG CB, p.25 as O'Deays. In both cases, especially Branwell's manuscript, the name appears to me to be O Dear.

75. PBB, [Branwell's Blackwood's] Magazine for

January 1829, [?Jan. 1829]: MS Lowell 1(8) p.3, Harvard. The poem is published in VN, *PBB*, p.3 where its origins in the National Anthem are identified. American politics were to feature in later issues of the magazine, see, for example, CB, 'An American Tale', YMM for Nov. 1829, 9 Sept. 1829: MS Lowell 1(4), Harvard, [CA, i, 83–5].

76. PBB, [Branwell's Blackwood's] Magazine for January 1829, [?Jan. 1829]: MS Lowell 1(8) p.4, Harvard. CA *EW*, p.35 suggests Charlotte was 'unimpressed' by the old tongue and did not use it but this letter, like her interpolation in Branwell's 'History of the Rebellion in My Fellows', appears to be by her.

77. PBB, Branwell's Blackwood's Magazine for June 1829, [?June 1829]: MS Lowell 1(7) pp.4–6, Harvard. This contains the second part of the story, so the first part must have appeared in an earlier issue, now lost. Charlotte's own version of the story, set in Paris, was written on two leaves of what appears to be a dismantled miniature book: CB, The Enfant, 13 July 1829: MS Bon 80(9), BPM, [CA, i, 34–6].

78. PBB, Branwell's Blackwood's Magazine for July 1829, July 1829: MS Lowell 1(9) p.21, Harvard.

79. CB, Fragment, 8 Aug. 1829: MS Bon 80(10), BPM, [CA, i, 41].

80. CB, Anecdtotes of the duke of Wellington, 8 July–2 Oct. 1829: MS Bon 81, BPM.

81. CB, 'Silence', YMM for Nov. 1830, 26 Aug. 1830: MS BS 12 pp.3–10, BPM [CA, i, 241–55, where it is wrongly dated to 16 Aug. 1830].

82. For spectral visions see CB, 'Military Conversations', YMM for Oct. 1829, 2 Sept. 1829: MS Lowell 1(5), Harvard, [CA, i, 74–6]; CB, 'The Keep of the Bridge', 13 July 1829: MS Berg, [CA, i, 36, 38]; CB, 'Liffey Castle', YMM for Aug. 1830, 12 Aug. 1830: MS Bon 84 pp.3–9, BPM, [CA, i, 216–20]. For premonitory dreams see CB, 'Strange Events', YMM for Dec. 1830, 29 Aug. 1830: MS in Law Colln, [CA, i, 257–60]. For fairy transformations see CB, 'Fairy Gift', Visits in Verreopolis, 18 Dec. 1830: MS in Law Colln, [CA, i, 319–27]. Blackwood's Magazine ran many series on the supernatural: see, for example, 'On Some Popular Superstitions in Wales', *Blackwood's Magazine*, iii, 1818, pp.170–96; 'Legends and Traditions of Southern Ireland', xviii, 1825, pp.55–61; 'Fairies, Brownies and Witches', xxiii, 1828, pp.214–17, 509–19; 'An Autumnal Night's Dream in Ireland', xxii, 1827, pp.685–91.

83. CB, 'An Extraordinary Dream', YMM for Dec. 1830, 2 Sept. 1830: MS Bon 86 p.7, BPM, [CA, i, 271–2]; 'The Buried Alive', *Blackwood's Magazine*, x, 1821, pp.262–4, in which the 'corpse' revives when about to be dissected by Resurrectionists. Branwell, too, was writing about Resurrectionists at the same time as Charlotte. In his first volume of 'Letters from an Englishman', James Bellingham falls into the hands of Dr Hume and is only just saved from being dissected alive by the timely intervention of the

Duke of Wellington: PBB, Letters from an Englishman, vol. i, 6 Sept. 1830: MS pp.14–17, Brotherton, [*M&U*, i, 97–102]. The Resurrectionists crop up again in CB, An Interesting Passage in the Lives of Some Eminent Men of the Present Time, 17–18 June 1830: MS Lowell 1(1), Harvard, [CA, i, 170–7].

84. See, for example, the revival of Arthur Wellesley in CB, Tales of the Islanders, vol. ii, 6 Oct. 1829: MS p.5, Berg, [CA, i, 103–4] and of Captain Tree in CB, The Poetaster, vol. ii, 12 July 1830: MS MA 2696 R-V, Pierpont Morgan, [CA, i, 196].

85. CB, Description of the Duke of Wellington's Small Palace situated on the Banks of the Indiva, 16 Jan. 1830: MS MA 2538, Pierpont Morgan, [CA, i, 130–3].

86. CB, 'Review of "The Chief Genius in Council" by Edward de Lisle', YMM, 9 Dec. 1829: MS Ashley 157 p.2, BL, [CA, i, 114]. As CA *EW* p.241 points out, passages such as these owe as much to the biblical visions of the New Jerusalem as to the *Arabian Nights' Entertainment*.

87. CB, 'Liffey Castle', YMM, 12 Aug. 1830: MS Bon 84 p.3, BPM [CA, i, 216].

88. CB, 'Conversations', YMM, 10 Dec. 1829: MS Ashley 157 p.10, BL, [CA, i, 118].

89. CB, 'Review of Causes of the Late War by the Duke of Wellington', YMM for Aug. 1829, 24 July 1829: MS Lowell 1(6), Harvard, [CA, i, 56].

90. CB, 'A Day at Parry's Palace', YMM for Oct. 1830, 22 Aug. 1830: MS Bon 85 pp.3–4, BPM, [CA, i, 230].

91. *Ibid.*, p.5 [CA, i, 229–33].

92. PBB, The Liar Detected, 19 June 1830: MS Bon 139 p.1, BPM. This was Branwell's reply to CB, An Interesting Passage in the Lives of Some Eminent Men of the Present Time, 17–18 June 1830: MS Lowell 1(1), Harvard, [CA, i, 170–7].

93. PBB, The Liar Detected, 19 June 1830: MS Bon 139 p.6, BPM.

94. CB, The Poetaster, vol. i, 3–6 July 1830: MS Lowell 1(2), Harvard, [CA, i, 181].

95. *Ibid.*, vol. ii, 12 July 1830: MS MA 2696 R-V, Pierpont Morgan, [CA, i, 194–7]. The literary allusions in 'The Poetaster' are discussed in Melodie Monahan (ed.), 'Charlotte Brontë's *The Poetaster*: Text and Notes', *Studies in Romanticism*, xx, 1981, pp.475–8.

96. PBB, The Monthly Intelligencer, 27 Mar.–26 April 1833: MS BS 117, BPM, [*M&U*, ii, 187–9]. The paper was modelled on the local *Leeds Intelligencer*.

97. PBB, 'The Nights', Branwell's Blackwood's Magazine, June 1829: MS Lowell 1(7) p.10, Harvard.

98. PBB, A Collection of Poems by Young Soult the Ryhmer, 30 Sept. 1829: MS BS 114 p.17, BPM, [VN *PBB*, p.25]. Volume ii of this work is MS BS 115, BPM, [VN *PBB*, pp.14–30]. For Chateaubriand see *Blackwood's Magazine*, ix, 1821, pp.187–91.

99. PBB, 'REVIEW OF BUDS commentary on

Ossian', Branwell's Blackwood's Magazine, July 1829: MS Lowell 1(9) pp. 14–15, Harvard. The Brontës actually owned a copy of James Macpherson's *Poems of Ossian* (London, J. Walker, 1819) upon which one of them, probably Branwell, wrote various derogatory comments such as 'poopooh nonsense Branwell poopoo' and 'Bombast': MS HAOBP:bb203, pp.220, 270, BPM.

100. PBB, Laussane: A Dramatic Poem by Young Soult, 18–23 Dec. 1829: MS Bon 138, BPM, [VN *PBB*, pp.37–46]. The manuscript is described as 'a dramatic poem' on the title page but as 'A Trajedy' on the front cover. The 'Horae Germanicae' series, which included translations of works by Goethe, Schiller and Müllner, ran for several years from 1819 in *Blackwood's Magazine*.

101. PBB, Caractacus: a dramatic poem, 26 June 1830: MS in Brotherton, [VN *PBB*, pp.48–62]; PBB, The Revenge: a Tradgedy in 3 Acts, 23 Nov.–18 Dec. 1830: MS BS 116, BPM, [VN *PBB*, pp.62–71]. The count's son in 'The Revenge' is named Werner, after Byron's tragic hero of that name: 'Werner' was reviewed by Timothy Tickler and Morgan O'Doherty in *Blackwood's Magazine*, xii, 1822, pp.10–19, 782–5. Another character, Lodbrog, was based on the king of Denmark of that name who was a contemporary of Charlemagne: see *Blackwood's Magazine*, xxxiii, 1833, pp.910–23.

102. PBB, The Revenge: a Tradgedy in 3 Acts, 23 Nov.–18 Dec. 1830: MS BS 116 p.11, BPM, [VN *PBB*, note to p.62]. The quotation from 'Caractacus' is slightly different: 'In Dramatic poetry the passions are the cheif thing and in Proportion as exelence in the depicting of these is obtained so the writer of the poem takes his class among Dramatic authors C BUD'S Synop[s]is of <the> Dramatic writing Vol 1. p.130.': PBB, Caractacus: a dramatic poem, 26 June 1830: MS p.1, Brotherton, [VN *PBB*, note to p.48].

103. PBB, Letters from an Englishman, in 6 vols, 6 Sept. 1830–2 Aug. 1832: MSS in Brotherton, [*M&U*, i, 97–158].

104. See, for example, Lane, *The Brontë Story*, p.115, which states categorically of Branwell that 'he was certainly no stranger to alcohol in his teens'.

105. The motto is introduced in part 6 of the 'Noctes Ambrosianae', *Blackwood's Magazine*, xii, .822, p.693.

106. 'Maxims of Morgan O'Doherty', pts 1 & 2, *Blackwood's Magazine*, xv, 1824, pp.597–605, 632–42. See also, for example, 'The Bishop of Bristol', *ibid.*, v, 1819, p.668.

107. CB, 'A Frenchman's Journal', YMM, second no. for Dec. 1830, 4 Sept. 1830: MS Bon 86 p.14, BPM, [VN *CB*, pp.59–60]; for further examples see VN *CB*, pp.7, 11.

108. Branwell's work is full of classical references and allusions from a very early age: to take one simple early example, the cast of characters for 'Nights' includes Epimanondas [sic] Johnson

(for the Theban general Epaminondas) and Cicero Stephenson (for the Roman orator): PBB, Branwell's Blackwood's Magazine, June 1829: MS Lowell 1(7) p.7, Harvard. All his learned characters are classicists, from Alexander Percy, his alter ego, to H. M. M. Montmorency, the revolutionary, whose library is full of appropriate books on ancient history; Percy's blue-stocking wife, Zenobia, reads Seneca's letters 'in the original' in her leisure hours: PBB, Life of Feild Marshal the Right Honourable Alexander Percy, vol. i, [Spring, 1834]: MS pp.7, 12–13, Brotherton, [Collins, pp.30, 55, 57]; PBB, Real Life in Verdopolis, vol. i, May 1833: MS p.2, Brotherton [Collins, p.127]; *ibid.*, vol. ii, 17 Aug. 1833: MS pp.1, 2, Brotherton, [Collins, pp.164–5]. Later Branwell wrote and rewrote a long poem on the battle of Thermopylae, as well as translating the first book of Horace's *Odes*.

109. See, for example, CB, 'An American Tale', YMM for Nov. 1829, 9 Sept. 1829: MS Lowell 1(4), Harvard, [CA, i, 83–4]: CB, 'Visits in Verreopolis', 11 Dec. 1829: MS in Law Colln, [CA, i, 299, 301].

110. The manuscript is split between the Taylor Colln, Princeton and MS BS 13(1), BPM, [VN *CB*, pp.64–9]. 'The Violet' contains allusions to 'Aeolian Music', 'Cim[m]erian shade', the River Eurotas and Mount Parnassus, as well as to the ancient writers Homer, Sophocles, Euripides, Aeschylus and Virgil. The violet, perhaps significantly, was the personal emblem of Napoleon: see *Blackwood's Magazine*, xiii, 1823, pp.695–8.

111. PB, [French Phrasebook], 1842: MS BS 178, BPM, [partial L&D, pp.302–3].

112. Charlotte's copy of *La Henriade*, inscribed 'Charlotte Bronte's Book price 3s purchased May: 1830 Anno Domini La Henriad[e], un Epique Poeme par Voltaire', is in the Houghton Library, Harvard. Her English translation of the first book, written in a miniature book, is MS Eng 35.5, Harvard.

113. CB, 'Journal of a Frenchman', YMM, 13 Aug. 1830: MS Bon 84 pp.11–15, BPM, [CA, i, 221–3]; the series is continued in YMM for Nov., 28 Aug. 1830: MS BS 12 pp.14–18 and YMM for Dec., no. i, 31 Aug. 1830: MS in Law Colln & YMM for Dec., 4 Sept. 1830: MS Bon 86 pp.9–10, 13–18, BPM, [CA, i, 250–4, 261–4, 276–9].

114. *Leeds Mercury*, 25 July 1829, p.3.

115. CB to PB, 23 Sept. 1829: MS Bon 159, BPM, [*L&L*, i, 82]. Jane Branwell Fennell, their mother's aunt, had died on 26 May 1829. Her tombstone, in Cross-stone churchyard, is inscribed with the following moving lines: 'Farewell blest saint thou dear and faithfull friend / Beloved in life lamented in thine end / Instructed long in sharp afflictions school / To make submission to the Lord thy rule / To find when every hope of life was past / Thy best thy choicest comforts were thy last / Thou now

with HIM eternally shall dwell / Blest saint thou dear and faithful friend.' For her burial, by Charles Musgrave, vicar of Halifax, see Register of Burials 1813–32, Cross-stone Church: p.170 no. 1353 [29 May 1829] Microfilm, WYAS, Calderdale.

116. CB to PB, 23 Sept. 1829: MS Bon 159, BPM, [*L&L*, i, 82].

117. CB, untitled note, 25 Sept. 1829: MS Bon 108, BPM.

118. PB to *Leeds Mercury*, 14 Nov. 1829, p.4. The Editor of the *Leeds Mercury*, Edward Baines jr, who had been one of the chief characters in the Young Men Plays, came to Keighley early in March 1830, to deliver a lecture 'On the moral influence of unrestricted commerce'. Between six and seven hundred people attended the lecture, if the newspaper's figures are to be believed, with many more being turned away for lack of room. It seems likely that Patrick, and possible that his children, would have been present: *Leeds Mercury*, 6 March 1830, p.3.

119. *Ibid.*, 1 May 1830, p.3; *Leeds Intelligencer*, 29 April 1830, p.3.

120. PB to *Leeds Intelligencer*, 6 May 1830, p.4. It was not until 1838 that the government finally adopted the position Patrick had campaigned for for so long, abolishing the death penalty for all crimes except murder or attempted murder, treason and piracy on the high seas. A measure of reform was adopted in 1832, which removed house-breaking, sheep-stealing and forgery from the list of capital offences, but there were still over 200 crimes for which the death penalty could be imposed.

121. *Leeds Mercury*, 17 April 1830, p.3. There had been an epidemic of smallpox in Haworth and its neighbourhood in the winter and early spring: one Haworth man, Jesse Murgatroyd, lost all his five children to the disease: *ibid.*, 23 Jan. 1830, p.3.

122. Patrick's last duty, before he was so ill that he had to take to his bed, was a funeral on 18 June. Thomas Plummer officiated at all the funerals between 20 June and 10 July, all the baptisms between 23 June and 10 July and the sole marriage on 21 June 1830: Registers, Haworth Church. Patrick described the details of his illness in a letter to Mrs Franks, 28 April 1831: MS BS 182 pp.2–3, BPM, [*L&L*, i, 86].

123. CB, 'The following strange occurence', 22 June 1830: MS Eng 35.5, Harvard, [*CA*, i, 177]. Mr Midgley, a Haworth contemporary of the Brontës, identified the mysterious caller as 'an eccentric rather well to do gentleman farmer' who eventually died in a lunatic asylum: Edward Harrison to Revd A. Wilkes, 26 Nov. 1879: MS BS ix, H p.3, BPM, [*BST*:12:63:204].

124. PB to Mrs Franks, 28 April 1831: MS BS 182 pp.2–3, BPM, [*L&L*, i, 86].

CHAPTER SEVEN

Title: inscription on the silver medal awarded to Charlotte at Roe Head: HAOBP: J25, BPM.

1. Pobjoy, *A History of Mirfield*, p.103. The building was absorbed into the large school run by the Fathers of the Community of the Resurrection at Mirfield but has recently been converted into Holly Bank School, a residential school for disabled children.

2. Leah and Maria Brooke were daughters of John Brooke, son-in-law of John Halliley, senior, and co-partner in Halliley, Brooke and Co., carpet manufacturers of Dewsbury; Hannah Haigh was probably a member of the family at Longlands where Patrick stayed overnight with John Firth in 1817: see above, p.848, n.52.

3. The pupils who can be identified as being at Roe Head in the period 1831–2 are as follows: Charlotte Brontë, Ellen Nussey, Mary and Martha Taylor, Susan Ledgard, Hannah Haigh and Maria Brooke, whose names are recorded in a list written by Charlotte inside the front cover of her copy of *Historical and Miscellaneous Questions*: MS HAOBP:bb215, BPM. These names correlate with those mentioned by Martha Taylor in 1832, to which she adds Miss Hall and Miss Allison: Martha Taylor to EN, 17 May 1832: MS in Texas, [*L&L*, i, 102]. Other references identify Amelia Walker, Mrs Atkin-son's niece, as a pupil at the same time: see, for instance, her name on one of Charlotte's drawings, dated June 1831, HAOBP:P.Br C62, BPM. There were only seven pupils at the school in the 1841 census, by which time it had removed to Dewsbury Moor: Census Returns for Dewsbury Moor, 1841: Microfilm, Kirklees. Ellen Nussey said that, during one half-holiday, the girls held a 'ball' but only had sufficient numbers for a quadrille and two Scotch reels, which implies that they only had enough to form four couples: EN, Reminiscences, *BST*:2:10:64. The Brookes were from Dewsbury, Ellen Nussey from Birstall, Mary and Martha Taylor from Gomersal and Hannah Haigh from Batley, all of which were within a three-mile radius of Roe Head.

4. PB to ECG, 20 June 1855: MS EL B121 p.4, Rylands, [*BST*:8:43:89]; *L&L*, i, 84 n.1, quoting 'a pupil'; CB to EN, May 1842: MS in Law Colln, [*L&L*, i, 260].

5. There were two ladies' boarding schools in Keighley, one in High Street and one in Skipton Road: Pigot, *National & Commercial Directory*, 1828–9, p.989. For schools in Bradford and Halifax, see *ibid.*, pp.908–9, 937.

6. Elizabeth Franks and Frances Atkinson had taken tea at least once with the 'Miss Woolers' at Purlwell in May 1829: Firth, 15 May 1829.

7. WG *CB*, pp.54, 67, probably following Yates, *The Father of the Brontës*, p.100 and Chadwick, pp.91–2, says that the Atkinsons paid Charlotte's school fees but there is no evidence to support this claim. The shortness of Charlotte's time at Roe Head suggests that eighteen months was all Patrick could afford. Ellen Nussey said that Charlotte regarded herself as 'an object of expense to those at home' and therefore worked hard at school out of a sense of moral obligation to her family. This also suggests that Patrick (or possibly Elizabeth Branwell) was paying for her education: EN, Reminiscences, *BST*:2:10:63–4. Elizabeth Franks seems to have played no part in the decision to send Charlotte to school: Patrick's letter to her, written after Charlotte had gone to Roe Head, gives her his news for the last year as if he had had no contact with her for some time: PB to Mrs Franks, 28 April 1831: MS BS 182, BPM, [*L&L*, i, 85–6].

8. MT to ECG, 18 Jan. 1856: MS n.l., [Stevens, pp.157–8]. This is the only source which ever refers to Charlotte having an Irish accent. If Mary Taylor was right, then the accent must have been lost during Charlotte's schooldays. Though Branwell was often labelled by his Irish ancestry (see, for example, below, pp.270, 904 n.71), no one ever claimed he had an Irish accent. Nor was one ever ascribed to Emily or Anne, though they had least contact with the world outside their home and might therefore have been expected to have picked up any brogue their father had retained after thirty years in England.

9. EN, Reminiscences, *BST*:2:10:59–60. According to the diary of her brother, he escorted Ellen to Roe Head on 25 January 1831: Henry Nussey, Journal, 1830–2: MS Egerton 3268A p.16, BL.

10. MT to ECG, 18 Jan. 1856: MS n.l., [Stevens, pp.158–9]; EN, Reminiscences, *BST*:2:10:62.

11. MT to ECG, 18 Jan. 1856: MS n.l., [Stevens, p.158].

12. *Ibid.*; EN, Reminiscences, *BST*:2:10:62.

13. MT to ECG, 18 Jan. 1856: MS n.l., [Stevens, pp.158–9].

14. Charlotte's copies of Richmal Mangnall's *Historical and Miscellaneous Questions* and Mr Tocquot's *Easy Guide to the ... French Language* (London, 1806), both inscribed 'C Brontë Jany 17 1831', are MSS HAOBP:bb215 & bb62, BPM. Her copies of W. Pinnock's *A Comprehensive Grammar of the English Language* (London, Poole & Edwards, 1830), inscribed 'C Bronte', and of Lindley Murray's *English Grammar* (York, Longman *et al.*, 1818), which has various annotations, are MSS HAOBP:bb46 & bb216, BPM. The last is inscribed with a number of different dates, including 'Jany 17 1832', 'July 29th 1832' and 'Augt 29th 1832', of which the first is possibly not genuine. It may be, therefore, that the book was acquired by Charlotte after she had left Roe Head when she began to instruct her sisters at home.

15. CB, silver medal for achievement: HAOBP:J25, BPM; *Le Nouveau Testament* (Edimbourg, G. Cowie & Co., 1829), MS HAOBP:bb6, BPM. The inscription has faded to the point of illegibility but is quoted from the entry in the Stock Book of the BPM.

16. CB, watercolour of wild roses 'from nature', 13 July 1830: HAOBP:P.Br C9.5, BPM; CB, watercolour copy of a portrait of her mother, Oct. 1830: HAOBP:P.Br C10.5, BPM; CB, watercolour 'Lycidas', March 1830: HAOBP:P:Br C13, BPM. In a way that is typical of Charlotte's copies, her portrait of her mother is 'prettified' by the addition of a frilly cap, puffed sleeves, curls and a less square chin than in the original; the result, which Charlotte presented to 'her dear Aunt' Branwell, is that Mrs Brontë appears as a young girl rather than the more matronly figure of the original. The 'Lycidas' picture was copied from a painting of 'The Dawn' by the Swiss artist, Fuessli, which was one of the pictures exhibited at Somerset House and reviewed by *Blackwood's Magazine*, xiv, 1823, p.10. Fuessli specialized in illustrating Shakespeare and Milton, 'The Dawn' being suggested by some lines from Milton's poem 'Lycidas', hence Charlotte's title. Another of Charlotte's watercolours at this time, 'Bessy Bell and Mary Gray', 15 Dec. 1830: HAOBP:P.Br C11, BPM, was an illustration to a poem which appeared in *Blackwood's Magazine*, ii, 1817, pp.165–6.

17. I have presumed that the girls at Roe Head used the same source as the contemporaneous boys at Woodhouse Grove School, as described by the artist James Smetham, who spent the years 1832–6 at the Grove and 'copied Raphael's cartoons from the *Penny Magazine*' but wasted the rest of his time there: *Woodhouse Grove School 1812–1962*, p.26. The Raphael cartoon labelled 'Amelia Walker' and apparently signed 'Charlotte Bronte 17 March 1830 [sic]' is HAOBP:P.Br C62, BPM. It was sold as lot 375, with lot 380 'Portrait of Susan Ledgerd [sic]', at Wooller Jennings' Sale of the Binns' family collection of Brontëana at Saltaire in 1886: the Binns family were relatives of Martha Brown, the Brontës' servant. For examples of Charlotte's drawings of scenes and botanical illustrations see CB, drawing of the tower at Haddington, June 1831: HAOBP:P.Br C16, BPM; CB, 'Annual Lavatera', signed 'Miss Brontë. Roe Head. Decr 15th 1831': HAOBP:P.Br C101, BPM. Charlotte's drawing of Roe Head, unsigned and undated but authenticated by her father, is virtually identical to those drawn by Anne Brontë and Susan Carter: HAOBP:P.Br Bon 32 & P. Br A9 & P136, BPM.

18. EN, Reminiscences, *BST*:2:10:62.

19. *Ibid.*, p.63.

20. MT to ECG, [1857]: MS n.l., [Stevens, p.163].

21. MT to ECG, 18 Jan. 1856: MS n.l., [Stevens, p.158].

22. EN, Reminiscences, *BST*:2:10:64–5.

23. *Ibid.*, pp.63–4. The half-holiday and 'coronation performance' were probably to celebrate the real coronation of William IV and his Queen, which took place on 8 September 1831: *Leeds Mercury*, 10 Sept. 1831, p.3.

24. EN, Reminiscences, *BST*:2:10:69; C. W. Hatfield & C. M. Edgerley, 'The Relatives of Miss Ellen Nussey', *BST*:9:49:253–6. For the fullest account of Ellen and her family see Whitehead. The Rydings is still standing, looking shabby and incongruous, having been swallowed up by a paint factory which has also destroyed its beautiful landscaped gardens.

25. For Joshua Taylor's bankruptcy see *Leeds Mercury*, 4 Feb. 1826 p.3; 18 Feb. 1826 p.3. See also, for a slightly different version, Whitehead, pp.20–1.

26. MT to ECG, 18 Jan. 1856: MS n.l., [Stevens, p.159]; MT to ECG, [1857]: MS n.l., [Stevens, p.162].

27. Mrs Abraham Hirst of Roberttown was always sent to escort Charlotte to and from Green House: Yates, *The Father of the Brontës*, pp.100–1.

28. EN, Reminiscences, *BST*:2:10:68. Though unnamed, the family may have been the Brookes, whose daughters Leah and Maria were at Roe Head with Charlotte; Mrs Brooke was sister to Mrs John Buckworth and daughter of John Halliley, senior. The whole family had known Patrick well in the past but were not sufficiently acquainted with his daughter to be aware of her exact age.

29. CB to Mrs Franks, May 1831: MS BS 38, BPM, [*L&L*, i, 87]. The presents may have been given for Charlotte's fifteenth birthday which fell on 21 April 1831. The letter is signed 'C Brontë', Charlotte using the diaeresis on her surname apparently for the first time.

30. The memorial, together with one from the gentlemen, merchants, 'yeomen' and tradesmen of what is now the Kirklees area, was signed on 6 December 1830: *Leeds Mercury*, 5 Feb. 1831, p.3. Stocks had been acquitted of the offences by 24 March 1831 but as late as July letters were still flooding in to the lord lieutenant on the subject of readmitting him to the magistracy; most were against the proposal: see *ibid.*, 24 March 1831, p.3 and also MSS in Harewood Archives, Lieutenancy Papers, Box I, WYAS, Leeds. Stocks was readmitted to the magistracy at the end of June, incurring thunderings from an editorial in the Tory *Leeds Intelligencer*, which disapproved of him and the support given him by the Whig *Leeds Mercury*: *Leeds Intelligencer*, 23 June 1831, p.3; 14 July 1831, pp.2–3.

31. PB to Mrs Franks, 28 April 1831: MS BS 182 pp.1–2, BPM, [*L&L*, i, 85–6]. Patrick was in what his Tory friends would consider unsavoury company on this question: Moses Saunders, the Baptist minister of Haworth, and Abraham Wildman, a notorious Radical and later Chartist also from Haworth, were among those agitating

for the passing of the Bill: *Leeds Intelligencer*, 17 March 1831, p.3.

32. CB to PBB, 17 May 1832: MS Grolier A pp.1–2, BPM, [WG *CB*, p.69]. From the formal wording of this letter, Margaret Smith suggests that it was a school exercise rather than a genuine letter home.

33. *Ibid.*, pp.1–3.

34. PBB, 'The History of the Young Men', vol. i, 15 Dec. 1830–7 May 1831: MS Ashley 2468, BL, [*M&U*, i, 63–95]. This is the first of the children's little books to be written in the minuscule hand but on much larger pages than had been used previously. Branwell was later to adopt this format for all his books.

35. PBB, Letters from an Englishman, vol. ii, 8 June 1831: MS in Brotherton, [*M&U*, i, 103–13]. The Marquis of Douro explains to Bellingham that 'White bread' was loaves made from arsenic and oil of vitriol and 'Prussian Butter' was prussic acid 'transformed by a process with which I am not acquainted' into butter. The children clearly had a running joke about these poisons as an advert for the sale by auction of '20 loaves of the best white BREAD impregnated with Prussian BUTTER', placed by 'Captain Make Thousands NOT EAT any more food for THE Remainder of their precious LIVES', appeared in CB, YMM for November 1829, 9 Sept. 1829: MS Lowell 1(4), Harvard, [*CA*, i, 87–8]. Adulteration of food, particularly flour by arsenic, was a serious problem at this time and many deaths among the poorer classes were attributed to it.

36. [EJB?], note on verso of title page of PBB, Letters from an Englishman, vol. ii, 8 June 1831: MS in Brotherton.

37. PBB, Letters from an Englishman, vol. iii, 9–11 June 1831: MS in Brotherton, [*M&U*, i, 113–24]. CA *EW*, p.74 argues that Branwell wrote almost all of his 'Letters from an Englishman' when Charlotte was at home and that it was Charlotte's enthusiasm (and presence) which encouraged him to write. This argument cannot be substantiated. The dates of the holidays at Roe Head are unclear, but from the few extant letters dating from this period and from 1835–8 when Charlotte was a governess at Roe Head/Dewsbury Moor, it would appear that there were only three annual holidays, corresponding to the end of the three terms. The summer holiday seems to have been the six weeks from around 17 June to the last week in July, so Branwell's 'Letters' must have been written before Charlotte's return home. The winter holiday began around 17 December and the new term began around 17 January. A possible Easter holiday during the month of April is implied in CB to EN, 10 May 1836: MS HM 24411 pp.1–2, Huntington, [*L&L*, i, 139].

38. CB, A Fragment, 'Overcome with that delightful sense of lassitude', 11 July 1831: MSS Bon 82 & Bon 87, BPM [VN *CB*, 86–91]; CB, 'Albion and

Marina', 12 Oct. 1830: MS at Wellesley, [CA, i, 285–97]. The setting, choice of name ('Albion' for the Marquis of Douro) and character of the heroine, Marian Hume, all seem to me to be extremely derivative and based on Patrick's own story *The Maid of Killarney.* Only the apparitions and the narrator Charles Wellesley's sardonic voice in the preface are wholly Charlotte's own creation. I disagree with CA *EW,* pp.74–5, who sees the fragment as an immediate resumption of the imaginary world and the result of Charlotte's brooding over the development of the plot while at school. Charlotte must have been at home a full three weeks before she wrote it and, if 'Albion and Marina' had been written in four hours flat, as Charlotte claimed, the fragment must have been abandoned very quickly through lack of interest.

39. CB, 'The trumpet hath sounded', 11 Dec. 1831: MS Autograph File (52M–174), Harvard, [VN *CB,* 91–2]. Most critics and biographers, following Ratchford, pp.49–50, see the poem as marking the sweeping away of the Glasstown kingdoms but such a cataclysmic event would certainly have inspired more writing than a single isolated poem. Both Charlotte's poem and Branwell's works on Rogue's revolution refer only to the destruction of the city, not the whole kingdom, which is still very much in being many years later and coexists with Angria. There was thus no need for a 'resuscitation' of Glasstown on Charlotte's return from Roe Head (Ratchford, pp.56ff.) as the kingdom had never been obliterated. For those who follow Ratchford's interpretation see, for example, VN *CB,* p.403; CA *EW,* pp.75–6. According to EN, Reminiscences, *BST:*2:10:70, Charlotte 'was very familiar with all the sublimest passages [of the Bible], especially those in Isaiah, in which she took great delight'. Byron's poem 'The Destruction of Sennacherib', one of his 'Hebrew Melodies' which were published in *Blackwood's Magazine,* is based on the story in Isaiah of the King of Assyria whose troops were slain overnight by the angel of God.

40. CB, 'O There is a land which the sun loves to lighten', 25 Dec. 1831: MS Bon 80(6), BPM, [VN *CB,* 93–4].

41. ECG, *Life,* pp.68–9.

42. EN, Reminiscences, *BST:*2:10:70 tells us that Charlotte was confirmed while at Roe Head – surprisingly, perhaps, as one would have thought Patrick would have wished to oversee his own daughter's confirmation. This is supported by Miss Wooler's great-nephew, who said that his great-uncle, the Reverend E. N. Carter, had given Charlotte her confirmation lessons: Reverend Max Blakeley, 'Memories of Margaret Wooler and her Sisters', *BST:*12:62:113. The Archbishop of York's tour of the area to consecrate new churches and hold confirmations took in Bradford, Halifax, Huddersfield (where he dined at the Franks'), Kirk-

burton, Heckmondwike, Liversedge, Brighouse, Huddersfield again and Birkenshaw, 21–7 September 1831: *Leeds Mercury,* 17 Sept. 1831, p.3. It seems most likely that Charlotte would have been confirmed on Saturday, 24 September, during the confirmation at Liversedge and that the occasion was the reason for the presentation of a Book of Common Prayer, inscribed 'The gift of the Rev W Morgan of Bradford, to Charlotte Brontë, 1831': Sotheby's Sale of the Effects of Arthur Bell Nicholls, 26 July 1907, lot 14.

43. The death of Ann Cook is the subject of CB to EN, 12 Jan. 1840: MS n.l., [*L&L,* i, 195]. ECG, *Life,* p.125 introduces the letter by saying that Ann was a former pupil of Charlotte's and 'had attached herself very strongly' to Anne Brontë, 'who, in return, bestowed upon her much quiet affection'.

44. CB to EN, 11 May 1832 [should be 1831]: MS BS 39 pp.2–3, BPM, [*L&L,* i, 89, misdated to 31 May 1831]. Unless the manuscript is purely a formal school exercise, as the tone and the fact that Ellen was still at school with Charlotte suggest, it must be misdated; Charlotte says it is the first letter she has ever addressed to Ellen, so it must predate her letter of 13 January 1832.

45. CB to EN, 13 Jan. 1832: MS p.3, Harvard, [*L&L,* i, 101–2].

46. Through Ellen's careful selection of which letters to preserve and which to show to Charlotte's biographers, not to mention her heavy-handed editing out of names, references to her own family and anything which appeared to her to reflect badly on her friend, Ellen wilfully manipulated those biographers who sought her assistance. Mrs Gaskell observed that the spirit of Charlotte's letters varied according to the correspondent she was addressing: ECG to WSW, 15 Dec. [1855]: [*C&P,* p.375].

47. EN, Reminiscences, *BST:*2:10:71.

48. PB to Mr Metcalfe, 30 June 1831 and Archbishop of York to PB, 27 June [1831]: MSS BS 183(a & b), BPM, [L&D, p.336].

49. PB to I. C. Wigram, Secretary of the National Society, 8 Aug. 1831: MS BS 183.5, BPM, [*BST:*16:85:351–2]. Edwin Smith preached in aid of the Sunday school at the afternoon and evening services on 14 August 1831: Haworth Church Hymn Sheet, 14 Aug. 1831: MS BS x, H, BPM. Thomas Crowther similarly raised £8 11s. 5d. preaching the sermons the previous year: *Leeds Intelligencer,* 21 Oct. 1830, p.3. Having instituted an annual Sunday school sermon, always preached by a visiting minister, Patrick purchased a copy of *Hymns for the Use of [the National] Sunday Schools* (Keighley, R. Aked, 1821) in which he wrote 'price 6d. To be kept, for the purpose, of selecting Hymns, for the Annual Sunday School Sermons – at Haworth – Those selected must be marked, in order to prevent any from being used a second time – as repetition must be avoided –': MS HAOBP:bb201, BPM. The plaque, over the entrance to the Sunday school,

is still there. It continues: 'It was erected AD 1832 by Voluntary Subscription and by a grant from the National Society in London. Train up a child in the way he should go and when he is old do not depart from it. Prov. xxii.6.'

50. [Benjamin Binns], *Bradford Observer*, 17 Feb. 1894, p.6, who says, 'I can vouch for the accuracy of the incident, for I witnessed it, and the boy was my own brother.' The teaching roles of Charlotte, Emily and Anne are vouched for by their former pupils, Mrs Ratcliffe (Martha Brown's sister), quoted in C. Holmes Cautley, 'Old Haworth Folk who Knew the Brontës', *The Cornhill Magazine*, 29, July–Dec. 1910, pp.77–8; Mr Midgley, quoted in Edward Harrison to Revd. A. Wilkes, 26 Nov. 1879: MS BS ix, H, BPM, [*BST*:12:63:203–4].

51. CB to EN, 21 July 1832: MS HM 24430 p.2, Huntington, [*L&L*, i, 103].

52. *Ibid.*, pp.1–3. Ellen seems to have returned to school for only a few lessons a week, not as a boarder.

53. *Ibid.*, pp.1–2. This description accords remarkably well with the pattern of 'usual occupations' of Flora, Patrick's heroine in *The Maid of Killarney*. From six to eight a.m. she read the Scriptures and other books of a religious character, at eight thirty she joined the family for prayers and then breakfasted; from nine to eleven she read history and *belles-lettres*, 'such works as were calculated to refine, without sullying the mind'. She walked or rode between eleven and twelve, from twelve to one supervised the preparations for dinner and the afternoon she devoted to fancy work 'or more useful domestic employment'. In the evening she gave an hour or two to recreation and concluded the day 'as she began it' with her devotions: PB, *The Maid of Killarney*, pp.86–7, [*Brontëana*, p.166].

54. CB to EN, 21 July 1832: MS HM 24430 p.2, Huntington, [*L&L*, i, 103]. The amount of social visiting that the Brontës did is consistently underplayed and, though four visits in just over a month may not seem much compared to the daily visiting of Ellen and Mrs Gaskell, it is still significantly more than Charlotte or her biographers would have us believe.

55. CB, The Bridal, 14 July–20 Aug. 1832: MS split between MA 2614, Pierpont Morgan and Bon 88, BPM, [*CA*, i, 335–8]. The prose section, significantly, in view of Charlotte's own position at the time, has the author going into the country 'being weary with study ... [and] ... tired of Verdopolis and all its magnificence'. Again I strongly disagree with Ratchford, pp.55, 57, who suggests that 'in contrast to her brother, [Charlotte] wrote with fresh assurance under the inspiration of recent experiences, her imagination seething with new conceptions'. This is the third or possibly the fourth reworking of the same story and exhibits all Charlotte's old Glasstown preoccupations, lush description, magic, false visions and interference of the

Genii. It even incorporates the evil genius Danasch, who is lifted from the *Arabian Nights*. There is an undated two-page fragment, which appears to be a draft of 'The Bridal', so Charlotte may have begun the story earlier and abandoned it either because it was not working or because she lost interest in it: CB, untitled fragment, 'About 9 months after my arrival at the Glasstown', n.d.: MS at KSC & Bon 112, BPM, [*CA*, i, 333–5].

56. CB, St John in the Island of Patmos, 30 Aug. 1832: MS, transcript by ABN, in Brotherton, [VN *CB*, pp.98–100]; CB, Lines on the Celebrated Bewick, 27 Nov. 1832: MS in private hands, [VN *CB*, pp.100–2].

57. PBB, The Fate of Regina, May 1832: MS pp.1–8, originally in BPM (see Brontë Society Catalogue, 1927, item no. 5), now in private hands, [VN, *PBB*, pp.76–9]. The first 166 lines of the poem are missing with the first pages of the manuscript notebook in which it is written. The notebook, which is of ordinary octavo size, contains five poems written at different times and copied into the book in an ordinary cursive hand rather than Branwell's more usual minuscule or rounded left-hand styles. This suggests that the notebook was a fair copy book and that 'The Fate of Regina' may be all that is left of a much longer manuscript story. For 'IIId Ode on the Celebration of the Great AFRICAN GAMES', 26 June 1832, see *ibid.*, pp.9–12, [VN, *PBB*, pp.79–83]. This poem is the second item in the notebook and may well have been intended as a continuation of 'The Fate of Regina'. The odd 'IIId' at the beginning of the title suggests it may have been book iii of that poem.

58. PBB, Ode to the Polar Star, 26 June 1832: MS, see note 57, pp. 14–15, [VN *PBB*, p.84].

59. PBB, Letters from an Englishman, vol. vi, 2 Aug. 1832: MS p. 15, Brotherton, [*M&U*, i, 157–8]. The MSS of vols iv, 3 Aug. 1832 and v, 3 Aug. 1832 are also in the Brotherton, [*M&U*, i, 125–37, 138–49].

60. CB to EN, 5 Sept. 1832: MS BS 39.5 p.3, BPM, [*L&L*, i, 104–5]; EN, Reminiscences: MS pp.48–50, KSC, [*BST*:2:10:71–3].

61. CB to EN, 18 Oct. 1832: MS n.l., [*L&L*, i, 107–8]; CB to EN, 1 Jan. 1833: MS BS 40, BPM, [*L&L*, i, 108–9].

62. CB to EN, 1 Jan. 1833: MS BS 40 pp.1–2 and 1 crossed, BPM, [*L&L*, i, 108–9]. This ritual of self-examination to see what improvements have taken place was shared with Anne who, in her diary paper of 1841, says, on reviewing the last four years, 'we ourselves have sustained very little alteration since that time. I have the same faults that I had then, only I have more wisdom and experience, and a little more self-possession than I then enjoyed': AB, Diary Paper, 30 July 1841: MS n.l., [*L&L*, i, 239].

63. CB to EN, 20 June 1833: MS HM 24404 p.3, Huntington, [*L&L*, i, 110].

64. PBB, The Pirate, 30 Jan–8 Feb. 1833: MS Bon

140, BPM, [*M&U*, i, 171–82]. A larger format had been introduced in PBB, The History of the Young Men, 15 Dec. 1830–7 May 1831: MS Ashley 2468, BL, [*M&U*, i, 62–95].

65. CB, Characters of the Celebrated Men of the Present Time, 17 Dec. 1829: MS in Law Colln, [CA, i, 128].

66. The first page of the manuscript is titled 'THE PIRATE. A Tale by The Author of Letters from an Englishman', i.e. James Bellingham, but the cover is inscribed 'THE PIRATE A TALE. By Captain John Flower'. Ratchford, p.59 accepts the Flower authorship; *M&U*, i, 171–2, by a curious misreading of Rogue's addressing Bellingham by the appellation 'Freind', ascribe the authorship to 'Everard' Bellingham. It is clear from the title and from the references to Bellingham & Co.'s ships being captured that the author is James Bellingham, the merchant.

67. PBB, The Pirate, 30 Jan.–8 Feb. 1833: MS Bon 140 p.2, BPM, [*M&U*, i, 172].

68. Rogue's piratical career seems to be modelled on that of Conrad, subject of Byron's poems *The Corsair* (1814) and *Lara* (1814). Rogue shares Conrad's proud and cynical expression too, see Byron's *Lara*, canto 1st, verse v: 'That brow in furrow'd lines had fix'd at last, / And spake of passions, but of passion past; / The pride, but not the fire, of early days, / Coldness of mien, and carelessness of praise; / A high demeanor, and a glance that took / Their thoughts from others by a single look; / And that sarcastic levity of tongue, / The stinging of a heart the world hath stung ...' See also James Hogg, *The Private Memoirs and Confessions of a Justified Sinner* (London, Longman & Co., 1824); this was the same 'Ettrick Shepherd' who contributed to *Blackwood's Magazine*.

69. Zenobia, a rival to Marian Hume for the love of the Marquis of Douro, made her first appearance as Zelzia Ellrington in Charlotte's 'Albion and Marina', written in October 1830, and reappeared in her 'The Bridal' of June 1832. The suddenness and incongruity of the match between Zenobia and Rogue is explained away by Branwell: 'I had often heard Rougue declare that of all the women in the world he most admired Zenobia Elrington, her too I had not less often heard say that she thought Alexander Rougue in her mind in spite of his conduct had the form and spirit of a Roman Hero': PBB, The Pirate, 30 Jan.–8 Feb. 1833: MS Bon 140 p.13, BPM, [*M&U*, i, 181].

70. CB, 'Fair forms of glistening marble stand around', 26 March 1833: MS Bon 80(4), BPM, [VN *CB*, 106–7]. This poem, which was apparently entitled 'Lord Ronan' and written by the Marquis of Douro, depicts Rogue on his deathbed having to surrender his soul to the evil spirit who has hitherto guided him. Branwell responded by treating the poem, not as an advancement of the story, but as a malicious invention by Douro which puts Rogue in a

flaming temper and compels his return to Glasstown: PBB, Real Life in Verdopolis, vol. ii, 17 Aug. 1833: MS pp.1, 20, Brotherton, [Collins, pp.162, 211].

71. CB, Something About Arthur, 1 May 1833: MS p.1, Texas, [CA, ii, pt i, p.10]. A flashman, according to Alexander's note, was a bully in a bawdy house or a whore's bully. Much of the description and slang used is based on the 'Noctes Ambrosianae'. There are several distasteful incidents of unjustified cruelty, such as Arthur's murder of Lieutenant Tree by tying his cravat 'to such good purpose that the prostrate Lieutenants Life came squirting out to <such good> in a stream of black blood from his eyes and mouth.': *ibid.*, MS p.12, Texas, [CA, ii, pt i, 23].

72. See, for example, Maria Sneachie, who, like Blanche Ingram in *Jane Eyre*, is 'a real, dazzling, brilliant, <im> smiling beauty, what large imperial eyes what a magnificent neck & brow, & how haughtily she lifts her fair head with its weight of glancing black ringlets': CB, 'A Peep into a Picture Book', Corner Dishes, 30 May 1834: MS HM 2577 p.2v, Huntington, [CA, ii, pt ii, 91]. Such portraits are strongly reminiscent of Diana Vernon, heroine of Walter Scott's *Rob Roy*. For the description of a typical male, see Charlotte's portrayal of the Marquis of Douro, below, pp.198–9. There is an interesting development in her portrayal of men, perhaps inspired by sarcasm from Branwell about their effete features. Warner Howard Warner, who is a typical hero of the imaginary worlds, is several times referred to as a hermaphrodite by the more hearty male characters: see, for example, CB, 'A Day Abroad', Corner Dishes, 15 June 1834: MS HM 2577 p.4, Huntington, [CA, ii, pt ii, 102–3].

73. CB, The Foundling, 31 May–27 June 1833: MS Ashley 159, BL, [CA, ii, pt i, 43–125]; CB, 'Lily Hart', The Secret & Lily Hart, 7 Nov. 1833: MS Rare PR 4167.543, Missouri–Columbia, [CA, ii, pt i, 269–315].

74. See, for example, CB, The Foundling, 31 May–27 June 1833: MS Ashley 159 pp.7v–9, BL, [CA, ii, pt i, 50, 103–18]; CB, 'The Secret', The Secret & Lily Hart, 7 Nov. 1833: MS Rare PR 4167.S43 p.8, Missouri–Columbia, [CA, ii, pt i, 297–8].

75. See, for example, Castlereagh and Julia in PBB, Real Life in Verdopolis, 2 vols, May–22 Sept. 1833: MS in Brotherton; for Mary Percy and Sir Robert Pelham see PBB, The Politics of Verdopolis, 23 Oct.–13 Nov. 1833: MS Bon 141, BPM.

76. The Genii play no role at all in any of Branwell's writings after his 'Ode on the Celebration of the Great African Games' of 26 June 1832. Their last appearance altogether is in 'The Pirate' when Alexander Rogue threw Sdeath overboard in an attempt to kill him. On touching the water he changed into the 'Cheif Genius

BRANII' and departed in flashes of fire with 'the Cheif Genii TALLI EMII & ANNII': PBB, The Pirate, 8 Feb. 1833: MS Bon 141 p.14, BPM, [*M&U*, i, 181]. They appear with a functional role for the last time in Charlotte's writings in 'The Foundling', when the four Chief Genii restore to life the Marquis of Douro, Ellrington and Montmorency: CB, The Foundling, 31 May–27 June 1833: MS Ashley 159, p.9, BL, [CA, ii, pt i, 116].

77. For example, both men are castigated for their part in allowing the defeat of the Glasstowners by Napoleon's invading armies, see PBB, An Historical Narrative of the War of Aggression, [Nov.–Dec. 1833]: MS Eng 869(2), pp.1, 4–5, 7, Harvard.

78. PBB, The Pirate, 8 Feb. 1833: MS Bon 141, BPM, [*M&U*, i, 171–82]; PBB, Real Life in Verdopolis, 2 vols, May–22 Sept. 1833: MSS in Brotherton, [Collins, pp.121–210]. The setting of the hideout, in a cavern amidst desolate moorland hills and reached by a tunnel under the river, is strongly reminiscent of the Haworth area and later descriptions of the countryside of Angria. It seems likely that Branwell's evocative description of the scenery here, which was so different from that of Verdopolis, may have given him the incentive to develop 'the provincial' as opposed to 'the metropolitan' in the creation of Angria. It also, of course, draws heavily on Walter Scott's *Rob Roy*.

79. CB, The Green Dwarf, 2 Sept. 1833: MS p.25, Texas, [CA, ii, pt i, 206]; Rogue flirts with the Marchioness of Douro in revenge for his own wife's evident passion for the marquis. See, for example, CB, The Foundling, 31 May–27 June 1833: MS Ashley 159 p.5, BL, [CA, ii, pt i, 78–9] & CB, 'Brushwood Hall/The Post Office' in Arthuriana, 27 Sept. 1833: MS MA 29, Pierpont Morgan, [CA, ii, pt i, 227–31].

80. CB, The Foundling, 31 May–27 June 1833: MS Ashley 159, BL, [CA, ii, pt i, 40–125]; PBB, Real Life in Verdopolis, 2 vols, May–22 Sept. 1833: MS in Brotherton, [Collins, pp.121–210].

81. *Leeds Mercury*, 2 Sept. 1833, p.5. According to the Lodge Minute Books, quoted in Feather, *A Centenary History of the Three Graces Lodge, 408, Haworth, 1792–1931*, p. 41, the festivities were to celebrate the removal from the public rooms of the Black Bull to new buildings in Lodge Street, Haworth. After a period of ten years, during which membership had fallen dramatically and meetings were only held intermittently, the Lodge affiliated to the United Grand Lodge of England in 1831 and thereafter enjoyed a revival of its fortunes: *ibid.*, pp.29–40. The Masonic overtones of the Elysium Society are later made more explicit, as, for example, when Charlotte refers to its members as 'Knights of the Mattock': CB, 'The Secret', The Secret & Lily Hart, 7 Nov. 1833: MS Rare PR 4167.S43 p.4, Missouri-Columbia, [CA, ii, pt i, 282]. Apart from its obvious Heavenly overtones, 'Elysium' was the

site of Ambrose's tavern in the 'Noctes Ambrosianae' in *Blackwood's Magazine*.

82. CB, The Foundling, 31 May–27 June 1833: MS Ashley 159 p.5, BL, [CA, ii, pt i, 75–6]; PBB, Real Life in Verdopolis, vol. ii, 17 Aug.–21 Sept. 1833: MS p.4, Brotherton, [Collins, p.168].

83. CB, The Foundling, p.6, [CA, ii, pt i, 85–6]; PBB, Real Life in Verdopolis, vol. i, pp.13–15, vol. ii, 10, pp.13–14 [Collins, pp.154–61, 185–7, 193ff.]; CB, 'The Post Office', Arthuriana, 20 Nov. 1833: MS MA 29 p.1, Pierpont Morgan, [CA, ii, pt i, 209].

84. PBB, The Monthly Intelligencer, 27 March–26 April 1833: MS BS 117 p.1, BPM [*M&U*, i, 183].

85. EN, Reminiscences: MS pp.52–3, opp. p.62, KSC, [*BST*:2:10:73–4, 79].

86. *Ibid.*, pp.53–4. In the MS Ellen includes a deleted phrase, 'She probably had been pretty.'

87. *Ibid.*, pp.54–6, 65–6.

88. *Ibid.*, pp.55–6.

89. Plait of AB hair, with PB autograph note, 22 May 1833: MS BS 171, BPM. Anne's hair had been fair as a baby, when Sarah Garrs cut off a lock in 1824: see above, p.134.

90. EN, Reminiscences: MS p.56, KSC, [*BST*:2:10:76]. See also Branwell's self-portraits in both 'The Pillar Portrait' and 'The Gun Group', and the various caricatures of his appearance in, for example, CB, My Angria and the Angrians, 14 Oct. 1834: MS in Law Colin, [CA, ii, pt ii, 249].

91. PBB, The Wool is Rising, 26 June 1834: MS Ashley 2469 p.12, BL.

92. Leyland, i, 87–9.

93. *Ibid.*, i, 117–18. There was even a series on boxing called 'Boxiana; or Sketches of Pugilism' in *Blackwood's Magazine*, v–xii, 1819–22. PBB, Real Life in Verdopolis, vol. i, p.15.

94. EN, Reminiscences: MS pp.54–60, 62, KSC, [*BST*:2:10:75–6, 79, 81]. Oatmeal porridge was regarded as the staple diet of the working class, hence Ellen's politely concealed surprise. The dog, the first to be mentioned at the parsonage, would appear to have been Grasper, whose picture Emily drew from life in delicate pencil work in January 1834: EJB, pencil drawing, 'Grasper – from life', Jan. 1834: HAOBP:P.Br.E10, BPM, [JB *ST*, no. 22]. I suspect that Ellen conflated this visit with other, later visits, as it seems extremely unlikely that Patrick, still without a curate at this time, would have had the time to spend his afternoons sitting with the newspapers. The fact that Aunt Branwell was reading them to him also suggests that this picture dates from some years later when Patrick had more leisure because he employed a curate and was gradually losing his sight because of the cataracts in his eyes: it would then be necessary to have the papers read to him.

95. EN, Reminiscences: MS pp.1–3, KSC. Typically Ellen claims this was the first time the Brontës entertained the Sunday school tea-

chers, but this had been one of Charlotte's first duties on her return from Roe Head: see above, p.184.

96. *Bradford Observer*, 17 Feb. 1894, p.6; Haworth Parsonage, Bill of Sale for 1 Oct. 1861: MS X, H, BPM; PBB, watercolour, Dec. 1830: HAOBP:P.Br.B8, BPM, inscribed by Branwell, 'Qeen [sic] Esther – Painted by Martin – and copied by P. B-Brontë – Decr. 1830 –'.

97. EN, Reminiscences: MS pp.3–16, KSC.

98. CB to EN, 11 Sept. 1833: MS HM 24405 p.3, Huntington, [*L&L*, i, 117].

99. *Ibid.*, pp.2–3.

100. ECG, *Life*, p.184; See also CB, *Shirley*, pp.497–513.

101. Characters of the Celebrated Men of the Present Time, 17 Dec. 1829: MS in Law Colln, [CA, i, 124–5].

102. PBB, Real Life in Verdopolis, vol. i, pp.14–15, ii, pp.13–14, [Collins, pp.156–61, 194–8]; PBB, An Historical Narrative of the 'War of Encroachment', 17 Nov.–17 Dec. 1833: MS Eng 869(1) pp.6–7, Harvard; PBB, An Historical Narrative of the War of Aggression, [Dec. 1833–Jan. 1834]: MS Eng 869(2) pp.8–10, Harvard.

103. CB, Arthuriana, 1 Oct.–20 Nov. 1833: MS MA 29, Pierpont Morgan, [CA, ii, pt i, 207–67]; PBB, The Politics of Verdopolis, 23 Oct.–15 Nov. 1833: MS Bon 141, BPM.

104. *Ibid.*, p.1. Charlotte quotes a passage from this

book before beginning a long poem on the death of Ellrington's wife: CB, 'Captain Flower's Last Novel', Arthuriana, 20 Nov. 1833: MS MA 29, Pierpont Morgan, [CA, ii, pt i, 262–7]. Later, she says of Percy Hall, 'The picture of the splendid & venerable pile of buildings that constitute the hall, the slopes of sunny verdure that surround it, the noble trees principally elms of the grandest dimensions, that cover those slopes with trembling gloom interlaced by continual bursts of light, must be imprinted in the heart of every one who has read <Real Life in> The Politics of Verdopolis & who has not?': CB, High Life in Verdopolis, 20 March 1834: MS Add 34255 p.9, BL, [CA, ii, pt ii, 36].

105. PBB, An Historical Narrative of the 'War of Encroachment', 17 Nov.–17 Dec. 1833: MS Eng 869(1), Harvard; PBB, An Historical Narrative of the War of Aggression, [Dec. 1833–Jan. 1834]: MS Eng 869(2), Harvard. Angria is first mentioned in the first of these stories, p.4, the villages of Northangerland and Zamorna, the site of the last great battle, in the second, p.16.

106. PBB, An Historical Narrative of the 'War of Encroachment', 17 Nov.–17 Dec. 1833: MS Eng 869(1) p.6, Harvard.

107. *Ibid.*, p.12.

108. PBB, An Historical Narrative of the War of Aggression, [Dec. 1833–Jan. 1834]: MS Eng 869(2) p.16, Harvard.

CHAPTER EIGHT

Title: the battle cry of the Angrians, from PBB, [The Rising of the Angrians], 24 Dec. 1835–23 March 1836: MS p.14, Princeton.

1. PB to ECG, 24 July 1855: MS EL B121 pp.4–5, Rylands, [*BST*:8:43:92].

2. CB, Richard Coeur de Lion & Blondel, 27 Dec. 1833: MS Ashley 170, BL, [VN *CB*, pp.124–8]. Patrick's note is written above the title of this poem in the manuscript. The poem purports to be the song sung by Blondel outside the castle where his master, Richard 1, is imprisoned and the king's response. CB, Death of Darius Codomanus, 2 May 1834: MS Bon 90, BPM, [VN *CB*, pp.137–42]. Darius Codomanus was a Persian king, treacherously murdered in 331 BC as he tried to withstand an attack by Alexander the Great. CB, Saul, 7 Oct. 1834: MS in Berg, [VN *CB*, pp.154–5]; the poem depicts Saul on the battlefield, sunk in depression and calling for David to come and sing for him. Though now separated, these poems were all part of one notebook which is reconstructed in VN *CB*, pp.xxxvi–xxxvii, 408, on the basis of its distinctive lined paper and Charlotte's handwriting. Patrick may have given Branwell a similar notebook as his poem, 'Thermopylae', for instance, is also written on lined paper in a

cursive hand: PBB, Thermopylae, 9 Aug. 1834: MS Bon 142, BPM, [VN *PBB*, pp.90–5].

3. PBB, The Wool is Rising, 26 June 1834: MS Ashley 2469 p.3, BL.

4. *Ibid.*, p.5. The Earl of St Clair, who had been executed in PBB, An Historical Narrative of the War of Aggression, [Dec. 1834–Jan. 1835]: MS Eng 869(2) p.10, Harvard, is revived without explanation here and in CB, High Life in Verdopolis, 20 Feb.–20 Mar. 1834: MS Add 34255 pp.2–3, BL, [CA, ii, pt ii, 12–13].

5. CB, Last Will & Testament of Florence Marian Wellesley, 5 Jan. 1834: MS MA 2696 R-V, Pierpont Morgan, [CA, ii, pt i, 317–20]. Marian's death of a broken heart is alluded to, for instance, in CB, High Life in Verdopolis, 20 Feb.–20 Mar. 1834: MS Add 34255 pp.4, 6, BL, [CA, ii, pt ii, 17, 26]. Mary Percy was about to marry Sir Robert Pelham – and the then Marquis of Douro was about to give her away – at the end of PBB, Politics in Verdopolis, 23 Oct.–13 Nov. 1833: MS Bon 141 p.18, BPM. Mary is the wife of Zamorna in CB, A Leaf from an Unopened Volume, 17 Jan. 1834: MS BS 13.2, BPM, [CA, ii, pt i, 321–78] but this purports to be many years in the future. She is his bride of three months' standing in CB, High Life in Verdopolis, 20 Feb.–20 Mar.

1834: MS Add 34255, BL, [CA, ii, pt ii, 3–81].
6. CB, A Leaf from an Unopened Volume, 17 Jan. 1834: MS BS 13.2, BPM, [CA, ii, pt i, 321–78]. Zamorna calls Finic 'misshapen abortion' and has him executed for plotting against him. The Negress, Sofala, also died of a broken heart when the marquis, as he then was, deserted her. On Charlotte's own chronology the affair was adulterous as the marquis was, at eighteen, already married to Marian Hume: *ibid.*, pp.19–20, [CA, ii, pt i, 375–7]. Helen Victorine is first referred to in CB, High Life in Verdopolis, 20 Feb.–20 Mar. 1834: MS Add 34255 p.6, BL, [CA, ii, pt ii, 26]. There she is un-named but her son, Ernest fitzArthur, is cared for by Mina Laury, Zamorna's mistress. By October 1834, Charlotte was suggesting that this, too, was not a proper marriage and that Ernest is illegitimate: though 'his inheritance will be wide & rich ... but, alas! alas! the broad bar sinister must be drawn through all': CB, 'A Brace of Characters', The Scrap Book, 30 Oct. 1834: MS Add 34255, BL, [CA, ii, pt ii, 340].
7. CB, High Life in Verdopolis, 20 Feb.–20 March 1834: MS Add 34255 p.10, BL, [CA, ii, pt ii, 40]; CB, The Spell, 21 June–21 July 1834: MS Add 34255 p.7, BL, [CA, ii, pt ii, 171]. Mina Laury's adulterous affair with Zamorna is already implicit in CB, High Life in Verdopolis, 20 Feb.–20 March 1834: MS Add 34255 pp.14–18, BL, [CA, ii, pt ii, 53–68]. It later became explicit in CB, Mina Laury, 17 Jan. 1838: MS at Princeton, [WG FN, 127–69].
8. CB, High Life in Verdopolis, 20 Feb.–20 March 1834: MS Add 34255 p.1, BL, [CA, ii, pt ii, 4]. The 'quotation' is taken from a supposed article in the *Verdopolitan Magazine* by Tree, which on internal evidence, Charlotte tells us, was actually written by Zamorna. It is used by Charles Wellesley to open his book, not because he approves of its sentiments but because it is appropriate to a book about lords and ladies. The complexity of the authorial pedigree is evidence of Charlotte's increasing sophistication in her use and awareness of the authorial voice.
9. PBB, The Wool is Rising, 26 June 1834: MS Ashley 2469 pp.8, 20, BL.
10. *Ibid.*, pp.7–8; CB, *The Professor*, pp.14–40.
11. CB, The Spell, An Extravaganza, 21 June–21 July 1834: MS Add 34255 pp.26–7, BL, [CA, ii, pt ii, 234–7].
12. PBB, The Life of feild Marshal the Right Honourable ALEXAN[D]ER PERCY, vol. i, [Spring 1834]: MS p.2, Brotherton, [Collins, p.12]. This volume is undated but the poem 'Augusta though Im far away' appears in Branwell's fair copy book and is dated to Spring 1834: PBB, Fair Copy Book of Poems, compiled 9 March 1837–12 May 1838: MS BS 125 pp.8–9, BPM, [JB SP, pp.23–4].
13. PBB, The Life of feild Marshal the Right

Honourable ALEXAN[D]ER PERCY, vol. i, [Spring 1834]: MS pp.3–6, Brotherton, [Collins, pp.17–27]. Percy's favourite hymns, which probably reflect Branwell's own preferences, are listed as ' 'Twas on that dark that doleful night', 'Why did my God and Saviour bleed', 'When I can read my title clear' and 'There is a land of pure delight': *ibid.*, p.6.
14. Perhaps because atheism was so alien to their own beliefs, the Brontës seem to have associated it with a rejection of the idea of life after death rather than simply a conviction that there is no God. Percy's first explicit avowal of atheism, for instance, reflects this idea and actually occurs in one of Charlotte's stories. In 'High Life in Verdopolis' he tells his daughter: 'The Grave, Corruption, Annihilation, are the only followers of Death. Mary you see in Zamorna & myself the perfection of created things. man is the master-piece of nature or \of/ him who commanded the existence of nature ... Dreamers think otherwise but I say "the first dark day of nothingness" comes after the heart is still & the eye glazed for ever.' The quotation is from Byron's *The Giaour*, l.70: CB, High Life in Verdopolis, 20 Feb.–20 March 1834: MS Add 34255 p.8, BL, [CA, ii, pt ii, 32]. The suggestion that Branwell himself was an atheist is made, for example, in WG *PBB*, pp.294–7.
15. PBB, An Historical Narrative of the War of Aggression, [Dec. 1834–Jan. 1835]: MS Eng 869(2) p.15, Harvard.
16. PBB, The Wool is Rising, 26 June 1834: MS Ashley 2469 p.8, BL.
17. PBB, The Life of feild Marshal the Right Honourable ALEXAN[D]ER PERCY, vol. i, [Spring 1834]: MS p.7, Brotherton, [Collins, p.34].
18. John Barnet, in James Hogg's *Confessions of a Justified Sinner* and Andrew Fairservice, in Walter Scott's *Rob Roy*, first published in 1817, are both a similar blend of pseudo-Calvinistic piety spoken, in these instances, in Scots dialect. The emergence of the theme of religious hypocrisy in Branwell's writing in the winter of 1834 and the spring of 1834 may reflect his father's very public clash with John Winterbotham, the minister of West Lane Baptist Chapel, which occurred at the same time.
19. PBB, The Life of feild Marshal the Right Honourable ALEXAN[D]ER PERCY, vol. i, [Spring 1834]: MS p.13, Brotherton, [Collins, p.57].
20. *Ibid.*, p.15; see, for example, Branwell's poems 'Augusta though Im far away', 'The Doubter's Hymn' and 'Thou art gone but I am here', which are all from *ibid.*, vol. i, pp.13–14, vol ii, pp.14, 16 [JB SP, pp.23–6].
21. Branwell's manuscripts from the second half of 1834 were divided up and sold piecemeal by T. J. Wise, making it extremely difficult to reconstruct the books he wrote. Neufeldt (ed.), *A Bib-*

liography of the Manuscripts of PBB is a much-needed tool for locating and identifying the scattered fragments. See pp.6–7 for the relevant MSS references. An edition of Branwell's juvenilia is greatly needed and would, I think, radically alter the accepted assessment of his literary ability and his influence on his sisters' work, which is usually derived from the very jaundiced views expressed in Ratchford.

22. CB, My Angria and the Angrians, 14 Oct. 1834: MS in Law Colln, [CA, ii, pt ii, 245]. Wiggins had already appeared as a caricature of Branwell in CB, 'A Day Abroad', Corner Dishes, 28 May–16 June 1834: MS HM 2577 pp.4–5v, Huntington, [CA, ii, pt ii, 104–15]. Branwell, who was not without a self-deprecating sense of humour, caricatured himself as a colour grinder to Sir Edward de Lisle at about this same time in PBB, The Wool is Rising, 26 June 1834: MS Ashley 2469, p.12, BL, see above, p.195.

23. CB, My Angria and the Angrians, 14 Oct. 1834: MS in Law Colln, [CA, ii, pt ii, 248–50].

24. CB to EN, 11 Feb. 1834: MS HM 24406 pp.1, 3, Huntington, [L&L, i, 118].

25. CB to EN, 20 Feb. 1834: MS HM 24407 p.1, Huntington, [L&L, i, 119].

26. Ibid., pp.2–3.

27. See, for example, Charlotte's letter to Ellen where she gives her a taste of the sort of letters Mary received in response to a complaint by Ellen: CB to EN, 13 March 1835: MS n.l., [L&L, i, 126–7].

28. [Benjamin Binns], Bradford Observer, 17 Feb. 1894, p.6. This is confirmed by the many accounts of concerts in Haworth in the local newspapers. The Brontës had many more opportunities to attend concerts than people living in small towns today.

29. Bradford Observer, 13 Nov. 1834, p.325. The age of the Haworth Philharmonic Society I have deduced from the opening of this review: 'It has been customary with this Society for more than half a century to meet together on the 5th of November, to enjoy a festival of vocal and instrumental music.' For further examples of concerts in Haworth, see Bradford Observer, 10 April 1834, p.77; 13 Nov. 1834, p.325.

30. The Band played, for instance, at Theodore Dury's Sunday school treat at Keighley on 30 July 1832 and at a Masonic celebration in Haworth on 2 September 1833: Leeds Mercury, 4 Aug. 1832, p.5; 7 Sept. 1833, p.5. The concert for the opening of the Haworth church organ was arranged by Mr Sunderland and included a performance by Mr Greenwood on the new organ, built by Mr Nicholson of Rochdale, which 'is allowed by many of the best judges to be of exquisite tone, sweetness, and power'. He was accompanied by Thomas Parker, singing 'in that style of excellence for which he is so remarkable'. Henry Heap, vicar of Bradford, and Charles Musgrave, the archdeacon of Halifax, both preached on the day of the opening of the

organ and the collections amounting to nearly £30 were taken on behalf of the fund: Leeds Mercury, 29 March 1834, p.7; Bradford Observer, 3 April 1834, p.69; 10 April 1834, p.77. Greenwood returned to Haworth to accompany Thomas Parker again on 12 April 1835 in a concert for the organ fund which raised £15: Leeds Mercury, 18 April 1835, p.5.

31. [Benjamin Binns], Bradford Observer, 17 Feb. 1894, p.6.

32. CB, My Angria and the Angrians, 14 Oct. 1834: MS in Law Colln, [CA, ii, pt ii, 251–2].

33. PBB, MS Music Book, 1 Nov. 1831–Jan. 1832: MS Bon 56, BPM. 'Oh no, we never mention her', by Thomas Bayly, is used to allude to Marian Hume in CB, Something About Arthur, 1 May 1833: MS p.24, Texas, [CA, ii, pt i, 40]. It was also used in AB, Tenant of Wildfell Hall, p.404 as a sly reference to Helen Huntingdon. I am grateful to Margaret Smith for this reference. For Branwell's ability to play the organ and love of oratorio see Leyland, i, 119–20.

34. The piano is in the Brontë Parsonage Museum: HAOBP: F13, BPM. For its provenance and a detailed description see JB ST, no.23. Gawkroger's, the music shop in Halifax, sold cheap mahogany pianofortes, both second-hand and new, ranging in price from £14 to £38: Halifax Guardian, 13 June 1840, p.2. For Sunderland still coming to give music lessons see EJB/AB, Diary Paper, 24 Nov. 1834: MS Bon 131 p.2, BPM, [JB ST, no. 11].

35. Paganini's concert, enthusiastically reviewed the following week, was advertised in the Leeds Mercury, 4 Feb. 1832, p.3. It doubtless inspired the references to him in the juvenilia, see, for example, CB, 'A Day Abroad', Corner Dishes, 15 June 1834: MS HM 2577 p.5, Huntington, [CA, ii, pt ii, 110–11]. For the concerts by Strauss and Liszt see Halifax Guardian, 20 Oct. 1838, pp.2, 3; 30 Jan. 1841, p.3. Mendelssohn had a particularly close relationship with the Halifax Choral Society, which introduced many of his works to this country; in gratitude he dedicated his setting of the 95th Psalm to the Society, which gave it its first performance in 1846: Bradford Observer, 30 April 1846, p.5.

36. Leeds Mercury, 30 Nov. 1833, p.5; 11 Jan. 1834, p.8; 10 Jan. 1835, p.3.

37. Leeds Intelligencer, 27 July 1833, p.3. A new court house was opened on 12 August 1833: Leeds Mercury, 17 Aug. 1833, p.5. The first stone of Keighley Church Sunday school, which was also to be a National and Infant School, was laid on 19 May 1834: Leeds Intelligencer, 24 May 1834, p.3. The opening of the new Keighley Mechanics' Institute was celebrated with a concert on 29 December 1834: Leeds Mercury, 11 Jan. 1835, p.8.

38. For Patrick's membership see Keighley Mechanics' Institute, Annual Report for year ending 8 April 1833, list of members: MS no. 213, Keighley. In January 1833, William Dearden was given a silver medal inscribed 'Presented to W S

Dearden, by the Committee of the Keighley Mechanics' Institute as a testimonial of their estimation of his highly interesting course of lectures on Ancient British Poetry': *Leeds Mercury,* 12 Jan. 1835, p.5. For a brief résumé of Dearden's career, see 'Warley Worthies', *Transactions of the Halifax Antiquarian Society,* (1916), pp.105–8. For the other lectures see *Bradford Observer,* 10 Dec. 1835, p.357; Ian Dewhirst, 'The Rev. Patrick Brontë and the Keighley Mechanics' Institute', *BST*:14:75:36.

39. ECG to unknown, [September 1853]: [C&P, p.249]. Charlotte told Mrs Gaskell that it took her six months at a time to finish one of these pencil copies of engravings out of annuals and blamed the detailed work for weakening her eyesight. This seems unlikely as she was already shortsighted when she attended Roe Head: see above, pp.172–3, 195. CB, pencil drawing entitled 'Santa Maria', 23 Sept. 1833: MS at Princeton; CB, pencil drawing entitled 'Geneva', 23 [Aug., changed to] Nov. 1834: HAOBP:P.Br. Bon 14, BPM. Both are copies of engravings by William Finden, many of whose illustrations Charlotte copied.

40. CB, pencil drawing of Lord Byron, [c.1833]: MS in private hands; CB, pencil drawing of Countess Blessington, 1833: MS in private hands; CB, pencil drawing of Lady Jersey, entitled 'English Lady', 15 Oct. 1834: HAOBP:P.Br. Bon 2, BPM; CB, watercolour based on the 'Maid of Saragoza', [c.1834]: HAOBP:P.Br. Bon 25, BPM. The portraits of Lady Jersey (in a book which Charlotte recommended to Ellen Nussey) and the 'Maid of Saragoza' were both copied from William Finden's engravings.

41. Charlotte's fictional hero, the Marquis of Douro, whose portrait she sketched many times, is an example. Though based on portraits of the Duke of Wellington, the features are softened and made almost feminine. See, for example, HAOBP:P.Br.B15, BPM which, though attributed to Branwell, is undoubtedly by Charlotte, and HAOBP:P.Br.C28r, BPM.

42. *Leeds Mercury,* 1 Nov. 1823, p.2; 29 Nov. 1823, p.3.

43. *Leeds Intelligencer,* 8 June 1833, p.3. Many of the greatest contemporary painters were displayed at the exhibition: Robinson's mentor, Sir Thomas Lawrence, and J. M. W. Turner, for example, both exhibited in 1828: *Leeds Mercury,* 24 May 1828, p.3. The 1826 exhibition consisted of ancient and modern masters from private collections, none of the pictures being for sale: *Bradford & Wakefield Chronicle,* 1 April 1826, p.3. For the 1834 exhibition see Leyland, i, 129–31; *Leeds Intelligencer,* 19 July 1834, p.4; 16 Aug. 1834, p.3; 28 June 1834, p.3; 12 July 1834, p.4.

44. WG *PBB,* p.79, but I have not been able to identify a contemporary source for the claim that Patrick paid two guineas a lesson. It seems unlikely to me that Branwell started his lessons with William Robinson so early. I believe it is more likely that Branwell was still receiving

lessons from Bradley in 1834 and that he only graduated to Robinson after he decided to apply to the Royal Academy in the autumn of 1835.

45. Susan Foister, 'The Brontë Portraits', *BST*:18:95:342–3. For Robinson's obituary see *Leeds Mercury,* 27 Oct. 1838, p.4.

46. Leyland, i, 135–6. The critic of the *Leeds Intelligencer,* reviewing the 1834 exhibition of the Northern Society for the Encouragement of the Arts, said that Robinson's portraits of children had 'very expressive, but somewhat hard features. Considering them as groups, they are formal and matter of fact; there is an absence of the imaginative which we are sure the artist can supply if he pleases. We would point to the works of Reynolds.': *Leeds Intelligencer,* 19 July 1834, p.4.

47. EN, *Reminiscences,* [*L&L,* i, 112].

48. ECG to unknown, [Sept. 1853]: [C&P, p.249]. The portrait was 'brought down' by Charlotte to show Mrs Gaskell on her visit to Haworth in 1853, implying it was not prominently displayed in the parsonage. When Mrs Gaskell saw it, the image of Branwell was not visible and she fancied that the 'great column, lit by the sun' divided Charlotte from her sisters' melancholy fate. Mrs Gaskell described it as 'not much better than sign-painting, as to manipulation; but the likenesses were, I should think, admirable ... from the striking resemblance which Charlotte, upholding the great frame of canvas, and consequently standing right behind it, bore to her own representation': ECG, *Life,* p.88. Much significance has been attached to the painting out of Branwell's portrait, which has variously been ascribed to dissatisfaction with his own image, a later fit of self-disgust and even to his family's wish to obliterate him from their collective memory and therefore arranging to have him painted out after his death. The conservators at the National Portrait Gallery, however, were convinced that the same hand painted the image in and out and that this was done at the same time as the rest of the portrait was painted: Susan Foister, 'The Brontë Portraits', *BST*:18:95:354 n.13. The fact that the image of Branwell is completely undamaged and carefully painted over does not support the theory that it was removed in a fit of pique or anger. Similarly, the landscape format of the second portrait, which lends itself to a much less crowded composition, suggests that Branwell (perhaps at his tutor's suggestion) removed his self portrait to create a more balanced grouping.

49. T. P. Foley, 'John Elliot Cairnes' Visit to Haworth Parsonage', *BST*:18:94:293; Arthur Bell Nicholls told Clement Shorter that he had destroyed all but the profile portrait when Shorter visited him in Ireland in 1895: Shorter, note on pp.123–4. There has been much speculation about the identity of the 'profile portrait', many people preferring to believe it is of Anne, because it is 'too pretty' to be of Emily, but there

is no doubt of the identification. The discovery of Martha Brown's photograph of the complete portrait confirmed the identifications made by John Greenwood on his tracings of the original, proving that the profile was of Emily and that Ellen Nussey's initialled identifications on the highly inaccurate reproduction of the portrait in Horsfall Turner's *Haworth Past and Present*, opp. p.137 were wrong: see Barker, 'The Brontë Portraits: A Mystery Solved', *BST*:20:1:3–11.

50. Again, the prominent displaying of the portrait which includes Branwell suggests that his family cannot have been responsible for the obliteration of his image in the 'Three Sisters' portrait.

51. CB, pencil portrait of Anne Brontë, 17 April 1833: HAOBP:P:Br.C17.5, BPM; CB, watercolour portrait of Anne Brontë, 17 June 1834: HAOBP:P.Br.C21, BPM; CB, watercolour portrait of Anne Brontë, [1834]: in private hands, on loan to BPM. It has been suggested that Charlotte was sharing her brother's lessons with Robinson, but in that case one would have expected her to produce some portraits in oils. A professional artist of his standing is unlikely to have instructed a girl in pencil or watercolour. There is also some doubt as to whether Robinson would have travelled to Haworth to give lessons: it seems more likely that Branwell would have had to travel to Leeds to Robinson's studio for instruction, something that Charlotte could not have done. Charlotte's interest in portraiture at this time confirms my belief that Branwell was still receiving lessons from John Bradley – lessons which Charlotte would have been able to share.

52. PB to Chas Dudley, Bible Society, 20 July 1833, 3 Sept. 1833: MSS in archives of Bible Society, ULC.

53. PB to Archbishop of York, July 1833: MS in Borthwick. This letter signifies Patrick's intention to appoint James Bardsley to be his curate at Haworth but the salary and date are left blank in the document. For the story of Bardsley's non-appointment to Haworth see C. W. Bardsley, *A Dictionary of English and Welsh Surnames* (London and New York, 1901), p.v. I am grateful to Margaret Smith for this reference. Bardsley officiated once in Haworth, at the burial of four-year-old Suzanna Feather on 2 September 1833. The entry in the register, originally signed 'James Bardsley' in Patrick's handwriting, was erased and Patrick wrote over it 'The ceremony was performed by Mr Bardsley': Register of Burials, 1813–36, Haworth Church. Bardsley was already the curate at Keighley by 19 May 1834, when he is reported as being present in that capacity at the ceremony to lay the foundation stone of the new Keighley Church Sunday school: *Leeds Intelligencer*, 24 May 1834, p.3.

54. Thomas Crowther preached at the afternoon and evening services on 21 July 1833: Haworth Church Hymn Sheets, 21 July 1833: MS BS x, H, BPM; William Morgan preached two sermons on 20 July 1834: *Leeds Mercury*, 26 July 1834, p.5.

55. See, for example, *Leeds Mercury*, 28 Dec. 1833, p.7.

56. John Winterbotham, in his letter to the *Leeds Mercury*, 8 March 1834, p.6, says that he is responding to 'the three letters of my friend to the Editor of the *Intelligencer*'. I have only been able to locate one of these, Patrick's letter of 7 January, signed 'P.B.', which was published in the *Leeds Intelligencer*, 18 Jan. 1834, p.4. Winterbotham replied to this letter in detail the following week in the *Leeds Mercury*, 25 Jan. 1834, p.6 and said that it was Patrick's second one. Another letter from Patrick, dated 17 February and signed 'P. BRONTE', was published in the *Leeds Mercury*, 22 Feb. 1834, p.6, but on content it does not seem to be the one Winterbotham called Patrick's third. I have been unable to find any letters or articles in the *Leeds Intelligencer*, *Leeds Mercury* or *Leeds Times*, either under Patrick's own name or initials or under a pseudonym, which fit Winterbotham's description of and quotations from Patrick's first and third letters. Nor can I find any letter or article in those papers which uses the phrases quoted by Winterbotham. Patrick cannot be 'A Yorkshire Rector', who had letters defending the Established Church in the *Leeds Mercury* and *Bradford Observer*, as he dates at least one of his letters from 'E—, nr W.': *Leeds Mercury*, 4 Jan. 1834 p.8. Nor can he have been 'A Churchman', as he had already written two letters before Patrick's identified one of 18 January: *Leeds Intelligencer*, 23 Nov. 1833, p.3; 4 Jan. 1834, p.3.

57. John Winterbotham to *Leeds Mercury*, 8 March 1834, p.6. Winterbotham was equally vitriolic and personal in his attack on the Reverend George Bull, 'the factory child's friend', see below, p.880 n.65.

58. PB to *Leeds Mercury*, 22 Feb. 1834, p.6.

59. John Winterbotham to *Leeds Mercury*, 8 March 1834, p.6.

60. Three days after his reply to Winterbotham was published in the *Leeds Mercury*, 22 Feb. 1834, p.6, Patrick wrote again to the paper stating that 'Having already taken my friendly leave of the Rev. John Winterbotham, and being willing to throw a mantle of charity over him, and all his motives and actions, I would farther observe, that unless forced by unexpected circumstances, I will not reply to any article bearing his signature, whether that article might, perchance, be the product of his own mind, or the result of a neighbourly co-operation of heads more learned than his own'. The subject of this letter was yet another renewal of his attack on the severity of the criminal code: a statesman who advocated such reform would, Patrick said, 'like Howard and Wilberforce, ... erect for himself a monument more durable

than brass, and more precious than gold'.: *Leeds Mercury,* 8 March 1834, p.3.

61. PB to Church Trustees, 1 Feb. 1834: MS Heaton B143 p.5, WYAS, Bradford, [L&D, p.337]; PB, deed between Incumbent and Church Trustees, 28 July 1834: MS BS 155, BPM. Patrick had complained of the problems that gave rise to the agreement in his letters to the Governors of the Queen Anne's Bounty in 1825: see above, pp.142–3.

62. PB to Earl of Harewood, 11 Aug. 1834: MS in Box 1, Lieutenancy Papers, Harewood Papers, WYAS, Leeds.

63. PB to Henry Heap, 27 Nov. 1834, forwarded to the Earl of Harewood with Henry Heap to Earl of Harewood, 2 Dec. 1834: MSS in Box 1, Lieutenancy Papers, Harewood Papers, WYAS, Leeds. Joseph Greenwood was sworn in at the Skipton Sessions on 28 June 1836: Justices' Qualification Oaths, 1819–37: MS in WYAS, Wakefield. I am grateful to Sarah Fermi for this reference.

64. PB to Henry Heap, 27 Nov. 1834, forwarded to the Earl of Harewood with Henry Heap to Earl of Harewood, 2 Dec. 1834: MSS in Box 1, Lieutenancy Papers, Harewood Papers, WYAS, Leeds. Contraventions of the Act were dealt with at assizes as far away as Skipton: see, for example, Jonas Hird, of Royd House, Haworth, caught by the factory inspectors and fined at Skipton Assizes for employing children for over twelve hours a day and allowing his foreman to make up his records of hours worked: *Leeds Mercury,* 13 Sept. 1834, p.8. Hartley Merrall was also fined for working his mill children in Haworth beyond the hours specified in the Factory Act: *Leeds Intelligencer,* 4 April 1835, p.3.

65. George Bull to *Leeds Mercury,* 13 Sept. 1834, p.5; John Winterbotham to *Leeds Mercury,* 20 Sept. 1834, p.6. The Reverend George Stringer Bull, vicar of Bierley, whom Winterbotham characteristically and unfairly dubbed 'the pugnacious parson', was better known as 'the factory child's friend'. Though a Tory by conviction, like Patrick, he was also a friend of the reformer Richard Oastler and of the Radical and Chartist Abraham Wildman. He worked tirelessly with them for the Ten Hours Bill, writing to the press and addressing public meetings, like the one in Keighley on 3 March 1835, where all three spoke in favour of the Bill: *Leeds Intelligencer,* 7 March 1835, p.3. Patrick was one of the signatories of a memorial to George Bull, praising his campaign for factory children: *Bradford Observer,* 17 Sept. 1840, p.2.

66. *Bradford Observer,* 20 Nov. 1834, p.333; *Leeds Mercury,* 22 Nov. 1834, p.7; Haworth Temperance Society membership cards, no. 77 Jonas Gregson, 26 Dec. 1834, no. 94 Mary Binns, 26 Dec. 1834, no. 191 Thomas Pickles, March 1835: MSS BS 146 (a–c), BPM. According to Babbage, *Report to the General Board of Health,* pp.11–12, the average consumption of beer per

head of population in Haworth was about one-ninth of a pint daily. Nancy Garrs complained that Aunt Branwell only allowed the parsonage servants half a pint of beer a day, which she considered 'close': Helen Arnold, 'The Reminiscences of Emma Huidekoper Cortazzo: a friend of Ellen Nussey', *BST*:13:68:227. The parsonage must have brewed its own beer as 'Brewing Utensils' were sold at the sale of effects in 1861: Catalogue of the Sale of Haworth Parsonage, first day of sale, 1 Oct. 1861, lot 32: MS BS x, H, BPM. Wine, which Patrick regularly ordered from the Thomas' firm of wine merchants in Haworth, was not a distilled liquor and presumably therefore excluded from the pledge.

67. CB to EN, 19 June 1834: MS n.l., [*L&L*, i, 120].

68. CB to EN, 4 July 1834: MS HM 24408 pp.2–3, Huntington, [*L&L*, i, 121]; CB to EN, 10 Nov. 1834: MS MA 2696 R-V p.3, Pierpont Morgan, [*L&L*, i, 123].

69. CB to EN, 4 July 1834: MS HM 24408 p.2 crossed, Huntington, [*L&L*, i, 122].

70. Charlotte's wide reading of Byron is reflected, for instance, in CB, High Life in Verdopolis, 20 Feb.–20 Mar. 1834: MS Add 34255, BL, [CA, ii, pt ii, 3–81], where she quotes from both Shakespeare and Byron at the beginning of each chapter. The high value that the Brontës attached to Byron is indicated by the fact that Branwell, on a trip to Liverpool in May 1835, spent some of his meagre savings on a copy of *Childe Harold's Pilgrimage* (Paris, 1827): MS HAOBP:bb15, BPM.

71. CB to EN, 4 July 1834: MS HM 24408 p.3 crossed, Huntington, [*L&L*, i, 122].

72. EJB/AB, Diary Paper, 24 Nov. 1834: MS Bon 131, BPM, [JB *ST*, no. 11].

73. CB to EN, 13 March 1835: MS n.l., [*L&L*, i, 126–7].

74. *Leeds Intelligencer,* 11 April 1835, p.3.

75. John Foster to *Leeds Mercury,* 18 April 1835, p.8.

76. CB to EN, 8 [March should be May] 1835: MS Bon 160, BPM, [*L&L*, i, 127–8].

77. 'O.P.Q.' to *Leeds Mercury,* 23 May 1835, p.7.

78. PB, *The Signs of the Times; or a Familiar Treatise on Some Political Indications in the Year 1835* (Keighley, R. Aked, 1835), price 6d., [*Brontëana,* pp.220–32].

79. Patrick was not acting out of pure self-interest in his defence of the church establishment; his own salary was not dependent on tithes or church rates so their abolition would not have affected his personal finances. He defended the 'fair commutation' of tithes, rather than their outright abolition, on the grounds that clergyman had 'as fair a claim on their dues, as any landed proprietor can have on his rents.': *ibid.,* p.12, [*Brontëana,* p.226]. Branwell reflected his father's views in his juvenilia, where he has Zamorna, in disguise as Colonel Hartford, defend the Established Church of the Glasstown Union: 'I am a Member of the Church of

Africa because I think it the best church in the Universe but poor is the best compared with the loftiness of the truth. And though I think that to seperate from my church because many of its Doctrines and much of its government is and are eron[e]ous would be to do more injury to religion than to uphold even its faults yet I will never cease to advocate the Doctrines I have founded and too endeavour to spread them as wide as my name may extend.': PBB, [Massacre of Dongola], [c. Dec. 1834–Jan. 1835]: MS p.9, Brotherton, [facsimile in *M&U*, ii, 71].

80. PB, *The Signs of the Times*, pp.16, 19, [*Brontëana*, pp.229, 231].

81. Northangerland's attacks on the ministry by letter and in Parliament are contained in PBB, [Northangerland's Letter to the Angrians], 12 Sept. 1834: MS pp.1–2, Brotherton and PBB, [The Opening of the Angrian Parliament], [Oct. 1834]: MS pp.4–8, Brotherton, [part in facsimile, *M&U*, ii, 467–9].

82. PBB, [History of Angria I], 15 June–25 July 1835: MS p.4, Rutgers, [facsimile *M&U*, ii, 103]. This, again, is only a fragment of a dismembered manuscript.

83. *Ibid.*, p.8.

84. CB to EN, 2 July 1835: MS HM 24410 pp.1–2, Huntington, [*L&L*, i, 209].

CHAPTER NINE

Title: Referring to Angria, from CB, 'All this day I have been in a dream', 11 Aug.–14 Oct. 1836: MS Bon 98(8) p.1, BPM.

1. CB to EN, 2 July 1835: MS HM 24410 p.3, Huntington, [*L&L*, i. 129].

2. PBB, draft letter to the Secretary for the Royal Academy, [Summer 1835]: MS in three fragments, MS Bon 147 pp.1v, 1v, 3v, BPM.

3. The idea was first suggested in 1914 by Chadwick, p.114: 'That he went to London is certain, though Mrs Gaskell did not get to know this; but he soon got through all the money his father had allowed him, giving useless excuses, such as that he had been robbed by a fellow-traveller. The old Vicar saw that Branwell was not to be trusted in London, and he was brought back.' Chadwick offers no authority or source for her information but this tale, which Gérin confidently attributes to 'Haworth folk who still remembered that deplorable return' is the main evidence of her long account of Branwell's disastrous visit to London: WG *PBB*, p.111. Gérin also states categorically 'That he went there, his friends Leyland, Grundy and Searle Phillips and many others later heard directly from himself': WG *PBB*, p.95. The evidence of Leyland, Grundy and Searle Phillips, as we shall see, is at best second hand and amounts to no more than a suggestion that Branwell spent a few days in London, not at the Royal Academy. Far from there being 'many others' who later heard the story from Branwell himself, no one else at all ever corroborated this version of events. Gérin's account has been accepted unquestioningly by all other biographers, including Du Maurier, pp.49–52; Bentley, *The Brontës and Their World*, pp.60–1; Lane, *The Brontë Story*, pp.114–19; Wilks, *The Brontës*, pp.76–7; Rees, *Profligate Son*, pp.45–7; Fraser, pp.100–2.

4. CB to EN, 2 July 1835: MS HM 24410 p.3, Huntington, [*L&L*, i, 129]; PB to Mrs Franks, 6 July 1835: MS BS 184 p.1, BPM, [*L&L*, i, 130].

5. Leyland, i, 144–5; Grundy, p.80.

6. PBB, 'Then shall I perish for ever' and 'While Charles Wentworth leant over a parapet', 28 May 1836: MSS in Brotherton, [*M&U*, ii, 182–5, 2nd fragment only]. These fragments, which begin and end abruptly, were once part of a larger manuscript. For their context see Neufeldt, *A Bibliography of the Manuscripts of PBB*, pp.9–21, esp.p.11(f). The story is cited, for instance, by Du Maurier, pp.51–2, WG *PBB*, pp.98–106 and Fraser, p.101.

7. PBB, draft letter to the Secretary for the Royal Academy, [Summer 1835]: MS in three fragments, MS Bon 147 pp.1v, 2v, 3v, BPM. I am grateful to Ms Helen Valentine, Curatorial Assistant of the Royal Academy, for checking the records on my behalf.

8. A portfolio of drawings 'from the skeleton' and 'from the antique' were required as proof of draughtsmanship from all potential probationers at the Royal Academy: Leyland, i, 142–3. According to a letter from Patrick to William Robinson, Branwell was going to Leeds to complete his course of lessons on 11 September: PB to William Robinson, 7 Sept. 1835: MS BS 185 p.2, BPM, [*L&L*, i, 132]. It seems likely that Branwell would have taken more lessons during the next two to two and a half years before he set up in business on his own in Bradford.

9. EN to ECG, 22 Oct. 1856: MS n.l., [Shorter, p.15].

10. The Brontë copy of *A Description of London* (London, William Darton, 1824), which is heavily annotated, is in the Brontë Parsonage Museum: MS HAOBP:bb35, BPM. An engraving of Westminster Abbey appears between pp.12–13.

11. January Searle [George Searle Phillips], 'Branwell Brontë', *The Mirror*, 28 Dec. 1872 p.278. Far from being confirmation of Branwell's supposedly disastrous trip to London, as WG *PBB*, p.95 asserts, this account explicitly makes clear that the visit never happened.

12. Leyland, i, 145, 202. 'Mr Woolven' is mentioned in no other contemporary source that I can find, including Grundy, though he is said to have worked on the Leeds and Manchester Railway.

There is no variant of this name in the 1841 census for Luddenden Foot: Census Returns for Midgeley & Warley, 1841: Microfilm, Halifax.

13. Extracts from Pierce Egan's *Boxiana*, the ninth of which was set in the Castle tavern, were printed in *Blackwood's Magazine*, v–xii, 1819–22. WG *PBB*, p.107 says that *Bell's Sporting Life*, was taken by Thomas Sugden at the Black Bull but gives no source for her information which is contradicted by the son of the Haworth tailor. He says that Branwell sent him over to the Shake Hands public house between Haworth and Oakworth every Sunday to collect *Bell's Sporting Life* for him to read: [Benjamin Binns] *Bradford Observer*, 17 Feb. 1894, p.6. Egan had begun the journal in 1824 under another title and in 1859 it was incorporated into *Sporting Life*. See also Pierce Egan, *Book of Sports* (London, 1832) for accounts of the Castle Tavern and its customers.

14. Huchison, *The History of the Royal Academy, 1768–1968*, p.49. I'm grateful to Mr P. B. Hearne for this reference.

15. PBB to the Editor of *Blackwood's Magazine*, 8 April 1836: MS 4042 p.1, NLS. Branwell was initiated as a Mason into the Three Graces Lodge of Haworth on 29 February 1836 and attended the next meeting on 28 March: Feather, *A Centenary History of the Three Graces Lodge*, p.43; MS Masonic Records, in private hands.

16. PBB to J B Leyland, [*c.*24 Jan. 1847]: MS pp.2–3, Brotherton, [*L&L*, ii, 124].

17. Wentworth appears only in the second volume of Branwell's great history of Angria which is dismembered and scattered over a number of locations. The fragments in which he appears, in chronological order, are: PBB, 'Then shall I perish for ever', [May 1836] and 'While Charles Wentworth leant over a parapet', 28 May 1836: MSS in Brotherton, [*M&U*, ii, 182–5, 2nd fragment only]; PBB, untitled fragment, wrongly bound as part of [A Narrative of the First War by Henry Hastings], 4–30 June 1836: MS pp.9–16, Texas; PBB, untitled & undated fragment, wrongly bound as part of [The Rising of the Angrians], 24 Dec. 1835–23 March 1836: MS pp.17–20, Princeton; PBB, 'This will never do thought I', 12 July 1837: MS BS 123, BPM; PBB, ' "All the same – where's a worse than myself." ', [July 1836]: MS Ashley 187 pp.2r–2v, BL. It is a measure of the lack of importance Branwell attached to Wentworth that he did not credit a single poem to him, even though he attributed poetry to less likely figures such as the pragmatic Warner Howard Warner.

18. PBB, 'Then shall I perish for ever', [May 1836]: MS p.1, Brotherton, [facsimile in *M&U*, ii, 180].

19. PBB, 'While Charles Wentworth leant over a parapet', 28 May 1836: MS pp.1, 2, Brotherton, [*M&U*, ii, 183]. Branwell 'took a half-year's-farewell of old friend whisky' and drank 'whisky-toddy as hot as hell!' at Kendal: PBB to John Brown, [13 March 1840]: MS n.l. but see chapter

12, note 6, [*L&L*, i, 198–9]; in a letter to Francis Grundy he says he can 'now speak cheerfully and enjoy the company of another without the stimulus of six glasses of whisky': PBB to Francis Grundy, 22 May 1842: MS n.l., [*L&L*, i, 263]. In what is presumed to be his last letter before his death, Branwell asked John Brown to contrive to get him five pence worth of gin: PBB to John Brown, [1848]: MS in Brotherton, [*L&L*, i, 224].

20. PBB, ' "All the same – where's a worse than myself." ' [Aug. 1837]: MS Ashley 187 pp.4r–4v, BL.

21. PBB, 'While Charles Wentworth leant over a parapet', 28 May 1836: MS p.2, Brotherton, [*M&U*, ii, 185].

22. Hastings belonged to the 'Devil's Own', the 19th Infantry Regiment of Angria, and was a loyal supporter of Zamorna, though in the summer of 1837 he threw his hand in with Northangerland and the Revolutionists, earning himself a proscription as a rebel: PBB, ' "All the same – where's a worse than myself." ' [Aug. 1837]: MS Ashley 187 pp.5r–5v, BL; PBB, 'I have lately remarked', 20 Oct. 1837: MS Bon 149(1) p.2, BPM.

23. The events following the battle of Loanga are described in a continuous section of manuscript which is divided between a number of different locations: see Neufeldt, *A Bibliography of the Manuscripts of PBB*, pp.8–9. The new chapter, which concludes the first volume, is also dismembered: PBB, untitled story by Henry Hastings, 3 Oct. 1835: MS MA 2696 R-V pp.17–18, Pierpont Morgan; PBB, [Rising of the Angrians], 7 Jan. 1836: MS pp.1–14, Princeton.

24. THE LIFE OF Feild Marshal the Right Honourable ALEXANDER PERCY, vol. ii, 3 June–17 Nov. 1835: MS p.7, Brotherton, [Collins, p.91]. For the existence of a third volume, now lost, see Neufeldt, *A Bibliography of the Manuscripts of PBB*, p.37.

25. THE LIFE OF Feild Marshal the Right Honourable ALEXANDER PERCY, vol. ii, 3 June–17 Nov. 1835: MS p.16, Brotherton, [Collins, p.116].

26. PBB, 'How fast that Courser fleeted by', 18 Dec. 1835: MS BS 118, pp.2–10, BPM, [VN *PBB*, pp.380–8]. This poem is an early draft of 'Misery. Scene 1st' which Branwell sent for publication in *Blackwood's Magazine* on 8 April 1836. Branwell produced Angrian prose and poetry virtually every month throughout 1836 and 1837. The manuscripts, nearly all unpublished, are scattered throughout various collections: see Neufeldt, *A Bibliography of the Manuscripts of PBB*, pp.9–21 and index p.155.

27. PBB to the Editor of *Blackwood's Magazine*, [8] Dec. 1835: MS 4040 p.3, NLS, [*L&L*, i, 133–4]. Though Branwell has left a space where he intended to insert the day of the month, the letter is postmarked 8 December. On p.1, he says, 'I have addressed you twice before, and now I do it again'.

28. *Ibid.*, pp.2–3.

29. See, for example, the letter of 'Solomon Timms' to the editor, asking him to publish a piece by his nephew and offering 'to stand any loss under a five-pound note; for, as I said before, money's no object': *Blackwood's Magazine*, xl, June 1840, p.795.

30. CB to EN, 2 July 1835: MS HM 24408 pp.2–3, Huntington.

31. *Jane Eyre*, for example, sets up as a schoolmistress under the aegis of her cousin, St John Rivers, after her marriage to Mr Rochester is prevented: CB, *Jane Eyre*, pp.359ff. Similarly, Paul Emanuel gives Lucy Snowe her own school before he leaves for the West Indies and is lost at sea: CB, *Villette*, pp.604ff.

32. John Buckworth, Patrick's former vicar at Dewsbury, had died in April 1835 and Thomas Allbutt, his curate, was appointed in his stead, enabling him to marry Marianne Wooler on 9 July 1835: *Leeds Mercury*, 4 April 1835, p.5; Yorkshire IGI.

33. PB to Mrs Franks, 6 July 1835: MS BS 184 p.1, BPM, [*L&L*, i, 130].

34. WG, *EJB*, p.53 says that Charlotte and Emily shared a bed but does not state her source. This seems extremely unlikely, as for discipline reasons alone it would have been inappropriate to allow a pupil and teacher to share a bed. The incidents of 'late talking' during Charlotte's own schooldays suggest that the teachers slept apart from the pupils but it is possible that Charlotte had a bed in the same dormitory as she refers to being disturbed by the young ladies coming for their curl papers: CB, 'All this day I have been in a dream', 11 Aug.–14 Oct. 1836: MS Bon 98(8) p.4, BPM, *M&U*, ii, 255.

35. Constantin Heger, quoted in ECG, *Life*, p.151.

36. The Gondals were already discovering the interior of Gaaldine in Emily's first 'diary note': EJB, Paper, 24 Nov. 1834: MS Bon 131, BPM, [JB *ST*, no.11]. At much the same time, the Verdopolitans were moving into Angria, so the implication is that the Gondal stories had reached a similar level of sophistication.

37. CB, 'All this day I have been in a dream', 11 Aug. 1836: MS Bon 98 p.2, BPM, [*M&U*, ii, 255]. There is a problem with the dating of this manuscript: it is dated 'Friday August 11th' at the top in minuscule and 'October 14th 1836' in longhand at the bottom. August 11th was on a Thursday in 1836, but as Charlotte frequently confused dates, it is not unlikely that she simply got the wrong date.

38. Chitham, *A Life of Emily Brontë*, p.87 suggests that the view was 'a soft and leafy prospect, but it was not moorland'. This is not entirely true. The valleys, wherever they were not industrialized, were certainly heavily wooded at the time but the hill tops, especially in the distance, were open moorland. The wild, uncultivated and sparsely populated moors around Huddersfield and Mirfield were the meeting place

for several generations of malcontents, from Luddites to Plug Rioters and Chartists.

39. CB, Prefatory Note to A Selection of Poems by Ellis Bell, 1850: EJB, *Wuthering Heights*, p.370.

40. CB, 'My Compliments to the weather' [Roe Head Journal], [*c.*March 1837]: MS Bon 98(6) pp.1–2, BPM.

41. Emily drew some rough sketches of cattle on 23 October, which are totally untypical of the Roe Head copy-book style, suggesting that she was home by this date: HAOBP:P.Br.E4 & 4v, BPM. Anne was apparently at Roe Head by 27 October 1835, when she drew the first in a series of pencil studies of trees; she drew another just over a fortnight later which, by implication, must have been from the same copy book which must have been at Roe Head: AB, pencil drawing of an Oak Tree, 27 Oct. 1835: HAOBP:P.Br.Bon 15, BPM; AB, pencil drawing of An Elm Tree, 13 Nov. 1835: HAOBP:P.Br.A4, BPM. Alone of her family, Anne seems to have tired of the imaginary worlds, writing in 1845, 'We have not yet finished our Gondal Chronicles that we began three years and a half ago. When will they be done? ... The Gondals in general are not in first-rate playing condition.': AB, Diary Paper, 31 July 1845: MS in private hands, [*L&L*, ii, 52–3]. I am grateful to William Self for sending me a photocopy of this manuscript and allowing me to quote from it.

42. CB to EN, 5–6 Dec. 1836: MS Bon 162, p.1, postscript at top of page, BPM, [*L&L*, i, 148]; CB, 'My Compliments to the weather' [Roe Head Journal], [*c.*March 1837]: MS Bon 98(6) p.7, BPM. According to Shorter's edition of ECG, *Life* (London, Smith, Elder & Co., 1905), p.147 n.1., Anne was presented with a copy of Watts' *On the Improvement of the Mind* (Dove's English Classics, 1826) inscribed 'Prize for good conduct. Presented to Miss A Brontë with Miss Wooler's kind love. Roe Head, December 14 1836'. I have been unable to locate this prize book.

43. See, for example, the three drawings of ruined towers done for her by her brother and sister and the lock of her hair preserved by her father: PBB, pencil drawing 'For Anne Brontë', 17 Nov. 1828: HAOBP:P.Br.B3, BPM; PBB, pencil drawing 'Copy – For Anne Brontë', 23 Feb. 1829: HAOBP:P.Br.B4, BPM; CB, pencil drawing 'for Anne x A Copy', 2 Sept. 1828: HAOBP: P.Br.C2; PB, note accompanying plait of AB hair, 22 May 1833: MS BS 171, BPM; PB to Mrs Franks, 6 July 1835: MS BS 184 p.1, BPM, [*L&L*, i, 130].

44. MT to ECG, 18 Jan. 1856: MS n.l., [Stevens, p.160].

45. A[nn] Cook, Anne Brontë's friend, is referred to in CB, 'I'm just going to write because I cannot help it' [Roe Head Journal], [Oct. 1836]: MS Bon 98(7) p.1, BPM; Miss Upton is referred to in CB to EN, 26 Sept. 1836: MS Bon 161 p.3, BPM, [*L&L*, i, 146] and Miss Caris, whom Charlotte 'always found ... an intelligent though

never an agreeable pupil', in CB to EN, 28 March 1848: MS Bon 199 p.1, BPM, [*L&L*, ii, 199]. Ellen Cook, Miss Lister & Miss Marriott are mentioned in CB, 'All this day I have been in a dream' [Roe Head Journal], 11 Aug. 1836: MS Bon 98 p.2, BPM, [*M&U*, ii, 255]; Ann and Ellen Cook, daughters of Thomas Cook, a banker and merchant in Dewsbury, were christened in June 1825 and on 5 December 1827 respectively: Pigot & Co., *National Commercial Directory* (1828–9), pp.921–2; Yorkshire IGI. It is worth noting that, according to the 1841 census, there were still only seven boarding pupils at the school, which had, by this time, removed to Dewsbury Moor. It was run by Catherine and Eliza Wooler, who are respectively described as having independent financial means and being a governess.

46. CB, 'About a week since I got a letter from Branwell' [Roe Head Journal], [autumn 1835]: MS Bon 92 p.1, BPM. Alexander, *A Bibliography of the Manuscripts of Charlotte Brontë*, p.21 dates this fragment to October 1837 but Northangerland's daughter was dead by September 1836. Northangerland's letter is written during his exile from Angria and received by Mary at Zamorna Palace, where she is still the wife of Zamorna, so it must date from the autumn of 1835, before her divorce.

47. CB, prose continuation of 'We wove a web in childhood', 19 Dec. 1835: MS HM 2578 pp.5–6, Huntington, [VN *CB*, p.170]. Though the implication of both the poem and the prose continuation is that they were written actually at Roe Head, the manuscript is clearly signed and dated in Charlotte's longhand at the end 'C Brontë Decbr 19th Haworth 1835'.

48. CB, 'We wove a web in childhood', 19 Dec. 1835: MS HM 2578 pp.2–3, Huntington [VN *CB*, p.166–7].

49. *Bradford Observer*, 24 Sept. 1835, p.269.

50. The family quarrel, which eventually resulted in the bankruptcy of the business, is discussed in Sarah Fermi, 'A "Religious" Family Disgraced', *BST*:20:5:289–95. Joseph Greenwood was the only member of his family to be a member of the Church of England (the others were all Baptists) and the only Tory. Mr Atkinson, the Lord Lieutenant's agent, informed him that in the absence of other information, he had looked up Joseph Greenwood in the poll books and discovered that he voted for Mr Wortley while all the other members of his family voted for Lord Morpeth, the Whig candidate who was elected. 'This may be taken as an indication of his politics – and I should think his recommendation by Mr Heap & Mr Bronte a good security for his general respectability.': Mr Atkinson to the Earl of Harewood, 4 Jan. 1836: MS in Harewood Papers, Lieutenancy Papers Box 1, WYAS, Leeds.

51. *Bradford Observer*, 24 Sept. 1835, p.269. The church rates covered the cost of paying for the bellringers, singers and the salaries of the two

clerks as well as such necessities as purchasing coal and candles to heat and light the church, communion wine and robes for the minister and his clerks. They were also supposed to pay for repairs and maintenance of the church building and yard. Much dissension was caused at the meeting by the disclosure that expenses under 'sundries' were for 'a bottle of wine here and another there, when the churchwardens had their meetings'.

52. Earl of Harewood to PB, 1 Oct. 1835: MS in Harewood Papers, Lieutenancy Papers Box 1, WYAS, Leeds. This letter refers to Patrick's letter of 23 Sept. 1835, which I have been unable to find. PB to Earl of Harewood, 6 Oct. 1835: MS in Harewood Papers, Lieutenancy Papers Box 1, WYAS, Leeds.

53. PB to Henry Heap, 26 Dec. 1835: MS in Harewood Papers, Lieutenancy Papers Box 1, WYAS, Leeds.

54. Henry Heap to Earl of Harewood, 28 Dec. 1835: MS in Harewood Papers, Lieutenancy Papers Box 1, WYAS, Leeds.

55. Justices' Qualification Oaths 1819–37: MS in WYAS, Wakefield. I am grateful to Sarah Fermi for this reference.

56. The population of the chapelry of Haworth (which included Stanbury and Oxenhope) was 5,835 in 1831 but had risen to 6,303 by 1841: Page, *Victoria History of the County of York*, iii, 533; Register of Burials 1813–36, Haworth Church. On 21 July 1834 Patrick personally baptized twenty-three children, on 19 and 20 July 1835 he christened twenty children each day; again, on 18, 19, 20 October of the same year he christened sixteen children each day: Register of Baptisms 1829–37, Haworth Church. The following year, 1836, Patrick published a short tract, *A Brief Treatise on the Best Time and Mode of Baptism* (Keighley, R. Aked, 1836) in answer to one by the Baptist minister of Hall Green, Moses Saunders, who sanctioned adult baptism. Patrick's treatise made a strong defence of infant baptism and the rising rate of Anglican baptisms in Haworth shows that he practised what he preached.

57. The Reverend Thomas Brooksbank Charnock (1800–47), son of James Charnock, the previous incumbent of Haworth, matriculated on 22 June 1819, and graduated BA in 1823 and MA in 1826 from University College, Oxford: Venn, *Alumni Oxonienses (1715–1886)*, i, 241. He committed suicide in 1847: see below, p.545. From the Haworth Church registers it is clear that he assisted Patrick occasionally from 1834 onwards and he also preached the Sunday school sermons at the afternoon and evening services on 19 July 1835: Haworth Church Hymn Sheet, 19 July 1835: BS x, H, BPM.

58. William Hodgson admitted he was born into a 'humble station in life' in his letter to *Leeds Mercury*, 31 Dec. 1836, p.7. Irish origins are suggested by his being called a 'potato eater' by the

Bradford Observer, 9 March 1837, p.45 but Winterbotham's sneers in *Leeds Mercury*, 17 Dec. 1836, p.8 may indicate that he was a local boy 'made good'. From the Haworth Church registers he would appear to have left for Colne after 11 May 1837: Register of Burials 1836–54, Haworth Church.

59. Hodgson first signs the registers as 'W Hodgson Curate', rather than simply 'W Hodgson', on 3 April 1836: Register of Baptisms 1827–37, Haworth Church. According to White's *Directory of the West Riding* (Sheffield, 1838), ii, 436, in 1837 Patrick was 'assisted by the Rev. Wm Hodgson to whom the Pastoral Aid Society has allowed an annuity of £50 granted in 1836'. As this sum was not adequate to cover his salary, it was augmented by a voluntary subscription in Haworth: Requisition to the Reverend William Hodgson, 30 April 1837: MS n.l., quoted in Clement Shorter, 'New Light on the Brontës', *BST*:1:8:18. It is possible that this method was also used to pay his salary when he first came to Haworth in December 1835.

60. *Ibid.*, p.16.

61. Hodgson is mentioned only once in the Brontë correspondence, when as 'Papa's former Curate' he visited Haworth bringing with him his own curate, the Reverend David Pryce, who subsequently proposed to Charlotte: CB to EN, 4 Aug. 1839: MS HM 24418 p.2, Huntington, [*L & L*, i, 184].

62. According to Olridge-de-la-Hey, Hodgson lodged with 'three coeval generations of women – mother, daughter, and granddaughter', a description which fits exactly with the 1841 census description of the family with whom a later curate, William Weightman, lodged at Cook Gate: Clement Shorter, 'New Light on the Brontës', *BST*:1:8:16; Haworth Census, 1841.

63. PB, *The Cottage in the Wood*, pp.3–4, [*Brontëana*, p.102].

64. CB to Robert Southey, 16 March 1837: MS n.l., [*L & L*, i, 158].

65. CB, 'Long since as I remember well', [Jan. 1836]: MS in William Carlos Williams Colln, pp.2, 5, 8, SUNY, [VN *CB*, pp.172, 175, 179]. In the right-hand margin of this section, someone, apparently Branwell, to judge by the hand, has written 'This hope's divine' and 'this' four times alongside pious sentiments.

66. PBB, [Rising of the Angrians], 24 Dec. 1835–7 Jan. 1836: MS at Princeton; PBB, 'This is the first day of January 1836', 7 Jan. 1836: the MS of this story is widely scattered but the opening, dated fragment is MS Ashley 187 p.1, BL.

67. CB, 'But once again, but once again', 19 Jan. 1836: MS in William Carlos Williams Colln, pp.17–18, 20, SUNY, [VN *CB*, p.187–8, 191].

68. Feather, *History of the Three Graces Lodge*, p.43, citing the minute book of the Lodge which has been lost; John Brown & Joseph Redman to Richard Hird, General Secretary to the Pro-

vincial Lodge of Free Masons, Wakefield, 8 Feb. 1836: MS BS ix, B p.1, BPM.

69. John Brown & Joseph Redman to Robert Carr, Deputy General Secretary, Provincial Lodge of Free Masons, Wakefield, 11 Feb. 1836: MS BS ix, B p.1, BPM.

70. Robert Carr to John Brown, 13 Feb. 1836: MS BS ix, B p.1, BPM; Feather, *History of the Three Graces Lodge*, p.43.

71. PBB to the Editor of *Blackwood's Magazine*, 8 April 1836: MS 4042, NLS, [VN *PBB*, pp.379–80].

72. PBB, 'Misery. Scene 1st [&] Scene. 2d', [8 April 1836]: MS 4042, NLS, [VN *PBB*, pp.99–114]; PBB to the Editor of *Blackwood's Magazine*, 8 April 1836: MS 4042 p.2, NLS, [VN *PBB*, p.380].

73. PBB, 'How fast that Courser fleeted by', 18 Dec. 1835: MS BS 118 pp.2–10, BPM, [VN *PBB*, pp.380–8]; PBB, 'Wide I hear the wild winds sighing', 2 March 1836: MS MA 2696, Pierpont Morgan, [VN *PBB*, pp.388–96]. Undated trial lines for these two scenes are also extant: see VN *PBB*, pp.388, 396–7. Branwell substantially revised both scenes before sending the poem off to *Blackwood's Magazine* on 8 April 1836.

74. PBB to the Editor of *Blackwood's Magazine*, 8 April 1836: MS 4042 pp.1–2, NLS, [VN *PBB*, pp.379–80].

75. *Ibid.*, p.2.

76. Feather, *History of the Three Graces Lodge*, p.44. Branwell only missed one Lodge meeting in August 1836 and two, in February and November, in 1837. Thereafter he never attended more than two meetings a year: Contemporary MSS notes of Lodge of Three Graces meetings in private hands.

77. Branwell's portrait of Michael Merrall has not been traced but is described in Leyland, i, 239–40; the unsigned and undated portraits in oils of William Thomas, Henry Foster and James Fletcher are nos HAOBP: P.Br.B22, B44 & B26 in the BPM. They may well date from 1838 when Branwell set up a studio in Bradford, but equally may predate that period as one would have expected Branwell to paint local figures before attempting to go further afield professionally. PBB, portrait in oils of Thomas Parker, 22 Dec. 1838: HAOBP:P.Br.B21, BPM; PBB, portrait in oils of John Brown, n.d.: HAOBP:P.Br.B20, BPM; PBB, portrait in oils of William Brown, n.d.: HAOBP:P.Br.B19, BPM.

78. PBB, portrait in oils of Maria Taylor, n.d.: original in private hands. I am grateful to Mr A. I. F. Parmeter for sending me a photograph of this portrait. ECG, *Life*, p.88.

79. These events are described in dismembered manuscripts often only a couple of pages long and bound out of order with unrelated fragments. They are scattered across a number of locations, the main references being to PBB, [A New Year Story], 7 Jan. 1836: MS Ashley 187, BL; PBB, [Rising of the Angrians], 24 Dec. 1835–23 March 1836: MS in Princeton; PBB, untitled

fragments, wrongly bound with [A Narrative of the First War], 4–30 June 1836: MS pp.9ff, Texas. There are also a number of shorter fragments in the BPM and Brotherton. For the sequence of fragments see Neufeldt, *A Bibliography of the Manuscripts of PBB*, pp.9–21.

80. PBB, [Rising of the Angrians], 24 Dec. 1835–7 Jan. 1836: MS p.7, Princeton.

81. CB, 'Well here I am at Roe Head' [Roe Head Journal], [Jan. 1836]: MS MA 2696 R–V pp.1–2, Pierpont Morgan, [*M&U*, ii, 123–4].

82. *Ibid.*, p.2.

83. CB, 'Well here I am at Roe-Head' [Roe Head Journal], 4 Feb. 1836: MS MA 2696 R-V, Pierpont Morgan; CB, My Angria and the Angrians, 14 Oct. 1834 was the last complete story Charlotte had written; CB, The Scrap Book, 15 Sept. 1834–17 March 1835 had simply been a collection of various fragments.

84. CB, Passing Events, 21–9 April 1836: MS MA 30 p.4, Pierpont Morgan, [WG *FN*, pp.38–9].

85. *Ibid.*, p.13, see also pp.11–14.

86. PBB, unrelated fragment at end of [Rising of the Angrians], beginning 'Oh not till you see your sins in so strong a light', [April 1836]: MS p.24, Princeton. See also PBB, 'O Lord God Creator of heaven and Earth', [April 1836]: MS pp.1–2, Brotherton, [*M&U*, ii, 171–2]. Though usually dated to May, this fragment must predate 'Passing Events' as Charlotte refers there to Northangerland's 'wandering & wild & terrible' sermon: CB, Passing Events, 21–9 April 1836: MS MA 30 p.14, Pierpont Morgan. Percy's first 'Methodist' speech is in PBB, An Historical Narrative of the War of Aggression, [Dec. 1834–Jan. 1835]: MS Eng 869(2) p.15, Harvard.

87. PBB, unrelated fragment at end of [Rising of the Angrians], beginning 'Oh not till you see your sins in so strong a light', [April 1836]: MS p.24, Princeton.

88. This attitude is still evident as late as the Brontës' published novels: the leader of the Luddite rioters in *Shirley*, for instance, is a drunken and hypocritical Methodist lay preacher (CB, *Shirley*, pp.128ff.) and Emily gives a piquant caricature of Methodism in her description of Jabes Branderham and the Seventy times Seven sermon (*Wuthering Heights*, pp.20–2).

89. CB to EN, [28 May 1836]: MS n.l., [*L&L*, i, 142]. This letter is wrongly conflated with one from CB to EN dated 10 May 1836, for which the manuscript is extant, in ECG, *Life*, p.93.

90. MT to ECG, 18 Feb. 1856: MS n.l., [Stevens, p.160]; CB to EN, 10 May 1836: MS HM 24411 p.2, Huntington, [*L&L*, i, 139], where Charlotte says, 'You seemed kindly apprehensive about my health. I am perfectly well now and I never was very ill.'

91. CB to Mrs Franks, 2 June 1836: MS 58 Cii p.3 (MS Q 091 F), Sheffield, [*L&L*, i, 143].

92. PB to Mrs Franks, 13 June 1836: MS BS 186 p.1, BPM, [*L&L*, i, 144].

93. John Firth Franks to George Moore Smith, n.d.: MS 58 Cvi, Sheffield. This extremely unreliable anecdote may actually relate to a visit during Charlotte's days as a pupil at Roe Head. John Firth Franks recollected 'being seated on the floor in my mother's dining room with my box of bricks, when the 3 misses Bronte walked in' and mentions that the visit was during an Easter vacation. Although it seems more likely that it relates to 1831, when the boy was five years old and likely to be playing with bricks, Charlotte would have been unaccompanied, whereas in 1836, when the boy was ten, she had Anne with her. John Firth Franks states specifically that 'Charlotte was then assistant mistress at the school in Mirfield parish', so I have reluctantly accepted this dating.

94. CB to EN, [July 1836]: MS 24412 p.2, Huntington, [*L&L*, i, 145].

95. *Ibid.*, p.3.

96. EJB, 'Cold clear and blue the morning heaven', [?Spring 1836]: MS Bon 127 p.16, BPM, [Hatfield, p.29].

97. CB, unrelated fragment appended to Passing Events, 24–8 June 1836: MS MA 30 pp.28–33, Pierpont Morgan. Though this was transcribed as part of 'Passing Events' by WG *FN*, pp.72–82 and in the *M&U*, ii, 160–8, a recent article has shown that it is in fact a separate piece: Jos Bemelmans, '*Passing Events* and Another Manuscript', *BST*:20, pt 3, 121–5.

98. The manuscripts containing these developments are dismembered and scattered throughout a number of locations. The principal manuscripts are PBB, unrelated fragment beginning 'Thy Flower deprived of warmth will wither & die', at end of untitled MS by Henry Hastings, 30 June 1836: MS pp.9–12, Texas; PBB, unrelated fragment beginning 'been I – "Yes – thats very well' at end of [Rising of the Angrians], [June 1836]: MS pp.17–20, Princeton; PBB, 'My Ancient Ship upon my Ancient sea', July 1836: MS Bon 146(1) and (2), BPM, [VN *PBB*, pp.116–18]. For a full list of the manuscripts, see Neufeldt, *A Bibliography of the Manuscripts of PBB*, pp.12–13.

99. CB, 'And when you left me what thoughts had I then', 19 July 1836: MS Bon 93, BPM, [VN *CB*, pp.194–209].

100. These form the so-called 'Roe Head Journal', but the term is misleading and inappropriate as it implies a consistent set of dated entries in a bound volume. In fact, the 'Journal' is composed of the autobiographical passages with which Charlotte introduced or ended Angrian fragments she wrote at Roe Head, some of which are undated. Many of them appear to have been written on a day subsequent to the events described, which perhaps explains the inconsistencies in dating. On both her dated pieces, Charlotte got the day or date wrong: both are supposed to be Fridays, but 4 February 1836

and 11 August 1836 were both Thursdays. The fragments, in chronological order, are as follows: 'About a week since I got a letter from Branwell', [autumn 1835]: MS Bon 92 pp.1–2, BPM; 'Well here I am at Roe-Head', [Jan. 1836]: MS MA 2696 R-V pp.1–2, Pierpont Morgan; 'Now as I have a little bit of time', 4 Feb. 1836: MS MA 2696 R-V p.2, Pierpont Morgan; 'All this day I have been in a dream', 11 Aug.–14 Oct. 1836: MS Bon 98(8), pp.1–4, BPM; 'I'm just going to write because I cannot help it', [c.Oct. 1836]: MS Bon 98(7) pp.1–2, BPM; 'My Compliments to the weather', [Feb.–March 1837]: MS Bon 98(6) pp.1–

3, 6–7, BPM. To this list, printed in Alexander, *A Bibliography of the Manuscripts of Charlotte Brontë*, p.56, I would also add the prose continuation of 'We wove a web in childhood', 19 Dec. 1835: MS HM 2578, Huntington, [VN *CB*, p.169–70].

101. CB, 'All this day I have been in a dream', 11 Aug.–14 Oct. 1836: MS Bon 98(8), pp.1–2, BPM.
102. *Ibid.*, p.2.
103. CB, 'I'm just going to write because I cannot help it', [c.Oct. 1836]: MS Bon 98(7), p.1, BPM.
104. *Ibid.*
105. CB, 'All this day I have been in a dream', 11 Aug.–14 Oct. 1836: MS Bon 98(8), p.4, BPM.

CHAPTER TEN

1. E. Metcalfe to the Bible Society, London, 23 July 1836: MS in archives of Bible Society, ULC. Moses Saunders and the other Baptists had apparently withdrawn their membership of the Bible Society: contrary to the Society's rules, Saunders later purchased 'certain dissenting publications of a controversial nature' for the library but was forced to remove them by the committee: *Leeds Intelligencer*, 15 April 1837, p.5.
2. *Bradford Observer*, 7 July 1836, p.181; 24 Nov. 1836, p.341.
3. *Ibid.*, 29 Sept. 1836, p.272.
4. PB to *Leeds Mercury*, 5 Nov. 1836, p.6.
5. 'Z' to *Leeds Mercury*, 17 Dec. 1836, p.8. Winterbotham's letter trying to raise support for a Bradford Anti-Church Rates Society is in the *Bradford Observer*, 15 Dec. 1836, p.366.
6. William Hodgson to *Leeds Mercury*, 31 Dec. 1836, p.7.
7. William Hodgson to *Leeds Intelligencer*, 31 Dec. 1836, p.8.
8. CB to EN, 29 Dec. 1836: MS BS 40.4 pp.1–2, BPM, [*L&L*, i, 149]. The weather was particularly severe that winter: four inches of snow had already fallen by 28 October: *Bradford Observer*, 2 Nov. 1837, p.317; in her letter Charlotte refers to the moors being 'blockaded with snow'.
9. ECG, *Life*, pp.108–9; CB to EN, 29 Dec. 1836: MS BS 40.4 p.1 crossed, BPM, [*L&L*, i, 150].
10. AB, Verses to Lady Geralda, Dec. 1836: MS lost, transcript in Symington Colln, Texas, [Chitham, pp.49–51].
11. Branwell's story, though once part of a single manuscript, is now broken up into various untitled fragments which are, in chronological order: 'from the interview between Greville and Percy', 16 Dec. 1836: MS Bon 145(3), BPM; 'And surely too died before his time that Child of Hope and promise', n.d.: MS in Brotherton, [facsimile in *M&U*, ii, 267–81]; 'The war which for a space did fail', 17 Dec. 1836: MS Bon 145(4), BPM; [Elegant Extracts], 17 Dec. 1836–6 Jan. 1837: MS pp.3–4, 1–2, Berg; [The End of the Angrian Revolution]: MS pp.1–2, Brotherton.
12. PBB, 'Through the hoarse howlings of the storm', 19 Sept. 1836: chap. 5 of [The Angrian

Adventure], 22 July 1836: MS p.15, Brotherton, [*M&U*, ii, 219].
13. 'I wonder if Branwell really has killed the Duchess – Is she dead, is she buried is she alone in the cold earth on this dreary night': CB, 'I'm just going to write because I cannot help it' [Roe Head Journal], [Oct. 1836]: MS Bon 98(7), p.1, BPM.
14. PBB, 'Thus then has departed from among us', 11 Nov. 1836: MS p.2, private hands. I am grateful to Mr Barrett for sending me photocopies of his manuscript and allowing me to quote from it.
15. CB, [The Return of Zamorna], Dec. 1836–Jan. 1837: MS in Law Colln, [*M&U*, ii, 284–5].
16. *Ibid.*, pp.282–314.
17. CB, 'Well the day's toils are over, with success', 9 Jan. 1837: MS Bon 100, BPM, [VN *CB*, 209–20]; PBB, 'ing awoke among the lines', n.d.: MS BS 111 pp.3–10, BPM. pp.1–2 of this manuscript are from an unrelated manuscript, 'Upon the very threshold of my subject', dated 14 April 1837.
18. CB, 'The Wood', Dec. 1836–Jan. 1837: MS n.l., [VN *CB*, pp.295–8]; CB, 'Well the day's toils are over, with success', 9 Jan. 1837: MS Bon 100, BPM, [VN *CB*, 209–20]; CB, 'Lady-bird!, ladybird! fly away home' [Jan. 1837]: MS part Berg, part Bon 127 pp.10–10v, BPM, [VN *CB*, 221–6]; CB, 'I never sought my mother's face': MS Bon 105, BPM, [VN *CB*, pp.226–7]; CB, 'On the bright scene around them spread' & '& few have felt the avenging steel', 17 Jan. 1837: pencilled inside front cover of Charlotte's copy of Mr Porny, *Grammatical Exercises, English and French* (London, F. Wingrave, J. Walker *et al.* 1810), HAOBP:bb47, BPM, [VN *CB*, pp.227–8].
19. Robert Southey to Caroline Bowles, quoted in *L&L*, i, 156. For Charlotte's letter to Hartley Coleridge, see below, p.337–8.
20. Robert Southey to CB, March 1837: MS n.l., [*L&L*, i, 155]. The first two sentences, which are not included in the standard printed versions, are printed in Smith, 'The Letters of Charlotte Brontë: some new insights into her life and writing', p.63; Robert Southey to Caroline Bowles, quoted in *L&L*, i, 156.

21. CB, *Shirley,* p.390.
22. CB to Robert Southey, 16 March 1837: MS n.l., [*L&L*, i, 157–8].
23. CB, note on letter wrapper from Robert Southey, 21 April 1837: MS BS 14.5, BPM, [*L&L*, i, 156]. The letter was sent to Haworth Parsonage where Emily readdressed it and forwarded it to Charlotte at Roe Head.
24. PBB to Editor of *Blackwood's Magazine*, 4 Jan. 1837: MS BS 135 pp.2, 3, BPM, [*BST*:16:81:20–1].
25. PBB to William Wordsworth, 10 Jan. 1837: MS pp.1–2, Wordsworth Trust, [*L&L*, i, 151–2].
26. PBB, The Struggles of flesh with Spirit Scene I – Infancy, n.d.: MS accompanying letter of PBB to William Wordsworth, 10 Jan. 1837: MS in Wordsworth Trust. Earlier versions of this poem are given in VN *PBB*, pp.120–6, 398–404. The poem was drafted as early as January 1836 though this version is substantially the same as the version Branwell composed in five days from 8–13 August 1836. Like 'Misery – Scene 1st' which Branwell had sent to *Blackwood's Magazine*, on 8 April 1836, the poem is part of a longer scheme depicting the life of Alexander Percy.
27. Robert Southey to Caroline Bowles, quoted in *L&L*, i, 156.
28. PBB, untitled notebook, 9 March 1837–12 May 1838: MS BS 125, BPM, [VN *PBB*, pp.xii–xiv].
29. Emily's earliest extant dated poems are 'Will the day be bright or cloudy', 12 July 1836 & 'High waving heather, 'neath stormy blasts bending', 13 Dec. 1836: MS Bon 127 pp.16, 18, BPM, [Hatfield, pp.29, 31]. Thereafter she seems to have written and preserved poems almost monthly. For Anne's earliest extant poem see note 10.
30. *Leeds Intelligencer*, 21 Jan. 1837, p.7. Although Patrick's authorship cannot be established beyond doubt, the sentiments are in keeping with Patrick's known views and the piece is signed 'P.B. Near Keighley, Jan. 14th, 1837'. 'P.B.' later submitted another poem, 'A solemn political hymn' to be sung to the tune of 'Auld Lang Syne', which urged the Church to withstand her attackers: *Leeds Intelligencer*, 3 Feb. 1838, p.7.
31. PBB, Minute Book of the Haworth Operative Conservative Society, 27 Jan.–12 Feb. 1837: MS BS 125 pp.81, 82, 83 and MS BS 146.5, BPM. Branwell wrote the minutes of the meetings on 27 January and 12 February in the notebook which, by 9 March, he had converted into a record of his poems. Provision for the purchase of a book for minutes was made at the initial meeting, so Branwell must have transferred his minutes to the new book by the middle of February. Branwell began his poems at the other end of the book and upside down to the minutes he had already written.
32. *The Times*, 27 Feb. 1837, p.6
33. *Ibid.*; *Leeds Intelligencer*, 25 Feb. 1837, p.8. Abraham Wildman supported a reform meeting in Keighley to petition Parliament to pass Russell's Reform Bill in 1831: *Leeds Intelligencer*, 17 March 1831, p.3; led a march of Keighley workmen to York where he addressed a meeting in favour of the Ten Hours Bill in 1832: *ibid.*, 26 April 1832, pp.2–3; and both chaired and addressed numerous meetings in Keighley in support of the Ten Hours Bill from 1833–5: *ibid.*, 3 Aug. 1833, p.3; 7 March 1835, p.3. He was known locally, like his friends Oastler and Bull, as the 'factory child's friend': *Leeds Mercury,* 21 March 1835, p.7. Abraham Leighton, according to the 1841 census, lived at no. 40 Main Street; though married he had no children and must have been better off than most wool-combers as he employed a household servant.
34. *Leeds Intelligencer*, 20 May 1837, p.7.
35. *Bradford Observer*, 2 March 1837, p.37. As a Whig paper, the *Bradford Observer* was in favour of abolition and therefore supported the meeting. The Tory *Leeds Intelligencer*, 4 March 1837, p.8, carried a witty but hostile report which may possibly have been written by Branwell.
36. *Bradford Observer*, 2 March 1837, p.37. *Leeds Intelligencer*, 4 March 1837, p.8. I have been unable to identify any pieces which Branwell may have submitted earlier to the *Leeds Intelligencer*, despite extensive searches.
37. *Bradford Observer*, 2 March 1837, p.37.
38. *Ibid.*, 9 Mar. 1837, p.45.
39. William Hodgson to *Leeds Intelligencer*, 4 March 1837, p.7. Hodgson's baptismal figures for 26–8 February are supported by the baptismal registers. At the end of December 1837 Moses Saunders performed the first Baptist 'wedding ceremony' in Haworth, the couple having to wait till the arrival of Thomas Umpleby, the Keighley registrar, before they could be legally married. Patrick himself is said to have attended and is delightfully described as appearing 'prim as a shrimp': *Halifax Guardian*, 9 Jan. 1838, p.2.
40. PBB, Declaration to the Rate Payers of Haworth, March 1837: MS BS 147, BPM; *Leeds Intelligencer*, 25 March 1837, p.5.
41. *Ibid.*, 1 April 1837, p.5.
42. *Bradford Observer*, 20 April 1837, p.93; 25 May 1837, p.133.
43. *Ibid.*, 20 April 1837, p.93.
44. PB to the *Leeds Intelligencer*, 22 April 1837, p.8.
45. A Requisition to the Revd William Hodgson, Assistant Minister of Haworth, Yorkshire, 30 April 1837: MS n.l., [C. K. Shorter, 'New Light on the Brontës', *BST*:1:8:18]; Register of Burials, 1836–54, Haworth Church.
46. *Bradford Observer*, 20 July 1837, p.197.
47. PB to Mrs Taylor, 19 July 1837: MS RMP 746(c), WYAS, Calderdale.
48. [Benjamin Binns], *Bradford Observer*, 17 Feb. 1894, p.6.
49. 'Midgley', quoted in Edward Harrison to Revd A. Wilkes, 26 Nov. 1879: MS BS ix, H, BPM, [*BST*:12:63:203]; *Bradford Observer*, 17 Feb. 1894, p.6.
50. CB, 'My Compliments to the weather' [Roe Head Journal], [*c.* Mar. 1837]: MS Bon 98(6), p.3, BPM.

51. EJB/AB, Diary Paper, 26 June 1837: MS BS 105, BPM, [JB *ST*, no. 6].
52. *Ibid.*
53. This has not prevented attempts to do so, most notably by Ratchford, *Gondal's Queen* and in her introductions to Hatfield. While doing sterling detective work, Ratchford made a number of assumptions and presents the reconstruction as much more concrete than it actually is. Her work should be read in conjunction with W. D. Paden, *An Investigation of Gondal* (New York, Bookman Associates, 1958).
54. Rev. J. Goldsmith, *A Grammar of General Geography* (London, Longman & Co., 1823): HAOBP:bb217, pp.170, 183, 159, 168, 187, 188, BPM, [JB *ST*, no.45].
55. See, for example, AB, 'Fair was the evening and brightly the sun', 1 July 1837: MS lost, transcript in Symington Colln, Texas, [Chitham, pp.52–9]; AB, 'That wind is from the North, I know it well', 26 Jan. 1838: MS MA 2696 R-V pp.1–3, Pierpont Morgan, [Chitham, pp.63–4]; EJB, 'There shines the moon, at noon of night –', 6 Mar. 1837: MS Add 43483, pp.1–2, BL, [Hatfield, pp.33–5].
56. EJB, 'A sudden chasm of ghastly light', 14 Oct. 1837: MS n.l., [Hatfield, pp.50–2]; EJB, 'Awake awake how loud the stormy morning', [Dec. 1837]: MS Bon 127, p.8, BPM, [Hatfield, pp.58–9]. Another, earlier battle is referred to in EJB, 'The battle had passed from the height', Aug. 1837: MS Bon 127 p.21, BPM, [Hatfield, p.45].
57. EJB, 'There shines the moon, at noon of night –', 6 March 1837: MS Add 43483, pp.1–2, BL, [Hatfield, p.34]. See also, EJB, 'O mother I am not regreting', 14 Dec. 1837: MS Bon 127, p.13, BPM, [Hatfield, pp.60–2].
58. Though the diary paper clearly says, 'Agustus Almeda', this appears to be a case of Emily's slip-shod writing. Augusta Almeda, as 'A.G.A.', is the author and subject of many of Emily's poems, including 'There shines the moon, at noon of night –', 6 Mar. 1837: MS Add 43483, pp.1–2, BL, [Hatfield, pp.33–5], 'Lord of Elbe on Elbe hill', 19 Aug. 1837: MS Bon 127 p.8, BPM, [Hatfield, pp.43–4] and 'O transient voyager of heaven!', Dec. 1837: MS in Berg, [Hatfield, pp.57–8].
59. See, for example, AB, 'That wind is from the North, I know it well', 26 Jan. 1838: MS MA 2696 R-V pp.1–3, Pierpont Morgan, [Chitham, pp.63–4]; EJB, 'The linnet in the rocky dells', 1 May 1844: MS Add 43483 p.45, BL, [Hatfield, pp.204–5].
60. PBB, 'Among all the descriptions I have read', 30 Dec. 1837: MS Bon 149(7) p.21, BPM.
61. *Ibid.*
62. CB, Tales of the Islanders, vol. i, 30 June 1829: MS p.3, Berg, [CA, i, 22]. The lists of Gondal names appear on manuscripts of poems: EJB, 'It was night and on the mountains', [July 1843]: MS Bon 127 p.11, BPM; AB, 'A prisoner in a

dungeon deep', [*c*.1844]: MS Bon 132 p.2, BPM; EJB, [list of Gondal characters], n.d.: MS in Texas.
63. David Moir (1798–1851) contributed poems and ballads regularly to *Blackwood's Magazine* between 1820 and 1844. Among his earliest published pieces are those most similar to Emily's: see, for example, his 'Hymn to the Moon', which begins 'How lovely is this silent scene! / How beautiful, fair lamp of Night, / On stirless woods, and lakes serene, / Thou sheddest forth thy holy light; /' (*Blackwood's Magazine* vi, 1820, p.681). See also, from 'Ballad Stanzas': 'I ponder on the time, when ours / It was in bliss to meet, / When future years seem'd strewn with flowers, / And grief itself grew sweet – / When fondly, wildly, I press'd thy hand, / And gazed in thine eyes of blue, / Till Earth became an enchanted land, / Which sorrow never knew ... /' (*Blackwood's Magazine* xxiv, 1828, p.498). As well as celebrating Walter Scott's home at Abbotsford, Delta also wrote several ballads about Douglas, who was incorporated into Gondal: see, for example, 'Sonnets on the Scenery of the Tweed', *Blackwood's Magazine* xxvi, 1829, pp.185–6; 'The Burial of Douglas', *ibid.*, xxv, 1829, p.105.
64. See, for example, AB, 'Fair was the evening and brightly the sun', 1 July 1837: MS lost, transcript in Symington Colln, Texas, [Chitham, pp.52–9]; EJB, 'Now trust a heart that trusts in you', Nov. 1837: MS Bon 127 p.17, BPM, [Hatfield, pp.53–4].
65. AB, 'That wind is from the North, I know it well', 26 Jan. 1838: MS MA 2696 R-V, pp.1–2, Pierpont Morgan, [Chitham, pp.63–4]. Emily wrote a similar poem, in which Augusta Almeda is comforted by the appearance of a wreath of snow while in prison: EJB, 'O transient voyager of heaven!', Dec. 1837: MS in Berg, [Hatfield, pp.57–8].
66. See, for example, above, pp.255–6.
67. EJB, 'I'll come when thou art sadest', [Nov. 1837]: MS Bon 127 p.7, BPM, [Hatfield, pp.56–7]. Charlotte later declared that her faculty of imagination had been her saviour in the dark months after her sisters' deaths: 'I am thankful to God who gave me the faculty – and it is for me a part of my religion to defend this gift and to profit by its possession': CB to WSW, 21 Sept. 1849: MS Gr F9 p.3, BPM, [*L&L*, iii, 24].
68. PBB, '"All the same – where's a worse than myself"', [July–Sept. 1837]: MS Ashley 187 p.21, BL.
69. PBB, 'of her who almost forty years ago', 31 Oct. 1837: MSS Bon 150 p.2, Bon 149 pp.7–8, 3–4, BPM.
70. PBB, 'Cease, Mourner, cease thy sorrowing for the Dead', *c.* 31 Oct. 1837: MS Bon 149(4), BPM, [VN *PBB*, pp.459–60]. Branwell later revised the poem several times and published a version of it in the *Bradford Herald*, 12 May 1842, p.4 and the *Halifax Guardian*, 14 May 1842, p.6.

71. PBB, 'I have lately remarked', 20 Oct. 1837: MS Bon 149(5), BPM.

72. *Ibid.*, p.6.

73. PBB, 'Among all the descriptions I have read', 30 Dec. 1837: MS Bon 149(7) p.21, BPM.

74. PBB, 'And the Weary are at Rest', n.d.: MS part in Berg and part at Princeton, [PBB, *And the Weary are at Rest*, (ed.) J. A. Symington (London, Privately Printed, 1924)].

75. CB, 'There is, reader, a sort of pleasure in sitting down to write' [Julia], 29 June 1837: MS in Texas, [WG *FN*, pp.87–121]. On 21 July Charlotte completed a second story beginning 'A day or two ago, in clearing out an old rubbish drawer', the manuscript of which is now lost: see CA *EW*, p.256.

76. VN *CB*, p.xxxviii.

77. CB, 'My Compliments to the weather' [Roe Head Journal], [Feb.–March 1837]: MS Bon 98(6), pp.1–3, 6–7, BPM.

78. The poem was originally two separate pieces, composed three days apart: CB, 'The room is quiet', 15 May 1837: MS Bon 94(1), BPM and CB, ''Tis not the air I wished to play', 12 May 1837: MS Bon 98(1) p.4, BPM. In the second manuscript, Charlotte emended 'spirit' to 'spring' and added an alternative last line, 'Beneath the strain of care'.

79. CB to EN, [4 Jan. 1838]: MS Bon 163 pp.1–3, BPM, [*L&L*, i, 163–4].

80. ECG, *Life*, pp.109–10; WG *AB*, p.98 places the incident before June 1837 when she believed the school relocated to Roe Head, but Edward Chitham, in Chitham and Winnifrith, *Brontë Facts & Brontë Problems*, p.32 argues convincingly that the move took place in early 1838. James de la Trobe (see below, note 81) said that his visits took place at Roe Head and Charlotte's letter to Ellen describing the incident is postmarked 5 January 1838, so December 1837 would seem to be the correct date.

81. James de la Trobe to William Scruton, n.d.: quoted in William Scruton, 'Reminiscences of the late Miss Ellen Nussey', *BST*:1:7:27. De la Trobe was minister of the Moravian chapel at Well House, Mirfield from 1836 to 1841 and later became a bishop: *ibid.*, p.26–7. He was the son of the headmaster of Fulneck School at Pudsey, a Moravian establishment which is still active today, and also ran his own school at Well House for children of all religious denominations: Pobjoy, *A History of Mirfield*, p.76; White, *History, Gazetteer & Directory of the West Riding of Yorkshire*, 1838, ii, 396–7.

82. James de la Trobe to William Scruton, n.d.: quoted in William Scruton, 'Reminiscences of the late Miss Ellen Nussey', *BST*:1:7:27.

83. WG *AB*, pp.28–39, 98–102.

84. Elizabeth Branwell attended Thornton Church when Patrick was minister there, was observed always going to and from Haworth Church alone and requested burial next to her sister in the Brontë family vault under Haworth Church: Firth, 28 July 1816; Elizabeth Branwell, Last Will & Testament, 30 April 1833: copy in MSS Copy Docs, BPM.

85. James de la Trobe to William Scruton, n.d.: quoted in William Scruton, 'Reminiscences of the late Miss Ellen Nussey', *BST*:1:7:27.

86. See, for example, CB to EN, 26 Sept. 1836: MS Bon 161, pp.2–3, BPM, [*L&L*, i, 146].

87. CB to EN, 10 Nov. 1834: MS MA 2696 R-V p.3, Pierpont Morgan, [*L&L*, i, 123].

88. CB to EN, 16 Feb. 1850: MS BS Gr.E17 p.3, BPM, [*L&L*, iii, 78]. John Firth Franks later said that 'Aunt' Atkinson told him 'that Charlotte B had shocked all her friends by a novel called Jane Eyre, in which she had slandered Canon Carus Wilson': John Firth Franks to George Moore Smith, n.d.: MS 58, Cvi, Sheffield.

89. Henry Nussey officiated at Dewsbury from September 1835 to 24 July, 1837, though he continued to take the occasional duty until December 1837: Registers of All Saints', Dewsbury. I am grateful to Margaret Smith for drawing my attention to Henry Nussey's curacy at Dewsbury. The only exception to the hardliners in this area was William Margetson Heald, vicar of Birstall 1836–75, who took over the incumbency from his father, also William Margetson Heald, who retired in 1836 when he had a stroke and died in January 1837. The father had entered holy orders late, having first trained as a physician; the son, who was also Chaplain of Trinity College, Cambridge, 1830–44, had been his father's curate in Birstall 1826–9. Both were Cambridge graduates: Venn, pt ii, iii, 309. Charlotte's liking for Heald jnr is evident from her sympathetic portrayal of him as the Reverend Cyril Hall in *Shirley* – the only clergyman to emerge unscathed in the book.

90. CB to EN, 10 May 1836: MS HM 24411 p.3, Huntington, [*L&L*, i, 139].

91. CB to EN, [early Oct. 1836]: MS HM 24383 p.3, Huntington, [*L&L*, i, 140]. The letter is undated, but Margaret Smith suggests that it was written in early October 1836 as it echoes the references to 'stupid pupils' and stormy weather in CB, 'I'm just going to write because I cannot help it' [Roe Head Journal], [*c.* Oct. 1836]: MS Bon 98(7) p.1, BPM.

92. CB to EN, 4 July 1834: MS HM 24408 pp.2–3, Huntington, [*L&L*, i, 121–2]; CB to EN, 1 Jan. 1833: MS BS 40 pp.2–3, BPM, [*L&L*, i, 108], where Charlotte wrote, 'You very kindly caution me against being tempted by the fondness of my Sisters to consider myself of too much importance.'

93. CB to EN, [Oct./Nov. 1836]: MS HM 24413 pp.2–3, Huntington, [*L&L*, i, 142–3]. The letter is undated, but Margaret Smith posits a date of Oct.–Nov. 1836 on the basis of the paper and the references to Calvin anticipating Charlotte's letter of 6 Dec. 1836. See also CB to EN, June 1837: MS n.l., [*L&L*, i, 160]. See also, for example, CB to EN, 20 Feb. 1837: MS n.l., [*L&L*, i, 153],

where Charlotte 'prayed fervently to be enabled to resign myself to *every* decree of God's will'.

94. CB to EN, 29 Dec. 1836: MS BS 40.4 p.3, BPM, [*L&L*, i, 150].

95. CB to EN, 20 Feb. 1837: MS n.l., [*L&L*, i, 153].

96. CB to EN, 5–6 Dec. 1836: MS Bon 162 pp.2, 3, 2 crossed, BPM, [*L&L*, i, 147]. The word 'your' was deleted by Ellen Nussey, which suggests to me that she was sensitive to the accusation that she had ever held Calvinist beliefs. Had the word simply been a casual reference, meaning 'the ones you have just mentioned' as Winnifrith argues, there would have been no need to eradicate it: Tom Winnifrith, 'Charlotte Brontë and Calvinism', *Notes & Queries*, new series, 17, 215 (Jan. 1970), pp.17–18.

97. PB to J. C. Franks, 10 Jan. 1839: MS BS 188 p.1, BPM, [*L&L*, i, 169].

98. Registers of All Saints', Dewsbury. Henry Nussey's journal suggests that he was worthy but rather dull and not very bright. Like his sister he seems to have been prone to much searching of his conscience and self-criticism. There are many passages of self-examination which are similar in tone and content to Charlotte's outpourings of this time, though they are less vehemently expressed. This seems to me to confirm that he and his sister were partially responsible for Charlotte's religious crisis. See: Henry Nussey, Journal, 1830–2, 1838–9: MS Egerton 3268 A, BL.

99. CB to EN, [Oct.–Nov. 1836]: MS HM 24413, p.3, Huntington, [*L&L*, i, 143].

100. James de la Trobe to William Scruton, n.d.: quoted in William Scruton, 'Reminiscences of the late Miss Ellen Nussey', *BST*:1:7:27.

101. AB to Reverend D. Thom, 30 Dec. 1848: MS at Princeton. See below, pp.580–1.

CHAPTER ELEVEN

Title: Referring to Emily's teaching post at Law Hill: 'This is slavery. I fear she will never stand it': CB to EN, 2 Oct. 1838: MS BS 40.3, pp.2–3, BPM, [*L&L*, i, 162].

1. CB, [Mina Laury II], 17 Jan. 1838: MS p.14, Princeton, [WG *FN*, p.143].

2. See CB, [Return of Zamorna], c. 24 Dec. 1836–Jan. 1837: MS in Law Colln, [*M&U*, ii, 282–314]. It should perhaps be pointed out that even though Mary Percy is now alive again, the story is not a reversion to earlier times but is set in contemporary Angria and takes into account, for instance, Northangerland's dying state introduced in Branwell's latest manuscripts.

3. CB, 'There's no use in weeping', 29 Jan. 1838: MS Bon 113(10), BPM, [VN, *CB*, pp.477–9].

4. *Bradford Observer*, 2 Nov. 1837, p.317; 25 Jan. 1838, p.9.

5. CB to EN, [5 May 1838]: MS Bon 164 p.3, BPM, [*L&L*, i, 165].

6. ECG, *Life*, p.109.

7. CB to EN, [5 May 1838]: MS Bon 164 p.3, BPM, [*L&L*, i, 165].

8. CB to MW, [Nov. 1846]: MS FM 3 p.2, Fitzwilliam. Charlotte later made strenuous efforts to assist a friend who was suffering from 'religious hypochondria': Smith, 'The Letters of Charlotte Brontë: some new insights into her life and writing', p.59. Several of Charlotte's fictional characters suffered from hypochondria. See, for example, Lucy Snowe during the Long Vacation in CB, *Villette*, pp.196–8.

9. CB to EN, 9 June 1838: BS 40.45 pp.1–2, BPM, [*L&L*, i, 166].

10. Walter Scott, *The Vision of Don Roderick; Rokeby* (Edinburgh, John Ballantyne & Co., 1811/13), inscribed by Margaret Wooler on the flyleaf: 'Presented to Miss Brontë with the Love and best wishes of a sincere friend – Heald's House. May 23d. 1838 –'. The book had evidently been a gift to Miss Wooler herself as the flyleaf has been glued to another page on which there is the inscription 'Decr 18[21? or 31?] Presented to Miss Wooler as a token of respect from A Friend': HAOBP:bb214, BPM.

11. CB to EN, 9 June 1838: BS 40.45 pp.3–4, BPM, [*L&L*, i, 167].

12. *Ibid.*, pp.2–3.

13. AB, 'Methought I saw him but I knew him not' and 'That wind is from the North, I know it well', 24, 26 Jan. 1838: MS MA 2696R-V pp.3–5, 1–3, Pierpont Morgan, [Chitham, pp.62, 63–4]; EJB, 'Weaned from life and torn away' and 'Ierne's eyes were glazed and dim', Feb. 1838: MSS in Berg, [Hatfield, pp.63–4]; EJB, 'But the hearts that once adored me', [Feb. 1838]: MS in Texas; EJB, fragmentary translations of *Aeneid* and notes on Greek tragedy, 13 March 1838: MSS at KSC.

14. PBB, THE LIFE OF WARNER HOWARD WARNER ESQR, Feb. 1838: MS Bon 152(1) p.2, BPM.

15. There is a memorial to a Haworth Currer in Kildwick Church, a few miles from Haworth between Keighley and Skipton, which Branwell may have seen and from which he may have taken the name.

16. PBB, a continuation of THE LIFE OF WARNER HOWARD WARNER ESQR, 8 March 1838: MS Bon 152(1) p.7, BPM.

17. CB, 'Amen! Such was the sound given in a short shout which closed the evening service at Ebenezer-Chapel' [Stancliffe's Hotel], 28 June 1838: MS Bon 114 pp.3, 4–5, BPM, [unpublished, but excellent detailed précis in CA *EW*, pp.171–8].

18. Mrs Gaskell, thinking Charlotte's description

of taking opium in *Villette* had to be drawn from personal experience, was surprised when Charlotte said she had never knowingly taken the drug but had merely imagined the effects: ECG, *Life*, p.368. The *Villette* experience, incidentally, which leads to a heightened awareness and almost compulsive physical activity, is totally at odds with this description. CA *EW*, p.173 argues that Charlotte was drawing on Branwell's experience of the drug to which, she says, he was probably introduced by his artist friends in Bradford and which he took as a comforter for his 'little success and little money' as a portrait painter there. This is not possible as Branwell did not go to live in Bradford until some time in July (see below, p.291) and did not experience failure immediately. Nor was there any reason for him to have sampled the drug prior to this as he had been at home where he suffered neither failure nor depression.

19. CB, 'In a distant retreat very far indeed from the turmoil of cities' [The Duke of Zamorna], 21 July 1838: MS in Law Colln, [*M&U*, ii, 373, 375].

20. Hymn sheets for the afternoon and evening services, 22 July 1838: Haworth Church hymn sheets, MS BS x, H, BPM. William Hodgson, Patrick's former curate, also came over from Colne to deliver the evening sermon for the same cause. Branwell dated the first draft of one of his best and longest poems, 'Sir Henry Tunstall', from 'Bradford July 31st 1838': PBB, 'Tis only Afternoon, yet midnights gloom', 31 July 1838: MS Ashley 176, BL, [VN *PBB*, pp.463–73]. The binders of the MS attributed it to Emily, a mistake followed by WG *EJB*, p.84 who believed it was a transcription by Emily of a Branwell poem; it is clear from the manuscript hand that it was both written and transcribed by Branwell himself.

21. *Bradford Observer*, 2 Jan. 1840, p.2; 2 June 1836, p.140. Kirby was a wholesaler of beer, not a beer seller which, at that time, was the poorest sort of public house. One of his little daughters became Branwell's particular favourite and was often allowed to dine with him in his private sitting room at his request: Leyland, i, 175.

22. Branwell's portraits in oil of Mr and Mrs Kirby and their niece, Margaret Hartley, all undated, are in the BPM: HAOBP.P.Br.B23, B24, B25, BPM. The portraits of Morgan and Heap do not appear to have survived, though they are mentioned by Leyland, i, 175. A watercolour portrait of Morgan does exist which is inscribed on the reverse in Patrick's hand, 'Portrait, of the Revd Wm Morgan – Price 10s.6d – By a profess'd Artist': HAOBP:P.Br.B12, BPM. This may have been a joking reference to Branwell but stylistically the portrait is unlike any of Branwell's other portraits, all of which are painted in oils. Morgan also appears to be quite a young man in the picture which suggests that it may belong to the Wellington period, rather than the 1830s

when Morgan was already in his fifties.

23. CB to EN, 24 Aug. [1838]: MS HM 24415 pp.1–2, Huntington, [*L&L*, i, 161, wrongly dated to 1837].

24. *Ibid.*, p.3. I am grateful to Margaret Smith for pointing out that the *L&L*, i, 161, wrongly transcribe the surname, which Ellen Nussey has deleted, as 'Carter' though the manuscript probably reads 'Cook'. Eighteen months after this letter, Charlotte was shocked to hear that Ann Cook had died: 'Ann Cook, it seems, is *dead*; when I saw her last she was a young, beautiful, and happy girl; and now "life's fitful fever" is over with her, and she "sleeps well." I shall never see her again. It is a sorrowful thought; for she was a warm-hearted, affectionate being, and I cared for her. Wherever I seek for her now in this world she cannot be found, no more than a flower or a leaf which withered twenty years ago. A bereavement of this kind gives one a glimpse of the feeling those must have who have seen all drop round them, friend after friend, and are left to end their pilgrimage alone. But tears are fruitless and I try not to repine': CB to EN, 12 Jan. 1840: MS n.l., [*L&L*, i, 195].

25. *Bradford Observer*, 9 Aug. 1838, p.3; 23 Aug. 1838, p.3. Richard Oastler and Fergus O'Connor addressed the protesters at the rally.

26. *Halifax Guardian*, 20 Oct. 1838, p.3 which reviewed the concert in glowing terms: 'The best description which could be given of the band, taking it as a whole, is that their performances are as those of one man and that man a Thalberg or a Paganini!' Strauss and his orchestra later gave a grand concert on 25 October in the New Assembly Rooms which was also rapturously received: *Halifax Guardian*, 20 Oct. 1838, p.2; 27 Oct. 1838, p.2. Halifax, like almost every area the Brontës were ever associated with, has its lobby which insists that the Law Hill area provided the background for *Wuthering Heights*. The house itself had been built by Jack Sharpe, who had been adopted by his uncle and proceeded to attempt the ruin and degradation of any members of the family who opposed him. The tale may well have been told to Emily and may have influenced her story, but the identification of Wuthering Heights with High Sunderland Hall, near Law Hill, simply because it had a carved gateway, overlooks all the other features of the house which do not fit in with the description of the farm in the novel. The idea that the half-timbered Shibden Hall, in the valley below Law Hill, is the model for Thrushcross Grange defies belief. The links were suggested as early as 1893 by Thomas Keyworth (see note 27, below). The most vociferous exponent was the Halifax authoress, Phyllis Bentley, in her many books on the Brontës but her views have been accepted and followed by Chitham, *A Life of Emily Brontë*, pp.104–9, 113, 119–21. For a full account of the Jack Sharpe story, see WG *EJB*, pp.75–80.

27. Thomas Keyworth, 'A New Identification of Wuthering Heights', *The Bookman*, March 1893, p.183; White, *History, Gazetteer & Directory of the West Riding of Yorkshire, 1837–1838*, p.407; White, *Directory of the ... West Riding of Yorkshire*, 1843, p.441. WG *EJB*, pp.71–2 believed that it was the Brooke connection which secured Emily the post, but she was relying on the mistaken idea that Emily went to Law Hill in September 1837, when Maria Patchett got married. She also suggests that there was a possible contact through Branwell who, according to Leyland, i, 154 (who was himself following the notoriously unreliable Grundy, p.76), was an usher in a school in Halifax in the autumn of 1837. This is intrinsically unlikely. The post of usher was reserved for unqualified teachers, being both extremely low grade and ill paid: both socially and academically it was far beneath Branwell's notice. In any case, a foray into the teaching profession in the middle of his artistic training and just before he set up as a professional portrait painter, is incomprehensible. The likeliest, if least romantic, reason for Emily's getting the Law Hill post was through an advertisement in a local paper. On 11 August the *Leeds Mercury* carried an advertisement which may have been placed by Miss Patchett. It read: 'WANTED, in a Ladies' Boarding School, a YOUNG FEMALE as TEACHER, competent to assist in all the useful Branches of Education. None need apply but such as are decidedly pious, & can give satisfactory references. Letters (Postpaid) to Y.Z. Mr Hartley's, Stationer, Halifax.': *Leeds Mercury*, 11 Aug. 1838, p.5.

28. Chadwick, pp.124, 127, 128; Thomas Keyworth, 'A New Identification of Wuthering Heights', *The Bookman*, March 1893, p.183.

29. CB to EN, 2 Oct. [1836 should be 1838]: MS BS 40.3 pp.2–3, BPM, [*L&L*, i, 162]. The date of this letter, and consequently of Emily's posting to Law Hill, has been frequently questioned. With typical carelessness, Charlotte dated it 'Dewsbury Moor – Octbr 2nd – 1836', but Miss Wooler's school was still at Roe Head in October 1836. The *L&L*, i, 161 therefore redated it to 1837, which was accepted by WG *EJB*, pp. 70–84 and others. This dating was challenged by Edward Chitham in Chitham and Winnifrith, *Brontë Facts and Brontë Problems*, pp.28–9. He suggested an 1838 date which, as Jennifer A. Cox pointed out in 'Emily at Law Hill, 1838: corroborative evidence', *BST*:18:94:267–70, is substantiated by the postmark, 'Oct. 6 1838', and internal evidence.

30. The details of the pupils and the Law Hill household are obtained from the 1841 census for Southowram which lists twenty pupils aged eleven to fifteen living at Law Hill as boarders. The two teachers, in addition to Miss Patchett who is described as the 'schoolmistress', were thirty-year-old Charlotte Hartley and twenty-five-year-old Jane Aspden. Three female and

one male servants also lived in the house which was a working farm: Census Returns for Southowram, 1841: Microfilm, Halifax; Chadwick, p.126.

31. *Ibid.*, pp.123–4, quoting Mrs Watkinson of Huddersfield, a former pupil.

32. EJB, 'Light up thy halls! 'Tis closing day;' 1 Nov. 1838: MS Add 43483 pp.24–6, BL, [Hatfield, pp.85–7].

33. EJB, 'A little while, a little while', 4 Dec. 1838: MS in Law Colln, [facsimile in *Poems of EJB & AB*, pp.303–4; Hatfield, pp.93–5]. When she decided to publish this poem, Charlotte made some emendations to the manuscript which I have not included in my transcript.

34. EJB, 'Loud without the wind was roaring', 11 Nov. 1838: MS in Law Colln, [facsimile in *Poems of EJB & AB*, p.302; Hatfield, p.92]. Though the sentiments appear more appropriate for Emily's own feelings at Law Hill, the references at the end of this poem to 'the loved and the loving' meeting on 'the mountain' again suggest a Gondal setting.

35. EJB, 'The bluebell is the sweetest flower', 18 Dec. 1838: MS in Law Colln, [facsimile in *Poems of EJB & AB*, pp.305–6; Hatfield, pp.97–9]. It is clear from Emily's description of the 'slight and stately stem,/The blossom's silvery blue' that she meant a harebell, which flowers in July, August and September around Haworth. This is very different from the bluebell, with its rows of dark blue, bell-shaped flowers growing off a single coarse stem, which is a spring flower. Interestingly, though Emily later correctly referred to it as a harebell in her evocative description of the graves of Edgar Linton, Cathy and Heathcliff in the closing passage of *Wuthering Heights*, Anne also called it a bluebell in one of her poems and *The Tenant of Wildfell Hall*. AB, 'A fine and subtle spirit dwells', 22 Aug. 1840: MS 2696 R–V pp.15–18, Pierpont Morgan, [JB *SP*, pp.85–6, 144].

36. *Leeds Intelligencer*, 28 July 1838, p.8. For the vestry meeting at which a church rate was adjourned, then defeated in a poll see *Bradford Observer*, 5 April 1838, p.3, 12 April 1838, p.3. It is possible that this church rate was levied for Bradford rather than Haworth as almost immediately after the meeting a deputation from Haworth waited on the vicar, Henry Heap, and offered to match the largest sum he had ever received by way of dues from the chapelry in the form of a voluntary subscription: *ibid.*, 12 April 1838, p.3. For the other prosecutions see *ibid.*, 1 Nov. 1838, p.3; 25 Nov. 1838, p.3.

37. PB to John Milligan, 9 Oct. 1838: MS BS 187, BPM, [*L&L*, i, 167–8]. John Milligan was only an apprentice to the Keighley surgeon, Mr Mitchell, when he won a prize presented by the Keighley Mechanics' Institute for an essay on 'Cleanliness, Temperance and Moral Improvement, as conducive to happiness' in 1831: *Leeds Mercury*, 9 April 1831, p.3. He was one of the

first people to recognize the appalling state of sanitary conditions in large towns and instigated an investigation into Keighley's public health: *Bradford Observer,* 7 Aug. 1845, p.7; 25 Mar. 1847, p.8. He achieved far more than local fame, however, when he won the gold medal of the Medical Society of London for his essay 'On the Influence of Civilisation on Health and Disease': *Bradford Observer,* 22 Feb. 1849, p.8.

38. PB to James Clarke Franks, 10 Jan. 1839: MS BS 188 pp.1–2, BPM, [*L&L,* i, 168–9].

39. *Bradford Observer,* 24 Jan. 1839, p.2. Heap was only forty-nine; he died on the same day as his youngest daughter, Anna Maria, aged seven, and they had a joint funeral: *Leeds Intelligencer,* 19 Jan. 1839, p.8. Like Patrick, Heap had been a sizar at St John's College, Cambridge, though he matriculated in 1814, eight years after Patrick left: Venn, pt ii, iii, 310.

40. *Leeds Intelligencer,* 14 Feb. 1839, p.2. It was even announced that after the death of 'the present incumbent' of Haworth, it was expected that the chapelry would be further divided into two separate district parishes, Haworth-cum-Stanbury and Oxenhope-cum-Near Oxenhope: *Leeds Mercury,* 6 April 1839, p.5; 21 Feb. 1839, p.2; *Halifax Guardian,* 23 Feb. 1839, p.3. Carus Wilson shared the hard-line attitude of the eventual appointee, Dr Scoresby, towards church dues and rates: he dismissed 'poor Heap' as 'a cypher ... in all his doings': William Carus Wilson to Dr Scoresby, 11 May 1840: MS in Unsorted Bundle, 1840, Whitby.

41. CB to EN, 24 May [1838]: MS HM 24415 p.4, Huntington, [*L&L,* i, 162].

42. *Ibid.,* pp. 1–2.

43. CB to EN, 20 Jan. 1839: MS BS 40.5 pp.1–2, 3, BPM, [*L&L,* i, 170].

44. *Ibid.,* p.2.

45. CB, 'A young gentleman of captivating exterior' [Henry Hastings], 24 Feb.–26 March 1839: MS in Widener Colln, Harvard, [WG *FN,* pp.177–270]. The second volume of the manuscript is missing, only the first and third volumes being extant in this collection. Gérin's repeated assertion (pp.173–5) that Henry Hastings is a portrait of a debauched Branwell now being loyally supported by his loving sister, is not supported by the facts.

46. PBB, 'Five years have now elapsed since the close of the Angrian wars' [Love and Warfare], 15 Dec. 1838–April 1839: MS MA 2696 R-V, Pierpont Morgan. There appear to be several sections missing from this manuscript, though each chapter is obviously part of the same story. The sections relating to Henry Hastings' assassination attempt were all written before 21 February 1839 and therefore predate Charlotte's third volume which is concerned with its aftermath.

47. CB, 'A young gentleman of captivating exterior' [Henry Hastings], 24 Feb.–26 March 1839: MS in Widener Colln, Harvard, [WG *FN,* pp.206, 181. It is possible that Elizabeth Hastings'

name may have been suggested to Charlotte by a tablet erected in 1745 in Mirfield Church, which she would have seen whenever she attended Edward Carter's services there. The plaque, which can still be seen on the wall of the ruined tower of the old church, records among a list of 'Pious and Charitable Benefactors', Lady Elizabeth Hastings, who left two pounds for a monthly sacrament to be held in Mirfield Church. Lady Elizabeth Hastings (1682–1739) was a well-known northern philanthropist who also founded scholarships to Bradford Grammar School and Queen's College, Oxford.

48. *Ibid.,* p.224.

49. *Ibid.,* p.243.

50. *Ibid.,* pp.243–4.

51. *Ibid.,* pp.256–7.

52. Henry Nussey, Journal, 26 Feb. 1839: MS Egerton 3268A p.62, BL, [*L&L,* i, 172].

53. CB to EN, 12 March 1839: MS Grolier E2 p.2, BPM, [*L&L,* i, 174]. Henry Nussey, like many clergymen, supplemented his income by taking pupils.

54. CB to EN, 26 Sept. 1836: MS Bon 161 p.3, BPM, [*L&L,* i, 146].

55. CB to EN, 12 March 1839: MS Grolier E2 p.2, BPM, [*L&L,* i, 174].

56. CB to Henry Nussey, 5 March 1839: MS in private hands, [*L&L,* i, 172–3]. I am grateful to William Self for permission to quote from this manuscript and Margaret Smith for allowing me to use her transcript of it.

57. CB to EN, 12 March 1839: MS Grolier E2 p.3, BPM, [*L&L,* i, 174].

58. Henry Nussey, Journal, [9 March 1839]: MS Egerton 3268A p.64v, BL, [*L&L,* i, 172]. Like his fictional counterpart, Henry Nussey also had plans to be a missionary which Charlotte mocked in a rather unkind fashion: see CB to EN, 15 Nov. 1843: MS MA 2696 R-V pp.2–3, Pierpont Morgan, [*L&L,* i, 308].

59. See, for example, WG *PBB,* p.147; Fraser, p.122. For Branwell's new chapter, dated from Haworth, see: PBB, '"Matilda" said I to the Countess' [Love & Warfare], 21–23 Feb. 1839: MS 2696 R-V pp.12–20, Pierpont Morgan. This chapter follows one begun on 4 February, but there is no indication whether this was written in Bradford or Haworth.

60. R. Bentley (ed.), *Q Horatius Flaccus ... opera* (Amsterdam, R. & J. Wetsten & W. Smith, 1728), pp.112, 143: HAOBP:bb208, BPM. When translating the Odes of Horace at Broughton-in-Furness, Branwell had to rely on memory: see his note at the end of the translations of five odes he sent to Thomas De Quincey in April 1840: 'There are doubtless many mistakes of sense and language – except the first – I had not when I <un> translated them, a Horace at hand, so was forced to rely on memory.': MS p.16, Harvard, [Japp, *De Quincey Memorials,* ii, 208–33].

61. PBB to J. H. Thompson, 17 May 1839: MS BS 136 p.1, BPM, [Leyland, i, 176].

62. Leyland, i, 175; White, *Directory of the ... West Riding of Yorkshire*, 1843, p.459. Though the list may include what we would now call decorators, it also included such eminent artists as Wilson Anderson.

63. *Leeds Mercury*, 1 Sept. 1838, pp.4, 5; *Leeds Intelligencer*, 1 Sept. 1838, pp.5, 8. The family were dependent on a charitable subscription for their survival: see *Leeds Mercury*, 27 Oct. 1838, p.4.

64. See, for example, Robinson, *Emily Brontë*, p.64; WG *PBB*, pp.146, 150; WG *FN*, pp.173–5.

65. PBB to J.H. Thompson, 24 Aug. 1839: MS BS 137 p.2, BPM, [*L&L*, i, 187].

66. PBB to J.H. Thompson, 17 May 1839: MS BS 136 pp.1–2, BPM, [Leyland, i, 176–7]; PBB to J.H. Thompson, 24 Aug. 1839: MS BS 137 p.3, BPM, [*L&L*, i, 187].

67. Trollope, *An Autobiography*, pp.50–1.

68. PBB to J.H. Thompson, 24 Aug. 1839: MS BS 137 pp.2–3, BPM, [*L&L*, i, 187], where Branwell refers to 'our poor Master' and Thompson's kindness to his widow. Branwell's letter of 17 May 1839 is addressed to Thompson as 'Artist Care of Mr Aglen Carver & Gilder', but by the time Branwell wrote again in August, Thompson had left him and taken up residence in the George Hotel at Bradford. Leyland, i, 202.

69. *Ibid.*, i, 203–4; Leyland's obituary, which chronicles his later decline, is printed in the *Halifax Guardian*, 10 May 1851, p.8.

70. Leyland, i, 187–8, 203; John James, *The History of Bradford and its Parish* (London, Longman & Co., 1866).

71. PBB to J.H. Thompson, 24 Aug. 1839: MS BS 137 p.2, BPM, [*L&L*, i, 187].

72. Margaret Hartley, original n.l., quoted in WG *PBB*, p.142.

73. Leyland, i, 178–9: the Bradford friend, as quoted by Leyland, described Branwell as 'a quiet, unassuming young man, retiring, and diffident, seeming rather of a passive nature, and delicate constitution, than otherwise': *ibid.*, i, 179.

74. EJB, 'The night was dark, yet winter breathed', 12 Jan. 1839: MS Bon 127 p.9, BPM, [Hatfield, pp.99–100]. There is no extant poem after this until EJB, 'What winter floods, what showers of spring', 27 March 1839: MS in Berg, [Hatfield, pp.101–2]. From the middle of April, Emily was once again in full poetic flow, indicating she was back in Haworth.

75. ECG, *Life*, p.110; Laura Watkinson, one of Emily's pupils who went to Law Hill in October 1838, states that Emily was 'a teacher during the winter, 1838–9': Chadwick, p.123.

76. CB to Henry Nussey, 5 March 1839: MS in private hands, [*L&L*, i, 173].

77. CB to EN, 12 March 1839: MS Grolier E2 p.2, BPM, [*L&L*, i, 174].

78. CB to EN, 15 April 1839: MS HM 24416 pp.1–2, Huntington, [*L&L*, i, 175].

79. AB, *Agnes Grey*, p.9.

80. Susan Brooke, 'Anne Brontë at Blake Hall', *BST*:13:68:250. Blake Hall, parts of which dated back to the seventeenth century, was demolished in 1954; the site is now part of a modern housing estate and commemorated by several road names.

81. J.T.M. Nussey, 'Notes on the background of three incidents in the lives of the Brontës', *BST*:15:79:333–4; EN to C.K. Shorter, 22 April 1896: MS in bound vol. of miscellaneous letters from EN, Shorter Colln, no. 6, Brotherton. Ellen says of Mrs Ingham, 'A sister was a pupil of Miss W[ooler's]. Formerly they were friends of ours & very kind to me when at school before Mr Ingham married – a family connection existed on his mother's side. Mrs I was an amiable conventional woman – her sister Harriet clever – but refractory, was a pupil in C's time of teacher.' For Ellis Cunliffe Lister's election to Parliament see *Leeds Mercury*, 22 July 1837, p.1.

82. Susan Brooke, 'Anne Brontë at Blake Hall', *BST*:13:68:241; CB to EN, 15 April 1839: MS HM 24416 pp.1–2, Huntington, [*L&L*, i, 175].

83. *Ibid.*, pp.1–2. No other source indicates that Anne suffered from any kind of stammer or hesitation of speech.

84. AB, *Agnes Grey*, pp.34–6; Susan Brooke, 'Anne Brontë at Blake Hall', *BST*:13:68:247.

85. CB to EN, 15 April 1839: MS HM 24416 pp.2–3, Huntington, [*L&L*, i, 175–6].

86. CB to EJB, 8 June 1839: MS n.l., [*L&L*, i, 179]. The temporary nature of the situation is here suggested by Charlotte hoping that Miss Hoby, the Sidgwicks' usual governess, would return after the family had been to Swarcliffe. For the Sidgwicks, see Rowley, *Old Skipton*, pp. 46–50.

87. The marriage took place on 10 January 1827 at Keighley Parish Church: Bishop's Transcripts, Keighley (3) 1824–38: Microfilm, Keighley. Knowle House is described as 'the only one superior mansion to greet the eye of the traveller as he entered the town'; now a funeral parlour, it only retains a faint vestige of its former grandeur: *Keighley Past and Present* (London & Keighley, 1858), p.101.

88. In June Mrs Collins told Emily that Mrs Sidgwick intended to keep Charlotte permanently, so she clearly knew all about the appointment: CB to EJB, 8 June 1839: MS n.l., [*L&L*, i, 179]. Mr Sidgwick had been the prime mover in building the new church in Lothersdale which opened in October 1838: the first incumbent was the Reverend Edward Nicholls Carter, who was married to Susan Wooler: 'DRW', *Christ Church Lothersdale 1838–1888: A Short History*, p.1.

89. Rowley, *Old Skipton*, pp.47–8; CB to EJB, 8 June 1839: MS n.l., [*L&L*, i, 178].

90. 'DRW', *Christ Church Lothersdale 1838–1888: A Short History*, p.1. The Carter children were Ellen aged four, Edward aged three and Susan aged one: when the 1841 census was taken they had moved to their new house at Oakcliffe, in the village, had another daughter, Catherine, and employed two servant girls: Census Returns for

Lothersdale, 1841: Microfilm, Skipton.

91. CB to EJB, 8 June 1839: MS n.l., [*L&L*, i, 178].

92. *Ibid.*, pp.178–9. Charlotte jokingly addresses the letter to 'Dearest Lavinia', probably a reference to the woman who works in the fields in James Thomson's 'Autumn' section of his poem *The Seasons*, published in 1730.

93. CB to EN, [30 June 1839]: MS 2696 R-V pp.1–3, Pierpont Morgan, [*L&L* i, 180].

94. C. K. Shorter, 'New Light on the Brontës', *BST*:1:8:19; Mrs Sidgwick's fifth child, Edward, was born on 18 August 1839 only a few weeks after Charlotte left the family.

95. *Ibid.*, *BST*:1:8:19; Benson, *The Life of Edward White Benson, sometime Archbishop of Canterbury*, i, 12.

96. ECG, *Life*, p.114; CB to EN, [30 June 1839]: MS 2696 R-V p.3, Pierpont Morgan, [*L&L* i, 181].

97. ECG, *Life*, pp.114–15.

98. CB to EJB, 8 June 1839: MS n.l., [*L&L*, i, 179].

99. CB to EN, 26 July 1839: MS HM 24417 p.2, Huntington, [*L&L*, i, 182]; *Leeds Intelligencer*, 27 July 1839, p.5.

100. CB to EN, 26 July 1839: MS HM 24417 pp.1–2, Huntington, [*L&L*, i, 182].

101. CB to EN, 4 Aug. 1839: MS HM 24418 p.1, Huntington, [*L&L*, i, 183].

102. Leyland, i, 238–9.

103. CB to EN, 4 Aug. 1839: MS HM 24418 p.2, Huntington, [*L&L*, i, 183].

104. *Ibid.*, pp.2–3. There is some confusion over the name of this curate. In her letters Charlotte referred to him as 'Mr Price', but the *L&L*, i, 184, 197 corrects this to 'Mr Bryce'. In fact, the name was 'Pryce': David Pryce, from County Wicklow, had been a fee-paying student at Trinity College, Dublin and had graduated the previous summer: Burtchaell and Sadleir, *Alumni Dublinensis*, p.684.

105. CB to EN, 4 Aug. 1839: MS HM 24418 p.4, Huntington, [*L&L*, i, 183]; CB to EN, [24 Jan. 1840]: MS MA 2696 R-V p.2, Pierpont Morgan, [*L&L*, i, 197].

106. CB to EN, 14 Aug. 1839: MS BS 42 pp.1–2, BPM, [*L&L*, i, 185–6]; CB to EN, [9 Aug. 1839]: MS BS 41 p.1, BPM, [*L&L*, i, 185].

107. EN, Reminiscences: MS p.27, KSC, [*L&L*, i, 188–9].

108. *Ibid.*, pp.29–30.

109. CB to EN, 24 Oct. 1839: MS HM 24419 p.2, Huntington, [*L&L*, i, 191].

110. CB to Henry Nussey, 28 Oct. 1839: MS BS 43 p.3, BPM, [*L&L*, i, 192]. Henry Nussey had seen the sea, 'emblem of eternity' as he called it, for the first time in 1832. His phlegmatic response was that it was one of the finest sights mortal eyes could behold, 'yet was not surprised at it, as it appeared much as I imagined it would': Henry Nussey, Journal, 17 July 1832: MS Egerton 3268A, BL.

111. They also visited two of Henry's former parishioners at Burton Agnes: CB to Henry Nussey, 28 Oct. 1839: MS BS 43 p.3, BPM, [*L&L*, i, 192]. The original of the painting is lost but WG *CB*, opp. p.156 reproduced a photograph of it which was in the Bayle Gate Museum at Bridlington.

112. EN, Reminiscences: MS pp.31–2, KSC, [*L&L*, i, 190]. Ellen could not remember where they had stayed, but I have identified the lodgings from a reference in one of Charlotte's letters to her having lost her spectacles at Bridlington and hoping that 'Madame Booth won't refuse to give them up': CB to EN, 24 Oct. 1839: MS HM 24419 p.2, Huntington, [*L&L*, i, 191]. According to Pigot & Co.'s *Directory of Yorkshire* (1842), p.37, Ann Booth was a lodging house keeper in Garrison Street, at Bridlington Quay. The description of Quay and its pier fits exactly with that given by Ellen in her account of their stay: *ibid.*, p.35.

113. EN, Reminiscences: MS p.33, KSC, [*L&L*, i, 190].

114. CB to EN, 24 Oct. 1839: MS HM 24419 p.2, Huntington, [*L&L*, i, 191].

115. EJB, 'I am the only being whose doom', 17 May 1839: MS p.1, Princeton, [Hatfield, p.36]. Hatfield mistakenly dates the poem to 1837 which has given rise to much speculation that the poem is a personal statement by Emily, who was then eighteen, like her fictional character. However, the manuscript is clearly dated 1839, when Emily was twenty, and the poem equally obviously belongs to the Gondal cycle. Emily wrote some thirty-seven poems during the year 1839, twenty-five of them in the latter part of the year: see Hatfield, pp.99–137. Charlotte is said to have written her novelette, which is usually referred to as 'Caroline Vernon', between July and December 1839, but the French themes running through it suggest to me that it belongs, in part at least, to 1840.

116. EJB, 'And now the housedog streched once more', 12 July 1839: MS 2696 R-V, Pierpont Morgan, [Hatfield, p.114].

117. EJB, 'Well, some may hate and some may scorn', 14 Nov. 1839: MS in Law Colln [facsimile in *Poems of EJB & AB*, p.314; Hatfield, pp.132–3].

118. *Bradford Observer*, 11 July 1839, p.3. Scoresby took up residence in Bradford on 4 October and preached his first sermon on 6 October: *ibid.*, 10 Oct. 1839, p.2.

119. *Ibid.*, 28 Nov. 1839, p.3; *Leeds Intelligencer*, 23 Nov. 1839, p.5.

120. Stamp, *William Scoresby: Arctic Scientist*, pp.141–2; William Morgan to Dr Scoresby, [9 Jan. 1840]: MS in unsorted bundle, 1840, Whitby. Morgan pronounced himself 'too fatigued to reply' to his vicar.

121. According to the registers, William Weightman took up office as assistant curate on 19 August 1839: see: Register of Baptisms, 1837–54, Haworth Church; Register of Burials, 1836–54, Haworth Church.

122. CB to EN, 21 Dec. 1839: MS HM 24420 p.2,

Huntington, [*L&L*, i, 193]; Haworth Census, 1841.

123. CB to EN, 21 Dec. 1839: MS HM 24420 pp.2–3, Huntington, [*L&L*, i, 194].

CHAPTER TWELVE

Title: Referring to Branwell as 'a distant relation of mine, one Patrick Boanerges': CB to EN, 29 Sept. 1840: MS n.l., [*L&L*, i, 216].

1. *Leeds Intelligencer*, 21 Dec. 1839, p.1. The Postlethwaites must have paid for three entries as the advertisement appeared again on 28 Dec. 1839, p.4 and 4 Jan. 1840, p.4.
2. An advertisement, which may have been placed by Branwell, appeared in the *Leeds Intelligencer*, 11 May 1839, p.4, stating that 'a gentleman 23 years of age, (a Member of the Established Church), [requires] a SITUATION in a respectable Family, to instruct Pupils in the Classics, the Elements of Mathematics, & the Useful branches of an English Education. A comfortable Home is more desired than pecuniary Remuneration. Reference, as to Respectability, Qualification, &c., can be given to a Clergyman'. As was normal practice, letters were to be addressed to 'A. B.', care of the Printer of the newspaper. Though Branwell was in fact nearly twenty-two when this advertisement was placed, he was always careless about giving his age: see, for instance, his enrolment with the Masons and his letter to Wordsworth. Patrick's copy of his Concordance, with its title page and publication details missing, but with his reading scheme for Branwell written in his hand on the flyleaves, is HAOBP:bb212, BPM. According to the notes in the Concordance, Branwell read at least the first three books of the *Aeneid* and the first four chapters of St Matthew's Gospel in Greek.
3. Branwell translated Odes xiv and xv on 30 April and 1 May, transcribing them into his fair copy book of poems on 12 May: MS BS 125 pp.77–9, BPM, [*VN PBB*, pp.524, 526].
4. CB to EN, [28 Dec. 1839]: MS in Beinecke, [*L&L*, i, 194–5].
5. Most sources, following Leyland, i, 245, say that Branwell attended the meeting of 25 December 1839 and that he acted as 'organist' on this occasion. However, this meeting was in 1838, when Branwell attended on only two occasions, 30 April and 25 December, acting as organist on Christmas Day. Leyland also says this was the last meeting Branwell attended, but this is also not the case: he attended twice in 1842 and once in 1847: contemporary MSS notes of meetings at the Three Graces Lodge, in private hands.
6. PBB to John Brown, [13 March 1840]. The original of this letter is lost, so my transcript is an amalgam of three different and incomplete copies: Lord Houghton, MS Commonplace Book, 1857–60, p.336, TC Cambridge; half of a copy, possibly by John Brown, MS BS 137.5,

BPM; the printed (and heavily edited) version in *L&L*, i, 198–9. I am immensely grateful to Ms Diana Chardin of Trinity College Library for discovering the references in Lord Houghton's Commonplace Book, drawing them to my attention and assisting me in transcribing Houghton's appalling hand.

7. PBB to J. Brown, [13 March 1840]: see note 6. WG *PBB*, p.166 suggests the family had county connections going back to the thirteenth century, but as Timothy Cockerill, 'A Brontë at Broughton-in-Furness', *BST*:15:76:34, pointed out, the Postlethwaites were second-generation merchants. Gérin also wrongly supposes that Robert Postlethwaite was a deputy lieutenant of Cumberland: this honour belonged to his father. He was, however, as she says, a magistrate: Mannex, *History, Topography and Directory of Westmoreland*, p.434. Postlethwaite's age is uncertain: according to Cockerill, he was baptized in 1786 but the census returns for Broughton West (which correctly identify the ages of his children) put him at fifty in 1841 and sixty-two ten years later: Census Returns for Broughton West, 1841: Microfilm, BFRL.
8. Mannex, *History, Topography and Directory of Westmoreland*, p.430. By the time Branwell arrived in Broughton, the woollen industry had been destroyed by mechanization and the town had fallen back on the production of hoops and baskets and quarrying blue slate. Broughton still held a prosperous weekly market and three annual sheep and cattle fairs.
9. For Branwell's comments on the Fishes, see PBB to J. Brown, [13 March 1840]: see note 6. A plaque over the door at High Syke House declares that it was built by the Robinsons in 1753. When I visited Broughton the house was for sale and, according to the particulars, all the timbers in the property were supplied from old sailing ships. WG *PBB*, p.167 says that Branwell lodged with a Dr Gibson, but there was no surgeon of that name in Broughton. The town had only two surgeons, Edward Fish of High Syke House and Robert Lightfoot, who was a single man lodging at the Black Cock Inn in Prince's Street: Census Returns for Broughton West, 1841: Microfilm, BFRL. Atkinson was clearly not in a position to be able to offer Branwell lodgings, so Edward Fish must have been his landlord.
10. The church in Branwell's day had 300 sittings and had been substantially altered in the eighteenth century; it was virtually demolished and rebuilt on the same site in 1874: Guide to the Church of St Mary Magdalene, Broughton-in-Furness, pp.2–3. In the church there is a window

dedicated to the Reverend John Postlethwaite, Branwell's pupil, who died in 1886, and his wife, Isabella, who died in 1875. For Branwell's drawing of the church see PBB, pencil drawing 'Broughton Church', 2 March 1840: HAOBP: P.Br.Bon 18, BPM. On the verso of this drawing is a wonderfully characteristic sketch, a self-portrait in profile.

11. William Wordsworth, 'The River Duddon: a series of sonnets', composed 1806–20, published in 1820; 'Written with a Slate Pencil on a Stone, on the Side of the Mountain of Black Comb', composed 1813, published 1815; 'View from the Top of Black Comb', composed 1813, published 1815; Hutchinson, *Wordsworth: Poetical Works*, pp. 296–303, 429, 174.

12. PBB to J. Brown, [13 March 1840]: see note 6. 'Prince William of Springhead' is William Cockcroft Greenwood, son and heir of Joseph Greenwood of Springhead. Like all his family, apart from his father, William appears to have been a Baptist, hence the reference to 'his friend, Parson Winterbotham'. Joseph purchased a single seat in pew 25 in the North gallery of Haworth Church in 1840 which confirms that he was the sole Anglican in his family: Joseph Whitehead, Pew Receipt for Joseph Greenwood, 13 May 1840: MS note in Register of Baptisms, to 1813, Haworth Church. I am grateful to Sarah Fermi for this last reference.

13. PBB to J. Brown, [13 March 1840]: see note 6. Enoch Thomas was the innkeeper of the King's Arms, William Hartley was a tinner and brazier, 'Billy' [William] Brown was John Brown's brother and, like him, a stonemason, and the 'Doctor' was the Haworth surgeon, Thomas Andrew: Haworth Census, 1841. I have not been able to identify the other men Branwell refers to as none of the existing copies of this letter gives their names.

14. PBB to J. Brown, [13 March 1840]: see note 6.

15. CB to EN, 12 Jan. 1840: MS BS 44 p.1, BPM, [*L&L*, i, 195]; CB to EN, [28 Dec. 1839]: MS in Beinecke, [*L&L*, i, 194].

16. WG *CB*, pp.164, 166–8, 211 introduced the idea that Anne was in love with Weightman and expanded it in her *AB*, 136–50, 173–5, 180–8. It has since been accepted, without qualification or question, by all subsequent biographers.

17. Son of William and Hannah Weightman, he was baptized in St Lawrence's Church, Appleby, on 29 May 1814: Westmorland IGI.

18. PB, *A Funeral Sermon for the late Rev. William Weightman* (Halifax, J. U. Walker, 1842) p.10, [*Brontëana*, pp.257–8]. I am grateful to Dr Ian Doyle and Dr Hall of the University of Durham library for supplying me with details of Weightman's career at University College. According to the University Warden's Book, Weightman matriculated on 24 October 1837 and resided each term till Easter 1839. For his degree see the University Calendars, 1839–43; *Leeds Intelligencer*, 23 June 1838, p.7; 25 July 1840, p.7, includes him

as being from University College, Durham, in a list of priests newly ordained by the Bishop of Ripon. Patrick's mistaken belief that Weightman was both a BA and an MA may have been based on reports in the *Leeds Intelligencer*, 21 Dec. 1839, p.5 that 'William Wightman' had just been admitted to the degree of MA: this Wightman, however, was a graduate of Queen's College, Oxford and a noted lawyer, who was receiving an honorary degree. Patrick also says that his curate went straight from school to university but this is impossible, given the fact that he was already twenty-four when he went to Durham; I cannot account for the missing years.

19. PB, *A Funeral Sermon for the late Rev. William Weightman*, p.10, [*Brontëana*, p.257]. Weightman was ordained priest in July 1840: *Leeds Intelligencer*, 25 July 1840, p.7. For the commencement of his duties in Haworth see Register of Baptisms, 1837–54 [19 Aug. 1839] and Register of Burials, 1836–54 [19 Aug. 1839].

20. PB, *A Funeral Sermon for the late Reverend William Weightman*, p.10, [*Brontëana*, pp.257–8].

21. In the 1841 census he appears as a twenty-five-year-old clergyman, lodging at Cook Gate, with Grace Ogden (sixty), a lady of independent means, Susanna Ogden (twenty-five) and Grace Ogden (nine): Haworth Census, 1841; CB to EN [17 March 1840]: MS HM 24421 p.2, Huntington, [*L&L*, i, 201].

22. EN, Reminiscences, [*L&L*, i, 201].

23. *Ibid*; CB to EN, [17 March 1840]: MS HM 24421 p.2, Huntington, [*L&L*, i, 201].

24. CB/EJB/AB/EN, 'A Rowland for your Oliver', [14 Feb. 1840]: MS n.l., printed in the *Whitehaven News*, 17 Feb. 1876, p.4, [VN *CB*, pp.271–2].

25. CB to EN, 12 March 1839: MS Grolier E2 p.3, BPM, [*L&L*, i, 174].

26. EN, Reminiscences, [*L&L*, i, 201].

27. CB, pencil portrait, [Feb. 1840]: HAOBP:P.Br.B35, BPM. The BPM identifies the portrait as being by Branwell and does not identify the sitter. For my arguments about the identity of both artist and sitter, see Barker, 'A possible portrait of William Weightman', *BST*:19:4:175–6. For the similarity in hairstyle to Branwell, see his self-portrait on the verso of PBB, pencil drawing 'Broughton Church', 2 March 1840: HAOBP: P.Br. Bon 18, BPM. For the Walton portrait see CB to EN, [7 April 1840]: MS HM 24422 p.3, Huntington, [*L&L*, i, 203].

28. *Ibid.*, pp.1–3, 3 crossed. I have been unable to locate the newspaper carrying the reports of the lectures to the Keighley Mechanics' Institute referred to by Charlotte. A report of the Church Rate meeting, naming no names, appeared in the *Bradford Observer*, 2 April 1840, p.2. The meeting refused to grant a rate but as the churchwardens had incurred expenses of £21 it was agreed to pay off their debts by means of collections in church, aided by the Dissenters.

29. CB to EN, [7 April 1840]: MS HM 24422 pp. 2–3, Huntington, [*L&L*, i, 203]. Charlotte only uses the nickname twice, here and in CB to EN [17 March 1840]: MS HM 24421 p.2, Huntington, [*L&L*, i, 201]. In future, when her relations with him had cooled, she refers to him as 'Mr Weightman'.

30. *Ibid.*, pp.1–2; MS HM 24422 p.1, Huntington, [*L&L*, i, 202]. CB to EN, [June 1840]: MS BS 46, BPM [*L&L*, i, 209–10]; CB to EN, [14 July 1840]: MS Bon 165, BPM, [*L&L*, i, 212–13].

31. See, for example, CB to EN, [30 April 1840]: MS 24423 p.1 crossed, Huntington, [*L&L*, i, 206]; CB to EN, 15 May 1840: MS n.l., [*L&L*, i, 206]; CB to Henry Nussey, 26 May 1840: MS in private hands, [*L&L*, i, 207–8].

32. CB to EN, 15 May 1840: MS n.l., [*L&L*, i, 206–7].

33. *Bradford Observer*, 2 April 1840, p.2. See also *Leeds Intelligencer*, 28 March 1840, p.5.

34. CB to EN, [7 April 1840]: MS 24422 p.3 crossed, Huntington, [*L&L*, i, 203]; *Bradford Observer*, 30 April 1840, p.2. Patrick is likely to have been persuaded to do the sermon when William Morgan paid a three-day visit in March. Charlotte found the 'fat Welshman's prosing' unendurable but William Weightman relieved the burden by listening with patience and good temper to all his long stories: CB to EN, [17 Mar. 1840]: MS 24421 p.2, Huntington, [*L&L*, i, 202].

35. CB to EN, 12 Jan. 1840: MS BS 44 pp.1–2, BPM, [*L&L*, i, 195–6]; CB to EN, [24 Jan. 1840]: MS MA 2696 R-V p.1, Pierpont Morgan, [*L&L*, i, 196].

36. Census Returns for Thorpe Underwoods, in the parish of Little Ouseburn, 1841: Microfilm, Harrogate. Anne is not included in the census of Thorp Green as she was on holiday at home in June 1841. The Inghams at Blake Hall employed only five live-in servants, as well as a governess, and a gardener who lived in a cottage in the grounds: Census Returns for Mirfield, 1841: Kirklees. For the value of the Robinson estate see Edmund Robinson, Draft Conveyance of Thorp Green Estate to Harry Thompson, 4 April 1866: MS in Robinson Papers no. 52, BPM.

37. White, *History, Gazetteer & Directory of the West Riding of Yorkshire*, 1838, ii, 789–90; Census Returns for Great Ouseburn & Little Ouseburn, 1841: Microfilm, Harrogate. The wealthiest family, the Thompsons, lived at Kirby Hall, just a mile away from Thorp Green, where they employed six male and nine female domestic servants who lived in and a gardener and lodge-keeper who lived in cottages on the estate: see Census Returns for Kirby Hall, in the parish of Little Ouseburn, 1841: Microfilm, Harrogate.

38. Anne was still at home on 17 March 1840 when Charlotte told Ellen 'Anne's cold is better – but I don't consider her strong yet': CB to EN, [17 Mar. 1840]: MS HM 24421 p.3, Huntington, [*L&L*, i, 202]. She is not mentioned again in Char-

lotte's letters until 9 May 1841 but she was clearly established at Thorp Green by 28 August 1840 when she wrote 'Lines Written at Thorp Green': MS in Law Colln, [facsimile in *Poems of EJB & AB*, p.355; Chitham, p.75]. Chitham, pp.10–11, makes a convincing case for arguing that Anne started her employment on 8 May 1840, the quarter day on which she was paid.

39. The ages of the Reverend Edmund and Mrs Robinson I have taken from the census returns: Census Returns for Thorpe Underwoods, in the parish of Little Ouseburn, 1841: Microfilm, Harrogate. Mrs Robinson's portrait, now belonging to Walsall Area Health Authority, is reproduced in *BST*:18:91: opp. p.28 [see plate 6c].

40. Lydia Robinson was born on 6 October 1825, Elizabeth on 16 November 1826, Mary on 21 March 1828 and Edmund on 19 December 1831: Georgiana Jane, born in 1838, died on 15 March 1841 aged two years eight months and three weeks: Register of Births, Little Ouseburn, 1814–69, Register of Deaths, [Hibbs, pp.304, 502 (f)].

41. Leyland, i, 250.

42. James Thorne, *Rambles by Rivers* (London, Charles Knight & Co., 1844), pp.36, 28, 26, 37: HAOBP:bb61, BPM. On the illustration of Seathwaite Chapel, p.23, Branwell wrote 'The bell rope' and drew a hand pointing to it.

43. PBB, 'Blackcomb', [Spring 1840]: MS n.l. Branwell published the poem under the pseudonym Northangerland, in the *Yorkshire Gazette*, 10 May 1845, p.7. Leyland, i, 251, gives much the same version with slightly different punctuation, [VN *PBB*, p.209].

44. PBB, 'Sir Henry Tunstall', 15 April 1840: MS bms Eng 1009(1) pp.7–8, Harvard, [VN *PBB* p.480]. The earlier version is PBB, ''Tis only Afternoon, yet midnights gloom', 31 July 1838: MS Ashley 176, BL, [VN *PBB*, p.463–73].

45. PBB, translations of Horace, *Odes*, Book I, nos. xv, xi, ix, xxxi, xix, 15 April 1840: MS bms Eng 1009(1) p.16, Harvard, [VN *PBB*, p.530].

46. It should be pointed out, however, that Japp, *The De Quincey Memorials*, ii, 212 considered the manuscripts had only been preserved because they were 'swallowed up in his vast piles of papers and never recovered till his death'. Japp published both 'Sir Henry Tunstall' and the translations: *ibid.*, ii, 208–33.

47. PBB to Hartley Coleridge, 20 April 1840: MS in Law Colln, transcript in Ratchford Papers, Texas, [VN *PBB*, pp.442–3].

48. PBB, 'At dead of midnight – drearily', 20 April 1840: MS in Law Colln, [VN *PBB*, pp.202–9]. For the earlier versions see VN *PBB*, pp.443–52.

49. PBB to Hartley Coleridge, 20 April 1840: MS in Law Colln, transcript in Ratchford Papers, Texas, [VN *PBB*, p.443].

50. When he came to translate the thirty-eighth ode of Book I, Branwell simply wrote, 'This ode I have no heart to attempt, after having heard Mr H Coleridges translation, on May day, at

Ambleside.': PBB, translation of the *Odes* of Horace, Book I: MS p.64, Brotherton, [facsimile in *M&U*, ii, 465]. Branwell also referred to the visit in his letter to Hartley Coleridge, 27 June 1840: MS n.l., [*L&L*, i, 210].

51. Timothy Cockerill, 'A Brontë at Broughton-in-Furness', *BST*:15:76:35; WG *PBB*, pp.174–5.

52. Lord Houghton, MS Commonplace Book, 1857–60, p.338, TC Cambridge.

53. PBB, 'Letter from a Father on Earth to his Child in her Grave', [3 April 1846], published in *Halifax Guardian*, 18 April 1846, p.6. According to Leyland, ii, 128, the lost manuscript of the poem was dated 3 April 1846.

54. The physical description is based on Branwell's self-portrait which he sketched on the back of his drawing of Broughton Church: PBB, pencil drawing 'Broughton Church', 2 March 1840: HAOBP: P.Br.Bon 18vo, BPM. Descendants of Mary Ann Judson, who was born at Buckley Farm, near Stanbury, in 1839, believe that she was the illegitimate daughter of Branwell by Martha Judson, a twenty-six-year-old married woman who already had four children by her husband. I am grateful to Phyllis Cheney, a descendant, for this information.

55. Census Returns for Broughton West, 1841: Microfilm, BFRL. The Fishes had left High Syke House by the time the 1851 census was taken and I have not been able to find out where they went. There are no records of any members of the Fish family in the Broughton Parish registers, though Mrs Fish, described in burial records as widow of the late Edward Fish, surgeon of Broughton, was buried in St Mary's Church at Ulverston aged eighty-one: Burial Register of St Mary's Church, Ulverston 1859–1965: MS BPR/2 I 1/40, CRO, Barrow-in-Furness. I am grateful to Eileen Maughan of CRO, Barrow-in-Furness for locating this reference. I was unable to find any further references to any members of the Fish family in any of the registers of St Mary's Church, Ulverston. On the offchance that Margaret Fish might have been sent to her mother's relations at Ulverston to give birth I also checked the baptismal records there for any child of hers, again without success.

56. Register of Baptisms, 1813–51, Church of St Mary Magdalene, Broughton-in-Furness: MS BPR/6 I 2/1 p.149 no. 1192, p.152 no. 1209, p.153 no. 1219, CRO, Barrow-in-Furness. I am indebted to Eileen Maughan of the Record Office for her initial searches and identifications of all the possible candidates in the Broughton parish registers and the 1841 census returns.

57. Census Returns for Broughton West, 1841, 1851: Microfilm, BFRL. After Armer's death, Eleanor returned to Broughton to marry William Park, a skinner: Register of Marriages, 1837–1915, Church of St Mary Magdalene, Broughton-in-Furness: MS BPR/6 I 3/3, 2 Oct. 1841, 1 Jan. 1849, CRO, Barrow-in-Furness. James Nelson is not referred to in the 1851 census, neither living with his mother and her family nor with his grandfather.

58. Census Returns for Broughton West, 1841, 1851: Microfilm, BFRL; Register of Burials, 1813–73, Church of St Mary Magdalene, Broughton-in-Furness: MS BPR/6 I 4/1, p.137 no. 1096, CRO, Barrow-in-Furness.

59. Census Returns for Broughton West, 1841: Microfilm, BFRL. The Mary Riley who was buried on 27 July 1845 was only eleven months old, according to her death certificate, so she cannot be the same as the one baptized on 21 March 1841: Register of Burials, 1813–73, Church of St Mary Magdalene, Broughton-in-Furness: MS BPR/6 I 4/1, p.106 no. 842, CRO, Barrow-in-Furness. I am grateful to Janet Crockett, Superintendent Registrar of Ulverston, for identifying the second Mary Riley.

60. He was at home by 27 June 1840 when he completed his fair copy of his translations, which he dated from Haworth: PBB, translation of the *Odes* of Horace, Book I: MS p.64, Brotherton, [*M&U*, ii, 465]. There is always the rather dull possibility that the Postlethwaites simply terminated Branwell's employment at Midsummer, 24 June, the customary pay-day, because they were not satisfied with the standard of his teaching. There is no evidence, contemporary or otherwise, to suggest that Branwell obtained his own recall from his father as suggested by WG *PBB*, p. 175. Another possibility, which cannot be overlooked, is that Branwell himself may have only intended to take the post for six months: in his letter to John Brown he mentioned his return at Midsummer and though I have taken this to be a reference to his expected holiday then, it is open to interpretation as a statement of intent to give up his job: PBB to J. Brown, [13 March 1840]: see note 6.

61. PBB to Hartley Coleridge, 27 June 1840: MS n.l., [*L&L*, i, 210–11].

62. *Blackwood's Magazine*, for instance, regularly included translations from the classics. See, for instance, the series, by William Hay, 'Translations from the Greek Anthology' which ran throughout 1836 and part of 1837, and was followed by 'The Latin Anthology' in 1838. Individual articles also dealt with classical subjects, like, for instance, Chapman's translation of Aeschylus' *The Eumenides*, which appeared in 1839.

63. Hartley Coleridge to PBB, 30 Nov.–1 Dec. 1840: MS, draft only, Texas, [VN *PBB*, pp.522–3]. I am grateful to Mrs A. H. B. Coleridge for permission to quote from this letter.

64. CB, 'When I concluded my last book' [Caroline Vernon]: [*c*. July 1839–Spring 1840]: MS in Widener Colln, Harvard, [WG *FN*, 277–367]. This manuscript appears to have been begun on Charlotte's return from Stonegappe as she says 'Scarce three moons have waxed & waned' since she wrote her last story, but there seems to have

been a break in the writing before the Parisian episode, so I have tentatively given it a later date than is usually suggested.

65. CB to EN, [20 Aug. 1840]: MS HM 24425 pp.2–3, Huntington, [*L&L*, i, 215].

66. CB, 'Alexander Percy was a man', [Spring 1840]: MS MA 2696 R-V, Pierpont Morgan, [part only in *BST*:10:50:18–24].

67. CB to Hartley Coleridge, [*c.*Nov./Dec. 1840]: MS MA 2696 R-V pp.1–3, Pierpont Morgan, [*BST*:10:50:16–17]. The fair copy of this letter is dated 10 December and is in Texas, [*TLS*, 14 May 1970, p.544]. According to ECG, *Life*, pp.126–7 and *L&L*, i, 211–12, this letter was to William Wordsworth, but Charlotte later told Monsieur Heger, 'Southey, et Coleridge – deux de nos meilleurs auteurs, à qui j'ai envoyé certains manuscrits en ont bien voulu témoigner leur approbation': CB to M. Heger, 24 July [1844]: MS Add 38732A p.3, BL, [*L&L*, ii, 10, 13]. The clear implication of this is that Charlotte only wrote to those two authors. Mrs Gaskell assumed the letter was to Wordsworth, knowing of Branwell's earlier letter to him and seeing the Ambleside postmark on the wrapper in which Charlotte's manuscript was returned. However, Ambleside was also Coleridge's nearest postal town and his encouragement of Branwell must have suggested him to Charlotte as a critic of her own work. The existence of the fair copy proves that the letter was addressed to Coleridge.

68. CB to EN, [2 June 1840]: MS HM 24424 p.1, Huntington, [*L&L*, i, 208]; CB to EN, [June 1840]: MS BS 46 p.1, BPM, [*L&L*, i, 209].

69. CB to EN, 20 Nov. 1840: MS HM 24426 p.3, Huntington, [*L&L*, i, 221–2]. Ellen Nussey has deleted six lines here about Mary Taylor which I have been unable to decipher.

70. CB to EN, [14 July 1840]: MS Bon 165 p.1, BPM, [*L&L*, i, 213]; CB to EN, [June 1840]: MS BS 46 p.1, BPM, [*L&L*, i, 213].

71. CB to EN, [14 July 1840]: MS Bon 165 p.1 crossed, BPM, [*L&L*, i, 213], says Weightman left Haworth that morning and 'I have no doubt he will get nobly through his examination he is a clever lad'. The record of the ordination is in the *Leeds Intelligencer*, 25 July 1840, p.7. Chitham, pp.18–19 flatly denies that Weightman had any examinations to pass, suggesting that this was part and parcel of his 'charming ... unreliable' character, his 'half-truths and exaggerations'. This seems unfair: all candidates for the priesthood had to undergo an oral examination before the ordaining bishop: see, for example, Patrick's comments to the Reverend Mr Campbell of Glenfield, that his fellow graduate of St John's, Robert Cox, would be unable to undergo the Bishop of Lincoln's examination: PB to Revd Mr Campbell, 12 Nov. 1808: MS in Parrish Colln pp.1–2, Princeton, [L&D, p.39].

72. CB to EN, 20 Aug. 1840: MS HM 24425 p.1, Huntington, [*L&L*, i, 214–15]. For further references to his time in Appleby see CB to EN,

[June 1840]: MS BS 46 p.3, BPM, [*L&L*, i, 209]; CB to EN, 29 Sept. 1840: MS n.l., [*L&L*, i, 217]. William Weightman signs the registers for the first time since July on 13 September, indicating that he returned about this time: Register of Baptisms, 1837–54, Haworth Church.

73. CB to EN, 29 Sept. 1840: MS n.l., [*L&L*, i, 217].

74. See, for example, the generously worded tribute on the memorial to Weightman erected in Haworth Church, quoted below, p.403; Register of Baptisms, 1837–54, Register of Marriages, 1837–70, Register of Burials, 1836–54, Haworth Church.

75. PB, *A Funeral Sermon for the Reverend William Weightman*, pp.8–9, 11, [*Brontëana*, pp.256–8].

76. *Leeds Mercury*, 1 Aug. 1840, p.5; *Bradford Observer*, 17 Sept. 1840, p.2; *Leeds Mercury*, 8 Aug. 1840, p.5.

77. *Ibid.*, 26 Sept. 1840, p.5; 17 Jan. 1852, p.10; 15 Aug. 1840, p.5.

78. *Halifax Guardian*, 5 Sept. 1840, p.4.

79. CB to EN, 12 Nov. 1840: MS n.l., [*L&L*, i, 219].

80. Until 25 September 1840, John Collins signed the Keighley registers without a title. Busfeild appears to have promoted him officially to 'Assistant Curate' as thereafter he signs in this capacity. His last signature occurs in the baptismal registers on 18 April 1841, his place then being taken by William Fawcett: Bishop's Transcripts, 1838–54, Keighley: Microfilm, Keighley. However, he appears in the Clergy Lists as Busfeild's curate 1843–6, and again, with no named curacy, in 1847: I am grateful to Margaret Smith for this information which fits in with the fact that Mrs Collins later had a second child by her husband and was abandoned by him in Manchester in 1847: see note 81.

81. CB to EN, [4 April 1847]: MS pp.2–3, Princeton, [*L&L*, ii, 130–1].

82. AB, 'A fine and subtle spirit dwells', 22 Aug. 1840: MS 2696 R-V pp.17–18, Pierpont Morgan, [Chitham, pp.73–4]. There is no doubt that Anne meant the harebell though she calls the flower a bluebell: see above, p.893 n.35.

83. AB, 'O! I am very weary', 28 Aug. 1840: MS in Law Colln, [facsimile in *Poems of EJB & AB*, p.355]. In this fair copy book, compiled in 1845, the poem is given the title 'Lines written at Thorp Green', apparently as an afterthought. When she amended and published the poem in the sisters' 1846 volume, she gave it the same title as Emily's poem, 'Appeal': *Poems 1846*, p.140.

84. WG *AB*, p.167, who wrongly dates the poem to 1841 and says it was only published posthumously, and Chitham, pp.169–70 both assert the autobiographical nature of the poem and associate it with Scarborough. The Robinsons do not feature in the list of visitors published in the *Scarborough Herald*, 13 Aug. 1840, p.3 though they were usually resident at this period in later years. It is possible that the Robinsons visited earlier but there are no earlier extant editions of the *Scarborough Herald* to confirm this. As Anne had only started her

job in May it is possible that Mrs Robinson did not allow her to take what was to become her usual summer holiday just before the Robinsons went to Scarborough. In *Agnes Grey*, Mrs Bloomfield cut short her governess' holiday, because she had only arrived so recently: this would be applicable to Anne's appointment at Thorp Green, but not to her earlier post at Blake Hall: AB, *Agnes Grey*, pp.31–2.

85. EJB, 'If greif for greif can touch thee', 18 May 1840: MS in Law Colln, [facsimile in *Poems of EJB & AB*, p.310–11]. In this manuscript notebook, the poem is untitled, but it shares the same metre and vocabulary as Anne's poem: see JB *SP*, pp.129–30, 145.

86. CB to EN, 12 Nov. 1840: MS n.l., [*L&L*, i, 218]. Charlotte also lost the chance of a post as governess to the Thornton family at Cottingley Hall because she could not undertake to teach music: Speight, *Chronicles and Stories of Old Bingley*, p.350. I am grateful to Sarah Fermi for this reference.

87. CB to EN, 12 Nov. 1840: MS n.l., [*L&L*, i, 218].

88. CB to EN, 17 March 1840: MS HM 24421 p.3, Huntington, [*L&L*, i, 202]; CB to EN, [June 1840]: MS BS 46 p.3, BPM, [*L&L*, i, 210]; CB to EN, 20 Aug. 1840: MS HM 24425 p.3, Huntington, [*L&L*, i, 215]. Charlotte's use of 'Charivari' and 'Ça Ira' seems to reflect her French reading at this time: *Punch* did not adopt the title 'The London Charivari' until 1841, so Charlotte was presumably quoting the French journal.

89. CB to EN, 20 Aug. 1840: MS HM 24425 p.2, Huntington, [*L&L*, i, 215]; CB to EN, [13 Aug. 1840]: MS Bon 166, BPM, [*L&L*, i, 213–14].

90. *Halifax Guardian*, 29 Aug. 1840, p.2.

91. CB to EN, 29 Sept. 1840: MS n.l., [*L&L*, i, 216].

The references are from the Bible, Mark 3:17, 2 Chronicles 8:4.

92. WG *PBB*, p.180. The clerk-in-charge, George Duncan, was engaged at an annual salary of £130, rising to a possible £150. Thomas Sugden, whom Branwell first offered as a surety in place of his aunt, was not landlord of the Black Bull, as Gérin claims, but a woolstapler: White, *Directory of the... West Riding of Yorkshire* (1843), p.372.

93. *Halifax Guardian*, 10 Oct. 1840, p.2; 19 Dec. 1840, p.3; 26 Dec. 1840, p.4.

94. *Ibid.*, 3 Oct. 1840, p.2; 20 Feb. 1841, p.1.

95. *Ibid.*, 17 Oct. 1840, p.2. Passions were roused to such an extent that the head waiter of the White Swan Hotel was later prosecuted for an assault on the guard of the rival Union Hotel omnibus: *ibid.*, 28 Nov. 1840, p.3.

96. White, *Directory of the... West Riding of Yorkshire* (1843), p.444.

97. Du Maurier, p.117 and WG *PBB*, pp.183–4 both quote the 'local tradition' for which I have been unable to find a contemporary source. White, *Directory of the... West Riding of Yorkshire* (1843), p.444 does not list a 'Pear Tree Inn' though it does identify Edward (not Ely) Bates as the owner of a beer-house.

98. A concert of sacred music was held in the Old Assembly Rooms (in the Talbot Inn, Halifax) on 9 September 1840 and there was a performance of the *Messiah* in the Oddfellows' Hall on 28 December: *Halifax Guardian*, 9 Nov. 1840, p.1; 28 Dec. 1840, p.2; 2 Jan. 1841, p.3. Two lectures by Mr Burns, a New Zealand chief in full regalia, were given in the Old Assembly Rooms: *ibid.*, 5 Dec. 1840, p.3. Halifax Theatre reopened under the management of Mr Skerrett in December: *ibid.*, 26 Dec. 1840, p.2; 2 Jan. 1841, p.3.

99. Leyland, i, 266–7.

CHAPTER THIRTEEN

Title: 'I hardly know what swelled to my throat as I read her letter... such a strong wish for wings – wings such as wealth can furnish': CB to EN, 7 Aug. 1841: MS HM 24428 p.2, Huntington, [*L&L*, i, 240].

1. CB to EN, [3 Jan. 1841]: MS Grolier E3 p.1, BPM, [*BST*:17:9035: 4–5].

2. CB to EN, [20 Nov. 1840]: MS HM 24426 pp.1, 2–3, Huntington, [*L&L*, i, 220–1].

3. Ellen enigmatically referred to Charlotte 'helping to cook a certain hash which has been concocted at Earnley', this being the home of Henry Nussey: CB to Henry Nussey, 11 Jan. 1841: MS BS 47 p.2, BPM, [*L&L*, i, 223].

4. CB to Henry Nussey, 26 May 1840: MS in private hands, [*L&L*, i, 208]. I am grateful to William Self for permission to quote from this manuscript and to Margaret Smith for the use of her transcript of it.

5. CB to Henry Nussey, 11 Jan. 1841: MS BS 47 p.3, BPM, [*L&L*, i, 224].

6. CB to EN, 3 March 1841: MS n.l., [*L&L*, i, 225–6].

7. *Ibid.*, p.226. Anne's salary was £10 per quarter: see Edmund Robinson, Cash Book, 1845–6: MS 93/2, Robinson Papers, BPM.

8. Monument to John White in St Wilfrid's Parish Church, Calverley. The entire inscription reads: 'Sacred to the memory of John White of Upperwood House, Rawdon Gentleman who died 30th October 1860 in the 70th year of his age & was interred near the east window of this church on the 6th day of the following month. This Monument is erected by his sorrowing widow in affectionate remembrance of his amiable upright and truly Christian demeanour in every relation of life.' For his children see *Brontë House – the First Fifty Years: 1934–1984*, (privately printed for Woodhouse Grove School, 1984), p.4.

When Upperwood House was demolished Brontë House, the preparatory school for Woodhouse Grove, was built in its grounds.

9. CB to EN, 3 March 1841: MS n.l., [*L&L*, i, 226].
10. CB to WSW, 12 May 1848: MS Grolier F3 pp.1–3, BPM, [*L&L*, ii, 212–13].
11. See below, p.354.
12. CB to EN, [21 March 1841]: MS BS 47.5 p.1, BPM, [*L&L*, i, 227–8].
13. CB to EN, [1 April 1841]: MS HM 24427 p.1, Huntington, [*L&L*, i, 228].
14. CB to EJB, 2 April 1841: MS n.l., [*L&L*, i, 230].
15. CB to EN, 4 May 1841: MS BS 48 p.1, BPM, [*L&L*, i, 230].
16. *Ibid.*, pp.1–3.
17. CB to Henry Nussey, 9 April 1841: MS in private hands, [*L&L*, i, 233]. I am grateful to William Self for permission to quote from this manuscript and to Margaret Smith for allowing me to use her transcript of it. Though Charlotte may have simply confused her dates in this letter when she told Henry Nussey that she had received an *invitation* to Brookroyd 'a fortnight since', it is probable that she meant she was *at* Brookroyd two weeks before. If this is not the case, then Charlotte may have visited Brookroyd for a second time in April.
18. CB to EN, [4 May 1841]: MS BS 48 p.3, BPM, [*L&L*, i, 231].
19. *Ibid.*, pp.3–4.
20. *Ibid.*, p.3; CB to EN, [10 June 1841]: MS BS 49 pp.3–4, BPM, [*L&L*, i, 234].
21. CB to EN, [1 July 1841]: MS p.1, in private hands, [*L&L*, i, 234]. I am grateful to Lynda Glading for allowing me to see this manuscript and quote from it. CB to EN, [3 July 1841]: MS Grolier E1 p.1, BPM, [*L&L*, i, 235]; CB to EN, 19 July 1841: MS Grolier E4 p.1, BPM, [*L&L*, i, 235].
22. W. Scoresby to all clergymen of Bradford Parish, Dec. 1840: MS in Unsorted Bundle, 1840, Scoresby Papers, Whitby; Petition to Joseph Shackleton from the inhabitants of Haworth, Dec. 1840: MS (two copies, one in Scoresby's hand) in Unsorted Bundle, 1840, Whitby.
23. *Bradford Observer*, 11 Feb. 1841, pp.3, 4.
24. PB to the *Leeds Intelligencer*, 13 March 1841, p.7.
25. William Morgan to Dr Scoresby, 3 April 1841: MS in Unsorted Bundle, 1841, Whitby. This 'letter' simply stated 'Mr Morgan respectfully thanks the vicar for his letter, and declines any further correspondence with him'. *Halifax Guardian*, 10 April 1841, p.3; 17 April 1841, p.2.
26. PB to the *Bradford Observer*, 13 May 1841, p.4.
27. *Ibid.*
28. John Winterbotham to *Bradford Observer*, 20 May 1841, p.4; 5 June 1841, p.4.
29. *Halifax Guardian*, 3 July 1841, p.3.
30. Accounts of the campaign in Haworth differ according to the political affiliation of the newspaper. The Tory *Leeds Intelligencer*, 3 July 1841, p.5 declared 'Never was there such a signal defeat of and discomfiture to the Whig party in Haworth' while the supplement to the Liberal *Leeds Mercury*, 3 July 1841, p.3 said that 'The visit of the Blue candidates to Haworth has strengthened much the Liberal cause.'

31. EJB, Diary Paper, 30 July 1841: MS in Law Colln, [facsimile in Shorter, p.146]. Emily's hawk is usually referred to as 'Hero' but, as Margaret Smith has pointed out, the name in this diary paper appears to be 'Nero', which is appropriate given the family propensity for naming pets after classical figures. Victoria and Adelaide, named after the Queen and her aunt, were the pet geese.
32. CB to EN, [1 July 1841]: MS in private hands, [*L&L*, i, 234]. The Robinsons are listed among the visitors in the *Scarborough Herald*, 22 July 1841, p.3. Details of Wood's Lodgings are given in an advertisement in the *Scarborough Record*, 7 June 1841, p.1.
33. AB, Diary Paper, 30 July 1841: MS in Law Colln, [*L&L*, i, 239].
34. CB to EN, 19 July 1841: MS Grolier E4 pp.1–2, BPM, [*L&L*, i, 235–6].
35. *Ibid.*, pp.2–3, 3, 4.
36. *Ibid.*, p.4.
37. *Ibid.*, p.3.
38. CB to EN, [2 Nov. 1841]: MS HM 24429 pp.1–2, Huntington, [*L&L*, i, 244–5].
39. CB to EN, 7 Aug. 1841: MS HM 24428 p.2, Huntington, [*L&L*, i, 240].
40. CB to Aunt Branwell, 29 Sept. 1841: MS n.l., [*L&L*, i, 242–3].
41. CB to EN, [2 Nov. 1841] MS HM 24429 p.3, Huntington, [*L&L*, i, 245].
42. CB to EJB, 7 Nov. 1841: MS n.l., [*L&L*, i, 247].
43. *Ibid.*, i, 246.
44. CB to EN, [2 Nov. 1841]: MS HM 24429 p.1, Huntington, [*L&L*, i, 244]; CB to EN, 10 Dec. 1841: MS p.3, Harvard, [*L&L*, i, 247].
45. CB to EN, 10 Jan. 1842: MS n.l., [*L&L*, i, 249].
46. The narrative poems include a reworking of Augusta Almeida's murder by Douglas: EJB, 'Were they shepherds, who sat all day', Jan. 1841–May 1844: MS Add 43483 pp.29–38, BL, [Hatfield, pp.150–61]; EJB, ''Twas night, her comrades gathered all', 17 Aug. 1841: *ibid.*, pp.20–2, [Hatfield, pp.168–9]; EJB, 'Weeks of wild delirium past –', 1 Sept. 1841: *ibid.*, pp.17–19, [Hatfield, pp.150–61, 168–9, 170–2].
47. EJB, 'Shall Earth no more inspire thee,', 16 May 1841: MS in Law Colln, [facsimile in *Poems of EJB & AB*, p.307; Hatfield, pp.163–4]. The nature-loving character, who is rejected by society, may be Douglas, the outlaw who killed Augusta. He appears in other poems.
48. EJB, 'I see around me tombstones grey', 17 July 1841: MS in Law Colln, [facsimile in *Poems of EJB & AB*, p.316; Hatfield. p.167].
49. EJB, *Wuthering Heights*, p.80. See also p.160, where the dying Catherine muses, 'the thing that irks me most is this shattered prison, after

all. I'm tired, tired of being enclosed here. I'm wearying to escape into that glorious world, and to be always there; not seeing it dimly through tears, and yearning for it through the walls of an aching heart; but really with it, and in it.'

50. EJB, 'And like myself lone, wholly lone', 27 Feb. 1841: MS in Berg, [Hatfield, p.161].

51. EJB, 'Riches I hold in light esteem', 1 March 1841: MS in Law Colln, [facsimile in *Poems of EJB & AB*, p.309; Hatfield, p.163].

52. CB to EN, 10 Jan. 1842: MS n.l., [*L&L*, i, 249].

53. CB to EN, [20 Jan. 1842]: MS HM 24480 p.4, Huntington, [*L&L*, i, 250].

54. See, for example, Chitham, p.15; CB to EN, [20 Jan. 1842]: MS HM 24430 pp.4, 1, Huntington, [*L&L*, i, 250].

55. *Ibid.*, p.2.

56. *Ibid.*, pp.2–3.

57. CB to EN, [17 Dec. 1841]: MS Bon 167, BPM, [*L&L*, i, 248].

58. CB to EJB, 2 April 1841: MS n.l., [*L&L*, i, 229]; Minutes of the Board of the Manchester and Liverpool Railway: MS LY 1/10, PRO.

59. Census Returns for Midgley township, 1841: Microfilm, Halifax.

60. Grundy, p.75.

61. PBB to Francis Grundy, 22 May [1842]: MS n.l., [Grundy, p.85]. Grundy dates this letter to 1845 but on content it clearly dates from 1842. Du Maurier, pp.118–32 and WG *PBB*, pp.187–204 are both convinced of Branwell's downfall, through debauchery, at Luddenden Foot.

62. Among Grundy's wilder exaggerations was a claim to have met all the Brontë sisters whom he described, *en masse*, as 'distant and distrait, large of nose, small of figure, red of hair, prominent of spectacles': Grundy, p.74. He described Branwell in similarly unflattering terms which are not borne out either by descriptions by other friends or by his portraits: 'Branwell was very like them, almost insignificantly small – one of his life's trials. He had a mass of red hair, which he never brushed high off his forehead, – to help his height, I fancy; a great, bumpy, intellectual forehead, nearly half the size of the whole facial contour; small ferrety eyes, deep sunk, and still further hidden by the never removed spectacles; prominent nose, but weak lower features. He had a downcast look, which never varied, save for a rapid momentary glance at long intervals. Small and thin of person, he was the reverse of attractive at first sight.': *ibid.*, p.75.

63. Leyland, i, 289–90; Grundy, p.76.

64. William Weightman's salary, paid by the Church Pastoral Aid Society, was £100 a year: *Halifax Guardian*, 20 Feb. 1841, p.4. On 21 February, William Weightman appropriately enough preached a sermon on behalf of the CPAS in Haworth Church and raised a 'liberal collection' for its funds: *Halifax Guardian*, 27 Feb. 1841, p.2.

65. The so-called 'Luddenden Foot Notebook' was mainly in use in the period 1840–2, but

Branwell continued to make entries as late as 1843. The manuscript is divided, the bulk of twenty-eight pages being MS BS 127, BPM and a further fourteen pages being in the Brotherton. For the concert note see PBB, [Luddenden Foot Notebook], 1840–2: MS p.2, Brotherton. The only concert of sacred music held in the Old Assembly Rooms on a Monday was the one on 11 November 1841: *Halifax Guardian*, 7 Nov. 1841, p.1; 14 Nov. 1841, p.3. Branwell notes the address of the 'Mottet Society' and that subscriptions, in the form of post office orders, should be sent to E. Rimbault, the Managing Editor: PBB, [Luddenden Foot Notebook], 1840–2: MS p.5, Brotherton.

66. *Halifax Guardian*, 30 Jan. 1841, p.3; 2 Jan. 1841, p.3; 18 Dec. 1841, p.4; 9 Jan. 1841, p.3. The second concert got appalling reviews. The singer from London 'took unwarrantable liberties' with the music, the drummer was a full beat behind the rest of the orchestra and 'The chorus was murdered outright': *ibid.*, 1 Jan. 1842, p.4.

67. Register of Members & Monthly Receipts, Luddenden Village Library, 1834–1914: MS SPL: 238, WYAS, Calderdale. See, for example, WG *PBB*, pp.194–5 for the 'local and well-substantiated tradition' (but unattributed) that Branwell used the library.

68. White, *History, Gazetteer and Directory of the West Riding of Yorkshire* (1838), ii, 414; *Halifax Guardian*, 26 Dec. 1840, p.2. White, ii, p.422 also lists two other subscription libraries in Halifax and the library of the Halifax Mechanics' Institute.

69. PBB, [Luddenden Foot Notebook], 1840–2: MS pp.1, 5, 9, Brotherton; MS BS 127 p.1. BPM.

70. This strange claim is made by Du Maurier, p.123 and followed by later biographers.

71. PBB, [Luddenden Foot Notebook], 1840–2: MS p.4, Brotherton. According to the 1841 census, George Thompson, a thirty-year-old corn dealer and maltster, lived at Middlefoot, between Luddenden and Luddenden Foot; there was a James Titterington, aged twenty-five, at High Lees who was a worsted weaver and Henry Killiner, aged thirty, the only porter, lived at Bankfield: Census Returns for Midgley & Warley, 1841: Microfilm, Halifax. A John Titterington was a worsted manufacturer and spinner in Sowerby Bridge: Robson, *Commercial Directory* (London, William Robson, 1840–1), ii, 194. I have not been able to identify the other name(s), 'R. Cal' (not Col as in Du Maurier, p.123 and WG *PBB*, p.197) and 'Rd [S?]al'; the latter name may be longer and has either faded or been unintentionally erased. 'At R. Cal last night' suggests an abbreviated form of an inn name, but the nearest I can get to this is the R[oyal] Oak. Du Maurier's premise that the two names are the same, 'Col', and a form of 'Coll' and 'McColl', Irish labourers 'who herded together, squatter fashion, near the canal at Luddenden Foot', is totally without foundation. There were no Irish in Luddenden Foot accord-

ing to the 1841 census (except, as it says, Branwell!) and there was only one Michael McCall, a fifteen-year-old labourer at Denholme, to represent the entire race of 'Cols'. The weavers, spinners, factory hands and watermen of Luddenden Foot were, almost without exception, Yorkshire born and bred.

72. Grundy, p.79. Grundy thought the poem 'necessarily an impromptu' but it was in fact an adaptation of one Branwell had written as early as 1836: see VN *PBB*, p.455.

73. Grundy, pp.80–1. According to Grundy, the fortune teller was a ninety-five-year-old woman, who was also consulted in jest by the 'three curates' of *Shirley* fame. In fact, there appears to have been a tradition of astrology in Haworth. A renowned Haworth astrologer, Jack Kaye, died in 1846, his obituary appearing in the *Leeds Intelligencer*, 30 Jan. 1846, p.5. Another is referred to in a curious book, *The Wild Moor*, written as a semi-fictional account of the area by the curate of Cross-stone. His story has two ladies going to Haworth to consult the astrologer and being taken instead to see Patrick Brontë: see Rev. James Whalley, *The Wild Moor: A Tale Founded on Fact* (Privately Printed, 1869), pp.70–3. I am grateful to Sarah Fermi for drawing my attention to this book.

74. Leyland, i, 290–2; *Halifax Guardian*, 10 Aug. 1861, p.4. Sowden was later to become a close friend of Arthur Bell Nicholls and performed the marriage ceremony for him and Charlotte Brontë. PBB, [Luddenden Foot Notebook], 1840–2: MS BS 127 p.18, BPM. The two names are written in Greek letters above and below the same drawing of a man reclining in a chair, so there is no indication which is the name of the sitter. John Murgatroyd, forty-five, was a corn miller at Brearley and the two John Murgatroyds who were stuff manufacturers, aged seventy and thirty, lived at Green Hedge and Victory respectively: Census Returns for Midgley & Warley, 1841: Microfilm, Halifax. I have been unable to trace George Richardson. There is no one of that name in the 1841 census for either Midgley or Warley and it was Henry, not George, Richardson who was the wharfinger for the Calder & Hebble Navigation at Sowerby Bridge as claimed by Du Maurier, p.117, 127.

75. Minutes of the Board of the Manchester and Liverpool Railway: MS LY 1/10, PRO.

76. Branwell knew John Frobisher well enough to send him a set of verses to put to music: PBB to John Frobisher, [Mar. 1846] and 21 March 1846: MSS in WYAS, Calderdale, [*BST*:12:65:410–11]. *Halifax Guardian*, 20 Feb. 1841, p.4, for instance, records a dinner held in his honour at the Swan Inn, Halifax, attended by J. B. Leyland; it seems likely that Branwell would have been among the fifty guests.

77. *Yorkshire Notes and Queries*, 1st series, vol.i, p.35; his cousin produced a literary and scientific magazine in Nottingham, called *Dearden's Mis-*

cellany, to which he contributed. Dearden had published a poem on J. B. Leyland's statue of 'African Bloodhounds', which was reviewed in the *Halifax Guardian*, 20 March 1838, p.3. Leyland, 'The Leyland Family', *Halifax Antiquarian Society Journal*, 1954, p.37. Leyland, i, 188. Branwell had friends in Ovenden, the Pearsons, with whom he stayed in 1846: see below, pp.512–13.

78. William Heaton, quoted in Leyland, i, 268–9. It should be pointed out, however, that nightingales are not to be found in the West Riding.

79. Leyland, 'The Leyland Family', *Halifax Antiquarian Society Journal*, 1954, p.37.

80. The fact that Leyland seems unaware that any of Branwell's poems were published was first pointed out by VN *PBB*, p.xxx.

81. *Halifax Guardian*, 22 May 1841, p.3. The fact that the editor's note is addressed to 'PBB', whereas the poem is published under the 'Northangerland' pseudonym, suggests that Branwell had sent the poem himself with a covering letter. Another example of this is extant, an undated letter to James Walker, the Editor and Publisher of the paper, which he signed 'Patrick, Branwell, Brontë'. I have been unable to date the letter or identify whether the poem was published. 'I send you a production which I know is too long for your columns during the sessions of parliament, so I must leave it <it> to your judgement whether or not you may think it worth your while to give it a place in the "Halifax Guardian".': PBB to the Editor of the *Halifax Guardian*, [n.d.]: MS HAS B21/38 p.4, WYAS, Calderdale.

82. *Ibid.*, 5 June 1841, p.4, [VN *PBB*, p.210].

83. The eight poems are 'Heaven and Earth' (23 Jan. 1838, published 5 June 1841, p.4); 'On the Callousness produced by Cares' (13 Dec. 1837, published 7 May 1842, p.6); 'On Peaceful Death and Painful Life' (20 Oct. 1837, published 14 May 1842, p.6); 'Caroline's Prayer' (31 July 1838, published 4 June 1842, p.6); 'Song' (27 Aug. 1837, published 11 June 1842, p.6); 'An Epicurean's Song' (11 Dec. 1837, published 9 July 1842, p.6) and 'The End of All' (15 Dec. 1837, published 5 June 1847, p.6): all of these were published under the 'Northangerland' name. For an anonymously published poem, 'Speak kindly to thy fellow man', published on 19 Sept. 1846, p.6, see below, p.933 n.18. The two poems on Angrian themes which are probably revisions of earlier work are 'On Caroline' (published 16 July 1842, p.6) and 'Real Rest' (published 8 Nov. 1845, p.6). The three original works are 'On Melbourne's Ministry' ([Aug. 1841], published 14 Aug. 1841, p.6], 'Penmaenmawr' ([Nov. 1845], published 20 Dec. 1845, p.6) and 'Letter from a Father on Earth to his Child in Her Grave' (3 April 1846, published 18 April 1846, p.6).

The same pattern is true of the poems Branwell submitted to the *Bradford Herald* in 1842, six out of eight being revisions of earlier works which were also published in the *Halifax*

Guardian, the two original poems were 'On Landseer's Painting' ([Aug. 1841], published 28 April 1842, p.4) and 'Noah's Warning over Methuselah's Grave' ([July–Aug. 1842], published 25 Aug. 1842, p.4). On the other hand, the only poem Branwell seems to have submitted to the *Leeds Intelligencer,* 'The Afghan War' (published 7 May 1842, p.7) and three of the four poems he sent to the *Yorkshire Gazette* were all new. For the *Yorkshire Gazette* poems see below, pp.464–5.

84. *Halifax Guardian,* 14 Aug. 1841, p.6; 18 Sept. 1841, p.5.

85. PBB, 'Oh thou whose beams were most withdrawn', 8 Aug. 1841: PBB, [Luddenden Foot Notebook], 1840–2: MS p.7, Brotherton, [VN *PBB,* p.212]. This poem is usually dated as being from 'Brearley Hill' but the manuscript clearly reads 'Brearley Hall'.

86. PBB, 'O God! while I in pleasures wiles', 19 Dec. 1841: PBB, [Luddenden Foot Notebook], 1840–2: MS BS 127 p.15, BPM, [VN *PBB,* p.219].

87. PBB, 'Amid the worlds wide din around', 11 Sept. 1841: PBB, [Luddenden Foot Notebook], 1840–2: MS BS 127 p.4, BPM, [VN *PBB,* p.214].

88. PBB, 'The desolate earth – The Wintry Sky', 15 Dec. 1841: PBB, [Luddenden Foot Notebook], 1840–2: MS BS 127 p.14, BPM, [VN *PBB,* p.216]. See also, my notes on this poem in JB *SP,* pp.116–17. PBB, LORD NELSON, [*c.*Sept. 1841]: PBB, [Luddenden Foot Notebook], 1840–2: MS BS 127 pp.3, 6–12, BPM, [VN *PBB,* pp.487–93]. After the title Branwell has written 'NELSONI MORS. H.K. White'. See also JB *SP,* pp.118–20.

89. The first list begins with Blind Maeonides, ie. Homer (omitted by VN *PBB,* p.454) and continues with David, King of Israel, Alexander of Macedon opposite whom Branwell has written 'the brightest Star that ever blazed away the night of war', William Shakespeare, Oliver Cromwell, Samuel Johnson, Robert Burns, Horatio Nelson, Napoleon Buonaparte bracketed with Michael Angelo, Sylla of Rome, Julius Caesar, Walter Scott, John Wilson, Henry Brougham (not Broughton, as in VN *PBB,* p.454), DANTON and Columbus: PBB, [Luddenden Foot Notebook], 1840–2: MS p.8, Brotherton, [VN *PBB,* p.454]. As Neufeldt points out, the names of Johnson, Burns and Nelson are marked with an asterisk and all feature heavily in Branwell's poems at this time. The bracket linking Buonaparte and Michael Angelo is also asterisked, suggesting a possible future poem on them. All the names were those of famous poets and writers or warriors, except Columbus, discoverer of America, John Wilson, founder of *Blackwood's Magazine* as well as being a poet in his own right, and Henry Brougham, a Whig politician who merits his place on the list as the founder of the *Edinburgh Review.* The second list relates more obviously to Branwell's poem, 'The desolate earth – The Wintry Sky' and includes 'Guido', possibly meant for the

Sicilian poet, Guido delle Colonne (omitted by VN *PBB,* p.454), Burns, Tasso, Galileo, Milton, Otway, Johnson, Cowper, Burns and Johnson again, deleted: PBB, [Luddenden Foot Notebook], 1840–2: MS BS 127 p.17, BPM, [facsimile in JB *ST,* no.36; VN *PBB,* p.454].

90. Grundy, p.86; Leyland, i, 288.

91. CB to EN, 20 Jan. 1842: MS HM 24480 p.3, Huntington, [*L&L,* i, 250]. I have been unable to find any variant of the name Woolven in any directory or of the 1841 census. In the census, Branwell's occupation is somewhat mysteriously given as 'C.L.', possibly for 'Clerk of the Line'; the only other person in the area with that occupation is William Spence, aged twenty-five, who lived with his wife, Susannah, and their one-year-old son near Brearley, so I have assumed that he was Branwell's assistant: Census Returns for Midgley & Warley, 1841: Microfilm, Halifax.

92. Minutes of the Board of the Manchester & Liverpool Railway: MS LY 1/10, PRO.

93. See, for example, the following prosecutions reported in the *Halifax Guardian.* William Babington, committed to prison for two months at the Railway's request, for failing to display the red flag when taking up track at Mytholmroyd, though no accident took place: 28 Nov. 1840, p.2; three men prosecuted for taking two cranes along the line without displaying lights or signals, thereby causing a crash at Sowerby Bridge: 16 Jan. 1841, p.4; Joseph Cobden, discharged and prosecuted for derailing a train at Brighouse because he forgot to change the points: 27 March 1841, p.2; four men arrested for causing a crash at Luddenden Foot when they travelled along the line on a truck after a drinking bout and ran into a train, causing serious injuries to two of them: 4 Dec. 1841, p.7. The drunken driver from Leeds, who had worked on the railway for ten years, was sentenced to two months' hard labour at Wakefield House of Correction: 6 March 1841, p.3.

94. PBB to Francis Grundy, 22 May 1842: MS n.l. [Grundy, p.85, wrongly dated to 1845]; CB to EN, 14 April [1846]: MS HM 24444 p.4, Huntington, [*L&L,* ii, 88].

95. *Bradford Observer,* 13 Jan. 1842, p.7.

96. *Ibid.* The proposal was made and seconded by two Dissenters, William Thomas and William Greenwood, junior, of Oxenhope. The churchwardens of Bradford incurred expenses of £53 4s. 11d. in getting the writ of Mandamus against Haworth: MS MM 55/6/3, WYAS, Bradford. As this was more than two-thirds of the total sum they were claiming as a rate, it is an indication of how serious the confrontation had become. PB to *Bradford Observer,* 3 Feb. 1842, p.4.

97. *Ibid.,* p.3. Patrick was away in Brussels when the goods were actually distributed, so presumably William Weightman was involved in his stead.

98. PB, French notebook, 1842: MS BS 178 p.1, BPM, [JB *ST,* no.15].

99. *Ibid.*, pp.9, 13. Though Patrick clearly meant 'secs', 'sec' and 'privé', the MS reads 'sees', 'see' and 'priver'.
100. EJB, diary paper, 30 July 1845: MS p.1, in private hands, [facsimile in Shorter, p.154; *L&L*, ii, 49]. I am grateful to William Self for sending me a photocopy of this manuscript and allowing me to quote from it.
101. ECG, *Life*, pp.200–1.
102. MT to ECG, [1857]: MS n.l., [Stevens, p.165].
103. CB to EN, 14 Oct. 1850: MS Bon 226 p.1, BPM, [*L&L*, ii, 169].
104. CB, *Villette*, pp.58–9.
105. *Ibid.*, p.58.
106. PB, French notebook, 1842: MS BS 178 p.22, BPM, [JB *ST*, no.15].
107. I am assuming that Charlotte followed the same arrangements on her return to Brussels the following year, and have taken my description of this first journey from her own account of the second journey: CB to EN, 30 Jan. 1843: MS p.1, TC Cambridge, [*L&L*, i, 292]; Ostend Police Registers, 1842, quoted in WG *CB*, p.185. Gérin says the party arrived about midnight on the Saturday and went straight to their hotel, assuming the voyage took only fourteen hours.
108. PB, French notebook, 1842: MS BS 178 pp.7, 16–17, BPM, [JB *ST*, no.15].
109. CB, *The Professor*, pp.49–50.
110. Brussels Police Registers, 1842, quoted in WG *CB*, p.186.
111. CB, *Villette*, p.131. Frederika Macdonald, who was at the Pensionnat Heger nineteen years after Charlotte, recognized the passages in *Villette* as a graphic description of the school and its surroundings: Macdonald, 'The Brontës at Brussels', *The Woman at Home*, pp.277–80.
112. Chadwick, pp.210–11.
113. *Ibid.*, pp.213–14.
114. Prospectus for 'Maison d'éducation pour les jeunes Demoiselles sous la direction de Madame Heger-Parent', 1842: MS BS x, H, BPM, [facsimile in Chadwick, opp. p.190]; Abraham Dixon, snr, to Mary Dixon, 24 July 1843: MS no.4, Dixon. I am grateful to Margaret

Smith for drawing my attention to this archive. In this letter, Abraham Dixon has had to abandon his plan to place Ellen Taylor at Mme Heger's and bear part of the expense: 'The terms are including Music, drawing and every other expense frs 1055 or £42 pr year as particularized below. There will also be the cost of her clothes in addition, which I will suppose cost much the same as in England.

Pension yearly	fcs 650
Music – 15 fcs pr mth	180
Drawing – 8 " "	96
Dancing 6 ms in winter	30
Washing	60
Servants	5
Use of bed & linen	34
	fcs 1055'

The terms for yearly pension and the use of bed & linen are identical to those quoted in the Prospectus, so one can assume that the other fees were also appropriate to Charlotte and Emily.
115. Constantin Heger, quoted in ECG, *Life*, p.146.
116. Prospectus for 'Maison d'éducation pour les jeunes Demoiselles sous la direction de Madame Heger-Parent', 1842: MS BS x, H, BPM, [facsimile in Chadwick, opp. p.190]. The prospectus stated 'Cet établissement est situé dans l'endroit le plus salubre de la ville … La santé des élèves est l'objet d'une surveillance active les parents peuvent se reposer avec sécurité sur les mesures qui ont été prises à cet égard dans l'établissement.'
117. Mrs Jenkins, quoted in Chadwick, p.225. The Dixons' address is quoted in Abraham Dixon, snr, to Mary Dixon, 24 July 1843: MS no.4, Dixon. The Jenkins' address is quoted in ECG to Laetitia Wheelwright, c.13 June 1856: [C&P, p.391].
118. [Benjamin Binns], *Bradford Observer*, 17 Feb. 1894, p.6.
119. PB, French notebook, 1842: MS BS 178 pp.21–2, BPM, [JB *ST*, no.15].

CHAPTER FOURTEEN

Title: Referring to life at the Pensionnat Heger: 'The difference in country and religion makes a broad line of demarcation between us and all the rest. We are completely isolated in the midst of numbers': CB to EN, May 1842: MS in Law Colln, [*L&L*, i, 260]

1. CB to EN, May 1842: MS in Law Colln, [*L&L*, i, 260]. The Taylors, by comparison, were making little progress in French because they were still awaiting the arrival of a French teacher: MT to EN, March–April 1842: MS p.3, Pierpont Morgan, [Stevens, pp.29–30].
2. Emily apparently wrote only two poems

throughout the nine months she spent in Brussels: Hatfield, pp.173–80.
3. CB to EN, May 1842: MS in Law Colln, [*L&L*, i, 260]; A few months later, Charlotte was describing the school as having ninety pupils: CB to EN, [July 1842]: MS HM 24431 p.2, Huntington, [*L&L*, i, 267].
4. CB to EN, May 1842: MS in Law Colln, [*L&L*, i, 260].
5. *Ibid.*, pp.260–1.
6. See, for instance, Charlotte's 'Cahiers de rough drafts', as she called them, in MS BS 17, BPM & in the Brotherton; ECG, *Life*, pp.151–2.
7. Macdonald, 'The Brontës at Brussels', *The*

Woman at Home, pp.283–4. This is borne out by the number of essays by both Charlotte and Emily which were preserved in Brussels by M. Heger.

8. CB, 'La jeune fille malade', 18 April 1842: MS in Parrish Colln, Princeton, [translation, *BST*: 12:62:98–9]. 'La Pauvre Fille', whose author Duthie, *The Foreign Vision of Charlotte Brontë*, p.26 identifies as Alexandre Soumet, is the first item in Charlotte's exercise book, MS Bon 115 pp.1–4, BPM.

9. CB, 'La Prière du Soir dans un camp', 26 April 1842: MS in Parrish Colln, Princeton. Chateaubriand's 'Prière du Soir à bord d'un vaisseau' occurs twice in Charlotte's book of French extracts, the first time in a much shortened form, the second in the form on which she based her exercise: MS Bon 115, pp.5–6, 11–14, BPM. The soldiers were men from General Abercrombie's brigade who defeated the remnants of Napoleon's Egyptian garrison at the battle of Aboukir in 1801 when Abercrombie himself was killed. Charlotte sketched a highly romanticized portrait of Abercrombie in Highland dress in one of her French exercise books: MS Bon 122, p.6 (loose leaf), BPM.

10. Chateaubriand's account of Eudore is in the same book of French extracts, MS Bon 115 pp.8–11, BPM. Chateaubriand's version begins 'Sous le règne de Galérius, un Chrétien nommé Eudore, fiancé à la jeune Cymodocée, allait être livré aux bêtes féroces': *ibid.*, p.8; Charlotte's version begins 'Sous le règne de Marie, reine d'Angleterre, une jeune fille nommée Anne Askew allait être menée au supplice': CB, 'Anne Askew Imitation', 2 June 1842: MS HM 2560 p.1, Huntington. Hers ends with the words 'Je suis protestante', echoing Chateaubriand's 'Je suis Chrétien'.

11. ECG, *Life*, p.154. The passage 'Mirabeau à la Tribune' by Victor Hugo is quoted at length in Charlotte's book of French extracts: MS Bon 115, pp.19–23, BPM.

12. CB, 'Imitation Portrait de Pierre l'Hermite', 31 July 1842: MS EL fB91 p.4, Rylands, [ECG, *Life*, pp.154–7]. 'La puissance de Pierre [l'hermite: added by M. Heger] n'était nullement une puissance physique, car la Nature, ou pour mieux dire, Dieu, est impartial dans la distribution de ses dons; il accorde à l'un [de ses enfants: added by M. Heger] la grace, la beauté, les perfections corporelles à l'autre, l'esprit, la grandeur morale. Pierre <donc: MH> était un homme petit, d'une physionomie peu agréable; mais il avait ce courage, cette constance, cet enthousiasme, cette énergie de sentiment qui écrase toute opposition et qui fait que la volonté d'un seul homme devien[ne: deleted by M. Heger and changed to: t] la loi de toute une nation.'

13. EJB, 'Portrait, Le Roi Harold avant la Bataille de Hastings', June 1842: MS Bon 129 pp.2–4, BPM, [WG *EJB*, pp.267–8; translation *BST*:11:57:98–9]. Gérin's transcript is not accu-

rate; the text was also heavily annotated by Monsieur Heger, whose many corrections are marked 'MH'. Where he put a line through many of Emily's words, without offering an alternative, I have marked this with brackets thus <pouvoir>; the underlinings are all by Monsieur Heger. The quoted passages read: 'Harold réunissait [dans: changed by MH to: en] lui<-même> [toute: added by MH] l'énergie, <la pouvoir>, [et: changed by MH to: rouler] les espérances [de la: changed by MH to: d'une] nation. Alors, il n'était plus un roi, il était un héros. <La situation> [lui: changed by MH to: l'] avait transormé, <car> en paix il aurait été sans doute comme presque tous les autres princes [assis sur un tranquille: changed by MH to: <végétant><de son epoque> indifferent et paisible sur son] trône <un des> [s'eut été: added by MH] un misérable [enseveli: changed by MH to: esclave confiné] dans son palais abîmé en plaisirs, trompé [de: changed by MH to: par ses] flatteurs sachant, pourvu qu'il ne [soit: changed by MH to: fut] pas tout à fait imbécille, que de tout son peuple il est [le: changed by MH to: l'homme le] moins libre … [Mais: added by MH] Harold, sur le champ de bataille, sans palais, sans ministres, sans courtisans, sans faste, sans luxe, n'ayant [au dessus de lui: added by MH] que le ciel de sa patrie <au dessus de lui pour toit>, et <cette terre> sous ses pieds, [cette terre: added by MH], qu'il tient de ses ancêtres, et qu'il n'abandonnera qu'avec la vie; Harold, entouré <de cette foule> de coeurs dévoués, <les représentatifs de millions plus>, [tous: changed by MH to: qui lui ont tous] confi[dé: changed by EJB to: dent] <a lui> leur sureté, leur liberté et leur existence <comme son peuple> – quelle différence! Aussi visible aux hommes [MH addition: ?Harold? illegible] qu'à son Créateur, l'âme [divine brille: changed by MH to: d'un illegible] dans ses yeux, une multitude [de: changed by MH to: des] passions humaines y [éveillent en même temps: changed by MH to: n'existe pas qu'à cette heure], mais elles sont exaltées, sanctifiées, presque déifiées – [le: changed by MH to: Son] courage n'a pas de témérité, [cette: changed by MH to: sa] fierté <n'a> pas d'arrogance, [cette: changed by MH to: son] indignation [n'a pas: changed by MH to: manque] d'[injustice: changed by MH to: colère], [cette: changed by MH to: son] assurance [n'a pas: changed by MH to: plus] de presomption. Il est intérieurement convaincu qu'aucun pouvoir [mortel: changed by MH to: humain] ne l'abattira – [La morte de: deleted by EJB] La Mort, seule, [MH comments illegible] peut emporter la victoire [de: changed by MH to: à] ses armes, <et> Harold <est> prêt [à succomber devant elle: MH comments illegible], parceque la touche de cette main est au héros comme le coup qui lui rendait la liberté était à l'esclave'.

14. ECG, *Life*, p.157. Emily's weaker French is readily apparent from the number of corrections inserted by M. Heger and from the number of English words she uses when a more appropriate French word exists.

15. CB, 'Le siège d'Oudenarde', [1842]: MS p.3, Swarthmore. The passage in French reads: 'Un combat affreux déchirait son coeur pendant quelques instants il ne disait pas mot – il couvrit [les: changed to: ses] yeux de ses mains et appuya son front sur les créneaux de la muraille bientôt il se réléva – sa figure était pâle, et ses lèvres livides – il repondit d'une voix ferme et sonore " <Ghent> "Que mes enfants meurent Dieu les recevra dans son sein, pour moi je n'ai qu'un devoir à remplir, c'est de rester fidèle à ma patrie – Ghentois je ne suis pas vaincu<e>, éloignez-vous" '.

16. *Ibid.*, pp.3–4 'Marcus Curtius s'élançant dans le gouffre béant qui <s'ouvrit> s'était ouvert au milieu du Forum n'était pas animé d'un courage plus sublime que le commandant d'Oudenarde sacrifiant ses sentiments comme père à ses principes comme patriote.' Marcus Curtius was a mythical Roman knight who, in obedience to an oracle which declared that this was the only way to save his country, leapt fully armed and on horseback into a fissure which had opened in the Roman Forum.

17. EJB, 'Le Siège d'Oudenarde', [1842]: MS p.1, Swarthmore. 'Même les femmes cette classe condamnée par les lois de la société, d'être un lourd fardeau en tout cas d'action et de danger, sur cette occasion, mettaient à côté leurs priviléges dégradants, et prenaient une part distinguée dans les travaux de défense.'

18. *Ibid.*, pp.2–3. 'Le commandant regardait ses fils dont les yeux pleins de larmes implorait son secours, à leurs côtés il voyait les soldats armés des glaives qui devraient finir leurs jours; un moment il hesitait, la nature luttait fortement avec l'honneur – son sein gonflait d'une emotion terrible mais enfin le patriote subjugait le père, il se tournait vers les Ghentois; "Prenez, dit il "la vie de ces pauvres enfants, je ne puis pas la balance contre la liberté de ma patrie, et pour leurs ames je les confie à Dieu. mon sentence est prononcé." '

19. *Ibid.*, p.3. 'les hommes qui pourraient sauter avec Martius Curtius dans une tombe vivante sont plus nombreux que ceux qui pourraient sacrifier <les> comme Lalaing les plus tendres affections du leur coeur pour l'amour de leur patrie –'.

20. EJB, 'Le Chat', 15 May 1842: MS p.1, Berg, [WG *EJB*, p.266; translation in *BST*:11:60:338]. 'Je puis dire avec sincérité que j'aime les chats… Un chat est un animal qui a plus des sentiments humaines que presque tout autre être.'

21. EJB, 'L'Amour Filial', 5 Aug.[1842]: MS Bon 130 p.2, BPM, [WG *EJB*, p.269; translation in *BST*:11:57:99–100]. This manuscript, without corrections, is obviously a final fair copy of the original. 'Les parents aiment leurs enfants, c'est un principe de la nature; la[sic] daim ne craint pas les chiens lorsque son petit est en danger, l'oiseau meurt sur son nid; cet instinct est une particule de l'âme divine que nous partageons avec tout animal qui existe, et Dieu n-a-t-il pas mis dans le coeur de l'enfant un pareil sentiment? Quelque chose vraiment il y a et cependant la voix tonnante leur crie: "Honorez vos parents ou vous mourerez!" '

22. *Ibid.*, p.4. 'L'heure viendra quand la conscience s'év<i>eillera alors il aura une rétribution terrible; quel médiateur plaidera alors pour le criminel? C'est Dieu qui l'accuse; Quelle puissance sauvera le miserable? c'est Dieu qui le condamne. Il a rejeté le bonjeur dans la vie mortelle pour s'assurer du tourment dans la vie éternelle – Que les anges et les hommes pleurent son sort – il était leur frère.'

23. CB, 'La Chenille', 11 Aug. 1842: MS in private hands, [*BST*:12:65:363, 365; translation, pp.362, 364]. 'la chenille passe une vie grossière, matérielle, elle mange, elle rampe aujourd'hui; elle a mangé, elle a rampé hier; elle mangera, elle rampera demain;': *BST*:12:65:363.

24. EJB, 'Le Papillon', 11 Aug. 1842: MS pp.2–3, Berg, [WG *EJB*, pp.271–2; translation in *BST*:11:60:340–1]. 'La nature est une problème inexplicable, elle existe sur un principe de destruction; il faut que tout être soit l'instrument infatigable de mort aux autres, ou qu'il cesse de vivre lui-même; et cependant, nous célébrons le jour de notre naissance, et nous louons Dieu d'avoir entré un tel monde.'

25. *Ibid.*, pp.4–5. 'Que la créature ne juge pas son Créateur, voila un symbole du monde à venir – comme la laide chenille est l'origine du splendide papillon, ainsi ce globe est l'embrion d'un nouveau ciel et d'une nouvelle terre dont la beauté la plus pauvre excédera infiniment ton imagination mortelle et quand tu verras le resultat magnifique de ce qui te semble maintenant si basse combien mépriseras tu ta présomption aveugle, en accusant Omniscience qu'elle n'avait pas fait périr la nature dans son enfance.'

26. CB, 'Le Palais de la Mort Matière', 16 Oct.[1842]: MS BS 21 p.8, BPM, [translation in *BST*:12:62:98]; 'La Guerre et l'Ambition ne sont que tes enfants; tous les démons qui perdent l'homme naissent de toi'. For Emily's essay see EJB, 'Matière. Le palais de la Mort', 18 Oct. 1842: MS BS 106, BPM, [*BST*:12:64:281–5; translation pp.280–4]. The date for Charlotte's essay cannot be 1843 as the translation claims, since Emily's essay was written only two days later. See also the article discussing the possible source by J. C. Maxwell, 'Emily Brontë's "The Palace of Death" ', *BST*:15:77:139–40; the source is undoubtedly French, as this was Monsieur Heger's invariable practice, so John Gay's fable 'The Court of Death' is extremely unlikely to be the original upon which the two essays were based.

27. EJB, 'Matière. Le palais de la Mort', 18 Oct. 1842: MS BS 106 pp.7–8, BPM, [*BST*:12:64:285; translation p.284]. The corrections and underlining are by M. Heger: 'j'ai une amie devant laquelle toute cette assemblée sera forcée à succomber; elle se nomme la Civilization: en <u>quelques</u> années elle viendra habiter cette terre avec nous et chaque siècle augmentira son pouvoir – et la fin elle détournera l'Ambition de votre service; elle jetera <u>sur</u> la colère le frein de la loi; elle arrachera les armes des mains du Fanatisme; elle [chassera: changed by MH to: confinera] la Famine parmi les sauvages: moi seule j'agrandirai et fleurirai sous son règne'.

28. ECG, *Life*, p.157 comments on how often Charlotte chose Old Testament scenes and characters to write about. Ellen Nussey was deeply upset by accusations of Charlotte's lack of piety: see, for example, EN, Reminiscences, *BST*:2:10:58–9.

29. Prospectus, 'Maison d'éducation pour les jeunes Demoiselles sous la direction de Madame Heger-Parent', [1842]: MS BS x, H, BPM, [facsimile in Chadwick, opp. p.190]; ECG, *Life*, p.150, quoting a French lady resident in Brussels.

30. *Ibid.*, p.157. Monsieur Heger said, 'Elle était nourrie de la Bible.'

31. CB, 'Sacrifice d'une veuve Indienne', 17 April 1842: MS BS 17, BPM. The subject, though probably dictated by Charlotte's source, was one which had given rise to much anguished correspondence from Indian missionaries to Evangelical magazines, including *The Cottage Magazine*, so Charlotte would have been well briefed on the matter. See also CB, 'La jeune fille malade', 18 April 1842: MS in Parrish Colln, Princeton, [translation, *BST*:12:62:98–9]; CB, 'Le Nid', 30 April 1842: MS in Berg, [translation, *BST*:16:83:213–14].

32. Constantin Heger, 'Conseil', at end of CB, 'Le Nid', 30 April 1842: MS p.4, Berg, [translation, *BST*:16:83:213–14]. 'Conseil – quelle importance faut-il donner aux détails, dans le développemt d'un sujet? – Sacrifier <u>impitoyablemt</u> tout ce qui ne contribue pas à la clarté, à la vraisemblance et à l'effet. accuser fortement tout ce qui donne du relief à la pensée principale, que l'impression soit alors colorée, pittoresque: Il suffit que le reste soit <u>à sa place, mais dans la demi-teinte</u>. C'en a qui donne au style, comme à la peinture, l'unité, la perspective, et <u>l'effet</u>. <u>Liser</u> la xiv. harmonie de Lamartine: <u>L'infini</u>, nous l'analyserons ensemble, <u>du point de vue des détails</u>. 4 Mai C Heger'.

33. Constantin Heger, marginal and other annotations on CB, 'Imitation Portrait de Pierre l'Hermite', 31 July 1842: MS EL fB91, Rylands, [ECG, *Life*, pp.154–7].

34. Charlotte's poetic style certainly reflected her verbose prose style, but this may not necessarily be true of Emily. It should be pointed out, for instance, that Emily's diary papers are just as uncontrolled as Charlotte's prose, flitting from subject to subject and running on at length.

35. ECG *Life*, p.151.

36. CB to WSW, 15 Feb. 1848: MS p.3, Pforzheimer, [*L&L*, ii, 189].

37. Chadwick, p.225.

38. ECG, *Life*, p.152.

39. CB to EN, [July 1842]: MS HM 24431 pp.2–3, Huntington, [*L&L*, i, 266–7].

40. Joseph Green, 'The Brontë–Wheelwright Friendship' (1915): Typescript, i, 23, in Brotherton; Chadwick, p.226; ECG, *Life*, pp.150–1. Ellen Nussey also commented on their changed appearance: 'none of the Brontës understood dress with its right and simple advantages till Charlotte and Emily had been in Brussels; they then began to perceive the elegance of a well-fitting garment made with simplicity and neatness <when and> they adapted the better style for themselves it was a manifest improvement': EN, Reminiscences: MS p.16, KSC.

41. CB to EN, [July 1842]: MS HM 24431 p.2, Huntington, [*L&L*, i, 267]. Though Monsieur Heger told Mrs Gaskell (ECG, *Life*, p.151) he found Emily 'egotistical and exacting compared to Charlotte' and that she exerted 'a kind of unconscious tyranny' over her elder sister, he evidently grew fond of her. On 13 September 1842 he presented her with a copy of the speech he had given at the distribution of prizes at the Athénée Royal on 15 August, signing it 'A Miss Emily Bro[n]të témoignage de sincère affection. C Heger Bruxelles 13 Septembre 1843': Constantin Heger, *Discours prononcés à la Distribution des Prix faite aux élèves de l'Athénée Royal de Bruxelles* (Brussels, Privately Printed, 1843), at Wellesley.

42. *Ibid.*, p.1.

43. CB, Preface to 'Selections from the Poems of Ellis Bell', 1850: MS n.l., [EJB, *Wuthering Heights*, p.370]. The three poems are EJB, 'In the same place, when Nature wore', 17 May 1842 [MS Add 43483 pp.53–4, BL], which was the only one completed, and two poems finished at home, 'How do I love on summer nights', 20 Aug. 1842–6 Feb. 1843 [*ibid.*, pp.8–10] and 'The evening passes fast away', 23 Oct. 1842–6 Feb. 1843 [MS in Law Colln, facsimile in *Poems of EJB & AB*, pp.316–17]: see Hatfield, pp.173–81.

44. Joseph Green, 'The Brontë–Wheelwright Friendship', i, 4–5, 10. I have followed Green's spelling of the name though Gérin calls it the Hotel 'Cluysenaar' in *CB*, p.221 and 'Cluysenaer' in *EJB*, p.130.

45. Laetitia Wheelwright to C. K. Shorter, Jan. 1896, quoted in Joseph Green, 'The Brontë–Wheelwright Friendship', i, 23–4.

46. Chadwick, p.227. The fact that the Brontës were in the first class of twelve pupils is recorded in a note by Laetitia Wheelwright in her copy of Mrs Gaskell: see Joseph Green, 'The Brontë–Wheelwright Friendship', i, 14; EJB, pencil drawing of

tree, [1842]: MS HAOBP:P:Br.E8, BPM. The drawing, described by Chadwick, p.227, was presented to the BPM by the de Bassompierre family of Belgium.

47. MT to EN, [24 Sept. 1842]: MS pp.3–4, Texas, [Stevens, p.38].

48. *Halifax Guardian*, 7 May 1842, p.5. He was found hanged in his own barn on 26 April.

49. *Bradford Observer*, 5 May 1842, p.8. He died on 30 April.

50. PBB to J. B. Leyland, 29 June 1842: MS in Brotherton, [*L&L*, i, 266]. Branwell's letter inviting Leyland to undertake the commission for £40 and to come to the parsonage before attending the committee meeting is: PBB to J. B. Leyland, 15 May 1842: MS in Brotherton, [*L&L*, i, 262–3].

51. *Halifax Guardian*, 30 July 1842, p.5; 27 Aug. 1842, p.5. See also, for Brown's role, PBB to J. B. Leyland, 12 July 1842: MS in Brotherton, [*L&L*, i, 269].

52. *Halifax Guardian*, 7 May 1842, p.5. Similar action was taken against the churchwardens of Wilsden. See also *Leeds Intelligencer*, 18 June 1842, p.7; *Bradford Observer*, 30 June 1842, p.6.

53. *Ibid.*, 30 June 1842, p.5; 21 July 1842, p.5; 28 July 1842, p.5. For the family details of the Winterbothams see Haworth Census, 1841. The *Nemesis* ran aground off New York: John Winterbotham to *Bradford Observer*, 13 Oct. 1842, p.6.

54. PBB, pen and ink sketch, n.d.: original enclosed with letter of PBB to J. B. Leyland, 15 May 1842: MS in Brotherton, [Symington and Hatfield, *The Leyland Manuscripts*, p.13].

55. PBB to Francis Grundy, 22 May 1842: MS n.l., [*L&L*, i, 263–4].

56. PBB to Francis Grundy, 25 Oct. 1842: MS n.l., [*L&L*, i, 272–3]; according to the visitor lists published in the *Scarborough Herald*, the Revd E. Robinson and his family were in residence at No.15, The Cliff by 7 July and had left by 18 August, though his mother and sister stayed on for a further week at No.3, The Cliff: *Scarborough Herald*, 1 July 1842, p.3; 18 Aug. 1842, p.3; 25 Aug. 1842, p.3.

57. PBB, 'On Landseer's painting – "The Shepherd's Chief Mourner"', *Bradford Herald*, 28 April 1842, p.4. The undated poem is in PBB, [Luddenden Foot Notebook], 1840–2: MS p.1, Brotherton, [VN *PBB*, p.222]. A fair copy, possibly the one sent to the *Bradford Herald*, is MS BS 132, BPM. PBB, 'On the callousness produced by cares', *Bradford Herald*, 5 May 1842, p.4; *Halifax Guardian*, 7 May 1842, p.6. The first version was written on 13 December 1837: PBB, 'Sonnet', 13 Dec. 1837: MS BS 125 p.60, BPM, [VN *PBB*, 457–8]. A fair copy, again possibly the one sent to one of the papers, is MS BS 133, BPM. PBB, 'The Afghan War', *Leeds Intelligencer*, 7 May 1842, p.7. The original manuscript of this poem is lost but Branwell apparently adapted some lines he had written on 25 April: PBB, 'When side by side at twilight sitting', 25 April 1842: [Luddenden Foot Notebook],

1840–2: MS BS 127 pp.21–3, BPM, [VN *PBB*, p.221].

58. PBB, 'ON PEACEFUL DEATH AND PAINFUL LIFE', *Bradford Herald*, 12 May 1842, p.4; *Halifax Guardian*, 14 May 1842, p.6. The poem was originally part of Branwell's 'Life of Alexander Percy' and was written in October 1837 as 'Percy's Last Sonnet': MS Bon 149 p.4, BPM and see above p.278. The fair copy is MS BS 131, BPM, [VN *PBB*, p.459].

59. PBB, 'Caroline's Prayer', *Bradford Herald*, 2 June 1842, p.4; *Halifax Guardian*, 4 June 1842, p.6; PBB, *Song*, *Bradford Herald*, 9 June 1842, p.4; *Halifax Guardian*, 11 June 1842, p.6; PBB, 'An Epicurean's Song', *Bradford Herald*, 7 July 1842, p.4; *Halifax Guardian*, 9 July 1842, p.6; PBB, 'On Caroline', *Bradford Herald*, 14 July 1842, p.4; *Halifax Guardian*, 16 July 1842, p.6. 'Caroline's Prayer' is taken from 'Sir Henry Tunstall', the earliest version of which was written on 31 July 1838: PBB, ''Tis only Afternoon, yet midnights gloom', 31 July 1838: MS Ashley 176 ll.352–71, BL, [VN *PBB*, pp.470–1]. 'Song' is a variant of Branwell's version of 'Should Old Acquaintance be forgot' which appears in the middle of a long poem written in August 1837: PBB, 'How Eden like seem Palace Halls', 27 Aug. 1837: MS BS 122 ll.258–77, BPM, [VN *PBB*, p.193]. 'An Epicurean's Song' was originally by Henry Hastings and written in December 1837, though like the rest of Branwell's published poems, it was printed under his pseudonym 'Northangerland': PBB, 'Song ... The present days Sorrow', 11 Dec. 1837: MS BS 125 pp.59–60, BPM, [VN *PBB*, 460–1]. 'On Caroline' does not have an extant manuscript, but Caroline and her sister, Harriet, had featured in Branwell's Angrian poetry since at least 1838, [VN *PBB*, pp.124, 443–52].

60. PBB to Francis Grundy, 9 June 1842: MS BS 138 pp.1–2, BPM, [*L&L*, i, 265].

61. *Ibid.*, p.1.

62. William Oakendale [Dearden] to *Halifax Guardian*, 15 June 1867, p.7. When Branwell met Dearden to read this poem, he discovered that he had brought the wrong manuscript. He therefore read aloud a long portion from it, possibly the descriptions of Darkwall, which Dearden, not unnaturally, later assumed to have been Wuthering Heights, giving rise to claims that Branwell, not Emily, had written the novel.

63. *Bradford Observer*, 27 June 1861, p.7.

64. PBB, 'Azrael. or the Eve of Destruction', [July–Aug. 1842]: MS BS 125 pp.70, 73, BPM, [VN *PBB*, p.233].

65. PBB, 'NOAH'S WARNING OVER METHUSELAH'S GRAVE', *Bradford Herald*, 25 Aug. 1842, p.4. The lines were printed as being 'from an unpublished poem'.

66. PBB to Editor of *Blackwood's Magazine*, 6 Sept. 1842: MS 4060, NLS, [VN *PBB*, p.462]. For a draft of this letter see MS BS 127 p.26, BPM.

67. PBB, 'The Triumph of mind over body',

[Sept.–Oct. 1842]: MS Bon 155, BPM, [VN *PBB*, pp.253–60].

68. Grundy, pp.45, 79. Harriet Martineau later wrote 'I know this; – that I have always been anxious to extend to young or struggling authors the sort of aid which would have been so precious to me in that winter of 1829–1830, and that, in above twenty years, I have never succeeded but once. I obtained the publication of "The Two Old Men's Tales," – the first of Mrs Marsh's novels: but, from the time of my own success to this hour, every other attempt, of the scores I have made, to get a hearing for young or new aspirants has failed': HM, *Autobiography*, p.146.

69. PBB to Francis Grundy, 25 Oct. 1842: MS n.l., [*L&L*, i, 273].

70. *Bradford Observer*, 25 Aug. 1842, p.5; *Halifax Guardian*, 20 Aug. 1842, pp.5–7. The Chartists had a six-point programme, 'The People's Charter', which called for universal male suffrage, equal electoral districts, removal of the property qualification for MPs, payment of MPs, secret ballot and annual general elections.

71. *Bradford Observer*, 18 Aug. 1842, p.6; *Halifax Guardian*, 20 Aug. 1842, p.7; 27 Aug. 1842, p.2; *Bradford Observer*, 25 Aug. 1842, p.5.

72. *Bradford Observer*, 8 Sept. 1842, p.5; [Landlord of the Black Bull], quoted in Reid, p.194.

73. PB to John White, 22 Sept. 1842: MS BS 189 pp.2–3, BPM.

74. PB, *Funeral Sermon ... for William Weightman*, pp.12–13, [*Brontëana*, p.259]. Weightman's illness cannot be precisely dated, but he performed his last official duty, a baptism, on 14 August 1842: Register of Baptisms, 1837–54, Haworth Church. This confirms Charlotte's comment that his illness was, like Martha Taylor's, of about a fortnight's duration: CB to EN, [10 Nov. 1842]: MS at Harvard, [*L&L*, i, 282].

75. William Weightman Funeral Card, 6 Sept. 1842: MS BS x, F, BPM; Register of Burials, 1836–54, Haworth Church.

76. PB, *Funeral Sermon ... for William Weightman*, pp.3, 16, [*Brontëana*, p.252].

77. William Weightman memorial in Haworth Church. The obituary was published in the *Leeds Intelligencer*, 8 Oct. 1842, p.7. Patrick's newly published sermon was praised as 'plain and touching in its language, simple yet expressive, [and] pays a well-deserved tribute to the memory of the preacher's beloved and lamented fellow labourer'; Weightman himself is described as 'admired and beloved for his sterling piety, his amiability, and cheerfulness, and the loss of so zealous and useful a Minister of Christ is deeply felt by those among whom he lived and laboured': *Leeds Intelligencer*, 29 Oct. 1842, p.7.

78. PBB to Francis Grundy, 25 Oct. 1842: MS n.l., [*L&L*, i, 272–3].

79. PBB to Francis Grundy, 29 Oct. 1842: MS n.l., [*L&L*, i, 273].

80. CB to EN, [10 Nov. 1842]: MS p.1, Harvard, [*L&L*, i, 282]; Register of Burials, 1836–54, Haworth Church [3 Nov. 1842]; Elizabeth Branwell, 'Last Will & Testament', 30 April 1833: MS (copy) in MS PROBATE, Borthwick, [*L&L*, i, 277]. The fact that Aunt Branwell chose to be buried in the church, rather than in the Methodist burial ground, is further evidence of the fact that she had become a member of the Church of England. Even if this was merely dictated by sentiment, her choice of executors was not and again reflects an impeccable Anglican pedigree. She chose her brother-in-law, Patrick Brontë, the vicar of Keighley, Theodore Dury, and one of the Haworth Church trustees, George Taylor of Stanbury. As Theodore Dury had left Keighley by the time she died, he sought and obtained a release from his duties as an executor.

81. CB to EN, [10 Nov. 1842]: MS p.1, Harvard, [*L&L*, i, 282].

82. *Ibid.*, p.2; MT to EN, 1 Nov. 1842: MS in Berg, [Stevens, pp.39–40]; CB to EN, [10 Nov. 1842]: MS p.2, Harvard, [*L&L*, i, 282].

83. Constantin Heger to PB, 5 Nov. 1842: MS n.l., [*L&L*, i, 278–9]. 'je n'ai pas l'honneur de vous connaître personnellement, et cependant j'éprouve pour votre personne un sentiment de sincère vénération, car en jugeant un père de famille par ses enfants on ne risque pas de se tromper, et sous ce rapport l'éducation et les sentiments que nous avons trouvés dans mesdemoiselles vos filles n'ont pu que nous donner une très haute idée de votre mérite et de votre caractère. Vous apprendrez sans doute avec plaisir que vos enfants ont fait du progrès très remarquable dans toutes les branches de l'enseignement, et que ces progrès sont entièrement dûs à leur amour pour le travail et à leur persévérance; nous n'avons eu que bien peu à faire avec de pareilles élèves; leur avancement est votre oeuvre bien plus que la nôtre; nous n'avons pas eu à leur apprendre le prix du temps et de l'instruction, elles avaient appris tout cela dans la maison paternelle, et nous n'avons eu, pour notre part, que le faible mérite de diriger leurs efforts et de fournir un aliment convenable à la louable activité que vos filles ont puisée dans votre exemple et dans vos leçons'.

84. *Ibid.*, p.279–80. 'Ce n'est pas, croyez-le bien, monsieur, ce n'est pas ici pour nous une question d'intérêt personnel, c'est une question d'affection; vous me pardonnerez si nous vous parlons de vos enfants, si nous nous occupons de leur avenir, comme si elles faisaient partie de notre famille; leurs qualités personnelles, leur bon vouloir, leur zèle extrême sont les seules causes qui nous poussent à nous hasarder de la sorte'.

85. CB to EN, [20 Nov. 1842]: MS at Harvard, [*L&L*, i, 283]; CB to EN, 25 Nov. 1842: MS n.l., [*L&L*, i, 283–4].

86. AB, 'In memory of a happy day in February',

Feb.–10 Nov. 1842: MS Bon 134 pp.2–3, BPM, [Chitham, pp.82–3].

87. AB, 'To Cowper', 10 Nov. 1842: MS MA 28 pp.2–3, Pierpont Morgan, [Chitham, pp.84–5].

88. CB to EN, 25 Nov. 1842: MS n.l., [*L&L*, i, 283–4]. Anne did not come back for the Christmas holidays, having taken time off for Aunt Branwell's funeral.

89. AB, 'To ———', Dec. 1842: MS MA 28 pp.4–6, Pierpont Morgan, [Chitham, pp.87–8].

90. See, for example, AB, 'The Captive's Dream', 24 Jan. 1838 and 'The lady of Alyerno's hall', 10 July 1838: MS MA 2698 R-V pp.3–5, Pierpont Morgan, [Chitham, pp.62, 66–8]. One love poem, whose MS is lost, 'Farewell to thee! but not farewell', associated with William Weightman by WG *AB*, p.188 and Chitham, pp.76–7, was actually published as a song in *The Tenant of Wildfell Hall*. This either suggests, as I believe, that it had nothing to do with Weightman or that Anne was remarkably clinical and detached in her use of apparently personal material for a work of public fiction. In any event, it negates Chitham's argument that Anne's poem of December 1842 was 'suppressed' and deliberately omitted from *Poems* by Currer, Ellis and Acton Bell because it was autobiographical.

91. *Bradford Observer*, 8 Dec. 1842, p.8.

92. *Ibid.*, 5 Jan. 1843, p.5; *Keighley Saturday Observer*, 31 Dec. 1842, p.8. Hoffman had played in Keighley at the beginning of December: *Bradford Observer*, 8 Dec. 1842, p.8.

93. *Ibid.*, 29 Dec. 1842, p.5. Charlotte may have been referring to this incident when she jokingly sent her 'Regards to the fighting gentry': CB to EJB, 29 May 1843: MS n.l., [*L&L*, i, 299].

94. Elizabeth Branwell, Last Will & Testament, 30 April 1833: MS (copy) in MS PROBATE, Borthwick, [*L&L*, i, 277]. Charlotte was left Aunt Branwell's Indian workbox, Emily her workbox with the china top and her ivory fan, Anne her watch and eyeglass with their chains etc. and Branwell her japanned dressing case. Their aunt's rings, silver spoons, books, clothes etc. were all to be divided among the three sisters as their father saw fit. Eliza Kingston was the only daughter of Elizabeth's sister Jane, who had married John Kingston and left him in America, returning with Eliza to live in Penzance. Like the Brontës, she had no financial security and was therefore a beneficiary of Aunt Branwell's will. Branwell was omitted deliberately as he was expected to be able to earn his own living.

95. The probate of Elizabeth Branwell's will was finally granted on 28 December 1842, William Morgan administering the oath to the executors as a commissioner for the Archbishop of York.

The estate was sworn to be under the value of £1,500: Elizabeth Branwell, probate papers, 21 Nov.–28 Dec. 1842: MS in MS PROBATE, Borthwick. According to the will the money from the estate was to be invested until the youngest legatee reached the age of twenty-one. The inventory of the residue of Aunt Branwell's property was drawn up by Patrick on 30 January 1843. It included ten whole and four half shares in the York & North Midland Railway Company, valued at £1,087, a promissory note valued at £30, a gold watch (presumably Anne's legacy) valued at £10 and the remaining books and jewellery valued at £20. A note added that one half railway share and all the money in the Bolitho & Sons Bank of Chiandower, near Penzance, had been spent on the funeral, probate and other expenses and that £124 worth of shares in certain mines in Cornwall were found to be worthless. Branwell's japanned dressing box was valued at 'not above 5/-'. Aunt Branwell's remaining valuables were listed thus: A gold eyeglass £1, 1 Garnet ring 5/-, 1 jet ditto 5/-, 1 agate ditto 7/-, 1 pair of small gold earrings 5/-, 7 silver teaspoons £1 8s. od., 2 silver tablespoons 18/-, A silver knife and fork 15/-, A silver butter-knife 5/-, 2 small jet brooches 3/-: PB, Inventory of the residue of the late Miss Elizabeth Branwell's property, 30 Jan. 1843: MS in private hands.

96. CB to EN, [10 Jan. 1843]: MS at Harvard, [*L&L*, i, 284]; CB to EN, [15 Jan. 1843]: MS Gr. E5, BPM, [*L&L*, i, 285].

97. CB to EN, 30 Jan. 1843: MS at TC Cambridge, [*L&L*, i, 291].

98. CB, *Villette*, p.61.

99. ECG, *Life*, p.168.

100. CB to EN, 30 Jan. 1843: MS at TC Cambridge, [*L&L*, i, 291].

101. ECG, *Life*, pp.168–9.

102. CB to EN, 6 March 1843: MS BS 50.4 pp.1–2, BPM, [JB *ST*, no.14].

103. *Ibid.*, p.3. Abraham Dixon snr to Mary Dixon, 24 July 1843: MS in Dixon.

104. CB to EN, 6 March 1843: MS BS 50.4 pp.1–2, BPM [JB *ST*, no.14]. At the bottom of the letter Charlotte drew a very revealing portrait of herself, a short, ugly figure with a head too big for her body, waving goodbye across the Channel to Ellen, who is ladylike prettiness personified. Ellen's name has been struck out and replaced with 'Mrs O. V[incent]' and she is hand in hand with a bespectacled man in a top hat who is labelled 'The Chosen'. A more compellingly graphic illustration of the way Charlotte perceived herself and her pretty friend could not be imagined.

CHAPTER FIFTEEN

1. See, for example, EJB, 'All blue and bright, in glorious light', 24 Feb. 1843: MS Add 43483 pp.27–9, BL, [Hatfield, pp.181–4]; EJB, 'Lie down and rest – the fight is done', 18 Dec. 1843: *ibid.*, p.55, BL, [Hatfield, p.191–2]; EJB, 'Where beams the sun the brightest', 1 May 1843: *ibid.*, p.42, BL, [Hatfield, p.186–7]; EJB, 'Yes holy be thy resting place', [July 1843]: MS Bon 127 p.6v, BPM, [Hatfield, p.189]; EJB, 'In the earth, the earth thou shalt be laid', 6 Sept. 1843: MS Add 43483 p.43, BL, [Hatfield, p.190]. For a discussion of the Brussels influence on Emily see: Musselwhite, *Partings Welded Together*, pp.75–108.

2. MT to EN, 16 Feb. 1843: MS p.1, Berg, [Stevens, p.43].

3. EN to Meta Gaskell, n.d.: MS no. 11, bound vol. of miscellaneous letters of EN, Brotherton. See also Martha Brown, quoted in Scruton, p.130.

4. CB to EJB, 29 May 1843: MS n.l., [*L&L*, i, 298]. Charlotte may have attempted to find another teacher as a printed circular for German lessons from Madame Hock, 'Une Dame Allemande, qui connait le français et l'anglais' who lived at No.35, Rue de la Montagne, was among Charlotte's effects: MS in private hands.

5. CB, Cahier d'of German Translations, 25 April 1843: MS Bon 117, BPM; Charlotte's translations of four poems by Schiller, 'Des Mädchens Klage', 'Der Alpenjager', 'Ritter Toggenburg' & 'Nadowessische Totenklage', are bound with CB, [William Wallace & other essays], [1843]: MS Ashley 160, BL, [VN *CB*, pp.365–70]. CB, Cahier d'Translations from English to German, May 1843: MS Bon 118, BPM. There are only four pages of German translations in this notebook, though at least two further pages have been torn out; the remainder of the book was later used by Charlotte for drafting her own poetry.

6. For Charlotte's translation of Scott's *Lady of the Lake*, canto iii, 16 see CB, 'Coronach pour un montagnard écossais', [Spring 1843]: MS bound with CB, 'L'Immensité de Dieu', [1843]: MS in Brotherton [poem only, VN *CB*, pp.364–5]. Her translation of Byron's *Childe Harold's Pilgrimage*, canto iv, 140–1, is in CB, [William Wallace & other essays], [1843]: MS Ashley 160, BL, [VN *CB*, pp.365–70]. Charlotte's translations of Louis Belmontet's 'Les Orphelins' as 'The Orphans', Feb. 1843, and Auguste Barbier's 'L'Idole' as 'Napoleon', March 1843, are in CB, Cahier d'of English Translations: MS MA 2696 R-V pp.1–5, 6–9, Pierpont Morgan, [VN *CB*, pp.485–7, 355–6]. Draft lines for the Napoleon poem are CB, 'Thy France O straight-haired Corsican' and 'O Corsican thou of the stern contour', [March 1843]: MS Bon 116 pp.1–2, BPM, [VN *CB*, pp.488–9].

7. *Manchester Athenaeum Album* (1850).

8. The importance of these *devoirs* and their subject matter, which is usually completely overlooked, is eloquently discussed in Lonoff, 'Charlotte Brontë's Belgian Essays: the Discourse of Empowerment', pp.387–409.

9. See above, p.386.

10. CB, 'La Chute des Feuilles', 30 March 1843: MS in private hands, [*BST*:6:34:241–2; a second, less accurate transcript with a translation by Phyllis Bentley is in *BST*:12:65:279]. The original poem by Millevoye is one of the items in CB, Copy Book, *c.*1842–3: MS Bon 115 pp.14–16, BPM. My French transcript, given below, is from M. H. Spielmann, 'An early essay by Charlotte Brontë', *BST*:6:34:241–2. The underlinings are again by M. Heger; his emendations are added in square brackets and marked 'MH'. 'Ayant ainsi préparé son canevas et [tracé: changed by MH to: arrêté] les premiers rudes [MH comment: (obscur) Le zéphyr soupire les autans se plaignent grondent hurlent râlent mugissent etc] contours de son esquisse, n'a-t-il pas soigneusement cherché les détails, rassemblé les images propres à faire ressortir son idée principale? N'a-t-il pas bien pesé chaque pensée, bien considéré chaque accessoire bien mesuré et ajusté chaque partie du grand Tout de manière que leur réunion ne [presentat nul pêché: changed by MH to: pêchat en rien] contre le [maître-principe de la composition: changed by MH to: de l'art d'écrire], le principe de l'Unité? Est-ce bien là le procédé que suivit Millevoye? Est-ce la méthode que suivent les grands poëtes? ["Souls made of fire and children of the Sun!": two translations offered by MH: Chers enfants d'Apollon, âmes faites du feu! & Chers enfants d'Apollon, de feu comme leur père!] Hélas! je ne sais pas: c'est à ces grands esprits seuls de répondre, mais il y a une chose que je sais bien parce que l'assurance [MH comment: obscur] en dépend plutôt de la raison que du génie c'est que pour les novices en littérature, pour ceux qui veulent imiter les grands maîtres cette méthode [c'est: changed by MH to: est] la seule qui [peut: changed by MH to: puisse; MH comment: (pourquoi?)] les conduire à un but tant soit peu eligible; peut-être [qu'en: changed by MH to: en] la suivant ne trouveront-ils jamais que du plomb dans leurs creusets, peut-être aussi si l'étincelle dormante du génie s'allume pendant l'opération, une nouvelle lumière éclairera leurs esprits, le vrai secret de l'Alchimie se révélera et leur plomb [se transmuera: MH comment: barbarisme déjà signalé] en or.'

11. *Ibid.* 'Je crois que la génie … n'a pas besoin de chercher des détails, qu'il ne s'arrête guère pour réfléchir, qu'il ne pense pas à l'unité: je crois que les détails viennent tout naturellement sans que le poëte les cherche, que l'inspiration tient la place de la reflexion et, quant à l'unité, je pense qu'il n'y a pas d'unité plus parfaite que celle qui résulte d'un coeur rempli d'une seule idée [MH

comment: excellent] ... La nature de génie tient à celle d'instinct, son opération est à la fois simple et merveilleuse; l'homme de génie produit [sans travail: MH marginal comment: il en sera de ce produit comme de tous les produits naturels: c'est de l'or en barres, d'autres façonneront cet or: Virgile, Ennius – Plaute – Molière, Daubenton, Buffon etc] et comme par un seul effort des résultats auxquels l'homme sans génie quelque savant, quelque persévérant qu'il soit ne pourrait jamais atteindre. [MH comment: très juste]'. Phyllis Bentley's transcription of the marginal comment is somewhat different: 'opération possible, mais il en sera de ce produit là comme de tous les produits naturels – C'est de l'or – d'autres la façonneront cet or en barres. Virgile-Ennius – Plaute-Molière – Daubenton-Buffon – C. H.': *BST*:12:65:381.

12. 'Le travail ne fait pas la poëte; l'homme ne fait pas son génie, il le reçoit du ciel – c'est incontestable.

La mécanique ne crée pas la force, elle en règle l'emploi, elle en centuple l'effet.

L'homme ne sait pas ce que c'est que le génie; c'est un don du ciel, c'est quelquechose de divin, dit-il – Il en est de même de la force.

Mais supposons deux hommes de même force, l'un sans levier, l'autre avec un levier: le premier soulevera 1,000 livres, le second en faisant même effort deracinera un [plantane: word supplied by Bentley].

Le levier, n'est-ce rien?

Sans voix point de chanteur, – sans doute – mais point de chanteur aussi sans art, sans imitation.

La nature fait le peintre – Que serait-il cependant sans l'étude de la perspective, de l'art des couleurs etc. [C. H.: supplied by Bentley]' 'Combien vaudraient, combien désireraient[dureraient: Bentley] ses tableaux?

Sans étude point d'art; sans art point d'effet sur les hommes puisque l'art est le résumé de ce que tous les siècles nous lèguent, de ce que l'homme a trouvé beau, de ce qui a fait effet sur l'homme, de tout ce qu'il a trouvé digne d'être sauvé de l'oubli.

Le génie sans l'étude et sans l'art, sans la connaissance de ce qui a été fait, c'est la Force sans le levier, c'est Démosthène sublime orateur, qui bégaie et se fait siffler. C'est l'âme qui chante en dedans mais qui n'a pu exprimer ses chants interieurs [qu'une voix rude et inculte: words supplied by Bentley]; C'est le sublime musicien enfin qui n'a qu'un piano discord p[ou]r faire entendre au monde les suaves mélodies qu'il entend résonner en lui.

Certes le lapidaire ne fait pas le diamant, mais sans le lapidaire le plus beau diamant est un caillou.

Poëte ou non, étudiez donc la forme. Poëte vous serez plus puissant et vos oeuvres vivront – Dans le cas contraire vous ne ferez pas de poésie mais vous en savourerez le mérite et les charmes.': M. H. Spielmann, 'An early essay by Charlotte Brontë', *BST*:6:34:245–6. I am grateful to Allegra Huston for suggesting the analogy between Calvinism and Charlotte's concept of genius.

13. CB, La Mort de Napoléon, 31 May [1843]: MS BS 20 p.2, BPM, [*BST*:12:64:275, omitting all MH's comments, with translation]. Monsieur Heger's comments are in square brackets; where he has made a deletion without offering an alternative, this is enclosed in <> brackets: 'un simple particulier, a-t-il le droit d'exprimer ses sentiments [insert by MH: de formuler son opinion] sur la vie ou la mort de Bonaparte? [sait il: changed by MH to: peut-il s'eriger] en juge<r>? Oui, quelque insignifiant que [<il>: changed to: un homme] soit il a le droit de [insert by MH: se] former une opinion et même de [l'exprimer: changed to: la dire]: ni roi, ni empereur n'a [l': MH addition]autorité de faire taire cette voix intérieure que [<parfois>: MH addition] tout homme entend parler dans son coeur et qui approuve ou condamne, non seulement ses propres actions, mais les actions [<de ceux> qui l'entourent: changed by MH to: d'autrui]. Ainsi on ne peut pas [ôter: changed by MH to: contester] à la médiocrité son droit de juger le génie, mais il [<n>: changed to: ne s] 'en suit pas que son jugement soit toujours juste'. Monsieur Heger allowed Mrs Gaskell to see and transcribe the revised version, incorporating his emendations and excising the introductory section on genius, when she visited him in Brussels: see ECG, *Life*, pp.172–5.

14. CB, La Mort de Napoléon, 31 May [1843]: MS BS 20 p.3, BPM, [*BST*:12:64:275]. '<La Médiocrité> peut [voir: changed by MH to: découvrir] les défauts du Génie, ses imprudences, sa témérité, son ambition, mais elle est trop froide, trop bornée, trop égoiste pour [connaître ses: changed by MH to: les apprécier les] luttes, ses souffrances, ses sacrifices; aussi elle est envieuse et ses vertus même lui paraissent sous un jour faux et terne.' This whole passage is crossed through by M. Heger.

15. Lonoff, 'Charlotte Brontë's Belgian Essays: the Discourse of Empowerment', p.396.

16. CB, La Mort de Napoléon, 31 May [1843]: MS BS 20 pp.10–12, BPM, [*BST*:12:64:279, 281]. 'J'ai dit que cet homme est [<le paire>: changed by MH to: l'égal] de Napoleon: en génie, oui; en [droiture de caractère, en: changed by MH to: comme mesure de caractère, comme] élévation de but il [n'est: changed by MH to: ne lui est] ni égal ni supérieur, il est d'une autre espèce. Napoleon Bonaparte [tenait à sa: changed by MH to: était avide de la] réputation <et aimait beaucoup la célébrité>, Arthur Wellesley ne se soucie ni de l'une ni de l'autre. L'opinion publique [<avait une>: changed by MH to: la popularité était chose de] grande valeur [pour: changed to: aux] Napoleon; pour Wellington

l'opinion publique est une [idée: changed by MH to: rumeur], un rien que le souffle de sa puissante volonté fait disparaître, comme une bulle de savon – Napoleon flattait le peuple [et: changed by MH to: Wellington le brusque; l'un] cherchait [les: changed by MH to: ses] applaud- issements; [<Wellington le brusque le>: changed by MH to: l'autre ne se soucie que de] sa [<propre conscience>] l'approuve c'est assez: changed by MH to: quand elle] toute autre louange l'obsède ... <Malgré> cette fierté [il est modeste: changed by MH to: ?s'en? ?exclut? pas chez lui modeste]; [parlont: MH addition] il se soustrait à [MH addition: l']éloge, il rejette le panégyrique, jamais il ne parle de [<lui>: changed by MH to: ses propres exploits], et jamais il ne souffre qu'un autre lui en parle: son caractère égale en grandeur et surpasse en vérité celui de tout autre héros, [MH addition: du monde] ançien ou moderne.'

17. Lonoff, 'Charlotte Brontë's Belgian Essays: the Discourse of Empowerment', p.396.

18. CB, 'Lettre d'un Pauvre Peintre à un grand Seigneur', 17 Oct. 1843: MS p.5, Berg, [Lonoff, 'On the Struggles of a Poor and Unknown Artist: a devoir by Charlotte Brontë', *BST*:18:95:377–9, which includes a transcript and a translation]. 'Milord, je crois avoir du talent. Ne vous indi- gnez pas de ma présomption, ne m'accusez pas d'amour-propre, je ne connais pas ce sentiment faible, enfant de la vanité; mais je connais bien un autre sentiment, le Respect pour moi-même, sentiment né de l'independance et de l'intégrité. Milord, je crois avoir du Génie. Cette déc- laration vous choque; vous la trouvez arrogante moi, je la trouve tout simple. N'est il pas convenu de tout le monde que sans génie nul artiste ne peut réussir? Donc ne serait-ce pas de l'imbécilité que de se vouer aux arts sans s'assurer qu'on a cette qualité si indispensable?'

19. *Ibid.*, pp.6–7. 'pendant toute ma première jeu- nesse la différence qui existait entre moi et la plupart des personnes qui m'entouraient, était pour moi une énigme embarrassante que je ne savais pas résoudre je me croyais inférieur à tous et je m'en chagrinais. Je croyais de mon devoir de suivre l'exemple que me donnait la [majorité de mes: changed by MH to: plupart] con- naissances, exemple sanctionné par l'ap- probation de la médiocrité prudente et légitime et cependant je me sentais incapable de sentir et d'agir comme sentait et agissait cette majorité ... Il y avait toujours de la superfluité en ce que je faisais; j'étais ou trop ému ou trop abattu; sans vouloir je laissais voir tout ce qui se passait dans mon coeur et il y passait quelquefois des orages: en vain j'essayais d'imiter la douce gaieté, l'hu- meur sereine et égale que je voyais sur les figures de mes compagnons et que je trouvais si digne d'admiration; tous mes efforts étaient inutiles; je ne pouvais pas mettre un frein au flux et reflux du sang dans mes artères et ce flux et reflux se marquaient toujours sur ma physionomie et sur

mes traits durs et peu attrayants; je pleurais en secret'.

20. *Ibid.*, pp.10–11. 'j'ai beaucoup souffert à Florence à Venise et à Rome et j'y ai gagné ce que je désirais posséder; une connaissance intime de tous les mystères mécaniques de la Peinture, un gout cultivé selon les règles de l'art. Quant au génie naturel, ni Titian ni Raffaelle ni Michel- Ange n'aurait su me donner ce qui vient de Dieu seul; le peu que j'ai, je le tiens de mon Créateur ...'

21. Constantin Heger, *Discours prononcés à la Dis- tribution des Prix faite aux élèves de l'Athénée Royal de Bruxelles Le 15 aout 1843* (Bruxelles, privately printed, 1843). A copy of this *Discours*, now in Wellesley, is inscribed on the flyleaf: 'A Miss Emily Bro[n]të témoignage de sincère affection C Heger Bruxelles 13 Septembre 1843'. It seems odd that Monsieur Heger should have taken the trouble to send a copy of this to Emily in Haworth, but he may have done so through Charlotte, who had copies of two of his lectures: CB to Constantin Heger, 24 Oct. 1844: MS Add 38732(B) p.4, BL, [*L&L*,ii, 18].

22. CB, 'Lettre d'un Pauvre Peintre à un grand Seigneur', 17 Oct. 1843: MS p.10, Berg, [*BST*:18:95:381]. 'Je ne manquais ni \de/ courage ni \de/ fortitude, aussitôt je me mis à travailler, quelquefois il est vrai le désespoir m'accablait un instant \car/ quand je voyais les oeuvres des grands maîtres de mon art je me sentis trop méprisable; mais la fièvre de l'emulation vint chasser cet abattement momentané et de cette conscience profonde d'infériorité, je puisais de nouvelles forces pour le travail – il naquit en moi une resolution fixe – "je veux tout faire, tout souffrir pour tout gagner –"'.

23. CB, *The Professor*, pp.122–3.

24. CB, *Villette*, pp.504–5; CB, *Shirley*, pp.485–90. Louis Moore also makes Shirley recite 'Le Cheval Dompté', a piece by Bossuet, which Charlotte herself had copied into her notebook: MS Bon 115 pp.38–9, BPM.

25. Constantin Heger to unknown, n.d.: MS n.l., [Edith Weir, 'New Brontë Material Comes to Light': *BST*:11:59:256–7].

26. Mr Westwood to unknown, 21 Nov. 1869–21 Feb. 1870: MS 52.298 pp.3–4, Brown. Mr Westwood's wife's cousin was also a former pupil and 'just one of those intellectual pupils whom he was wont to single out for preference. –' Monsieur Heger had not only told her Charlotte's story but also shown her Charlotte's letters. 'He is a finished specimen of a Jesuit,' Westwood com- mented, 'but with all that a worthy & warm- hearted man ... He remembers her with affec- tion, Madame Beck with wrath. –': *ibid.*, pp.4, 2.

27. CB to EN, 6 March [1843]: MS BS 50.4 p.2, BPM, [*L&L*, i, 293–4].

28. *Ibid.*, p.2.

29. CB to EN, [April 1843]: MS HM 24432 p.2, Huntington, [*L&L*, i, 295].

30. *Ibid.*, p.2.

31. CB to PBB, 1 May 1843: MS Ashley 161 pp.2–3, BL, [*L&L*, i, 297].

32. *Ibid.*, pp.3–4. Monsieur Heger's gift, a New Testament in German, published in London, has been preserved: *Das Neue Testament* (London, C. Bagster, 1835): HAOBP:bb98, BPM. It is inscribed in Charlotte's hand, in a mock Gothic script, on the flyleaf, 'Herr Heger hat mir dieses Buch gegeben Brussel Mai 1843 CB'. The gift coincides with, and may have prompted, Charlotte's resumption of German lessons.

33. CB to EJB, 29 May 1843: MS n.l., [*L&L*, i, 299].

34. Charlotte told Emily, 'Mdlle Blanche's character is so false and so contemptible I can't force myself to associate with her. She perceives my utter dislike and never now speaks to me – a great relief': CB to EJB, 2 Sept. 1843: MS n.l., [*L&L*, i, 303].

35. *Ibid.*, i, 299.

36. CB to EN, [*c*.June 1843]: MS 2696 R-V pp.3–4, Pierpont Morgan, [*L&L*, i, 308–9, wrongly dated to 15 Nov. 1843]. This undated letter is usually attributed to 15 November; I am grateful to Margaret Smith for redating it to *c*.June 1843 on the grounds that Charlotte belatedly returned the portrait referred to on 6 August.

37. Abraham Dixon snr to Mary Dixon, 24 July 1843: MS in Dixon; Mr Jenkins' duties seem to have been taken, temporarily at least, by either his brother, David Jenkins, now incumbent of Pudsey, or, more likely, his nephew, who was curate at Batley. At the beginning of August Charlotte heard 'a voice proceed from the pulpit' of the Chapel Royale '– which instantly brought all Birstal and all Batley before my mind's eye –'; though she could not see him, it was Mr Jenkins who later called round with news that Ellen's sister, Sarah, had died and that Ellen herself had gone to Harrogate: CB to EN, [6 Aug. 1843]: MS BS 50.6 pp.1–2, 4, BPM, [*L&L*, i, 302].

38. The Wheelwrights' departure is mentioned in CB to EN HM 24433 p.2, 13 Oct. 1843: MS Huntington, [*L&L*, i, 306]. Susanna Mills is not mentioned in any of Charlotte's correspondence but she wrote to the *South Wales Echo* in May 1901 to say that she had been a contemporary of Charlotte, Emily and the Wheelwrights at the Pensionnat Heger. She offered no insights or memories of them, though she did say that she remembered them well. The letter is quoted in a footnote in Shorter, *The Brontës: Life and Letters*, i, 233. Charlotte's opinion of Maria Miller is given in a letter to Laetitia Wheelwright, 16 June 1852: MS divided, pp.1–2 containing the references to Maria Miller n.l., pp.3–4 in Brotherton, [*L&L*, iii, 338–9]. Maria was particularly friendly with Laetitia Wheelwright at the school and the family considered her to be the original of Ginevra Fanshawe in *Villette*. Joseph Green, 'The Brontë–Wheelwright Friendship', i, 33.

39. CB to EN, [6 Aug. 1843]: MS BS 50.6 pp.1–2, BPM, [*L&L*, i, 301–2].

40. CB to EJB, 2 Sept. 1843: MS n.l., [*L&L*, i, 303–4].

41. *Ibid.* p.304.

42. CB, *Villette*, pp.199–200.

43. *Ibid.*, pp.201–2.

44. CB to EJB, 1 Oct. 1843: MS n.l., [*L&L*, i, 305–6]. Tiger was the family cat.

45. CB to EN, 13 Oct. 1843: MS HM 24433 p.2, Huntington, [*L&L*, i, 306–7].

46. CB, *Villette*, p.440. The passage in *Villette* tells how M. Paul, 'accidentally hearing me one day acknowledge an ignorance of some branch of education (I think it was arithmetic) which would have disgraced a charity-schoolboy, as he very truly remarked, he took me in hand, examined me first, found me, I need not say, abundantly deficient, gave me some books, and appointed me some tasks'. This ties in with Charlotte's sudden embarkation on arithmetic lessons. In her Cahier d'Arithmétique, she noted that her Professor was Monsieur Heger; only eight pages out of the exercise book were completed, however, suggesting that the lessons did not last long: CB, Cahier d'Arithmétique, Sept. 1843: MS Bon 119, BPM.

47. Charlotte's last two extant *devoirs* were written in October: CB, Athènes sauvée par la Poësie, 6 Oct. 1843: rough draft MS Bon 120, BPM, [translation only in *BST*:12:62:90–6]; an amended copy, dated 22 December 1843, is in CB, Cahier d'of English Translations, [1843]: MS in Pierpont Morgan. For CB, Lettre d'un Pauvre Peintre à un grand Seigneur, 17 Oct. 1843, see above pp.417–18.

48. CB to EN, 13 Oct. 1843: MS HM 24433 p.2, Huntington, [*L&L*, i, 306–7]. Charlotte's copy of Russell's *General Atlas of Modern Geography*, with the note inside the back cover, is MS 2696 R-V, Pierpont Morgan.

49. CB to Mary Dixon, 16 Oct. 1843: MS p.2, Princeton. CB to EN, [*c*.June 1843]: MS 2696 R-V p.2, Pierpont Morgan, [*L&L*, i, 308, wrongly dated to 15 Nov. 1843]. Charlotte adds, 'This opinion is for you only mind –'; see also CB to EN, 13 Oct. 1843: MS HM 24433 p.2, Huntington, [*L&L*, i, 306].

50. CB to EJB, 19 Dec. 1843: MS n.l., [*L&L*, i, 309–10].

51. CB to Laetitia Wheelwright, [Dec. 1843]: MS in Kentucky. 'Denk op my on ik zal op u denken N Vrindinne Pensez à moi et je penserai toujours à vous Votre amie Charlotte.' This note purports to be in Charlotte's autograph but appears to me to be a copy in another hand. Abraham Dixon snr to Mary Dixon, 30 Dec. 1843: MS in Dixon. This letter was actually given to Charlotte to deliver to Mary in England, thus avoiding the huge postal charges of sending from Brussels.

52. CB to EN, 23 Jan. 1844: MS p.2, Law Colln, photograph in Mildred Christian Colln, BPM, [*L&L*, ii, 3].

53. *Ibid.*, p.2. Charlotte's determination to set up her own school had also wavered. In this letter she also tells Ellen she has decided not to leave home in order to commence a school, because of her father's increasing blindness.

54. *Ibid.*, p.2. One of her former pupils, Mathilde, actually wrote to Charlotte from Brussels, making her admiration and affection for her teacher absolutely clear. As she also quotes a letter from Charlotte to herself in which she had said, 'I shall not cease to think of you with affection and even esteem', Charlotte's loathing for her Belgian pupils, as expressed in *The Professor* and *Villette*, cannot have been universal: 'Mathilde' to CB, n.d.: MS ix, M, BPM, found in Charlotte's writing desk.

55. CB to PB, 2 June 1843: MS n.l., [*L&L*, i, 300]. Tabby's physical frailty is suggested by Charlotte's comment that 'I am exceedingly glad to hear that you still keep Tabby. It is an act of great charity to her, and I do not think it will be unrewarded, for she is very faithful, and will always serve you, when she has occasion, to the best of her abilities.'

56. *Bradford Observer*, 9 March 1843, p.5; Register of Burials, 1836–54, Haworth Church. On 12 March, Smith simply signed his name; seven days later he signed it again using his official title 'curate'.

57. *Leeds Intelligencer*, 18 March 1843, p.5.

58. *Bradford Observer*, 30 March 1843, p.5. A report in the paper in July stated that the Haworth Church clock had been found bound up with cords to prevent it telling the time, a move prompted by the pro-church rate party who were angry at their recent defeat in attempting to lay a rate. It is clear, however, that Patrick now made no effort to hold church rate meetings, relying instead upon voluntary subscriptions. The story has evidently been confused with Keighley, where Busfeild had unsuccessfully attempted to lay a rate and had indeed ordered the church clock to be stopped so that the Dissenters could not have the benefit of its services. It was not restarted till the beginning of November: *Bradford Observer*, 13 July 1843, pp.5, 7; 13 Aug. 1843, p.5. Busfeild engaged in further petty persecutions, stopping his subscription to the newspaper reading rooms of a Mr Crabtree because he had displayed an anti-church rate poster there: *ibid.*, 20 July 1843, p.6.

59. PB to the *Leeds Intelligencer*, 27 May 1843, p.6.

60. PB to the *Halifax Guardian*, 29 July 1843, p.3. The letter was written a month earlier, on 29 June, in response to a discussion with the editor when Patrick attended the last annual visitation of the Archdeacon of Craven.

61. PB to Hugh Brontë, 20 Nov. 1843: MS BS 191 pp.1–4, BPM, [L&D, 334–5]. Patrick is obliged to ask Hugh for their brother William's address and sends greetings to his 'Brothers, and Sisters, and all old Friends, who may now be living', both of which imply that he had lost contact with his Irish roots. William merited his own

letter from Patrick, perhaps because he had previously fought as a United Irishman in the engagement at Ballynahinch: see above, p.4.

62. PB to *Leeds Mercury*, 15 July 1843, p.6. The details of the duel were given during the prosecution of the surviving protagonists, recorded in the *Leeds Intelligencer*, 2 Sept. 1843, p.8.

63. PB to *Leeds Intelligencer*, 2 Sept. 1843, p.8.

64. PB to *Leeds Intelligencer*, 22 July 1843, p.8. The Dissenters' chief objections to the National Education Bill are neatly summarized in the biography of a leading Bradford Nonconformist: G. W. Conder, *Memoir and Remains of the Late Rev. Jonathan Glyde, Pastor of Horton Lane Chapel* (London, Farquhar Shaw, 1858), pp.106–11.

65. Patrick was a signatory to a bill calling for the inauguration of a Bradford Church Institution: *Bradford Observer*, 6 July 1843, p.8. See also letter of William Morgan to *Bradford Observer*, 13 July 1843, p.8. The vicar and all the incumbents of the parish signed the bill, except William Morgan.

66. PB to the National Society, 4 Aug. 1843: MS n.l., [Brian Wilks, 'Schools and Schooling in the Lives and Literature of the Brontë Family', *BST*:18:95:355].

67. *Bradford Observer*, 26 Oct. 1843, p.8.

68. *Bradford Observer*, 28 Dec. 1843, p.5; *Leeds Intelligencer*, 3 Feb. 1844, p.5. The importance of the opening of the Church Day school was immediately recognized by the Dissenters in the township. A month later the Wesleyan Methodists opened their own day school in Haworth, run on the Glasgow training system and offering 'a good English and commercial education': *Bradford Observer*, 29 Feb. 1844, p.5.

69. PB to principal inhabitants of Haworth, 28 Jan. 1844: MS RMP 746a, WYAS, Calderdale. This copy is not in Patrick's hand – a reflection of his poor eyesight – and was sent to Mrs Taylor of Stanbury.

70. PB to the National Society, 1844, [Brian Wilks, 'Schools and Schooling in the Lives and Literature of the Brontë Family', *BST*:18:95:355]. The quotation is from Proverbs, ch.3 v.17.

71. William Scoresby to PB, 4 Jan. 1844: MS Heaton B143 p.6, WYAS, Bradford. Patrick sent this letter on to one of the trustees, Robert Heaton, whose address he wrote on its wrapper. *Halifax Guardian*, 3 Feb. 1844, p.5; *Bradford Observer*, 8 Feb. 1844, p.8. The latter paper later declared that the original endowment, providing £20 a year, which was to be divided in the ratio £18 for the maintenance of the schoolmaster and £2 for distribution among the poor, was now worth £80; with more generosity than accuracy it therefore argued that £62 should now be distributed among the poor: *ibid.*, 23 May 1844, p.5.

72. *Bradford Observer*, 8 Feb. 1844, p.8; PB to *Bradford Observer*, 15 Feb. 1844, p.5. Some months later, Isaac Constantine, a Haworth Baptist, endeavoured to resurrect the issue by demanding to know whether Patrick would bury anyone bap-

tized outside the Established Church; Patrick replied in eight lines, stating categorically that he would continue to bury Baptists as he had always done: *Bradford Observer*, 18 April 1844, p.7; 25 April 1844, p.7.

73. PB to *Leeds Mercury*, 16 March 1844, p.6.

74. Bishop of Ripon to William Scoresby, 27 Nov. 1843: MS in Unsorted Bundle, 1843, Whitby. The bishop told Scoresby 'Mr Brontë seems very anxious about Oxenhope District – and I am quite willing to make him wait a little while, if there be a prospect of a general Measure for the whole Parish of Bradford, under Sir Robert Peel's Bill – or, do you think that Oxenhope stands upon such clear, unexceptionable ground, that it might be proceeded with, without interfering with the general Plan –'. PB to *Leeds Intelligencer*, 17 Feb. 1844, p.7. At the very time Patrick was writing, building work was commenced on a new church at Oakworth, which fell partly into Haworth and Keighley districts. When it opened it would reduce Patrick's burden of parish duties in that area: *Bradford Observer*, 15 Feb. 1844, p.5. Registers of Baptisms, 1837–54, Marriages, 1837–70, Burials, 1836–54, Haworth Church. James Chesterton Bradley, who is often cited as being Patrick's assistant curate at this period, in fact provided very little help: he performed only one marriage on 25 February 1843 and two burials as far back as 3 November and 1 December 1842. Thomas Crowther preached the afternoon and evening sermons in aid of the Sunday school on 23 July 1843 and performed eight baptisms on the same day: Haworth Church Hymn Sheets, 23 July 1843: MS BS x, H, BPM; Register of Baptisms, 1837–54, Haworth Church. James Smith preached for the benefit of the church singers in Haworth Church on 15 October 1843: *Bradford Observer*, 19 Oct. 1843, p.5.

75. PB to ?Joseph Greenwood?, 4 Oct. 1843: MS n.l., [*L&L*, i, 305–6].

76. CB to EN, 23 Jan. 1844: MS pp.2–3, Law Colln, photograph in Mildred Christian Colln, BPM, [*L&L*, ii, 3].

77. *Ibid.*, p.1.

78. *Ibid.*, p.3.

79. PBB, Thorp Green, 30 March 1843: PBB, [Luddenden Foot Notebook], 1840–2, Brotherton [VN *PBB*, p.260]. This was only a first draft: l.3 originally read 'And nothing calls to mind this day' and l.5 'Unthought of cares unwelcome fears'.

80. PBB, pen and ink sketch of his 'Old Hall' lodgings, Thorp Green, 25 Aug. 1844: HAOBP:P.Br.B13, BPM. Beneath the drawing Branwell has written 'P B Brontë. 1844. Aug 25th.' and 'This is only a rough pen and ink sketch of my lodgings – the "Old Hall" built about 1680 – or 85.' On the verso there is a pencil sketch of a number of men with guns.

81. CB to PBB, 1 May 1843: MS Ashley 161 p.1, BL, [*L&L*, i, 296]. The case concerned a forged

codicil to the will of a Haworth Church trustee, John Beaver. As a witness to the original will, Patrick was called to give evidence at the York Assizes and appeared there between 11 March, when he was sworn in, and 20 March, when the trial began: see Sarah Fermi and Dorinda Kinghorn, 'The Brontës and the Case of the Beaver Forgery', *BST*:21:1, 2:19; *Bradford Observer*, 9 March 1843, p.5; *Leeds Intelligencer*, 11 March 1843, p.5. Patrick was deeply concerned about two of his parishioners, William Thomas and Enoch Thomas, landlord of the King's Arms, who, as an executor and a witness to a codicil, were traumatized by their involvement in the case. See PB to William Thomas, 1 Aug. 1843: MS pp.1–3, Columbia, [*L&D*, p.339] and PB to George Taylor, 29 Feb. 1844: MS n.l., [*L&D* p.340].

82. AB, A Word to the Calvinists, 28 May 1843: MS MA 28 p.18, Pierpont Morgan, [Chitham, pp.89–91]. The poem was first published in the sisters' 1846 edition of *Poems*, under the title 'A Word to the Elect'.

83. AB, [Song Book], June 1843: MS Bon 133, BPM, [JB *ST*, no.24].

84. The Robinsons first appear in the list of visitors in the *Scarborough Herald* on 6 July 1843, p.3 and appear weekly thereafter; they had left by 3 August, though Mrs Robinson senior stayed on for a further two weeks: *ibid.*, 3 Aug. 1843, p.3; 24 Aug. 1843, p.3.

85. AB, 'Eternal power of earth and air', 10 Sept. 1843: MS MA 28 pp.8–11, Pierpont Morgan, [Chitham, pp.91–2]. This poem was also chosen by Anne for inclusion in the 1846 volume of poems, where it appeared under the title 'The Doubter's Prayer'.

86. AB, The Captive Dove, 31 Oct. 1843: MS MA 28 pp.11–13, Pierpont Morgan, [Chitham, pp.92–3]. A note on the MS says that this poem was 'mostly written in the Spring of 1842'. Emily had written a poem on the same subject, 'The Caged Bird', on 27 February 1841. Both poems were included in the sisters' 1846 volume of *Poems*. I have argued that the poems both belong to the Gondal cycle in JB *SP*, pp.131, 147.

87. AB, Home, [Nov. 1843]: MS n.l., [Chitham, pp.99–100]. The poem was chosen by Anne for inclusion in the 1846 volume of *Poems*, as was a slightly earlier poem, 'The Consolation', which in terms of style and content is very similar to 'Home': AB, The Consolation, 7 Nov. 1843: MS MA 28 pp.13–16, Pierpont Morgan, [Chitham, pp.94–5]. It should be noted that 'The Consolation' was attributed by Anne to 'Hespera Caverndel', indicating it was part of the Gondal cycle. It is a strong possibility that the comparatively large number of poems Anne produced in the latter part of 1843 were the result of her seeking comfort in writing a Gondal chronicle. This would suggest that the poems should not be taken as being purely autobiographical though they clearly reflected

Anne's own preoccupations at the time. It is also worth pointing out that Anne obviously considered that her work produced during this year was some of her best as she included so many of the items in *Poems* by Currer, Ellis and Acton Bell.

88. AB, Music on Christmas Morning, [25 Dec. 1843]: MS n.l., [Chitham, pp.96–7]. The poem was published in the sisters' 1846 volume of poems.

89. AB, The Student's Serenade, Feb. 1844: MS in Berg, [Chitham, pp.98–9]; The Gondal origins of the poem are suggested by the fact that its authorship is attributed to 'Alexander Hybernia'. Anne had acquired several books over the autumn of 1843 and the spring of 1844 in connection with her teaching duties. Her copy of Rabenhorst's *Pocket Dictionary of the German and English Languages* (London, Longman, Brown & Co., 1843) is inscribed on the flyleaf 'Anne Brontë September 14th 1843': HAOBP:bb50, BPM. Similarly, her *Deutsches Lesebuch* (London, Dulau & Co., 1837) is inscribed on its flyleaf 'Anne Brontë Thorp Green March 7th 1844': HAOBP:bb52, BPM. She had bought R. Valpy's *Delectus Sententiarum et Historiarum* (London, Longman & Co., 1842) about the same time, inscribing it 'Anne Brontë Thorp Green November – 1843': HAOBP:bb226, BPM. As Branwell was already Edmund Robinson's tutor by the time she bought this book, Anne cannot have acquired it in order to teach her only male pupil so she must have offered her girls rudimentary Latin.

90. EJB, Gondal Poems, Feb. 1844: MS Add 43483, BL. A note above the title says 'Transcribed February 1844': the first poem is dated 6 March 1837, the last 13 May 1848. EJB, untitled copybook of poems, Feb. 1844: MS in Law Colln, [facsimile in *Poems of EJB & AB*, pp.301–29]. Again there is a note above the first poem stating 'Transcribed Feb[r]uary 1844': the first poem is dated 11 November 1836, the last 25 January 1846. It is often used as an argument for ascribing Emily's poems to autobiographical experience rather than Gondal fantasy that the poems in the second book are 'non-Gondal'. This is clearly not the case. Though the first three poems are the three she wrote at Law Hill, a large number of the subsequent ones have an indisputable Gondal context. This view has recently received support from Derek Roper, 'Emily Brontë's Lover', *BST*:21:1&2:25–31.

91. EJB, Castle Wood, 2 Feb. 1844: MS in Berg, [Hatfield, pp.194–5]. The authorial character of this poem is strongly reminiscent of the one in Emily's earlier poem, 'I am the only being whose doom'. See for example, EJB, 'How few, of all the hearts that loved,', 11 March 1844: MS Add 43483 pp.39–40, BL, [Hatfield, pp.201–2]; EJB, 'The linnet in the rocky dells', 1 May 1844: *ibid.*, p.45, BL, [Hatfield, pp.204–5]; EJB, 'Come, the wind may never again', 2 Oct. 1844: *ibid.*, pp.48–9, BL, [Hatfield, pp.207–8].

92. EJB, 'The linnet in the rocky dells', 1 May 1844: MS Add 43483 p.45, BL, [Hatfield, pp.204–5].

93. EJB, To Imagination, 3 Sept. 1844: MS in Law Colln, [facsimile in *Poems of EJB & AB*, p.323; Hatfield, p.206].

94. *Bradford Observer*, 8 Feb. 1844, p.8; 24 Oct. 1844, p.5. The lectures on medical botany were a popular series but the lecture on Chartism attracted little support: *ibid.*, 29 Feb. 1844, p.5; 28 April 1844, p.5. There were also regular concerts in Keighley: see, for example, *ibid.*, 22 Feb. 1844 p.5; 2 Jan. 1845, p.8. For the closure of the library see *ibid.*, 8 April 1844, p.5.

95. *Leeds Intelligencer*, 27 July 1844, p.7; CB to Mrs Taylor, [17 July 1844]: MS n.l., [*L&L*, ii, 6]. The letter is simply dated 'Wednesday morning' and is usually assigned to June 1844, but it seems logical that Charlotte would invite the Rands and Mrs Rand's mother, Mrs Bacon, to take tea after the examinations; the invitation is for 'Friday afternoon' which was the day of the examinations. I have therefore dated the letter to 17 July 1844.

96. *Leeds Intelligencer*, 27 July 1844, p.7.

97. *Bradford Observer*, 25 July 1844, p.5; Haworth Church Hymn Sheets, 21 July 1844: MSS BS xi, H, BPM; J. Hodgson Ramsbotham to *Leeds Intelligencer*, 18 April 1857, p.7. Redhead told his son-in-law about his former reception at Haworth on the way to preach the sermons. The two sermons raised £18 6s. ¾d., a comparatively large sum. It is instructive to compare this with the sums raised by the Dissenting bodies for their Sunday Schools in the township. The five Methodist chapels raised nearly £91 between them for their schools, the four Baptist chapels just over £65 and the Primitive Methodists or Ranters nearly £9: *ibid.*, 28 Aug. 1844, p.5. The figures are eloquent evidence of the scale of Dissenting support in the township and reveal just what Patrick was up against as the sole supporter of the Establishment.

98. *Bradford Observer*, 25 July 1844, p.5. A preliminary survey of the line had been virtually completed by the end of October and, despite a one in twenty gradient, it was widely expected that the line would be profitable because of the large number of factories and quarries along its length: *ibid.*, 24 Oct. 1844, p.5.

99. CB to EN, [4 March 1844]: MS Princeton, [*L&L*, ii, 4]; CB to EN, [25 March 1844]: MS BS 50.8, BPM, [*L&L*, ii, 5]; EN, Reminiscences: MS pp.62–3, KSC, [*BST*:2:10:81]; CB to EN, 7 April 1844: MS at Harvard, [*L&L*, ii, 5].

100. A scrap of paper with a picture of a man apparently drowning and the punning printed legend 'HIGH WATER AT THE ISLE OF MAN and BURY-HEAD', is in Emily's writing desk. Beneath this, someone, possibly Emily, has written 'Likewise at Bolton Bridge on Thursday June 20th 1844', suggesting they witnessed someone falling in. In her diary for July 1844, Ellen noted that they were playing at

'high water', which seems to be a reference to the same incident: EN, Diary, 1844: MS at Texas, [13, 22 July 1844].

101. *Ibid.*, 8, 10, 13, 21 July 1844. According to her diary, Ellen arrived at Haworth on 1 July and left on 22 July. For Anne's and Branwell's holidays see CB to EN, [23 June 1844]: MS BS 52, BPM, [*L&L*, ii, 6]. The Robinsons stayed at No.7, The Cliff for a month: they were there by 11 July and had gone by 15 August: *Scarborough Herald*, 11 July 1844, p.3.; 15 Aug. 1844, p.3.

102. CB to EN, [29 July 1844]: MS Grolier E6 p.3, BPM, [*L&L*, ii, 7, wrongly dated to 16 July 1844]. As Ellen was still at Haworth on 16 July, Margaret Smith posits the more likely date of 29 July, which supports Charlotte's 'Monday morning' dating.

103. CB to EN, [2 Oct. 1844]: MS MA 2696 R-V p.2, Pierpont Morgan, [*L&L*, ii, 16 where it is wrongly treated as a separate letter from p.1 and dated to 15 Aug. 1844]. Here Charlotte says, 'Mr Smith leaves in the course of a fortnight – he will spend a few weeks in Ireland previously to settling at Keighley.' This is borne out by the registers, which he signed for the last time on 13 October: Register of Baptisms, 1837–54, Register of Burials, 1836–54, Haworth Church.

104. CB, *Shirley*, p.8. It was undoubtedly fair comment when Charlotte ended her novel with the remark about 'Peter Malone': 'Were I to give the catastrophe of your life and conversation, the public would sweep off in shrieking hysterics, and there would be a wild cry for sal-volatile and burnt feathers. "Impossible!" would be pronounced here: "untrue!" would be responded there. "Inartistic!" would be solemnly decided. Note well! Whenever you present the actual, simple truth, it is, somehow, always denounced as a lie': *ibid.*, p.632.

105. CB to EN, 26 Feb. 1848: MS HM 24457 pp.2–3, Huntington, [*L&L*, ii, 193]. The last that was heard of him was that he had moved south and was working as a lumberjack in Minnesota. His fictional reputation was defended by his fellow curate, J.C. Bradley, and his nephew, Robert Smith, both of whom seem to have been unaware of the cause of his original flight from Keighley: see *L&L*, iii, 3–4.

106. CB to Constantin Heger, 24 July [1844]: MS Add 38732(a) p.3, BL, [*L&L*, ii, 10]. 'Emilie n'aime pas beaucoup l'instruction mais elle s'occuperait – toujours du ménage et, quoiqu'un peu recluse, elle a trop bon coeur pour ne pas faire son possible pour le bien être des enfants –'.

107. CB to EN, [c.10 Aug. 1844]: MS HM 24434 pp.1–2, Huntington, [*L&L*, ii, 8, wrongly dated to 20 July 1844]. The *L&L* dates this letter to 20 July but this is impossible as Ellen was still at Haworth then. In her diary Ellen records 'Heard from Charlotte' on 11 August, so Margaret Smith tentatively redates this letter to 10 August; CB to EN, [c.22 Aug.] 1844: MS n.l., [*L&L*, ii, 15,

wrongly dated to 29 July 1844]. Charlotte refers to Henry Nussey's appointment to Hathersage in this letter, but Ellen did not hear of it until 21 August. I am grateful to Margaret Smith for redating this letter.

108. Card of Terms for 'Misses Bronte's Establishment', [July 1844]: original preserved in CB's writing desk: HAOBP: H219, BPM. The terms were considerably more expensive than similar establishments in the area. A Ladies' seminary at Union House, Warley, conducted by Miss Greenwood, for example, advertised annual board and education fees of £18 18s. for girls under twelve, £21 for girls over twelve and £15 (£3 15s. per quarter) for weekly boarders. Additional charges were made for French, music, drawing 'etcetera', for which 'the best masters than can be procured' would be required to attend the seminary regularly. The school was under the aegis of Miss Greenwood's father or brother, the Revd B. Greenwood, who ran the well-known Spring Garden Academy for boys at Warley: *Halifax Guardian*, 1 Jan. 1842, p.1. I have been unable to find any newspaper advertisements for the Brontës' proposed school.

109. CB to EN, [2 Oct. 1844]: MS MA 2696 R-V p.1, Pierpont Morgan, [*L&L*, ii, 17].

110. CB to EN, 14 Nov. 1844: MS HM 24435 pp.2–3, Huntington, [*L&L*, ii, 20].

111. CB to M. Heger, 24 July [1844]: MS Add 38732(a) pp.4, 2 BL, [*L&L*, ii, 11]. 'Oh c'est certain que je vous reverrai un jour – il le faut bien – puisque <la> aussitôt que j'aurai gagné assez d'argent pour aller à Bruxelles j'y irai – et je vous reverrai si ce n'est que pour un instant.'

112. *Ibid.*, p.3. 'Je ne connaîtrais pas cette lethargie si je pouvais écrire – autrefois je passais des journées, des semaines, des mois entiers à écrire et pas tout à fait sans fruit<s> – puisque Southey, et Coleridge – deux de nos meilleurs auteurs, à qui j'ai envoyé certains manuscrits en ont bien voulu témoigner leur approbation – mais à present j'ai la vue trop faible pour écrire – si j'écrirais beaucoup je deviendrais aveugle. Cette faiblesse de vue est pour moi une terrible privation – sans celà savez-vous ce que je ferais Monsieur? – j'écrirais un livre et je le dédierais à mon maître de litérature – au seul maître que j'ai jamais eu – à vous Monsieur. Je vous ai souvent dit en français combien je vous respecte – combien je suis redevable à votre bonté, à vos conseils, je voudrais le dire une fois en Anglais – Cela ne se peut pas – il ne faut pas y penser – la carrière des lettres m'est fermée – celle de l'instruction seule m'est ouverte – elle n'offre pas les mêmes attraits – c'est égal, j'y entrerai et si je n'y <av> vais pas loin, ce ne sera pas manque de diligence.'

113. Only four letters are extant but Charlotte asks M. Heger if he has received her letter at the beginning of May (which has not survived) and refers to another 'that was less than reasonable'.

M. Heger seems only to have written in response to letters from Charlotte and she refers to his letters as if she had received a number of them: CB to M. Heger, 24 July [1844]: MS Add 38732(a) p.1, BL, [*L&L*, ii, 11]. CB to M. Heger, 24 Oct. 1844: MS Add 38732 pp.1–2, BL, [*L&L*, ii, 19]. All the surviving letters have been torn into pieces and sewn back together again, bearing out the claim that Mme Heger retrieved them from the waste bin and reconstituted them in order to learn what Charlotte had written. There are no extant letters from M. Heger to Charlotte.

CHAPTER SIXTEEN

1. CB to EN, 13 June 1845: MS HM 24439 pp.2–3, Huntington, [*L&L*, ii, 38].
2. PB to B. Terry, 24 Feb. 1845: MS 6/21, Whitby. The meeting on 28 February and the address, signed by 3,000 parishioners, were reported in the *Bradford Observer*, 6 March 1845, p.6.
3. Haworth Church Hymn Sheets, 20 July 1845: MS BS xi, H, BPM. Scoresby gave the evening sermon and P. Eggleston, curate of Heptonstall but soon to be curate of Keighley, gave the afternoon one. The hymn sheet does not specify the cause for which the sermons were preached, referring only to the 'aforesaid Institution', but that Sunday was customarily devoted to the Sunday school collections.
4. Though varying dates are given for Arthur Bell Nicholls' early career, including his birth, I have followed his own version, given in ABN, Application for a Missionary Appointment, 23 Jan. 1845: MS in archives of the USPG. See also, 'Reminiscences of a Relation of Arthur Bell Nicholls', *BST*:15:79:246. According to the *Alumni Dublinensis*, he entered Trinity College, aged eighteen, as a pensioner paying normal fees, on 4 July 1836. He was the son of William Nicholls, a farmer, of Antrim and his previous teacher had been Dr Bell: Burtchaell and Sadleir, *Alumni Dublinensis*, p.619. Quite why it should have taken him seven years to graduate, I have been unable to discover, but this was not uncommon.
5. CB to Mrs Rand, 26 May [1845]: MS 2696 R–V, Pierpont Morgan, [*L&L*, ii, 35]. Arthur Bell Nicholls was ordained deacon by the Bishop of Lichfield on behalf of the Bishop of Ripon on Trinity Sunday 1845: ABN, Application for a Missionary Appointment, 23 Jan. 1845: MS in archives of the USPG; Registers of Baptisms 1837–54, Marriages 1837–70, Burials 1836–54, Haworth Church.
6. PB to Joseph Rushworth, 21 April [1845]: MS BS 192, BPM, [*L&L*, ii, 31]. The letter was dictated to a clerk and only the signature is in Patrick's own hand. According to the *Leeds Intelligencer*, 5 July 1845, p.5, recording the placing of the order, the little bell had been placed in the church tower in 1664, the middle one in 1742 and the tenor bell in 1747 – both the latter bells dating from Grimshaw's incumbency. See also *Bradford Observer*, 3 July 1845, p.5 and, for the installation, 6 Nov. 1845, p.8. For an example of the Haworth ringers entering a competition see *Leeds Intelligencer*, 21 March 1846, p.5.

7. *Ibid.*, 31 July 1845, p.5.
8. CB to Constantin Heger, 24 Oct. 1844: MS Add 38732(B) p.3, BL, [*L&L*, ii, 18]. Included in her 'little library' were the complete works of Bernardin St Pierre, the *Pensées* of Pascal, a book of poetry, two books in German and 'worth all the rest', as Charlotte told Monsieur Heger, two of his own Discourses, given at the presentation of prizes at the Athénée Royal.
9. CB to Constantin Heger, 8 Jan. [1845]: MS Add 38732(D) p.1, BL, [*L&L*, ii, 21]. 'Mr Taylor est revenu, je lui ai demandé s'il n'avait pas une lettre pour moi – "Non, rien". "Patience" – dis-je – Sa soeur viendra bientôt. Mademoiselle Taylor est revenue "Je n'ai rien pour vous de la part de Monsieur Heger" dit elle "ni lettre ni message"'; *ibid.*, pp.1–2. 'Jour et nuit je ne trouve ni repos ni paix – si je dors je fais des rêves tourmentants où je vous vois toujours sévère, toujours sombre et irrité contre moi – Pardonnez-moi donc Monsieur si je prends la partie de vous écrire encore – Comment puis je supporter la vie si je ne fais pas un effort pour en alléger les souffrances? Je sais que vous serez impatiente quand vous lirez cette lettre – vous direz encore que je suis exaltée – que j'ai des pensées noires &c. Soit Monsieur – je ne cherche pas à me justifier, je me soumets à toutes sortes de réproches – tout ce que je sais – c'est que je ne puis pas – que je ne veux pas me résigner à perdre entièrement l'amitié de mon maître – j'aime mieux subir les plus grandes douleurs physiques que d'avoir toujours le coeur, lacéré par les regrets cuisants. Si mon maître me retire entièrement son amitié je serai[s:del] tout à fait sans espoir – s'il m'en donne un peu – très peu – je serai contente – heureuse, j'aurais un motif pour vivre – pour travailler – Monsieur, les pauvres n'ont pas besoin de grand chose pour vivre – ils ne demandent que les miettes de pain qui tombent de la table des riches – mais si on leur refuse ces miettes de pains – ils meurent de faim – Moi non plus je n'ai pas besoin de beaucoup d'affection de la part de ceux que j'aime – je ne saurais que faire d'une amitié entière et complète – je n'y suis pas habituée – mais vous me témoigniez, autrefois, <u>un peu</u> d'intérêt quand j'étais votre élève à Bruxelles – et je tiens à conserver ce <u>peu</u> d'intérêt – j'y tiens comme je tiendrais à la vie.'
10. ECG to EN, 9 July 1856, [C&P, p.394]. The

letters could not be found; Mrs Gaskell suspected Mr Nicholls had destroyed them but it is more likely that Charlotte did so before her marriage. See below, p.807.

11. ECG to Emily Shaen, 7–8 Sept. 1856, [C&P, p.409]. 'I believed him to be too good to publish those letters – but I felt that his friends might really with some justice urge him to do so, –'.

12. CB, 'At first I did attention give' [Jan. 1845]: MS in Berg, [VN *CB*, p.274]. A revised version of the latter part of the poem was included as a song in *Jane Eyre*, pp.274–5. See also, CB, Gilbert, [Spring 1845]: MS Bon 118 pp.1v–8v, BPM, [VN *CB*, p.274]. The poem, telling the story of a self-centred man who rejects his devoted lover, was first published in *Poems* by Currer, Ellis & Acton Bell (Aylott & Jones, 1846), pp.60–75.

13. CB to EN, [6 Jan. 1845]: MS BS 53.5, BPM, [*L&L*, ii, 21].

14. CB to EN, 20 Feb. 1845: MS n.l., [*L&L*, ii, 25]. The letter mentions that Charlotte does not know the address of Ellen's lodgings and that she is therefore sending the letter via the Hudsons of Easton Farm.

15. MT to ECG, 18 Jan. 1856: MS n.l., [Stevens, p.161].

16. CB to EN, 20 Feb. 1845: MS n.l., [*L&L*, ii, 25–6].

17. CB to EN, 24 April 1845: MS HM 24438 pp.2–3, Huntington, [*L&L*, ii, 33–4].

18. CB to EN, 2 April 1845: MS HM 24437 pp.3–4, Huntington, [*L&L*, ii, 30].

19. MT to ECG, 30 July 1857: MS n.l., [Stevens, p.133]. The text says a 'walking nightmare' but, as Margaret Smith has pointed out, this is probably a misreading for the more appropriate 'waking nightmare'; MT to CB, 5 April 1850: MS at Texas, [Stevens. p.87].

20. MT to ECG, [1857]: MS n.l., [Stevens, pp.165–6]. Charlotte's definition of a 'sister of charity' appears in her portrayal of Miss Ainley in CB, *Shirley*, p.182.

21. *Halifax Guardian*, 5 Sept. 1840, p.5. The statistics, taken from the *Scotsman*, calculated a woman's chances of marrying. Taking 100 as the total number of chances she would have over the years, the table offered the following figures: 14½% aged 15–20, 52% aged 20–25, 18% aged 25–30, 6½% aged 30–35, 3½% aged 35–40, 2½% aged 40–45 and 1½% aged 45–50.

22. CB to Margaret Wooler, 23 April 1845: MS FM 1, pp.1–2, Fitzwilliam, [*L&L*, ii, 31–2].

23. *Ibid.*, p.2.

24. The probate papers of both Emily and Anne are stamped by the York & North Midland Railway Company and the Reeth Consolidated Mining Company, indicating that they still had shares in them: EJB, Grant of administration of estate of to PB, 5 Feb. 1849: MS Bon 73, BPM; AB, Grant of administration of estate of to PB, 5 Sept. 1849: MS Bon 74, BPM. On her death

Aunt Branwell had ten whole shares in the York & North Midland Railway worth £93 10s. each and four half shares worth about £38 each. Her shares in the Reeth Mines in Cornwall, for which she had paid £124, had never afforded a dividend and on her death were considered worthless: Elizabeth Branwell, inventory of the Residue of the late Miss Elizabeth Branwell's property, 30 Jan. 1843: MS in private hands.

25. CB to EN, 24 March 1845: MS in Law Colln, [*L&L*, ii, 28].

26. AB, Diary Paper, 31 July 1845: MS p.2, in private hands, [*L&L*, ii, 52].

27. CB to EN, 13 June 1845: MS HM 24439 pp.2–3, Huntington, [*L&L*, ii, 38]. The marriage, at which Ellen was a bridesmaid, is mentioned in CB to EN, 1 June 1845: MS BS 54 p.2, BPM, [*L&L*, ii, 36]. For the arrangements for Hathersage see: CB to EN, [18 June 1845]: MS HM 24440 p.1, Huntington, [*L&L*, ii, 39]; CB to EN, [*c*.27 June 1845]: MS Bon 168 pp.1–2, BPM, [*L&L*, ii, 41, wrongly dated to 24 June 1845].

28. *Ibid.*, p.1.

29. EJB, Diary Paper, 30 July 1845: MS p.1, in private hands, [*L&L*, ii, 50–1].

30. *Leeds Intelligencer*, 13 April 1844, p.5; 24 Aug. 1844, p.5.

31. CB, 'The Missionary', [Spring 1845]: MS n.l., [VN *CB*, pp.291–4]. Neufeldt dates this, and several other 'story poems' also published in *Poems* by Currer, Ellis & Acton Bell, to the Spring of 1845. I think there is a good case for dating it slightly later, to the period of the Hathersage visit. CB to EN, [*c*.June 1843]: MS 2696 R-V pp.2–3, Pierpont Morgan, [*L&L*, i, 308, wrongly dated to 15 Nov. 1843]. In this letter Charlotte remarked 'his notion of being a Missionary is amusing – he would not live a year in the climates of those countries where Missionaries are wanted –'.

32. The brasses are still to be seen in St Michael's Church today. See also G. A. Lester, *The Eyre Brasses of Hathersage* (reprint from G. A. Lester, *Brasses and Brass-Rubbing in the Peak District*), (Midsummer Publications, n.d.).

33. Though there are many contenders for the original of Thornfield, North Lees Hall is the only one which best fits the description in the novel of a three-storey gentleman's manor house with battlements, with a rookery behind, a large meadow in front and hills in the distance: CB, *Jane Eyre*, p.100. Charlotte may well have been inside the Hall as in another chapter she gives a graphic description of the Apostles Cupboard, a highly individual piece of furniture belonging to the Eyres, which is now in the Brontë Parsonage Museum: HAOBP: F32, BPM. This and the other Hathersage locations were all 'identified' as early as the 1890s: see, for instance, J. J. Stead, 'Hathersage and *Jane Eyre*', *BST* 1:4:26. It should be borne in mind, however, that Charlotte always said that she only allowed

reality to suggest, never to dictate, her fictional creations.

34. Local tradition has it that Charlotte arrived at the George Inn by public coach from Sheffield, but it seems more likely that Ellen met the omnibus at Sheffield with her own private transport as she had done when expecting Charlotte the previous week: CB to EN, [*c.*27 June 1845]: MS Bon 168 p.1, BPM, [*L&L*, ii, 40, wrongly dated to 24 June 1845]. I am grateful to Margaret Smith for redating this letter; on the evidence of the letters, she dates Charlotte's visit to Hathersage from *c.*3–26 July 1845.

35. EN to Mary Gorham, 22 July 1845: MS pp.2, 4, BS viii, BPM; M. F. H. Hulbert, *Discovering Hathersage Old Vicarage* (Hathersage PCC, 1985), pp.10–11.

36. CB to EN, [18 June 1845]: MS HM 24440 p.2, Huntington, [*L&L*, ii, 39]; EN to Mary Gorham, 22 July 1845: MS p.2, BS viii, BPM.

37. *Ibid.*, p.3.

38. EJB to EN, 16 July 1845: MS BS 108 p.1, BPM [*BST*:12:63:193, wrongly dated to 18 July 1845]. The last sentence, valediction and signature have been cut off and are now missing; a transcription of this section, possibly in Ellen's own hand, is written on p.3 of the letter.

39. Haworth Church Hymn Sheet, 20 July 1845: MS BS x, H, BPM. The hymn sheet refers to Eggleston as being 'of Heptonstall', but he was soon to be appointed curate of Keighley: *Leeds Mercury*, 26 July 1845, p.9.

40. The five poems published in *Poems* were ' "Enough of Thought, Philosopher', 3 Feb. 1845: MS in Law Colln, [facsimile in *Poems of EJB & AB*, pp.324–6; Hatfield, pp.220–2]; 'Cold in the earth and the deep snow piled above thee!', 3 March 1845: MS Add 43483 pp.52–3, BL, [Hatfield, pp.222–3]; 'Death, that struck when I was most confiding', 10 April 1845: MS in Law Colln, [facsimile in *Poems of EJB & AB*, p.327; Hatfield, pp.224–5]; 'Ah! why, because the dazzeling sun', 14 April 1845: MS in Law Colln, [facsimile in *Poems of EJB & AB*, p.327; Hatfield, pp.225–7]; 'How beautiful the Earth is still', 2 June 1845: MS in Law Colln, [facsimile in *Poems of EJB & AB*, p.328; Hatfield, pp.231–3].

41. EJB, Diary Paper, 30 July 1845: MS pp.1–2, in private hands, [*L&L*, ii, 50].

42. I think it is dangerous to argue that all Anne's religious poems, particularly those written during the spring and early summer of 1845, are autobiographical. There are many parallels in both storyline and mood between the poems written by Anne and Emily at this time. We also know from Emily's 1845 diary paper that they were then both writing about the First Wars between the Royalists and Republicans. The subject matter naturally lent itself to the contemplation of blighted hopes and expressions of despair at the separation of families and lovers by the political divide. Anne's poem 'I love the silent hour of night', which is usually regarded as a personal lamentation for William Weightman, is closely paralleled by Emily's 'Cold in the earth and the deep snow piled above thee!' also written at this time. Similarly, Anne's 'Oppressed with sin and wo' and 'When sinks my heart in hopeless gloom' find strong echoes in Emily's 'How beautiful the Earth is still', the first and last poems being written on consecutive days in June. The fact that Anne's heroes and heroines look to God rather than hope or imagination for comfort is simply a reflection of her character. If, as I suspect, most of Anne's poems of this period belong in a Gondal setting, then the depth of her own despair at Thorp Green may have been unduly exaggerated.

43. AB, 'Call me away; there's nothing here,', 24 Jan. 1845: MS in Law Colln, [facsimile in *Poems of EJB & AB*, p.344; Chitham, p.107]. I cannot agree with Chitham that this poem reflects the Branwell–Mrs Robinson situation. The lovers are clearly a Gondal Romeo and Juliet and as we know from Emily's diary paper that both she and Anne were writing about the First Wars it seems likely that one came from a Royalist family, the other from a Republican one.

44. AB, 'Oppressed with sin and wo', 1 June 1845: MS Bon 134 p.4, BPM, [Chitham, p.114].

45. AB, Diary Paper, 31 July 1845: MS p.1, in private hands, [*L&L*, ii, 52]. I am grateful to William Self for a photocopy of this manuscript and permission to quote from it. It has been suggested that Anne's 'passages in the life of an Individual' may possibly be an early version of *Agnes Grey* but Emily's diary paper of the same date says that Anne is working on a book by Henry Sophona; a masculine narrator makes it unlikely that this was a forerunner of *Agnes Grey*.

46. AB, Diary Paper, 31 July 1845: MS pp.1–3, in private hands, [*L&L*, ii, 52–3].

47. The myth of Emily's sympathy and secret support for a beleaguered Branwell relies on two principal sources: Emily's poem ' "Well, some may hate and some may scorn' which expresses pity for a man of 'ruined hopes' and 'blighted fame' who has died unlamented and the tradition that Emily used to put a lighted lamp in the parsonage window to guide the drunken Branwell home from the Black Bull. The poem belongs to 1839 (see above, p.317) and there is no contemporary source for the tradition which, if true, would have meant that Emily was encouraging Branwell's vices, a scenario which is inherently unlikely.

48. EJB, Diary Paper, 30 July 1845: MS pp.2–3, in private hands, [*L&L*, ii, 51]. I am grateful to William Self for a photocopy of this manuscript and permission to quote from it.

49. *Ibid.*, p.1, [*L&L*, ii, 49, omitting the phrase regarding Branwell]. Emily's apparent lack of concern about the situation is even more striking because in the original manuscript, which

may have been copied out from rough drafts, she transposed the first sentence of the next paragraph into her statement about Branwell. What she actually wrote was 'Branwell <went our first long Jo> left – July 1845.'

50. AB, Diary Paper, 31 July 1845: MS p.1, in private hands, [*L&L*, ii, 52].

51. Mildred Christian, 'Branwell Brontë and the Robinsons of Thorp Green': unpublished typescript, [*c*.1965], in Mildred Christian Papers, BPM; Du Maurier, pp.163–4.

52. ECG to George Smith, 2 Oct. 1856: [C&P, p.418].

53. CB to EN, 31 July 1845: MS Grolier E6 p.3, BPM, [*L&L*, ii, 43]. Charlotte wrote to Ellen's mother three days earlier, declining an invitation to Brookroyd but giving no hint of Branwell's affairs: CB to Mrs Nussey, 28 July 1845: MS BS 54.5, BPM, [*L&L*, ii, 41–2, wrongly dated to 23 July].

54. ECG, *Life*, pp.197, 194.

55. George Smith, 'Recollections': (Typescript) MS Acc 6713, Box 5, Item 4, p.105, NLS, quoted in Mildred Christian, 'Branwell Brontë and the Robinsons of Thorp Green', pp.20–2.

56. PBB to F. H. Grundy, Oct. 1845: MS n. l., [Grundy, pp.87–8]. Grundy's transcript is clearly inaccurate: he misreads 1845 as 1848, for example, and omits all the names. Mrs Robinson was the cousin of Sir George Trevelyan and Grundy may have accidentally transposed this to 'Lord'. The last two omissions indicated in the quoted text are Grundy's own and may well be crucial for they would seem to have contained further personal revelations about Mrs Robinson.

57. See, for example, Mildred Christian, 'Branwell Brontë and the Robinsons of Thorp Green', p.55. WG *PBB*, p.226 is a proponent of the idea that Branwell was living through his Northangerland persona.

58. Lord Houghton Commonplace Book, 1857–60, pp.338–9: MS at TC Cambridge.

59. CB to EN, 23 Jan. 1844: MS in Law Colln, photograph in Mildred Christian Papers, BPM, [*L&L*, ii, 3].

60. In his letter of January 1840 to John Brown, (see above, pp.323, 897 n.6) Branwell suggests that 'Beelzebub means to make a walking-stick of yours [prick]', which I take to mean he was implying that Brown was promiscuous.

61. ECG to George Smith, 29 Dec. 1856, [C&P, p.432].

62. Lydia Robinson eloped with Henry Roxby on 20 October 1845 and married him the same night at Gretna Green: Hibbs, p.16(k). For Elizabeth's breach of promise see Robinson Papers, BPM and for her and Mary's broken engagements see: CB to EN, 28 July 1848: MS Grolier E14 p.3, BPM, [*L&L*, ii, 239–40]. Though breaking an engagement might not seem a very important matter now it was then one of the most serious offences a young girl

could commit. The subject is one which crops up with great frequency in the novels of Anthony Trollope.

63. Jacob, the twin brother of Esau, was so named because he was born holding on to his brother's heel. The name therefore literally meant 'he takes by the heel' and came to mean 'the supplanter': Genesis, ch.25, v.26.

64. Lord Houghton Commonplace Book, 1857–60, p.339: MS at TC Cambridge.

65. Census Returns for Thorpe Underwoods, 1841: Microfilm, Harrogate; Hibbs, p.511(l). See MS 89, Robinson Papers, BPM; WG *PBB*, p.237; Mildred Christian, 'Branwell Brontë and the Robinsons of Thorp Green', pp.42–5.

66. *Ibid.*

67. Leyland, ii, 36; Census Returns for Great Ouseburn, 1841: Microfilm, Harrogate. A memorial to Dr Crosby in Great Ouseburn church is at odds with the role he later played as a go-between for Mrs Robinson; it suggests he too may have been duped by the lady. The memorial says: 'This tablet is erected by subscription in memory of the late John Crosby Esqr Surgeon Great Ouseburn who died December 1st 1859 aged 62 years. His universal kindness, professional ability, benevolent disposition & active usefulness, during a residence here of 30 years warmly endeared him to a large circle of friends who deeply lament his sudden removal.'

68. ECG, *Life*, p.188.

69. CB to EN, 13 Jan. 1845: MS HM 24436 p.4, Huntington, [*L&L*, ii, 25]; CB to Constantin Heger, 24 Oct. 1844: MS Add 38732B p.2, BL, [*L&L*, ii, 18]. Charlotte actually says 'mes soeurs se portent bien mais mon pauvre frère est toujours malade'.

70. WG *PBB*, p.233 claims 'no greater proof of his mental preoccupation at Thorp Green can be found than in the almost total cessation of creative writing which marked those years'. Flintoff, 'Some Unpublished Poems of Branwell Brontë', pp.241–52. This important article not only makes out an excellent case for there being a 'Thorp Green' notebook, but also partially reconstructs it.

71. PBB, 'Oer Grafton Hill the blue heaven smiled serene', [*c*.summer 1843/1844]: MS n.l., sold at Sotheby's Sale, 13 Dec. 1993, lot 40; photograph in HT43 (212), BPM, [VN *PBB*, p.261].

72. PBB, 'I saw a picture, yesterday,', [*c*.1843/1844]: MS in Brotherton, [VN *PBB*, p.262].

73. PBB to J. B. Leyland, [25 Nov. 1845]: MS p.1, Brotherton, [*L&L*, ii, 72].

74. *City of York Directory: 1843* (Hull, W. H. Smith, 1843), pp.84, 100, 115; Edmund Robinson, Cash Book, 1845: MS 93/2, Robinson Papers, BPM; see below, note 78 for evidence of Branwell's subscription to the library.

75. *Yorkshire Gazette*, 10 May 1845, p.7.

76. PBB, The Emigrant, 26 May 1845: MS BS 128, BPM, [VN *PBB*, p.263]; *Yorkshire Gazette*, 7 June 1845, p.7.

77. AB, Diary Paper, 31 July 1845: MS p.1, in private hands, [*L&L*, ii, 52].

78. PBB to Mr Bellerby, 3 June 1845: MS in private hands. The books were obviously intended for Branwell's own pleasure, not for teaching purposes, and they reveal that his tastes had changed little since his childhood. He requests any two volumes of the following works: Freycinet's *Voyage Autour du Monde*, *Blackwood's Magazine* for 1843 and 1844, the *Quarterly Review* and *Frazer's Magazine* for 1844, Brougham's *Sketches*, William Miller's *Biography* (*recte Memoirs*; Miller was a soldier in the Peninsular War), any one or two volumes of the *Annual Biography* from 1837 and Davy's *Ceylon*.

79. Edmund Robinson, Cash Book, 1845: MS 93/2, Robinson Papers, BPM; Hibbs, p.15(g); see below, note 82.

80. CB to EN, 13 June 1845: MS HM 24439, Huntington, [*L&L*, ii, 37–9]; CB to EN, 18 June 1845: MS HM 24440 p.1, Huntington, [*L&L*, ii, 39]; CB to EN, [*c*.27 June 1845]: MS Bon 168 p.2, BPM, [*L&L*, ii, 41, wrongly dated to 24 June 1845].

81. WG *PBB*, pp.239–40; Du Maurier, p.162. The actual date of Branwell's dismissal remains unclear though the weight of evidence points to 17 July 1845. According to his sisters' diary papers, Branwell went to Liverpool on Tuesday, 29 July: he claimed in his October letter to Grundy that on receiving his dismissal he had passed 'eleven continuous nights of sleepless horror' which 'reduced me to almost blindness' resulting in his going to Wales: this confirms the 17 July date. Only Charlotte's letter of 31 July to Ellen, saying that Branwell had received his dismissal 'last Thursday', i.e. 24 July, contradicts this: but Charlotte was clearly agitated when she wrote the letter and is likely to have reported the news as she heard it on her return without taking account of the week that had passed since then. I am grateful to Margaret Smith for her argument in favour of the 17 July date.

82. It should be pointed out that inclusion on a list does not mean that the visitor arrived on that date; the lists cover the visitors arriving and departing during the previous week and no specific dates are given for anyone. Both the *Scarborough Record* and the *Scarborough Herald* initially refer to the family as 'Rev E Robinson, Mrs Robinson and the Misses Robinson', implying that Edmund had been left behind. The *Herald* then apparently notes his arrival when it adds 'Master Robinson' to the list printed on 24 July. Neither the *Record* nor the other paper, the *Scarborough Gazette*, mentions Edmund by name at any time. All three papers give different and conflicting dates of arrival

for the various members of the Robinson party. According to the *Scarborough Record*, published on a Saturday, the 'Rev E Robinson Mrs & Misses Robinson' had arrived at their lodgings at No. 7A, The Cliff by 5 July; their listing remains unchanged each week, with no reference to Edmund, until 2 August when it becomes the 'Rev E Robinson & fam[ily]': *Scarborough Record*, 5 July 1845, p.4; 12 July 1845, p.4; 19 July 1845, p.4; 26 July 1845, p.4; 2 Aug. 1845, p.4; 9 Aug. 1845, p.4. The change seems to have been dictated by the constraints of column space rather than the arrival of a new member of the family. The *Scarborough Herald*, on the other hand, which was published on a Thursday, noted that Mrs Robinson senior (Mr Robinson's widowed mother) was staying at No. 2, The Cliff from 10 July but does not record the arrival of 'Robinson Rev E & Mrs Robinson 3 Misses' until 17 July, twelve days after the event. This is the only paper to note 'Master Robinson' separately but it begins to list him on 24 July, a week after the date given by Gérin and Du Maurier and a week before the *Record* altered its listing: *Scarborough Herald*, 10 July 1845, p.3; 17 July 1845, p.3; 24 July 1845, p.3; 31 July 1845, p.3; 7 Aug. 1845, p.3. Mrs Robinson senior stayed on another week as she is listed 14 Aug. 1845, p.3. The *Scarborough Gazette*, which, like the *Record*, was published on a Saturday, notes both the arrival of Mrs Robinson senior and 'Robinson Rev E Mrs & fam[ily]' in the list of 12 July and repeats this description each week until the family depart at the beginning of August: *Scarborough Gazette*, 12 July 1845, p.2; 19 July 1845, p.2; 26 July 1845, p.2; 2 Aug. 1845, p.2. This paper also notes Mrs Robinson senior stayed on another week (9 Aug. 1845, supplement) but, like the *Herald*, moves her from No. 2 to No. 3, The Cliff from 26 July.

83. Hibbs, p.15(g).

84. Edmund Robinson, Cash Book, 1845: MS 93/2, Robinson Papers, BPM, [5, 16 July 1845].

85. *Yorkshire Courant*, 10 July 1845, pp.7–8.

86. Mrs Rhodes pp. Mrs Taylor to J. A. Erskine Stuart, 5 March 1887: MS BS xi, 48 pp.1–2, BPM; George Smith, 'Recollections': (Typescript) MS Acc 6713, Box 5, Item 4, p.105, NLS, quoted in Mildred Christian, 'Branwell Brontë and the Robinsons of Thorp Green', pp.21–2. For the location of the boathouse see O.S. map of Scarborough, 1850.

87. George Whitehead notes that 'Robert Pottage left and finish'd all up at Thorp Green Feb. 13th 1846' followed almost immediately by 'Richard Bowser began gardening at Thorp Green February 16th'; later he notes 'Robert Pottage (Gardener) died July 10th 1849': Hibbs, 18(j), 18(l), 516(g). See also Edmund Robinson, Cash Book, 1845: MS 93/2, Robinson Papers, BPM, [5 July 1845]. The payment occurs after those for other servants.

88. PBB to F. H. Grundy, Oct. 1845: MS n.l.,

[Grundy, pp.87–8]. Branwell also said that one of Mr Robinson's executors had threatened to shoot him if he saw him: PBB to J. B. Leyland, [June 1846]: MS p.1, Brotherton, [*L&L*, ii, 95].

89. Edmund Robinson, Cash Book, 1845: MS 93/2, Robinson Papers, BPM.

90. Fraser, pp.231–3. This is the best weighing up of the evidence for and against the Branwell/Robinson affair on the evidence then available. Mrs Gaskell reports that Mrs Robinson also had a clandestine meeting in Harrogate with Branwell 'some months after' his dismissal. She offered to elope with him but a 'strange lingering of conscience' prevented him from doing so. Though one might suspect that this was simply a confusion with the story of the younger Lydia Robinson's elopement with Henry Roxby, Mr Robinson's cash book notes expenditure of two pounds on expenses at Harrogate on 3 September 1845: ECG, *Life*, p.195; Edmund Robinson, Cash Book, 1845: MS 93/2, Robinson Papers, BPM, [3 Sept. 1845].

91. CB to EN, 31 July 1845: MS Grolier E6 pp.3–4, BPM, [*L&L*, ii, 43].

92. Mrs Rhodes pp. Mrs Taylor to J. A. Erskine Stuart, 5 March 1887: MS BS xi, 48 p.2, BPM.

93. CB to EN, 31 July 1845: MS Grolier E6 p.4, BPM, [*L&L*, ii, 43].

94. There is a rough outline sketch of mountains, the largest of which is labelled 'PENMAENMAWR', across the top half of the page on which Branwell wrote his poem, 'Cannot my soul depart –', [c.29 July–3 Aug. 1845]: MS p.1, Brotherton, [VN *PBB*, pp.275–6]. Mountains are also sketched in outline across PBB, 'Penmaenmawr', [Nov. 1845]: MS pp.2–3, Brotherton, [VN *PBB*, pp.276–8]; a revised version was published in the *Halifax Guardian*, 20 Dec. 1845, p.6. A three-day pleasure excursion to Liverpool organized by the Bradford Tea-Totallers' Association in September 1845 attracted 1,400 trippers: *Bradford Observer*, 28 Aug. 1845, p.5; 11 Sept. 1845, p.5; *Halifax Guardian*, 13 Sept. 1845, p.5.

95. PBB, 'Cannot my soul depart –', [c.29 July–3 Aug. 1845]: MS in Brotherton, [VN *PBB*, pp.275–6]. There is an indecipherable cancelled line between ll.21 and 22. Lydia Gisborne was, of course, Mrs Robinson's maiden name. The poem is written on a page which Flintoff identifies as being from the missing Thorp Green notebook: Flintoff, 'Some Unpublished Poems of Branwell Brontë', pp.241, 244–5.

96. PBB to J. B. Leyland, 4 Aug. 1845: MS p.1, Brotherton, [*L&L*, ii, 57].

97. PB to ECG, 2 April 1857: MS EL fB91 p.3, Rylands, [*BST*:8:44:126–7]. Patrick regarded Mrs Gaskell's picture of Mrs Robinson in her *Life* as a masterpiece.

98. Grundy, p.90; EJB, Diary Paper, 30 July 1845: MS p.2, in private hands, [*L&L*, ii, 50–1].

99. CB to EN, 31 Dec. 1845: MS n.l., [*L&L*, ii, 74].

For Joseph Nussey's alcoholism see Whitehead, pp.102, 106, 122–3, 127.

100. CB to EN, 8 Sept. [1845]: MS BS 55 pp.1–2, BPM, [*L&L*, ii, 60]; CB to EN, 23 Jan. [1846]: MS HM 24442 p.4, Huntington, [*L&L*, ii, 75].

101. CB to MW, 30 Jan. 1846: MS FM 2 p.3, Fitzwilliam, [*L&L*, ii, 76–7].

102. AB, Diary Paper, 31 July 1845: MS p.2, in private hands, [*L&L*, ii, 52].

103. CB to Constantin Heger, 18 Nov. 1845: MS Add 38732C pp.1–2, BL, [*L&L*, ii, 67]. 'Je vous dirai franchement, qu'en attendant, j'ai tâché de vous oublier, car le souvenir d'une personne que l'on croit ne devoir plus revoir et que, pourtant, on estime beaucoup, harasse trop l'esprit et quand on a subi cette espèce d'inquiétude pendant un ou deux ans, on est prêt à tout faire pour retrouver le repos. J'ai tout fait, j'ai cherché les occupations, je me suis interdit absolument le plaisir de parler de vous – même à Emilie mais je n'ai pu vaincre ni mes regrets ni mon impatience – c'est humiliant cela – de ne pas savoir maîtriser ses propres pensées, être esclave à un regret, un souvenir, esclave à une idée dominante et fixe qui tyrannise son esprit.'

104. *Leeds Intelligencer*, 11 Oct. 1845, 2nd supplement, p.4; PBB to Manchester & Hebden Bridge & Keighley & Carlisle Junction Railway, [c. Oct. 1845]: MS BS 139, BPM.

105. CB to EN, [4 Nov. 1845]: MS p.2, Berg, [*L&L*, ii, 65–6].

106. PBB to F. H. Grundy, [June 1846]: MS n.l., [Grundy, p.89]; PBB to J. B. Leyland, 4 Aug. 1845: MS p.1, Brotherton, [*L&L*, ii, 57]; PBB to J. B. Leyland, 19 Aug. 1845: MS p.1, Brotherton, [*L&L*, ii, 58–9]; *Halifax Guardian*, 23 Aug. 1845, p.5.

107. *Halifax Guardian*, 8 Nov. 1845, p.6.

108. PBB to J. B. Leyland, [25 Nov. 1845]: MS pp.1–2, Brotherton, [*L&L*, ii, 72].

109. *Halifax Guardian*, 20 Dec. 1845, p.6.

110. *Ibid*.

111. PBB to J. B. Leyland, [Aug.–Sept. 1845]: MS p.1, Brotherton, [*L&L*, ii, 137]. The letter is undated and not postmarked but is usually ascribed to July 1847; in terms of handwriting and signature ('P. B. Brontë'), however, an 1845 date seems more likely. In a letter of 10 September, Branwell urges Leyland to 'never mind the lines I put into your hands' which would tie in with the contents of this letter: PBB to J. B. Leyland, 10 Sept. [1845]: MS p.1, Brotherton, [*L&L*, ii, 60]. Both letters contain sketches; the first of a cross with 'POBRE!' written upon it and Branwell's note 'The best Epitaph ever written – It is <writt> carved on a rude cross, in Spain, over a murdered traveller – and simply means "Poor Fellow!" '; the second of two pugilists, 'Bendigo' (William Thompson) and Benjamin Caunt, labelled 'Bendigo 'taking a sight'. "Alas! Poor Caunt!" '

112. PBB to J. B. Leyland, 10 Sept. [1845]: MS pp.1–2, Brotherton, [*L&L*, ii, 60].

113. PBB, 'Among all the descriptions I have read', 30 Dec. 1837: MS Bon 149(7) p.5, BPM.

114. PBB, And the Weary are at Rest, [Aug.–Sept.

1845]: MS p.65, Princeton, [*And the Weary are at Rest* (Privately printed, 1924), p.59].

115. *Ibid.*, pp.80–1.

CHAPTER SEVENTEEN

Title: [EJB], CB to WSW, [Sept. 1848]: MS Ashley 164 p.5, BL, [*L&L*ii,256]

1. CB, *Biographical Notice*, pp.359–60.
2. *Ibid.*, p.360.
3. Though Charlotte enjoyed anonymity when she was writing, she also craved the public recognition which allowed her to move in literary circles: this is suggested by the fact that she allowed her true identity to become known immediately after the deaths of Emily and Anne.
4. CB, *Biographical Notice*, pp.359–60.
5. For Miss Currer's local philanthropy see, for instance, *Leeds Intelligencer*, 4 Dec. 1824, p.1; *Leeds Mercury*, 21 July 1838, p.7; *Bradford Observer*, 15 July 1847, p.8. PBB, THE LIFE OF WARNER HOWARD WARNER ESQR, Feb. 1838: MS Bon 152, p.2, BPM. For the Ellis family see, for instance, the account of the celebrations among his workpeople for the marriage of William Ellis junior: *Leeds Mercury*, 5 July 1845 (supp.), p.9. For Ellis Cunliffe Lister-Kay's obituary see *ibid.*, 26 Nov. 1853, p.5; *Bradford Observer*, 1 Dec. 1853, p.5. The words 'ACTON' and 'OUSEBURN', written by Branwell in capital letters, occur on a page from his missing Thorp Green notebook: PBB, 'Penmaenmawr', [Nov. 1845]: MS p.2, Brotherton. For the new bells see *Bradford Observer*, 6 Nov. 1845, p.8.
6. The three Charlotte poems for which there are no extant manuscripts are 'Preference', 'Gilbert' and 'The Missionary', the last two possibly dating from as recently as her trip to Hathersage in the summer of 1845.
7. CB to Miss Alexander, 18 March 1850: MS p.3, Brotherton, [*L&L*, iii, 86]. See also CB to WSW, [Sept. 1848]: MS Ashley 164 pp.4–5, BL, [*L&L*, ii, 256].
8. CB to ECG, 26 Sept. 1850: MS MA 2696 R-V pp.2–3, Pierpont Morgan, [*L&L*, iii, 162].
9. AB, Self Congratulation, based on the MS '"Maiden, thou wert thoughtless once', 1 Jan. 1840: MS MA 2696 R-V pp.23–6, Pierpont Morgan, [Chitham, pp.71–2.] Anne contributed the following poems: (dates are the dates of MS composition and where the MS is undated but attributed to a year, the title is marked with an asterisk). 1840: 'Appeal' & 'Self-Congratulation'; 1842: 'To Cowper' & 'Lines composed in a Wood on a Windy Day'; 1843: 'Music on Christmas Morning',* 'The Doubter's Prayer', 'A Word to the Elect', 'Past Days', 'The Consolation' & 'The Captive Dove'; 1844: 'A Reminiscence', 'Home',* 'The Student's Serenade' & 'Fluctuations'; 1845: 'The Arbour',* 'Vanitas Vanitatum, Omnia Van-

itas', 'The Penitent', 'Stanzas', 'If this be all', 'Memory' & 'Views of Life'.

10. Emily contributed the following: (dates are the dates of MS composition and where the MS is undated but attributed to a year, the title is marked with an asterisk). 1839 'Sympathy'* & 'Stanzas to —'; 1840: 'Stanzas'; 1841: 'The Old Stoic'; 1842/3: 'Self-Interrogation'; 1843: 'Hope' & 'How clear she shines'; 1844: 'Faith and Despondency', 'A Death Scene', 'Song', 'A Day-Dream', 'To Imagination', 'Plead for Me', 'Honour's Martyr' & 'My Comforter'; 1845: 'Stars', 'The Philosopher', 'Remembrance', 'Anticipation', 'The Prisoner' & 'Death'.

Six poems, 'Faith and Despondency', 'Remembrance', 'A Death-Scene', 'Song', 'The Prisoner' and 'Honour's Martyr', were taken from EJB, notebook titled Gondal Poems, transcribed Feb.1844: MS Add 43483, pp.45, 47–8, 49–50, 51–2, 52–3, 59–62, BL. The remaining fifteen were taken from EJB, untitled notebook, transcribed Feb.1844: MS in Law Colln, [facsimile in *Poems of EJB & AB*, pp.309, 310, 313, 314, 316–17, 318, 318–19, 319–20, 321–3, 323, 324, 324–6, 326–7, 327, 328].

11. CB to WSW, [Sept. 1848]: MS Ashley 164 p.5, BL, [*L&L*, ii, 256].

12. EJB, 'Cold in the earth – and the deep snow piled above thee!', 3 March 1845: MS Add 43483 pp.52–3, BL; EJB, Remembrance, *Poems*, (1846), pp.31–2.

13. EJB, The Prisoner, *Poems*, (1846), pp.76–9; EJB, Julian M— and A.G. Rochelle ['Silent is the House – all are laid asleep'], 9 Oct. 1845: MS Add 43483 pp.60–1, BL. The published version is composed of lines 13–44 and lines 65–92 of the manuscript: see JB *SP*, pp.131–2 for a discussion of this and another extract from the same poem published by Charlotte in 1850 under the title 'The Visionary'.

14. See *ibid.*, pp.116, 128–9, 131–2.

15. EJB, 'Enough of Thought, Philosopher,', 3 Feb. 1845: MS in Law Colln, [facsimile in *Poems of EJB & AB*, pp.325–6]; EJB, The Philosopher, *Poems* (1846), p.25. The text quoted is the printed version; when Emily transcribed the poem she apparently cancelled the last four lines and substituted those used in the 1846 edition.

16. The last dated lines which have been preserved are EJB, 'Why ask to know what date what clime', 13 May 1848: MS Add 43483 p.68, BL, [Hatfield, pp.252–3].

17. EJB, 'No coward soul is mine', 25 Jan. 1846: MS in Law Colln, [facsimile in *Poems of EJB & AB*, p.329; Hatfield, pp.243–4].

18. The exact date of the poem is difficult to read; it may be 'Jan 25' or possibly 'Jan 23' but it is

certainly not 'Jan 2' as in Hatfield's reading. The poem was probably begun in December as the initial letter of 'Jan' has been written over a capital 'D'. Two versions of 'Why ask to know what date what clime', dated 14 Sept. 1846 and 13 May 1848, were written into the 'Gondal Poems' notebook [MS Add 43483 pp.62–8, BL], but these would appear to have been working drafts rather than fair copies of completed poems.

19. CB to WSW, [Sept. 1848]: MS Ashley 164, pp.5–6, BL, [*L&L*, ii, 256].

20. CB, *Biographical Notice*, p.360; Chambers' could find no record of their correspondence with Charlotte when Mrs Gaskell wrote to them ten years later: ECG, *Life*, p.199.

21. CB to Aylott & Jones, 28 Jan. 1846: MS Bon 169 p.1, BPM, [*L&L*, ii, 81].

22. CB to Aylott & Jones, 31 Jan. 1846: MS Bon 170 pp.1–2, BPM, [*L&L*, ii, 81–2]; CB to Aylott & Jones, 6 Feb. 1846: MS Bon 171 p.1, BPM, [*L&L*, ii, 82]. For the further enquiries about its safe arrival see CB to Aylott & Jones, 15 Feb. 1846: MS Bon 172 p.1, BPM, [*L&L*, ii, 82]; CB to Aylott & Jones, 16 Feb. 1846: MS Bon 173 p.3, BPM, [*L&L*, ii, 83].

23. *Ibid.*, pp.1–3; CB to Aylott & Jones, 21 Feb. 1846: MS at Princeton; CB to Aylott & Jones, 3 March 1846: MS Bon 174 p.1, BPM, [*L&L*, ii, 83].

24. CB to EN, 13 Feb. 1846: MS n.l., [*L&L*, ii, 78]. The decision to go must have been taken suddenly because on 30 January she had written to Miss Wooler saying that she had not visited Ellen for more than a year and implying she had no plans to do so: CB to MW, 30 Jan. 1846: MS FM 2, Fitzwilliam, [*L&L*, ii, 76]. The fact that a day after she wrote this letter she heard that Aylott & Jones had accepted *Poems* for publication may have made her change her mind.

25. EJB to EN, 25 Feb. 1846: MS bms Eng 870 (98) p.1, Harvard, [*L&L*, ii, 78].

26. CB to [Eliza Kingston], [6 Feb. 1846: should be 3 March 1846]: MS BS 56 p.2, BPM, [*BST*:12:64:300]. The date of this letter is clearly wrong. Charlotte intended to reply to her cousin on 6 February, dating the letter appropriately, but then delayed writing until after her return from Brookroyd on 2 March: CB to EN, 3 March 1846: MS Bon 175 pp.2–3, BPM, [*L&L*, ii, 84]. I am grateful to Margaret Smith for confirming the redating of this letter.

27. CB to EN, 3 March 1846: MS Bon 175 pp.3–4, BPM, [*L&L*, ii, 84]; PBB, notice of a shooting match, 2 March 1846: MS BS 148, BPM. As Branwell was presumably one of the nine subscribers who put up five shillings each, he must have used part of his father's sovereign for this purpose.

28. CB to Aylott & Jones, 11 March 1846: MS Bon 176 p.1, BPM, [*L&L*, ii, 84]; CB to Aylott & Jones, 13 March 1846: MS Bon 177 p.1, BPM, [*L&L*, ii, 85].

29. CB to Aylott & Jones, 6 Feb. 1846: MS Bon 171 p.1, BPM, [*L&L*, ii, 82].

30. CB to Aylott & Jones, 28 March 1846: MS Bon 178 p.1, BPM, [*L&L*, ii, 85].

31. See, for example, CB to Mr Rand, 22 Jan. 1846: MS at Knox. Charlotte explains at the beginning of the letter, 'Papa's sight is still very bad – and consequently he wishes me to answer your last letter in his stead.' She records his interpolations throughout the letter.

32. CB to WSW, 2 Oct. 1848: MS MA 2696 R-V p.3, Pierpont Morgan, [*L&L*, ii, 262]; January Searle, 'Branwell Brontë', *The Mirror*, 28 Dec. 1872, pp.278–9. There are a number of anomalies in this piece, not least that Branwell supposedly told the author that the number of visitors to Haworth had increased dramatically since the publication of *Jane Eyre* even though Charlotte's identity as its author did not become known till 1849, after Branwell's death; William Oakendale [Dearden] to *Halifax Guardian*, 15 June 1867, p.7.

33. CB to Aylott & Jones, 7 May 1846: MS Bon 183 p.3, BPM, [*L&L*, ii, 93].

34. See, for example, CB to WSW, 15 Dec. 1847: MS Bon 195 p.1, BPM, [*L&L*, ii, 162].

35. CB to Aylott & Jones, 11 April 1846: MS Bon 180 pp.1–2, BPM, [*L&L*, ii, 87–8].

36. PBB to J. B. Leyland, [28 April 1846]: MS pp.2–4, Brotherton, [*L&L*, ii, 91–2].

37. CB to WSW, 2 Oct. 1848: MS MA 2696 R-V p.3, Pierpont Morgan, [*L&L*, ii, 262].

38. PBB to John Frobisher, [March 1846] and 21 March 1846: MSS in WYAS, Calderdale, [*BST*:12:65:410]; PBB to John Frobisher, 21 March 1846: MS in WYAS, Calderdale, [*BST*:12:65:410]; JB *SP*, pp.17–18, 107.

39. PBB to J. B. Leyland, [28 April 1846]: MS p.2, Brotherton, [*L&L*, ii, 91]. Branwell refers to his 'prosecuting enquiries about situations suitable to me whereby I could have a voyage abroad' in this letter; PBB, endorsement of bill for 2/6d. for an advertisement in the *Halifax Guardian*, 9 April 1846: MS BS 149, BPM.

40. *Halifax Guardian*, 18 April 1846, p.6, [VN *PBB*, p.280]. Leyland, ii, 128 says that the manuscript was dated 3 April 1846.

41. *Ibid.*

42. Leyland, ii, 111, 132, 242–9. Leyland had already produced a bust of Branwell the previous summer: see PB to J. B. Leyland, [25 Nov 1845]: MS pp.2–3, Brotherton, [*L&L*, ii, 73]; Leyland, ii, 85. For references to the medallion see, for example, PBB to J. B. Leyland, [28 April 1846]: MS p.2, Brotherton, [*L&L*, ii, 91]. In October 1846 Branwell drew a sketch of it and wrote 'Is the medallion cracked that Thorwaldsen executed of AUGUSTUS CAESAR?', the last name being written round the sketch in the manner of a Roman coin. Bertel Thorwaldsen (1768–1844) was a Danish sculptor, specializing in statues and bas-reliefs of classical mythology, who is regarded as the leader of the classical revival: PBB to J. B. Leyland, [Oct. 1846]: MS p.2, Brotherton, [*L&L*, ii, 113]. The medallion itself is now in the dining room of the BPM.

The incomplete manuscript of 'Morley Hall' is MS BS 134, BPM which is printed in Leyland, ii, 246–9, but this short text of only ninety lines does not square with Branwell's own reference in October 1846 to Morley Hall being 'in the eighth month of her pregnancy and expects ere long to be delivered of a fine thumping boy': PBB to J.B.Leyland, [Oct. 1846]: MS pp.1–2, Brotherton, [*L&L*, ii, 113]. Another, longer manuscript may be missing.

43. CB to Aylott & Jones, 7 May 1846: MS Bon 183 p.3, BPM, [*L&L*, ii, 93]; Two first editions of *Poems* are in the BPM: MS Bon 294 & HAOBP:bb235, BPM.

44. I have been unable to locate Charlotte's copy. The collector, William Law, writing to the Honorary Secretary of the Brontë Society, claimed ownership of Anne's copy inscribed 'A Brontë May 7th 1846' and Emily's copy: William Law to Butler Wood, 9 March 1895: MS DB28/21, WYAS, Bradford. A copy, said to be Emily's and inscribed with her name and the same date, is item X821.B78.1848, Illinois. As the title page bears the Smith, Elder & Co. imprint, however, this is clearly not the rare 1846 edition but that of 1848, suggesting that the signature is a forgery. The manual emendations to the text and the insertion of dates of composition are not an indication that the book even belonged to a Brontë as the emendations are those proposed in the printed list of errata published with the book and the dates were available after Clement Shorter's editions of the poems were published in 1923. The intriguing possibility arises that the book may be a forgery by the notorious T.J.Wise, who worked closely with Shorter and forged other rare first editions. CB to Aylott & Jones, 7 May 1846: MS Bon 183 p.1, BPM, [*L&L*, ii, 93]. The ten recipients of review copies were *Colburn's New Monthly* [*Athenaeum*], *Bentley's Miscellany* [*Literary Gazette*], *Hood's Magazine* [*Critic*], *Jerrold's Shilling Magazine* [*Times*], *Blackwood's Magazine*, *The Edinburgh Review*, *Tait's Edinburgh Magazine*, *The Dublin University Magazine*, *Daily News* and *Britannia Newspaper*. The names in brackets were added in another hand, possibly by someone at the publisher's, after Charlotte's titles.

45. CB to Aylott & Jones, 11 May 1846: MS Bon 184 pp.1–2, BPM, [*L&L*, ii, 93]; CB to Aylott & Jones, 25 May 1846: MS Bon 185 pp.1–2, BPM, [*L&L*, ii, 94].

46. *Yorkshire Gazette*, 30 May 1846, p.5.

47. PBB, Lydia Gisborne, 1 June 1846: MS BS 128.5, BPM, [Flintoff, 'Some unpublished poems of Branwell Brontë', p.248]. Flintoff points out that the poem is written on a leaf from the missing Thorp Green notebook. Branwell also wrote 'Lydia' in Greek letters and drew a tombstone in the margin of his poem 'Juan Fernandez', which is usually dated to Jan. 1847, though it may have been written the previous

summer: PBB, Juan Fernandez, n.d.: MS Bon 154, BPM, [VN *PBB*, pp.288–90].

48. PBB to J.B.Leyland, [24 Jan. 1847]: MS p.1, Brotherton, [*L&L*, ii, 123].

49. CB to EN, 17 June 1846: MS Grolier E11 pp.1–2, BPM, [*BST*:17:90:356–7].

50. Release from the executors of the will of the Revd Edmund Robinson to his son Edmund Robinson, reciting the will of 2 Jan. 1846, 14 Jan. 1853: MS 30, Robinson Papers, BPM.

51. See, for instance, Du Maurier, pp.188–91; Joan Rees, *Profligate Son*, pp.132–3.

52. Edmund Robinson, Cash Book, 1845: MS 93/2, Robinson Papers, BPM. Mrs Robinson and Mr Robinson on her behalf spent £30 11s. at Scarborough between 5 July and 7 August 1845.

53. WG *PBB*, pp.262–4 confuses references in Branwell's letters to the coachman and George Gooch, the latter being a railway acquaintance who had been employed as an engineer on the construction of the Summit Tunnel: *Halifax Guardian*, 6 March 1841, p.3. In 1847 Gooch and Grundy were both working near Haworth on the Bradford to Keighley line, so Branwell was in contact with them both: *ibid.*, 6 March 1847, p.4. The Thorp Green coachman, as is clear from the Robinson cash book, was William Allison.

54. Hibbs, 25(b), 26(k). William Allison left and went to live with Sir Edward Scott, Mrs Robinson's second husband, in February 1847, having been at Thorp Green for four years. He returned on 14 April to fetch his family so the arrangement was clearly to be made permanent.

55. ECG, *Life*, p.197.

56. PBB to J.B.Leyland, [June 1846]: MS pp.1–2, Brotherton, [*L&L*, ii, 95].

57. PBB to J.B.Leyland, [June 1846]: MS pp.1–2, Brotherton, [*L&L*, ii, 98].

58. *Ibid.*, p.2.

59. PBB to J.B.Leyland, [June 1846]: MS p.2, Brotherton, [*L&L*, ii, 96]. A sketch accompanying this letter depicted a martyr tied to the stake in the middle of the fire and titled 'Myself' in Branwell's hand.

60. CB to EN, [17 June 1846]: MS Grolier E11 p.2, BPM, [*L&L*, ii, 96–7]; CB to EN, 14 April [1846]: MS HM 24444 p.4, Huntington, [*L&L*, ii, 88–9].

61. PBB to F.H.Grundy, [June 1846]: MS n.l., [Grundy, p.89].

62. Anonymous Review in *Critic*, 4 July 1846, [JB *SP*, p.148].

63. *Ibid.*, p.148.

64. Anonymous Review in *Athenaeum*, 4 July 1846, [JB *SP*, pp.147–8].

65. Anonymous Review in *Critic*, 4 July 1846, [JB *SP*, pp.148–9].

66. CB to WSW, 9 Oct. 1847: MS p.2, Brotherton, [*L&L*, ii, 148]; CB to Aylott & Jones, 10 July 1846: MS Bon 186 pp.1–2, BPM, [*L&L*, ii, 102]. The other journals to receive copies of *Poems* were *Frazer's Magazine*, *Chambers' Edinburgh*

Journal, the *Globe* and the *Examiner*. Aylott & Jones advised against further expenditure on advertisements as the season was 'unfavourable': CB to Aylott & Jones, 18 July 1846: MS Bon 188 p.1, BPM, [*L&L*, ii, 103].

67. *Halifax Guardian*, 10 Oct. 1846, p.6.

68. Anonymous Review in *Dublin University Magazine*, Oct. 1846, [JB *SP*, p.150].

69. CB to the Editor of the *Dublin University Magazine*, 6 Oct. 1846: MS Bon 190 pp.1–2, BPM, [*L&L*, ii, 112].

70. CB to J. G. Lockhart, 16 June 1847: in HAOBP:bb235, BPM.

71. L&L, ii, 136. Ebenezer Elliott's copy of the book, though not the accompanying letter, is MS Bon 294, BPM. Elliott (1781–1849) was a Sheffield master founder and a lyric poet, though he was best known as the 'Corn-Law Rhymer' for his advocacy of a repeal of the Corn Laws.

72. CB to Aylott & Jones, 23 July 1846: MS BS 104/15, BPM, [*L&L*, ii, 103–4].

73. CB, *Biographical Notice*, p.361.

74. PBB to J. B. Leyland, 10 Sept. [1846]: MS p.2, Brotherton, [*L&L*, ii, 61].

75. CB to Aylott & Jones, 6 April 1846: MS Bon 179 p.1, BPM, [*L&L*, ii, 87]; CB, *The Professor*, 27 June 1846: MS in Pierpont Morgan, [CB, *The Professor*, p.xxviii]; CB to Henry Colburn, 4 July 1846: MS divided, p.1 at Princeton, p.2 in Pennsylvania.

76. [Martha Brown] ECG to John Forster, [Sept. 1853], [C&P, p.247]; ECG, *Life*, p.215.

77. CB, Preface to *The Professor*, [1850]: MS MA 32, Pierpont Morgan, [CB, *The Professor*, p.1]. Charlotte had expressed a similar idea as early as 1833, in her story 'Brushwood Hall': 'But let me resume my narrative – I must remember that an English merchant is its hero and <hereafter> henceforth rigorously reject everything allied to the sentimental': CB, Arthuriana, 20 Nov. 1833: MS MA 29 p.4, Pierpont Morgan, [*CA*, ii, 218].

78. See above, p.203–4, 206.

79. Walter Scott's *Rob Roy* was first published in 1817 and was clearly a Brontë favourite. See above, pp.273–4.

80. PBB, THE POLITICS OF VERDOPOLIS, Oct.–Nov. 1833: MS Bon 141 p.15, BPM. For a discussion of Gondal poetry anticipatory of *Wuthering Heights* see JB *SP*, pp.117, 120, 122–8.

81. PBB, The Life of feild Marshal the Right Honourable ALEXAN[D]ER PERCY, [Spring 1834]: MS in Brotherton, [Collins, pp.23–4, 34–6]; CB, The Foundling, 31 May–27 June 1833: MS Ashley 159 p.6, BL, [*CA*, ii, 87–8].

82. For examples, see JB *SP*, pp.117, 120, 122–8.

83. CB, Editor's Preface to the New Edition of *Wuthering Heights*, 1850: MS n.l., [EJB, *Wuthering Heights*, pp.365, 366].

84. AB, *Agnes Grey*, p.1.

85. ECG, *Life*, p.215, quoting Harriet Martineau's obituary of Charlotte in the *Daily News*, 1 April 1855.

86. AB, *Agnes Grey*, p.138.

87. CB, *Biographical Notice*, p.361.

88. This was argued by Tom Winnifrith in 'Wuthering Heights: One Volume or Two', in Chitham and Winnifrith, *Brontë Facts and Brontë Problems*, pp.84–90.

89. ECG, *Life*, pp.209–10. The Parish Registers confirm that Arthur Bell Nicholls effectively took all the duties throughout this year.

90. CB to EN, 10 July 1846: MS Gr.E10 pp.2–3, BPM, [*L&L*, ii, 101].

91. *Bradford Observer*, 16 Jan. 1846, p.8; *Leeds Mercury*, 17 Jan. 1846, p.9. The *Bradford Observer*, 19 Feb. 1846, p.8 announced the appointment of William Crowther, second son of the Reverend Thomas Crowther of Cragg Vale, but he declined to accept it and, on 2 March, James Cranmer was appointed in his stead. He was sacked in 1848 for neglecting 'to attend properly to the school': Minutes of the Trustees of Haworth Free Grammar School, 1838–63: MS in Keighley [9 Feb., 2 March 1846, 10 March 1848]. I am grateful to Sarah Fermi for this reference.

92. *Leeds Intelligencer*, 6 June 1846, p.7. The Ancient Order of Foresters held their thirteenth annual meeting on Whit Tuesday at the Wesleyan Chapel but were addressed by one of their own number. For the opening of the school see *Bradford Observer*, 25 June 1846, p.5. The Revd J. B. Grant wrote a furious letter to the *Leeds Mercury* denouncing the ceremony which was held during his absence from the parish for a few days and without his prior knowledge. The Revd Thomas B. Charnock, son of the former minister of Haworth, attracted his particular opprobrium because he had officiated at the ceremony and, probably more significantly, because he was credited with originating the scheme. In fact, as Grant pointed out, Charnock had worked with Patrick Brontë and William Weightman as long ago as 1841 to obtain grants for a school in Oxenhope but these had lapsed when the requisite local fund had failed to attract subscribers. 'With the present school he has had nothing to do except as a subscriber, the originators of it being Mr George Feather, Mr John Sutcliffe, and myself', Grant pompously claimed. *Leeds Mercury*, 4 July 1846, p.12. The letter is excellent first-hand evidence for the accuracy of Charlotte's portrayal of Grant as Joseph Donne in *Shirley* who was unsurpassed in the art of begging for his little school, church and parsonage, all of which owed their erection to his ability in this field: CB, *Shirley*, pp.633–4.

93. *Bradford Observer*, 2 April 1846, p.8.

94. *Ibid.*, 23 July 1846, p.5; *Leeds Intelligencer*, 25 July 1846, p.7; Haworth Church Hymn Sheet, 19 July 1846: MS BS x, H, BPM; *Bradford Observer*, 23 July 1846, p.5.

95. *Leeds Intelligencer*, 25 July 1846, p.7; 8 Aug. 1846, p.7.

96. CB to MW, [Nov. 1846]: MS FM 3 p.1, Fitzwilliam, [*L&L*, ii, 116]; CB to EN, 9 Aug. 1846:

MS HM 24445 p.2, Huntington, [*L&L*, ii, 105].

97. E. Mansfield Brockbank, *Sketches of the Lives and Work of the Honorary Medical Staff of the Manchester Infirmary* (Manchester, MUP, 1904), pp.269–71.

98. Slater, *General and Classified Directory and Street Register of Manchester and Salford*, p.55; CB to EN, 9 Aug. 1846: MS HM 24445 pp.2–3, Huntington, [*L&L*, ii, 105–6]. Charlotte says she found 'a Mr Wilson' to act as surgeon, suggesting she did not know of his reputation before she went to Manchester. Oddly enough, Mr Wilson had featured as a surgeon to the Infirmary in an article, 'A Week at Manchester', in *Blackwood's Magazine*, xlv, 1839, pp.490–1.

99. CB to EN, 21 Aug. 1846: MS HM 24496 pp.1–2, Huntington, [*L&L*, ii, 106–7]; ECG, *Life*, p.210. The landlady seems to have been absent for some considerable time; according to the local directories, John Robinson, a book-keeper, was

living there in 1845 and Thomas Bell, an 'agent', in 1847: Slater, *General and Classified Directory and Street Register of Manchester and Salford*, p.9, and *ibid.*, 1845 (Street Directory), p.10.

100. CB to EN, 26 Aug. [1846]: MS HM 24447 p.1, Huntington, [*L&L*, ii, 108].

101. Patrick Brontë's annotated copy of Thomas John Graham, *Modern Domestic Medicine*, (London, 1826): MS HAOBP:bb210 p.226, BPM.

102. CB to EN, 26 Aug. [1846]: MS HM 24447 p.1, Huntington, [*L&L*, ii, 108].

103. Graham, *Modern Domestic Medicine*. MS HAOBP:bb210 pp.226–7, BPM.

104. CB to EN, 26 Aug. [1846]: MS HM 24447 p.2, Huntington, [*L&L*, ii, 108]; CB to EN, 31 Aug. 1846: MS in Beinecke, [*L&L*, ii, 109]. See also CB to EN, 24 July 1846: MS p.1, Rosenbach, [*L&L*, ii, 109].

CHAPTER EIGHTEEN

Title: CB to Henry Colburn, 4 July 1846: MS p.1, Princeton.

1. CB to WSW, 28 Oct. 1847: MS MA 2696 R-V p.2, Pierpont Morgan, [*L&L*, ii, 150].

2. CB, *Jane Eyre*, pp.255–6.

3. CB to EN, [13 Sept. 1846]: MS Bon 189 p.2, BPM, [*L&L*, ii, 110].

4. [HM], Obituary of Charlotte Brontë in the *Daily News*, 6 April 1855, [Allott, p.303].

5. CB to EN, 31 Aug. 1846: MS at Yale, [*L&L*, ii, 109]; CB to EN, [13 Sept. 1846]: MS Bon 189 p.1, BPM, [*L&L*, ii, 109]; CB to EN, [22 Sept. 1846]: MS HM 24446 pp.1–2, Huntington, [*L&L*, ii, 110]; CB to EN, 26 Aug. 1846: MS HM 24447 p.2, Huntington, [*L&L*, ii, 108].

6. CB to EN, [29 Sept. 1846]: MS BS 57 p.1, BPM, [*L&L*, ii, 111]; PB marginal notes in his copy of Thomas John Graham, *Modern Domestic Medicine*. MS HAOBP: bb210 38, pp.226–8, BPM, [JB *ST* no.42].

7. CB to EN, [17 Nov. 1846]: MS Gr.E12 p.2, BPM, [*BST*:17:90:358]; Nicholls' absence and Patrick's activity are confirmed by the entries in the Baptismal and Burial Registers of Haworth Church; Patrick received occasional help from J. B. Grant of Oxenhope and Philip Eggleston, curate of Keighley.

8. [HM], Obituary of Charlotte Brontë in the *Daily News*, 6 April 1855, [Allott, p.303–4].

9. CB, Preface to *The Professor*, [*c.*1850]: MS MA 32, Pierpont Morgan, [CB, *The Professor*, p.2].

10. George A. Wade, 'Charlotte Brontë as I knew her: a chat with the Rev J C Bradley', *Great Thoughts*, 17 Oct. 1908, pp.278–9: copy in typescript in C.K.S. Colln, Brotherton. Bradley identified the house as belonging to the Greenwoods, suggesting it was Spring Head he had in mind. Ellen Nussey claimed that the story was inspired by rumours of a ghostly lady stalking

the attics of Roe Head, [EN, Reminiscences, *BST*:2:10:68–9] and there is still an attic room in the upper storey of Norton Conyers, near Ripon, which Charlotte may have visited while a governess with the Sidgwicks, which is said to have suggested the mad woman's cell. CB to EN, [17 Nov. 1846]: MS Gr.E12 pp.2–3, BPM, [*BST*:17:90:358].

11. AB, Mirth and Mourning, 15 July 1846: MS HM 2576 pp.8–11, Huntington, [Chitham, pp.130–1]; AB, 'Weep not too much my darling;', 28 July 1846: *ibid.*, pp.11–14, [Chitham, pp.132–3]; AB, The Power of Love, 13 Aug. 1846: MS Bon 135 pp.3–7, BPM, [Chitham, pp.134–5]; AB, 'I dreamt last night; and in that <nig> dream', 14 Sept. 1846: *ibid.*, pp.7–16, [Chitham, pp.136–40]; AB, 'Gloomily the clouds are sailing', 6 Oct. 1846: MS Bon 136 pp.12–14, BPM, [Chitham, pp.140–1].

12. EJB, 'Why ask to know the date – the clime', 14 Sept. 1846: MS Add 43483 pp.62–7, BL, [Hatfield, pp.244–52]. For Anne's poem, written the same day on the same subject, though with a different point of view, see AB, 'I dreamt last night; and in that <nig> dream', 14 Sept. 1846: MS Bon 135 pp.7–16, [Chitham, pp.136–40].

13. Part of the time may have been occupied in sittings for Leyland's medallion portrait of Branwell: see above, pp.491, 929 n.42.

14. Mary Pearson, Commonplace Book, [1841–7]: MS pp.55–6, Texas; Census Returns for Ovenden, 1841: Microfilm, WYAS, Calderdale. Mary's age at the time of Branwell's visit is uncertain. The census describes her and two of her sisters as being fifteen in 1841, which is extremely unlikely, but as she is listed first of the children she may have been the eldest. By 1847, the year after Branwell's visit, she was old enough to have taken over the running of the Ovenden Cross though she was still unmarried:

White, *Directory of the ... West Riding of Yorkshire* (1847), p.466.

15. Mary Pearson, Commonplace Book, [1841–7]: MS p.48, Texas, [VN *PBB*, p.458]. 'Why hold young eyes the fullest fount of tears' had already appeared in the *Bradford Herald* and *Halifax Guardian* in May 1842: see above, p.905 n.83. An earlier version of 'When all our cheerful hours seem gone for ever', (p.50) was included in the letter PBB to J. B. Leyland, 28 April 1846: MS p.4, Brotherton,]VN *PBB*, p.144]. The epitaph, written under a sketch of Branwell as a corpse and a tombstone, read 'MARTINI LIUGI IMPLORA ETERNA QUIETE!'; beneath this Branwell has written '"Martin Luke implores for eternal rest!" (Italian epitaph.)': PBB to J. B. Leyland, [Jan. 1847]: MS in Brotherton, [*L&L*, ii, 120]. As Leyland pointed out, Branwell must have been aware that Lord Byron, one of his literary heroes, had seen a Bolognese tomb inscribed 'Implora pace!' and had expressed a wish to have only these same words upon his own grave. He would also have known Mrs Hemans' poem of the same title inspired by reading this remark: Leyland, ii,256. Branwell seems to have made a study of epitaphs after his dismissal from Thorp Green: an earlier letter ended with a sketch of a cross inscribed 'POBRE!' and the words 'The best Epitaph ever written – It is <writt> carved on a rude cross, in Spain, over a murdered traveller – and simply means "Poor Fellow!"': PBB to J. B. Leyland [n.d., but because the signature is accented rather than having the diaeresis it must date post-July 1845 and pre-28 April 1846]: MS p.1, Brotherton, [*L&L*, ii, 137, wrongly ascribed to 'circa July 1847'].

16. Mary Pearson, Commonplace Book, [1841–7]: MS p.52, Texas.

17. *Ibid.*, p.54, [VN *PBB*, p.283].

18. *Ibid.*, pp.49, 51. A further four cuttings from the *Halifax Guardian* containing Branwell's poems 'On Peaceful Death', 'Real Rest', 'Caroline's Prayer' and 'Should Life's first feelings' appear on pp.24, 28, 35. I am grateful to Victor Neufeldt for this information. On p.53, opposite Branwell's self-portrait, there is a clipping from the *Halifax Guardian* of a poem entitled 'Speak Kindly': though uncharacteristically anonymous, the sentiments and metre are typical of Branwell and the whole poem is strongly reminiscent of his 'The man who will not know another', [VN *PBB*, pp.220, 455]. I think the poem must be by Branwell and I suspect that his name was left off in error. As the poem is unpublished a transcript is appended. 'Speak kindly to thy fellow man, / Who droops from weight of woe! / He sinks beneath deep sorrow's ban / With cares thou canst not know: / Oh! kindly speak, for deadly grief / Is gnawing at his heart; / It may be thine to give relief, / And act a brother's part! / Perchance, from thee, a single word, / Spoken in accents kind, / May a sweet transient

joy afford / To his o'ercharged mind; / And though his careworn heart is filled / With heaviness and gloom, / It may cause peace and hope to gild / His passage to the tomb! / Turn not the wanderer away, / E'en though the weight of sin / Hath quench'd his spirit's heavenly ray, / And darken'd all within! / Oh! chide him not – nor coldly spurn / His now repentant tears; / For from that one good spark may burn / A flame in after years! / Yes! kindly speak – and bid his soul / From its dejection rise, / Push back the waves which round him roll, / And point him to the skies: / Stay not to ask his grade, nor how / He into evil ran, – / It is enough for thee to know / He is thy fellow man.'

19. PBB to J. B. Leyland, [Oct. 1846]: MS pp.2–3, Brotherton, [*L&L*, ii, 114].

20. PBB to J. B. Leyland, [Jan. 1847]: MS p.1, Brotherton, [*L&L*, ii, 121].

21. CB to EN, 13 Dec. 1846: MS HM 24450 pp.2–3, Huntington, [*L&L*, ii, 117–18].

22. PBB to J. B. Leyland, [Jan. 1847]: MS p.1, Brotherton, [*L&L*, ii, 121].

23. PBB to J. B. Leyland, [c.24 Jan. 1847]: MS p.1, Brotherton, [*L&L*, ii, 123].

24. *Ibid.*, p.4.

25. On 12 May 1847 Charlotte told Ellen that Branwell had 'got to the end of a considerable sum of money of which he became possessed in the Spring': CB to EN, 12 May [1847]: MS p.2, Berg, [*L&L*, ii, 132]. Twenty pounds a time is the sum mentioned by Mrs Gaskell as being the amount Branwell received from Mrs Robinson: ECG, *Life*, p.196.

26. PBB to J. B. Leyland, [24 Jan. 1847]: MS pp.2–3, Brotherton, [*L&L*, ii, 123–4].

27. MT to ECG, [1857]: MS n.l., [Stevens, p.164].

28. CB to EN, 14 Oct. 1846: MS HM 24449 pp.4–5, Huntington, [*L&L*, ii, 115]; CB to EN, [24 March 1847]: MS Bon 191 pp.3–4, BPM, [*L&L*, ii, 130].

29. CB to EN, 13 Dec. 1846: MS HM 24450 p.1, Huntington, [*L&L*, ii, 117]. For the unseasonably mild weather in Haworth throughout the year see *Bradford Observer*, 5 Feb. 1846, p.5; 13 June 1846, p.8; 3 Sept. 1846, p.8.

30. CB to EN, 13 Dec. 1846: MS HM 24450 p.1, Huntington, [*L&L*, ii, 117].

31. *Leeds Mercury*, 17 Jan. 1846, p.9; *Bradford Observer*, 5 Feb. 1846, p.5; 20 Aug. 1846, p.8; 3 Sept. 1846, p.8; ECG, *Life*, p.32. Mrs Gaskell does not identify the strike but this was the most bitter and protracted of Patrick's incumbency and the strikers would certainly have needed his assistance 'by all the means in his power to "keep the wolf from their doors," and avoid the incubus of debt'. In supporting the wool-combers against the mill-owners, Patrick incurred the wrath of the most powerful and influential section of his congregation but persevered in pursuit of what he believed was right.

32. *Bradford Observer*, 3 Sept. 1846, p.8; 24 Sept. 1846, p.8; 26 Nov. 1846, p.5; 31 Dec. 1846, p.8.

33. *Ibid.*, 19 Nov. 1846, p.8; 11 Feb. 1847, p.8. The rector peevishly refused John Milligan's services in the investigation, presumably fearing he would be too radical in his views. *Leeds Intelligencer*, 27 Feb. 1847, p.8; *Bradford Observer*, 25 March 1847, p.8. Milligan had earlier lectured 'On the moral and intellectual conduct of England and her people', attacking the immorality, drunkenness, prostitution and poverty of the metropolis while praising its fine buildings and famous literary and scientific men: *ibid.*, 14 Jan. 1847, p.8.

34. *Ibid.*, 31 Dec. 1846, p.8. Though it is possible that Patrick was aligning himself with Scoresby's opponents (Morgan and Boddington both declined to attend also), it is more likely that it was simply the distance and bad weather which kept him from attending so soon after his cataract operation. *Ibid.*, 4 Feb. 1847, p.5.

35. *Halifax Guardian*, 6 March 1847, p.4.

36. PB to the *Leeds Intelligencer*, 27 March 1847, p.8.

37. PB, marginal notes in his copy of Thomas John Graham, *Modern Domestic Medicine*. MS HAOBP:bb210, contents page, BPM.

38. PB to the *Leeds Mercury*, 5 June 1847, p.7. Later in the year, Charlotte told Ellen Nussey that she 'had always consoled myself with the idea of having my front teeth extracted and rearranged some day' under the influence of ether, but having heard of its effects on Ellen's friend, Catherine Swaine, she would 'think twice before I consented to inhale; one would not like to make a fool of oneself': CB to EN, [29 Nov. 1847]: MS HM 24456 p.4, Huntington, [*L&L*, ii, 157–8].

39. PB to the *Leeds Intelligencer*, 25 Sept. 1847, p.6. Patrick had conducted a personal crusade on behalf of clever, pious young men in his parish for many years, offering William Hodgson a curacy, for example, and supporting their applications for betterment. See, for example, his testimonial for the Revd W. R. Thomas who wished to become an emigrant teacher: PB to The Secretary of the Society for the Propagation of the Gospel, 22 June 1850: MS file DOS 1961, USPG.

40. PB, Church Reform, Nov. 1847: MS pp.1–2, in private hands. This copy, in Patrick's hand, was preserved by Arthur Nicholls; another copy, in an unidentified hand, is MS BS x, H, BPM.

41. CB to EN, 28 Dec. 1846: MS HM 24451 pp.2–3, Huntington, [*L&L*, ii, 119].

42. CB to EN, 19 Jan. 1847: MS BS 57.5 pp.2–4, BPM, [*L&L*, ii, 122]. Ellen has deleted her sister-in-law's name in the manuscript.

43. CB to EN, 1 March 1847: MS pp.2–3, Law Colln, photograph in Mildred Christian Colln, BPM, [*L&L*, ii, 128.].

44. *Ibid.*, p.3.

45. The Robinsons finally left Thorp Green on 3 March 1847, Mrs Robinson to go 'among her relations', the children into lodgings in York until 10 March when they joined their mother at Great Barr Hall: Hibbs, pp.25(e), 26(f).

According to Whitehead, the Misses Robinson had been on a protracted visit 'among their relations' from 16 November 1846 to 8 February 1847: *ibid.*, p.24(a).

46. CB to EN, 1 March 1847: MS p.3, Law Colln, photograph in Mildred Christian Colln, BPM, [*L&L*, ii, 128].

47. CB to EN, 12 May [1847]: MS p.3, Berg, [*L&L*, ii, 132].

48. CB to EN, [14 May 1847]: MS pp.2–3, Columbia, [*L&L*, ii, 133]; *Bradford Observer*, 18 March 1847, p.4. Two of Branwell's friends from his railway days, Francis Grundy and George Gooch, were engineers on this new line: *Halifax Guardian*, 6 March 1847, p.4.

49. CB to EN, 17 May 1847: MS n.l., [*L&L*, ii, 133].

50. CB to EN, 20 May [1847]: MS Bon 192 pp.1–3, 4 crossed, BPM, [*L&L*, ii, 134]. Ellen eventually came to stay at Haworth from 20 July to 12 August 1847, her visit only being memorable for her involvement in a carriage accident at its close: CB to EN, 12 Aug. 1847: MS Bon 193 p.1, BPM, [*L&L*, ii, 140]. I am grateful to Margaret Smith for identifying the period of Ellen's visit which must have coincided with Charlotte's receiving Smith, Elder & Co.'s letter about *The Professor*: see below, p.525–6.

51. CB to EN, 25 May 1847: MS n.l., [*L&L*, ii, 134–5]; CB to EN, 5 June 1847: MS HM 24453 p.4, Huntington, [*L&L*, ii, 135].

52. PBB to J. B. Leyland, [16 July 1847]: MS p.1, Brotherton, [*L&L*, ii, 137].

53. *Halifax Guardian*, 5 June 1847, p.6. The first draft of the poem is PBB, 'Upon that dreary winters night', 15 Dec. 1837: MS Bon 151, BPM, [VN *PBB*, pp.518–21]. There is a particularly poignant change in the first verse where the poet's anticipated suffering 'through many an hour' is changed to 'not hours, but years'.

54. See, for example, PBB, 'The westering sunbeams smiled on Percy Hall', [May–June 1847]: MS n.l., [Leyland, ii, 259–63; VN *PBB*, pp.291–2]; PBB 'Might rough rocks find neath calmest sea' [1847]: MS in Brotherton, [VN *PBB*, p.294].

55. CB, *Biographical Notice*, p.361; G. Larken, 'The Shuffling Scamp', *BST*:15:80:400; CB to WSW, 18 Sept. 1850: MS S-G 40 p.1, BPM, [*L&L*, iii, 160]. According to Charlotte, Newby mentions 'in his letter to my sister' that '"the sale of 250 copies would leave a surplus of 100£ to be divided"': *ibid.*, p.1. In another letter Charlotte claimed Newby had undertaken to print 350 copies of *Wuthering Heights* and *Agnes Grey* but then declared he had only printed 250; Emily and Anne's deposit of £50 should therefore have been returned to them but they never received a penny: CB to WSW, 13 Sept. 1850: MS MA 2696 R-V p.1, Pierpont Morgan, [*L&L*, iii, 156].

56. CB to Smith & Elder, 15 July 1847: MS S-G 1 pp.1–2, BPM, [*L&L*, ii, 139]. The fact that this

was her seventh attempt to secure a publisher is noted in CB to G. H. Lewes, 6 Nov. 1847: MS Add 39763 p.2, BL, [*L&L*, ii, 153].

57. Smith, p.84; CB to Smith, Elder & Co., 2 Aug. 1847: MS S-G 2 pp.1–2, BPM, [*L&L*, ii, 139–40]. George Smith later gave a more colourful account of this incident: 'Before ... our letter was despatched, there came a letter from "Currer Bell" containing a postage-stamp for our reply, it having been hinted to the writer by "an experienced friend" that publishers often refrained from answering communications unless a postage-stamp was furnished for the purpose!": Smith, p.85. In fact, Charlotte's letter makes no mention of the advice of an 'experienced friend' (which is intrinsically unlikely as Charlotte had no one to consult and had already been in communication with publishers for the last eighteen months) and merely states as a postscript, 'I enclose a directed Cover for your reply.'

58. *Ibid.*, pp.84–5.
59. CB, *Biographical Notice*, p.361.
60. CB to Smith, Elder & Co., 7 Aug. 1847: MS S-G 3 p.1, BPM, [*BST*:18:92:101–2].
61. *Ibid.*, p.2.
62. CB to Smith, Elder & Co., 24 Aug. 1847: MS in private hands, [*L&L*, ii, 141]; Smith, p.87.
63. *Ibid.*, pp.87–8; ECG, *Life*, pp.225–6.
64. CB to Smith, Elder & Co., 12 Sept. 1847: MS S-G 1B p.2, BPM, [*BST*:18:92:102]; ECG, Receipt for £800, 10 Feb. 1857: MS S-G 105b, BPM and see also, Smith, Elder & Co. Publication Ledgers, vol.i, p.369, John Murray. Mrs Gaskell received a further £50 for the continental copyright on 4 April 1857 and another £200 on the publication of the fourth edition in a single volume: *ibid.*, pp.369, 477.
65. CB to Smith, Elder & Co., 12 Sept. 1847: MS S-G 1B pp.2–3, BPM, [*BST*:18:92:102–3].
66. *Ibid.*, pp.1–2.
67. *Ibid.*, pp.3–4. Charlotte's request for the return of *The Professor* caused some consternation at Smith, Elder & Co., as it was thought she might attempt to send off the manuscript elsewhere: see CB to Smith, Elder & Co., 18 Sept. 1847: MS S-G 3B p.2, BPM, [*BST*:18:92:103].
68. *Ibid.*, p.1; ECG, *Life*, p.225.
69. CB to EN, [25 Sept. 1847]: MS MA2696 R-V, Pierpont Morgan, [*L&L*, ii, 143].
70. AB to EN, 4 Oct. 1847: MS BS 3 pp.1–5, BPM, [*BST*:12:63:193]. Crab-cheese, a kind of apple curd or jam, was reputed to have medicinal qualities. Charlotte later apologized to Ellen for having 'inoculated you with fears about the east wind': CB to EN, 7 Oct. 1847: MS HM 24455 p.2, Huntington, [*L&L*, ii, 146].
71. *Ibid.*, p.3. Arthur Nicholls was in the throes of evicting the washerwomen of Haworth from the churchyard, so this may have accounted for his unpopularity at the time.
72. CB to EN, 29 June 1847: MS HM 24454 p.4, Huntington, [*L&L*, ii, 137]; CB to EN, [15 Oct.

1847]: MS pp.1–2, WYAS, Kirklees, [*L&L*, ii, 148].
73. Gilbert Markham's letter, round which the story is built, is dated at the end of the book 10 June 1847 but as the novel was not published until July the following year, it is possible that this was actually the date Anne began to write the book: AB, *Tenant of Wildfell Hall*, p.471; CB to EN [4 April 1847]: MS pp.2–3, Princeton, [*L&L*, ii, 130–1].
74. CB, *Biographical Notice*, p.362.
75. CB to MW, 30 Jan. 1846: MS FM 2 pp.3–4, Fitzwilliam, [*L&L*, ii, 77].
76. AB, *Tenant of Wildfell Hall*, p.31.
77. AB, Preface to Second Edition of *Tenant of Wildfell Hall*, 22 July 1848, [AB, *Tenant of Wildfell Hall*, p.4].
78. CB, *Biographical Notice*, p.363.
79. AB, Preface to Second Edition of *Tenant of Wildfell Hall*, 22 July 1848, [AB, *Tenant of Wildfell Hall*, pp.3–4].
80. CB to EN, 7 Oct. 1847: MS HM 24455 pp.1–2, Huntington, [*L&L*, ii, 146].
81. CB, *Biographical Notice*, p.363.
82. T. C. Newby to Ellis Bell, 15 Feb. 1848: MS Bon 1, BPM, [in EJB writing desk] [JB *ST*, p.43].
83. John Hewish, 'Emily Brontë's Second Novel', *BST*:15:76:28; Unsigned Review, *Examiner*, Jan 1848, pp.21–2, [Allott, p.221].
84. CB, *Biographical Notice*, p.364; see also CB, Editor's Preface to *Wuthering Heights*, [1850] [EJB, *Wuthering Heights*, pp.365–9].
85. CB to Smith, Elder & Co., 24 Sept. [1847]: MS S-G 4 p.1, BPM, [*L&L*, ii, 142]; see also CB to Smith, Elder & Co., 29 Sept. 1847: MS S-G 5 p.1, BPM, [*L&L*, ii, 143].
86. CB to Smith, Elder & Co., 8 Oct [1847]: MS S-G 6 p.1, BPM, [*L&L*, ii, 144, wrongly dated to 2 Oct. and attributed to C Brontë instead of C Bell]; CB to Smith, Elder & Co., 12 Sept. 1847: MS S-G 1B p.2, BPM, [*BST*:18:92:102].
87. CB to Smith, Elder & Co., 19 Oct. 1847: MS p.1, Princeton, [*L&L*, ii, 149].
88. CB to Smith, Elder & Co., 26 Oct. 1847: MS S-G 7 pp.1–2, BPM, [*L&L*, ii, 149–50].
89. W. M. Thackeray to WSW, 23 Oct. 1847: Ray, *The Letters and Private Papers of William Makepeace Thackeray*, ii, 318–19.
90. CB to WSW, 28 Oct. 1847: MS MA 2696 R-V pp.1–2, Pierpont Morgan, [*L&L*, ii, 150].
91. *Ibid.*, p.4. Charlotte's unusually deprecatory remarks about her novel ('It has no learning, no research, it discusses no subject of public interest') may have been prompted by the somewhat patronizing comment in the *Athenaeum* that *Jane Eyre* 'deserves high praise, and commendation to the novel-reader who prefers story to philosophy, pendantry, or Puseyite controversy': see Allott, p.72; unsigned review by G. H. Lewes, *Westminster Review*, Jan. 1848, pp.581–4, [Allott, p.87].
92. Unsigned review, *Critic*, 30 Oct. 1847, pp.277–8, [Allott, p.73]; unsigned review by A. W. Fon-

blanque, *Examiner*, 27 Nov. 1847, pp.756-7, [Allott, p.76]; unsigned review, *Era*, 14 Nov. 1847, p.9, [Allott, pp.78-9]. 'The perusal of the "Era" gave me much pleasure': CB to WSW, 17 Nov. 1847: MS p.1, Princeton, [*L&L*, ii, 155].

93. CB to WSW, 11 Dec. 1847: MS p.2, Harvard, [*L&L*, ii, 160].

94. Unsigned review, *Era*, 14 Nov. 1847, p.9, [Allott, p.79]; unsigned review, *Spectator*, 6 Nov. 1847, pp.1074-5, [Allott, p.75]; CB to Smith, Elder & Co., 13 Nov. 1847: MS S-G 8 pp.1-2, BPM, [*L&L*, ii, 155].

95. CB, *Jane Eyre* (Clarendon Edn), pp.xiv, xvii, xix. The Smith, Elder & Co. Ledgers are missing for the period of the publication of *Jane Eyre* but the print runs for the first editions of *The Professor* and *Life* were both in the region of 2,500: Smith Elder & Co., Publication Ledgers, ii, 882; i, 369; John Murray.

96. CB to WSW, 10 Nov. 1847: MS n.l., [*L&L*, ii, 154].

97. Smith, pp.3-14; L. Huxley, *The House of Smith, Elder* (London, Privately Printed, 1923), pp.22-4. Most of these works were known and read at the parsonage, so the name of Smith, Elder & Co. would not have been unfamiliar to the Brontës.

98. Smith, pp.85-7. George Smith described William Smith Williams' skills as a book-keeper as 'most primitive', citing the way he used to strike a balance at the bottom of each page in his ledger to avoid the necessity of having to carry his figures forward.

99. G. Larken, 'The Shuffling Scamp', *BST*: 15:80:400, 406.

100. Trollope, *An Autobiography*, pp.74-5.

101. *Ibid.*, p.75.

102. CB to WSW, 17 Nov. 1847: MS p.2, Princeton, [*L&L*, ii, 155-6].

103. CB to WSW, 14 Dec. 1847: MS p.3, Princeton, [*L&L*, ii, 162]; CB to WSW, 21 Dec. 1847: MS p.2, Pforzheimer, [*L&L*, ii, 165].

104. Unsigned review, *Spectator*, 18 Dec. 1847, p.1217, [Allott, p.218]. Smith Williams, who had worked for the *Spectator* as its theatre critic, had found himself hampered by the 'chilly temperament' of the editor who used to declare impressively 'The "Spectator" is *not* enthusiastic, and must not be': Smith, p.86; unsigned review, *Athenaeum*, 25 Dec. 1847, pp.1324-5, [Allott, p.218].

105. Unsigned review, *Atlas*, 22 Jan. 1848, p.59, [Allott, p.231]; see also, *Britannia*, 15 Jan. 1848, pp.42-3, [Allott, pp.224-5]. Copies of both reviews were found in Emily's writing desk: Bon 1, BPM.

106. See, for example, *Britannia*, 15 Jan. 1848, pp.42-3, [Allott. pp228]. G. W. Peck in the *American Review*, June 1848, pp.572-85 objected most strongly to the profanity which 'offends against both

politeness and good morals', [Allott, p.236]. Curiously, he also attacked Emily's one instance of substituting a dash for what she herself, in the actual text of the book, had called 'an epithet as harmless as duck, or sheep, but generally represented by a dash'. Clearly not appreciating that this was intended to be humorous, Peck declared that it showed 'a conscious determination to write coarsely', the author 'knew the word to be a low word, though not an immodest one, and he determined to show his bold independence by using and defending it': [*ibid.*, p.238]. Stung by such criticism, Charlotte leapt to Emily's defence in her editorial preface to *Wuthering Heights*, published in 1850: 'The practice of hinting by single letters those expletives with which profane and violent persons are wont to garnish their discourse, strikes me as a proceeding which, however well meant, is weak and futile. I cannot tell what good it does – what feeling it spares – what horror it conceals': EJB, *Wuthering Heights*, pp.365-6.

107. Unsigned review in *Britannia*, 15 Jan. 1848, pp.42-3, [Allott, p.225]; see also, *Douglas Jerrold's Weekly Newspaper*, 15 Jan. 1848, p.77, [Allott, p.228].

108. Unsigned review in *Britannia*, 15 Jan, 1848, pp.42-3, [Allott, p.224]; unsigned review, *Literary World*, April 1848, p.243, [Allott, p.234].

109. Unsigned review, *Douglas Jerrold's Weekly Newspaper*, 15 Jan. 1848, p.77, [Allott, p.228]; [G. W. Peck], *American Review*, June 1848, pp.572-85, [Allott, p.241].

110. Unsigned review in *Britannia*, 15 Jan. 1848, pp.42-3, [Allott, p.226]; unsigned review, *Atlas*, 22 Jan. 1848, p.59, [Allott, p.233].

111. CB to WSW, 11 Dec. 1847: MS p.2, Harvard, [*L&L*, ii, 160]; CB to Smith, Elder & Co., 10 Dec. 1847: MS BS 60 p.1, BPM, [*BST*:16:82:111].

112. CB, Preface to *Jane Eyre*, 21 Dec. 1847: MS in Rosenbach, [CB, *Jane Eyre*, pp.3-4]. The emendations included the change in title from 'edited by Currer Bell' to 'by Currer Bell', which was intended to stop press speculation that 'Currer Bell' was one and the same as 'Ellis' and 'Acton Bell': CB to WSW, 31 Dec. 1847: MS p.1, Princeton, [*L&L*, ii, 170].

113. *Ibid.*, pp.1-2. 'I read my preface over with some pain: I did not like it: I wrote it when I was a little enthusiastic, like you about the French Revolution;': CB to WSW, 11 March 1848: MS p.3, Harvard, [*L&L*, ii, 198].

114. CB, Preface to *Jane Eyre*, 21 Dec. 1847: MS in Rosenbach, [CB, *Jane Eyre*, p.5]. Charlotte had earlier drafted another preface which, on second thoughts, she withdrew because 'I fear it savours of flippancy': CB to WSW, 21 Dec. 1847: MS p.1, Pforzheimer, [*L&L*, ii, 165].

115. CB to WSW, 28 Jan. 1848: MS p.2, Berg, [*L&L*, ii, 183].

CHAPTER NINETEEN

Title: Referring to Branwell: ECG, *Life*, p.224.

1. AB to EN, 26 Jan. 1848: MS BS 4 pp.1–2 crossed, BPM, [*BST*:12:63:195; *L&L*, ii, 175, wrongly dated to 4 Jan. 1848]. Anne's underlining of 'nothing (to speak of)' is suggestive: it indicates that Anne may have known that Ellen was aware of the sisters' authorship but, in deference to Emily, preserved the show of secrecy.

2. CB to EN, [15 Oct. 1847]: MS p.1, WYAS, Kirklees, [*L&L*, ii, 148]; CB to EN, 11 Jan. 1848: MS p.3, Law Colln, photograph in Mildred Christian Colln, BPM, [*L&L*, ii, 178]; J. B. Grant to J. B. Leyland, 24 Dec. 1847: MS HAS B21/38 p.3, WYAS, Calderdale. This letter acknowledges the safe receipt of the bosses which are 'rather large' and promises payment the following week.

3. PBB to J. B. Leyland, [Jan. 1848]: MS p.3, Brotherton, [*L&L*, ii, 177]. Branwell sent his apologies to the landlady of the Talbot 'if I did anything, during temporary illness, to offend her'.

4. *Ibid.*, p.1. Branwell also called himself 'Sanctus Patricius Branuellius Brontëio', i.e. St Patrick, in PBB to J. B. Leyland, [Jan. 1847]: MS p.1, Brotherton, [*L&L*, ii, 121]. Phidias, Leyland's pseudonym, was a fifth-century Greek sculptor, regarded as the greatest of the ancient world. A Firedrake is a meteor, or, in German mythology, a fiery dragon, but the significance of this pseudonym is lost on me as I have been unable to identify 'Drake'. Patrick Reid was a twenty-year-old Irishman convicted with his accomplice, Michael McCabe, of the robbery and horrific murders of an elderly couple, James and Ann Wraith, and their twenty-year-old servant girl, Caroline Ellis, who were found with their throats slashed by a razor. The case was notorious not only for the shocking nature of the crime but also because of the anti-Irish feeling it aroused; despite this, the first jury acquitted Reid and a second one had to be empanelled to hang him. On the gallows he confessed his guilt but confirmed McCabe's innocence; the latter's sentence was therefore commuted to transportation for life. The case was covered by all the papers: see, for example, *Leeds Mercury*, 24 July 1847, p.7; 31 July 1847, p.14; 24 Dec. 1847, p.5; 15 Jan. 1848, p.11 (supplement); 5 Feb. 1848, p.5. With unbelievable ghoulishness, a waxwork depicting the triple murder was displayed in Bradford at the end of January, shortly after Reid's execution: *ibid.*, 29 Jan. 1848, p.9.

5. CB to EN, 11 Jan. 1848: MS p.3, Law Colln, photograph in Mildred Christian Colln, BPM, [*L&L*, ii, 178]; John Greenwood, Diary: MS in private hands, photocopy of relevant page in MSS Copy Docs, BPM, ['John Greenwood and the Brontës', *BST*:12:61:37–8].

6. CB to EN, 11 Jan. 1848: MS p.3, Law Colln, photograph in Mildred Christian Colln, BPM, [*L&L*, ii, 178]; ECG, *Life*, pp.197–8.

7. PB marginal notes in Graham's *Modern Domestic Medicine*. MS HAOBP:bb210 pp.392–3; CB to EN, 11 Jan. 1848: MS p.3, Law Colln, photograph in Mildred Christian Colln, BPM, [*L&L*, ii, 178].

8. *Halifax Guardian*, 30 Oct. 1847, p.5; Register of Burials, 1836–54, Haworth Church, 29 Oct. 1847, no.1637. Patrick's taking the service was unusual as Mr Nicholls took virtually all the duties at this time. As a suicide, Charnock could have been refused church burial.

9. ECG, *Life*, p.230; CB to Smith, Elder & Co., 1 Dec. 1847: MS S-G 11 p.1, BPM, [*L&L*, ii, 158]; Mrs Gaskell wrongly dates this incident to 1846.

10. ECG to Catherine Winkworth, [25 Aug. 1850]: [C&P, p.126].

11. *Ibid.*, p.126. Mrs Gaskell here places the incident three months after the publication of *Jane Eyre*, which is appropriate as its success was assured with the printing of a second edition; she also claims to be reporting the conversation verbatim, as told to her by Charlotte. In her *Life*, p.230, Mrs Gaskell adapted this account and introduced subtle changes to it, making Patrick say 'My dear! you've never thought of the expense it will be! It will be almost sure to be a loss, for how can you get a book sold? No one knows you or your name.' She also makes him describe the book as 'much better than likely'. Though Mrs Gaskell assumes only the girls were told, it is possible that Branwell was also informed by his father.

12. CB to WSW, 4 Jan. 1848: MS HM 26008, Huntington [*L&L*, ii, 174].

13. Mary and Phoebe Crowther were nos 230 and 244 in the Admissions Register of the Clergy Daughters' School, 1824–39: MS in CRO, Kendal. Thomas Crowther's 'disparaging remarks' were made to Arthur Bell Nicholls: ABN to *Halifax Guardian*, 18 July 1857, p.3 (referring to 'Mrs Baldwin's own father'). Crowther was fifty-four in 1848: see his memorial tablet, Church of St John the Baptist in the Wilderness, Cragg Vale. Patrick himself was already aware of his daughter's authorship, so he cannot have been the 'elderly clergyman'. Thomas Plummer, the only other likely candidate, had died several years ago: see *Leeds Intelligencer*, 7 Dec. 1839, p.5. I am grateful to Margaret Smith for this reference.

14. CB to WSW, 14 Dec. 1847: MS pp.1–2, Princeton, [*L&L*, ii, 161].

15. CB to G. H. Lewes, 6 Nov. 1847: MS Add 39763 pp.1–4, BL, [*L&L*, ii, 152–3].

16. CB to G. H. Lewes, 12 Jan. 1848: MS Add 39763 pp.1–3, BL, [*L&L*, ii, 178–9].

17. *Ibid.*, p.4.

18. CB to WSW, 28 Jan. 1848: MS p.3, Berg, [*L & L*, ii, 184].
19. CB to WSW, 14 Dec. 1847: MS pp.2–3, Princeton, [*L & L*, ii, 161–2]. Charlotte embarked on a recasting of *The Professor*; see CB, draft preface to *The Professor*, [Nov.–Dec. 1847]: MS Bon 109, BPM, [CB, *Jane Eyre*, Clarendon Edition, Appx 3, pp.295–6].
20. CB, [John Henry], n.d.: MS at Princeton, [CB, *Shirley*, Clarendon Edn. Appx D, pp.805–35].
21. CB to WSW, 5 Feb. 1848: MS Gr F1 p.1, BPM, [*L & L*, ii, 186]. For the production see Donna Marie Nudd, 'Bibliography of Film, Television and Stage Adaptations of *Jane Eyre*', *BST*:20:3:171. I am grateful to Dr Patsy Stoneman of the University of Hull for drawing my attention to this reference.
22. CB to WSW, 15 Feb. 1848: MS p.1, Pforzheimer, [*L & L*, ii, 189]; CB to WSW, 25 Feb. 1848: MS E.9.4 pp.2–3, Boston, [*L & L*, ii, 191]. Charlotte could not prevent the translation but was advised by Williams not to give it her formal sanction: CB to WSW, 28 Feb. 1848: MS p.1, Harvard, [*L & L*, ii, 193]; CB to GS 17 Feb. 1848: MS S-G 13 p.1, BPM, [*L & L*, ii, 190].
23. CB to WSW, 21 Dec. 1847: MS p.1, Pforzheimer, [*L & L*, ii, 165].
24. CB to WSW, 13 Jan. 1848: MS in private hands, [*BST*:18:92:117]; CB to EN, 12 June 1850: MS HM 24471 pp.3–4, Huntington, [*L & L*, iii, 118]. Charlotte sent Julia Kavanagh a copy of the second edition of *Jane Eyre*, knowing she had found the book '*suggestive*' and saying 'I know that suggestive books are valuable to authors': CB to WSW, 22 Jan. 1848: MS Bon 196 p.3, BPM, [*L & L*, ii, 182]; CB to Miss Kavanagh, 2 Feb. 1848: MS p.1, Law Colln, photograph in Mildred Christian Colln, BPM, [*L & L*, ii, 185].
25. CB to R. H. Horne, 15 Dec. 1847: MS p.1, Princeton, [*L & L*, ii, 163]; CB to WSW, 21 Dec. 1847: MS p.1, Pforzheimer, [*L & L*, ii, 165]; CB to Smith, Elder & Co., 25 Dec. 1847: MS S-G 12 pp.1–2, BPM, [*L & L*, ii, 168] where Charlotte punningly remarks, on finding the contents of Leigh Hunt's book as attractive as the cover, 'the *Honey* is quite as choice as the Jar is elegant'.
26. CB to WSW, 21 Dec. 1847: MS p.2, Pforzheimer, [*L & L*, ii, 165].
27. CB to WSW, 5 Feb. 1848: MS Gr F1 p.3, BPM, [*L & L*, ii, 187]; see also above, p.533 for T. C. Newby's letter to Emily re her second book; Newby published Anne's second novel, *The Tenant of Wildfell Hall*, in July 1848: see below, p.537. CB to GS, 17 Feb. 1848: MS S-G 13 p.1, BPM, [*L & L*, ii, 190].
28. CB to Amelia Ringrose, 24 Dec. [1847]: MS p.3, Brotherton, [*L & L*, ii, 167]; CB to EN, 28 Jan. 1848: MS p.1, Berg, [*L & L*, ii, 184].
29. See, for example, CB to EN, [Dec. 1847]: MS in Fales, [*L & L*, ii, 164]; CB to EN 11 Jan. 1848: MS in Law Colln, photograph in Mildred Christian Colln, BPM, [*L & L*, ii, 177–8]; by the end of February Charlotte was worried that

Ellen was offended at her lack of contact: CB to EN, 26 Feb. 1848: MS HM 24457 p.1, Huntington, [*L & L*, ii, 192]; CB to EN, 28 Jan. 1848: MS p.1, Berg, [*L & L*, ii, 184].
30. *Ibid.*, p.3.
31. PBB to J. B. Leyland, [17 June 1848]: MS p.1, Brotherton, [*L & L*, ii, 223].
32. ECG, *Life*, p.87; CB to WSW, 11 March 1848: MS pp.1–3, Harvard, [*L & L*, ii, 197].
33. CB, Note to the Third Edition of *Jane Eyre*, 13 April 1848, [CB, *Jane Eyre*, p.6].
34. CB to EN, 28 April 1848: MS Bon 201 p.1, BPM, [*L & L*, ii, 207]; CB to EN, 3 May 1848: MS n.l., [*L & L*, ii, 211–12].
35. MT to CB, [June–24 July 1848]: MS pp.1–2, Pierpont Morgan, [Stevens, pp.73–5]. The manuscript of this letter, the second half of which is in the Berg, is postmarked in Wellington on 24 July 1848 and in Keighley on 14 December 1848, from which information (confirmed by postmarkings on other letters) I have concluded that the letters took six months to travel to and from New Zealand.
36. Mary Taylor also had her secrets from Ellen: Charlotte told Ellen she had received an almost identical letter from Mary except that Charlotte's contained 'an allusion or two to points on which she enjoins secrecy but which concerns herself alone' which prevented her sending the letter to Ellen: CB to EN, 5 June 1847: MS HM 24453 p.2, Huntington, [*L & L*, ii, 135].
37. CB to WSW, 25 Feb. 1848: MS E.9.4 pp.1–2, Boston, [*L & L*, ii, 190]; CB to WSW, 28 Feb. 1848: MS pp.3–4, Harvard, [*L & L*, ii, 194]; CB to WSW, 29 March 1848: MS pp.2–3, Harvard, [*L & L*, ii, 201].
38. CB to MW, 31 March 1848: MS FM 4 pp.2–4, Fitzwilliam, [*L & L*, ii, 202].
39. *Halifax Guardian*, 1 April 1848, pp.4–5; *Bradford Observer* 13 April 1848, p.8; *Halifax Guardian*, 3 June 1848, p.3; 27 May 1848, p.5.
40. CB to WSW, 20 April 1848: MS Ashley 166 pp.1–2, BL, [*L & L*, ii, 203].
41. ECG, *Life*, p.276. It is possible, of course, that Charlotte abandoned the attempt, begun in the characterization of William Farren, after reading *Mary Barton*.
42. CB to WSW, 12 May 1848: MS Grolier F3 p.5, BPM, [*L & L*, ii, 215–16].
43. CB to WSW, 15 June 1848: MS Egerton 2829 pp.14, 15, BL, [*L & L*, ii, 220–1].
44. MT to CB, [June–24 July 1848]: MS p.1, Pierpont Morgan, [Stevens, p.74].
45. CB to WSW, 22 June 1848: MS Bon 203 p.7, BPM, [*L & L*, ii, 226]; Newby advertised that *The Tenant of Wildfell Hall* would be published on 27 June and the book appears in lists of new publications on Saturday 1 July 1848: AB, *The Tenant of Wildfell Hall*, Clarendon edn, p.xix. CB to MT, 4 Sept. 1848: MS E.L. f.B.91 pp.2–3, Rylands, [Stevens, p.177].
46. *Ibid.*, p.2. This description hardly tallies with George Smith's later recollection that his letter

said 'we should be glad to be in a position to contradict the statement, adding at the same time we were quite sure Mr Newby's assertion was untrue': Smith, p.89.

47. CB to MT, 4 Sept. 1848: MS E.L. f.B.91 p.3, Rylands, [Stevens, p.177].

48. CB, Cash Book, [1848–9]: MS BS 22 p.2, BPM, [*BST*:5:29:277]; CB to MT, 4 Sept. 1848: MS E.L. f.B.91 pp.3–4, Rylands, [Stevens, pp.177–8].

49. Smith, p.89.

50. CB to MT, 4 Sept. 1848: MS E.L. f.B.91 pp.4–6, Rylands, [Stevens, p.178].

51. *Ibid.*, pp.6–7.

52. Smith, pp.88, 91. The suggestion that Charlotte's head was too large for her body is borne out in her caricatured self-portrait drawn in 1843: See plate 11a.

53. *Ibid.*, p.91.

54. CB to MT, 4 Sept. 1848: MS E.L. f.B.91 p.11, Rylands, [Stevens, p.181].

55. *Ibid.*, pp.11, 9.

56. *Ibid.*, p.9. See also ECG, *Life*, p.251.

57. *Ibid.*, p.252.

58. CB to MT, 4 Sept. 1848: MS E.L. f.B.91 p.9, Rylands, [Stevens, p.180]; ECG, *Life*, pp.251–2.

59. CB to MT, 4 Sept. 1848: MS E.L. f.B.91 p.10, Rylands, [Stevens, p.180].

60. *Ibid.*, pp.10–11. George Smith was amused by Charlotte's description of his house as 'a very fine place – the drawing-room especially – looked splendid to us', writing in his autobiography 'The house in which we lived is occupied by a hairdresser, and you may purchase cosmetics and hairpins in what used to be the dining-room, and have your hair cut, curled, singed, and shampooed in the little room in which I read the manuscript of "Jane Eyre"': Smith, pp.102–3.

61. CB to MT, 4 Sept. 1848: MS E.L. f.B.91 pp.11–12, Rylands, [Stevens, p.181]; CB to WSW, 8 July 1848: MS Grolier F4 p.1, BPM, [*L&L*, ii, 230]. This letter, accepting Williams' invitation, is the first to which Charlotte put her real name rather than her pseudonym. Thereafter she always used her real name in her correspondence with Smith, Elder & Co.

62. On 10 April 1849 Mary wrote to Charlotte saying, 'I've been delighted to receive a very interesting letter from you with an account of your pop visit to London &c. ... I wish you would give me some account of Newby, & what the man said when confronted with the real Ellis[sic] Bell': MT to CB, 10 April 1849: MS Bon 256 p.1, BPM, [Stevens, p.85]. No later letter ever mentions an account of the meeting with Newby and Charlotte's preoccupations with her sisters' ill health may have prevented her ever getting round to giving it.

63. CB, Cash Book, [1848–9]: MS BS 22 pp.2–3, BPM, [*BST*:5:29:277–8].

64. EN, Reminiscences, *L&L*, ii, 228.

65. CB to EN, 26 June 1848: MS HM 24463 p.2, Huntington, [*L&L*, ii, 227]. With characteristic

obtuseness, Ellen thought that the reference to her naivety meant that Charlotte had failed to realize that Ellen had recognized her as the author of *Jane Eyre*; in fact, it meant that Charlotte was amused by her gauche attempt to get her to confess her authorship.

66. *Ibid.*, pp.2–4. For the Taylor–Mossman relationship see Joan Stevens, 'A note on Mossmans', *BST*:16:81:47–50. Charlotte heard nothing from Hunsworth for many months after this visit and suspected that Joe Taylor had taken offence at her refusal to confide in him: CB to EN, 10 Dec. 1848: MS p.4, Harvard, [*L&L*, ii, 293]. According to Ellen, he was later responsible for making an 'open secret' of Charlotte's authorship: see EN, Reminiscences, *L&L*, ii, 228.

67. CB to WSW, 31 July 1848: MS pp.3–4, Princeton, [*L&L*, ii, 241].

68. Unsigned review, *Athenaeum*, 8 July 1848, pp.670–1, [Allott, p.251].

69. Unsigned review, *Spectator*, 8 July 1848, pp.662–3, [Allott, p.250].

70. CB to WSW, 31 July 1848: MS pp.3–4, Princeton, [*L&L*, ii, 241].

71. AB, Preface to second edition of *The Tenant of Wildfell Hall*, 22 July 1848: MS n.l., [AB, *The Tenant of Wildfell Hall*, p.5]. For the date of the second edition see AB, *The Tenant of Wildfell Hall*, Clarendon Edn, p.xxii.

72. CB to GS, 7 Sept. 1848: MS S-G 17 pp.1–2, BPM, [*L&L*, ii, 254]; CB to WSW [Sept. 1848]: MS Ashley 164 p.4, BL, [*L&L*, ii, 256].

73. CB to WSW, 18 Aug. 1848: MS BS 65.1 p.1, BPM, [*BST*:12:64:301]. Through force of habit, Charlotte signed the letter 'Currer Bell' adding a postscript: 'I forget my own name – but it does not signify; <me> you know me better as C. Bell than as C Brontë.'

74. PBB to J. B. Leyland, [17 June 1848]: MS p.1, Brotherton, [*L&L*, ii, 223].

75. CB to EN, 28 July 1848: MS Grolier E14 pp.4, 1 crossed, BPM, [*L&L*, ii, 240].

76. ECG, *Life*, p.197.

77. PBB to John Brown, [summer 1848]: MS p.1, Brotherton, [*L&L*, ii, 224].

78. Grundy, pp.90–1.

79. *Ibid.*, p.91.

80. *Ibid.*, pp.91–2.

81. CB to Ann Nussey, 14 Oct. 1848: MS BS 65.5 p.2, BPM, [*L&L*, ii, 265]; CB to EN, 9 Oct. 1848: MS Ashley 2452 p.2, BL, [*L&L*, ii, 264].

82. Leyland, ii, 278; Tabitha Ratcliffe, quoted in C. Holmes Cautley, 'Old Haworth Folk who knew the Brontës', *Cornhill Magazine*, 29, July–Dec. 1910, p.78; CB to EN, 9 Oct. 1848: MS Ashley 2452 p.1, BL, [*L&L*, ii, 264].

83. CB to WSW, 6 Oct. 1848: MS Bon 204 pp.2–3, BPM, [*L&L*, ii, 262–3]; Leyland, ii, 278–9.

84. CB to WSW 6 Oct. 1848: MS Bon 204 pp.2–3, BPM, [*L&L*, ii, 263]; CB to EN, 9 Oct. 1848: MS Ashley 2452 p.2, BL, [*L&L*, ii, 264]; Leyland, ii, 279–80. According to Mrs Gaskell, Branwell had

resolved to die standing on his feet, declaring in his last illness that as long as there was life there was strength of will to do what it chose; in his death throes he insisted on getting to his feet and died standing up, his pockets full of Mrs Robinson's letters: ECG, *Life*, pp.197, 254. Both Mrs Gaskell and Leyland, whose account I have preferred, quoted 'one who attended Branwell in his last illness', the likely informant in both cases being John Brown or his daughter, Martha, the Parsonage servant. I suspect, however, that Mrs Gaskell got her account second hand from Ellen Nussey, who quotes Branwell as saying 'You have only to will a thing to get it' in 1839: EN, Reminiscences: MS p.27, KSC. It is inherently unlikely that Branwell claimed strength of will on his deathbed, and it seems probable that the description of his death agonies were simply embroidered for and by village gossip. Martha Brown herself flatly contradicted the suggestion that Branwell died with his pockets full of Mrs Robinson's letters, though unwittingly lending credence to the story by saying that the letters 'were mostly from a gentleman of Branwell's acquaintance, then living near the place of his former employment': Leyland, ii, 284. Clearly Martha did not realize the role played by Dr Crosby in Branwell's affair with Mrs Robinson. Though Branwell was thirty-one at his death, his funeral card and the newspapers all wrongly stated his age to be thirty: PBB, Funeral Card, MS BS x, F, BPM; *Bradford Observer*, 28 Sept. 1848, p.5; *Leeds Mercury*, 30 Sept. 1848, p.8; *Leeds Intelligencer*, 30 Sept. 1848, p.5 where a printing error reduced Branwell to twenty years old.

85. CB to WSW, 2 Oct. 1848: MS MA 2696 R-V p.3, Pierpont Morgan, [*L&L*, ii, 262]. This is Charlotte's claim; she obviously did not remember being at her mother's deathbed.
86. CB to WSW, 6 Oct. 1848: MS Bon 204 pp.3–4, BPM, [*L&L*, ii, 263].
87. CB to WSW, 2 Oct. 1848: MS MA 2696 R-V pp.1–3, Pierpont Morgan, [*L&L*, ii, 261].
88. *Ibid.*, p.3.
89. CB to EN, 9 Oct. 1848: MS Ashley 2452 p.3, BL, [*L&L*, ii, 264]; CB to WSW, 2 Oct. 1848: MS MA 2696 R-V p.3, Pierpont Morgan, [*L&L*, ii, 262].
90. AB to WSW, 29 Sept. 1848: MS Ashley 155, BL, [*L&L*, ii, 260–1].
91. Register of Burials, 1836–54, Haworth Church: no.1756 (28 Sept. 1848).
92. PBB, Death Certificate, 24 Sept. 1848: MS BS x, D, BPM. Charlotte herself told a friend that Branwell had been 'long in weak health – and latterly consumptive – though we were far from apprehending immediate danger': CB to Laetitia Wheelwright, 15 March 1849: MS pp.1–2, in private hands, [*L&L*, ii, 315]. I am grateful to Roger Barrett for a photocopy of this letter and permission to quote from it. Ironically, given the volume and frequently lyrical quality of the poetry Branwell had written over the years, his last effort appears to have been a vituperative and obscene attack on Wheelhouse, whose attentions had evidently not been appreciated: PBB, 'While holy Wheelhouse far above' & 'Say Dr Wheelhouse is a jewel', [1848]: PBB, [Luddenden Foot Notebook], [1840–2]: MS pp.3–6, Brotherton [VN *PBB*, pp.298–9].
93. Grundy, p.92.

CHAPTER TWENTY

Title: CB to WSW, 13 June 1849: MS Ashley 172 p.3, BL, [*L&L*, ii, 340].

1. CB to WSW, 2 Oct. 1848: MS 2696 R-V p.1, Pierpont Morgan, [*L&L*, ii, 261].
2. CB to WSW, 25 June 1849: MS BS 70 p.3, BPM, [*L&L*, ii, 349].
3. CB to WSW, 18 Oct. 1848: MS n.l., [*L&L*, ii, 266].
4. CB to EN, 29 Oct. 1848: MS Grolier E15 pp.2–3, BPM, [*BST*:17:90:359].
5. CB to WSW, 2 Nov. 1848: MS BS 66 p.1, BPM, [*L&L*, ii, 269]; CB to GS, 7 Nov. 1848: MS S-G 18 p.2, BPM, [*L&L*, ii, 270–1]; CB to WSW, 25 June 1849: MS BS 70 p.7, BPM, [*L&L*, ii, 350].
6. CB to WSW, 2 Nov. 1848: MS BS 66 p.3, BPM, [*L&L*, ii, 269].
7. *Ibid.*, pp.2–3.
8. CB to WSW, 22 Nov. 1848: MS Ashley 2452 pp.1–2, BL, [*L&L*, ii, 286–7].
9. CB to EN, 23 Nov. 1848: MS Grolier E16 pp.1–2, BPM, [*BST*:17:90:360–1].
10. *Ibid.*, p.2.

11. CB to EN, [27 Nov. 1848]: MS p.1, Princeton, [*L&L*, ii, 289]; CB to WSW, 7 Dec. 1848: MS Grolier F6 p.1, BPM, [*L&L*, ii, 289–90]; CB to WSW, 9 Dec. 1848: MS Grolier F5, BPM, [*L&L*, ii, 291–2]; CB to EN, [19 Dec. 1848]: MS in Pennsylvania, [*L&L*, ii, 293].
12. CB to WSW, 7 Dec. 1848: MS Grolier F6 pp.1–2, BPM, [*L&L*, ii, 290].
13. CB to EN, 28 July 1848: MS Grolier E14 pp.3–4, BPM, [*L&L*, ii, 240].
14. *Ibid.*, p.4; CB to EN, 18 Aug. 1848: MS Grolier E13 pp.3–4, BPM, [*L&L*, ii, 246–7].
15. CB to EN, 23 Nov. 1848: MS Grolier E16 p.3, BPM, [*BST*:17:90:361].
16. *Ibid.*, pp.2–3; Henry Clapham/Mary Robinson, Draft Marriage Settlement, 18 Oct. 1848: MS 23, Robinson Papers, BPM; CB to EN, 10 Dec. 1848: MS p.3, Harvard, [*L&L*, ii, 293].
17. CB to EN, 23 Nov. 1848: MS Grolier E16 p.3, BPM, [*BST*:17:90:361].
18. CB to EN, 10 Dec. 1848: MS p.3, Harvard, [*L&L*, ii, 293].
19. Unsigned review, *Sharpe's London Magazine*,

Aug. 1848, pp.181–4, [Allott, pp.263, 265].

20. Unsigned review, *Rambler*, Sept. 1848, pp.65–6, [Allott, pp.268, 267].

21. E. P. Whipple, *North American Review*, Oct. 1848, pp.354–69, [Allott, p.248]; CB to WSW, 22 Nov. 1848: MS Ashley 2452 pp.2–3, BL, [*L&L*, ii, 287].

22. CB to EN, 10 Dec. 1848: MS pp.1–2, Harvard, [*L&L*, ii, 292–3]. Graham's *Modern Domestic Medicine*, p.239, points out that diarrhoea occurs in the third and last stage of consumption and, as with Emily, 'Till this period, and occasionally, indeed, through it, the patient supports his spirits, and flatters himself with ultimate success.'

23. CB, *Biographical Notice*, p.363.

24. Robinson, *Emily Brontë*, p.228. The incident is uncorroborated and no contemporary source is given. ECG, *Life*, pp.257–8.

25. Tabitha Ratcliffe, quoted in C. Holmes Cautley, 'Old Haworth Folk who knew the Brontës', *Cornhill Magazine*, xxix (July–Dec. 1910), p.78. The comb is in the BPM, having been acquired from the Brown family via the Dixon sale: HAOBP: H121, BPM.

26. Martha Brown, quoted in ECG to [?John Forster], [Sept. 1853]: MS pp.12–13, Brotherton, [C&P, p.246]; CB to EN, [19 Dec. 1848]: MS in Pennsylvania, [*L&L*, ii, 293].

27. ECG, *Life*, p.258. Dr Wheelhouse's presence is presumed from the fact that he signed the death certificate as being 'in attendance': EJB, Death Certificate, 19 Dec. 1848: MS BS x, D, BPM. An ulcerated throat and mouth, inflicting hoarseness of the voice, were a recognized symptom of the final stages of consumption according to Graham's *Modern Domestic Medicine*, p.239.

28. The first person to suggest that Emily died on the sofa was Robinson, *Emily Brontë*, p.230, who describes how Emily 'tried to rise, leaning with one hand upon the sofa. And thus the chord of life snapped'. This sounds suspiciously like the accounts of Branwell's death. Charlotte's references to Emily's dying-bed and her dying in the arms of those who loved her, suggest a more conventional place of death: CB to WSW, 25 June 1849: MS BS 70 p.1, BPM, [*L&L*, ii, 348]; CB to WSW, 13 June 1849: MS Ashley 172 pp.3–4, BL, [*L&L*, ii, 340]. See also CB to EN, 23 Dec. 1848: MS p.1, Berg, [*L&L*, ii, 294].

29. CB to WSW, [20 Dec. 1848]: MS in Scripps. I am grateful to Margaret Smith for drawing my attention to this unpublished manuscript.

30. WSW to CB, 21 Dec. 1848: MS pp.1–4, 6–7, in private hands.

31. CB to WSW, 25 Dec. 1848: MS Ashley 2452 p.1, BL, [*L&L*, ii, 294].

32. *Ibid.*, p.3.

33. *Bradford Observer*, 21 Dec. 1848, p.5; *Halifax Guardian*, 23 Dec. 1848, p.8; *Leeds Intelligencer*, 23 Dec. 1848, p.5; *Leeds Mercury*, 23 Dec. 1848, p.8. All the newspapers place Emily in her twenty-ninth year, as does the funeral card, which is printed with the name of Joseph Fox, Confectioner, who

presumably supplied the funeral tea: EJB, Funeral Card, 19 Dec. 1848: MS BS x, F, BPM. Two pairs of white funeral gloves, issued at the funerals of unmarried women, and associated with Emily's burial, are in the Brontë Parsonage Museum: HAOBP: D60 & D62. Plaited necklaces and bracelets, made from Emily's and Anne's hair, are also there: HAOBP: J12, J43 & J51. Mourning jewellery, made from the hair of the deceased, was a popular memento of the dead in the days before photography became cheap and commonplace.

34. Register of Burials, 1836–54, Haworth Church: no.1775 (22 Dec. 1848). The entry is recorded by Arthur Bell Nicholls. Martha Brown told Mrs Gaskell the details of the funeral procession: ECG to [?John Forster], [Sept. 1853]: MS p.13, Brotherton, [C&P, p.246]. For Keeper see CB to WSW, 25 June 1849: MS BS 70 p.1, BPM, [*L&L*, ii, 348]; ECG, *Life*, p.259.

35. CB to EN, 23 Dec. 1848: MS p.1, Berg, [*L&L*, ii, 294].

36. CB to WSW, 25 Dec. 1848: MS Ashley 2452 p.3, BL, [*L&L*, ii, 295].

37. CB to WSW, 7 Dec. 1848: MS Grolier F6 pp.3–4, BPM, [*L&L*, ii, 290]; CB to WSW, 14 Aug. 1848: MS p.6, Berg, [*L&L*, ii, 245]. In this second letter Charlotte says, 'My sister Anne wishes me to say that should she ever write another work, Mr Smith will certainly have the first offer of the copyright.'

38. By July 1853 only 279 copies out of the 961 purchased from Aylott & Jones at 6d. each, had been sold: G. D. Hargreaves, 'The Publishing of "Poems by Currer, Ellis and Acton Bell"', *BST*:15:79:299; unsigned review, *Spectator*, 11 Nov. 1848, pp.1094–5, [Allott, pp.64–6].

39. AB, The Three Guides, 11 Aug. 1847: MS Bon 136, BPM, [Chitham, pp.144–50]; *Fraser's Magazine*, Aug. 1848, pp.193–5; ECG, *Life*, p.203. This was not, as Chitham claims, the only one of Anne's poems to appear in print during her lifetime other than in *Poems*, and it was not, as he concludes, the poem Ellen thought was published in *Chambers's Journal* while she was staying at Haworth. Anne probably learnt that her poem, 'The Narrow Way', had been published in *Fraser's Magazine* from the *Leeds Intelligencer*, 30 Dec. 1848, p.7, which printed the poem in its poetry column under the heading 'From Fraser's Magazine for the present Month'.

40. AB, 'Believe not those who say', 24 April 1848: MS Ashley 54 pp.9–10, BL, [Chitham, *Poems of AB*, pp.161–2]. I have followed the version printed in the *Leeds Intelligencer*, 30 Dec. 1848, p.7.

41. Unsigned review, *Sharpe's London Magazine*, Aug. 1848, pp.181–4, [Allott, p.265]; AB to the Reverend David Thom, 30 Dec. 1848: MS pp.2–3, 6–7, Princeton. Though Anne's letter suggests she had discovered the idea of Universal Salvation for herself, I suspect that she was probably influenced by her father. Though he could not preach the doctrine openly, because Ang-

lican clergymen who did so were liable to be deprived of their livings, his liberal attitude towards, for instance, criminals (see above, pp.158, 168) suggests that he did not believe in eternal damnation. It is also significant, I think, that Charlotte was also a believer in Universal Salvation. In 1850 she rounded on Miss Wooler who had dared to repeat clerical criticism of Charlotte's books: 'I am sorry the Clergy do not like the doctrine of Universal Salvation; I think it a great pity for their sakes, but surely they are not so unreasonable as to expect me to deny or suppress what I believe the truth!': CB to MW, 14 Feb. 1850: MS FM 8 p.2, Fitzwilliam, [*L&L*, iii, 75].

42. CB to EN, 10 Dec. 1848: MS p.2, Harvard, [*L&L*, ii, 293].

43. EN, Reminiscences, *BST* 8:42:21.

44. CB to WSW, 2 Jan. 1849: MS p.2, Berg, [*L&L*, ii, 298]; CB to GS, 22 Jan. 1849: MS S-G 20 pp.3–4, BPM, [*L&L*, ii, 302–3].

45. CB to EN, 10 Jan. 1849: MS HM 24463 pp.1–2, Huntington, [*L&L*, ii, 298–9]; CB to EN, 15 Jan. 1849: MS pp.1–2, Berg, [*L&L*, ii, 299].

46. CB to WSW, 18 Jan. 1849: MS Bon 205 p.4, BPM, [*L&L*, ii, 301].

47. AB, 'A dreadful darkness closes in', 7–28 Jan. 1849: MS Bon 137 pp.1–2, BPM, [JB *ST*, no.26]. The poem exists in rough draft only and has several versions of some words and lines. The second verse has two cancelled readings, 'rolling' and 'gathering', and one alternative, 'blinding', to describe the mist. In the fifth verse, 'pure' is an alternative for 'keen', in the sixth 'breaking' for 'bleeding' and in the seventh 'For' for 'O'.

48. *Ibid.*, pp.1–2. The third verse quoted here has an alternative second line, 'What ever be' in the place of 'What'er' and 'may be' instead of 'my written'.

49. CB to WSW, 18 Jan. 1849: MS Bon 205 pp.1–2, BPM, [*L&L*, ii, 300]. Ellen had returned home, leaving her box behind, by 9 January: see CB to EN, 10 Jan. 1849: MS HM 24463 pp.1–3, Huntington, [*L&L*, ii, 298–9]. In this same letter, Charlotte states that she had rejected the offer of a visit from the Taylors as she felt unable to receive them properly.

50. CB to WSW, 18 Jan. 1849: MS Bon 205 pp.1–2, 3–5, BPM, [*L&L*, ii, 300]. The fifth page of this letter is missing.

51. CB to EN, 15 Jan. 1849: MS pp.3, 2, Berg, [*L&L*, ii, 299–300]; CB to EN, [30 Jan. 1849]: MS MA 2696 R-V p.3, Pierpont Morgan, [*L&L*, ii, 304].

52. *Ibid.*, p.1. Charlotte told Ellen to purchase a thirty-shilling respirator; CB to WSW, 1 Feb. 1849: MS Grolier F7 p.2, BPM, [*L&L*, ii, 305].

53. CB to GS, 22 Jan. 1849: MS S-G 20 pp.1–2, BPM, [*L&L*, ii, 302]; CB to EN, [30 Jan. 1849]: MS MA 2696 R-V pp.2–3, Pierpont Morgan, [*L&L*, ii, 304].

54. CB to WSW, 1 Feb. 1849: MS Grolier F7 pp.1–

4, BPM, [*L&L*, ii, 305–6]; CB to WSW, 18 Jan. 1849: MS Bon 205 pp.3–4, BPM, [*L&L*, ii, 301].

55. CB to WSW, 1 Feb. 1849: MS Grolier F7 p.4, BPM, [*L&L*, ii, 306].

56. CB to WSW, 4 Feb. 1849: MS BS 67 pp.2–3, BPM, [*L&L*, ii, 307].

57. CB to James Taylor, 1 March 1849: MS n.l., [*L&L*, ii, 312–13].

58. CB to WSW, [2 March 1849]: MS p.2, Harvard, [*L&L*, ii, 313].

59. CB to EN, 18 June 1845: MS HM 24440 p.2, Huntington, [*L&L*, ii, 39–40].

60. CB to WSW, [2 March 1849]: MS p.2, Harvard, [*L&L*, ii, 313]; CB to WSW, [2 April 1849]: MS Bon 208 pp.1–2, BPM, [*L&L*, ii, 319].

61. CB, *Shirley*, p.632. When describing 'the premature and sudden vanishing of Mr Malone from the stage of Briarfield parish' she added a weighted comment in similar vein: 'you cannot know how it happened, reader; your curiosity must be robbed to pay your elegant love of the pretty and pleasing': *ibid.*, p.634.

62. CB to Laetitia Wheelwright, 15 March 1849: MS p.3, in private hands, [*L&L*, ii, 315–16]. I am grateful to Roger Barrett for a photocopy of this letter and permission to quote from it.

63. PB to Mr Rand, 26 Feb. 1849: MS Bon 252, BPM, [*L&L*, ii, 311]. The Rands had left Haworth for Stalybridge in the spring of 1845: CB to Mrs Rand, 26 May [1845]: MS 2696 R-V, Pierpont Morgan, [*L&L*, ii, 35]; PB to Mr Rand, 5 June 1845: MS n.l., [*L&L*, ii, 37].

64. CB to EN, 29 March 1849: MS Bon 207 pp.3–4, BPM, [*L&L*, ii, 318].

65. *Ibid.*, p.4; AB to EN, 5 April 1849: MS BS 5 pp.1–5, BPM, [JB *ST*, no.28].

66. *Ibid.*, pp.2–8.

67. CB to EN, 12 April 1849: MS Bon 209 pp.1–2, BPM, [*L&L*, ii, 324].

68. PB, marginal annotation in Graham's *Modern Domestic Medicine*: MS HAOBP:bb210, p.247; CB to EN, 12 April 1849: MS Bon 209 pp.2–3, BPM, [*L&L*, ii, 324] where Charlotte adds that they will go in 'a month or six weeks hence' if Anne continues to wish for the change as much as she does at present; four days later Charlotte was already deferring the journey to six or eight weeks hence: CB to WSW, 16 April 1849: MS p.2, Princeton, [*L&L*, ii, 325].

69. *Ibid.*, p.2; CB to WSW, 8 May 1849: MS MA 2696 R-V p.3, Pierpont Morgan, [*L&L*, ii, 329]. Of the servants Charlotte remarks, 'One of them [Tabby] is indeed now old and infirm and unfit to stir much from her chair by the kitchen fireside – but the other is young and active and even she has lived with us seven years.'

70. CB to EN, 12 April 1849: MS Bon 209 pp.1–2, BPM, [*L&L*, ii, 324].

71. CB to EN, 1 May 1849: MS MA 2696 R-V pp.1–3, Pierpont Morgan, [*L&L*, ii, 327–8].

72. CB to EN, [12] May 1849: MS pp.1–2, Harvard, [*L&L*, ii, 330]. For Fanny Outhwaite's death,

aged fifty-four, on 14 February 1849 see *Leeds Intelligencer*, 17 Feb. 1849, p.5.

73. CB to MW, 16 May 1849: MS FM 7 pp.1–3, Fitzwilliam, [*L&L*, ii, 331]; CB to EN, 16 May 1849: MS HM 24468 p.1, Huntington, [*L&L*, ii, 332].

74. Ellen's presence at Haworth prior to the Brontës' departure is presumed from the fact that Charlotte notes the purchase of three train tickets from Keighley to Leeds, costing 10/- in all: CB, Cash Book, [1848–9]: MS BS 22 p.11, BPM; CB to EN, 16 May 1849: MS HM 24468 p.1, Huntington, [*L&L*, ii, 332]. This is confirmed by Ellen's diary. An entry on Wednesday, 23 May, 'To Scarbro' with CB & AB' is deleted and replaced with 'To Leeds'; the next day she records 'to Haworth – at York – the George Hotel': EN, [Diary], [1849]: in *A Christian Remembrancer* (London, R. A. Suttaby, 1849): HAOBP:bb112, BPM.

75. CB to EN, 16 May 1849: MS HM 24468 p.1, Huntington, [*L&L*, ii, 332]; CB to WSW, 4 June 1849: MS Ashley 2452 pp.2–3, BL, [*L&L*, ii, 338].

76. *Ibid.*, p.1; CB to WSW, 27 May 1849: MS n.l., [*L&L*, ii, 332–3].

77. A list of items titled 'To be bought' appears on the opposite page to the relevant expenditure in Charlotte's cash book: CB, Cash Book, [1848–9]: MS BS 22 p.10, BPM; Charlotte refers to the 'dreary mockery' of buying such items in CB to EN, [12] May 1849: MS p.2 crossed, Harvard, [*L&L*, ii, 331]; Ellen identifies the George Hotel as their quarters in York and, according to Charlotte's cash book, the stay cost them £2 6d.: EN, [Diary], [1849]: HAOBP:bb112, BPM [24 May 1849]; CB, Cash Book, [1848–9]: MS BS 22 p.11, BPM.

78. EN, 'A short account of the last days of dear A.B.', n.d.: MS pp.1–2, KSC, [ECG, *Life*, p.271]. Mrs Gaskell's quotation from this manuscript appears to have been selective as there are omitted passages. Ellen appears to have added to her account in the 1870s as the version quoted by T. W. Reid in his *Charlotte Brontë* includes these and further details which are not in this manuscript. CB to WSW, 27 May 1849: MS n.l., [*L&L*, ii, 332].

79. EN, Reminiscences, Reid, p.95; EN, 'A short account of the last days of dear A.B.': MS p.3, KSC, [ECG, *Life*, p.271].

80. EN, [Diary], [1849]: HAOBP:bb112, BPM, [27 May 1849]; CB, Cash Book, [1848–9]: MS BS 22 p.12, BPM.

81. CB to WSW, 27 May 1849: MS n.l., [*L&L*, ii, 333].

82. EN, 'A short account of the last days of dear A.B.': MS pp.4–7, KSC, [ECG, *Life*, p.272].

83. EN, Reminiscences, Reid, p.96.

84. *Ibid.*; EN, 'A short account of the last days of dear A.B.': MS pp.8–11, KSC, [ECG, *Life*, pp.272–3].

85. CB to WSW, 13 June 1849: MS Ashley 172 p.2,

BL, [*L&L*, ii, 339]; EN, 'A short account of the last days of dear A.B.': MS p.10, KSC, [ECG, *Life*, p.273].

86. *Ibid.*, pp.11–12 [end missing], [ECG, *Life*, p.273–4]; CB to WSW, 30 May [1849]: MS p.1, Berg, [*L&L*, ii, 337].

87. AB, Death Certificate, 28 May 1849: MS BS x, D, BPM. Curiously, even though a doctor had been in attendance during Anne's final hours, he neither certified nor registered the death. For Miss Wooler's role see ECG, *Life*, p.274; Max Blakeley, 'Memories of Margaret Wooler and her Sisters', *BST*:12:62:114.

88. *Scarborough Gazette*, 31 May 1849, pp.1, 3. The same edition, p.2, included Charlotte's and Ellen's names among the Scarborough visitors. In the deaths column, Anne's address is given as Brookroyd, Birstall, near Leeds, suggesting Ellen had supplied the information. The death was reported correctly a week later in the West Riding papers: *Bradford Observer*, 5 June 1849, p.8; *Halifax Guardian*, 9 June 1849, p.8; *Leeds Mercury*, 2 June 1849, p.8; *Leeds Intelligencer*, 2 June 1849, p.5.

89. CB to PB, 29 May 1849: MS n.l. but referred to in ECG, *Life*, p.274.

90. Register of Burials, 1841–1900, St Mary's Church, Scarborough, [p.238 no 30]: photocopy, Scarborough. In the week after Anne's burial it was reported that a stray cannonball from the civil war and a bell had both been found embedded in the north walls of St Mary's Church during their demolition: *Leeds Mercury*, 9 June 1849, (supp.) p.11.

91. ECG, *Life*, p.274; Max Blakeley, 'Memories of Margaret Wooler and her Sisters', *BST*:12:62:114.

92. CB to WSW, 4 June 1849: MS Ashley 2452 pp.1–2, BL, [*L&L*, ii, 337].

93. CB to WSW, 30 May 1849: MS p.1, Berg, [*L&L*, ii, 337]; CB to WSW, 4 June 1849: MS Ashley 2452 p.3, BL, [*L&L*, ii, 338].

94. CB to WSW, 13 June 1849: MS Ashley 172 p.2, BL, [*L&L*, ii, 339].

95. CB to WSW, 4 June 1849: MS Ashley 2452 p.3, BL, [*L&L*, ii, 338]; CB to WSW, 13 June 1849: MS Ashley 172 p.2, BL, [*L&L*, ii, 339].

96. CB to Martha Brown, 5 June 1849: MS BS 69 p.1, BPM, [*L&L*, ii, 338]; CB to WSW, 27 May 1849: MS n.l., [*L&L*, ii, 339]; CB to WSW, 13 June 1849: MS Ashley 172 p.2, BL, [*L&L*, ii, 339].

97. CB to WSW, 4 June 1849: MS Ashley 2452 p.2, BL, [*L&L*, ii, 338].

98. CB to WSW, 13 June 1849: MS Ashley 172 p.4, BL, [*L&L*, ii, 340]; CB to EN, 6 June 1852: MS HM 24496 pp.1–2, Huntington, [*L&L*, iii, 336].

99. CB to PB, [7 June 1849]: MS fragmented [*BST*:20:1:44–5]. This letter, which Patrick unaccountably cut up into at least seven pieces to distribute among autograph hunters, has been brilliantly reconstructed by Margaret Smith from the surviving fragments in numerous different locations: see *BST*:20:1:44–5. Charlotte later complained of five errors in

the gravestone lettering: in her transcript of the inscription for her father she says 'Here lies the Remains…', which may account for one mistake; another, which was never altered, was that Anne's age was given as twenty-eight – an error that also appears in the burial register.

100. CB to WSW, 13 June 1849: MS Ashley 172 pp.1, 3–4, BL, [*L&L*, ii, 339–40].

101. *Ibid.*, p.4; CB to Martha Brown, [18 June 1849]: MS in private hands. I am grateful to the late Lady Graham of Norton Conyers and Mrs Sarah Greenwood for allowing me to see this manuscript and transcribe it; CB to EN, 4 July 1849: MS BS 71.2 p.1, BPM, [*L&L*, iii, 6].

102. CB to EN, [23 June 1849]: MS pp.1–3, Law Colln, photograph in Mildred Christian Colln, BPM, [*L&L*, ii, 347].

103. CB to ECG, 27 Aug. 1850: MS n.l., [*L&L*, iii, 150]; CB, 'There's little joy in life for me', 21 June 1849: MS HM 2575, Huntington, [JB *SP*, p.22]. Charlotte had similarly attempted to write a poem after Emily's death: see CB, 'My darling thou wilt never know', 24 Dec. 1848: MS HM 2574, Huntington, [JB *SP*, p.21].

104. CB to EN, [23 June 1849]: MS p.3, Law Colln,

photograph in Mildred Christian Colln, BPM, [*L&L*, ii, 347].

105. CB to WSW, 25 June 1849: MS BS 70 pp.2–3, BPM, [*L&L*, ii, 349].

106. CB to EN, 14 July 1849: MS p.4, Law Colln, photograph in Mildred Christian Colln, BPM, [*L&L*, iii, 8]; CB to WSW, 25 June 1849: MS BS 70 pp.2, 6–7, [*L&L*, ii, 348–9].

107. CB to EN, 14 July 1849: MS pp.3–4, Law Colln, photograph in Mildred Christian Colln, BPM, [*L&L*, iii, 8].

108. CB to WSW, 26 July 1849: MS Bon 210 pp.2–3, BPM, [*L&L*, iii, 9]; the *Quarterly Review* had claimed that if the author of *Jane Eyre* was a woman she must be one who had 'for some sufficient reason, long forfeited the society of her own sex': see below, pp.605–8.

109. CB to WSW, 25 June 1849: MS BS 70 p.4, BPM, [*L&L*, ii, 349]. Margaret Smith points out the 'tragic associations of the phrase', which is quoted from Macbeth's 'Canst thou not minister to a mind diseased, / Pluck from the memory a rooted sorrow' in her article, 'The Letters of Charlotte Brontë', p.61.

110. CB to WSW, 26 July 1849: MS Bon 210 p.3, BPM, [*L&L*, iii, 9].

CHAPTER TWENTY-ONE

Title: CB to WSW, 1 Nov. 1849: MS MA 2696 R-V p.2, Pierpont Morgan, [*L&L*, iii, 29].

1. CB, *Shirley*, p.421.
2. *Ibid.*, p.442.
3. ECG, *Life*, p.277.
4. CB to WSW, 3 July 1849: MS BS 71 p.5, BPM, [*L&L*, iii, 6].
5. CB to WSW, 12 May 1848: MS Grolier F3, pp.2,4, BPM, [*L&L*, ii, 213–14].
6. CB to WSW, 3 July 1849: MS BS 71 pp.2–3, BPM, [*L&L*, iii, 5].
7. For the preparations for Ann Nussey's marriage to Robert Clapham see CB to EN, 27 July 1849: MS HM 24466 p.2, Huntington, [*L&L*, iii, 10]; CB to EN, 23 Aug. 1849: MS n.l., [*L&L*, iii, 13]. See also Whitehead, pp. 152–3. For Mercy's jealousy see CB to EN, [13 Sept. 1849]: MS Bon 213 p.3, BPM, [*L&L*, iii, 19].
8. CB, *Shirley*, pp.179, 181–3, 174.
9. Mary Taylor denounced Charlotte for this attitude: 'I have seen some extracts from Shirley in which you talk of women working: And this first duty, this great necessity you seem to think that some women may indulge in – if they give up marri\a/ge & don't make themselves too disagreeable to the other sex. You are a coward & a traitor A woman who works is by that alone better than one who does not & a woman who does not happen to be rich & who still earns no money & does not wish to do so, is guilty of a great fault – almost a crime – A dereliction of duty which leads rapidly & almost certainly to

all manner of degradation': MT to CB, [April 1850]: MS Bon 257 p.2, BPM, [Stevens, pp.93–4]. Charlotte was to do the same in *Villette*, much to Harriet Martineau's annoyance, see below, pp.718–20.

10. CB to EN, 4 July [1848 shd be 1849]: MS BS 71.2 p.1, BPM, [*L&L*, iii, 6]. Charlotte mistakenly dated this letter to 1848 but the mourning border and contents make it clear that it belongs to 1849. CB to EN, 14 July 1849: MS p.3, Law Colln, photograph in Mildred Christian Colln, BPM, [*L&L*, iii, 8]; CB to EN, 23 Aug. 1849: MS n.l., [*L&L*, iii, 13].

11. CB to EN, [27 July 1849]: MS HM 24466 pp.1–2, Huntington, [*L&L*, iii, 10]. For the spread of English cholera in the district see *Leeds Intelligencer*, 22 Sept. 1849, p.8; 29 Sept. 1849, p.5; *Bradford Observer*, 27 Sept. 1849, p.5.

12. CB to EN, [24 Sept. 1849]: MS pp.1–2, Harvard, [*L&L*, iii, 24]; CB to EN, 28 Sept. 1849: MS Bon 215 p.1, BPM [*L&L*, iii, 25].

13. CB to WSW, 29 Aug. 1849: MS p.1, Law Colln, photograph in Mildred Christian Colln, BPM, [*L&L*, iii, 15]; CB to WSW, 21 Aug. 1849: MS pp.1–2, Brotherton, [*L&L*, iii, 12]; CB to WSW, 24 Aug. 1849: MS Bon 211 p.1, BPM, [*L&L*, iii, 13].

14. *Ibid.*, pp.1–3.

15. CB to James Taylor, 3 Sept. 1849: MS n.l., [*L&L*, iii, 17]; CB to EN, [4 April 1851]: MS Grolier E21 pp.2–4, BPM, [*L&L*, iii, 220–1, wrongly dated to 5 April 1851 comparing Taylor's first and second visits; CB to GS, 14 Sept. 1849: MS S-G 22 p.2, BPM, [*BST*:18:92:104].

16. CB to James Taylor, 20 Sept. 1849: MS p.1, Texas, [*L&L*, iii, 22]. The visiting clergyman was Patrick's friend, the Revd. Thomas Crowther, who preached twice in Haworth Church on Sunday 16 September to raise money towards defraying the cost of gas lighting in the church: *Leeds Intelligencer*, 22 Sept. 1849, p.5. The letters to Smith Williams are CB to WSW, 15 Sept. 1849: MS EL 400, Rylands, [*L&L*, iii, 21]; CB to WSW, 17 Sept. 1849: MS Bon 214, BPM, [*L&L*, iii, 21].

17. *Ibid.*, p.1.

18. CB to WSW [*c.* 16 Sept. 1849]: MS Bon 212 pp.1–2, BPM, [*L&L*, iii, 17, where it is dated to 10 Sept., but it must postdate CB's letter asking him if he agrees with Taylor's criticisms]; CB to WSW, 13 Sept. 1849: MS n.l., [*L&L*, iii, 20].

19. CB to WSW, 15 Sept. 1849: MS EL 400, Rylands, [*L&L*, iii, 21].

20. CB to WSW, 2 Jan. 1849: MS p.1, Berg, [*L&L*, ii, 298].

21. CB to WSW, 16 Aug. 1849: MS Grolier F8 p.4, BPM, [*L&L*, iii, 12]; CB, 'A Word to the "Quarterly"', 29 Aug. 1849: MS S-G 96 p.1, BPM, [*BST*:16:85:329].

22. *Ibid.*, pp.3–7.

23. CB to WSW, 31 Aug. 1849: MS n.l., [*L&L*, iii, 15–16]; CB to GS, 31 Aug. 1849: MS S-G 21 p.1, BPM, [*L&L*, iii, 16]; CB to WSW, 4 Sept. 1849: MS BS 71.5, BPM.

24. CB, *Shirley*, pp.375–6; 'A word to the "Quarterly". Charlotte Brontë's rejected Preface to "Shirley"', *BST*:16:85:337.

25. CB to WSW, 16 Aug. 1849: MS Grolier F8 p.4, BPM, [*L&L*, iii, 12]; CB to WSW, 21 Sept. 1849: MS Grolier F9 p.2, BPM, [*L&L*, iii, 23].

26. CB to GS, 26 Oct. 1849: MS S-G 31 p.3, BPM, [*BST*:18:92:107].

27. CB to WSW, 21 Sept. 1849: MS Grolier F9 pp.1–2, BPM, [*L&L*, iii, 23].

28. *Ibid.*, p.2.

29. *Ibid.*, p.1; CB to WSW, 19 Sept. 1849: MS BS 71.6, BPM, [*L&L*, iii, 29]; CB to WSW, 1 Oct. 1849: MS n.l., [*L&L*, iii, 26].

30. CB to EN, [20 Oct. 1849]: MS Bon 216 pp.1–2, BPM [*L&L*, iii, 28]. According to a note in Charlotte's cash book, the dentist was Mr Atkinson of 30 Portland Crescent; she also called on Mr Gray of 14 Park Row, Leeds: CB, Cash Book, [1848–9]: MS BS 22 p.9, BPM.

31. CB to EN, [22 Jan. 1849]: MS HM 24464 p.2, Huntington, [*L&L*, ii, 303]; ECG, *Life*, p.277. Mary Taylor was equally blasé about featuring in her friend's novel: 'On Wednesday I began Shirley & continued in a curious confusion of mind till now principally abt the handsome foreigner who was nursed in our house when I was a little girl. – By the way you've put him in the servant's bedroom. You make us all talk much as I think we shd have done if we'd ventured to speak at all – What a little lump of perfection you've made me! There is a strange feeling in reading it of hearing us all tallking

[sic]. I have not seen the matted hall & painted parlour windows so plain these 5 years. But my Father is not like. He hates well enough & perhaps loves too but he is not honest enough. It was from my father I learnt not to marry for money nor to tolerate any one who did & he never wd <te> advise any one to do so or fail to speak with contempt of those who did.' MT to CB, 13 Aug. 1850: MS pp.1–2, Berg, [Stevens, p.97]. Mary inclined to the same curious opinion which generally (and uniquely) afflicts those who live in 'Shirley Country', namely that *Shirley* was a better and more interesting book than *Jane Eyre*.

32. CB to WSW, 1 Nov. 1849: MS MA 2696 R-V pp.2–3, Pierpont Morgan, [*L&L*, iii, 29].

33. *Ibid.*, pp.3–4; unsigned review, *Daily News*, 31 Oct. 1849, p.2, [Allott, pp.117–18]; CB to WSW, 1 Nov. 1849: MS MA 2696 R-V p.4, Pierpont Morgan, [*L&L*, iii, 30].

34. Unsigned review, *Atlas*, 3 Nov. 1849, pp.696–7, [Allott, p.120]; unsigned review, *Critic*, 15 Nov. 1849, pp.519–21, [Allott, p.141]; unsigned review [probably W. G. Clark], *Fraser's Magazine*, Dec. 1849, pp.691–4, [Allott, p.154].

35. CB to WSW, 5 Nov. 1849: MS n.l., [*L&L*, iii, 33].

36. [A. Fonblanque], *Examiner*, 3 Nov. 1849, pp.692–4, [Allott, pp.125–9]. For a similar range of criticism see *ibid.*, pp.117–70.

37. See, for example, the reviews in the *Britannia*, *Fraser's Magazine* and the *Westminster Review*, [Allott, pp.139, 153, 158].

38. ECG, *Life*, p.277.

39. CB to WSW, 15 Nov. 1849: MS HM 24392 pp.2–3, Huntington, [*L&L*, iii, 35].

40. CB to G. H. Lewes, 1 Nov. 1849: MS Add 39763(1) pp.1–2, BL, [*L&L*, iii, 31].

41. CB to WSW, 5 Nov. 1849: MS n.l., [*L&L*, iii, 34].

42. [G. H. Lewes], *Edinburgh Review*, Jan. 1850, pp.153–73, [Allott, 163, 165, 167].

43. CB to WSW, 10 Jan. 1850: MS pp.1–2, Berg, [*L&L*, iii, 66].

44. CB to G. H. Lewes, [Jan. 1850]: MS Add 39763(7), BL, [*L&L*, iii, 67].

45. CB to G. H. Lewes, 19 Jan. 1850: MS Add 39763(8) pp.1–3, BL, [*L&L*, iii, 68].

46. ECG to Eliza Fox, 26 Nov. 1849: [C&P, p.90]. Dr Epps was the London physician whom Charlotte had consulted about Emily's symptoms: see above, p.572.

47. CB to WSW, [*c.*16 Nov. 1849]: MS p.1, Brotherton, [*L&L*, iii, 40, wrongly dated to 20 Nov. 1849 but Charlotte says she received Mrs Gaskell's letter 'this morning' and her own reply is dated 17 Nov. 1849].

48. CB to ECG, 17 Nov. 1849: MS BS 71.7(a), BPM, [*BST*:17:90:349].

49. ECG to [Catherine Winkworth], [late Nov. 1849]: [C&P, p.93].

50. CB to WSW [*c.*16 Nov. 1849]: MS pp.2–3, Brotherton, [*L&L*, iii, 40: see note 47].

51. CB to WSW, 24 Nov. 1849: MS n.l., [*L&L*, iii, 45]; CB to WSW, 22 Nov. [1849]: MS p.2, Berg, [*L&L*, iii, 41]; CB to WSW, 19 Nov. 1849: MS p.4 crossed, Berg, [*L&L*, iii, 39].

52. CB to WSW, 22 Nov. [1849]: MS pp.3–4, Berg, [*L&L*, iii, 41].

53. CB to G.H. Lewes, 1 Nov. 1849: MS Add 39763(6) p.1, BL, [*L&L*, iii, 31].

54. CB to WSW, 15 Nov. 1849: MS HM 24392 p.3, Huntington, [*L&L*, iii, 35–6].

55. CB to GS, 19 Nov. 1849: MS S-G 28 pp.1–2, BPM, [*L&L*, iii, 37–8].

56. *Ibid.*, pp.2–3; CB to EN, 16 Nov. 1849: MS p.4, Harvard, [*L&L*, iii, 37]; CB to EN, 26 Nov. 1849: MS Bon 217 p.2, BPM, [*L&L*, iii, 43].

57. MT to ECG, [1857]: MS n.l., [Stevens, p.166].

58. CB to GS, 14 Sept. 1849: MS S-G 22 pp.1–2, BPM, [*BST*:18:92:104]; CB to GS, 20 Sept. 1849: MS S-G 23 pp.1–2, BPM, [*BST*:18:92:104–5]; CB to GS, 22 Sept, 1849: MS S-G 24 pp. 1–3, BPM, [*BST*:18:92:105–6].

59. CB to GS, 4 Oct. 1849: MS S-G 26 pp.1–2, BPM, [*L&L*, iii, 27]. See also CB to GS, 27 Sept. 1849: MS S-G 25, BPM, [*BST*:18:92:106]. Charlotte's concern at her father's reaction to the news was surely misplaced: he had already had to deal with the probates of both Emily's and Anne's estates, which included shares in the same railway, the latter only in the previous month, so he must have been aware of the true state of his daughter's finances. See EJB, Probate Papers, 31 Jan. 1849: MS PROBATE, Borthwick; EJB, Administration Papers, 5 Feb. 1849: MS Bon 73, BPM; AB, Probate Papers, 5 Sept. 1849: MS PROBATE, Borthwick; AB, Administration Papers, 5 Sept. 1849: MS Bon 74, BPM.

60. CB to EN, [4 Dec. 1849]: MS MA 2696 pp.2–3, Pierpont Morgan, [*L&L*, iii, 53].

61. *Ibid.*, p.3; CB to EN, [9 Dec. 1849]: MS in Berg [*L&L*, iii, 55].

62. CB to EN, [4 Dec. 1849]: MS MA 2696 R-V p.1, Pierpont Morgan, [*L&L*, iii, 53]; CB to MW, 14 Feb. 1850: MS FM 8 pp.5–6, Fitzwilliam, [*L&L*, iii, 76].

63. *Ibid.*, pp.6–7.

64. CB to EN, [9 Dec. 1849]: MS in Berg, [*L&L*, iii, 55]; CB to WSW, 19 Dec. 1849: MS pp.1–3, Princeton, [*L&L*, iii, 61].

65. CB to Laetitia Wheelwright, 17 Dec. [1849]: MS BS 72 pp.1–2, BPM, [*L&L*, iii, 59].

66. CB to EN, [9 Dec. 1849]: MS in Berg, [*L&L*, iii, 56]; CB to WSW, 19 Dec. 1849: MS pp.3–4, Princeton, [*L&L*, iii, 61–2].

67. W.M. Thackeray, 'The Last Sketch', *Cornhill*, i, Jan.–June 1860, p.486.

68. CB to PB, 5 Dec. 1849: MS pp.1–3, Berg, [*L&L*, iii, 54, wrongly dated to 4 Dec. 1849].

69. ECG, *Life*, p.287. For the reference to *Jane Eyre*, where the smell of Mr Rochester's cigar warns Jane that he is nearby, see CB, *Jane Eyre*, p.250. CB to PB, 5 Dec. 1849: MS p.3, Berg, [*L&L*, iii, 54, wrongly dated to 4 Dec. 1849].

70. HM, *Autobiography*, pp.323–5.

71. Lucy Martineau to Jack Martineau, 10 Dec. 1849: MS pp.3–4, in private hands, Barker, '"Innocent & Un-Londony": Impressions of Charlotte Brontë': *BST*:19:1&2:46–7].

72. HM, *Autobiography*, p.326. Catherine Wink-worth, a friend of Miss Martineau's, knew by 5 December 1849 that 'the author is herself threatened with consumption at this time, and has lost two sisters, Ellis and Acton Bell, by it. Their real name is Brontë, they are of the Nelson family': Catherine Winkworth to Eliza Paterson, 5 Dec. 1849: Shaen (ed.), *Memorials of Two Sisters*, p.53. The reference to the Brontës being of the Nelson family ties in with the gossip G.H. Lewes was spreading.

73. ECG to Anne Shaen, [?20 Dec. 1849]: [C&P, p.97]; Lucy Martineau to Jack Martineau, 10 Dec. 1849: MS pp.4–5, in private hands, Barker, '"Innocent & Un-Londony": Impressions of Charlotte Brontë': *BST*:19:1&2:47].

74. *Ibid.*, p.4. For a typically garbled version, based on this letter or a personal interview, see ECG to Anne Shaen, [?20 Dec. 1849]: [C&P, pp.96–7]. Mrs Gaskell wrongly describes the meeting as taking place in Hyde Park Square: 'when lo! and behold, as the clock struck, in walked a little, very little, bright haired sprite, looking not above 15, very unsophisticated, neat & tidy. She sat down & had tea with them; her name being still unknown; she said to HM, "What did you really think of 'Jane Eyre'?" HM. I thought it a first rate book, whereupon the little sprite went red all over with pleasure. After tea Mr & Mrs RM. withdrew and left sprite to a 2 hours tete-a-tete with HM, to whom she revealed her name & the history of her life. Her father a Yorkshire clergyman who has never slept out of his house for 26 years; she has lived a most retired life; – her first visit to London, never been in society, and many other particulars which HM. is not at liberty to divulge any more than her name, which she keeps a profound secret; but Thackeray does *not*'.

75. CB to PB, 5 Dec. 1849: MS p.3, Berg, [*L&L*, iii, 54, wrongly dated to 4 Dec. 1849].

76. CB to Laetitia Wheelwright, 17 Dec. [1849]: MS BS 72 pp.1–2, BPM, [*L&L*, iii, 59]; ECG *Life*, p.288–9.

77. Unsigned review, *The Times*, 7 Dec. 1849, [Allott, pp.288–9]; [Mrs Smith], ECG, *Life*, p.287.

78. CB to MW, 14 Feb. 1850: MS FM 8 p.5, Fitzwilliam, [*L&L*, iii, 76].

79. CB to WSW, 19 Dec. 1849: MS pp.5–6, Princeton, [*L&L*, iii, 62].

80. CB to Laetitia Wheelwright, 17 Dec. [1849]: MS BS 72 pp.1–2, BPM, [*L&L*, iii, 59].

81. CB to GS, 17 Dec. 1849: MS S-G 30 pp.1–2, BPM, [*L&L*, iii, 58–9]. For the other letters see CB to Laetitia Wheelwright, 17 Dec. [1849]: MS BS 72, BPM, [*L&L*, iii, 59] and CB to Mrs

Smith, 17 Dec. 1849: MS S-G 29, BPM, [*L&L*, iii, 58].

82. CB to GS, 26 Dec. 1849: MS S-G 31 p.1, BPM, [*BST*:18:92:106–7, wrongly dated to 26 Oct. 1849].

83. *Ibid.*, pp.3–5. Knowing George Smith's tastes as well as she did, it is probably significant that Charlotte herself acquired 'the prettiest little pink drawn-silk' bonnet for one of her later trips to London: see HAOBP: D141, BPM.

84. CB to GS, 15 Jan. 1850: MS S-G 33 pp.2–3, BPM, [*L&L*, iii, 67].

85. CB to WSW, 19 Dec. 1849: MS p.1, Princeton, [*L&L*, iii, 61]; CB to WSW, 19 Nov. 1849: MS pp.1–2, Berg, [*L&L*, iii, 38].

86. CB to EN, 19 Dec. 1849: MS p.3, Berg, [*L&L*, iii, 60, wrongly dated to 18 Dec. 1849]; CB to EN, 22 Dec. 1849: MS part in Yale, [*L&L*, iii, 63].

87. 'P. B.', 'A Christmas Hymn', *Leeds Intelligencer*, 22 Dec. 1849, p.7; 'P. B.', 'Our Church, it is pure and unstain'd,', 18 Dec. 1849: MS BS x, B, BPM.

88. CB to EN, 22 Dec. 1849: MS part in Yale, [*L&L*, iii, 63].

89. CB to Amelia Ringrose, 16 Nov. 1849: MS p.1, Brotherton, [*L&L*, iii, 36]; CB to EN, 16 Nov. 1849: MS pp.1–3, Harvard, [*L&L*, iii, 67]; CB to EN, [9 Dec. 1849]: MS in Berg, [*L&L*, iii, 56].

90. CB to EN, 22 Dec. 1849: MS part in Yale, [*L&L*, iii, 62–3].

91. CB to WSW, 3 Jan. 1850: MS BS 73 pp.2–3, BPM, [*L&L*, iii, 63].

92. William Margetson Heald to EN, 8 Jan. 1850: MS BS ix, H, BPM, [*L&L*, iii, 64–5].

93. CB to EN, [19 Jan. 1850]: MS p.2, Law Colln, photograph in Mildred Christian Colln, BPM, [*L&L*, iii, 69]. Arthur Bell Nicholls is said to have presented Charlotte with a Book of Common Prayer on the publication of *Shirley* but this letter implies he knew nothing of Charlotte's authorship until after her return from London. The book is Rare Book Rit.d.775.1., UCL.

94. CB to EN, [28 Jan. 1850]: MS p.4, Harvard, [*L&L*, iii, 71]. Arthur Nicholls received a more favourable portrayal than his fellow curates in

Shirley, being described as 'decent, decorous, and conscientious' and credited with making the Sunday and Day Schools flourish 'like green bay-trees' under his sway; nevertheless, as Mr Macarthey, he was still a victim of Charlotte's acerbic wit. 'Being human, of course he had his faults; these, however, were proper, steady-going, clerical faults; what many would call virtues: the circumstance of finding himself invited to tea with a Dissenter would unhinge him for a week; the spectacle of a Quaker wearing his hat in the church – the thought of an unbaptized fellow-creature being interred with Christian rites – these things could make strange havoc in Mr Macarthey's physical and mental economy; otherwise, he was sane and rational, diligent and charitable': CB, *Shirley*, p.634.

95. CB to EN, [5 Feb. 1850]: MS pp.1–2, Berg, [*L&L*, iii, 73].

96. *Ibid.*, p.2.

97. CB to EN, [16 Feb. 1850]: MS Grolier E17 p.2, BPM, [JB *ST*, no.1].

98. CB to WSW, 3 April 1850: MS pp.3–4, Berg, [*L&L*, iii, 89, where it is wrongly transposed into the middle of a letter from CB to WSW of 19 March 1850]; CB to EN, 30 March 1850: MS HM 24469 pp.3–4, Huntington, [*L&L*, iii, 91].

99. John Berry to the Editor, *Boston Weekly Museum*, 2 March 1850, [*BST*:16:83:206]; CB to EN, 30 March 1850: MS HM 24469 p.2, Huntington, [*L&L*, iii, 90–1].

100. CB to WSW, 3 April 1850: MS pp.5–6, Berg, [*L&L*, iii, 89: see note 98].

101. CB to WSW, 22 Feb. 1850: MS HM 24393 p.4, Huntington, [*L&L*, iii, 80].

102. CB to EN, [16 Feb. 1850]: MS Grolier E17 pp.5–7, BPM, [JB *ST*, no.1]. Most printed sources, following the misreading in *L&L*, iii, 78, identify the rumbustious parson as the Revd John Barber, vicar of Bierley, but even though the name in the manuscript has been deleted, it is still clearly legible as that of Andrew Cassels of Batley.

103. *Bradford Observer*, 28 Feb. 1850, p.5.

CHAPTER TWENTY-TWO

Title: Referring to Charlotte, 'This was her notion of literary fame – a passport to the society of clever people': MT to ECG, [1857]: MS n.l., [Stevens, p.166].

1. CB, 'I have never had time for much writing', 23 Jan. 1850: MS Bon 124(1) BPM, [CB, *Villette*, Clarendon Edn, Appx.1, pp.753–5]; see also the three ensuing fragments, MSS Bon 124(2–4), BPM, [*ibid.*, pp.755–64].

2. CB to EN, [16 Feb. 1850]: MS Grolier E17 p.3, BPM, [JB *ST*, no.1].

3. *Ibid.*, p.3; CB to MW, 14 Feb. 1850: MS FM 8 pp.3–4, Fitzwilliam, [*L&L*, iii, 75].

4. CB to EN, [16 Feb. 1850]: MS Grolier E17 pp.4–5, BPM, [JB *ST*, no.1].

5. *Dictionary of National Biography*, x, 1138–40; CB to Lady Kay Shuttleworth, 5 Feb. 1850: MS p.1, Harvard.

6. CB to EN, 5 March 1850: MS n.l., [*L&L*, iii, 81].

7. CB to EN, 19 March 1850: MS pp.1–2, Law Colln, photograph in Mildred Christian Colln, BPM, [*L&L*, iii, 86].

8. CB to WSW, 16 March 1850: MS p.3, Law Colln, photograph in Mildred Christian Colln, BPM, [*L&L*, iii, 82]. See also CB to EN, 19 March 1850: MS pp.3–4, Law Colln, photograph in Mildred Christian Colln, BPM, [*L&L*, iii, 87].

9. CB to WSW, 16 March 1850: MS p.3, Law Colln, photograph in Mildred Christian Colln, BPM [*L&L*, iii, 82]; CB to Lady Kay Shuttleworth, 22 March 1850: MS in private hands, [*BST*:16:84:274].

10. CB to EN, 19 March 1850: MS pp.4–5, Law Colln, photograph in Mildred Christian Colln, BPM, [*L&L*, iii, 87–8].

11. CB to Thornton Hunt, 16 March 1850: MS Bon 218, BPM, [*L&L*, iii, 85]; CB to GS, 16 March 1850: MS S-G 34 pp.1–2, BPM, [*L&L*, iii, 83].

12. CB to EN, 28 Jan. 1850: MS p.3, Harvard, [*L&L*, iii, 71]; CB to Mr Lovejoy, 5 Feb. 1850: MS BS 75, BPM; CB to Miss Alexander, 18 March 1850: MS in Brotherton, [*L&L*, iii, 86]. Charlotte still signed the note 'C Bell' and did not give Miss Alexander the satisfaction of her address or real name.

13. CB to WSW, 19 March 1850: MS n.l., [*L&L*, iii, 88]; CB, 'List of books from Smith & Elder', 18 March 1850: MS BS 23, BPM. As this is the only extant list of books in a Smith, Elder & Co. parcel, it is worth transcribing the whole: Southey's *Life*, [Julia Kavanagh] *Women in France, Hungarian Lady, Letters of Chas Lamb, Self-Culture*, Hazlitt's *Essays*, [Emerson] *Representative Men*, [Meinhold] *Amber Witch*, [Jane Austen] *Sense & Sensibility*, [Jane Austen] *Emma*, [Jane Austen] *Pride & Pred* [sic], *Marian*, William Carleton *Tithe Proctor, Life of Mahomet*, Valerius [Maximus] [*Facta et Dicta Memorabilia*], *Woman's Friendship*, [Samuel Brown] *Galileo Galilei*, G. H. Lewes *The Noble Heart*, Scott *Suggestions [on Female Education], Woman & her Master*.

14. CB to WSW, 12 April 1850: MS HM 24394 pp.4–5, Huntington, [*L&L*, iii, 99].

15. CB to WSW, 3 April 1850: MS p.7, Berg, [*L&L*, iii, 94]; CB to EN, [12 April 1850]: MS BS 75.6 pp.1–2, BPM, [*L&L*, iii, 100].

16. Petition from the principal Inhabitants of Haworth to the General Board of Health, 28 Aug. 1849: MS n.l., [L&D, p.432].

17. PB to the Secretary to the General Board of Health, 5 Feb. 1850: MS n.l., [L&D, p.433]; For the results of Babbage's investigation see above, pp.95–6; Babbage Report, pp.12, 26–7.

18. CB to EN, [12 April 1850]: MS BS 75.6 pp.1–2, BPM, [*L&L*, iii, 100]; CB to Amelia Ringrose, 6 April 1850: MS p.2, Brotherton, [*L&L*, iii, 97].

19. CB to EN, [12 April 1850]: MS BS 75.6 p.2, BPM, [*L&L*, iii, 100].

20. *Leeds Mercury*, 6 April 1850, p.5.

21. CB to EN, [12 April 1850]: MS BS 75.6 pp.2–4, BPM, [*L&L*, iii, 100]; CB to Lady Kay Shuttleworth, 18 May 1850: MS BS 76 p.2, BPM, [*BST*:13:67:144].

22. CB to EN, [15 April 1850]: MS HM 24470 pp.1–2, Huntington, [*L&L*, iii, 101].

23. *Ibid.*; CB to EN, [24 April 1850]: MS Grolier E18 p.1, BPM, [*L&L*, iii, 102]; CB to Amelia Ringrose, [28 April 1850]: MS p.1, Brotherton, [*L&L*, iii, 106]. The letter to Ellen asks 'what are the results of the operation', which the *L&L*

unaccountably transcribes as 'tooth extraction'; the letter to Amelia refers to a 'dentist-operation'.

24. CB to EN, [24 April 1850]: MS Grolier E18 pp.1–3, BPM, [*L&L*, iii, 102]; CB to EN, [29 April 1850]: MS Bon 219 pp.1–2, BPM, [*L&L*, iii, 107]; CB to EN, 31 Jan. 1850: MS p.2, Pforzheimer, [*L&L*, iii, 72].

25. CB to EN, [7 Feb. 1850]: MS pp.1–3, Kentucky, [*L&L*, iii, 73–4, wrongly dated to 5 Feb. 1850].

26. CB to Amelia Ringrose, 31 March 1850: MS p.4, Brotherton, [*L&L*, iii, 92]; CB to Amelia Ringrose, 6 April 1850: MS p.3, Brotherton, [*L&L*, iii, 97–8].

27. CB to EN, [12 April 1850]: MS BS 75.6 p.4, BPM, [*L&L*, iii, 100]; CB to EN, [29 April 1850]: MS Bon 219 p.3, BPM, [*L&L*, iii, 107].

28. *Ibid.*, pp.1–3.

29. CB to EN, 11 May 1850: MS pp.3–4, Princeton, [*L&L*, iii, 109]; CB to John Driver, 16 May 1850: MS in Maine. Although I have been unable to identify Mr Driver, it seems likely he was related to the Revd Jonas Driver who lent the Brontës newspapers [see above, p.419]; a personal acquaintance is implicit in Charlotte's valedictory 'my own and my Father's united regards to yourself and Mrs Driver'.

30. CB to Lady Kay Shuttleworth, 18 May 1850: MS BS 76 pp.1–2, BPM, [*BST*:13:67:144]; CB to EN, 21 May 1850: MS n.l., [*L&L*, iii, 110]; CB to Lady Kay Shuttleworth, 21 May 1850: MS pp.1–2, Harvard.

31. CB to James Taylor, 22 May 1850: MS p.2, Princeton, [*L&L*, iii, 111].

32. *Ibid.*, pp.3–4.

33. The Smiths had moved from Westbourne Place to Gloucester Terrace in March 1850: see CB to GS, 16 March 1850: MS S-G 34 p.4, BPM, [*L&L*, iii, 84 omitted]. The passage omitted from the printed text offers George Smith 'my excessive sympathy in that painful operation of a "removal" to which you allude – and a much sincerer sympathy to your Mother and Sisters – for you I daresay have not been allowed to suffer much'. CB to Mrs Smith, 25 May 1850: MS S-G 5b p.3, BPM, [*L&L*, iii, 113]. The baby-socks are wrongly enclosed with MS S-G 6b, BPM; they are referred to in CB to Mrs Smith, 9 Jan. 1850: MS S-G 4b pp.3–4, BPM, [*L&L*, iii, 66].

34. CB to Mrs Smith, 25 May 1850: MS S-G 5b p.3, BPM, [*L&L*, iii, 113]; CB to Lady Kay Shuttleworth, 29 May 1850: MS BS 77 pp.1–2, BPM, [*BST*:13:66:39].

35. CB to EN, 3 June 1850: MS pp.1–2, Princeton, [*L&L*, iii, 115].

36. CB to GS, 18 April 1850: MS S-G 35 p.1, BPM, [*L&L*, iii, 101]; CB to GS, 27 July 1850: MS S-G 38 p.2, BPM, [*L&L*, iii, 127]; CB to WSW, 6 May 1850: MS pp.1–2, Harvard, [*L&L*, iii, 108].

37. CB to Martha Brown, 12 June 1850: MS Law Colln, [*L&L*, iii, 120]; CB to PB, 4 June 1850: MS n.l., [*L&L*, iii, 116–17]. Though Charlotte clearly tailored her news to suit her recipients,

Martha's letter is the only one to carry anything more than the bare fact that Charlotte had attended the Opera – she does not even indicate which opera she saw.

38. CB to EN, [12 June 1850]: MS HM 24471 p.2, Huntington, [*L&L*, iii, 117]: Smith, p.92.

39. CB to EN, [12 June 1850]: MS HM 24471 pp.1–2, Huntington, [*L&L*, iii, 117]; Smith, p.92.

40. *Ibid.*, p.101; G. H. Lewes to GS, n.d.: MS n.l., [*L&L*, iii, 172].

41. CB to EN, [12 June 1850]: MS HM 24471 p.3, Huntington, [*L&L*, iii, 118]. With her startling ability to rewrite the past, in a letter to George Smith fifteen months later Charlotte was to say of Lewes, 'I felt what he was through the very first letter he sent me – and had no wish ever to hear from – or write to him again – You appear to me something very different – <u>not</u> hard – <u>not</u> insolent – <u>not</u> coarse – <u>not</u> to be distrusted – all the contrary': CB to GS, 15 Sept. 1851: MS S-G 56 p.3, BPM, [*BST*:18:92:110].

42. G. W. Cross (ed.), *George Eliot's Life: as related in her letters and journals* (Blackwood, 1885), i, 307.

43. CB to EN, [12 June 1850]: MS HM 24471 pp.3–4, Huntington, [*L&L*, iii, 118].

44. *Ibid.*, pp.5–6. Charlotte now instinctively shrank from the family, excepting only Smith Williams himself and his eldest daughter from her mysterious comment to Ellen that 'others do not see – or at least do not mention – what I seem to see in that family –'.

45. *Ibid.*, p.2; W. M. Thackeray, 'The Last Sketch', *Cornhill*, i, Jan.–June 1860, p.487; Smith, pp.92, 100.

46. Thackeray Ritchie, *Chapters from Some Memoirs*, [*L&L*, iii, 49]. Mrs Brookfield also said that the Carlyles were present, though one would have expected Charlotte to mention a meeting with the eminent historian and his wife. Charlotte does refer to meeting another lady novelist, Geraldine Jewsbury, in London during this visit and she may well have been present on this occasion: Brookfield, *Mrs Brookfield and Her Circle*, ii, 355–6; CB to EN, [15 July 1850]: MS p.3, Law Colln, photograph in Mildred Christian Colln, BPM, [*L&L*, iii, 50].

47. Thackeray Ritchie, *Chapters from Some Memoirs*, [*L&L*, iii, 48]. Fragments of the dress, which was cut up to give as mementoes to souvenir hunters, are preserved in the BPM: see, for example, HAOBP: D59, BPM. As it was now over a year since Anne's death, Charlotte would have come out of mourning a few days before her trip to London.

48. Brookfield, *Mrs Brookfield and her Circle*, ii, 305. Mrs Brookfield confuses the various meetings of Thackeray and Charlotte: she describes the hairpiece in relation to their first meeting in December 1849, but it was not purchased until the end of April 1850. She also describes the dinner party in Young Street as taking place after Thackeray's lectures, but these took place in 1851 and Anne Thackeray Ritchie places the

dinner party in 1850: Charlotte herself refers to going to dine there in her letter CB to EN, [12 June 1850]: MS HM 24471 pp.2–3, Huntington, [*L&L*, iii, 118]. For the purchase of the hairpiece see CB to EN, [29 May 1850]: MS Bon 219 p.4, BPM, [*L&L*, iii, 107]; CB to EN, [11 May 1850]: MS p.4, Princeton, [*L&L*, iii, 109].

49. Thackeray Ritchie, *Chapters from Some Memoirs*, [*L&L*, iii, 48].

50. *Ibid.*, [*L&L*, iii, 48–50];Smith, p.98.

51. *Ibid.*, pp.98–9.

52. Susan Foister, 'The Brontë Portraits', *BST*:18:95:350.

53. Stirling, *The Richmond Papers*, p.60.

54. Smith, p.104.

55. Mary Taylor to ECG, [1857]: MS n.l., [Stevens, p.133].

56. Sidney Lee, 'Charlotte Brontë in London', *BST*:4:19:116. The commission did not prevent requests for permission to publish Charlotte's portrait; the very day she sat to Richmond she wrote refusing one such request: CB to James Hogg, 13 June 1850: MS Egerton 2697 p.28, BL, [*L&L*, iii, 120].

57. CB to EN, 21 June 1850: MS Grolier E19 p.1, BPM, [*L&L*, iii, 121].

58. *Ibid.*, p.2.

59. CB to EN, 19 Dec. 1849: MS p.2, Berg, [*L&L*, iii, 60, wrongly dated to 18 Dec. 1849]. Aware of the criticisms of *Jane Eyre*, Mrs Smith expected Charlotte to be a man-eater – and was disappointed. 'Mrs Smith is rather a stern woman – but she has sense and discrimination – She watched me very narrowly – when I was surrounded by gentlemen – she never took her eye from me – I liked the surveillance – both when it kept guard over me amongst many or only with her cherished and valued Son – She soon – I am convinced – saw in what light I viewed both her George and all the rest – Thackeray included.'

60. CB to EN, 21 June 1850: MS Grolier E19 pp.2–3, BPM, [*L&L*, iii, 121].

61. Smith, pp.91, 92, 96, 101.

62. CB to Mrs Smith, 28 June 1850: MS S-G 8b pp.1–2, BPM, [*L&L*, iii, 122].

63. CB to Laetitia Wheelwright, 30 July 1850: MS p.2, Berg, [*L&L*. iii, 128]; CB to GS, 27 June 1850: MS S-G 36 p.1, BPM, [*L&L*, iii, 121].

64. Smith, p.104; CB to WSW, 20 July 1850: MS Bon 221 pp.1–2, BPM, [*L&L*, iii, 125].

65. CB to Laetitia Wheelwright, 30 July 1850: MS pp.2–3, Berg, [*L&L*, iii, 128].

66. CB to EN, 5 July 1850: MS in Eton College Library, [*L&L*, iii, 123].

67. PB to EN, 12 July 1850: MS BS 194 pp.2–3, BPM, [*BST*:12:63:198]; see also CB to Martha Brown, 12 June 1850: MS in Law Colln, [*L&L*, iii, 119]. For the anecdote see [Benjamin Binns], *Bradford Observer*, 17 Feb. 1894, p.6.

68. PB to EN, 12 July 1850: MS BS 194 pp.1–2, BPM, [*BST*:12:63:198].

69. CB to EN, [15 July 1850]: MS pp.2–3, Law

Colln, photograph in Mildred Christian Colln, BPM, [*L&L*, iii, 123].

70. PB to EN, 12 July 1850: MS BS 194 p.4, BPM, [*BST*:12:63:198].

71. CB to EN, 18 July 1850: MS Bon 220 pp.2–3, BPM, [*L&L*, iii, 125]; CB to WSW, 20 July 1850: MS Bon 221 p.2, BPM, [*L&L*, iii, 125–6]; CB to GS, 27 July 1850: MS S-G 38 p.2, BPM, [*L&L*, iii, 127].

72. CB to EN, 1 Aug. 1850: MS Bon 222 pp.2–3, BPM, [*L&L*, iii, 129]; PB to GS, 2 Aug. 1850: MS File 10 no.1, John Murray.

73. CB to GS, 1 Aug. 1850: MS n.l., [*L&L*, iii, 130].

74. *Ibid.*; PB to GS, 2 Aug. 1850: MS File 10 no.1 pp.2–3, John Murray, [*L&L*, iii, 131].

75. CB to GS, 1 Aug. 1850: MS n.l., [*L&L*, iii, 130]; CB to GS, 5 Aug. 1850: MS S-G 37 pp.2–3, BPM, [*L&L*, iii, 132].

76. CB to EN, 7 Aug. 1850: MS Bon 223 pp.1–2, BPM, [*L&L*, iii, 133]. The actual subject of Charlotte's embargo is not mentioned; I have presumed it is the question of a possible marriage with George Smith, knowing Patrick's anxiety on the subject and judging from Charlotte's refusal to give an unspecified promise to Ellen in a previous letter on the grounds that 'Who that does not know the future can make promises? Not I': CB to EN, 1 Aug. 1850: MS Bon 222 p.3, BPM, [*L&L*, iii, 129].

77. CB to EN, 23 Oct. 1850: MS HM 24476 p.4, Huntington, [*L&L*, iii, 174].

78. CB to EN, 26 Aug. 1850: MS part HM 24473 p.4, Huntington and part in Berg, [*L&L*, iii, 149]. Manners published his *English Ballads and Other Poems* in 1850; Smythe was a brilliant journalist: both were models for Disraeli's ideal Conservative in *Coningsby*.

79. CB to EN, 16 Aug. 1850: MS HM 24472 p.4, Huntington, [*L&L*, iii, 139].

80. CB to PB, [20 Aug. 1850]: MS BS 79 pp.1–2, BPM, [*L&L*, iii, 139–40, wrongly dated to 19 Aug. 1850]. For descriptions of the drive and house, which has been demolished and replaced, see ECG to Catherine Winkworth, [25 Aug. 1850]: MS p.2, Brotherton, [C&P, p.123].

81. *Ibid.*, p.3.

82. *Ibid.*, pp.5–11.

83. *Ibid.*, pp.8, 10–12. With characteristic exaggeration of what Charlotte must have told her, Mrs Gaskell said Charlotte expected a lonely death because she had no friend or relative in the world to nurse her and her father 'dreaded a sick room above all places'. This was patently untrue: Patrick was an assiduous visitor of the dying, witness, for example, his daily attendance on both William Weightman and Charlotte herself, and Ellen Nussey would willingly have nursed her friend if she was dying, as she did on the occasions she was ill.

84. ECG to Eliza Fox, [27] Aug. 1850: [C&P, p.130]; CB to EN, 26 Aug. 1850: MS HM 24473 p.4, Huntington, [*L&L*, iii, 148].

85. ECG to Catherine Winkworth, [25 Aug. 1850]: MS p.4, Brotherton, [C&P, p.124]; ECG to Charlotte Froude, [*c.*25 Aug. 1850]: [C&P, p.129]. Francis Newman, who later became a Unitarian like Mrs Gaskell, was an opponent of his Catholic brother and both ladies liked his book, *The Soul*, which had been published the previous year. ECG to Eliza Fox, [27] Aug. 1850: [C&P, p.130].

86. CB to James Taylor, 6 Nov. 1850: MS p.4, Texas, [*L&L*, iii, 178–9].

87. CB to James Taylor, 15 Jan. 1851: MS pp.2–3, Texas, [*L&L*, iii, 199].

88. CB to EN, 26 Aug. 1850: MS HM 24473 p.1., Huntington, [*L&L*, iii, 147]; CB to MW, 27 Sept. 1850: MS FM 9 pp.2–3, Fitzwilliam, [*L&L*, iii, 163–4].

89. ECG to Eliza Fox, [27] Aug. 1850: [C&P, p.130]; CB to EN, 26 Aug. 1850: MS HM 24473 pp.3–4, Huntington, [*L&L*, iii, 148].

90. *Ibid.*, p.1.

91. CB to ECG, 27 Aug. 1850: MS n.l., [*L&L*, iii, 149].

92. CB to EN, 1 Aug. 1850: MS Bon 222 p.2, BPM, [*L&L*, iii, 129]; CB to EN, 2 Sept. 1850: MS HM 24474 pp.2–4, Huntington, [*L&L*, iii, 152]. Charlotte's opinion, expressed here, coincides with Mary Taylor's: 'His passion for marryin[g] seems just to have come because it is the only thing serious enough to excite him – if that were done what would there be left?': MT to CB, 5 April 1850: MS p.1, Texas, [Stevens, p.88].

93. CB to EN, 2 Sept. 1850: MS HM 24474 p.2, Huntington, [*L&L*, iii, 151–2]; CB to EN, 14 Sept. 1850: MS HM 24475 p.1, Huntington, [*L&L*, iii, 158]. Charlotte was wrong in saying that there had been a lapse in correspondence for nine months: she had written to James Taylor, mentioning the receipt that morning of a letter from him, on 22 May 1850: MS p.3, Princeton, [*L&L*, iii, 111]; CB to James Taylor, 5 Sept. 1850: MS pp.2–3, Texas, [*L&L*, iii, 154].

94. [Sydney Dobell], unsigned review, *Palladium*, Sept. 1850, pp.161–75, [Allott, pp.277–83]. In the light of Charlotte's comment to Mrs Gaskell that Shirley was a portrayal of Emily as she might have been if she had had health and fortune, it is surprising that she did not react to Dobell's remark that 'To make Shirley Keeldar repulsive, you have only to fancy her poor': Allott, p.282.

95. CB to WSW, 5 Sept. 1850: MS pp.3–4, Princeton, [*L&L*, iii, 156].

96. CB to GS, 3 Dec. 1850: MS S-G 42 p.2, BPM, [*L&L*, iii, 185]. For further details of the negotiations with Newby see CB to GS, 18 Sept. 1850: MSS S-G 39 and 40, BPM, [*L&L*, iii, 158–60]; CB to GS, 31 Oct. 1850: MS S-G 41 pp.4–5, BPM, [*L&L*, iii, 177].

97. CB, *Biographical Notice*, pp.364–5. Charlotte withdrew a more explicit condemnation of the critics in her last paragraph 'for I believe it was not expressed with the best grace in the world':

CB to WSW, 16 Oct. 1850: MS Bon 277 p.1, BPM, [*L&L*, iii, 171].

98. EJB, 'I do not weep, I would not weep,', 19 Dec. 1841: MS Add 43483 pp.43–4, BL, [Encouragement, 1850, l.14]; EJB, 'A little while, a little while', 4 Dec. 1838: MS in Law Colln, [facsimile in *Poems of EJB & AB*, pp.303–4] [Stanzas, 1850, l.40].

99. EJB, 'Loud without the wind was roaring', 11 Nov. 1838: MS in Law Colln, [facsimile in *Poems of EJB & AB*, pp.301–2] [Stanzas, 1850, l.32]; EJB, 'In summer's mellow midnight', 11 Sept. 1840: MS in Law Colln, [facsimile in *Poems of EJB & AB*, pp.308–9] [The Night-Wind, 1850, ll.33–6].

100. EJB, 'Silent is the House – all are laid asleep', 9 Oct. 1845: MS Add 43483 pp.59–62, BL, [The Visionary, 1850]. There was a precedent for this in that Emily had used ll.13–44 for the 1846 edition of *Poems*, rounding off the extract with a newly composed verse. The other three poems to which Charlotte added lines are : EJB, 'Aye there it is! It wakes tonight', 6 July 1841: MS in Law Colln, [facsimile in *Poems of EJB & AB*, p.309] ['Ay – there it is – it wakes tonight', 1850, to which CB added 5 lines at the end]; EJB, 'Listen! when your hair, like mine,', 11 Nov. 1844:

MS Add 43483 pp.46–7, BL [The Elder's Rebuke, 1850, of which CB printed only the first 28 lines, adding 6 of her own at the end]; EJB, 'Child of Delight! with sunbright hair', [28 May 1845]: MS Add 43483 pp.57–8, BL ['Child of delight, with sun-bright hair', 1850, in which CB inserted four lines before Emily's last verse].

101. AB, 'I have gone backward in the work', 20 Dec. 1841: MS Bon 134(2), BPM [Despondency, 1850, in which CB omitted the fifth verse].

102. AB, 'Blessed be Thou for all the Joy', 10 Nov. 1842: MS Bon 134(1), BPM [In Memory of a Happy Day in February, 1850, l.47]; AB, 'My God! O let me call Thee mine!', 13 Oct, 1844: MS Bon 133 pp.72–3, BPM [A Prayer, 1850, l.9]. Charlotte presumably intended a parallel with William Cowper's famous poem, 'The Castaway', with which all the family were familiar.

103. AB, 'A dreadful darkness closes in', 7–28 Jan. 1849: MS Bon 137, BPM, ['I hoped that with the brave and strong', 1850, omitting ll.1–16, 29–36, 41–52 and substituting ll.25–8].

104. CB to EN, 23 Oct. 1850: MS HM 24476 pp.2–3, Huntington, [*L&L*, iii, 173].

105. CB to WSW, 2 Oct. 1850: MS HM 24397 p.2, Huntington, [*L&L*, iii, 166–7].

CHAPTER TWENTY-THREE

Title: CB to ECG, 6 Nov 1851: MS EL fB91 p.2, Rylands, [*L&L*, iii, 286].

1. [Jane Forster] to Mrs Gaskell, 3 Oct. 1850, quoted in ECG, *Life*, pp.319–21. The assumption that Mrs Forster was the writer of this letter is derived from her use of 'W— ' to stand for her husband William, her friendship with Mrs Gaskell and Harriet Martineau, both of whom could have introduced her to Charlotte, and a reference in one of Charlotte's letters to the Forsters making 'another of their sudden calls here': CB to EN, 5 Oct. 1852: MS in Berg [*L&L*, iv, 10].

2. CB to John Stores Smith, 25 July 1850: MS 2696 R-V p.1, Pierpont Morgan, [*L&L*, iii, 126]. See also *BST*:16:81:22–3 for Smith's account of his visit written in 1868.

3. *Ibid.*, pp.25–8. Smith's description of Patrick is somewhat suspect: he 'remembered' him being blind, which he was not, and that he rambled on in senile fashion about his daughters' deaths and Charlotte's unexpected success. According to Smith, Charlotte had met Dickens during her recent visit to London (a fact not recorded elsewhere) and, while admiring his genius, disliked him personally.

4. 'K. T.' to CB, [c.8 Nov. 1850]: MS Bon 230 p.2, BPM, [*BST*:9:47:48, wrongly dated to 9 Nov. 1850]; CB to 'K. T.', 9 Nov. 1850: MS HM 20069 p.2, Huntington.

5. 'K. T.' to CB, 13 Nov. 1850: MS Bon 230 (2) pp.4, 8, 9; CB to 'K. T.', 21 Nov. 1850: MS p.2, Princeton,

[*L&L*, iii, 181]. A draft of this letter is in Bon 230(3), BPM. 'K. T.' to CB, 25 Nov. 1850: MS Bon 230(4), BPM, [*BST*:9:47:93–6]; CB to 'K. T.', 6 Dec. 1850: MS pp.1–2, Harvard. A draft of this letter is in Bon 231, BPM, [*BST*:9:47:96–7]. 'K. T.' admitted his age was thirty in his final letter to Charlotte, 11 Dec. 1850: MS Bon 231 p.2, BPM, [*BST*:9:47:98].

6. CB to EN, [14 Oct. 1850]: MS Bon 226 p.2, BPM, [*L&L*, iii, 169]; CB to EN, 16 Aug. 1850: MS HM 24472 p.3, Huntington, [*L&L*, iii, 139].

7. CB to G.H. Lewes, 17 Oct. 1850: MS Add 39763(9) p.2, BL, [*L&L*, iii, 172–3]. Charlotte returned the books in her box to Smith, Elder & Co.: CB to [WSW], 21 Oct 1850: MS in private hands.

8. CB to WSW, 25 Oct. 1850: MS HM 24398 p.1, Huntington, [*L&L*, iii, 174]; see also CB to James Taylor, 6 Nov. 1850: MS pp.3–4, Texas, [*L&L*, iii, 178].

9. CB to WSW, 9 Nov. 1850: MS p.1, Brotherton, [*L&L*, iii, 179].

10. PB to the *Leeds Intelligencer*, 19 Oct. 1850, p.6. For examples of speculation about Papal intentions see articles and editorials in *Bradford Observer*, 1 Aug. 1850, p.5; *Halifax Guardian* 23 Nov. 1850, pp.3, 4.

11. *Leeds Intelligencer*, 23 Nov. 1850, p.5. Patrick & Arthur Bell Nicholls were not listed among the signatories calling for the meeting but Arthur attended the meeting and presumably gave his sanction to the resolution: *ibid.*, 30 Nov. 1850, pp.7–8.

12. CB to GS, 31 Oct. 1850: MS S-G 41 pp.2–5, BPM, [*L&L*, iii, 176].

13. CB to EN, 26 Nov. 1850: MS Bon 229 p.1, BPM, [*L&L*, iii, 184]; CB to ECG, 13 Dec. 1850: MS EL fB91 pp.1–2, Rylands, [*L&L*, iii, 187, part only]; CB to EN, 18 Dec. 1850: MS HM 24477 p.1, Huntington, [*L&L*, iii, 189]. HM to G. H. Lewes, 10 Dec. 1850: [Sanders (ed.), *Harriet Martineau: Selected Letters*, p.120]. Miss Martineau had first invited Charlotte nearly a year before, shortly after their first meeting in London, and had reissued the invitation several times since then: CB to WSW, 3 Jan. 1850: MS BS 73 p.3, BPM, [*L&L*, iii, 63]; CB to EN, 26 Nov. 1850: MS Bon 229 p.1, BPM, [*L&L*, iii, 184].

14. The house is still standing and relatively untouched by the passage of time.

15. CB to PB, 21 Dec. 1850: MS BS 80.5, p.3, BPM, [*L&L*, iii, 190]; CB to EN, 18 Dec. 1850: MS HM 24477 p.2, Huntington, [*L&L*, iii, 189].

16. CB to EN, 21 Dec. 1850: MS p.2, Harvard, [*L& L*, iii, 190]. Lady Kay Shuttleworth was near her confinement, Sir James still suffering the ill effects of stress.

17. Matthew Arnold to Miss Wightman, 21 Dec. 1850: [Russell (ed.), *Letters of Matthew Arnold 1848–88*, p.13]; CB to James Taylor, 15 Jan. 1851: MS p.3, Texas, [*L&L*, iii, 199].

18. HM, *Autobiography*, p.350; Matthew Arnold to Miss Wightman, 21 Dec. 1850 [Russell (ed.), *Letters of Matthew Arnold 1848–88*, p.13]; CB to James Taylor, 11 Feb. 1851: MS p.1, Texas, [*L&L*, iii, 208].

19. HM, *Autobiography*, pp.380–1; ECG *Life*, Haworth edition, p.500.

20. *Ibid.*, p.500; CB to James Taylor, 15 Jan. 1851: MS p.5, Texas, [*L&L*, iii, 200].

21. CB to WSW, 1 Jan. 1850 [should be 1851]: MS Grolier F10 p.2, BPM, [*L&L*, iii, 193, wrongly dated to 3 Jan. 1851].

22. *Ibid.*, p.2; CB to EN, 21 Dec. 1850: MS p.1, Harvard, [*L&L*, iii, 190]; CB to PB, 21 Dec. 1850: MS BS 80.5, p.1, BPM, [*L&L*, iii, 190].

23. CB to EN, 27 Dec. 1850: MS n.l., [*L&L*, iii, 191]; CB to WSW, 1 Jan. 1850 [should be 1851]: MS Grolier F10 p.1, BPM, [*L&L*, iii, 193, wrongly dated to 3 Jan. 1851]. Charlotte clearly began to tackle her letters the day after her return home, dating her letters to both Smith Williams and Taylor to 1850 instead of 1851, and referring in the one to Smith Williams to returning home 'yesterday' [not 'yesterday week' as in *L&L*, iii, 193]; only the letter to Ellen, telling of her safe arrival, was completed on that day, the rest having to wait until 1 January 1851.

24. CB to EN, 27 Dec. 1850: MS n.l., [*L&L*, iii, 191]. See, for example, unsigned review, *Examiner* 21 Dec. 1850, p.815, [G. H. Lewes] unsigned review, *Leader*, 28 Dec. 1850, p.953 and unsigned review, *Athenaeum*, 28 Dec. 1850, pp.1368–9, [Allott, pp.288–95].

25. CB to WSW, 1 Jan. 1850 [should be 1851]: MS Grolier F10, BPM, [*L&L*, iii, 193–4, wrongly

dated to 3 Jan. 1851]; CB to James Taylor, 1 Jan. 1850 [should be 1851]: MS in Texas, [*L&L*, iii, 192–3]; CB to ECG, 4 Jan. 1851: MS n.l., [*L&L*, iii, 194].

26. CB to GS, 7 Jan. 1851: MS S-G 43 pp.2–3, BPM, [*L&L*, iii, 195].

27. CB to EN, [8 Jan. 1851]: MS Bon 223 pp.1–2, BPM, [*L&L*, iii, 197]; CB to EN, [20 Jan. 1851]: MS pp.2–3, Law Colln, photograph in Mildred Christian Colln, BPM, [*L&L*, iii, 202].

28. CB to EN, [14 Oct. 1850]: MS Bon 226, BPM, [*L&L*, iii, 169]; CB to EN, [20 Jan. 1851]: MS p.1, Law Colln, photograph in Mildred Christian Colln, BPM, [*L&L*, iii, 201]; CB to EN, 30 Jan. 1851: MS Grolier E20 p.3, BPM, [*L&L*, iii, 205, this paragraph omitted].

29. *Bradford Observer*, 2 Jan. 1851, p.5. The same notice appeared in the *Westmoreland Gazette*, 21 Dec. 1850, p.2. CB to EN, 30 Jan. 1851: MS Grolier E20 p.2, BPM, [*L&L*, iii, 204–5].

30. 'A Mountaineer of the Wild West' to CB, [post 10 Dec. 1850]: MS in private hands. The 'Wild West' at this time referred to Ireland rather than America.

31. John Abbott to CB, 22 Feb. 1851: MS in private hands. Abbott had met Dr Scoresby, the former vicar of Bradford, a few years previously when the latter was on his travels, and had learnt something of his old Yorkshire friends from him.

32. CB to WSW, 1 Feb. 1851: MS HM 24399 pp.1–2, Huntington, [*L&L*, iii, 206].

33. CB to GS, 5 Feb. 1851: MS S-G 45 pp.2–3, BPM, [*L&L*, iii, 207].

34. CB to EN, [20 Jan. 1851]: MS pp.3–4, Law Colln, photograph in Mildred Christian Colln, BPM, [*L&L*, iii, 202]. George Smith later gave up the idea of the trip down the Rhine, see CB to GS, 31 March 1851: MS S-G 47 p.2, BPM, [*L&L*, iii, 216].

35. CB to GS, 5 Feb. 1851: MS S-G 45 pp.3–4, BPM, [*L&L*, iii, 207].

36. CB to GS, 11 March 1851: MS S-G 46 p.2, BPM, [*L&L*, iii, 210].

37. CB to EN, 26 Feb. 1851: MS Bon 234 p.3, BPM, [*L&L*, iii, 209].

38. CB to ECG, 25 March 1851: MS EL fB91 p.2, Rylands.

39. Sydney Dobell to CB, [?March 1851]: MS n.l., [*L&L*, iii, 217–19].

40. CB to Sydney Dobell, [?April 1851]: MS n.l., [*L&L*, iii, 219–20]; Sydney Dobell to CB, 17 April [1851]: MS n.l., [*L&L*, iii, 226].

41. CB to EN, [4 Dec. 1849]: MS 2696 R-V p.3, Pierpont Morgan, [*L&L*, iii, 53]; CB to EN, 30 Jan. 1851: MS Grolier E20 p.4, BPM, [*L&L*, iii, 205].

42. CB to James Taylor, 22 March 1851: MS in Texas, [*L&L*, iii, 213–14]; CB to James Taylor, 24 March 1851: MS in Texas, [*L&L*, iii, 214].

43. CB to EN, 9 April 1851: MS BS 81 pp.2–3, BPM, [*L&L*, iii, 222].

44. CB to EN, [4 April 1851]: MS Grolier E21 pp.1–2, BPM, [*L&L*, iii, 220, wrongly dated to 5

April]. The manuscript is dated 'Friday Evening – 6 o'clock'; Friday was 4 April, not 5 April, though Charlotte added a postscript on Saturday morning.

45. CB to EN, 23 April 1851: MS Grolier E22 pp.2–3, BPM, [*L&L*, iii, 229].

46. CB to EN, 5 May 1851: MS HM 24478 p.2, Huntington, [*L&L*, iii, 230–1]. The manuscript was originally dated 24 April 1851, but Charlotte crossed this through and redated it.

47. *Ibid.*, p.2; CB to EN, 14 Sept. 1850: MS pp.1–2, Rochester, [*L&L*, iii, 157]. The second half of this letter is MS HM 24475, Huntington.

48. CB to EN, [21 May 1851]: MS HM 24480 p.2, Huntington, [*L&L*, iii, 236]; CB to EN, [5 May 1851]: MS HM 24478 pp.2–3, Huntington, [*L&L*, iii, 231].

49. CB to EN, [4 April 1851]: MS Grolier E21 pp.2–3, BPM, [*L&L*, iii, 221, wrongly dated to 5 April].

50. CB to EN, 9 April 1851: MS BS 81 p.2, BPM, [*L&L*, iii, 222]; MT to EN, 11 March 1851: MS p.1, Berg, [*L&L*, iii, 212].

51. CB to EN, 12 April 1851: MS Bon 235 pp.1–2, BPM, [*L&L*, iii, 223].

52. PB to Secretary to the General Board of Health, 12 Feb. 1851: MS n.l., [L&D, p.433]; PB to Secretary to the General Board of Health, 1 April 1851: MS n.l., [L&D, p.434].

53. L&D, p.435; PB to Secretary to the General Board of Health, 10 July 1851: MS n.l., [L&D, p.436]. Objectors included the Merrall brothers, William & Richard Thomas, Tobias Lambert and Joseph Hartley.

54. PB to Reverend A. P. Irwine, District Secretary of Church Pastoral Aid Society, 15 April 1851: MS pp.2–3, n.l., photocopy in MSS Copy Docs, BPM. See also PB to The Secretary, Church Pastoral Aid Society, 24 Feb. 1851: MS in private hands. Patrick's letter suggests that Arthur Nicholls cannot have been the rabid Puseyite he is usually depicted as being by Charlotte and Mrs Gaskell.

55. CB to Amelia Taylor, 12 April 1851: MS n.l., [*L&L*, iii, 223]; See, for example, 'I wish Amelia had her business well over and was hearty and happy with her chit on her knee – or yelping in that bascinet you are to <by> buy': CB to EN, 12 April 1851: MS Bon 235 p.2, BPM, [*L&L*, iii, 223–4]; 'I wish the female had its nest furnished with the expected nestling – I believe it would then be more interesting – the small egotism rather repels me just now': CB to EN, 10 May 1851: MS HM 24479 p.3, Huntington, [*L&L*, iii, 232].

56. CB to Mrs Smith, 17 April 1851: MS S-G 96 p.1, BPM, [*L&L*, iii, 225].

57. CB to GS, 19 April 1851: MS S-G 48 pp.1, 2–3, BPM, [*L&L*, iii, 227–8]. Mrs Gaskell and Harriet Martineau are inferred from Charlotte's description of them as 'Two ladies – neither of them unknown to fame – whom I reverence for their talents and love for their amiability'. Mrs Gaskell had procured Charlotte an invitation to the Shaens at Crix in December 1850, Miss Martineau one to Sydney Dobell's in Gloucestershire in March 1851.

58. CB to EN, 12 April 1851: MS Bon 235 pp.2–3, BPM, [*L&L*, iii, 224]; CB to EN, 23 April 1851: MS Grolier E22 pp.1–2, BPM, [*L&L*, iii, 228].

59. CB to EN, 10 May 1851: MS HM 24479 p.3, Huntington, [*L&L*, iii, 232].

60. CB to GS, 12 May 1851: MS S-G 10b p.3, BPM, [*L&L*, iii, 233]; CB to Mrs Smith, 20 May 1851: MS S-G 11b p.2, BPM, [*L&L*, iii, 234]. To Mrs Smith Charlotte made the enigmatic remark: 'I will not say much about being glad to see you all. Long ago, when I was a little girl, I received a somewhat sharp lesson on the duty of being glad in peace and quietness – in fear and moderation; this lesson did me good and has never been forgotten.'

61. CB to ECG, 10 May 1851: MS EL fB91 p.2, Rylands; CB to EN, [22 May 1851]: MS Bon 236 p.1, BPM, [*L&L*, iii, 237, dated to 26 May, but EN has dated the MS 22 May].

62. CB to EN, 23 April 1851: MS Grolier E22 p.2, BPM, [*L&L*, iii, 228]. The date of the visit was fixed in CB to Mrs Smith, 20 May 1851: MS S-G 11b p.2, BPM, [*L&L*, iii, 234]; subsequently it was altered to 28 May, see CB to EN, 2 June [1851]: MS p.1, Berg, [*L&L*, iii, 240].

63. CB to EN, [21 May 1851]: MS HM 24480 p.2, Huntington, [*L&L*, iii, 236]; CB to PB, 29 May 1851: MS pp.1–2, Berg, [*L&L*, iii, 238–9]; CB to EN, 2 June [1851]: MS p.1, Berg, [*L&L*, iii, 240].

64. CB to PB, 30 May 1851: MS pp.1–2, Harvard, [*L&L*, iii, 239, wrongly dated to 31 May 1851]; CB to EN, 2 June [1851]: MS pp.1–2, Berg, [*L&L*, iii, 240].

65. Smith, p.99; ECG, *Life*, p.335; CB to PB, 30 May 1851: MS p.2, Harvard, [*L&L*, iii, 239, wrongly dated to 31 May 1851].

66. *Ibid.*, pp.2–3; CB to EN, 2 June [1851]: MS p.3, Berg, [*L&L*, iii, 241]. For his gifts to Charlotte see CB to WSW, 12 April 1850: MS HM 24394 p.2, Huntington, [*L&L*, iii, 98] & CB to GS, 19 April 1851: MS S-G 48 pp.3–4, BPM, [*L&L*, iii, 228]; ECG, *Life*, pp.335–6. As Mrs Gaskell points out, Charlotte later used this incident and her own reactions to it in *Villette*, where Paul Emanuel confronts Lucy Snowe and demands to know her opinion of his lecture.

67. CB to EN, 2 June [1851]: MS p.2, Berg, [*L&L*, iii, 240]; Smith, pp.99–100. George Warrington was the friend who shared Arthur Pendennis' chambers and was one of the few influences to the good on his life in Thackeray's novel, *Pendennis*.

68. CB to PB, 30 May 1851: MS pp.3–4, Harvard, [*L&L*, iii, 240]; CB to EN, 2 June [1851]: MS pp.3–4, Berg, [*L&L*, iii, 241].

69. CB to PB, 7 June [1851]: MS MA 2696 R-V pp.2–3, Pierpont Morgan, [*L&L*, iii, 243]; CB to Amelia Taylor, 7 June 1851: MS pp.2–3, Brotherton, [*L&L*, iii, 244].

70. CB to PB, 14 June 1851: MS Ashley 167 p.2, BL, [*L&L*, iii, 246]; CB to EN, 24 June 1851: MS HM 24482 p.3, Huntington, [*L&L*, iii, 251]; CB to PB, 26 June 1851: MS BS 81.6, p.3, BPM, [*L&L*, iii, 252].

71. CB to MW, 14 July 1851: MS FM 10 p.3, Fitz-william, [*L&L*, iii, 262]. Charlotte made an exception to this statement of those with a large range of scientific knowledge; with Sir David Brewster she had perceived 'he looked on objects with other eyes than mine'.

72. CB to Amelia Taylor, 11 June [1851]: MS p.2, Brotherton, [*L&L*, iii, 245]; CB to EN, 24 June 1851: MS HM 24482 p.2, Huntington, [*L&L*, iii, 251].

73. CB to Sydney Dobell, 28 June [1851]: MS n.l., [*L&L*, iii, 253]; CB, *Villette*, p.322. Consciously playing on the biblical origin of the name Rachel, Charlotte called her fictional actress Vashti, after the wilful queen of King Ahasuerus in Esther, ch.1. CB to Amelia Taylor, 7 June [1851]: MS p.2, Brotherton, [*L&L*, iii, 245].

74. *Ibid.*, p.3; CB to PB, 14 June 1851: MS Ashley 167 pp.2–3, BL, [*L&L*, iii, 246–7]; CB to Sydney Dobell, 28 June [1851]: MS n.l., [*L&L*, iii, 253].

75. CB to PB, 17 June 1851: MS n.l., [*L&L*, iii, 248–9].

76. CB to EN, 24 June 1851: MS HM 24482 p.2, Huntington, [*L&L*, iii, 251].

77. CB to EN, 11 June 1851: MS pp.1–2, Berg, [*L&L*, iii, 245–6]; CB to EN, 19 June [1851]: MS HM 24481 p.3, Huntington, [*L&L*, iii, 250].

78. CB to ECG, [June 1851]: MS HM 26010 pp.2–3, Huntington, [*L&L*, iii, 248]; CB to EN, 19 June [1851]: MS HM 24481 p.1, Huntington, [*L&L*, iii, 249]; CB to EN, 24 June 1851: MS HM 24482 p.1, Huntington, [*L&L*, iii, 251].

79. *Ibid.*, pp.2–4. Charlotte was also invited to a private viewing of the Earl of Ellesmere's picture collection: CB to PB, 26 June 1851: MS BS 81.6 p.2, BPM, [*L&L*, iii, 252].

80. CB to PB, 14 June 1851: MS Ashley 167 p.4, BL, [*L&L*, iii, 247]; CB to EN, 24 June 1851: MS HM 24482 pp.1–2, Huntington, [*L&L*, iii, 251].

81. CB to Richard Monckton Milnes, 17 June [1851]: MS pp.1–2, TC Cambridge; CB to EN, 24 June 1851: MS HM 24482 p.2, Huntington, [*L&L*, iii, 251].

82. CB to Mrs Gore, 28 June [1851]: MS p.1, Brotherton, [*L&L*, iii, 254]. For the gift of the book see CB to GS, 1 Aug. 1850: MS n.l., [*L&L*, iii, 130] and CB to Mrs Gore, 27 Aug. 1850: MS pp.1–2, Berg, [*L&L*, iii, 150, part only]. See also CB to Mrs Gore, 21 June [1851]: MS Bon 237 p.1, BPM, [*L&L*, iii, 250].

83. CB to EN, 2 June [1851]: MS p.5, Berg, [*L&L*, iii, 241].

84. Glynn, *Prince of Publishers*, pp.45–7; CB to EN, 24 June 1851: MS HM 24482 p.4, Huntington, [*L&L*, iii, 251]. See also Smith, p.15.

85. CB to EN, 24 June 1851: MS HM 24482 p.4, Huntington, [*L&L*, iii, 251].

86. CB to GS, 2 July 1851: MS S-G 56 p.1, BPM, [*L&L*, iii, 258]; Smith, p.95.

87. J.P. Browne, Phrenological Estimate of a Gentleman, 29 June 1851: MS S-G 101 p.2, BPM, Glynn, *Prince of Publishers*, pp.70–1].

88. J.P. Browne, Phrenological Estimate of a Lady, 29 June 1851: MS S-G 100 pp.1–3, BPM, [Smith, pp.93–5].

89. CB to GS, 8 July 1851: MS S-G 51 pp.5, 3–4, BPM, [*L&L*, iii, 260].

90. CB to ECG, [June 1851]: MS HM 26010, Huntington, [*L&L*, iii, 247–8]; CB to ECG, 18 June [1851]: MS at Harvard.

91. CB to GS, 1 July 1851: MS S-G 49 pp.1–2, BPM, [*L&L*, iii, 255]. The Gaskells rented Plymouth Grove for £150 a year – little short of Patrick's entire annual income: ECG to Eliza Fox, [?April 1850]: [C&P, pp.107–8].

92. CB to Mrs Smith, 1 July 1851: MS p.2, Brotherton, [*L&L*, iii, 254]; CB to ECG, 6 Aug. 1851: MS EL fB91 p.6, Rylands, [*L&L*, iii, 269].

93. CB to Mrs Smith, 1 July 1851: MS p.2, Brotherton, [*L&L*, iii, 254].

94. CB to PB, 14 June 1851: MS Ashley 167 p.4, BL, [*L&L*, iii, 247].

95. CB to GS, 8 July 1851: MS S-G 51 pp.6–7, BPM, [*L&L*, iii, 260–1].

96. CB to MW, 14 July 1851: MS FM 10 pp.1–2, Fitzwilliam, [*L&L*, iii, 261].

97. CB to EN, 31 Dec. 1851: MS HM 24487 p.2, Huntington, [*L&L*, iii. 303]; *Leeds Intelligencer*, 26 July 1851, p.7. The two sermons raised £21 3s. 9d. for the Sunday schools.

98. CB to EN, [27 July 1851]: MS p.2, TC Cambridge, [*L&L*, iii, 265]. Charlotte enjoined Ellen to burn the note after she had read it: not for the first or last time, Ellen disobeyed her; Henry Robinson to CB, 23 July 1851: MS n.l., typescript in Brotherton, [*L&L*, iii, 264–5].

99. CB to EN, [27 July 1851]: MS p.2, TC Cambridge, [*L&L*, iii, 265].

100. *Halifax Guardian*, 2 Aug. 1851, p.5; CB to EN, 10 Sept. 1851: MS BS 82.7 p.2, BPM, [*L&L*, iii, 275].

101. CB to EN, 1 Sept. 1851: MS HM 24484 p.3, Huntington, [*L&L*, iii, 273].

102. CB to EN, 17 Sept. 1851: MS MA 4500, Pierpont Morgan, [*L&L*, iii, 276]; CB to EN, 10 Sept. 1851: MS BS 82.7 pp.1–3, BPM, [*L&L*, iii, 275, part only]; CB to EN, [20 Sept. 1851]: MS BS 83 pp.1–2, BPM, [*L&L*, iii, 277].

103. CB to EN, 25 Nov. [1851]: MS BS 84 p.2, BPM; CB to EN, 8 Dec. 1851: MS BS 84.5 p.3, BPM, [*L&L*, iii, 298, wrongly dated to Dec. 1851].

104. CB to GS, 8 Sept. 1851, MS S-G 55 pp.2–3, BPM, [*L&L*, iii, 274]. Charlotte had already turned down the offer of a series from the *New York Tribune*: CB to Charles A. Dana, 11 Jan. 1851: MS in private hands.

105. CB to GS, 9 Aug. 1851: MS S-G 54 pp.1–3, BPM, [*L&L*, iii, 269–70]; CB to GS, 31 July 1851: MS S-G 52 pp.1–2, BPM, [*L&L*, iii, 265–6]; CB

to GS, 4 Aug. 1851: MS S-G 53 pp.1, 3–4, BPM, [*L&L*, iii, 266–7].

106. CB to EN, 1 Sept. 1851: MS HM 24484 p.3, Huntington, [*L&L*, iii, 273]. William Morgan was a great tractarian. In his life of John Crosse, he describes visiting Haworth with the Religious Tract Society's publication which had adopted William Grimshaw's letter 'Is it well with you' as its text. He distributed it among the poor of Haworth and on his frequent visits afterwards was beset by people running after him for copies of the tract: Morgan, *The Parish Priest Pourtrayed*, p.42. CB to EN, 5 May 1851: MS HM 24478 p.4, Huntington, [*L&L*, iii, 231].

107. *Bradford Observer*, 4 Sept. 1851, p.5. The buildings had cost £1,600 and were also used as the church Sunday school; *ibid.*, 30 Oct. 1851, p.5; *Halifax Guardian*, 1 Nov. 1851, p.5; *Bradford Observer*, 6 Nov. 1851, p.5. William Morgan was still rector of Hullcott when he died in Bath, aged seventy-six, on 25 March 1858: *ibid.*, 1 April 1858, p.8.

108. CB to MW, 22 Sept. 1851: MS n.l., [*L&L*, iii, 280–1]; CB to EN, 3 Oct. 1851: MS p.1, Harvard, [*L&L*, iii, 282]. The Ladies' Book Club in Penzance had been an assiduous supporter of 'Currer Bell', purchasing each of the novels almost as soon as they were published: Record of the Ladies' Book Club, Penzance, 1770–1912: MS in Penzance, [3 Dec. 1847 (*Jane Eyre*); 8 Nov. 1849 (*Shirley*); 29 March 1853 (*Villette*); 4 May 1857 (*Life of CB*)].

109. CB to MW, 22 Sept. 1851: MS n.l., [*L&L*, iii, 280–1]; CB to EN, 3 Oct. 1851: MS pp.1–2, Harvard, [*L&L*, iii, 282].

110. CB to MW, 21 Oct. 1851: MS FM 11 pp.2–3, Fitzwilliam, [*L&L*, iii, 283]; CB to EN, 19 Nov. 1851: MS HM 24485 pp.1–2, Huntington, [*L&L*, iii, 291].

111. CB to ECG, 6 Nov. 1851: MS EL fB91 p.2, Rylands, [*L&L*, iii, 286]; CB to EN, [30 Oct.

1851]: MS Bon 238 p.1, BPM, [*L&L*, iii, 285]; CB to Mrs Forster, 28 Oct. 1851: MS p.1, in private hands.

112. CB to EN, [4 Nov. 1851]: MS pp.1–2, Harvard, [*L&L*, iii, 285–6]; CB to James Taylor, 15 Nov. 1851: MS 2696 R-V p.2, Pierpont Morgan, [*L&L*, iii, 289].

113. CB to EN, [4 Nov. 1851]: MS p.2, Harvard, [*L&L*, iii, 285]; CB to EN, 19 Nov. 1851: MS HM 24485 pp.2–3, Huntington, [*L&L*, iii, 291]; CB to EN, 2 June [1851]: MS p.4, Berg, [*L&L*, iii, 241]. For Smith Williams' opinion of James Taylor see CB to WSW, 1 Jan. 1852: MS n.l., [*L&L*, iii, 304].

114. CB to GS, [*c*.Nov. 1851]: MS S-G 91 pp.1–2, BPM, [*L&L*, iii, 292]. Charlotte observed this trait in Smith's letter to Harriet Martineau: 'this speciality is perceptible only in the slightest degree – quite imperceptible for Miss [M] but it is there – and more or less you have it always': *ibid.*, p.2.

115. CB to GS, 15 Sept. 1851: MS S-G 56 pp.2–3, BPM, [*BST*:18:92:110]. The repeated phrase which is deleted is evidence that Charlotte had drafted this letter before sending it and had made an error in copying it.

116. CB to GS, 22 Sept. 1851: MS S-G 57 pp.2–3, BPM, [*L&L*, iii, 280].

117. CB to GS, 20 Nov. 1851: MS S-G 60 pp.2–3, BPM, [*L&L*, iii, 293].

118. CB to GS, 28 Nov. 1851: MS S-G 61 p.5, BPM, [*L&L*, iii, 295].

119. CB to EN, [30 Oct. 1851]: MS Bon 238 p.1, BPM, [*L&L*, iii, 285].

120. CB to Mrs Smith, 29 Jan. 1852: MS S-G 12b pp.2–3, BPM, [*L&L*, iii, 311].

121. CB to EN, 17 Dec. 1851: MS HM 24486 pp.1–2, Huntington, [*L&L*, iii, 300].

122. CB to EN, 8 Dec. 1851: MS BS 84 pp.1–2, BPM, [*L&L*, iii, 298].

123. CB to EN, 17 Dec. 1851: MS HM 24486 p.2, Huntington, [*L&L*, iii, 300].

CHAPTER TWENTY-FOUR

1. CB to EN, 31 Dec. 1851: MS HM 24487 p.1, Huntington, [*L&L*, iii, 302]. The dates of Ellen's stay are unclear – Charlotte later referred to it as being in early January 1852 (CB to Laetitia Wheelwright, 12 April 1852: MS p.1, Princeton, [*L&L*, iii, 330]) but in her letter to Ellen dated Thursday [18 Dec. 1851] Charlotte expects her to arrive on Saturday [20 Dec. 1851]; she had apparently returned home before Monday, 29 December: CB to EN, [18 Dec. 1851]: MS BS 85, BPM, [*L&L*, iii, 301]; CB to EN, 31 Dec. 1851: MS HM 24487 p.1, Huntington, [*L&L*, iii, 302].

2. CB to MW, 20 Jan. [1851 should be 1852]: MS FM 12 p.2, Fitzwilliam, [*L&L*, iii, 308].

3. CB to EN, [14 Jan. 1852]: MS Bon 240 p.1, BPM, [*L&L*, iii, 306]; CB to EN, 16 Jan. 1852: MS HM 24488 pp.2–3, Huntington, [*L&L*, iii, 306–7].

4. CB to Laetitia Wheelwright, 12 April 1852: MS p.2, Princeton, [*L&L*, iii, 330–1].

5. W.E. Forster to Richard Monckton Milnes, [Jan. 1852] quoted in Pope-Hennessy, *Monckton-Milnes: The Flight of Youth, 1851–1885*, pp.65–6.

6. PB to Richard Monckton Milnes, 16 Jan. 1852: MS pp.1–2, TC Cambridge.

7. CB to EN, 16 Jan. 1852: MS HM 24488 p.1, Huntington, [*L&L*, iii, 306].

8. CB to EN, 24 Jan. 1852: MS HM 24489 pp.1–2, Huntington, [*L&L*, iii, 309–10]. According to this letter, Charlotte arrived at Brookroyd on 27 January 1852.

9. CB to ECG, 6 Feb. 1852: MS EL fB91 p.1, Rylands, [*L&L*, iii, 312, part only]. The quotation, which Charlotte often used in her letters and novels, is from Christ in the Garden of

Gethsemane: see Matthew ch.26 v.27.
10. CB to MW, 17 Feb. 1852: MS FM 13 p.3, Fitz-william, [*L&L*, iii, 317–18]. According to this letter, Charlotte also met Margaret Wooler's brother, William, and his family, during this visit but when and where is not clear.
11. CB to GS, 29 Jan. 1852: MS S-G 66 p.1, BPM, [*L&L*, iii, 310].
12. CB to GS, 1 Jan. 1852: MS S-G 65 pp.1–2, BPM, [*L&L*, iii, 303]; CB to GS, 31 Dec. 1851: MS S-G 64 pp.1–4, BPM, [*L&L*, iii, 301–2].
13. CB to HM, 10 Dec. 1851: MS S-G 62 pp.1–3, BPM, [*L&L*, iii, 299]; CB to GS, 19 Dec. 1851: MS S-G 65 pp.1–2, BPM, [*L&L*, iii, 301]; HM, *Autobiography*, p.382. In Charlotte's defence it should be pointed out that Miss Martineau may have misrepresented her enthusiasm for 'Oliver Weld'. In a letter to George Smith on the subject, Charlotte complained 'There is a pec-uliar property in her which must sooner or later be recognised as a great inconvenience by such of her acquaintance as admire her intellectual powers and her many excellent personal qual-ities without being able to agree in her views; she is prone to mistake liking for agreement, and with the sanguine eagerness of her charac-ter thinks to sweep you along with her in her whirlwind course. This will not do.': CB to GS, 31 Dec. 1851: MS S-G 64 pp.2–3, BPM, [*L&L*, iii, 302]; CB to EN, 5 March 1852: MS HM 24492 p.3, Huntington, [*L&L*, iii, 320].
14. CB to GS, 29 Jan. 1852: MS S-G 66 pp.1–2, BPM, [*L&L*, iii, 310–11]; CB to Mrs Smith, 29 Jan. 1852: MS S-G 12b pp.1–2, BPM [*L&L*, iii, 311].
15. CB to GS, 14 Feb. 1852: MS S-G 68 pp.1–4, BPM [*L&L*, iii, 314].
16. CB to GS, 19 Dec. 1851: MS S-G 63 p.1, BPM, [*L&L*, iii, 301]; CB to EN, 23 March 1852: MS HM 24494 pp.3–4, Huntington, [*L&L*, iii, 325].
17. CB to EN, 16 Feb. 1852: MS HM 24490 pp.2–3, Huntington, [*L&L*, iii, 315–16]; CB to EN, 5 March 1852: MS HM 24492 p.3, Huntington, [*L&L*, iii, 320].
18. CB to EN, 7 March 1852: MS HM 24493 p.2, Huntington, [*L&L*, iii, 321]. See also CB to EN, [24 Feb. 1852]: MS p.1, Princeton, [*L&L*, iii, 318].
19. CB to MW, 12 March 1852: MS FM 14 pp.1–2, Fitzwilliam, [*L&L*, iii, 323].
20. CB, *Villette*, Clarendon Edn, pp.xx, xxxi.
21. CB, *Villette*, p.193.
22. CB to ECG, 22 May 1852: MS EL fB91 pp.2–3, Rylands; CB to Mrs Gore, 28 May 1852: MS Bon 244 p.1, BPM, [*L&L*, iii, 335].
23. The dates for Ellen's visit to Sussex are hazy. The original intention was that she would go in May and a reference to her niece, Georgiana, suggests she was in London with her brother by the beginning of June: CB to EN, 6 June 1852: MS HM 24496 pp.3–4, Huntington, [*L&L*, iii, 337]. Charlotte hoped that she had arrived safely

home in CB to EN, 5 Oct. 1852: MS p.1, Berg, [*L&L*, iv, 10]. For James Taylor's silence see CB to EN, 7 March 1852: MS HM 24493 p.3, Huntington, [*L&L*, iii, 321] and CB to EN, 4 [March should be May] 1852: MS HM 24491 pp.3–4, Huntington, [*L&L*, iii, 319, wrongly dated March]. For the silence from Cornhill see CB to EN, 1 July 1852: MS 1532 p.2, Guildhall, [*L&L*, iii, 341]. Charlotte later found out that George Smith's silence was due to extra-ordinary pressure of work: CB to GS, 19 Aug. 1852: MS S-G 73 pp.2–3, BPM, [*L&L*, iv, 5].
24. *Leeds Intelligencer*, 17 April 1852, p.7. William Cartman had substituted for Arthur Bell Nich-olls while the latter was away in Ireland: see CB to PB, 7 June 1851: MS MA 2696 R-V p.1, Pierpont Morgan, [*L&L*, iii, 340].
25. MT to CB, [postmarked Keighley 27 Oct. 1852]: MS p.2, Berg, [Stevens, pp.108–9].
26. CB to EN, 4 [March should be May] 1852: MS HM 24491 pp.1–2, Huntington, [*L&L*, iii, 319, wrongly dated March]. This letter is an instance of Charlotte's unreliable dating. She has clearly written 'March 4th/52' but this must be wrong as the news of Ellen's death could not have reached England before 24 April 1852 and Charlotte sent on this letter and two others from Hunsworth referring to Ellen's death to Ellen Nussey on 18 May, implying that the letters had only just been received: CB to EN, 18 May 1852: MS Bon 243 pp.1–3, BPM, [*L&L*, iii, 333]. For a discussion of the dating see Stevens, pp.106–7.
27. CB to MW, 12 March 1852: MS FM 14 p.3, Fitzwilliam, [*L&L*, iii, 323]; CB to EN, 7 March 1852: MS HM 24493 p.2, Huntington, [*L&L*, iii, 321].
28. CB to EN, 6 June 1852: MS HM 24496 p.2, Huntington, [*L&L*, iii, 336–7]. The exact dates of Charlotte's visit to Filey are not known. She is likely to have arrived on or shortly before 28 May, the anniversary of Anne's death, as she dated her letter from Filey to Mrs Gore, 28 May 1852: MS Bon 244, BPM, [*L&L*, iii, 335].
29. CB to PB, 2 June 1852: MS MA 2696 R-V pp.2–4, Pierpont Morgan, [*L&L*, iii, 335].
30. *Halifax Guardian*, 29 May 1852, p.5; CB to PB, 2 June 1852: MS MA 2696 R-V p.4, Pierpont Morgan, [*L&L*, iii, 335–6]. For the reasons why Charlotte and Patrick had a general aversion to Butterfield see below, p.700.
31. CB to MW, 23 June 1852: MS FM 15 p.2, Fitz-william, [*L&L*, iii, 339].
32. CB to EN, 1 July 1852: MS 1532 p.2, Guildhall, [*L&L*, iii, 341].
33. CB to MW, 23 June 1852: MS FM 15 pp.2–3, Fitzwilliam, [*L&L*, iii, 339–40]; CB to EN, 6 June 1852: MS HM 24496 p.2, Huntington, [*L&L*, iii, 337]. Charlotte says Filey 'Bridge' in her letter, but she clearly meant the local landmark, the Brig.
34. *Ibid.*, p.1.
35. CB to MW, 23 June 1852: MS FM 15 p.3, Fitz-

william, [*L&L*, iii, 340]; CB to EN, 1 July 1852: MS 1532 p.3, Guildhall, [*L&L*, iii, 341].

36. CB to PB, 2 June 1852: MS MA 2696 R-V p.5, Pierpont Morgan, [*L&L*, iii, 336]; PB, Account Book, *c.1855–61*: MS BS 173 p.13, BPM.

37. CB to EN, 1 July 1852: MS 1532 p.3, Guildhall, [*L&L*, iii, 341]. Harriet Martineau, like Charlotte, was a student of phrenology, hence the reference to Joe Taylor's 'organ of combativeness and contradiction'.

38. The suggestion that 'Tim' might be derived from 'Timon' comes from *Villette* where, more appropriately, Ginevra Fanshawe refers to Lucy Snowe as 'Timon' and 'Tim': CB, *Villette*, p.292, 591. I am grateful to Allegra Huston for suggesting a reason why the name might have been appropriate.

39. CB to EN, 11 May 1852: MS HM 24495 p.2, Huntington, [*L&L*, iii, 333]; CB to EN, 23 March 1852: MS HM 24494 p.3, Huntington, [*L&L*, iii, 325]. See also CB to MW, 21 Oct. 1851: MS FM 11 p.4, Fitzwilliam, [*L&L*, iii, 284].

40. CB to EN, 22 April 1852: MS at Yale, [*L&L*, iii, 332].

41. CB, *Villette*, pp.595–6; CB to EN, 5 March 1852: MS HM 24492 p.2, Huntington, [*L&L*, iii, 320]. The youthful sufferer in *Villette* survived five 'brushes with death'; tragically, however, Emily Martha Taylor died just before her seventh birthday in August 1858, nine months after her father and only two years before her mother: Stevens, p.117 n.1.

42. CB to EN, 26 July 1852: MS pp.1–3, Haverford, [*L&L*, iv, 2]; CB to EN, 3 Aug. 1852: MS HM 20069 pp.1–2, Huntington, [*L&L*, iv, 3]; CB to EN, 12 Aug. 1852: MS pp.1–2, Brotherton, [*L&L*, iv, 3–4].

43. Richard Butterfield, the Merralls, Joseph Greenwood, Mrs Ferrand *et al.*, Petition to the General Board of Health, 10 Dec. 1851: MS n.l., [L&D, pp.436–7]. William Ranger came to Haworth on 30 July 1852 in response to this petition: *ibid.*, p.437.

44. CB to EN, 25 Aug. 1852: MS HM 24498 p.1, Huntington, [*L&L*, iv, 5]; CB to MW, 2 Sept. 1851: MS FM 16 pp.1–2, Fitzwilliam, [*L&L*, iv, 6–7]. Mr Nicholls took all the parish duties throughout August and most of September: see Haworth Church Registers.

45. CB to GS, 19 Aug. 1852: MS S-G 73 pp.2–3, BPM, [*L&L*, iv, 5].

46. CB to EN, 25 Aug. 1852: MS HM 24498 pp.3–4, Huntington, [*L&L*, iv, 6]. A deleted word, which I am unable to decipher, is replaced by 'burden'.

47. CB to EN, [24 Sept. 1852]: MS HM 24499 pp.2–3, Huntington, [*L&L*, iv, 9]. Charlotte simply thanked Ellen for a copy of *The Times* reporting the death and comments 'what it said on the mighty and mournful subject was <u>well</u> said – All at once the whole Nation seems now to take a just view of that great character'. Wellington died on 14 September 1852.

48. CB to MW, 2 Sept. 1852: MS FM 16 p.2, Fitzwilliam, [*L&L*, iv, 7].

49. CB to EN, 5 Oct. 1852: MS pp.1–2, Berg, [*L&L*, iv, 10].

50. See, for example, CB to EN, 12 Aug. 1852: MS pp.3–4, Brotherton, [*L&L*, iv, 4]. CB to EN, 25 Aug. 1852: MS HM 24498 pp.2–3, Huntington, [*L&L*, iv, 5–6]; CB to EN, 5 Oct. 1852: MS Berg, [*L&L*, iv, 10].

51. CB to EN, 9 Oct. 1852: MS MA 4500, Pierpont Morgan, [*L&L*, iv, 10].

52. CB to MW, 21 [Sept. changed to Oct.] 1852: MS FM 17 pp.3–4, Fitzwilliam, [*L&L*, iv, 12].

53. CB to EN, 26 Oct. 1852: MS n.l., [*L&L*, iv, 13]; CB to WSW, 26 Oct. 1852: MS Eng lett e 30 p.187, Bodleian.

54. CB to EN, 1 July 1852: MS 1532 pp.2–3, Guildhall, [*L&L*, iii, 341]; CB to WSW, 3 April 1852: MS HM 24401, Huntington, [*L&L*, iii, 327–8]. For the July letter asking about the forthcoming edition of *Shirley* see CB to WSW, 28 July 1852: MS in Buffalo, [*L&L*, iv, 2–3].

55. CB to GS, 30 Oct. 1852: MS S-G 74 pp.1–2, BPM, [*L&L*, iv, 13].

56. CB to EN, 16 Nov. 1849: MS p.2, Harvard, [*L&L*, iii, 37].

57. CB, *Villette*, pp.368–70.

58. CB to GS, 30 Oct. 1852: MS S-G 74 pp.1, 4, BPM, [*L&L*, iv, 13].

59. CB to GS, 3 Nov. 1852: MS S-G 75 pp.1–3, BPM, [*L&L*, iv, 16].

60. CB to WSW, 6 Nov. 1852: MS Grolier F11 pp.1–3, BPM, [*L&L*, iv, 18].

61. *Ibid.*, p.3.

62. CB, *Villette*, Clarendon Edn, p.xxxiv.

63. CB to GS, 3 Nov. 1852: MS S-G 75 p.2, BPM, [*L&L*, iv, 16]; CB to GS, 10 Nov. 1852: MS S-G 76 p.1, BPM, [*L&L*, iv, 18, wrongly described as a letter to WSW]. The single-volume edition of *Shirley* was published in November 1852, though it bears an 1853 imprint on its title page: see the *Athenaeum*, 20 Nov. 1852, p.1259 for an advertisement describing it as '*Now ready*'. The announcement of 'A NEW NOVEL, BY CURRER BELL' appeared on the page opposite the title page. I am grateful to Margaret Smith for this information.

64. CB to GS, 10 Nov. 1852: MS S-G 76 pp.1–2, BPM, [*L&L*, iv, 18, wrongly described as a letter to WSW]. Charlotte had told Smith Williams in October that the third volume would be ready in two or three weeks' time: CB to WSW, 26 Oct. 1852: MS Eng litt e 30 p.187, Bodleian.

65. CB to GS, 20 Nov. 1852: MS S-G 13b pp.1–3, BPM, [*L&L*, iv, 20].

66. CB to EN, 22 Nov. 1852: MS pp.1–2, Harvard, [*L&L*, iv, 20–1].

67. CB to Mrs Smith, 25 Nov. 1852: MS S-G 15b p.2, BPM, [*L&L*, iv, 21].

68. CB to GS, 1 Dec. 1852: MS S-G 77 p.1, BPM, [*BST*:18:92:III].

69. CB to GS, 6 Dec. 1852: MS S-G 78 pp.1–2, BPM, [*L&L*, iv, 22].

70. *Ibid.*, pp.2–3.
71. CB to EN, 9 Dec. 1852: MS Montague, [*L&L*, iv, 24]. The 'female character' referred to is most likely to be Paulina who had been the subject of Charlotte's previous letter to George Smith: CB to GS, 6 Dec. 1852: MS S-G 78 p.3, BPM, [*L&L*, iv, 23].
72. *Ibid.*, p.3; CB to EN, 9 Dec. 1852: MS Montague, [*L&L*, iv, 24].
73. CB to GS, 6 Dec. 1852: MS S-G 78 pp.3–4, BPM, [*L&L*, iv, 23, this paragraph omitted]. For Miss Wooler's visit see CB to MW, 7 Dec. [1852]: MS FM 18 pp.1, 2, Fitzwilliam, [*L&L*, iv, 23–4]. For Charlotte's return see CB to EN, 9 Dec. 1852: MS Montague, [*L&L*, iv, 24].
74. CB to MW, 27 Jan. 1853: MS FM 19 pp.3–5, Fitzwilliam, [*L&L*, iv, 39].
75. HM to ECG, quoted in *L&L*, iv, 39 n.1.
76. CB to Mrs Smith, 10 Dec. 1852: MS Bon 246 p.1, BPM, [*L&L*, iv, 25].
77. CB to EN, 15 Dec. 1852: MS pp.1–4, Berg, [*L&L*, iv, 29–30]. It was not true that Patrick was opposed to the very idea of Charlotte marrying; he had supported James Taylor's proposal.
78. CB to EN, [27 July 1851]: MS p.2, TC Cambridge, [*L&L*, iii, 265].
79. CB to PB, 2 June 1852: MS MA 2696 R-V p.3, Pierpont Morgan, [*L&L*, iii, 335–6]; CB to EN, 10 July 1846: MS Grolier E10 p.3, BPM, [*L&L*, ii, 101], where she also counters rumours of her engagement to Mr Nicholls.
80. Anon., quoted in C. Holmes Cautley, 'Old Haworth Folk who knew the Brontës', *Cornhill Magazine*, xxix, July–Dec. 1910, p.79; Mrs Widdop junior, quoted in Whiteley Turner, *A Spring-Time Saunter Round and About Brontëland* (Halifax, Halifax Courier Ltd, 1913), p.212. The dog, which features in many of the stories about Mr Nicholls, actually belonged to Patrick who purchased it from Mr Summerscale, the master of the National School, in the summer of 1855: PB, Account Book, [*c*.1855–61]: MS BS 173 p.1, BPM.
81. CB to EN, 18 Dec. 1852: MS pp.3, 1–2, Berg, [*L&L*, iv, 30–1].
82. *Ibid.*, p.2; CB to EN, 2 Jan. 1853: MS p.3, Law Colln, photograph in Mildred Christian Colln, BPM, [*L&L*, iv, 32].
83. *Ibid.*, p.2.
84. CB to Mrs Smith, 30 Dec. 1852: MS S-G 16b pp.1–2, BPM, [*L&L*, iv, 31–2].
85. CB to EN, 9 Dec. 1852: MS Montague, [*L&L*, iv, 25].
86. CB to EN, 11 Jan. 1853: MS HM 26001 pp.1–3, Huntington, [*L&L*, iv, 33]. In Smith, p.15, he described the punishing routine he followed at this time, dictating to two clerks while two others were occupied in copying. 'It was a common thing for me and many of the clerks to work until three or four o'clock in the morning, and occasionally, when there was but a short interval between the arrival and

departure of the Indian mails, I used to start work at nine o'clock of one morning, and neither leave my room nor cease dictating until seven o'clock the next evening, when the mail was despatched.'
87. CB to GS, 26 March 1853: MS S-G 81 p.2, BPM, [*L&L*, iv, 55].
88. CB to EN, 11 Jan. 1853: MS HM 26001 pp.3–4, Huntington, [*L&L*, iv, 33].
89. CB to EN, 19 Jan. 1853: MS HM 26002 p.2, Huntington, [*L&L*, iv, 35]; Smith, p.91.
90. CB to GS, 30 Oct. 1852: MS S-G 74 p.3, BPM, [*L&L*, iv, 14].
91. CB to ECG, 12 Jan. 1853: MS EL fB91 p.3, Rylands, [*L&L*, iv, 34–5].
92. *Ibid.*, p.3.
93. Ellen's copy is referred to in CB to EN, 28 Jan. 1853: MS p.2, Law Colln, photograph in Mildred Christian Colln, BPM, [*L&L*, iv, 40]. Miss Wooler's inscribed copy is in Louis Clarke Case 4g, Fitzwilliam. A sale notice of Dr Forbes' copy is to be found in this book; Dr Forbes had escorted Charlotte round the Bethlehem Hospital: CB to EN, 19 Jan. 1853: MS HM 26002 p.2, Huntington, [*L&L*, iv, 35].
94. CB to ECG, 24 Feb. 1853: MS EL fB91 p.3, Rylands.
95. See also CB to EN, 28 Jan. 1853: MS p.3, Law Colln, photograph in Mildred Christian Colln, BPM, [*L&L*, iv, 41]. George Smith acknowledges the mutual unease created by *Villette* in Smith, p.95.
96. PB to CB, [*c*.11–19 Jan. 1853]: MS BS 196 pp.1–2, BPM, [*BST*:12:63:198–9].
97. [PB] 'Old Flossy' to CB, [*c*.11–19 Jan. 1853]: MS BS 193 pp.1–2, BPM, [*BST*:12:63:197].
98. ABN to Secretary of the Society for the Propagation of the Gospel, 28 Jan. 1853, with accompanying questionnaire: MSS in the archives, USPG.
99. Revd Sutcliffe Sowden to Secretary of the Society for the Propagation of the Gospel, 31 Jan. 1853: MS pp.2, 4, USPG. Sowden had also been Branwell's friend from the latter's days in the Calder Valley.
100. Revd Joseph B. Grant to Revd W. J. Bullock, Society for the Propagation of the Gospel, 1 Feb. 1853: MS p.1, USPG.
101. Revd William Cartman to Secretary of the Society for the Propagation of the Gospel, 31 Jan. 1853: MS pp.1–2, 4, USPG.
102. PB to Revd W. J. Bullock, Society for the Propagation of the Gospel, 31 Jan. 1853: MS pp.1–2, USPG.
103. ABN to Secretary of the Society for the Propagation of the Gospel, 28 Jan. 1853: MS p.1, USPG.
104. CB to EN, 28 Jan. 1853: MS p.3, Law Colln, photograph in Mildred Christian Colln, BPM, [*L&L*, iv, 40].
105. CB to EN, 22 Nov. 1852: MS p.1, Harvard, [*L&L*, iv, 20].
106. [Albany Fonblanque or John Forster]

unsigned review in the *Examiner*, 5 Feb. 1853, pp.84–5, [Allott, p.175]; unsigned review in the *Literary Gazette*, 5 Feb. 1853, pp.123–5, [Allott, p.178].

107. See, for example, unsigned review in the *Athenaeum*, 12 Feb. 1853, pp.186–8, [Allott, p.188]; unsigned review in the *Critic*, 15 Feb. 1853, pp.94–5, [Allott, p.192]. Even Harriet Martineau thought Paulina and her father the best drawn characters in the book: HM, Review in the *Daily News*, 3 Feb. 1853, p.2, [Allott, p.174].

108. Unsigned review in the *Spectator*, 12 Feb. 1853, pp.155–6, [Allott, p.182].

109. Unsigned review in the *Guardian*, 23 Feb. 1853, pp. 128–9, [Allott, p.193]; CB to WSW, 9 March 1853: MS HM 26009 p.2, Huntington, [*L&L*, iv, 50–1].

110. HM, Review in the *Daily News*, 3 Feb. 1853, p.2, [Allott, pp.172–4]. In her autobiography, Miss Martineau recounted how she and Charlotte had disagreed about Catholicism when it appeared as an issue in her abandoned novel, 'Oliver Weld'. Miss Martineau had claimed credit for the Catholics as far as their good works extended. To this Charlotte replied, 'Their good deeds I don't dispute; but I regard them as the hectic bloom on the cheek of disease. I believe the Catholics, in short, to be always doing evil that good may come, or doing good that evil may come': HM, *Autobiography*, p.382.

111. ABN Copy of HM to CB, [Feb. 1853]: MS HM 93 p.5, Birmingham. This is Mr Nicholls' transcript from Miss Martineau's original letter and not the bowdlerized version which she gave Mrs Gaskell from memory for inclusion in later editions of ECG, *Life*, Haworth Edition, pp.595–8.

112. CB to HM, [Feb. 1853]: MS n.l., [*L&L*, iv, 42]. Charlotte added the postscript, 'To differ from you gives me keen pain.'

113. W. M. Thackeray to Lucy Baxter, 11 March 1853, [Allott, pp.197–8].

114. CB to G. H. Lewes, [Jan. 1850]: MS Add 39763(7), BL, [*L&L*, iii, 67].

115. CB to GS, 26 March 1853: MS S-G 81 pp.2–3, BPM, [*L&L*, iv, 55].

116. CB to MW, 13 April 1853: MS FM 21 pp.3–4, Fitzwilliam, [*L&L*, iv, 58].

CHAPTER TWENTY-FIVE

Title: Referring to Charlotte: 'she wants some Tomkins or another to love her and be in love with. But you see she is a little bit of a creature without a penny worth of good looks … buried in the country, and eating up her own heart there, and no Tomkins will come': W. M. Thackeray to Lucy Baxter, 11 March 1853, [Allott, pp.193–4].

1. CB to EN, 15 Feb. 1853: MS HM 26003 p.2, Huntington, [*L&L*, iv, 45].

2. PB to GS, 7 Feb. 1853: MS File 10 no.2, John Murray, [*L&L*, iv, 44–5]; PB to Edward Baines, 7 Feb. 1853: MS in private hands; see also CB to GS, 16 Feb. 1853: MS S-G 80 pp.3–4, BPM, [*L&L*, iii, 46, omitted]. The *Leeds Mercury* no longer reviewed books but long extracts appeared in the *Leeds Intelligencer*, 19 Feb. 1853, p.3.

3. This inscribed copy of *Jane Eyre* is now HAOBP:bb236, BPM. The distinction in accents on the Brontë name suggests that the Irish Brontës had not yet adopted the diaeresis which the Haworth Brontës had used consistently for many years. Patrick himself only used the diaeresis after Charlotte became famous and when he remembered to do so; the distinction here is therefore particularly significant.

4. CB to [WSW], 29 March 1853: MS BS 87 pp.3–4, BPM, [*BST*:12:65:409, wrongly described as being to George Smith]. For Mr Grant see CB to EN, 10 March 1853: MS p.1, Law Colln, photograph in Mildred Christian Colln, BPM, [*L&L*, iv, 51].

5. CB to GS, 16 Feb. 1853: MS S-G 80 p.2, BPM, [*L&L*, iv, 46].

6. CB to GS, 26 Feb. 1853: MS S-G 17b p.1, BPM, [*L&L*, iv, 47]. The portrait joined Smith's other gifts, the portraits of Wellington [HAOBP:P44, BPM] and Charlotte herself [National Portrait Gallery], in the dining room of the parsonage, where it still hangs today: HAOBP:P45, BPM. When she had seen the portrait of Thackeray for the first time, Charlotte had stood silent for a few minutes then simply stated, 'There came a Lion out of Judah': Smith, pp.100–1.

7. CB to GS, 26 March 1853: MS S-G 81 p.4, BPM, [*L&L*, iv, 56].

8. CB to WSW, 23 March 1853: MS pp.2–3, Texas, [*L&L*, iv, 54, part only].

9. ECG, *Life*, p.366; CB to WSW, 23 March 1853: MS p.3, Texas, [*L&L*, iv, 54, part only].

10. See, for example, CB to WSW, 9 March 1853: MS HM 26009, Huntington, [*L&L*, iv, 50–1]. The first two pages of a letter written two weeks later are full of comment on the current prosperity of Smith Williams' son who had emigrated to Australia: Charlotte had not taken such an interest in any member of the Williams family since securing an introduction to Mrs Gaskell for another son, Frank Williams, who was an aspirant artist: CB to WSW, 23 March 1853: MS pp.1–2, Texas, [*L&L*, iv, 54, omitted]. For Frank Williams' introduction see: CB to WSW, 6 Nov. 1851: MS HM 24400, Huntington, [*L&L*, iii, 286]; CB to ECG, 6 Nov. 1851: MS EL fB91 p.1, Rylands, [*L&L*, iii, 286, omitted].

11. CB to EN, 4 March 1853: MS Grolier E23 pp.1–2, BPM, [*L&L*, iv, 49].

12. ECG, *Life*, p.377.

13. CB to EN, 4 March 1853: MS Grolier E23 pp.4–5, BPM, [*L&L*, iv, 49–50].
14. CB to MW, 12 April 1854: MS FM 26 pp.4–5, Fitzwilliam, [*L&L*, iv, 114]; CB to EN, 4 March 1853: MS Grolier E23 pp.2, 3, BPM, [*L&L*, iv, 49–50].
15. *Bradford Observer*, 17 March 1853, p.5; CB to EN, 6 April 1853: MS Grolier E24 pp.2–3, BPM, [*L&L*, iv, 56]; CB to EN, 18 April 1853: MS pp.3–4, Law Colln, photograph in Mildred Christian Colln, BPM, [*L&L*, iv, 60].
16. CB to WSW, 23 March 1853: MS p.3, Texas, [*L&L*, iv, 54, omitted].
17. CB to EN, [22 March 1853]: MS p.4, Law Colln, photograph in Mildred Christian Colln, BPM, [*L&L*, iv, 53]; *Leeds Intelligencer*, 2 April 1853, p.7. The collections after the sermons were for the church organist; the paper notes the efficiency of the choir and that 'Haworth has been celebrated for vocalists and music, and musical composers for upwards of a century.'
18. ABN to the Secretary of the Society for the Propagation of the Gospel, 1 April 1853: MS pp.1–2, USPG. He had already put off a proffered interview in London in February 'owing to the solicitation of friends' who had led him to doubt the 'desirableness of leaving the Country at present–': ABN to the Secretary of the Society for the Propagation of the Gospel, 26 Feb. 1853: MS pp.1–2, USPG. Charlotte reported rumours that Nicholls had found another curacy in CB to EN, 6 April 1853: MS Grolier E24 p.3, BPM, [*L&L*, iv, 56].
19. *Ibid.*, pp.3–6.
20. CB to ECG, 24 Feb. 1853: MS EL fB91 p.4, Rylands; CB to ECG, 14 April 1853: MS BS 89 p.1, BPM, [*L&L*, iv, 59]. This letter arranges the visit for the 21st, but CB to EN, 23 April 1853: MS n.l., [*L&L*, iv, 64] refers to her arrival 'yesterday'.
21. CB to ECG, 22 May 1852: MS EL fB91 pp.3–4, Rylands, [*L&L*, iii, 334, omitted].
22. ECG, *Life*, pp.379, 380. I assume the ghost story relates to the Upjohn house at Gorleston where Ellen was due to visit. CB to EN, 19 May 1853: MS p.2, Berg, [*L&L*, iv, 65] refers to her being made comfortable there 'unless the house is really haunted as Mr Clapham supposed'. That the letter was one from Ellen is made clear by CB to EN, 23 April 1853: MS BS 81.5 p.1, BPM, [*L&L*, iv, 64].
23. ECG, *Life*, pp.379–80.
24. ECG to [?John Forster], [?late April 1853]: [C&P, p.231]; ECG, *Life*, p.380.
25. *Ibid.*, pp.380, 381; ECG to [?John Forster], [?late April 1853]: [C&P, p.230]; CB to GS, [May 1853]: MS S-G 81b p.6, BPM, [*L&L*, iv, 67]. This quotation is used by Mrs Gaskell to illustrate Charlotte's argument at the time.
26. Brian Kay and James Knowles, 'The "Twelfth Night" Charlotte Saw', [*BST*:15:78:242–3].
27. ECG to [?John Forster], [?late April 1853]: [C&P, p.230]. Mrs Gaskell went on to say, '– and I was so sorry for her! She has had so little kindness &

affection shown to her; she said that she was afraid of loving me as much as she could, because she had never been able to inspire the kind of love she felt'. If this was correctly reported, it was an odd remark, particularly in the light of Mr Nicholls' sufferings at the time. However, since the loss of her sisters, Charlotte had craved affection almost obsessively and had indeed remarked to Ellen, whose expected letter had not arrived, causing Charlotte considerable unease: 'This won't do, I'm afraid of caring for you too much': CB to EN, [26 Oct. 1852]: MS n.l., [*L&L*, iv, 12]. Ellen's love for her friend was unquestioned but formed only a part of her busy life.
28. CB to ECG, [April 1853]: MS n.l., [*L&L*, iv, 64]; ECG to [?John Forster], [?late April 1853]: [C&P, p.231].
29. CB to EN, 31 Oct. 1852: MS HM 24500 pp.1, 2, Huntington, [*L&L*, iv, 14]; for Patrick's reaction see CB to EN, [early Nov. 1852]: MS at Wellesley, [*L&L*, iv, 15].
30. MT to EN, May–21 July 1853: MS pp.1–2, Berg, [Stevens, p.116]. The best account of the whole Upjohn saga is to be found in Stevens, pp.110–17.
31. CB to EN, 13 June 1853: MS n.l., [*L&L*, iv, 71].
32. CB to EN, 16 May 1853: MS pp.2–4, Princeton, [*L&L*, iv, 65].
33. CB to EN, 19 May 1853: MS pp.2–3, Berg, [*L&L*, iv, 66].
34. ABN to Clement K. Shorter, 18 June 1895: MS in Brotherton.
35. CB to EN, 19 May 1853: MS p.3, Berg, [*L&L*, iv, 66].
36. *Leeds Intelligencer*, 28 May 1853, p.8. The paper reported that Merrall's speech was 'kind and feeling' and that during Nicholls' eight years 'his zeal and energy in behalf of the church and schools, as well as his kind and judicious conduct to all, have won him the respect and esteem of the parishioners: so it is with sincere regret that they are parting with him'. The gold watch, inscribed inside the cover, 'Presented to the Revd. A. B. Nicholls B.A. by the teachers scholars and congregation of St Michael's Haworth Yorkshire May 25th 1853', is now in the BPM: HAOBP: J1, BPM.
37. CB to EN, 27 May 1853: MS Grolier E25 pp.3–5, BPM, [*JB ST*, no.3].
38. Mr Nicholls performed his first duty, a burial, on 11 August but he may have been there earlier as the previous curate took his last duty on 24 June. The duties were very light – Mr Nicholls only performed six baptisms and seven burials in the nine months he was there – so an exact date of arrival cannot be ascertained: Register of Baptisms, 1813–74, Register of Burials, 1813–38, St Peter's Church, Kirk Smeaton: MSS D69/6, D69/10, WYAS, Wakefield; WG *CB*, p.524 suggests that Mr Nicholls' departure was delayed because Patrick had to find a new curate and Nicholls a new post. It is clear from Nicholls' missionary application, however, that he was

contracted to remain at Haworth until the end of May: ABN to the Secretary of the Society for the Propagation of the Gospel, 28 Jan. 1853: MS in USPG. What he did between leaving Haworth and taking up the Kirk Smeaton posting I have not been able to discover. I suspect he spent at least part of the time in Ireland.

39. CB to EN, 27 May 1853: MS Grolier E25 p.3, BPM, [JB *ST*, no.3]; Register of Burials, 1836–54, Haworth Church; Register of Baptisms, 1837–54, Haworth Church.

40. ECG to [John Forster], [late April 1853]: [C& P, p.231]. Charlotte may have deliberately given the impression that she would not write for some time so that she could write at leisure and without the pressure of a deadline; she had, of course, fulfilled her contractual obligation to Smith, Elder & Co. so was not required to write another book. For the two page fragment of 'Willie Ellin' that she wrote at this time see CB, 'I will not deny that I took pleasure', May 1853: MS Eng 35.4, Harvard, [*BST*:9:46:4–5].

41. CB to WSW, 28 May 1853: MS HM 24402 p.1, Huntington, [*L&L*, iv, 69]; CB to Mrs Holland, 28 May 1853: MS BS 89.2, BPM, [*BST*:17:87:123].

42. CB to ECG, 1 June 1853: MS n.l., [*L&L*, iv, 70]. Ellen was still at Oundle on 20 June, though planning an imminent return home via Haworth: CB to EN, 20 June 1853: MS BS 90 pp.1–3, BPM, [*L&L*, iv, 72, partial].

43. CB to ECG, 1 June 1853: MS n.l., [*L&L*, iv, 70]; PB to ECG, [*c.*6–12 June 1853]: MS EL B121, Rylands, [*BST*:8:43:84–5]; CB to GS, 12 June 1853: MS S-G 83 p.1, BPM, [*BST*:18:92:112]. See also, CB to EN, 13 June 1853: MS n.l., [*L&L*, iv, 71].

44. CB to EN, 16 June 1853: MS Bon 247 p.1, BPM, [*L&L*, iv, 71]; CB to GS, 14 July 1853: MS S-G 85 pp.3–4, BPM, [*L&L*, iv, 78]. Apart from temporary attacks, before his cataracts were operated upon and when he had his stroke, Patrick was never actually blind, retaining enough vision to be able to write occasional letters till his death.

45. *Ibid.*, p.3: see also CB to GS, 3 July 1853: MS S-G 84 pp.4–5, BPM, [*L&L*, iv, 75], where Patrick's declared intention was to stay in private lodgings in London.

46. *Ibid.*, pp.2–3, [*L&L*, iv, 75, omitted].

47. [Anne Mozley], unsigned review in the *Christian Remembrancer*, April 1853, pp.401–43, [Allott, p.203]. Anne Mozley could have guessed something of the trauma Charlotte had gone through if she had read the Biographical Notice prefixed to the 1850 edition of *Wuthering Heights & Agnes Grey*.

48. [Elizabeth Rigby], unsigned review in *Quarterly Review*, Dec. 1848, pp.153–85, [Allott, p.111]. See above, pp.605–8.

49. CB to the Editor of the *Christian Remembrancer*, 18 July 1853: MS n.l., [W. Robertson Nicoll, 'Charlottë Bronte and one of her Critics', *The*

Bookman, Nov. 1899; *L&L*, iv, 79, partial]. The letter was published in full in the July 1857 issue in an article based on ECG, *Life*.

50. *Christian Remembrancer*, Oct. 1853, [W. Robertson Nicoll, 'Charlotte Brontë and one of her Critics', *The Bookman*, Nov. 1899].

51. CB, 'In other countries and in distant times', 22 June 1853: MS Eng 35.4, Harvard, [*BST*:9:46:5–19]; CB, ' "Stop" – said the expectant victim earnestly', [?June 1853]: MS Bon III, BPM, [*BST*:9:46:19–23].

52. *Leeds Intelligencer*, 30 July 1853, p.8; Haworth Church Hymn Sheet, 24 July 1853: MS BS, x, H, BPM.

53. Charlotte was making arrangements for Ellen to visit in CB to EN, 20 June 1853: MS BS 90 pp.1–3, BPM, [*L&L*, iv, 72, partial] but whether the visit actually took place is not clear. It seems likely that it did as there was as yet no quarrel between the friends.

54. CB to EN, 11 April 1854: MS p.1, Pforzheimer, [*L&L*, iv, 112]. Though not explicitly mentioned, Mr Nicholls' visit in July is inferred from Charlotte's statement: 'Matters have progressed thus since last July. He renewed his visit in Septbr –'. No other biographer mentions this visit. The accepted version, which is to be found, for instance, in WG *CB*, p.527 and Fraser, p.444 quotes Katie Winkworth: 'He wrote to her very miserably; wrote six times, and then she answered him – a letter exhorting him to heroic submission to his lot, &c. He sent word it had comforted him so much that he must have a little more, and so she came to write to him several times': Catherine Winkworth to Emma Shaen, 8 May 1854 [Shaen (ed.), *Memorials of Two Sisters*, p.115; *L&L*, iv, 124]. The two versions are not mutually incompatible but are difficult to place in sequence.

55. MT to EN, 24 Feb. 1854: MS Ashley 5768 p.2, BL, [Stevens, p.120], mentioning that Ellen's letter was written on 12 August.

56. CB to EN, 20 June 1853: MS BS 90, BPM, [*L&L*, iv, 72, partial] is apparently the last extant letter before CB to EN, 1 March 1854: MS Montague, [*L&L*, iv, 107]. Mary Hewitt refers to a [lost] letter from Charlotte to Ellen ending the quarrel in Mary Hewitt to EN, 21 Feb. [1854]: MS in Brotherton, [*L&L*, iv, 103]. There is one letter which implies a meeting with Ellen in Leeds where Charlotte purchased mops, carpets, a rug, crockery and glass. It is dated only 'Thursday Morning' by Charlotte, but Ellen attributes it to 6 October 1853. It is possible, as Margaret Smith suggests, that Charlotte met Ellen in Leeds on her return from Hornsea on Thursday, 13 October 1853. The nature and timing of the purchases, however, suggest to me that the letter has been misdated by several months: the annual spring clean and Mrs Gaskell's visit were both over and this was before Charlotte became engaged. For the letter see: CB to EN, [?13 Oct. 1853]: MS Bon 248, BPM,

[*L&L*, iv, 97–8, wrongly dated to 6 Oct. 1853].

57. CB to MW, 12 Dec. 1853: MS FM 25 p.2, Fitzwilliam, [*L&L*, iv, 101]. Significantly, this letter is incomplete, ending with the words 'My heart …' immediately after the sentence quoted in my text. This seems to me further evidence of a comprehensive attempt to destroy all references to the quarrel in Charlotte's correspondence: Miss Wooler would willingly have acquiesced to such a request from Ellen, just as she did with regard to James Taylor references for Mr Nicholls.

58. Mary Hewitt to EN, 21 Feb. [1854]: MS in Brotherton, [*L&L*, iv, 103].

59. CB to EN, 11 April 1854: MS p.1, Pforzheimer, [*L&L*, iv, 112].

60. CB to MW, 30 Aug. 1853: MS FM 22 pp.2–4, Fitzwilliam, [*L&L*, iv, 81–2].

61. *Ibid.*, pp.3–6.

62. *Ibid.*, p.1; CB to MW, 8 Sept. 1853: MS FM 23 pp.1–2, Fitzwilliam, [*L&L*, iv, 84–5].

63. CB to ECG, [31 Aug. 1853]: MS in private hands, [*L&L*, iv, 83–4]; CB to EN, 11 April 1854: MS p.1, Pforzheimer, [*L&L*, iv, 112].

64. CB to MW, 30 Aug. 1853: MS FM 22 p.4, Fitzwilliam, [*L&L*, iv, 82].

65. See, for example, CB to MW, 12 Dec. 1853: MS FM 25, Fitzwilliam, [*L&L*, iv, 101].

66. PB to ECG, 15 Sept. 1853: MS EL B121 pp.2–3, Rylands, [*BST*:8:43:85]; See CB to ECG, 1 June 1853: MS n.l., [*L&L*, iv, 70], quoted above, p.731.

67. CB to ECG, 16 Sept. 1853: MS EL fB91 p.1, Rylands, [*BST*:8:43:86].

68. *Ibid.*; ECG to [unidentified], [end Sept. 1853] [C&P, pp.247–8]. This letter is quoted in ECG, *Life*, pp.383–5, where it appears as 'part of a letter I wrote at the time'. I suspect, however, that this is actually an edited, reordered and polished version of her extant letter to someone, possibly John Forster, which was actually written at the time: see ECG to [?John Forster], [end Sept. 1853]: MS in Brotherton, [C&P, pp.242–7].

69. *Ibid.*, pp.1, 3–5.

70. *Ibid.*, pp.2–3.

71. *Ibid.*, pp.3, 5–8, 11.

72. *Ibid.*, pp.12–14.

73. ECG, *Life*, pp.387, 388.

74. *Ibid.*, p.386; ECG to [?John Forster], [end Sept. 1853]: MS p.9, Brotherton, [C&P, p.245]. See, for example, her remarks on Patrick's dining alone which gave her the impression he normally took all his meals alone: *ibid.*, p.3.

75. ECG to Richard Monckton Milnes, 29 Oct. [1853]: [C&P, pp.252–3]. According to the letter, Mrs Gaskell, a Unitarian, had also tried to find Mr Nicholls a place as curate to Dr Hook, the widely respected Anglican Bishop of Leeds, but he had no vacancies available.

76. CB to ECG, [25 Sept. 1853]: MS n.l., [*L&L*, iv, 96].

77. CB to Francis Bennoch, 29 Sept. 1853: MS BS 91 p.3, BPM, [*BST*:13:67:142]; *Bradford Observer*, 6 Oct. 1853, p.5. Both sermons were in aid of Stanbury Sunday schools and between them raised £7.

78. CB to MW, 18 Oct. 1853: MS FM 24 pp.2, 3–4, Fitzwilliam, [*L&L*, iv, 99, wrongly dated to 8 Oct. 1853].

79. See, for example, the Revd William Fawcett (not J. T. C. Fawcett, vicar of Kildwick, as stated in *L&L*, iv, 98, 350), who stayed four days at the parsonage from 15 to 18 October, preaching on the Sunday and baptizing four infants during the service: *ibid.*, p.1; Register of Baptisms, 1837–54, Haworth Church.

80. CB to ECG, 15 Nov. 1853: MS in private hands, [*BST*:12:65:428–9, photograph only]. This letter proves Charlotte planned the visit prior to learning of George Smith's engagement and not as a response to it as is suggested by Fraser, pp.451–2.

81. For Charlotte's disappointment over the payment for *Villette* – she considered it 'not quite equitable' – see CB to MW, 7 Dec. 1852: MS FM 18 pp.1–2, Fitzwilliam, [*L&L*, iv, 23]. For the power of attorney see CB to GS, 27 July 1850: MS S-G 38 p.2, BPM, [*L&L*, iii, 127].

82. CB to GS, 6 Dec. 1852: MS S-G 78 p.1, BPM, [*L&L*, iv, 22].

83. CB to Emily Shaen, 21 Nov. 1853: MS in Brotherton, [*L&L*, iv, 99–100].

84. CB to Mrs Smith, 21 Nov. 1853: MS S-G 86 p.2, BPM.

85. Draft letter Mrs Smith to CB, [c.22–3 Nov. 1853]: MS S-G 87 p.1, BPM, [Fraser, p.452]. For George Smith's own account in his memoirs of meeting and falling in love with Elizabeth Blakeway at a ball on 5 April 1853 and his proposal and acceptance the following November, see Glynn, *Prince of Publishers*, pp.77–9.

86. CB to Emily Shaen, Thursday morning [24 Nov. 1853]: MS in Brotherton, [*L&L*, iv, 99–100]. It is clear from this letter that Charlotte received Mrs Smith's letter that morning, the day she was due to go to London, and cancelled her visit immediately. Mrs Gaskell was clearly intrigued both by the purpose of the visit and the reasons for its cancellation, obliging Charlotte to fend her off with the equally oracular 'circumstances give me no present warrant to dwell on the point … The change of plan with regard to my London journey was regulated only by commonplace causes': CB to ECG, 27 Dec. 1853: MS EL fB91 p.4, Rylands, [*BST*:12:62:121–2].

87. CB to WSW, 6 Dec. 1853: MS Grolier F12 p.1, BPM, [*L&L*, iv, 100].

88. CB to GS, 10 Dec. 1853: MS S-G 88 p.1, BPM, [*BST*:18:92:113].

89. CB to MW, 12 Dec. 1853: MS FM 25 p.1, Fitzwilliam, [*L&L*, iv, 101]; CB to ECG, 27 Dec. 1853: MS EL fB91 p.2, Rylands, [*BST*:12:62:122].

90. CB to EN, 11 April 1854: MS pp.1–2, Pforzheimer, [*L&L*, iv, 112].

91. *Ibid.*, p.2; CB to EN, [28 March 1854]: MS p.3, Princeton, [*L&L*, iv, 111].

92. *Leeds Intelligencer*, 7 Jan. 1854, p.8. The severe

weather prompted William Cartman to give Patrick a pair of heel spikes to buckle under his shoes and prevent him slipping on the ice: writing to thank him, Patrick declared the device 'another prop to Old-Age –': PB to William Cartman, 27 Jan. 1854: MS BS 197 pp.1–2, BPM, [*L&L*, iv, 101]. The heel spikes are now in the BPM: HAOBP:H61, BPM.

93. Richard Monckton Milnes to ECG, 30 Jan. 1854: MS fms Am 1943.1 (131) pp.1–3, Harvard. Milnes may have succeeded in securing some augmentation of income for Mr Nicholls because Mrs Gaskell later wrote 'thanking you most truly about Mr Nicholls. I am sure you will keep the secret; and if you want a steam-engine or 1000 yards of calico pray employ me in Manchester': ECG to Richard Monckton Milnes, [?early June 1854]: [C&P, p.299].

94. For the ending of the three-month strike at Merralls' mill see *Halifax Guardian*, 7 Jan. 1854, p.4 and 14 Jan. 1854, p.5 for the ending of a five-month strike at Lunds' mill in Keighley; for the water dispute see 18 Feb. 1854, p.5 and also *Leeds Intelligencer*, 21 May 1853, p.5, *Bradford Observer*, 19 May 1853, p.5; for Patrick's invitation to a CPAS meeting in Bradford see: CB to Revd James Caspar, 21 Feb. 1854: MS BS 198, BPM. The CPAS meeting was held in the splendid surroundings of the newly built and opened St George's Hall in Bradford: *Halifax Guardian*, 4 March 1854, p.6.

95. *Ibid.*, 4 March 1854, p.5; 18 March 1854, p.5.

96. CB to Francis Bennoch, 27 Jan. 1854: MS BS 92 p.2, BPM, [*BST*:13:67:143].

97. CB to Sydney Dobell, 3 Feb. 1854: MS n.l., [*L&L*, iv, 102].

98. See, for example, William Wooler, who consulted Charlotte on publishing his manuscripts. She advised him that Smith, Elder & Co. were unlikely to publish his work because they dealt chiefly in fiction, warned him against publishing at his own risk and suggested he make the disposal of the copyright 'an indispensable preliminary' so as to avoid loss: CB to William Wooler, 31 March 1853: MS BS 88, BPM, [*BST*:16:82:110]. Writing to his sister, Margaret Wooler, a few weeks later she hints that the manuscripts were advocating political progress: CB to MW, 13 April 1853: MS FM 21 p.4, Fitzwilliam, [*L&L*, iv, 58–9].

99. CB to Henry Garrs, 22 Feb. 1854: MS BS 93 p.1, BPM; CB to Henry Garrs, 17 March 1854: MS BS 94 p.3, BPM. Abraham Holroyd, recalling this story for William Scruton in the 1880s, gave it a very different slant. According to him, Henry Garrs came first to him for advice and, on learning the relationship with the Brontë servants, Holroyd advised him to consult Charlotte. He therefore travelled to Haworth the next day, Charlotte recognized him instantly ('Why, you are Nancy's brother') despite never having met him, listened to his plans and advised him against publishing, citing the difficulties *Poems* had encountered. Later, though unwell, she dictated a letter to her father urging him not to publish. A few weeks afterwards, five pounds came from the Earl of Carlisle, clearly procured through her intervention: Scruton, pp.114–15. Though one can see where the story came from, it is contradicted in all its most important aspects by these letters: there is no suggestion of any personal meeting, certainly not before the first letter, both letters are in Charlotte's own hand and her advice was to publish. Henry Garrs later sent Patrick copies of his patriotic verses on the Crimean War: PB to Henry Garrs, 2 April 1856: MS BS 202, BPM.

100. CB to T.C. Newby, 18 March 1854: MS BS 94.1, BPM.

101. CB to EN, 1 March 1854: MS Montague, [*L&L*, iv, 107]; CB to EN, 7 March 1854: MS HM 26004, Huntington, [*L&L*, iv, 107–8]; CB to EN, [22 March 1854]: MS Bon 249, BPM, [*L&L*, iv, 109–10]. Charlotte attempted to conceal the fact that she was expecting a visit from Mr Nicholls by telling Ellen in this last letter that she could not go to Miss Wooler at Hornsea because of 'a prior engagement this month': *ibid.*, pp.1–2.

102. CB to EN, [28 March 1854]: MS pp.2–3, Princeton, [*L&L*, iv, 110]. This letter was evidently a reply to one from Ellen turning down the invitation to Haworth.

103. CB to EN, [1 April 1854]: MS BS 94.5 pp.1–2, BPM, [*L&L*, iv, 111]; CB to ECG, 3 April 1854: MS EL fB91 p.2, Rylands.

104. CB to EN, 11 April 1854: MS p.3, Pforzheimer, [*L&L*, iv, 112].

CHAPTER TWENTY-SIX

Title: [CB] 'Oh! I am not going to die, am I? He will not separate us, we have been so happy': ECG, *Life*, p.400.

1. CB to EN, 11 April 1854: MS pp.3–5, Pforzheimer, [*L&L*, iv, 112–13].

2. CB to MW, 12 April 1854: MS FM 26 p.3, Fitzwilliam, [*L&L*, iv, 114].

3. CB to EN, 15 April 1854: MS BS 95.2 p.3, BPM, [*L&L*, iv, 115]; CB to ECG, 18 April 1854: MS n.l., [*L&L*, iv, 116]; CB to EN, 28 April 1854: MS BS 95.4 pp.1–2, BPM, [*L&L*, iv, 120].

4. CB to EN, 15 April 1854: MS BS 95.2 pp.2–4, BPM, [*L&L*, iv, 115].

5. *Leeds Intelligencer*, 22 April 1854, p.6. 'The meeting deeply regretted the inability of their reverend incumbent, the Rev. P. Brontë, to be present, he

having for some time been in a weak state of health.'

6. PB to Revd James Cheadle, 18 April 1854: MS BS 198.5, BPM; CB to MW, 12 April 1854: MS FM 26 p.4, Fitzwilliam, [*L&L*, iv, 114].

7. CB to Francis Bennoch, 11 April 1854: MS BS 95, BPM, [*BST*:13:67:143–4]; CB to EN, 15 April 1854: MS BS 95.2 p.1, BPM, [*L&L*, iv, 114–15].

8. CB to EN, 11 April 1854: MS p.3, Pforzheimer, [*L&L*, iv, 112]; CB to EN, [22 May 1854]: MS Grolier E27 pp.2–3, BPM, [*L&L*, iv, 126]. For part of the costs of conversion, amounting to £9 15s. 17d., see CB, Expenses of House Repairs, 22 April 1854: MS p.1, in private hands.

9. CB to GS, 18 April 1854: MS S-G 89 pp.1–3, BPM, [*BST*:18:92:113–14].

10. CB to GS, 25 April 1854: MS S-G 90 pp.1–4, BPM, [*L&L*, iv, 118–19].

11. *Bradford Observer*, 20 April 1854, p.5; *Leeds Intelligencer*, 22 April 1854, p.8; CB to ECG, 26 April 1854: MS EL fB91 p.2, Rylands, [*BST*:12:62:123, wrongly dated to 1864]. Patrick himself preached on the Day of National Humiliation and Prayer: CB to EN, 28 April 1854: MS BS 95.4 p.1, BPM, [*L&L*, iv, 120].

12. *Ibid.*, pp.2–3. Catherine Winkworth repeated similar remarks made by Charlotte during a conversation they had at Mrs Gaskell's a few days after this letter: 'He is a Puseyite and very stiff; I fear it will stand in the way of my intercourse with some of my friends. But I shall always be the same in my heart towards them. I shall never let him make me a bigot. I don't think differences of opinion ought to interfere with friendship, do you?': Catherine Winkworth to Emma Shaen, 8 May 1854, [Shaen (ed.), *Memorials of Two Sisters*, p.113]. The reference, which caused Mr Nicholls to groan, was to 'The present successors of the apostles, disciples of Dr Pusey and tools of the Propaganda, were at that time being hatched under cradle-blankets, or undergoing regeneration by nursery-baptism in wash-hand-basins': CB, *Shirley*, p.6.

13. CB to EN, 28 April 1854: MS BS 95.4 pp.2–3, BPM, [*L&L*, iv, 120].

14. ECG to John Forster, [17 May 1854]: [C&P, p.289]. Mrs Gaskell was wrong in thinking Patrick 'sightless'; though his eyesight was poor, he was not blind.

15. ECG to Richard Monckton Milnes, 20 April [1854]: [C&P, pp.277–8]. It seems unlikely that Mr Nicholls ever received any financial benefit from Mrs Gaskell's intervention: he turned down the posts offered and does not seem to have received a pension. This letter also suggests the benefit was purely psychological: 'I can't help fancying your kind words may have made him feel that he was not so friendless as he represented <himself> & believed himself to be at first; and might rouse his despondency up to a fresh effort.' For the letter to John Forster, describing Mr Nicholls' puzzlement, see ECG to John Forster, [17 May 1854], [C&P, p.289].

16. Catherine Winkworth to Emma Shaen, 8 May 1854: [Shaen (ed.), *Memorials of Two Sisters*, pp.112–13].

17. *Ibid.*, pp.114, 115.

18. CB to EN, 6 May 1854: MS Bon 250 pp.1–2, BPM, [*L&L*, iv, 120–1]; for references to 'grandmamma' see, for example, CB to Amelia Taylor, [Dec. 1854]: MS p.2, Brotherton, [*L&L*, iv, 163].

19. CB to EN, 6 May 1854: MS Bon 250 p.1, BPM, [*L&L*, iv, 121]; CB to EN, 15 April 1854: MS BS 95.2 pp.1–2, BPM, [*L&L*, iv, 115]. The trip to Halifax is implied by the fact that Charlotte later told Ellen 'I got my dresses from Halifax a day or two since – but have not had time yet to take the cord off the box – so I don't know what they are like': CB to EN, [11 June 1854]: MS Grolier E28 p.3, BPM, [*BST*:17:90:369].

20. CB to EN, 14 May 1854: MS HM 26005 pp.2–3, Huntington, [*L&L*, iv, 125]; CB to EN, 7 June 1854: MS HM 26007 p.3, Huntington, [*L&L*, iv, 129].

21. CB to EN, [11 June 1854]: MS Grolier E28 p.2, BPM, [*BST*:17:90:369, wrongly referring to 6 weeks' leave]; CB to EN, [16 June 1854]: MS Grolier E29 pp.1–2, BPM, [*L&L*, iv, 130]. Charlotte was being most unfair to George de Renzy as he apparently returned to Haworth to help out while Patrick was on his own. Among the substitutes Mr Nicholls found were William Mayne, incumbent of Ingrow, near Keighley (30 June), George de Renzy himself (21 July) and Joseph Grant (29 July): Register of Burials, 1836–54, Haworth Church. George de Renzy also performed five baptisms on 16 July and Thomas Crowther ten on 23 July, the day he preached the Sunday school sermons and raised £18 12s.: Register of Baptisms, 1854–76, Haworth Church; *Leeds Intelligencer*, 29 July 1854, p.6. Patrick himself performed the only marriage during the honeymoon period, on 10 July: Register of Marriages, 1837–70, Haworth Church.

22. CB to EN, [22 May 1854]: MS Grolier E27 pp.3–4, BPM, [*L&L*, iv, 126–7]. According to Martha Brown, there was another strong reason, which suggests that Patrick feared the effect of pregnancy. When the specialist pronounced that there was no hope for Charlotte, Patrick had come down to the kitchen and said, 'I told you, Martha, that there was no sense in Charlotte marrying at all, for she was not strong enough for marriage': Martha Brown, quoted in Chadwick, p.477.

23. CB to EN, 27 May 1854: MS HM 26006 pp.1–3, Huntington, [*L&L*, iv, 127].

24. CB, Marriage Settlement, 24 May 1854: MS BS x, B, BPM. This manuscript is transcribed and discussed in Juliet R. V. Barker, 'Subdued Expectations: Charlotte Brontë's Marriage Settlement', *BST*:19:1&2:33–9.

25. The small discrepancy between this sum and the £1684 7s. 6d. which Charlotte thought she had invested may be an error or, more likely, the cost of setting up and stamping the settlement

deeds: see *ibid.*, p.35. Charlotte had originally suggested that George Smith should remain responsible for remitting the dividends but had deferred to Joe Taylor's opinion on the matter: CB to Mr Carr, 22 May 1854: MS BS 95.6, BPM.

26. CB to EN, 15 April 1854: MS BS 95.2 p.3, BPM, [*L&L*, iv, 115]. In my original article I felt that the clause reflected Charlotte's unease about Mr Nicholls' motives in marrying her. Fraser, p.463 suggests that Patrick was more likely to have insisted on the arrangement for Charlotte's protection. I now believe that Charlotte was trying to ensure that her father would not lose financially by her marriage; she wanted to give him the security of her capital if she died before him.

27. CB to EN, [11 June 1854]: MS Grolier E28 pp.3, 1–2, BPM, [*BST*:17:90:369]. A deleted couple of lines on p.2 seem to indicate great irritation: '<He was very tiresome on the last time – he was here – he would (keep me?) <u>while</u>>.'

28. CB to EN, 27 May 1854: MS HM 26006 p.4, Huntington, [*L&L*, iv, 128]; CB to EN, 7 June 1854: MS HM 26007 p.4, Huntington, [*L&L*, iv, 129]; CB to EN, [11 June 1854]: MS Grolier E28 p.3, BPM, [*BST*:17:90:369]; CB to EN, [16 June 1854]: MS Grolier E29 pp.2–4, BPM, [*L&L*, iv, 131]. See also CB to MW, 16 June 1854: MS FM 27 pp.1–2, Fitzwilliam, [*L&L*, iv, 131].

29. [John Robinson], 'Love Story of Charlotte Brontë: Wedding recollected', *Keighley News*, 27 Oct. 1923, p.8. John Robinson was eighty-six years old when he was interviewed, on the occasion of his diamond wedding anniversary.

30. CB to MW, 22 Aug. 1854: MS FM 29 p.4, Fitzwilliam, [*L&L*, iv, 148]. The wedding dress was preserved by Mr Nicholls who bequeathed it to his niece, Miss Charlotte Brontë Nicholls, with the instruction that she should burn it before she died so that it could not be sold: his wishes were carried out in 1954, but Miss Nicholls' own niece, Margaret Ross, saw it and described it, enabling a copy to be made which was displayed in the Brontë Parsonage Museum in 1967: *Yorkshire Post*, 19 June 1967, p.5. The bonnet and lace mantle (which is described as a veil but is too large to be one) are in the BPM: HAOBP:D2 & HAOBP:D97, BPM, [JB *ST*, no.53]. ECG, *Life*, p.395.

31. CB to MW, 16 June 1854: MS FM 27 pp.2–3, Fitzwilliam, [*L&L*, iv, 131]. No other guests were invited. The eighteen names on Charlotte's list were to receive wedding cards, informing them of the marriage, not invitations as suggested in Fraser, pp.465–6. ECG, *Life*, p.395.

32. See, for example, CB to Martha Brown, 28 July 1854: MS BS 96 p.1, BPM, [*L&L*, iv, 143].

33. CB/ABN, Marriage Certificate, 29 June 1854: MS BS Copy Docs, BPM; ECG, *Life*, p.395; [John Robinson], 'Love Story of Charlotte Brontë: Wedding recollected', *Keighley News*, 27 Oct. 1923, p.8; EN to GS, 28 March [1860]: MS File 7 no.4, John Murray. The dress, which is

actually a skirt and top, is in the BPM: HAOBP: D74 (1&2), BPM, [JB *ST*, no.51]. For notices of the wedding in the local press see *Halifax Guardian*, 1 July 1854, p.8; *Leeds Intelligencer*, 1 July 1854, p.8; *Bradford Observer*, 6 July 1854, p.5.

34. CB to EN, [29 June 1854]: MS p.1, Berg, [*L&L*, iv, 133–4]. This is the first extant letter to bear Charlotte's married name 'C. B. N[icholls]'; there is apparently no surviving letter from Charlotte to Patrick at this time, though she must have written to him at the same time as to Ellen.

35. CB to Catherine Wooler, 18 July 1854: MS FM 33 p.2, Fitzwilliam, [*L&L*, iv, 136].

36. CB to MW, 10 July 1854: MS FM 28 pp.2–4, Fitzwilliam, [*L&L*, iv, 134]. See also Charlotte's comment, 'I was also greatly surprised to find so much of English order and repose in the family habits and arrangements': CB to Catherine Wooler, 18 July 1854: MS FM 33 p.3, Fitzwilliam, [*L&L*, iv, 136].

37. CB to MW, 10 July 1854: MS FM 28 pp.3–5, Fitzwilliam, [*L&L*, iv, 134].

38. *Ibid.*, p.4; ABN to Revd George Sowden, 10 Aug. 1854: MS BS 247, BPM, [*L&L*, iv, 148]; CB to Catherine Winkworth, 27 July 1854: MS p.2, Brotherton, [*L&L*, iv, 137, photograph & transcript].

39. CB to Catherine Wooler, 18 July 1854: MS FM 33 p.3, Fitzwilliam, [*L&L*, iv, 136]. The West End Hotel, run by a widow, Mrs Shannon, and her three daughters, was the second best hotel in Kilkee. It had an illustrious clientele, including Lord John Manners, who visited earlier, and the Dowager Lady Charlotte O'Brien of Dromoland Castle, who was there at the same time as the newly-weds. Other visitors, including Jonathan Binns in 1837 and the future Poet Laureate, Alfred Austin, in 1894, complained about the quality of the food – presumably one of the things Charlotte would have carped at. I am grateful to Thomas J. Byrne for all this information.

40. CB to Catherine Winkworth, 27 July 1854: MS pp.2–3, Brotherton, [*L&L*, iv, 137–8, photograph & transcript]. Mr Nicholls was actually equally impressed with the sea at Kilkee, singling it out as a particularly memorable part of the honeymoon tour: 'the finest shore I ever saw – Completely girdled with stupendous cliffs – it was most refreshing to sit on a rock & look out on the broad Atlantic boiling & foaming at our feet –': ABN to Revd George Sowden, 10 Aug. 1854: MS BS 247 p.3, BPM, [*L&L*, iv, 148].

41. CB to EN, 28 July 1854: MS n.l., [*L&L*, iv, 143]. I have reordered the list of places to follow what seems more likely to have been their route.

42. CB to Catherine Winkworth, 27 July 1854: MS p.4, Brotherton, [*L&L*, iv, 138, photograph & transcript].

43. CB to Martha Brown, 28 July 1854: MS BS 96

pp.1–2, BPM, [*L&L*, iv, 143]; CB to EN, 28 July 1854: MS n.l., [*L&L*, iv, 143].

44. CB to EN, 9 Aug. 1854: MS pp.2–4, Law Colln, photograph in Mildred Christian Colln, BPM, [*L&L*, iv, 145]. As yet unused to her new name, Charlotte signed the letter '<CBron> Nicholls'.

45. CB to MW, 22 Aug. 1854: MS FM 29 p.4, Fitzwilliam, [*L&L*, iv, 148]; CB to MW, 29 Aug. 1854: MS Bon 251 p.2, BPM, [*L&L*, iv, 150].

46. CB to MW, 19 Sept. 1854: MS FM 30 p.4, Fitzwilliam, [*L&L*, iv, 152–3].

47. CB to EN, 9 Aug. 1854: MS p.2, Law Colln, photograph in Mildred Christian Colln, BPM, [*L&L*, iv, 145].

48. CB to MW, 22 Aug. 1854: MS FM 29 pp.2–3, Fitzwilliam, [*L&L*, iv, 149].

49. CB to MW, 19 Sept. 1854: MS FM 30 pp.2–3, Fitzwilliam, [*L&L*, iv, 152]. Among the visiting clergy was Dr Burnett, vicar of Bradford, who came to preach the sermons on behalf of the Society for the Conversion of the Jews on 17 September; the collection raised a meagre £2 5s. which, together with Patrick's annual subscription of 5/-, was sent to the Bradford treasurer: *ibid.*, p.2; PB, Account Book, *c.*1845–61: MS BS 173 p.6, BPM, [wrongly dated by Patrick to 16 September, the day before the sermon].

50. See, for example, CB to MW, 19 Sept. 1854: MS FM 30, Fitzwilliam, [*L&L*, iv, 152–3].

51. CB to EN, 29 Aug. [1854]: MS Bon 251 p.1, BPM, [*L&L*, iv, 150]; CB to EN, 7 Sept. 1854: MS p.2, Pforzheimer, [*L&L*, iv, 150], also signed '<CBron> Nicholls'; CB to EN, 14 Sept. 1854: MS Montague, [*L&L*, iv, 151].

52. *Ibid.*; CB to EN, 11 Oct. 1854: MS MA 2696 R-V p.1, Pierpont Morgan, [*L&L*, iv, 154]; CB to EN, 9 Aug. 1854: MS p.3, Law Colln, photograph in Mildred Christian Colln, BPM, [*L&L*, iv, 145].

53. CB to ECG, 30 Sept. 1854: MS EL fB91 p.3, Rylands, [*L&L*, iv, 154, omitted]; ECG, *Life*, p.397; ECG to various, [11–30 Oct. 1854]: [C&P, pp.305–22]. Mrs Gaskell was also reluctant to visit 'because it required a little courage to face Mr Nicholls, as she had told me he did not like her intimacy with us as dissenters, but that she knew he *would* like us when he had seen us': ECG to GS, 4 June [1855]: [C&P, p.347].

54. CB to EN, 11 Oct. 1854: MS MA 2696 R-V pp.2–3, Pierpont Morgan, [*L&L*, iv, 154].

55. CB to EN, [20 Oct. 1854]: MS MA 2696 R-V pp.1–4, Pierpont Morgan, [*L&L*, iv, 155].

56. CB to EN, 31 Oct. 1854: MS BS 96.5 pp.3–4, BPM, [*L&L*, iv, 156–7].

57. See, for example, CB to EN, 7 Nov. 1854: MS MA 2696 R-V pp.2–3, Pierpont Morgan, [*L&L*, iv, 158]: 'As to my own notes, I never thought of attaching importance to them, or considering their fate – till Arthur seemed to reflect on both so seriously.' A sharp exchange, through Clement Shorter, over forty years

later, revealed the fact that Charlotte had not kept Ellen's letters: 'Pray tell Mr Nicholls that if he has found letters written by me to Charlotte before marriage, that I request that in faith to his wife's wishes he will seal and send them to me at once – She most emphatically declared her intention of destroying everything of the kind. He had better show himself even thus late a man of honour': EN to C. K. Shorter, 10 April 1895, MS in bound vol. of miscellaneous letters, Brotherton. Mr Nicholls' reply was more temperate: 'You may tell Miss Nussey that her letters never came into my possession; in fact I cannot remember having ever seen a <scrapp> scrap of her hand-writing. I presume my wife burned them as soon as read': ABN to C. K. Shorter, 26 April 1895: MS in bound vol. of ABN letters to C. K. Shorter, Brotherton.

58. EN to ABN [Nov. 1854]: MS in Texas, [*L&L*, iv, 157]; this letter was addressed to 'Revd The Magister'. How the note came back into Ellen's hands is not clear: there was no reason for Mr Nicholls to return it to her as it was addressed to him personally. It is possible that Clement Shorter was responsible. Ellen later actually lied about her response to this request, telling William Scruton, for instance, that her reply was 'Miss Nussey's compliments to Mr Nicholls and she will thank him to mind his own business': William Scruton, 'Personal Reminiscences of Miss Ellen Nussey', *Yorkshire Notes & Queries*, vol. iii, no.8, p.293.

59. CB to EN, 7 Nov. 1854: MS MA 2696 R-V p.2, Pierpont Morgan, [*L&L*, iv, 158, partial]. Ellen deleted the first sentence of this quote in the manuscript, substituting her own phrase 'Arthur wishes you would burn my letters', which appears in the printed versions. This was a deliberate attempt on Ellen's part to obfuscate the fact that she had reneged on her promise to burn Charlotte's letters.

60. CB to EN, 7 Nov. 1854: MS MA 2696 R-V p.3, Pierpont Morgan, [*L&L*, iv, 158].

61. CB to EN, 14 Nov. 1854: MS Ashley 168, BL, [*L&L*, iv, 158–9]; CB to MW, 15 Nov. 1854: MS FM 31 pp.3–4, Fitzwilliam, [*L&L*, iv, 160]. Charlotte chose to view the offer as 'a gratifying proof of respect for my dear Arthur': *ibid.*, p.3.

62. CB to EN, 14 Nov. 1854: MS Ashley 168 pp.1–3, BL, [*L&L*, iv, 158–9]; CB to EN, 21 Nov. 1854: MS pp.2–3, Berg, [*L&L*, iv, 161]. Charlotte's comments on this matter, in particular her insistence that 'Mr S— is most anxious that the affairs should be kept absolutely quiet – in the event of disappointment it would be both painful and injurious to him if it should be rumoured at Hebden Bridge that he has had thoughts of leaving. Arthur says if a whisper gets out – these things fly from parson to parson like wild-fire', are clear evidence that her husband was *not* censoring her letters at this time as Ellen later claimed.

63. CB to MW, 15 Nov. 1854: MS FM 31 pp.2–3, Fitzwilliam, [*L&L*, iv, 160].

64. *Ibid.*, pp.1–2; CB to EN, 14 Nov, 1854: MS Ashley 168 p.3, BL, [*L&L*, iv, 159].

65. CB to Amelia Taylor, [Dec. 1854]: MS pp.1–2, Brotherton, [*L&L*, iv, 163].

66. CB to Amelia Taylor, [Dec. 1854]: MS p.3, Brotherton, [*L&L*, iv, 166].

67. CB to EN, 21 Nov. 1854: MS p.1, Berg, [*L&L*, iv, 161]; CB to EN, 29 Nov. 1854: MS Ashley 2452(5) p.3, BL, [*L&L*, iv, 162]; CB to MW, 6 Dec. 1854: MS FM 32 pp.1–2, Fitzwilliam, [*L&L*, iv, 163–4].

68. *Ibid.*, p.2; CB to EN, 7 Dec. 1854: MS Grolier E30 pp.1–4, BPM, [*L&L*, iv, 164].

69. *Ibid.*, p.3; CB to Mr Ingham, [Dec. 1854]: MS BS 98, BPM, [*L&L*, iv, 171, partial, wrongly dated to Jan. 1855].

70. CB to MW, 6 Dec. 1854: MS FM 32 pp.3–4, Fitzwilliam, [*L&L*, iv, 164].

71. CB to unidentified, 13 Dec. 1854: MS in private hands. I am grateful to the Headmaster of Woodhouse Grove School, Rawdon, for allowing me to see this letter. ABN to Messrs Heaton, 13 Dec. 1854: MS Heaton B143 p.4, WYAS, Bradford. Both letters are in Patrick's name, including the signature, but are in Charlotte's and Arthur's hands respectively. The addressee of Charlotte's letter is hidden by the frame. Haworth's response was slow to the Royal Proclamation setting up the Patriotic Fund, which had been reported in the *Leeds Intelligencer*, 14 Oct. 1854, p.5 and *Bradford Observer*, 19 Oct. 1854, p.7. Bradford had held its meeting at the end of October and raised over £3,000: *Halifax Guardian*, 4 Nov. 1854, p.5; 2 Dec. 1854, p.5.

72. CB to EN, 26 Dec. [1854]: MS BS 97 p.2, BPM, [*BST*:16:81:19].

73. *Bradford Observer*, 21 Dec. 1854, p.5; 4 Jan. 1855, p.6; *Halifax Guardian*, 13 Jan. 1855, p.5.

74. ABN to GS, 11 Oct. 1859: MS File 8 no. 3 pp.2–3, John Murray, [*BST*:19:3:102].

75. CB, 'Emma', 27 Nov. 1853: MS at Princeton, [CB, 'The Last Sketch', *Cornhill Magazine*, i, Jan.–June 1860, pp.487–98].

76. CB to EN, 19 Jan. [1854]: MS BS 99 pp.1–2, BPM, [*L&L*, iv, 170–1]. The date of the visit is uncertain, but there is nothing in the parish registers between 6 and 16 January, suggesting that it probably took place at some time between those dates.

77. ECG, *Life*, p.398; CB to EN, 29 Nov. 1854: MS Ashley 2452(5) pp.1–2, BL, [*L&L*, iv, 161–2]; CB to EN, 7 Dec. 1854: MS Grolier E30 p.2, BPM, [*L&L*, iv, 164–5]; CB to EN, 26 Dec. 1854: MS BS 97 p.2, BPM, [*BST*:16:81:19].

78. CB to EN, 19 Jan. 1855: MS BS 99 pp.2–3, BPM, [*L&L*, iv, 171].

79. CB to Amelia Taylor, [21 Jan. 1855]: MS pp.3–4, Brotherton, [*L&L*, iv, 172].

80. *Ibid.*, p.1.

81. ABN to EN, 23 Jan. 1855: MS pp.1–2, Brotherton, [*L&L*, iv, 173]; ABN to EN, 29 Jan. 1855:
MS p.1, Brotherton, [*L&L*, iv, 173]; ABN to EN, 1 Feb. 1855: MS p.1, Brotherton, [*L&L*, iv, 173].

82. PB to Sir James Kay Shuttleworth, 3 Feb. 1855: MS pp.1–2, Brotherton.

83. ABN to EN, 14 Feb. 1855: MS pp.1–2, Brotherton, [*L&L*, iv, 174].

84. CB, Last Will & Testament, 17 Feb. 1855: MS in Borthwick.

85. Tabitha Aykroyd, gravestone, Haworth Churchyard; Register of Burials, 1854–84, Haworth Church [21 Feb. 1855].

86. CB to EN, [21 Feb. 1855]: MS BS 101 p.1, BPM, [*L&L*, iv, 175].

87. CB to EN, [Feb. 1855]: MS BS 100 p.1, BPM, [*L&L*, iv, 175]. Mary Hewitt's baby had been born in December 1854: CB to EN, 7 Dec. 1854: MS Grolier E30 pp.2–3, BPM, [*L&L*, iv, 165].

88. CB to Amelia Taylor, [Feb. 1855]: MS BS 103 p.1, BPM, [*L&L*, iv, 176].

89. CB to Amelia Taylor, [Feb. 1855]: MS BS 102 p.1, BPM, [*L&L*, iv, 176]; ECG, *Life*, p.399.

90. CB to EN, [Feb. 1855]: MS BS 100 p.1, BPM, [*L&L*, iv, 175].

91. ABN to EN, 15 March 1855: MS pp.1–2, Brotherton, [*L&L*, iv, 176–7].

92. ECG, *Life*, p.400.

93. *Leeds Intelligencer*, 17 March 1855, p.3; 24 March 1855, p.7; Register of Burials, 1854–84, Haworth Church [27 March 1855].

94. PB to EN, 30 March 1855: MS pp.1–3, Princeton, [*L&L*, iv, 177].

95. ABN to EN, 31 March 1855: MS BS 247.2, BPM, [*L&L*, iv, 177–8]; ABN to Mary Hewitt, 11 April 1855: MS pp.2–3, Brotherton, [*L&L*, iv, 178].

96. CB, death certificate, 31 March 1855: copy in MS Copy Docs, XA, C, BPM. The dispute over the cause of Charlotte's death has raged for many years owing chiefly to Mr Nicholls' reluctance to cite pregnancy as the cause of her illness in his letter to Ellen of 14 February 1855 and the 'phthisis' declaration of the death certificate – a cause normally associated with tuberculosis. Verdicts have ranged from a severe wasting disease or tuberculosis alone to a hydatidiform mole (a rare complication in which the fertilized ovum develops into a bag of cysts instead of a foetus). For a summary of the arguments see H.W. Gallagher, 'Charlotte Bronte: A Surgeon's Assessment', *BST*:18:95:368–9. There can be no doubt that Charlotte was pregnant: her family and friends had ample opportunity to contradict that express statement in Mrs Gaskell's *Life*, p.399 and Charlotte herself implied as much when comparing her own case to Mary Hewitt's: see above, p.771, n. 87. All her symptoms suggest that she was suffering from a classic case of hyperemesis gravidarum (severe vomiting in pregnancy). In modern medical practice, this would lead to early screening for hydatidiform mole, multiple pregnancy and urinary infec-

tion, all of which can cause hyperemesis. The severe sickness, which usually lasts until about the fifteenth week, can now be treated with intravenous feeding and anti-emetics, but sometimes an abortion is still necessary to save the mother's life. The feverish symptoms exhibited by Charlotte are consistent with a urinary infection as the cause and this would now be treated successfully with antibiotics. In Charlotte's case, her small frame and thinness would have led to a more rapid and severe deterioration in her condition. By fifteen weeks, she would have been so worn and emaciated by the constant vomiting, which in itself would have caused poisoning of her body fluids as her kidneys failed, that the death certificate verdict of 'phthisis', general wasting, would have been appropriate. I am grateful to Ian Beck, Consultant Gynaecologist and Obstetrician, for this information and opinion.

97. EN to GS, 1 June [1860]: MS File 7 no.5, John Murray; EN to GS, 28 March [1860]: MS File 7 no.4, John Murray.

98. PB to ECG, 27 Aug. 1855: MS EL B121 p.3, Rylands, [*BST*:8:43:96].

99. Register of Burials, 1854–84, Haworth Church. William Cartman, headmaster of Skipton Grammar School, and one of Patrick's oldest friends, later delivered the funeral sermon on the text 'And all wept and bewailed her' from Luke ch. 8 v. 52: Whiteley Turner, *A Spring-Time Saunter Round and About Brontëland*, p.199.

100. CB to Amelia Taylor, [21 Jan. 1855]: MS p.4, Brotherton, [*L&L*, iv, 172].

101. EN to GS, 1 June [1860]: MS File 7 no.5, John Murray.

102. See, for instance, CB to WSW, 25 April 1850: MS HM 24395 pp.1–2, Huntington, [*L&L*, iii,

103]; CB to WSW, 6 May 1850: MS p.2, Harvard, [*L&L*, iii, 108]; Mrs Gaskell also reports that Charlotte took her several times to see John Greenwood when she stayed in Haworth and that Charlotte asked her to send a message to him when she stayed in Manchester: ECG to GS, 4 June [1855]: [C&P, p.346]. This hardly constitutes the sort of intimate friendship to which Greenwood himself seems to have laid claim.

103. ECG to John Greenwood, 4 April [1855]: [C&P, pp.335–6]. It is clear from the date of this letter (the same day as Charlotte's funeral) and the fact that Mrs Gaskell learnt of Charlotte's death from John Greenwood, rather than anyone at the parsonage, that Mrs Gaskell was not invited to the funeral as suggested in L&D, p.477.

104. PB to ECG, 5 April 1855: MS EL B121 pp.1–3, Rylands, [*BST*:8:43:86–7].

105. ECG to John Greenwood, 12 April [1855]: [C&P, p.337].

106. HM to John Greenwood, April 1855: MS n.l., but printed in a newspaper cutting held as MS HM 107, Birmingham. A note on the cutting says it is from a correspondent of *Harper's Weekly* but it would seem more likely to be from the *Daily News*, a paper with which Miss Martineau had connections. Greenwood clearly knew nothing of the estrangement between Charlotte and Harriet Martineau which is further evidence that his claims to friendship with Charlotte were exaggerated.

107. [HM], Obituary of Charlotte Brontë, *Daily News*, 6 April 1855, [Allott, pp.302, 304]. Miss Martineau's admirable magnanimity towards Charlotte may have been due, at least in part, to the fact that she believed herself to be mortally ill at the time.

CHAPTER TWENTY-SEVEN

1. Register of Burials, 1854–84, Haworth Church. Sowden conducted burials on 3, 4 (Charlotte's), 7 (two) and 8 April; *Leeds Intelligencer*, 14 April 1855, p.6. The collections were in aid of the organist.

2. *Leeds Mercury*, 14 April 1855, p.7. The *Halifax Courier* mentioned that the Institute now had 116 members and 600 volumes in its library: *Halifax Courier*, 14 April 1855, p.5.

3. PB to GS, 20 April 1855: MS File 10 no.3, John Murray, [*L&L*, iv, 179]. For Arthur Nicholls' response to Mary Hewitt's letter of sympathy see ABN to Mary Hewitt, 11 April 1855: MS in Brotherton, [*L&L*, iv, 178].

4. [Matthew Arnold], 'Haworth Churchyard', *Fraser's Magazine*, May 1855, pp.527–30, [Allott, p.308]. Arnold published the poem anonymously but wrote to tell his mother that 'There will be some lines of mine in the next Fraser (without name) on poor Charlotte Brontë': Matthew Arnold to his mother, 25 April 1855,

[Russell (ed.), *Letters of Matthew Arnold (1848–1888)*, p.44]. The poem referred to his meeting Charlotte Brontë in Harriet Martineau's company during her visit to Ambleside in December 1850.

5. Matthew Arnold to ECG, 1 June 1855, [Allott, p.306]: 'I am almost sorry you told me about the place of their burial. It really seems to me to put the finishing touch to the strange cross-grained character of the fortunes of that ill-fated family that they should even be placed after death in the wrong, uncongenial spot'. Arnold's references to Patrick and Arthur were contained in two verses: 'See! in the desolate house / The childless father! Alas – / Age, whom the most of us chide, / Chide, and put back, and delay – / Come, unupbraided for once! / Lay thy benumbing hand, / Gratefully cold, on this brow! / Shut out the grief, the despair! / Weaken the sense of his loss! / Deaden the infinite pain! / Another grief I see, / Younger; but this the

Muse, / In pity and silent awe / Revering what she cannot soothe, / With veil'd face and bow'd head, / Salutes, and passes by.': [Allott, p.308].

6. See, for example, *Leeds Intelligencer,* 7 April 1855, p.5; *Westmoreland Gazette,* 21 April 1855, p.6; *Halifax Courier,* 21 April 1855, p.6.

7. *Literary Gazette,* 14 April 1855, p.235 no.1995.

8. The story was reprinted in the *Bradford Observer,* 10 May 1855, p.5; *Leeds Intelligencer,* 12 May 1855, p.5; *Halifax Guardian,* 12 May 1855, p.8. The story even reached Mary Taylor in New Zealand: MT to EN, 19 April 1856: MS p.1, Berg, [Stevens, p.126].

9. ECG to John Greenwood, 5 May [1855]: [C&P, pp.342–3]. To her credit, Mrs Gaskell rose stoutly to Arthur's defence, pointing out that it was too early to press such things on the bereaved and responding to the snide suggestion that he had fawned on a wealthy man by saying: 'I know of better curacies being offered to him, & one living indeed, <which> \the refusal of which/ also seems to prove that he is not a worldly man, so that I can not understand how he should slight any one for another, inferior in character & attainments, but superior in fortune. A man who could do that would have snatched at opportunities of improving his own worldly condition': ECG to John Greenwood [after 5 May 1855]: [C&P, pp.343–4].

10. MW to ABN, 30 April 1855: MS pp.1–4, in private hands. For the assumption that the letter was about James Taylor, see EN to GS, 27 Feb. 1869: MS File 7 no.17, John Murray. Charlotte's letter to Miss Wooler must have fallen in the period when Charlotte had heard twice from Taylor in India and was troubled about her response: see above, pp.686–7.

11. *Ibid.*

12. *Sharpe's London Magazine,* June 1855, pp.339–42.

13. EN to ABN, 6 June 1855: MS in private hands, [*L&L,* iv, 189].

14. ECG to Catherine Winkworth, [25 Aug. 1850]: [C&P, pp.123–6]; ECG to unknown, [*c.25* Aug. 1850]: [C&P, p.127]. See above p.651.

15. ABN to EN, 11 June 1855: MS n.l., [*L&L,* iv, 189–90].

16. ECG to ECG, 16 June 1855: MS EL B121 pp.1–3, Rylands, [*BST*:8:43:87–8; *L&L,* iv, 190–1], wrongly dated to 16 July 1855].

17. ECG to GS, 4 June [1855]: [C&P, 347–8]; see also ECG to GS, 31 May 1855, [C&P, p.345]: 'Sometime, it may be years hence – but if I live long enough, and no one is living whom such a publication would hurt, I will publish what I know of her, and make the world (if I am but strong enough in expression,) honour the woman as much as they have admired the writer.'

18. ECG to GS, 18 June [1855]: [C&P, 349].

19. PB to ECG, 20 June 1855: MS EL B121 pp.7, 6, Rylands, [*BST*:8:43:90].

20. ECG to Marianne Gaskell, [27 July 1855]: [C&P, p.364].

21. PB to Henry Garrs, 2 April 1856: MS BS 202 pp.1–2, BPM.

22. ECG to EN, [24] July [1855]: [C&P, p.361].

23. ABN to EN, 24 July 1854: MS pp.2–4, Brotherton, [*L&L,* iv, 191]. In her letters Mrs Gaskell also used the phrase 'if you would allow *us* [my italics] to see as much of her correspondence with you as you might feel inclined to trust me with': ECG to EN, 24 July 1855: MS n.l., [*L&L,* iv, 192: C&P, p.261, however, has 'me'].

24. EN to ECG, 26 July 1855: MS n.l., [*L&L,* iv, 193].

25. EN to GS, 1 June [1860]: MS File 7 no.5, John Murray. Ellen later told T.J. Wise that she had burnt the remaining 200 letters which had not been selected for Mrs Gaskell: EN to T.J. Wise, 18 Nov. 1892: MS in 'Brontëana' file of bound miscellaneous EN correspondence, no.1, Brotherton. Mrs Gaskell said she had 'a series of 350 to one friend' who could only be Ellen: ECG to GS [?late Oct. 1855]: [C&P, p.372]. Mrs Gaskell's visit on or about 13 August is referred to in ECG to EN, 11 Aug. [1855]: [C&P, pp.869–70]; ECG to EN, 6 Sept. [1855]: [C&P, p.870].

26. *Ibid.,* p.871.

27. ECG to EN, 25 Sept. 1855: [C&P, pp.871–2]; ECG to MW, 12 Nov. [1855]: [C&P, p.372].

28. ECG to GS, 10 Oct. 1855: [C&P, p.371]; ECG to GS, 20 Oct. 1855: [C&P, p.371]; ECG to EN, 3 Nov. 1855: [C&P, p.874]; ECG to WSW, 15 Dec. [1855]: [C&P, p.375].

29. ECG to John Greenwood, [*c.5* Aug. 1855]: [C&P, p.368]. Mrs Gaskell had asked Martha to take her to the church to see the Brontë memorial tablets, thinking it would be too painful to ask Arthur, but he insisted on accompanying her and she did not like to transcribe them in his presence: ECG to John Greenwood, 25 July [1855]: [C&P, p.362]; ECG to unknown, 23 Aug. [1855]: [C&P, p.369]; ECG to EN, 25 Sept. 1855: [C&P, p.872].

30. PB, Account Book, *c.*1848–61: MS BS 173 pp.17, 1, BPM. The dogs cost three pounds each and had been bred from a Newfoundland bitch, originally the property of Mr Ferrand of Harden Grange at Bingley.

31. PB to Martha Brown, 9 June 1855: MS BS 201 p.2, BPM.

32. PB to Sarah Newsome, 12 June 1855: MS BS 201.5 pp.2–4, BPM.

33. PB, Last Will and Testament, 20 June 1855: Copy in MS Bon 75, BPM, [*L&L,* iv, 245–6]. Revealing once again the unpleasantly vindictive side of her nature, Ellen Nussey put the worst possible construction on the will, snidely informing George Smith that her own 'unfavourable impressions' of Arthur 'afterwards deepened still more through what seemed a most selfish appropriation of everything to himself in permitting Mr Brontë to execute a Deed of Gift solely in his favour when near relations on both Mr & Mrs Brontës side were still living': EN to GS, 27 Feb. 1869: MS

File 7 no.17, John Murray. As Ellen was well aware – and Patrick indeed stated in his will – he owed his relations nothing, neither side having shown anything other than the rarest interest in his family.

34. Register of Burials, 1854–84, Haworth Church [4 Sept. 1855; 6 June 1856; 13 Aug. 1855]; Register of Baptisms, 1854–76, Haworth Church [1 July 1855; 27 Nov. 1855; 30 March 1856]

35. ECG to Mrs Alcock, 13 Aug. 1855: [C&P, p.368]; ECG to EN, 11 Aug. [1855]: [C&P, pp.869–70]; ECG to EN, 6 Sept. [1855]: [C&P, p.870]; ECG to EN, [c.20 Oct. 1855]: [C&P, p.873]; EN to ECG, 15 Nov. [1855]: MS n.l., [L&L, iv, 196]. Ellen's twelve-page account of Anne's last days is now in the library of KSC.

36. ECG to EN, [c.20 Oct. 1855]: [C&P, p.873]. 'I think I dare not ask Mr Brontë for those letters unless I go over and see him.' Ellen evidently prepared the way for Mrs Brontë's letters were provided: ABN to EN, 24 Dec. 1855: MS p.4 [end missing], Brotherton, [L&L, iv, 198, partial]. Patrick's letters to Mrs Gaskell, dated 20 June 1855, 24 July 1855, 30 July 1855 and 27 Aug. 1855, are in MS EL B121, Rylands, [BST:8:43:88–97].

37. ABN to EN, 24 Dec. 1855: MS pp.2–3, Brotherton, [L&L, iv, 197].

38. PB to ECG, 23 Jan. 1856: MS EL B121, Rylands, [BST:8:43:97].

39. MT to EN, 4–8 Jan. 1857. MS p.2, Berg, [Stevens, p.130]. 'I wish I had kept Charlotte's letters now though I never felt it safe to do so until latterly that I have had a home of my own. They would have been much better evidence than my imperfect recollection & infinitely more interesting. A settled opinion is very likely to look absurd unless you give the grounds for it & even if I could remember them it looks as if there might be other facts which I have neglected which ought to have altered it.' MT to ECG, 18 Jan. 1856: MS n.l., [Stevens, pp.157–62].

40. ECG to GS, [?29 April 1856]: [C&P, p.388]; ECG to Laetitia Wheelwright, [?30 April 1856]: [C&P, p.388]; ECG to GS, [?1 Aug. 1855]: [C&P, p.366]. WG CB, p.520 says that Charlotte pledged George Smith to refuse and prevent a French translation of *Villette* but that a pirated edition, which got into the Hegers' hands, appeared in 1855. The evidence points to the contrary: as early as April 1853 Mrs Gaskell knew that George Smith had got Charlotte £100 for a French translation of *Villette*. ECG to [?John Forster]: [C&P, p.231].

41. Constantin Heger to ECG, 22 May 1856: MS EL fB91, Rylands; ECG to EN, 9 July 1856: [C&P, p.394]; ECG to Emily Shaen, [7, 8 Sept. 1856]: [C&P, p.409]; ECG, *Life*, pp.179–81, suggesting Charlotte's growing hostility towards Roman Catholicism and her fears about Branwell and her father's failing sight.

42. ECG to EN, 9 July 1856: [C&P, pp.395–6]; EN to ECG, [July 1856]: MS n.l., [L&L, iv, 205].

43. ECG to EN, 9 July 1856: [C&P, pp.394–5]; Marianne Gaskell, pp.ECG to EN, 15 July 1856, [C&P, p.881].

44. EN to ECG, [July 1856]: MS n.l., [L&L, iv, 204–5].

45. PB to William Gaskell, 23 July 1856: MS BR f823.81 G, pp.1, 2, Archives Dept., Manchester. Accompanying notes give a résumé of William Gaskell's sermon, delivered at the Cross Street Chapel on 4 May 1856.

46. Marianne Gaskell, pp.ECG to EN, 25 July 1856, [C&P, p.882].

47. ECG to GS, [?25 July 1856]: [C&P, pp.398–9]; See ECG to EN, 9 July 1856: [C&P, p.395] for a previous attempt to get the portrait photographed.

48. ECG to GS, [?25 July 1856]: [C&P, p.398]. Mrs Gaskell also described them as being curiously like some manuscripts of William Blake's she had recently seen.

49. ECG to GS, [1 Aug. 1856]: [C&P, pp.400–1].

50. ECG to Emily Shaen, [7, 8 Sept. 1856]: [C&P, p.410]; ECG to GS, 13 Aug. [1856]: [C&P, p.403]; ECG to Emily Shaen, [7, 8 Sept. 1856]: [C&P, pp.409–10]; ECG to GS, [1 Aug. 1856]: [C&P, p.401].

51. ECG to Emily Shaen, [7, 8 Sept. 1856]: [C&P, p.410]; ABN to GS, 21 Aug. 1856: MS File 8 no.22, John Murray, [BST:19:3:99].

52. ABN to GS, 20 Sept. 1856: MS File 8 no.23, John Murray, [BST:19:3:99].

53. ECG to GS, 17 March [1858]: [C&P, p.496]; EN to T. W. Reid, quoted in Fraser, p.478. Ellen later told Reid that Arthur's 'whole anxiety … was that she should cease entirely to be the author' and that 'she was compelled to place a severe strain upon herself in order to comply with her husband's wishes, and once, as we have seen, her strength of self-repression gave way, and she indulged in the forbidden luxury of work with the pen': Reid, p.186.

54. ABN to GS, 1 Oct. 1856: MS File 8 no.1, John Murray, [BST:19:3:100]; ECG to Emily Shaen, [7, 8 Sept. 1856]: [C&P, p.410]; ABN to GS, 26 Sept. 1856: MS File 8 no.24, John Murray.

55. ECG to GS, 2 Oct. [1856]: [C&P, p.417].

56. *Ibid.*; ABN to GS, 4 Oct. 1856: MS File 8, no.25, John Murray, [BST:19:3:100].

57. PB to ECG, 3 Nov. 1856: MS EL B121 pp.3–6, Rylands, [BST:8:43:99–100].

58. *Ibid.*, pp.6–7.

59. ECG to GS, 11 Dec. [1856]: [C&P, p.425]; ECG to [?WSW], [?19 Jan. 1856]: [C&P, p.439].

60. See, for example, PB to ECG, 23 Jan. 1856: MS EL B121 pp.2–4, Rylands, [BST:8:43:97–8]; ABN to EN, 24 Dec. 1855: MS pp.2–3, Brotherton, [L&L, iv, 197]; EN to GS, 1 June [1860]: MS File 7 no.5, John Murray.

61. ECG to GS, 19 Aug. [1856]: [C&P, p.405].

62. ECG to GS, [c.15 Nov. 1856]: [C&P, pp.420–1].

63. ECG to GS, 22 Nov. [1856]: [C&P, p.422]; ABN to GS, 1 Dec. 1856: MS File 8 no.27, John Murray; ABN to GS, 28 Nov. 1856: MS File 8 no.26, John Murray.

64. *Ibid.*, pp.1–2.

65. ABN to GS, 3 Dec. 1856: MS File 8 no.28, John Murray.

66. ABN to GS, 1 Dec. 1856: MS File 8 no.27, John Murray.

67. ECG to GS, 11 Dec. [1856]: [C&P, p.425].

68. ECG to GS, [?early Nov. 1856]: [C&P, p.420]; ECG to GS, [?Dec. 1856]: [C&P, p.427].

69. ECG to GS, 26 Dec. [1856]: [C&P, pp.429–30]. 'I suppose Mr Williams thought that I was going to print that part relating to his being like a "faded Tom Dixon". If I had no delicacy of feeling, I have at least a consciousness of what would \or ought to/ interest readers, and I should have certainly scored out, so that no one could have read it through my marks all that related to any one's appearance, style of living &c, in whose character as indicated by these things the public were not directly interested.' The proofs came much too slowly for Mrs Gaskell's liking: see her letters to George Smith [C&P, pp.436–8].

70. ECG to GS, 26 Dec. [1856]: [C&P, p.430]; ECG to GS, 29 Dec. 1856: [C&P, pp.431–4]. Mrs Gaskell signed a receipt for £800 for the copyright of the *Life*, on 2 February 1857: MS S-G 105b, BPM.

71. ECG to GS, 4 Feb. [1857]: [C&P, p.442]; ECG to GS, 6 Feb. 1857: [C&P, p.443]; ECG to GS, [?11 Feb. 1857]: [C&P, p.446]. Arthur's comment on the engraving was 'Haworth Church and Parsonage are commonplace enough, but not quite such queer things as they are represented in the view': ABN to GS, 2 April 1857: MS File 8 no.32 p.3, John Murray.

72. Smith, Elder & Co. Ledgers, vol.i, p.369, John Murray. To the cost of purchasing the copyright (£800) were added £50 for printing in English on the Continent, 10 guineas for permission to publish the Richmond portrait of Charlotte and 22 guineas to Armytage for engraving the portrait and Mrs Gaskell's drawing.

73. [John Skelton], unsigned review, *Fraser's Magazine*, May 1857, pp.569–82, [Allott, p.331].

74. Unsigned review, *Christian Remembrancer*, July 1857, pp.87–145, [Allott, p.364].

75. [Margaret Sweat], unsigned review, *North American Review*, Oct. 1857, pp.293–329, [Allott, pp.379–80].

76. Charles Kingsley to ECG, 14 May 1857: [Allott, p.343].

77. [W. C. Roscoe], unsigned review, *National Review*, June 1857, pp.127–64, [Allott, p.346].

78. *Ibid.*, [Allott, p.347].

79. G. H. Lewes to ECG, 15 April 1857: [Walker, *Letters Addressed to Mrs Gaskell by Celebrated Contemporaries*, p.38]; Charles Kingsley to ECG, 14 May 1857: [Allott, p.343]; William Gaskell to EN, 15 April 1857: [*L&L*, iv, 222].

80. The *Spectator*, quoted in the *Bradford Observer*, 9 April 1857, p.7.

81. G. H. Lewes to ECG, 15 April 1857: [Walker, *Letters Addressed to Mrs Gaskell by Celebrated Contemporaries*, p.38].

82. PB to GS, 30 March 1857: MS File 10 no.4, John Murray, [*L&L*, iv, 220]; PB to ECG, 2 April 1857: MS EL fB91 pp.3–4, Rylands, [*BST*:8:44:126].

83. ABN to GS, 2 April 1857: MS File 8 no.32 pp.1–3, John Murray.

84. See, for example, the *Bradford Observer*, 30 April 1857, p.7.

85. *Ibid.*; 'J. W. E.', 'A Pilgrimage to Haworth', *Bradford Observer*, 30 April 1857, p.7; *Leeds Intelligencer*, 2 May 1857, p.7.

86. PB to William Gaskell, 7 April 1857: MS EL B121 pp.1–3, Rylands, [*BST*:8:44:127–8]. The 'Eccentrick Movements' were burning hearth rugs and sawing the backs off chairs.

87. G. H. Lewes to ECG, 15 April 1857: [Walker, *Letters Addressed to Mrs Gaskell by Celebrated Contemporaries*, p.38]; J. Hodgson Ramsbotham to *Leeds Intelligencer*, 18 April 1857, p.7. Mrs Gaskell declared, 'I don't see any great difference' between this account and her own: ECG to EN, 16 June [1857]: [C&P, p.453].

88. ECG to GS, 2 Oct. [1856]: [C&P, p.418].

89. ECG to GS, 26 Dec. [1856]: [C&P, pp.428–9].

90. ECG to GS, 29 Dec. [1856]: [C&P, p.432]; *The Times*, 30 May 1857, p.5. The retraction also appeared in the *Athenaeum*, 6 June 1857: I am grateful to Margaret Smith for this reference. The letters themselves are dated 26 and 27 May, so they predate Mrs Gaskell's return, though the publication of the retraction did not.

91. ABN to GS, 23 May 1857: MS File 8 no.30 pp.2–3, 5–6, John Murray; ABN to *Halifax Guardian*, 6 June 1857, p.6. W. W. Carus Wilson's letters, quoting Miss Andrews, were published in the *Leeds Intelligencer* and *Leeds Mercury* on 16 May 1857.

92. ABN to GS, 1 June 1857: MS File 8 no.33 pp.1–3, John Murray. The fullest range of correspondence was published in the *Halifax Guardian* with letters appearing each week from May to the end of July 1857.

93. ABN to GS, 6 June 1857: MS File 8 no.31 pp.1–3, John Murray; PB to GS, 9 June 1857: MS File 10 no.8 pp.1–2, John Murray.

94. PB to GS, 15 June 1857: MS File 10 no.7, John Murray.

95. As Mary Crowther, age fourteen, pupil no.230, she was admitted on 12 January 1830: Admissions Register of the Clergy Daughters' School, 1824–39: MS in CRO, Kendal. In common with many other entries, her Christian name appears to have been wrongly entered.

96. PB to the Editor of the *Halifax Guardian*, 22 July 1857: MS Bon 253, BPM, [*L&L*, iv, 311]; *Halifax Guardian*, 25 July 1857, p.8. The editor wearily complained that he had received for insertion that week alone '1. Another letter of four pages

(note size) from Mr Wilson. 2. A letter of a little more than three pages foolscap from the Rev. Mr Nicholls. 3. A letter (note size) of four pages from the "E" of Mr Nicholls' last letter. And last, but not least, a letter of six closely-written foolscap pages from Mrs Baldwin'.

97. Sarah Baldwin to the Readers of the *Halifax Guardian* [Advertisement], 1 Aug. 1857, p.6. Arthur seems to have written privately to Mrs Baldwin to rebuke her for refusing to accept the editor's conclusion. This prompted a furious reply from her, which I quote as an example of the vituperative nature of her correspondence: 'You could not expect after your <u>grossly abusive</u> letters to me that I should <u>submit</u> to such a closing of the Controversy ... Surely it would have been a greater adorning to your Gown to have adopted a <u>less Crooked</u> Course than you have been led to do by some few <u>prejudiced</u> minds – I am sorry you could condescend to such <u>Coarseness</u>, as to partake of my Father's hospitality as you have done, then make such <u>mean</u> remarks about him [Arthur had quoted Thomas Crowther as making disparaging remarks about the Clergy Daughters' School when he withdrew his youngest child] – Your mind seems to be fully made up to believe nothing but <u>evil</u> – I am no partizan nor in any way interested as you so <u>meanly</u> insinuate – Your <u>hard</u> words have not excited in me any <u>angry</u> feeling: <u>contempt</u> I <u>do</u> feel, more especially that you could condescend to be so *little* as by any such evidence <as your> to give reality to fiction –': Sarah Baldwin to ABN, [c.8 Aug. 1857]: MS in private hands.

98. ABN to *Halifax Guardian*, 8 Aug. 1857, p.3; William Baldwin to ABN, 13 Aug. 1857: MS p.2, in private hands.

99. PB to GS, 9 June 1857: MS File 10 no.8, John Murray. See also PB to GS, 16 July 1857: MS BS 203 pp.1–2, BPM where he states he has written to Mrs Gaskell with a list of the anecdotes which he wished to have expunged from the next edition, but has only had a reply from Marianne as Mrs Gaskell herself was ill. See also PB to ECG, 30 July 1857: MS EL B121 pp.1–4, Rylands, [*BST*:8:44:129–30].

100. *Ibid.*, pp.1–4.

101. William Dearden to *Bradford Observer*, 13 Aug. 1857, p.7 and 20 Aug. 1857, p.8.

102. PB to ECG, 20 Aug. 1857: MS EL B121 pp.2–4, Rylands, [*BST*:8:44:132].

103. HM to *Daily News*, 24 Aug. 1857, quoted in *Bradford Observer*, 27 Aug. 1857, p.8.

104. William Dearden to *Bradford Observer*, 3 Sept. 1857, p.8; PB to William Dearden, 31 Aug. 1857: MS BS 205 pp.1–3, BPM, [*BST*:12:63:200].

105. PB to ECG, 31 Aug. 1857: MS EL B121 p.3, Rylands, [*BST*:8:44:134].

106. William Dearden to *Bradford Observer*, 3 Sept. 1857, p.8. Dearden also persuaded Francis Leyland, brother of Branwell's great friend, and William Brooksbank, who had accompanied him on his two visits to Haworth, to write corroborative accounts of his conversation with Patrick. Dearden could not believe that Patrick had not demanded changes to the next edition in his first letter to Mrs Gaskell. In a letter to Catherine Winkworth, Miss Martineau explained how Mrs Gaskell had sent her Patrick's letter on the publication of her biography: 'The old monster!', Miss Martineau commented, 'Any thing so appalling as one sentence in it I am sure I never saw come from a human hand. Beautiful as the book is in many ways, I do mourn that Mrs G. ever came in the way of that awful family': HM to Catherine Winkworth, 13 June [1857]: [Sanders (ed.), *Harriet Martineau: Selected Letters*, p.143]. I am at a loss to identify the sentence of which Miss Martineau complains.

107. Article in the *Spectator*, reprinted in the *Bradford Observer*, 3 Sept. 1857, p.7.

108. ECG to EN, 16 June [1857]: [C&P, p.454]; ECG to GS, 3 June [1857]: [C&P, p.449].

109. PB to ECG, 9 Sept. 1857: MS EL B121 pp.2–3, Rylands, [*BST*:8:44:135].

110. PB to HM, 5 Nov. 1857: MS HM 90, Birmingham; HM to PB, 5 Nov. 1857: MS HM 89, Birmingham.

111. ABN to HM, 6 Nov. 1857: MS HM 91 pp.2–3, Birmingham. Arthur also informed Miss Martineau that he had supplied Mrs Gaskell with a copy of the letter and Charlotte's reply to it.

112. HM to ABN, [c.7 Nov. 1857]: MS HM 105 pp.1–4, Birmingham.

113. ABN to HM, 9 Nov. 1857: MS HM 93 p.3, Birmingham.

114. HM to ABN, 10 Nov. 1857: MS HM 94, Birmingham; ABN to HM, 11 Nov. 1857: MS HM 95, Birmingham; PB to HM, 11 Nov. 1857: MS HM 96 pp.1, 4, Birmingham.

115. HM to ABN, 13 Nov. 1857: MS HM 98, Birmingham; John Greenwood to ABN, 12 Nov. 1857: MS HM 97, Birmingham; ABN to HM, 14 Nov. 1857: MS HM 99 pp.2–3, Birmingham.

116. HM to ABN, 13 Nov. 1857: MS HM 98, Birmingham; ABN to HM, 14 Nov. 1857: MS HM 100, Birmingham.

117. According to HM to Mr Graves, 23 Nov. 1857: MS BS ix, M, BPM, [*BST*:18:95:396], Arthur had earnestly requested her to burn his last letter which was 'wholly; self-excusing ... he desired to obtain my good opinion before we parted'. See also HM to Mr Graves, 16 Nov. [1857]: MS BS ix, M, BPM, [*BST*:16:83:199].

118. PB to ECG, 30 July 1857: MS EL B121 p.3, Rylands, [*BST*:8:44:129].

CHAPTER TWENTY-EIGHT

Title: PBB poem, 'The End of All', published in the *Halifax Guardian*, 5 June 1847, p.6.

1. ABN to GS, 9 May 1857: MS File 8 no.29 pp.1–2, John Murray; ABN to GS, 23 May 1857: MS File 8 no.30 p.1, John Murray. Arthur's foreword, dated 22 September 1856, appeared after Charlotte's preface in the first edition [CB, *The Professor*, Clarendon Edn, p.4]; CB, Draft Preface to *The Professor*, [*c.*,Nov. 1849]: MS MA 32, Pierpont Morgan, [CB, *The Professor*, pp.1–2]. The manuscript of the book, which was originally entitled *The Master* and is dated 27 June 1846, is MS MA 31, Pierpont Morgan.

2. Smith, Elder & Co. Publication Ledgers, ii, 882 (*The Professor*); i, 406–8 (*Jane Eyre*); ii, 944–5 (*Shirley*); ii, 944–6 (*Villette*); ii, 997 (*Wuthering Heights & Agnes Grey*), John Murray. A cheap edition of *The Professor*, with the addition of some poems, was published in August 1860: I am grateful to Margaret Smith for this reference.

3. [E. S.Dallas], unsigned review, *Blackwood's Magazine*, July 1857, pp.77–94, [Allott, p.361]; [W. C.Roscoe], unsigned review, *National Review*, June 1857, pp.127–64, [Allott, pp.355–6]. This latter opinion echoes that of Mrs Gaskell, who thought it the only justification for publishing the novel: ECG to Emily Shaen, 7, 8 Sept. 1856: [C&P, p.410]. For those who doubted the wisdom of publishing *The Professor* see, for example, [W. C.Roscoe], unsigned review, *National Review*, June 1857, pp.127–64, [Allott, p.355]; unsigned review, *Athenaeum*, 13 June 1857, pp. 755–7, [Allott, pp.344–5]; [Margaret Sweat], unsigned review, *North American Review*, Oct, 1857, pp.293–329, [Allott, pp. 383–4].

4. ABN to GS, 27 June 1857: MS File 8 no.2 p.2, John Murray.

5. *Bradford Observer*, 7 May 1857, p.5.

6. ABN to GS, 23 May 1857: MS File 8 no.30 p.3, John Murray. Elizabeth Greenwood, for example, who had been seduced by her brother-in-law, William Sugden, during her sister's pregnancy, was readily identifiable from Mrs Gaskell's description: see Sarah Fermi, 'A "Religious" Family Disgraced', *BST*:20:5:289–95.

7. ABN to GS, 23 May 1857: MS File 8 no.30 pp.6–7, John Murray.

8. *Bradford Observer*, 2 July 1857, p.5; *Leeds Intelligencer* 4 July 1857, p.7.

9. 'J. W. E.', 'A Day at Haworth', [Aug. 1857], *Bradford Observer*, 19 Nov. 1857, p.8; J. Copley, 'An early visitor to Haworth [Walter White]', *BST*:16:83:220–1.

10. PB to ECG, 31 Aug. 1857: MS EL B121 p.4, Rylands, [*BST*:8:44:135].

11. *Leeds Intelligencer*, 22 Aug. 1857. p.7; PB to ECG, 24 Aug. 1857: MS EL B121 p.4, Rylands, [*BST*:8:44:133]. The invitation is inferred from a scrap of paper dated 'Bolton Abbey Aug 27 1857',

bearing the ducal coronet, on the verso of which is written 'I venture to propose that/ in September which is a good/ time for seeing this [lacuna] he': Duke of Devonshire to [ABN]: 27 Aug. 1857: MS in private hands.

12. 'J. W. E.', 'A Day at Haworth', [Aug. 1857], *Bradford Observer*, 19 Nov. 1857, p.8.

13. Edward White Benson's account of the visit was published in *The Times*, 22 Sept. 1933, reprinted in *BST*:8:44:136. See also E. W. Benson to 'Lightfoot', 25 Jan. 1858 [Benson, *The Life of Edward White Benson*, i, 133], announcing his visit that day. He became Archbishop of Canterbury in 1882.

14. PB to Sir Joseph Paxton, 16 Jan. 1858: MS MA 2696 R-V pp.2–3, Pierpont Morgan, [*L&L*, iv, 228–9]. The 'mercenary' may actually have been Mrs Gaskell who, in September 1857, stayed at Chatsworth, where Sir Joseph acted 'quite the master of the place' on behalf of the deaf and wheelchair-bound duke: she was quite capable of suggesting that the duke should donate towards the Haworth subscription fund: ECG to Marianne Gaskell, [13, 14 Sept. 1857]; [C&P, pp.470–3].

15. PB to the Revd James Cheadle, 29 Aug. 1857: MS BS 204.5, pp.1–2, BPM.

16. PB to Mrs Nunn, 1 Feb. 1858: MS n.l., [*L&L*, iv, 229–30]; PB to Mrs Nunn, 26 Oct. 1859: MS n.l., [*L&L*, iv, 236–7].

17. PB to the Revd Robinson Pool, 18 March 1858: MS BS 206 p.1, BPM, [*L&D*, p.203].

18. *Bradford Observer*, 1 April 1858, p.4. Morgan's funeral sermon was preached at his former church, Christ Church in Bradford, on 11 April 1858, by the Revd Joshua Fawcett, 'one of Mr Morgan's oldest friends in the parish': *ibid.*, 8 April 1858, p.5.

19. *Ibid.*, 1 April 1858, p.5; *Leeds Intelligencer*, 3 April 1858, p.7; *Bradford Observer*, 6 May 1858, p.5. The new tablet was erected on 1 April 1858. See also Meta Gaskell to a friend, 25 Oct. 1860: MS Ashley 2829, BL, [*L&D*, p.521] for William Brown's account of having to break up and bury the old memorials. J. B. Leyland, who might otherwise have secured the commission, had died on 26 January 1851: *Halifax Guardian*, 10 May 1851, p.8.

20. James Hoppin, *The Old Country: Its Scenery, Art and People* (*c.*1858–9), quoted in *BST*:15:79:329–30. The date of Hoppin's visit is deduced from the fact that Patrick was still preaching and that he remarks on the 'new marble tablet'. Patrick's attack of bronchitis is mentioned in PB to the Revd Robinson Pool, 18 March 1858: MS BS 206 p.3, BPM, [*L&D*, p.203].

21. James Hoppin, *BST*:15:79:329–30.

22. [Henry Jarvis Raymond], [*c.*1858–9], quoted in Reid, pp.194–5.

23. See, for example, PB to unidentified, 10 Nov. 1858: MS in Texas; PB to Franklin Bacheller, 22

Dec. 1858: MS MA 2696 R-V, Pierpont Morgan, [*L&L*, iv, 232]; PB to Mrs Abba Woolson, 16 July 1859: MS 3158/1–3, TC Dublin. All three letters enclosed scraps from the same letter: for a reconstruction of the original letter and locations of the other scraps, see Margaret Smith, 'A Reconstructed Letter', *BST*:20:1.42–7.

24. *Leeds Intelligencer*, 10 Oct. 1857, p.6; L&D, p.438.

25. See, for example, the report in the *Halifax Courier*, 18 April 1858, p.2.

26. *Bradford Review*, 23 Oct. 1858, p.2. The concert was held on 18 October 1858. Tom Parker sang at a benefit concert for a widow and her children at the Hall Green Baptist Chapel on Christmas Eve, 1860: *Halifax Courier*, 5 Jan. 1861, p.5.

27. Thackeray was lecturing on 'The Four Georges' in the Mechanics' Institutes of Bradford and Halifax in the winter of 1856: *Bradford Observer*, 11 Dec. 1856, p.5; 18 Dec. 1856, p.8; *Halifax Guardian*, 13 Dec. 1856, p.5; 14 Feb. 1857, p.7. Despite his proximity to Haworth, he did not visit Patrick and Arthur at the parsonage. Dickens was giving readings from his novels in the same towns as early as December 1854: see *Bradford Observer*, 21 Dec. 1854, p.5; 14 Oct. 1858, p.5; 27 Oct. 1859, p.5; *Halifax Guardian*, 18 Nov. 1854, p.5; *Halifax Courier*, 18 Sept. 1858, p.5. John Ruskin gave the inaugural lecture at the new school of the Bradford Mechanics' Institute: *Bradford Observer*, 3 March 1859, p.5.

28. *Ibid.*, 6 Jan. 1859, p.5; *Bradford Review*, 8 Jan. 1859, p.4; *Leeds Mercury*, 8 Jan. 1859, p.7 (Keighley). Massey's lecture was drawn entirely from the first edition of the *Life of Charlotte Brontë*. He returned again with his lecture to Bradford in 1860 and printed an article on Charlotte in Abraham Holroyd's publication, *The Bradfordian*, the following year: *Bradford Review*, 20 Oct. 1860, p.4; *Leeds Mercury*, 20 Oct. 1860, p.7; *Bradford Observer*, 3 Jan, 1861, p.5.

29. Patrick wrote to thank Milligan for the gift: its timing, so soon after the lecture, does not appear to be entirely coincidental: PB to John Milligan, 25 Jan. 1859: MS BS 208, BPM, [*L&L*, iv, 232–3]. *Bradford Review*, 15 June 1861, p.6.

30. Eight copies were sent to the parsonage: Martha Brown to Abraham Holroyd, 10 Aug. 1859: MS BS ix, B, BPM, [*L&L*, iv, 235]. Holroyd, who was friendly with the Garrs family, had visited Haworth in the summer of 1853, shortly after his return from the United States. Having read *Jane Eyre* and *Shirley* there, he was determined to meet Charlotte and travelled over one Sunday to attend Haworth Church. He waited for her at the end of the service and presented her with a copy of the Common Prayer Book used in the Episcopal churches in the United States. As a child, living in Clayton, he remembered hearing Patrick preach at the Old Bell Chapel in Thornton: Abraham Holroyd, quoted in Scruton, pp.111–15.

31. ECG to GS, 17 March [1858]: [C&P, p.495]; ECG to GS, [?1 Oct. 1859]: [C&P, p.577].

32. ABN to GS, 11 Oct. 1859: MS File 8 no.3, John Murray, [*BST*:19:3:102]; ABN to GS, 14 Oct. 1859: MS File 8 no.4, John Murray, [*BST*:19:3:102–3].

33. ABN to GS, 17 Oct. 1859: MS File 8 no.5 pp.1–2, John Murray; ABN to GS, 11 Nov. 1859: MS File 8 no.7 p.1, John Murray, [*BST*:19:3:103].

34. *Ibid.*, p.2; ABN to GS, 23 Dec. 1859: MS File 8 no.8, John Murray.

35. ABN to GS, 25 Jan. 1860: MS File 8 no.9, John Murray; ABN to GS, 27 Jan. 1860: MS File 8 no.10 p.2, John Murray.

36. PB to GS, 26 March 1860: MS n.l., [*L&L*, iv, 238]; ABN to GS, 11 April 1860: MS File 8 no.13 p.2, John Murray; CB, 'The Last Sketch', *Cornhill Magazine*, i, Jan.–June 1860, pp.485–98.

37. The following correspondence in the Smith, Elder & Co. Archives at John Murray refers to poems being offered for publication, some of them for the reissue of *The Professor*. ABN to GS, 31 Jan. 1860: MS File 8 no.11; ABN to GS, 11 April 1860: MS File 8 no.13; ABN to GS, 30 May 1860: MS File 8 no.15; ABN to GS, 22 June 1860: MS File 8 no.16; ABN to GS, 30 Oct. 1860: MS File 8 no.17; ABN to GS, 23 Nov. 1860: MS File 8 no.19; ABN to GS, 4 April 1861: MS File 8 no.18. Emily's 'The Outcast Mother' was published in the *Cornhill Magazine*, i, Jan.–June 1860, 616 and Charlotte's 'Watching and Wishing' and 'When Thou Sleepest' in ii, July–Dec. 1860, p.741 and iv, July–Dec. 1861, p.178 respectively.

38. Lord Houghton, MS Commonplace Book, 1857–60: MS in TC Cambridge. For Richard Monckton Milnes reading the manuscripts in Mrs Gaskell's possession as she wrote the *Life*, see Reid, *The Life, Letters and Friendships of Lord Houghton*, i, 527. Though Mrs Gaskell, Arthur and Patrick seem to have been unaware of it, Monckton Milnes had a prized collection of pornography, which may explain his pursuit of and interest in John Brown's letters from Branwell. See Robert B. Martin, *Tennyson: the Unquiet Heart* (1980), pp.96, 420, 541. I am grateful to Margaret Smith for this reference.

39. Francis Leyland claimed to possess 112 letters from Branwell to his brother, J.B. Leyland, though only a fraction of these are extant and have been printed: Anonymous Memo. 'Visit to Mr Leyland', n.d.: MS BS x, V, BPM, [*BST*:12:63:200–2]; ABN to Richard Monckton Milnes, 21 Dec. 1860: MS pp.1–2, TC Cambridge.

40. Register of Marriages, 1837–70, Haworth Church [24 Feb. 1857]; Register of Baptisms, 1854–76, Haworth Church [26 April 1857]; Register of Burials, 1854–86, Haworth Church [26 Oct. 1858]. Patrick baptized Brontë Greenwood on 14 November 1859. The story is only told from the Greenwood point of view and is repeated in ECG to WSW, 20 Dec. 1860: [C&P, pp.641–2]; Meta Gaskell to a friend, 25 Oct. 1860: MS Ashley 2829, BL, [L&D, pp. 521–2]. Meta says the child was baptized at six months, but according to the date of birth she gives and the baptismal date in the register, he was nine months old.

41. *Bradford Observer*, 9 Aug. 1860, p.5 correcting a report in the *Halifax Courier*, 4 Aug. 1860, p.4 that Patrick had taken a final leave of his parishioners on 21 July 1860. The 30 October 1859 date for Patrick's last sermon is confirmed by William Wright, Memo, 12 Aug. 1860: MS BS ix, W, BPM. The *Halifax Courier's* dating is accepted by L& D, p.518 who did not see the correction that followed.

42. See, for example, ABN to GS, 27 Jan. 1860: MS File 8 no.10 p.4, John Murray. For the severity of the winter and its effect on Patrick see ABN to Richard Monckton Milnes, 21 Dec. 1860: MS pp.2–3, TC Cambridge; ABN to GS, 29 Feb. 1860: MS File 8 no.12 pp.2–3, John Murray.

43. *Bradford Observer*, 9 Aug. 1860, p.5; 16 Aug. 1860, p.5; Register of Baptisms, 1854–76, Haworth Church [5 Aug. 1860].

44. *Halifax Courier*, 21 July 1860, p.4; *Bradford Observer*, 9 Aug. 1860, p.5. The denial of the report seems to have originated with Arthur or at least to have been authorized by him.

45. *Bradford Observer*, 13 Sept. 1860, p.5.

46. PB to ECG, 2 Oct. 1860: MS EL B121, Rylands, [*BST*:8:44:137]; Meta Gaskell refers to 'a few tremulous, feeble lines' from Patrick saying he would be glad to see the Gaskells if they called: Meta Gaskell to a friend, 25 Oct. 1860: MS Ashley 2829, BL, [L&D, p.519].

47. L&D, pp.519–21; ECG to WSW, 20 Dec. 1860: [C&P, p.641]. For Mrs Gaskell's gratitude for Patrick's support in the wake of the publication of the *Life*, see: ECG to GS, [23 Aug. 1857]: [C& P, p.468].

48. ECG to WSW, 20 Dec. 1860: [C&P, p.641]; Meta Gaskell to a friend, 25 Oct. 1860: MS Ashley 2829, BL, [L&D, p.522].

49. ABN to GS, 30 Oct. 1860: MS File 8 no.17 p.2, John Murray; ABN to GS, 23 Nov. 1860: MS File 8 no.19 p.2, John Murray; *Bradford Review*, 12 Jan. 1861, p.8; *Bradford Observer*, 17 Jan. 1861, p.5.

50. PB, Account Book, *c.*1848–61: MS BS 173 p.3, BPM.

51. *Halifax Courier*, 16 Feb. 1861, p.5; 23 March 1861, p.5.

52. ABN to GS, 4 April 1861: MS File 8 no.18 pp.1–2, John Murray; Venn, iv, 573.

53. ABN to GS, 25 June 1861: MS File 8 no.20 p.2, John Murray; *Bradford Review*, 8 June 1861, p.5. For other obituaries, nearly all quoting extensively from the *Life of Charlotte Brontë*, see: *Leeds Mercury*, 11 June 1861, p.3; *Bradford Observer*, 13 June 1861, p.5; *Halifax Guardian*, 15 June 1861, p.5; *Leeds Intelligencer*, 15 June 1861, p.5; *Halifax Courier*, 15 June 1861, p.5. Freed from the constraints which Patrick had imposed on him during his lifetime, William Dearden took the opportunity to write an obituary which defended Patrick against Mrs Gaskell's claims: William Dearden to the *Bradford Observer*, 27 June 1861, p.7.

54. *Leeds Intelligencer*, 15 June 1861, p.5.

55. *Ibid.*; *Bradford Review*, 13 June 1861, p.2; *Halifax Guardian*, 15 June 1861, p.5.

56. According to L&D, pp.527, 529, Arthur had to apply to the Secretary of State for permission to bury Patrick in Haworth Church. An order of Council had been issued on 28 July 1856 which, with immediate effect, closed all graveyards and burial grounds in the parish of Bradford. An important clause, which I would have thought applied to the Brontë vault and would therefore have made it unnecessary to apply to the Secretary of State, was an exemption for 'private vaults and graves which can be opened without the disturbance of remains, in which each coffin shall be embedded in powdered charcoal, and separately entombed in an airtight manner': *Halifax Guardian*, 2 Aug. 1856, p.5. The inscription on the tablet, which is still in Haworth Church, is from a long passage on the resurrection.

57. 'N' to *Bradford Review*, 12 Oct. 1861, p.5.

58. *Halifax Guardian*, 29 June 1861, p.5. Dr Burnett's sermon was on the text 'For the Lord himself will descend from heaven with a cry of command, with the archangel's call, and with the sound of the trumpet of God. And the dead in Christ will rise first; then we who are alive, who are left, shall be caught up together with them in the clouds to meet the Lord in the air; and so we shall always be with the Lord': 1 Thessalonians ch.4. vv.16–17.

59. *Halifax Guardian*, 10 Aug. 1861, p.4. Sutcliffe Sowden's obituary gives a pleasant picture of the man who had been a friend to Branwell Brontë during his days in the Calder Valley and to Arthur since 1847. 'Mr Sowden was about 46 years of age ... Of a quiet and somewhat retiring disposition, he won the respect and esteem of all – churchmen and dissenters alike. In him the church has lost a faithful and diligent servant, and the poor a generous friend. Of a philosophical turn of mind, Mr Sowden was noted as a geologist and an ardent lover of nature. Excursionists into the deep and lovely valleys of this secluded district looked forward to his company with much anticipation and delight.' He had been vicar of Hebden Bridge since October 1841: *ibid.*, 17 Aug. 1861, p.5.

60. *Ibid.*

61. 'N' to *Bradford Review*, 12 Oct. 1861, p.5

62. See, for example, WG *CB*, p.567; L&D, p.529.

63. ECG to WSW, 20 Dec. 1860: [C&P, pp.641–2]; Meta Gaskell to a friend, 25 Oct. 1860: MS Ashley 2829, BL, [L&D, pp.521–2]; Charles Hale to his mother, 11 Nov. 1861: ['An American Visitor at Haworth 1861', *BST*:15:77:128–9]. Hale confuses the Greenwoods with the Browns and states that he heard the story from Mrs Gaskell. Immediately after the publication of Mrs Gaskell's biography there was some hostility towards Arthur in the township: the gossips accused him of supplying her with her lurid anecdotes about Haworth and he was under the impression that Sarah Baldwin, through Nancy Ogden, was trying to stir up ill-feeling in the parish against

him: ABN to GS, 23 May 1857: MS File 8 no.30 p.3, John Murray; William Baldwin to ABN, 13 Aug. 1857: MS pp.3, 5, in private hands.

64. See, for example, Ernest Raymond, quoted in Reid, pp.194–6 and Walter White, 'An Early Visitor to Haworth', *BST*:16:83:219–21. See also the local people quoted in C. Holmes Cautley, 'Old Haworth Folk who Knew the Brontës', *Cornhill Magazine*, 29, July–Dec. 1910, pp.76–84 and Whiteley Turner, *A Spring-Time Saunter Round and About Brontë Land*, p.212.

65. 'N' to *Bradford Review*, 12 Oct. 1861, p.5.

66. *Bradford Observer*, 29 March 1860, p.5; *Bradford Review*, 31 March 1860, p.5. When Wade was presented with a testimonial by his former parishioners at Daisy Hill, in Bradford, a post he had resigned in expectation of getting the incumbency of Girlington, Dr Burnett announced that 'he disbelieved the charges against Mr Wade, & expressed the fullest confidence in him. He felt it to be due to himself to demand, at an early period, an explanation of the "insuperable difficulty" which it had been alleged stood in the way of the election of Mr Wade to the incumbency of Girlington Church': *ibid.*

67. L&D, p.531.

68. Arthur's signature as 'O[fficiating] M[inister]', rather than 'curate', appears in the Register of Burials, 1854–84, Haworth Church [25 June 1861–4 Aug. 1861] and Register of Baptisms, 1854–76, Haworth Church [23 June 1861–18 Aug. 1861]. For newspaper reports that Arthur's appointment was expected see, for example, the *Halifax Courier*, 16 Feb. 1861, p.5.

69. Arthur signed himself 'O. M.' on 11 August 1861 when he baptized two children, but this may have been from habit; he had reverted to 'curate' in the baptismal register by 18 August. For the public announcement of Wade's appointment see: *Halifax Courier*, 21 Sept. 1861, p.5.

70. *Bradford Observer*, 26 Sept. 1861, p.4.

71. *Halifax Guardian*, 28 Sept. 1861, p.8; *Bradford Review*, 26 Sept. 1861, p.2; Register of Baptisms, 1854–76, Haworth Church [22 Sept. 1861].

72. Haworth Parsonage, Notice of Sale, 1 Oct. 1861: MS BS x, H, BPM; Haworth Parsonage, Auction Catalogues, 1–2 Oct. 1861: MS BS x, H, BPM, [Joanna Hutton, 'The Sale at Haworth Parsonage', *BST*:14:75:46–50, extracts only].

73. Charles Hale to his mother, 11 Nov. 1861: ['An American Visitor at Haworth 1861', *BST*:15:77:128]. Arthur signed the registers for the last time on 17 September 1861, the last duties recorded before Wade arrived for his inaugural sermon: Register of Baptisms, 1854–76, Haworth Church [17 Sept. 1861]; Register of Burials, 1854–84, Haworth Church. His last marriage had been on 29 July 1861, but Joseph Grant officiated at a wedding on 21 September 1861: Register of Marriages, 1837–70, Haworth Church.

74. Marjorie Gallop, 'Charlotte's Husband: Sidelights from a Family Album', *BST*:12:64:298–9;

'Reminiscences of a Relation of Arthur Bell Nicholls', *BST*:15:79:346; [Ethel Selkirk] quoted in *BST*:11:60:374; Martha Brown, Gravestone, Haworth Churchyard; Martha Brown, Funeral Card, 19 Jan. 1880: MS in private hands.

75. [Ethel Selkirk] quoted in *BST*:11:60:374. Arthur's new home, where he lived until his death, was Hill House, Banagher, which is still there.

76. Marjorie Gallop, 'Charlotte's Husband: Sidelights from a Family Album', *BST*:12:64:298–9; 'Reminiscences of a Relation of Arthur Bell Nicholls', *BST*:15:79:346–8; [Ethel Selkirk] quoted in *BST*:11:60:374.

77. Marjorie Gallop, 'Charlotte's Husband: Sidelights from a Family Album', *BST*:12:64:299; ABN, Gravestone, Banagher Churchyard. The inscription in full reads: 'In Loving Memory of The Revd Arthur Bell Nicholls, formerly curate of Haworth, Yorkshire, who died at the Hill House Banagher, December 2nd 1906, aged 88. Also of Mary Anna, his wife who died at the Hill House Banagher, February 27th 1915, aged 83'. I am grateful to Vicki Fattorini for supplying me with photographs of the church and gravestone.

78. Sotheby's Sales of Books and Manuscripts, 26 July 1907, 19 June 1914.

79. It was not until the last decade or so of his life that he was harassed by the acquisitive Clement Shorter and his notorious forger friend, T. J. Wise. The story of how they acquired Arthur's manuscripts (and Ellen Nussey's) is a nefarious one which I hope to tell at some future date.

80. She died, in the midst of regaling her family with an anecdote, on 12 November 1865: Uglow, *Elizabeth Gaskell: A Habit of Stories*, pp.609–10.

81. James Taylor is buried in the Bombay cemetery where his tomb is briefly inscribed 'James Taylor. Died April 29, 1874, aged 57', [*L&L*, iv, 312]; William Smith Williams' death is referred to in GS to EN, 10 May 1878: MS n.l., [*L&L*, civ, 265]. For George Smith himself see Smith, pp.60–4.

82. Constantin Heger died, aged eighty-six, on 6 May 1896; Madame Heger predeceased him, dying on 9 January 1890, [*L&L*, i, 251 n.1.].

83. Wooler Family Tree, BPM; Max Blakeley, 'Memories of Margaret Wooler and her Sisters', *BST*:12:62:114.

84. Stevens, pp. 142–7. Mary Taylor's novel, *Miss Miles*, which she was writing when Charlotte was working on *Shirley*, was not published until 1890. Its subtitle, *A Tale of Yorkshire Life Sixty Years Ago*, was a recognition of the fact that, by then, its message had lost much of its startling unorthodoxy. The book was reprinted, with an introduction by Janet H. Murray, by Oxford University Press in 1990.

85. EN to T. J. Wise, Nov. 1892, MS in Brotherton, [Stevens, pp. 147–8].

86. EN to GS, 1 June [1860]: MS File 7 no.5, John

Murray. See also EN to GS, 15 Aug. 1860: MS File 7 no.8, John Murray.

87. EN to GS, 20 Feb. 1869: MS File 7 no.18, John Murray.

88. EN to GS, 16 Feb. 1869: MS File 7 no.13, John Murray.

89. ABN to [?Clement K. Shorter], 12 July 1898: MS p.2, Fales.

90. The only pieces which Ellen succeeded in publishing were her own memoir of the Brontë family, [Ellen Nussey], 'Reminiscences of Charlotte Brontë', *Scribner's Monthly*, May 1871, reprinted in *BST*:2:10:58–83 and some excerpts from Charlotte's letters in *Hours at Home*. For her failed proposals to publish the letters in the *Cornhill* and as a private publication, edited by J. Horsfall Turner, see Whitehead, pp.214–15, 230–40.

91. See, for example, William Scruton, 'Reminiscences of the Late Miss Ellen Nussey', *BST*:1:7:24–42; 'M. C.', 'Memories of Ellen Nussey', *BST*:11:56:40–1; Helen Arnold, 'The Reminiscences of Emma Huidekoper Cortazzo: A Friend of Ellen Nussey', *BST*:13:68:228–30.

92. *Bradford Observer*, 29 Nov. 1897, p.4.

93. PB to ECG, 30 July 1857: MS EL B121 p.3, Rylands, [*BST*:8:44:129].

94. Uglow, *Elizabeth Gaskell: A Habit of Stories*, p.399.

ANCILLARY SOURCE
INFORMATION

Full bibliographical details are given below for printed sources to which several references are made in the notes. Principal printed sources are listed on pp. 833–4. Bibliographical details of all other printed sources, including articles, are given in full in the relevant note.

Alexander, Christine, *A Bibliography of the Manuscripts of Charlotte Brontë* (Brontë Society/Meckler Publishing, 1982)

Anon., *Memoir of the Rev. John Buckworth, M.A., late vicar of Dewsbury, Yorkshire* (London, Hatchard & Co., 1836)

Armytage, Edith B. (ed.), *The Parish Registers of Hartshead* (Yorkshire Parish Register Society, 1903)

Babbage, Benjamin Herschel, *Report to the General Board of Health on a Preliminary Inquiry into the Sewerage, Drainage, and Supply of Water, and the Sanitary Condition of the Inhabitants of the Hamlet of Haworth* (London, HMSO, 1850)

Baines, Edward, *History, Directory and Gazetteer of the County of York* (Leeds, 1822)

Bardsley, C. W., *A Dictionary of English and Welsh Surnames* (London and New York, 1901)

Benson, A. C., *The Life of Edward White Benson, sometime Archbishop of Canterbury* (London, Macmillan, 1900)

Bentley, Phyllis, *The Brontës and Their World* (London, Thames & Hudson, 1969)

Bielby, A. Ronald, *Churches and Chapels of Kirklees* (Huddersfield, Kirklees Libraries and Museums Service, 1978)

Birrell, Augustine, *The Life of Charlotte Brontë* (London, Walter Scott, 1887)

Brookfield, Charles & Frances, *Mrs Brookfield and Her Circle* (London, Pitman, 1905)

Burtchaell, G. D. & Sadleir, T. U. (eds), *Alumni Dublinenses* (Dublin, Alex Thom & Co., 1935)

Carus, William, *Memoirs of the Life of Charles Simeon* (London, Hatchard, 1847)

Carus Wilson, William, *A Child's First Tales* (Kirkby Lonsdale, 1836)

Charlesworth, M. L., *A Choice of Churches* (Shrewsbury, n.d.)

Chitham, Edward, *The Brontës' Irish Background* (London, Macmillan, 1986)

Chitham, Edward, *A Life of Emily Brontë* (Oxford, Basil Blackwell, 1987)

Chitham, Edward & Winnifrith, Tom, *Brontë Facts and Brontë Problems* (London, Macmillan, 1983)

Conder, George William (ed.), *Memoir and Remains of the late Rev. Jonathan Glyde, Pastor of Horton Lane Chapel* (London, Farquhar Shaw, 1858)

Craven, Joseph, *A Brontë Moorland Village* (Keighley, Rydal Press, 1907)

Davids, Shirley & Moore, Geoff, *Haworth in Times Past* (Chorley, Countryside Publications, 1983)

'DRW', *Christ Church Lothersdale 1838–1888: A Short History* (Leeds, privately printed, 1988)

Duthie, Enid, *The Foreign Vision of Charlotte Brontë* (London, Macmillan, 1975)

Evans, George, *Wellington: a portrait in old photographs and picture postcards* (Market Drayton, S. B. Publications, 1990)

Feather, W., *A Centenary History of the Three Graces Lodge, 408, Haworth, 1792–1931* (Keighley, Feather Bros, [1931])

Fennell, John, *A Sermon Preached at the Funeral of the Rev. John Crosse* (Bradford, T. Inkersley, 1816)

Flintoff, Eddie, 'Some Unpublished Poems of Branwell Brontë', *Durham University Journal*, lxxxi (1989)

Forrest, H. E., *Old Churches of Shrewsbury* (Shrewsbury, Wilding & Son, 1920)

Galloway, F. C., *A Descriptive Catalogue of Objects in the Museum of the Brontë Society at Haworth* (Bradford, Brontë Society, 1896)

Glynn, Jenifer, *Prince of Publishers: A Biography of George Smith* (London, Allison & Busby, 1986)

Haig, Alan, *The Victorian Clergy* (London, Croom Helm, 1984)

Harland, Marian, *Charlotte Brontë at Home* (New York, G. P. Puttnam's Sons, 1899)

Hewish, John, *Emily Brontë: a Critical and Biographical Study* (Macmillan, 1969)

Horsfall Turner, J., *Haworth Past and Present* (Bingley, privately printed, 1879)

Hulbert, Charles, *The Manual of Shropshire Biography; Chronology and Antiquities* (Shrewsbury, printed and published by the author, 1829)

Hutchinson, S. C., *The History of the Royal Academy, 1768–1968* (London, 1968)

Hutchinson, Thomas (ed.), *Wordsworth: Poetical Works* (Oxford, OUP, 1990)

Japp, Alexander, *De Quincey Memorials* (London, Heinemann, 1891)

Kipling, Lesley & Hall, Nick, *On the Trail of the Luddites* (Pennine Heritage Network, n.d.)

Kirke White, Henry, *The Remains of Henry Kirke White* (London, Longman & Co., 1823)

Lane, Margaret, *The Brontë Story* (Otley, Smith, Settle, 1990)

Leyland, Mary, 'The Leyland Family', *Halifax Antiquarian Society Journal*, 1954

Lloyd Evans, Barbara & Gareth, *Everyman Companion to the Brontës* (London, J. M. Dent, 1985)

Lonoff, Sue, 'Charlotte Brontë's Belgian Essays: the Discourse of Empowerment', *Victorian Studies*, vol.32, no.3 (Indiana University, 1989)

McCrea, Marjorie, *A History of the Parish Church of All Saints Wellington, Shropshire* (Wellington, 1987)

Macdonald, Frederika, 'The Brontës at Brussels', *The Woman at Home*, July 1894

Mannex, P. J., *History, Topography and Directory of Westmoreland* (London, Simpkin Marshall & Co., 1849)

Monahan, Melodie (ed.), 'Charlotte Brontë's *The Poetaster* Text and Notes', *Studies in Romanticism*, xx, 1981

Morgan, William, *The Parish Priest: pourtrayed in the life, character and ministry of the Rev. John Crosse, A. M.* (London, Rivingtons, 1841)

Musselwhite, David, *Partings Welded Together: Politics and Desire in the Nineteenth Century English Novel* (London, Methuen, 1987)

Neufeldt, Victor (ed.), *A Bibliography of the Manuscripts of Patrick Branwell Brontë* (New York, Garland Publishing, 1993)

Page, William (ed.), *Victoria History of the County of York* (London, University of London, 1974)

Pearce, John (ed.), *The Wesleys in Cornwall: Extracts from the Journals of John and Charles Wesley* (Truro, Bradford Barton Ltd, 1964)

Pearse Chope, R. (ed.), *Early Tours in Devon and Cornwall*, repr. and with a new introduction by Alan Gibson (Newton Abbot, David & Charles, 1967)

Peters, Margot, *Unquiet Soul* (New York, Doubleday, 1975)

Pobjoy, H. N., *A History of Mirfield* (Driffield, The Ridings Publishing Co., 1969)

Pobjoy, H. N. & M., *The Story of the Ancient Parish of Hartshead-cum-Clifton* (Driffield, The Ridings Publishing Co., 1972)

Pollack, John, *Wilberforce* (London, Constable, 1977)

Pollard, Arthur, *The Landscape of the Brontës* (Exeter, Webb & Bower, 1988)

Pollard, Arthur & Hennell, Michael (eds), *Charles Simeon (1759–1836): Essays in Commemoration of his Bicentenary* (London, SPCK, 1959)

Pool, P. A. S., *The History of the Town and Borough of Penzance* (Penzance, The Corporation of Penzance, 1974)

Pope-Hennessy, James, *Monckton-Milnes: The Flight of Youth, 1851–1885* (London, Constable, 1951)

Pritchard, F. C., *The Story of Woodhouse Grove School* (Bradford, 1978)

Ramsden, J., *The Brontë Homeland* (London, Roxburghe Press, [1898])

Ratchford, Fannie, *Gondal's Queen* (Austin, University of Texas Press, 1955)

Ray, Gordon N. (ed.), *The Letters and Private Papers of William Makepeace Thackeray* (1947)

Rees, Edgar A., *Old Penzance* (Penzance, privately printed, 1956)

Rees, Joan, *Profligate Son: Branwell Brontë and his Sisters* (London, Robert Hale, 1986)

Reid, T. W., *The Life, Letters and Friendships of Lord Houghton* (London, Cassell, 1890)

Robinson, A. Mary F., *Emily Brontë* (London, W. H. Allen, 1883)

Rowley, K. Geoffrey, *Old Skipton* (Clapham, Old Dalesman Publishing, 1969)

Ruskin, John, *Praeterita* (Oxford, OUP, 1978)

Russell, G. W. (ed.), *Letters of Matthew Arnold 1848–88* (London, Macmillan, 1895)

Sale, Geoffrey, *The History of Casterton School* (Casterton School, 1983)

Sanders, Valerie (ed.), *Harriet Martineau: Selected Letters* (Oxford, Clarendon Press, 1990)

Scargill, Christopher & Lee, Richard, *Dewsbury As It Was* (Nelson, Hendon Publishing, 1983)

Scott, R. F. (ed.), *Admissions to St John's College* (Cambridge, 1931)

Scruton, William, *Pen and Pencil Pictures of Old Bradford* (Otley, The Amethyst Press, 1890, repr. 1985)

Shaen, Margaret J. (ed.), *Memorials of Two Sisters: Susanna and Catherine Winkworth* (London, Longman & Co., 1908)

Shorter, Clement K., *The Brontës and their Circle* (London, J. M. Dent, [1914])

Shorter, Clement K., *The Brontës: Life and Letters* (London, Hodder, & Stoughton, 1908)

Slater, Isaac, *General and Classified Directory and Street Register of Manchester and Salford* (Manchester, Isaac Slater, 1847)

Slugg, J. T., *Woodhouse Grove School: Memorials and Reminiscences* (London, 1885)

Smith, Margaret, 'The Letters of Charlotte Brontë: some new insights into her life and writing', *Conference Papers: Brontë Society–Gaskell Society Joint Conference 1990* (Keighley, Brontë Society, 1991)

Speight, Harry, *Chronicles and Stories of Old Bingley* (London, Elliot Stock, 1898)

Stamp, Tom & Cordelia, *William Scoresby: Arctic Scientist* (Whitby, Caedmon Press, c.1976)

Stirling, A. M. W., *The Richmond Papers* (London, Heinemann, 1926)

Symington, J. A. & Hatfield, C. W., *The Leyland Manuscripts* (Privately printed, 1925)

Thackeray Ritchie, Anne, *Chapters from Some Memoirs* (London, Macmillan & Co., 1894)

Trollope, Anthony, *An Autobiography* (Oxford, OUP, 1980, repr. 1987)

Turner, Whiteley, *A Spring-Time Saunter Round and About Brontëland* (Halifax, Halifax Courier Ltd, 1913)

Uglow, Jenny, *Elizabeth Gaskell: A Habit of Stories* (London, Faber & Faber, 1993)

Walker, Ross (ed.), *Letters Addressed to Mrs Gaskell by Celebrated Contemporaries* (Manchester University Press, 1935)

White, William, *History, Gazetteer and Directory of the West Riding of Yorkshire 1837–8* (Sheffield, 1838)

White, William, *Directory of the ... West Riding of Yorkshire* (Sheffield, 1843)

Wilks, Brian, *The Brontës* (London, Hamlyn, 1975)

Winnifrith, Tom, *The Brontës and Their Background* (London, Macmillan, 1973)

Wood, Margaret M., *Hartshead & District in Times Past* ([Chorley] Countryside Publications, 1985)

Woodhouse Grove School 1812–1962: 150 Years of Memories and Recollections (Leeds, Woodhouse Grove, 1962)

Wright, William, *The Brontës in Ireland* (London, Hodder & Stoughton, 1893)

Yates, W. W., *The Father of the Brontës: his life and work at Dewsbury & Hartshead* (Leeds, Fred R. Spark & Son, 1897)

Branwell's map of the Glasstown Confederacy

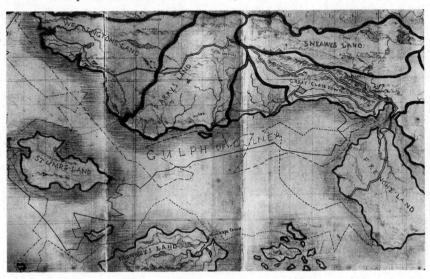

CHARACTERS AND PLACES IN THE JUVENILIA

Almeda, Augusta: wilful and beautiful Queen of Gondal, overthrown by rebellion but regains crown only to be assassinated

Angria: kingdom with English characteristics carved out of the interior of Africa by Arthur Wellesley and Alexander Percy in wake of French invasion

Ardrah, Arthur, Marquis of: heir to Parrysland and leader of Reform Ministry which splits Verdopolitan Union over disputed status of Angria

Ashantees: originally wooden ninepins, representing native Africans, traditional enemies of the Young Men; allies of Verdopolitan Reform Ministry and Northangerland during course of Angrian civil war

Bellingham, James: English merchant, chronicler of his travels in Africa; PBB pseudonym

Bud, Captain John: dramatic poet, editor of Ossian, historian of Verdopolis and Angria; tutor and biographer of Alexander Percy; PBB pseudonym

Douro, Marquis of: *see* Wellesley, Arthur

Ellrington, Viscount: *see* Percy, Alexander

Ellrington, Zenobia: blue-stocking rival to Marian Hume for affection of Arthur Wellesley; marries Alexander Percy as his third wife but remains in love with Wellesley; devotes herself to Percy after his final defeat

Fidena, John, Duke of: heir to Sneakiesland; as Mr Seymour woos and secretly marries Lily Hart; leader of Constitutionalists in Verdopolis, supports Angrians against Reform Ministry, and restores order to Verdopolis and Angria after civil war

Flower, John (Baron Richton): follower of Fidena; chronicler of Angrian wars; PBB pseudonym

Glasstown: *see* Verdopolis

Glasstown Confederacy: *see* Verdopolitan Union

Gaaldine: large island in South Pacific, divided into four kingdoms

Gondal: large island in North Pacific, capital Regina; later subject to civil war between Royalists and Republicans

Gravey: *see* Parry

Hastings, Elizabeth: loyal sister of Henry, whom she shelters and tries to protect from his pursuers; a school-teacher, she loves William Percy

Hastings, Henry: Angrian soldier and writer, joins Alexander Percy in revolt and proscribed; attempts assassination of Arthur Wellesley

Hume, Marian ('Marina'): child bride and

innocent second wife of Arthur Wellesley; dies when neglected by husband

Laury, Mina: peasant girl, first love of Arthur Wellesley; remains his loyal mistress and nurse to his children after his marriage and throughout his changing fortunes

Montmorenci, Hector: friend, ally and partner in crime of Alexander Percy

Napoleon Bonaparte (Sneaky): Branwell's chief Young Man, founder of Sneakiesland; invades Verdopolitan Union from Frenchysland; character gives rise to Rogue

Northangerland, Earl of: *see* Percy, Alexander

Parry, Edward W. (Gravey): Emily's chief Young Man, founder of Parrysland

Percy, Alexander (Rogue, Alexander Rogue, Viscount Ellrington, Earl of Northangerland, 'Mr Ashworth'): arch demagogue, revolutionary and politician of Verdopolis and Angria; friend then bitter foe of Arthur Wellesley; PBB favourite pseudonym

Percy, Edward: estranged elder son of Alexander Percy by Mary Henrietta: makes fortune as mill owner in Angria

Percy, Mary (Duchess of Zamorna): daughter of Alexander Percy, third wife of Arthur Wellesley: a victim of their quarrel she is exiled to Alnwick where she dies of a broken heart

Percy, Mary Henrietta (*née* Wharton): second wife of Alexander Percy, mother of Edward, William and Mary

Percy, William: estranged younger son of Alexander Percy, employed by his brother in counting house of Angrian Mill

Quashia: leader of Ashantees, sometime ally of Alexander Percy

Rogue, Alexander: *see* Percy, Alexander

Ross, John (Waiting Boy): Anne's chief Young Man, founder of Rossesland

Sdeath, Patrick Robert: servant and evil genius of Alexander Percy, whose father and wife he murders

Segovia, Augusta Romana di: beautiful and ambitious atheist, the great love and first wife of Alexander Percy, murdered by Sdeath

St Clair, Earl of: disguises self as Mr Leslie to woo his future wife; leader of Aristocratic Party in Verdopolis; victim of Alexander Percy plot and as Prime Minister, executed during Arthur Wellesley's military coup

Sydney, Edward ('The Foundling'): foundling child revealed to be long lost son and heir of Duke of York; leader of Aristocratic Party in Verdopolis

Thurston, Maria: beautiful but neglected wife of owner of Darkwall; falls in love with Alexander Percy

Townshend, Charles: a reincarnation of Charles Wellesley, the sardonic reporter of Angrian events: succeeds him as CB favourite pseudonym

Tree, Captain: Verdopolitan writer and reporter, CB pseudonym

Twelves: *see* Young Men

Verdopolis (Verreopolis, Glasstown): each of the African kingdoms had its own Glasstown capital. The Great Glasstown, head of the Verdopolitan Union and seat of its Parliament, stood at the mouth of the River Gambia

Verdopolitan Union (Glasstown Confederacy): federal association of Young Men's kingdoms in Africa

Victorine, Helen: first wife of Arthur Wellesley, dies of a broken heart when neglected by her husband

Warner, Warner Howard: native Angrian aristocrat, remains loyal to Arthur Wellesley during civil war and defeats Alexander Percy

Wellesley, Arthur ('Albion', Marquis of Douro, Duke of Zamorna, King of Angria): elder son of Duke of Wellington whom he replaces as Charlotte's main character. At first a clean-cut hero, becomes a philanderer with high political ambitions; friend, then bitter foe of Alexander Percy

Wellesley, Charles: younger son of Duke of Wellington; sardonic observer and reporter of his brother's career; CB favourite pseudonym

Wellington, Duke of: Charlotte's chief man in the plays of the Islanders and Young Men; a presiding hero throughout her juvenilia

Wentworth, Charles: wealthy young Angrian, visitor to Verdopolis, joins Alexander Percy against Verdopolitan Reform Ministry

Young Men (Twelves): based on the twelve wooden toy soldiers given to Branwell by Patrick in June 1826: founders of the kingdoms of the Verdopolitan Union in Africa

Young Soult: poet and tragedian of Verdopolis; caricatured as Henry Rhymer by Charlotte; PBB pseudonym

Zamorna, Duke of: *see* Wellesley, Arthur

Zenobia, Alexandrina: Gondal heroine, forcibly separated from her lover by civil war, imprisoned and deserted by her friends

INDEX